Women's Works, volume 1

# WOMEN'S WORKS

Volume 1:
900 –1550

FIRST EDITION



First publication 2013.

Typeset in Times New Roman

---

*Library of Congress Cataloging in Publication Data*

Foster, Donald W., ed., with Michael W. O'Connell, Christine M. Reno, and Harriet Spiegel
Women's Works: Volume 1: 900 – 1550

1. English Literature – Medieval – Reformation. 2. Women Writers. 3. Canu Heledd, trans. D. Foster; 4. Exeter Book, trans. D. Foster. 5. Marie de France, Fables, trans. Harriet Spiegel; Lay le Frein, anon. trans.; 6. Katherine of Sutton, trans. Michael O'Connell. 7. Trotulas; childbirth; midwives; 8. Julian of Norwich. 9. Margery (Brunham) Kempe. 10. Lollardy. 11. Awisia Moon. 12. Margery Baxter. 13. Julian Barnes (Berners). 14. Margaret of Anjou. 15. Findern Manuscript. 16. Paston Letters. 17. Floure and the Leaf. 18. (Queen) Elizabeth of York. 19. Margaret Beaufort. 20. Gwerful Mechain. 21. Christine de Pizan. 22. English nunneries. 23. Elizabeth Barton, Holy Maid of Kent. 24. Coffin-Welles Anthology. 25. (Queen) Catherine of Aragon. 26. (Queen) Anne Boleyn. 27. Margaret Douglas (Stuart). 28. Mary Shelton (Heveningham). 29. (Queen) Jane Seymour. 30. (Queen) Anne of Cleves. 31. (Queen) Katherine Howard. 32. *The Birth of Mankind; or, the Woman's Book.* 33. (Queen) Katherine Parr. 34. Anne Askew. Et al. 35. Songs and occasional verse.

Foster, Donald W. (1950 – ). Title.
O'Connell, Michael W. (1943 - )
Reno, Christine M. (1942- )
Spiegel, Harriet (1949 - )

ISBN-10: 0-988-28200-3
ISBN-13: 978-0-9882820-0-1
Library of Congress Control Number: 2013935660

---

Wicked Good Books online address: www.wickedgoodbooks.com

*Gwen, ireiddwen gain raddol*

## CONTRIBUTORS

**DONALD W. FOSTER**, main editor of *Women's Works*, is the Jean Webster Professor of Dramatic Literature in the Department of English at Vassar College. He received his doctorate in English from the University of California in 1985 and has taught at Vassar since 1986. Prior to *Women's Works,* Prof. Foster published three books and some forty articles on a wide range of topics, from classical literature to terrorism. He is currently at work with other scholars on *The Player's Shakespeare,* paperback editions designed for actors, directors, and students of drama.

**MICHAEL O'CONNELL** is Professor Emeritus in English literature at the University of California, Santa Barbara, where he has taught since 1970. He received his Ph.D. from Yale University in 1971. He is the author of *Mirror and Veil: The Historical Dimension of Spenser's* Faerie Queene (1977), *Robert Burton* (1986), *The Idolatrous Eye: Iconoclasm and Theater in Early Modern England* (2000), *Three Florentine Sacre Rappresentazioni: Texts and Translations* (2011), as well as articles on Spenser, Catullus, Petrarch, Shakespeare, Milton, and Handel. Professor O'Connell is currently at work on a project about the relations between the late medieval theater and the Elizabethan stage. To *Women's Works,* Volume 1, Prof. O'Connell has contributed the chapter on Katherine of Sutton, and translated the Easter Play of the Nuns of Barking Convent.

**CHRISTINE RENO** is Professor of French and Francophone Studies at Vassar College. She received her Ph.D. in Romance Languages from Yale University in 1972. She has published numerous scholarly articles on Christine de Pizan, and on other texts ranging from paleography in medieval manuscripts to women in Voltaire. With Liliane Dulac she has published a new critical edition of the *Advision,* for Champion, and with Gilbert Ouy and Inès Villela-Petit, a study of Christine de Pizan's manuscript workshop titled *Album Christine de Pizan* (Brepols, 2012). To *Women's Works,* Volume 1, Prof. Reno has contributed "Christine de Pizan in England," while also providing much invaluable assistance with Anglo-Norman and Old French manuscripts.

**HARRIET SPIEGEL** is Professor Emeritus in Literature at the California State University at Chico. She received her doctorate in English from Brandeis University in 1976. She taught English and Medieval literature literature for many years and has published a highly acclaimed edition and translation of the medieval Fables of Marie de France, several of which appear in Volume 1 of Women's Works, by the gracious permission of Prof. Spiegel and the University of Toronto Press. Her edition of Chaucer's Troilus and Criseyde, co-edited with Professor James Dean of University of Delaware, will soon be published by Broadwell Press.

# WOMEN'S WORKS

Volume 1: 900 – 1550 CE

---

Edited by

Donald W. Foster

With Michael O'Connell,

Christine Reno, and Harriet Spiegel

WICKED GOOD BOOKS

NEW YORK

## About the Imprint

Wicked Good Books, founded in 2012, is a not-for-profit cooperative, representing a consortium of scholars, artists, and writers. WGB is committed to book projects that significantly advance human knowledge, or that challenge received ideas about culture.

Submissions: Books intended either for the classroom or for scholarly reference are subject to the usual process of peer review, which may take up to six months. Books intended for the general market will be will be accepted from authors whose previous books have sold at least 10,000 copies; or by invitation.

10% of all retail royalties from WGB titles are donated to the educational foundation or charity of the author's choice.

Registered high school and college students with a family income of under $50,000 may apply for a free copy of any title in the WGB booklist.

Website: http://www.wicked-good-books.com

**Every copy purchased of *Women's Works,* vol. 1, generates a donation to the Fistula Foundation and to the Global Fund for Women**

About two million women, most of them child brides, suffer physical and social misery from untreated obstetric fistula, an injury caused by unrelieved obstructed labor. The condition is curable but most victims are too poor to afford the surgery. Founded in 2000, **the Fistula Foundation** is dedicated to the treatment and prevention of obstetric fistula. In addition to its global education programs, the organization supports medical treatment in Afghanistan, Angola, Bangladesh, Cameroon, Ethiopia, Kenya, Liberia, Niger, Nigeria, Senegal, Somaliland, Tanzania, Uganda. Chad, Sudan, and the Republic of Congo.

Year after year, the Fistula Foundation has received the highest rating from nonprofit watchdog groups. The editors of *Women's Works,* and the Fistula Foundation, are grateful for your support.

Website: http://www.fistulafoundation.org/

The **Global Fund for Women** is a publicly supported grant-making foundation that advances women's human rights by funding women-led organizations worldwide. The Global Fund for Women funds local, regional and national organizations that empower women and girls to live free of prejudice and violence and to achieve success. Active in nearly 200 countries, the Global Fund for Women continues to advance the international women's movement and to promote equal education and social justice, worldwide.

Website: http://www.globalfundforwomen.org

# Women's Works

## Volume 1: 900 – 1550


WELCOME to *Women's Works* xxiii

**BRYTHONIC PERIOD** (to 1066 CE) 1

THE RED BOOK OF HERGEST 3

Canu Heledd: The Songs of Heledd (ninth century) 4

**ANGLO-SAXON PERIOD** (c. 410 – 1066) 11

THE EXETER BOOK 13

Wulf: Wolf (tenth century) 15

Heofung: Lamentation (tenth century) 16

Charms (tenth century) 19

Æcerbot: Field Blessing 19

To Induce Delayed Labor 20

After the Quickening 20

After a Stillbirth or Infant Death 20

To Produce Breast Milk 20

**ANGLO-NORMAN PERIOD** (1066 – 1215) 21

MARIE DE FRANCE (late twelfth century) 23

From *The Fables,* trans. Harriet Spiegel 24

The Wolf and the Lamb 24

The Dog and the Ewe 25

The Sun Who Wished to Wed 26

The Wolf and the Sow 26

The Wolf and the Dog 27

The Peasant Who Saw Another with his Wife 28

The Fox and the Bear 29

The Eagle, the Hawk, and the Crane 30

Lay le Frein (anon. 14th-century English trans., Lai le Fresne) 31

**LATE MEDIEVAL PERIOD** (1215 – 1500) 37

CHRISTINE de PIZAN (1363 – c. 1430) 38

Christine de Pizan in England, by Christine Reno 38

Prologue to *The Feats of Arms and Chivalry* (Englished 1489) 40

*The Body of Policy* (1407, Englished 1521) 41

*The City of Ladies* (1405, Englished 1521) 44

KATHERINE of SUTTON (fl. 1363-1376) 49

Easter Play of the Nuns of Barking Convent, trans. Michael O'Connell 51

HOLY SISTERS 54

Abbey of Barking 56

Priory of Rothwell 58

Priory of Markyate 59

Priory of Sewardsley 61

Priory of Stainfield 62

Priory of Heynings 63

Priory of Legbourne 64

Priory of Grace Dieu 65

Priory of Ankerwicke 68

Priory of Catesby 71

Priory of Littlemore 74

Abbey of Godstow 77

Priory of Nun Cottam 82

Elstow Abbey 83

Form of Confession 89

JULIAN OF NORWICH (1342-1417) 90

From *Revelations to One who Could not Read a Letter* (1393) 91

MARGERY BRUNHAM KEMPE (1373 - c. 1439) 96

From *The Book of Margery Kempe* (1430-38) 99

KATHERINE of KENT (fl. 1420s?) 119

For Nun Would I Never be None (c. 1425) 120

LOLLARD WOMEN 125

AWISIA MOON (fl. 1428-1431) 126

The Abjuration of Awisia Moon (1431)

MARGERY BAXTER (fl. 1428-1431) 128

The Story of Margery Baxter (1431; pub. 1563)

MARGARET of ANJOU (1430-1482), Queen of Henry VI 131

(Duke of Suffolk, To Serve the Flower [ca. 1447/8]) 132

(Duke of Suffolk, from *The Assembly of Ladies*, [1447/8]) 133

To Robert Kent (n.d., 1445/1450) 138

To the Master of St. Giles in the Fields Beside the City of London 138

To Dame Jane Carew (1447/1450) 139

To the Executors of Cardinal Beaufort's will (18 March, 1447/8) 139

To Nicholas Straunge of Iseldon [Islington] (3 May c. 1450) 139
To Sir John Forester, Knight (n.d.) 140
To William Gastrik, respecting the marriage of his daughter (1446-1448) 140
To the Sub-prioress and Brethren of the Monastery at Nuneaton (1446/7) 141
To the Citizens of London (1461) 143
(Balthasar of Syrie, to England [c. 1470], parody) 144

THE FINDERN MANUSCRIPT (c. 1460s) 145
(Farewell to My Betrothed) 147
Margery Hungerford, Without Variaunce 147
Sorrow 147
Goodbye 147
Alas, Why 147
Of a Star 148
Continuaunce 149
Men 149
Absence 149
Love Cycle 150
Good Fortune 150

THE PASTON WOMEN 151
MARGARET PASTON to John Paston I (14 December [1441]) 152
MARGARET PASTON to John Paston I (28 September [1443]) 153
(Richard Calle to MARGARET PASTON II [August? 1469]) 156
MARGARET PASTON to Sir John Paston (10/11 September 1469) 157
MARGARET PASTON to Sir John Paston (12 September 1469) 157
(Sir John Paston to Margaret Paston [15 Sept. 1469]) 157
MARGARET PASTON to Sir John Paston (30 September 1469) 158
ELIZABETH BREWS to John Paston III (ca. January 1476/7) 159
MARGERY BREWS to John Paston III (9 or 10 Feb. 1476/7) 160
ELIZABETH BREWS to John Paston III (9 or 10 Feb. 1476/7) 161
MARGERY BREWS PASTON to John Paston III (14? Feb. 1476/7) 162
MARGARET PASTON to Dame Elizabeth Brews (11 June 1477) 164
"MARGARET PASTON" to John Paston III (29 June 1477) 165
MARGARET PASTON to Sir John Paston (11 August 1477) 165

THE LEAF POET 167
The Floure and the Leaf (ca. 1486) 171

ELIZABETH OF YORK (1466-1503), Queen of Henry VII 179
(Humphrey Brereton, *Song of the Lady Bessie* [1485]) 181
Epithalamion (1486) 185
Letter to Isabella, Queen of Castile (1497) 188
Communion Prayer (1500) 190

MARGARET BEAUFORT (1443-1509) 192
To Thomas Butler, earl of Ormond (c. 1597) 193
To her son, Henry VII (1499) 194

To her son, Henry VII (1500/1) 195
(Henry VII to Margaret, countess of Richmond and Derby [1501]) 196
From "The Mirror of Gold to the Sinful Soul" (c. 1504) 197
"The Lady Margaret her Vow" (1504) 199

Lady [MARGARET?] BRIAN (fl. 1486-1489) 200
(Newton to Lady Brian: *Go, little bill...* ) 201
(Newton to Lady Brian: I *pray you M, to me be true…*) 201
(Newton to Lady Brian: *O ye, my empress…*) 201
(Newton to Lady Brian: *Beauty of you burn in my body abides…*) 201
Lady Brian's Farewell: *Farewell, that was my love so dear...* 202
(Newton's farewell: *Alas, a thousand sighs, alas…*) 202

THE WELSH TRADITION (15th century) 203
(Gruffudd ap Dafydd ap Grono: To Gwenllian) 203
GWENLLIAN ferch Rhirid Flaid: Englyn in reply to Dafydd 203
(Tudur Penllyn: Seisnig Saesnes) 204
GWERFUL ap FYCHAN: Snow 205

GWERFUL MECHAIN (c. 1462 - c. 1505) 206
Eight Englynion: 208
1. Llanc ym min y llwyn: Boy in the Bush 208
2. Y Gwahaniaeth: The Difference 208
3. Dyferu Wlyb: Dripping Wet 208
4. I'w Thad: To her Dad (on his young girlfriend) 208
5. I'w Gwr am ei Churo: To her Husband for Striking Her 208
6. Pwyllwch: Keep Calm 208
7. Dianc y Bardd: The Artful Dodger 208
8. Swydd Wag: Vacancy 208
Cywydd y Cedor: Cywydd of the Bush 209
I Wragedd Eiddigeddus: To Jealous Wives 211
Conversation between Two Poets 211
Cywydd i ateb Ieuan Dyfi: In reply to Dyfi for his cywydd to Anni Goch 212

SONGS AND OCCASIONAL VERSES (1300-1550) 214
Dame Alice Kyteler: A Charm for Wealth 215
By the Prayers of St. Dorothy: *What manner of evil thou be...* 216
Isabel Mure: Benedicite 216
Mother Mary's Lament: *Why have ye no ruth on my child...* 217
Jesu my Leman: *Jesus Christ mine leman sweet...* 217
Jesu my Spouse: *Jesu, my spouse good and true...* 217
Lullay: *Little child, why weepest thou so sore?...* 218
Corpus Christi Lullaby: *The falcon hath born my make away...* 219
Dame Courtesy's Book for Children: *Whosoeuer will thrive or thee...* 220
The Irish Dancer: *Ich am of Irelaund,...* 222
Black is Beautiful: *Some men sayon that I am black...* 223

Trolly-Lolly: *Of serving men I will begin…* 223
As I Could Wish: *The man that I loved alder-best…* 224
Reply to her Lover: *Ensamples fair ye find in Nature…* 225
Double Dealing: *Your counterfeiting with double dealing…* 227
Why is it?: *O blessed Lord, how may this be,…* 228
Night is Long: *Merry it is while summer y-last…* 228
Fragment: *Welaway, why did I so?…* 228
Fragment: *Who shall to my leman say…* 228
Fragment: *Welaway that Ich ne span…* 228
Fragment: *Barrèd girdle, woe ye be…* 228
Fragment: *Alas, how should I sing?…* 229
Fragment: *And I were a maiden…* 229
The Sooth I See: *I loved a child of this country…* 229
Alas, What Remedy? *Grievous is my sorrow…* 230
Lady Bryan's Lament: *The last time I the well woke…* 233
Come, Death: *I will no more go to the plough…* 234
Led I the Dance: *Led I the dance, a Mi'summer Day…* 234
The Serving Maid's Holiday: *Web ne reel, ne spin Ich ne may…* 236
To My True Love and Able: *Unto you, most froward…* 237
Women's Work: *Jesu that art gentle, for joy of thy dame…* 238
Jamie: *He that will be a lover…* 242

VERNACULAR TROTULAS 243
From *The Knowing of Woman's Kind in Childing* (c. 1390, ms. c. 1510) 245
From *Science of Cirurgie* (c. 1380) 245
From *The Book of Rota* (c. 1550) 247
From *Woman's Privy Sickness* (c. 1490) 248
From *Liber Trotuli* (c. 1525) 252

JULIAN BARNES (fl. 1480s?) 253
From *The Book of Hunting* (1450><1486) 255

**REFORMATION PERIOD** (1500-1550) 259

THE COFFIN-WELLES ANTHOLOGY (1515-38) 260
(From her suitor: *Please it your grace dear heart, to give audience…*) 262
Maiden to her suitor: *"I love so sore"? I would fain discern...* 263
(From her suitor: R*ight gentle heart of green flowering age...*) 264
To her suitor: *Green flowering age, of your manly countenance...* 266
To her suitor: *O resplendent flower, print this in your mind...* 267
(From her suitor: *O my lady dear, both regard and see...*) 267
To her suitor: *Right best beloved and most in assurance...* 268
(From her suitor: *O love most dear, O love most near my heart...*) 270
To her suitor: *Even as merry as I make might...* 271
(From her suitor: *Sweetheart, I love you more fervent...*) 271
A Letter Sent by One Young Woman to Anoder 272

MARY OSTREWYK (c.1470-1547) 274
Certain Prayers Shewed unto Mary Ostrewyk (1530) 274
ELEANOR (SUTTON) SOMERSET (c. 1489 – 1526/49), Countess of Somerset: 275
Book-Plates (ca. 1525) 275
Book-plates, 14th-18th centuries) 275
CATHERINE of ARAGON (1485-1536), Queen of Henry VIII 276
Letter to Princess Mary (April 1534) 277
Letter to Henry VIII (7 Jan. 1535/6) 278
ELIZABETH BARTON (1506?-1534), Holy Maid of Kent 279
Prophecies 281
Scaffold Speech 282
Inventory 282
ANNE BOLEYN (c. 1501-1536), Queen of Henry VIII 283
Letter to Cardinal Wolsey (1528, facs.) 284
(Birth Announcement, 7 Sept. 1533) 285
(Book of Hours, 1534) 287
(E. Hall: The Arrest of Anne Boleyn, 2 May 1536) 289
(W Kingston, Constable: prison reports) 290
Last Letter (6 May 1536) 295
Scaffold speech (19 May 1536) 296
MARGARET DOUGLAS (STUART) (1515-1578), Countess of Lennox 297
Margaret Tudor to Henry VIII (12 August 1536) 298
The Douglas (Howard) correspondence (1536-1537) 299
(T. Howard, holograph, *Now may I mourn, as one of late...*) 299
(T. Howard, holograph, *To mourn, of right, it is my part...*) 299
(T. Howard, holograph, *Who hath more cause for to complain...*) 300
(T. Howard, holograph, *Alas, that men be so un-gent...*) 300
(T. Howard, holograph, *What thing should cause me to be sad...*) 300
M. Douglas, ent. Howard, *I may well say, with joyful heart...* 301
(T. Howard, holograph, *To your gentle letters, an answer to recite...*) 301
Dame Agnes Jordan to Lord Cromwell (6 November 1536) 302
Margaret Douglas to Lord Cromwell (December 1536) 303
(T. Howard, holograph, *If reason govern fantasy...*) 304
(T. Howard, holograph, *What helpeth hope of happy Hap...*) 304
(T. Howard, holograph, *This rooted grief will nought but grow…*) 305
(T. Howard, holograph, *Some say I love. Some say I mock…*) 305
(T. Howard, entered by E. Knyvet, *O miserable sorrow, withouten cure…*) 305
(T. Howard, ent. M. Douglas, *There is no cure for care of mind...*) 306
(T. Howard, ent. M. Douglas, *Thy promise was to love me best...*) 306
(T. Howard, ent. M. Douglas, *How Should I?...*) 307
(T. Howard, ent. M. Douglas, *I see the|e change from that that was...*) 307
(T. Howard, ent. M. Douglas, *As for my part I know nothing...*) 307

(T. Howard, ent. M. Douglas, *And this (by this) ye may...*) 308
(T. Howard, ent. M. Douglas, *What needeth life when I require...*) 308
(T. Howard, ent. M. Douglas, *To my mishap, alas, I find...*) 308
Margaret Douglas, holograph, *My heart is set not to remove...* 309
Margaret Douglas, holograph, *When I bethink my wonted ways...* 309
Margaret Douglas, holograph, *Fancy framèd my heart first...* 310
Margaret Douglas, ent. Mary Shelton, *I am not she, by proof of sight...* 311
Margaret Douglas, ent. Mary Shelton, *To counterfeit a merry mood...* 311
Margaret Douglas, holograph, *Might I as well within my song belay...* 311
Margaret Douglas, holograph, *The sudden chance did make me muse...* 311
Margaret Douglas, ent. Mary Shelton, *My youthful days are past...* 312
Margaret Douglas, holograph, *Now that ye be assembled here...* 313
Margaret Douglas, holograph, *Lo, in thy haste...* 314
Margaret Douglas to her father, the earl of Angus (1548/9) 314

MARY SHELTON (HEVENINGHAM) (c. 1513-1570/1) 319
The Shelton (Knyvet) correspondence (1536-1541) 321
(E.K., *Suff'ring in sorrow, in hope to attain,...*) 321
Shelton, On E.K.'s "Service" 321
(E.K., *Bound am I now and shall be still...*) 322
(E.K., *My fearful hope from me is fled...*) 323
Shelton, *Your "fearful hope" cannot prevail ...* 324
(E.K., *Too dear is bought the doubleness...*) 324
(E.K., *To men that knows ye not...*) 325
(E.K., *If that I could in verses 'close...*) 325
(E.K., *In places where that I company...*) 326
(E.K., *Mine unhappy chance ...*) 326
(E.K., *Wily, no doubt, ye be awry...*) 326

JANE SEYMOUR (1508-1537), Queen of Henry VIII 328
Birth Announcement (1537) 330

ANNE of CLEVES (1515-1557), Queen of Henry VIII 331
Letter of consent: to Henry VIII (1540) 334
Letter of consent: to her brother, the Duke of Cleves (1540) 335
Letter to Queen Mary (1554) 336

BIRTH OF MANKIND; or, THE WOMAN'S BOOK (1540) 338
An Admonition to the Reader 340
Dedication to Queen Katherine Howard 340
Who be Unperfecter, the One than the Other 341
The Pricks of Nature 341
No Joy without Some Sorrow 342
The Terms be of so Wholesome Blood 342
The Due Fashion of Birth 342
Of Easy and Uneasy, Difficult, or Dolorous Deliverance 343
On the Management of Normal Childbirth 343

On the Rupturing of the Forewater 344
On the Management of Abnormal Presentation 344
Of the Nurse and her Milk 344
Remedies of Dandruff of the Head 345
To Take away Hair 345
To Clear and Clarify the Skin 345
To Supple and Mollify the Ruggedness of the Skin 345
To Keep and Preserve the Teeth Clean 345
Of Stinking Breath 345
Of the Rank Savor of the the Armhole 345

KATHERINE HOWARD (c. 1520-1542), Queen of Henry VIII 346
Confession to Archbishop Cranmer (7 Nov. 1541) 349
Examination before the Privy Council (12 Nov. 1541) 351
Letter to Thomas Culpepper (1541) 352

KATHERINE PARR (1512-1548), Queen of Henry VIII 355
Letter to Henry VIII (July 1544) 356
*Prayers Stirring the Mind* (1545) 357
Katherine Parr to Lord Thomas Seymour (mid-February 1546/7) 363
Lord Thomas Seymour to Dowager Queen Katherine (March 1546/7) 363
Dowager Queen Katherine to Lord Thomas Seymour (April 1547) 363
Lord Thomas Seymour to Dowager Queen Katherine (17 May 1547) 364
Dowager Queen Katherine to Lord Thomas Seymour (c. 24 May 1547) 364
Dowager Queen Katherine to Lord Thomas Seymour (c. 25 May 1547) 364
Lord Thomas Seymour to Dowager Queen Katherine (c. 31 May 1547) 365
Dowager Queen Katherine to her husband (11 June 1548) 365
The Confession of Elizabeth Tyrwhitt concerning the Death of Katherine Parr 366

ANNE ASKEW (KYME) (c. 1521–1546) 367
The First Examination (pub. 1546) 369
The Ballad which Anne Askew Made 374
From The Latter Examination (pub. 1547) 375

TIMELINE of Women's History 378

TEXTUAL NOTES 388

BIBLIOGRAPHY OF WORKS CITED 407

ACKNOWLEDGMENTS 413

The Names and First-Line indices for vol. 1 appear at the rear of volume 2

## Also available: *Women's Works*, vols. 2-4

Each volume contains the best extant writing by and for women readers, with up-to-date biographies and cultural context. All literary writings are reproduced in modern orthography, edited directly from the earliest and best manuscripts and printed texts. Translations are supplied for texts in Old English, Norman French, Welsh, and Latin.

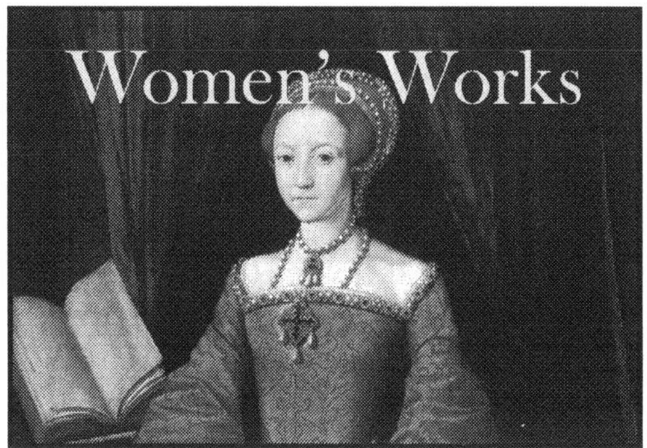


### *Volume 2: 1550 - 1603*

### THE ELIZABETHAN AGE


JANE I (1537-1553), Queen of England
From The Apology of Lady Jane
God Save the Queen
Queen Jane to William Parr
By the Queen
Lady Jane, to Master Harding
A Certain Communication
To her father
To her sister Katherine
(Anon., "The End of the Lady Jane Dudley")

MARY I (1516-1558), Queen of England
Prayer of St. Thomas
Letter of Submission
Interview with the Bishop of London
Letter to the Privy Council
To the People of Norfolk
To the Bishop of Winchester
Queen Mary I defending her Spanish marriage
To Princess Elizabeth
Pardon to "All … as would desist from their purpose"
Circular letter, to muster troops
To the Earl of Sussex, to oppose the rebels
Queen Mary's speech at the Guildhall
To Prince Philip
To the Sheriff and Deputies of the County of Norfolk
To Cardinal Pole
(Giovanni Michieli, "Mary, Queen of England")
The Last Will and Testament Of Mary I

ELIZABETH I (1533-1603), Queen of England
From Elizabeth, trans., *A Glass for the Sinful Soul*
The Thomas Seymour scandal, correspondence
Princess Elizabeth to King Edward VI
Princess Elizabeth to King Edward VI
Princess Elizabeth to Princess Mary
Princess Elizabeth to King Edward VI
Princess Elizabeth to Queen Mary
Written on a Wall at Woodstock
Verses She Wrote with her Diamond
Hoc est corpus meum
Accession speech
Proclamation to Forbid Preaching
Oration on marriage and succession
The Doubt of Future Foes
Genus infoelix vitae
Written in her French Psalter
Oration in the Parliament House
On Monsier's Departure
Dame Pleasure
A Rhyme Royal
(W. Ralegh, "Fortune hath taken away my love...")
Queen Elizabeth's Reply
Elizabeth to the Earl of Leicester
Elizabeth to Mary Queen of Scots
(James of Scotland to Queen Elizabeth)
Elizabeth to James VI of Scotland
Armada Speech to the Troops at Tilbury
A Godly Prayer and Thanksgiving
Elizabeth to of Navarre
Privy Addition: A Prayer for the Cadiz Voyage
From Seneca's *Hercules Oetæus*
From Boethius's *Consolation of Philosophy*
A Precious Token of Her Highness's Great Wit
The Golden Speech

CATRIN FERCH GRUFFYUDD ab Hywell (16th C.)
On the Cold Summer of 1555

ALIS FERCH GRUFFYUDD ab Ieuan (16th C.)
On a husband: Englyn ateb (reply to her father )
On her Father's Remarriage
(Englyn ateb: his reply)
Englyn ateb: To her Lover (on her sister Gwen)

GWERFUL of Fferi: Asking for a Harp

JOANE (FITZALAN) LUMLEY (1536 - 1578)
From *Iphigenia*

CUNNING WOMEN:
From trials at Chelmsford, Essex (1566)

ISABELLA WHITNEY (1520? - 1587)
From *Copy of a Letter*
I.W. to her Unconstant Lover
From *A Sweet Nosegay*
The Author to the Reader
from *A Hundred and Ten Flowers*
A Careful Complaint by the Unfortunate Author
Is. W., Being Weary of Writing
Her Will and Testament
A Communication which the Author Had to London
The manner of her will
From *A Gorgeous Gallery*
"The Lamentation of a Gentlewoman"
Anonymous: Go, Cause the Bell to Toll

ELIZABETH TYRRWHIT (c. 1519 - 1578)
From *Morning and Evening Prayers*
A Hymn of the State of All Adam's Posterity
Certain Godly Sentences

FRANCES (MANNERS) NEVILLE (c. 1530 - 1576)
A Prayer against the Fellowship of the Ungodly
An Acrostical Hymn

MARY CHEKE (c. 1530-1616)
John Harington, the younger, "Of a Certain Man"
Lady Mary Cheke, "Of a Certain Woman"

MARGARET TYLER (fl. 1578)
From *A Mirror*: On the Education of Women

KATHERINE (COOKE) KILLIGREW (1530-1583)
To Her Sister Mildred

CUNNING WOMEN:
From trials at Chelmsford, Essex (1579)
From trials at Windsor, Berkshire (1579)
From trials at St. Osyth, Essex (1582)

MARY STUART (1542-1587), Queen of Scots
Farewell letter

ELIZABETH DOUGLAS MAXWELL (1558 – 1637)
E.D. in praise of Master William Fowler Her Friend
E.D. in Commendation of the Author

ANNE (DACRE) HOWARD (1557-1630)
Oratio Alianor Percy

JANE ANGER, pseud. (1589)
*Jane Anger: Her Defense of Women*

CUNNING WOMEN:
From trials at Chelmsford, Essex (1589)

KATHERINE (EMMES) STUBBES (1571-1590)
From P. Stubbes, *A Crystal Glass*
A Most Wonderful Conflict

MARY (SIDNEY) HERBERT (1561-1621)
Selections from *Antony*
From *The Psalms*
To ... Elizabeth
To the Angel Spirit
Psalm 58: Si Vere Utique
Psalm 64: Exaudi, Deus
Psalm 71: In Te Domine Spera
Psalm 119: Beati Immaculati
Psalm 120: Ad Domine
Psalm 131: Domine, non est
Psalm 137: Super Flumina
The Doleful Lay of Clorinda
A Dialogue

CUNNING WOMEN:
From trials at Burton Staffordshire (1596)
Alice Goodridge, the Witch of Stapenhill
BRIDGET de VERE (NORRIS) (1584-1631)
Lady B. to N.

ELIZABETH (SIDNEY) MANNERS (1585-1612)
I Know Not What
From the Bright Manuscript
Song: Careless Content
Harden that Heart
Summer of Love

PENELOPE (DEVEREUX) RICH (1563-1607)
To her Majesty in the Behalf of the Earl of Essex

FRANCES (HOWARD) SEYMOUR (1578-1639)
(from John M., *Philip's Venus*)
(from Hecatonphila, pseud., *The Art of Love*)
(Sir George Rodney, Elegia)
The Countess of Hertford's Reply
(Sir George Rodney before he killed himself)

TÊTE-À-TÊTE
The Courting of Thomas Whithorn (1550s)
From *A Poetical Rhapsody* (1602)
Anon., Sonnet: Upon Her Acknowledging His Desert
Anon., Her Answer in the Same Rhymes
Anon., A Dialogue Between The Lover And His Lady
Anon., Her Answer

### *Volume 3: 1603 - 1625*

## THE JACOBEAN PERIOD

ANNE (CLIFFORD) HERBERT (1590 - 1676)
From *A Memorial of the Life of Me*
Death of Queen Elizabeth, Coronation of King James

ANNE (CLIFFORD) HERBERT (1590 - 1676)
From *A Memorial of the Life of Me*
The Death of Elizabeth and Coronation of James

ELIZABETH MELVILLE (c. 1580 - c. 1640)
(C. Marlowe, The Passionate Shepherd to His Love)
(W. Ralegh, The Nymph's Reply)
A Call to Come to Christ
A Triple Talent
Ane Godly Dream (Scots and English)

CECILY BOULSTRED (1584-1609)
(B. Jonson: To Mistress Boulstred)
(B. Jonson: Song: To Celia)
(B. Jonson: Song to Celia)
(B. Jonson: Shall I not my Celia Bring?)
(B. Jonson: On the Court Pucelle)
(F. Anthony: An Apology or Defense)
(E. Herbert: Epitaph. Caecil. Boulser)
(J. Donne: Elegy on Mistress Boulstred)
(J. Donne: Elegy XI)
(B. Jonson: Epitaph)
C. Boulstred: News of my Morning Work
(T. Carew: Know, Celia)

LUCY (HARINGTON) RUSSELL (1581-1627)
Elegy on Mistress Boulstred

ROSE (LOCKE) HICKMAN (1526 - 1613)
Certain Old Stories by an Aged Gentlewoman

MARGARET CUNNINGHAM (c. 1587 – c. 1631)
A Part of the Life of Margaret Cunningham
The True Copy of a Letter

AEMILIA (BASSANO) LANYER (1569 -1645)
To the Doubtful Reader
From *Salve Deus Rex Judaeorum*
To the Virtuous Reader
To the Queen's Most Excellent Majesty
To the Lady Elizabeth's Grace
The Author's Dream: to Mary, Countess of Pembroke
On Beauty: to Anne Clifford, Countess of Cumberland
From the Preamble
An Apology for Women
On Anne Clifford
The Description of Cookham

The PENDLE WITCHES (d. 1613)
Fr. *A Wonderful Discovery of Witches in Lancaster*

ELIZABETH (TANFIELD) CARY (1585? - 1639)
*The Tragedy of Mariam, Fair Queen of Jewry*

MARY (GREY) DRAYTON (1585-1643)
On the Decease of My Incomparable Sister
A Funeral Pyramid
To the Soul

PENELOPE GREY (SALTER) (b. 1591)
Parodia

ANNE (GREY) MASTERS (1595-1645)
To Her Soul-Loved Sister

DOROTHY (KEMPE) LEIGH (1561-1613)
From *The Mother's Blessing*

MARY OXLIE (REDHEAD) (fl. 1616)
To William Drummond

ELIZABETH ARNOLD (fl. 1616)
Against the Painting of Women

RACHEL SPEGHT (PROCTOR) (1598 - c. 1661)
From *A Muzzle for Melastomus*
*Mortality's Memorandum*, part 1: The Dream

ESTHER SOURNAM, Esther Hath Hanged Haman

MARY (SIDNEY) WROTH (1587 - c. 1652)
From *Love's Victory*
From *Pamphilia to Amphilanthus*
From *The Countess of Montgomery's Urania*
Lyrics from *Urania*
(Sir Edward Denny: To Pamphilia)
Railing Rhymes Returned

ELIZABETH (KNYVET) CLINTON (1575 - 1638)
*The Countess of Lincoln's Nursery*

JOAN, MARGARET, and PHILLIPA FLOWER; ANNE BAKER, JOAN WILLIMOT, and ELLEN GREEN (d. 1619)
The Sisters of Belvoir Castle

ELIZABETH SAWYER (d. 1621)
Witch of Edmonton

ELIZABETH JENNINGS (b. 1610)
The Bewitchment of Elizabeth Jennings

BESSIE CLARKSON (1603 - 1625)
The Conflict in Conscience of Bessie Clarkson

SONGS AND OCCASIONAL VERSES
Farewell
He is Gone
I Know Not What
Marrying Maiden
Love Lamenting
King James: The Dryer-Up of Doubts (1623)
A Lady: An Answer to the Wiper-Away (1623)
Anon., Saint Elizabeth (1624)
King Charles: A Gracious Answer (1642)

***Volume 4: 1625 - 1650***

**THE CAROLINE PERIOD**

ANNA (NORMAN) LEY (c.1599-1641)
On the Death of King James
Upon the Great Plague, following the Death of King James

ANNE (HARRIS) SOUTHWELL (1573-1636)
From *Sir Thomas Overbury His Wife*
Answer to the Very Country News (1614)
Certain Edicts from a Parliament in Utopia (1615)
From *The Precepts* (Folger MS) (1624-1632)
Of Wit and Wealth
On Servants
The Miser
The Huntsman
The Male Scold
Precept I
Precept II
Precept IIII

Precept IV
Precept V
Precept VII
Precept VIII
From *The Precepts* (British Library MS) (1626)
Precept III
Precept IV
Pleasure's Vassal
Anger
Dialogue
Sonnet: Beauty, honor, youth
Sonnet: O how happy
All Things
To Her Husband
On Marriage
A Letter to Doctor Adam
In Defense of Poetry
An Elegy
An Epitaph upon Cassandra MacWilliams
Blest Necessity
Omnia Vincit Amor
On Fortune
A Paraphrase upon Seneca
An Abstract of Plutarch
An Epitaph upon Frances Howard, Countess of Somerset

MABEL SWINNERTON (fl. 1623)
Testimony against Dr. John Lamb (1623; pub. 1628)
Elizabeth Cary, On the Duke of Buckingham

THE TUCHET WOMEN
Lady Amy (Mervyn) Blount, Psalm 25
Mervyn Tuchet, attrib., On Himself
Anon, An Answer
Anne (Stanley) Tuchet, attrib., The Lady's Answer

MARTHAMOULSWORTH (1577 - 1646)
The Memorandum of Martha Moulsworth (1632)

DIANA PRIMROSE
*A Chain of Pearl* (1630)

SIBILLA (COLE) DOVER (c. 1580-1653)
To Her Modest Mirth-Making Friend (1636)

LUCY (PERCY) HAY (1599-1660)
(Extracts fr. Herrick, Herbert, Cecil, Carew, Waller, Habington, Cartwright, Donne, de Voiture, Davenant)
(Fr. Toby Matthew, *The Character of Lady Lucy*)
(John Suckling, Here Lies Don Alonzo)
(John Suckling, Upon My Lady Carlisle's Walking)

HENRIETTE MARIE (1609-1669)
Civil War Letters (1642-1644)

THE WOMEN'S PEACE MARCH (8-9 August 1643)
The Petition of Many Civilly-Disposed Women

GRACE (BROWN) CARY (c. 1595-1668)
*England's Forewarning* (1644)

HESTER (LEY) PULTER (1605-1678)
On the King's Most Excellent Majesty (c. 1642)
Aurora (c. 1643/4)
To Sir W.D. on the Unspeakable Loss (c. 1643/4)
To my Dear Jane, Mary, Penelope Pulter (1645)
Upon the Death of my Dear and Lovely Daughter, Jane Pulter (1646)
On the Same (1646)
To My Solitary Soul (c. 1643/4)
Of a Young Lady at Oxford (1646)
Upon the Imprisonment of his Sacred Majesty (1647)
The Invitation into the Country (1647)
Made When I was Sick (1647)
The Perfection of Patience and Knowledge (c. 1648)
Universal Dissolution (1648)
A Flight of Fancy (1648)
On Charles the First, his Horrid Murther (1649)
Upon the Horrid Murther (1649)
Solitary Confinement (c. 1649)
A Dialogue between Two Sisters (c. 1650)
Dust, to Earth (c. 1650)
The Circle (c. 1650)

ANNE (DUDLEY) BRADSTREET (c. 1612-1672)
From *The Tenth Muse* (1650)
Prologue (1650)
In Honor of that High and Mighty Princess Queen Elizabeth (1643)
Dialogue between Old England and New (1642)

JANE CAVENDISH (CHEYNE) (1623-1669)
From the Poetry Book (1644-1645)
Dedication
The Great Example
Passion's Letter to my Lord my Father
Passion's Contemplation
Passion's Delate
A Song in Answer to Your Lordship's Satire
The Cure
On a False Report of your Lordship's Landing
Wit's Waggery
On a Noble Lady
The Pert One: or otherwise, My Sister Brackley
The Quintessence of "Cordial"
A Song (Maid, wife, or widow)
Thanks Letter
An Answer to the Verses Mr. Carew Made to Lady Carlisle
Passion's Invitation
On an Acquaintance
1.-3. On a Noble Lady
On the Lord Viscount Brackley
On my Sweet Sister Brackley
Love's Universe
Misfortune's Weather-glass
The Captive Burial
The Cautious Man, or Wit's Wonder
A Song (I would love's language…)
On an Honorable Lady (Frances Cavendish)
On My Dear Mother
On my Dear Brothers and Sister
Hope's Preparation
*A Pastoral* (with Elizabeth Egerton, 1645)
*The Concealed Fancies* (1646)

ELIZABETH (CAVENDISH) EGERTON (1627-63)
From the *Loose Papers* (1648 ff; compiled 1663)
Considerations concerning Marriage
Spoken upon the Receiving a Cake of Perfume
On a Sight of the Countess of Bridgewater's Picture
A Commendation of the Society of Dear Friends
A Prayer in the Sickness of my Girl Frank
A[nother] Prayer in the Sickness of my Girl Frank
A Prayer when I was with Child
A Prayer in Time of Labor
A Prayer after I was Brought to Bed
A Prayer for my Husband
A Prayer when I was with Child
A Prayer when I continued with Child
Upon occasion of the Death of my Boy Henry
Upon recovery out of a sickness after delivery
A Prayer and Resolution against Despair
When I lost my dear girl Kate
On the same occasion
On the same
A Prayer When I was with Child (of Stuart)
A Prayer when I was with Child
(John Egerton: [Death Notice])
(Jane Cavendish: On the Death of my Dear Sister)

MARY (SWINHOE) MOORE (c. 1618 - 1679)
*Wonderful News from the North* (1650)

MARY (TICKELL) OVERTON (1615 – after 1655)
The Appeal and Petition of Mary Overton (1649)
The Petition of Divers Well-Affected Women (1649)
The Petition of Divers Well-Affected Women (1649)
The Petition of Divers Well-Affected Women (1653)

MARIE (JACKSON) CAREY (c. 1609 - c. 1681)
On the Death of My Fourth and Only Child
On the Death of My Fifth Child
Upon the Sight of my Abortive Birth

ELIZA (fl. 1644-1652)
From *Eliza's Babes*
To my Sisters
To the Reader
And now, my Babes,
Psalm 56, verse 10
The Virgin's Offering
My Wishes
To the Queen of Bohemia
To the King (Writ 1644)
The Invincible Soldier
To a Friend, for her Naked Breasts
To a Friend at Court
My Robes
The Dart
The Heart
The Giver Engaged to the Receiver
The Defiance
The Bride
The Gift
On the Sun
Upon the Loss of my Brother
On Marriage
My Second Part
The Change
Being Called a "Stoic"
To My Husband
On Sudden Death
A Question
To General Cromwell
Questions and Answers
The Support
To a Lady that Bragged of Her Children
The Royal Priesthood
This on my Tomb
The Secure Pavilion

ANNE GREEN (1628 – 1650 and 1650 - 1659)
William Burdet, *Wonder of Wonders*
Richard Watkins, *News from the Dead* (1650)

••••••••••••••••••••••••••••••••••••

Robert Campin, Mother and Child before a firescreen (c. 1440). Courtesy of the National Gallery

# WELCOME to *Women's Works*

*Mulier in silentio discat cum omni subiectione. Docere autem mulieri non permitto neque dominari in virum sed esse in silentio. Adam enim primus formatus est deinde Eva; et Adam non est seductus mulier autem seducta in praevaricatione fuit. Salvabitur autem per filiorum generationem si permanserint in fide et dilectione et sanctificatione cum sobrietate.*
—Biblia Sacra Vulgata (late 4th century)

*Let a woman learn in silence, with al subjection. But to teach, I permit not vnto a woman, nor to haue dominion ouer the man: but to be in silence. For Adam was formed first, then Eue. And Adam was not seduced: but the woman being seduced was in prevarication. Yet shal she be saued, by generation of children, if they continue in faith & loue and sanctification with sobrietie.*
—Rheims New Testament (1582)

*I said, he oughte to fynd no faute in poore women,*
*excepte they had offended the lawe.*
—Anne Askew (1546)

NE lasting impression that students receive from their classroom curriculum – even at the university level, even in the twenty-first entury – is that men produce culture, while women produce sons. History is the record of kings and warfare. The women who tidied up when the killing was done, or who penned competing narratives, receive at most a footnote. Heroic literature narrates what alpha males achieved on the battlefield or suffered at the hands of inscrutable gods. Women's heroic labors in the birthing chamber (more dangerous than military service), and their literature of the childbed, are by tradition excluded from the syllabus. The great epics were written by men – the *Odyssey*, *Beowulf*, *The Faerie Queene*, *Paradise Lost*, to name a few – while women plied their needle and preserved their honor, or looked pretty and played the whore. To men are credited the most memorable lyrics, the wittiest satires, the grandest stageplays and 100 Great Books. Women's lot, it has been supposed, was not to write, but to be written *about,* to be celebrated in verse as the objects of male desire, or to be honored as the mother of a messiah or the consort of a king.

As a result of this pervasive gender bias in primary, secondary, and higher education, very few English-speaking women today know much about their own cultural past, and very few men know the first thing about history from women's point of view.

Late in the last century, a great and collaborative work of recovery was undertaken by literary scholars to exhume women poets, storytellers, and playwrights whose works of genius were lurking, dusty and undiscovered, in the archives of major research libraries. The first sizable collection to appear was Germaine Greer's *Kissing the Rod* (1988), which commenced with Jacobean religious doggerel and included nothing early than 1604. Since that time, scholars have uncovered dozens of writers whose lives and works are no less engaging, for their time, than those of Jane Austen or Dorothy Lessing or Toni Morrison. But their stories have not yet been adopted for the classroom, or for the book club, or for bedside reading. There are many reasons for that, none of them good ones.

The first (and, to a lay reader, most obvious) obstacle is academia's fetish for original spelling. Countless gleanings from early women's literary production now lie scattered across academic journals or upon university bookshelves, chiefly in "diplomatic" (exact) transcriptions. These texts have received all the benefits of scholarship except an actual readership. Who but a scholar reads the Bible or Shakespeare or *Frankenstein* in original typography? Yet early women writers have been reproduced since 1980 chiefly in critical old-spelling editions, either in journals or in books that cost more than $100 per volume and are read by few: scholars for research purposes consult facsimiles of the original, available from such digital resources as *Early English Books* and *Perdita Manuscripts*, while undergraduate students and lay readers find the original printed texts inaccessible and largely unintelligible, and the original manuscripts illegible and unavailable. The message that students receive, when invited to read the Western canon in a modern edition and to view an early women writer in original orthography, is that the woman's text is a cultural fossil, a museum artifact of interest to pedants, but not quite the same thing as literature.

The opposite extreme, exhibited by editors of anthologies, has been to select a few token-hits of early women's writing, and to reissue them in a version ruthlessly "modernized," with altered syntax and word-substitutions; with a two-paragraph editorial introduction that typically compliments the writer and describes her work as "important"; when in fact the anthologized version has no more importance for study of language and literature than a SparkNotes paraphrase.

With the strong showing of feminists in higher education in the 1990s, it was widely hoped that the canon could be split open – and it was. Today, all texts are fair game for study in the English classroom, from any era, any clime, and almost any venue, not excluding comic books, television screenplays, videogames, and pop music. That is as it should be: critical thinking is no less essential when one reads a Britney Spears lyric than when reading Shakespeare. But the expectation that early women's literature would thereby find a permanent and valued place in academia's ever-ballooning curriculum has all but evaporated. Scholarship continues to thrive well enough, but classroom study of early women writers is about where it stood one hundred years ago. The Oxford anthology of *Early Modern Women's Writing* includes nothing earlier than 1560, while the Columbia anthology commences with the report of a speech by Elizabeth I in 1588. The *Meridian Anthology of Early Women Writers: British* contains nothing earlier than 1660. The more rangy *Norton Anthology of Literature by Women* includes two lays of Marie de France in translation; a few brief extracts from Julian of Norwich, Margery Kempe, and Julian Barnes; and the "Ballad" of Anne Askew. The *Longman Anthology of Literature by Women* includes two lyrics from the Exeter Book; four letters (two from Queen Matilda, two from Margery Paston); plus brief extracts from Margery Kempe and the two Julians – all of these selections having been dumbed down with excessive and unnecessary "modernization." That's *it* – plus very little else from the reigns of Elizabeth, James, Charles, and the Interregnum. The implicit lesson: Although English literature begins with *Beowulf,* early women's writing begins with Aphra Behn or Jane Austen.

Needless to say, much of women's culture from the Celtic, Anglo-Saxon, Norman, late Medieval, and Reformation periods has been irretrievably lost. Few women were either permitted or able to record their words: denied formal schooling, deprived of tutoring, women endured illiteracy as one of many lifelong penalties imposed on them for the fault of having been born without a penis. As a result, women's lore – spinning and sewing, horticulture and cooking, midwifery and holistic medicine, charms and incantations, songs and poems and stories – had to be transmitted orally; and the male clerics whom we may thank for preserving secular literature rarely deigned to record verse or prose that was obviously by, or for, the daughters of Eve. What has survived is very hit-or-miss, often no more than a rhymed couplet of women's verse quoted in a sermon, or a posy scrawled on the flyleaf of a prayerbook.

That said, our grief for what has been lost may tempt us to overpraise what we do discover in ancient archives, or even to recuperate women's literary remains in ways not justified by the available evidence. The well-known medieval lyric, "I am Rose" provides a case in point. This surprising poem, which survives in a unique copy in Cambridge University Library MS Hh.6.11 (c. 1280), is catalogued in the *Index of Middle English Verse* under the genres, "Women as speakers/narrators" and "Laments." It has been reproduced in anthologies of Middle English poetry, republished on dozens of Websites, and even set to music. Scholarly transcriptions vary—

**I am Rose**
Ed. Carlton Brown (1943)

I am Rose wo is me
sutere kat ignete þe
þat i wacs þat weylawey
cherles hand me þristet ay

**I am Rose**
Ed. Rossill Robbins (1955)

I am Rose, wo is me,
Sutere þat I suete þe.
I wacs þat weylawey
cherles hand me þristet ay.

–as do modern paraphrases:

**I am Rose**
Ed. Brian Stone (1964)

I am Rose, woe is me
Though sweeter than the sweet I be.
I grow in grief and misery:
For hand of churl has done for me.

**I am Rose**
Ed. Gunnvôr Silfrahárr (2003)

I am Rose, alas for me,
Sweeter than the sweet I be.
I wax in pain and misery:
A churlish hand has pluckèd me.

The poet has been tentatively identified in published scholarship as one "Rose *Souter*," or perhaps the wife of a *cobbler* named Rose, who had a *suitor* among the clergy. But here is what MS Hh.6.11 actually says (at left), with a parallel text in conservatively normalized spelling and punctuation (at right):

| | |
|---|---|
| I am rose wo is me | I am rose: woe is me, |
| sutere þat i snete þe | Sutere, that I snittè thee! |
| þat \ i wacs / weylawey | That I wax, welaway! |
| cherles hand me þristet ay | Churl's hand me thristeth aye. |

Mangled by editors, this thirteenth-century Rose has indeed been been *thrusted* aye and again: "Sutere" does not signify *sweeter*. Nor does it reference a *suitor*. Nor is it Rose's surname or trade. Nor is *Rose* her Christian name. Nor is "I am rose" even a women's poem. The *Oxford English Dictionary,* every undergraduate English major's favorite reference work, clarifies the text's meaning:

- *suter*, from Latin *sutor,* shoemaker, from Roman times a proverbial botcher; *MED, OED,* "a term of abuse" (as in: "horsoned *suters*!" [1478]; "called him *sowter,* and gave him opprobrious words" [1575]; "Creishie *soutter*! … Minch moutter!" [1585]).
- *churl,* OED n.4 (f. 1275): "peasant, rustic, boor"; n.5, "base fellow, villein")
- *snite*, OED v.2 (fr. 1100): "to clean or clear the nose from mucus, esp. by means of the thumb and finger only" (as in these wise proverbs: "Therfor sayth Salamon, *Whoso ouer-harde snythyth the noos, he draueth blode*" [1422]; "Pi[c]ke not youre nose.., Snyff nor snitynge hyt" [1475]; "Even yet among the Persians it is held a shamefull thing...to snit the nose" [1632]).
- *thrist,* OED *thrust,* v.1 (fr. 1100): "to expel, eject"; v.6: "to enter, pierce, or penetrate some thing or…extend (a limb or member [or finger]) into some place" [such as a nose].
- *welawey,* OED intj.1 (fr. 888): "exclamation of sorrow or lamentation"
- *wax,* OED v.5 (fr. 971): "To rise, swell; to flow out in a flood"

Hence:

I am rose[-nosed]. Woe unto me, a botcher, that I picked thee!
Now I've got a gusher, welaway! My churlish hand has always gotta be poking!

This rose-red ditty, half as old as the kingdoms of Wessex and Mercia, has an identifiable source. It translates a Latin riddle, preserved (in part) along with the English text, and preserved (in full) in a manuscript housed in the Bibliothèques d'Amiens Métropole (MS 460), where it is attributed to a monk:

*Heu, rosa! cur crevi? manus angit rustica!*
*Heu, rosa!* (*Cur rosa sum? villani mulceo nasum.*) [1]
—Albertus, monacus Clarevallis (c. 1270-80)

*Woe, a rose*! *why am I blown*? *picked by a boorish hand!*
*Woe, a rose*! *Why am I a "rose"? I fondle the nose of a villein* [*rustic*].
—Albert, a monk of Clairvaux, trans. DWF (2013)

The original author of "I am rose" is not an English-speaking woman of the British Isles, but a French monastic; and the "I" who speaks is not a courtly woman with a broken heart, but a bumpkin with a nose-bleed. If "*Heu, rosa*!" has a place in our literary tradition, it is not as a precursor to Gertrude Stein's 1939 lyric, "I am rose," but to Janet Clinker's 1787 praise of broad-shouldered Scottish hussies: "If a puir man want a perfect wife, let him wale [*choose*] a weel-blooded hissie, wi' braid shouders and thick about the haunches, that … snites the snotter frae their nose."[2]

(*Moral*: When revising the canon to include Rose Souter or Marie de Meulan or W.S. or any other real or supposed author, we do well to establish a reliable text, and to have an accurate notion of what it means, and perhaps even to ask ourselves who wrote it, before foisting it on our colleagues and students.)

Every item in *Women's Works* has been freshly and accurately edited from the earliest authoritative manuscripts, augmented with commentary that places the original work in its cultural and biographical context. The resulting collection, though hardly comprehensive, provides enough new material to keep thoughtful readers entertained and serious scholars occupied for quite some time. Not all of the texts selected for inclusion are known to have been written by women (a few were certainly written by men,

---

[1] *mulceo* ] to stroke, fondle; with phonological pun on *mulco*: to thrash, handle roughly.

[2] Janet [i.e., Humphrey] Clinker, *The History of the Haverel Wives* (1787), ed. 1903, 54-55.

either to or for women readers). And yet, one reason that the clergy so bitterly condemned women's speech, so often, is precisely because their female contemporaries had so much to say: Volume one presents a smorgasbord of narrative verse, elegy, riddle, fable, romance, satire, song, correspondence, essay, medical handbook, court testimony, autobiography, and occasional verse. And each succeeding volume is as rich as and varied as Volume one. Clearly, if women of medieval Britain did not produce epic battles or epic poems, neither did they remain silent for the first thousand years of our literary history.

Most of the poetry in these pages and much of the prose was first composed to be read aloud for an intimate audience. Various helps are therefore here supplied, so that extracts from *Women's Works* can be heard with pleasure, whether in the classroom or the family room. Spelling and punctuation have been normalized (without paraphrase or word-substitutions).[1] Parallel translations are supplied for texts originally written in Welsh, Old English, or Anglo-Norman French. Difficult words are glossed at the bottom of the page, not banished to a glossary at the rear. Accent marks are added to assist metrical fluency: an acute accent indicates a stressed syllable (*cóntent, contént*), while a grave (back-slashed) accent indicates an unstressed syllable (*blessèd, learnèd* [2 syllables.]; *blessed, learned* [1 syllable]); *demand* is pronounced as in modern English while medieval *demandé* is pronounced as in French, three syllables with the last being accented; etc. (No musical settings are supplied for the song lyrics: readers may wish to invent their own.) With a bit of rehearsal, there is no text in *Women's Works* that resists delivery by anyone with a high school education and a sense of play.

A quarter-century in development, *Women's Works* has reached print none too soon, appearing at a moment when "the English major" is in decline across America and throughout the United Kingdom. To sustain enrollments (or perhaps to commit disciplinary *seppuku*), departments of English have beefed up their course-offerings in media studies and journalism but without making many new hires in literatures earlier than the nineteenth century. And since graduate students generally gravitate to those fields where they find job openings, doomsayers predict that "English literature," a generation from now, may be a thing of the past in more ways than one, with English departments having been converted to writing programs, and Literature reduced to a discipline for specialists. Such jeremiads sound far-fetched until one considers a recent study by the Jenkins Group, which indicates that eighty percent of U.S. families no longer buy or read books; and that 42% of American college graduates never read another complete book after the bachelor's degree. If current trends continue, students may soon be paying $60,000 a year in tuition and fees but without reading any text earlier than their own birth date, or longer than a tweet. (The editors of *Women's Works* are less pessimistic. Most of the texts included here had their first trial run among students at Vassar College, where the readings met with passionate enthusiasm. The death of Literature has been predicted many times, most often from the culture police who hold to the Great required Books school of thought. But great literature, including the women's texts contained herein, will never lack for readers so long as there remain teachers and students with a passion for learning, and who love the English language.)

Readers who have gotten thus far will recall that *Women's Works* opens with an epigraph quoting holy Scripture, one of several passages where the Word enjoins feminine silence. Translated by scholars at the English College (Douai), the Rheims New Testament (1582) was the first Bible in vernacular English that "popish" laymen were permitted to read, without sin. For added clarity, or perhaps just to express their solidarity with St. Paul, the English College attached a lengthy footnote to the apostle's dictum, with a dire warning: "Women are much given to reading, disputing, chatting, and jangling of the holy Scriptures, yea, and to teach also, if they might be permitted; but Saint Paul utterly forbiddeth it … [T]he woman taught but once: that was when, after her reasoning with Satan, she persuaded her husband to transgression; and so she undid all mankind; and in the ecclesiastical writers we find that women have been great promoters of every sort of heresy" (1 Timothy 2:11-14 [1582] fn.).

The hope of the editors is that women readers will find in these pages much to dispute, chat, and jangle about; and that *Women's Works* will be blessed with readers who (like those early women readers and writers) become teachers of reason, and great promoters of every sort of heresy against the status quo.

DWF

---

[1] Editorial interpolations, emendations and substantive variants are recorded in the Textual Notes (pp. 389-407) and signaled in the edited text by brackets or a degree symbol: [*interpolation*], *emendation*°.

# BRYTHONIC Period (to 1066)

*In ben ba dech de mnāiph, ba sí opair dognid, techt ar cenn catha cathrōi, dāil dūnaid, fechta slōgaid, gonæ airligh. A tīagh looin for indara tāib dī, al-lenban for in tōib n-ailiu. A fidcheis fria hais. Trīcha traigeth ina hairdi. Corrān īaroinn for indara cinn dī, conidh edh doberedh ar trilis na bandscāile aili arsin cad n-araile. A fer inna díaidh; cūaille airbed inna lāim oc a sroigled ar cenn catha. Ar ba cenn mnaa nō dācich noberthe i tarilbhath in tan sin.*

—Adomnán of Iona, *Cain Adomnáin* (c. 697) [1]

*The work that the best women had to do was to go to battle and battlefield, engage and camp, muster and fight, wound and slay. She would carry, on one side, her bag of provisions, her babe on the other, her wooden pole upon her back. Thirty traigeth long it was, and had on one end an iron hook, which she would thrust into the tunic of some woman in the enemy host; her husband behind her, carrying in his hand a fence-stake and flogging her on to courage. For in those days the head of a woman, or her two breasts, were taken as trophies.*

—trans. DWF

HE CELTS, by the third century BCE, registered their influence from Turkey in the east to Portugal in the west, and from the Mediterranean to the British Isles. But the notion that "the Celts are the fathers of Europe" – that there once existed, at the heart of the Continent, a grand and sophisticated iron-age Celtic culture which shrank to a western rump in Great Britain – is a myth constructed by nineteenth- and twentieth-century historians. The distribution of Celtic languages in southwest Europe indicates rather a trail of agriculturalists who dispersed 7,000 years ago from Anatolia, migrating along the north coast of the Mediterranean to Italy, France, and Spain, eventually to Britain. Celtic arrival in what is now England is often said to correspond with the appearance of chariot burials, from about the sixth century BCE. By the third century, the Britons dominated what is now England and Wales; by which time Celtic peoples on the Continent were under retreat from the Germanic tribes and coming under the rule of Rome. Julius Caesar's conquest of Gaul in the 50s BCE left only the British Isles under independent Celtic control.

In 43 CE, Claudius invaded the island, with the object of total conquest. By the early 80s, the Romans had established the province of "Britannia" and pushed as far as Scotland ("Caledonia"). The Britons at the time had no written language, but the Romans, who did, have much to say about them. The reputed sexual freedom of the continental Celts (noted already by Aristotle in the fourth century CE), and the fierceness of their women in battle, are much noted. Diodorus Siculus (fl. 60-30 BCE), possibly borrowing a line from military recruiters, alleges that the boys of Britannia "will offer themselves to strangers and take offense if the offer is refused."[2] Athenaeus (second century CE), and Ammianus (fourth century) harp on the same string, reporting that the men slept openly with one another, often preferring boys even though their women were strong, tall, and beautiful. Celtic women seem to have been accorded a corresponding freedom. Divorce could be requested by either husband or wife and was easily obtained, after which both parties were free to remarry. Nor was marriage thought to entail exclusive rights. Cuckoldry and bastardy were not such points of anxiety among the Britons as among the Romans: in the determination of a legitimate heir, robustness trumped monogamous wedlock, as Edmund argues in *King Lear*. In this regard, Cassius Dio cites "a very witty remark" made by the wife of the Scots prince, Silver-Leg ("Argentocoxus") to Julia Augusta (58 BCE - 29 CE): "When the empress jested with her (after the treaty) concerning the free intercourse of her sex with men in Britain, the foreigner replied: 'We fulfill the demands of nature much more satisfactorily than you Roman women: we consort openly with the best men, whereas you let yourselves be debauched in secret by the vilest.'"[3]

The Celts both male and female were indeed robust, powerfully built, and stood a full head taller than most Roman soldiers, many of whom returned from the front bearing tales (as surviving reports attest) of the women's ferocity in battle. Among the most justly famous of their women warriors is Boudica (Welsh "Buddug"), queen of the Iceni tribe (in what is now roughly Norfolk). Her husband Prasutagus had ruled the Iceni as a nominally independent ally of Rome. When he died, he named Boudica as regent, leaving his kingdom jointly to his daughters and to the Roman Emperor, the Icenis' acknowledged overlord. Instead, as Tacitus tells us, Catus Decianus annexed the kingdom as if conquered, subjugated the nobles, flogged Boudica, and raped her daughters. Awaiting her moment, Boudica raised an army,

---

[1] Ed. Kuno Meyer (1905); 2-3; *Tricha traigeth* ] thirty feet; but the measure of the Irish foot is unknown; perhaps about $8^1/_2$ modern inches (which would still make her *fidcheis*, or staff, more than twenty modern feet long).

[2] Diodorus Siculus (fl. 60-30 BCE), *Bibliotheca Historica*, 5:32, trans. DWF.

[3] Cassius Dio (c. 165-235), *Historia Romana*, 5:7777, trans. DWF.

and in 60-61 CE led a revolt that began with the sacking and demolition of the provincial capital, Camulodunum (Colchester). Next to fall was Londinium, followed by Verulamium (St. Albans). Dio's vivid account describes a ritual in which Boudica before battle invoked the goddess Andraste for victory and released a hare from within her robes, whose running through the camp cheered the Britons, who understood it to represent the flight of the Romans. Seventy to eighty thousand Roman subjects were slain by Boudica's army, with the usual terrors: the noblest women (reports Dio) were impaled on spikes and had their breasts cut off and stitched to their mouths. Suetonius met the resistance somewhere in the West Midlands. A better military tactician, the Roman commander, though greatly outnumbered, defeated Boudica and slaughtered Britons by the tens of thousands, including vast crowds of women and children stationed in wagon-trains as a last line of defense. Boudica's death marked the end of armed insurgency against the Roman occupation.

Sometime between 400 and 700 CE, in what is now Scotland and northern England, the Welsh became culturally distinct from the Cornish, the Bretons, and the tribes of the Hen Ogledd (Old North). From this period there developed the Welsh dialect and the literary tradition represented by *Y Cynfeirdd* ("The Early Bards"). Depending on the patronage of kings, these professionals – the bard Taliesin is regarded as the first in the line – produced chiefly poetry of praise. Saga poems associated with Llywarch Hen (Llywarch the Elder) and Heledd (the sister of Kynddylan) date from the ninth century, having roots in the seventh (though few textual witnesses survive earlier than the fourteenth century). Llywarch Hen is a legendary hero, a sixth-century prince of the northern Brythonic kingdom of Rheged who is said to have lost his lands, plus dozens of sons and a few daughters, in battles with the invading Saxons. Other poems lament the fall of Pengwern, the kingdom of Kynddylan (in what is now Shropshire).

The *Beirdd yr Tywysogion* ("Bards of the Princes"), also called *Y Gogynfeirdd*, ("the Less Early Bards") were members of a guild who worked from the time of the Norman invasion of England until 1282, when the defeat of the Welsh kingdom of Gwynedd by England's Edward I ended eight centuries of independent rule. Welsh poets therafter were obliged to seek patronage among land-owning aristocrats. The *Beirdd yr Uchelwy* ("Bards of the Nobility") date from the fall of Gwynedd until 1536, when Welsh law was fully replaced by English law, and the Union established. This fertile period produced both praise and satire, much of both being written in the popular meter of the *cywydd.*[1]

Alongside the court poet worked the king's storyteller, a tradition represented by the "Mabinogion," eleven tales, preserved in two manuscripts: the Red Book of Hergest (which also contains the earlier Song of Heledd) and the White Book of Rhydderch. Written in Middle Welsh, the common literary language from the late eleventh century to the fourteenth, the Mabinogion preserve much pre-Christian Celtic mythology and draw upon the developing legends of King Arthur.

Despite rich troves of extant verse from as early as the sixth century, the Welsh tradition has remained untaught and virtually unknown in the literature classrooms of England and America, which typically take Beowulf as the starting point of our literary tradition, and Chaucer as "the father of English poetry." The Canu Heledd here serves as an apt starting point for a parallel women's tradition in English that remains almost as widely unknown as the Welsh.

DWF

---

[1] Traditional Welsh poetic meters consist of 24 different forms, called *Y Pedwar Mesur ar Hugain*. All require *cynghanedd* – complex structural arrangements of sound, each having a set number of syllables per line, off-rhymes, and internal rhymes that anticipate end-rhymes (features impossible to replicate in English translation). As set down in the fourteenth century by the masters Einion Offeiriad and Dafydd Ddu Athro, the Measures are divided into three classes: the *engyln* or stanza; the *awdl* or ode; and the *cywydd* or harmony. The oldest is the popular *englyn*, consisting of three or four lines. (Well suited to epigrammatic statement and compact imagery, individual *englynion* often exhibit the beauty and compression of the Japanese *haiku.*) Eight different types of *englyn* are given among the traditional forms, with varying degrees of complexity in the obligatory *cynghanedd.* The *awdl* originally had a single end-rhyme throughout, which could stand alone or be embedded in a longer work. Eventually, the monorhyme gave way to *awdlei* in monorhyme sections of 20-40 lines, in various meters. An innovation of the fourteenth century was the inclusion of *englynion* at the beginning or end of the *awdl,* or between sections. Poets of the late medieval period tended to reserve the *awdl* for serious and ceremonial occasions. The *cywydd,* used for much popular verse including dialogues and satires, was written in rhymed couplets (occasionally, in triplets), with seven-syllable lines, one line rhyming on a stressed syllable, the other on an unstressed one. By the end of the fourteenth century, the *cywydd* meter had become a standard for all genres and subject matter, with no set length.

## Canu Heledd (tenth century)

| | |
|---|---|
| *Heledd hwyedic y'm gelwir, ...* | *I shall be known as wandering Heledd...* |
| *Ys ysgawn gan rei vy ruch.* | *When nothing remains, I shall travel light.* |
| —lines 235, 198 | |

THE RED BOOK OF HERGEST (*Llyfr Coch Hergest*) is a Welsh anthology compiled near the end of the fourteenth century, probably in a monastery. Preserved today in the Bodleian Library (Jesus College MS 111), the vellum manuscript derives its name from the color of its leather binding and from its later association with Hergest Court. *The Red Book* contains ancient Welsh prose, notably the tales of *Mabinogion*, and verse attributed to *y Gogynfeirdd* ("the Less Early Poets"). Its poetry dates from the ninth and tenth centuries but with roots in an oral tradition as early as the seventh. Much of its verse is concerned with the Anglo-Saxon conquest.

Following Rome's withdrawl from Britain in the fifth century, Germanic tribes arrived in wave upon wave – Saxons from northern Germany, Jutes and Angles from the region of Denmark.[1] Settling at first on the eastern shores, the "Lloegrwys" (as the medieval Britons called the tribes of England) battled their way up the Thames River, destroying all that stood in their way. Against overwhelming force, the Celtic Britons had only a few memorable victories, later mythologized as triumphs of King Arthur. Those who stayed and fought were killed or captured, with young captives only being kept alive, as slaves. Those who fled found refuge in North Wales or Ireland, or crossed the Channel and settled in Armorica (the Brittany coast).

The Cornovii – a name by which two or three Celtic tribes were known in Roman Britain – stood their ground in the lowland border regions of Wales. Powys was governed by King Kyndrwyn "the Stubborn," whose seat was at Pengwern in what is now Shropshire, on the modern Welsh border. After Kyndrwyn's death, his sons, chief of whom was Kynddylan, formed an alliance against the Anglo-Saxons. They are believed to have joined forces with Penda of Mercia, which places them at the Battle of Maes Cogwy on 5 August 642, when the Christian king Oswald of Northumbria was defeated and slain.

That was the Celts' last great victory. About 655, Kynddylan and his brothers are said to have met the Lloegrwys at the ford of the River Tren (i.e., the Tern). Their resistance proved futile. Invading Powys-land, the English burned Pengwern to the ground. Kynddylan was slain, together with his many brothers and sisters. Only Heledd escaped.

From at least the tenth century onward, perhaps from the seventh, there developed a bardic tradition of lamenting the fall of Pengwern and the death of King Kynddylan, whose reign came to represent a Golden Age before the English arrived. Among the greatest of the extant exemplars is the cycle of poems known as "Canu Heledd," sung by Kynddylan's sister – verses written for a woman's voice, to the accompaniment of a harp, and luckily preserved in the *Red Book of Hergest*. In these elegiac poems, Heledd grieves for her slain family and mourns the fall of Pengwern, reduced now to a smoking ruins.

The "Canu Heledd" was not composed in any originary sense by an "author," least of all by the male scribe who recorded its lyrics into the *Red Book of Hergest* in the latter fourteenth century. The surviving Canu Heledd represents a single inscription of an elegiac tradition rooted in pre-history and branching across time.[2] Composed for a woman's voice, the "Canu Heledd" is like Heledd herself a survivor, a figure of inexpressible grief transfigured into music for the harp, and heart.

DWF

---

[1] The Jutes, who occupied portions of what is now Kent, Hampshire, and the Isle of Wight, were wiped out or assimilated by their Anglo-Saxon rivals in the latter seventh century.

[2] Heledd figures in the Welsh *Triads* as an unrestricted guest of King Arthur and one of the Tri Eniryavl – the three driven mad by grief; elsewhere as the originator of wise sayings (e.g.,"Have you heard what Heledd sang, the daughter of Cyndryn of great wealth? Prosperity cannot come of pride ... nor is it generosity that causes poverty").

## Canu Heledd

Anon., Book of Hergest

SEFWCH ALLANN vorynnyon! a syllwch werydre
Gyndylan: Llys Benngwern, neut tande?
Gwae ieueinc a eidun brotre.
UN PRENN a govit
Arnaw odieinc ys odit,
Ac a vynno Duw derffit.
KYNDYLAN, callon iäen,
Gaeaf, a want twrch trwy y benn,
Cu a rodeist yr cwrwf Trenn!
KYNDYLAN, callon godeith,
Wannwyn, o gyflwyn am gyvyeith,
Yn amwyn Tren, tref diffeith.
KYNDYLAN, befyrbost kywlat,
Kadwynawc, kildynnyawc cat.
A mucsei Tren, tref y dat.
KYNDYLAN, beuyrbwyll ovri,
Kadwynawc kynndynnyawc llu,
Amucsei Tren hyt tra vu.
KYNDYLAN, callon milgi,
Pan disgynnei yg kymelri,
Cat, calaned a ladei.
KYNDYLAN, callon hebawc,
Buteir ennwir gynndeiryawc
Keneu Kyndrwyn, kyndȳnnyawc.
KYNDYLAN. callon gwythhwch,
Pan disgynnei ym priffwch,
Cat, kalaned yn deudrwch.
KYNDYLAN, gulhwch, gynnifiat,
Llew, blei dilin disgynnyat,
Nyt atuer twrch tref y dat.
KYNDYLAN hyt tra attat
Yd adei, y gallon mor wylat
Gantaw, mal y gwrwf y gat.
KYNDYLAN Powys borffor,
Wychyt, kell esbyt, bywyt ior,
Keneu Kyndrwyn, kwynitor.
KYNDYLAN, wynn uab Kyndrwyn,
Ny mat wisc baraf am y drwyn,
Gwr ny bo gwell no morwyn?
KYNDYLAN, kymwyat wyt
Ar meithyd nabydyd° lwyt
Am Trebwll twll dy ysgwyt.
KYNDYLAN, kae di y riw
Yn y daw Lloegwrwys hediw,
Amgeled am un ny diw.
KYNDYLAN, kae di y nenn
Yn y daw Lloegyrwys drwy Dren,
Ny elwir coet o un prenn!
KAN VYGCALLON i mor dru
Kyssyllu ystyllot du,
Gwynn gnawt Kyndylan, kyngran canllu.

• • •

## The Song of Heledd

Trans. DWF

STAND FORTH, maidens! And behold the land
Of Kynddylan: the court of Pengwern is on fire.
Alas, for the lad who seeks his brothers!
A TENDRIL, a single tree,
May yet escape.
Whatever God hath willed, must be.
KYNDDYLAN, with a heart of winter-ice,
Who could pierce the head of a boar,
You have drunk deep of the ale of Tren!
KYNDDYLAN, with a heart like the fires of spring,
By the common oath, reputed of all,
Defended Tren, that now-desolate town.
KYNDDYLAN, bright pillar of the marches,
Armor-clad, steadfast in fight,
Protected Tren, the town of his father.
KYNDDYLAN, bright spirit gone out,
Armor-clad, stubborn in war,
Protected Tren as long as he lived.
KYNDDYLAN, with the heart of a hound
Plunging into the havoc,
Carved carnage upon the foe.
KYNDDYLAN, with the heart of a hawk,
A ravenous bird of prey:
The stubborn son of Kyndrwyn.
KYNDDYLAN, having the heart of a boar,
When he charged into the fray,
Created carnage in double heaps.
KYNDDYLAN, a ravaging boar,
A lion in pursuit of the wolves.
To his father's town, the boar will not return.
KYNDDYLAN – as long as he lived,
It was to his heart a merriment,
To be in the thick of the fight!
KYNDDYLAN of Powys, purple-robed,
A harbor to guests, an anchor to life,
Kyndrwyn's son is to be – bewailed.
"KYNDDYLAN, blest son of Kyndrwyn,
What good are men with a beard under nose
Who can do no more than a maid?
"KYNDDYLAN, maker of grief.
To grow grey is not your intent:
At Trebwll, shields must be shattered.
"KYNDDYLAN, stay upon the rise
Till the Lloegriaus come,
Why worry yourself over one?
"KYNDDYLAN, keep thou your place
Till the Lloegriaus enter the Tren:
One tree does not make a wood!"
MY HEART breaks with grief:
Black lumber encases the blest-pale
Corpse of Kynddylan, our centurion.

• • •

• • •

STAVELL GYNDYLAN ys tywyll
Heno, heb dan heb wely.
Wylaf wers, tawaf wedy.
STAVELL GYNDYLAN ys tywyll
Heno, heb dan heb gannwyll.
Namyn Duw, pwy a'm dyry pwyll?
STAVELL GYNDYLAN ys tywyll
Heno, heb dan heb olevat,
Etlit° a'm daw amdanat.
STAVELL GYNDYLAN ys tywyll
Y nenn, gwedy gwen gyyweithyd.
Gwae, ny wna da a'e dyvyd.
STAVELL GYNDYLAN neut athwyt
Heb wed. Mae ym bed dy yscwyt
Hyt tra vu ny bu dollglwyt.
STAVELL GYNDYLAN ys digaryat
Heno, gwedy yr neb pievat,
Owi, a angheu byrr y'mgat!
STAVELL GYNDYLAN nyt esmwyth
Heno, ar benn carrec hytwyth,
Heb ner, heb niver, heb amwyth.
STAVELL GYNDYLAN ys tywyll
Heno, heb dan, heb gerdeu–
Dygystud devrud dagreu.
STAVELL GYNDYLAN ys tywyll
Heno, heb dan, heb devlu.
Hidyl [vyn neigyr] men yt gynnu.
STAVELL GYNDYLAN a'm gwan
Y gwelet, heb doet, heb dan;
Marw vy glyw, buw mu hunan.
STAVELL GYNDYLAN ys peithwac
Heno, gwedy ketwyr bodawc,
Elvan Kyndylan kaeawc!
STAVELL GYNDYLAN ys oergrei
Heno, gwedy yr° parch a'm buei.
Heb wyr, heb wraged a'e katwei.
STAVELL GYNDYLAN ys araf
Heno, gwedy colli y hynaf.
Y mawr drugawc Duw! pa wnaf?
STAVELL GYNDYLAN ys tywyll
Y nenn, gwedy dyva o Loegyrwys
Kyndylan ac Elvan Powys.
STAVELL GYNDYLAN ys tywyll
Heno, o blant Kyndrwynin°,
Kynon a Gwiawn a Gywyn.
STAVELL GYNDYLAN a'm erwan
Pob awr gwedy, mawr ymgyvyrdan
A weleis ar dy benntan!

• • •

• • •

THE HALL OF KYNDDYLAN is dark
Tonight, no fire in the hearth, no bed.
I'll weep a while – and then, be still.
THE HALL OF KYNDDYLAN's dark
Tonight, no hearth-fire, no taper-light.
(Save God, who will keep me sane?)
THE HALL OF KYNDDYLAN is dark
Tonight, no light, no merry blaze.
The spreading silence surrounds thee.
THE HALL OF KYNDDYLAN – its roof
Is black – no more, the blest assembly.
O, this was no way to end.
THE HALL OF KYNDDYLAN has
No form. In the dirt, its shield lies.
No breach, no crack, was there whilst he lived.
IN KYNDDYLAN HALL is no love
Tonight, now that its keeper is gone.
O, Death, leave not me alone!
IN KYNDDYLAN HALL, no comfort
Tonight, atop the mighty rock –
No lord, no feast, no troops.
THE HALL OF KYNDDYLAN's dark
Tonight, no fire in the hearth, no songs –
Only tears, to tear the cheeks.
THE HALL OF KYNDDYLAN is dark
Tonight. No fire in the hearth, no host.
My grief swells up where it falls.
THE HALL OF KYNDDYLAN wounds me
To see it – no warm hearth, no roof..
My lord is dead. I'm breathing still.
THE HALL OF KYNDDYLAN is a ruin
Tonight, the site where warriors vied–
Elvan, and gold-wearing Kynddylan!
THE HALL OF KYNDDYLAN's cold
Tonight. Lost, the honors that were mine –
Lost are the men, lost is the women's care.
THE HALL OF KYNDDYLAN is still
Tonight, having lost its lord.
Great merciful God! what's to be done?
THE HALL OF KYNDDYLAN – dark is its roof
Since Lloegriaus brought to the grave
Kynddylan and Elvan of Powys.
THE HALL OF KYNDDYLAN is dark
Tonight. Erased is the line of the Kyndrwynin,
Kynon and Gwiawn and Gwyn.
THE HALL OF KYNDDYLAN, hour by hour,
Makes a hurt of my heart: gone, the joys
That we knew by its glowing hearths.

• • •

ERYR Eli ban y lef:
[Heno,] lewssei [ef] gwyar° llynn,
Creu callon Kyndyllan wynn.
ERYR Eli gorelwi
Heno, y gwaet gwyr gwynn novi.
Ef y goet trwm hoet y mi.
ERYR Eli a glywaf
Heno, creulyt yw, nys beidyaf.
Ef y goet, twrwm hoet arnaf.
ERYR Eli gorthrymet
Heno, diffrynt Meissir mygedawc,
Dir Brochuael, hir rygodet.
ERYR Eli echeidw myr
Ny threid pyscawt yn abyr.
Gelwit gwelit owaet gwyr.
ERYR Eli gorymda coet
Kyuore kinyawa.
A'e llawch llwydit y draha.
ERYR penngwern penn garn ,
Llwyt aruchel y atleis,
Eidic amgic [a gereis].
ERYR penngwern Penngarn,
Llwyt aruchel y evan,
Eidic am gic Kynndylan.
ERYR penngwern Pengarn,
Llwyt aruchel y adaf,
Eidic amgic a garaf.
ERYR penn gwern pell galwawt
Heno, ar waet gwyr gwylat,
Rygelwir Trenn tref difawt.
ERYR penngwern – pell gelwit
Heno, ar waet gwyr gwelit,
Rygelwir Trenn tref lethrit.

• • •

EGLWYSSEU BASSA – y orffowys
Heno, y diwed ymgynnwys,
Cledyr kat, callon Argoetwys!
EGLWYSSEU BASSA ynt ffaeth
Heno, vyn tavawt a'e gwnaeth –
Rud ynt wy rwy vy hiraeth.
EGLWYSSEU BASSA ynt yng
Heno, y etived Kyndrwynin°,
Tir mablan Kyndylan wynn.
EGLWYSSEU BASSA ynt tirion
Heno, y gwnaeth eu meillyon,
Rud ynt wy, rwy vyng callon.
EGLWYSSEU BASSA collassant eu breint,
gwedy yr° diva o Loegyrwys
Kyndlan ac Elvan Powys.
EGLWYSSEU BASSA ynt diva
Heno, y chetwyr ny phara.
Gwyr a wyr a mi yma.
EGLWYSSEU BASSA ynt barvar
Heno, a minneu wyf dyar!
Rud ynt wy, rwy vyggalar.

THE EAGLE of Eli cries shrilly
Tonight. He has swallowed streams of blood –
The heart-blood of blessed Kynddylan.
THE EAGLE of Eli is screaming
Tonight, wading in warriors' blood.
He is in the wood; to me, a heavy grief.
THE EAGLE of Eli, I hear him
Tonight, bloody, he'll not be defied:
He is in the wood, my unbearable grief.
THE EAGLE of Eli, most dreadful
Tonight, over Meissir's lovely vale,
The land of Brochwael, in deep distress.
THE EAGLE of Eli o'erlooks the sea.
He'll not tear fish from the streams:
He shrieks for the blood of men.
THE EAGLE of Eli surveys the wood,
Seeking to surfeit on blood—
He thrives on the violence of men.
THE EAGLE of Pengwern with gray horn-beak,
Too shrill is his piercing voice,
A glutton for flesh [that I loved.]
THE EAGLE of Pengwern with gray horn-beak,
Too shrill his cry,
He gluts on Kynddylan's flesh.
THE EAGLE of Pengwern with gray horn-beak,
Too sharp his claws.
He gluts on the flesh of my love.
THE EAGLE of Pengwern, he calls
Tonight. For warriors' blood, he waits.
Tren shall be called the land of loss.
THE EAGLE of Pengwern, he calls
Tonight. For warriors' blood, he waits.
Tren shall be known as the vale of death.

• • •

BASSA CHURCH lies at rest
Tonight, collapsed upon itself,
Shelter in war, heart of the folk of Argoed!
BASSA CHURCH lies crumbled
Tonight. My very own tongue is the cause –
It, too, is red: too great is my grief.
BASSA CHURCH is a prison
Tonight, for the heir of the Kyndrwynin,
For blest Kynddylan, a burial ground.
BASSA CHURCH land is fallow
Tonight – its clover is wet with blood.
Ruddy, the ground: too full is my heart.
BASSA CHURCH holds no sanctuary
Now, with the Lloegriaus' killing of
Kynddylan, and Elvan of Powys.
BASSA CHURCH lies a ruin
Tonight: its war-men live no more,
The folk and men by whom I am known.
BASSA CHURCH is aglow
Tonight, and I can only weep.
It, too, is red: my grief overflows.

• • •

Y DREF WENN ym bronn y coet,
Ysef yw y hefras eiryoet,
Ar wyneb y gwellt y gwaet.
Y DREF WENN yn y thywyr –
Y hefras, y glas vyvyr,
Y gwaet a dan draet y gwyr.
Y DREF WENN yn y dyffrynt –
Llawen y bydeir, wrth gynanrud
Kat: ygwerin, neurderynt.
Y DREF WENN rwng Trenn a Throdwyd,
Oed gnodach ysgwyt tonn, yn dyvot o gat
Nogyt ych yechwyd.
Y DREF WENN rwng Trenn a Thraval.
Oed gnodach y gavet, ar
Wyneb [y] gwellt noc eredic brynar.

• • •

GWYNN Y BYT FFREUER mor yw diheint.
Heno, gwedy colli kenveint
O anffawt vyn tavawt yt llesseint°.
GWYNN Y BYT FFREUER! mor yw gwann
Heno, gwedy agheu Elvan,
Ac eryr Kyndrwyn, Kyndylan.
NYT ANGHEU FFREUER a'm de
Heno, am damorth brodyrde.
Duhunaf wylaf uore.
NYT ANGHEU FFREUER a'm gwna heint,
O dechreu nos hyt deweint,
Duhunaf wylaf bylgeint.
NYT ANGHEU FFREUER a'm tremyn
Heno, am gwna grudyeu melyn,
A chochen dagreu dros erchwyn.
NYT ANGHEU FFREUER a erwinaf
Heno, namyn my hun, yn wan glaf,
Vym brodyr a'm tymyr a gwynaf.
FFREUER WENN – Brodyr a'th uaeth,
Ny hannoedynt o'r diffaeth.
Wyr ny uegynt vygylyaeth.
FFREUER WENN, Brodyr a'th vu:
Pann glywynt gywrenin llu
Ny echyvydei ffyd ganthu.
MI A FFREUER a Medlan,
Kyt ytuo cat ym pob mann,
Ny'n tawr: ny ladawr an rann.

• • •

Y MYNYD kyt a tuo uch.
Nyt eidigafaf ydwyn vym buch.
Ys ysgawn gan rei vy ruch.
AM HAVAL ar avaerwy,
Yd aa Tren yn y Trydonwy,
Ac yd aa Twrch ym Marchnwy.
AM HAVAL° ar elvyden,
Ydaa Trydonwy yn Tren,
Ac yd aa Geirw yn Alwen.

• • •

BLEST TOWN in the bosom of th' wood –
This was always its end:
On the face of its grass, the blood.
BLESSÈD TOWN in the countryside –
Its destiny, a gray-green memory,
Blood beneath the feet of men.
BLESSÈD TOWN in the valley –
Joyful its troop in the heat of fight,
In carnage: its people now have perished.
BLEST TOWN between Trodwyd and Tren,
The shattered shield returned from field
As often as evening ox to barn.
BLEST TOWN between Traval and Tren.
More common was blood on its grassy turf
Than the ploughing of fallow land.

• • •

FAIR FREUER! How painful 'tis
Tonight, after this loss of kin.
By the fault of my tongue were they slain.
FAIR FREUER! Such sorrow
Tonight, after the death of Elvan,
And Kynddylan, the eagle of Kyndrwyn.
'TIS NOT FREUER'S FATE torments me
Tonight, but the death of our valiant brothers.
I lie awake, I weep at dawn;
NOT FREUER'S FATE that pierces with pain –
From dusk till the dead of night
I like awake, I weep with the sun.
'TIS NOT FREUER'S FATE that grieves me
Tonight, that yellows my cheek, and
Reddens the tears that o'erflow the bed;
NOT FREUER'S FATE that torments me
Tonight, but myself, being feeble and sick:
I mourn for my brothers, my land.
FAIR FREUER – belovèd of brothers,
No offspring of the ignoble were they,
But warriors who harbored no fear.
FAIR FREUER, They were your brothers, too:
Whenever they heard of a mighty host
Their confidence never failed.
FREUER AND ME, and Median:
While battles raged at every turn,
We had no fear: our side would not be slain.

• • •

THE MOUNTAIN, though it be high,
I'll not graze there, to prolong my life.
When nothing remains, I shall travel light.
JUST AS upon the boundary,
Tren receives the Roden,
And the Twrch falls into the Marchnwy,
JUST SO, upon the land.
The Roden descends to the Tren,
The Geirw falls into the Alwen.

KYNN BU VYG kylchet croennen°
Gavyr galet, chwannawc y gelein;
Ry'm goruc y nuedw ued Bryum. [1]
KYNN BU VYG kylchet croenen
Gavyr galet, kelyngar y llillen,
Ry'm goruc y uedw ued Trenn.
GWEDY VYM brodyr o dymyr Hafren,
Y am dwylan Dwyryw,
Gwae vi, Duw, vy mot yn vyw!
GWEDY MEIRCH hywed a chochwed
Dillat, a phlwawr [mawr] melyn,
Mein uyg coes ny'm oes dudedyn.

• • •

GWARTHEC Edeirnyawn ny buant
Gerdennin, a cherd neb nyt aethant,
Ym buw; Gorwynnyonn [gwr anchwant].
GWARTHEC Edeirnyawn ny buant,
Gerdennin. a chant neb ny cherdynt,
Ym byw Gorwynnyon, gwr eduynt°.
GWARTHEGYD GWERTH gwyla negyd.
Ar a dyvo dra, gwarth a'e deubyd.
Mi a wydwn a oed da:
Gwaet am y gilyd, gwrda.
BEI GWREIC GYRTHMWL, bydei gwan [2]
Hediw. Bydei bann y disgyr:
Hi gyva, diva y gwyr.
TYWARCHEN ERCAL ar erdywal, wyr.
O etived Moryal:
A gwedy rys macrysmal.

• • •

HELEDD HWYEDIC y'm gelwir,
"O Duw, pa diw yt° rodir;
Meirch vym brodyr° ac eu tir?"
HELED HWYEDIC a'm kyveich:
"O Duw, padiw yt° rodir gurumseirch.
Kyndylan a'e bedwardeg meirch?"
NEUR SYLLEIS olygon ar dirion dir
O orsed orwynnyon.
Hir hwyl heul; hwy vyghouyon.
NEUR LLYSSEIS [olygon] o dinlleu
Ureconn, Ffreuer werydre,
Hiraeth am damorth vrodyrde. [3]
MARCHAWC o Gaer adanaw,
Nyt oed hwyr a gwynnyon,
Gwr o Sanneir. [4]
LLAS VYM BRODYR ar vnweith,
Kynan, Kynndylan, Kynnwreith;
Yn amwyn Tren, tref diffeith.
NY SANGHEI WEHELYTH ar nyth
Kyndylan. Ny thechei droetued vyth.
Ny vagas y uam uab llyth.

MY COVERS, THEN, were made of the hide
Of the hardy goat – intent I was on carnage,
Being made drunk on the beer of Bryurn. [1]
MY COVERS, THEN, were made of the hide
Of the hardy goat, the kid who's fond of holly:
I, too, was made drunk on the mead of Tren.
NO MORE, my brothers of Severn's vale,
From the banks of both the Rhiws –
(Alas, God, that I survive!)
AFTER THE HORSES, trapped out in red, lie broken,
After the waving of yellow plumes,
My legs are thin. No covers remain.

• • •

THE CATTLE of Edeyrniawn never strayed,
With none did they wander away,
In the lifetime of Gorwynion, great man of war.
THE CATTLE of Edeyrniawn, then, never strayed,
No company carried them off, not
When Gowrynion, wise war-man, had life.
THE HERDSMAN knows only shame and contempt.
He who suffers, wins no respect.
I know what is good:
For the blood of one warrior, another.
WERE GYRTHMWL A WOMAN, she'd be weak [2]
This day. Shrill would be her cry:
She would wail the loss of her heroes.
ERCAL'S SOIL covers men of courage.
Dirt now lies upon Moryal's line:
The earth, having fed, returns them to dust.

• • •

I SHALL BE KNOWN as wandering Heledd.
O God, to whom are given
My brothers' horses, and their land?
WANDERING HELEDD's greeting:
"O God, to whom are given the dark trappings
Of Kynddylan and his fourteen steeds?"
I HAVE GAZED with mine eyes on fallow land
From the mound of Gorwynion.
Long, the course of the sun; longer, my remembrance.
I HAVE GAZED with mine eyes, from
Wrecon, upon Freuer's heritage:
I grieve that our valiant brothers are dead. [3]
A HORSEMAN from Caer beneath him,
He was slow to complain,
That man of Sannair. [4]
SLAIN WERE MY BROTHERS, at once,
Kynan, Kynddylan, Kynwraith –
In defending Tren, a town laid waste.
PRINCES DARED NOT tread on the nest
Of Kynddylan. He would not retreat one inch.
His mother nursed no weakling son.

---

[1] Cf. lines 138, 171; Heledd may have called for war, prophesying victory; *gelyn:carnage...holly* ] blood-drops

[2] *Gyrthmwl* ] possibly a herdsman, though the name probably derives from Gwyrth-Mael, *prince of miracles.*

[3] *Wrecon* ] Wroxeter

[4] *Caer* ] Chester; *Gwr o Sanneir : man of Sannair* ] uncertain text, possibly corrupt

BRODYR, a'm bwyat ny vall,
A dyvynt ual gwyal coll;
O un y un edynt oll.
BRODYR, a'm bwyat a duc
Duw ragof: vy anffawt a'e goruc.
Ny obrynynt ffaw yr ffuc.

• • •

TENEU AWEL tew lletkynt,
Pereid y rycheu; ny phara
Ae goreu, [tru] ar a vu nat ydynt.
AS CLYWO a Duw a dyn,
As clywo y ieveinc a hyn,
Mevyl barveu madeu Hedyn.
YM BYW Hedyn° ehedyei
Dillat yn aros gwaedvei,
A'r glas vereu haf nwyfei.
RYVEDAF dincleir na diw
Yn ol, kilyd kelvyd, clyw!
Yg gwall tyrch torri cneu kynw.
NY WN y° ae nywl ae mwc,
Ae ketwyr yn kyuamwc.
Ygweirglawd, aer yssyd drwc.
EDEWEIS y weirglawd aer ysgwyt.
Digyvyng, dinas y gedyrn,
Goreu gwr, Garanmael.
KARANMAE, kymwy arnat.
Atwen dy ystlen° o gat.
Gnawt man ar gran kyniviat.
KYMWED ognaw llaw hael,
Mab Kynndylan clot avael,
Dywedwr Kynndrwynin, Caranmael.
OED DIHEID ac oed [dihat],
Oed diholedic tref tat,
A geissywys Caranmael yn ynat.
KARANMAEL, kymwed ognaw,
Mab Kyndylan clot arllaw,
Nyt ynat kyt mynat ohonaw.
Pan wisgei GARANMAL gatpeis Gyndylan,
A phyrydyaw y onnen,
Ny chaffei Ffranc tranc oe benn.

• • •

AMSER Y BUUM° vras vwyt
Ny dyrchafwn vy mordwyt
Yr gwr a gwynei claf gornwyt.
BRODYR a'm bwyat inneu
Nys cwynei glevyt cornnwydeu;
Un Elvan, Kyndylan deu.
NY MAT WISC BRIGER nyw dirper o wr
Yn dirvawr gywryssed.
Nyt oed levawr vym broder.

BROTHERS I had who never were forlorn.
They grew straight as the hazel tree.
One by one, they fell.
BROTHERS I had, taken from me
By God: my own misfortune, the cause.
They would not purchase fame by deceit.

• • •

A LIGHT BREEZE, and a thick storm.
Furrows remain. Those who made them, are gone.
Those who have been, exist no more.
LET IT BE HEARD by God and man,
Let it be heard by young and old:
Disgrace on their beards for failing Hedyn!
IN THE LIFETIME of Hedyn, he shot forth,
Enduring all upon the field,
With the grey-blue blades of a lord he provoked.
I WONDER at that which approaches:
Skillful defenders, listen!—
In dens of the boar, pigs breaking nuts:
IS THAT NOT MIST? Is it smoke?—
Or is it warriors, engaged in fight?
On farmland, slaughter is a terrible thing.
I'VE HEARD In the fields the clatter of shields.
A fortress cannot contain the strong,
The best of men, Caránmaèl.
CARANMAEL, you are pressed by the foe.
I know your course of fight:
On the cheeks of a warrior dwell many scars.
MIRTH-MAKING, extending a liberal hand,
The son of Kynddylan, retainer of praise,
The last son of Kyndrwyn, Caranmael.
THEY WERE FORSAKEN, deprived,
Their heritage lost, those who
For their vengeance, Caranmael sought.
CARANMAEL, mirth-making,
Praise-giving Kynddylan's son,
Was no avenger, though that was his wish.
When CARANMAEL wore armor of Kynddylan,
When he shook his ashen spear,
The Franks from him had no relief.

• • •

IN THE DAYS when I fared on rich repast,
I scorned to lift up my thighs
For a man who complained of his scabs.
BROTHERS, too, I had
Who would not complain of the plague.
Elvan, for one. Kynddylan, too.
'TIS NOT GRACEFUL HAIR that becomes
A man engaged the heat of a fight.
My brothers were not men who fussed.

ONYT RAC AGHEU ac aeleu,
Mawr agloes glas uereu,
Ny bydaf levawr inneu.

• • •

MAES MAODYN neus cud rew.
O diva da y odew
Ar ued Eirinved eiry tew.
TOM ELWITHAN neus gwlych glaw,
Maes Maodyn y danaw?
Dylyei Gynon y gwynaw.

• • •

PEDWAR PWN BRODER a'm bu,
Ac y bob un penn teulu.
Ny wyr Tren perchen y du.
PEDWAR PWN BRODER a'm buant.
Ac y bob un, gorwyf nwyvant.
Ny wyr Tren perchen kugant.
PEDWAR PWN TERWYN o adwyn
Vrodyr a'm buant o Gyndrwyn.
Nyt oes y Drenn berchen mwyn.

SAVE ONLY FOR DEATH and its torment,
And the wound of the grey-bladed spear,
Neither shall I lament.

• • •

THE PLAIN OF MAODYN lies covered with frost
Since the man of goodwill was destroyed:
On the mound of Eirinwed, thick the snow.
The BARROW OF ELWYDDAN, soaked with rain
And, below, the plain of Maodyn:
Kynon must be lamented as well.

• • •

FOUR NOBLE BROTHERS, I knew:
Each was the head of a host.
Tren knows no keeper now.
FOUR NOBLE BROTHERS, had I.
Full of vigor, each of them.
No kind keeper has Tren, tonight.
FOUR TRUE BROTHERS, comely
And bold had I, from Kyndrwyn.
No more has Tren a keeper of joy.

In *The Red Book of Hergest*, the Canu Heledd ends with two corrupt stanzas, the text and translation of which are uncertain; the point of which seems to be that Heledd will seek death in the woods rather than be captured by the invading tribes and be made a concubine or slave:

GOSGO yghot, adot arnat.
Nyt wyt bylgeint gyvot.
Neum gwant ysgwr o gwrr dy got.
GOSGO di yghot athecf— [325]
Nyt wyt ymadrawd dibech.
Nyt gwiw clein yth grein y grech.

FLY infidelity, the mark of death.
You'll not rise at dawn
To feel the piercing lust of those men.
FLY to the wood and hide yourself—
Better that, than yield to shame.
Nor is it worth to stoop, to grovel, and weep.

Seven additional Heledd stanzas are preserved in the Black Book of Carmarthen. Though formally imperfect and possibly corrupt, the stanzas sung by Heledd for her sisters and for her brother Cynddylan, provide a poignant alternative ending for the Canu Heledd of the Red Book of Hergest:

**Chwiorydd Heledd**

AMSER Y BUANT addfwyn,
I cerid merched cyndrwyn:
Heledd, Gwladus a Gwenddwyn.
CHWIORYDD a'm bu° diddan.
Mi a'u colleis oll achlan:
Ffreuer, Medwyl a Medlan.
CHWIORYDD a'm bu hefyd,
Mi a'u collais oll i gyd:
Gwledyr, Meysir a Cheinfryd.

**Sisters of Heledd**

IN THE DAY when each was fair,
Belov'd were the daughters of Kyndrwyn:
Heledd, Gwladus, and Gwenddwyn.
MY SISTERS, enchanting they were:
I lost them all, each one,
Freuer, Meddwyl and Meddlan.
SISTERS had I more,
I have lost them all:
Gwledyr, Ceinfryd, and Meisir.

**Cynddyllan y Cynwraith**

LLAS CYNDDYLAN, llas Cynwraith,
Yn amwyn Tren, tref ddiffaith.
Gwae fi, fawr aros eu llaith.

**Kynddyllan and Kynwraith**

KYNDDYLAN WAS SLAIN, Kynwraith was killed,
Defending Tren, a desolate town.
The woe is mine, their death, ever to endure.

# ANGLO-SAXON Period (410 - 1066)

*Hluꝺe ƿæꞃan hẏ, la, hluꝺe, ða hẏ oꝼeꞃ þone hlæƿ ꞃiꝺan,*
*ƿæꞃan anmoꝺe, ða hẏ oꝼeꞃ lanꝺ ꞃiꝺan.*
*Scẏlꝺ ðu ðe nu, þu ðẏꞅne nið ᵹeneꞅan moꞇe.*
*Uꞇ, lẏꞇel ꞅpeꞃe, ᵹiꝼ heꞃ inne ꞅie!*
*Sꞇoꝺ unꝺeꞃ linꝺe, unꝺeꞃ leohꞇum ꞅcẏlꝺe,*
*þæꞃ ða mihꞇiᵹan ƿiꝼ hẏꞃa mæᵹen beꞃæꝺꝺon*
*anꝺ hẏ ᵹẏllenꝺe ᵹaꞃaꞅ ꞅænꝺan...*
—Wið færstice feferfuige (9th century)
B.L. MS Harleian 585, fols. 75-6

*Loud they were, yes, loud, when over the hill they rode,*
*Fierce they were, when over the land they rode.*
*Shield thee now, that this violence thou may'st escape.*
*Out, little spear, if herein you be!*
*I stood under linden, under a light shield,*
*When the mighty women their power prepared*
*And sent their screaming spears...*
—Charm for a sudden stitch (trans. DWF)

SAXONS made their presence felt in Roman-occupied Britain from the second century, with periodic raids on the eastern coast. Picts and Scots made frequent incursions from the north (which motivated both Hadrian's and the Antonine walls, as lines of defense). In the early fifth century, when Rome abandoned the island, Britain was left unprotected. In the power vacuum that ensued, the Britons while fighting amongst themselves hired Germanic mercenaries to defend the northern border – but that expediency led to their own undoing. The Angles and Saxons loved the island so well that they invaded *en masse* and took possession, employing essentially the same strategy in Britain that would be used by their devout descendants centuries later, in North America, and with a similar result: throughout much of Britain, the native culture and language were extirpated. By the mid-ninth century, what is now called England (Angle-land) was almost entirely Anglo-Saxon, the Britons retreating to the north and west. On land that had been inhabited by Celts for a millennium, very little evidence of their presence survived after the conquest besides the earth-mounds (and place-names, but not many of those: even *Stonehenge*, built long before the Celts, derives its name from Old English).

As with the Britons, Anglo-Saxon women were permitted and often required to serve on the battlefield as combatants, cheerleaders, or decoys. What Tacitus writes of Germania appears to have been true of Anglo-Saxons as well: Women, he wrote, "are to each man the most sacred witnesses to his courage; these, his most generous backers. The soldier brings his wounds to mother and wife, who shrink not from counting and even demanding his gashes, and who provide food and encouragement to the warriors. Tradition has it that armies already faltering and giving way have been rallied by their women who, with earnest cries and their bosoms laid bare, have vividly represented the terrors of captivity – which the Germans fear with extreme dread in behalf of their women... Their men, who believe there to be a sanctity and prescience in the [female] sex, neither despise their advice nor take their answers lightly."[1]

Anglo-Saxon women were afforded limited self-determination, and (though often overstated today) significant agency under the law. Marriage was a mixed bag: Noble women had at least the right to choose whom they would marry or refuse. (Some daughters, *freoþuwebban* ["peace-weavers"], were still married for political reasons, with or without the maiden's consent.) From the early seventh century onward, as Christianity spread, the clergy of the new religion enjoined wives to obey their husbands, and encouraged husbands to discipline their wives with physical beatings. Women's sexual pleasure was condemned, even within marriage; adultery by either party was punished. Divorce was rarely sought, and rarely permitted.

That said, wealthy wives retained limited autonomy, even with respect to child-bearing (Queen Aethelflaed after having a child refused to bear a second); nor could a husband legally repudiate a wife for a failure to bear children. If the husband died first, Anglo-Saxon law required that the widow remain unmarried for a year; but it also her guarded her rights in communal property and child-custody.

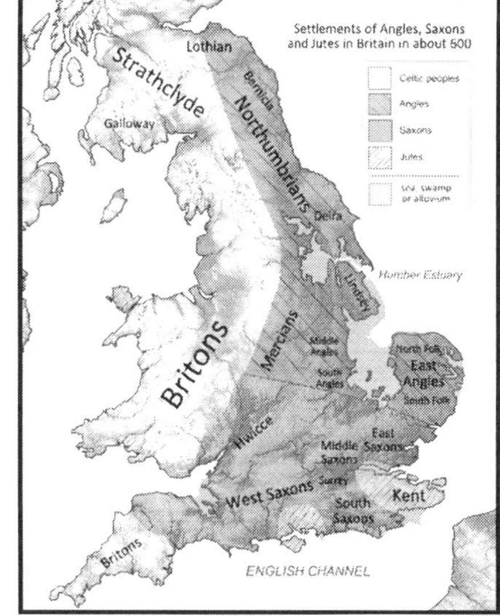

fr. W.R. Shepherd, *The Historical Atlas* (1926)

[1] Tacitus (56-117 CE), *Germania*, chaps. 7-8, trans. DWF.

A noblewoman could inherit, alienate, and bequeath land in her own right; and a bride with real estate retained a limited interest after marriage, including the right to choose her heirs as she pleased (even to disinherit her children). About a fourth of the extant wills from Anglo-Saxon England were made by women, from which it appears that many noblewomen were not only literate but well-read: mention is made of their private libraries. The Church denied women the right to teach, take oaths, or serve as a judge. But many aristocratic women participated fully in public affairs and, to a limited degree, in the legal system. Correspondence survives in which we find noblewomen serving as advocates and property agents, for themselves and others.

Little is known of the conditions of life for Anglo-Saxon serfs and slaves, the invisible majority. That bondwomen were at the disposal of men, quite literally, is illustrated in legislation under Æthelbert (king of Kent, 590-616), which stipulates that if a man rapes a female slave, he must pay sixty shillings to her "owner," as wergild for having damaged his property; thirty shillings, if the victim was not still a virgin.

Some free Anglo-Saxon women earned a comfortable income by cloth-making (the skills of weaving and embroidery being passed from one generation of professionals to the next). Others sold goods at market, or worked by commission as "cunning women." A privileged few who decided not to marry could join a convent – the most prestigious of which, Barking Abbey, afforded its inmates the medieval equivalent of a university education, with training in history, grammar, rhetoric, and Latin.

During the ninth and tenth centuries, the seven Anglo-Saxon kingdoms were under constant stress from attacks by the Danes, who eventually conquered all but Wessex. It was Alfred the Great (849-899) who finally drove back the Danes and established a united kingdom. Mindful of falling standards of literacy and learning (one result of the Viking invasions), Alfred also initiated a plan of educational reform that focused on the production of manuscripts written in English rather than Latin. (Many Old English manuscripts that survive from the tenth century represent translations, commissioned by Alfred, from Latin texts.) Our rich extant corpus of Old English also includes some 30,000 lines of poetry, in a range of genres, chiefly in four manuscripts: the Beowulf manuscript, the Vercelli Book, the Junius Manuscript, and the Exeter Book.

Much of what we know about England for the period 410-1066 comes from the Anglo-Saxon Chronicle, a collection of annals begun in the ninth century, probably in Wessex under the patronage of Alfred the Great. Multiple copies were placed in monasteries across England, where they were independently augmented. Nine copies survive, one of which was still being updated as late as 1154, nearly a full century after the Norman Conquest brought the Anglo-Saxon period to a close.

DWF

Replica of a ceremonial helmet from Sutton Ho, near Woodbridge, the site of two Anglo-Saxon cemeteries, of the 6th and early 7th centuries.
(Courtesy of the British Museum)

Remains of a bejeweled Anglo-Saxon woman buried with a sacrificial cow, late fifth century, uncovered in 2012 by students from Manchester Metropolitan University and the University of Central Lancashire. (Photocredit: BBC)

# Women's verse in *The Exeter Book*

*Þæt mon eaþe tosliteð*
*þætte næfre gesomnad wæs*
– *Wulf*, 18-19

THE tradition of women's wordcraft, in English, begins with the feminine voice in "Wulf," an Anglo-Saxon lyric that has become widely known – though not well understood – as "Wulf and Eadwacer." The Wikipedia article on this ancient text begins, "*Wulf and Eadwacer* is an Old English poem of famously difficult interpretation. It has been variously characterized, (modernly) as an elegy, (historically) as a riddle, and (in speculation on the poem's pre-history) as a song or ballad with refrain. The poem's complexities are, however, often asserted simply to defy genre classification, especially with regard to its narrative content..." It opens like a riddle, which in Old English typically begin, "Ic (ge)seah" (*I saw*), indicating a creature's identity to be discovered; "Ic gefrægn" (*I have heard*) or "Ic wat" (*I knew*). To say, however, that "We do not yet know what 'Wulf' means" would be a misleading statement: its "meaning" is not located outside the text, or in the text itself, but rather in the interpretive work of the singer or her audience, the scribe or his readers. We have no reason to suppose that "Wulf" ever referenced "real-life" people or events or creatures which, if known, would lead us to the original composer's intention; and to suppose that "the meaning" inhabits the words on the page, as a fixed though hidden quantity, like a buried gem, is naïve.

Far from meaningless, "Wolf" may be among the most meaning-full verse in the history of our literature; for it can be read as a 117-word statement about meaning itself: the singer presents her auditors (or the scribe, his readers) with an invitation, quite possibly a *dare*, to produce coherence from a thoughtfully constructed ambiguity.

"Wolf" survives in the *Codex Exoniensis,* or "Exeter Book," a manuscript anthology compiled by monks ca. 960-990 CE. By the mid-eleventh century, the volume was owned by Leofric, first Bishop of Exeter (d. 1072); who donated it to the Cathedral library. The Exeter Book is our largest extant collection of Anglo-Saxon verse: in addition to songs, religious and elegiac poetry, the Exeter Book contains some ninety Anglo-Saxon riddles; and it has been said that "Wulf" is one of them. But a "riddle," like a mystery novel, is a declarative text: it begins with a question that leads to an answer. Riddles – whether for performance by an ancient scop, or read in a book, or posted to the Internet – supply necessary hints while leading to a solution, an "answer" that is supplied either by the text itself, or by a canny auditor. "Wulf," however, is a puzzle without a solution.

Insistently interrogative, the poet/singer defeats every effort by her audience to localize its referentiality. Like Shakespeare's *Hamlet,* or Thomas Pynchon's *Crying of Lot 49,* the poem raises questions that the poem itself "knows" cannot be answered. For instance:

Is "Wulf" (*wolf*) a proper name? a term of endearment? or a *canis lupis*?

Does *my tribe* reference the speaker's native family and tribe? or is it a folk to whom she is now consigned – as the bride of an arranged exogamous marriage? as a girl captured in a raid? as an exile?

If Wolf should come to the speaker's island, will he be received by her people as a help, or as a helping to be torn and devoured?

Whose isle is inhabited by a *murderous* folk: his or hers, or both?

Is Wolf, on that distant island, an exile? a prisoner? a premarital romantic interest of the speaker? the speaker's lost son? an imagined gallant who could rescue the narrator from an unhappy marriage?

Does the singer reference *eadwacer* as a proper name, or as an unnamed *protector of wealth*?

Is it implied that Wolf has prior knowledge of the speaker's sickness – her deprivation, her lack (or refusal) of food, of her heart's longing – or do the proffered symptoms merely underscore the singer's futile inability to be heard or seen or pitied by her absent (or present) significant Other?

Is it Wolf, or Eadwacer, or both, or the same man, who has wrapped the speaker in his arms? And what aspect or condition of that embrace has she found pleasant ("wyn") or loathsome ("lað")?

If two – or even three – different men are produced in the mind of the audience, which one is the singer's friend; and which, her foe? And which is the husband? (The ambivalent feeling of the woman-narrator toward the male Other finds expression in her ambiguity.)

Near the close, a fourth (or at least a third) figure enters the narrative: the inauspicious offspring: "Our pitiful cub / Wolf [or wolf] shall bear to the woods": With *Wolf* far distant and inaccessible, shall a *wolf* appear in his place, to claim the child? Is the stated abduction figured as a worry, a prediction, a hope, or a threat? Has the child (whelp) already been born, or is it still in utero? Is the infant to be doomed (or rescued) because it is unwanted, or coveted? Will the singer's song – a song unsung, with Wolf – be undone *by* the taking of her cub?

**Of Ladies and Lords**. *Lady* in Old English begins as a compound word, a contraction of *hlaf* (loaf, bread) + *dige* (kneader [*fem.*]); and *lord*, as a contraction of *hlaf,* + *weard* (keeper, ward, guard). Over the centuries, *hlaf-weard* becomes *hlavord, hlaord, laord, lord. Hlæfdige* becomes *hlafedig, hlefwedi, levedy, leuedy, leudi, lady*. The etymologyical ancestor of the modern English *lady* is thus the Anglo-Saxon maker of bread; while the modern English *lord* descends from the Anglo-Saxon male responsible the food supply, whether as master of a household, or as an imaginary bread-giver in the heavens. *Woman* derives from Old English *wifman* (fr. *wif,* woman, + *manna,* human being) and not from the ubiquituous but spurious early modern etymology that she is called "*Woeman*, because she is a *woe* unto *man.*"

A final puzzle: How cannot it be *easy* to "undo" what was "never united"? – and who will do the undoing?

The illogic of the singer's final assertion works much like the syllogism that closes Shakespeare Sonnet 116: "If this be error and upon me prov'd, / I never writ, nor no man ever loved." The narrator insists upon the survival of an ideal that exists only as imagined in the speaker's own words, not in the world "out there." From the singer's point of view, the statement is self-referential, and perhaps self-congratulatory. Still disunited are the various clues, planted in lines 1 through 18, of which the song, "Wulf," is comprised: the text seems self-aware that its statements of fact cannot be brought together in a coherent frame of reference. "Wolf" at the close thereby asserts its own lack of referentiality, its own passive-aggressive putting-asunder of whatever, or whomever, its interpreters may have joined together. He who attempts to discover and conquer the singer's implied sense – dozens of critical essays have assayed the poem's "meaning" – do not get it.

To suppose historicity – to hypothesize that some originary scop, or hausfrau, had in mind a specific Wolf, a real-life Eadwacer, two geographically specific islands, and an unhappy love-life – is a pointless game of pretend. Nothing in the text implies that "Wulf" was originally composed to memorialize, or to entertain, an Anglo-Saxon king or warrior or celebrity or legend. Moreover, even if there were some occasion that originally called for the poem's invention, that cannot be why the poem was preserved (when so much else was lost or forgotten). The *language* of "Wulf" was more familiar to singers and auditors of the tenth and eleventh centuries than to our own generation; but the text presented them with no more *information* than it presents to us: the singer tells no single story, but calls up a range of possible narratives, all of which arise from what it means to live as a woman in a man's world ("Sindon wælreowe"), a ferocious folk, a culture of valiant bloodshed.

A poem, it has often been said, can mean many things – but it cannot mean just *any*thing. So, too, with "Wolf": from the text's statements of fact, a finite number of internally consistent narratives can be constructed. But what this remarkable lyric ultimately achieves, in its dogged resistance to closure, is more than a set of imagined stories. The speaker or singer of "Wulf" delivers an emotion, the distilled experience of isolation, of powerless despair, a song of falling in the woods when there is no one to hear. "Wolf" offers no solution, but instead constructs feminine longing for a resolution that cannot be had, a hymn that cannot be sung, by him. Seen in this light, the text offers something more than a riddle, or elegy, or martial epic can do: it creates, for the attentive audience, the quintessential experience of the feminine; the apprehension of being trapped within a masculinist culture while desiring something more, something other than *this*, a harmony that cannot be and a subject self whose subjectivity cannot be predicated.

DWF

## [Wulf]

Leoꝺum iꞅ minum ꞅƿẏlce him mon lac ᵹiꝼe ƿillað hẏ hi
ne aþecᵹan ᵹiꝼhe onþꞃeaꞇ cẏmeð unᵹelic iꞅ uꞅ · ƿulꝼ
iꞅ on ieᵹe icon oþeꞃꞃe ꝼæꞅꞇ iꞅ þæꞇ eᵹlonꝺ ꝼenne bi
ƿoꞃƿen ꞅinꝺon ƿælꞃeoƿe ƿeꞃaꞅ þæꞃ on iᵹe ƿillað hẏ
hine aþecᵹan ᵹiꝼ he on þꞃeaꞇ cẏmeð unᵹelice iꞅ uꞅ
ƿulꝼeꞅ ic mineꞅ ƿiꝺ laꞅꞇum ƿenum ꝺoᵹoꝺe ƿōn hiꞇ ƿæꞅ
ꞃeniᵹ ƿeꝺeꞃ onꝺ ic ꞃeo ꞇuᵹu ꞅæꞇ þōn mec ꞅe beaꝺu caꝼa
boᵹum bileᵹꝺe ƿæꞅ me ƿẏn toþōn ƿæꞅ me hƿæþꞃe eac
lað ƿulꝼmin ƿulꝼ ƿena me þine ꞅeoce ᵹeꝺẏꝺon þine
ꞅelꝺ cẏmaꞅ muꞃnenꝺe moꝺ naleꞅ meꞇe liꞅꞇe ᵹehẏꞃeꞅꞇ þu,
eaꝺ ƿaceꞃ unceꞃne eaꞃne hƿelp biꞃeð ƿulꝼ ꞇoƿuꝺa þæꞇ
mon eaþe ꞇoꞅliꞇeð þæꞇꞇe næꝼꞃe ᵹeꞅomnaꝺ ƿæꞅ unceꞃ ᵹieꝺꝺ
ᵹeaꝺoꞃ ·]

## [Wulf]

Leodum is minum    swylce him mon lac gife
Willað hy hine aþecgan    gif he on þreat cymeð
Ungelic is us
Wulf is on iege    ic on oþerre
Fæst is þæt eglond    fenne biworpen
Sindon wælreowe    weras þær on ige
Willað hy hine aþecgan    gif he on þreat cymeð
Ungelice is us
Wulfes ic mines widlastum    wenum dogode
Þonne hit wæs renig weder    ond ic reotugu sæt
Þonne mec se beaducafa    bogum bilegde
Wæs me wyn to þon    wæs me hwæþre eac lað
Wulf min Wulf    wena me þine
Seoce gedydon    þine seldcymas
Murnende mod    nales meteliste
Gehyrest þu, Eadwacer    Uncerne ear[m]ne hwelp
Bireð wulf to wuda
Þæt mon eaþe toslitеð    þætte næfre gesomnad wæs
Uncer giedd geador

## Wolf

To my tribe it's as if    he's a helping for them
If he comes to the troop    they'll partake of that gift
Our lots are unlike
Wolf is on one isle    I on another
That isle is a fastness    begirt by a fen
A ferocious folk    inhabit the isle
If he comes to the troop    they'll partake of that gift
Our lots are unlike
I have longed for my Wolf    with far-reaching desire
When the weather was rainy    and I sat in my tears
When the man brave in battle wrapped me in his arms
It was winsome for me    but loathsome as well
Wolf my Wolf    'twas my thoughts of thee
So seldom seen    my mourning mind
That made me sick    not lack of food
Hearest thou Eadwacer[?]    Our pitiful cub
Wolf shall bear to the wood
What was never united    is easily undone [1]
Our song together

trans. DWF

---

[1] *is easily undone* ] lit., one easily slits asunder.

## [Heofung]

## [Heofung]

Ic þis giedd wrece bi me ful geomorre minre sylfre sið
ic þæt secgan mæg hwæt ic yrmþa gebad siþþan icuppeox
niwes oþþe ealdes no ma þon nu a ic wite wonn minra
wræc siþa ærest min hlaford gewat heonan of leodū
ofer yþa gelac hæfde ic uht ceare hwær min leod fru
ma londes wære · ða ic me feran gewat folgað secan
wineleas wrecca for minre wea þearfe · ongunnon ꝥ
þæs monnes magas hycgan þurh dyrne geþoht ꝥ hy
todælden unc þæt wit gewidost inworuldrice lifdon
lað licost 7mec longade · het mec hlaford min her
heard niman ahte ic leofra lyt onþissum lond ste
de holdra freonda forþon is min hyge geomor ·
ða ic me fulgemæcne monnan funde heard sælig ne
hyge geomorne mod miþende morþor hycgende
bliþe gebæro ful oft wit beotedan ꝥ unc ne ge dælde
nemne deað ana owiht elles eft is þæt onhworfen is
nu swa hit nowære freond scipe uncer seal ic feor ge
neah mines fela leofan fæhðu dreogan heht mec
mon wunian onwuda bearwe under ac treo in þā ·
eorð scræfe · eald is þes eorð sele eal ic eom oflongad ·
sindon dena dimme duna up hea bitre burg tunas
brerum beweax ne wic wynna leas ful oft mec her wra
þe begeat from siþ frean frynd sind oneorþan leofe
lifgende leger weardiað þon icon uhtan ana gonge
under ac treo geond þas eorð scrafu þær ic sittan
mot sumor lang ne · dæg þæric wepan mæg mine
wræc siþas earfoþa fela forþon ic æfre ne mæg þære
mod ceare minre gerestan · ne ealles þæs longaþes þe
mec onþissū life begeat ascyle geong mon wesan geo
mor mod heard heortan geoþoht swylce habban sceal
bliþe gebæro eac þon breost ceare sin sorgna ge dreag
sy æt him sylfū gelong eal his worulde wyn sy ful wi
de fah feorres folc londes þæt min freond siteð
under stan hliþe storme behrimed wine werig mod
wætre beflowen ondreor sele dreogeð se min wine
micle mod ceare he ge mon to oft wyn licran wic
wabið þam þe sceal oflangoþe leofes abidan ·7

# A Lamentation (ca. 900 CE)

*Ic þis giedd wrece*
*bi me ful geomorre...*
– [*Heofung*], 1-2

FOR many generations, scholars stated as fact that Anglo-Saxon women did not produce poetry. Hence, two lyrics in the *Codex Exoniensis* – known as "Wulf and Eadwacer" (fol. 100-01) and "The Wife's Lament" (fol. 115), though composed for a woman's voice – and though produced and sung in an oral culture for a largely illiterate audience – must have been originally produced by male scops.

That circular argument avoids the obvious. We have no record of female poets in Anglo-Saxon "Angle-lond"; but neither have we any evidence that male scops routinely adopted a feminine "I" for their own performance.

Medieval verse for a woman's voice survives outside the Exeter Book. "The Wife's Lament" closely resembles the German *frauenlied*, of which numerous examples have survived. The evidence of continental exemplars, though sparse, suggests that women throughout the medieval period sang songs, and composed, and improvised, and passed lyrics along to the next generation, just as men have done. That only a small number of Anglo-Saxon elegies and lays, by *anyone*, were eventually put into writing is our loss; but the mere fact that so little has survived tells us nothing about the circulation and transmission of songs by lay people, male and female, who neither belonged to a religious order, nor enjoyed professional status as a king's jester, musician, scop, or scribe.

It has been said that no Anglo-Saxon woman who *did* compose verse is likely to have produced anything quite so formally correct and deeply moving as "Wulf" or "The Wife's Lament." But that, too, is a specious argument. On the available evidence, it may require less faith to credit originary female composition of these poems, than to suppose there existed an Anglo-Saxon male with the ability to shed his phallocentric speaking position so effectively as to evoke feminine despair, a singer with a longing heart but without agency.[1]

["The Wife's Lament"] – the title assigned by modern critical convention to a second untitled woman's song in The Exeter Book – is a misnomer, an interpretive move even more reductive than ["Wulf *and* Eadwacer."] To assume that the song must represent the grief of a forsaken wife is to ignore the singer's own words. The imposed title supposes a woman whose life has been rendered incomplete, and her happiness ended, by the loss of her spouse. But the husband who has gone missing from the singer's life is himself figured as radically unsatisfactory – peremptory, unhappy, and violent. So, too, is the kinship circle that provides a social context for the singer's misery: "never since childhood" has she known joy. Yes, she remembers a time when love for her man – her husband, or another – made obedience seem less onerous. But happiness is figured here as skin deep, the blithe demeanor of men who smile, and smile, and smile, even while plotting the next round of internecine or intertribal violence.

**English in an Indo-European language**

| Sanskrit | Greek | Latin | Old Eng. | Mod. Eng. |
|---|---|---|---|---|
| *bharami* | *phero* | *fero* | *bera* | *bear* |
| *bratar* | *phrater* | *frater* | *brōþor* | *brother* |
| *pitá* | *patḗr* | *pater* | *fater* | *father* |
| *padam* | *póda* | *pedem* | *fōt* | *foot* |
| *tryah* | *tris* | *tres* | *þrēo* | *three* |

If "Wolf" is a masterpiece of ambiguity, "The Wife's Lament" is a study in ambivalent feeling. The narrator can imagine something very like "romantic love" – or at least, the mutually satisfied desire of "loving companions alive on the earth / in their bed." But in actual practice, the endless feud, the meddling of powerful kin, the hypocrisy of revenge, the routine disposal of women as objects of exchange reduce love to a longing for that which cannot be had. Whatever the original circumstance of its composition may have been, "The Wife's Lament" reads less like empathic ventriloquism by a male scop than like a feminine critique of a society inimical to woman's happiness. Insofar as a title is needed for a remarkable poem that survived for nearly a thousand years without one, the modern English translation is here called, simply, "A Lamentation."

DWF

[1] The gender of the speaker has been debated. See Bambas (1963), Stevens (1968), Lucas (1969), Mandel (1987), Desmond (1990), Klinck (1994) (in Bibliography of Works Cited).

## [Heofung]

Ic þis giedd wrece bi me ful geomorre
minre sylfre sið ic þæt secgan mæg
hwæt ic yrmþa gebad siþþan ic up [a]weox
niwes oþþe ealdes no ma þonne nu
a ic wite wonn minra wræcsiþa
Ærest min hlaford gewat heonan of leodum
ofer yþa gelac hæfde ic uhtceare
hwær min leodfruma londes wære
ða ic me feran gewat folgað secan
wineleas wræcca for minre weaþearfe
Ongunnon þæt þæs monnes magas hycgan
þurh dyrne geþoht þæt hy todælden unc
þæt wit gewidost in woruldrice
lifdon laðlicost ond mec longade
Het mec hlaford min her [eard] niman
ahte ic leofra lyt on þissum londstede
holdra freonda forþon is min hyge geomor
Đa ic me ful gemæcne monnan funde
heardsæligne hygegeomorne
mod miþendne morþor hycgend[n]e
bliþe gebæro ful oft wit beotedan
þæt unc ne gedælde nemne deað ana
owiht elles eft is þæt onhworfen
is nu [fornumen] swa hit no wære
freondscipe uncer s[c]eal ic feor ge neah
mines felaleofan fæhðu dreogan
Heht mec mon wunian on wuda bearwe
under actreo in þam eorðscræfe
eald is þes eorðsele eal ic eom oflongad
sindon dena dimme duna uphea
bitre burgtunas brerum beweaxne
wic wynna leas ful oft mec her wraþe begeat
fromsiþ frean frynd sind on eorþan
leofe lifgende leger weardiað
þonne ic on uhtan ana gonge
under actreo geond þas eorðscrafu
þær ic sitta[n] mot sumorlangne dæg
þær ic wepan mæg mine wræcsiþas
earfoþa fela forþon ic æfre ne mæg
þære modceare minre gerestan
ne ealles þæs longaþes þe mec on þissum life begeat
A scyle geong mon wesan geomormod
heard heortan geoþoht swylce habban sceal
bliþe gebæro eac þon breostceare
sinsorgna gedreag sy æt him sylfum gelong
eal his worulde wyn sy ful wide fah
feorres folclondes þæt min freond siteð
under stanhliþe storme behrimed
wine werigmod wætre beflowen
on dreorsele dreogeð se min wine
micle modceare he gemon to oft
wynlicran wic wa bið þam þe sceal
of langoþe leofes abidan

10th century

## Lamentation

This song have I wrought of my full-wretched self
of mine own subjection of this I can speak
what woes I've endured though not since childhood
early or late more misery than now
I have suffered ever the way of the exile
First when my lord went forth from his folk
over sea-salt waves I was saddened ere dawn
not knowing in the land where my lord might be
As I considered my cruel condition
I sought for service a friendless exile
His kin then began to conspire in secret
scheming how to sunder us twain
so we lived in the world in misery apart
with yearning my heart was oppressed
My lord bade me take up my dwelling-place here
even though I lack friends in this land
who are loyal and dear thus mournful my heart
I found for myself my best-suited mate
of hard misfortune of heavy heart
concealing his purpose devising death
blithe in demeanor we two often swore
that nothing should part us save death alone
but all that has changed it is different now
as if our companionship never had been
needs must I endure both far and near
the fatal feud of my dearly beloved
I was ordered to dwell in a copse in the wood
under the oak in this hole of the earth
this earth-hall is old all is heartache to me
dark are the dales high are the hills
sharp are the hedges grown over with briars
a dwelling all joyless full oft am I cruelly
gripped by the going away of my lord
loving companions alive on the earth
lie together abed while at daybreak alone
I pass under the oak through holes of earth
there must I sit through the summer-long day
there may I mourn for my lot in exile
my uncountable hardships for I may not rest
from this heart-ache of mine or still the desire
the longing in me that my life has begot
Ever must that young man be somber in spirit
ever hard the thought of his heart
though blithe in demeanor with a breast full of cares
and endless distress let all of his joys
in the world depend on himself all alone
let him be cast adrift in a far-distant land
that my friend may sit under a craggy cliff
as my ill-minded mate chilled by the storm
encompassed by water in a dwelling of gloom
with sorrowful mind remembers too often
a happier home woeful is he who
abides in desire for the one that is loved

trans. DWF

## Æcerbot

*Her ys seo bot, hu ðu meaht þine æceras betan gif hi nellaþ wel wexan oþþe þær hwilc ungedefe þing on gedon bið on dry oððe on lyblace....*

*þonne nime man uncuþ sæd æt ælmesmannum and selle him twa swylc, swylce man æt him nime, and gegaderie ealle his sulhgeteogo togædere; borige þonne on þam beame stor and finol and gehalgode sapan and gehalgod sealt.*

*Nim þonne þæt sæd, sete on þæs sules bodig. Cweð þonne:*

*Erce, Erce, Erce, eorþan modor,*
*geunne þe se alwalda, ece drihten,*
*æcera wexendra and wridendra,*
*eacniendra and elniendra,*
*sceafta hehra scirra wæstma,*
*and þæra bradan berewæstma,*
*and þæra hwitan hwætewæstma,*
*and ealra eorþan wæstma.*
*Geunne him ece drihten*
*and his halige þe on heofonum synt,*
*þæt hys yrþ si gefriþod wið ealra feonda gehwæne,*
*and heo si geborgen wið ealra bealwa gehwylc,*
*þara lyblaca geond land sawen.*
*Nu ic bidde ðone waldend, se ðe ðas woruld gesceop,*
*þæt ne sy nan to þæs cwidol wif ne to þæs cræftig man*
*þæt awendan ne mæge word þus gecwedene.*

*þonne man þa sulh forð drife and þa forman furh onsceote/ Cweð þonne:*

*Hal wes þu, folde, fira modor!*
*Beo þu growende on godes fæþme,*
*fodre gefylled firum to nytte. ...*

*Nim þonne ælces cynnes melo and abacæ man innewerdre handa bradnæ hlaf and gecned hine mid meolce and mid haligwætere and lecge under þa forman furh. Cweþe þonne:*

*Ful æcer fodres fira cinne,*
*beorhtblowende, þu gebletsod weorþ*
*þæs haligan noman þe ðas heofon gesceop*
*and ðas eorþan þe we on lifiaþ;*
*se god, se þas grundas geworhte, geunne us*
*growende gife,*
*þæt us corna gehwylc cume to nytte.*

*Cweð þonne III:*

*Crescite in nomine patris, sit benedicti. Amen and Pater Noster þriwa.*

10th century

## Field Blessing

Here is the remedy, how to better thine acres if they will not grow well, or if some unwholesome thing has been done to it by a sorcerer or a poisoner. ...

Take unknown seeds from beggars and give them twice as much as was taken from them, and let all his plough tools be gathered; then let him bore a hole in the plough-beam; therein put incense and fennel and hallowed soap and hallowed salt.

Then take the seed, set it on the plough's body.
Say then:

Erce, Erce, Erce, Earth mother,
May the all-ruler grant you, the eternal Lord,
Fields growing and thriving,
Flourishing and fruitful,
Bright shafts of millet-crops
And broad crops of barley
And white crops of wheat
And all the crops of Earth.
May the eternal Lord grant him
(And his holy ones who are in Heaven),
That his produce be fortified against every foe
And secure against all harm
From poisons sown throughout the land.
Now I pray the Master who shaped this world
That no speaking woman, nor crafty man, [1]
May weaken the words that are uttered here.

Then you drive forth the plough and cut the first furrow. Say then:

Hale may thou be, Earth, mother of all;
Be thou fruitful in God's embrace,
Filled with food for our folk's need....

Then take each kind of flour and bake a loaf as broad as the palm of your hand, and knead it with milk and with holy water, and lay it beneath the first furrow. Say then:

Field full of food, for humankind,
Bright blooming, be thou blessed,
In the holy name of the one who shaped heaven,
And the earth on which we live,
May the god who wrought the ground grant us
gift of growing,
That each kind of seed may come to good.

Then say thrice:

Grow in the name of the father, be blessed,
amen. And Our Father three times.

trans. DWF

---

[1] *speaking-woman* ] "cwidol wif," i.e., a cunning woman who can utter curses or refute charms.

### To Induce Delayed Labor

Se wifman, se hire cild afedan ne mæg, gange to gewitenes mannes birgenne and stæppe þonne þriwa ofer þa byrgenne and cweþe þonne þriwa þas word:

þis me to bote     þære laþan lætbyrde,
þis me to bote     þære swæran swærbyrde,
þis me to bote     þære laðan lambyrde.

And þonne þæt wif seo mid bearne and heo to hyre hlaforde on reste ga, þonne cweþe heo:

Up ic gonge,     ofer þe stæppe
mid cwican cilde,     nalæs mid cwellendum,
mid fulborenum,     nalæs mid fægan.

The woman who cannot bring her child to term must go to a dead man's grave, and step three times over the grave and say these words three times:

This, my remedy against the loathed late birth,
This, my remedy against the grievous dismal birth,
This, my remedy against the loathed lame birth.

And when that woman is with child and she goes with her lord to rest, then she must say:

Up I go, stepping over thee
With a living child, not with a dying one,
With a full-born child, not with a doomed one.

### After the Quickening (first felt movements)

And þonne seo modor gefele þæt þæt bearn si cwic, ga þonne to cyrican, and þonne heo toforan þan weofode cume, cweþe þonne:

Criste, ic sæde,     þis gecyþed!

And when the moder feels that the bairn is quick, she must go then to church, and when she comes before the altar, then she must say: [1]

To Christ, I have said, this is made known!

### After a Stillbirth or Infant Death

Se wifmon, se hyre bearn afedan ne mæge, genime heo sylf hyre agenes cildes gebyrgenne dæl, wry æfter þonne on blace wulle and bebicge to cepemannum and cweþe þonne:

Ic hit bebicge,     ge hit bebicgan,
þas sweartan wulle     and þysse sorge corn.

The woman who cannot sustain her bairn must take a piece from the grave of her own child, wrap it up in swart wool and sell it to merchants. And then she must say: [2]

I sell it, you must sell it,
This swart wool and the seeds of this sorrow.

### To Produce Breast Milk

Se wifman, se n[e] mæge bearn afedan, nime þonne anes bleos cu meoluc on hyre handæ and gesupe þonne mid hyre muþe and gange þonne to yrnendum wætere and spiwe þær in þa meolc and hlade þonne mid þære ylcan hand þæs wæteres muð fulne and forswelge. Cweþe þonne þas word:

Gehwer ferde ic me þone mæran     maga þihtan,
mid þysse mæran     mete þihtan;
þonne ic me wille habban     and ham gan.

þonne heo to þan broce ga, þonne ne beseo heo, no ne eft þonne heo þanan ga, and þonne ga heo in oþer hus oþer heo ut ofeode and þær gebyrge metes.

The woman who cannot feed her bairn must then take the milk of a cow of one color in her hand, sip then with her mouth and go then to running water and spew the milk into it. And then with the same hand she must scoop a mouthful of water and swallow it. Let her then say these words:

Everywhere I carried this strong great one with me,
Strong because of this great food;
Such a one I will to have and go home with.

When she goes to the stream, then she must not look around, nor again when she goes from there, and let her then go to a house other than from where she began, and there take meat. [3]

10th century

trans. DWF

[1] *moder* ] mother; *bairn* ] child; *quick* ] quickened, made alive.

[2] *grave of her own child … sell it* ] an item from the burial of a previous child; *swart* ] black.

[3] *meat* ] food, nourishment.

# The ANGLO-NORMAN Period (1066-1215)

[1.]
De le franceis, ne del rimer,
Ne me dait nuls hom blamer,
Kar en engletere fu ne,
E norri ordine, et aleue;
De vne vile si nome
Ou ne est burg ne cite...

[2.]
Of þe vrenche noþer of þyme
no man schulde blame me
for I was bore in Ingelond
and norschud and ordred
of a lytul town þat is nat nemned
noþer burh ne cite...

[3.]
Of the French, n'other of rhyme, [1]
no man should blame me
for I was bore in Englond
and nour'shed and ord'red [and alive]
of a little town that is not nam'ned
n'other burgh ne city...

THE NORMAN CONQUEST of England dates from 14 October 1066, when Duke William of Normandy defeated and killed King Harold II of England at the Battle of Hastings. Crowned on Christmas day, King William rewarded his followers with lands confiscated from the lords who had fought for Harold. As reinforcements arrived from France, the Normans extended their control, building fortifications across the country. Life may have changed little for the English-speaking serfs under the new ruling elite, but for the Anglo-Saxon aristocracy the Norman Conquest was catastrophic. William "the Conqueror" claimed ownership of all land that came under his control, and he disposed of it to his supporters as he saw fit. The former landowners were forced to die or fly. Wives and daughters of the wealthy who did not escape were married off to Normans. By these means, the Anglo-Saxon lords that had ruled England for centuries were wholly displaced in a single generation by the *nouveau riche*. The Domesday Book records a massive redistribution of wealth: by 1075, all earldoms were held by Normans; by 1086, Normans owned virtually all of England south of the River Tees; and by 1096, the last of the English bishops had died, leaving the Church entirely under Norman control as well.

Anglo-Norman, a dialect of Old French, abruptly displaced Old English as the language of the ruling class. This resulted in a two-tier, bilingual, society whose influence is still registered in modern English. To the French elite, a member of the Anglo-Saxon underclass was a *villein* (O.F. serf or peasant), a term of contempt: hence modern *villain*. Old English *cnafa* ("male child, boy," *OED* n.1.) by 1225 becomes Middle English *cnavè* ("menial servant," *OED* n.2.). By 1275, *knave* denotes both a member of the English servant-class, and "an unprincipled man, given to dishonorable and deceitful practices; a base and crafty rogue" (*OED* n.3). The Normans were *noble* (from O.F. *noble*: magnificent, virtuous, distinguished). The Normans were *royal* (O.F. *roial*: exceptional, first class, of the highest order). For a *virgin,* look again to the Normans (O.F. *virgine*); your *whore* is Anglo-Saxon (Late O.E. *hóre*).[2] From Norman aristocrats, we receive *virtue* (O.F. *vertu*); and from the Anglo-Saxons, *sin* (O.E. *syn*). For *merit, courage,* and *chastity*, we may thank the gracious Normans (O.F. *merite, corage, chastete, gracious*); from the native poor we get *hunger filth, shit* (O.E. *hungor, fýlþ, scitte*), and anatomical obscenities.

In Anglo-Saxon England, there were of course differences in power and wealth; but "man" (O.E. *manna, monn*) denoted every human being, irrespective of age or sex. Old English *ceorl* (M.E. *cheorl,* human male) under Norman rule denotes a native Anglo-Saxon; hence, a *churl,* a base knave. A "well-born" man was now a *gentle* man (O.F. *gentilz hom,* M.E. *gentleman*). By the mid 14th century, *gentle* also connotes *well-bred, excellent, superior*. By the late fifteenth century (Norman influence having waned), *gentile* could denote any English-speaker but a *vile* Jew – though to be *gentle*, you still had to be *well-born*.

| **Old English** | **Norman** | **Modern English** | |
|---|---|---|---|
| **English** | **French** | *On hoof* | *On plate* |
| Cealf | Veau | Calf | Veal |
| Cu | Cow | Cow | Beef |
| Oxa | Beuf | Ox | Beef |
| Scepe | Mouton | Sheep | Mutton |
| Lamb | Mouton | Lamb | Mutton |
| Swin | Bacon | Swine | Bacon |
| Swin | Porc | Swine | Pork |
| Deor | Venaison | Deer | Venison |

Twelfth-century social distinctions between the servants and the served are preserved in our words for livestock and meat.

[1] Late 14th-C Anglo-Norman French; 2. nearly contemporary English translation, same manuscript; 3. original English text normalized (2013); 4. modern English: *No man should criticize either my French or my rhymes, for I was born in England and nourished and trained* [*and lived*] *in a little town that can be called neither a borough nor a city* (2013). St. John's Coll. (Cambridge) MS no. G.30, p. 413.

[2] Cf. Old Norse *hór* (adultery); Mid. Low German *horre* , Mid. Dutch *huerre* , Old High German *huorra* (adulterer); during the early Christian era, the act of adultery became localized in the transgressive female body (*whore*).

Because the ethnic identity of England's aristocrats from 1066 differed from that of the native poor, Norman rule greatly advanced the ideology of biological superiority, within Britain, of a segregated ruling class. Personal identity could no longer be subsumed by membership in a community or tribe. In the determination of one's innate worth as a human being, not even land-ownership figured as strongly as *race* (O.F. *rais, raiz*: root[s], genealogical descent).[1] But nothing mattered so much as one's gender. The Normans not only imported feudalism but were more attentive than the Anglo-Saxons had been to the misogynistic doctrines of continental Christianity, encoded in Church canon law, which declared women to be essentially evil, good only for child-bearing, and a continual threat to the salvation of men. Norman clerics, influenced by the patristic tradition, represent marriage as a necessary evil, thereby to contain sinful lust and to legitimize heirs. Norman women as daughters of Eve therefore lacked privileges that were accorded to noblewomen of the Anglo-Saxon period.[2] Canon law allowed for girls to be betrothed at age 7, the legal age of "consent" (typically, to the highest bidder); and to be physically wedded at age 12, often to a man three times her age. Marriage was conducted as a property transaction, with the husband having full proprietary rights to wife, children, land, and goods. Without the consent of her husband, a woman could not validly express even her last will for the disposition of her jewelry and personal effects. Wealthy widows and nuns had a small measure of freedom, but even they were obliged to keep their heads covered and to manifest their shamefastness and submission at all times.[3]

In *The Owl and the Nightingale*, a late twelfth-century poem, two female birds debate whether it is best to be joyful or sorrowful. Having surveyed the field, the melancholy owl has much unhappiness to report amongst married women in Norman England: "For it y-tideth frequently / That man and wife don't well agree. / And therefore comes his guilty lust: / He loves another woman t' thrust. / He spends upon her all his gold, / He swiveth one not his to hold: / And hath at home his rightful spouse, / Barren walls and empty house, / Left thinly clad, without a shred, / Without much food and poorly fed. / And when he cometh home to wife, / She dare not speak, upon her life. / He chides and yells as he were wood [=mad], / And never brings home other good. / Whate'er she does, gives him a fit / Whate'er she speaks to him, is shit. / And oft, when she's done no misdeed, / She gets his fist right in her teeth." There were surely happy marriages as well, in the Norman period – the Owl herself concedes that "Many a chapman [=merchant], many a knight, / Loveth and holds his wife aright. / And so doth many a bondsman."[4] But under Norman law, when a husband became abusive, or turned violent, the wife had no more right to complain than if he had kicked his ploughhorse or broken the teeth of a curry comb.[5]

Literary works have come down to us from only two women writers of the Norman period: Clemence of Barking (a nun who wrote *La Vie de sainte Catherine*, c. 1160s, a fairly conventional hagiography of St. Catherine of Siena); and the extraordinary Marie de France (who seems also, in light of recent scholarship, to have been a nun of Barking Abbey, a sister of Thomas à Becket). At the close of the twelfth century, Marie wrote: "Amur n'est pruz se n'est egals" (*Love is not honorable unless based on equality.*)[6] That may explain why both Clemence and Marie, and other well-born women, chose to eschew marriage and to spend their adult lives in a sisterhood.

DWF

---

[1] *race* (OED n.2, n.3) is distinct from *race* (OED n.1, rush, run, from Scandinavian *ras*).

[2] For a concise survey, see Pauline Stafford, "Women and the Norman Conquest" (1994).

[3] "Women must cover their heads because they are not the image of God. They must do this as a sign of their subjection to authority and because sin came into the world through them. …Because of original sin they must show themselves submissive" —*Decretum Gratiani* (c.1140), on which Church Law was based (*Causa* 33, qu. 5, ch. 19).

[4] "Foꞃ hıꞇ ıꞇẏꝺ oꝼꞇe anꝺ ılome / Þaꞇ pıꝼ ⁊ peꞃe beoþ unıꞅome; / ⁊ þeꞃꝼoꞃe pe peꞃe ᵹulꞇe, / Þaꞇ leoꝼ ıꞅ oþeꞃ pẏmmonn ꞇo pulꞇe, / ⁊ ꞅpeneþ on þaꞃe al þaꞇ he haueþ, / ⁊ ꞅẏpeþ þaꞃe þaꞇ nohꞇ naueþ, / an haueþ aꞇꞇom hıꞅ ꞃıᵹꞇe ꞅpuꞅe, / popeꞅ peꞅꞇe, ⁊ leꞃe huꞅe, / pel þunne ıꞅch[ꞃ]uꝺ ⁊ ıueꝺ pꞃoþe, / an leꞇ heo buꞇe meꞇe ⁊ cloþe. / Ƿan he comeþ ham eꝼꞇ ꞇo hıꞅ pıue, / ne ꝺaꞃ heo noᵹꞇ a poꞃꝺ ıꞅchıꞃe: / he chıꝺ ⁊ ᵹꞃeꝺ ꞅpuch he beo poꝺ, / an ne bꞃınᵹþ [hom] non oþeꞃ ᵹoꝺ. / Al þaꞇ heo ꝺeþ hım ıꞅ unpılle, / al þaꞇ heo ꞅpekeþ hıꞇ ıꞅ hım ılle: / an oꝼꞇ hpan heo noᵹꞇ ne mıꞅꝺeþ, / he haueþ þe ꝼuꞅꞇ ın hıꞃe ꞇeþ…. / Monı chapmon ⁊ monı cnıhꞇ / luueþ ⁊ [halꝺ] hıꞅ pıꝼ aꞃıhꞇ, / an ꞅpa ꝺeþ monı bonꝺeman" (B.L. MS Cotton Caligula A.ix, fols. 243v-244v, lines 1521-39, 1575-7). Trans. DWF.

[5] The standard thirteenth-century commentary on church canon law justifies the exclusion of women's testimony: "What is flightier that smoke? A breeze. What is flightier than a breeze? The wind. What is flightier than the wind? A woman. What is more flighty than a woman? Nothing" (Bernard of Botone, *Glossa Ordinaria*, trans. DWF).

[6] Marie de France, "Equitan," line 137, trans. DWF.

# Marie de France (fl. 1160-1215)

*Me numerai pur remembrance:*
*Marie ai num, si sui de France.*
*Put cel estre que clerc plusur*
*Prendreient sur eus mun labur.*
*Ne voile que nul sur li le die!*
*E il fet que fol ki sei ublie!*

I'll give my name for memory:
I am from France, my name's Marie.
And it may hap that many a clerk
Will claim as his what is my work.
But such pronouncements I want not!
It's folly to become forgot!

—from the Epilogue to *The Fables*

ARIE DE FRANCE is known to history only from the works that she wrote. A French émigré, she may have been active in the court of Henry II (where her name was known); or she may have been a remarkably urbane nun, whose poetry circulated among twelfth-century literati. Nine centuries later, Marie continues to receive acclaim for her Lais, a collection of twelve narrative poems that she composed in Anglo-Norman French.

Among the most popular of Marie's work in her lifetime were her fables of "Ysopet," 103 of which survive, represented by twenty-five manuscript copies. Her *Espurgatoire* is a faithful French translation of a Latin treatise on St Patrick's Purgatory, by the Cistercian monk Henry of Saltrey; Marie dedicated the work to "H[ugh,] abbot of Sartis" (in Wardon, Bedfordshire). June Hall McCash has argued persuasively that the author of the Lays and Fables is the same Marie who composed a saint's life called *La Vie seinte Audree* (a life of Æthelthryth, a.k.a. Saint Audrey of Ely).

The poet's biography has proved elusive. It is generally agreed that Marie was born in France, perhaps in the Bretagne; that she was of noble, perhaps royal, descent; that she spent most or all of her adult life in England; and that her work circulated among the courtiers of Henry II and his queen, Eleanor of Aquitaine. Marie dedicated her Fables to a "Count William" – possibly William Longsword, illegitimate son of King Henry II; and she dedicated her Lais to a "noble king," probably Henry himself.

Various candidates named Marie have been put forward by historians. The abbeys at Reading (Berkshire) and Shaftesbury (Dorset) were among the wealthiest and most exclusive nunneries; both have been associated with literary production, chiefly devotional or hagiographic; both in the latter twelfth century had abbesses named Marie (Dame Marie of Shaftesbury was the illegitimate daughter of Geoffrey Plantagenet, count of Anjou; she was thereby half-sister to Henry II). A third nominee is Marie I of Boulogne (1136-1182), abbess of Romsey (Hampshire) and daughter of King Stephen (d. 1154). A fourth candidate, Marie de Meulan, is said to be the eighth child of Waleran de Beaumont, and wife of Hugh Talbot. Waleran's fief was in the French Vexine (modern Eure), which is where Marie de Meulan spent her childhood. The *Deus Amanz* of Marie de France is the tale of two young lovers of the Vexine who die on a peak above Pitres.[1] Marie de Meulan thus remained an attractive candidate until it was shown that this Marie was not the author, but the product, of fiction: Marie de Meulan never existed.[2] The reigning champion, for the moment at least, seems to be Dame Marie of Barking abbey (fl. 1173-1175), a sister of Thomas à Becket.

If Marie de France was a nun, she was a sister who knew how to enjoy herself. The *joie de vivre* of her lays and fables has little in common with the sacred writings usually associated with the abbeys. Surprisingly sophisticated, often bawdy, Marie's Muse takes a more avid interest in adultery than in chastity, and more pleasure in jousting than in theological disputes. Her outlook in the lays is insistently aristocratic and secular. She seems fully conversant with the milieu of the royal court, writing of tournaments and courtly love-games with the eye of a spectator. And yet, Marie weaves into her fables a strong thread of protest against a system of social privilege whereby the poor and dispossessed are victimized by the rich, without recourse to justice – unless a woman intervenes. (Marie typically represents women as the wittier and more resourceful sex, being inferior to men in nothing but brute force.)

Eight of Marie's fables are here presented in the parallel text of Harriet Spiegel, whose French text and highly acclaimed English translations are reprinted with the permission of Prof. Spiegel and the University of Toronto Press.

DWF

---

[1] See Yolande de Pontfarcy (1995).

[2] See Carla Rossi (2009).

## *The Fables*

Edited and translated by Harriet Spiegel

### 2. **Del lu et de l'aignel**

Ci dit del lou e de l'aignel,
Ki beveient a un clincel.
Li lus en la surse beveit
E li aignels aval esteit.
Irïement parla li lus,
Que mut esteit cuntrarïus,
Par maltalent parla a lui,
"Tu me fes," dist il, "grant ennui!"
Li aignel ad respundu:
"Sire, de quei?"
"Dunc ne veiz tu?
Tu m'as ceste ewe si trublee,
N'en puis beivre ma saülee.
Arere m'en irai, ceo crei,
Cum jeo vinc ça, murant de sei."
Li aignelez dunc li respunt,
"Sire, ja bevez vus amunt.
De vus me vient ceo que ai beü."
"Quei!" fet li lus, "maudiz me tu?"
Cil li a dit: "N'en ai voleir!"
Li lus respunt, "Jeo en sai le veir.
Cest memes me fist tun pere
A ceste surse, u od luì ere –
Ore ad sis meis, si cum jeo crei."
"Que retez ceo," fet il, "a mei?"
Ne fu pas nez dunc, si cum jeo quit."
"E ke pur ceo?" li lus ad dit;
"Ja me fez tu ore cuntrere
E chose que ne deussez fere."
Dunc prist li lus l'aignel petit,
As denz l'estrangle, si l'ocit.

Issi funt li riche seignur,
Li vescunte e li jugeür
De ceus qu'il unt en lur justise:
Faus acheisuns par coveitise
Treovent asez pur eus confundre;
Suvent les funt a pleit somundre:
La char lur tolent e la pel,
Si cum li lus fist a l'aignel.

### 2. **The Wolf and the Lamb**

This tells of wolf and lamb who drank
Together once along a bank.
The wolf right at the spring was staying
While lambkin down the stream was straying.
The wolf then spoke up nastily,
For argumentative was he,
Saying to lamb, with great disdain,
"You give me such a royal pain!"
The lamb made this reply to him,
"Pray sir, what's wrong?"
"Are your eyes dim?
You've so stirred up the water here,
I cannot drink my fill, I fear.
I do believe I should be first,
Because I've come here dying of thirst."
The little lamb then said to him,
"But sir, 'twas you who drank upstream.
My water comes from you, you see."
"What!" snapped the wolf. "You dare curse me?"
"Sir, I had no intention to!"
The wolf replied, "I know what's true.
Your father treated me just so
Here at this spring some time ago –
It's now six months since we were here."
"So why blame me for that affair?
I wasn't even born, I guess."
"So what?" the wolf responded next;
"You really are perverse today –
You're not supposed to act this way."
The wolf then grabbed the lamb so small,
Chomped through his neck, extinguished all.

And this is what our great lords do,
The viscounts and the judges too,
With all the people whom they rule:
False charge they make from greed so cruel.
To cause confusion they consort
And often summon folk to court.
They strip them clean of flesh and skin,
As the wolf did to the lambkin.

### 4. **Del chien e de la berbiz**

Ci cunte de un chien menteür,
De males guisches, tricheür,
Que une berbiz enpleida.
Devant justise la mena,
Si li a un pain demandé,
Qu'il li aveit, ceo dit, [a]presté.
La berbiz tut le renea
E dit que nul ne li [a]presta!
Li juges al chien demanda
Si nul testimoine en a.
Il li respunt qu'il en ad deus,
Ceo est li scufles e li lus.
Cil furent avant amené.
Par serment unt afermé
Que ceo fu veirs que li chiens dist.
Savez pur quei chescun le fist?
Qu'il en atendeient partie,
Si la berbiz perdist la vie.
Li jugere dunc demanda
A la berbiz qu'il apela.
Pur quei il ot le pain neié
Que li chiens li aveit baillé,
Menti en ot pur poi de pris –
Ore li rendist einz qu'il fust pis!
La cheitive n'ot dunt rendre:
Dunc li covient sa leine vendre.
Yvern esteit, de freit fu morte.
Li chiens i vient, sa leine en porte,
E li escufles d'autre part,
E puis li lus, trop li est tart
Que la chars fust entre eus detreite,
Kar de viande eurent suffreite.
Ne la berbiz plus ne vesqui;
Sis sire del tut la perdi.

Par cest essample nus veut mustrer:
E de meint hume le puis prover,
Ki par mentir e par tricher
Funt les povres sovent pleider;
Faus testimoines sovent traient,
De l'aveir as povres les [a]paient;
Ne lur chaut que li las devienge,
Mes que chescun sa part tienge.

### 4. **The Dog and the Ewe**

This story's of a dog's deceit,
An evil, cunning dog, a cheat.
He sued a ewe – he held a grudge –
And brought the ewe before a judge.
He sought from her a loaf of bread
Which he had lent her, so he said.
The ewe denied it resolutely –
He'd lent her nothing, absolutely!
The judge then asked the dog if he
Had witnesses to back his plea.
The dog replied that he could cite
Two witnesses: the wolf and kite.
To prove his case, he brought in both.
Each swore and stated under oath
That all the dog had said was true.
Why did they act this way, those two?
Each one was waiting for his share,
If death should be her sentence there.
At this the judge then asked the ewe,
The one he sent his summons to,
"Why do you still deny the bread,
That which the dog has lent," he said.
"Why lie about such petty stuff –
Return it or the going's rough!"
The poor thing couldn't, she had naught:
She had to sell her woolen coat.
She froze to death in winter's grip.
The dog was there, her fleece to strip.
The kite came for his share of fleece;
The wolf was anxious for his piece.
They could not wait her flesh to eat,
For they'd been hankering after meat.
No life was left to that poor ewe;
Her lord entirely lost her, too.

This example serves to tell
What's true for many men as well:
By lies and trickery, in short,
They force the poor to go to court.
False witnesses they'll often bring
And pay them with the poor folks' things.
What's left to the poor? The rich don't care,
As long as they all get their share.

### 6. **De soleil ki volt femme prendre**

Par essample fet ci entendre
Que li soleil volt femme prendre.
A tute creature le dist
E que chescune se purveïst.
Les creatures s'asemblerent;
A la Destinee en alerent,
Si li mustrerent del soleil,
Que de femme prendre quert conseil.
La Destinee lur cumande
Que veir dïent de la demande,
E ceo que vis lur en esteit.
Cele parla ki meuz saveit:
"Quant li soleil," fet ele, "est hauz
El tens d'esté, est il si chauz
Qu'il ne lest rien fructifiër
Terre e herbe fet sechïer,
E s'il a esforcement –
E cumpaine a sun talent –
Nule riens nel purra suffrir.
Desuz lui vivre no garir."
La destinee respundi:
"Veir avez dit. Laissum l'issi,
Cum il ad esté, grant tens a,
Kar ja par mei n'esforcera."

Issi chastie les plusurs
Qui sur eus unt les maus seignurs,
Que pas nes deivent esforcier
N'a plus fort de eus acumpainier
Par lur sens ne par lur aveir,
Mes desturber a lur poeir.
Cum plus est fort, pis lur fet;
Tuz jurs lur est en mal aguet.

### 6. **The Sun Who Wished to Wed**

Apply this story to your life:
The sun once wished to take a wife.
He told all creatures his intent:
Each should prepare for the event.
The animal community
Thus met and went to Destiny.
The sun, they told her, would be wise
To seek advise in choosing wives.
Destiny asked them to attest
The truth concerning sun's request:
What did they think of this affair?
Thus spoke the wisest of them there:
"The summer sun's so hot," she said,
"That when the sun's high overhead,
No trees can blossom or bear fruit;
The earth is parched, no plants take root.
If reinforcement he acquires,
A partner sharing his desires,
We'll not be able to survive,
For under them no life could thrive."
Said Destiny, "It seems to me
You speak the truth. We'll let it be
As it has been since long ago.
I won't allow his strength to grow!"

Thus everyone should cautioned be
When under evil sovereignty:
Their lord must not grow mightier
Nor join with one superior
To them in intellect or riches.
They must do all they can to thwart this.
Stronger the lord, the worse their fate:
His ambush always lies in wait.

### 21. **Del lu e de la troie**

Jadis avint que un lus erra
Par un chemin, si encuntra
Une truie ki preinz esteit.
Vers li ala a grant espleit
E dist que pes li vot duner,
Ore se hastast de purceler –
Car ses purceus voleit aveir.
Cele respunt par grant saveir:
"Sire, cument me hastereie?
Tant cum si pres de mei vus veie,
Ne me puis pas deliverer;
Tel hunte ai de vus esgarder.
Ne savez mie que ceo munte?
Tutes femeles unt grant hunte,
Si mains madles les deit tucher
A tel busuin ne aprismer!"

### 21. **The Wolf and the Sow**

Once long ago a wolf strolled down
A path and chanced to come upon
A sow who was with piglets big.
He hastily approached the pig.
He'd give her peace, he told the sow,
If quickly she'd bear piglets now –
Her piglet babes he wished to have.
With wisdom, this response she gave:
"My lord, how can you hurry me?
When you, so close to me I see,
I cannot bear my young outright;
I'm so ashamed when in your sight.
Do you not see the implication?
All women suffer degradation
If male hands should dare to touch
At such a time, or even approach!"

Idunc s'en va li lus mucier,
Ki les purcels voleit manger,
E la troie s'en est alee,
Que par engin s'est delivree.

Cest essample deivent oïr
Tutes femmes e retenir:
Que pur sulement mentir
Ne laissent lur enfanz perir!

With this the wolf hid in retreat
Who'd sought the baby pigs to eat.
The mother pig could now proceed
Who through her cleverness was freed.

All women ought to hear this tale
And should remember it as well:
Merely to avoid a lie,
They should not let their children die!

### 26. **Del lu e del chien**

Un lu e un chien s'encuntrerent
Par mi un bois u il alerent.
Li lus ad le chien esgardé.
E puis si l'ad areisuné.
"Frere," fet il, "mut estes beaus!
E mut est luisant tis peaus!"
Li chiens respunt: "Ceo est veritez;
Jeo manguz bien, si ai asez,
E süef gis puis tut le jur;
Devant les piez mun seignur
Puis chescun jur runger les os,
Dunt jeo me faz e gras e gros.
Se vus volez od mei venir
E vus li voliez obeïr –
Si cum jeo faz – asez averez
Plus viande que ne vodrez."
"Si ferai, veirs," li lus respunt.
Dunc s'acumpainent, si s'en vunt.
Einz que a vile fussent venu,
Garda li lus, si a veü
Cum li chien porta sun coler;
Sa chaëne le vit traïner.
"Frere," fet il, "merveilles vei
Entur tun col, mes ne sai quei."
Li chiens respunt, "C'est ma chaëne,
Dunt humme me lie la semaine.
Kar suventefeiz mordereie
A plusurs riens mesfereie,
Que mes sires veut garantir;
Si me fet liër [e] retenir.
La nuit vois entur la meisun,
Que n'i aprisment li larun."
"Quei!" fet li lus, "est il issi
Que aler ne poëz fors par li!
Tu remeindras, jeo m'en irai;
Ja chaëne ne choiserai!
Meuz voil estre lus a delivre
Que en cheine richement vivre,
Quant uncore pois estre a chois.
Va a la vile, jeo vois al bois!"
Par la chaëne est departie
Lur amurs e lur cumpainie.

### 26. **The Wolf and the Dog**

A wolf and dog met on the way
While passing through the woods one day.
The wolf looked closely at the dog,
And then began this dialogue:
"Brother," he said, "you look so fine!
And oh, such fur! How it does shine!"
The dog replied, "That's very true;
I eat quite well, a great deal, too.
Each day I make my cozy seat
While resting at my master's feet
Where daily I gnaw bones, and that
Is what makes me so big and fat.
If you would like to come with me,
If to obey him you'll agree –
And act like me – you'll have from this
More food than you could ever wish."
"I'll do that! Sure!" the wolf replied.
Together off they went, allied.
Before they'd at the town arrived,
The wolf looked at the dog and eyed
The way the dog a collar wore
And how a dragging chain he bore.
"Brother," he said, "how odd is that
Thing 'round your neck – I know not what."
"That's my chain-leash," the dog replied,
"With which all through the week I'm tied;
For his possessions I would chew on,
And many items I would ruin.
My master wants them all protected,
And that's why I'm tied and restricted.
At night, around the house I peer
And make sure no thieves draw near."
"What!" cried the wolf. "By this you mean
You can't go out except with him!
Well, you can stay! I won't remain.
I'll never choose to wear a chain!
I'd rather live as a wolf, free,
Than on a chain in luxury.
I still can make a choice, and so
You fare to town; to woods I'll go."
A chain thus brought the termination
Of friendship and fraternization.

## 44. **Del vilein ki vit un autre od sa femme**

D'un autre vilein voil ci cunter,
Que od sa femme vit aler
Vers la forest sun dru od li.
Aprés eus vet; cil s'en fuï,
Si s'est dedenz le bois musciez,
E cil returne tut iriez.
Sa femme leidist e blasma;
E la dame li demanda
Pur quei parlast issi vers li,
E ses baruns li respundi
Qu'il ot veü sun lecheür,
Ki li fist hunte e deshonur,
E aler od li vers la forest.
"Sire," fet ele, "si vus plest,
Pur amur Deu, dites me veir!
Quidastes vus humme veeir
Aler od mei? Nel me celer!"
"Jel vi," fet ele, "el bois entrer."
"Lasse," fet il, "morte sui!
Demain murrai u uncore hui! –
A ma aiole avient tut autresi –
E a ma mere – ker jel vi:
Un poi devant lur finement,
(Ceo fu sceü apertement)
Que uns bachelers les cundueient,
E que od eus autre rien n'aveint.
Ore sai jeo bien, pres est ma fins.
Mandez, sire, tost mes cusins,
Si departirums nostre aveir;
N'os el secle plus remaneir!
Od tute la meie partie
Me metrai en une abeïe."
Li vileins l'ot, mercie li crie.
"Lessez ester, ma bele amie!
Ne departez de mei einsi!
Mençunge fu quanque jeo vi."
"N'i os," fet ele, "plus arrester,
Kar de m'alme m'estuet penser,
Ensurketut pur la grant hunte,
Dunt tu as fet si grant cunte.
Tuz jurz me sereit repruvé
Que vilement avereie vers vrus erré
Se vus ne me jurez serement,
Si quil veient mi parent,
Que n'en veïstes hume od mei.
Puis afierez la vostre fei
Que jamés mot n'en sunerez
Ne jamés nel me repruverez."

## 44. **The Peasant Who Saw Another with his Wife**

Another peasant I'll tell about
Who saw his wife once venture out
Into the forest with her lover.
He chased; the man ran off for cover
And hid among the shrubbery.
The peasant went back angrily;
He cursed his wife, took her to task.
What could the lady do but ask
Why he addressed her in this way.
Her husband answered her, to say
Her paramour he had just seen,
And thus disgraced and shamed he'd been.
He'd seen them go among the trees.
"My lord," she said, "now if you please,
For love of God, tell me the truth!
You think you saw a man forsooth
Go off with me? Now be quite honest!"
"I saw him go into the forest."
"Oh, woe!" she said. "I'm dead! For I
Tomorrow – even today – shall die!
It happened to my grandmother –
I saw it, yes – and to my mother,
That just before the time they died
(This was well known both far and wide),
A young man led the two away
Though they'd no cause to go that way.
I know for sure, my end is near
My lord, call all my cousins here.
Now let's divide our goods of worth;
I dare not waste my time on earth!
With all the share that comes to me,
I'll go into a nunnery."
The peasant heard and cried for peace.
"My lovely sweetheart dear, now cease!
Do not take leave of me this way!
It was a lie I saw today!"
"To wait here longer, I don't dare,"
She said, "my soul must be my care.
Especially after this dishonor
You've done to me by your false rumor –
People will ever chastise me
For wronging you so wickedly.
Unless you swear an oath to me,
Which all my relatives can see,
That you saw no man with me there.
Upon your faith you must now swear
That you'll not speak of this again
And will from chiding me abstain."

"Volunters, dame," il li respunt.
A un muster ensemble vunt:
La li jura ceo que ele quist –
E plus asez qu'il i mist.

Pur ceo dit hum en repruver
Que femmes seivent enginner;
Les veziëz e li nunverrable
Unt un art plus que ke diable.

"Gladly, lady!" he gave consent.
Together to a church they went.
He swore to all she'd asked him for –
Whatever he could do – and more.

And so, forewarned all men should be
That women know good strategy.
They've more art in their craft and lies
Than all the devil can devise.

### 70. **Del gupil e de l'urse**

D'un gupil nus recunte e dit,
Que une urse trova e vit.
Forment li preia e requist
Que ele suffrist que li fesist.
"Teis!" fet ele, "mauvais gupilz!
Mut par iés cheitifs e vilz!"
"Jeo sui," fet il, "tel cum jeo suil –
Sil te ferai estre tun voil."
"Fui!" fet ele, "leis me ester!
Se jeo t'en oi ja mes parler,
Tenir te purras pur bricun;
Jeo te baterai od mun bastun!"
Tant l'a li gupilz enchalcié,
Que l'urse s'est mult curucié.
Aprés curut pur lui ferir,
E il fuï, pur li trahir –
Tant qu'il meine en un buissun.
E les espines tut envirun
L'unt entaché e encumbré,
E par la pel l'unt detiré,
Si ke ne pot avant aler
Pur nule rien ne returner.
Dunc revient li gupil pa derere;
Sur li sailli cume trichere.
L'urse cumence a criër,
Puis si li prist a demander:
"Mauvais gupil! Quei fras tu?"
Li gupilz li ad tost respundu:
"Ceo que t'oi," fet il, "preié,
Dunt tu m'aveies manacié."

Ceo deit ester e remaner,
Que li pruz hum dira pur ver:
As veziëz est bien avis,
Que lur parole est en tel pris
Cum li engins de meinte gent –
Que par cunsel venquent suvent.

### 70. **The Fox and the Bear**

And now you'll hear what did betide
When fox one day a she-bear spied.
Urgently fox did beg and pray
For her to let him have his way.
"Shut up! You wicked fox!" she said;
"You are contemptible and bad!"
"That's just the way I am," said he;
"I'll make you want it, too – you'll see."
"Get out of here! Now let me be!
If I hear more such talk," said she,
"You will be thought a thieving knave,
And I will beat you with my stave!"
The fox kept trying to engage her
Till finally he did enrage her.
She chased the fox so she could strike.
The fox kept running, as a trick –
Into a bush he led the bear.
A mass of thorns all round her there
Stuck to the bear, entangled her,
And made a frazzle of her fur,
So she could not gain any ground
Try how she might, nor turn around.
The fox approached her from the rear;
Cheat that he was, he jumped on her.
At this, the bear began to cry,
And then she questioned him this way:
"You wicked fox! What will you do?"
The fox made this reply thereto:
"Just what I'd asked you for," said he,
"When earlier you threatened me."

And it must always be this way –
As worthy men forsooth will say:
Wise people think it's clearly true
That their words will be equal to
Some other people's stratagems.
Yet they'll be vanquished by these schemes.

### 81. De l'egle, de l'ostur, e de la grue

Uns egles esteit mut iriez
Envers un ostur e curucez.
Tuz les oiseus fet asembler;
Aprés l'ostur les fist voler,
Saver s'il le purreient prendre.
Mes ne lur volt pas atendre:
El crus d'un chesne s'esteit mis.
Les oiseus l'unt entur asis.
Puis esgardent ki l'a[s]saudra
E ki avenir i purra.
Dunc i unt la grue enveié,
Pur le lung col l'unt preié.
La grue lance bek avant,
E li ostur demeintenant
L'aveit par la teste saisie.
La grue fu si esbaïe,
Que li mesavient par derere.
Tuz les oiseus fist trere arerer –
Que entur lui venu esteient
E ki aider a li voleient.
Tuz les ordea e mesbailli,
E il s'en fueient desur li.
Quant ele ot sa teste fors mise,
Purpensa sei que en nule guise
Ne volst el païs arester,
Ainz passera, ceo dist, la mer
Pur la hunte que ele aveit fete,
Que li sereit tuz jurs retrete.
Quant ele fu en mer entree,
Si ad une maue encuntree.
Si li demanda e enquist
U ele alot. E cele li dist
Que de sun païs ert fuïe,
Si li cunta sa vileinie.
Dunc ad la maue respundue,
Demanda li si ele est venue
Senz cel usteil qui la huni.
E la grue li respundi:
"Einz l'ai," fet ele, "ensemble od mei!"
"Dunc te lo jeo par dreite fei
Que ti t'en vois en ta cuntree,
Quant de celui n'es delivree;
Greinur mal peot il ailurs fere."
La grue se mist el repeire.

Cest essample ad pur ceo cunté:
Cil que sunt plein de mauveisté
E en lur cuntree mesfunt,
Puis la guerpissent, si s'en vunt.
Pur nent lessent lur païs,
Aillurs funt il autel u pis!
Lur mauvais quor deivcnt changer,
Ne mie lur mauveis quor lesser.

### 81. The Eagle, the Hawk, and the Crane

An eagle once was irritated
About a hawk, infuriated!
He called for all the birds to flock
And bid them all fly after hawk
To see if they could capture him.
But hawk wished not to wait for them
And hid within a hollow oak.
But then the birds surrounded hawk
And they began to talk about
Which one should strike, who'd draw hawk out.
It was crane who received their beck,
And this was because of her long neck.
And when the crane thrust forth her beak,
The hawk who was extremely quick,
Seized the crane's head and held on tight.
The crane was taken so with fright,
She had a mishap at her rear.
The birds all moved away from her –
Those who'd been round her, in attendance,
And who had wished to give assistance.
She'd covered them with excrement
So up they flew and off they went.
Then when she got her head back out,
There's one thing she was sure about:
She'd not stay in this land, she said –
She'd go across the sea instead,
For the disgraceful thing she'd done –
Which she'd soon hear from everyone.
And then when she had reached the sea,
She met a seagull there, and he
In parley with her, asked the crane
Where she was going. She explained
That from her land she'd had to flee
And told of her atrocity.
The seagull, hearing what she'd done,
Now asked the crane if she had come
Without her implement of shame.
She could in answer but exclaim:
"I have it with me still!" said she.
"Then I must conscientiously
Advise you to go home forthwith
Since you've not gotten rid of it.
It may yet do worse things elsewhere."
And so crane started home from there.

Now this example should address
Those who are full of wickedness,
Who've done wrong in their native home
And think they'll leave it all and roam.
For nothing do they take this course;
They'll do elsewhere the same or worse!
One must first change his wicked heart–
One can't forsake it and depart.

## The Lais

MARIE DE FRANCE in her twelve *Lais* celebrates the ideals of courtly love. As in the Fables, she favors the octosyllabic couplet, which well suits her sparkle and wit. Her lais are concise (*Eliduc*, the longest, is only about a sixth as long as the verse romances being written by Marie's contemporary, Chrétien de Troyes); and most are pointed, but the implicit moral is often a surprising one: in Marie's ethic, the imperatives of true-love trump those of Christian monogamy, most especially when a young woman is married against her will to an old or jealous husband. Marie's lais found a wide and enduring readership; prompted many allusions and adaptations; and were translated into English, Middle High German, and Old Norse. The Lais may be read today in more than a dozen languages.[1]

Five extant manuscripts contain one or more of the lais. All twelve appear together only in Harley 978 (a thirteenth-century manuscript housed in the British Library); wherein the lais are accompanied by a 56-line prologue addressed to the king, probably Henry II (d. 1189). The tales in Harley 978 may be arranged as intended by Marie. It has been observed, for example, that the odd lays – *Guigemar, Le Fresne* ("The Ash"), *Lanval, Yonec, Milun*, and *Chevrefoil* ("The Honeysuckle") – celebrate love that manifests itself in unselfish loyalty and service (tales that end, not always luckily, but happily, in a validation of truelove). The even lays – *Equitan, Bisclavret* ("The Werewolf"), *Les Deux Amants* ("The Two Lovers"), *Laüstic* ("The Nightingale"), *Chaitivel* ("The Unhappy One"), and *Eliduc* – feature selfish and sometimes violent lovers who end badly.

Marie wrote chiefly for Norman aristocrats. Some 115 years after her death, an anonymous English translation of her *Lai le Fresne* was included in a volume known today as the Auchinleck manuscript, prepared for English gentry c.1330. Badly damaged, the Auchinleck text lacks lines 121-33 and 341-408; these were ingeniously reconstructed from Harley 978 by Henry William Weber in 1810. What follows is a modern-spelling edition of the Auchinleck text, as supplemented by Weber's reconstruction (in italic).

[1] A digital facsimile of MS Harl. 978 has been published by the British Library online. The best print edition is Jean Rychner, ed., *Les lais de Marie de France* (Paris, Champion, 1966). For a jaunty and faithful rendering of eight lais, see Judith P. Shoaf, trans., *The Lais of Marie de France* (1991-96), online.

## Lay le Frein

WE READETH oft and findeth y-writ
(And this clerkès well it wit),
Lays that be'n in harping
Be'n y-found of ferlie thing. [2]
Some be'th of war and some of woe,
And some of joy and mirth also,
And some of treachery and of guile,
Of old avéntures that fell while,
And some of bords and ribawdy,
And many there be'th of faèry. [3]
Of all thingès that men sayeth
Most o' love, forsooth, they be'th. [4]
In Brittany by oldè time
These lays were wrought, so sayeth this rhyme
When kingès might our [song]° y-hear
Of any marvels that there were
They took an harp in glee and game,
And maked a lay, and gave it name.
Now o' these avéntours° weren y-fall,
I can tell some, ac noughtè all. [5]
Ac hark'neth, lordings, sooth to sayen,
Ich'll tell you° "Lai le Frein." [6]
Befell a case in Brittany
Whereof was made a° lay "le Freine"
In English for to tellen, ywis, [7]
Of "An Ash," forsooth it is –
An ensample fair with all
That some [past] time was befall.
In th' West country woned tway knights
And loved 'hem well in allè rights;
Rich men, in 'heir bestè life
And either of 'hem had wedded wife. [8]
That o' knight made his leu'dy mild
That she was wonder-great with child. [9]
And when her time was comen tho,
She was deliv'red out of woe. [10]

[2] *clerkes well it wit* ] clerics know well; *ben ... thing* ] Lays when harped are found to be a marvelous thing.

[3] *fell while* ] happened once upon a time; *bords and ribawdy* ] jokes and ribaldry; *faèry* ] (3 sylls.); *be'th of faèry* ] are about faery lore.

[4] *Of all the subjects men discourse about (as poets or audience), most are of love.*

[5] *weren y-fall* ] that happened; *ac noughte all* ] but not all.

[6] *Ac hark'neth* ] But listen.

[7] *ywis* ] verily, certainly.

[8] *woned tway* ] dwelt two; *in all rights* ] completely; *either* ] each (both).

[9] *o'* ] one; *leu'dy* ] lady, gentlewoman; *she* ] for fem. singular, MS uses *sche* and *hye* (trans. "[*she*]") interchangably; *wonder great* ] amazingly big.

[10] *tho* ] then.

The knightè thankèd God almight'
And cleped his messenger, on height. [1]
"Go," he said, "to my neighbor swith,
And say I greet him felè sith, [2]
And pray him that he come to me,
And say he shall my gossib be." [3]
The messenger go'th, nought° foryet,
And fint the knightè at his meat. [4]
And fair he gretè in the hall,
The lord, the leu'dy, the meiny all. [5]
And sithen on knees, down him set
And the Lord full fair he gret: [6]
"He bade that thou shouldst to him te
And for love, his gossib be." [7]
"Is his leu'dy delured with sound?" [8]
"Ya, sir, y-thanked be God the stound." [9]
"And whether a maid-child,° other a knave?" [10]
"Túay *sons*, sir! God 'hem save!" [11]
The knight thereof was glad and blithe
And thonkèd Goddès sondè swithe
Graunted his errand in all thing,
And yaf him a palfrey for his tidíng. [12]
Then was the leu'dy of the house
(A proud dame and an envious),
Hoker-fullich mís-seggíng,
Squeàmous and eke scorníng. [13]
(To each woman she had envíe).
She spake these words of felony:
"Ich have wonder, thou messenger,
Who was thy lordès' counselor,
To teach him about to send
And tell shame, in each-on-end,
That his wife two° childer y-bore! [14]
Well may each man wit therefore
That tway men her han had in bower;
That is 'heir *bothè* dishonour!" [15]
The messenger was sore ashamed.
The knight himself was sore agramed,
And rebuked his leuèdy
To speak any woman villany. [16]
And each [one°] thereof might hear
Cursed her, all [women°] y-fere,
And besought God in Heaven
For his holy namè seven
That yif [she euer should child]° abide
A worse aventure, *her*° betide! [17]
Soon thereaft' befell a case
That herself with child was:
When God willed, she was unbound
And deliverèd, all with sound:
*Two* maiden childer she had y-bore!
When [she] it wist, woe her° therefore! [18]
"Alas," she said, "that this hap coom!
Ich have y-yoven mine owèn doom. [19]
(Forboden biddè Ich woman [20]
To speak another° harm upon!)
Falselich, another I 'gan deem. [21]
The selfè hap is on *me* seen!
Alas," she said, "that I was born!
Withouten end, Ich am forlorn. [22]
Or Ich mot siggen, sikerly,
That tway men han y-lie me by,
Or Ich mot sigge in all my life
That I belied my neighbor's wife. [23]
Or Ich *mot* – (that God it shield!)
Help to slay mine owen child.
Oon of these three° Ich mot nede
Sigge, other done in deed. [24]
Yif Ich say I had bi-leman°
Then Ich leigh myself upon,
And eke they will that me see
Hold me wor' than common be. [25]

---

[1] *cleped* ] called; *on height* ] in haste.

[2] *swith* ] straightway; *fele sith* ] fully then.

[3] *gossib* ] gossip, i.e., godparent.

[4] *nought foryet* ] forgetting nothing; *fint* ] found; *meat* ] food, meal.

[5] *gretè* ] greeted; *meiny* ] household.

[6] *sithen* ] at that time; *gret* ] greeted.

[7] *te* ] go; *gossib* ] godparent.

[8] *del'ured with sound* ] delivered, with safety.

[9] *the stound* ] at the present time.

[10] *other a knave* ] or a boy?

[11] *Tuay* ] (two syls.) two.

[12] *thonked ... swith* ] thanked God's sending (dispensation) greatly; *yaf...palfrey* ] gave him a riding-horse (it was considered good luck to give a gift on news of a newborn).

[13] *Hoker-fullich missegging* ] scornfully provoking; *squeamous* ] contemptuously; *eke* ] also.

[14] *each-on-end* ] everywhere.

[15] *wit therefore* ] thereby realize; *bower* ] bedchamber; *'heir both dishonour* ] a dishonor to them both.

[16] *agramed* ] outraged.

[17] *thereof might hear* ] who heard of her insult; *y-fere* ] together; *His holy namè seven* ] by God's seven names (Elyon, El, Elohim, Jehovah, Yahweh, Adonai and Shaddai).

[18] *wist* ] realized; *woe her* ] how sorry she was.

[19] *y-yoven* ] given judgment on myself.

[20] *bitte* ] bid; or *bitè* (be it); Ich; or, each (*MS* bite ich).

[21] *deem* ] condemn, judge.

[22] *Withouten ... forlorn* ] I am forever lost.

[23] *Or Ich mot sigge sikerly* ] Either, I must say, certainly.

[24] *Sigge, other done in deed* ] say, or do in fact.

[25] *bi-leman* ] (double-sweetheart) paramour; *leigh ... upon* ] belie, slander myself; *eke* ] also; *wor'* ] worse.

And yif Ich 'knowledge to each man
That Ich leigh the leu'dy upon,
Then Ich worth, of old and young,
Be held leighster and false of tongue. [1]
Yet, me is best takè my chaunce,
And slay my child, and do penaunce."
  Her midwife, [she] clepèd her to.
"Anon," she said, "this child fordo,
And ever say thou, where thou go,
That Ich have oon child, and ne moe." [2]
  The midwife answered thurchout all
That [she] *nil*, no [she] *ne* shall!– [3]
  *[The leu'dy had a maiden free,*
*Who there y-nurtured had y-be,*
*And fostered fair full many a year.*
*She saw her keep this sorry cheer,*
*And weep, and sigh, and cry, "Alas!"*
*And thought to helpen her in this case.*
*And thus she spake, this maiden ying:* [4]
*"So n'ould y-weepen for no kind thing*
*But this o' child will I off-bear*
*And in a co'vent leave it yare.* [5]
*Ne shall thou be ashamed at all;*
*And whoso findeth this child small,*
*By Mary, blissful queen above,]* [6]
May help it, for God'is love." [7]
  The leu'dy graunted anon thereto,
And would well that it were y-do. [8]
She took a rich baudekine
That her lord brought from Co'stantine
And lapped the little [child°] therein,
And took a ring of goldè fin,
And whoso her found should have in mind
That it were coomen of richè kind. [9]
  The maid took the child her mid
And stole away in an eventide,
And passèd o'er a wild heath. [10]
Thurch field and thurch [the] wood [she] g'eth
All the winterlongè night –
The weather clear°, the moon was light –
So that [she] coom by a forest side;
She wax all weary and 'gan abide. [11]
Soon thereafter°, she 'gan hark
Cockès crow and houndès bark.
She arose and thither would.
Near and near she 'gan behold
Walls, and house felè [she] sey,
A church with steeple fair and high. [12]
Then n'as there n'other street° no town,
But an house of religioun,
An order of nunnès well y-dight
To servè God both day and night. [13]
  Abode the maiden no lengóre,
But yede her to the chirchè door,
And on knees she sat a-down,
And said (weepand) her orisoun: [14]
  "O Lord," she said, "Jesu Crist,
That sinful man bedès hearest,
Underfong [thou°] this presént,
And help this seely innocent
That it mot y-christ'ned be,
For Mary' love, thy moder free!" [15]
  [She] lookèd up and by her sey
An ash by her, fair and high,
Well y-bowed, of mickle pris;
The body was hollow as many oon is. [16]
Therein she laid the child for cold,
In the pel as it was befold,
And blissèd it with all her might. [17]
  With that it 'gan to dawè light.
The fowlès up and sung on bough,
And acre men yedè to the plough.
The maiden turned again anon,
And took the way [she] had ere gone.
  The porter of the abbey 'rose,
And did his office in the close,
Rung the bells and tapers light,
Laid forth books and all ready dight. [18]

---

[1] *'knowleche* ] acknowledge to everyone; *leigh* ] belie, slander; *worth ... beheld* ] will be considered; *leighster* ] liar, slanderer.

[2] *che ... to* ] called unto her; *fordo* ] put to death.

[3] *thurchout* ] throughout; *nil...shall* ] will not, nor ever shall commit infanticide.

[4] *ying* ] young.

[5] *co'vent* ] convent; *yare* ] quickly.

[6] lines 121-33: ed. DWF from Webster's Middle English reconstruction, from the Anglo-Norman, of lines missing in the damaged manuscript; again at 341-408.

[7] *God'is* ] God's (MS Godes, old genitive).

[8] *would ... y-do* ] wished well it were done.

[9] *kind* ] kinfolk.

[10] *mid* ] with.

[11] *wax* ] grew.

[12] *fele* ] many; *sey* ] saw.

[13] *y-dight* ] called.

[14] *lengore* ] longer.

[15] bedès ] beads, i.e., prayers; *Underfong* ] undertake, accept; *seely* ] simple, guileless.

[16] *ash* ] an ash tree (le fresne); mickle pris ] great worth (price); excellence.

[17] *pel* ] the embroidered, rich mantle.

[18] *dight* ] prepared.

The churchè door he undid –
And sey anon in the stead
The pel liggen in the tree! –
And thought well that it might be
That thieves had y-robbed somewhere,
And gone thereforth and le't it there.
Thereto he yede and it unwound,
And the maidenchild therein he found.
He took it up between his hond,
And thonkèd Jesu Cristès sond. [1]
Home° to his house he it brought,
And took it his doughter, and her besought
That [she] should keep it as she can,
(For she was milche and couth thereon). [2]
She bade it suck – ac it n'ould,
For it was nighè dead for cold! [3]
Anon [a] fire she a-lit
And warmèd it, well a-plit. [4]
She gave it suck upon her barm,
And sithen laid it to sleep warm. [5]
And when the Massè was y-done,
The porter to th'abbess coom full soon:
"Madame, what rede ye of this thing? [6]
Today, right in the morníng,
Soon after the firstè stound,
A little maiden-child Ich found
In the hollow ash there-out,
And a pel, her° about.
A ring of gold also was there. [7]
How it come thither I n'ot near." [8]
The abbess a-wond'red° of this thing.
"Go," [she] said, "on heighíng,
And fetch it hither, I pray thee. [9]
It is welcome to God and to me.
Ich'll it help as I can
And sig it is my kinswomán."
The porter anon it 'gan forth bring,
With the pel and with the ring.
The abbess let clepe a priest anon,
And let it christen in fontston°. [10]
And for it was in an ash y-found,
She clep'd it "Frein," in that stound. [11]
(The French of the ashè is a *fresne*
After the language of Bretagne;
Forth "Le Fresne" men clepeth this lay
More than "Ash" in ech countrèy.)
Thus Frein thrived from year to year –
The abbess' *niece*, men wenn'd it were. [12]
The abbess her 'gan teach and beld. [13]
By that [she] was of twelve winter eld,
In all Englond, there n'as none
A fairer maiden than [she] was oon. [14]
And when [she] couth ought of manhead
[She] bade the abbess her wis and rede
Which were her kin, one or other,
Fader or moder, suster or brother. [15]
The abbess her in counsel took
To tellen her, [she] nought forsook,
How [she] was founden, in all thing;
And took her the cloth and the ring,
And bade her keep it in that stead. [16]
And therewhiles she lived, so she did!
Then was there in that country
A rich knight of land and fee,
Proud and young and jollivè,
And had nought yet y-wedded wife. [17]
He was stout, of great renown,
And was y-clepèd Sir Gyroun. [18]
He heard praise, that maiden free,
And [sigge]° he would her see.
He dight him in the way anon
And, jollive-lich, thither he coom;
And bade his man sigge veriment
He should to-ward a tournament. [19]
The abbess and the nunnès all
Fair him grete in the guest hall
And damsel Frein, so hend of mouth,
Grete him fair as [she] well couth. [20].

[1] *sond* ] sending, gift.

[2] *milche* ] nursing, had milk.

[3] n'ould ] would not.

[4] *a-plit* ] straightaway.

[5] *barm* ] bosom.

[6] *rede* ] advise.

[7] *stound* ] hour (can also mean amazement).

[8] *n'ot* ] know not.

[9] on heighing ] in haste.

[10] *let clepe* ] let (a priest) be called; *fontston* ] bapismal font.

[11] *in that stound* ] at that very hour.

[12] *wenn'd* ] believed.

[13] *beld* ] edify, beautify.

[14] *that* ] the time.

[15] *couth ought of manhead* ] knew something of human nature/manhood; *wis and rede* ] advice and counsel.

[16] *took* ] gave; *stead* ] place.

[17] *land and fee* ] real estate and moveable property; *jollive* ] jolly, full of *joie de vivre.*

[18] *stout* ] proud.

[19] *dight him* ] readied himself; *jollive-lich* ] jovially, joyful-like; *sigge veriment* ] say verily, truthfully; *should to-ward* ] had to attend.

[20] *hend of mouth* ] courteous of speech; *Grete ... couth* ] greeted him elegantly, as she well knew how.

And swithè° well he 'gan devise
Her semblaunt and her gentryise,
Her lovesome eyen, her rudd so bright,
And comm'ced to love her anon right
And thought how he might take on
To have her to his lemán. 1
He thought, "Yif Ich come here to
More than Ich have y-do',
The abbess will souchy guile
And void her, in a little while." 2
He compassed another enchesoun:
To be *brother* of that religìoun. 3
"Madame," he said to the abbess,
"I love ye° well in all goodness.
Ich'll yivè, oon and other,
Lands and rents, to become your brother,
That ye shall ever fare the bet'
When I come, to have recet." 4
At few words, they be'n at oon;
He graithès him and forth is gone. 5
Oft he coom by day and night
To speakè with that maiden bright,
So that (with his fair behest
And with his glosing) attè last
[She] graunted him to do'en his will,
When he will, loud and still. 6
"Leman," he said, "thou must let be
The abbess, thy niece, and go with me. 7
For Ich am rich, of swich power
Thee find bett' than thou hast here." 8
The maiden grant and to him tryst,
And stole away, that no man wist;
With her, tookè [she] no thing
But her pellè and her ring. 9

When the abbess 'gan espy
That [she] was with the knight away,
She made mourning in her thought,
And her bement, and gainèd nought. 10
So long [Frein] was in his castéll
That all his meiny loved her well.
To rich and poor, she 'gan her 'dress,
That all her lovèd, more and less.
And thus she led with him her life
Right as she'ad been his wedded wife. 11
His knightès coom and to him spake,
And Holy Church commandeth eke,
Some lordès doughter for to take,
And his leman all forsake;
And said him "were well more fair
In wedlock to getten him an heir
Than lead his life with swichè oon
Of whose° kin he knewè none."
And said, "Here besides is a knight
That hath a daughter fair and bright
That shall bear his heritage:
Taketh *her* in marrìage!" 12
Loath him was, that deed to do,
Ac attè last he graunt thereto. 13
The forward was y-maked aright,
[They°] were at oon, and trothè plight. 14
Alas, that he no had y-wit,
Ere the forward were y-smit
That [she] and his lemán also
Sistren were and twinnès too! 15
Of o' father begetten they were,
Of o' moder born y-fere.

[1] *swithe ... devise* ] very well began to observe; *semblaunt* ] semblance, appearance; *gentryise* ] gentleness, graciousness; *lovesome eyen* ] lovely eyes; *rudd* ] complexion; *comm'ced* ] commenced*to his leman* ] for his sweetheart.

[2] *More ... y-do'* ] more than I've already done; *souchy guile* ] suspect trickery; *void her* ] put her [Frein] away (from my sight).

[3] *compassed another encheson* ] devised another excuse; *be...religion* ] to join that monastery as one of the monks.

[4] *Ich'll ... other* ] I'll give to one and all; *recet* ] reception, place of refuge, resort.

[5] *at oon* ] of one mind; *graithes him* ] prepares himself.

[6] *behest* ] promises, vow; *glosing* ] flattery.

[7] *Leman* ] lover, sweetheart.

[8] *Thee find bett* ] (You'll) find better prosperity.

[9] *grant...tryst* ] granted … trusted, met by appointment; *no man wist* ] no one knew; *pelle* ] mantle.

[10] *bement ... nought* ] lamented, to no avail.

[11] *'gan her 'dress* ] began to communicate; *Right as* ] just as if.

[12] *beside* ] living nearby.

[13] *Ac atte last* ] but at the last.

[14] *forward* ] prenuptial agreement.

[15] *y-wit* ] knowledge.

That [she] so were, n'wistè none,
For sooth I say, but God alone. 1
The new bride was gra'ed withal
And brought home to the lordès hall. 2
Hir fader coom with her, also
The leu'dy her moder, and other moe.
The bishop of the land withouten fail
Coom to do the 'spousial.
[*That maiden bride in bower bright,*
*Le Codre she was y-hight.*
*And there the guests had gamen and glee,*
*And said to Sir Gyroun joyfully:*
*"Fairer maiden n'as never seen –*
*Better than Ash, is Hazel y-ween!"*
*(For in Romaunce Le Frein "ash" is,*
*And Le Codre "hazel," y-wis.)*
*A great feast then 'gan they hold*
*With glee and pleasaunce manifold.*
*And moe than all servaunts, the maid*
*Y-hight Le Frein, as servant, sped.*
*All-be her heart well-nigh to-broke,*
*No word of pride ne grame she spoke.* 3
*The leu'dy marked her simple cheer,*
*And 'gan to love her, wonder dear.* 4
*Scant could she feel more pine or ruth*
*Were it her owen child, in sooth.*
*Then to the bower the damsel sped,*
*Where graithèd was the spousal bed.* 5
*She deemed it was full foully dight,*
*And ill-beseemed a mai' so bright.* 6
*So to her coffer quick she cam,*
*And her rich baudekyn out-nam,*
*Which from the abbess she had got*
*(Fairer mantle n'as there not),*
*And deftly on the bed it laid—*
*Her lord would thus be well-apaid.* 7
*Le Codre and her mother, there,*
*Insame unto the bower 'gan fare,*
*But when the leu'dy that mantle sey,*
*She well nigh swoonèd away.*
*The chamberlain she clepèd tho,*
*But he wist of it no moe.* 8
*Then came that hendy maid, Le Frein,*
*And the leu'dy 'gan to her say'n,*
*And askèd whose mantle it were.*
*Then answerèd that maiden fair:*
*"It is mine, without lesíng;*
*I had it together with this ring.* 9
*Mine aunt told me a ferli case*
*How in this mantle y-fold I was,*
*And had upon mine arm this ring,*
*When I was y-sent to nourishing."* 10
*Then was the leu'dy astonied sore:*
*"Fair child! My daughter, I thee bore!"*
*She swoonèd, and was well-nigh dead,*
*And lay sikéand on that bed.* 11
*Her husband was fettè tho,*
*And she told him all her woe,*
*How of her neighbor she had mis-sayn,*
*For she was deliuer'd of childer twain;*
*And how two children herself she bore:*
*"And that o' child I off-sent thore,*
*In a convent y-fostered to be;*
*And this is she, our daughter free;*
*And this is the mantle, and this the ring*
*You gave me of yore as a love-tokening."*
*The knight kissed his daughter hend*
*Oftimes, and to the bishop wend:*
*And he undid the marriage straight,*
*And wedded Sir Gyroun alsgate*
*To Le Frein, his leman, so fair and hend.* 12
*With them Le Codre away did wend,*
*And soon was spoused with game and glee,*
*To a gentle knight of that countréy.*
*Thus ends the lay of tho' maidens bright,*
*Le Frein and Le Codre y-hight.*]

*finis*

[1] *n'wiste none* ] no one knew.

[2] *gra'ed* ] graithed, adorned.

[3] *grame* ] resentment.

[4] *leu'dy* ] lady, the mother of Frein and Codre.

[5] *graithed* ] adorned.

[6] *foully dight* ] not elegant enough; *mai'* ] maiden (so bright as Codre).

[7] *out-nam* ] brought out the embroidered pell in which baby Frein had been wrapped.

[8] *cleped tho* ] called then (to her).

[9] *lesing* ] lying.

[10] *ferli case* ] marvelous event.

[11] *sikeand* ] sighing.

[12] *alsgate* ] instead.

# **LATE MEDIEVAL Period** (1215-1500)

> they vysyte y$^{e}$ syke & comfort thē / they renne to pore people & serche th hospytalles & bury y$^{e}$ deed bodyes. Mesemeth y$^{t}$ these be y$^{e}$ werkes of womē ... And what thynge is there in y$^{e}$ worlde more sweter & more amyable than is a woman well set in ordre.
>
> —*the Boke of the Cite of Ladyes* (1521), Ee2r

THE DECLINE of Anglo-Norman dominance is usually dated from 1215, when King John was forced to sign the Magna Carta (the "Great Charter"), endorsing certain rights claimed by his rebellious barons, with attendant limitations on his personal rule. In actual practice, the document never did much to contain the arbitrary power of King John or of any other British monarch; but in the seventeenth century the Magna Carta would acquire symbolic importance as a proclamation of inalienable liberties, such as the right of freemen to a trial by their peers, when accused; freedom from oppressive taxation; and nominal separation of Church and State.

Edward I (1239-1307) reigned from 1272, holding to the Norman the principle that all real property, currency, and liberties are held from the Crown. He crushed rebellion at home; subjugated the Welsh; continued the conflict with France; launched brutal assaults on Scotland; and paid for his wars by expelling Jews from the kingdom, confiscating their property and their accounts receivable.

In the years 1315 to 1317, the Great Famine struck much of northwest Europe, including England. The enduring food shortage reduced England's population, due to malnutrition and related illness, by an estimated ten percent. A greater misery was around the corner. In 1347, a merchant ship returning from China arrived in Sicily with black rats carrying *yersinia pestis* bacteria. By 1351, as much as half of Europe's population had perished from the Black Death ("the Great Mortality" as it was then called), the most devastating pandemic in recorded history. All Christendom became a death camp from which there was no escape. In some urban areas and among the overcrowded poor, fatalities were as high as eighty percent. In segregated Jewish communities on the Continent, where Mosaic cleanliness laws were observed, the death rate was much lower – until they were blamed for the plague, whereupon the Jewish death rate in many areas was 100%. The epidemic subsided in 1351, returning to England in 1361 to take another fifth of the population – and would reappear in lesser waves for the next five hundred years.

Not even the Black Death could keep England and France from fighting. The Hundred Years' War (1337-1453) took its pointless toll not only among soldiers but on thousands of uncounted noncombatant poor, whose property and food and livestock were endlessly pillaged by the armies of both nations.

The Church, meanwhile, had grown flamboyantly corrupt, but amassed incalculable wealth from bequests of land, masses for the dead, and the sale of indulgences (on word that suffering on earth was nothing compared to the Purgatorial torments that God had in store for those who did not ante up).

Hunger, plague, and war produced a chronic labor shortage, which brought some gains for those who survived. A surplus of property – land, housing, moveables – led to a redistribution of wealth, closing the gap between the wealthiest aristocrats and everyone else. Peasants migrated to the cities, risking the plague in order to achieve a higher standard of living; which in turn led to the decay of feudalism. The labor shortage led also to increased opportunities for women, who were taught the trades of their fathers and husbands, and permitted to work in the shops.

The fourteenth century despite its many miseries produced Geoffrey Chaucer (1343-1400), one of the wittiest poets of all time, described often as the father of English literature; and Christine de Pizan (c. 1364 - c. 1430) who without having set foot in Britain might well be called its matriarch. Well into the sixteenth century, women of the privileged classes – those few who had both an education and a library, including the aristocratic nuns of Barking Abbey – did most of their reading in French. In 1476 when the printing press came to England, Christine de Pizan was among the first authors to appear, in English, in the London bookshops; only to be neglected thereafter. Throughout the twentieth century, the English literature curriculum marched inexorably from *Beowulf* to Chaucer to Shakespeare to Milton, no heckling admitted from Christine de Pizan in the *poulailler*; but the fifteenth-century French of *Le Livre de la Cité des Dames* arguably did more than the vernacular English of the Wife of Bath to enable women's cultural production of the generations to follow. Christine's work effectively challenged the dominant discourse, paving the way in the sixteenth century not only for women's literature, but for the temporary regency of Katherine Parr, the legitimacy of Queen Mary, and the absolute sovereignty of Queen Elizabeth.

DWF

## **Christine de Pizan** (c. 1364 – c. 1430), in England

I can not vnderstande this repugnaunce … For knowe wel y[t] all this euill saynges generally of wome̅ hurteth y[e] sayers & not y[e] wome̅.
—*The Cyte of Ladyes,* Englished 1521, sigs. B2v, B4v.

BORN in Venice and raised at the Parisian court of Charles V "the Wise," where her father, Thomasso da Pizzano, was royal physician and astrologer, Christine de Pizan is the first European woman known to have made a living by writing. She began her career when she was widowed at age 25 after a happy ten-year marriage to a notary and royal secretary, Etienne du Castel. In her *Vision* (1405-1406), she reveals with an allegory-piercing frankness that her husband's death, with all its incumbent sorrow and financial problems, actually opened the door to a life she valued more. Her professional activity also brought new vexations familiar to countless women writers who succeeded her: accusations that she used ghost writers, and false rumors regarding romantic involvements.[1]

Christine owed her career not only to her husband's early death but also to the exceptional education she received from her father, including instruction in Latin. A voracious reader, she had privileged access not only to her father's manuscripts but also to the royal and ducal libraries. Astonishingly productive, the most prolific writer of her generation in France, she also was an entrepreneur who supervised the copying and distribution of her works. Her patrons included the royal couple Charles VI and Isabeau of Bavaria, and court figures and nobles of all ranks and political allegiances, including the most famous bibliophile of the age, John, Duke of Berry. She relates that her readers were eager for "new things" produced by a woman's pen.[2]

Christine de Pizan was known in England at the very beginning of her career. As early as 1402, Hoccleve adapted her *Epistre au dieu d'amours* (*Epistle to the God of Love*) in his *Letter of Cupid.* An important conduit for her early manuscripts was the Earl of Salisbury, who took part in negotiations involving the marriage of Charles VI's daughter, Isabelle, to Richard II.[3] After Richard's overthrow and Salisbury's murder in 1400, Henry IV came across the manuscripts she had sent Salisbury and found a place for her son at court. Christine sent Henry additional manuscripts as a ploy to obtain her son's safe return;[4] among these was certainly a copy of her allegorical treatise on knighthood, the *Epistre Othea* (*Epistle of Othea*), for which she composed a special preface for him.[5]

Some ten per-cent of the 213 or so known surviving manuscripts of Christine de Pizan's works in French are currently located in England. Some are known to have been copied there,[6] a larger number were brought from the continent. Among the manuscripts brought to England, the most noteworthy is undoubtedly the monumental British Library, Harley MS 4431 containing thirty works presented to the French Queen in January, 1414 ; the volume, now divided in two, was brought to England in 1425 by the Duke of Bedford, regent of France.[7] It passed by inheritance to Anthony Woodville, second Earl of

[1] Christine de Pizan, *The Vision of Christine de Pizan*, trans. Glenda McLeod and Charity Cannon Willard (Woodbridge, Suffolk and Rochester, NY: D. S. Brewer, 2005), chaps. II.22, III.6 and 18.

[2] *Ibid.*, III.11.

[3] James C. Laidlaw, "Christine de Pizan, the Earl of Salisbury and Henry IV," *French Studies*, 36. (1982), 129-43. Isabelle was six at the time of the marriage and Richard a widower of twenty-nine.

[4] *The Vision of Christine de Pizan*, III.11.

[5] Laidlaw, "Christine de Pizan, the Earl of Salisbury and Henry IV." Lydgate's *Troy Book* (ca. 1415) reveals the direct influence of Christine's text; see Jocelyn Wogan-Browne *et al.*, *The Idea of the Vernacular: An Anthology of Middle English Literary Theory, 1280-1520* (University Park: Pennsylvania State Univ. Pr., 1999), 305. The *Othea* was very popular in both England and France; Edward IV would later own two copies in anthologies he commissioned: B.L. MS Royal 4 E. ii (fol. 272-316) and 17 E. v (fol. 291-331v). Sir John Paston had the French text copied by the scrivener William Ebesham, and the work was twice translated into English before the age of print, once by Stephen Scrope, secretary to Sir John Fastolf, between 1444 and 1450, and some decades later by Anthony Babyngton.

[6] See important articles by Carol M. Meale: "'alle the bokes that I haue of latyn, englisch and frensch': laywomen and their books in late medieval England," in *Women and Literature in Britain 1150-1500*, ed. Meale (Cambridge Univ. Press, 1993), 128-58 and "Patrons, Buyers and Owners: Book Production and Social Status," in Jeremy Griffiths & Derek Pearsall, eds., *Book Production And Publishing in Britain, 1375-1475* (Cambridge Univ. Press, 2000), 201-38.

[7] Harley MS 4431 is today one of the great treasures of the British Library and the subject of an international research project directed by Prof. James Laidlaw of the University of Edinburgh; see www.pizan.ed.ac.uk.

Rivers, who translated the version of the *Moral Proverbs* contained therein; this translation was one of the first works printed by Caxton in 1478.[1]

Christine's book on the art of warfare, the *Fais d'armes et de chevalerie* (1410) captured the interest of the military leader Sir John Talbot, who had it included in the luxury codex he commissioned in Rouen and presented to Margaret of Anjou on the occasion of her marriage to Henry VI in 1445.[2] The work was partially translated in around 1451 and later revised by William Worcester, Sir John Fastolf's secretary, in his *Boke of Noblesse.* A full translation, titled *The Book of Fayttes of Armes and of Chyualrye*, was completed by none other than Caxton in around 1489 at the behest of Henry VII. By the time of Caxton's translation, fully half the manuscripts had expunged every reference to the female author from the work; luckily, or wisely, Caxton used a manuscript that did not, but he did take the trouble to remove some unflattering remarks Christine had made about the English.[3]

The *Book of the Body Politic* (1521) is a translation of the 1407 *Livre du Corps de Policie*, a work describing the functions of all classes in society, from princes to peasants, that draws heavily upon the French translation of Valerius-Maximus' first-century *Facta et dicta memorabilia* (*Memorable Deeds and Sayings*). First translated in manuscript form around 1470, probably by Anthony Woodville,[4] the *Corps de Policie* was again translated and printed by John Skot in 1521 under the title *Body of Polycye*.

The *Cité des dames* (ca. 1405, Englished 1521) was also the object of early interest in England. An allegorical fortress meant as a refuge for potentially all women, the *City of Ladies* is considerably more feminist than Boccaccio's *De mulieribus claris* (*Concerning Famous Women*), on which it is based. French copies of the work were owned by Edward IV's parents, Richard, third duke of York and his wife Cecily Neville; Alice Chaucer, granddaughter of the poet; and Anne Harling of Suffolk, widow of John, fifth lord Scrope of Bolton.[5] In 1521, Henry Pepwell published a translation of the *City of Ladies* by Brian Anslay.[6] As has been speculated, Anslay's translation may well have been commissioned to prepare the English public for the eventual rule of young Mary Tudor, who could be imagined growing up as strong a leader as Christine's heroines.[7] Further impetus to the spread of this work's message was provided by the sets of six large tapestries depicting the "Citie of ladies" bequeathed by Henry VIII in 1547 to his children Elizabeth and Edward VI.[8]

Christine de Pizan became the most widely read woman author in fifteenth-and early sixteenth-century England, and continued to be read in both French and English.[9]

Christine Reno

---

[1] Woodville's translation would be reprinted by Richard Pynson in 1526 in his three-volume edition of Chaucer. See the Christine de Pizan section compiled by Angus J. Kennedy in the *Encyclopedia of Literary Translation into English*, ed. Olive Classe (London: Fitzroy Dearborn, 2000), 2 vols, 1.282-4.

[2] British Library, Royal MS 15 E. vi. See Michel-André Bossy, "Arms and the Bride: Christine de Pizan's Military Treatise as a Wedding Gift for Margaret of Anjou," in Marilynn Desmond ed., *Christine de Pizan and the Categories of Difference* (Minneapolis and London: Univ. of Minnesota Press, 1998), 236-56.

[3] A.T.P. Byles, ed., *The Book of Fayttes of Armes and of Chyualrye, trans. and printed by William Caxton from the French original by Christine de Pisan* (London: Oxford UP, 1932) EETS 189; Kraus Reprint, 1988, pp. xiv-xvi, liii.

[4] *The Middle English Translation of Christine de Pisan's 'Livre du Corps de Policie', ed. from MS C.U.L. Kk. 1.5*, ed. Diane Bornstein (Heidelberg: Carl-Winter, 1977), esp. pp. 17-36.

[5] See Meale, "Patrons, Buyers and Owners", p. 208 and Karen K. Jambeck, "The Library of Alice Chaucer, Duchess of Suffolk: A Fifteenth-Century Owner of a *Boke of le Citee de Dames,*" *The Profane Arts of the Middle Ages /Les Arts Profanes au Moyen Age*, 7 (Autumn 1998), 106-35. Cecily Neville's copy survives as B.L. MS Royal 19 A. xix).

[6] Maureen Cheney Curnow notes that Anslay most likely based his translation on Royal MS XIX A. xix, to which he would have had access as a member of Henry VIII's household; "*The Boke of the Cyte of Ladyes*, an English Translation of Christine de Pisan's *Le livre de la cité des dames,*" *Les bonnes feuilles* 3 (1974), 116-37 at p. 125.

[7] Hope Johnston, "How *Le Livre de la cité des dames* first came to be printed in England," in *Desireuse de plus avant enquerre… Actes du VI*[e] *Colloque international sur Christine de Pizan (Paris, 20-24 juillet 2006),* ed. Liliane Dulac, Anne Paupert *et al.*, (Paris: Champion, 2008), 389.

[8] See Susan Groag Bell, *The Lost Tapestries of the City of Ladies: Christine de Pizan's Renaissance Legacy* (Berkeley: Univ. of California Pr., 2004) esp. pp. 39, 164, 167. Other sets were owned by Margaret of Austria (bequeathed to Mary of Hungary), Anne of Brittany, Francis I and James V of Scotland. No material vestige of the tapestries has survived.

[9] Jennifer Summit, *Lost Property. The Woman Writer and English Literary History, 1380-1589* (Chicago and London: University of Chicago Press, 2000), 61.

## Here beginneth the Book of *Feats of Arms and of Chivalry* (Englished, 1489)

*And the first chapter is the Prologue, in which Christine of Pise excuseth herself to have dare enterprise to speak of so high matter as is contained in this said book.*

BECAUSE that *Hardiness* is so much necessary to enterprise high things (which, without that, should never *be* enprised), that same is covenable to me at this present work: to put it forth without other thing – seeing the littlehood of my person, which I know not deign ne worthy to treat of so high matter, ne durst not only *think* what blame Hardiness causeth when she is foolish! I, then (nothing moved by arrogance in foolish presumption, but admonested of veray affection and good desire of noble men in th'office of arms) am *exhorted*, after mine other escriptures passed (like as he that hath to-foren beaten down many strong edifices is more hardy to charge himself defy or to beat down a castle or fortress, when he feeleth himself garnished of covenable stuff thereto necessary). [1]

Then, to enterprise to speak in this present book of the right honorable office of arms and of chivalry (as well, in things which thereto be'n convenient, as in *droits*; which thereto be appertainent, like as the *laws*); and divers authors declaren it to the purpose, I have assembled the matters and gad'red in divers books for to produce mine intention in this present volume. [2]

But as it appertaineth this matter to be more executed by feat of diligence and wit, than by subtleties of words polished; and also, considered that they that be'n excer'sing and expert in th'art of chivalry be not commonly clerks, ne instruct in science of language, I intend not to treat but to the most plain and intendible language; that I shall move to that end, that the doctrine given by many authors (which, by the help of god, I purpose to declare in this present book) may be, to all men, clear and intendible. [3]

And because that this is thing not accustomed, and out of usage to *women* (which commonly do not intermit but to spin on the distaff and occupy them in things of household), I suppli' humbly to the said right high office and noble 'state of Chivalry; that in contemplation of their Lady Minerva born of the country of Greece, whom the ancients for her great cunning reputeden a goddess, the which found (like as old writings sayen; and as I have other times said; and also the poet Boece reciteth in his *Book of Clear and Noble Women*, and semblably reciten many other) the art and manner to make harness of iron and steel; which will not have, ne take it for none evil, if I, a *woman*, charge myself to treat of so like a matter; but will ensue th' ensignment and teaching of Senec', which sayeth, "Reck thee not what they say, so that the words be good." [4]

And therefore (and to purpose, in manner poetic), it pleaseth me t'address such a prayer to the foresaid lady: *O Minerva, Goddess of arms and of chivalry, which by virtue of high intendment above all other women, foundest and institutest – among th'other noble arts and sciences which of thee took their beginning – th'usage to forge of iron and steel armors and harness, propice and covenable to cover and targe the body of man against the strokes of darts, noyous shot, and spears in battle; feats of arms, helms, shields, targes, and other harnesss defensible, fro' the first comen, institutest and gavest manner and order to arrange battles and t'assail and fight in manner. Adored Lady and high Goddess, be thou not displeased that I, simple and little woman (like as nothing unto the greatness of thy renowm in cunning) dare presently comprise to speak of so magnifique an office as is th'office of arms; of which first, in the said*

---

[1] *enprised* ] undertaken; *covenable* ] suitable, appropriate; *Hardiness* ] boldness, fortitude, personified as a woman; *deign* ] fit; *other thing* ] other qualification or authority; *admonisted* ] admonished encouraged (to write, by my own high motives); *office* occupation or service; *extorted ... fortress* ] My successful writings (escriptures) that are already on record encourage me to take on a more daunting labor, no less than the warrior, made confident by his former conquests, assaults a strong fortress; *to-foren* ] heretofore; *garnished* ] equipped.

[2] *droits* ] legitimate perquisites; *laws* ] the principles or rules of chivalry.

[3] *clerks* ] clerics, scholars; *instruct* ] instructed; *intendible* ] intelligible, accessible; thus, *I, with my diligence and wit, shall undertake what could not be done by scholars who lack both expertise in arms, and the science of language, to compose a reader-friendly discourse on this challenging topic*; *doctrine* ] instruction.

[4] *intermit but to* ] occupy themselves except to; *distaff* ] a cleft staff used for winding wool or flax; *suppli'* ] supplicate, appeal; *'state* ] estate; *the which found* ] she who founded, invented; Boece, *Book of Clear and Noble Women* ] Boccacio, *De Claris Mulieribus,* one of Christine's most valued sources; *semblably reciten* ] similarly reported; *harness* ] armor and accoutrements; *ensue th' ensignment* ] appeal to the teaching (O.F. *enseignement*); cf. Seneca, *Ad Serenum de Tranquilitate Animi* ("Never shall I be ashamed to quote an unesteemed author if the words are good"); cited again in the *Body of Policy.*

*renowmèd country of Greece, thou gavest th'usage. And insomuch it may please thee to be to me favorable – that I may be somewhat consonant in the nation where thou wast born, which (as then) was named the Great Greece, the country beyond the Alps or mountains; which now is said 'Pulia and Calabrè in Italy, where you were born – and I am, as you were, a woman Italian.* [1]

## From *The Body of Policy* (Englished, 1521)

**Anonymous Tudor translation of Christine's *Le Livre du Corp de Policie*** (c. 1407)

People well-counseled, or people that be eurous, I say to you, the disciples of study and of wisdom… [2]

EARCH out the highness of the clear rejoicing star! that is, to know the star of *science*, taking diligently the good treasure of that clear and healthful fountain. Fulfill yourself of that pleasant refection that may so much avail you and bring you to worship. For what thing is more worthy to man than science and the highness of cunning? Certainly, thou that desirest it, and employest thyself thereto, hath chosen a glorious life! [3]

For by that, thou mayest comprehend the election of virtue and the eschewing of vice, like as it stirreth to the one and defendeth from the other. For there is nothing more parfit than the truth and clearness for to understand and know the parfitness of things, which cannot be understond without cunning of science. For a wise man would take pain to get the least savor of the relics of wisdom. And certainly I dare well say, whatsoever any man sayeth, that there is joy ne treasure semblable to the treasure of understonding. Wherefore ye champions of sapience, if ye will do any labor or pain, I counsel you that ye labor to *get science*. For an' ye have it and use it well, ye be noble, ye be rich, ye be all parfit. [4]

And this is plainly showed in the doctrine of philosophers which showest and teachest the way to come by wisdom to the treasure of pure and parfit sufficiaunce. A prudent philosopher that was called Cleanthes had such a desire to taste of the great goodness of sapience, and loved it so well, notwithstanding that he was so poor, that he could not find the means to come thereto but by great labor that he had in the night, and that was this: he drew water all the night, which was necessary to the use of the scholars. And so by that mean he got his living. And in the day, he intended to the study and to the lessons of Chrysippsus (which was a solemn philosopher); to that intent that he might be fulfilled of the cunning of this wise man; and by that teaching and long continuance became a sovereign man. Wherefore meseemeth, truly, that this man was worthy to have great laud, as well for the constance of his labor as for the great science that he got. Wherefore Seneca sayeth in an epistle that Cleanthes, by his great labor, holp himself to "come to the perfection of science." [5]

Yet to the purpose: to love science and to be diligent to learn it (for the great goodness that may fall to him that list to labor therefore), we will speak a little of other philosophers, for to sharpen the appetite of them that study for to learn: The philosopher Platon loved science so much that through the diligence that he made for to get it, he filled himself with wisdom and doctrine. This Platon was master to Aristotle and was in the time of Socrates the philosopher – and he profited so greatly in doctrine that for the nobleness of his wit was counted the wisest man living. And that he loved science he showed it well, for he went all about for to search out all the doctrine of books, namely in Italy. Wherefore Valere speaketh of his great diligence and desire that he had for to know and understond: that the great thought that he took, for to get books togeder, was for nothing else but that science and cunning might be cast abroad by him through all the world. [6]

---

[1] *propice* ] propitious; *helms* ] helmets; *targes* ] shields; *darts* ] arrows, javelins; *noyous shot* ] hurtful bullets; *renowm* ] renown, fame; *the traditional story is that Minerva was born from the head of her father Jupiter; in Christine's redaction, Minerva was born in greater Hellas, in the region of Apulia and Calabria.*

[2] *eurous* ] lucky, prosperous, successful.

[3] *science* ] knowledge, academic discipline; *refection* ] refreshment, nourishment; *worship* ] respect, admiration.

[4] *is joy ne* ] is neither joy nor; *semblable* ] can compare with.

[5] *parfit sufficiaunce* ] perfect sufficiency; *Cleanthes* ] (331 – 232 BCE), Greek Stoic; this and various other anecdotes are drawn from Valerius Maximus, *Factorum et dictorum memorabilium libri novem,* in the French translation by Simon de Hesdin and Nicolas de Gonesse's (*Les Fais et les Dis des Romains et de autres gens*, 1375-1401); *Chrysippus* ] (c. 280 - 207 BCE), Greek Stoic; *Seneca* ] Lucius Annaeus Seneca (c. 4 BCE - 65 CE), Rome Stoic philosopher and author of closet tragedies; a moralist; *holp* ] i.e., helped.

[6] *namely in Italy* ] searching as far away (from Athens) as Italy.

This solemn philosopher died in the age of eighty-and-eight years – and happened well at his death the great love that he had to all manner of books, for they found lying by him the books of a woman that was a poet, which was named Sappho (and wrote of love, in pleasant and goodly verses, as 'Orace° sayeth). And peradventure he looked upon them for taking of his pleasure in her° pleasant sayings. [1]

And yet there is contained, in the book of Valere, of the philosopher Democritus, which was a famous man in natural philosophy. And as Aristotle telleth in the first book of *Generation and of Corruption*, and chargeth of all things; that is to say, he would give commendation to the saying of Democritus. And therefore Aristotle commendeth him greatly, in divers places, for his natural philosophy; and allowed greatly his opinions. Also Valere commendeth much the said philosopher for because he dispraised riches greatly (which oftentimes hath done many men much hurt and letting in getting of philosophy), and sayeth that this Democritus might have greatly abounded in riches if he had would; for his fader was so passingly rich that he fed all the host of King Xerxes. Yet notwithstanding all that riches, he drew him to study. And when the goods fell unto him, he distributed them to his friends and to the poor people and unneth left him anything to live upon. [2]

Secondly, Valere commendeth him inasmuch as he never desired worldly honors, which impeacheth greatly to conquer sapience. And as he dwelled long in Athens he employed all his time in exercise of doctrine and lived there long time unknown in the said city (like as himself witnesseth in one of his volumes): for he chose° to live solitarily, for to be out of noise and strife which letteth greatly speculation. Then it appeared that he had great desire of cunning, for he eschewed to his power all manner things that might lett him fro' the getting of science. [3]

Yet to the same purpose: that men should love science and study, Valere speaketh of the philosopher Carneades, saying that he was the weary° knight that labored sciences for eighty years. He lived in philosophy and he was marvelously conjoined to the works of doctrine – that it seemed oftentimes, as he sat at his meat, that he took his refection in studying of doctrine! – so that Melissa his servant was fain oftentimes to take him by the hand and put it to his meat, seeing the great study that he was in. This said philosopher set by nothing in the world, but only by virtue.[4]

Of many other philosophers and shewers of wisdom a man might speak of (but for shorting of this matter, I will pass over). And these matters heretofore I have brought to mind, to the intent that I may reduce and bring to knowledge of the good students (such as desire to learn science and virtue): for it is no doubt but the sciences make a man to be gracious and well-governed, but if it be such one as is undiscrete and weeneth himself that he knoweth all sciences (but in *themself* they show it not, but *teach* it to other). And such manner of men as teacheth sapience and do nothing themself of the same, be'n likened to such as die for hunger, and their good lying by them; and other men help themself with that good. (And such men be more blameworthy when they do amiss, than other.) [5]

Yet of the same: for because that this fair matter is right covenable to be known (and also that every man hath not the book of Valere for to gader out to their pleasaunce all the matters that he speaketh of), it liketh me yet to speak of the good purpose that 'longeth to study; for because I have said heretofore that the students ought to do great diligence in the getting of science; as Valere reciteth and showeth how that diligence, well-modered (without to great excess), shall bring a man in great exercise of cunning; and assigneth the cause why he sayeth so. [6]

Scevola, which was an excellent legister at Rome, composed certain laws which other legisters useth yet; and after his great occupation and study would take recreation of divers plays. And that a man *should* do so, Valere showeth that it is reason, and sayeth that the nature of things will not suffer a man

---

[1] *taking* ] to acquire a pleasant style for his own wise sayings; *Sappho* ] Valerius Maximus reports that Plato died reading *Sophron* (Sophron of Syracuse, 5th C BCE, a writer of mimes); following a mistake in the French translation, Christine suggests that Plato spent his last hours studying the work of the famous woman poet.

[2] *Democritus* ] (460 - c. 370 BCE), a pre-Socratic philosopher noted for his cheerfulness, and for his original formulation of atomic theory; detested by Plato; *first book* ] *De Generatione et Corruptione,* Book 1; *allowed* ] accepted as true; *letting* ] hindrance; *Xerxes* ] king of Persia (486 – 465 BCE).

[3] *letteth greatly speculation* ] greatly hinders scientific inquiry; *lett* ] obstruct.

[4] *Carneades* ] (214 -129 BCE), a Skeptic; *refection in* ] nourishment from; *meat* ] food, dinner.

[5] *shewers* ] guides; *but if it be such* ] except in the case of; *good* ] money.

[6] *well-modered* ] well-moderated (French *modérer*), perhaps with a glance at well mothered (ME *moder*).

continually to be in labor;[1] that is to say, he must needs at some time have rest in idleness. But this "idleness" should not be that a man should cease fro' all bodily labors. But it is to understond that a man should be occupied in some joyful disport, by the which his understonding may be the fresher. For by long studying, all the sensitive virtues of man be made weary and dull. And also, they be not brought again to their rest and tranquility by ceasing of *all manner* works. For they that be travailed in study, if they be not occupied with some gladness, they should be full of melancholy (for the spirit that hath been in so great labors of study before). And if they go to bed so, they shall suffer pain in their sleep (as in dreaming, and otherwise). And therefore, the remedy of that travail is for to rejoice his spirit with some goodly play and disport. And in like wise as the pleasant meats please more at some time when they be intermeddled with gross meats, in like wise the work of study is the better nourished when a man at some time applyeth° himself to play and disport.

And therefore Caton sayeth, "Intermeddle thy works among with disports°." Also Aristotle sayeth in the third book of *Ethics*, "A man in his labor should use virtuously, as well play, as labor." To the which thing Senec' accordeth in his book of *Tranquility of Courage*, and sayeth that "the lusty and well-bearing fields be soon hurt by continual fertility, without they be otherwise refreshed." Likewise, continual labor in any science hurteth the courage of any person, and engend'reth frenzy. And therefore Nature giveth man inclination of disport and play otherwhiles; for the cause also, they that 'stablished the laws in old time ordained certain feasts: to that intent, that all manner of people should assemble for to disport and play and leave their labor. To this purpose is said of Socrates (which no part of science was hid fro'), that he was not ashamed when he was mocked of Achipiades for because that he found him playing with little children. But he did so for because that the recreation which he had among them should sharp and refresh his wit and make it more quick to the study. And for that cause, as old as he was, he learned to play on the harp. [2]

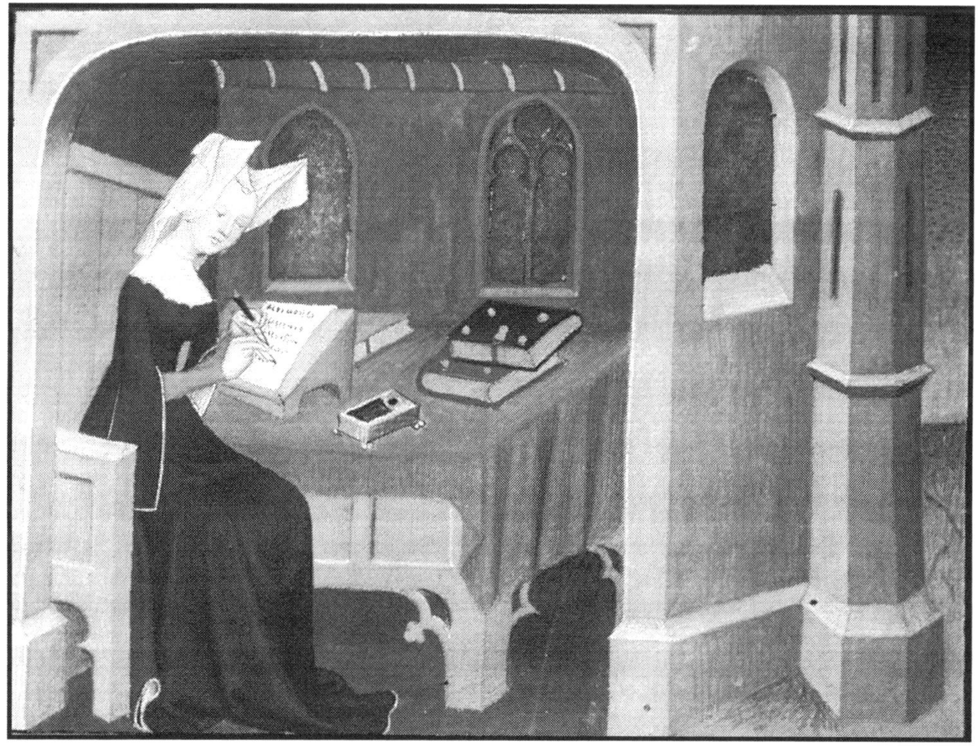

Christine de Pizan in her study (Brussels, MS KBR 10309, f. 3r)

[1] *Scaevola* ] Quintus Mucius Scaevola, ak.a. Pontifex (died 82 BCE), founder of the scientific study of Roman law.; *legister* ] legislator; *reason* ] reasonable.

[2] *Caton* ] Dionysius Cato (3d century CE), to whom is ascribed Cato's *Distichs,* proverbial wisdom and morality in Latin couplets that Christine imitates with her *Moral Proverbs*; *Senec'* ] another allusion to Seneca's *Ad Serenum de Tranquillitate Animi*; *otherwhiles* ] at other times (when not studying); *Achipiades* ] i.e., Alcibiades.

## From *The City of Ladies* (Englished, 1521)

*Here beginneth the first chapter, which telleth how and by whom the City of Ladies was first begun to build—*

**AFTER the manner that I have much in usage, and to that thing which the exercise of my life is most disposed; that is, to *know*, in the haunting of study —**

N A DAY, as I was sitting in my little cell (divers books of divers matters about me), mine intent was, at that time, to travail and to gather into my conceit the weighing of divers sentences of divers authors by me° long time before studied. I 'dressed my visage toward those foresaid books, thinking (as for the time) to leave in peace *subtle* things;[1] and, to disport me, for to look upon some pleasant book of the writing of some *poets*. [2]

And as I was in this intent, I searched about me after some *pratty* book; and, of adventure, there° came a strange book into my hands that was taken to me to keep. I opened this book, and I saw by the entitulation that it called him "Matholeus" – then, in *laughing*, because (I had not seen him, and oftentimes I had heard speak of him) that he should not speak well of the reverence of women. I thought that, in manner of solace, I would visit him. And yet I had not looked long on him, but that my good moder that bare me called me to the refection of supper, whereof the hour was come. [3]

Purposing to see him in the morning, I left him at that time – and in the morrow following, I sat me again to my study, as I did of custom. I forgat it not, and° put my will to effect that came to me that night before – to visit the foresaid book of Matheolus.

And then I began to read and to proceed in him – but, as meseemed, the matter was not right "pleasant" to people that delighted them not in *evil-saying*; nor it was of no profit to any edifying of virtue, seeing the words and the matters dishonest, of which it touched.

Visiting here and there, and so come° to the end, I left him, and took heed of more higher matters and of more profit. Yet the sight of this foresaid book – howbeit that he was of none authority – it engendered in me a new thought, which was made great marvel to grow in my courage and thinking: What might be the cause, and whereof it might come, that so many divers men (clerks and others) have been, and *be*,° inclined to say, by mouth and in their treatise and writings, so many slanders and blames of women and of their conditions? – and not only one or twain (nor this "Matheolus" – which, among others, hath no manner of reputation, and treateth in manner of scorn), but generally in *all* treatises of philosophers, poets, and all rhetoricians (which should be long, to rehearse all their names) speaketh, as it were, by one mouth, and accordeth all, in semble conclusion, determining that "the conditions of women" be'n fully inclined to all vices.[4]

These things thinking in me right deeply, I began to examine myself and my conditions as a woman natural; and in like wise I discuted of other women whose company I haunted – as well of princesses and of great ladies, as of mean gentlewomen, right great plenty, which of their graces have told me their privities and strait thoughts – to know by my judgment, in conscience and without favor, if it° might be true that so many notable men of one another witnesseth; yet notwithstanding that, for things that I might *know* (as long as I have sought and searched), I could not perceive that such judgments might be true against the natural conditions or manners of women.[5]

---

[1] *'dressed my visage* ] addressed my attention; *subtle* ] profound.

[2] *to gather ... sentences* ] to gather into comprehension my considered collection of quotes, *sententiae,* from various authorities already studied.

[3] *pratty* ] pretty; *of adventure* ] by chance; *to keep* ] to take care of; *he should not* ] subjunctive; *i.e.*, that I should find he did not; *Matheolus* ] Mathieu of Boulogne, author of *Liber lamentationum Matheoluli* (*The Lamentations of Matheolus*) (c. 1295), a commentary on marriage alleging that women make men's lives miserable; *in manner of solace* ] i.e., just to amuse myself; *moder* ] mother

[4] *Visiting here and there* ] browsing, poking around; *semble* ] the like.

[5] *discuted* ] pondered; *haunted* ] frequented, kept; *without favor* ] impartially, without bias; *privities and strait thoughts* ] secrets and confidential thoughts.

I argued strongly against these women, saying that it should be too great a thing, that so many famous men, so solemn clerks of so high and great understanding, so clearly saying in all things, as it seemed, that should have spoken or written *lyingly* (and in so many places! – that of pain, I found *any* moral volume, whatsoever the author were, that ere I had read it to the end but some chapters or certain clauses were of blaming of them). This only short reason made me to conclude that mine understanding, for his simpleness and ignorance, ne could not know my great defauts—and semblably of other women, that always it accorded that it was so, *truly*. And so I reported me more to the judgment of *other,* than to that I felt or know of my *self.* [1]

Thus, in this thought, was I as a person half from himself. And there came before me right great foison of ditties and proverbs, of many divers authors, to the purpose that I remembered in myself one after another, as it were a well springing. And in conclusion of all, I determined that God made a foul thing, when He formed woman; in marveling how so worshipful a Workman deigned ever to make one so abhominable work, which is the vessel (as by saying of them), and the draught and herbegage, of all evil and of all vices. [2]

Then, I being in this thought, there sprang in me a great displeasance and sorrow of courage, in dispraising myself and all womankind, so as if that should be showed in nature. And I said such words in my complaints: "Ha, Lord God! How may it be? For if I err not in the faith, I ought not doubt that thine infinite wisdom and very parfit goodness had nothing made but that 'all were good'; and formest not thou thyself woman, right singularly? and then thou gave her all such inclinations that pleased thee, that she should have. And how may it be, that thou should have failed in anything? Alway, see here so many great occasions, thus judged determined, and concluded against them! I cannot understand this *repugnance*! And if it be so, good Lord God – that it be *true* that womankind haboundeth in so many abhominations, as many men witnesseth (and thou sayest thyself, that 'The witness of many is for to believe' – by the which, I ought not doubt but that it should be true) – alas, good Lord, why hadst thou not made me to be born into this world in the *masculine* kind, to that intent that mine inclinations might have been all to have served thee the better? and that I should not have erred in anything? and might have been of so great perfection, as they say that *men* be? Yet, sith it is so, that thy debonaireness stretcheth not so much toward me, then spare my negligence in thy service, good Lord God, and be not displeased. For that servant that receiveth least rewards of his Lord least is bound to his service." [3]

Such words and moe enow I said, right long, in my sorrowful thought to God, and in my lamentation (so as she that, by my folly, held me right evil content of that, that God made me to be born into this world, in kind of "woman"). [4]

**Part 1, chap. 2.** *Christine telleth how three ladies appeared to her and how she that went before reasoned with her first and comforted her of the displeasure that she had—*

S I WAS IN THIS SORROWFUL THOUGHT, the head downcast as a shameful person, the eyes full of tears, holding mine hand under my cheek, leaning upon the pommel of my chair, suddenly I saw come down upon my lap a streamen of light, as it were of the same, and that I° was in a dark place, in which the sun might not shine at that hour. Stert then, as though I had been waked of a dream (and 'dressing the head to behold this light, fro' whence it might come), I saw before me standing three ladies crowned, of right sovereign reverence. Of the which, the shining of their clear faces gave light unto me and to all the place there. As I was marveling – neither man nor woman with me; considering the door close upon me, and they thider came; doubting lest it had been some fantasy, for to have tempted me – I° made the sign of the cross in my forehead, full of dread. [5]

And then she which was the first of the three, in laughing, began thus to reason with me: "Dear daughter, dread thee not! For we be not come hider for nothing that is *contrary* unto thee, nor to do thee to be *encumbered*; but for to *comfort* thee, as those that have pity of thy trouble; and to put thee out of the ignorance that so much blindeth thine understanding; and that thou puttest fro' thee that thou *knowest* (of

---

[1] *his simpleness* ] the simplicity of my academic understanding; *know ... defauts* ] apprehend my own faulty observation; *semblably* ] likewise; *reported me* ] referred myself; *that I felt* ] that which I felt.

[2] *foison* ] abundance; *ditties* ] common sayings; *the draught and herbegage* ] the fount and lodging.

[3] *showed in nature* ] essentially true; *veray parfit* ] truly perfect.

[4] *moe enow* ] more than enough.

[5] *Stert* ] Startled.

very certain science), to give *faith to the contrary* (to that which thou feelest not, ne see'st not, ne knowest, otherwise than by plurality of strange opinions). Thou resemblest the fool (of the which was made a jape) which was sleeping in the mill and was clothed in the clothing of a woman; and to make resemblance, those that mocked him witnessed that he *was* a woman – and so he believed more *their false sayings* than the certainty of his *being*. How is it, fair daughter, and where is thy wit become? Hast thou forgotten now how that fine gold proveth him in the furnace? – that he changeth not his *virtue*, but is more pliant, to be brought to divers fashions. And knowest thou not that the most marvelous things be most debatous and most arguous? If thou wilt advise thee in the same wise, to the most high things that be'n – that is, to know the celestial things – behold, if these great 'philosophers' that hath been (that *thou* arguest, against thine own kind!) have determined *false*, and to the contrary of truth; and as they repugn, one against another – as thou thyself hast seen in the book of *Metaphysic* (whereas Aristotle reproveth their opinions), and rehearseth the same wise of Plato, and of others; and note this again, if Saint Austin and other doctors of the Church have done so? The same wise, Aristotle (in *some* parties, albeit that he be called 'the prince of philosophers,' and in whom 'philosophy natural and moral was sovereign').° And it seemeth thou° trowest that all all the words of 'philosophers' be'n articles of the faith of Jesu Crist, and that they may not err! [1]

"And as to these 'poets' of which thou speakest: knowest not thou well, that they have spoken in many things in manner of *fables*, and do intend so much to the *contrary* of that that their sayings showeth? (and it may be taken after the rule of grammar, which is named *antiphrasis*); the which intendeth thus (as thou knowest well), as one should say, "Sith *one* is a shrew," that is to say, that "*He* is good." And so, by the contrary.

"So I counsel thee that thou do thy profit of their sayings, and thou understand it so (whatsoever be their *intent* in such places whereas they blame women). And peradventure this same man (that is, Matheolus) in his book understood the same. For there be many things, whoso taketh them after the *letter*, it should be pure heresy and shame to him that sayeth it! – and not only to him, but to others; and the same wise, of *The Romaunt of the Rose,* on whom is put great faith because of the authority of the maker.[2]

"This thing proveth clearly, by experience, that the contrary is true of the shrewdness that they purpose, and yet° to *be* in that estate, to the great charge and blame of *women*. For who was ever that husband that ever suffered such mastery of his wife that she should have leave to say so many villainies and injuries as they put upon women, that *they* should say! I believe (whatsoever thou hast seen in writing) that thou° sawest it never, at the eye. So they be pure lesings, right shrewdly colored. [3]

"Thus I say, in concluding, my lief friend, that folly caused ye this present opinion. Now come again to thyself. Take thy wit, and trouble ye no more for such fantasies. For know well that all this evil sayings generally of women hurteth the sayers and not the women." [4]

**Part 2, chap. 12:** *Here Rightwisness sayeth that she hath achieved the stonework of the city and it is time to people it.*

[*Lady Rightwisness*:°] "Now meseemeth, right dear friend, that our building is well-lift up of our City of Ladies, and the high masonry all along the large streets, and the royal palaces, strong buildings of dungeons and defensible towers lifted right high, that it may be seen afar. So it is time fro' henceforth that we begin to people this noble city – to the intent that she be not waste nor void, but inhabited of ladies of great excellence (for we will none other people). O how fortunate shall the citizens of our city be! For they shall have no need to have dread nor doubt to be dislodged of their possession by straungers. For this is the propriety of our work: that the owners shall not need to be put out. [5]

"And now there is a new feminine royalm begun, but it is much more worthier than that other was: for it shall [not°] need that the ladies lodged here go out of their land, for to conceive ne bring forth new heirs to maintain their possession by divers ages fro' line to line. For it shall suffice enough forever, of them

---

[1] *a jape* ] a trick or prank.

[2] *Romaunt of the Rose* ] title of the English trans. to which young Chaucer contributed. Christine's reference is to the French original, Jean de Meun's popular but stridently misogynistic continuation of Guillaume de Lorris' *Roman de la Rose* (c. 1275).

[3] *lesings* ] lies, falsehoods, slanders.

[4] *lief* ] beloved.

[5] *dungeons* ] not, originally, prisons but the great towers of a castle, situated in the innermost court and well fortified.

that we shall put in it now: for this is the destiny of them, that *they shall never die*. And without fail, they shall abide in the same age, beauty, and freshness – be they young or old that we shall put therein. [1]

"And when we have peopled it with noble citizens, Dame Justice my sister shall come after, that shall bring thither the Queen (above all other women most excellent); accompanied with princesses of great dignity which shall inhabit the most high places and high dungeons. For it is good reason that when the Queen shall come thither, that she find the city garnished and peopled of noble ladies that should receive her with great worship as their sovereign lady and empress of all their kind.

"Yet what citizens shall we put there? Shall they be unstable women, or defamed? Certainly, nay! But they shall be all worshipful women and of great authority – for more fair people, ne more great array, may not be in a city than good women and worshipful.

"Now rise, lief friend! Now put thee in business and go before, and let us seek them."

**Part 2, chap. 13:** *Here Christine asketh of Dame Rightwisness if ... the life of marriage is hard to bear for the occasion of women...; and Rightwisness answereth ... of the great love of women to their husbands*

Then in going to seek the foresaid ladies by the ordinance of Dame Rightwisness, in going I said: "These words, Madame, without fail, ye and Reason have assoiled, and concluded so well and so fair my questions and demaunds, that I cannot reply no more. And I hold me right well informed of that that I sought. And by you two, I have learned enough how all things able ought to be done and learned (as much in strength of bodies, as in wisdom of understanding – and if all virtues be possible, to be executed by women!). But yet I pray you, that ye would tell and certify me if it be true, that these men say (and so many authors beareth witness); through the which I am in right a great thought that the life of the order of marriage be to men 'heavy' and environed of 'so-great tempest,' by the blame and importunity of women and of their 'ravenous grief'; (as it is written in many books, and people enow witnesseth it). And that 'They love their husbands and their company so little that nothing 'noyeth them so *much*!' —by the which, to 'void such inconveniences, many have counseled the wise men that they marry not, certifying that few of them [who are wives°] be true in their party. And also, Valere writing° to Ruffin and Theophrastus in his book sayeth that 'No wise man ought to take a wife, for there is but little love in women, but great charge and jangling.' And 'If the man do it to be the better served and kept in his sickness, more better and more truly a true *servaunt* shall keep him and serve him, and shall not cost him so much.' And 'If the woman be sick, the husband is in great sorrow and dare not speak one word nigh her.' And – enough of such things he telleth, which should be too long to rehearse! Wherefore I say, mine own Lady, that if these things be true, these defaults be so great that all the grace and virtues that [women°] may have be brought to nought, and quenched." [2]

*Answer*. "Certes, dear friend, so as thou thyself hath said sometime to that purpose: that *One may lead a process well at his ease that pleadeth without party*. And I promise thee that the books that so sayeth, women made them not! But I trow that he that would make a new book (that were *true*!) of the debates of marriage, an' that he were informed of the truth, one should find other tidings. Alas, dear friend, how many women be there as thou knowest thyself that useth their weary life in the bond of marriage by the hardness of their husbands in more greater penaunce than [if°] they were esclaves among the Saracens! Ha, God, how many hard beatings without cause and reason! How many villainous wrongs and outrageous bondages suffereth many of these good and worshipful women (which all cry not out on harrow!); and such that die for hunger and for mis-ease! – and their husbands be'n at the tavern and in other dissolute places, and yet the poor women shall be beaten at their coming home, and *that* shall be their supper. And to say that these husbands be'n any thing sorrowful for the 'sickness' of their wives? I pray thee, my Love, where be they? [3]

"And without that that I say more to thee, thou mayest know well, that these slaunders said against women, whoso sayeth it, they were (and be!) things found and said of *violence*, and against truth. For the husbands be the masters over the women, and not the women their masteresses. So they would never suffer such authority of their wives.

---

[1] *royalm* ] realm, queendom.

[2] *assoiled* ] solved, made clear; *Valere...to Ruffin* ] Walter Map, *Dissuasio Velerii ad Rufinum* (cf. Wife of Bath on Jankyn's *Book of Wikked Wyves*).

[3] *esclaves* ] slaves; *Saracens* ] as Muslims were known in Christian Europe during the medieval period; *to cry out on harrow* ] to call out in distress, or to denounce someone's actions (obsolete by 1600).

"But I promise thee, that all marriages be not maintained in such contents (it were great damage!). For there be'n some that liveth in peaceableness, love, and truth togeder, by that that the parties be good and discrete and reasonable. Though it be not, of evil husbands, there be'n right good, worshipful, and wise; and the° women that meeteth with them liveth as to the glory of the world, in right a good hour for them. And that, thou mayest well know by thyself, and thou hadst such one that in thy judgment none other man passed him in all bounty, peaceableness, truth, and good love; of the which, the sorrows of that that death took him away from thee shall never part from thine heart."

**Part 2, chap. 36.** *Here it speaketh against them that say that is not good that women should learn letters...*

After these things beforesaid, I, Christine, said thus: "Madame, I see well that many great wealths cometh by women. And if any evil have followed by any evil women, nevertheless it seemeth me that there be'n many moe wealths come by *good* women, and in the same wise by *wise* women – *and* by them that have learned sciences, of whom there is mention made before; by the which, I marvel greatly of the opinion of some men that say that they would 'not in no wise' that their daughters or wives or kinswomen should learn sciences; and that it should "apair their conditions."

*Answer.* "Thou mayest see well, by *that*, that all the opinions of men be not founded upon Reason! – and that they have wrong. For it ought not to be presumed that of knowing the science moral, and they that learn virtue, the conditions of them ought not to be 'impaired' by that! But it is no doubt that they [are°] *nobled* thereby, and amended. How is it thought that he that learneth a good lesson of doctrine should 'impair'? This thing is not to say, ne to sustain... [T]here be not many men that be wise, of the opinion abovesaid. Thy fader, that was a natural philosopher, had not that opinion that 'Women should not learn letters' – but insomuch that he saw she inclined to learning (as thou knowest well), he had great pleasure of it, and by the 'blame' of thy moder (which by the common opinion of women) thou were tarried in thy youth to enter more in the deepness of sciences. But as the proverb sayeth, 'That [which°] Nature giveth may not be taken away.' So it may not hurt – the feeling of cunning that thou hast gad'red togeder the little drops; of the which, I trow, that thou weenest be not of little valor; but thou holdest them in great treasure (and without fail, thou hast cause!)."

I, Christine, answered: "That [which°] you say is as true as the Pater noster!"

**Part 2, chap. 44.** *Here it speaketh against them that sayeth women would be ravished...*[1]

Then I, Christine, said thus: "Madame, I believe it well that ye say, and I am sure that there be'n enow fair women chaste and that can keep them from the await of the deceivers; yet it grieveth me of that, that many men say: that 'Women would be ravished,' and that 'It displeaseth them not, though they say the contrary with their mouth.' But it were a great thing to make me to believe it that it were agreeable to them."

*Answer.* "Doubt it not, fair friend, that it is no pleasance to these chaste ladies of heart and thought to be 'ravished,' but it to them right great sorrow, above all other. And that it be true, there be many of them that have showed it by fair ensamples, as of Lucrece the right noble woman of Rome. [....] Some say, for because of her there was a law made that if any man that ravished a woman, [he°] should die – the which law is convenable and just."

[Conclusion,] **Part 2, chap. 19**

Christine speaketh to all princesses, ladies, and to all women ... which loveth, loved, and shall love virtue and good conditions – as much [to°] those that been passed as those that be'n now, and those that are to come: "Be ye glad! And make joy in our new City – which (thanks be God!) is all builded for the most part, and near-hand peopled. Yield ye thanks to God, which hitherto hath conduited me with great labor and study; and would that a worshipful lodging (for a perpetual dwelling as long as the world shall last) were made by me in the cloister of a city 'stablished; to which I am come hitherto, hoping to go forth to the conclusion of my work, by the help and comfort of Dame Justice, which after her promise shall be to me help without being weary, till it be closed and all parfitly made. Now pray for me, my most 'douted ladies!"[2]

Bib. Nat. (Paris) MS. Fr. 598, fol. 43r

[1] *would be ravished* ] want to be raped.

[2] *'douted* ] redouted, awesome, reverend.

# Katherine of Sutton (fl. 1363-1376)

*Heu! misere, cur contigit*
*videre mortem Salvatoris?*

— Easter play, Barking Convent

THE EASTER PLAY OF BARKING CONVENT is the earliest surviving drama written by a woman in England. It is also the earliest record of women playing the female roles in a dramatic representation and the only certain record of such playing until the Restoration drama in the later seventeenth century. A prefatory note in the manuscript tells us that the play was devised by Lady Katherine of Sutton, who was the abbess of the Barking convent between 1363 and 1376. Though little else is known of her, Lady Katherine was one of a long line of noblewomen who served as abbesses of the convent, including a kinswoman, Yolande de Sutton, and three queens and two princesses. Through her office the abbess of Barking was also a baroness with the duty of sending knights and soldiers to serve the king in war.

The play itself is a liturgical drama, performed annually in the context of the celebration of the Easter ritual in the church of the convent. Its audience consisted of nuns of the convent (some 35 to 40 women) joined by the lay men and women who flocked to its church for the celebration of major feasts. As the manuscript note explains, Lady Katherine conceived the play to stimulate the emotional involvement of these laypeople with the events commemorated in the feast. The first part portrays the descent of Christ to Limbo where he releases the souls of the just who have been imprisoned from the time of Adam's sin until the redemption; this story is not in the canonical gospels of the New Testament, but was part of a well-known tradition reaching back to the fourth-century apocryphal Gospel of Nicodemus. This section concludes in a symbolic and liturgical mode with the priest taking the Eucharist from the Easter tomb, (that is, a special repository where it was placed on Good Friday), and displaying it "risen" before the congregation. The procession that follows is specifically said to figure the return of Jesus' disciples to Galilee, where the Gospel of Mark says they were to encounter the risen Lord. The second part is directly related to the oldest stratum of liturgical drama, the "Quem quaeritis" trope from the Easter liturgy. Dramatizing the early morning visit to the tomb by the three women (traditionally called "the three Maries") told in the Gospels of Matthew, Mark, and Luke, it had centered on the question "Whom do you seek?" ("Quem quaeritis?") asked by the angel they encounter in the tomb. When they answer "Jesus of Nazareth," the angel's response, "He is risen," had traditionally led to the rejoicing which concluded earlier dramatic representations. But here it is followed by a dramatization of the encounter of Mary Magdalen (one of the "three Maries") with the risen Jesus, told in the Gospel of John. In this play, then, fittingly for a community of women, it is Mary Magdalen who announces the resurrection to the clergy who portray Jesus' male disciples; she is then joined by them and by the choir of the convent in the final affirmation of the resurrection and the solemn hymn "Te Deum laudamus" ("We praise you, O God") which concluded the representation.

St. Cuthberga, stained glass, *Wimbourne Minster*

Like the liturgical drama that had been performed by monastic communities since the mid-twelfth century, the aim of the play was not a "realistic" representation of events and emotions, but a stylized portrayal of emotion through the resources of musical chant and gesture. In fact Lady Katherine (and perhaps those in the convent who assisted her) did not script the dialogue of the play but drew on earlier Easter plays and assembled it from the Latin antiphons, verses, portions of hymns, and so forth that were the common fund of liturgical offices sung in monasteries and convents. But the degree of freedom with which they ranged over this material is indicated by the fact that eight verses spoken in the play cannot be identified from the known sources. (Commonly the verses were not written out in full, but only indicated by their beginning or "incipit.") The most tantalizing of these missing verses is indicated by the incipit "Te suspiro" ("I sigh after you") which suggests a love song sung by Mary Magdalen for the dead Jesus just before he appears to her; the poem may indeed have been adapted from a secular love song. (In the present translation, the missing portions of the verses are indicated by asterisks.) Because this chanted and sung "dialogue" was in Latin, it would not have been comprehensible in itself to most of the congregation. But because it was also mimed through the gestures of the actor/singers, and because it was a familiar story, it would presumably have been not only understood but found deeply moving by those watching and those participating. Similarly costuming was not designed to be a realistic approximation either of biblical or contemporary clothing, but was drawn from liturgical vestments available.

Despite the closeness to liturgical enactment implied by the elements of chant, vestments, and the display of the Eucharistic host, the play can be understood as genuinely representational. The principals are variously said "to figure" and "to represent" the biblical characters. Moreover, the basic purpose of the drama was to move the audience toward emotional engagement and identification with the sacred narrative. What is significant about the Barking play is the elaboration of the parts of the three Maries who come to the tomb and the fact that the "Christicolae" – the seekers after Christ – were played by women rather than by male clerics. Since nuns were specifically understood as "brides of Christ," their taking on the roles of these earliest mourners-turned-joyful-celebrants of the risen Lord seems especially appropriate. In poetry, drama, and visual art from the medieval period through the seventeenth century, the Magdalen figures centrally as the penitent sinner who became the chaste but passionate lover of Christ. In this play it is she, along with the other Maries, who becomes the mediator between the risen Jesus and still unknowing disciples. The women who portrayed the Magdalen and the Maries in turn mediated the experience of the risen Lord for their sisters, the clergy, and people of Barking.

Michael O'Connell

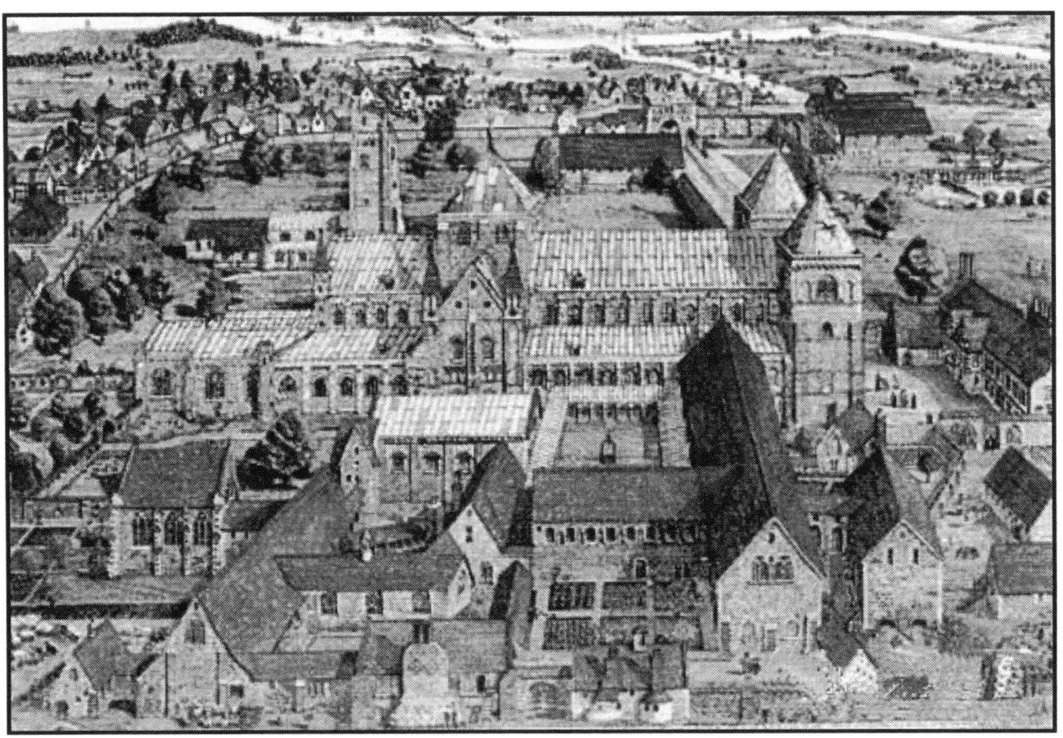

Barking Abbey as it may have looked ca. 1500
Painted by Sir Charles Nicholson 1932

### The Easter Play of the Nuns of Barking Convent

*Realizing that according to the ancient custom of the Church the Resurrection of the Lord was celebrated before matins and before any ringing of the bells on Easter day, and having seen how the congregation of people in her times had grown cold in their devotions and that human indolence was increasing greatly, our venerable lady, Lady Katherine of Sutton, then bearing the office of pastoral care, wanted to dispel that sluggishness entirely and to excite more fully the devotion of the faithful at that most solemn celebration.*[1] *So with the unanimous consent of her sisters she instituted that the celebration of the Lord's resurrection would occur after the third response of matins on Easter day and that the procession would be established in the following way.*

#### Part One

*First, let the lady abbess go with all the convent and with certain priests and clergy wearing copes, each priest and cleric carrying a palm and an unlit candle in his hand, and let them enter the chapel of Saint Mary Magdalen.*[2] *Portraying the souls of the holy patriarchs before the coming of Christ descending to the lower world, let them shut the entrance of that chapel. Then let the celebrating priest come to the chapel wearing an alb and a cope and accompanied by two deacons, one carrying a cross with the banner of the Lord hanging from its top and the other bearing a censer in his hand, and by other priests and clergy with two boys carrying waxen tapers.*[3] *Let the priest who will portray Christ in his descent to the lower world and his breaking of the gates of Hell begin three times the antiphon*:

Raise up your gates, you princes, and be lifted up, you everlasting doors, and the King of glory will enter in.

*Let him begin this antiphon each time in a higher voice, which the clergy shall each time repeat, and each time he says it let him knock at the door with the cross to portray the breaking of the gates of Hell. At the third knocking let the door open.*

*Then let him proceed in with his ministers. Meanwhile let a priest coming forth in the chapel begin the antiphon*:

From the gates of Hell—

*to which let the cantrix with all the convent respond—*[4]

Bring out my soul, O Lord.

*Then the celebrating priest will bring forth all those in the chapel, and let the other priest begin the antiphon*:

Lord, you have rescued—

*And the cantrix will respond with—*

My soul from the lower world.

*Then let all go out from the chapel, that is, from the limbo of the patriarchs, and let the priests and clergy sing*:

When Christ, the king of glory, came to vanquish Hell, and the chorus of angels advanced before him to raise the gates of the princes of the underworld, the nation of saints held captive in death cried out with a tearful voice, "You whom we have been waiting for in darkness come most welcome to lead from prison this night all those who have been enchained. Our sighs called out to you, and our great torments sought you out. You have been hope for those in despair, a great consolation in our torments."

*Let them go in procession through the middle of the choir, each carrying a palm and a candle to signify the victory snatched from the enemy, with the lady abbess, the prioress, and all the convent following as if they are the ancestors. And when they have come to the sepulchre, let the celebrating priest incense the sepulchre, then go into the sepulchre as he begins:*[5]

When Christ rose—

*Then let the cantrix respond with—*

from the tomb, he returned victorious from the abyss, driving the tyrant forth in chains and unlocking Paradise. We beseech you, creator of all, in this Easter joy, defend your people from death's blow. Glory be to you, O Lord, who have risen from the dead, with the Father and the Holy Spirit, forever and ever!

---

[1] *matins* ] the office, together with the lauds, that constitutes the first of the seven canonical hours.

[2] *copes* ] a long ecclesiastical vestment worn over the alb or surplice.

[3] *alb* ] a long white linen robe with tapered sleeves worn by a priest at Mass.

[4] *cantrix* ] vocal soloist and leader of the choir.

[5] *sepulchre* ] a burial vault.

*And during this time he will carry the body of the Lord [that is, the sacramental host] from the tomb and then in front of the altar and facing the people, holding in his hands the body of the lord enclosed in a crystal monstrance, he begins:*[1]

Christ rising—

*Then let the cantrix respond—*

from the dead now dies no more. Death will have no further dominion over him, for he lives, lives in God, alleluia, alleliua!

*And when they have completed this antiphon let them go in procession to the altar of the Holy Trinity in solemn fashion, that is, with censers and tapers, and let the convent follow singing that antiphon with this verse and the following short verse:*

Let the Jews say now how the soldiers guarding the tomb lost the king from beneath the stone. Why did they not serve the rock of justice? Either let them yield up his buried body, or adore him as risen, saying with us, alleluia, alleluia!

Say to the nations that the Lord has reigned from the wood of the cross, alleluia, alleluia, alleluia!

Prayer: God, who gave your son for us ***

*This procession thus figures the way in which Christ went into Galilee after his resurrection with his disciples following.*

### Part Two

*When these things have been done, let three sisters chosen before by the lady abbess go and remove their black clothing in the chapel of St. Mary Magdalen and put on the whitest of cloaks, with white veils placed upon their heads by the lady abbess. Thus prepared and holding silver flasks in their hands, let them say the Confiteor [a prayer of confession] to the abbess, and when they have been absolved by her let them stand in a place appointed with candelabra. Then let her who is playing the role of Mary Magdalen sing this verse:*

Once God's ***

*When this is finished, let the second nun, who portrays Mary the mother of James, respond with the other verse:*

Then approaching alone ***

*Let the third Mary, taking the part of Salome, sing the third verse:*

Let me go with you ***

*After this let the choir, with weeping and submissive voice, sing these verses as they advance:*

Alas, what sorrow and lamentation for the Comforter whom we have lost assails our grieving hearts within us. The cruel nation of the Jews gave him over to death.

*These verses finished, let the Magdalen sing this verse alone:*

Alas, unhappy women, why did it happen that we should see the death of the Savior?

*Let the mother of James respond:*

Alas, our consolation—that he should endure death!

*And Salome:*

Alas, the redemption of Israel – that he should want to suffer so!

*The fourth verse let all three sing together, namely:*

But for now, come, let us hasten quickly to the tomb to anoint the most holy body of our beloved.

*Then let the Maries, as they leave the choir, say together:*

But alas, who will roll back the stone for us from the entrance of the tomb?

*When then they have come to the sepulchre, let a cleric wearing a white alb and stole sit before the sepulchre bearing the figure of that angel who rolled back the stone from the mouth of the tomb and sat upon it. And let him say to them:*

Whom do you seek in the sepulchre, O followers of Christ?

*Let the women respond:*

We seek Jesus of Nazareth, who was crucified.

*The angel then says in reply:*

He is not here. He has risen as he said. Go and announce that he has risen from the grave. Come and see the place where the Lord was laid, alleluia, alleluia!

*When he has said this, let them go into the sepulchre and kiss the place where the crucified one was laid. Let Mary Magdalene meanwhile take the cloth which had been over his head and carry it with her. Then let the other cleric sitting in the sepulchre in the role of the other angel say to the Magdalen:*

---

[1] *monstrance* ] a receptacle in which the host is held.

Woman, why are you crying?

*She then says*:

Because they have taken away my Lord, and I do not know where they have laid him.

*Then let the two angels singing together say to the women*:

Why do you seek the living among the dead?

*Then still doubting the resurrection of the Lord, let the women say by turns as they weep*:

Alas! what sorrow, what agonies of pain we feel now that we have lost the presence of our beloved master! Alas! who has taken his dearly loved body from tomb?

*After this let Mary Magdalen, sighing, sing:*

I sigh after you, etc. ***

*Then to the left of the altar let the figure of Christ appear, saying to her*:

Woman, why are you crying? Whom do you seek?

*But let her, thinking that he is the gardener, respond*:

Sir, if you have taken him away, tell me where you have laid him, and I will take him away.

*Let the figure of Christ respond*:

Mary!

*Then let her, recognizing him, prostrate herself at his feet, saying*:

Rabboni!

*But let the figure of Christ, pulling back from her, say*:

Do not touch me, for I have not yet ascended to my Father. But go to my brethren and say to them: I am ascending to my Father and your Father, to my God and your God.

*When the figure of Christ has disappeared, let Mary communicate her joy to her companions, singing with a joyful voice these verses*:

Rejoice and be glad, etc. ***

*When this is finished, let the figure of Christ hasten to meet the three women together on the right side of the altar, saying*:

Hail! Do not be afraid! Go and announce to my brethren that they must go into Galilee where they will see me.

*Then prostrate at his feet, let them embrace his feet and kiss them. When this has been done, let them sing these verses alternately with Mary Magdalen beginning*:

Jesus the Nazarene, etc. ***

*When these verses are completed, then let the Maries, standing on the step before the altar and turning toward the people, sing this response, with the choir making response to them*:

Alleluia! The Lord has risen from the sepulchre, who hung for us upon the cross, alleluia!

*When this is finished, the priests and clerics go forth in portrayal of Christ's disciples saying*:

O cursed people ***

*Then let one of them approach Mary Magdalen and say to her*:

Tell us, Mary, what did you see on the way?

*Let her then respond*:

I saw the sepulchre of the living Christ, the glory of his rising, the angelic witnesses, the headcloth and the shroud.

*With her finger let her point to the place where the angel sat, and let her offer to them the headcloth to be kissed, adding this verse*:

Christ our hope has risen! He will go before his followers into Galilee.

*Then let these last verses be added by the disciples and the choir*:

The truthful Mary is more to be believed than the lying crowd of Jews, for we know that Christ has truly risen from the dead. Have mercy on us, victorious king!

*Then let the Magdalen begin, joined by the clergy and choir*:

Christ rising from the dead now dies no more.
Death will have no further dominion over him, for he lives, lives in God, alleluia, allelulia!

*When this has been done, let the hymn "Te Deum laudamus" be solemnly sung, the priest first beginning. And meanwhile let the priests put on again their own clothes in the chapel and passing through the choir with candles let them go pray at the sepulchre, where they shall make a brief prayer. Then let them return to their own place until the Abbess gives them the signal to go out to rest.*

—Trans. Michael O'Connell

# Holy Sisters (1200 – 1539)

*They token her leve and forthe they went;*
*And to eche of hem was geven grete hyre,*
*And therefore they were so fervent*
*To seke owte nunryes in every schyre.*
–Katherine of Kent, 13-16

ROM the earliest Anglo-Saxon monasteries until the Dissolution of religious houses under Henry VIII, England's nunneries were idealized as houses of devotion. On the Continent, some abbeys provided care for lepers or the dying, and helped to dispose of plague victims. English nuns were not expected to engage in charity and rarely did so in any organized way. But neither were English sisterhoods caught up in the ghastly masochism of many European monasteries—where nuns sought and obtained approbation of their father-confessors through anorexia, marathon self-flagellation, the ingestion of scabs and spittle of lepers, self-mutilation of the genitals, and the like. With respect to mortification of the flesh, the Middle English *Ancrene Wisse* (early thirteenth century) aims at pious moderation:

### Rule for Anchoresses°

The nun must not treat herself too gently ["Ne grope herself none too softlich"], lest she deceive herself. She will not be able, for her life, to keep herself pure ["clene"], nor to hold herself aright in chastity without two things (as Saint Ailred wrote to his sister): The one is, to pain her flesh with fasting, with watching, with flagellations, with wearing of coarse garments, with a hard bed, with illness, and with much labor ["swink"]. The other thing is heartly-feeling: as devotion, ruefulness, mercy, heart-pity, love, modesty, and other such virtues....Between delights and ease and fleshly overplus, who was ever chaste? Who ever bore fire within her that did not burn? Shall not a pot that boils briskly be less overladen, or have cold water mixed therein, or the fire withdrawn? The belly ["womb"] that boils always with meats, more so with drink, conveys its heat to that unruly member to which it is so near a neighbor....

Next to your flesh wear no flaxen cloth unless it be of hard and coarse hempen. Whoever will, may have a stamin; and whoever will, may be without it.[1] Ye shall lie girded under one warmer. Wear no iron, nor haircloth, nor porcupine-hides, nor flog yourselves therewith, nor with a scourge of leather thongs, nor leaded.[2] Do not with holly or briars be-bloody yourself without the leave of your confessor. Do not, all at one time, use too-fulsome flagellation. Overshoes may be thick and warm. In summer ye have leave to go and to sit barefoot, and to wear vamp-less stockings, and whoso liketh may sleep in them. Some women may, well enough, wear knickers ["brech"] of haircloth full-well tied and the strapples a-down to her feet, laced full-tight.... (trans. DWF)

• • •

The convent's day was divided into seven offices or "hours," beginning with the night office at 2 a.m. – at which time the nuns according to the Rule were summoned from their beds to the choir, where they recited *Matins* (morning prayers) and lauds (hymns of praise). Arising again at dawn, the sisters had an hour to wash and dress before *Primes*. A simple breakfast of bread and beer was followed at intervals by the services called *Tierce, Sext*, and (after mid-day dinner) *None*. Reading was permitted in the morning. The afternoon was devoted to assigned labors. Then came *Vespers*, a light supper, and *Compline*; after which, the nuns were obliged to retire in procession, immediately and without speaking, to the dorter for prayers and rest. All meals were to be eaten together in the frater.

Strict silence was to be observed, speech being permitted (under the more liberal orders) during afternoon chores. Hand-gestures were the legislated form of communication. The Sion Rule prescribes a common-form sign language: If incense were needed for the mass, the sacristan would "put her two fingers unto her nosthrils." At meals, to request a serving of milk, a nun was to pull on "her left little finger, in manner of milking"; for mustard, "hold her nose in the upper part of her right fist, and rub it"; for salt, "fillip with her right thumb and forefinger over the left thumb"; and for fish, "wag her hand displayed sidelings, in manner of a fish-tail." A table of 106 signs in the Sion Rule is coupled with a warning that "it is never lawful to use them without some reason and profitable need: for oft-time more hurteth an evil

---

[1] *stamin* ] an undergarment made of coarse worsted worn by ascetics.

[2] *iron* ] Caterina of Cardona wore iron chains which cut into her flesh, and flogged herself daily with chains and hooks, sometimes for hours at a time. Evangelista del Giocondo pressed her flesh with iron pincers until the blood would flow and is said to have scourged herself until the floor and even the walls were besmeared with blood; so, too, Catherine of Siena, who self-flagellated with iron chains three times a day; Francesca Bussa de Ponziani wore a tight iron-studded band around her hips; etc.; for which they received high approbation and were cited as pious examples.

sign than an evil word, and more offense it may be to God." To express anger or reproof with a hand-gesture or spitting was forbidden, as was pushing in line: "none shall jut upon other willfully, nor spit in any place reprievably (nor spit upon the stairs going up or down unless it be treaded out").[1] The nuns were generally civil to one another without reminders; but most English nunneries were careless in their observance of the prescribed religious discipline. From at least the thirteenth century onward, the offices were slackly attended; and the rules for silence and self-mortification, largely disregarded.

Depending wholly on their endowments and rents, the nunneries received no financial assistance from the diocese. Impoverished convents – which was most of them, north of the Thames – led a hard-scrabble existence. When destitute, the nuns could apply for exemption from diocesan taxation; or seek a license to leave their cloister (in groups) to beg for food and alms; but the Church supplied no financial aid. Thus developed the custom, condemned by the bishops but universally practiced, of leasing rooms to secular women, chiefly moneyed widows who desired the safety or society of conventual life without taking holy orders.

Virtually all English nuns, from the earliest times until the Dissolution, came from aristocratic or at least affluent families. Novitiates, taking Christ as their spouse, were expected to bring a dower. The wealthiest and most exclusive houses – Barking, Sion, Shaftesbury – received a substantial endowment with each newcomer. The less prestigious abbeys, having to settle for less, became a dumping-ground for unwanted children. A father could dispose of extra daughters by placing them in a needy religious house for a fraction of the sum required for marriages to men of the father's own social class. Not infrequently, male heirs cheaply placed unwed sisters in an abbey and pocketed the dowers provided in the father's will. The poor nunneries were often obliged as well to contract with aristocrats to care for their elderly parents or unwanted children with handicaps or behavior problems. (Children born out of wedlock to the nuns themselves were tolerated as residents until age 8-12 for boys, 10-14 for girls; at which time, if a home or sponsor could not be found for them, they were turned out as beggars, by injunction.)

The abbess was typically the most well-born and well-connected inmate, a source of pride even when funds were lacking (A case in point: For twenty-one years, Dame Isabel de Stanley, Prioress of cash-strapped King's Mead, Derby, refused to pay a rent demanded from her house by the Abbot of Burton. When at last the Abbot sent his bailiff to distrain for it, she spoke her mind: "Weenest these churls to overlead me, or sue the law again' me? They shall not be so hardy but they shall aby upon their bodies, and be nailed with arrows. For I am a gentlewoman, comen of the greatest of Lancashire and Cheshire; and that, they shall know right well!")[2]

The abbess or prioress was appointed by election, a source of contention when that right was short-circuited by intervention from the diocese. But the bishops rarely took much interest in the day-to-day affairs of the sisterhood except to ensure that the nuns' affairs were not sexual ones. Strict (often ineffectual) commands were issued forbidding sisters from speaking with men other than servants or visiting kin, and then (ideally) only in the presence of a chaperone. Rules were invoked as well to ensure that the nuns slept each in her own bed, lest in their feminine frailty they succumb to unspeakable temptations.

Periodic visitations from the bishop entailed a thorough inquest, each nun being sworn to answer all questions truthfully. The inquests examined finances, religious discipline, and sex; and found usually that the first two were in short supply. On the evidence of the nuns' (limited) sexual freedom,[3] the English convents have been condemned by historians both academic and religious, as if sexual activity were a grave offense among young women who were denied marriage, education, and income, many of whom did not wish to become nuns in the first place. The bishops certainly thought so: Nuns who had given birth to a child since the last visitation were typically imprisoned for up to a year in an unheated cell, one ankle shackled, sometimes on a prescribed fast of bread and water, three days a week.

By the sixteenth century, most English convents functioned largely as secular communes. All but a few were in debt. Many were in sorry decay. The 1535/6 Suppression of Religious Houses Act closed more than one hundred nunneries (all but 21 having less than the £200 annual income required to stave off the king's commissioners); the second Act of 1539 closed the remainder. The Crown confiscated all property and retired the nuns on pensions of as little as five shillings per year.

DWF

---

[1] Ed. DWF from George J. Aungier, *History of Syon Monastery* (London, 1840), pp. 298, 320, 385, 405-9; Eileen Power, *Medieval English Nunneries,* c. *1275-1535* is a useful starting point for any study of English conventual life.

[2] Lysons (1817), 5.113, temp. Henry VI.

[3] See, for example, the Archbishops' Registers for the diocese of York, 1280 -1360, summarized in *VCH Yorkshire*.

## Work Orders

By the Cellaress of Barking Convent (c. 1300)

***This is the Charge 'longing to the Office of the Cellaress of the Monastery of Barking, as hereafter followeth*°:**

First she must look, when she cometh into her office, what is owing to the said office by divers farmers and rent-gaderers, and see that it be paid as soon as she may.... [1]

*Buying of Grains:* [The Cellaress] must purvey yearly, for three quarters, malt for the tuns: of St. Ae'lburga and Christmas, each of them, twelve bushel; and then must she pay to the brewer of each tun, twenty pence.

• And then must she purvey for a quarter-and-seven bushels of wheat: for pittance of William Dun, Dame Maud Leveland, Dame Alice Merton, Dame Maud the king's daughter; and for rishew in Lenten (and to bake with else on Sheer Thursday).

• And then must she pay to the baker for baking (of every pittance, six pence). And also she must purvey for one bushel of green beans for the co'vent ayenst Midsummer. [2]

*Buying of Store:* And she must purvey for twenty-two good oxen by the year for co'vent.

*Providance for Advent and Lenten*: Also, she must purvey for two cades of herrings that be red, for the co'vent in Advent, and for seven cades of red herring, for the co'vent in Lenten; and also for three barrels of white herring,... 112 lb. almonds, ...eighteen salt fish,...fourteen or else fifteen salt salmons,...three pecks and 24 lb. figs,...one peck raisins..., and also for 28 lb. rice, for the co'vent in Lenten; and for eight gallons mustard, for the co'vent. [3]

*Rishew Silver:* And also she must pay to every lady of the co'vent (and also to the Prioress, to two Cellaresses and Kitchener, for their doubles), for their rishew silver, by sixteen times payable in the year, to every lady (and doubles), at each time, halfpenny. (But it is paid now but at two times, that is to say, at Easter and Michaelmess.) Also, she must pay to every lady of the co'vent, and to the said four doubles, to each lady and double, tuppence for their crispses and crumb-cakes (alway paid at Shrovetide).[4]

*Anniversaries:* And also, she must pay for five anniversaries, that is to say, Sir William Vicar, Dame Alice Merton, Dame Maud the king's daughter, Dame Maud Leveland, and William Dunn; and also, to purvey for twelve gallon good ale, for the pittance of William at the day of anniversary.[5]

*Offerings and Wages, and Gifts of the Cellaress:* And also she must pay in offering to two Cellaresses by year, twelve pence; and then shall she pay to the steward of household, what time he bringeth home money from the courts, at each time, twenty pence.

• And then shall she give to the Steward of household, at Christmas, twenty pence; and to my Lady's gentlewoman, twenty pence; and to every gentleman, sixteen pence; and to every yeoman as it pleaseth her to do, and grooms in like case.

---

[1] Omitted here is a detailed list that follows, enumerating accounts receivable from farmers, lessees, and collectors in London, and in thirteen outlying suburbs.

[2] *tuns* ] large casks of beer (or wine); *Ae'lburga* ] Aethelburga (d. 675), first abbess of Barking (her feast was celebrated on 11 October); *pittance* ] an additional allowance of food or drink at particular festivals, or on the anniversary of the benefactor's death, in return for the saying of masses; *William Dun,* an associate of Robert le Moyne, canon of St. Paul's, 1246-1256, temp. Henry III.] *Dame Alice Merton* ] prioress, 1276-1291; *Dame Maud the king's daughter* ] daughter of King John, abbess 1247-1252; *Maud Leveland* ] abbess, 1258-1275; *rishew* ] a dish of finely chopped fruit or meat mixed with spices, formed into balls or patties, and fried in oil; for recipe, see E. Power, op.cit., n.1657 *Sheer Thursday* ] the Thursday in holy week, also called Maundy Thursday; *ayenst Midsummer* ] in preparation for the solstice feast.

[3] *providance* ] provision; *cades* ] a *cade* (barrel) of herring held six *great hundreds* of six score each; *red herring* ] i.e., smoked; *white herring* ] fresh or salted; *almonds* ] used for making almond-milk, a substitute during Lent, when milk was a forbidden luxury.

[4] *rishew silver* ] an allowance of cash for the purchase of rishews or other goods; *Michaelmess* ] Michaelmas, 29 Sept., the Feast of St. Michael and the beginning of the second quarter of the Church year; *kitchener* ] the officer in a monastery or abbey who had charge of the kitchen; *crispes* ] crisp pastries made by dropping batter into boiling fat; *Shrovetide* ] the Sunday, Monday, and Tuesday just before Lent, a time of feasting and merriment.

[5] *anniversaries* ] celebrated to commemorate the death of benefactors; with a special mass, and prayers said for their souls; for the which, the nuns were paid an extra pittance of food or cash; *the pittance of William* ] on the anniversary of patron William Vicar's death, each nun was given an extra pittance (allowance) of good ale, to toast his salvation.

• And then must she buy a sugar-loaf for my Lady at Christmas;
• And also, she must pay to her clerk, for his wages, thirteen shillings fourpence; to her yeoman-cook, 26 shillings eightpence; and she shall pay for a gown to her groom-cook and her pudding-wife, by the year, two shillings.[1]

*Pittance of the Co'vent:* And also she must purvey for three case of mutton for the co'vent, for the pittance of Sir William Vicar; also, she must purvey for a peck of wheat and three gallons milk, for furmety on Saint Ae'lburga's day. Also, she must purvey four bacon-hogs for the co'vent, for pittance of Dame Alice Merton, and Dame Maud the king's daughter, at two times in winter; and she must buy six grices, six sows for the co'vent, and also six inwards; 100 eggs to make white puddings; also, bread, pepper, saffron for the same puddings; also to purvey three gallons good ale for besoignes. And also to purvey marrow-bones to make white-worts for the co'vent. [2]

• And then must she purvey at Saint Andrew-tide a pittance of fish for my Lady and the co'vent; [3]
• And then must she pay at Shrovetide to every lady of the co'vent, and to four doubles, for their crispes, and for the crumb-cake, to every lady and double, tuppence.
• And then must she purvey for my Lady Abbess, ayenst Shrovetide, eight chickens; also buns for the co'vent at Shrovetide. [4]
• Also four gallons milk for the co'vent, the same time; and then must she purvey for every Sunday in Lenten, pittance-fish for the co'vent; and also, to be sure of twelve stub-eels and twelve shaft-eels to bake for the co'vent on Sheer Thursday; and also one pottle Tyre for my Lady Abbess the same day, and two gallons of red wine for the co'vent the same day; and also to purvey three gallons of good ale for the co'vent every week in Lenten, and to have one gallon red wine for the co'vent on Easter even. [5]

• And also to purvey for three case of mutton for the co'vent, for the pittance of William Dunn: and also to purvey for every lady of the co'vent, and five double to every lady, and double dimidium-goose delivered at the Feast of the Assumption of our Lady. [6]

*Egg silver:* And also she must pay to thirty-seven ladies of the co'vent for their egg-silver fro' Michaelmas till All-Hallow Day, to every lady by the week, one penny three-farthings; and then to every lady by the week, fro' All-Hallow Day till Advent, one penny farthing; and then to every lady by the week fro' Advent Sunday till Childermas Day, one penny farthing. [7]

And then, to every lady for the same egg-silver by the week, fro' Childermas Day unto Ash Wednesday, penny farthing; and then fro' Easter unto Michaelmas to every lady by the week, one penny three-farthings; and then must she pay to each lady for the egg-silver for each vigil falling within the year, halfpenny; and then must she pay to the priory each week in the year, except Lenten, 32 eggs, or else tuppence three farthings, in money for them, every week (except four week in Advent) ...

*Buying of Butter:* And then must she purvey for feast-butter of Saint Ae'lburga for thirty-seven ladies (and four doubles, that is to say, the Prioress, two Cellaresses, and the Kitchener), to every lady and double, one gobbet, every dish containing three gobbets: and then must she pay to the said ladies and doubles for the storying-butter by five times in the year (that is to wit, in Advent, and three times after Christmas), to each lady and double, at every, halfpenny; and also she must purvey for the said ladies and doubles for the feast-butter at Easter and Whitsuntide (like as she did at Saint Ae'lburga's tide); also she must purvey for the said ladies of the co'vent, and the said four doubles, and the priory for their fortnight butter fro' Trinity Sunday unto Holy Round day, that is to said, to every lady double, and priory, at each fortnight between the said two feasts one gobbet butter, three gobbets making a dish; and also she must purvey to the said ladies with their doubles to the feast-butter of Assumption of our Lady, to every lady and double, one gobbet butter.

---

[1] *my Lady's gentlewoman* ] the prioress's lady-in-waiting; *grooms* ] male servants; *yeoman-cook* ] hired assistant cook; *pudding-wife* ] sausage-maker.

[2] *furmety* ] (also *frumenty*) a dish made of hulled wheat boiled in milk, seasoned with cinnamon and sugar; *grices* ] piglets; *puddings* ] sausages; *besoignes* ] doing business; white-worts ] pot vegetables.

[3] *Andrew-tide* ] feast of St. Andrew, 30 November.

[4] *ayenst* ] in preparation for.

[5] *stub-eels ... shaft-eels* ] large and small eels; *pottle Tyre* ] one half-gallon of sweet wine (imported from Tyre).

[6] *dimidium* ] half.

[7] *egg-silver* ] an allowance paid to the sisters ostensibly so that they could purchase their own eggs; *All-Hallow Day* ] All Saints Day, 1 November; *Childermas* ] Feast of the Holy Innocents, 28 December.

*Hiring of Pasture:* And then must she be sure of pasture for her oxen in time of year, as her servants can inform her.

*Mowing and Making of Hay:* And also to see her hay be mow and made in time of the year, as earing requireth.

*Costs of Reparations:* And then must she see that all manner of houses within her office be sufficiently repaired as well without (at her farms, manors) as within the monastery....

*Instructions follow for the amount of food to be purchased for each major feast, with detailed servings per capita of almonds, rice, figs, raisins, red and white herring, saltfish, salmon, mutton, pork, bacon, chicken, goose-meat, and eggs; or a cash gratuity; each sister being allotted precisely the same amount except the officers, who were given a double-helping of each (the surplus from which, one supposes, may have been used by the officers as gratuities and not to fatten themselves).*

• • •

**Rothwell Priory**

THE AUGUSTINIAN PRIORY at ROTHWELL, Northamptonshire, dedicated to John the Baptist, was founded sometime before 1262 by Richard Clare, earl of Gloucester, who died before fully establishing the convent. The house was never well endowed. By the early fifteenth century, the number of sisters had dwindled from fourteen to eight. On account of their poverty, Bishop Dalderby in 1318 licensed the nuns to beg.

Very little else is recorded of this small and moneyless convent. During the latter half of the fourteenth century, the sisters rebuilt the priory church (consecrated in 1379). In 1385, the nuns were granted the appropriation of the neighboring rectory of Desborough, to alleviate their poverty; a portion of which living was payable to the Bishop of Lincoln. But a mandate of Pope Boniface IX to the abbot of Pipewell in 1392 indicates that the nuns of Rothwell were at that time still destitute, and begging for food and alms.

Bishop Repingdon in 1414 issued a mandate to the prioress desiring her to re-admit Joan, an apostate canoness who had abandoned the convent. The prioress at first refused to receive the delinquent, alleging that Joan by her own confession had for three years lived in sin with one William Suffewick. The bishop thereupon cited the prioress for disobedience and again enjoined her to readmit the apostate sister, who was to do penance for three years while being confined with iron chains within the priory; on Wednesdays her fare should be bread and cheese and pulse; on Fridays, bread and cheese only (Archer, 88v). It is not recorded whether Joan the canoness is the same Joan who eight years later was twice abducted from the convent and raped, nor whether Suffewick was her assailant.

**Mandate of Solemn Excommunication with Lighted Candles, etc., for violence done, etc., [c. March 1421/2]°** (Latin. Trans. DWF)

Richard [Fleming], by the sufferance of God bishop of Lincoln –

To our beloved sons, the official of our archdeacon of Northampton and the dean of Rothwell: Health, grace and blessing. [1]

...It hath been brought to our attention, the which we relate with sorrow, that certain followers of the wickedness of Satan, yea, degenerate sons of holy Mother Church yet sons of everlasting damnation, led (yea, led astray) by the spirit of the Devil – we do not know their names – descended by night like pirates upon a place of religion set apart to God, i.e., the priory of the nuns of Rothwell aforesaid. Forcing and breaking open the enclosures and cloister-precinct, and the windows and barred doors of the same priory, they seized with violence a certain woman named Joan, of gentle and honest reputation, who was dwelling chastely under the rule and governance of the prioress of the said priory.

While she struggled and protested as much as she was able, they brought her away by force and violence out of the said priory to a house situated far from the society of all humankind. There one of them (said to be the leader of the rest and the prime mover of this wickedness), when he was alone with the said woman in the said house, saw that he could not accomplish the criminal purpose which he intended. He then called his accomplices, who with ropes and cords spread her legs – and as terrible as it may be to speak and hear, it was more horrendous and horrible in actuality – he thus fulfilled his desire, setting aside the shame of all humanity; so that, like a tyrant and beyond the endurance of Nature, nay rather, beyond that from which Nature itself would shrink, he wickedly overpowered and violated the same [Joan] against her will.

---

[1] The archdeacon of Northampton at this time was Robert Fitzhugh, son of Henry V's chamberlain; the identity of dean of Rothwell (which included 44 parishes) is unknown. The prioress of Rothwell was possibly Alice Langton, elected in 1395 (Ryland, et al, *V.C.H. Northamptonshire* [1906], 2.138).

This actor and head of so great a crime and baseness, not content with this wickedness but hardened in the sin which he had begun, crowned his evils with an evil truly worse, indeed, worse than all: Behold, like a tyrant and pirate he entered the same priory a second time, with a far greater multitude of like-minded followers, a company of untamed and savage men; who with drawn swords and divers other offensive weapons, fell again upon the same woman, as if they were snatching a prey.

[Joan°] was then in the presence of the prioress and the nuns in the hall of the said priory. Exceeding the evils already noted, and disregarding all reverence of their persons and the place, those men daringly laid their wicked, sacrilegious and violent hands upon her, and upon the prioress and nuns of the said place. These honorable members of the church, women hallowed to God, tried gently to appease their baseness and savagery, insofar as their sex as women allowed. But the men cudgeled them with cruel blows, threw them to the ground, and trampled them underfoot; kicked them violently and without mercy; and pulled the garments of their nun's habits over their heads. Then, like robbers having seized their prey, they carried off the said woman, dragging her with them out of the priory – to the grievous scandal of all, our holy Mother Church, and to the grave danger of their own souls and to the exceeding tearful example of very many others; incurring thereby their own damnation and the sentence of excommunication, which in this case has been decreed with aforethought by divers fathers against those men.

Such excess of crime, such boldness of sinful daring, causes devotion to be withdrawn from Holy Church and thereby sets a dangerous precedent for the future. In order that the freedom from punishment of men so grievously guilty may not serve as an example to others, we therefore (by the right of our pastoral office, and acting by the authority of the sacred canons whereof we are the agents appointed by law) earnestly enjoin and command you, all and several, in virtue of obedience (and under pain of excommunication which we intend to pronounce against your persons if you shall not perform our commandment, both together and as individuals), requiring that no one shall wait for the other, nor the other use his fellow as an excuse: [that you] declare excommunicate all and individually the guilty perpetrators of these grievous crimes, or any of them, and all who openly or secret afford aid, assistance, help, counsel, consent or favor to them for the perpetration of so huge iniquities, and ratify or approve such things when done or perpetrated…

*Bishop Fleming's successor, William Gray, visited Rothwell on 22 July 1442; at which time the priory housed seven nuns – Margaret Staple, prioress, Margaret Claybrook, Joan Burghe, Agatha Holme, Margaret Cross, Agnes Marsh, and Joan Chase; all of whom reported that all things were well. The nuns at that time had stock of a hundred sheep and just six marks in unpaid debts.*

*Few additional records survive for Rothwell, which remained poor, and dependent on charity. Small bequests are found among Northamptonshire wills in the reign of Henry VIII. (One 1521 will bequeaths "to the convent off Nunnys a Browne Kowe"* [Cox, 128]).

*Having income of less than £200, the Rothwell nunnery came under the earlier measure for suppression of religious houses. The Valor of 1535 shows that it possessed no properties other than the site of the buildings, and a garden and an orchard, plus the Desborough income; with net annual revenue of £5 19s. 8½d. (hardly enough to feed even one adult).*

*The house of Rothwell was dissolved, and the nuns dismissed to fend for themselves, sometime before 11 February 1537/8. In 1545, the priory building and lands were granted by the Crown to Henry Lee.*

• • •

**Markyate Priory**

THE BENEDICTINE PRIORY of MARKYATE, Bedfordshire, founded in 1145, was situated in a woods that belonged to the Dean and Chapter of St. Paul's, London. Dedicated to the Trinity, Markyate is most often referenced in the historical record as "Holy Trinity in the Wood."

In the mid-thirteenth century, the Friars Preachers came to Dunstable to help build the convent's church. The prioress, Agnes Gobion, "out of pure charity," sent them a certain number of loaves each day for their better nourishment. But the friars thereafter would not permit her to withdraw the largesse; they sent to Rome and had the dole of daily bread from Markyate Priory confirmed to them, for ever.

In 1297, it came to the attention of Bishop Sutton that the apparitor of Dunstable had cited "certain persons of both sexes living in the priory of Markyate" for sexual congress, whereby the house had incurred scandal. Three years later, Bishop Dalderby put the entire house under penance to punish four nuns who had flatly refused to comply with his injunction requiring them not to leave the cloister precincts.

The house at Markyate remained poor and therefore receives little notice in the ecclesiastical records except when sexual offenses were reported; as with the scandal of 1433, when the bishop received word that the prioress herself, Lady Denise Lowelich, for the past five years had co-habited with the abbey's male steward, as his bedpartner. Bishop Gray appointed a special commissary to investigate. [1]

**The Commission to Investigate Lady Denise Lowelich, Prioress of Markyate, 25 May 1433°**
(Latin. Trans. DWF)

William [Gray], by the sufferance of God bishop of Lincoln—

To our beloved son, Master Robert Thornton, licentiate in laws: Health, grace, and blessing.

Some time ago, when by our right as Ordinary we made actual visitation of the priory of the Holy Trinity of the Wood by Markyate (of the order of St. Benedict, of our diocese), we made anxious inquiry concerning the state of the said priory and the concerns of religion there; and we discovered in that visitation certain crimes, transgressions, and offenses due for correction; by occasion whereof and for the end of a more healthful and thrifty governance of the said priory in matters both spiritual and temporal, we enjoined upon the prioress and convent of that place certain injunctions and commands to be observed, under heavy penalties and censures.

But it has lately come to our attention, amidst abundant and blatant gossip, and the notorious fact made public, that more grievous offenses than we discovered in that visitation were unhappily taking place and being done in that priory, even before the commencement of the said [inquiry]; which the said prioress and her sisters, with aforethought, concealed from us at the time of our visitation, contrary to the institutes of the holy canons.

And [we have learned] that since our visitation, Sister Katherine Titsbury, a nun of that place, moved by the Devil, has departed into apostasy in the default of the said prioress, who neglects our said injunctions and commands, nor causes them to be observed by the others, her sisters; but herself scorns them, even though the injunctions were healthful; and at the present she rejects them with contempt. Therefore, by the content of this present [commission,] and by our office, we authorize you (of whose faithfulness and diligence we have full confidence in the Lord), using the power of any canonical compulsion whatsoever, to investigate: … and also to depose, remove, and suspend the said prioress from her dignity …

Given under our seal *ad causas* in our residence at the Old Temple in London, on the 14th day of April in the year of our Lord 1433 (and the second year of our translation [as bishop].)

**Robert Thornton, commissary, to William Gray, bishop of Lincoln, June 1433°:**
(Latin. Trans. DWF)

I came in person to the said priory of the Holy Trinity of the Wood, by Markyate …

I appointed Lady Denise Lowelich (prioress of the said priory) and the rest of the nuns of the said priory, all and several, to appear in the chapter house; and assigned the third hour of the same day, after breakfast…. When this hour came, the aforesaid Lady Denise Lowelich, prioress, and the rest of her fellow nuns and sisters, all and several, appeared before me in person. I there read aloud certain articles which are written here below, translating and explaining the articles in the mother tongue. And before the entire chapter, in the mother tongue, I presented the charges against the aforesaid Lady Denise, the said prioress; doing so of my mere office for the mere correction of her soul: [2]

IN THE NAME OF GOD, Amen. I, Robert Thornton, commissary of the reverend father in Christ and lord, the Lord William [Gray], by the grace of God bishop of Lincoln, proceeding by the mere virtue of my office specially committed to me in this behalf, do present the following charges against you, Lady Denise, prioress of the priory of the Holy Trinity of the Wood, of the order of St. Benedict, by Markyate, of the diocese of Lincoln:

First, that you have loosed the reins of chastity and shamelessly cast away the modesty of a nun and the meekness of your sex, cleaving in the flesh to one Richard, late steward of the said priory, with incestuous, adulterous, and sacrilegious embraces, within the said priory and elsewhere. [3]

---

[1] *Lowelich* ] MS spellings, Loweliche and Lewelyche; alt. spellings for *Lovelace* or *Loveless.*

[2] *third hour* ] i.e., third hour after dawn, about 9 a.m.

[3] *incest* ] sexual congress between priests (fathers), prioresses (mothers), monks (brothers) and nuns (sisters) was figured by the Church as "incest," in a rhetorical effort to discourage copulation.

Also, that you unchastely continued with the said Richard the steward in these crimes of incest, adultery, and sacrilege for five years and more, until the death of the said Richard; to the grievous offense of God, (to whom you pledged your purity); to the evil reputation of religion; and as a damnable example both to your fellow nuns and very many other people.

Also, that the place was thereby belabored in public talk and rumor during the said time, by all and sundry in the town of Markyate and other places, near and far, in the diocese of Lincoln and elsewhere....

*When thus confronted, Lowelich denied the charges against her. But she was unable to enlist five sisters present who would say under oath that they believed the allegations were untrue. Thornton granted Lowelich a recess of three hours to rally support. When the hour came and mother Denise was still unable to produce five sisters who would speak in her defense, Thornton on authority of the bishop forced her to resign. Her punishment is unrecorded but probably entailed imprisonment in chains within the cloister walls, as was usual in such cases.*

...Before me, [Robert Thornton,] in the said chapter house, and in presence of her fellow nuns all and several of the said priory, and other witnesses, Lady Denise (of her own free will and certain knowledge, as she said), submitted herself to the grace and ordinance of my lord, the bishop of Lincoln; and offered herself in readiness to resign the said priory into the hands of the said reverend father; and said aloud in the mother tongue with good delivery: "I submit myself to the grace and regulation of my lord the bishop of Lincoln, and into the hands of the said reverend father I submit my resignation from the same priory, estate, dignity and office of the same priory."

Thereafter, she made in fact an unequivocal renunciation, taken down in writing, as follows:

"In the name of God, Amen. I, Denise Lowelich, prioress of the priory of the Holy Trinity of the Wood, freely, of my own accord, absolutely resign the aforesaid priory into the sacred hands of the most reverend father in Christ and lord, the Lord William Gray, by the grace of God bishop of Lincoln, diocesan of the place; and [resign] the dignity, estate, and office of the same priory; with lowly supplication that his fatherhood aforesaid will deign to admit this my resignation."

—There being present at that time, in the same place, all and severally, the nuns of the said priory, i.e., ladies Margaret Stuckley, the sub-prioress; Anne Willoughby; Jane Askam; Jane Marchande, Isabel Reconge, Alice Lydiate, Jane Wyrral, Isabel Clark, Katherine Titsbury, Margaret Lowelich; also, Sir James Sodelomb, perpetual vicar of the parish church of Kensworth, of the diocese of Lincoln; and John Punsonby, of the diocese of York (witnesses specially called and summoned to the premises).

*In the century following, no further visitations from the bishops are recorded. Markyate (having revenue of less than £200, ) was surrendered to the Crown under the Act of 1536. Then prioress Joan Zouche was assigned a pension of twenty marks, which she first received on 10 February 1536/7. On the site was built a house called Markyate Cell, later famous as the home of Lady Katherine (Ferrers) Fanshaw (1634–1660), the legendary "Wicked Lady," a highwaywoman who terrorized Nomansland Common in Hertfordshire before bleeding to death from gunshot wounds sustained during a robbery.*

• • •

**Priory of Sewardsley**

THE CISTERCIAN PRIORY of SEWARDSLEY, Northamptonshire, was founded in the reign of Henry II by Richard de Lestre, lord of the manor. The house had little land and was poorly endowed, not generating enough income to feed the four or five nuns in residence at one time.

In 1300, Joan de Fynnemere abandoned her destitute sisters and returned to secular life; for which Bishop Dalderby punished her with greater excommunication. Fearing further defections, Dalderby then granted an indulgence from Purgatory to anyone who would bestow alms on the house, to relieve the plight of the remaining nuns; an indulgence that the bishop renewed in 1319.

The bishop's incentive was unproductive. In 1366, ill-nourished and poorly dressed, the prioress requested and obtained from the diocese a license for the sisters to beg for food and alms.

If one may read between the lines of Bishop Gray's unusually severe denunciation in 1435, the nuns of Sewardsley—four or five impecunious women living in a ruinous structure—were by that time reduced to prostitution. The prioress was then Alice Basynge, who was elected in 1432 and resigned in 1439.

**Commission of Inquiry to Investigate the Priory of Sewardsley, 23 February 1434/5°**
(Latin. Trans. DWF)

William Gray, by divine permission [bishop] of Lincoln, etc. –

To our beloved son, Master John Lichbarrow, our commissary general in our archdeaconries of Northampton and Leicester: health, grace, and blessing.

By the report of many trustworthy persons it has often come to our hearing that the prioress and nuns of the priory of Sewardsley of our diocese, having renounced the world and all of its pompous processions, having betrothed themselves to serve the Lord of virtues, the true spouse of the faithful soul, beneath the monastic habit and regular discipline; have instead pursued the enticements of the flesh; abandoned the path of religion; and have cast aside all restraints of modesty and chastity. Giving their minds to debauchery, they have been committing in damnable wise, publicly, and (as it were) in open view of everyone, acts of adultery, incest, sacrilege and fornication; to the death of their own souls, the reproach of religion and as a mischievous example to others.

Wishing therefore to be more surely informed concerning the perpetrators of the aforesaid offenses, and with the instrument of our jurisdiction utterly to cut away the brambles of those vices in the said priory – so that the blood of the same offenders may not be required at our hands in the Last Judgment – we authorize you and command you to go down to the said place as our deputy; and by our authority to make diligent and faithful inquiry of the truth in all respects concerning the life, reputation, and behavior of the said prioress and nuns; and [to inquire after] the aforesaid crimes, misdeeds, sins and trespasses which it is said are being committed by them; [to investigate] their whole circumstance; to examine separately the several persons of the same prioress and nuns, as well other trustworthy men who possess more perfect knowledge of the premises … and, having dispatched the said business, to certify, plainly and openly, with all due haste, whatever you are able to discover by these inquiries … Given under our seal *ad causas* in our palace of Liddington, on the twenty-third day of the month of February, in the year of our Lord 1434[/5] and the fourth year of our translation.

*The outcome of the 1435 investigation is unrecorded.*

*The bishops thereafter make no note of Sewardsley until 1530, when Prioress Eleanor Scaresbrig died. To succeed her, the nuns elected Sister Agnes Carter. But their choice was declared void by the bishop, who described Lady Agnes as "mulier corrupta, apostate, et unius prolis mater"* (*The woman has been corrupted, is apostate, and the mother of one child*). *Elizabeth Campbell, appointed by the bishop in place of Lady Agnes, was the last prioress of the house. At the dissolution she received an annuity of £5. The site and lands of Sewardsley were then leased by the Crown to Thomas Broke of London; and in 1550 the property was granted to Richard Fermor.*

• • •

**Stainfield Priory**

THE BENEDICTINE PRIORY OF STAINFIELD, Lincolnshire, was founded by William or Henry de Percy, in or before the reign of Henry II. The convent appears to have been well managed. In 1392 Bishop Bokyngham forbade merchants to hawk their wares in the convent's church or churchyard; and one finds the usual complaints, following bishops' visitations, concerning secular women being permitted to lodge with the nuns in their dorter. But rarely was Stainfield cited for lax religious observance or for sexual promiscuity.

**Commission for the Enclosure of an Anchoress, 23 January 1435/6°**

In 1435, Beatrice Frank, a nun in good standing at the Benedictine priory of Stainfield, asked to be relieved of her original calling and oath, in order to become a recluse, in a cell to be built against the parish church of Winterton, there to be enclosed until her death.

On 15 January 1435/6, William Gray bishop of Lincoln commissioned the abbot at the monastery of Blessèd Mary of Thornton "to examine the said sister Beatrice and her purpose and intent. And if you find her persistent in her purpose and intent, firm and steadfast, and in other respects apt and fit for this purpose and in no wise wavering, and if her desire of an anchorage arises from a pure heart, a good conscience, and faith unfeigned…; and if you know that the consent and agreement of the general folk among whom she will have her conversation are agreeable in this matter; then [you may] license and authorize in our stead the same sister Beatrice to be removed from the said priory to her desired end…; commanding you, when the said business is dispatched, to certify us concerning your whole proceeding…"

The abbot of Thornton interviewed the candidate on 21 January; at which time he examined her motives and past behavior. The abbot duly warned Beatrice "concerning the perils of them that choose such a life and afterwards repent thereof." Finding her resolute, and having craved "the life of an anchorite almost from the time of her youth," the abbot gave his approval.

The prioress of Stainfield likewise wrote to the bishop in support of Beatrice's application:

**Margaret Hull, by the permission of God prioress of the priory of Stainfield, of the order of St. Benedict, of the diocese of Lincoln—°**

To our beloved daughter and sister, sister Beatrice Frank, fellow nun and sister of us and our said priory, publicly and expressly professed in the same:

With much approval in the Lord of your purpose to change your condition to a stricter life under the rule or order of an anchorite, and desire to be shut up in a cell adjacent to the parish church of Winterton, of the said diocese of Lincoln, where you may have more freedom to contemplate your Creator – which, as we steadfastly believe, has been divinely inspired in you, not lightly or impetuously, but out of an honest heart and faith unfeigned, thereby to win the fruit of a more holy life – we grant you special license by the purport of these present [documents] to have agency to remove to such life and be shut up in the said cell, as you have often asked of us, toward that end; with the will and consent of the most reverend father in Christ and lord, the Lord William [Gray], by the grace of God bishop of Lincoln, diocesan of these places. And after sufficient deliberation, we release you by these presents from the bond of the obedience wherewith you were and are bound to us and our said priory, to the end of your removal and enclosure aforesaid, and not for any other purpose or in any other manner. In witness of which, the seal of our office is attached to these presents. Given in the chapter house of our priory aforesaid, etc.

Margaret Hull, Prioress

*On St. Vincent's Day, before the high altar of the Winterton church, Beatrice Frank publicly made her new profession, reading it openly and clearly, under oath, promising moreover her continued chastity and obedience. When Mass was concluded, those present enclosed her in a cell constructed on the north side of the church: "Making fast the door thereof with bolts, bars and keys, we then left her in peace and calm of spirit and, as it is believed by most, in the joy of her Savior. ... Given at Thornton on the 23d of January, in the year of our Lord 1435[/6]"* (Thompson, 1.114-5).

*Four years later, on 25 July 1440, Bishop Gray visited Stainfield, at which time the priory housed 22 professed nuns, "All of whom made their appearance, save only Alice Bennington; who, being out of her mind, is kept in chains"* (3.2.345). *The 21 sisters who attended the visitation reported to the Bishop that all things were well.*

*No further record survives of Beatrice Frank.*

*The priory of Stainfield was dissolved a century later, in 1536. The prioress Elizabeth Bursby received a small pension, and the sisters 20s. apiece to buy secular apparel. The lands and house were granted to Robert Tyrrwhit, who built Stainfield Hall on the site.*

• • •

**Heynings Priory**

THE CISTERCIAN PRIORY of HEYNINGS, situated in Knaith, Lincolnshire, was founded by Rayner de Evermue, Lord of Knaith, early in the reign of King Stephen. Patronage of the house remained with the lords of Knaith throughout most of its history. The house had a meager endowment and remained extremely poor.

Bishop Alnwick visited the abbey in April 1440. His report:

**Visitation of the bishop of Lincoln to the priory of Heynings, 7 April 1440°**
(Latin. Trans. DWF)

Lady JOAN HOTHUM, ... the prioress says that all things are well (*omne bene*).

Lady ISABEL BURTON, the sub-prioress, says that all things are well.

Lady KATHERINE HOGHE says that several of the nuns are sleepy and come late to matins and the other canonical hours. She says also that the house is in debt, due to the large repairs that have been done within and without, and also due to the scarcity of corn for several years.

Lady ELLEN COTUM says all things are well.

Lady ALICE PORTER says that the prioress when she makes corrections is a respecter of personage: those whom she loveth, she passes over lightly; those whom she dislikes, she harshly punishes. She says also that the prioress hath reproached her sisters, telling them that if they say *aught* to the bishop, she will lay on them such punishment that they shall not easily endure it. (*The prioress denieth the second part of the article: she also denieth the first part of the article.*)

[Lady Porter] sayeth also that the prioress doth not report on the state of the house, in common; and she says that the prioress urgeth her secular serving-women (whose speech she credits more than that of her sisters), to reprove the nuns; and for this cause quarrels do spring up between the prioress and her sisters.

Also she says that the prioress has had thick trees chopped down without need. (*To this,* [*the prioress*] *says that she caused none to be felled save for the manifest advantage, and with the express consent of the convent.*)

Also she says that sisters Ellen Brigg and Agnes Bock have often recourse to Lincoln, and there make long tarrying. (*They deny recourse, as is alleged in the article.*)

Lady AGNES BOCK says that all things are well.

Lady ELLEN BRIGG says all things are well.

Lady KATHERINE BENNET says all things are well.

Lady CUSTANCE BURNHAM says all things are well.

Lady JOAN ASHTON says all things are well.

Lady AGNES SUTTON says that her friends made agreement with the prioress and convent for twelve marks that she should be received as a nun; and the said money was paid before her admission. She says that no one is admitted until the sum agreed on for reception be paid.

(*The prioress made answer that nothing is demanded but what has been freely offered. Let an injunction be made that no demand be made henceforth save of those who are willing to give something of their free will.*) [1]

Lady KATHERINE PACKINGTON says all things are well.

Lady ISABEL PUDSEY says all things are well.

Sister ALICE LEGET, lay sister converse, says that the infirmary is occupied by secular folk, to the great disturbance of the sisters. ([*Note*:] *Let an injunction be made.*)

Also she prayeth that the cloister doors may be shut and opened at the appropriate hours, forasmuch as they stand open too late. (*Let an injunction be made.*)

Also she says that secular serving-women do lie among the sisters in the dorter, and specially one who did buy a corrody there. (*Let an injunction be made.*) [2]

Also she says that the nuns do hold "drinkings" at night, in the guest-chamber, even after compline has ended, especially when their friends come to visit them. (*Let an injunction be made that such "drinkings" shall be prohibited.*)

Sister AGNES DAUGHTRY, lay sister converse, says all things are well.

(*Excepting such as are already boarders in that place, my lord* [*bishop*] *hath ordained that the* prioress shall receive none new who have passed, if males, their twelfth, and if females their fourteenth, year. Having reserved his power of correction, etc, and making injunctions, my lord dissolved the visitation.)

*Heynings priory was surrendered to the crown in 1539 by Joane Sanford, prioress; at which time there were twelve nuns, with annual revenue of less than £50. Dr. John London alleges that many of the nuns at Heynings, having been professed very young, had succumbed to inchastity and were delighted that they might now return to the world and marry. But at least six of the twelve lived on till 1553 and continued to receive their small pensions as unmarried women. The Heynings real estate was granted to Sir Thomas Henneage.*

**Legbourne Priory**

THE CISTERCIAN PRIORY OF LEGBOURNE, Lincolnshire, was founded by Robert FitzGilbert about 1150. The first recorded bishop's visitation was that of John Deping in 1440, who reserved most of his criticism for the prioress. Here follow a few extracts from the interviews of 1440, a century before the dissolution.

**Visitation of Master John Deping, Canon of Lincoln, to Legbourne Priory, 3 July 1440°.** (Latin. Trans. DWF)

Lady JOAN PULVERTOFT, the prioress, says on examination that at the time of her confirmation and installation, the house was £63 in debt, and now only £14....

Lady JOAN FRANCES says that every nun receiveth, daily, one loaf and one pottle of beer; one pig a year; eighteen pence for beef, daily, in Advent and at Lent; two herrings and a little butter in summer; and sometimes two stone of cheese a

[1] This pretense of dowerless admission was a diplomatic fiction; no one was admitted as novitiate without at least a small dower to cover room, board, and clothing.

[2] *corrody* ] fr. the 12th century, privileges sold to a secular person for residence at an abbey or religious house. A full corrody included food, drink, and lodging. Some corrodies also included clothing, laundering, and even a regular cash allowance. Corrodians sometimes stayed on after the principal was exhausted.

year and eightpence a year for raiment; and no more. Also she says that the vicar of Louth is the confessor for the convent, though not appointed by my lord [bishop] so far as she is aware. Also she says that several of the prioress's kindred have often access to the priory; she knows not, however, whether the house be burdened thereby.

Lady JOAN GYNEY, dwelling in the household of the prioress, receiveth food only from the house and nothing at all for her raiment. She says that the prioress, after she received my lord's mandate for the visitation, called together the chapter and told them if there were aught in need of correction among them, they should tell it to her; because (quoth she) it was more suitable that they should correct themselves than that others should do so.... Also she says that the tenements and houses producing rent which belong to the priory are exposed to ruin by reason of the carelessness of the prioress and bailiff, and will soon fall to pieces unless a remedy be applied....

Lady JOAN PAVY ... says that Margaret Ingoldesby, a secular woman, lieth at nights in the dorter among the nuns, bringing her birds, by whose continual chattering silence is broken and the sleep of the nuns, disturbed.

Lady JOAN FRESHNEY says that the prioress allows secular women, both boarders and servants, to lie by night in the dorter among the nuns, against the Rule....

Lady ALICE STANE says that all things are well.

Lady SIBYL PAPELWICK says that the prioress... is over-harsh, and to some over-kind and indiscreetly partial. Also she says that the prioress is useless in the governance of matters temporal, nor doth she care whether or not they prosper, but instead disposeth all to her own use as though the [resources] were her own, even the common goods of the house.

*Injunctions were issued accordingly, with the usual penalties enjoined for disobedience.*

*A century later, upon receiving news of the 1536 Act of Suppression, the nuns of Legbourne hoped that their house might be spared, in that their patron was Thomas, Lord Cromwell, chief minister of Henry VIII. The abbess, Joan Missenden, wrote (in English) to Cromwell in 1536, begging him to exert his influence for a reprieve:*

**Joan Missenden to Thomas, Lord Cromwell:** °

Right honorable, our most singular master and founder (our duty in the humblest wise presupposed, with daily prayer as your perpetual and religious beadwomen), please it your goodness to understond that whereas almighty God hath endued you with just title, "Founder of the Priory of Legbourne," to the great comfort of me and all my sisters, we do and shall always submit ourselves to your most righteous commandment and order, only putting our comfort in your goodness.

And whereas we do hear that a great number of abbeys shall be punished, suppressed and put down because of their mis-living, and that *all* abbeys and priories under the value of £200 be at our most noble prince's pleasure to be suppressed and put down, yet if it may please your goodness, we trust in God ye shall hear no complaints against us, n'other in our living nor hospitality-keeping. In consideration whereof, if it may please your goodness in our great necessity to be a mean and a suitor for your own poor priory, that it may be preserved and stand, you shall be a more higher founder to us than he that first founded our house.

We have none other comfort nor refuge but only unto your goodness, and we wholly submit ourselves to the pleasure of God, to the pleasure of our prince, and to the pleasure of you our founder; and howsoever it shall please God that we shall be ordered, we shall continue your faithful and daily beadwomen, as knoweth our Lord, who ever preserve you to your most comfort.

Your own daily beadwomen,
Jane Missenden, prioress,
and sisters of the priory of Legbourne

*The petition was unsuccessful. The priory of Legbourne was dissolved in September; whereupon mother Joan received a pension of £7 a year; and the nine remaining nuns, 20s. each, to buy themselves secular apparel. The property was granted to Thomas Henneage.*

• • •

**Grace Dieu Priory**

THE AUSTIN PRIORY OF GRACE DIEU, Leicestershire, was founded between 1235 and 1241 by Rose de Verdon, who endowed the convent with the manor and advowson of Belton, and with the manor of Kirkby in Kesteven. The sisters for their white habits were called the White Nuns of Saint Augustine. Among the abbey's restrictions, unusual for English monasteries, was a rule forbidding the women, after taking vows, to leave the abbey's walled precincts; a rule that by 1441 was no longer observed.

A surviving account book for the years 1414-1418 indicates that there were fourteen nuns then resident, together with long-term guests, chiefly daughters of local families. Twenty-two male and eight female servants helped with the livestock, buildings and grounds, food-preparation, laundry, and medical care. Income came chiefly from rents: much of Belton was leased to tenant farmers; and female guests were charged for their room and board. Additional income was supplied by the abbey's large herds of livestock (meat, leather, dairy products), and by the sale of firewood. The priory seems to have been well ordered and self-sustaining. Each nun received an annual allowance of six shilling eight pence for clothing.

But when William Alnwick, bishop of Lincoln, visited Grace Dieu in January 1440/1, he got an earful: Alice Dunwich, prioress since 1418, was accused of favoritism, and of failing to render account of the convent's affairs to the other nuns. The cellaress was said to be too familiar with the convent's male chaplain, and lax in her choir attendance. The priory was in debt, the infirmary unstaffed, and the buildings in need of repair.

The interviews:

**Visitation of the Bishop of Lincoln to Grace Dieu Priory, 21 January 1440/1**°
(Latin. Trans. DWF)

Lady ALICE DUNWICH, prioress, says that at her installation the house was forty-eight pounds in debt; and now, thirty-eight pounds.

She says that the refectory is not stored, nor has it been kept for seven years. The nuns every day sit in company at table in her hall, along with secular folk. They have reading-time during meals. She says that there are two households only in the convent, namely, in her own hall, and in the infirmary where three sit together at table.

She says that she sometimes giveth leave that nuns may go visit their friends, for six days. Those nuns who are officers go to the offices by themselves.

A male child of seven years sleeps in the dorter, with the cellaress.

She says also that during her tenure three corrodies have been sold.[1] One was to the vicar of Whitwick for £20; another to a lady, for fifty marks.

She says that the cloister is not maintained, nor hath it been kept closed for a long time. (The cellaress and sub-cellaress serve as bursars, receiving and disbursing all of the house's revenues.)

Lady AGNES ROTEBY, the sub-prioress, says that the prioress doth not show herself impartial to all, but is too harsh to some and over-kind to others.

She says that the prioress by reason of old age and incapacity hath abdicated her governance of all matters temporal. Nor doth she take part in divine service, so that she is of no use whatever. And if she maketh any corrections, she doth so with chiding and abusive speech; so that, under this prioress, religious discipline is almost altogether forsaken.

She says that certain nuns the prioress calls her "disciples." These keep always close to her. To them, and to the prioress, secular folk have frequent access, with whom these pupils hold indiscreet conversation.

She says also that the prioress makes no reckoning yearly before her sisters in common; and that the treasures of the house are put in pawn without the knowledge of the convent (but she knows not to whom, or wherefore); insomuch that they have not a single goblet remaining from which to drink.

Among the secular folk that sit at table with her, the prioress maketh common the secrets of their religious life, to the convent's great scandal.

She says that Margaret Bellers taketh all their temporal affairs into her own hands, never consulting with her fellow treasurer, or with anyone else of the convent. According to the Rule, they ought to be assured of the general state of the house, and informed of the accounts, four times in the year, in common. Because this is no longer done, the nuns remain ignorant of the state of their own convent.

Also she says that from the time of the last visitation there hath been no love among them: from that time ever since, the prioress hath reviled the nuns for the matters disclosed by them in that visitation. She says also that the prioress hath her own boarders, one of whom came to the place just within the last three days, the daughter of one Villiers.

She says that Bellers, the cellaress, cometh not to choir, either by day or by night – not even on Sundays or feast-days. She says further that the cellaress, too early in the morning, all alone, visits the offices and the other out-buildings where men are employed.

Sometimes, during the autumn season, the nuns help the secular folk to garner their grain. But Bellers departeth with the chaplain to their autumn tasks, to mow hay and to harvest; insomuch that one day, she rode back at evening behind him on the same horse. Sith then, Bellers

---

[1] *corrodies* ] an annual payment of food, firewood, free lodging, or other provision given by religious houses to the lord of the parish or other patron.

and the chaplain have been, and remain, too free in their conversation. She says further that the said chaplain (named Henry) neglecteth to say the canonical hours, and at the altar behaveth himself without devotion, for he cleaneth the stables and goeth to the altar with unwashen hands, nor maketh he any bow before or after Mass. He dwelt sometime at Loughborough, where he was not of good report.

(*Note: It should be remembered to make mention to the prioress, and all, that they receive not any boarders.*)

Lady ELIZABETH JORDAN says that the prioress for twenty-three years hath withheld from the office of the infirmary twenty shillings donated for that purpose by one Knyvington, of the county of Derby.

She says also that their maltstress is a Frenchwoman of very unseemly conversation; and that the secular serving-folk hold the nuns in disrespect; and chiefly are they rebellious in their words against the kitchener. She prays that they may be restrained.

Lady PHILIPPA JECK says that all corrections are made with such great harshness and with so much ado, that charity and loving-kindness are banished from the house. She says also that the infirmary is in such a ruinous state that the nuns cannot abide there without great discomfort.

Lady ALICE ROWBY says that Bellers trusteth so mightily in her own judgment that she doth despise all others.

Lady AGNES POUTRELLE says all things are well.

Lady ISABEL JORDAN says all things are well.

Lady ELIZABETH SHERBURN says that Poutrelle clepeth herself the prioress's "disciple," and whatever she heareth or see'th among the nuns, she doth straightway tell to the prioress, who rebuketh them most shamefully. And she says that Isabel Jordan is the same way. [1]

Lady MARGARET BELLERS, the cellaress, says that Lady Margaret Chesham, her subcellaress, at the commandment of the prioress, lieth in the infirmary and cometh neither to the matins at night, nor to the other hours; and with this excuse, that they have no serving-woman in the infirmary.

Also she says that the servants of the house come not together for meals, but in scattered parties and severally; to the great waste of the house. What would be enough for four is set before one or two.

Lady MARGARET CROSS says that all things are well.

Lady MARGARET CHESHAM referreth herself to the words of the sub-prioress and the others that follow her.

Lady JOAN GERMAIN says that all things are well.

Lady CUSTANCE LONDON says that no satisfaction hath been made of her necessary nun's habit.…Also, that Bellers in autumn goes out to work alone with Sir Henry, he reaping the harvest and she binding the sheaves; and returneth late in the day, riding behind him on the same horse. She is over friendly with him and has been, ever since the doings aforesaid.…

[*Respondents*:]

An article having been laid to her charge that she cometh not to choir at night, CHESHAM says that she hath been appointed by the prioress to be of service in the infirmary to three old nuns who lie therein every night (and she with them, in the same way). She careth for them night and day, washing them and doing all else like a laywoman. She prayeth therefore to be restored to dorter, and to the choir and the other regular observances. She shall willingly watch, by day, that fit service be done to the [elderly nuns].…

That Sir HENRY the chaplain busies himself with unseemly tasks, cleansing the stables, and then goeth to the altar without washing, staining his vestments:

He appeared and, such article having been laid to his charge, he expressly denieth the allegations contained therein. Howbeit, he was sworn that henceforth he will not commit whatever he hath done heretofore, going to country places with Bellers alone, harvesting, and making hay, and making stacks in the barns.

He expressly denieth his solitary roaming in the fields with the said Bellers; howbeit he confesses that he hath been in the fields with the others and Bellers, carting hay and helping to pile the sheaves in stacks in the barn.

That he is without devotion and disrespectful at the altar and hath an evil name at Loughborough, where he formerly dwelt, and elsewhere: He hath been sworn to behave himself devoutly and reverently henceforth, as also at the altar in making his bow after and before his Masses.

• • •

---

[1] *Sherburn* ] prioress 1485-1493, succeeding Alice Dunwich; *clepeth* ] calls, names.

*When the interviews were ended, Bishop Alnwick had harsh words for prioress Alice Dunwich, concluding that "love, charity, peace and concord are utterly excluded and exiled fro' you; and nothing among you but privy envy, hate, simulations, discords, upbraids and rebukes." The bishop on pain of cursing and impeachment commanded mother Alice to bring her house into order; whereupon Dunwich in her own defense replied that "charity and loving-kindness were utterly banished, and strivings, hatreds, backbitings and quarrellings have ever flourished," on account of what the nuns said of her at the previous visitation, conducted by Bishop William Grey (d. 1436); "wherefore she hath held them, and holdeth, them in hatred."*

*The bishop, "in order that these things should altogether be utterly driven out and peace, concord, charity and love one to another be restored among them, warned the said prioress a first, second and third time peremptorily, under pain of excommunication and under pain of her final and perpetual deprivation and removal from the office and estate of prioress of that place, that henceforth, from that moment forward, she broach not anew, in any way, the disclosures made either at the last visitation of his predecessor, or at this of his own"; but that she "treat and cherish her sisters with motherly and sisterly love"; or "we shall proceed agains' you to the execution of the pains afore-written as far as law will demaund."*

*Grace Dieu was next visited by the bishop's commissary in 1518, at which time the nuns again complained of mismanagement of the house.*

*At a visitation by the chancellor of the diocese in 1528 the fourteen nuns present reported that all was well.*

*The last visitation came on the eve of the Dissolution, in 1535; at which time the income of the house was assessed at £92, with fifteen resident nuns, and thirty-six servants (twenty-seven male, nine female). The buildings were found to be in good repair, though inelegant. Two of the fifteen nuns were reprimanded for sexual incontinence. And the convent was said to reverence what the nuns believed to be the girdle and tunic of Saint Francis of Assisi.*

*A commission of local gentry, that same year, defended the White Nuns of St. Augustine at Grace Dieu, affirming that all fifteen were virtuous, and that all wished a reprieve, believing theirs to be the only remaining house of Austin nuns in England.*[1] *The prioress, Agnes Liderland, in 1536 obtained a license to continue. But the respite was brief. Grace Dieu was surrendered to the crown in October 1538. The abbey's income in its final year came to £73. 11*s. *8*d. *The buildings and lands were granted to Humphrey Foster.*

• • •

**Ankerwick Priory**

THE BENEDICTINE PRIORY OF ANKERWICK in Buckinghamshire was founded about 1160 and dedicated to Saint Mary Magdalene. A detailed report survives of Bishop Alnwick's visitation of 1441, which took place some ten months after his visit to Grace Dieu:

**Visitation of the bishop of Lincoln to Ankerwick Priory, 10 October 1441** °
(Latin. Trans. DWF)

LADY CLEMENCE MEDFORD, the prioress, says that the nuns are sometimes moved against her for small cause. Also, she says that the nuns are wont to drink almost every day, contrary to the rule, and do hold drinkings after compline.

Lady ISABEL STANDEN, the sub-prioress, says that all is well.

[1.] Lady MARGERY KIRKBY says that all of the houses and buildings within the priory are in ruinous condition, and that three useful and necessary houses are flattened to the ground through carelessness and neglect of the prioress; to wit, the sheepfold, which was consumed by fire (by the fault of the prioress, who was then at a wedding at Bromhall); another house, wherein dairy stuff is made; also a barn, of which the timber, because it was not gathered together, is now burned up. (*The prioress confesseth being at the wedding; she confesseth the burning; also the rest of the article.*)

[2.] Also: that the prioress alone keepeth (and her entire tenure hath kept) the common seal of the house, so that she can do therewith whatever she will, without the knowledge and advice of the nuns. (*The prioress confesseth that she alone hath kept the seal for her term, at set times, years and days; and sometimes, with other her fellow-nuns, so long as there have been any of discretion.*)

[3.] Also: the vestments used to be notable, and many in number. Where they are gone, or

[1] In fact, several other, less wealthy, Augustinian convents survived until 1539. Burnham (Bucks.), Canonsleigh and Cornworthy (Devon), Aconbury and Limebrook (Hereford), Grimsby (Lincoln), Halliwell (London), and Holystone (Northumberland).

whether they be there, is not known; but it is believed that they are alienated from the house. (*The prioress says that there abide in the house all things that she received from the last prioress, touching the which she hath shown a schedule concerning the delivery of the vestments and jewels.*)

[4.] Also: they had four chalices, and now there is one only. (*The prioress confesseth that there were four, whereof two are in the house. The third is in pawn to Thomas Stanes; the fourth hath been broken up, also with the consent of the convent.*)

[5.] Also: the prioress hath caused a silver censer and a silver chalice, the heaviest which they had, to be broken up; therewith to make a cup for use at table; and she gave the chalice and censer as broken silver to one brother William Tuddington, a monk of Chertsey, that he might take order for the making of the said cup therewith; and because the prioress had been given to understand that he had paid for the making of the chalice, and she had not the wherewithal to pay him, the said cup remaineth in the hands of the said monk. (*She confesseth the article, but says she first had communication with the convent, who all say that agreement was not held in chapter touching this, nor was the consent obtained of all, but only that the greater number had no knowledge of the action before it was taken.*)

[6.] Also: she says that there used to be beautiful psalters kept in the house, ten in number, certain whereof the prioress hath given away and alienated. (*The prioress confesseth that she lent three, one to the prioress of Bromhall. "Without the consent of the convent," she denieth.*)

[7.] Also: that in the year last past, in a place called [Brack]ley Park, two miles distant from the priory, she sold an hundred oaks, without need and without meeting to ask consent of the convent. (*She denieth that article.*)

[8.] Also: at Alderbourne, she caused beeches to be felled at an unseasonable time, so that they will never grow again, and so are come to nought, for good and all. (*She denieth the article.*)

[9.] Also: the prioress hath never rendered an account of her receipts and expenses, and yet she alone receiveth, payeth, and provideth all things, even dispatching weighty business and leases, not communicating with the convent. And whereas she says that the house at the time of her installation was three hundred marks in debt, this deponent says outright that then it was only thirty pounds in debt, and that amount was paid from other sources and in no wise from the goods of the priory or of the former prioress. (*She confesseth that she hath never rendered an account. She confesseth also that she alone hath received and doth administer all things without the knowledge of the convent. She denieth that she hath made leases, unless with the knowledge of the convent.*)

10. Also: she caused Rowell Wood, situated at Parnish, to be felled unseasonably, suffering the boughs there to remain after felling; wherefore it is unlikely that the wood will grow again to the profit of those now living. (*She denieth the article.*)

11. Also (*see the first*): she says that the prioress hath destroyed an entryway (to wit, a gatehouse), through which needful stuff was brought in, and peasepods and other waste were carried out. And now that this entry is blocked up, they are carried out through the church, to the great scandal of the house. (*She confesseth the whole article, but says that* [*it was done*] *for greater seemliness, to keep outside the cloister pigs and other beasts which formerly, coming in through that entry, did befoul it.*)

12. Also: through default of the prioress, six nuns have now left the house in apostasy. (*She confesseth that this many nuns have left, yet without her foreknowledge.*)

13. Also: that she hath appropriated to herself in the dorter four nuns' places, and hath blocked up the view towards the Thames, which was a great comfort to the nuns. (*She confesses the appropriation of those places, and confesseth blocking up the view, because she saw that men stood in the narrow space close to the window to converse with the nuns.*) [1]

14. Also: the prioress weareth rings of gold, sumptuous, with divers precious stones; and also, girdles that are o'er-silvered and gilded. Also, she weareth silken veils and she set her veil too high above her forehead, leaving her forehead uncovered, to be seen of all. And she wears furs of Vares. (*She confesseth the use of several rings and girdles and silken veils and the high carriage of her veils; she confesseth also the use of furs of Vares. She has sworn that she will reform these things, having now taken her oath thereto.*) [2]

---

[1] *dorter* ] dormitory.

[2] *furs of Vares* ] prob ably, of the English grey squirrel.

15. Also: she weareth shifts [made] of cloth of Rennes, which doth cost sixteen pence the ell. (*She denieth the article.*) [1]

16. Also: she weareth kirtles laced with silk, and tiring-pins of silver and silver-gilt, and hath caused all the nuns to wear the like. (*She confesseth the article so far as regards her own wearing; she hath sworn that she will reform these things and hath sworn to perform her penance, etc.*)

[17.] Also: she weareth above her veil a cap-of-estate that is furred with budge on the sails. (*She confesses thereto; but it is because of divers infirmities in her head; she hath sworn, as above, that she will reform these things.*) [2]

[18.] Also: for three years' space she hath not furnished adequate habits to the nuns, insomuch that the nuns go about in patched cloth. (*The bareness of the nuns was observed by my lord* [*the bishop*].)

[19.] Also: at great cost to the house, the prioress did invite to this visitation several outside folk from the neighborhood; saying to them, "Stand on my side in this time of visitation, for I do not wish to resign." (*She confesseth the entertainment of her friends, but says it was not for that purpose.*)

20. Lady JULIAN MESSENGER says that their hay and other grains are stored in the church, for the lack of barns, which in the neglect of the prioress have gone to ruin. (*She confesseth the storage.*)

Also: during the prioress's second year in this place, the sheepfold of the house burned up, and she hath never made repair thereof since; wherefore their hay is stored as aforesaid; nor doth she make *any* repairs. And, albeit some [donors] have given somewhat for maintenance, the prioress keepeth for herself what she will of what is given, without making the necessary repairs. (*She says that repairs have been done in her time, touching which she hath shown my lord a schedule whereby it appeareth that those repairs were done about the church.*)

Also: the copses are destroyed in default of the prioress, as aforesaid; and herein she agreeth in all things with Kirkby.

[21.] Also: the prioress bringeth into the priory divers strangers, both male and female, folk unknown [to the convent] and maintaineth them at the common cost of the house. And some that are almost witless, and others that are disabled, she maketh nuns. (*She denieth the article.*)

[22.] Also: she treateth the nuns her sisters in harsh wise, even when their friends come to visit them.

[23.] Also: the younger nuns have not a governess to instruct them in reading and song. (*Provision of the sub-prioress,* [*Juliane Messenger,*] *hath now been made to them.*)

24. Also: the prioress cometh rarely to matins or masses; and when she cometh, she upbraideth the nuns and chideth them.

25. Also: they had not serving-folk in the brewhouse, bakehouse, or kitchen, from last year's Feast of the Nativity of St. John the Baptist, to the Michaelmas next following; insomuch that this deponent, with the aid of other her sisters, prepared the bread, beer and victuals and, with them, served the nuns in her own person.

(*See 18.*) Sister Thomasine Talbot says that the prioress hath not provided this deponent with bed-clothes, insomuch that she lieth in a bed of straw; and when my lord [bihop] had commanded this deponent to lie in the dorter, and this deponent asked bed-clothes of the prioress, she said chidingly to her, "Let him who gave you leave to lie in the dorter provide you with raiment."

(*See 22.*) Also: when the nuns' friends come down to the priory to see the nuns, the prioress behaves irritably, when giving leave to the nuns to talk with them.

(*See 14.*) Also the prioress hath on her neck one long silken band, (in English, a "lace"), which hangeth down below her bosom; and thereon pendant, a golden ring with a diamond. And she hath all the archives and the common seal of the house in her keeping. (*She confesseth she wore the lace and ring, but in jest.*)

26. Also: many times, when the prioress cometh to choir at the end of the canonical hours, she requireth the nuns to begin those hours over again.

(*See 18.*) This deponent hath no kirtle appointed for her to wear.

Sister AGNES DYCHERE asketh that sufficient provision be made to her in cloth for her bed and body, that she may be covered from the cold; and also, sufficient edibles, that she may have strength to undergo the burden of religious observance and divine service; for these hitherto have not been so supplied to her.

---

[1] *cloth of Rennes* ] Rennes linen, the finest available, woven in Brittany.

[2] *budge* ] lambs' wool.

She and the other young nuns have not a governess in reading, song, or religious exercise.

Also, she says that the prioress requireth the nuns to sing more psalms than is the manner accustomed in the place, beyond all measure.

Sister MARGARET SMITH also speaketh of the failure to repair; of the charters and common seal of the house; etc. Also, she says that the prioress is very harsh and is too excessive in her corrections. Also. the prioress serveth not this deponent with sufficient provision of bed-clothes. She, too, asks to have a governess in reading, song, and religious observance.

Having examined these – and passing by the other three (to wit: sisters Isabel Coke, Elizabeth London, and Ellen Morton), on account of their tender age and slender discretion, in that the eldest of them is not more than thirteen years of age – my lord adjourned his said visitation and the business thereof, even as it then stood and remains, until the day of Monday next before the Feast of All Saints…

*In the next recorded visitation to Ankerwick, in 1519, Bishop Atwater had harsh words: he learned that one sister was cohabiting with her lover in the house of a relative, while another sister had abandoned the priory, her whereabouts unknown.*

*Magdalen Downs, then a novice, was prioress in 1536 when Ankerwick Priory was surrendered to the Crown. After the dissolution, she married. The real estate was granted to Lord Windsor.*

• • •

**Catesby Priory**

THE CISTERCIAN PRIORY OF CATESBY was founded about 1175 by Robert de Easeby. Various saints' relics were kept there. On the death in 1267 of William de Mauduit, earl of Warwick, his body was buried at Westminster Abbey, but his heart sent to be interred at Catesby Abbey. The first recorded bishop's visitation was in 1442, during the tenure of prioress Margate Wavere; at which time bishop William Alnwick found much that displeased him.

**Visitation of the bishop of Lincoln to Catesby Priory, 17 July 1442**°
(Latin. Trans. DWF)

The Visitation of the Priory of the Nuns of Catesby, of the Order of Citeaux, of the diocese of Lincoln, performed in the chapter-house there on the 17th day of the month of July, in the year of our Lord 1442, by the reverend father in Christ and lord, the Lord William, by the grace of God bishop of Lincoln, in the 16th year of his consecration and the sixth of his translation [to bishop].

In the first place, as the said reverend father was sitting in his capacity of judge, as a tribunal for the business of the said visitation, on the day and in the place aforesaid, there appeared before him the prioress and convent of the aforesaid place, in readiness as was apparent to undergo this visitation.

At that time, first and before all else, the Word of God was set forth in accordance with the process that was to take place and the company that heard it, in the vulgar tongue by the honorable Master John Beverley, professor of Holy Writ, [speaking] upon this text, "Go forth, ye daughters of Sion, and behold King Solomon," etc.

And when this was done, the prioress delivered to my lord [bishop] the certificate of the mandate [which had been addressed] to her for the commencement of this visitation, in these words, "To the reverend father in Christ," etc.; the which having been read through, the prioress displayed her title, and a bull confirming the foundation [of the house], and swore obedience and fealty. And then the same reverend father proceeded to his preparatory inquiry, as follows.

Sister [prioress] MARGARET WAVERE says that sister A[gnes Allesl]ey has six or seven young folk of both sexes that do lie in the dorter.

[Also she says] that secular folk have often recourse to the nuns' chambers within the cloister, and conversations and entertainments take place there without the knowledge [of the prioress].

She says that she herself has four nuns in her "household," and there are three additional "households" of nuns within the cloister.

She says that divine service is not said at the due hours according to the rule, and she says that silence is not observed in the due places.

The nuns do send out messages and receive [letters] sent to them, without the permission of the prioress.

She says that when these seculars visit, they disclose the secrets of the house in neighborhood roundabout.

Also, the nuns do dispatch servants of the priory on their affairs and receive the persons for whom they have sent; with whom the nuns parley and converse, whereof the prioress is unaware.

Also she says that Isabel Benett is defamed with Sir William Smith, former chaplain in that place, and did conceive by him and bore his child, and that [the prioress] hath not punished her, because she dared not.

Also, the said Isabel is disobedient to the prioress. Likewise, the other nuns are sometimes obedient, sometimes not. Nor do the nuns wear their veils down to their [eyebrows], but do keep their foreheads exposed.

Sister JULIANE WOLF says that there should be two lamps burning in the upper church and choir in time of divine service.

Also she says that the prioress does not show to the convent the accounts of her administration.

Also, she says that the prioress has pawned the treasures of the house, to wit, for a period of ten years a cup for the body of Christ, which still remains in pawn, and also other pieces of silver.

Also, she says that the prioress did threaten that, if the nuns disclosed anything in the visitation, they would pay for it with imprisonment.

Also she says that the prioress is wont to go by herself to the town of Catesby to the gardens with one man alone, a priest named William Taylor.

Also Isabel Wavere, the prioress's mother, rules almost the whole house together with Joan Coleworth, the kinswoman of a certain priest, and these two do carry the keys of all the offices.

Also, when guests come to the house, the prioress sends out the young nuns to make their beds, the which is a scandal to the house, and perilous.

Also the prioress does not give the nuns satisfaction in the matter of raiment and money for food; and she says that touching the premises the prioress and the nuns' are in debt for three quarters of the year.

Also the buildings and tenements both within and without the priory are ruinous, and many have fallen to the ground because of default in repairs.

Lady ISABEL BENETT says that when the prioress is enraged against any of the nuns, she calls them "whores" and pulls them by the hair, even in choir.

Also she says that the prioress was herself defamed with Sir William Taylor. (*The man appeared in person before my lord [bishop] in the church of Brampton; and the article having been laid to his charge, he denies the crime at any time. Wherefore, at his own request, my lord appointed him the Saturday next after the festival of [Saint] Margaret, in the church of Rothwell, to clear himself with five chaplains of good report, who have knowledge of his behavior, etc.*).

The nuns know nothing of the receipt and expenses of the house, nor of the state of the convent, because the prioress hath never rendered an account.

These ten years the prioress hath made no repairs except in one part of the cloister....

Also she says that divine service is chanted with such great speed that no pauses are made.

Also, the prioress is so harsh and headstrong that she may in no wise be appeased.

Also, the prioress's mother knoweth well the secrets of the chapter and doth publish them in the town. So, too, doth the prioress publish them.

Also, in the last visitation, made by the lord William Gray, the prioress said that for a purse and certain amount of money, a clerk of the said bishop disclosed [to her] what each nun had said in that visitation.

Sister AGNES ALLESLEY says that the prioress sows discord amongst the sisters, saying, "Such an one said thus and thus about you," if she to whom she speaks hath transgressed in aught.

Also she says as above concerning the scandal of the prioress and Sir William Taylor (who now dwells at Boughton, near Northampton); and she says that the overmuch familiarity between them was a cause of scandal, because [the prioress] did go out of a morning to the offices, alone except for that chaplain; and even after the prioress was warned of the public scandal, the said chaplain after his departure did come to the house thrice within a month.

The revenues of the house, thirteen years ago, were worth sixty pounds a year and now scarce fifty pounds; and this decrease hath come to pass from the evil administration of the prioress; the matter of Sir William Taylor; neglect in the repair of tenements and the failure to obtain tenants, etc.

Also two sheepfolds have stood unthatched these two years. Therefore the timber has begun to rot and the lambs yeaned therein have died, due to the wetness.

Also she says that at the time of the prioress's installation, the house was but a little or nothing in debt. Also, at the same time [the prioress] found table-linen suitable to serve the king, and a set of twelve silver spoons. Now all has disappeared, and the spoons and the other vessels which are in the house belong to the prioress's mother.

Sister ALICE KEMPE says that, because the nuns at the last visitation disclosed what should be disclosed, the prioress whipped some of them; and that the prioress is too cruel and harsh with the nuns, "and loves them not."

Also if perchance the nuns transgress, she rebukes and reproaches them in the presence of secular visitors, and even during the divine office, and without restraint....

Sister AGNES HALWEY says that the prioress in choir, and outside, doth pull the veils from the nuns' heads, and she calleth them "beggars" and "whores."

Also, [Sister Alice] is young and would fain learn religious discipline and other things, but the prioress sets her to making of beds, to sewing and spinning and other chores.

Also, she says that she hath caught William Taylor and the prioress in the act of fornicating together, for she saw him lying on top of her, and she on her back.

The prioress denieth the article of cruelty with respect to calling them whores and beggars; she denieth also having laid violent hands upon the nuns. As to her not having rendered an account, she confesseth it, and with the excuse that she hath not a clerk who can write. As to the burden of debt, she referreth herself to the account presently to be rendered. As to the neglect of the sheepfolds, she referreth herself to the visible evidence. As to the pawning of the chalice, she says that that was done with the consent of the convent, for the payment of tithes. As to the felling of trees, she says that it was turned to the convent's profit, partly with and partly without the knowledge of the house. As to the disclosures in the last visitation and the reproaching of those who made them, and the whippings, she denieth the article. As to threatening them lest they should make disclosures [in this visitation,] she denieth the article. As to the publishing of the secrets of their religion, she denieth the article. As to her mother and Joan Coleworth, she denieth the article. As to the bed-making and other chores, she denieth the article. As to the withholding of food and raiment from the nuns, she confesseth it, in part. As to the decay of the outer tenements, she says that they are partly in repair and partly not. As to the sowing of discord, she says that she might have done so: she is uncertain. As to this – that for a purse, and cash, that she knew all the disclosures at the last visitation, she flatly denieth the article. As to Sir William Taylor, she denieth the crime, at any time.

She hath until the morrow to clear herself of that she hath denied, [on the testimony] of four sisters; and to receive punishment for those she hath confessed.

–At which [appointed] time she brought forward not one compurgator. Therefore, she was declared to have made default in purgation. And having presented nothing, she was pronounced convicted as charged. She forswore the said man and all familiar converse with the same, henceforward.

Isabel Benett confesseth her crime, but [says] it was not with Sir William Smith. Notwithstanding, she foreswore him and all familiar converse with him henceforward; and hath until tomorrow to hear her punishment. (Note: She thereafter cleared herself, with [compurgators] Julian Wolf, Elizabeth Langley, Alice Holywell, and Alice Kempe.)

[*Addenda*:] As to the lamps, the prioress says that they shall be provided.

As to the chaplains, the prioress says that none can be had, but she will do her diligence that they be obtained.

Ladies Isabel Benett and Agnes Allesley, nuns of Catesby, will not obey or hearken to the injunctions of the lord bishop, and especially that concerning giving up their [private] chambers,' asserting that they are not subject [by their Rule] to the said constraint.

Also the said Lady Isabel on Monday last past spent the night with the Austin friars at Northampton and did dance and play the lute with them in that place until midnight; and on the night following, she passed the night with the friars preachers at Northampton, luting and dancing in the same manner.

And then [the bishop] adjourned his visitation....

*In a document signed the next day, 18 July 1442, Bishop Gray issued lengthy injunctions upon the prioress and nuns, on penalty of greater excommunication and imprisonment if they failed to obey in all points.*

*Less than three years later, in January 1444/5, Margaret Wavere was impeached and removed from office by the diocesan. The bishop at that time commissioned an audit of the accounts, which was conducted by sisters Agnes Allesley and Isabel Benett. Allesley was appointed next prioress; and after her death, Bennett; during whose tenure there appears to have been no further trouble; or at least, no further visitations from a bishop.*

*A century later, under the first Act of Dissolution, the priory of Catesby was visited by Dr. John Tregonnell, who in his subsequent report to Cromwell (27 September 1535) singled out the priory of Catesby as a well-ordered house. ("The prioress and sisters are free from suspicion.") Tregonnell, a lawyer for the king in the affairs of Sir Thomas More and Anne Boleyn, was one of the most relentless of the monastic visitors. His testimony in favor of Catesby cannot be due to partiality.*

*Upon learning that her house was slated for dissolution and promised to a local landowner, prioress Joan Berkeley set about to save her covent, appealing to Queen Anne Boleyn; who generously offered to donate to the Royal Exchequer the substantial sum of £2000 pounds if Cromwell would spare the priory of Catesby.*[1]

*Mother Joyce wrote to Cromwell (in English), begging that her priory be exempted*:

**Joyce Berkeley to Lord Cromwell (April 1536)°:**

To the right honorable and my most especial good master, Master Secretary:

Pleaseth it your mastership to call to your remembrance that Dr. [Richard] Gwent informed you yesternight, that the queen's Grace hath moved the king's Majesty for me, and hath offered his highness two thousand marks in recompense of that house of Catesby – and hath as yet no perfit answer. If it may like you now in great sorrow and pensiveness to be so good master to me as to obtain that the king's Grace do grant that the house may stand, and get me years of payment for the two thousand marks, you shall have a hundred marks of me to buy you a gelding; and my prayers during my life, and all my sisters during their lives. (I trust you have not forgotten the report that the commissioners did send unto you of me and my sisters.)

Master Onley says that he hath a grant of the house. But my very trust is in God, and [in] you to help forward that the queen's grace may obtain her request that it may stand.

And thus I beseech almighty God send you ever such comfort at your need, as it was to my heart yesternight when Doctor Gwent did send me word that you would move the king's grace for me this morning again.

Your most bounden of all creatures,
Joyce, late prioress of Catesby

*The prioress's timing and choice of royal patronage proved unlucky: Queen Anne having had a miscarriage in January, she was arrested for treason on May 2nd; and on May 19th, beheaded. In the interim, the local commissioners (perhaps still unaware of Anne Boleyn's sudden fall) visited Catesby priory and dispatched to Cromwell a review that was suitable for framing (in English)*:

**Commissioners in Northamptonshire to Lord Cromwell (12 May 1536)°**

...The house of Catesby we found in very perfect order; the prioress a sure, wise, discreet, and very religious woman with nine nuns under her obedience, as religious and devout and as good obedience as we have in time past seen or belike shall see. The said house standeth in such a quarter much to the relief of the king's people and his Grace's poor subjects there likewise much relieved. ... Wherefore if it should please the king's Highnesses to have remorse that any such religious house shall stand, we think his grace cannot appoint any house more meet to share his most gracious charity and pity on than the said house of Catesby. Further, ye shall understand that as to her bounden duty towards the king's Highness in this his affairs, also for discreet entertainment of us his commissioners and our company, we have not found nor belike shall find any such of greater discretion...

From Catesby the 12th day of this present month of May.

Edmund Knightly, John Lane, George Gifford, Robert Burgoyne.

*Receiving this letter within days of Queen Anne's execution, Cromwell nonetheless showed it to Henry VIII; but the king upon reading the report became irate, accusing the four commissioners of having taken bribes from Berkeley or her supporters.*[2]

*In the end, neither the offer of two thousand crowns from the fallen queen, nor the horse promised by mother Berkeley, moved Cromwell to reverse the order for dissolution: by year's end, the priory of Catesby was surrendered to the Crown. Plate was seized to the value of £29; furniture, vestments, and other goods, £400; lead torn from the roofs, £110; and £3 for the broken metal of two bells. Mother Joyce and her nine nuns and twenty-six dependents were turned out. To the prioress was granted a pension of £20. The buildings and lands were granted to John Onley, esq.*

• • •

**Littlemore Priory**

THE BENEDICTINE PRIORY OF LITTLEMORE was founded by Robert de Sandford during the reign of King Stephen. The Knights Templar were the abbey's patrons from about 1280 until its dissolution (for cause) in 1525. Poorly en-

---

[1] Of the smaller houses that were exempted from dissolution under the first Act, many or most negotiated pretection, in payments ranging from £20 to £400, funds that may have come from donors acting in the nuns' behalf. A. Gasquet, *Henry VIII* vol. 2.47 ff.

[2] George Gifford to Cromwell (19 June 1536), MS Cotton. Cleop. E.iv, fol. 213.

dowed, the abbey receives little notice in the historical record until the date of its first recorded visitation: in June 1445, while Bishop Alnwick visited Godstow, his commissary Dr. John Derby visited Littlemore, where he found the abbey in a sorry state of disorder: the nuns no longer slept in the dorter, for fear the roof would cave in. They ate meat seven days a week, kept divine service only at their own convenience, and disregarded the rules for silence. The prioress and sub-prioress slept in their own private households, always with a bedpartner. Secular women were taken as lodgers, and men, as visitors. The convent had become a virtual open house for monks and Oxford students. The inquest:

**Visitation to Littlemore Abbey by Dr. John Derby, commissary to the bishop of Lincoln, 1 June 1445**° (Latin. Trans. DWF)

Lady ALICE WAKELEY, the prioress, says that the nuns do not lie by night in the dorter because they are afeared of the ruinous state of the building. Also she says that … boarders in the house each pay fourpence a week. The house's cook is a secular man.

Lady AGNES PIDDINGTON, the sub-prioress, says that Agnes Marcham, a "nun" (not expressly professed), of twenty-eight years of age, hath continued for twelve years wearing the habit of the professed, while refusing to make sworn public profession.

Lady ALICE BILLESDON says that all things are well.

Lady JOAN MAYNARD says that the said Agnes Marcham is very quarrelsome and rebellious and will not do her work like the others.

Lady ISABEL SYDNALE says that she herself lieth every night in the same bed with the sub-prioress.

Lady CHRISTINE CORDBERD lieth at night in the same bed with the prioress; and agreeth with the sub-prioress [about Marcham].

Lady AGNES MARCHAM says that she entered religion in the said place in the thirteenth year of her age and hath stayed in the priory, wearing the habit of the professed, for thirteen years. She says that she hath no intent to make express profession while she remaineth in that place, because of the evil reputation which is current roundabout concerning that place; and also because of the barrenness and poverty which in likelihood will overtake the place on account of its slender revenues.

Also she says that a certain monk of Rievaulx (who is a student at Oxford and is of the Cistercian order) hath common and frequent access to the priory, eating and drinking with the prioress and spending the night therein sometimes for three, sometimes for four, days on end. [1]

Also she says that Master John Herars, master in arts, a scholar of Oxford and a kinsman of the prioress, hath access in like manner to the priory, breakfasting, supping and spending the night therein.

Also, she says that Sir John Somerset, parish chaplain of Sandford, who boards with the prioress, hath common and frequent access to the chequer of the said Joan Maynard, and sits therein by himself and is with the said Joan by herself, in manner suspect. [2]

Also she says that the nuns do eat meat in the refectory every day, whenever they eat therein.

*Bishop Alnwick, upon receiving Dr. Derby's report, fired off an angry letter to Alice Wakeley, demanding immediate reform* (*in English*):

*Quod iaceant separalim el non in vno* [*On lying separately, not in one*]: In the first, for as mickle as we find detect[ed], in our said visitation, that diverse of you, [against] the Rule of your order, and also the common law, do lie two-and-two togeder in one bed by night, we charge, enjoin, [and] commaund you and each one of you, under pain of the great curse – the which we intend to give on each one of you that obeys not to this our injunction – that fro' henceforth each one of you lig separately in one bed by herself, housing all togeder, to such time as your dorter (which, as it is said, is in plight to fall) be sufficiently repaired; so that ye, Prioress, see that each one of your susters have a separate bed by herself, and that nightly they and none other secular, woman ne child, lig with them in the same house.

And also: that every suster of yours, and ye also, use your veils hanging [to] your brows.

Also we enjoin you, Prioress, under pain of privation from your state and dignity, that for as mickle as ye and your said place are grievously noised and sclaundered for the gre[at and] common access of secular people, and specially of scholars of Oxonford, and in-special one dan John, [monk] of Rievaulx of the Order of Citeaux, schooling at Oxonford, that fro' henceforth ye suffer no secular person ne other, and in especial the said monk, to have any recourse or access to your said place or to any singular person thereof, ne there to abide by night, ne that ye suffer none

[1] *Rievaulx* ] a Cistercian abbey near Helmsley in North Yorkshire.

[2] *chequer* ] a room for keeping the accounts.

of your susters, and in especial Dame Joan Maynard, to speak with any secular persons ne religious but all only in [manner] so that ye see and hear what they do and say, and that their speaking togeder be not long but in few words. [1]

Also we charge you and each one of you (under pain of cursing above-said) that ye, ne none of you, receive no subjournants man ne woman within your place over the age of a man of nine year, ne woman of twelve year; ne not [even] them withouten special leave of us or our successors, bishops of Lincoln, asked, and had. [2]

*Quod diebus ieiunandi reficiant et commedant simul in refectorio* [*On days of fasting and eating together in the refectory*:] Also we charge you under like and the same pain that fro' henceforth every Wednesday, Friday, and Saturday, and on days when fasting is commaunded by the kirk or your order, that ye eat together in your refectory and that those days there be fish or white meat or other such, as is used in your place since time of old.

Written under our seal *ad causas* in the monastery of Oseney, the fourth day of June, the year of our Lord 1445…

• • •

LITTLEMORE ABBEY was next visited in 1517, by Dr. Edmund Horde, commissary to Bishop Atwater; at which time only six nuns remained – Katherine Wells, prioress; Julian Beauchamp; Anne Willy; and the three Winter sisters, Julian, Jane, and Elizabeth. The prioress and one of the nuns had given birth. The five nuns had a running battle with mother Katherine; and none of them was especially well behaved. From the interviews:

**Wednesday, 17 June 1517, by the commissary, Master Edmund Horde, doctor of decretals for William Atwater, bishop of Lincoln. Discovered in the Visitation**° (Latin. Trans. DWF)

In the first place, the nuns say that the prioress enjoined them on virtue of obedience that they disclose nothing to the commissioner; warning them that she will punish them severely for whatever information reaches her.

Also, it was found that the said prioress has had a daughter by incestuous intercourse with Sir Richard Hewes, chaplain (now in Kent), and that she feeds her daughter in the monastery.

They say also: that the said Sir Richard visits this monastery two or three times a year, staying overnight with the prioress like a man in bed with a wife of his own.

Also…that the said prioress has been withdrawing from the monastery many utensils, cloth, pots, candlesticks, basins, sheets, pillows, featherbeds, etc., for her daughter's marriage.

…that the said Sir Richard was with the said prioress at the Feast of the Purification of the Blessèd Mary last past, and lay in bed with her at night; and the nuns would have taken them in the act, were it not that Sir Richard's servingman was there in the prioress's parlor.

…that the prioress gave to Sir Richard the convent's silver gilt chalice, worth five marks.

…that they many times exhorted the said prioress to abstain from the society of the said Sir Richard. But she said that she would not, because "We are in love, and are pleased to love."

…that a lady of the house, Julian Winter, was disgraced with John Wicksley, a married man of Oxford, and bore his child, which they believe was occasioned by the ill example of the prioress.

…that all of the buildings are falling to ruin.

…that almost all the convent's treasures are now pawned.

…that the prioress is most excessive in her punishments; and especially when they rebuke her sinful life, she confines the nuns in the stocks.

…that they lack food and clothing, and have no stipend.

…that one girl who intended to enter religious life as a novice, when she saw the bad behavior of the prioress, she left and in some places made public the prioress's bad behavior.

…that the said Sir Richard Hewes intends to return to the convent by the Feast of St. Peter ad Vincula, as indicated in his letters.

…that the prioress has leased tenements under the common seal and pocketed the rents.

The nuns pray for a quick remedy, saying that if the prioress learns of their petition against her, they will leave the convent for fear of her punishments.

*A year later, on 2 September 1518, Bishop Atwater came to Littlemore in person "to effect some reformation"; by which time the scandal had become suitable stuff for a stage play. The prioress testified first*:

[1] *dan* ] an honorable title used chiefly for members of religious orders, equivalent to Mr.

[2] *subjournants* ] sojourners, temporary residents.

**Visitation to Littlemore Abbey by William Atwater, bishop of Lincoln, 2 Sept. 1518°** (Latin. Trans. DWF)

[*Allegations of Katherine Wells, prioress*]

Lady Elizabeth Winter is not obedient to the prioress or willing to be corrected by the prioress although delinquent. She plays and wrestles with the boys in the cloister, but obstinately refuses correction.

Lady Elizabeth was placed by the prioress in the stocks, for correction; but three other ladies, Anne Willy, Juliana Winter, and Joan Winter, straightaway broke the doors and keys of the parlor and dormitory, and together started a fire, and refused to admit the prioress into the parlor. And finally, when she [the prioress] sent for the sergeants and others in the Oxford vicinity for help and counsel, the four nuns broke a window and escaped secretly in the night and resorted to [the house of] a certain English [friend], and remained there for two or three weeks in continuing apostasy.

Lady Juliana Winter was impregnated by John Wicksley and gave birth to a child two years ago, and still has common conference with laymen, and is unwilling to abstain from familiar conversation with the men, despite warnings from the prioress..

The same four nuns last named are always playing around in divine service; they laugh during high Mass, even at the elevation [of the Eucharis]t; and all of them are obstinately disobedient.

[*The nuns in turn complained about Wells:*]

The four nuns aforenamed [say that] the lady Prioress has punished them too bitterly for their disclosures at the time of the last visitation [June 1517], and has words that are harsh and threatening.

Lady Anne Willy (as she says) was placed by the prioress in the stocks once a month within the past year, without cause.

Lady Juliana Beauchamp told Anne Willy, in the year the following words, *viz.*: "I am ashamed to hear of the evil rule of my Lady."

The lady Prioress is too excessive: she severely struck one on the head in the chapter-house of the cloister and in the household of Elizabeth Winter, with the fists and feet, punishing her with the same excessive severity, before this Feast of the Passion last past.

She sold an entire wood belonging to the priory.

Sir Richard Hewes, chaplain, now residing in Kent, was again with the prioress, in the same place, at the feast of the Passion last past.

*The doings at the abbey were now the talk of all Oxfordshire. Mother Katherine Wells was summoned to stand trial before the Church court. The hearing lasted for several days, concluding with the bishop's ruling that she deserved deprivation of her office. Wells was allowed to continue as prioress, provided that she consulted often with Edmund Horde; but she was not permitted to take part in the punishment of the other sisters accused of sin.* [1]

*Littlemore Priory was dissolved in February 1525, a decade before the general dissolution. Katherine Wells, still prioress at that time, was awarded a pension of £6 13s. 4d. The property was granted to William Owen and John Bridges.*

• • •

**Godstow Abbey**

THE BENEDICTINE ABBEY AT GODSTOW, Oxfordshire, was founded in 1133. Its church was dedicated in 1139, in a ceremony attended by King Henry I. Throughout the twelfth century, Godstow was one of the most distinguished and wealthy of aristocratic nunneries. It was at Godstow in 1176 that the fair Rosamund, mistress of Henry II, was buried. (Bishop Hugh visiting Godstow in 1191 and finding Lady Rosamund's tomb being venerated as a shrine, he required that her body be removed from its resting place beneath the high altar and buried outside.)

Monastic rule appears to have been closely observed until the latter thirteenth century. The first notable trouble was over the abbey's colonization of public lands previously available to the poor for hunting and gathering. In 1281, King Edward I ordered the arrest of the prioress for having enclosed 60 acres of the demesne of the king and of the common pasture of the citizens of Oxford. Losing that cause, the prioress turned around and enclosed another 40 acres of land. She was again cited; but this time she was able to show a grant from Henry II deeding the parcel to the abbey.

As the nearby University of Oxford grew, religious discipline at hospitable Godstow Abbey became less rigorous.

In 1290, Archbishop Peckham excommunicated persons unknown for having intercepted a carriage and for kidnapping sister Agnes de

[1] For a transcript of the charges and depositions, see Bowker (1967): 46-51. Latin.

Shene. Shortly after, Agnes, too, was excommunicated, together with a second nun, a kinswoman of the Countess of Warwick, after the bishop discovered that the kidnapping was in fact an elopement.

Though the convent owned much property, the expensive tastes of its mostly aristocratic clientele, and many servants, caused the house to run into debt. From 1284 until the dissolution, the sisters of Godstow were repeatedly cited, not only for the usual offenses – lax attendance at service, and the lodging of secular women within the cloister – but for apostasy, inchastity, and profligate spending.

William Grey, bishop of Lincoln, visited Godstow abbey on 16 July 1432 and was alarmed by what he discovered: the convent had become party central for Oxford scholars. The abbess was then Elizabeth Pitt (d. 1434). Finding the situation unimproved after two years, on the succession of Elizabeth Felmersham, Gray re-issued his injunctions on the nuns of Godstow, again commanding the nuns to exclude secular visitors and female lodgers. To ensure compliance, he required the porter to take a solemn oath to admit no secular person without special permission.

**Injunctions of Bishop William Gray to Godstow Abbey, 7 June 1434°**
(Latin. Trans. DWF)

Injunctions and ordinances made in the monastery of Godstow, of the order of St. Benedict, of the diocese of Lincoln, by the reverend father in Christ, [and] lord, the Lord William, by the grace of God bishop of Lincoln, in his visitation held by the same in the said monastery during the year of our Lord 1432 and in the second year of his translation [as bishop]:

In the first place: that all the nuns, at least all who are able, attend every night at matins in choir; and that they attend in choir at masses, vespers, and the other hours; so that, even if they chant not the service, they may read some good thing, practice contemplation or meditate, according to the ancient and laudable custom of the monastery.

• Also, that at the least twelve nuns take their meals every day in the frater; and that the said frater be duly repaired with all speed. [1]

• Also, that silence be kept by all the nuns without distinction at the appropriate times and places; and that those who transgress herein be severely punished according to the Rule, without discrimination by rank.

• Also, that strangers who come to the monastery be directly brought into the abbess's hall by the gatekeeper of the monastery; where, after the reason of their coming has been ascertained by the abbess – if they have come to see one of the nuns, to converse with her – the abbess shall send for her forthwith, and shall herself hear (if she have leisure, or another ancient and discreet nun shall by appointment of the same abbess [hear]), what conversation is held between them and what they say; so that the visit of strangers may be quickly dispatched, and they may so depart, and in no wise shall pass the night there unless they be the father or mother, brother and sister, of that nun for whose sake they have so come to the monastery.

• Also, that the gatekeeper take an oath, in the presence of the abbess and her council, to guard the great gates of the monastery, diligently and faithfully, and to permit no strangers to enter except on conditions aforesaid [i.e., with the permission of the prioress].

• Also, that adult [secular] women be altogether removed from lodging within the convent during the coming year since they disturb the nuns and provide a bad example by reason of their dress and their visitors.

• Also, that the present bailiff of the monastery, who boasteth that there is not one virtuous woman in the convent, may have no private conversation with any nun whomsoever.

• Also, that there be no reveling or drinks after compline, but when it is over all the nuns shall go together to the dorter and lie there throughout the night .... [2]

• Also, that the [guest] beds be altogether removed from the nuns' dormitory rooms, other than those for the children; and that no nun may receive any secular [person] for any recreation in the dorter, under threat of excommunication. For the scholars of Oxford say that the nuns give them whatever manner of solace they desire....

• Also, that no secular person, nor any friar or other man of religion enter the cloister precincts or the nuns' dorter after compline or before the bell rings for prime....

• Also, that all of the doors of the nuns' dorter towards the outer court, through which it is possible to enter into the cloister precinct when the other doors of the cloister are shut, be altogether bricked up, or that there be placed upon the doors such means of barring or shutting them that all approach or entrance through those doors may be excluded to secular persons.

---

[1] *frater* ] dining commons.

[2] *dorter* ] dormitory.

• Also, that the access of the scholars of Oxford to the convent be altogether curtailed and suppressed....
• Also, that [neither] the gatekeeper of the priory, nor any other secular person, convey any gifts, payments, letters, or tokens from the nuns to any scholars of Oxford or other secular person whomsoever, or bring back any from such scholars or persons to the nuns; not even skins said to contain wine, without the view and knowledge of the abbess, and with her special permission asked and received; under pain of expulsion from his office and from the said monastery, forever; and if any nun shall disobey, she shall undergo imprisonment for a year.

• • •

On 29 May 1445, at the same time that his commissary, John Derby, was conducting his eye-popping visitation to Littlemore, Bishop Alnwick visited Godstow, where the religious discipline had actually improved somewhat since the previous visitation (1434). Both the newly elected and retiring abbessses, Alice Lumley (d. 1446) and Elizabeth Felmersham, professed their vigilance in keeping the cloister off-limits to the university boys. Felmersham requested specific injunctions from the bishop to help her maintain discipline:

**Visitation of the bishop of Lincoln to Godstow Abbey, 29 May 1445°** (Latin. Trans. DWF)

LADY ELIZABETH FELMERSHAM, the abbess, says that the house can spend 400 marks a year.

She prayeth that injunctions be issued to the end that they receive no boarders, and that secular women may not lie in the dorter, and that the convent grant no corrodies.

She says that there are, in the monastery, several separate households of nuns; wherefore seculars have frequent access to the nuns, both during the divine office in choir, and at the refectory during mealtime. The nuns without asking leave of the abbess are able to converse with the seculars who visit the monastery. And she says that she cannot prevent Oxford students from having common access, in her despite, to the monastery and to the cloister precincts.

Lady ALICE LUMLEY, the prioress, says that the nuns, in turn, on pretense of visiting their friends, have frequent access to visit the city of Oxford....

Lady JULIAN WESTON prayeth that the conduit may be speedily repaired: by reason of default in repair, they suffer great scarcity of water within the cloister. Also she prayeth that their bread and beer, which are sometimes quite poor, be improved....

Lady ISABEL CLINTON, the sacrist and bursar, says that the abbess doth not lie in the dorter.

Lady ALICE HENLEY says that Sir Hugh Sadler of Oxford, chaplain, hath had often access to Lady Alice Longsby, whom he hath professed to be his "kinswoman"; and under such pretense holds often conversation with sister Longsby. She says also that there are four separate households of nuns in the monastery.

Lady ALICE LONGSBY says all things are well.

Lady MARGARET MORE says that Lady Amy Hardelle is the doorkeeper of the cloister.

Lady ELIZABETH HULTON says all things are well.

Lady ELIZABETH FORTHEY says all things are well.

Lady AMY HARDELLE says that Lady Katherine Okeley holdeth too much conversation with the strangers that come to the monastery – in the church, in the chapter-house, at the church-door, the hall-door, and divers other places; nor is she obedient to the orders and commands of the abbess according to the Rule.

Also she says that Lady Alice Longsby is wont to hold parley, in a manner exceedingly suspect, in the church of the convent with Sir Hugh Sadler, priest; this, despite the prohibition of the abbess (*for the which, there was enjoined upon her the penance of imprisonment, and of punishment according to the Rule, and to keep to the refectory and cloister for a year*).

Also she says that John Norris, the steward, receiveth from the house a yearly wage of ten marks – and he hath been of profit to the monastery in *nought*.

Lady MARY BREWLEY says all things are well.

Lady MARY BROWDIE says all things are well. Howbeit she says that, whereas they should have four priests constantly in the monastery, sometimes they have but two or three; and yet, although such priests are wanting, allowance is made to the abbess for the pay and board of four priests.

Lady MARGARET GRENHURST says that all things are well.

Lady AGNES WILD says that swine come into the churchyard and root up the earth and befoul the churchyard in other wise.

Also she says that secular servants and various other secular women do ease themselves in the privy appointed for this purpose to the nuns only. She prayeth therefore that seculars be forbidden to do so, and another place be appointed them to this end, outside the cloister.

Lady ALICE, nun, says that sister Maud, a laywoman, is exceeding rebellious to the abbess, and that she hath obtained, without the abbess's knowledge, a bull from the apostolic See to the prejudice of the monastery.

Lady KATHERINE OKELEY says that all things are well.

• • •

*In his ensuing injunctions, Bishop Alnwick forbade secular persons all access to the nuns during choir, and during meals; he commanded the sisters to eat together in the refectory as one household, all at one time, with no secular adults present, either male or female. Under no circumstance were the nuns to have private conversations with any clergyman or layman or Oxford student except in the presence of "two ancient nuns." And leaves of absence to see family were to last no more than three days. Visits to Oxford were forbidden.*

*Over the near term, the quality of life at Godstow improved somewhat. In 1447, perhaps in gratitude for favors rendered, a clerk of Oxford left a generous bequest to repair the buildings. Religious discipline, meanwhile, became more rigorous. In 1450, then prioress Alice Henley commissioned a vernacular translation of the abbey's Latin Register, or "Books of Remembrance"; thereby to provide present and future inmates with an English breviary of hymns and prayers; also, a record of their cartulary (deeds and charters), and a detailed catalogue of the offenses that entailed imprisonment within the convent, or greater excommunication. The anonymous clerk who made the translation for mother Alice supplies a prologue in which he defends his project as useful and instructive, in that the sisters of Godstow were "in englissh bokys well y-lernyd" but could not read Latin:*

From **the Prologue to the English Register of Godstow Abbey (c. 1450)°**

The wise man taught his child gladly to read books and 'hem well understond; for in defaut of understonding is oft-times caused negligence, hurt, harm and hindrance (as experience proveth in many a place). And forasmuch as women of religion, in reading books of Latin, be'n excused of great understanding, where it is not 'heir moder tongue; therefore, howbeit that they would read 'heir Books of Remembrance of 'heir Muniments writ in Latin, for defaut of understonding they took oft-times great hurt and hindrance,...it were right necessary, as it seemeth to the understonding of such religious women, that they might have, out of 'heir Latin books, some writing in 'heir moder tongue...as followeth this simple translation....

*A century later, Godstow Abbey had a good reputation among the locals. The royal commissioners who visited Godstow in 1538 reported that "that most of the young gentlewomen of the country were sent there to be bred, so that the gentry of the country desired the king would spare the house"* (Burnett, 1.368).

*But to no avail: on 4 November 1539, Dr. John London came to Godstow to enforce the abbey's surrender. Abbess Katherine Bulkeley refused to admit him. The next day, she wrote to Cromwell to complain of Rev. London*:

**Abbess Katherine Bulkeley to Lord Cromwell, 5 November 1536°** (English)

Pleaseth it your honor with my most humble duty to be advertised, that where it hath pleased your lordship to be the very mean to the king's majesty for my preferment, most unworthy to be abbess of this the king's monastery of Godstow; in the which office, I trust I have done the best in my power to the maintenance of God's true honor, with all truth and obedience to the king's majesty; and was never moved nor desired by any creature, in the king's behalf or in your lordship's name, to surrender and give up the house; nor was never minded nor intended so to do, otherwise than at the king's gracious commandment or yours; to the which I do, and have ever done, and will submit myself most humbly and obediently; and I trust to God that I have never offended God's laws, n'other the king's, whereby that this poor monastery ought to be suppressed. And this notwithstanding, my good lord, so it is that Dr. London, which (as your lordship doth well know) was against my promotion, and hath ever since borne me great malice and grudge like my mortal enemy) is suddenly comed unto me, with a great rout with him; and here doth threaten me and my sisters, saying that he hath the king's commission to suppress the house, spite of my teeth. And when he saw that I was content that he should do all things according to his *commission*, and showed him plain that I would never surrender to *his* hand, being my ancient enemy; now he begins to entreat me, and to inveigle my sisters one by one, otherwise than ever I heard tell that any of the king's subjects hath been handled; and here tarrieth and continueth, to my great cost and charge; and will not take my answer: that I will not surrender till I know the king's gracious commandment, or your good lordship's.

Therefore I do most humbly beseech you to continue my good lord, as you ever have been; and to direct your honorable letters to remove him hence. And whensoever the king's gracious commandment, or yours, shall come unto me, you shall find me most ready and obedient to follow the same.

And notwithstanding that Doctor London, like a untrue man, hath informed your lordship that I am a "spoiler" and a "waster," your good lordship shall know that the contrary is true. For I have not alienated one ha'p'orth of the goods of this monastery, moveable, or unmovable, but have rather increased the same; nor never made lease of any farm or piece of ground belonging to this house other than hath been in times past always set under convent seal for the wealth of the house. And therefore, my very trust is that I shall find the king as gracious lord unto me, as he is to all other his subjects, seeing I have not offended; and am and will be most obedient to his most gracious commandment at all times; with the grace of Almighty Jesus, who ever preserve you in honor long to endure to his pleasure. Amen. [1]

At Godstow the 5th day of November [1536].
Your most bounden beadswoman,
Katherine Bulkeley, abbess there

*Mother Katherine was perhaps surprised when her prayer was answered: Dr. London was instructed to back off. The abbess again wrote to Cromwell, this time to express her gratitude and to affirm that she and her entire convent were prepared to subscribe to the new articles of faith:*

[1] *ha'p'orth* ] half-pennyworth.

**Abbess Katherine Bulkeley to Thomas, lord Cromwell, 26 Nov. 1536°**

To the right honorable and my very singular good lord, my Lord Privy Seal

My most singular good Lord,

My most humble duty, this be specially to thank you for that it pleaseth you to direct your letters for the stay of Dr. London which was here, ready to suppress this poor house against my will and all my sisters; and had done it indeed if you had not so speedily sent contrary commandment; for the which your goodness you shall be well assured (as I am ready most bounden) of a poor maiden's prayer my life; seeing I have no other riches to recompense you withal.

And where it pleased you to direct your letters since that time to me and my sisters for the preferment of Master Dr. Owen to our demesne and stock, this be to certify your lordship that we have accomplished the same with all favor and gentleness as I trust he will report and give your lordship thanks therefore: for no man living under the king could have had it of us with our good wills, saving your lordship. [2]

And, therefore, as my very trust and comfort is in you, I beseech you to continue my good lord, as I trust you shall never have cause to the contrary. For your lordship shall be well assured that there is n'other pope nor purgatory, image nor pilgrimage, ne praying to dead saints, used or regarded amongst us. But all superstitious ceremonies set apart, the very honor of God and the truth of His Holy Words, as far as the frail nature of women may attain unto, is most tenderly followed and regarded with us. Not doubting but this garment and fashion of life doth nothing prevail toward our justifying before God; by whom, for His sweet son Ihesus' sake, we only trust to be justified and saved, who ever preserve your honor to His pleasure. Amen.

At Godstow, this 26th day of November [1536].
Your most bounden beadswoman,
Katherine Bulkeley, abbess there

*The reprieve was brief: as per the king's command, Godstow abbey was surrendered to Sir John Williams 17 November, 1539. The abbess received a pension of £50 and her sixteen sisters an allowance for new clothes. The abbey and lands were granted to Henry VIII's physician, George Owen.*

[2] *demesne and stock* ] real estate holdings and store (of other communal belongings).

### Nun Cotham Priory

THE PRIORY OF NUN COTHAM, Lincolnshire, of the Cistercian order, was founded in King Stephen's reign by Alan de Moncels. Poorly endowed, the sisters sold corrodies (room and board) to single women and widows who did not wish to take orders, a practice that the bishops condemned in the visitations of 1382, 1440, and 1519 – injunctions that the nuns disregarded. But Bishop Longland in his visitation of 1530 found that religious life at Nun Cotham had deteriorated. Prioress Joan Thompson was said to be conducting business as if the abbey and its stock were her personal property, and an open house for her kinfolk to receive free food, lodging, and goods. The sisters were quarreling. And the bishop found that Nun Cotham's tradition of hospitality to secular women was being extended as well to amorous men.

### Bishop Longland's Injunctions to the Priory of Nun Cotham, 30 April 1530° (in English)

John Longland by the sufferance of God bishop of Lincoln, to our well-beloved sisters in Christ, the prioress and convent of Nun Cotham, of our diocese of Lincoln, sendeth greeting, grace and blessing.

And forasmuch as in our ordinary visitation of late exercised within that house, divers things appeared and were detected worthy of reformation, we therefore for the honor of God and redress of the same and maintenance of good religion there send to you these injunctions following, which we will and command you to keep under the pains ensuing...

Forasmuch as by your negligent sufferance divers of your sisters hath wandered abroad in the world, some under the pretense of pilgrimage, some to see their friends and otherwise; whereby hath grown many inconveniences, insolent behaviors, and much slander as well to your house as to those sisters (as by the text of my said visitation doth evidently appear); I charge you, lady Prioress, therefore, and all your successors, that from henceforth ye neither license ne suffer any [of] your sisters to go out of your monastery without a great urgent cause by you known and two of your senior sisters approved afore your said license so given; and that they tarry not out of the monastery in the nighttime; and to have in company one otherwise, [a] sober and discreet sister, that so the one may testify of the other['s] honest conversation ... and no more to be absent as in times past they have been wont to use, being content if six have been present, the residue to go at liberty where they would, some at Thornton, some at Newsome, some at Hull, some at some other place, at their pleasures, which is in the sight of good men abhominable, high displeasure to God, rebuke, shame, and reproach to religion – and due correction to be done, according unto your religion, from time to time.

Also, we charge you, Lady Prioress, under pain of excommunication, that ye from henceforth no more suffer Sir John Ward, Sir Richard Calverly, Sir William Johnson, nor Parson [Alot] the parson of Scotton, ne Sir William Sele, to come within the precincts of your monastery; that if they by chance do [so] unwares to you, that ye straight banish them and suffer not them there to tarry, nor none of your sisters to commune with them or any of them; and that ye void out of your house Robert Laurence, and he no more to resort to the same....And that ye suffer not any men-children to be brought up nor taught within your monastery, nor any person young ne old to lie within your dorter but only religious women; and that every sister do lie alone, according to the laws; and the door of the said dorter nightly to be shut, and light nightly to burn in the same...And that ye cause the cloister doors to be shut half-hour before eight of the clock every night at the uttermost, and so to stand shut and not opened till six of the clock in the morning; and no secular men to enter into the said cloister without your especial license; and that ye know them that so shall enter....[1]

Item, I charge you, ladies all, under pain of disobedience and of the law, that ye and every of you do truly observe your religion, serve God, keep your divine service devoutly and all other rites, observances, and ceremonies appertaining unto your said religion as well within the church, chapter house, fratry, dorter, as *cloister,* and that ye be obedient in all lawful commandments unto your lady prioress, and observe and keep very charity amongst you, and to leave all dissension, rancor, malice, and debate; and to unite yourselves in God by clean, chaste, and religious living, and no more to wander abroad in the countries as ye have used, neither by the pretense of pilgrimages, nor visitation of your friends, whereby much slander hath risen to your house, and many inconveniences; and to occupy yourselves when your service is done in some good

---

[1] *Alot* ] Rev. John Alot (d. 1533).

occupations and labors, so to avoid idleness (the mother and nourisher of all vice) and to flee all ill company; and no suspect persons to have any resort to you nor ye to them. And thus doing, ye shall have the blessing of God, and mine.

Item, I will and command you, Lady Prioress, that these mine injunctions be every month hereafter once openly read in your chapter house in presence of all your sisters, under pain of excommunication; and charge you, ladies all, by the virtue of your obedience, from henceforth no more to write any letter or letters or cause any to be written or sent to any person or persons, without special license of the prioress, for the time being, and she to see the contents of the same, afore. In witness whereof hereunto we have put our seal, when at our manor of Woburn the last day of April in the year of our Lord God a thousand five hundred and one and thirty.

*Nun Cotham was surrendered to the Crown on 9 July 1539. Prioress Joan Thompson received a pension of £6; her twelve sisters annuities varying from £2 to 30s. The house and site were granted to William Skipwith.*

• • •

### Elstow Abbey

THE BENEDICTINE ABBEY OF ELSTOW, Bedfordshire, was founded about 1078 by Judith of Lens, a niece of William the Conqueror and the widow of Earl Waltheof. Tradition has it that Judith endowed the abbey as an act of contrition after having betrayed her husband to his death, following the revolt of the earls.

Elstow was considered a royal foundation at least as early as the thirteenth century; its patronage remained with the Crown until the dissolution. Most of the nuns were daughters of nobility with friends about the court who found every excuse to visit the abbey, and to stay on as lodgers. That the sisters extended hospitality to their secular friends was a constant worry to the bishops, who complained for generations that Elstow was too worldly. As early as 1270 Bishop Gravesend remarks that the nuns of Elstow generated "more frequent reports of disgraceful acts than in any other house beneath our rule." [1]

Nowhere was the world-savviness of the Elstow sisters more publicly apparent than in the abbey's litigiousness: from the twelfth through the early fourteenth centuries, the nuns of Elstow were continually involved in litigation, chiefly disputes over land. Not all of those suits were successful. But the abbey was a favorite among landowners when writing their wills, and its real estate holdings steadily grew. By the fourteenth century, Elstow had rental income that extended to twelve counties.

The abbey's vast wealth, and the family connections of the nuns, made it difficult for the bishops to insist upon reform. Injunctions were enjoined upon the nuns of Elstow throughout the fourteenth and fifteenth centuries, all or most of which commands and strictures appear to have been cheerfully disregarded: the nuns of Elstow remained one of the most independent and independently minded of English sisterhoods.

The injunctions issued to Elstow in January 1422 are representative of the bishops' concerns expressed in directives periodically throughout the late Medieval period. Of special interest in that Bishop Fleming in his prologue adopts a more florid and literary prose style than in his injunctions to less exclusive nunneries. At the time of Fleming's visit, the abbess was Lady Joan Trayle, elected in 1409.

#### Bishop Fleming's Injunctions to Elstow Abbey, 17 Jan. 1421/22°

(Latin. Trans. DWF)

Richard [Fleming], by sufferance of God bishop of Lincoln—

To our beloved in Christ, the abbess and convent of the monastery of Elstow, of the order of St. Benedict, of our diocese: Health, grace, and blessing.

In our recent visitation to you at the said monastery, we discovered, in the head and members, transgressions and offenses notoriously in need of reformation. And so that the brightness of religion be not eclipsed by the dark overshadowing of those transgressions and offences (even as a light set upon a candlestick may give light to all that are in the house), we now follow the footsteps of the lord William of honest memory, former archbishop of Canterbury, at the time of his [1382] visitation (by his right as metropolitan); we dispatch to you by these present letters certain of our injunctions and mandates (below); strictly enjoining upon you, all and severally, under the penalties and censures written below, that you observe the same without breach, all and sundry, so far as they pertain to you or to individual persons of the said monastery.

---

[1] Trans. DWF from Raine, *Historical Letters and Papers from the Northern Registers* ed. (Rolls Ser.), pp. 33-4, and *Register of W. Giffard* (Surtees Soc.) p. 164.

First of all: from manifest inference and the certainty of our own observation we have learned that the stay of visitors (especially of married persons) in the said monastery hath caused serious wrack to the purity of religion as well as to the sweetness of honest conversation and character (the fragrance of which, in our judgment, far surpasseth that of temporal goods, and the destruction of which far exceedeth the waste of temporal wealth); and as it is likely to cause more serious harm, in future: We therefore ordain, enjoin and command you who are now abbess, and the other several persons who shall be abbesses in the said monastery – under penalty of deprivation, beside the other penalties written below, which it is our will you shall likewise incur, if you do contrary to that which we command – that henceforward you neither admit nor allow to be admitted, or receive to lodge or stay within the limits of the cloister, any persons male or female, how honest soever they be, who are beyond the twelfth year of their age, nor any other persons soever, and married persons in particular, within the precincts of the same monastery, unless you have procured express and special license in the cases premised from ourselves or from our successors, who for the time being shall be bishops of Lincoln. …

Also, we ordain that every nun of the said monastery have each Monday, Wednesday and Saturday, one dish of meat or fish appropriate to the season, of the value of every dish one penny…. Also, that each nun have five measures of the best ale each week; and that there be no difference between the bread of the abbess and the bread of the convent…

Also, that no nun convicted, publicly defamed, or manifestly suspect of the crime of unchastity, be deputed to any office within the monastery, and *especially* not that of gatekeeper, until her innocence, [or] purgation be sufficiently established…

Also, that henceforth no secular, nor any man of religion, be admitted after the hour when the gates of the cloister-precincts are to be shut; nor may he enter those precincts, unless he be a great and noble person; and then, only if it be for a cause that is manifestly honest and important.

Also, that no nun admit secretly into her chamber any secular men or men of religion; and if they be admitted, she must not keep them there very long.

Also, that the gates be shut and opened at the proper times, as required of the rule.

Also, that no nun have access to the town of Bedford or to the town of Elstow, or to other towns or neighboring places; nor let any have a meal outside the monastery, unless for a manifest and unavoidable reason to be approved by the judgment of the abbess, and unless she first ask and obtain license of the same.

Also, that no nun go out of the cloister precinct unless she first obtain special leave and permission from the prioress, and then only for a most pressing reason; and she shall have in her company at least one nun of mature age and discretion and of good reputation, to bear witness of her behavior….

Also we enjoin and command that no nun presume to wear silver pins in her hair, or silken gowns, or several rings on her fingers (save one only, the ring of her profession), under the pain written below….

Therefore we warn you, abbess, nuns, sisters, and lay sisters of the said monastery (those who are now, or shall be), for the first, second, and this third time peremptorily, under pain of the greater excommunication which, if you do not responsibly and effectually obey these warnings, we shall lay upon you (what has gone before – our threefold and canonical admonition aforesaid in this particular, and your own delay, fault, fraud, and transgression deservedly requiring it). We enjoin in these writings, now as then, and then as now, that you, and each one of you, keep these injunctions without breach, insofar as they concern you, all and individually, the premises, ordinances, injunctions and commands. And the punishment of all and several, who in any manner shall incur our sentences before delivered, we specially reserve to ourselves and our successors and to our vice-regents.

• • •

JOAN TRAYLE, abbess of Elstow, died in 1429 and was succeeded by Blanche Battesford, who was no more strict than her predecessor. Richard Fleming, bishop of Lincoln, died in January 1431/2. He was succeeded by William Gray; who during his first year in office revisited Elstow—and found more guest lodgers than nuns under orders, few of whom were observing the daily devotions and services required of the Rule. The Bishop enjoined a new set of injunctions upon Lady Battesford and her sisters, upon pain of "greater excommunication," which entailed complete isolation from other Christians as well as being barred from the bread of the Eucharist.

**Bishop Gray's Injunctions to Elstow Abbey [October or November, 1432]°**
(Latin. Trans. DWF)

William [Gray,] by sufferance of God bishop of Lincoln—

To our beloved daughters, the abbess and convent of the monastery of Elstow, of the order of Saint Benedict, of our diocese: health, grace, and blessing.

For the reformation of the transgressions of our subjects…

First of all, we enjoin upon you, all and severally, under pain of excommunication, that the convent, and that each one of you, keep silence at the due hours and places, as required in your regular observance. Also, that at least two-thirds of the convent observe frater every day….[1]

Further, since the usual number of nuns of the said monastery has so diminished, that those who are now received are scarcely enough for the chanting of divine service by night and day according to the requirement of your Rule, we desire and enjoin upon you, the abbess, in virtue of obedience and under the penalties written above and below, that (with what speed you can), you cause the number of nuns in the said monastery to be increased in proportion to your resources….

As we see from mutual cohabitation of one with another, secular women (especially married women, from their performance of conjugal relations) may incite and facilitate fleshly desire even for religious women, we therefore enjoin upon you, all and individually, in virtue of obedience and under the penalties written above and below, that you remove entirely these secular persons, all and severally, who are now staying within the cloister precincts of the said monastery; not admitting or receiving the same or others to stay in that manner within the cloister precincts; and in no wise may you admit males past their tenth year, or females past their fourteenth, or married persons….

Furthermore, since faults unpunished incite others to wrongdoing; and as it was revealed and reported to us (in the course of our said visitation) that one Lady Pernell, a nun of the same monastery, being several times guilty of fleshly delinquencies, sad to say, and is now alleged to be leading an apostate life in secular habit outside the said monastery; we enjoin upon you the abbess, in virtue of obedience and under the penalties written above and below, that you search out with all diligence and care the said apostate, and bring her back to the fold of the Lord; and when she is brought back, that you punish her according to the regular observances of your order, in sisterly wise and with motherly piety, so that not her fault, but her punishment, may be a lasting example to others.

Next following, we enjoin upon you the abbess, and the several presidents of the order in the said abbey, in virtue of obedience and under the pains written above and below, that you [admit] no secular persons whatsoever, howsoever honest they be, to the cloister precinct of the said abbey, except for a lawful and honest reason approved by your judgment, abbess, or by the judgment of one of the presidents, and only if they be in honest company, so that no sinister suspicion may thereby arise; and that you allow no nun to have frequent access to any places outside the convent, without the companionship of another nun of mature discretion and of good reputation, and [unless she be] with honorable companions.

• • •

Fast forward one hundred years. Because Elstow was a large house, it had both an abbess and a prioress (the higher rank). On 9 August 1529, after the death of Agnes Gascoigne, abbess, in July, the nineteen nuns of Elstow assembled in their chapter house to elect her successor. Matilda Shelton and Anne Preston nominated Cecilia Starkey; Alice Boyfield nominated Elizabeth Boyfield. Shelton, Preston, and Alice Boyfield thereby became "scrutineers" (non-voting observers), according to the Rule. Starkey and Elizabeth Boyfield, not allowed to vote for themselves, both voted for the unpopular subsacrist, Helen Snow. Of the others, all but two of the eldest nuns – Lady Barbara Gray and Prioress Anne Wake – voted for Boyfield.

Dissatisfied with the outcome, Wake complained on the spot to the bishop's director of the election, Edward Rayne: "Well," she said, "some of these young nuns be to blame."

Asked to elaborate, the elderly prioress replied: "For they would not show me so much: for I asked divers of them, before this day, to whom they would give their voices, but they would not show me."

"What said they to you?" asked the director.

"They said to me," replied Lady Anne, "they would not *tell* to whom they would give their

[1] *frater* ] eating together in the commons.

voices, till the time of th'election – and then they would give their voices as God should put into their minds – but this is by *counsel*! And yet it would have beseemed them to have shown as much to me as to the others.... What, should the young nuns give voices? Tush! they should *not* give voices!"

Matilda Shelton, subprioress, proclaimed Elizabeth Boyfield the new Abbess of Elstow, duly elected by the "more and sounder part of the convent." The younger majority chose Helen Snow and Katherine Wingate as proctors to obtain confirmation of Boyfield's election from the Bishop of Lincoln, John Longland. Unwilling to accept defeat, Anne Wake and the defeated Cecilia Starkey addressed a complaint to the bishop.

Hearing both sides, Bishop Longland counseled the two elderly nuns to accept the outcome, and confirmed Boyfield as the new abbess.

But the trouble had just begun.

By the time Bishop Longland visited Elstow on 25 August 1530, the house had become thoroughly secularized, operating as a kind of ladies' lodge. The nuns did not dine in commons but in private households, with their secular friends. The sisters dressed much as well-to-do lay women, with superfluous jewelry, gowns with low-cut bosoms, scarlet stomachers, and shoes that were cut to expose the feet and ankles. Instead of veils, the nuns wore cornered crests (q.v., Hans Holbein's portrait of Jane Seymour, pp. 328). When the lady abbess, Elizabeth Boyfield, walked in procession from the precincts, she leant upon the arm of her valet and was followed by a train of servants, after the manner of an English countess. Boyfield's female "chaplain," Katherine Wingate, had not attended matins for six years, and she took her meals in the abbess's buttery with the male steward and a few favored guests. Bishop Longland was vastly displeased.

**Injunctions of the bishop of Lincoln to Elstow Abbey, [October] 1530°.** (English.)

John Longland by the sufferance of God bishop of Lincoln—

To our well-beloved sisters in charity, the abbess and convent of Elstow, of our diocese of Lincoln – sendeth greeting, grace and blessing.

And forasmuch as in our ordinary visitation of late exercised within that monastery divers things appeared and were detected worthy reformation we therefore, for the honor of God and redress of the same and maintenance of good religion there, send to you these injunctions following; which we will and command you to keep under the pains ensuing:

First, forasmuch as the very order of Saint Benedict his rules are not there observed in keeping the fratry at mealtimes, where the sisters should be as well-fed spiritually with Holy Scripture as bodily with meat, but customably they resort to certain places within the monastery called "the households," where much insolency is used, contrary to the good rules of the said religion, by reason of resort of secular persons, both men, women, and children (and many other inconveniences hath thereby ensued)—

In consideration whereof, and for that we will the said religion to prosper according unto the foundation of the house and the rules of the same, we enjoin and straitly command under the pain of disobedience that the lady abbess and your successors see that no such households be then kept from henceforth but only one place which shall be called the Misericorde where shall be one sad lady of the eldest sort overseer and masteress to all the residue that thither shall resort....[1]

Over this, it is ordered under the said pain and injunction that the lady abbess [Elizabeth Boyfield] have no moe sisters from henceforth in her household but only four, with her "chaplain" [Katherine Wingate], and likewise weekly to change, till they have gone by course through the whole number of sisters, and so ayen to begin and continue....

*Those nuns who were not in rotation to dine in the Misericorde or in the Abbess's household were commanded to eat in the common frater, where fish, bread, and beer were served.*

*The bishop further commanded that all sisters resume attendance at Matins, Mass, Compline, and other divine service; all nuns returning to the dorter, following compline, no later than half past seven. Under no circumstance were men to be admitted to the dorter, and never within the precincts unless for good cause and with license of the prioress. Exterior doors and passages were ordered to be kept shut and barred except when the nuns needed to pass, as to and from the choir and fratry.*

*Finding the physical plant in sad shape, the bishop gave Boyfield one year to make necessary repairs.*

---

[1] *sad* ] grave, sober-minded; *Misericorde* ] chamber in a monastery where there was a licensed relaxation of the Rule, especially with respect to meat and drink. Additional instructions follow, mandating a rotation of nuns permitted to dine in the Misericorde, with the "sad" overseer to be changed quarterly.

Moreover, forasmuch as the Lady Abbess and Convent of that house be all one religious body, united by the rules and profession of holy Saint Benedict, and it is not convenient any religious [sisters°] to be dissevered or separate, we will and enjoin that from henceforth none of the said Abbess's servants nor no other secular person or persons, whatsoever he or they be, go in any procession before the said Abbess between her and her said Convent under pain of excommunication, and that the Lady Abbess nor any of her successors hereafter be led by the arm or otherwise in any procession there as in time passed hath been used, under the same pain.

Also we will, command, and enjoin to Dame Katherine Wingate, the said Lady Abbess's Chaplain, under pain of contempt, that nightly she rise and be at Matins within the said morning with her other religious sisters there, and that from henceforth she do not sup nor breakfast in the buttery of the said Abbess, neither with the steward nor any other secular person or persons (under the same pain above expressed).

Beyond this, we ordain and by way of injunction command, under pain of disobedience, from henceforth that no lady ne any religious sister within the said monastery presume to wear their apparels upon their heads under such lay fashion as they have now of late done, with cornered crests, neither under such manner of height showing their foreheads more like lay people than religious...and that their gowns and kirtles be closed afore and not so deep-voided at the breast, and no more to use red stomachers but other sadder colors in the same.

• • •

*On 17 December 1530, the bishop's commissary, Robert Gostwick, returned to Elstow and was met with a majority verdict of all's well ("Omne bene"); with dissenting opinions from Anne Wake, prioress, and Cecilia Starkey, Boyfield's defeated rival. Discontents Barbara Gray and Alice Bowles, for one reason or another, were either not interviewed, or their comments not recorded. Gostwick returned to Lincoln with a report that favored the Boyfield faction.*

**The Rebellion**

On 27 June 1531, acting on evidence of continued strife between the abbess and the prioress, Bishop Longland returned to Elstow in person.

The attendant inquiry indicates that Lady Barbara Gray (Anne Wake's ally and friend), together with Alice Bowles, had smuggled out letters of complaint against Boyfield's administration, not showing their correspondence to the abbess as Boyfield expressly demanded.

When the bishop responding to those letters visited Elstow, it was the expectation of Wake, Gray, and Bowles that he would depose Boyfield and appoint a new abbess. Instead the bishop deposed Wake, appointing Helen Snow as the new prioress. Boyfield he censured for her failure to enforce the injunctions, and suspended her; but permitted her to continue her duties as the acting abbess, until further notice.

When this unexpected coup was announced in the chapter house at Wednesday matins, the convent was shell-shocked. Boyfield's chaplain, Katherine Wingate, made the announcement, then asked all of her sisters to rise.

Barbara Gray and Alice Bowles remained seated. The chaplain waited, perhaps casting a look at Boyfield, wondering what should be done.

Boyfield felt secure enough in her office not to endure insubordination: upon seeing her two elder sisters refuse to rise, she "went out of her stall to bid them so do" (with a gesture) – at which point the indignant Bowles blurted out her anger, in the midst of divine service, that "Ye have made her *prioress* that made *ye* abbess!" – breaking her silence, a violation of the Rule of Saint Benedict, which requires all nuns not at the high altar to keep silence during divine service except for the purpose of singing and chanting the liturgy.

At long last, Barbara Gray and Alice Bowles stood up – and exited their stalls, and walked out of the chapter house. Others followed.

In all, twelve sisters – more than half the convent, and most of those who happened to attend matins that night – left the house without waiting for a benediction. Boyfield went to the door and called out after them to return: of the ten who left, only Katherine Cornwallis returned.

Not all of those who left were of the same party, but all were of one mind that the bishop had no right to violate the sacred Rule of Saint Benedict. Rallying around their elderly prioress, they cast defiance in the bishop's teeth.

On word of this outrage, the bishop's Vicar General, Dr. John Rayne, returned post-haste to Elstow, to examine the disputants and to put out the fire. [1]

---

[1] For a similar dispute at Stratford caused by a bishop's interference with an election, see Wood, *Letters,* vol. I, nos. 30-31, pp. 68-70: the bishop "hath been with us yesterday and ... he sayeth the prioress shall continue and be prioress still, in spite of our teeth and of their teeths that say nay to it ... he commanded her to assault us and to punish us, that other may beware by us."

**Visitation of the Vicar General of Lincoln to Elstow Abbey, 1 July 1531°** (in Latin and English; English trans. DWF in italics)

*Lady* BARBARA GRAY, *asked* if she did ask license of my Lady Abbess to write letters to her friends: She says that she did ask license to write to her friends; and my lady Abbess said, 'If ye show me what ye write, I am content.' And she said again, 'I have done my devoir to ask license – and if ye will needs see it, I will write no letters.' [*Asked if she left the chapter house*: She admits it.] That if it were to do again, she would so do, and those, [because] my lord [bishop] did command my lady Snow to be prioress. She says that she cannot find in her heart to obey her as prioress; and that she will rather go out of the house (by my lord [bishop]'s license) ere she will obey her. She says there was none did counsel her to go forth of the chapter house, and that she will *never* obey her as prioress, for her heart cannot serve her; but said she will show no cause at this time wherefore she cannot love her, saying that "The prioress makes every fault a deadly sin, and [jud]ges every one of them ill except herself, and [if she] do take an opinion, she will keep it [whether] it be right or wrong."

*Lady* ALICE BOWLES, *asked* if she did ask license of the Abbess to write, she says she did ask license to write and my lady Abbess said, "My lord [bishop] hath given us so-strait commandment that 'None should write without ye show it to me, what ye do write.' And she says she made answer again to th'abbess, "It hath not been so in times past, and I have done my duty. I will not write now at this time." *Asked if she left the chapter house, she admits she departed*; but she says that nobody did move her to go forth. She says that she "must needs now obey the prioress, at my lord's commandment"; also saying that "my lady Snow is not meet for that office" (but she would show no cause wherefore).

*Lady* CECILIA STARKE *asked if she left the chapter house,* says that she went forth of the chapter house; but she says she gave no occasion to any of her susters to go forth. And says she knew not how many of her susters went forth whilst she come into the dorter; [also] saying that she cannot find in her heart nor will not accept and take my lady Snow as prioress. She stated that she "cannot find in her heart nor will not accept and take my lady Snow as prioress."

*Lady* MATILDA SHELTON, *subprioress, asked why she left the chapter on Wednesday last past against the mandate of the abbess, says that she left for a necessary cause and did not know of the departure of the other nuns, or their reason, until she saw them in the dormitory.*

*Lady* MARGARET NICHOLSON, *asked if she left the chapter house, admitteth that she did so,* because she would not consent that my lady Snow should be prioress; *and says* that there was none that did counsel her to leave. She says that "My lady abbess did command them to tarry, that not withstanding they went forth, *lady* Cecilia Starkey, *lady* Anne Preston, *lady* Alice Blackwell, *lady* Margery Preston, *lady* Alicia Bowles, *lady* Alicia Foster, and *lady* Elizabeth Sincler."

MARGERY PRESTON, *asked if she left the chapter house, says that she left* with other of her sisters, and she says that she went forth of the chapter house because the prioress was put forth of her office, and for no malice that she bears to my lady Snow; and she says that she is well content to obey my lady Snow as prioress. And she desires my lord [bishop] to be good lord to the old prioress because of her age.

*Lady* ALICE FOSTER, *asked if she left the chapter house, admits that she left*; and says that they were commanded by the abbess to tarry still. But she and other went forth because the old prioress was put down wrongfully and my lady Snow put in against their wills; [also] saying that she will never agree to her as long as she lives. She says the sub-prioress went forth of the chapter-house first, and then she and other followed.

*Lady* ANNA ERDES *says* that "My lord [the bishop of Lincoln] did not command us to take my Lady Snow as prioress, but he said: 'If ye will not take her as prioress, I will make her prioress myself.'" She says she was one of them that went forth of the chapter house because my lady Snow is not able to be prioress; saying that they "were wont to have the prioress chosen by the abbess and the convent, not by my lord [the bishop], after Saint Bene't's rule"; and that she will take my lady Snow as prioress "as other will do, and no otherways."

*Lady* ANNA PRESTON *says* that she will never agree to my lady Snow to be prioress, and that she and other went out of the chapter house because she would not agree nor consent to have her to be prioress. And she will never take her as prioress as long as the old prioress lives.

*Lady* ELIZABETH SINCLER *says that she left the chapter house* because my lady Snow was made prioress against their will, and th'old unlawfully prioress put out; and says she will never take my lady Snow as prioress so long as the other lives; saying that she ill take th'old prioress as prioress as long as she lives and no other, And she says "If my lord [bishop] command us to take my lady Snow to be prioress," she had "liefer go forth of the house to some other place," and will not tarry there [at Elstow].

*Lady* ALICE BLACKWELL *says* that she was one of them that went forth of the chapter house, because the old prioress was put out of her office; for she says after their custom and their Rule of Saint Benne't, the prioress should have been elect by the abbess and the convent and not by my lord.

*Lady* KATHERINE CORNWALLIS *says* that she was going forth of the chapter-house with other of her susters and then, when she heard my lady abbess command them to tarry, she did tarry behind, but she says that she thinks that none of the other susters that went forth did hear her, but only she; and she is "sorry that th'old prioress is put out of her office." She says that "my lady abbess did tarry still, and *Lady* Alice Boyfield, *Lady* Snow, *Lady* Katherina Wingate, *Lady* Dorothy Commaforth, *Lady* Elizabeth Repton, and *Lady* Elizabeth Stanismore."

• • •

After these interviews, the Vicar General that same afternoon called the nuns together; at which time he commanded all and severally to obey both the abbess and the new prioress.

Barbara Gray and Alice Bowles were assigned a penance for their disobedience: on pain of greater excommunication, and until such time as the lord bishop relaxed their punishment: "First, that they should both keep silence, as silence ought to be kept by the religion." Also, "he commaunded them both that n'other of them should come within the house called the Misericorde" (where meat was served), "and that they should have their refections in the frater and in no other place." Also, "that n'other of them should write any letters to [any] person or persons, nor cause to be written, whiles they [wait] my lord's further pleasure." And henceforth, both in processionals and in other places, sisters Gray and Bowles were to take "the lowest places of all their susters."

*Elstow was surrendered to the Crown on 26 August 1539, at which time the house had an annual income of nearly £300. A pension of £50 was awarded to the abbess, Elizabeth Boyfield; £4 to the prioress, Helen Snow; 66 shillings to quondam prioress, Anne Wake; and smaller sums to the twenty-three nuns then resident. On being turned out of the abbey, some of the sisters went to live in nearby Bedford: the burial of three of them is recorded in the parish register of the Church of Saint Mary. The buildings and much of the land in 1553 was granted to Sir Humphrey Radcliff.*

**Form of Confession**°

*The form of confession reproduced here in modern spelling is believed to have been in use at Grace Dieu at the time of the priory's dissolution, but it may have been known, in one form or another, for more than two centuries, and at many convents:*

O good Lord, that knowest all thing,
Whom I offend fro' day to day,
Thy sweet mercy yet on me spring,
And my defauts, to know alway.
To thy mercy be I meek aye
And be in full hope to have it.
With all my mend thus I thee pray:
To thine own love, make thou me knit.

In all these that I have done, in thought, word, and deed, sleeping and waking, sitting or standing, walking or talking, in church or out of church, holy day or workday, mis-spending my time and mis-spending my body and soul, nought setting my love and my affection upon God almighty; ne keeping His commaundments so lovely and so truly as I should; but have been unkind to my Lord in sinning of the seven deadly sins, in mis-spending of my five wits, nought fulfilling the seven works of mercy, neither bodily ne ghostly with such pity and compassion of mine even-Christen as I should do; ne had so full belief ne such reverence in the seven sacraments, with so full love in working as I should; ne I have took° heed so heartily to the observaunces of religion as I should: to keep sight, silence, ne mine inclines so devoutly ne so ghostly, as I should, for God's love; but yif I did, I did more for praising, vain-glory, or 'ypocrisy, so that all thing that I have spoke or done for the most partie I have done for the world, feigning holiness full often in speech and in countenaunce, showing an outward as I were true, being full of false inward unnumbered wicked thoughts words, and deeds, rather to sin than virtue. I cry God mercy will all mine heart, and our Lady Saint Marie, Saint Augustine, and all the saints in Heaven, and thee, my ghostly Fader, *mea culpa,* now and ever. [1]

Jesu, blessèd be thy name.
Amen.

[1] *sight, inclines* ] observance, with bows of genuflection.

# Julian of Norwich (1342-1417?)

*Botte for I am a womann, schulde I therfore leve*
*that I schulde nought tell yowe the goodenes of god...?*
— from the short text (ca. 1373), chap. 6

JULIAN OF NORWICH, anchoress, entered a small stone cell sometime in her thirties and remained there until she died at age 75. An "anchorite" (m.) or "anchoress" (f.) is a person in religious orders who chooses to live as a recluse – typically, in the medieval period, in a tiny cell or "anchorhold," in near-total seclusion. Mass was observed and received through an opening in the sanctuary wall called a "hagioscope" or "squint." Food was served to the inmate, and the chamberpot passed in and out, through a larger opening in the outside side wall. It was through this outer opening that laymen could commune with the incarcerated mystic. Anchorites ate simple food, chiefly bread and beer, and slept on rushes, curled in a fetal position because there was no room to stretch out. It was not an easy life; some, no doubt, went mad; but the anchorite having once sworn to live as a recluse suffered excommunication if those vows were broken.

Julian is somewhat extraordinary in that she has provided a first-person narrative of her experience. As a young woman, she prayed that God would send her a "sekeness" – a disease that would put her in mind of Christ's suffering. When the illness came in May 1373, it nearly killed her. But Julian during her suffering also experienced a series of blissful visions of divine love. Illiterate, she dictated her experience to a scribe. The "short text," written soon after her recovery, is usually referenced as the Julian's *Book of Showings*. The "long text," of *Revelations,* is a later elaboration (wherein she states that "twenty year save three months" passed before she fully understood the meaning of her original visions – 1393 is therefore the earliest date for the long text). Preserved by nuns of Paris and Cambrai in three seventeenth-century manuscripts, the long text was first printed by Serenus Cressy in 1670.

The anchoress reveals no details of her early life but implies that she was in her own home at the time of her revelations. Before taking the oath to be a recluse, she would have been required to take holy orders and to live as a nun in good standing for some years. A plausible reconstruction: Julian remained a secular person until age 30; at which time she had her illness and attendant revelations. As a maid or widow wishing to devote her future life to God, she entered a convent – possibly at the nearby Benedictine priory of Carrow, whose sisterhood held the advowson of St Julian's Church. There, a cleric recorded her revelations. After some years, having proved by her holy life to be a suitable candidate for an anchorage, Julian would have had to apply to the bishop of Lincoln to be released from her vows to the sisterhood in order to become a recluse. (Approval was dependent on the bishop's conviction that the candidate had a spiritual calling from God and the physical and mental fortitude to endure solitary confinement.)

Anchorites, in renouncing the self, typically adopted the name of a saint – anchoresses often taking the name of a male saint. Whatever her original birth name may have been, the inspiration for our author's adopted identity seems to have come from the Church at Conisford in Norwich, whose patron saint was Julian the Hospitaller, also known as Julian the poor; where she spent most of her adult life in a 3-foot by 4-foot cell.

A bequest in 1394 to "Julian anchorite" indicates that she was probably, by that time, revered. Small bequests were recorded for Julian in 1404, 1415, and 1416, two of which included a gift for her maids Sarah and Alice, who assisted Julian with her food and sanitary needs. The scribe in the *Book of Showings* speaks of Julian as a "devout woman," that "is recluse at Norwich and yet is on-live, anno domini 1414." That is the same year in which she was visited by Margery Kempe of Bishop's Lynn, who wished to hear about Julian's "many wonderful revelations ... for the anch'ress was expert in swech things, and good counsel could yeven." Julian's death probably occurred in 1417, when she was 75 years old. A contemporary of Chaucer and Christine de Pizan, Julian of Norwich exerted her own quiet influence. Withdrawing from the world in turbulent times – war with France, the Black Death, the Peasants' Revolt, the Church's massacre of Jews, Henry Bolingbroke's usurpation, Wycliffe's heresy – Julian with her faith in a maternal God remained optimistic. Her most endearing revelation: *"All shall be well, and all shall be well. And all manner of thing shall be well."*

Destroyed by Nazi bombs during World War II, St. Julian's Church, extensively restored, reopened in 1953 as a shrine church for Julian the anchoress. Her anchorhold has been rebuilt on its medieval foundation. The Friends of Julian, in a hall at the street corner, operate a lending library and a souvenir shop.

DWF

## From *Revelations to One Who Could Not Read a Letter*

### Of the time of these Revelations, and how she asked three petitions

[2.] These Revelations were shewed to a simple creature (that could no letter) the year of our Lord 1373, the eighth° day of May – which creature desired, afore, *three*° gifts of God: the *first* was mind of his passion; the *second* was bodily sekeness in youth, at thirty years of age; the *third* was to have (of God's gift) three wounds.[1]

As in the *first*, methought I had some feeling in the passion of Christ – but yet I desired more, by the grace of God. Methought I would have been that time with Mary Magdalene, and with other that were Christ's lovers; and therefore I desired a bodily sight wherein I might have more knowledge of the bodily pains of our saviour and of the compassion of° our Lady and of all his true lovers that seen, that time, his pains; for I would be one of them and suffer with him. Other sight nor shewing of God desired I never none, till the soul was departed fro' the body.[2]

The cause of this petition was that, after the shewing, I should have the more true mind in the passion of Christ.

The *second* came to my mind with contrition, freely desiring that sekeness were° so hard as to death, that I might in that sekeness underfongen all my rites of holy Church, myself weening that I should die, and that all creatures might suppose the same that seen me. For I would have no manner comfort of eardtly life. In this sekeness I desired to have all manner pains, bodily and ghostly, that I should have if I should die, with all the dreads and tempests° of the fiends, except the outpassing of the soul. And this I meant for I would be purged (by the mercy of God), and after liven more to the worship of God because of that sekeness – and that, for the more speed in my death (for I desired to be soon with my God).[3]

These two desires, of the passion and the sekeness, I desired with a condition, saying thus:° "Lord, thou wotteth what I would, if it be thy will that I have it; and if it be not thy will, good Lord, be not displeased, for I will nought but as thou wilt."[4]

For the *third*, by the grace of God and teaching of holy Church I conceived a mighty desire to receive three wounds in my life, that is to say, the wound of very *contrition*, the wound of kind *compassion*, and the wound of willful *longing to God*. And all this last petition I asked without any condition.[5]

These two desires foresaid passèd fro' my mind, and the third dwelled with me continually.

### Of the sekeness obtained of God by petition

[3.] And when I was thirty years old and half, God sent me a bodily sekeness, in which I lay three days and three nights; and on the fourth night I took all my rites of holy Church, and weened not a-livèd till day. And after this I languorèd forth two days and two nights, and on the third night I weened oftentimes to have passèd; and so weened they that were with me. And in youngeth yet, I thought't° great sweem° to die – but for nothing that° was in earth that me likèd to liven for, ne for no pain that I was afeared of (for I trusted in God of his mercy); but it was to have lived, that I might have loved God better and longer time, [so] that I might have the more knowing and loving of God in bliss of Heaven. For methought all the time that I had lived here – so little and so short in reward of that endless bliss – I thought't° nothing. Wherefore I thought: "Good Lord, may my living-no-longer be to thy worship!" And I understood by my reason and by my feeling of my pains that I should die; and I assented fully, with all the will of my heart to be at God's° will.[6]

Thus I 'durèd till day – and by then my body was dead from the middès downwards, as to my feeling. Then was I stirred to be set upright (un-

---

[1] *that ... letter* ] that could neither read nor write; *mind of his passion* ] mindfulness of his suffering; *sekeness* ] sickness; *wounds*] contrition, compassion, and longing (not physical wounds).

[2] As in ] As for; *passion* ] suffering; *Methought ... time* ] I wished that I could have been living at that time; *seen* ] had seen; *the soul* ] i.e., my soul *fro* ] from.

[3] *second* ] i.e., the second petition; *underfongen* ] 1. receive; 2. comprehend; *weening* ] supposing; *freely desiring ... me* ] I freely wished for a deathly illness, so severe that I might be given Last Rites, and so that it might appear – to me and to all who saw me – that I would surely die; *would have no manner* ] wished to have no manner of; *eardtly* ] earthly; *all manner ... ghostly* ] every manner of suffering, both fleshly and spiritual; *fiends* ] devils; *except ... soul* ] all except death itself; *this ... purged* ] this I desired in order to be cleansed.

[4] *thou wotteth what I would* ] you know what I desire.

[5] *very contrition* ] true repentance; *kind* ] natural.

[6] *weened*] thought; *languored forth* ] lingered on; *in youngeth yet* ] being still young; *sweem* ] sorrow; *but for nothing* ] but not on account of anything; *reward* ] regard.

der-leanend with help) for to have more freedom of my heart to be at God's will, and thinking on God, while my life would last. [1]

My curate was sent for to be at my ending; and by then he came, I had set my eyen, and might not speak. He set the cross before my face and said, "I have brought thee the image of thy maker and saviour. Look thereupon and comfort thee therewith." [2]

Methought I was well, for my eyen were set uprightward into Heaven, where I trusted to come by the mercy of God; but nevertheless I assented to set my eyen in the face of the crucifix if I might; and so I did (for methought I might longer duren to look even-forth than right up). [3]

After this my sight began to failen, and it was all dark about me in the chamber, as it had be' night – save in the image of the cross, wherein I beheld a common light, and I wist not how. All that was beside the cross was ugly to me, as if had be' mickle occupied with the fiends. [4]

After this, the other partie of my body began to dyen (so far forth that unnethès I had any feeling), with shortness of ond;° and then I weened soothly to have passèd. [5]

And in this, suddenly all my pain was taken fro' me! – and I was as hale (and namely in the other partie of my body) as ever I was aforen. I marvelèd at this sudden change, for methought it was a privy working of God, and not of kind. And yet by the feeling of this ease I trusted never the more to liven; ne the feeling of this ease was no full ease to me, for methought I had liefer° ha' be' deliverèd of this world. [6]

Then came suddenly to my mind that I should desire the second wound of our Lord's gracious gift: that my body might be fulfilled with mind and feeling of his blissèd passion. For I would that his pains were my pains, with compassion and afterward longing to God. But in this I desired never bodily sight nor shewing of God, but compassion as a kind soul might have with our Lord Jesus (that for love would be'n a deadly man!); and therefore I desired to suffer with him. [7]

**Here beginneth the First Revelation of the precious crowning of Christ . . .**

[4.] In this, suddenly I saw the red blood tricklen down fro' under the garland, hot and freshly and right plenteous – as it were in the time of his passion that the garland of thornès was pressèd on his blissèd head [that was] right so both God and man, the same that suffered thus for me. I conceived truly and mightily that it was himself shewed it me, without any mean. [8]

And in the same shewing suddenly the Trinity fulfilled the heart most of joy. And so (I understond) it shall be in Heaven without end to all that shall come there. For the Trinity is God, God is the Trinity. The Trinity is our maker and keeper. The Trinity is our everlasting lover, everlasting joy and bliss, by our Lord Jesus Christ. And this was shewed in the First, and in all; for where Jesus appeareth, the blissèd Trinity is understond, as to my sight. And I said, "Benedicite Domine!" This I said for reverence in my meaning, with a mighty voice; and full greatly was astonièd, for wonder and marvel that I had, that he (that is so reverend and dreadful!) will be so homely° with a sinful creature living in wretched flesh.° [9]

This I took for the time of my temptation – for methought (by the sufferance of God) I should be tempted of fiends ere I died. With this sight of the blissèd passion, with the godhead that I saw in mine understonding, I knew well that it was strength enow to me, yea, and to all creaturers living, again' all the fiends of Hell and ghostly temptation. [10]

In this he brought our blissèd lady to my understonding. I saw her ghostly, in bodily likeness, a simple maid and a meek, young of age and little waxen above a child, in the stature that she was

---

[1] *'dured* ] endured; *middes* ] middle; *under-leanend* ] underpropped.

[2] *then* ] when; the time that; *set my eyen* ] set my eyes on Heaven; *might* ] could.

[3] *duren to look* ] 1. bear to look; 2. endure by looking; *even-forth* ] straight ahead.

[4] *as it had be' night* ] as if it were night; *wist* ] knew; *mickle . . . fiends* ] greatly filled with devils.

[5] *partie* ] part; *dyen* ] die; *unnethes* ] scarcely; *ond* ] wind, breath; *soothly* ] truly, actually.

[6] *hale* ] healthy, whole; *namely* ] especially; *kind* ] i.e., nature; *yet ... this ease* ] yet, by the time I felt this respite; *liefer ha'be'delivered of* ] rather have been delivered from.

[7] *blissèd* ] blessed; *deadly* ] mortal.

[8] *garland* ] Christ's crown of thorns; *mean* ] intermediary.

[9] *the heart* ] i.e., my heart; *the First* ] i.e., the first "shewing" or revelation; *understond* ] understood; *as to my sight* ] as I see it; *Benedicite Domine* ] Bless ye the Lord; *homely* ] familiar.

[10] *enow* ] enough; *creaturers* ] creatures; *again'* ] against; *ghostly* ] spiritual.

when she conceived with child. Also God shewèd in partie the wisdom and the truth of her soul, wherein I understood the reverend beholding that she beheld her God and maker, marveling with great reverence that he would be born of her that was a simple creature of his making. And this wisdom and truth – knowing the greatness of her° maker and the littlehood of herself that is made – causèd her say full meekly to Gabriel, "Lo me, God's handmaid!" In this sight I understood soothly that she is mair than all that God made beneath her in worthiness and grace; for aboven her is nothing that is made but the blissèd manhood° of Christ, as to my sight. [1]

**How God is to us everything that is good, tenderly wrappend us...** [2]

[5.] In this same time our Lord shewed to me a ghostly sight of his homely loving: I saw that he is to us everything that is good and comfortable for us. He is our clothing, that for love wrappeth us, halseth° us, and all-becloseth° us for tender love, that he may never leave us; being to us all thing that is good, as to mine understonding. [3]

Also in this he shewed a little thing, the quantity of an hazel-nut, in the palm of my hand; and it was as round as a ball. I lookèd thereupon with eye of my understonding, and thought, "What may this be?" And it was generally answered thus, "It is all that is made!" I marvelèd how it might lasten, for methought it might suddenly have fallen to nought, for little. And I was answered in my understonding: "It lasteth, and ever shall, for God loveth it." And so all thing hath the being – by the love of God. [4]

In this little thing I saw three properties. The first is that God made it. The second is that God loveth it. The third, that God keepeth it. But what is to me soothly the maker, the keeper, and the lover, I cannot tell – for till I am substantially onèd to him, I may never have full rest ne very bliss; that is to say, till° I be so fastenèd to him, that there is right nought that is made betwix my God and me.... [5]

**The Tenth revelation is that our Lord Jesus sheweth in love his blissèd heart, cloven in two, enjoyend** [6]

[24.] Then with a glad cheer our Lord looked into his side and beheld, enjoyend; and with his sweet looking he led forth the understonding of his creature, by the same wound, into his side within. And then he shewèd a fair delectable place, and large enow for all mankind that shall be save to resten in peace and in love. And therewith he brought to mind his dear-worthy blood and precious water, which he let pour all out for love. And with the sweet beholding he shewèd his blissful heart even cloven on two. And with this sweet enjoying he shewèd unto mine understonding, in partie, the blissèd godhead, stirring then the pure soul for to understond, as it may be said, that is to mean, the endless love that was without beginning, and is, and shall be ever.

And with this our good Lord said full blissfully, "Lo, how that I lovèd thee!" – as if he had said, "My darling, behold and see thy Lord, thy God, that is thy maker and thine endless joy. See what liking and bliss I have in thy salvation; and for my love, enjoy now with me." And also, for more understonding, this blissèd word was said: "Lo, how I lovèd thee! Behold and see that I lovèd thee so mickle ere I died for thee, that I *would* die for thee; and now I *ha'* died for thee, and suff'red willfully, that I may. And now is all my bitter pain and all my hard travail turnèd to endless joy and bliss, to me and to thee. How should it now be that thou should anything pray me that liketh me, but if I should full gladly grant it thee? For my liking is thy holiness and thine endless joy and bliss with me." [7]

This is the understonding, simply as I can say, of this blissèd word, "Lo, how I lovèd thee!" This shewèd our good Lord for to make us glad and merry.

**[God the Mother]**

[58.] [I]n our making, God (all-mighty) is our kindly Fader; and God (all-wisdom) is our kindly Moder; with the love and the goodness of the holy Ghost – which is all one God, one Lord. And in

---

[1] *little waxen above a child* ] grown hardly much taller than a child; *beholding that* ] beholding with which; *mair* ] more; *manhood* ] humanity.

[2] *wrappend* ] enwrapping.

[3] *halseth* ] holds, embraces.

[4] *for little* ] for its being so little; *the being* ] its being.

[5] *oned* ] (o-ned) united, made one with; *right...betwix* ] nothing that comes between.

[6] *cloven in two, enjoyend* ] cut in two, (with) rejoicing.

[7] *save* ] 1. saved; or 2. safe *The latter reading is not the obvious one, because it suggests a belief in universal salvation, which was a damnable heresy; but Julian elsewhere wavers on the points of eternal damnation, hell, and purgatory (e.g., chaps. 32-33)*; *mickle*] greatly; *that I may* ] in order to die for you; *liketh* ] pleaseth.

the knitting and in the oning he is our very true spouse, and we his lovèd wife and his fair maiden; with which wife he is never displeasèd. For he sayeth, "I love thee, and thou lovest me, and our love shall never be departed on two."° [1]

I beheld the working of all the blissèd Trinity, in which beholding I saw and understood these three properties: the property of the faderhead, the property of the moderhead, and the property of the lordhead, in one God. In our Fader almighty we have our keeping and our bliss as anempts our kindly° substance, which is to us by our making, without beginning. And in the Second Person in wit and wisdom we have our keeping as anempts our sensuality; our restoring and our saving; for he is our moder, brother, and savior. And in our good Lord, the holy Ghost, we have our rewarding and our yielding° (for our living and our travail), and endlessly° overpassing all that we desiren, in his marvelous courtesy, of his high plentivous grace.... [2]

[59.] And all this bliss we have by mercy and grace – which manner of bliss we might never have° had, ne knowen, but if that properties of goodness (which is God) had been contraried whereby we have this bliss. For wickedness hath been suff'red to risen contrary to the goodness, and the goodness of mercy and grace contraried again' the wickedness, and turnèd all to goodness and to worship, to all these that shall be savèd. For it is the property in God which doth good again' evil. Thus Jesus Christ, that doth good again' evil, is our very Moder. We have our being of him, where the ground of moderhead beginneth, with all the sweet keeping of love that endlessly followeth. As verily as God is our Fader, as verily, God is our Moder; and that shewèd he in All ...[3]

[60.] ... Our kind Moder, our gracious Moder, for he would all wholly become our Moder in all-thing: he took the ground of his work full low and full mildly in the maiden's womb. And that he shewèd in the First [Shewing], where he brought that meek maid aforn the eye of mine understonding in the simple stature as she was when she conceivèd; that is to say, our high God is sovereign wisdom of all. In this low place he raisèd him and dight him full ready in our poor flesh, himself to doen the service and the office of moderhead in all-thing. [4]

The moder's service is nearest, readiest, and seckirest, for it is most of truth.° This office ne might, ne couth, ne never none doen to the full, but° he alone. We witten that all our moders bear° us to pain and to dying; and what is that but our very Moder, Jesus – he alone° beareth us to joy and to endless living (blissèd mote he be!). Thus he sustaineth us within himself, in love – and travailed into the full time that he would suffer the sharpest throes and the grievousest pains that ever were or ever shall be, and died at the last. And when he had [so] done, and so borne us to bliss, yet might not all this maken asseth to his marvelous love; and that he shewèd° in these high overpassing words of love: "If I might suffer more, I would suffer more." [5]

He might ne more dyen, but he would not stinten of working. Wherefore then, him behoveth to feeden us, for the dearworthy love of moderhead hath made him debtor to us. The moder may given her child sucken her milk, but our precious Moder, Jesus, he may feeden us with himself – and doth [so], full courte'sly and full tenderly, with the blissèd sacrament that is precious food of very life; and with all the sweet sacraments he sustaineth us full mercifully and graciously; and so meant he in this blissèd word where that he said: "I it am, that holy Church preacheth thee and teacheth thee"; that is to say, "All the health and life of sacraments, all the virtue and grace of my Word, all the goodness that is ordainèd in holy Church for thee, I it am." [6]

The moder may layen the child tenderly to her breast, but our tender Moder, Jesus, he may homely leaden us *into* his blissèd breast, by his sweet open side, and shewen therein partie of the godhead and the joys of Heaven, with ghostly seckirness of endless bliss. And that, shewèd he in the Tenth° [Shewing], giving the same understonding in this sweet word where he sayeth, "Lo! how I love thee," beholdend into his side, enjoyend. [7]

---

[1] *one* ] (*pronounced* oon); *oning* ] ( =one-ing; *pron.* o-ning) uniting, atoning; *departed on two* ] separated.

[2] *blissèd* ] blessèd; *anempts* ] anent; regards; *Second Person* ] Jesus as the Son of God; *wit* ] understanding; *plentivous* ] plentiful.

[3] *might never ... but if that properties* ] might never have had, nor known, were it not that the properties.

[4] *dight him* ] arrayed himself; *doen* ] do.

[5] *seckirest* ] securest, most sure; *ne might ... doen* ] may no one—nor ever could anyone—ever do; *We witten* ] We understand; *mote* ] may; *asseth* ] satisfaction; *yet might not all this maken asseth* ] yet not even this could satisfy.

[6] *stinten of* ] leave off; *him behoveth* ] it behoves him.

[7] *open side* ] because wounded with a spear on the cross; *ghostly seckirness* ] spiritual assurance; *beholdend ... enjoyend* ] looking upon his wound with rejoicing.

This fair lovely word *moder*, it is so sweet and so kind of the self that it may ne verily be said of none but of him (and to her that is very moder of him and of all). To the property of moderhead 'longeth kind love, wisdom, and knowing – and it is good. For though it be so, that our bodily forthbringing be but little, low, and simple in regard of our ghostly forthbringing, yet it is he that doth it in the creatures by whom that it is done. The kind, lovend moder that wote and knoweth the need of her child, she keepeth it full tenderly (as the kind and condition of moderhead will). And as it waxeth in age, she changeth her working, but not her love. And when it is waxen of more age, she suff'reth that it be bristinèd in breaking down of vices, to maken the child receiven virtues and graces. [1]

This working, with all that be fair and good, our Lord doth it in 'hem by whom it is done. Thus he is our Moder in kind by the working of grace in the lower part, for love of the higher part. And he willeth° that we know it, for he will have all our love fastenèd to him. And in this I saw that all our debt that we owen, by God's bidding, be faderhead and moderhead, for God's faderhead and moderhead is fulfillèd in true loving of God; which blissèd love Christ worketh in us. And this was shewèd in All, and namely in the high plentivous words where he sayeth: "I it am that thou lovest." [2]

**The good Lord shewèd that this book should be otherwise performèd than at the first writing . . .**

[86.] This book is begun by God's gift and his grace, but it is not yet performèd, as to my sight.

For charity pray we all togeder° (with God's working), thankend, trustend, enjoyend. For thus will our good Lord be prayed, as by the understonding that I took in all his own meaning and in the sweet words where he sayeth full merrily, "I am ground of thy beseeking." For truly I saw and understood in our Lord's meaning that he shewèd it for he will have it knowen more than it is; in which knowing, he will give us grace to loven him and cleaven to him. For he beholdeth his heavenly treasure with so great love on earth that he will give us more light and solace in Heavenly joy, in drawing of our hearts, for sorrow and murkness which we aren in. [3]

And fro' that time that it was shewèd, I desired oftentimes to witten what was our Lord's meaning. And fifteen year after, and more, I was answerèd in ghostly understonding, sayend thus: "Wouldst thou witten thy Lord's meaning in this thing? Wit it well: *Love* was his meaning. Who shewèd it thee? Love. What shewèd he thee? Love. Wherefore shewèd it he? For Love. Hold thee therein and thou shalt witten and knowen more in the same. But thou shalt never knowen ne witten therein other thing, without end." Thus was I learnèd° that Love was our Lord's meaning. [4]

And I saw full seckirly in this and in all, that ere God made us he lovèd us; which love was never slackèd, ne° never shall. And in this love he hath done all his work; and in this love he hath made all things profitable to us; and in this love our life is everlastend. In our making we had beginning; but the love wherein he made us was in him from without beginning; in which love we have our beginning. And all this shall be seen in God, without end – which Jesus mote grant us! Amen. [5]

Lady Wearing a Gauze Headdress
by Rogier van der Weyden (c. 1435)
Staatlichen Museum (Berlin)

---

[1] *of the self* ] in itself; *so* ] true; *in regard of* ] in comparison to; *lovend* ] loving; *wote* ] witteth; understands; *waxeth* ] grows; *bristined* ] burst open.

[2] *'hem* ] them; *he will have* ] he wishes to have; *in All* ] i.e., in all twelve of my revelations.

[3] *thankend ... enjoyend* ] thanking, trusting, rejoicing; *beseeking* ] beseeching; *murkness* ] murkiness, darkness; *aren* ] be, are.

[4] *learned* ] taught.

[5] *seckirly* ] certainly; *which ... us* ] which blessing may Jesus grant us.

# Margery (Brunham) Kempe (1373 – c.1439)

*A Ser seyd þe clerkys her wot we wel þ$^{t}$ sche hath*
*a deuyl w$^{t}$inne hir for sche spekyth of þ$^{e}$ gospel.*
—from *The Boke of Margerie Kempe*, fol. 60r.

MARGERY KEMPE was the daughter and heir of John Brunham (d. 1413) of Bishop's Lynn, Norfolk, a prosperous merchant who was five times mayor and six times MP. In what must have been a marriage either of true-love or convenience, Margery at age twenty married penniless John Kempe, Jr., an apprentice leather-worker who in 1393 was admitted to the freedom of the Skinners Company.

Following her first pregnancy, Margery suffered severe depression, aggravated by a priest who frightened her with damnation when she mentiond but declined to explain a persistent and secret sin, possibly masturbation, that she had never disclosed in confession. (The Lollards of Norwich taught that priestly confession was unnecessary to receive God's forgiveness.) Given to bouts of weeping and visions of devils, unable care for her newborn, Margery received the usual diagnosis for mental illness – demon possession – and the usual treatment: for six of the nine months she was ill, Margery was kept in chains, in a storeroom; which did not help. In her confinement, Margery cut and scratched herself, and bit her hand so hard that she carried the stigmatum for the rest of her life. She recovered at last when Jesus in the likeness of a beauteous man came and sat on her cot, speaking words of comfort; whereupon Margery returned to her housekeeping duties – and began looking for opportunities to make her mark on the world.

Women married to journeymen typically worked as assistants in their husband's shop, but Margery had higher ambitions than to dress animal skins for a living. Married to a man who loved her but could not afford the wardrobe and state to which she had been accustomed as a merchant's daughter, Margery set out to invest her dowry in a profitable business. In the municipal records of Bishop's Lynn ("King's Lynn," since Henry VIII), John Kempe in 1403-5 is mentioned as a brewer: Margery's autobiography indicates that this was actually her own undertaking, with her own capital, against her husband's advice – one of several attempts by the plucky Mrs. Kempe to generate income, thereby to support her delight in fashionable dress. When the business failed, Margery internalized the criticism of her neighbors, but not enough to prevent her from trying again, this time by investing in a millworks. When that business also failed, Margery's thoughts turned toward distinctive religious experience.

Mother of Sorrows, c. 1480, Master of the Stötteritz Altar
*Cummer Museum of Art and Gardens* (*Jacksonville*)

Several times in the course of her marriage, the Lord urged Margery to abstain from "communing fleshly" with her husband – an activity that Margery reports they both enjoyed – in order to exercise spiritual discipline. After sixteen years of marriage, having given birth fourteen times, Margery was strong in favor of this experiment; John was not.

In her autobiography, Margery makes almost no mention of her children, her thoughts being fixed now on penance for her sins. She advised John that God had again called her to sexual abstinence, this time with a caveat: for John to engage in conjugal relations with her against her will, could cause him to suffer sudden death. This was a tough sell, but Margery in 1412 persuaded John, out of fear, not to "meddle" with her in bed for a new record of eight weeks; at which time he finally demanded better terms. After consultation with the Lord, Margery accepted John's offer: she would eat meat with him on Fridays, as the Lollards did, despite the Church's insistence on fish; and she would pay his debts before leaving on a pilgrimage to the Holy Land. She would swear to sexual abstinence, and he would not compromise her vow.

In 1413 Margery visited Julian of Norwich to seek reassurance concerning her conversations with God about these matters. She then sought permission from Philip Repyngdon, bishop of Lincoln, to become a vowess (common enough), and to dress all in white, like a vestal virgin, thereby to signify her sexual purity (unusual, for a married woman). Repyngdon sent her to Thomas Arundel, archbishop of Canterbury, who received her kindly and may have given his blessing. Shortly afterward, Margery left Yarmouth on a pilgrimage to the Holy Land, dressed in white. She traveled via Constance and Venice, living principally on alms. In Jerusalem, she visited the holy sites identified by Crusaders. It was at the Holy Sepulchre that Margery received the gift of uncontrollable weeping which was to become the hallmark of her spiritual ministry. On her return trip, passing through Venice, Assisi, and Rome, Margery visited churches where she kneeled before the crucifix, and bellowed her sorrow, sometimes for hours on end; which caused much hostility. But it was a successful trip. In Rome, while at the Venerable English College, Margery met a former servant of the visionary St. Bridget of Sweden; and thereafter she had many marvelous visions, including one in which she beheld herself married to the triune Godhead.

Returning to England in the summer of 1415, Margery delighted in pilgrimages to shrines throughout the counties, creating a scene wherever she went with her spiritual ministry of loud weeping. Church authorities were puzzled by Margery's theology. Unlike the Lollards, she adored religious images. But her eccentricities were so far outside conventional expressions of religious devotion that it was unclear to diocesan authorities whether she was ruled by God or Satan. Confronted with a married woman who had left home and her husband's rule in order to dress like a virgin and gallivant about the countryside, the clergy were deeply suspicious. Margery was questioned many times by inquisitors, on threat of burning at the stake as a heretic; but she was never found guilty of Lollardy.

In 1417 Margery set off again, this time on a pilgrimage to the shrine of St. James at Santiago de Compostela in northwest Spain. On her return she visited the shrine of the holy blood at Hailes, in Gloucestershire, proceeding next to Leicester. In one of her first altercations with secular power, the mayor of Leicester accused Margery, in Latin, of being a "cheap whore, a lying Lollard," and threatened her with prison. Margery insisted on her right to hear his accusations in English, whereupon she capably defended herself – not only against the mayor's allegations, but against sexual assault – only to be imprisoned for three weeks following additional interrogations by the mayor, the Dean of Leicester, and the abbot of the local Augustinian priory. Trouble followed Margery to York, where she was examined by the minster clergy and brought before Archbishop Henry Bowet. Margery's 1417 progress, if that's what it can be called, became a litany of arrest and interrogation – from Plymouth to Gloucester to Leicester to York to Cawood to Beverly to London to Canterbury. But she had supporters among churchmen as well: these included the Dominican anchorite of Lynn; Robert Springolde, her parish priest and confessor; Thomas Heveningham, prior of the Lynn monastery; Richard Caister, vicar of St. Stephen's, Norwich; and William Southfield, a Carmelite of Norwich – clergymen who believed that God revealed himself in visions to individuals (a concession dangerously close to the Protestant belief that laypersons, women included, could interpret Scripture through the indwelling Spirit of God).

In the 1420s Kempe remained in Lynn, often ill; but she continued to live apart from her husband, both to avoid temptation and to escape cynical gossip. About 1430, John Kempe fell down the steps in his own home, sustaining a brain injury that was blamed, by some, on his absent wife. Margery, 57, dutifully returned to his residence and nursed him, rejoicing in her care-giving as penance for the joy she had in his body when they were young.

Bishop's Lynn had a thriving Hanseatic colony of Baltic traders (whose wharves and a fifteenth-century warehouse can still be seen today by tourists). The Hanseatic League shipped timber, furs, resin, tar, flax, honey, wheat, and rye to England, in exchange for cloth and manufactured goods. One of Margery's sons – perhaps, by 1430, her only surviving son – had married the daughter of a Hanseatic trader and settled in Danzig, on the Baltic Coast. Hearing of his father's disability, this unnamed son returned to England, whereupon he and his mother collaborated in a writing project. Confined now at home to care for her dying husband, but having led an extraordinary life, Margery wished to record her memoirs; her son agreed to serve as her amanuensis. But he died before the work of transcription was complete, followed soon after by John's death. And when Margery sought a substitute amanuensis, she discovered that no one could read her son's illegible handwriting. The manuscript was set aside.

In April 1433, again feeling the travel bug, Kempe left Ipswich to accompany her widowed daughter-in-law back to Danzig, on the Baltic Coast. Because Margery went without her confessor's permission, God sent a storm that blew their ship off course to Norway. Eventually the two women reached Danzig; after which Margery traveled alone, with many tribulations, first to Brandenburg (to see the miraculous

Holy Blood of Wilsnack); then to Aachen (to behold the famous relics of St. Mary's cloak, baby Jesus' swaddling clothes, St. John the Baptist's beheading cloth, and Christ's loincloth). Crossing the Channel from Calais, Margery returned home via Sion Abbey. She reached Lynn about September 1534; whereupon she was reconciled with her confessor, and returned to her autobiography project.

In July 1436, Kempe persuaded a local priest to serve as her new amanuensis. It took some time for them to recast her son's draft into legible English. Completing Book 1 in April 1538, Margery and her priest undertook a sequel covering the years 1431-34. Extracts from Margery's book were printed by Wynkyn de Word, c. 1501, again by Henry Pepwell twenty years later (where the anonymous author is described, mistakenly, as "a devoute ancres"). *The Book of Margery Kempe* survives in a single manuscript copy, made in 1450 by an East Anglian scribe named Salthows. Later in the 15th century it was owned by the Yorkshire Carthusian priory of Mount Grace, later by the Butler-Bowdon family of Lancashire. It was Hope Emily Allen, in 1934, who first made the connection between the Butler-Bowdon manuscript and the excerpts published in 1501. The manuscript is housed today in the British Library.

In 1438, about the time her autobiography was completed, a "Margeria Kempe" was admitted to the prestigious Trinity Guild of Lynn. Margery was then nearly 70 years old. The date of her death is unrecorded. But having completed her autobiography, "sche wist wel that it was trewth that owyr Lord seyd to hir, er[e] sche went owt of Inglond: *Dowtyr, I schal makyn al the werld to wondryn of the*[*e*]!"

DWF

In the early 15th century, Bishop's Lynn (now King's Lynn) was a port of considerable importance, with a thriving international market and wealthy trade guilds. (John Kempe belonged to the Skinner's Company, one of the less prestigious.) The guild for each profession promoted the work, standards, and rights of its members. Each had a guildhall commensurate with the company's wealth. The halls served also as centers of religious, civic, and social activity. Four times a year, each brotherhood gathered its members and their spouses, dressed in their best robes, to march in procession and attend Mass. At dramatic festivals, the guilds participated in the mystery plays (dramatic recreations of Bible stories). The guilds also provided charitable assistance to members in need, and contributed to Lynn's walls, defenses, and sea banks. Funds were collected from fees, fines, and rents. In the late 14th century, as the Black Death ravaged England, the guilds assumed increasing importance, in Lynn as elsewhere. In 1373, the year of Margery's birth, Bishop's Lynn had 38 guilds. Twenty years later, there were sixty.

When Margery was three years old, wool traders of Lynn founded a guild devoted to St. George – a saint of Middle Eastern origins adopted by Crusaders who was later made the patron saint of England. St. George was believed to answer prayers to cure the plague, which made him a popular fellow. Under a charter granted by Henry IV in 1406, the guild of St. George built a hall that is now the oldest surviving guildhall in England (above right). Commenced in 1410 (a few years before Margery made her pilgrimage to the Holy Land), and completed in 1420 (after her return), St. George's Guildhall is made of brown brick, a structure 29 feet wide and 107 feet long, having a great room on the upper floor that served originally as a dining commons.

The guilds were dissolved in 1537-1547 by Henry VIII, who disapproved of their conversative adherence to Rome and mistrusted their organizational power. For some centuries after the dissolution, theatrical productions were performed in the Great Hall of St. George's (the earliest recorded performance occurred there in 1442. a few years after Margery's death.) The building serves today as an arts centre.

The Guildhall of the Holy and Undivided Trinity (below) was built in 1422-1428 at a cost of £200 after the previous structure was gutted by fire in 1421. Under Elizabeth, Trinity was converted to a prison. The original entrance, which had a dog-leg external staircase against the west wall, was replaced in 1624 with the elaborate porch shown here.

From ***The Book of Margery Kempe***

## THE FIRST BOOK

### Chapter 1

WHEN this creature was twenty year of age or some deal more, she was married to a worshipful burgess° and was with child within short time, as kind would. And, after that she had conceived, she was labored with great accesses till the child was born, and then – what for labor she had in childing, and for sickness going beforn – she despaired of her life, weening she might not liven.[1]

And then she sent for her ghostly fader, for she had a thing in conscience which she had never shewèd beforn that time in all her life; for she was ever letted by her en'my, the devil, evermore saying to her, while she was in good hale her needed no confession but doen penaunce by herself alone and all should be forgiven, for God is merciful enow. And therefore this creature oftentimes did great penaunce – in fasting bread and water, and other deeds of alms, with devout prayers – save she would not shewen it in confession. [2]

And when she was any time sick or diseased, the devil said in her mind that she should be dampnèd, for she was not shriven of that defaut. Wherefore, after that her child was born, she (not trusting her life) sent for her ghostly fader, as y-said beforn, in full will to be shriven of all her lifetime as near as she could. And when she came to the point for to sayen that thing which she had so long concealèd, her confessour was a little too hasty and 'gan° sharply to under-nemine her, ere then she had fully said her intent – and so she would no more sayen for naught he might do. And anon – for dread she had of dampnation on the to'side and his sharp reprieving on that other side – this creature went out of her mind, and was wonderly vexèd and labourèd with spirits half-year, eight weeks, and odd days. [3]

And in this time she sey (as her-thought) devils open 'heir mouths all enflamèd with brenning lows of fire as they should ha' swall'wèd her in – sometime ramping at her, sometime threating her, sometime pulling her and haling her, both night and day, during the foresaid time. And also the devils cried upon her with great threat'nings and boden her she should forsake her Christendom, her faith, and denyen her God, his moder, and all the saints in Heaven, her good works and all good virtues, her fader, her moder, and all her friends. [4]

And so she did. She slaund'red her husbond, her friends, and her own self. She spake many a reprievous word and many a shrewèd word. She knew no virtue ne goodness. She desirèd all wickedness. Like as the spirits tempted her to say and do, so she said and did. She would ha' fordone herself many a time at 'heir stirrings and ha' been dampnèd with 'hem in Hell (and into witness thereof, she bot her own hand so violently that it was seen all her life after). And also she rove her skin on her body again' her heart with her nails spetously (for she had none other instruments) – and worse she would ha' done, save she was bounden and kept with strength both day and night, that she might not have her will. [5]

---

[1] *married* ] to John Kempe of Lynn; *burgess* ] freeman or citizen of the borough; *kind* ] nature; *accesses* ] attacks of illness; *beforn* ] before; *weening* ] supposing.

[2] *ghostly fader* ] (fā-der) spiritual father; priest (cf. *moder, weder, togeder, hider, wheder, gader, slider,* etc.); *letted* ] hindered; *hale her* ] health she; *but doen* ] but only to do; *enow* ] enough.

[3] *dampnéd*] damned; *shriven* ] got absolution for oneself by confessing; *defaut* ] fault; *as y-said* ] as it was said; *'gan* ] began (frequent); *under-nemine* ] reprove, undermine; *ere then* ] before; *naught* ] anything; *to'side* ] one side; *reprieving* ] reproving.

[4] *sey* ] saw; *her-thought* ] she thought; as it seemed to her (cf. the more familiar *methought* or *methinks*); *'heir* ] their; *brenning lows* ] burning waves; *should ha' swall'wed* ] might have swallowed; *ramping* ] raging with violent gestures; *threating* ] threatening; *haling* ] dragging.

[5] *boden* ] bade; *reprievous* ] scolding; *shrewed* ] ill-tempered; vicious; *no ... ne* ] neither ... nor; *fordone* ] killed; *'hem* ] them; *bot* ] bit; *it* ] the scar; *rove* ] rived, scratched deeply; *again'* ] against; *spetously* ] spitefully; *save* ] except that; *that* ] so that (frequent).

And when she had long been laboured in these and many other temptations (that men weened she should never ha' scapèd, ne livèd), then on a time, as she lay alone and her keepers were fro' her, our merciful Lord Christ Jesu (ever to be trusted, worshiped be his name!), never forsaking his servaunt in time of need, appearèd – to his creature which had forsaken him – in likeness of a man, most seemly, most beauteous, and most amiable that ever might be seen with man's eye; clad in a mantle of purple silk, sitting upon her bedside; looking upon her with so blissèd a cheer that she was strengthèd in all her spirits. He° said to her these words: "Doughter, why hast thou forsaken me, and I forsook never thee?" [1]

And anon as he had said these words, she saw verily how the air openèd as bright as any levin, and he stey up into the air, not right hastily and quickly, but fair and easily, that she might well beholden him in the air till it was closèd again. [2]

And anon the creature was stabelèd in her wits and in her reason as well as ever she was beforn, and prayed her husbond (as so soon as he came to her) that she might have the keys of the buttery to taken her meat and drink as she had done beforn. Her maidens and her keepers counseled him he should deliver her no keys, for they said she would but give away swech good as there was,

[1] *fro* ] from; *Christ Jesu* ] (krīst′ yes'-oo); *blissèd* ] blessed; *strengthed* ] strengthened.

for she wist not what she said (as they weened).[3]

Nevertheless, her husbond – ever having tenderness and compassion of her – commaunded they should deliver to her the keys. And she° took her meat and drink as her bodily strength would serven her, and knew her friends and her meiny and all other that came to her to see how our Lord Jesu Christ had wrought his grace in her (so blissèd mote he be that ever is near in tribulation!). When men weenen he were far fro'hem, he is full near, by his grace. Sithen, this creature did all other occupations as fell for her to do, wisely and sadly enow, save she knew not verily the draught of our Lord. [4]

## Chapter 2

And when this creature was thus graciously comen again to her mind, she thought she was bounden to God and that she would be'n his servant. Nevertheless, she would not leaven her pride ne her pompous array that she had usèd before-time, neither for her husbond ne for none other man's counsel. And yet she wist full well that men saiden her full much villainy, for she wearèd gold pipès on her hevyd and her hoods, with the tippets were daggèd. Her cloaks were daggèd and layed with divers colours between the dags, that it should be the more staring to men's sight, and herself the more be'n worshiped. And when her husbond would speak to her, for-to leaven her pride, she answerèd shrewdly and shortly, and said that she was comen of worthy kin'red – him seemèd never for to have wedded her – for her fader was sometime mayor of the town N. and sithen he was alderman of the high guild of the Trinity in N., and therefore she would saven the worship of her kin'red, whatsoever any man said. [5]

[2] *air* ] sky; *levin* ] lightning; stey ] rose.

[3] *as so soon as* ] as soon as; *buttery* ] storeroom for liquor and other provisions; *swech good as there was* ] such goods as were there; *wist* ] knew.

[4] *of her* ] for her; *meiny* ] household; mote ] may; *weenen* ] suppose; *Sithen* ] After that; *sadly enow* ] solemnly enough; *draught* ] (= drawing-forth) spiritual calling.

[5] *pipès* ] piping on a gentlewoman's headdress; *hevyd* ] head; *tippets* ] long hanging slips forming part of the hood; *daggèd* ] cut along the margin into ornamental, pointed "dags"; *shrewdly* ] shrewishly; *kin'red* ] kindred; *him seeméd ... wedded her* ] it seemed he should not have married her; *N.* ] King's Lynn, in Norfolk (*the anonymity is dropped further along in her narrative*); *whatsoever* ] no matter what.

She had full great envy at her neighbours that they should be'n arrayed so well as she. All her desire was for to be worshiped of the people. She would not beware by any's chastising, ne be content with the goods that God had sent her, as her husbond was, but ever desirèd more and more.

And then, for pure covetise and for to maintain her pride, she 'gan to brewen – and was one of the greatest brewers in the town N., a three year or four, till she lost much good, for she had never ure thereto. For though she had never-so-good servaunts, and cunning in brewing, yet it would never prieven with 'hem. For when the ale was as fair-standing under barm as any man might see, suddenly the barm would fallen down, that all the ale was lost, every brewing after other, that her servaunts weren ashamèd and would not dwellen with her.[1]

Then this creature thought how God had pun'shed° her before-time and she could not beware, and now eftsoons by losing of her goods – and then she left, and brewèd no more. And then she askèd her husbond mercy for she would not foll'wen his counsel aforetime; and she said that her pride and sin was cause of all her pun'shing and she would amend that she had trespassèd, with good will. [2]

But yet she left not the world all whole, for now she bethought her of a new huswifery. She had an horse-mill. She got her twain good horse, and a man to grinden men's corn, and thus she trusted to getten her living. This provision durèd not long – for in short time after, on Corpus Christi Even, fell this marvel: This man being in good hale of body, and his twain horse crask and likend (that well hadden drawen in the mill before-time), as now he took one of these horse and put him in the mill as he had done before, and this horse would draw no draught in the mill for nothing the man might do. The man was sorry and assayed with all his wits how he should doen this horse drawen. Sometime he led him by the head, sometime he beat him, and sometime he cherished him; and all availed not, for he would rather goen backward than forward. Then this man set a sharp pair spurs on his heels and rode on the horse' back for to doen him drawen, and it was never the better. When this man saw it would be in no way, then he set up this horse again in the stable and gave him meat, and he et well and freshly.

And sithen he took the other horse and put him in the mill. And like as his fellow did, so did he – for he would not draw for anything that the man might do. And then this man forsook his service and would no lenger abiden with the aforesaid creature. [3]

Anon as it was noised about the town of N. that there would neither man ne beast doen service to the said creature, then some saiden she was accursèd. Some saiden God took open vengeance upon her. Some saiden [one thing], and some said another. And some wise men, whose mind was more grounded in the love of our Lord, said it was the high mercy of our Lord Jesu Christ, clepèd and callèd her fro' the pride and vanity of the wretched world. And then this creature, seeing all these adversities coming on every side, thought it weren the scourges of our Lord, that would chastise her for her sin. Then she askèd God mercy° and forsook her pride, her covetise, and desire that she had of the worships of the world, and did great bodily penaunce, and 'gan to enter the way of everlasting life, as shall be said after. [4]

Medieval grain mill, turned by an ox or horse

[1] *covetise* ] covetousness; *good* ] money; *ure* ] experience; *prieven with 'hem* ] succeed for them; *barm* ] yeasty foam that rises to the surface of fermenting malt liquors; *that…that* ] so that…and so that.

[2] *eftsoons*] soon afterwards; *foll'wen* ] follow; *amend that* ] amend in that which.

[3] *huswifery* ] housewifery; domestic enterprise; *twain* ] two; *crask and likend* ] fattened and in good condition; *doen this horse drawen* ] make this horse to draw; *Sometime* ] for a while.

[4] *clepéd and calléd* ] having named and called.

## Chapter 3

On a night, as this creature lay in her bed with her husbond, she heard a sound of melody so sweet and delectable, her-thought, as she had been in Paradise. And therewith she stirred out of her bed and said, "Alas that ever I did sin – it is full merry in Heaven!" This melody was so sweet that it passèd all the melody that ever might be heard in this world withouten any comparison, and caused this creature when she heard any mirth or melody afterward for to have full plentivous and habundaunt tears of high devotion, with great sobbings and sighings after the bliss of Heaven, not dreading the shames and the spites of the wretched world. [1]

And ever after this draught she had in her mind the mirth and the melody that was in Heaven – so much that she could not well restrain herself fro' the speaking thereof. For where she was in any company, she would say oftentime, "It is full merry in Heaven!" And they that knew her governaunce before-time and now heard her speaken so much of the bliss of Heaven said unto her, "Why speak ye so of the mirth that is in Heaven? Ye know it not, and ye have not be' there no more than we" – and were wroth with her, for she would not hear ne speak of wordly things as they didden (and as she did beforntime). [2]

And after this time she had never desire to commoun fleshly with her husbond, for the debt of matrimony was so abhominable to her that she had liever, her-thought, eten° or drinken the wooze, the muck in the channel, than to consenten to any fleshly commouning, save only for obedience. And so she said to her husbond, "I may not deny you my body, but the love of mine heart and mine affection is drawen fro' all eardly creatures and set only in God." [3]

He would have his will – and she obeyed with great weeping and sorr'wing for that she might not liven chaste. And oftentimes this creature counseled° her husbond to liven chaste and said that they oftentimes, she wist well, had displeasèd God by 'heir inordinate love and the great delectation that they hadden, either of 'hem, in using of other – and now it were good that they should, by 'heir bothens will and consenting of 'hem bothen, pun'shen and chastisen 'hemselfe willfully, by abstaining fro'heir lust of 'heir bodies. Her husbond said it were good to doen so, but he might not yet: he should, when God would. And so he usèd her as he had do' before – he would not spare. And ever she prayed to God that she might liven chaste – and three or four year after, when it pleasèd our Lord, he made a vow of chastity (as shall be written after), by the love of Jesu.... [4]

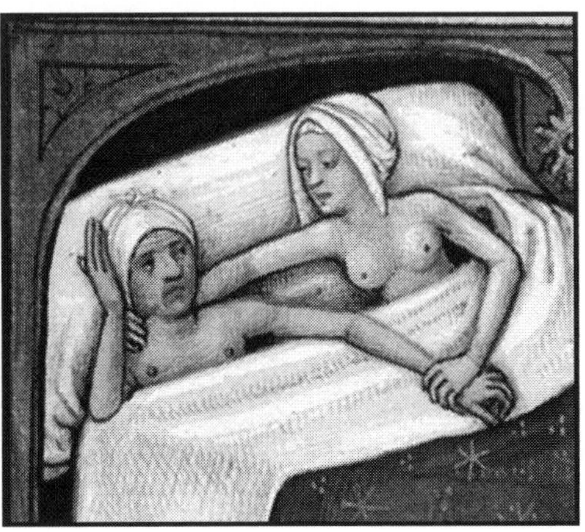

## Chapter 4

The first two year when this creature was thus drawen to our Lord, she had great quiet of spirit as for any temptations. She might well 'dure to fasten – it grievèd her not. She hated the joys of the world. She felt no rebellion in her flesh. She was strong, as her-thought, that she dredd no devil in Hell, for she did so great bodily penaunce. She thought that she lovèd God more than he her (she was smit with the deadly wound of vainglory and felt it not!), for she desirèd many times that the crucifix should loosen his hands fro' the cross and halsen her, in token of love. Our merciful Lord Christ Jesu, seeing this creature's presumption, sent her (as is writ before) three year of great temptation.... [5]

---

[1] *plentivous* ] plenteous.

[2] governaunce ] mode of living; *wordly* ] worldly.

[3] *woose* ] ooze, scum; *commoun* ] commune (*also*, to make common); *commoun fleshly* ] have intercourse; *liever* ] (comp. of *lief*) ] rather; *eardly* ] earthly.

[4] *delectation* ] great pleasure; *pun'shen and chastisen 'hemselfe* ] to punish and chastise themselves; *he should when God would* ] he would, when God willed him to do so; *do'* ] done.

[5] *as for* ] as regards; *might well 'dure to fasten* ] could well endure fasting; *dredd* ] dreaded; *smit* ] smitten; *halsen* ] embrace; *writ* ] written.

In the second year of her temptations it fell so that a man which she lovèd well said unto her – on St. Margaret's Even before evensong – that for anything he would lie by her and have his lust of her body, and she should not withstond him; for, if he might not have his will that time, he said, he should else have it another time – she should not choose. (And he did it for to prieve her what she would do, but she weened that he had meant full earnest as that time, and said but little thereto.) So they parted asunder as-then and wenten bothen for to hear evensong (for 'heir church was of Saint Margaret). [1]

This woman was so labored with the man's words that she might not hearen her evensong, ne say her paternoster, or thinken any other good thought, but was more labored than ever she was before. The devil put in her mind that God had forsaken her, and else should she not so been tempted. She 'lievèd the devil's 'suasions° and 'gan to consenten for because she could thinken no good thought. Therefore weened she that God had forsak her. And, when evensong was do', she went to the man beforesaid, that he should have his lust (as she weened that he had desired) – but he made swech simulation that she could not know his intent, and so they parted asunder for that night. [2]

This creature was so labored and vexèd all that night that she wist never what she might do. She lay by her husbond – and for to commoun with him, it was so abhominable unto her that she might not 'duren it (and yet was it lawful unto her, in lawful time, if had she would). But ever she was labored with the other man for to sin with him (inasmuch as he had spoke to her). [3]

At the last, thor'we inopportunity of temptation and lacking of discretion, she was overcomen, and consented in her mind, and went to the man to witten if he would then consenten to her. And he said he ne would, for all the good in this world; he had liever been hewen as small as flesh to the pot. [4]

She went away all shamèd and confusèd in herself, seeing his stableness and her own unstableness. Then thought she of the grace that God had given her before-time, how she had two year of great quiet in soul, repentaunce of her sin with many bitter tears of compunction, and parfit will never to turn again to her sin, but rather to be dead, her-thought. And now she saw how she had consented, in her will, for to doen sin. Then fell she half in despair. She thought she would ha' been in Hell for the sorr'we that she had. She thought she was worthy no mercy (for her consenting was so willfully do'), ne never worthy to doen him service for she was so false unto him. [5]

Nevertheless, she was shriven many times and often, and did her penaunce (whatsoever her confessour would enjoin her to do), and was governed after the rules of the Church. That grace God gave this creature (blissèd mote he be!) – but he withdrew not her temptation (but rather increasèd it, as her-thought). And therefore weened she that he had forsaken her, and durst not trusten to his mercy but was labored with horrible temptations of lethery and of despair nigh all the next year foll'wing (save our Lord of his mercy, as she said herself, gave her each day for the most partie two hours of compunction for her sins, with many bitter tears). And sithen she was labored with temptations of despair as she was before, and was as far fro' feeling of grace as they that never felt none – and *that* might she not bearen, and therefore alway she despairèd. Save for the time that she felt grace, her labors were so wonderful that she could evil fare with 'hem, but ever mournen and sorr'wen as though God had forsaken her. [6]

---

[1] *evensong* ] evening mass; *withstond* ] withstand; *prieve* ] prove; test; *as* ] at; *said . . . thereto* ] she said very little in reply; *as-then* ] for that time; *for to* ] in order to; *of St. Margaret* ] ded. to St. Margaret and therefore observing a special mass each year on St. Margaret's Eve.

[2] *paternoster* ] Lord's prayer ("Our Father . . ."); *lievéd* ] believed; *'suasions* ] persuasions; *forsak* ] forsook; *simulation* ] dissimulation; pretence.

[3] *'duren* ] endure; *yet was it lawful...if she had would* ] yet it was lawful (being married) and in lawful time (not during menstruation), had she so desired.

[4] *thor'we* ] through; *inopportunity* ] importunity, unseasonableness; *lacking* ] lack; *witten* ] learn; know; *ne* ] never; *liever* ] rather; *hewen as small as flesh to the pot* ] chopped as small as meat for the broth.

[5] *repentaunce* ] and repentance; *parfit* ] perfect; *sorr'we* ] sorrow.

[6] *lethery* ] litherness; wicked lethargy; *partie* ] part; *might . . . not bearen* ] could not endure; *Save* ] except; *wonderful* ] awful.

## Chapter 11

It befell upon a Friday on midsummer even in right hot weder, as this creature was coming fro' York-ward bearing a bottle with beer in her hand and her husbond a cake in his bosom, he askèd his wife this question: "Margery, if 'here come a man with a sword and would smite off mine head less-then I should commoun kindly with you as I have do' before, sayeth me truth of your conscience – for ye say ye will not lie – whether would ye suffer mine head to be smit off or else suffer me to meddle with you again as I did sometime?" [1]

"Alas, sir," she said, "why move ye this matter and have we been chaste this eight weeks!" [2]

"For I will weet the truth of your heart." [3]

And then she said with great sorr'we, "Forsooth, I had liever see you be slain than we should turn again to our uncleanness." [4]

And he said again, "Ye aren no good wife."

And then she askèd her husbond what was the cause that he had not meddled with her eight weeks before, sithen she lay with him every night in his bed. And he said he was so made a-feared when he would ha' touchèd her that he durst no more doen. [5]

"Now, good sir, amend you, and ask God mercy! – for I teld you near three year sithen that ye should be slain suddenly, and now is this the thrid year, and yet I hope I shall han my desire. Good sir, I pray you, graunt me that I shall asken, and I shall pray for you, that ye shall be savèd thor'we the mercy of our Lord Jesu Christ, and ye shall have more meed in Heaven than if ye wearèd an hair or an habergeon: I pray you, suffer me to make a vow of chastity in what bishop's hand that God will." [6]

"Nay," he said, "that will I not graunt you, for now may I usen you withouten deadly sin and then might I not so." [7]

Then she said again, "If it be the will of the holy Ghost to fulfillen that I have said, I pray God ye mote consent thereto; and if it be not the will of the holy Ghost, I pray God ye never consent thereto." [8]

Then went they forth to-Bridlington-ward in right hot weder, the forensaid creature having great sorr'we and great dread for her chastity. And, as they came by a cross, her husbond set him down under the cross, cleping his wife unto him and saying these words onto her: "Margery, graunt me my desire, and I shall graunt you your desire: My first desire is that we shall lyen still togeder in o' bed as we han do' before; the second, that ye shall pay my debts ere ye go to Jerusalem; and the thrid, that ye shall eten and drinken with me on the Friday as ye were wont to doen." [9]

"Nay sir," she said, "to break the Friday I will never graunt you while I live."

"Well," he said, "then shall I meddle you again."

She prayed him that he would give her leave to make her prayers, and he graunted it goodlike. Then she kneelèd down besiden a cross in the field and prayed in this manner with great habundaunce of tears: "Lord God, thou knowest all thing. Thou knowest what sorr'we I have had to be chaste in my body to thee all this three year, and now might I han my will and I dare not, for love of thee. For if I would breaken that manner of fasting which thou commaundest me to keepen on the Friday withouten meat or drink, I should now han my desire! – but, blissèd Lord, thou knowest I will not contraryen thy will, and mickle now is my sorr'we less-then I find comfort in thee. Now, blissèd Jesu, make thy will knowen (to me, unworthy) that I may foll'wen thereafter and fulfillen it with all my mights." [10]

---

[1] *midsummer even* ] evening of the summer solstice, 21 June; *less-then* ] (i.e., less-than) unless; *kindly* ] naturally; *suffer* ] allow.

[2] *and* ] when

[3] *will weet* ] wish to know.

[4] *forsooth* ] truly.

[5] *eight weeks before* ] for the past eight weeks, during which time Margery resumed sleeping with her husband while remaining abstinent; *sithen* ] since; *durst no more doen* ] no longer dared touch her.

[6] *teld* ] told; *three year sithen* ] three years ago; *that ... suddenly* ] that you would be slain by God if, because of you, I could not serve him in celibacy for three years (as threatened in chap. 9, MS fol. 11); *thrid* ] third; *han my desire* ] have my wish to remain celibate; *grant me that* ] grant me that which; *meed* ] reward; *an hair* ] a hair-cloth shirt, worn for the mortification of the flesh as a sign of repentance; *habergeon* ] coat of mail, likewise worn for penance (apart from its primary use for bodily protection in battle).

[7] *not so* ] not do so.

[8] *thereto* ] i.e., to my taking a vow of absolute celibacy.

[9] *to-Bridlington-ward* ] toward Bridlington (an ancient market town in Yorkshire, about a mile from the coast); *forensaid* ] aforesaid (Margery); *cleping* ] clasping, or calling; *desire* ] i.e., desire to take a vow of celibacy; *o' bed* ] one bed; *han do'* ] have done; *thrid* ] third; *as ye were wont to doen* ] as you used to do

[10] *goodlike* ] kindly; *contraryen* ] resist; *mickle ... thee* ] much now is my sorrow unless I find comfort in thee.

And then our Lord Jesu Christ with great sweetness spake to this creature, commaunding her to goen again to her husbond and prayen him to graunten her that she desired, "and he shall han that he desireth. For, my dear-worthy doughter, this was the cause that I bade thee fasten – for thou should'st the sooner obtain and getten thy desire! – and now it is graunted thee. I will no lenger thou fast. Therefore I bid thee, in the name of Jesu, eat and drink as thine husbond doth." [1]

Then this creature thankèd our Lord Jesu Christ of his grace and his goodness, sithen rose up and went to her husbond, saying unto him, "Sir, if it like you, ye shall graunt me my desire, and ye shall have your desire. Graunteth me that ye shall not comen in my bed, and I graunt thou to quit your debts ere I go to Jerusalem. And maketh my body free to God, so that ye never make no challenging in me to asken no debt of matrimony after this day while ye liven, and I shall eten and drinken on the Friday at your bidding." [2]

Then said her husbond again to her, "As free mote your body be'n to God as it hath been to me!"[3]

This creature thankèd God greatly, enjoying that she had her desire, praying her husbond that they should say three paternoster in the worship of the Trinity for the great grace that he had graunted 'hem. And so they did, kneeling under a cross – and sithen they eten and droonken togeder in great gladness of spirit. This was on a Friday on midsummer even. [4]

Then went they forth to-Bridlington-ward and also to many other countries and spoken with God's servaunts, bothen ankorès and recluses, and many other of our Lord's lovers, with many worthy clerks, doctours of divinity, and bachelors also in many divers places. And this creature, to divers of 'hem, shewèd her feelings and her contemplations (as she was commaunded for to doen, to witten if any deceit were in her feelings).[5]

## Chapter 13

On a time, as this creature was at Canterbury, in the church among the monks, she was greatly despised and reprievèd for-cause she wept so fast (bothen of the monks and priests and of secular men), near all o' day both aforenoon and afternoon, also insomuch that her husbond went away fro' her as he had not ha' knowen her, and left her alone among 'hem, choose her as she could, for other comfort had she none of him as that day.[6]

So an eld monk, which had been treasurer with the queen while he was in secular clothing, a rich man, and greatly dredd of much people, took her by the hand, saying unto her, "What canst thou sayen of God?" [7]

"Sir," she sayeth, "I will both speak of him and hearen of him" – rehearsing the monk a story of Scripture. [8]

The monk said, "I would thou were closèd in an house of stone, that there should no man speak with thee!"

"Ah, sir," she said, "ye should maintain God's servaunts, and ye aren the first that helden agains' 'hem. Our Lord amend you!"

Then a young monk said to this creature, "Either thou hast the holy Ghost or else thou hast a devil within thee, for that thou speakest here to us it is holy Writs – and that, hast thou not of thyself."

Then said this creature, "I pray you, sir, give me leave to tellen you a tale."

Then the people said to the monk, "Let her say what she will."

And then she said, "There was once a man that had sinned greatly agains' God, and when he was shriven his confessour enjoinèd him, in partie of penaunce, that he should o' year hire men to chide him and reprieven him for his sins, and he should given 'hem silver for 'heir labor.[9] And on a day he came among many great men (as now be'n here – God save you all!), and stood among

---

[1] *that . . . that* ] that which . . . that which; *I ... fast* ] I no longer require you to fast on Fridays.

[2] *sithen* ] then; *like you* ] please you; *quit* ] pay off.

[3] *mote* ] must.

[4] *enjoying* ] rejoicing; *sithen* ] ever after.

[5] *countries* ] counties; *ankorès* ] achorites; *clerks* ] clerics; scholars; *our Lord's lovers* ] ascetics and votaries; *bachelors* ] those who had taken the first, or lowest, degree in divinity.

[6] *for-cause* ] because; *o' day* ] one day *as he had not* ] as if he had not; *choose her as she could* ] without allowing her any choice in the matter.

[7] *eld* ] old; *dredd* ] dreaded; *eld ... people* ] identified by Hope E. Allen as John Kynton, who was chancellor to Queen Joanna, wife of Henry IV, prior to becoming a monk at Christ Church, Canterbury.

[8] *rehearsing* ] repeating to.

[9] *in partie of penaunce* ] as part of his penance; *o'year* ] one year.

'hem (as I do now among you) despising him, as ye do me; the man, laughing or smiling and having good game at 'heir words. The greatest master of 'hem said to the man, 'Why laughest thou, brothel, and art thou greatly despised?' [1]

"'Ah, sir, I have a great cause to laugh – for I have many days put silver out of my purse and hired men to chide me for remission of my sin, and this day I may keep my silver in my purse! I thank you all.'

"Right so I say to you, worshipful sirs. While I was at home in mine own country, day by day with great weeping and mourning I sorr'wed for I had no shame, scorn, and despite, as I was worthy. I thank you all, sirs, highly, what forenoon and afternoon I have had reasonably this day (blissèd be God thereof!)." [2]

Then she went out of the monastery, they foll'wing and crying upon her, "Thou shalt be brent, false Lollar! 'here is a cartful of thorns ready for thee, and a tun to bren thee with!" [3]

And the creature stood withouten the gates at Canterbury, for it was in the evening, much people wondering on her. Then said the people, "Take and bren her!" And the creature stood still, tremmeling and hwaking full sore in her flesh withouten any eardly comfort, and wist not where her husbond was become. [4]

Then prayed she in her heart to our Lord, thinking on this manner: "Hider came I, Lord, for thy love. Blissèd Lord, help me and have mercy on me." [5]

And anon after she had made her prayers in her heart to our Lord, there coomen twain fair young men and said to her, "Damsel, art thou none 'eretic ne no Lollar?" [6]

And she said, "No, sirs, I am neither 'eretic ne Lollar."

Then they askèd her where was her inn. She said she wist never in what street, nevertheless it should be at a Deuchman's house. Then this twain young men brought her home to her hostel and made her great cheer, praying her to pray for 'hem; and there found she her husbond.... [7]

**Chapter 18**

...And then she was boden by our Lord for to goen to an anch'ress in the same city which hight Dame Julian. And so she did, and shewèd her the grace that God put in her soul of compunction, contrition, sweetness and devotion, compassion with holy meditation and high contemplation, and full many holy speeches and dalliaunce that our Lord spake to her soul, and many wonderful revelations which she shewèd to the anch'ress to witten if there were any deceit in 'hem, for the anch'ress was expert in swech things, and good counsel could yeven. [8]

The anch'ress, hearing the marvelous goodness of our Lord, highly thankèd God with all her heart for his visitation, counseling this creature to be obedient to the will of our Lord God and fulfillen with all her mights whatever he put in her soul – if it were not again' the worship of God and profit of her even-Cristen; for, if it were, then it were not the moving of a good spirit but rather of an evil spirit. "The holy Ghost moveth never a thing again' charity, and if he did, he were contrarious to his own self, for he is all charity.[9] Also he moveth a soul to all chasteness, for chaste

St. Julian's Church, Norwich

[1] *brothel* ] degenerate (person); *and* ] when.

[2] *for I had* ] because I had; *as ... worthy* ] as I deserved; *reasonably* ] in good measure.

[3] *brent* ] burnt; *Lollar* ] Lollard; from Middle Dutch *lollaerd*, a mumbler (of prayers); the Lollardites were disciples of John Wycliffe (1320?-1384), an English reformer. Margery's parish priest, William Sawtrey, was a Lollard; in 1401, he was burned in a tun at Smithfield.; *'here* ] There; *tun* ] a large wine-cask

[4] *withouten* ] outside; *on her* ] at her; *tremmelling and hwaking* ] trembling and quaking; *was become* ] had gone.

[5] *Hider* ] Hither.

[6] *none 'eretic ne no Lollar* ] neither heretic nor Lollard

[7] *never* ] not; *Deuchman's house* ] possibly Prussian; *praying* ] asking.

[8] *ankress* ] anchoress (*fem. of* anchorite); a religious recluse; *which hight* ] who was called; *dalliaunce* ] fellowship; *yeven* ] give.

[9] *even-Cristen* ] fellow Christian; *contrarious* ] contrary.

livers be clepèd 'the temple of the holy Ghost,' and the holy Ghost maketh a soul stable and steadfast in the right faith and the right belief: 'And a double man in soul is ever unstable and unsteadfast in all his ways. He that is evermore doubting is like to the flood of the sea, the which is moved and borne about with the wind, and that man is not like to receiven the gifts of God.' [1]

"What creature that hath these tokens, he [may and ought] steadfastlike believen that the holy Ghost dwelleth in his soul. And much more, when God visiteth a creature with tears of contrition, devotion, or compassion, he may and ought to 'lieven that the holy Ghost is in his soul. Saint Paul sayeth that the holy Ghost asketh for us with mournings and weepings unspeakable; that is to sayen, he maketh us to asken and prayen with mournings and weepings so plentivously that the tears may not be numerèd. There may none evil spirit given these tokens, for Jerome° sayeth that tears tormenten more the devil than doen the pains of Hell. [2]

"God and the devil be'n evermore contrarious, and they shall never dwellen togeder in oon place, and the devil hath no power in a man's soul. Holy Writ sayeth that the soul of a rightful man is the seat of God, and so I trust, sister, that ye be'n. I pray God graunt you perséveraunce. Setteth all your trust in God and feareth not the language of the world, for the more despite, shame and reprief that ye have in the world, the more is your merit in the sight of God. Patience is necessary unto you, for in that shall ye keepen your soul." [3]

Much was the holy dalliaunce that the anch'ress and this creature hadden by commouning in the love of our Lord Jesu Christ many days that they were togeder....

## Chapter 39

Another time, right as she came by a poor woman's house, the poor woman clepèd her into her house and did her sitten by her little fire, giving her wine to drink in a cup of stone. And she had a little man-child sucking on her breast, the which suckèd a while on the moder's breast. Another while, it ran to this creature (the moder sitting full of sorr'we and sadness). Then this creature brast all into weeping, as though she had seen our Lady and her Son in time of his Passion —and had so many of holy thoughts that she might never tellen the halvendel, but ever sat and wept plentivously a long time; that the poor woman, having compassion of her weeping, prayed her to ceasen (not knowing why she wept). Then our Lord Jesu Christ said to the creature, "This place is holy." And then she rose up and went forth.... [4]

Bishop blessing an anchoress

## Chapter 46

Sithen yede she forth to Leice'ter, and a good man also, Thomas Marchale (of whom is written beforn). And there she came into a fair church where she beheld a crucifix that° was pit'ously painted and lamentable to behelden, thor'we which beholding the passion of our Lord ent'red her mind, wherethor'we she gan melten and allto-relenten, by tears of pity and compassion. Then the fire of love° kindled so yerne in her heart that she might not keepen it privy – for wheder she would or not, it causèd her to breaken out with a loud voice and cryen marvelous-like, and weepen and sobben full hidous-like, that many a man and woman wond'red on her therefor. [5]

When it was overcomen, she going out at the church door, a man took her by the sleeve and said, "Damsel, why weepest thou so sore?"

"Sir," she said, "it is not you to tell." [6]

And so she and the good man, Thomas Marchale, went forth and took her hostel and there eten 'heir meat. When they had eten, she prayed Thomas Marchale to writen a letter and senden to her husbond that he might fetten her home. And while the letter was in writing, the 'osteler came up to her chaumber in great haste, and took away her scrip, and bade her comen yerne and speaken with the mayor. And so she did. [7]

---

[1] *clepèd*] called; *temple of the holy Ghost* ] I Cor. 6:19; *And a double man ... the gifts of God* ] Jam. 1.6-8.

[2] *steadfastlike* ] steadfastly; *plentivously*] abundantly; *numerèd* ] numbered.

[3] *ben evermore contrarious* ] are ever at odds.

[4] *did her sitten* ] made her to sit; *Another while ... sadness* ] After a while, the child came over to Margery as the mother sat watching, full of sadness; *brast* ] burst; *the halvendel* ] the half of it.

[5] *yede* ] went; *Leice'ter* ] Leicester (pron. *Lesseter*); *melten* ] melt into tears; *pit'ously . . . behelden* ] piteously portrayed and lamentable to behold; *wherethor'we* ] wherethrough, so that; *allto-relenten* ] to dissolve thoroughly; *yerne* ] earnestly; *marvelous-like* ] marvelously; *hidous-like* ] hideously.

[6] *not you to tell* ] i.e., not fit to tell you.

[7] *fetten* ] fetch; *scrip* ] a small bag, wallet, or satchel, esp. one carried by a pilgrim, a shepherd, or a beggar; *yerne* ] directly; *mayor* ] probably John Arnesby, mayor of Leicester 1416/17.

Then the mayor askèd her of what country she was and whose doughter she was.

"Sir," she said, "I am of° Lynn in Norfolk, a good man's doughter of the same Lynn, which hath been mayor five times of that worshipful bur'gh and alderman also many years, and I have a good man, also a burgess of the said town of° Lynn, to mine husbond." [1]

"Ah," said the mayor, "Saint Kat'erine teld what kin'red she came of, and yet are ye not like, for thou art a false strumpet, a false Lollar, and a false deceiver of the people, and therefore I shall have thee in prison."

And she said again, "I am as ready, sir, to goen to prison for God's love as ye aren ready to goen to church."

When the mayor had long chidden her and said many evil and horrible words unto her, and she (by the grace of Jesu) had reasonably answerèd him to all that he could sayen, then he commaunded the jailer's man to leaden her to prison.

The jailer's man, having compassion of her with weeping tears, said to the mayor, "Sir, I have none house to put her in, less-then I put her among men."

Then she, movèd with compassion of the° man which had compassion of her, praying for grace and mercy to that man as to her own soul, said to the mayor, "I pray you, sir, put me not among men, that I may keepen my chastity and my bond of wedlock to mine husbond, as I am bounden to do."

And then said the jailer his own self to the mayor, "Sir, I will be bounden to keep this woman in safe ward till ye will have her again."

Then was there a man of Boston, and said to the good wife there she was at hostel: "Forsooth," he sayeth, "in Boston this woman is holden an holy woman and a blissèd woman." [2]

Then the jailer took her into his a-ward and led her home into his own house and put her in a fair chaumber, shetting the door with a key and commending his wife the key to keepen. Nevertheless, he let her goen to church when she would and did her eten at his own table and made her right good cheer for our Lord's love (thankèd be almighty God thereof!). [3]

[1] *bur'gh* ] borough.

[2] *Boston* ] a borough in Lincolnshire; *and said* ] who said; *there* ] where.

[3] *a-ward* ] keeping; *commending* ] commanding; *did her eten* ] made her to eat.

**Chapter 47**

Then the steward of Leice'ter, a seemly man, sent for the said creature to the jailer's wife, and she (for her husbond was not at home) would not let her goen to no man, steward ne other. When the jailer knew thereof, he came his proper person and brought her before the steward. The steward, anon as he sie her, spake Latin unto her, many priests standing abouten to hear what she should say, and other people also.[4]

She said to the steward, "Speaketh English, if you liketh, for I understond not what ye say."

The steward said unto her, "Thou liest falsely, in plain English."

Then said she unto him again, "Sir, asketh what question ye will in English, and thor'we the grace of my Lord Jesu Christ I shall answeren you reasonably thereto."

And then askèd he many questions, to the which she answerèd readily and reasonably, that he could getten no cause again' her.

Then the steward took her by the hand and led her into his chaumber and spake many foul, rebawdy words unto her, purposing and desiring, as it seemèd her, to oppressen her and forlyen her. And then had she much dread and much sorr'we, crying him mercy. She said, "Sir, for the reverence of almighty God, spareth me, for I am a man's wife." [5]

And then said the steward, "Thou shalt tell me whether thou hast this speech of God or of the devil, or else thou shalt goen to prison."

"Sir," she said, "for to goen to prison I am not a-feared, for my Lord's love, the which much more suff'red for my love than I may for his. I pray you doeth as you thinketh the best."°

The steward seeing her boldness, that she dredd no prisoning, he strugglèd with her, shewing unclean tokens and ungoodly countenaunce, wherethor'we he frayed her so much that she teld him how she had her speech and her dalliaunce of the holy Ghost and not of her own cunning. [6]

And then he, all astounèd of her words, left his business and his lewdness, saying to her as many man had do' beforn, "Either thou art a right good woman or else a right wicked woman" – and deliverèd her again to her jailer, and he led her home again with him.... [7]

[4] *steward of Leice'ter* ] possibly Sir Robert Babthorp; *his proper person*] himself; *anon ... her* ] as soon as he saw her.

[5] *rebawdy* ] ribald; obscene; *forlyen* ] violate.

[6] *frayed* ] frightened.

[7] *astounèd* ] astonished; *he led* ] i.e., the jailer led.

## Chapter 48

On a Wednesday the said creature was brought into a church of All Hall'wen in Leice'ter, in which place before the high autar was set the abbot of Leice'ter with some of his chanons, the dean of Leice'ter, a worthy clerk. There were also many freres and priests, also the mayor of the same town with much other of lay people. There was so much people that they strooden upon stools for to behelden her and wonderen upon her. [1]

The said creature lay on her knees, making her prayers to almighty God that she might han grace, wit, and wisdom so to answeren that day as might be'n most pleasaunce and worship to him, most profit to her soul, and best example to the people.

Then there came a priest to her and took her by the hand and brought her beforn the abbot and his assessours sitting at the autar, the which didden her swearen° on a book that she should answeren truly to the articles of the faith, like as she felt in 'hem. And first they rehearsèd the blissful sacrament of the autar, charging her to sayen right as she believèd therein. [2]

Then she said, "Sirs, I believe in the sacrament of the autar on this wise: that what man hath taken the order of priesthood, be he never so vicious a man in his living, if he say duly tho' words over the bread that our Lord Jesu Christ said when he made his maundy among his disciples there he sat at the supper, I believe that it is his very flesh and his blood, and no material bread – ne never may be unsaid, be it once said."[3]

And so she answerèd forth to all the articles, as many as they would asken her, that they were well pleasèd.

The mayor which was her deadly enemy, he said, "In faith, she meaneth not with her heart as she sayeth with her mouth."

And the clerks saiden to him, "Sir, she answereth right well to us."

Then the mayor allto-rebukèd her and rehearsèd many reprievous words and ungoodly, the which is more expedient to be concealèd than expressèd. [4]

"Sir," she said, "I take witness of my Lord Jesu Christ, whose body is here present in the sacrament of the autar, that I never had part of man's body in this world in actual deed by way of sin, but of mine husbond's body, whom I am bounden-to by the law of matrimony, and by whom I have borne fourteen childeren. For I do you to witten, sir, that there is no man in this world that I love so much as God, for I love him aboven all thing. And, sir, I tell you truly, I love all men in God, and for God." Also furthermore she said plainly to his own person, "Sir, ye aren not worthy to be'n a mayor, and that shall I prieven by holy Writ, for our Lord God said himself ere he would taken vengeaunce on the cities, 'I shall comen down and seen' – and yet he knew all thing. And that was nought else, sir, but for to shew men as ye be'n that ye should doen none execution in punishing but if ye had knowing beforn that it were worthy for to be done. And, sir, ye han do' all the contrary to me this day – for, sir, ye han causèd me much despite for thing that I am not guilty in. I pray God forgive you it." [5]

Then the mayor said to her, "I will witten why thou goest in white clothes, for I trow thou art comen hider to han away our wives fro us and leaden 'hem with thee." [6]

"Sir," she sayeth, "ye shall not witten of my mouth why I go in white clothes: ye aren not worthy to witten it. But, sir, I will tellen it to these worthy clerks with good will, by the manner of confession. Avise 'hem if they will tell it you!" [7]

Then the clerks prayed the mayor to goen down fro'hem with the other people; and when they weren gone, she kneelèd on her knees before

---

[1] *church of All Hall'wen* ] the Church of All Saints, which yet stands on Highcross Street; *autar* ] altar; *chanons* ] canons; priests who serve in a cathedral; *freres* ] friars.

[2] *didden her swearen* ] made her to swear; *blissful sacrament of the autar* ] blessed sacrament of the eucharist.

[3] *what man* ] whatever man; *tho words* ] those words; *maundy* ] eucharist, the Last Supper; *there he sat* ] where he sat.

[4] *allto-rebukèd* ] severely rebuked; *the which is more expedient to be concealed than expressed* ] i.e., the mayor's words are better left unrepeated.

[5] *do you to witten* ] would have you know; *comen down and seen* ] prior to the destruction of Sodom (*see* Gen. 18:20-21 ff.); *prieven* ] prove; *ye should doen none execution in punishing ...* ] i.e., one should determine guilt or innocence before administering punishment.

[6] *trow* ] believe.

[7] *by the manner of confession* ] in confidence, as to a priest; *Avise* ] consult with.

the abbot, and the dean of Leice'ter, and a frere prechour (a worshipful clerk), and teld these three clerks how our Lord by revelation warnèd her and bade her wearen white clothes ere she came at Jerusalem. [1]

"And so have I told my ghostly faders. And therefore they han chargèd me that I should goen thus, for they dare not doen again' my feelings, for dread of God; and if they durst, they would, full glad-like. And therefore, sirs, if the mayor will witten why I go in white, ye may say, if you liketh, that my ghostly faders bidden me goen so, and then shall ye make no leesings, ne he shall not know the truth." [2]

So the clerks clepèd up again the mayor and telden him in council that her ghostly faders had chargèd her to wearen white clothes and she had bounden her to 'heir obedience.

Then the mayor clepèd her to him, saying, "I will not letten thee goen hence for thing that thou canst sayen, less-then thou will goen to my lord of Lincoln for a letter – inasmuch as thou art in his jurisdiction – that I may be dischargèd of thee." [3]

She said, "Sir, I dare speak to my lord of Lincoln right well, for I have had of him right good cheer afore this time." [4]

And then other men askèd her if she were in charity with the mayor, and she said, "Yea, and with all creatures." [5]

And then she, obeying her to the mayor, prayed him to be'n in charity with her (with weeping tears) and forgiven her anything that she had displeasèd him (and he gave her goodly words for a while, that she weened all had been well and he had been her good friend, but afterward she wist well it was not so); and thus she had leave of the mayor for to goen to my lord of Lincoln and fetten a letter by the which the mayor should be excusèd. [6]

## Chapter 52

[*Lincoln.*] On the next day she was brought into the archbishop's chapel, and there coomen many of the archbishop's meiny, despising her, calling her "Lollar" and "heretic," and sworen many an horrible oath that she should be brent. [7]

And she (thor'we the strength of Jesu) said again to 'hem, "Sirs, I dread me ye shall be brent in Hell withouten end, less-then ye amend you of your oath-swearing, for ye keep not the commaundments of God. I would not swearen as ye doen for all the good of this world!" [8]

Then they yeden away as they had been ashamèd. She then, making her prayer in her mind, askèd grace so to be demeanèd that day as was most pleasaunce to God and profit to her own soul and good example to her even-Cristen. [9]

Our Lord, answering her, said it should be right well.

At the last, the said archbishop came into the chapel with his clerks, and sharply he said to her, "Why goest thou in white? Art thou a maiden?"

She, kneeling on her knees beforn him, said, "Nay, sir, I am no maiden. I am a wife."

He commaunded his men to fetten a pair of fetters, and said she should be'n fetterèd, for she was a false heretic.

And then she said, "I am none heretic, ne ye shall none prieve me." [10]

The archbishop went away and let her stonden alone. Then she made her prayers to our Lord God almighty (for to helpen her and succoren her again' all her enemies, ghostly and bodily), a long while, and her flesh tremmellèd and hwakèd wonderly, that she was fain to putten her hands under her clothes, that it should not be'n espied. [11]

Sithen, the archbishop came again into the chapel with many worthy clerks, amongs' which was the same doctour which had examined her beforn and the monk that had preachèd again' her a little time beforn in York. Some of the people askèd wheder she were a Christen woman or a Jew; some said she was a good woman, and some

[1] *frere prechour* ] preaching friar; i.e., a Dominican; the Dominicans (also called the Black Friars) had a monastery in King's Lynn, Margery's home town.

[2] *doen* ] act; *if ... glad-like* ] if they dared to forbid me, they would gladly do so; *make no leesings* ] tell no lies.

[3] *letten* ] allow; *less-then* ] unless; *lord of Lincoln* ] Philip Repyngdon, bishop of Lincoln 1405 - 1419.

[4] *afore this time* ] the Kempes took vows of chastity before Bishop Repyngdon in the summer of 1413.

[5] *were in charity with* ] felt charitably towards.

[6] *obeying her* ] submitting herself; *excused* ] i.e., for not burning or hangint Margery Kempe as a heretic

[7] *meiny* ] household.

[8] *good* ] material good.

[9] *yeden away as* ] went away as if.

[10] *ne ye shall none prieve me* ] nor shall ye prove me one.

[11] *succored* ] give aid; *tremmelled and hwaked wonderly, that* ] trembled and quaked so terribly that.

said nay. [1]

Then the archbishop took his See, and his clerks also, each of 'hem in his degree, much people being present. And in the time while the people was gadering togeder and the archbishop taken his See, the said creature stood all behinden, making her prayers (for help and succor again' her enemies) with high devotion – so long that she melted all into tears. And at the last she cried loud therewith, that the archbishop and his clerks and much people had great wonder of her, for they had not heard swech crying beforn. When her crying was passèd, she came beforn the archbishop and fell down on her knees, the archbishop saying full boistously unto her, "Why weepest thou so, woman?" [2]

She, answering, said, "Sir, ye shall willen some day that ye had wept as sore as I!"

And then anon, after the archbishop put to her the articles of our faith – to the which God gave her grace to answeren well and truly and readily withouten any great study so that he might not blamen her – then he said to the clerks, "She knoweth her faith well enow. What shall I doen with her?"

The clerks saiden, "We knowen well that she can the articles of the faith, but we will not suffer her to dwellen among us, for the people hath great faith in her dalliaunce, and peraventure she might perverten some of 'hem." [3]

Then the archbishop said unto her, "I am evil informèd of thee: I hear sayen thou art a right wicked woman."

And she said again, "Sir, so I hear sayen that ye aren a wicked man. And, if ye be'n as wicked as men sayen, ye shall never come in Heaven less-then ye amend you while ye be'n here."

[1] *Sithen* ] After that.

[2] *See* ] episcopal seat, throne; *boistously* ] boisterously.

[3] *can* ] knows; *peraventure* ] peradventure, perhaps.

Then said he full boistously, "Why, thou —,° what say men of me!"

She answerèd, "Other men, sir, can tell you well enow." [4]

Then said a great clerk with a furrèd hood, "Peace, thou speak of thyself and let him be'n."

Sithen said the archbishop to her, "Lay thine hand on the book here beforn me and swear that thou shalt goen out of my diocese as soon as thou may."

"Nay, sir," she said, "I pray you, give me leave to goen again into York to take my leave of my friends."

Then he gave her leave for one day or two. She thought it° was too short a time, wherefore she said again, "Sir, I may not goen out of this diocese so hastily, for I must tarryen and speaken with good men ere I go, and I must, sir, with your leave, goen to Bridlington and speaken with my confessour, a good man, the which was the good prior's confessour that is now canonized." [5]

Then said the archbishop to her, "Thou shalt swearen that thou ne° shalt teachen ne challengen the people in my diocese."

"Nay, sir, I shall not swearen," she said, "for I shall speaken of God and under-nemine 'hem that swearen great oaths wheresoever I go, unto the time that the Pope and holy Church hath ordained that no man shall be so hardy to speaken of God – for God almightly forbiddeth not, sir, that we shall speak of him. And also the gospel maketh mention that when the woman had heard our Lord preachèd, she came beforn him with a loud voice and said, 'Blissèd be the womb that thee bare and the teats that gave thee sucken.' Then our Lord said again to her, 'Forsooth, so are they blissèd that hearen the word of God and keepen it.' And therefore, sir, me-thinketh that the gospel giveth me leave to speaken of God." [6]

"Ah sir," said the clerks, "here wot we well that she hath a devil within her, for she speaketh of the gospel." [7]

Aswithe a great clerk brought forth a book and laid Saint Paul for his partie agains' her, that no woman should preachen. [8]

[4] At Oxford, Repyngdon had been a supporter of the reformer, John Wycliffe; but in 1382 he abjured reformist doctrines, after which he became a strict churchman and a persecutor of Lollards.

[5] John of Bridlington, canonized by Pope Boniface IX in 1401, was the last Englishman to be canonized before Sir Thomas More and John Fisher in 1935.

[6] *hardy* ] bold.

[7] *wot* ] know.

[8] *Aswithe* ] immediately; *partie* ] part.

She, answering thereto, said, "I preach not, sir, I come in no pulpit. I use but communication and good words, and that will I do while I live."

Then said a doctour which had examinèd her before-time, "Sir, she teld me the worst tales of priests that ever I heard."

The bishop commaunded her to tellen that tale.

"Sir, with your reverence, I spake but of o' priest by the manner of example – the which, as I have learnèd, went wile in a wood, thor'we the sufferaunce of God for the profit of his soul, till the night came upon him. He, destitute of his harbor'we, found a fair arbor, in the which he rested that night, having a fair peartree in the mids' all flourishèd with flowers, and belshèd, and blooms full delectable to his sight; where came a bear, great and boistous, hugely to beholden, shaking the peartree and felling down the flowers. Greedily this grievous beast et and devourèd tho' fair flowers – and when he had eten 'hem, turning his tail-end in the priest's presence, voided 'hem out again at the hinder° partie. [1]

"The priest, having great abhomination of that loathly sight, conceiving great heaviness for doubt what it might mean, on the next day he wand'red forth in his way all heavy and pensive – whom it fortunèd to meeten with a seemly aged man like to a palmer or a pilgrim, the which enquirèd of the priest the cause of his heaviness. The priest, rehearsing the matter beforn-written, said he conceivèd great dread and heaviness when he beheld that loathly beast defoulen and devouren so fair flowers and blooms and afterward so horribly to devoiden 'hem before him at his tail-end, and he not understanding what this might mean. [2]

"Then the palmer, shewing himself the messenger of God, thus a-reasoned him, 'Priest, thou thyself art the peartree, some deal flourishing and flowering thor'we thy service-saying and the sacraments minist'ring, though thou do undevoutly, for thou takest full little heed how thou sayest thy matins and thy service, so it be blabberèd to an end. Then goest thou to thy Mass withouten devotion, and for thy sin hast thou full little contrition. Thou receivest there the fruit of everlasting life, the sacrament of the autar, in full feeble disposition. Sithen, all the day after thou mispendest thy time – thou givest thee to buying and selling, chopping and changing, as it were a man of the world. Thou sittest at the ale, giving thee to gluttony and excess, to lust of thy body, thor'we lechery and uncleanness. Thou breakest the commaundments of God thor'we swearing, lying, detraction, and backbiting, and swech other sins using. Thus by thy misgovernaunce, like onto the loathly bear, thou devourest and destroyest the flowers and blooms of virtuous living, to thine endless damnation and many man's hind'ring (less-then thou have grace of repentaunce and amending).'" [3]

Then the archbishop likèd well the tale and commended it, saying it was a good tale. And the clerk which had examined her before-time in the absence of the archbishop, said, "Sir, this tale smiteth me to the heart."

The foresaid creature said to the clerk, "A worshipful doctour, sir, in place where my dwelling is most, is a worthy clerk, a good preacher, which boldly speaketh again' the misgovernaunce of the people and will flatter no man. He sayeth many times in the pulpit, 'If any man be evil-pleasèd with my preaching, note him well, for he is guilty.' And right so, sir," said she to the clerk, "fare ye by me – God forgive it you."

The clerk wist not well what he might say to her. Afterward the same clerk came to her and prayèd her of forgiveness that he had so been again' her. Also he prayèd her specially to pray for him.

And then anon after, the archbishop said, "Where shall I have a man that might leaden this woman fro' me?"

A-swith there stirred up many young men, and every man said of 'hem, "My lord, I will goen with her!" [4]

The archbishop answerèd, "Ye be'n too young. I will not have you."

Then a good sad man of the archbishop's meiny askèd his lord what he would given him and he should leaden her. The archbishop profferèd him five shillings° – and the man askèd a noble. The archbishop, answering, said, "I will not waren so much on her body." [5]

"Yes, good sir," said the said creature, "our Lord shall rewarden you right well again."

---

[1] *went wile* ] went astray; *harbor'we* ] harbor; *destitute of his harbor'we* ] lacking his usual shelter; *belshèd* ] embellished; *tho* ] those.

[2] *palmer* ] a pilgrim having been to the Holy Land; *heaviness* ] despondency; what this might mean ] *Margery modifies the obvious inference that the foul priest is like the bear, consuming what is good (the Gospel) and turning it to excrement.*

[3] *so it be* ] so long as it be; *chopping and changing, as it were* ] shopping and exchanging as if you were.

[4] *a-swith* ] swiftly.

[5] *sad* ] sober, solemn; *and* ] if; *noble* ] an English gold coin worth 6 shillings 8 pence; *waren* ] spend.

Then the archbishop said to the man, "See, here is five shillings, and lead her fast out of this country."

She, kneeling down on her knees, askèd his blessing. He, praying her to pray for him, blissèd her and let her go.

Then she, going again to York, was received of much people and of full worthy clerks, which enjoyed in our Lord that had gooven her not-lett'red wit and wisdom, to answeren so many learnèd men withouten villainy or blame (thanking be to God!). [1]

## Chapter 53

Sithen, that good man which was her leader brought her out of the town, and then went they forth to Bridlington to her confessour, which hight Sleytham, and spake with him and with many other good men which had cheerèd her before-time and done much for her. Then she would not abiden there but took her leave for to walk forth in her journey. And then her confessour askèd her if she durst not abiden for the Archbishop of York – and she said, "No, forsooth." Then the good man gave her silver, beseeching her to pray for him. [2]

And so she yede forth unto Hull. And there on a time, as they went in procession, a great woman all-to despised her; and she said no word thereto. Many other folk said that she should be set in prison, and maden great threating. And notwithstanding all 'heir malice, yet a good man came and prayed her to meat, and made her right good cheer. Then the malicious people, the which had despisèd her beforn, came to this good man and bade him that he should do her no good, for they held that she was no good woman.

On the next day at morr'wen her host led her out at the town's end, for he° durst no lenger keepen her. And so she went to Hessle, and would ha' gone over the water at Humber. Then happèd she to finden there two frere prechours, and two yeomen of the Duke of Bedford's. The freres teld the yeomen that woman she was, and the yeomen arrested her as she would ha' taken her boat, and 'rested a man that went with her also – "For our lord," they said, "the duke of Bedford, hath sent for thee. And thou art holden the greatest Lollar in all this country – or about London, either. And we han sought thee in many a country, and we shall han an hundred pound for to bring thee beforn our lord." [3]

She said to 'hem, "With good will, sirs, I shall goen with you where ye will leaden me."

Then they brought her again into Hessle, and there men callèd her "Lollar," and women came renning out of 'heir houses with 'heir rocks, crying to the people, "Brenneth this false heretic!" So, as she went forth to-Beverley-ward with the said yeomen and the freres befornsaid, they metten many times with men of the country, which said unto her, "Damsel, forsake this life that thou hast, and go spin and card as other women doen, and suffer not so much shame and so much woe. We would not suffer so much for no good in eard." [4]

Then she said to 'hem, "I suffer not so much sorr'we as I *would* do for our Lord's love – for I suffer but shrewèd words, and our merciful Lord Christ Jesu (worshiped be his name!) suffered hard strokes, bitter scourgings, and shameful death at the last, for me and for all mankind, blissèd mote he be! And therefore it is right nought, that I suffer, in regard to that he suffered." And so, as she went with the foresaid men, she teld 'hem good tales – till one of the duke's men which had arrested her said unto her, "Me over-thinketh that I met with thee, for meseemeth that thou sayest right good words." [5]

Then said she unto him, "Sir, overthinketh ne repenteth you not that ye met with me. Doeth your lord's will, and I trust all shall be for the best, for I am right well pleasèd that ye met with me."

He said again, "Damsel, if ever thou be saint° in Heaven, pray for me."

She answerèd, saying to him again, "Sir, I hope ye shall be a saint yourself, and every man that shall come to Heaven."

So they yeden forth till they coomen into Beverley, where dwellèd one of the men's wifes that had arrested her. And thider they ledden her, and tooken away fro' her her purse and her ring. They ordained her a fair chamber and an honest bed therein, with the necessaries, locking the door with the key and bearing away the key with 'hem.

---

[1] *enjoyed* ] rejoiced; *that had gooven* ] who had given; *not-lett'red* ] unschooled.

[2] *hight* ] was called; *durst not abiden for* ] dared not remain on account of.

[3] *country* ] region, county.

[4] *rocks* ] distaffs (the staff that held the unspun flax or wool); *in eard* ] on earth.

[5] *that ... that* ] that which ... that which; *Me over-thinketh* ] I regret.

Sithen, they tooken the man whom they arrested with her, which was the archbishop's man of York, and put him in prison; and soon after that same day came tidings that the archbishop was comen into the town where his man was put in prison. It was teld the archbishop of his man's prisoning, and anon he did him be letten out. Then that man went to the said creature with angry cheer, saying, "Alas that every knew I ye! I have been prisonèd for thee."

She, comforting him, said again, "Haveth meekness and patience, and ye shall have great meed in Heaven therefore." So yede he away fro' her. [1]

Then stood she looking out at a windown, telling many good tales to 'hem that would hearen her, insomuch that women wept sore and said with great heaviness of 'heir hearts, "Alas, woman, why shalt thou be brent?"

Then she prayèd the goodwife of the house to given her drink, for she was evil for thrist – and the goodwife said her husbond had borne away the key, wherefore she might not comen to her, ne given her drink. And then the women tooken a ladder, and set up to the windown, and gooven her a pint of wine in a pot and took her a piece, beseeching her to seten away the pot privily, and the piece, that when the goodman coom he might not espy it. [2]

### Chapter 54

The said creature, lying in her bed the next night foll'wing, heard with her bodily ears a loud voice, cleping, "Margery!" With that voice she woke, greatly afearèd, and, lying still in silence, she made her prayers as devoutly as she could for the time. And soon our merciful Lord, over-all present, comforting his unworthy servaunt, said unto her, "Doughter, it is more pleasing unto me that thou suffer despites and scorns, shames and repriefs, wrongs and dis-ease, than if thine head were smit off three times on the day every day in seven year! And therefore, doughter, fear thee not what any man can sayen unto thee, but in mine goodness. And in thy sorr'wes, that thou hast sufferèd therein, hast thou great cause to joyen, for when thou comest home into Heaven, then shall every sorr'we turnen thee to joy." [3]

On the next day she was brought into the chapital-house of Beverley, and there was the archbishop of York, and many great clerks with him, priests, chanons, and secular men. Then said the archbishop to the said creature, "What, woman, art thou come again? I would fain be deliverèd of thee".... [4]

Then said his steward and many moe with him, crying with a loud voice to the archbishop, "My° lord, we pray you, let her go hence at this time, and if ever she come again, we shall bren her ourself!"

The archbishop said, "I 'lieve there was never woman in Englond so feared withal as she is and hath been." Then he said to the said creature, "I wot not what I shall doen with thee."

She said, "My lord, I pray you, let me have your letter and your seal into record, that I have excusèd me again' mine enemies and nothing is attied agains' me, neither herrour ne heresy that may be'n prievèd upon me (thankèd be our Lord!); and John, your man, again to bringen me over the water." And the archbishop full goodly graunted her all her desire (our Lord reward him his meed!), and deliverèd her purse with her ring and her beads which the duke's men of Bedford had taken fro' her beforn. [5]

The archbishop had great marvel where she had good to goen with abouten the country. And she said good men gave it her, for she should pray for 'hem. [6]

Then she, kneeling down, received his blissing and took her leave with right glad cheer, going out of his chamber. And the archbishop's men prayed her to pray for 'hem, but the steward was wroth (for she lough and made good cheer), saying to her, "Holy folk should not laugh." [7]

She said, "Sir, I have great cause to laugh, for the more shame I suffer, and despite, the merrier may I be'n in our Lord Jesu Christ!"...

### Chapter 75

As the said creature was in a church of Saint Margaret to say her devotions, there came a man kneeling at her back, wringing his hands and shewing tokens of great heaviness. She, perceiving his heaviness, askèd what him ailèd. He said it stood right hard with him, for his wife was newly deliverèd of a child and she was out her mind.

---

[1] *meed* ] reward.

[2] *evil for thrist* ] sick with thirst; *gooven* ] gave; *piece* ] cup; *seten away ... the piece* ] hide the pot of wine and the cup.

[3] *over-all* ] everywhere; *repriefs* ] reproofs; *in* ] for.

[4] *chapital-house* ] chapter-house.

[5] *attied* ] formally charged; *herrour* ] error.

[6] *good* ] money.

[7] *lough* ] laughed; *wroth* ] angry.

"And, dame," he sayeth, "she knoweth not me, ne none of her neighbours. She roareth and crieth so that she maketh folk evil a-feared. She will both smiten and biten, and therefore is she manacled on her wrists."

Then askèd she the man if he would that she went with him and saw her, and he said, "Yea, dame, for God's love."

So she went forth with him to see the woman. And when she came into the house, as soon as the sick woman that was alienèd of her wit saw her, she spake to her sadly and goodly and said she was right welcome to her; and she was right glad of her coming and greatly comforted by her presence: "For ye aren," she said, "a right good woman, and I beheld many fair aungels about you, and therefore, I pray you, goeth not fro' me, for I am greatly comforted by you." [1]

And when other folk came to her, she crièd and gapèd as she would han eten 'hem and said that she saw many devils abouten 'hem. She would not sufferen 'hem to touchen her by her good will. She roarèd and crièd so, both night and day for the most part, that men would not suffer her to dwellen amongs' 'hem, she was so tedious to 'hem. Then was she had to the furthest end of the town, into a chamber, that the people should not hearen her cryen. And there was she bounden hands and feet with chains of iron, that she should smiten nobody.

And the said creature went to her each day, once or twice at the least-way; and while she was with her, she was meek enow and heard her speaken and dallyen with good will, withouten any roaring or crying. And the said creature prayèd for this woman every day – that God should, if it were his will, restoren her to her wits again. And our Lord answerèd in her soul and said she should faren right well. Then was she more bold to prayen for her recuring than she was beforn; and each day, weeping and sorr'wing, prayèd for her recure till God gave her her wit and her mind again – and then was she brought to church and purified as other women be (blissèd mote God be'n!). It was, as 'hem thought that knewen it, a right great miracle.... [2]

## Chapter 76

It happèd on a time that the husbond of the said creature (a man in great age, passing three-score year), as he would ha' coomen down of his chamber barefoot and bare-leg, he slidderèd or else failèd of his footing and fell down to the ground fro' the greces, and his hevyd under him grievously broken and bruisèd, insomuch that he had in his hevyd five teints many days while his hevyd was in wholing. [3]

And, as God would, it was known to some of his neighbours (how he was fallen down off the greces), peraventure thor'we the din and the lushing of his falling. And so they coomen to him and founden him lying with his hevyd under him, half on life, all rowèd with blood, never like to ha' spoken with priest ne with clerk but thor'we high grace and miracle. [4]

Then the said creature, his wife, was sent for, and so she came to him. Then was he taken up and his hevyd was sewèd, and he was sick a long time after, that men weened that he should ha' be' dead.

And then the people said, if he died his wife was worthy to be'n hangen for his death, forasmuch as she might ha' kept him and did not. (They dwellèd not togeder, ne they lay not togeder, for – as is written beforn – they bothen, with one assent and with free will of 'heir either, hadden made a-vow to liven chaste). And therefore to enschewen all perils they dwellèd and sojourèd in divers places where no suspicion should be'n had of 'heir incontinence (for first they dwellèd togeder after that they had made 'heir vow, and then the people slaund'red 'hem and said they usèd 'heir lust and 'heir liking as they didden beforn 'heir vow-making). And when they wenten out on pilgrimage, or to see and speaken with other ghostly creatures, many evil folk whose tongues were 'heir own hurt,° failing the dread and love of our Lord Jesu Christ, deem'den and saiden that they went rather to woods, groves, or valleys, to usen the lust of 'heir bodies, that the people should not espyen it ne witten it. [5]

---

[1] *as soon ... welcome to her* ] when the woman who was out of her mind saw Margery, the woman spoke to Margery, etc.; *sadly* ] soberly; *goodly* ] kindly; *aungels* ] angels.

[2] *at the least-way* ] at least; *dallyen* ] keep fellowship; *recuring . . . recure* ] recovery.

[3] *greces* ] stairs; *hevyd* ] head; *teints* ] medicated linen plugs; *wholing* ] healing.

[4] *lushing* ] crash; *on life* ] alive; *rowèd* ] streaked.

[5] *enschewen* ] eschew, avoid; *sojourèd* ] sojourned; stayed as temporary residents; *liking* ] pleasure; *deem'den* ] supposed.

They, having knowlach how prone the people was to deemen evil of 'hem, desiring to avoiden all occasion (inasmuch as they might goodly), by 'heir good will and 'heir bothens consenting, they parted asunder as touching to 'heir board and to 'heir chaumb'res, and wenten to board in divers places. And this was the cause that she was not with him (and also that she should not be letted fro' her contemplation). And therefore, when he had fallen and grievously was hurt (as is said beforn), the people said if he dièd it was worthy that she should answeren for his death. [1]

Then she prayèd to our Lord that her husbond might liven a year and she to be deliverèd out slaunder if it were his pleasaunce. Our Lord said to her mind, "Doughter, thou shalt have thy boon, for he shall liven – and I have wrought a great miracle for thee that he was not dead. And I bid thee take him home and keep him for my love."

She said, "Nay, good Lord, for I shall then not tenden to thee as I do now." [2]

"Yes, doughter," said our Lord, "thou shalt have as much meed for to keepen him and helpen him in his need at home as if thou were in church to maken thy prayers. And thou hast said many times that thou wouldst fain keepen me. I pray thee now keep him for the love of me, for he hath sometime fulfillèd thy will and my will both, and he hath made thy body free to me that thou should'st serven me and liven chaste and clean, and therefore I will that thou be free to helpen him at his need, in my name." [3]

"Ah, Lord," said she, "for thy mercy graunt me grace to obeyen thy will and fulfill thy will and let never my ghostly en'mies han no power to lett me fro' fulfilling of thy will." [4]

Then she took home her husbond to her and kept him years after, as long as he livèd, and had full much labor with him – for in his last days he turnèd childish again and lackèd reason, that he could not doen his own easement to goen to a sedge, or else he would not, but as a child voided his natural digestion in his linen clothes there he sat by the fire or at the table, wheder it were, he would sparen no place. And therefore was her labor much the more in washing and wringing and her costage in firing, and letted her full much fro' her contemplation, that many times she should han irkèd her labor save she bethought her how she in her young age had full many delectable thoughts, fleshly lusts, and inordinate loves to his person. And therefore she was glad to be punishèd with the same person, and took it much the more easily, and servèd him and helpèd him, as her-thought, as she would ha' done Christ himself. [5]

**Chapter 88**

When this book was first in writing, the said creature was more at home in her chamber with her writer and said fewer beads (for speed of writing) than she had done years beforn. And when she came to church and should hearen Mass, purposing to sayen her matins and swech other devotions as she had usèd aforetime, her heart was drawen away fro' the saying and set much on meditation.

She being a-feared of displeasaunce of our Lord, he said to her soul, "Dread thee not, doughter, for as many beads as thou wouldest sayen I accept 'hem as though thou said'st 'hem, and thy study that thou studiest – for to do writen the grace that I have shewèd to thee – pleaseth me right much, and he that writeth, both. For though ye were in the church and wept bothen togeder as sore as ever thou did'st, yet should ye not pleasen me more than ye doen with your writing; for, doughter, by this book many a man shall be turnèd to me and believen therein...." [6]

---

[1] *knowlach* ] knowledge; *chaumb'res* ] chambers; *letted fro* ] hindered in.

[2] *delivered out* ] delivred from; *tenden* ] attend.

[3] *meed* ] reward.

[4] *lett* ] prevent, hinder.

[5] *sedge* ] privy-stool; *there he sat* ] where he sat; *wheder it were* ] wherever he was; *costage in firing* ] expense for fuel; *letted* ] hindered; *irked* ] resented.

[6] *She being* ] In that she was; *For though ye* ] For even if you.

## Chapter 89

Also, while the foresaid creature was occupièd about the writing of this treatise, she had many holy tears and weepings, and oftentimes there came a flaume of fire about her breast full hot and delectable (and also he that was her writer could not sometime keepen himself fro' weeping!). And often in the meantime, when the creature was in church, our Lord Jesu Christ with his glorious moder and many saints also coomen into her soul and thankèd her, saying that they were well pleasèd with the writing of this book. And also she heard many times a voice of a sweet brid singing in her ear, and oftentimes she heard sweet sounds and melodies that passèd her wit for to tellen 'hem. And she was many time sick while this treatise was in writing – and as soon as she would goen about the writing of this treatise, she was hale and whole suddenly in a manner. And often she was commaunded to maken her ready in all haste....

Sometime she was in great heaviness for her feelings (when she knew not how they should be'n understonden) many days togeder, for dread that she had of deceits and illusions, that her-thought she would that her hevyd had be' smit fro' the body – till God of his goodness declarèd 'hem to her mind. For sometime, that she understood *bodily*, it was to be'n understonden *ghostly* – and the dread that she had of her feelings was the greatest scourge that she had in eard (and specially when she had her first feelings), and that dread made her full meek; for she had no joy in the feeling till she knew by experience whether it was true or not. But ever blissèd mote God be'n! – for he made her alway more mighty and more strong in his love and in his dread and gave her increase of virtue, with persévéraunce. [1]

Here endeth this treatise, for God took him to his mercy that wrote the copy of this book, and, though that he wrote not clearly ne openly to our manner of speaking, he in his manner of writing and spelling made true sentence – the which, thor'we the help of God and of herself that had all this treatise in feeling and working, is truly drawen out of the copy into this little book. [2]

[1] *that her-thought ... body* ] that she thought she would like to have her head smitten off; *sometime that* ] sometimes, that which; *eard* ] earth.

[2] *copy* ] the original MS by Margery's son, illegible and apparently corrupted with Prussian diction; the priest has finished transcribing the original narrative under Margery's direction, after the son's death; *this little book* ] the newly copied and revised manuscript.

Mater Dolorosa, by Rogier van der Weyden (c. 1435), *Museo del Prado* (*Madrid*)

## THE SECOND BOOK

## Chapter 10

This creature, of whom is treated beforn, usèd many years to beginnen her prayers on this manner: ... When she had said "Veni creator spiritus" with the verses, she said on this manner, "The holy Ghost I take to witness; our Lady, Saint Mary, the moder of God; all holy court of Heaven; and all my ghostly faders here in eard, that, though it were possible that I might han all knowing and understanding of the privities of God by the telling of any devil of Hell, I would not. And as wistly as I would° not knowen, hearen, seien, feelen, ne understonden in my soul in this life more than is the will of God that I should knowen, so wistly God mote helpen me in all my works, in all my thoughts, and in all my speeches, eating and drinking, sleeping and waking.... [3]

"As for my crying, my sobbing, and my weeping, Lord God almighty, as wistly as thou knowest what scorns, what shames, what despites, and what repriefs I have had therefor, and, as wistly as it is not in my power to weepen, neither loud ne still, for no devotion ne for no sweetness, but only of the gift of the holy Ghost, so wistly, Lord, excuse me again' all this world to knowen and to

[3] *Veni creator spiritus* ] "Come, Creator Spirit," a hymn addressed to the holy Ghost; *privities* ] secrets; *seien* ] seeing; *wistly* ] surely.

trowen that it is thy work and thy gift for magnifying of thy name and for increasing of other men's love to thee, Jesu. [1]

"And I pray thee, sovereign Lord Christ Jesu, that as many men mote be turnèd by my crying and my weeping as me han scornèd therefor, or shall scornen, into the word's end – and many moe, if it be your will. And, as anemst any eardly man's love, as wistly as I would no love han but God to loven above all thing, and all other creatures loven for God and in God, also wistly quench in me all fleshly lust and in all tho' that I have beholden thy blissful body in. And give us thine holy dread in our hearts, for thy wounds' smart. [2]

"Lord, make my ghostly faders for to dreaden thee in me and for to loven thee in me, and make all the world for to han the more sorr'we for 'heir own sins for the sorr'we that thou hast gooven me for other men's sins. Good Jesu, make my will thy will, and thy will my will, that I may no will han but thy will only....

"I cry thee mercy, blissful Lord, for the king of Englond and for all Cristen kings and for all lords and ladies that aren in this world. God, set 'hem in swech governaunce as they may most pleasen thee° and be'n lords and ladies in Heaven, withouten end.

"I cry thee mercy, Lord, for the rich men in this world that han thy goods in wielding; give 'hem grace for to spenden 'hem to thy pleasing...[3]

"I cry thee mercy, Lord, for all false heretics and for all misbelievers, for all false tithers, thieves, vowtries, and all common women, and for all mischievous livers. Lord, for thy mercy have mercy upon 'hem if it be thy will and bring 'hem out of 'heir misgovernaunce the sooner, for my prayers. [4]

"I cry thee mercy, Lord, for all tho' that aren tempted and vexèd with 'heir ghostly enemies, that thou of thy mercy will° give 'hem grace to withstonden 'heir temptations and deliver 'hem thereof when it is thy most pleasaunce.

"I cry thee mercy, Lord, for all my ghostly faders, that thou vouchsafe to spreaden as much grace in 'heir souls as I would that thou didst in mine.

"I cry thee mercy, Lord, for all my childeren, ghostly and bodily, and for all the people in this world, that thou make 'heir sins to me by very contrition as it were mine own sins, and forgive 'hem as I would that thou forgive me. [5]

"I cry thee mercy, Lord, for all my friends and for all mine enemies, for all that aren sick specially, for all lazaries, for all bedrid men and women, for all that aren in prison, and for all creatures that in this world han spoken of me either good or ill or shall doen into the world's end. Have mercy upon 'hem and be as gracious to 'heir souls as I would that thou were to mine. [6]

"And they that han said any evil of me, for thy high mercy, forgive it 'hem; and they that han said well, I pray thee, Lord, reward 'hem (for that is thor'we 'heir charity and not thor'we my merits); for though thou suffered'st all this world to vengen thee on me and to haten me for I have displeasèd thee, thou didst me no wrong.... [7]

"I pray my Lady – which that is only the moder of God, the well of grace, flower and fairest of all women that ever God wrought in eard, the most worthiest in his sight, the most lief, dear, and dear-worthy unto him, best worthy to be'n heard of God, and the highest that hath deservèd it in this life – benign Lady, meek Lady, charityful Lady, with all the reverence that is in Heaven and with all your holy saints, I pray you, Lady, offer ye thanks and praisings to the blissful Trinity for love of me, asking mercy and grace for me and for all my ghostly faders, and perseveraunce into our lives' end in that life we° may most pleasen God in.... [8]

"Gra'mercy, Lord, for all tho' sins that thou hast kept me fro' which I have *not* do'; and gra'mercy, Lord, for all the sorr'we that thou hast gooven me for tho' that I *have* do'; for these graces and for all other graces which aren needful to me and to all the creatures in eard. And for all tho' that faithen and trusten, or shall faithen and trusten in my prayers into the world's end, swech grace as they desiren, ghostly or bodily, to the profit of 'heir souls, I pray thee, Lord, graunt 'hem – for the multitude of thy mercy. Amen." [9]

---

[1] *excuse* ] defend; *trowen* ] believe.

[2] *that as many ... moe* ] that the number who repent due to my weeping will be as great, greater than, the number who have scorned me for it; *word's* ] world's; *anemst* ] as regards; *no love han but God to loven* ] have no love but a love for God; *all tho* ] all those; *for thy wounds' smart* ] for the sake of your painful wounds suffered on the cross.

[3] *wielding* ] possession.

[4] *vowtries* ] adulterers.

[5] *make 'heir sins* ] charge their sins.

[6] *lazaries* ] lepers.

[7] *vengen* ] avenge.

[8] *lief* ] beloved; *charityful* ] charitable.

[9] *gra-mercy* ] grant mercy.

# Katherine of Kent (fl. 1420s)

*Than my fader was fulle fayne*
*And callede hem to hym alle in fere*
*And seyde, "How sped ye there ye were,*
*How faren the nunnes that ye cam tylle?"*
(lines 26-29)

NUN WOULD I NEVER BE NONE narrates the spiritual journey of a woman of county Kent. She may not actually be from Kent, which is the point of departure and return for the action. Her true name may not be Katherine, although her father calls her by that name in the text. She may not even be real – both the speaker and her dream vision could be constructions of a clever male poet with an axe to grind. But the narrator, in her modest sincerity and dutiful obedience to a jolly father, presents a compelling narrative in a voice that sounds remarkably authentic.

A pious teen in a wealthy family, Katherine dreams of joining a convent. Her father withholds his consent, having learned, from the bishop's commissioners who visit the religious houses, that the nunneries of England have grown corrupt. Obedient but broken-hearted, the disappointed narrator turns to the Lord in prayer. Retiring one spring morning to the family gardens, she falls asleep; whereupon she has a vision much like "The Assembly of Ladies" and "The Flower and the Leaf," except that her dream illuminates the Catholic sisterhood rather than the royal court. Lady Experience has come to Katherine to give her a tour of a representative English convent: a nunnery governed by dames Sloth, Vainglory, Envy, Love Unordinate, Lust, Wanton, Nice [fastidious], and the worst, Dame Disobedient. Charity and Patience, marginal virtues in this house, must dwell apart in an outer chamber. Dame Devout has been evicted. Chastity is ready to pack her bags, and most of her sisters will be happy to see her go.

If Katherine's first sorrow was her father's refusal to get her to a nunnery, a greater disappointment comes upon learning that conventual life is nothing like her ideal. Katherine hints that Experience has given her an eyeful, more than she may with modesty disclose but enough to justify her decision, which has brought her into line with the will of both her earthly and heavenly Fathers: "nun would I never be none, / For such defauts that I have see'!" She worries that some readers will say that she "soon forsook a perfit way / And forfeited what might have been / For a fantasy or dream"; but Katherine is content that her inspiration came directly from God and is none of her own vain imagination. Nor is her decision final: "if they might amended be, / And forsake 'heir sin both day and night," she would be ready, father willing, to try again. Katherine closes her narrative with a homily to naughty nuns whose lax religious discipline have spoiled her original dream, exhorting the sisters of England to mend their ways and to follow the example of the female saints.

"Nun would I never be none" survives as a unique copy in a well-worn manuscript of the early fifteenth century, where it appears among articles both for and against the reform movement. Some verses in the collection venerate the Virgin Mary, or attack the Lollards, or applaud Rome for its response to heresy in Bohemia (where John Hus was burned at the stake in 1415 for having criticized the Church's sale of indulgences). Other articles are stridently reformist, denouncing England's corrupt clergy and monastics. The volume's compiler appears to have been a spiritual person committed to religious orthodoxy as set forth by Rome, but troubled by the failure of the Church to embody its own ideals. In choosing "Nun would I never be nun" for inclusion, he deletes much of the narrative frame: the poem's prologue (which evidently told of the bishops' dispatching commissaries to visit the nunneries), and its conclusion (doubtless affirming holiness and chastity without taking religious orders) are omitted: the scribe begins *in medias res* and breaks off in mid-stanza, but not before Katherine has been given opportunity to share her dream.

Portrait of a Woman called the Nun (1506-10), by Ridolfo Ghirlandaio
*Galleria degli Uffizi (Florence)*

DWF

## For Nun Would I Never be None

By Katherine of Kent

…And when they had received 'heir charge,
They sparèd neither mud ne mire,
But rode o'er° Inglond, broad and large,
To seek out nunneries in every shire.
'heir hearts were alway on 'heir *hire*,
(That showed they well in 'heir workíng,
For they were as fervent as any fire
To execute 'heir lord's biddíng.) 1

And shortly to say, no man abode
That on this errand should be sent:
Into divers shires divers men rode,
And one of 'hem began in Kent.
They tooken 'heir leave and forth they went.
And to each of 'hem was given great hire,
And therefore were they° so fervént
To seek out nunneries in every shire. 2

But the townès' names I overpass,
For an' I should tell all in-fere,
[And every nunnery, by the Mass!°]
It were a long tale for to hear.
But on a book I dare well swear,
In good faith and on womanhood,
None was forgot, far ne near,
Thorough Inglond, long and broad. 3

But when they were come home again
That roden out message to bear,
Then my fader was full fain
And called 'hem to him, all in-fere,
And said, "How speed ye, there ye were?
How faren the nuns that ye came till?"
"Well, sir!" quod they; "and made us cheer,°
And your desire they woll fulfill!" 4

"I thank 'hem, sirs, iwis," quod he.
"Now am I glad, so God me speed."
And then my fader looked on me.
"Damsel," quod he, "now take good heed:
For your *intent*, God do you meed:
Ye said [that°] ye would be a nun.
But ye may not fulfill in deed
The purpose that ye have begun." 5

"Fader," quod I (and sore I wept),
"Woll ye me hear with wordès few?
I trow my will shall be accept
Before our sovereign Lord Ihesú!
To° him I am and woll be true
With all my will and observaunce,
And° woll not change him for no new,
For I love him without° variaunce. 6

"And truly me repents° full sore
That my will may not be had."
My° fader lough and said no more,
But went his way and was full glad.
But then mourned I, and was right sad,
And in my heart I was full woe:
"Alas," I thought, "my chaunce is bad!
I trow that Fortune be my foe." 7

Then it befell in a morn° of May,
In the same year as I said before,
My pensiveness would not away
But ever waxèd more and more.
I walked alone and weptè sore
With sighings and a° mourning cheer,
I said but little and thought the more,
(For what I thought, no man might hear).

Pietro Lorenzetti, detail (1341). Uffizi Gallery

---

[1] *spared* ] avoided; *fire* ] with pun on *fere,* companion, mate.

[2] *abode* ] dallied.

[3] *an'* ] (and) if; *in-fere* ] together, all at once; *And…Mass* ] conjectural emendation for missing line; *Hit* ] it (frequent); *Through* ] through.

[4] *fain* ] eager, pleased, desirous; *desire … fulfill* ] will satisfy a man's (sexual) desire.

[5] *iwis* ] surely; *meed* ] reward.

[6] *trow* ] believe; *Ihesu* ] (yay-*soo*) Jesus; *no new* ] for any other (human) lord.

[7] *lough* ] laughed.

And in a garden I sported me
Every day at divers hours,
To behold and for to see
The sweet effect of April showers,°
The fair herbès and gentle floures
And birds° singing on every spray,
But my longing and my dolours
For all this sport would not away. [1]

The birds sat on the bowès green
And sang° full merrily and made good cheer;
'heir feaders were full fair and sheen
And all made merry in 'heir manère.
Then went I in° a fair herbère,
And set me on my knees alone.
To God I made my [pitous°] prayèr,
And on this wise I made my moan: [2]

"Lord God, that allè virtue hast
And hadst withouten beginning,
Keep me that I may liven° chaste
Fro' the° corruption of sinning;
For though my fader and all my kin
Forsake me thus in necessity,
Yet I hope such grace to win
That our Lord Ihesu woll receive me.

"Sovereign Lord omnipotent,
Now be my comfort, sweet Ihesu.
Before thee all thing is presént,
All that was, and all that is,
All that shall be after this.
Thou knowest all thing, both most and lest.
Now Ihesu king of Heaven bliss,
Wiss me, thy servant, what is best. [3]

"For now I am all desolate,
And of good counsel destitute.
Lord, to my mourning be mediate,
For thou art only my refute,
To thee for comfort I make my suit,
To have that joy that lasteth aye,
For her love that bare that fruit,
Sweet Ihesu, *miserere mei*! [4]

"I can no more, but trust in thee
In whom is all wisdom and wit;
And thou wost what is best for me,
For all thing in thy sight is pit.
Lo, here I, thine handmaid, sit
Despisèd and in point to spill.
My cause to thee, Lord, I commit:
Now do to me after thy will." [5]

And at that word for faint I fell
Among the herbès fresh and fine.
Unto a bench of camomile
My woeful head I did incline,
And so I lay in full great pine,
And could not cease but alway weep,
And sore I sighèd many a time
And prayed my Lord he would me keep. [6]

And at the last a sleep was brought
And all alone in this gardene.
Then° come a fair lady, as methought,
And called me by name, "Kat'rine,"
And said, "Awake, doughter mine,
And to my talking take intent.
To bring thine heart out of pine,
And to comfort thee, now have I meant.

"Katerine," she said, "look up and have."
Then° I beheld well her figúre:
I pray to God in Heaven her save,
For it was the most goodly creatúre
That ever I saw, I you ensure,
As I woll tell you ere I go,
For I beheld well her feature,
Her beauty, and her clothing also.

And methought I was as waking tho,
As I am now withouten lesing;
And I beheld that lady so
That I forgat all my mourning,
For it was to me a wonder thing
That lady to behold° and see:
She was so fair without° lesing
Both of clothing and of beautié, [7]

This that was so goodly 'rayed°.
Comforteth° me in divers wise,
And spake to me ["Be not dismayed,"°]
And bade me anon I should arise.
Methought I rose and kneelèd thrice,
And said to her with great reverence,
"What is your name, dame emprized?"
She said, "My name is *Experience*." [8]

"And, daughter, my teaching may not fail,
For what so I teach, it is full true,
And now at this time for thine avail
I am come hither on thee to rue;

---

[1] *spray* ] branch.

[2] *sheen* ] shining; *herbiere* ] herbary, garden.

[3] *Wiss* ] Inform.

[4] *only my refute* ] my only refuge; *miserere mei* ] have mercy on me.

[5] *wost* ] wottest, knowest; *in point to spill* ] about to be ruined.

[6] *pine* ] grief, sorrow.

[7] *tho* ] then; *lesing* ] lying or exaggeration.

[8] *dame emprized* ] honored lady.

And with the help of Christ Ihesu
I hope it shall be for the best,
For such things as I shall thee shew,
I trow it shall set thine heart in rest."

"Thank you, lady," quod I then,
"And thereof heartily I you pray;
And I, as lowly as I can,
Woll do you service night and day;
And what ye bid me do or say
To you I promise° obedience.
Bring° me out of this careful way,
My good dear Lady Experience."

Methought° she took me by the hond
As I kneeled upon my knee
And up anon she bade me stond°
And on this wise [she°] said to me:
"Kat'rine, this day shalt thou see
An house of women regular.
And diligent look that thou be,
And note right well what thou seest there." [1]

Methought°she led me forth a pace
Thorough a meadow fair and green,
And soon she brought me to a place,
(In Earth is none so fair, I wene)
Of royal building so I mean,
It shined without so fair and clear!
—But sin had made it full unclean
Within, as ye shall after hear. [2]

"What place is this that stondeth here,"
Quod I to her that did me lead.
"Kat'rine," she said, "we will go near,
And what thou° seest, take good heed."
Then at the gatès in we yede,
Boldly as though we had be' at home,
And I thought: "Now Christ us speed."
Then to the cloister soon we come, [3]

For it was a house of nuns in truth,
Of divers orders, both old and young,
But not well governed (and that was ruth!)
After the rule of sad living.
For where that self-will is reigning,
Th' which causeth discord and debate,
And reason hath none entering,
That house may not be fortunate! [4]

For Aristotle, whoso readeth,
In the first book of his *Morality*,
Plainly sayeth that "Every man needeth
To beware of th' unreasonability
That comes of° sensuality,
And not his beastly conditions sue,
But let reason have th' sovereignty,
And so he shall purchase vertúe."

But what in that place I saw
That to religion should not 'long,
Peraventure ye would desire to know,
And who was dwelling 'hem among.
Somewhat shall I tell you with tongue,
And somewhat counsel keep I shall,
(So I was taught when I was young,
To hear and see, and say not all.)

There° was a lady° hight Dame Pride –
In great reputation they her took.
And poor Dame Meekness sat beside,
To her unnethes any would look,
But all as who see'th° her forsook
And sat not by her, neither most ne lest.
(Dame Hypocrite look'd° upon a book
And beat herself upon the breast.) [5]

On every side then looked up I,
And fast I cast mine eye about
If I could see, behold, or espy,
I would have seen Dame Devout:
She° was with but° few o' that rout,
For Dame Sloth and Dame Vainglory
By violence had put her out –
Then in my heart I was full sorry.

But Dame Envy was there dwelling
Which° can seethe strife in every state,
And 'nother lady was there woning
That hight Dame Love Unordinate;
In that place both early and late
Dame Lust, Dame Wanton, and Dame Nice,
They were so there 'habited, I wete,
That few took° heed to God's servíce. [6]

---

[1] *women regular* ] those who have taken vows to follow the rules of their conventual order (unlike "women secular").

[2] *wene* ] suppose, imagine.

[3] *yede* ] went.

[4] *ruth* ] too bad, regrettable; *sad* ] sober, serious; *may not* ] can never.

[5] *hight* ] called; *unnethes any* ] hardly anyone; *neither most ne lest* ] neither the greatest nor lowliest.

[6] *seethe* ] keep boiling hot; *every state* ] anyone's condition or status; *'habited* ] resident (with pun); *wete* ] wit, know.

Dame Chastity, I dare well say,
In that convent had little cheer,
But oft in point to go her way,
She was so little belovèd there.
But some her loved in heart full dear,
And there weren that did not so,
And some set no thing by her,
But gave her good leave for to go. [1]

And at that place I saw much more,
But all I think not to descry
But woll° say as I said before,
And 'tis° a point of courtesy:
For whoso chattereth like a pie
And telleth all° he see'th and heareth°,
He'll be put out of company
And show the goose, thus wisdom° leareth. [2]

And in that place full busily
I walkèd while I might endure,
And saw [myself°] how Dame Envy
In every corner had great cure;
She bare the keys of many a door.
And then Experience to me come
And said, "Katerine, I thee ensure,
This lady is but seld° fro' home."

Dame° Patience and Dame Charity°
In that nunnery full sore I sought,
I'd° fain have wist where they had be',
For in that convent were they not;
But an out-chamber for 'hem was wrought,
And there they dwelt° withouten strife,
And many good women to them sought
And were full willful of 'heir life. [3]

Also another lady there was
That hight Dame Disobedient,
And she set nought by her Prioress.
And then methought [that°] all was shent,
For subjects° should e'er be diligent
Both in word, in will, and deed,
To please 'heir sovereigns with good intent,
And 'hem obey, else God forbid. [4]

Of° all th' defauts that I could see
Through showing of Experience,
It was the one most° grievèd me:
The wanting of obedience.
For it should be choice in conscience,
All religious rule witnesseth the same,
When I saw in her° no reverence,
I might no longer 'bide, for shame.

For they setten not by Obedience,
And then for woe mine heart 'gan bleed,
Ne had they° her in no rev'rence,
But few or none to her took heed.
And then I sped me thence, at° great speed,
That convent was so full of sin!
And then Experience did me lead
Out at the gates there we come in.

And when we were both without,
Upon the grass we set° us down,
And then beheld° the place about,
And there we talkèd as us list.
I prayed° Experience [me°] to have wist
Why she showed me this nunnery.
She said, "Now we be'n here in rest,
I think for to tellen thee why.

"Thy first desire and thine intent
Was to be'n a nun professed.
And for thy fader would not consent,
Thine heart wi' mourning was sore oppressed,
And thou wist not what to do was best.
I said I'd° cease thy grièvaunce,
And now for the most part in every cost
I've° showed thee nunnès' governaunce. [5]

"For as thou see'st within yond° wall
Such be'n the nuns in every ward –
As for the most part, I say not *all*,
God forbid, for then it were hard,
For *some* be'n devout, holy, and to-ward,
And holden the right way to bliss;
And some be'n feeble, lewd, and froward –
Now God amend that is amiss!

---

[1] *cheer* ] welcome, goodwill; *in point to* ] about to.

[2] *descry* ] reveal, disclose; *pie* ] magpie; proverbially noisy; *show the goose* ] look foolish; *leareth* ] teaches.

[3] *willful* ] in control (of their own lives).

[4] *shent* ] ruined.

[5] *cost* ] way, course

"And now, Katerine, I have all do'
For thy comfort that s'longeth to me,
And now let us arise and go
Unto the herbere, there I come to thee."
Then in this herbere she let be me.
I thanked her with great reverence,
I pray to God y-blest be she,
This fair Lady Experience.

And when she was gone, I waked anon.
I thought° how I may governed be,
For nun would I never be none,
For such defauts that I have see'!
(But if they might amended be,
And forsake 'heir sin both day and night,
God give me grace that day to see!
And else it woll not be a-right.)

But peraventure some would° say,
And to his conceit so it should seem,
That I soon forsook° a perfit way
[And forfeited what might have been°]
For a fantasy or dream°.
Dream° was it none, ne fantasy!
'Twas° unto me a gracious mean
[To keep me from apostasy.°] 1
.......................................

Holy Writ w[ell doth agree°]
Plainly go read it wh[en ye will°]
And it is writt'n in Genesy,
In the four-and-thirty chapitil,
How Dinah, for she bode not still
But went out to see things in vain,
She was defouled against her will,
Wherefore° thousands of folk° were slain. 2

Your barb, your wimple, and your veil,
Your mantle and your devout clothing,
Maketh men withouten fail
To wene ye holy be° in living.
And so it is an holy thing
To be'n in habit regular.
Then, as by outward array in seeming,
Be'th so within, my ladies dear. 3

A fair garlond of ivy green
Which hangeth at a tavern door,
It is a false token as I wene.
But if there be wine, good and sour,
Right so but ye, your vices forbear,
And let all lewd custom be broken,
So God me speed, I you ensure,
Else your habit is no true token. /.../ 4

Now, ladies, heed° this exhortation
That I've taught you in this lore,
Behold° the goodly° conversation
Of good women here before,
Full holy virgins many a store,
Which° liveden here religiously,
And now in joy and bliss therefore
They have possession endlessly:

Saint Clare and Saint Edith also,
Scholastica° and Saint Brigit,
Saint Radegund, and many moe
That were° professed in nuns' habit.
They full busy were with all 'heir wit
To beware of sin, and flee therefro',
And now forever they be'n quit
From all manner sorrow and woe.... 5

*finis*

Holbein, *Dance of Death* (1538)

---

[1] *conceit* ] understanding; *And ... been* ] Conjectural emendation for line om. in MS copytext; *mean* ] way, course of action; *To...apostasy* ] Conjectural emendation; damaged MS (stanza 44, part of 43 and are lacking).

[2] *Genesy* ] Genesis; *chapitil* ] chapter 34.

[3] *barb* ] covering for the breast; *wimple* ] linen head-covering.

[4] All that remains of stanzas 47-8 in the damaged MS: "...yng ... nde gode levyng, /...yf they be wythin the contrary / In Holy Schrypture wythowte lesyng / They bene called the chyldryn of false ypocrasy."

[5] MS breaks off in the middle of the next stanza with a list of seven saints.

# LOLLARD Women (1400 – 1532)

*Margery stretching out her armes abrode, said ...*
*thys is the true crosse of Christ.*
– testimony of Joan Cliffland

OLLARD, a loan-word from Middle Dutch *lollaerd*, "mumbler," enters the English language in the 1380s as a derisive epithet for the followers of John Wycliffe (c. 1320-1384); a free thinker whose criticism of Church corruption, and whose distribution of vernacular English Bibles (in manuscript), won broad support, even from such great lords as John of Gaunt. Henry IV after deposing Richard II resolved to crush the Lollard movement. In 1399, he inaugurated an English Inquisition on the Continental model, licensing Bishops to burn at the stake those who held unauthorized theological opinions. William Sawtrey, a priest of Lynn, Norfolk, was the first to die under the new statute. Like many Lollards, Sawtrey believed that the Eucharist bread, when blessed by the priest, did not turn into the flesh of Jesus ("transubstantiation"), but remained bread; he criticized the veneration of images and relics (sources of Church revenue); and he opined that the Church's boundless wealth should be used to aid the poor. The bishops harassed Father Sawtrey for two years before burning him at the stake at Smithfield in March 1401.

As the movement grew, so did the persecution, which forced the movement underground. The Lollard Bible was banned in 1407. Lollards were rounded up, interrogated and forced to renounce their faith. After uprisings of 1414 and 1431, dozens of leaders were burned and their property forfeited to the Crown. (Dependents of convicted heretics were turned out of doors into the street.) Sir John Oldcastle, leader of the 1414 rebellion, fled but was caught and burned alive, suspended on chains above the flames (Following Oldcastle's death, most aristocrats abandoned the movement to merchants, the trades, and peasants.)

A remarkable feature of the Lollard movement was the active participation of women (a fact often cited by the orthodox clergy as a sign of Lollard sinfulness). Among early notables to suffer were Anna Palmer (fl. 1393-1394), an anchoress of St. Peter's, Northampton, who was summoned to appear before the bishop of Lincoln on fifteen charges of heresy (which she refused to answer) and one charge of inchastity (which she denied). This dangerous anchoress was said to have fomented misbelief in secret conventicles that gathered at her cell. When she appeared before the bishop, Dame Anna denounced him as the antichrist and his clerks as the devil's disciples. Christina More (fl. 1412-14), a widow of Bristol, kept a Lollard chaplain, hosted Bible readings, and was prosecuted in connection with the 1414 rebellion. Lady Jane Young, widow of London mayor Sir John Young, is believed have been martyred along with her mother, Joan Boughton, burnt at Smithfield in 1494. How many women perished cannot be calculated: the names of the women martyrs often went unrecorded.

William Alnwick, bishop of Norwich, vowed that any Lollard found in his diocese would soon "hop headless or fry a faggot." His crusade against Norfolk Lollards is copiously documented; from which, two heretics – Awisia Moon and Margery Baxter – emerge as figures of special note. Awisia's husband, Thomas Moon, was an affluent shoe merchant of Loddon accused of providing financial support to Lollard priests and fugitives. Margery was the wife of William Baxter, a carpenter. Both women were outspoken supporters of William White, an itinerant preacher who denied transubstantiation; urged priests to marry; condemned capital punishment; rejected the legitimacy of war; and was widely revered in Norfolk. In 1428, after Bishop Alnwick burned White at the stake and suppressed his books, the Moons and Baxters helped to keep the local movement alive. Awisia – whom Margery Baxter calls the "most distinguished and wisest woman" – hosted Bible readings, discussions, and dinners. One such event was said to be a Lenten feast at which meat was served. Tried and convicted in August 1430, the Moons like most first-time offenders renounced their beliefs under threat of death and damnation. And, like many other forced confessions, Awisia's signed "abjuration" was prepared by the diocese (based on answers she made during interrogations). The Moons' penance included a series of six public floggings.

Margery and William Baxter (fl. 1428-1431) were brought to trial in October 1428, convicted, forced to recant, and like the Moons subjected to weekly floggings. But Margery the following April was arrested as a relapsed heretic; at which time others were enlisted to testify against her. Evidently, the radicalism of Margery Baxter went well beyond controversies over the Eucharist, striking at the foundations of ecclesiastical authority: Margery had declared the Church heretical for amassing wealth; for deceiving and exploiting the uneducated masses; and for putting true Christians to death, such as her friend and mentor, William White. In her anger over White's death, Margery predicted "assuredly that the vengeance of God will speedily come" upon "the cursed Pope, Cardinals, Archbishops and Bishops, and 'specially the bishop of Norwich." But Margery was mistaken: vengeance belonged to the Church.

From ***The Abjuration of Awisia Moon*** (1431)

In the name of God to-fore you, the worshipful fader in Christ, William, by the grace of God bishop of Norwich:

I, Hawisia Moon, the wife Thomas Moon of Lod[don] of your diocese, your subject, before this time I have be' right homely and privy with many heretics, knowing them for heretics. And them I have received and harboured in our house, and them I have concealed, comforted, supported, maintained and favoured with all my power – which heretics' ... (including significant, many entitled 'Sir,' [and] priests of Seething [and] Loddon); ... have oft-times kept, held and continued schools of heresy in privy chambers and privy places of ours; in the which schools I have heard, conceived, learned and reported the errours and heresies which be written and contained in these indentures, that is to say:

First, that the sacrament of bapti'm done in water, in form customed in the Church, is "but a truffle and not to be pondered." ("All Christès' people is sufficiently baptized in the blood of Christ, and so Christès' people need no other bapti'm.")

Also: that the sacrament of confirmation done by a bishop "is of none avail, ne necessary to be had. For as much as when a child hath discretion, and can and will understand the Word of God, it is sufficiently confirmed by the holy Ghost and needeth none other confirmation."

Also: that "confession should be made only to God, and to none other priest, for no priest hath power to remit sin, ne to assoil a man of any sin." [1]

Also: that "No man is bound to do no penaunce which any priest enjoineth him to do for 'heir sins which they have confessed unto the priest, for sufficient penaunce for all manner of sin is every person to abstain him from lying, backbiting and evil-doing, and no man is bound to do none other penaunce."

Also: that "No priest has power to make Christès' very body at Mess in form of bread, but that after the sacramental words said at Mess of the priest, there remaineth only material bread."

Also: that "The Pope of Rome is fader *Anti-Christ*, and false in all his working, and hath no power of God more than any other lewd man, but if he be more holy in living. Ne the Pope hath no power to make bishops, priests, ne none other orders. And he that the people callen *the Pope of Rome* is no 'pope' but a false extortioner and a deceiver of the people."

Also: that "He only that is most holy and most perfect in living in earth is very *pope*. And these Sing-Messes that be clepèd *priests* be'n no priests, but they be lecherous and covetous men and false deceivers of the people; and with their subtle teaching and preaching, singing and reading piteously they peel the people of their good. And therewith they sustain 'heir *pride*, 'heir *lechery*, 'heir *sloth*, and all other vices. And alway they make new laws and new ordinaunces, to curse and kill cruelly all other persons that holden against 'heir vicious living."

Also: that "Only consent of love betwix' man and woman, without contract of words, and without solemnization in church, and without sym-bride asking, is sufficient for the sacrament of matrimone." [2]

Also: "It is but a truffle to anoint a sick man with material oil consecrate by a bishop, for it sufficeth every man at his last end only to have mend of God."

Also: that "Every man may lawfully withdraw and withhold tithes and offerings from priests and curates, and give them to the poor people, and that is more pleasing to God."

Also: that "The temporal lords and temporal men may lawfully take all possessions and temporal goods from all men of Holy Church, and from all bishops and prelates, both horse and harness, and give their good to poor people. And thereto the temporal men be *bound*, in pain of deadly sin." [3]

Also: that "It is no sin, any person to do the contrary of the precepts" of Holy Church.

Also: that "Every man and every woman being in good life, out of sin, is as good priest and has as much power of God in all thing as any priest ordered, be he Pope or bishop." [4]

Also: that censures of Holy Church, "Sentences and cursings, ne of suspending, given by prelates or ordinaries, be not to dread ne to be feared, for God *blesseth* the cursings of the bishops and ordinaries." [5]

---

[1] *1 Tim.* 2:5; *assoil* ] absolve.

[2] *sym-bride asking* ] the asking of banns, an announcement of intended marriage, so that those who know of an impediment may have opportunity to object.

[3] *be bound* ] secular powers are *obliged* to seize the church's wealth and to share it with the poor.

[4] *ordered* ] ordained.

[5] *ordinaries* ] ordained bishops and archbishops.

Also: that "It is not lawful to swear in any case, ne is it lawful to pleaden, for anything." [1]

Also: that "It is not lawful to slay a man for any cause, ne by process of law to damn any traitor (or any man for any treason or felony) to death; ne to put any man to death for any cause; but every man should leave all vengeance only to the sentence of God." [2]

Also: that "No man is bound to fast in Lenten, Embren Days, Fridays, ne vigils of saints"; but all such days and times, "it is lawful to all Christès' people to eat flesh and all manner meatès, indifferently at 'heir own lust, as oft as they have appetite as any other days" which be not commanded to be fasted.

Also: that "No pilgrimage oweth to be do' ne be made. For all pilgrimage-going serveth of nothing but to give priests good that be too rich, and to make gay tapsters and proud 'ostlers."

Also: that "No worship ne reverence oweth be do' to any images of the crucifix, of our Lady ne of none other saints. For all such images be but idols and made by working of man's hand. But worship and reverence should be do' to the image of God, which only is man." [3]

Also: that "All prayer oweth be made only to God and to none other saints, for it is doubt if there be any such saints in Heaven as these Sing-Messes approven and commaunden to be worshiped and prayed to here in Earth.

"Because of which, and many other errors and heresies, I am called to-fore you, worshipful fader, which have cure of my soul."

[signed] ✝ [and set with her signet ring.] [4]

¶ The picture of the burning and hanging of diuers persons counted for Lollardes, in the first yeare of the raigne of king Henry the fift.

From Foxe, *Actes and Monuments of the Christian Church*. Executions of 1414, after the Oldcastle uprising

[1] *not lawful to swear* ] Mat. 5:33-37; *pleaden* ] litigate; Mat. 5:25.

[2] *Rom.* 12:19.

[3] "So God created man in his own image, in the image of God created he him; male and female created he them" (*Gen.* 1:27); the Lollards disdained sacred man-made images as idolatry.

[4] Awisia Moon could read but could not write.

**MARGERY BAXTER, wife of William Baxter Wright in Martham, the same year accused, against whom one Joan Cliffland was brought in by the bishop and compelled to depose.**

[*On the first day of the month of April in the year of our Lord 1429, Joan Cliffland, wife of William Cliffland, dwelling in the parish of St. Mary the Less in Norwich, was summoned and appeared in person before the reverend father in Christ and lord, William (Alnwick) by the grace of God the lord bishop of Norwich, sitting in judgment in the chapel of his palace. On the said lord's direction, by a corporal oath she swore upon God's Holy Gospels to answer truthfully to all and everything that was asked of her concerning the matter of the faith. When the oath had been thus taken, Joan Cliffland said*:] [1]

First, that the said Margery Baxter, the wife of William Baxter, wright, [lately dwelling] in Martham in the diocese of Norwich, whilst sitting and sewing with this witness, in her room next the fireplace, in the presence of this witness, and of Joan Grimell and Agnes Bethom, servants to this witness, did inform this deponent [and her servants] that [they] should in no case swear, saying to her in English, "Dame, beware of the bee! For every bee will sting, and therefore take heed you swear not, neither by God, neither by our Lady, ne by none other saint, and if ye do the contrary, the Bee will sting your tongue, and venom your soul."

Item, this deponent being demanded by the said Margery what she did every day at church, she answered that [first, after entering the church,] she [usually] kneeled down and said five *Pater nosters* in worship of the crucifix and as many *Ave Maries* in worship of our Lady, [mother of Jesus]; whom Margery rebuked, saying, "You do evil to kneel or pray to such images in the churches, for God dwelleth not in such churches, [nor has ever departed,] neither shall [he] come down out of Heaven and will give [or grant] you no more reward for such *prater* than a candle lighted and set under the [lathwork] cover of the font will give light by night to those which are in the church, [for there is no greater worship to be shown to images in churches or images of the crucifix than to the gallows from which they hung your brother";] saying moreover in English, "Lewd wrights of stocks hew and form such crosses and images. And after that, lewd painters gleir them with colours. And if you desire so much to see the true cross of Christ, I will show it you, at home, in your own house."

—Which this deponent being desirous to see, the said Margery stretching out her arms abroad, said to this deponent: "*This* is the true cross of Christ! And this cross, thou ought'st and mayest every day behold, and worship, [here] in thine own house. And therefore it is but vain to run to the church to worship dead crosses and images."

[This witness testifies that the aforesaid Margery asked her what she believed with respect to the sacrament of the altar.]

Joan Cliffland told Margery that she "believed the sacrament of the altar, after the consecration, to be the very body of Christ, in *form* of bread."

To whom Margery replied: "Your belief is nought. For if every such sacrament were God and the very body of Christ, there should be an infinite number of Gods, because that a thousand priests and more, do every day make a thousand such 'Gods'; and afterward, eat them, and void them out again by their hinder parts, filthily stinking under the hedges – where as you may find a great many such 'Gods,' if you will seek for them. And therefore, know for a certainty that, by the grace of God, it shall never be *my* God! – because it is falsely and deceitfully ordained by the priests in the Church, to induce the simple people to idolatry. For it is only material bread."

Moreover,...that "Thomas of Canterbury, whom the people call° *saint* Thomas, was a false traitor and dampned in Hell – because he injuriously endowed the churches with possessions, and raised up [and promoted] many heresies in the Church which seduce the simple people. And therefore, if God be blessed, the said Thomas is accursed. And those false priests that say that he suffered his death patiently before the altar do lie. For as a false cowardly traitor, he was slain in the church door, as he was flying away...."

Moreover,...that "The cursed Pope, Cardinals, Archbishops and Bishops – and specially, the bishop of Norwich – and others that support and maintain heresies and idolatry, reigning and ruling over the people, shall shortly have the very same, or worse, mischief fall upon *them*, than that cursed man, Thomas of Canterbury, had. For they falsely and cursedly deceive the people with their false mammetries and laws, to extort money (of the simple people) to sustain their pride, riot and idleness. And know assuredly that the vengeance of God will speedily come upon them which have most cruelly slain the children of God—[that is, holy] father Abraham, and William White, [the most holy and] true teacher of the law of God, and John Waddon, with many other godly men of the

[1] *on...faith* ] phrasing in brackets trans. DWF, from the Tanner transcript; omitted fr. 1563 trans. by John Foxe.

party of Christ's law] – which vengeance had [already] come upon the said Caiaphas, the bishop of Norwich (and his ministers, which are members of the Devil), before this time, if the Pope had not sent over those false pardons unto these parties, which the said Caiaphas had falsely obtained to induce the people to make procession for the state of them and of the church. Which pardons brought the simple people to cursed idolatry." [1]

[Item, the said Margery said to this deponent that "No child or baby born to Christian parents ought to be baptized in water according to customary practice because such an infant is sufficiently baptized in the mother's womb; and therefore, it is superstition and idolatry when these false and accursed priests dip babies into the font in churches, which they do only to extort money from the people, to support the priests and their concubines."

Also, the aforesaid Margery said to this witness then present that "Consent of mutual love between man and woman alone is sufficient for the sacrament of marriage, without any exchange of vows and without solemnization in the churches."

Item, that ... "Every faithful man or woman is not bound to fast in Lent, [on the Ember days, Fridays,] or other days appointed for fasting" by the Church; and that every man may lawfully eat flesh and all other meats upon the said days and times"; and that "It were better to eat the fragments left upon Thursday at night, on the fasting days, than to go to the market and bring themselves in debt to buy fish"; and that "Pope Silvester made the Lent."

Item,...that "William White [who] was falsely condemned for an heretic [is a great saint in Heaven and a most holy teacher ordained and sent from God, and that she prayed every day to that holy man William White; and she will pray to him every day of her life, as he is worthy to intercede for her before the God of Heaven"]; and that "he was a good and holy man." And that he willed her to follow him to the place of execution, whereas she saw, "when he would have opened his mouth to speak unto the people, to instruct them, a *devil* – one of the Bishop Caiaphas' servants – strake him of the lips, and stopped his mouth, that he could in no case declare the will of God." [2]

Item, ... that the said Margery taught her that "she should not go on pilgrimage, neither to our Lady of Falsingham, nor to any other saint or place." [3]

[Also, that this Margery said that Thomas Moon's wife is a woman most learnèd, and an intimate follower in the doctrine of William White ...]

Also, ... that the said Margery desired her that she and Joan her maid would come secretly in the night to her chamber, and there she should hear her husband read the law of Christ unto them; which law is written in a book that her husband was wont to read to her by night, and that her husband is well learnèd in the Christian verity. Also, that the same Margery had talked with a woman named Joan West, and that the said woman is in "a good way of salvation."

Also, that the said Margery said to this deponent, [Joan Cliffland:] "Joan, it appeareth by your countenaunce that you intend to disclose this, that I have said unto you." And this deponent sware that she would never disclose it, without the said Margery gave her occasion. Then said Margery unto this deponent, "If thou do accuse me unto the Bishop, I will do unto thee as I did once unto a certain friar Carmelite of Yarmouth, which was the best-learnèd friar in all the country."

Then this deponent desired to know what she had done to the friar; unto whom Margery answered that she had *talked* with the said friar – rebuking him, because he did beg; saying that it was no alms to give him *any* good thing except he would leave his habit and go to the plow. And so, he should please God more than following the life of some of those friars!

Then the friar required of the said Margery whether she could teach him or tell him anything else. Then the said Margery (as she affirmed to

---

[1] *mammetries* ] worship of idols or images.

[2] Foxe, who disapproves of praying to any martyr, Protestant or Catholic, omits from his 1563 translation this report of Margery's religious practice.

[3] Cf. the statements attributed to Margery's fellow defendant, William Hardy, in his forced aburation of 4 November 1430: "No pilgrimages should be carried out to the Lady of Falsingham, the Lady of Foulpit, and to Thomas of Cankerbury" [i.e., our Lady of Walsingham, our Lady of Woolpit, and Thomas à Becket of Canterbury] nor to any other saints or images; ... No worship or reverence ought to be offered to any images of 'our Lady' or of any other saints, nor ought greater reverence be paid to the *images* of the cross than ought to be paid to the gallows which men are hanged upon; for all such images are nothing but idols, and the makers of them are accursed." "The 'four doctors' – Augustine, Ambrose, Gregory, and Jerome – which the church of Rome as approved as 'saints,' were *heretics*, and their teachings, which *Christ's* people call a doctor's *draught*, are overt heresies" (Nov. 4, 1430).

this deponent) declared to this friar the Gospels in English, and then the friar departed from her. [1]

After this, the same friar accused the said Margery of heresy, and she, understanding that the friar had accused her, accused the friar again, that he would have known her carnally, and because she would not consent unto him, the friar had accused her of heresy. And moreover, she said, that her husband would have killed the friar therefore; and so the friar for fear held his peace, and went his way for shame.

This witness reports that Margery said also that she had oftentimes been feignedly confessed to the dean of [St. Mary in] the Fields, because he should think her to be a woman of good life; and therefore he gave the said Margery oftentimes money.

Then this deponent asked her, whether she had confessed her sins to a priest or not. And she answered that she had never *offended* any priest; and therefore she would never confess herself to any priest, neither obey him, because they have no power to absolve any man from their sins – for that they offend daily, more grievously than other men. [And this Margery said further that every man and every woman that be of Margery's persuasion are themselves good priests, and that Holy Church dwells in the places where all those dwell who are of her faith. Margery said,] therefore, that "Men ought to confess themselves only unto God, and to no priest."

Item, the said Margery said to this deponent that the people did "worship devils which fell from Heaven with Lucifer; which devils, in their fall to the Earth, entered into the images which stand in the Churches, and have long lurked and dwelled in them; so that the people worshiping those images commit idolatry."

Item, she said more to this deponent that holy bread and holy water were but "trifles of no effect or force," and that the bells are to be cast out of the church, and that they are excommunicate which first ordained them.

Moreover, that she should not be burned, although she were convict of Lollardy, for that she had "a charter of salvation" in her body['s womb].[2]

[Also, the same Margery said that she "vanquished in judgment the lord bishop of Norwich, and Henry Inglese, and the lords abbots along with them."]

Also, the said deponent sayeth that Agnes Betham her servant – being sent to the house of the said Margery, the Saturday after Ash Wednesday (the said Margery not being within) – found a brass pot standing over the fire with a piece of bacon and oatmeal seething in it, as the said Agnes reported to this deponent.

There were also, besides this deponent, divers other sworn and examined upon the said Margery – as John Grimley and Agnes Betham, servants to William Cliffland – which all together confirmed the former depositions.

*finis*

John Foxe reports, "Thus much we have thought good to note as concerning Margery Baxter – which we have gathered out of the old monuments and registers. But what became of her after this her accusation, because we find no mention made in the said registers, we are not able to declare" (408).

Those first-time offenders who confessed to having eaten meat on Fridays (when only fish was permitted) were obliged thereafter to fast on only bread and water each Friday (on pain of excommunication for repeat offenders). Most confessed offenders were flogged; some were condemned to as many as seven years in monastery prisons. Relapsed heretics were burned at the stake. No record of Margery's sentence survives. But given the radical opinions ascribed to her and the fact that she was on trial for relapse; and given the bishop's professed pleasure in burning and beheading dissenters, it's very doubtful that she escaped the flames.[3]

On the edge of Thorpe Wood, on a church-owned parcel just across the river from the Bishop's Palace, a theater of execution was cut into the hill so that Alnwick and his colleagues could observe executions in comfort and safety. On at least one sixteenth-century Norwich map, the site is captioned "the Lollards' Pit," the "place where men [and women] are customablie burnt."

In 1532, Thomas Harding became the last offender to die as a "Lollard," but the killing continued: the last known Christian executed by sentence of the Roman Catholic Church for holding unautorized opinions was Cayetano Ripoll, in 1826.

---

[1] *The bishop's transcript blurs Cliffland's information: the friar, first asking if Margery could teach him "anything else," made a sexual advance, seeking to "have known her carnally." Margery "said that her husband would have killed the friar, therefore. And so the friar, for fear, held his peace and went his way with shame ... And because she would not consent unto him, the friar had accused her of heresy."*

[2] *charter of salvation* ] Margery believed she would not be put to death while pregnant.

[3] *Norwich.* Georg Braun & Franz Hogenberg (1588).

# **Margaret of Anjou** (1430-1482),
Queen of Henry VI

*Humble et loiall.*
– Queen Margaret's motto

MARGUERITE d'ANJOU, queen consort of King Henry VI (and regnant queen during his madness), was born in the duchy of Lorraine, an imperial fief east of France. At her birth, Henry V of England was already eight years dead, of dysentery. Having invaded and conquered France, he died on 31 August 1422 without having seen his son and namesake, Henry VI, just nine months old. Two months later, France's Charles VI died. That made baby Henry not just king of England but king of France (as per the 1420 Treaty of Troyes). In his minority, the dukes of Bedford and Gloucester – Henry V's brothers – governed England and managed the ongoing war effort.

With the appearance of Joan of Arc, momentum swung to the French; her campaign led to the rescue of the Dauphin, child Henry's *roi rival*, crowned Charles VII on 17 July 1429. The English burned Joan of Arc as a heretic, but as the war dragged on, the French continued to recover lost ground.

At age 16, when his mother died, Henry VI assumed his role as regnant king of England and (titular) king of France. A gentle and religious lad, he favored peace but had no idea how to achieve it. Henry Beaufort, bishop (later Cardinal) of Winchester, and William de la Pole persuaded his teenaged Majesty that his best bet was to do as his father had done, taking to wife a French princess. A prime candidate: Margaret of Anjou, age 9, who would be ripe for plucking at age 14.

Margaret was the second daughter of Isabella, Duchess of Lorraine, by her husband René I of Naples (known as "Good King Rene," titular king of Jerusalem and Aragon, including Corsica, Majorca, and Sicily). Viewed from birth as a pawn in European diplomacy, Margaret now became a bargaining chip in the costly and endless French-English wars. The negotiations, which de la Pole conducted from 1539 to 1544, proved difficult; Charles VII (Margaret's uncle) drove a hard bargain. He finally agreed to the marriage on condition that he be excused from providing his niece with a dowry; in return, Charles would receive from England free title to the lands of Maine and Anjou.

Henry VI of England, 22, and Margaret of Anjou, 14, were betrothed in May 1444. In November, Pole departed again for France to collect the bride. He returned to England in April with Henry's queen at his side and with a peace treaty in hand, the terms of which were kept secret for fear of riots. Margaret and Henry were married on 23 April 1445.

William Pole was created Earl of Pembroke in 1447 and Duke of Suffolk in 1448. (His wife Alice de la Pole, a granddaughter of Geoffrey Chaucer, thereby became a duchess.) A favorite of both Henry and Margaret, Suffolk from 1445 until shortly before his death was the principal power behind a weak and otherworldly king; during which interval, the new duke also became fabulously rich from royal grants. The acquisitiveness of William de la Pole led to rumors that he had gone so far as to conquer the heart and bed of Queen Margaret, 36 years his junior. That gossip was doubtless politically motivated; but his relationship with Margaret while avuncular was extremely close. Chronicler Edward Hall calls Suffolk "the queen's darling," and everyone knew that the queen was his. Nor was he ashamed to say so: Suffolk wrote at least two poems in Margaret's praise: "How the Lover is Set to Serve the Flower" and "The Assembly of Ladies." The first (one of the duke's best poems) draws on the courtly gender-game of the Flower and the Leaf, a mode of poetic discourse in which the flower was associated with short-lived feminine beauty, and the leaf with the chivalric male who provides protection and nourishment. Because the common field daisies of England were called "margarets," the queen's name lent itself to Suffolk's Muse, and to his representation of Margaret as England's own *fleur-de-marguerite.*

"The Assembly of Ladies" survives in three manuscripts and was first printed (wrongly ascribed to Chaucer) in 1532. Influenced by Christine's *City of Ladies* but without Christine's originality and wit, Suffolk's "Assembly" is a dream narrative that celebrates the humility and loyalty of women relative to the pride and faithlessness of men – possibly with reference to real-life figures at court. Five ladies (including the narrator) and four gentlewomen appear before Lady Loyalty (a figure for Margaret), in order to submit petitions against their lame lovers. The tedious middle section of the narrative, in which the women present their various bills of complaint without consequence, is here omitted.

DWF

*Les roys de france et dangleterre*
*Affin de toute noize abatre*
*Firent abstinence de guerre.*

The kings of France and England agree to quiet their quarrel with an abstinence from war

Bibliothèque Nationale, Paris MS Français 5054 fol. 126v

*Comment la fille de cecille fut mariee au roy dangleterre*:

How the daughter of Sicily was married to the king of England.

## How the Lover is Set to Serve the Flower

[By William de la Pole]

MINE heart is set, and all mine whole intent,[1]
To serve this flower in my most humble wise
As faithfully as can be thought or meant,
Without feigning or sloth in my servíse;
For, wit thee well, it is a paradise
To see this flower when it begin to spread
With colours fresh ennewèd white and red. 2

And for the faith I owe unto this flower
I must, of reason, do my observáunce
To flowrès all, both now and every hour,
Sith Fortune list that it should be my chaunce
If that I could do service or plesaunce.
Thus am I set, and shall be till I starve,
And for o' flower all other for to° serve. 3

So woulde God that my simple cunníng
Were súfficiaunt this goodly flower to praise –
For as to me is none so rich a thing
That able were this flower to counterpeise.
O noble Chaucer, passèd be'n thy days,
Of poetry y-namèd worthiest,
Of° making in all other days the best. 4

Now thou art go,' thine help I may not have,
Wherefore to God I pray right specially
(Sith thou art dead and buried in thy grave)
That on thy soul him list to have mercíe.
—And to the monk of Bury now speak I
(For thy cunning is such, and eke thy grace,
After Chaucer to occupy his place), 5

Beseeching thee my pen to° enlumíne,
This flower to praise (as I before have meant)
And off these letters let thy colours shine,
This bill to further after mine intent:
For glad am I that fortune list assent
So to ordain that it should be mine ure
The flowers to chese as by mine aventúre. 6

Whereas ye say that "love is but dotáge,"
Of veray reason that may not be true:
For every man that hath a good couráge
Must lover be. This would I that ye knew:
Who loveth well, all vertue will him 'sue;
Wherefore I rede and counsail you express,
As for this matére, take none heaviness. 7

---

[1] *Mine heart* ] perhaps with a pun on *Mine art.*

[2] *ennewed* ] revived, renewed.

[3] *Sith fortune list* ] Since it is Fortune's wish; *o'* ] one.

[4] *to counterpeise* ] to equal, to be a match for.

[5] *go'* ] gone; *monk of Bury* ] Lydgate; *eke* ] also.

[6] *Beseeching ... enlumíne* ] "This is certainly a burlesque of Lydgate's style" (MacCracken); *ure* ] custom, experience; *chese* ] choose.

[7] *of veray reason* ] with sound logic; *Who ... 'sue* ] (*pursue*) in parody on Lydgate's "Who sueth vertu, vertu he shall leere" (MacCracken).

"These clerkès wise," ye say, "were brought full low,
And made full tame for all their subtlety."
Now am I glad it shall right well be know'
That love is of so great autority!
Wherefore, I let you wit as seemeth me,
It is your part in every manere wise
Of true lovers to further the servíse! 1

And of women ye say right as ye list
(That "truth in 'hem may but awhile endure"!)
And counsail eke that men should 'hem not tryst
And how they be "unsteadfast of natúre."
What causeth this? for every creàture
That is guiltie, and knoweth 'hem*self* culpáble,
Deemeth all other their case sembiláble! 2

And, by your books, I put case that ye knew
Much of this matere which that he ye have moved;
Yet God defend that everything were true
That clerkès write! – for then might this be proved
That ye have said – which will not be believed,
I let you wit, for trysteth verily:
In your conceit it is an 'eresy. 3

Ah, fie, for shame! O thou envious man,
Think whence thou came, and whither to repair!
Hast'ou not said eke that "these women can
Laugh, and love not"? Pardíe, it is not fair!
Thy corrupt speech infecteth all the air.
Knock on thy breast, repent thee° now and ever
Ayen therewith, and say thou saidst it never. 4

Think fully this, and hold it for no fable:
That faith in women hath his dwelling place;
For out of her came nought that was unable,
Save man that cannot well-say in no place!
O thou unhappy man, go hide thy face.
The court is set! thy falsehood shall be° tried.
Withdraw, I rede, for now thou art espied. 5

If thou be wise, yet do this after me:
Be not too hasty; come not in presénce.
Let thine attorney sue and speak for thee.
Look if *he* can excuse thy negligence!
And furthermore, yet must thou recompense
For all that ever thou hast said before
Have mind of this, for now I write no more. 6

*finis*

## The Assembly of Ladies

[By William de la Pole]

IN SÉPTEMBRE, at falling of the leaf
(The fresh seasóun was altogeder done
And of the corn was gad'red in the sheaf),
In a gardén, about twain after noon,
There were ladíes walkíng as was their wone,
Four in numbér (as to my mind doth fall),
And I the fiftè, simpelest of all. 7

Of gentil women four there were also
Disporting 'hem everich after their guise,
In cross allíes walkíng by two and two,
And some alone after their fantasies.
Thus occupied we were in divers wise,
And yet, in truthe, we were not alone –
Thére were knights and squires many oon. 8

Whereof I serve? (oon of 'hem askèd me).
I said again (as it fell in my thought),
"To walk about the maze, in certainty,
Ás a woman that no-thing ne° wrought."
He askèd me again whom that° I sought
And of my colour why I was so pale.
"Forsooth," quod I, "and thereby lieth a tale!" 9

---

[1] *wit* ] know; *as seemeth me* ] as it seems to me.

[2] *right as ye list* ] whatever you please; *hem* ] them; *That ... endure* ] Cf. Lydgate's poem, "They that nowhile endure" (MacCracken); *tryst* ] trust; *sembiláble* ] ( = semblable) to be the same.

[3] *put case* ] suppose.

[4] *Hast'ou* ] Hast thou; *Pardíe* ] By God!; *Ayen* ] against or again.

[5] *his* ] its; *Four out of her ... no place* ] For nothing bad ever came from woman but truthless man, a creature who speaks well nowhere; *rede* ] advise; *espied* ] found out.

[6] *do this after me* ] follow my advice.

[7] *gad'red* ] gathered; *twain* ] two (hours); *wone* ] custom, habit.

[8] *gentil women four* ] complainants; their respective mottoes: "It goes without saying," (627), "I trust in God" (645), "Be assured" (666), and "Well counseled" (675); *Disporting ... guise* ] each one entertaining herself after her own fashion or inclination; *cross-alleys* ] crossing or branching paths laid out in design and bordered usually with a rail on each side; *many oon* ] many-a-one.

[9] *Whereof ... me* ] One of the knights asked me of my purpose (possibly with respect to the narrator's allegiance in a courtly recreation); *maze* ] a garden maze, as at Hampton Court and Hatfield.

"That must me wit," quod he, "and that anon!
Tell on, let see, and make no tarrying."
"Abide," quod I, "ye be an hasty oon!
I let you wit, it is no little thing –
But for because ye have a great longíng
In your desire this process for to hear
I shall you tell the plain of this matére. 1

It happèd thus that in an after-noon
My fellawship and I, by oon assent,
When all our other busyness was done,
To pass our time, into this maze we went
And took our ways eche after our° intent.
Some went inwárd and weened they had gone out;
Some stood amids and lookèd all about; 2

And, sooth to say, some were full far behind—
And right anon, as far forth as the best!
Other there were, so mazèd in their mind,
All ways were good for 'hem, both east and west—
Thus went they forth and had but little rest;
And some their courage did them so assail
For veray wrath they stepped over the rail!

And as they sought 'hemself thus to and fro
I gat myself a little avauntáge.
Áll for-wearièd, I might no further go,
(Though I had won right great for my viáge);
So coom I forth into a strait passáge,
Which brought me to an herber fair and green,
Made with benchés full craftily and clean; 3

Thát, as méthought, might no creàture
Devise a better by proportìoun –
Safe it was closèd well, I you ensure,
With masonry of compass enviróun
Full secretly, with stairès going down
In mids the place, with turning wheel, certáine,
And úpon that a pot of marjolain; 4

With margarets growíng in ordinaunce
To shew 'hemself as folk went to and fro;
That to behold, it was a great plesáunce,
And how they were accompanied with moe,
*Ne m'oublie-mies* and *sovenez* also.
The poor pensees ne were not dislodgèd there –
No, no, God wot, their place was everywhere. 5

The floor beneath° was pavèd fair and smooth
With stonès square of many divers hue
So well joinèd that, for to say the sooth,
All seemèd oon, who that none other knew.
And underneath, the streamès, new and new,
As silver new-bright springing in such wise
That whence it coom, ye could it not devise. 6

A little while thus was I alone
Beholding well this delectáble place.
My fellawship were coming everichoon,
So must me need abide as for a space,
Remembering of many divers case
Of timè past, musing with sighès deep,
I set me down and there I fell in sleep. 7

And as I slept, methought there coom to me
A gentil woman meetly of statúre;
Of great worship she seemèd for to be,
Attired well, not high but by measúre,
Her countenance full sad and full demure,
Her colours blue, all that she had upon.
There coom no moè but herself alone. 8

Her gown was well enbrouded, certainlie,
With sovenez° after her own devise;
On the purfill her worde, by and by,
*Bien loialment*, as I could me avise.
Then prayed I her in every manere wise
That of her name I might have rémembraunce.
She said she was calléd Perséveraunce. 9

---

1 *That . . . anon* ] I must learn of that, and right away; *matére* ] matter.

2 *eche* ] each; *weened* ] thought, supposed.

3 *hemself* ] themselves; *great* ] greatly, right well; *víage* ] (*voyage*) venturing; *And as ... clean* (lines 43-9) ] i.e., the poet, having gotten ahead of the rest, although exhausted, found the last narrow passage that led to the enclosed arbor in the center of the maze.

4 *Safe ... well* ] it was enclosed securely; *stairès* ] steps down to the sunken center of the arbor; *In mids* ] In the middle of; *turning wheel* ] a turn-style; *marjolain* ] marjoram.

5 *margarets* ] the common field-daisy; *moe* ] (*more*) other flowers; *Ne m'oublie-mies and sovenez* ] forget-me-nots (a figure for constancy in love and for unrequited love) and remember-mes (germander speedwell); *pensees* ] pansies (*from O.F.* pensee, *thought*); *dislodged there* ] removed from the herber; *God wot* ] God knows.

6 *stonès square* ] the decorated tiles with which the arbor was paved; *divers* ] various; *All seemed oon* ] the floor-tiles seemed one piece; *streames* ] i.e., streams jetting from a spring-fed fountain in the middle.

7 *alone* ] i.e., while waiting for the other ladies to find the arbor at the center of the maze; *everichoon* ] every one; *So . . . space* ] so I had to wait for a while.

8 *meetly* ] well-proportioned, of medium height; *sad* ] solemn, dignified; *demure* ] sober, mature; *blue* ] signifying constancy and truth.

9 *enbrouded* ] embroidered; *sovenez* ] embroidered. with sovenez, the flower she has adopted as her emblem

So furthermore to speak then was I bold:
Where she dwelt, I prayed her for to say –
And she again full courteisly me told,
'My dwelling is and hath be' many a day
With a ladíe.' 'What lady, I you pray?'
'Of great estate, thus warn I you,' quod she.
'What call ye her?' 'Her name is Loyalty.' [1]

'Ín what office stand ye, or in what degree?'
Quod I to her. 'That would I wit full fain.'
'I am,' quod she, '(unworthy though I be)
Of her chamber her usher, in-certaine.
This rod I bear as for a token plain,
Like as ye know the rule in such servíse
Pertaining is unto to the same office. [2]

She chargèd me by her commaundèment
To warn you and your fellaws everichoon
That ye should come there as she is presént
For a counsáil, which shall be now anon,
Or seven dayès be'n comen and gone.
And furthermore she bade that I should say,
Excuse there might be none nor no° delay. [3]

Another thing was nigh forgete behind
Which in no wise I would not but ye knew!
Remembre it well, and bear it in your mind –
All your felláws (and ye) must come in blue,
Éverich your matére for to sue,
With more (which I pray you think upon) –
Your wordès on your sleevès everichoon. [4]

And be not ye abashèd in no wise
(As many be'n in such an high presénce).
Make your request as ye can best devise
And she gladlié will yeve you audience.
There is no grief nor no manére offence
Wherein ye feel your heart is sore° displeased
But with her help right soon ye shall be'n eased.' [5]

'I am right glad,' quod I, 'ye tell me this;
But there is none of us that knoweth the way.'
'And of your way,' quod she, 'ye shall not miss.
Ye shall have oon to guide you day by day
Of my felláws – I can no better say –
Such oon as shall tell you the way full right;
And *Diligence* this gentil woman hight, [6]

A woman of right famous governaunce
And well cherish'd, I say you for certáine.
Her fellawship shall do you great plesáunce,
Her port is such, her manere true and plain;
She with glad cheer will do her busy pain
To bring you there. Farewell, now have I done.'
'Abide,' quod I, 'ye may not go so soon!' [7]

'Why so?' quod she, 'and I have far to go
To yeve warníng in many divers place –
To your felláws, and so to other moe –
And well ye wot I have but little space.'
'Yet,' quod I, 'ye must tell me this case,
If we shall any men unto us call?'
'Not one,' quod she, 'may come among you all.' [8]

'Not one?' quod I, 'Ay, benedicité!
What have they° done? I pray you, tell me that.'
'Now, by my life, I trow but well,' quod she,
'But euer I can believe there is somewhat,
And for to say you truth, more can I not;
In questions I may no-thing be too large,
I meddle me no further than my charge.' [9]

'Then thus,' quod I, 'do me till undrestond,
What place is there this lady is dwellíng?'
'Forsooth,' quod she, 'and oon sought all a-lond,
Fairér is none, though it were for a king –
Devisèd well, and that in everything!
The towrès high full plesaunt shall ye find,
With fannès fresh turníng with every wind;

---

or device; *devise* ] heraldic device or emblem; *purfill* ] purfle; decorated hem; *word* ] motto; *Bien loialment* ] "well-loyally".

[1] *again* ] in reply.

[2] *That . . . fain* ] I earnestly wish to learn that; *usher* ] the usher of the chamber supervised the provision of food and service in the lord or lady's chamber; *in-certaine* ] certainly.

[3] *there as* ] there where; *might* ] must.

[4] *nigh forgete* ] almost forgotten; *wordes* ] mottos

[5] *yeve* ] give.

[6] *hight* ] is called.

[7] *port* ] comportment, demeanor.

[8] *well ye wot* ] well you know that.

[9] *benedicité* ] bless ye (the Lord)!; *large* ] open; *Now ... charge* (150-54) ] So far as I know, they have done well, but I remain willing to believe that there is something about men that cannot be trusted, and more than that I cannot say (without fear of giving offense).

The chambres and parlours both of o' sort,
With bay° windóws goodlíe as can be thought;
As for dauncíng and other wise disport,
The galleries right wonderfully wrought,
That well I wot, yif ye were thither brought
And took good heed thereof in every wise,
Ye would it think a veray paradise.' 1

. . . . . . . . . . . . . . . . . . . . . . . . . . . .

Then went we forth aftér *Perseveraunce.*
To see the prease. It was a wonder case;
Therefore, to pass, it was great cumberaunce,
The people stood so thick in every place.
'Now stond ye still,' quod she, 'a little space,
And for your ease somewhat shall I assay
Yif I can make you any better way.' 2

And forth she go'th among 'hem everichoon,
Making a way that we might thorough pass
More at our ease. And when as° she had done,
She beckoned us to come there as she was –
So after her we followed more and lass.
She brought us straight unto the chamberlain;
There left she us and then she went again. 3

We salwèd her as reason would it so,
Full humbely beseeching her goodnéss,
In our matéres that we had for to do,
That she would be good lady and mastrésse.
'Ye be'n welcóom,' quod she, 'in soothfastness,
And so what I can do you for to pleasex
I am readíe, that may be for your ease.' 4

We followed her unto the chamber door:
'Susters,' quod she, 'come in ye after me.'
– But wit ye well, there was a pavèd floor,
The goodliest that any wight might see;
And furthermore about then lookèd we
On echè corner and on every wall,
The which was made of beryl and crystál; 5

Wheron was graven of stories many oon:
First, how Phyllis of womanly pitíe
Died pitously for love of Demephon.
Next after was the story of Thisbé
– Hów she slew herself under a tree.
Yet saw I more: how (in right° pitous case)
For Antony, was slain Cleópatras.
That other side, was how that Melusine°
Untruly was deceivèd in her bain.
There was also Anélida the queen
Upon Arcite how sore she did complain!
All these stories were graven there, certáine,
And many moe than I rehearse you here
(It were too long to tell you all in-fere). 6

Ánd because the wallès shone so bright,
With fine umple they were all over-spread,
To that intent folk should not hurt their sight
And thorough that the stories might be read.
Then furthermore I went as I was led
And there I saw withouten° any fail
A chaìr set with full rich áppareil; 7

And five stages it was set from the ground,
Of cassidone full curiously wrought,
With four pommels of gold and veray round
Set with saphéres as fine as might be thought.
Wot ye what, yif it were thorough sought
(As I suppose) from this countríe till Ind,
Another suchè it were hard to find. 8

For wit ye well, I was right nearè that,
So as I durst beholding by and by.
Above there was a richè cloth of state,
Wróughte with the needle full straunglíe,
Her word thereon, and thus it said trulíe:
*A endurer*, to tell in wordès few,
With great letters, the better for to shew. 9

Thus as we stood, a door opened anone;
A gentil woman, seemly of statúre,
Bearing a mace, coom out, herself alone –
Trulíe, me-thought, a goodly creàture!
She spak no-thing too loud, I you ensure,
Nor hastily, but with goodlíe warníng:
'Make room!' quod she. 'My lady is comíng.' 10

With that anon I saw Perseveraunce,
How she held up the tappet in her hand.
I saw also in right good ordinaunce
This great lady within the tappet stand,
Comíng outward, I will ye understand,
And after her, a noble company –
I could not tell the number, sikerly. 11

---

[1] *do ... undrestond* ] make me to understand; *is there* ] is it where; *all a-lond* ] throughout the land; *o' sort* ] ( = *one sort*) of equal elegance; *galleries* ] covered walks alongside a manor house.

[2] *prease* ] press, throng; *wonder* ] wondrous.

[3] *thorough* ] through; *lass* ] less; *more and lass* ] high and low, one and all.

[4] *salwèd* ] saluted; *soothfastness* ] truth.

[5] *wight* ] person, spirit.

[6] *Melusine* ] from *The Romance of Partenay; bain* ] bath; *Anélida...Arcite* ] Cf. Chaucer, "Anelida and Arcite," lines 211-350; *in-fere* ] together.

[7] *umple* ] gauze; *To that intent* ] so that; *thorough* ] so.

[8] *stages* ] steps; *cassidone* ] may denote either chalcedony or (as is more likely here) a kind of marble; *pommels* ] rounded knobs; *Ind* ] ( = *India*) the Orient.

[9] *full straunglíe* ] very curiously; *Her word* ] the motto of Lady Loyalty; *A endurer* ] "(Ever) to endure!"

[10] *mace* ] metal staff of office, resembling a battle-mace.

[11] *tappet* ] cloth at entrance, lifted to enter; *sikerly* ] surely.

Óf their names I would no-thing inquere
Further than such as we would sue unto,
Sauf o' ladíe which was the chauncelor –
*Atemperaunce*, soothlíe, her name was so
– For us needeth with her have much to do
In our matéres and alway more and more.
Ánd, so forth, to tell you furthermore, [1]

Of this ladíe, her beauties to descrive
My cunning is too simple, verily –
For never yet the days of all my live
So inly fair I have none seen, trulíe,
In her estate, assurèd utterly!
There lackèd nought, I dare you well ensure,
That 'longèd to a goodly creàture.

And furthermore to speak of her array,
I shall you tell the manere of her gown:
Of cloth of gold full rich, it is no nay,
The colour blue of a right good fashióun,
In tabard-wise, the sleevès hanging down;
And what purfill there was and in what wise,
So as I can, I shall it you devise – [2]

After a sort, the collar and the vent,
Like as ermíne is made in purfilling;
With great pearls full fine and orient
Théy were couchéd all after oon worchíng,
With díamonds instead of powdering;
The sleevès and purfillès of assize,
Théy were made full° like in every wise; [3]

About her neck a serp° of fair rubíes
In white flowrès in right fine enèmail;
Upon her head, set in the freshest wise,
A circle with great balas of entail –
That (in earnest to speak, withouten fail)
For young and old and every manere age
It was a world, to look on her viságe! [4]

Thus comíng to sit in her estate,
In her presénce we kneelèd down echoon,
Presenting up our bills and, wot ye what,
Full humbly she took 'hem, by oon and oon.
When we had done, then coom they all anone
And did the same, eche after her° manére,
Kneeling at oons and rising all in-fere. [5]

. . . . . . . . . . . . . . . . . . . . . . . . . . . . . . .

What did she then, suppose you, verily?
She spake herself and said in this manére:
'We have well seen your billès by and by
And some of 'hem full pitous for to hear.
We will therefore ye knowen this all in-fere:
Within short time our court of parlement
Here shall be hold in our paláys presént, [6]

And in all this wherein ye find you grieved
There shall ye find an open remedy –
In such wissè as ye shall be relieved
Of all that ye rehearse here truèly.
As of the date ye shall know verily,
Then ye may have a space in your coming,
For Diligence shall bring it you° by writing.' [7]

We thankèd her in our most humble wise,
Our fellawship echoon by oon assent,
Submitting us lowlíe till her servíse,
For as us-thought we had our travel spent
In such wissè as we held us content.
Then eche of us took other by the sleeve,
And forthwithal – as we should take our leave –

All sodainly the water sprang anone
In my viságe, and therewithal I woke –
'*Where am I now*?' thought I, '*all this is gone*!'
All amazed – and up I 'gan to look.
With that anon I went and made this book,
Thus simpèly rehearsing the substáunce
Because it should not out of rémembraunce." [8]

"Now verily, your dream is passing good
And worthy to be had in rémembraunce! –
For though I stand here as long as I stood
It should to me be none encumberáunce,
I took therein so inly great plesáunce!
But tell me now, what ye the book do call,
For me must wit." "With right good will ye shall: [9]

"As for this book, to say you veray right
And of the name to tell the certaintíe,
'L'assemblée des Damès' – thus it hight.
How think ye that the name is?" "Good, pardíe!"
"Now go, farewell, for they call after me,
My fellaws all, and I must after soon.
Read well my dream, for now my tale is done." [10]

---

[1] *Sauf o' ladie* ] save ( = *except*) one lady; *Atemperaunce* ] lady Temperance ( = *self-control*).

[2] *tabard-wise* ] like a herald's coat; *purfill* ] trimming.

[3] *After a sort* ] same sort; *vent* ] slit in gown closed with a broach and bejeweled; *oon worching* ] one working, the same design; *of assize* ] of the same fashion.

[4] *serp* ] collar; *enemail* ] enamel; *balas* ] a rose-red balas-ruby; *of entail* ] delicately cut; *That* ] so that.

[5] *bills* ] petitions; *her* ] i.e., her own.

[6] *parlement* ] 1. talk, conversation; 2. judicial assembly; *hold* ] held; *paláys* ] palace.

[7] *such wisse* ] such wise, such manner.

[8] *viságe* ] face; a companion has thrown water in her face, to awaken her); *this book* ] having told her story to the knight, the narrator gives him a manuscript copy.

[9] *Now verily ... me must wit* (lines 743-49a) ] spoken to the narrator by the knight; *me must wit* ] I must know.

[10] *'L'assemblée des Dames' - thus it hight* ] "The assembly of Women" - thus it is called.

Margaret, a prolific letter-writer, learned English quickly and soon found a niche for herself as a benefactor to lovers, the unemployed, and the dispossessed. The several dozen letters to have survived from Margaret's pen, represented here by a small sampling, provide a self-portrait very unlike the homicidal and adulterous hell-*chatte* of the *Henry VI* plays or the shrill termagant of *Richard III*. Shakespeare's dramatically pejorative assessment of the queen's life and character has had a pernicious effect upon her reputation, and even upon historians who should know better. The Margaret of history, though French and widely hated by Henry's English subjects, was indefatigable in helping young men to the marriage altar, the unemployed to preferment, the sick and impecunious to charitable relief. That she took an active role in politics and combat following the mental collapse of King Henry was motivated by the same zeal to defend the rights of others, specifically, of her own husband and son.

Margaret of Anjou, fr. an illuminated manuscript by the Talbot Master

[***To Robert Kent*** (n.d., 1446x1448)°]

BY THE QUEEN
Well-beloved,

We greet, &c., And let you wit that our well-beloved servant, Thomas Shelford, whom – for his virtues and the agreeable service that he hath done unto us herebefore, and in especial now late in the company of our cousin of Suffolk – we have taken into our chamber, there to serve us about our person, hath reported unto us that, for the good and virtuous demeaning that he hath heard of a gentle woman being in your governance, which was daughter to oon "Hall of Larkfield," he desireth "full heartily to do her worship by way of marriage" (as he sayeth). [1]

Wherefore we desire and pray you heartily that, setting apart all instances or labours that have or shall be made unto you (for any other person whatsoever he be), ye will by all honest and lawful means be well willed unto the said marriage, entreating the said gentlewoman unto the same; trusting to God's mercy that it shall be both for her worship and avail in time to come. And if ye woll do your tender diligence to perform this our desire, ye shall therein deserve of us right good and especial thank, and cause us to show unto you therefore the more especial favour of our good grace in time to come.

Yiven, etc. [2]
To Robert Kent

[***To the Master of St. Giles in the Fields Beside the City of London*** (n.d., 1446x1448)°]

BY THE QUEEN
Trusty, etc.

And forasmuch as we be informed that oon Robert Upham°, of the age of seventeen year, late chorister unto the most reverend fader in God, our bel uncle the cardinal (whom God assoil), at his college at Winchester, is now by God's visitation become lepour– [3]

We desire therefore and pray you – sith he hath none other succour ne livel'ood to live upon, but oonly of almès of Christen people (as it is said) that, at reverence of our blessèd Creatour, and in contemplation of this our prayer, ye will accept and receive him into your hospital of Saint Giles, unto such finding and livel'ood as other persons there in such case be accustomed to have, as we trust you. In which thing ye shall not oonly do a right meritory deed to God's pleasire, but deserve also of us right especial thank, etc.

To the Master of St. Giles in the field beside the City of London.

---

[1] *demeaning* ] conduct, behavior (*OED* demeanour, n.).

[2] *Yiven* ] given (dictated).

[3] *bel* ] beautiful (punning on Cardinal *Beau*fort's surname); *assoil* ] absolve from sin; *lepour* ] infected with leprosy, a greatly feared disease that often led to social isolation.

[***To Dame Jane Carew*** (1447x1449)°]

BY THE QUEEN
Right dear and well-beloved,

We greet you well. And forasmuch as our trusty and well-beloved squire, Thomas Burnby, shewer of our mouth, as well for the great zeal, love, and affection that he hath unto your person, as for the womanly and virtuous governance that ye be renowned of, "desireth with all his heart to do you worship by way of marriage, before all creatures living" (as he sayeth). [1]

We, desiring th' increase, furtherance and preferring of our said squire, for his manifold merits and deserts as for the good service that he hath done unto my lord and us, and yet there in daily continueth, pray you right affectuously that, at reverence of us, ye will have our said squire towards his said marriage especially recommended, inclining you to his honest desire at this time. The rather by contemplation of this our prayer, wherein we trust verily ye shall moe purvey right well for yourself (to your great worship and heart's ease), and cause us to have you both in such tenderness and favor of our good grace, that by reason ye shall hold you right well content and pleased. And how ye think to be disposed to our pleasire in this party, ye will ascertain us by the bringer of these, as our single trust is in you. [2]

Yiven, etc., at Eltham, the [date], etc.
To Dame Jane Carew

[***The Queen to the Executors of Cardinal Beaufort's last will and testament*** (18 March 1447/8)°] [3]

BY THE QUEEN
Most worshipful fader in God, our right well-beloved cousin, right trusty and well-beloved,

We greet you well. And forasmuch as my lord's servant and ours, Piers Preston, yeoman of the crown, hath letten us wit that oon W[illiam] Frutest and Agnes Knoughton, poor creatures and of virtuous conversation, purposing to live under the law of God in th'order of wedlock, have made togeder a lawful contract likely by their discretions to be of sad and commendable rule, if they were put forth and relieved by some almès at this time. Whereupon my said lord's servant and ours right humbly hath besought us that it would please us to have them towards you, in seeing unto them of alms of the goods of our bel uncle the Cardinal (on whose soul God have mercy), especially recommended. [4]

We, at insistence and humble supplication of our said servant, and in especial the meritory in relievement of the said poor creatures of so virtuous purpose and laudable intention (as it is rehearsed), desire and heartily pray that ye will – at reverence of us, and for the merit of our said uncle's soul – have them in such tenderness and favor, in departing with them of the said almès, that they may perceive this our letters unto them valuable; and that they fare the better by contemplation of this our prayer, as our full trust is in you. In which thing, etc. [5]

At Windsor the 18th day of M[arch]

To th'archbishop of York, Cardinal; th'earl of Dorset; and Richard Waller: Executors of our uncle late Cardinal of England

[***To Nicholas Straunge of Islington°, on the Marriage of his daughter Katherine*** (n.d., 1446x1448)°]

BY THE QUEEN
W[ell-beloved,]

Forasmuch as we have understand[ing], by certain our servants right nigh attending about our person, how, albeit that T[homas] Bugdon hath now late made a lawful contract with Kat'rine your daughter, and heartily desireth to do her worship by way of marriage (as well for his duty and lawful contract as "for the great zeal, love and affection that he hath unto her person, before all creatures living," as it is said); yet

---

[1] *shewer of our mouth* ] The *shewer* superintended the arrangement of the table, the seating of guests, and the tasting and serving of the dishes; often spelled *sewer*.

[2] *affectuously* ] earnestly, ardently; *moe purvey* ] to prepare, supply, more; *the bringer of these* ] the letter-carrier (will fill you in on the details).

[3] *Beaufort* ] Henry Beaufort (?1375-11 April 1547).

[4] *sad* ] serious, sober-minded.

[5] *meritory* ] possessing merit; deserving, praiseworthy (*OED* adj.).

ye, of willfulness and by sinister excitation, not having regard unto the said contract, will not apply you, ne condescend unto the said marriage, ne give thereto your benevolence ne assent; but rather, induce your said daughter to the contrary – against God, the church, and all truth (as unto us is reported), to our great marvel.

We therefore desire and pray you (and also on God's behalf exhort and *require* you, if it so be), that then ye incline you to th'accomplishment of the marriage without seeking any formal delay or impediment, otherwise than right law and good conscience asken and requiren in this partè. Demeaning herein in such goodly wise that the said T[homas] may, at reverence of us, be unto you especially recommended, and fare the better by contemplation of this our prayer.

As we trust you, etc.

Yiven, etc. at Placentia the 3d day of May
To Nicholas Strange of Islington°

### [*A Letter of Reproof to Sir John Forester, Knight* (n.d., 1446x1448)°]

BY THE QUEEN
Trusty and well-beloved,

We let you° wit that, this same day there have be' before us a great multitude both of men and women, our tenants of our lordship of Hertingfordbury, complaining them that ye have (and yet be, daily) about to destroy and undo them forever – insofar forth that ye have do' many of them to be wrongfully indicted, now late, of felony before the crowner, by your own familiar servants and adherents, not knowing the truth of the matter. And many of them ye do keep in prison, and the remnant of our tenants dare not abide in their houses for fear of death and other injuries that ye daily do them; and all by color of a farm that ye have there of *ours* that, as it is said, for your own singular lucre, ye wrongfully engross towards you all our tenants' livelihood there, not only unto great hindering and undoing of our said tenants, but also unto great derogation and prejudice of us and our said lordship, whereof we marvel greatly; and, in especial, that ye that be *judge* would take so peaceably the wrongful destruction of our said tenants. [1]

Wherefore we will, and expressly exhort and require you, that ye leave your said labors and business, in especial against us and our said tenants, unto time that ye have communed and declared you in this matter before us. And that the meanwhile, ye do suffer our tenants that be in prison to be mainprized, under sufficient surety; and the remnant of our tenants, guiltless, that be fled for fear of your destruction, may come home unto our said lordship. And if any of our tenants have offended against the law, our intent is that the truth known, he shall be painfully punished and chastised, as the case requireth. And how ye think to be disposed therein ye will ascertain us, by the bringer of this, whereto we shall trust; as ye desire to stand in the tender and favorable remembrance of our grace therefore, in time coming.

Yiven, etc. at Winds[or], the etc. [2]
To John Forester, Knight

### [*To William Gaskrik° respecting the marriage of his daughter* (n.d., 1446x1448)°]

BY THE QUEEN
Trusty and well-beloved—

Forasmuch as our well-[beloved] servant Thomas Fountains, yeoman of my lord's crown, as well for the womanly and virtuous governance that your daughter is renowned of, as for the great zeal, love and affection that he hath unto her person, "before all creature living desireth with all his heart to do her worship by way of marriage" (as he sayeth); whereupon my said lord [the king] hath tenderly written unto you for his recommendation in his behalf (which we suppose verily that ye have clearly conceived and well imprinted in your remembrance). We – desiring also th'increase, weal, and furtherance of my said lord's servant and ours, to th'accomplishment of my said lord's intention in his honest desire at this time, as well for his many and great virtues and good conditions, and also for the good and true service that he hath done unto my said lord and us, and yet therein daily continueth – pray right affectuously that, at reverence of us, sith your daughter is in your rule and governance (as reason is), ye will give your good as-

---

[1] *crowner* ] coroner; originally, an officer charged with maintaining the rights of the private property of the Crown; *lucre* ] derogatory term for money; *take so peaceably* ] tolerate (when in fact you are the actual instigator).

[2] *mainprized* ] released from prison.

sent, benevolence, and friendship t'induce and t'excite your said daughter t'accept my said lord's servant and ours to her husband, to the good conclusion and tender exploit of the said marriage, as our full trust is in you; in which thing ye shall moe do us right great pleasance, and cause us to have you and yours, in such things ye shall moe have for to do towards us in time coming, in such tender remembrance of our good grace, that by reason ye shall hold you well content and pleased by God's might; which have you in his blessèd keeping. [1]

At our manor of P[lacentia] the —, etc.
To William Gaskrik

[***From the Queen, recommending Dame Maud Everingham to be Prioress of Nuneaton*** (n.d., 1446/7)°]

BY THE QUEEN
Dear and well-beloved in God,

We greet you well, and we suppose verily that it is clearly in your remembrance how that we have now late written unto you for the recommendation of our right well-beloved Dame Maud Everingham to be accepted and elited for your prioress there, what time ye shall next be destitute of a prioress. And it is now so that we understand that your prioress is passed to God's mercy; whereupon my most 'doubted lord writeth unto you at this time, right especially for the recommendation of the said Dame Maud unto th'election of your prioress there. Wherefore we desire and pray you eftsoons that, in accomplishment of my lord's request and ours in this party, ye will have the same Dame Maud in your next election right tenderly recommended, and choose her to be your prioress and governor, by consideration of her many virtues, religious governance, and good fame, that she is renowned of; and the rather by contemplation of this our prayer; as our full trust is in you. In which thing ye shall, etc. Yiven, etc. [2]

To the Sub-prioress of Nuneaton
To the Master and Brethren of Nuneaton [3]

• • •

Additional letters in the same vein as these have survived by the dozens. Margaret writes to Catherine de la Pole, abbess of Barking, asking that favor be shown to Mr. and Mrs. Robert Osborne, tenants in an abbey-owned residence, who sought employment at Barking. She writes to the archbishop of Canterbury and Lord Chancellor, seeking pardon for "a poor widow, Alice Marwarth"; and seeks relief for John Goldston, wrongly arrested for debt (as surety to his friend Richard Read), for a bond not in default. Etc. Many who required relief from poverty or abuse, or needed employment or safe passage, or help with a marriage contract, found in Queen Margaret an earnest advocate. That she was an "Amazonian trull," the "she-wolf of France" with "a tiger's heart wrapp'd in a woman's hide," is theatrical propaganda.

But Margaret soon had her hands full with matters of greater consequence than matchmaking or letters of recommendation. The King's favorite churchman, Cardinal Beaufort, and the nation's favorite duke, Humphrey of Gloucester, both died in 1447, leaving the queen's favorite, William de la Pole, the most powerful man in England at a time when the English occupation of France was on the of collapse.[4] English losses in Brittany (1449), Normandy (1450), and Gascony (1453) left England with no foothold on the Continent but Calais. Margaret's favorites – the dukes of Somerset and Suffolk – were blamed not only for the secret surrender of Maine in 1448, but for the loss of Normandy. The duke of Suffolk fast became the most hated man in England; and Queen Margaret, the most hated woman. According to the Yorkist narrative, Englishmen shed their blood on French soil to maintain the right of Henry V; whose

---

[1] *increase* ] growth in wealth, prosperity, honor; offspring; *sith* ] since, seeing that (*OED* since, adv. 4); *moe* ] more (MS *mowe*).

[2] *elited* ] chosen, elected for office (*OED* elite v.); *'doubted* ] redoubted, i.e., respected; *Yiven* ] Given (dictated).

[3] *Master and brethren* ] the priory of Nuneaton had at this time both a monastery and an abbey, and was subordinate to the abbey of Fontrevrault, Anjou. The monks were nominal overseers of the activities of the nunnery. Margaret's support for Maud Everingham proved unfortunate. Appointed prioress of Nuneaton in 1447, Dame Maud proceeded to enrich herself at the convent's expense. In 1462, Nuneaton was taken into royal receivership, "on account of the bad and wasteful governance of Maud the Prioress." The appointed custodians impeached Maud and appointed Dame Elizabeth Barton. But Maud contrived to retain control of all revenues and continued to waste them as before.(Early Chancery Proceedings, bundle. 28, No. 282). When Henry VI was briefly restored to the crown in 1470/1, Maud forcibly ousted Elizabeth and retained control of the house until her death in 1499.

[4] Shakespeare represents Gloucester's death as a murder, ordered by Queen Margaret and the duke of Suffolk.

son on bad advice gave away two entire provinces in exchange for a French wife; whose allies then permitted France to take back the rest of their conquered country.

When Richard of York returned from Ireland, Parliament impeached and imprisoned both Somerset and Suffolk for criminal mismanagement of the occupation; and advanced Richard, duke of York, to within striking distance of the crown by naming him the heir apparent. Suffolk was to be banished for five years; but on his departure for Calais in a ship owned the Duke of Exeter, its crew beheaded him — acting, as widely believed, on orders of the Duke of York. Suffolk's bloated and headless corpse was discovered on a beach near Dover and given to his wife Alice for burial in Suffolk.

Henry, a gentle man, could never understand why his nobles, in such a nice place as Windsor Castle or Placentia (Greenwich) Palace, on such a scept'red isle as Britain, could not get along; or why they always wanted to kill one another. He did not understand why the good Lord helped his father to conquer France, only to help the French take it back again. These problems, with the added stressors of a bankrupt government, a decadent aristocracy, and a commons always in revolt about one thing or another, left King Henry quite literally astounded: he regressed into something like catatonic schizophrenia, as if he were in a trance, wholly unresponsive. Cared for at Windsor, he was fed and dressed by attendants.

On 13 October 1453, some 10-12 weeks after the king succumbed to madness, Margaret gave birth to a son, whose birth threw a roadblock in the duke of York's advance to the throne. York nonetheless made his move: it took some months and much wrangling to accomplish, but in March 1453/4, with the king still out of commission, a Parliament packed with his allies appointed Edward of York to be Lord Protector of the Realm and Chief Councilor until such time as the King recovered. Margaret was denied the right to serve as regnant queen. Parliament stopped short of disinheriting the prince. (The Yorkists had whispered abroad that Margaret's son was a bastard begot by Edmund Beaufort, Duke of Somerset, or by James Butler, Earl of Wiltshire; but Parliament didn't buy it.)

Historian Robin Storey has quipped that "If Henry's insanity was a tragedy, his recovery was a national disaster" (p. 159). Recovering on Christmas Day 1454, Henry taking the helm quickly alienated York and his allies, reinstating Somerset; not noting until too late that York had mustered an army and was marching on London. The stage was now set for the Wars of the Roses. Fighting commenced on 22 May 1455, with the first battle of St. Albans; where York with his then-ally Richard Neville, Earl of Warwick (the "Kingmaker"), scored an easy victory over Henry and Margaret's hastily mustered troops. Fewer than fifty men died that day, but the fallen included Somerset, the king's closest remaining ally. Also killed were Warwick's sworn enemies Henry Percy, earl of Northumberland; and Thomas, Baron Clifford. The King was captured and soon released – but the experience left him again in a helpless funk.

Margaret now stepped in to govern Henry's kingdom and to keep the opposition at bay. She had at first some measure of success: York fled to Ireland; his son Edward and the earl of Warwick fled to Calais; but rebellion remained in the air. Returning to England in 1460, the Yorkist leaders captured the king at Northampton; whereupon Henry was forced to do what Parliament had not dared: under compulsion, he disinherited his son and named Richard of York as heir to the crown. Margaret (with Prince Edward) retreated to Wales and Scotland, to raise troops.

In a Lancastrian victory at Wakefield on 30 Dec. 1460, Richard of York and his son Rutland were killed. (Contra Shakespeare's version, Margaret was not present and killed no one.) Edward of York (fourth duke, later, Edward IV) now became the new Yorkist candidate for king. Warwick taking control of London declared him Edward IV, king of England.

Margaret on this news marched her supporters and Scottish mercenaries south toward the capital. Warwick spread word that she intended to pillage all England south of the Trent. Upon receiving this intelligence, the queen drafted a proclamation in her own hand, whereby she reassured London of her intentions:

**Margaret of Anjou, Queen, to the Citizens of London** (Feb. 1460/1)

Right trusty and well-beloved, we greet you heartily well:

AND WHEREAS the late duke of [York°,] of extreme malice long hid under color, imagining by divers and many ways and means the destruction of my lord's good grace ([*King Henry*], *whom God of his mercy ever preserve*!)

– hath now late, upon an untrue pretense, feigned a title to my lord's crown, and royal estate, and pre-eminence (*contrary to his allegiance, and divers solemn oaths of his own offer made, uncompelled or constrained*);

– and fully purposed to have deposed him [the king] of his regality (*ne had been* [*but for*] *the sad, unchangeable, and true dispositions of you and other his true liegemen; for the which your worshipful dispositions, we thank you as heartily as we can!*) [1]

– and howbeit, the same untrue, unsad, and unadvised person, of very pure malice, disposed to continue in his cruelness, to the utterest undoing (if he might) of us, and of my said lord's son and ours, the prince (*which, of God's mercy, he* [*the duke of York*] *shall not be of power to perform, by the help of you and all other my lord's faithful disposed subjects*). [2]

– hath thrown among you (*as we be certainly informed*) divers untrue and feigned matters and surmises; and in especial, that we and [prince Edward,] my lord's said son and ours, should newly draw towards you with an unseen power of strangers, disposed to rob and to despoil you of your goods and havings; [3]

We will that ye shall know for certain, that:

– at such time as we or our said son shall be disposed to see my lord (as our duty is, and so binds us to do); ye, nor none of ye, shall be robbed, despoiled, nor wronged by any person that at that time we, or our son, shall be accompanied with; or [by] any other sent in our or his name.

– praying you, on our most hearty and desirous wise, that above all earthly thing ye will diligently intend to the surety of my lord's royal person in the mean time; so that, through the malice of his [the king's] said enemy, he be no more troubled, vexed, or jeoparded; and so doing, we shall be unto you such Lady as, of reason, ye shall be largely content. Yiven under our signet, etc.

Margarete

• • •

Scribal copies of Margaret's missive would have been posted throughout the city but for another battle: Warwick to block her way mustered troops north of the city. Margaret made a wide outflanking maneuver, took Warwick by surprise, cut him off from London, and on 17 February defeated him at the second battle of St. Albans. She regained custody of the King, then turned back north to defeat "King" Edward in Yorkshire—but failed. On 29 March 1461, at Towton, Margaret and the Lancastrians were soundly defeated by the Yorkists in a ten-hour battle that is said to be the bloodiest ever fought on English soil, leaving tens of thousands dead. Henry, Margaret, and Prince Edward fled to Scotland. Edward of York was crowned at Westminster on 28 June.

Warwick now fell to the task of finding King Edward IV a continental marriage that would strengthen his alliances. Instead Edward secretly married his lover, Elizabeth Woodville, a commoner, and showered favors on her kin, making many friends but alienating his brother George (duke of Clarence) and the earl of Warwick; who fell out with Edward IV and in 1470 allied themselves with the Lancastrians. The wars resumed, King Edward fled to France, and Warwick the kingmaker reseated Henry on the throne.

Edward IV from exile offered Margaret his daughter (Elizabeth of York) to be married to her son (Prince Edward), a marriage would unite the red rose of Lancaster with the white rose of York and put an end to the dynastic conflict. Unimpressed, Margaret declined to wed her son to the daughter of her enemy. Looking to match the prince with Warwick's daughter, Anne Neville, Margaret said no and may have laughed Edward's offer to scorn: In the same manuscript with Margaret's letters of matchmaking is an political parody from 1570, a mock marriage proffer in which a braggart "Balthasar," exiled king of Syria, offers to wed his daughter to the prince of Wales. If not written by Margaret herself, the parody was evidently penned for her amusement: no copy survives but with her correspondence.

---

[1] *sad* ] solemn, sober-minded.

[2] *unsad* ] unreliable, giddy; *shall not be of power to perform* ] i.e., because he was killed at Wakefield.

[3] *havings* ] property.

## [Balthasar, King of Syrie, to Margaret of Anjou (c. 1570)°]

I, BALTHASAR, by the grace of Mohownd King of kings, Lord of lords, soudan of Syrie, emperor of Babylon, steward of Hell, porter of Paradise, constable of Jerusalem, flower of all the world, and cousin to the great God— [1]

And if ye list to wit *why* that I am *King of kings*? – for I have, under my protection, 38 kings crowned! And I am *Lord of lords*, and *soudan of Syrie*, and *emperor of Babylon*? – for I wedded the emperor's daughter, the which was heir to her fader. Then, why that I am porter of Paradise, where that no man can come in without my license? – for I keep the streams and the water that *rens* to Paradise! Why that I am *steward of Hell*? – for I have domination of mammets and wicked spirits, and certain clerks within my realms that may bring them down to me in what likeness that I will have them. And why that I am *flower of all the world*? – for I may well say that I have in my keeping that [which] all Christen people believeth on; for that is, to wit, the Holy Cross that your Lord died on! (the which may not be gotten without my license). [2]

And why that I am *cousin to the great God*? – for I am a Christen man (as ye be in England). For using of Lollar'y I might not abide in England. And then I went to Rome; and from Rome, to Rhodes, and I perverted to the Soudan, in faith. And for because that I was a personable man, I was put to the Soudan his house; and there I was made usher of his hall and steward of his lands. And then died the Soudan, and I wedded his wife; and died she, and I wedded the emperor's daughter of Babylon; and thus became *soudan of Syrie*. [3]

And then I sent greeting to your king of England and of France, and to Edward prince of Wales. And if he will wed my daughter, I will become Christen man, and all my regions and my realms. And they that will not convert *with* me, shall be brent. And I will give with my daughter eight millions of gold and pay within five Sundays. And I shall deliver him the Holy Cross that your Lord died upon, and the spear that struck him to the heart, and many other relics that I have in my keeping; and shall make him emperor of eighteen kings' lands.

• • •

Refusing all other proffers, Margaret betrothed Prince Edward to Anne Neville. The marriage was solemnized 13 Dec. 1470, at Angers. The honeymoon, however, was brief: Margaret returned to England on 14 April 1471, the same day on which Warwick was killed at Barnet. On 4 May, Margaret was defeated at Tewkesbury: Prince Edward was killed and Margaret imprisoned. On 21 May, the day after Edward IV returned to London, King Henry was murdered in the Tower. A year later, Anne Neville married Edward IV's brother, Richard duke of Gloucester (later, Richard III). Margaret remained a prisoner for five years. Ransomed at last to France, she lived out her years as a poor relation of the French king (her father's property having passed to the Crown, not to her). She wrote a brief will on 2 August 1482 and died in Anjou on the 25th, aged 52. She was interred next to her parents in Angers Cathedral. [4]

DWF

Wheel of Fortune (fr. *Hortus Deliciarum,* the Garden of Delights, 12th century)

Illumination from the MS records of the London Skinners' Fraternity of Our Lady's Assumption, to which Margaret was admitted in 1475, the last year of her captivity before she was ransomed to France. Margaret kneels before a *prie-dieu,* on which is set an open Bible, a sceptre, and a crown, with the caption, "The Qween Margarete sūty/me Wyff and Spowse to kyng Harry the sexthe." At left (Margaret's right): Katherine Vaux.

[1] *Mahownd* ] Mohammed; *soudan of Syrie* ] sultan of Syria.

[2] *to wit* ] to know; *rens* ] run, flow; *mammets* ] idols.

[3] *Lollar'y* ] Lollardy (Balthasar pretends to be a persecuted Lollard who fled to Roman Catholicism, then to Islam); *might not abide* ] was not permitted to remain.

[4] During the French Revolution, an anti-monarchist mob removed and scattered Margaret's bones. The coffin of her father Rene, though undisturbed by the Revolutionaries, was opened in 1895 and his skeleton photographed. Margaret's remains, never recovered, escaped the photo shoot.

## The Findern Manuscript (1446 – c.1550)

*Ther for y take myn auentoure I wisse*
*As sche that hath for sakene Ioyus all*
(fol. 153v)

THE FINDERN manuscript (Cambridge University Library MS Ff.1.6) was compiled by an affluent family of Derbyshire during the reigns of Henry VI, Edward IV, Edward V, Richard III, Henry VII, Henry VIII, and perhaps Edward VI. From 1446 onward, at least forty different hands contributed, beginning with poetry and ending a century later with household accounts. Among the women whose names appear early on are two self-professed party girls, Elizabeth Cotton and Elizabeth Francis, who transcribed the anonymous romance, *Sir Degrevant* (fols. 96r-109v). At the end, the two Elizabeths lay claim to their contribution with the medieval equivalent of a social media message:

**[Postscript]**

Give 'hem Heaven for to see
That loveth gamen and glee
And guests to feed—
Elizabeth Cotton
Elizabeth Francis

Local Derbyshire records indicate that the families of Findern, Francis, Cotton, Hungerford, and Shirley were related by bonds of marriage, real estate, and common interests. Elizabeth Francis, who married a Findern, may be the poetry-lover who first undertook the book project. But the "Findern manuscript" is so called only by convention; no one knows to which Derbyshire family the book originally belonged, or when and how it changed hands. Little or nothing is known of the women whose names figure in the manuscript – among whom are Margery Hungerford, Anne Shirley, Frances Crucken, and possibly a mistress "Lewistoun," and Anne or Agnes Godwin.[1] The manuscript has been linked to a book of hours preserved in the library of St. John's College, Cambridge, a volume that was inscribed by Margaret Beaufort, mother of Henry VI, to an Anne Shirley ("My good lady Shyrley, pray for me that gevythe yow thys boke, I hertely pray yow / Margaret, moder to the kynge"); but that Anne Shirley (the second wife of Sir Ralph Shirley, d. 1517) may have been later.

*Magdalena Reading* by Ambrosius Benson (c. 1530) Courtesy of the National Gallery

The compilers of the Findern anthology draw on a range of sources and genres, having literary interests that centered on the vicissitudes of love. Chaucer is represented by Anelida's Complaint (from Anelida and Arcite); the Parliament of Fowls; Complaint unto Pity; the Complaint of Venus; and extracts from the Legend of Good Women. Gower supplies extracts from Confessio Amantis (the Lover's Confession). From Lydgate comes the Wicked Tongue and a Treatise for Laundresses. Also included is the Book of Cupid; or, The Cuckoo and the Nightingale, by Thomas Clanvowe (a contemporary of Chaucer and Gower); Richard Roos's popular translation of Alain Chartier's La Belle Dame sans Merci; and Thomas Hoccleve's version of Christine de Pizan's "L'Epistre au Dieu d'Amours." Intermixed are twenty-four unique poems of anonymous authorship, as many as fourteen of which may have been written by women, either by the book's owner or by visitors to the household from as far away as London.

---

[1] There are several Margery Hungerfords among prominent families of the period, including Margaret ("Margery") of Botreaux (d. Feb. 1477/8), the wife of Robert Lord Hungerford; whose inheritance included her father's "best legend of the lives of the saints" and a cup that once belonged to John of Gaunt; but no known Margery Hungerford has geographical or family ties to the other names mentioned in the manuscript.

The poems of unknown authorship (only some of which are reproduced here) present an interpretive challenge for the editor or reader: here is a collection that is known to include verse by men and women, copied into the book by women and men, all of whose contributions are recorded without concern for authorship. Is it possible, in any of the anonymous verses, to distinguish between a woman's voice and a man's? Even if phrasing or pronouns appear that indicate gender, is it possible to distinguish an "authentic" feminine voice from male ventriloquism (or vice versa)? or heterosexual from homosexual affection? Does a poem read, or mean, differently if its text assumed to written/copied/revised, or at least spoken, by a woman rather than by a man? Because most poems are recorded in the Findern manuscript without caption, title, or *finis* (sometimes in the same hand, sometimes not), how can we even know where each poet or speaker falls silent, and the next begins? And what difference does that make?

The first selection below – ["Farewell to my Betrothed,"] three stanzas, caption added – is spoken by a man, if one can assume heteronormativity in the poet's address to "my lady sovereign." But the stanzas immediately following are indeterminate: Does the heading, "Margery Hungerford, without Variance" imply that the ensuing lines were written *by*, *to*, or *about* Margery Hungerford? (Actual correspondence was often but not always signed at the top, addressed at the bottom.) Two seven-line stanzas, rhyming ABABBAA ("rhyme royal"), are addressed to the loved one. These are followed in turn by an ABAB quatrain in the same scribal hand, which may represent a new, unrelated, poem; or a continuation of the preceding, either by the same or a different speaker. Since the quatrain has either a male speaker, or a perhaps a woman speaking as a cruel rival, its relation to the preceding stanzas may determine the perceived gender of the speaker in stanzas 1 and 2. And even if all three stanzas are construed as intended for the same voice, that interpretive move can tell us nothing about the gender of the author(s), since all three stanzas may have been composed by a male or female poet, but for more than one speaker in the tradition of the dialogue poem; in which case ["Farewell to my Beloved"] may be by the same poet, may perhaps even be the same *text,* as the two, or three, ensuing stanzas. Moreover, the heading, "Margery Hungerford W$^{t}$ owte variance," may not even be *correct*, from the original author's point of view: it was added later, in a different fifteenth-century hand, above the text. The caption may, then, be unrelated to the verse, or a conjectural attribution, or other context that was once apparent to local readers, although not to us.

"What matter, who's speaking?" asked Foucault, quoting [Samuel, not Thomas à] Beckett. If the original scribes cared nothing for attribution, why should we? – especially if we already know that we cannot *know* who's speaking?

Such interpretive cruxes may in the end tell us less about the primary text than about our own critical practice. In literary scholarship (even in indexes of Middle English verse in manuscript), courtly or erotic verses addressed to a lover that do not expressly denote gender are assumed to be heteronormative, by a male poet, with a male speaker addressing a female auditor; often with invented modern captions (such as "The Lover to his Lady") that serve to eliminate gender ambiguity. The reverse has lately been true as well: both verse and prose texts have been claimed for women that were almost certainly written by men, including even sly misogynist satires.

The Paston letters supply a similar puzzle in a verse epistle in 56 lines, beginning, "My right good Lord, most knightly gentil knight..." (c. 1484). John Fenn in his 1823 edition of the Paston Letters assigns this charming poem a female author, a female speaker, and a male auditor; which determines, in his edition, its meaning, captioned thus (by Fenn): "VERSES written by a Lady in the reign of Henry VI or Edward IV, to an absent Lord with whom she was in love."[1] Fenn neglected to note, however, that the original text is entirely in the hand of John Paston III, including cancellations and corrections: Although the speaker sounds full of erotic feeling for a good lord, knightly gentle, the text was at least revised by Paston, and was probably his original composition. And yet, John Paston III was a heterosexual known to have begotten a daughter out of wedlock; while most of the letters or verses composed by the Paston women were taken down or transcribed by men. So who knows? Fenn could be right.

*Gender* is constructed not only in the cultural milieu that produced the text, it is constructed in our own interpretive assumptions and conscious choices when exploring such conundrums as the Findern manuscript.

DWF

---

[1] Ed. Fenn (1823), 2.304v-10v (transcription) and 2.305r-11r (normalized text).

**[Farewell to my Betrothed]** (fol. 20r)
***I may well sygh for greuous ys my payne…***

I may well sigh, for grievous is my pain
Now to depart from you thus suddenly!
My fair sweetheart, ye cause me to complain–
For lack of you I stand full pitously,
All in discomfort (withouten remedy)
  Most, in my mind, my lady sovereign–
  Alas, for woe, departing hath me slain!

Farewell, my mirth and chief of my comfort!
My joy is turnèd into heaviness
Till I again [un]to you may resort.
As for the time, I am but recureless,
Like to a figure which that is heartèless–
  With you hit is, God wit, I may not feign!
  Alas, for woe, departing hath me slain! 1

Yet, notwithstanding, for all my grièvaunce
Hit shall be taken right patiently,
And think hit is to me but a plesaunce
For you to suffer a great deal more truèly.
[I] will never change but keep unfeigningly
  With all my might to be both true and plain–
  Alas, for woe, departing hath me slain!

**Margery Hungerford, Without Variance** (fol. 20v)
***Where y haue chosyn stedefast woll y be…***

Where I have chosen, steadfast woll I be,
Neuer to repent in will, thought, ne dede,
Yóu to serve what ye commaunde me,
Neuer hit withdrawe for no manere dreade.
Thus am I bound by youre godlihead
  Which hath me caused and that in euery wise
  While I endure° to do you my servíce. 2

Yóur desert can none odére deserve
(Which is in my remembraunce, both day and night);
Afore all creatures, I you love and serve
While in this world I have strength and might—
Which is in duty, of very due right,
  By promise made, with faithful assuráunce
  Euer you to serve withouten variaunce. 3

Ye are to blame to set your heart so sore
Sithen that ye wot that hit is recureless
T'increase your pain more and more
Sin' that ye wot that she is merciless.

[1] *recureless* ] without remedy, unavoidable; cf. "hit is recureless," below, possibly by the same male poet; *hit* ] it (frequent).

[2] *Neuer* ] never (*one syll,* nyoor'); *serve* ] -erv- *pron.* -arv-; *what* ] in whatever; *hit* ] it; *hit withdrawe* ] withdraw from serving you; *godlihead* ] goodly (handsome) appearance, goodly (virtuous) character; *wise* ] (*wiss*'-eh); *cf.* service (sar-*viss*'-eh), *line 7.*

[3] *odere* ] other.

**[Sorrow]** (fol. 153r)
***This ys no lyf a las $y^t$ y do lede…***

This is no life, alas, that I do lead
It is but death as in life's likèness,
Endless sorrow, assurèd out of dread,
Past all despair and out of all gladness.
Thus well I wot I am remediless
For me nothing may comfort nor amend,
Till death come forth and make of me an end.

**[Goodbye]** (fol. 153v-144r)
***Yit wulde I nat the causer faryd a mysse…***

Yet would I not the causer fared amiss
For all the good that ever I had, or shall.
Therefore I take min aventure, iwis,
As she that hath forsaken joyès all
And to all pain is both soiét and thrall.
Lo, thus I stand, withouten wordès moe
All void of joy and full of pain and woe. 4

Now ye that bathe in mirth and [in] pleasaunce
Have mind on me that was sometime in ease
And had the world at mine own ordinaunce
Which now is turnèd into all dis-ease.
Now glad were she that Fortune so could please,
That she might stand in very sécureness
Never to feel the stroke of unkindness.

Departing is the ground of displeasunce,
Most in my heart of anything earthèly
I you ensure, holy in remembraunce.
Within myself I think it verily–
Which shall continue with me daily.
Since that ye must needs depart me fro'
It is to me a very deadly woe.

**[Alas, Why?]** (fol. 137v-138r)
***Alas alas and Alas why…***

Alas, alas, and alas – Why
Hath Fortune done so cruellíe
Fro me to take away the sight
Of that that geret' my heart light? 5

Óf all thing that in earth is
To me hit was the moste bliss
When that I was in [thy] presénce
To whom my heart doth reverence,

[4] *soiet* ] subject; a person under the rule of another.

[5] *geret'* ] (geareth) makes.

And euer shall – for weal or woe,
Or dread of friend, or life also,
Hit shall me neuer other a-start
But ye, to have my wholè heart – 1

Sáve when I come to the death
There needès oute must the breath
That keepeth the life [of] me within,
Ánd then fro' you must I twin. 2

And till the day hit [take] me o'er,
Right faithfully I you ensure
Thát there shall no earthly° thing
Ón my part make départing.

Thus am I set in stable wise
To live and dure in your servíce
Withoute feigning of my heart
Though I feel neuer-so-great smart.

**[Of a Star]** (fol. 143v-144r)

For to pent,
And after repent,
Hit were folíe. 3
Odere ways than troth
Me were full loath,
Truly. 4
I sweat for feint
Lest I be shent
To appear 5
The rémembráunce
Of my pleasáunce
Compilèd here: 6
Of a star
Without compare°,
Be likèness 7
In the beams,°
That hit yseems°
Most of swetèness,
And more oriaund,
And pure gloryaund
In beautíe; 8
Of all oder
Hit is the moder
In mine e'e. 9
In a cloud of blue
Hit did neuer remue
The sp'ere, 10
But euer in oon,
Bright hit shone,
Streaming clear – 11
But euer me meant
On me hit blent
With laughing cheer. 12
Hit to behold
Was I neuer a-cold,
The lonesome lere – 13
The streams thereof
Away drove
Euer the rack. 14
A wicked wind
Rose behind
At my back – 15
Hit was so loud,
Hit blew a cloud
Upright;
Hit was so black,
Hit did o'ertake
My sight.
But euer I pray,
Both night and day
(When I may speak),
The cloud so dim
Away to swim,
In pieces break, 16
That I may see
The star so free,
Shining bright
In the west,
That goeth to rest
Euery night.

---

[1] *weal* ] wellness; *neuer odere* ] (nyoor' o-dîr') never other; *Hit shall ... / heart* ] No amount of dread could make me give my whole heart to anyone but you.

[2] *There* ] Then; *twin* ] separate.

[3] *pent* ] paint (deceive).

[4] *troth* ] truth, faithfulness.

[5] *for feint* ] on account of faintness; *shent* ] hurt or disgraced; *appear* ] to appear like.

[6] *Lest ... remembraunce* ] lest I be made like the dream that is recounted here.

[7] *Be likeness* ] is a similarity.

[8] *oriaund* ] orient; brilliant; *gloryaund* ] glorious.

[9] *moder* ] mother; the highest and best; *Of all oder* ] among all other beauties; *e'e* ] eyes.

[10] *cloud* ] sky; *remue* ] remove from, leave (the pole star as a figure for her own constancy in love, while her mate wanders); *spere* ] sphere.

[11] *euer in oon* ] *ever in one*, one place, unchanging.

[12] *blent* ] ( = *blended, mingled*) shined upon; but with a continuing identification between pole star and poet; *me meant* ] as it seemed to me; *perhaps also*, it (the star) *signified me, could illustrate my situation*).

[13] *lonesome lere* ] lesson in solitude? *perhaps read*, lonesome lerer ( = *lonesome scholar*).

[14] *streams* ] beams; *rack* ] mass of clouds.

[15] *wind* ] perhaps a figure for her lord's displeasure.

[16] *dim* ] dark.

**[Continuaunce]** (fol. 138v-139r)

Continuaunce
Of remembraunce
Without ending
Doth me penaunce
And great grievaunce
For your parting.
So deep ye be
Graven'd, pardie,
Within mine heart
That a-fore me
Euer I you see
In thought covert.
Though I ne 'plain
My woeful pain
But bear it still,
It were in vain
To say again 1
Fortune's will

**[Men]** (fol. 56)

***What so men seyn…***

Whatso men sayen,
Love is no pain
To them, certáine,
But variaunce,
For they constrain
Their hearts to feign,
Their mouths to 'plain
Their displeasáunce 2
Which is indede
But feignèd dread
(So God me spede!),
And doubleness, 3
Their oaths to bede,
Their lives to lede,
And profereth mede
New-fangleness. 4
For when they pray,
Ye shall have *nay*!
Whatso they say,
Beware for shame,
For euery day
They wait their prey
Whereso they may,
And make but game. 5
Then seemeth me
Ye may well see
They be so free
In euery place, 6
Hit were pitíe
But they should be
Begelèd, pardíe,
Withouten grace! 7

**[Absence]** (fol. 69v)

***My woo full hert this clad in payn…***

My woeful heart thus° clad in pain,
Wote not well what do nor sayen,
Long absence grieveth me so. 8
For lack of sight near am I slain;
All joy mine heart hath in disdain,
Comfórt fro' me is go' 9
Then, though I would me aught complain
Of my sorr'we and great pain,
Who should comfórt me do? 10
There is no thíng can make me° fain,
But the sight of him again
That causes [all] my woe. 11
None but he may me sustain.
He is my comfort in all pain.
I love him and no moe.
To him I woll be true, and plain,
And euer his owne, in certáine,
Till death depart us two. 12
My heart shall I neuer fro' him refrain;
I gave hit him without constrain,
Euer to continue so. 13

---

[1] *say again* ] gainsay, speak out against.

[2] *'plain* ] complain (of their distress as lovers).

[3] *feigned dread* ] pretended anxiety; *So God me spede* ] so help me!

[4] *doubleness* (12-17) ] *bede* (v.1) to bring to bed, (v.2) to string like beads; *profereth* (v.1) prefer, profer (bring forth, speak of, produce), (v.2) proffer; mede (n.1) meed of (reward), (n.2) maid; *bede* and *lede*, if read as nouns, link men's *oaths* to *bed*, their *lives* to *lead*; etc.

[5] *game* ] 1. play, a big joke; 2. victims of the hunt.

[6] *seemeth me* ] it seems to me.

[7] *Begeled* ] beguiled, deceived by us women (*perhaps also with a hint that deceitful men should* "be geld," castrated); *pardie* ] by god!

[8] *Wote* ] knows; *what do nor sayen* ] what to do or say; *grieveth* ] (*grē′*-wit).

[9] *go'* ] gone.

[10] *aught* ] somewhat.

[11] *fain* ] rejoice; *with a pun on* feign.

[12] *moe* ] ( = *more*) others; *plain* ] guileless (*with pun on* [com]plain [v.], *lament*); *in certaine* ] for sure.

[13] *constrain* ] constraint.

### [**Love Cycle**] (fols. 135r-136r )

[I.]
Come home, dear heart, [your°] tarrying
Causeth me to weep, both wail and wring,
Also to live euer in distress,
So great there may no wight express.
All my joy ye turn to mourning.
Sorr'we is in my heart digging:
To death, I trow, he woll° me bring,
In woeful trance, without redress.

When I have of you some tiding,
Great joy I have, without failing,
Right as me ought, with rightwisness;
But yet may not mine heaviness
Depart from me till your coming.

[II.]
To you, my joy and my wordly pleasáunce,
I woll shrive me, with dreadful countenaunce
Of chiding, which your letter be'reth witnéss—
Thereto constrained by my woeful distress,
Askíng you absolution and penáunce. 1
What woll ye more of me but répentáunce?
God woll himself have thereof suffisáunce!
Mercíe I seek, and ask aye fóryevenéss. 2

By sáint Martín, and ye knew my grieváunce!—
Th' which I suff'red with long continuaunce,
Dreading ye were of my woes roughtèless.
That was to me a grievous heaviness—
Yet ask I mercíe to be in patiénce. 3

[III.]
There may arrest me no pleasáunce,
And hour by hour I feel grieváunce;
I n'ot to whom I may complain,
For he that may my woe restrain
Woll have of me no rémembráunce.
Sith I am under his governaunce,
He should set me such ordinaunce
As I might have ease of my pain. 4

Methinketh he might have consciénce
And of my woes some suffisaunce,
Consid'ring that I am so plain
To him euer – with joy, or pain.
Let *him* have thereof repentaunce!

[IV.]
Welcóme be ye, my soveraign,
The causer° of my joyful pain!
For the while ye were away,
Mine heart said nought but "wellaway!" 5
No more I do my mirthès feign,
But in gladnéss I swim and bain—
[My heart no more is clad in pain.]
Ye have my mourning driven away. 6

Of your comíng I am so fain
That mirthès doen my sorr'we stain,
And make among them such a fray
That rest may they with me no day.
Gladnéss ye have brought me again! 7

### [**Good Fortune**] (fol. 137r)
***Sith Fortune hath me set thus in this wyse…***

Sith Fortune hath me set thus in this wise
To love you best I° callèd be:
You to serve and truly please
Is my desire and heartès ease.

R. Campin, Mérode Altarpiece (*Cloisters*)

---

[1] *wordly* ] worldly; also, consisting merely of words; *I woll ... countenaunce* ] Your fearful displeasure (evident in your letter) I will endure while confessing myself to you and seeking absolution (as if to a priest); *be'reth* ] beareth (*pron. as 1 syll.*, breth).

[2] *What ... me* ] What more do you want from me?; *God ... suffisaunce* ] True repentance is a sufficient restitution even for our offenses against God; *ask aye foryeveness* ] forever beg your forgiveness.

[3] *and ye* ] if only you; *roughteless*] heedless.

[4] *n'ot* ] ( = *ne wot*) know not; *set ... ordinaunce* ] so arrange or provide for me.

[5] *wellaway* ] an exclamation of sorrow or grief.

[6] *bain* ] bathe.

[7] *mirthes . . . stain* ] joys obliterate my griefs.

## The PASTON LETTERS (selections, 1441-1478)[1]

*for to do þe grettyst labure þat any woman*
*on lyue myght, I wold not forsake yowe.*
—Margery Brews to John Paston III

AGNES PASTON, mother of four boys by William Paston, JP, labored for years to find a suitable match for their only daughter, Elizabeth. The effort to marry Bessie to a wealthy landowner, which commenced about 1443 (a year before the father's death), took sixteen years to complete. The sticking point was not that Elizabeth lacked beauty, brains, charm, or a dowry. The "lett" (obstacle) was that none of her suitors was of sufficient quality to meet the social and financial objectives of her widowed mother.

Most aristocratic men of the fifteenth century preferred to wed a girl not much older than fourteen, the legal age for consummation under Church canon law. When Bessie Paston reached age twenty and still no husband, Dame Agnes settled on Stephen Scrope (c. 1399-1472), the stepson of Sir John Fastolf (1378-1459). A widower in his 50s, Scrope was a "simple person" (weak-minded? innocent?);[2] and badly disfigured by an illness of fourteen years. The upside: older than Agnes herself and in middling health, he seemed likely soon to die and thereupon leave his bride a prosperous widow. [3]

There were quarrels. Elizabeth, to her mother's chagrin, resisted the match, and may indeed have told Dame Agnes to marry the old man herself. But Scrope had no interest in the mother. He wanted the girl.

Passing mention in the Paston letters indicate that William and Agnes while raising their five children exercised corporal punishment, with a rod, as set forth in Scripture. But with Elizabeth's disobedience over the proposed match to Stephen Scrope, the physical abuse became persistent and severe.

In June 1449, Elizabeth Clere, Fastolfe's niece and a close friend of Agnes Paston, wrote in confidence to the eldest Paston son (John I), lamenting that his sister Bessie at age 20 "was never in so great sorrow as she is nowadays," for "she may not speak with no man who soever come, ne not may see ne speak with my man (ne with servants of her moder's but that she beareth her an hand otherwise than she meaneth); and she hath sin' Easteren the most part be' beaten once in the week or twice, and sometimes twice on a day, and her head broken in two or three places."

Mastress Clere implored John Paston not to disclose the source of his information: "I pray you," she wrote in closing, "*bren* this letter, that your men, ne none other men see it. For an' my cousin your moder knew that I had sent you this letter, she should never love me."[4]

In the end, Elizabeth Paston surrendered to her mother's will, only to be saved from an unwanted marriage when the negotiations hit a snag over some unidentified question concerning Scrope's indentures. So it was back to square one.

In the years that followed, several men sought Bessie Paston's hand in marriage, if only to lay their own hands on her generous dowry of 400 marks, as stipulated in her father's will. But none of those men was land-rich enough for Agnes Paston to close on the deal. Elizabeth, deemed a spinster, was finally disposed of at age 29: Mother Agnes arranged a marriage for Bessie with Robert Poynings, a convicted felon who had been sword-bearer and carver to the infamous rebel, Jack Cade. Poynings (having been pardoned) was not without money and property; and Elizabeth reports further, in a letter to her mother

---

[1] Agnes (Berry) Paston (c. 1405-1479); Elizabeth (Paston) Poynings Brown (1429-1488); Margaret (Mautby) Paston (c. 1426-1484); Elizabeth (Debenham) Brews (c. 1440- c. 1502); Margery (Paston) Calle (c. 1446-1482); Margery (Brews) Paston (c. 1463-1495).

[2] Elizabeth Clere to John Paston I (29 June [1449]); °for citations, see Text Notes.

[3] Scrope (1852): 264-83.

[4] ibid., E. Clere; *beareth...meaneth* ] bluffs her intention (as at cards); *sin' Easteren* ] since Easter; *bren* ] burn.

during her first year of married life, that "he is full kind to me."° But the marriage lasted for just two years: Poynings took up arms for the Yorkist cause and was slain at the second Battle of St. Albans. [1]

Nor were Elizabeth's troubles yet over: in 1467, one Sir Robert Fiennes, with the complicity of Henry Bourchier (then steward of the household to Edward IV), forcibly evicted Elizabeth and her seven-year-old son from her home; imprisoned her steward; and confiscated her lands. Elizabeth appealed to King Edward, who issued a royal writ commanding Fiennes to vacate and to restore Elizabeth's property.

About 1471, Elizabeth married Sir George Browne, by whom she had a son and a daughter. That second marriage abruptly ended in 1483 when King Richard III beheaded Sir George for his involvement in Buckingham's rebellion.

The story ends with a happy mystery. Elizabeth Paston Poynings Browne – the widow of two proclaimed traitors – was at the time of her death possessed of a great fortune in lands, jewels, plate, and other goods. Her 1487 will makes generous bequests not only to her three children and many domestic servants, but to churches, poor houses, the bedridden, and to inmates of Newgate, Marshalsea, King's Bench, and Ludgate prisons. She commends her soul to God, makes her benefactions, and asks that her body be buried in the Church of the Blackfriars in London, beside her beloved second husband, Sir George. Having outlived three of her four brothers, Elizabeth in her will makes no mention of her unhappy childhood, nor so much as mentions the name, *Paston*.

THE FOUR SONS of William and Agnes Paston had smoother sailing than Elizabeth, most especially John, the eldest son and heir. On a spring morning in 1440, William Paston received a letter from Agnes containing news that she wrote in her own hand, in haste, not waiting for a secretary: Their son John (1421-1466) had expectations of a marriage with Margaret Mautby, the effervescent daughter and heiress of John Mautby, a neighboring landowner. This fortuitous match, which would advance the Pastons' acquisition of Norfolk real estate, was clapped up quickly and lasted for a quarter century.

If John and Margaret Mautby Paston had a child in their first eighteen months of marriage, it did not survive. But by mid-December 1441, Margaret had a very noticeable baby bump from the child who would become John Paston II. As the holidays approached, Margaret wrote to her husband, who was in London on business, reminding him that she needed a new gown and sash for her maternity and lying-in:

### [Margaret (Mautby) Paston to John Paston I (14 December [1441])]°

To my right reverend and worshipful husbond, John Paston:

Right reverend and worshipful husbond,

I recommaund me to you, desiring heartily to hear of your welfare, thanking you for the token that ye sent me by Edmund Parries, praying you to wit that my moder sent to my fader to London for a gown-cloth of musterdevillers, to make of a gown for me. And he told my moder and me when he was come home that he charged *you* to buy it, after that he were come out of London. I pray you, if it be not bought, that ye will vouchsafe to buy it and send it home as soon as ye may – for I have no gown to wear this winter but my black and my grenadine, and that is so cumbrous that I am weary to wear it. [2]

As for the girdle that my fader behested me, I spake to him thereof a little before he yede to London last, and he said to me that the fault was in you, that ye would not think thereupon, to do-make it (but I suppose that is not so; he said it but for a 'scusation). I pray you, if ye dare take it upon you, that ye will vouchsafe to do-make it agains' ye come home, for I had never more need thereof than I have now – for I am waxed so fetys that I may not be girt in no bar of no girdle that I have, but of one.[3]

---

[1] Elizabeth Paston Poynings to Agnes Paston I (3 Jan. [1458/9]). Elizabeth's purpose in writing on this occasion was to ask that the first installment of 100 marks (as stipulated in her father's will and promised by her mother) will be paid soon. The tone of her letter is respectful but icy.

[2] *to wit* ] to know; *musterdevillers* ] mixed grey woollen cloth widely used in the fourteenth and fifteenth centuries (by corruption of *Montivilliers,* Normandy, where such cloth originated).

[3] *girdle* ] a belt or sash worn around the waist; *behested* ] promised; *yede* ] went; *'scusation* ] excuse; *waxed so fetys* ] a joke: 1. grown so *featous* (*OED* "well-formed, well-proportioned, handsome"); 2. grown so *fette* ("fat," "plump"); *bar* ] an ornamental transverse band on a girdle.

Elisabeth Peverel hath lay sick fifteen or sixteen weeks of the sciatica, but she sent my moder word, by Kate, that she should come hider when God sent time, though she should be carried in a barrow! [1]

John of Damm was here, and my moder discovered me to him. And he said, by his troth that he was not gladder of nothing that he heard this twelvemonth, than he was thereof.

(I may no longer live by my craft – I am discovered of all men that *see* me!) [2]

Of all oder things that ye desired that I should send you word of, I have sent you word of in a letter that I did write on Our Lady's Day, last was. [3]

The Holy Trinity have you in His keeping. Written at Oxned, in right great haste, on the Thursday next before Saint Thomas Day. [4]

I pray you that ye will wear the ring with the image of Saint Margaret that I sent you for a remembrance, till ye come home.

(Ye have left *me* such a remembrance, that maketh me to think upon you both day and night, when I would sleep!) [5]

Yours,

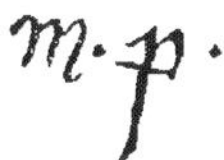

Though John Paston's career as a barrister and justice of the peace kept him often in London, his marriage appears to have been entirely affectionate. One autumn, upon hearing that John was laid up with an ulcerous sore and unable to travel, Margaret wrote of her longing to be with him: in fact, she would rather John were home again than to be given a costly new gown, of scarlet:

**Margaret Paston to John Paston I (28 September [1443]°)**

Right worshipful husbond,

I recommaund me to you, desiring heartily to hear of your welfare, thanking God of your a-mending of the great dis-ease that ye have had. And I thank you for the letter that ye sent me – for, by my troth, my moder and I were nought in heart's ease, from the time that we wost of your sickness till we wost verily of your a-mending. [6]

My moder hath behested anoder image of wax (of the weight of *you*!) to our Lady of Walsingham, and she sent four nobles to the four orders of friars at Norwich to pray for you. And I have behested to go on pilgrimage to Walsingham and to St. Leuonard's for you. By my troth, I had never so heavy a season as I had fro' the time that I wost of your sickness, till I wost of your a-mending, and yet mine heart is in no great ease, ne nought shall be, till I wot that ye be'n very whole. ...[7]

I pray you heartily that [ye°] woll vouchsafe to send me a letter as hastily as ye may (if writing be none dis-ease to you), and that ye wollen vouchsafe to send me word how your sore doth.

---

[1] *though ... barrow* ] even if she has to be carried in a wheelbarrow.

[2] *discovered me to him* ] disclosed that I'm pregant (but now, all who see me, discover it, without being told).

[3] *Our Lady's Day* ] 8 December (feast of the conception of the Virgin Mary).

[4] *Saint Thomas Day* ] 21 December.

[5] *such a remembrance* ] another joke: departing for London, he left her pregnant.

[6] *wost* ] knew (also *wot, wit, weet*).

[7] *Our Lady of Walsingham* ] a shrine to the virgin in Walsingham, Norfolk, where it was believed the Virgin appeared to Lady Richeldis de Faverchis in 1061; chandlers made images of wax that served as a substitute for those persons in need of prayer; *nobles* ] gold coins, a sum equivalent to £1 6s. 8d; *behested* ] promised; *St. Levonard's* ] the church of the Priory of St. Leonard's, another popular resort of pilgrims, featuring shrines of the Virgin, the Cross, and St. Andrew.

If I might have had my will, I should ha' seen you ere this time. I would ye weren at home – if it were your ease; and your sore might be'n as well looketh to here as it is there ye be'n now – liefer than a new gown, though it were of scarlet!

I pray you – if your sore be whole and so that ye may endure to ride, when my father come to London that ye woll asken leave, and come home when the horse shall be sent home again. For I hope ye shall be kept as tenderly here as ye be'n at London!

I may none leisure have, to do-written half a *quarter* so much as I should sayen to you if I might speak with you! (I shall send you anoder letter as hastily as I may.) I thank you that ye would vouchsafe to remember my girdle, and that ye would write to me at this time, for I suppose that writing was none ease to you. Almight' God have you in His keeping, and send you health. Written at Oxnead, in right great haste, on St. Michael's Even.

Yours,

M. Paston

[*postcript*:] My moder greeteth you well and sendeth you God's blissing and hers°; and she prayeth you, and I pray you also, that ye be well dieted of meat and drink, for that is the greatest help that ye may have now, to your healthward. (Your son fareth well, blissèd be God!)

Despite a high mortality from childhood diseases and the plague, seven children of John Paston I to Margaret Mautby survived to adulthood: two sons, both named John (not unusual, at the time), followed by two daughters (Margery and Anne) and three younger sons (Edmund, Walter, and William II). But the last years of John Paston I were unquiet ones. When the Norfolk magnate, Sir John Fastolf, died in 1459, he named Sir William Yelverton as his executor, and John Paston, co-executor, as his sole heir. This, in a last will and testament that Yelverton claimed was a rank forgery. Proclaiming himself the intended heir, Yelverton sold the Fastolf estates of Cotton and Helleston to Alice (Chaucer) de la Pole, the duchess dowager of Suffolk; the manor of Drayton, to her son, William de la Pole, 2nd duke of Suffolk.

Litigation ensued. Before the dispute was resolved, the duke of Suffolk with 500 men took Cotton, Helleston, and Drayton by force of arms. John Paston in 1465, and many of his servants, were cast into prison and kept there for months while the powerful duke took possession of the confiscated manors.

Yelverton next sold Fastolf's highly prized Caister Castle to Thomas Mowbray, duke of Norfolk; claiming the unsold lands for himself: Yelverton rode from one remaining Fastolf manor to another, commanding the tenants to pay their rents, not to John Paston, but to his own agents; else face eviction.

In 1466 John Paston died suddenly in London, age 44, in his chamber at the Inns of Court. Margaret blamed his death on the legal troubles.

Her eldest sons, John II and John III, hung out together for a time. At the 1468 wedding of King Edward's sister Margaret, in Bruges, the Paston boys (now 26 and 24) served in the wedding train. Shortly after, King Edward knighted of John the elder – which was quite the social coup, in a family of peasants that by its own scrappy determination had fought its way to respectability. John III returned to Norfolk, and in his brother's behalf took possession of Caister Castle. The duke of Norfolk on this news raised a militia, to throw him out: Caister, he said, was his.

Looking to her eldest son for guns, crossbows, and men, Dame Margaret wrote to him in London, Sir John was rubbing shoulders and other parts with members of the court, thanks to his employment as a champion jouster in the royal tournaments. Trusting to the courts, he wished not to be bothered with talk of mounting an armed conflict with one of Britain's most powerful men.

Then came another unlooked-for catastrophe: at the height of these troubles, Margaret's only daughter, Margery, secretly pledged herself in marriage to Richard Calle, long-time Paston bailiff for the collection of rents. This outrage was beyond endurance. Dame Margaret vowed that her late husband's name would not be dishonored, nor her upwardly mobile family tainted by intermarriage with one of her own servants, a commoner who owned no real estate.

Margaret had once hoped to wed Margery to the son of Sir John Howard, or to the son of Sir John Cleys. Those two matches fell through; but she was well along in negotiations with John Strange, gent., who in his nephew's behalf had a proffer on the table of £60 jointure and 40 marks per year of inheritance; against Margery's dowry of 400 marks. But the girl's self-appointed betrothal with Richard Calle was a deal-breaker.

Sir John, when he heard of his sister's betrothal to Richard Calle, accused John III of negligence in supervising his sister's behavior. The younger John wrote back, stating that even "if my father, whom God assoil, were alive and had consented thereto, *and* my moder, *and* ye both," Richard Calle "should never have *my* goodwill for to make my sister to sell candle and mustard in Framlingham."°[1]

Under canon law, the plighted troth of two consenting parties, aged 12 or more, was binding and could not be revoked. Margaret moved to prevent the marriage from being consummated: Richard Calle she suspended from service, and Margery she kept in seclusion, demanding that she renounce her pledge. But Margery remained true; and with Calle waiting in the wings, all other marriage plans for Margery were thereby rendered futile: when the banns were called, an impediment would be raised by the Pastons' own bailiff.

In August 1469, amidst these family woes, and with anarchy spreading throughout England, the Duke of Norfolk, accompanied by William Yelverton and a private militia, marched on Caister Castle. John III with thirty men barricaded themselves inside, outnumbered a thousand to one and vastly outgunned.

The duke was unwilling to fire cannon-shot at a structure that he wished to possess; but neither did John Paston have the resources to withstand a siege: unless the king intervened, or Sir John raised an army, Caister would be lost.

Dame Margaret was now on her own in dealing with the marriage crisis – she was on the outs with her bailiff; John III was holed up in the castle, surrounded by a hostile force of three thousand men, commanded by one of the most powerful men in England; and her eldest was having fun in London, disinclined to defend his own prime real estate, trusting that the courts would sort it out.

Added to all of that were the money troubles: Dame Margaret did not anticipate the loss of rents that would ensue without Calle, her capable and indispensible bailiff, whose job it was to collect payments due from her hard-pressed tenants; and when asked to do resume, he refused; whereupon some tenants paid Yelverton instead.

Dame Margaret in desperation returned Calle to the payroll; but under no circumstance would she permit him to speak with her daughter, much less accept him as her son-in-law.

Richard Calle comported himself throughout this ordeal with patience and courtesy. But with Margery approaching her third year as a domestic prisoner, his patience wore thin. Incommunicado for more than two years, he smuggled his bride a letter:

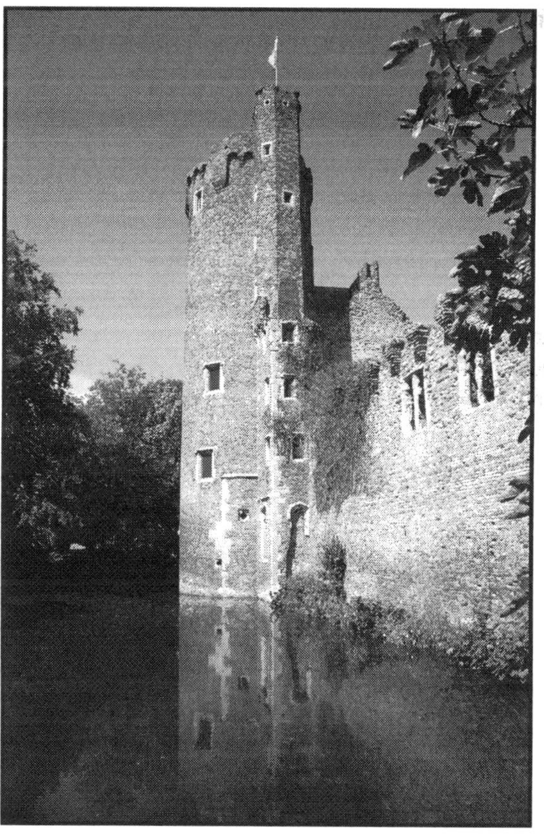

Caister Castle today

[1] John Paston III to Sir John Paston (May 1469), MS Add. 34889, fol. 77; *assoil* ] absolve of sin.

## [Richard Calle to Margaret Paston (August 1469)]°

My own lady and mistress, and before God very true wife,

I with heart full sorrowful recommaund me unto you as he that cannot be merry, nor nought shall be till it be otherwise with us than it is yet. For this life that we lead now is n'other pleasure to God nor to the world, considering the great bond of matrimony that is made betwix' us, and as also the great love that hath be' (and as I trust, yet is) betwix' us – and as on my part, never greater. Wherefore I beseech almighty God comfort us as soon as it pleaseth Him, for we that ought of very right to be most together, are most asunder.

Meseemeth it is a thousand year ago, sin' that I spake with you. I had liefer than all the good in the world, I might be with you. Alas, alas, good lady! Full little remember they what they do, that keep us thus asunder.... But what, lady? Suffer as you have do', and make you as merry as ye can, for iwis, lady, at the long way God woll, of His rightwisness, help His servaunts that mean truly and would live according to His laws, &c. [1]

I understond, lady, ye have had as much sorrow for me as any gentlewoman hath had in the world – as (would God!) all that sorrow that *ye* have had had rested upon *me*, so that ye had be' discharged of it! for iwis, lady, it is to me a death to hear that ye be entreated otherwise than ye ought to be. This is a painful life that we lead....

(I pray you, let no creature see this letter. As soon as ye have read it, let it be brent, for I would no man should see it, in no wise.) ...

I remit all this matter to your wisdom. Almighty Jesu preserve, keep, and give you your heart's desire, which I wot well should be to God's pleasure, &c.

This letter was written with as great pain as ever wrote I thing in my life, for in good faith I have be' right sick, and yet am not verily well – God amend it.

Richard Calle

On 8 September 1469, the dispute over the betrothal was presented for adjudication before Walter Hart, lord Bishop of Norwich: Calle begged to be united with his bride; Dame Margaret Paston demanded annulment. (The elder brothers did not attend: John III was tied up at Caister Castle, nearly out of food and ammunition; and Sir John remained in London.)

At the inquest, the bishop interrogated Richard and Margery separately, asking each to repeat the exact words spoken in their long-ago pledge; thereby to determine whether the betrothal was binding in the eyes of God. Richard remained firm for love. Before asking Margery, this bishop delivered a litany of the evils that would ensue–including the loss of her dowry and excommunication from her family–if she indeed gave her trothplight without parental consent.

Margery "boldly" repeated her vow, adding: "if tho' words made it not sure ... she would *make* it sure, ere-then she went thence; for she said she thought in her conscience she was bound, whatsoever the words weren." [2] Possibly vexed by Margery's resolve and Margaret's displeasure, the bishop said he needed two weeks before pronouncing the Church's decision.

Dame Margaret's decision was rendered straightaway: When Margery returned home to Oxnead (under escort of the bishop's men), she was met at the gate by Rev. John Glois, the Pastons' chaplain, who announced to Margery that she was henceforth excommunicate from her family. Because of her disobedience, never again would she be received by her mother, nor by her brothers, nor by any of her mother's friends or kin.

Returning to Norwich, the hapless bride threw herself on the mercy of the bishop. Though his lordship had forewarned Margery what would happen, if she persisted in her commitment to Calle, he condescended to find temporary lodging for her, first at the home of Roger Best (a grocer, alderman, and sometime sheriff of Norwich); then at the Blackborough convent, near Lynn.

John III could not be reached for comment. But to Sir John II in London, mother Margaret sent the sorry news, together with a note of consolation for the irrevocable loss of a sister:

---

[1] *liefer* ] rather; *good* ] gold, money.

[2] Margaret Paston to Sir John Paston (10-11 Sept. 1469), B.L. 34889, fol 83v.

### [Margaret Paston to Sir John Paston (10/11 Sept 1469)°]

...I pray you, and require you, that ye take it not pensively, for I wot well it goeth right near your heart, and so doth it to mine, and to other. But remember you, and so do I, that we have lost of her but a *brothel*; and set it the less to heart. For, an' she had be' *good* – whatso *ever* she had be'! – it should ha' been as it is. For an' he [Richard Calle] were *dead* at this hour, she should never be at my heart as she was! .... Wot it well: she shall full sore repent her lewdness, hereafter. And I pray God, she mot so. [1]

On or about the same day that Dame Margaret expelled her daughter from Oxnead, her long-time steward, John Daubney, was slain at Caister by the silent shot of a sniper's crossbow. The duke to force a surrender was now firing at will, not just with crossbows, but cannon-shot. The plight of John Paston III and his 29 men was grown desperate.

Margaret wrote again to her eldest, this time in high rage: Sir John's little brother was defending Sir John's own castle against the powerful duke of Norfolk. His little sister, now dead to the family, had absconded with her bailiff. Her steward was shot dead. And Sir John remained in London, competing in tournaments and sleeping with Anne Haute, doing nothing to help:

### [Margaret Paston to Sir John Paston (12 Sept 1469)°]

[*no address*] I greet you well, letting you wit that your brother and his fellowship stand in great jeopardy at Caister, and lack victual... Daubney and Berney be dead and divers other greatly hurt, and they fail gunpowder and arrows. And the place [is°] sore broken with guns of the t'other party; so that, but they have *hasty* help, they be like to lose both their lives *and* the place – to the greatest rebuke to *you* that ever came to any gentleman – for every man in this country marveleth greatly that ye suffer them to be so long in so great jeopardy without help or other remedy.

A Paston servant named Writtle was dispatched to Sir John London with news of the siege, and the urgent letter from his mother. But if Margaret ever doubted that her elder son was a knucklehead, his next move removed all doubt: Sir John patronized his mother a scoffing reply and a request for money:

### [Sir John Paston to Margaret Paston (15 Sept 1469)°]

Moder,

Upon Saturday last, was Daubney and Berney were on-live and merry – and I suppose that there coom no man out of the place to you sin' that time, that could have ascertained to you of their deaths! And as touching the "fierceness" of the Duke or of his people showed sin' that time that Wretyll departed, I trow it was concluded that truce and abstinence of war should be had ere he departed; which shall 'dure till Monday next coming. And by that time, I trow that truce shall be taken till that day sevennight after, by which time I hope of a good direction shall be had.... But as to say that they *shall* be rescued: if all the land that I have in England and friends may do it, they *shall* (and God be friendly!); and that, as shortly as it may goodly and well be brought about. And the greatest default earthly, is *money* (and some friends and neighbors, to help); wherefore I beseech you to send me comfort what money ye could find the means to get (or 'chevise upon surety sufficient, or upon livel'ood to be in mor'gage ere yet sold, and what people by likel'ood your friends and mine, could make upon a short warning; and to send me word in all the haste as it is needful. [2]

---

[1] *a brothel* ] a degenerate (originally, *brothel* was a person, and *bordel,* a place; *brothel-house* was then shortened to *brothel*); *mot so* ] may indeed (suffer for her "lewdness" in having pledged to marry without parental permission).

[2] *'chevise* ] achieve, accomplish; *surety* ] collateral; *livel'ood* ] livelihood; i.e., entailed rental income.

But Moder, I feel by your writing that ye deem in me I should not do my duer without ye wrote to me some "heavy tidings." And, Moder, if I had need to be quickened with a *letter* in this need, I were of myself too slow a fellow! But, Moder, I ensure you that I have heard ten times worse tidings sin' the assiege began, than any letter that ye wrote to me (and sometime°, I have heard right *good* tidings, both!). But this I ensure you: that they that be within [Caister] have no worse rest than I have, ne casteth more "jeopardy." But whether I had good tidings or ill, I take God to my witness that I have done *my* devoir as I would be done for in like case, and shall do till there be an end of it. [1]

Wretyll was dispatched back to Sir John in London, with more heavy tidings, and another a letter from his mother.

**[Margaret Paston to Sir John Paston (30 Sept 1469)°]**

To Sir John Paston, in haste:

I greet you well and send you God's blissing and mine; letting you wit that methinks° by the letter that ye sent me by Robin that you think that I should write you fables and imaginations. But I do not so. ... for certain, Daubney is dead, God assoil his soul, whereof I am right sorry and that it had pleased God that it might be oderwise....

Item, as for money, I could get but £10 upon pledges, and that is spent for your matters here, for paying of your men that were at Caister (and other things); and I wot not where to get none, n'other for surety nor for pledges. And as for mine own livel'ood, I am so simply paid thereof that I fear me I shall be fain to borrow for myself, or el' to break up household, or both.

And as for the yielding of Caister, I trow Wretyll hath told of 'pointments how it is delivered. I would that had be' so ere this time, and then there should not ha' be' so mickle hurt as there is in divers ways, for many of our well-willers aren put to loss for our sakes, and I fear me it shall be long ere it be recompensed again, and that shall cause other to do the less for us hereafter. I would ye should [send°] to your brother word, and some other that ye truth, to see to your own livel'ood, to set it in a rule, and to gather trust thereof that may be had in haste; and also of Sir John Fastolf's livel'ood (that may be gathered in peaceable wise). For as for Richard Call, he woll no more gather it but if ye command him; and he would fain make his account and have your good mastership (as it is told me)...and he sayeth he will not take none new master till ye refuse his service. Remember that your livel'ood may be set in such a rule that ye may know how it is, and what is owing to you. For by my faith, I have holpen as much as I may, and more, saving myself. And therefore take heed, ere it be worse.

This letter was begun on Friday was seven-night and ended this day next after Michaelmas Day. God keep you an give you grace to do as well as I would ye did. And I charge you, beware that ye set no land to mortgage, for if any a'vise you thereto, they aren not your friends. Beware betimes by mine a'vise, etc. I trow your brother will send you tidings.

In haste—

Having returned to his mother's home in defeat, John's thoughts turned once again to marriage, though with diminished financial resources. As early as 1467, John the younger had sought a match with Mastress Alice, the youngest daughter of Sir Geoffrey Boleyn; but the girl's widowed mother would have none of him. And Alice Boleyn was already his fourth or fifth failure to find a soulmate.

On 1 March 1469/70, John wrote to his elder brother: "I pray, get us a wife somewhere, for *melius est nubere in domino quam urere*."°[2] Sir John took the matter under advisement.

---

[1] *devoir* ] duty, area of responsibility, appointed task.

[2] Paston quotes St. Paul's view of marriage as a necessary evil, a last resort against the sins of lust and masturbation (1 Cor. 7:9).

When the popular earl of Warwick (Richard Neville, "the Kingmaker") broke from Edward IV to support the return of Henry VI, many of the Norfolk gentry followed, including (eventually) the Paston boys, who took up arms for the Lancastrian cause at the Battle Barnet (14 April 1471), a decisive engagement that left Warwick dead, Edward IV securely on the throne, and John Paston III out of commission with an arrow wound in his fore-arm.

At Tewkesbury on 4 May, Edward's army crushed the Lancastrians, taking captive Margaret of Anjou and killing her son, prince Edward. On the night of May 21st, her husband King Henry died in the Tower of London, of "melancholy." Edward (who doubtless issued the command for his rival's fatal sadness) was re-crowned the next morning, before Henry's blood had cooled.

The Wars of the Roses appeared at last to have ended, with a total victory for the Yorkists.

John the younger's thoughts turned again to marriage. Mastress Katherine Dudley, of independent means, declined; a Lady Grisacres, and Lady Elizabeth Bouchier, and "Stockton's daughter" were promised to others. He next tried for the daughter of Eberton, a wealthy London draper. That, too, fell through, despite much kibitzing from his elder brother; who (while cohabiting with Anne Haute and their illegitimate daughter) was himself scouting for a wife. In a March 1477, writing to his younger brother on the issue of holy matrimony, Sir John mentions his current flame, a certain Mastress Barley: "She is a little one! She may be a woman hereafter, if she be not old now: her person seemeth thirteen year of age; her years, men say, be'n full eighteen. She knoweth not of the matter, I suppose; nevertheless, she desired to see me, as glad as I was to see her."° But the girl's father was unable or unwilling to offer Sir John a satisfactory jointure, and the moment passed.

John III first heard of Margery Brews of Topcroft "by many and divers persons, and especially by my right trusty friend Richard Stratton."°[1] About December 1477, he chose Stratton, a mutual friend of the Paston and Brews families, to carry a discreet letter of inquiry to the maid. Although they had never met., they had perhaps seen one another at church. Margery, pushing fourteen, returned a green flag for Paston to approach her parents with an offer.

The lovesuit at first went swimmingly: Paston's mother, and Margery's, were thrilled with the prospect. (Sir John, in London, was not yet consulted.) Paston by invitation paid a visit to Topcroft, whereupon Margery's mother, Dame Elizabeth Brews, presented her husband's terms: a jointure of £100, plus a loan of £100, to be repaid at the rate of £20 per year, the repayments to come from some other source than the marriage money – i.e., from the Paston side.

That spelled trouble: John Paston II as a younger brother lacked substantial income. He returned home without a contract.

In the meantime, Margery's mother, Dame Elizabeth Brews, consulted with her father, who was willing to chip in. She then wrote again to Paston, inviting him to meet with her husband for further negotiations:

### [Dame Elizabeth Brews to John Paston III (ca. January 1476/7)°]

Right worshipful cousin,

I recommaund me unto° you, &c. And I sent mine husbond a bill of the matter that ye know of, and he wrote anoder bill to me again, touching the same matter. And he would that ye should go unto my mastress your moder, and assay if ye might get the whole £20 into your hands; and then he would be more glad to marry with you, and will give you an° £100. And, cousin, that day that she is married, my fader will give her 50 mark. But, an' we accord, I shall give you a greater treasure: that is, a witty gentlewoman, and (if I say it) both good and virtuous – for if I should take money for her, I would not give her for a *thousand* pound! But, cousin, I trust you so much that I would think her well beset on you, and ye were worth much more.[2]

---

[1] Margery (Brews), later Paston: not to be confused with Margery (Paston) Calle, now eight years married and still excommunicate from her mother and brothers.

[2] *mine husbond* ] Sir Thomas Brews, father of Margery; *bill* ] letter; *my mastress* ] courteous form of address, corresponding to *Mrs.* in modern English; *£20* ] i.e., for the first payment on the loan, without having to touch his received capital; *mark* ] 1 mark = 8 oz. of silver; *and we accord* ] if we can agree on a marriage settlement (*and* = *if*; again below); *and ye* ] even if you.

And, cousin, a little after that ye were gone, coome a man fro' my cousin Derby, and brought me word that such a chance fell that he might not come at the day that was set (as I shall let you understond more plainly, when I speak with you, &c.). But, cousin, an' it would please you to come again what day that ye will set, I dare undertake that they shall keep the same day, for I would be glad that mine° husbond and ye might accord in this marriage – that it might be my fortune to make an° end in this matter between my cousins and you, that each of you might love other in friendly wise, &c. [1]

And, cousin, if this bill please not your intent, I pray you that it may be brent, &c. No more unto you at this time, but almighty Jesus preserve you, &c.

By your cousin,
Dame Elizabeth Brews
(Unto my right worshipful cousin, John Paston, be this letter delivered, &c.)

*Communications were interrupted by the weather. But as soon as she was able, Margery's mother rode with servants to Norwich, and met there with Paston to discuss the contract. She returned home more convinced that ever that John Paston was her daughter's soulmate.*

*As Valentine's Day approached, Dame Elizabeth permitted Margery to correspond with her suitor, her message being written by a secretary (and doubtless inspected by mother Brews before posting):*

### [Margery Brews to John Paston III (9/10 February 1476/7)°]

Right reverent and worshipful, and my right well-beloved Valentine,

I recommaund me unto you full heartily, desiring to hear of your welfare, which I beseech almighty God long for to preserve, unto His pleasure and your heart's desire. And if it please you to hear of my welfare, I am not in good hale of body nor of heart, nor shall I be till I hear from you:

For there wottes no creàture
What pain that I endure;
And, for to be dead?
I dare it not discu'er! [2]

And my lady my moder hath laboured the matter to my fader full diligently, but she can no more get than ye know of (for the which, God knoweth, I am full sorry). But if that ye love me – as I trust verily that ye do – ye will not leave me therefore; for if that ye had not half the livel'ood that ye have, for to do the greatest labour that any woman on-live might, I would not forsake you. [3]

And if ye command me, to keepé me true,
Whereuer I go, iwis I will do
All my might you to lovè and never no moe.
And if my friends say that I do amiss,
They shall not me lett, so for to do.
Mine heartè me bids ever more to love you [4]

---

[1] "[T]he causey ere ye come to Bokenham Ferry is so overflown that there is no man that may unneth pass it, though he be right well horsed" (J.P. III to Margaret Paston, 8 March 1476/7). B.L. 43490, fol. 26.

[2] *wottes* ] knows; *discu'er* ] discover, experience.

[3] *get* ] learn; *if that* ] even if; *therefor* ] because of my father's delay; *livel'ood* ] livelihood, annual income; *on-live* ] alive.

[4] *iwis* ] surely; *no moe* ] no others; *lett* ] hinder, dissuade.

Truly over all earthily thing –
And if they be never so wroth, I tryst
It shall be better in time comíng. [1]

No more to you at this time, but the holy Trinity have you in keeping. And I beseech you that this bill be not seen of none earthily creature save only yourself, &c. And this letter was indite at Topcroft, with full heavy heart, &c. [2]

By your own

Margery Brews
(Unto my right well-beloved Valentine, John Paston, squire, be this bill delivered, &c.)

*With Margery's letter came one from her mother, inviting Paston to return to Topcroft and to stay over for a few days so that he and Sir Thomas might come to terms:*

**[Dame Elizabeth Brews to John Paston III (9 or 10 February 1476/7)°]**

Cousin,

I recommaund me unto you, thanking you heartily for the great cheer that ye made me and all my folks the last time that I was at Norwich. And ye promised me that ye would never break the matter to Margery unto such time as ye and I were at a point – but ye have made her such advocate for you that I may never have rest night nor day, for calling and crying upon to bring the said matter to effect, &c.

And, cousin, upon Friday is St. Valentine's Day, and every brid chooseth him a make. And if it like you to come on Thursday at night, and so purvey you that ye may abide there till Monday, I trusty to God that ye shall so speak to mine husbond; and I shall pray that we shall bring the matter to a conclusion, &c. [3]

For, cousin,

It is but a simple oak
That is° cut down at the first stroke! [4]

For ye will be reasonable, I trust to God (which have you ever in his merciful keeping, &c.).

By your cousin,

Dame Elizabeth Brews
(otherwise shall be called, by God's grace!) [5]
(To my worshipful cousin, John Paston, be this bill delivered, &c.)

---

[1] *if . . . wroth* ] even if they (my friends) become angry as never before; *tryst* ] trust.

[2] *indite* ] composed, dictated

[3] *brid* ] bird; *make* ] mate.

[4] cf. letter from Thomas Kela to John Paston (Feb. 1477): "And I harde my lady sey þ^t it was a febill oke, þ^t was kut down at the first stroke" (B.L. MS Add 43490, fol. 25; Davis 2.436).

[5] *otherwise* ] i.e., instead of "cousin," "mother".

## [Margery Brews to John Paston III (14? Feb. 1476/7)°]

Right worshipful and well-belovèd Valentine,

In my most 'umble wise, I recommaund me unto you, &c. And heartily I thank you for the letter which that ye sent me by John Bekarton, whereby I understond and know that ye be purposèd to come to Topcroft in short time, and without any errand or matter but only to have a conclusion of the matter betwix' my fader and you (I would be most glad of any creature on-live, so that the matter might grow to effect); and thereas ye say, *An' ye come and find the matter no more to-ward than ye did aforetime, ye would no more put my fader and my lady my moder to no cost nor business, for that cause, a good while after* – which causeth mine heart to be full heavy; and if that ye come and the matter take to none effect, then should I be much more sorry, and full of heaviness). [1]

Piero DiCosimo, Maddelena, 1490s
*Galleria Nazionale d'Arte Antica* (*Rome*)

And as for myself, I have done and understond in the matter [all°] that I can or may, as God° knoweth; and I let you plainly understond that my Fader will no more money part withal in that behalf but an hundred pound and fifty mark – which is right far fro' the accomplishment of your desire. [2]

Wherefore, if that ye could be content with that good (and my poor person), I would be the merriest maiden on ground. And if ye think not yourself so satisfied (or that ye might have much more good, as I have understond by you afore), good, true, and loving Valentine, that ye take no such labour upon you as to come more for that matter, but let it° pass, and never more to be spoken of, as I may be your true lover and bead-woman during my life. No more unto you at this time, but almighty Jesus preserve you, both body and soul, &c. [3]

By your Valentine, Margery Brews
(To my right well-beloved cousin,
John Paston, squire, be this letter delivered, &c.)

Love was in the air, but complications remained. Sir John was now seeking a match with Lady Wargrave, a propertied widow who seemed an apt bride, not for himself (much too old), but for his younger brother. Dame Wargrave was being courted as well by John Clopton and Sir Thomas Grey. Sir John's efforts in his brother's behalf were interrupted when a Brews manservant, John Bekerton, arrived from England with a letter, in which little brother confessed his love-interest in Margery Brews and begged Sir John's aid in meeting her father's terms.

---

[1] *thereas ye say, and ye come* ] in which [letter] you say, if you come; *to-ward* ] advantageous; *mech* ] much.

[2] *understond* ] understood; *that I can* ] as much as I can.

[3] *good* ] money; *as . . . life* ] as I may still live to love you and pray for you even if you refuse my father's offer.

Sir John was noncommittal: "I have received your letter," he replied in a letter of 9 March, "and you[r] man, J[ohn] Bekerton; by whom I know all the matter of Mastress Brews, which if it be as he sayeth, I pray God bring it to a good end....Bekerton telleth me that she loveth you well. If I died, I had liefer ye had her than the Lady Wargrave (nevertheless, she singeth well with an harp); Clopton is afeared of Sir T[homas] Grey, for he is a widower now late, and men say that he is acquainted with her of old."° Sending his good wishes, Sir John insisted only that his own major slice of the family pie remain untouched: he would not have any part of his inheritance entailed to facilitate his brother's marriage.

The same day that Sir John wrote his brother from Calais, John III in Norwich wrote a nervous follow-up letter, not waiting for Bekerton's return from France: "touching myself and Mastress Margery Brews," he reports to Sir John, "I am yet at no certainty, her fader is so hard; but I trow I have the goodwill of my lady her moder (and her!). But as the matter proveth, I shall send you word, with God's grace, in short time."°

Sir Thomas Brews, seeking his daughter's happiness, improved his offer, promising the couple the jointure of £100, plus (a.) "their board, free, as for two or three year"; or (b.) "300 mark without their board, payable by fifty mark yearly, till the sum of 300 mark be full paid"; or (c.) 400 mark, received from Sir Thomas over time (50 mark per year for eight years), plus a loan of £100;[1] provided in each instance that the repayment not be paid from the dowry but from some other income. Margery's parents (doubtless on the groom's cue) suggested that the deal could be closed if Margaret Paston assigned to the young couple the full income, for life, derived from one or two of her manors (actual ownership to be retained by Margaret, and by Sir John, her heir). "And if these or any of the conclusions may be taken," said Sir Thomas, "I am agreeable to make the bargain sure; or else, no more to be spoken of."[2] Take it, or cut bait.

Once again, Paston left Topcroft without a deal. He simply did not have enough personal income to meet the proffer.

Not wishing to see her son's heart broken, Dame Margaret came to the rescue, offering to make John III the assign for all of her rents from her manor of Swainsthorp, for term of life; plus ten mark out annually out of her Sparham rents. This proffer would not diminish her real property or Sir John's inheritance, though it would take a big bite out of her own disposable income.

On hearing of this maternal largesse, Sir John fired off at least two unhappy letters, one to his brother, the other to his mother. Writing to John the younger, Sir John absolved himself of any obligation to part with a single acre of his own inheritance, yet chastised John III for seeking for himself and his bride a portion of their mother's income:

...your mind is troubled. I pray you, rejoice not yourself too much in hope to obtain things that all your friends may *not* ease you of – for if my moder were disposed to give me and any woman in England the best manor that she hath, to have it to me and my wife and to the heirs of our two bodies begotten, *I would not take it of her*, by God! 'Stablish yourself on a good ground, and grace will follow. Your matter is far spoken of, and blown wide. And if it prove no better, I would that it had never be' spoken of. Also: that matter noiseth me that I am "so unkind" that I "lett all togeder." I think not a matter happy nor well handled, nor politicly dealt with, when it can never be finished without an inconvenience – and to any such bargain I keep *never* to be condescending – nor, of counsel. [3]

If I were at the beginning of such a matter, I would have hoped to have made a better conclusion (if they mock you not!). This matter is driven thus far forth without my counsel: I pray you, make an end without my counsel. If it be well, I would be glad; if it be oderwise, it is pity. I pray, you trouble me no more in this matter.°

---

[1] *400 mark* ] roughly £270 (In England a mark was two-thirds of a pound or 13s. 4d.).

[2] This memorandum, the hand of John Paston, appears to represent his notes during the discussion with Sir Thomas (B.L. MS Add. 27445, fol. 108).

[3] *lett* ] prevented, blocked.

*Sir John's letter to his mother was more courteous, but unyielding. He refused to give his blessing to a contract that he had no legal power to forestall; but Sir John grudgingly acquiesced, citing the example of the Pope: he might tolerate the indiscretion but he would certainly not issue a license or nihil obstat.*[1]

*By mid-June the prenuptials were still unsigned. Margaret Paston reached out once again to Elizabeth Brews with a personal letter.*

### [Margaret Paston to Dame Elizabeth Brews (11 June 1477)°]

Right worshipful and my chief lady and cousin,

As heartily as I can, I recommaund me to you. Madam, liketh you to understand that the chief cause of my writing to you at this season is this: I wot well it is not unrememb'red with you the large communication that divers times hath been had, touching the marriage of my cousin, Margery your daughter, and my son John; of which I have been as glad (and now latewards, as sorry) as ever I was for any marriage in mine life. And where, or in whom, the default of the breech is, I can have no parfit knowledge; but, madam, if it be in me or any of mine, I pray you, assign a day when my cousin your husbond and ye think to be at Norwich towards Salle – and I will come thider to you. And I think, ere ye and I depart, that the default shall be known° where it is, and also that (with your advice and help and mine togeders) we shall take some way, that it shall not break – for if it did, it were none honour to neither parties (and in chief to them in whom the default is), considering that it is so far spoken.[2]

And, madam, I pray you that I may have parfit knowledge by my son Yelverton (bearer hereof) when this meeting shall be, if ye think it expedient – and the sooner the better, in eschewing of worse. For, madam, I know well, if it be not concluded in right short time, that as for my son, he intendeth to do right well by my cousin Margery, and not so well by himself – and that should be to me (nor, I trust, to you) no great pleasure, if it so fortuned (as God defend! Whom I beseech to send you your liefest desires.).[3]

Madam, I beseech you that I may be recommaunded by this bill to my cousin your husbond, and to my cousin Margery (to whom I supposed to have given another name, ere this time!).

Written at Maltby, on Saint Barnaby'is Day.[4]
By your Margaret Paston
(To the right worshipful and my very good lady and cousin, Dame Elizabeth Brews)

No reply was immediately forthcoming. Throughout the month of June, both Margery's parents were ill, Dame Elizabeth Brews remaining confined to her bed and unable to discuss the matter with her husband; during which time Sir Thomas refused to budge an inch.

As June drew to a close, Margery's mother was sufficiently recovered to send a letter of regret to Margaret Paston, stating that she could get no other offer from her husband than was already on the table. They seemed to have reached an impasse.

It was now John's turn to conspire with his mother. He drafted two letters in her voice, one addressed to Margery's mother, the other to himself; and he requested ("it if please you") to have a secretary copy and send both letters after him to Topcroft, under his mother's signature. Dame Brews would open the one. He would open the other and with a bit of theatre disclose its contents. In the one to Dame Elizabeth Brews, "Margaret Paston" expresses her dismay that the match is not yet concluded, though she has already overextended her resources to make it happen. In the ventriloquised letter to John himself, his "moder, M.P.," expresses her exasperation, seeming ready to call it quits:

---

[1] Sir John Paston to Dame Margaret Paston (28 March 1477), B.L. MS Add. 27445, fol. 23.

[2] *wot* ] know; *divers* ] various; *parfit* ] perfect, complete; *default of the breech* ] fault for this break in our negotiations.

[3] *Yelverton* ] William Yelverton, married to her daughter Anne; *in eschewing of worse* ] to avoid something worse; *as God defend* ] May God forbid!; *liefest* ] dearest.

[4] *Saint Barnaby'is* ] ( = *old possessive form*, Barnaby his) St. Barnabas's Day.

### ["Margaret Paston" to her son, John Paston III (29 June 1477), by John Paston°]

I greet you well—

And send you God's blissing and mine, letting you wit that I understand well by my cousin Dame Elizabeth Brews's letter (which I send you herewith, whereby ye may understand the same) that they intend not to perform those proffers that ye told me they promised you (trusting that ye told me none otherwise than *was* promised you!). Wherefore I charge you (on my blissing) that ye be well ware how ye bestow your mind, without ye have a substance whereupon to live, for I would be sorry to wit you miscarry – for if ye do, in your default look never after help of me – and also I would be as sorry for *her* as for any genty-woman living, in good faith! – wherefore I warn you, be ware in any wise. And look ye be at Maltby with me as hastily as ye can, and then I shall tell you more. And God keep you. [1]

Written at Maltby, on Saint Peter's Day.
Your moder,
M.P.

A month later, with no wedding day in sight, Dame Margaret in her own person appealed to Sir John for a loan to his brother – only to learn that her eldest, always a prodigal spender, had borrowed 400 marks, with his inherited manor of Sporle as security; much of it to cover legal expenses in his (successful) litigation to recover Caister Castle, following the death of Norfolk, Sir John had three years to repay the loan, or Sporle would be forfeited (which, if it should happen, he wrote, "ye were never like to se me merry after, so God help me!" – Sir John's way of saying to his mother: *Please die, soon*). As salt in the wound, Sir John asked his mother for a gift of £20 so that he might repay an overdue loan to one Master Cockett. Plus, he had a mistress and a daughter to support. In a word, he was caught a bit short, for the moment and could do nothing more for his brother ("I have granted him as much as I may" [7 Aug. 1477°]). Mother Margaret was unequivocal in her reply:

### [Margaret Paston to Sir John Paston (11 August 1477)°]

...I put you in certain that I woll never pay [Cockett a] penny of that duty that is owing to him, though he sue me for it – not of my own purse! For I woll not be compelled to pay your debts agains' my will – and though I would, I may not. Wherefore I a'vise you to see me saved harmless against him (for your own advantage, in time coming)...And take this for a full conclusion in this matter, for it shall be none otherwise for me than I write here to you. [2]

...It causeth me to be in great doubt of you, what your disposition will be hereafter for such livelihood as I have been disposed, before this time, to leave you after my decease: for I think verily that ye will be disposed hereafter to sell (or set to mortgage) the land that ye should have after me, your mother – as gladly, and rather than, that livelihood that ye have after your father.

It grieveth me to think upon your guiding (after the great good that ye had in your rule!) since your father died (whom God assoil!); and so simply spent as it hath been! God give you grace to be of sad and good disposition hereafter – to His pleasance, and comfort to me, and to all your friends, and to your worship and profit hereafter. [3]

And as for your brother William, I would ye should purvey for his funding. For as I told you the last time ye were at home, I would no longer fund him at my cost and charge. His board and his school hire is owing since Saint Thomas's Day afore Christmas; and he hath great need of gowns and other gear that were necessary for him to have, in haste. I would ye should remember it, and purvey them. For as for me, I will not.

---

[1] *blissing* ] blessing; *without ye have a substance* ] unless you have a sufficient income; *wit* ] know.

[2] *though ... may not* ] even if ... cannot.

[3] *your rule* ] your upbringing; *assoil* ] absolve from sin.

I think ye set but little by my blessing, and if ye did ye would have desired it in your writing to me. [May] God make you a good man to His pleasance.

Written at Mautby the day after Saint Lawrence, the year of the reign of King Edward IV, the 17$^{th}$ year.

In the end, true love found a way: John Paston and Margery's father came to terms, and signed. The wedding, unrecorded, probably took place in September.

On 21 January 1477/8 John wrote to his elder brother, "Sir, as for my 'huswife,' I am fain to carry her to see her fader and her friends now this winter – for I trow she will be out of fashion, in summer!"° – and to his mother, on 3 February: "Your daughter of Swainsthorpe recommendeth [her°] to you ... lowly beseeching you of your blissing... Your daughter sendeth you part of such poor stuff as I sent her fro' London, beseeching you to take it in gree, though it be little plenty that she sendeth you." Margery had recently developed a craving for figs: "But as for dates, I will say truth: ye have not so many, by two pound, as were meant unto you – for she thinks at this season dates 'right good meat' – whatsoever it meaneth!" [1]

The baby, born in June, was christened William IV, after his great-grandfather, husband of Agnes.

The few extant letters from Margery to John during their married life, when her husband was away on business, are full of mundane business but replete with affection. In one, she writes, "My mother-in-law thinketh long she hear no word from you. She is in good hale (blissèd be God!), and all your babies also. I marvel *I* hear no word from you (which grieveth me, full evil!).... Sir, I pray you, if ye tarry long at London, that it will please [you] to send for me, for I think [it] long sin' I lay in your arms" (1 Nov.).° In another, written the very next day, Margery offers to speak in John's behalf to the duchess of Norfolk, in that "one word of a woman should do more than the words of twenty men – if I could rule my tongue and not speak of mine uncle. And if ye commaund me so for to do, I trust I should say nothing to my lady's displeasure, but to your profit" (4 Nov.).° In a third letter, she jests, "I pray God no ladies no more overcome you, that ye give no longer respite in your matters" (21 Jan. 1485/6).°

In November 1479, a few months after his nephew William was christened in Norfolk, Sir John Paston died in London, of the plague. Dame Margaret died in 1484. Now the principal heir, John II came at last into possession not only of his brother's and mother's estates, but of Caister Castle.

William Paston IV was John and Margaret's only child to live to adulthood (and the only grandchild of William and Agnes to carry on the Paston surname). Dame Margaret died in 1484, Margery in 1495, John III in 1504. The family is remembered today for the rich trove of letters that they left behind, more than a thousand of which are preserved today in the British Library, thereby to provide us with a window onto daily life in the turbulent fifteenth century. Scholars today can be grateful that Margaret Paston and her kin did not correspond, back when, by email.

♡ *Be yow$^{re}$ s$^{er}$ua$^{nt}$ & bedewom̄*
*Margery Paston*

♡ *By your servant & beadwoman*
*Margery Paston*

[1] *in gree* ] with goodwill.

# The Leaf Poet (fl. c. 1485)

*The Queen in white yt was of great beauty*
*Tooke by the hond the queen yt was in grene*
*And said suster I haue right great pity*
*Of your annoy and of the troublous tene*
*Wherein ye and your company haue bene*
*So long alas,...*

— fr. first publication (1598), lines 386-91

HE FLOURE AND THE LEAFE, a verse allegory from the late Medieval period, first saw print in Thomas Speght's 1598 edition of the *Workes* of Geoffrey Chaucer. The narrator, unable to sleep, rises from bed before dawn. Retiring in solitude to an arbor, she listens with pleasure to the merry notes of a (male) goldfinch and a (female) lark; whose songs are made the more glorious when "there came singing, lustily, / A world of ladies" (136-7). Dressed in white surcoats, richly bejeweled, each woman wears a chaplet of green leaves in her hair, either of *agnus castus* (virginal chastity), *woodbind* (loyalty); or *laurel* (triumph). One majestic woman, who holds in her hand a branch of agnus castus, goes "in mid the company / Sole by herself" – with "heavenly figured face / So plesaunt," "That of beautíe she passed 'hem everichoon" (324, 164-8). "To my sight, truly," reports the narrator, "She lady was of all the company" (174-5). Following the women, there comes a large company of men on horseback. Dressed in white surcoats, the knights wear chaplets of either laurel or oak-grain, to signify their honor and valor in combat.

This society of lords and ladies, being devoted to the Leaf, spend their day both pleasantly and virtuously: the ladies dance and sing for their own merriment, "most womanly." The men, when they enter, hold a jousting match, with the ladies in audience: "And to behold their rule and governaunce, / I you ensure, it was a great plesáunce."

Intruding on this scene comes a lusty company of men and women dressed all in green and wearing identical chaplets. These revelers are of Lady Flora's party. And party, they do: to the accompaniment of minstrels, they wear themselves out dancing, then collapse on the green to hear a bargeret of "Si doucè est la Margarete."

The courtly recreations are cut short, first by a blast of scorching heat, then by a violent storm. "The wind began so sturdily to blow / That down goeth all the flourès everichoon / So that in all the mead there laughed not oon" (362-64).

The company of the Leaf takes refuge under a massive laurel tree, possibly a figure for Edward IV. ("They feltè nothing of the great affray / That they in green without had in y-be" [373-5]).

The company of the Floure, less fortunate, are drenched to the skin.

Comfort ensues: when the tempest has passed, the queen in white (the Lady of the Leaf) reaches out to the queen in green (the Lady of the Floure), and graciously offers a healthy and low-calorie repast of salads; inviting those of the Floure "To sup with her, and eke, for anything, / That she should with her all her people bring" (418-19). Both sides together now resume "so plesauntly singíng / That ít would have comfórted any wight" (432-33) – at which point, the male goldfinch returns, alighting in the hand of the Lady of the Floure.

As the knights and ladies ride away to recover from the storm, the narrator reports, "I dressed me forth, and happed to meet anone / Ríght a fair Ladíe, I you ensure / And she coom riding by herself alone, / All in white, with semblaunce full demure" (456-59).

Turning to the narrator (now identified for the first time as a young maiden), the Lady of the Leaf exclaims: "My doughter, gramercíe!"

The narrator-maid inquires of the Lady how to interpret the spectacle she has just seen; who replies with somewhat predictable observations concerning the character and pursuits of the respective parties. The Lady then presses the poet to say whom she will serve, the Leaf or Floure? (573-4).

The maiden-narrator modestly announces her decision (the Leaf); for which she is applauded:

"That is," quod she, "right well done, certainly,
And I pray God to honour you avaunce [1]
(And keep you fro' the wicked remembráunce
Of Male Bouch, and all his cruelty)" (577-80)

The cult of the Flower and the Leaf, a courtly game that commenced in the fifteenth century, was known to Chaucer; who in his Prologue to *The Legend of Good Women* asks for diligent readers, "Whether ye ben with the leef or with the flour" (72). Other references to the cult are found in Deschamps and Charles d'Orléans. Derek Pearsall speculates: "Knights and ladies would declare their adherence to the Flower or the Leaf and maintain the propriety of their choice with no doubt elegant and sophisticated casuistry" (1990, 1). But the metaphors were strongly gendered: the leaf on the stem nurtures and protects the flower; the flower provides beauty and grace; the flower fades, the leaf perseveres. Or (as in this poem), the choice is between serving the leafy tree, a tower of strength and vertú, or the lovely flower, a thing of pleasure (and, by implication, sexual congress).

For nearly 300 years *The Floure and the Leafe* was admired as one of Chaucer's most charming poems. In 1778, when a pioneer Medieval scholar named Thomas Tyrwhitt suggested that it might not be Chaucer's, he was derided. A century later, Henry Bradshaw argued from internal evidence that *The Floure and the Leafe* was too late to be Chaucer's. Bradshaw's evidence carried the day; after which, scholars and teachers lost interest in the poem. As if by way of embarrassment for academia's having mistaken its paternity, *The Floure and the Leafe* thereafter was never anthologized; rarely if ever was it taught in the classroom; and rarely ever after has it been discussed in critical literature, except as a feminine curiosity. (The MLA Bibliography, from 1925 to 1975 lists one publication on *The Floure and the Leafe*: a concordance).

And yet, the poem's author exhibits a considerable range of cultural knowledge. Pearsall observes: "there are many echoes of Chaucer, Lydgate, and the French poets (Guillaume de Lorris, Guillaume Machaut, Jean Froissart, and Eustache Deschamps), particularly in the elaborate seasonal and garden setting" (1990, 1). Nor is the verse any less graceful now, or the narrator less *charmant*, than when the poem was thought to be of Chaucer's creation. But the intrinsic merits of *The Floure and the Leafe* have not been sufficient to recover the readers that it lost when it was booted from the Chaucer canon.

C. S. Lewis writes of the Leaf Poet with patronizing condescension:

> If she cannot claim wisdom, she has a great deal of good sense and good humour, and is guided by them to write a poem more original than she herself, perhaps, suspected. A similar merit, and a similar limitation, appear in her execution. She describes what interests her, selecting rather by temperament than by art; and she finds considerable difficulty in getting the right number of syllables into each line. (247-8)

From Lewis onward, *The Floure and the Leafe* has remained largely unread.

More productive, perhaps, than the question, *Did a woman write it*? are the questions, What does the poem mean? Or rather, How are its meanings shaped by its own narrative conventions? by its cultural context? by the speaking position of both the narrator and the producer of the tale?

Derek Pearsall, who has done more than anyone to revive interest in *The Floure and the Leafe,* observes that the narrative may be read as a conventional allegory, one that moralizes "adherence to the Flower and the Leaf in terms of a contrast between perseverance and fidelity in love, and fashionable fickleness and flirtation; and between honor and valor in battle, and idleness" (1990, 1). On this reading, the company of the Leaf are the virtue crowd: the men are brave, the women are chaste. Then come those others, a company of revelers dressed in green, a great throng of girls with their beaux, given to idle pleasures. When the storm of tribulation comes, those of the Leaf are sheltered, while the fun-loving Flower crowd get hammered. Read thus, service to the Leaf represents behavior that is both privileged and safe.

Whatever the author's original intention may have been (always an interpretive problem, for students of allegory), *The Floure and the Leafe* lends itself not only to moral but to political metaphor. Without presuming to know by whom, or for whom, the poem was first written or performed, students of the fifteenth century may find it helpful to use the text to illuminate the situation of a particular woman, at a particular moment in history: Elizabeth of York, just before her union with Henry Tudor, earl of

---

[1] *avaunce* ] in advance.

Richmond – a royal marriage that was said by Tudor historians to have united the white rose of Lancaster with the red rose of York; and which is idealized even today as the happy ending for a dynastic conflict that had lasted thirty years, cost tens of thousands of lives, and produced untold misery for those at the bottom of the social ladder as the big boys up top played king of the hill.

In 1483, Margaret Beaufort sent a proposal to Elizabeth Woodville (who with her children had taken sanctuary from Richard III in Westminster Abbey). The gist of Margaret's letter is recorded by Edward Hall (1548): "the time was come that her son [Henry Tudor] should be joined in marriage with Lady Elizabeth [of York], daughter and heir to King Edward; and that King Richard – being taken and reputed of all men for the common enemy of the realm, should out of all honour and estate be dejected, and of his rule and kingdom be clearly spoiled and expulsed." [1]

Margaret's proposal was one of mutual advantage: Her son was the House of Lancaster's last best hope – King Edward had dispensed with all other Lancastrian claimants – but Henry was descended on both the mother's and father's sides from bastards. He therefore had at best a weak claim to the crown.

The princess Elizabeth was daughter to Edward IV (now deceased); a sister of Edward V (missing or murdered); and a niece of Richard III (the usurper); she therefore had a strong claim to the succession, though a woman. But with the Buckingham rebellion having failed, only in alliance with Henry Tudor could Elizabeth of York ever hope to become queen. And without Henry's military intervention, the princess Elizabeth, her mother and siblings, might soon have no future at all.

Elizabeth Woodville, queen dowager, was persuaded by Margaret's argument: Richmond was her best chance to depose her hated brother-in-law and to place princess Elizabeth on the throne. The entire House of Lancaster, united with the Woodville faction of the House of York, would destroy the usurper. Win-win: Richard III would die childless, the English succession would be restored to the line of Edward IV through the Woodvilles; and a Lancaster would become king.

Exiled in Brittany, Henry Tudor was willing: he had everything to gain and nothing to lose. Margaret's plan required only the consent of the queen dowager, Elizabeth Woodville, who with her six daughters was barely subsisting, under constant guard, in Westminster Abbey. She, too, said yes.

The princess Elizabeth's thoughts on the subject are unrecorded. But *The Floure and the Leafe* may shed some light on the historical moment, as an allegorical tribute both to dowager queen Elizabeth Woodville (in the figure of *Diana*, the beautiful matron of honor, the Lady of the Leaf, dressed in white), and Margaret Beaufort (*Flora,* the Lady of the Flower, whose emblem is the daisy, or "sweet Margaret"); the entire story being told from the perspective of Princess Elizabeth (qua narrator), at a moment of decision. On this reading, the white-clad ladies and knights of the leaf, whose women are chaste and whose men wear chaplets of loyal woodbind, are associated not only with single life but with the house of Edward IV and white rose of York; while the company in green is associated with the House of Lancaster. On this view, the storm that engulfs both sides but pummels Lady Flora's troop stands conveniently for the Wars of the Roses. The male goldfinch who appears at the end to alight in the hand of Flora, adumbrates the return of Henry Tudor from exile – not to his bride, precisely, but to his mother Margaret. And those chaplets "Made of goodly floures, white and red," signal sexual as well as political union.

The narrator, a young virgin standing alone, is faced at the end with a puzzle: what to make of this scene?

One thing seems clear enough: all agency in this dream-vision (all but the violent storm) arises from women; most especially, from the virtuous women of the Leaf, whose diplomacy and grace are requited by the women of the adverse party. Reversing convention, the men here figure only as spectacle, as objects for the feminine gaze, or as singers in a general chorus of joy when the storm has ended.

A new question arises: If Elizabeth of York may be figured as the "I" of the narrative, what can we know of the author?

Not much. Pearsall concludes: "Whether the poem is actually by a woman is a question which no ingenuity, it seems, could solve, though prejudice might point a way. The poem is pervaded by an extraordinary charm and sweet reasonableness: it breathes through and softens even distressing moments and potentially severe moral judgments. It reads like a poem that Jane Bennett (of *Pride and Prejudice*) might have written."[2] Recognizing that the question, *Is it by a woman,* cannot be answered (as a point of

[1] Edward Hall, *The Union of the Two Noble and Illustre Famelies of Lancastre* [*and*] *Yorke* (London, 1548), fol. 35v.

[2] Pearsall (1990), 1.

history), Pearsall therefore moves instinctively to a point of criticism: when, if ever, can the sex of the author be seen in, or through, the gender of his or her first-person narrator?

A female tale-teller in verse narratives of the medieval and early modern period is not unheard of, but rarely do we find a male author who when writing "as" a woman is able to abandon or conceal his phallocentric speaking position (which may be true even here, insofar as the poet's emphasis on chastity represents masculine anxiety and not feminine affirmation). In the *Assembly of Ladies* (c. 1445?), a female narrator celebrates the ladies of Henry VI's court (Margaret of Anjou, in particular), but the author's point of view remains coherently masculine, and partisan. In *The Floure and the Leafe,* however, the author's voice, no less than the narrator's, keeps to a register that is persuasively feminine.

Whether *The Floure and the Leafe* can be assigned to one woman in particular – Elizabeth of York – is a question whose answer depends on its date of composition: we have no proof that *The Floure and the Leafe* was even written during her lifetime.[1] If the narrative is seen as referencing the game-changing events of 1483-1485, then the implied author may be Elizabeth herself, faced with a critical decision: shall I consent to this match, proposed by my own mother and by the mother of Henry Tudor? The future course of the English nation depended on her answer.

As *The Floure and the Leafe* draws to its happy close – and as the two companies of men and women raise their voice in song – the closure is less complete than it seems: the narrator, in contemplation of the scene, stands outside the symbolic union, as an uncommitted observer. She is given a choice. That question is not: "Will you join us?" (in a newly reconstituted commonwealth). Much less: "Will you take, for your lawfully wedded lord, to love, serve, and obey, this *goldfinch*?" The maid-narrator is asked, rather: "But to whom do ye owe / Your servicè? and which woll ye honóur, / Tell me, I pray, this year, the Leaf or Floure?" (572-74).

As moral allegory, the narrator's choice is predictable and coherent: she chooses to align herself with the chaste, virtuous, and safe party of the Leaf, associated on the one hand with virginity and on the other with dowager queen Elizabeth and the house of York.

Princess Elizabeth, presented with a choice, *did* eventually marry Henry Tudor. Forsaking the agnus castus, she chose to wear a "chapèlet on her head, / Which did right well upon the shining hair, / Made of goodly flourès, white and red." Her marriage is said to have united the house of Lancaster and the House of York in a mighty line of Tudor monarchs. But all of that, of course, lies beyond the vision of the narrator, and beyond the narrative's present moment.

If there were a poetic sequel to the allegory, it would look less like a glorious union of houses than like one more usurpation: Lending their support to the Lancastrian cause, Elizabeth Beaufort and the Woodvilles achieved the objective of deposing Richard. Henry Tudor and Elizabeth of York were united in holy matrimony; but Henry, not Elizabeth, was made sovereign. The young queen his bride was made to serve Margaret Beaufort not only as a second mother, but as her only mother: King Henry arrested and banished Elizabeth Woodville, confining her in Bermondsey Abbey for the rest of her life; and he did so without a peep of recorded protest from his wife Elizabeth, who became a gracious model of femininity: Elizabeth of York went on to serve *l'Margaraet douce*, and history, and future readers, as a silent but lovely marginal illumination; and as the mother of Henry VIII.

The narrator of *The Floure and the Leafe* wisely makes no love-commitments. Indeed, her choice to serve the Leaf implies a conscious rejection of marriage, in favor of extended chastity. For women of the fifteenth and many other centuries, that was not always a bad decision. Insofar as *The Floure and the Leafe* reflects the situation of Elizabeth of York c. 1484, a twin resistance to political marriage and sexual consummation may be reflected even in the author's own figuration: unlike fairy tales, where the princess and the toad (or werewolf or dragon) may live happily-ever-after, pursuant to the latter's transfiguration into human form, *The Floure and the Leafe* imagines no such fairy-tale ending. Consummation is happily precluded: the male goldfinch rests in the hand of Lady Flora; the female nightingale rests in the hand of Lady Diana. But the poet abstains from presenting to the maid a desiring and desirable prince in shining armor. The maid ends her tale as she began, neither asleep nor dreaming, but with eyes wide open, standing alone.

DWF

---

[1] *The Floure and the Leafe* cannot be much later than 1590 (as indicated both by internal linguistic evidence and by the text's association with items in the late fifteenth-century manuscript, MS Longleat 258).

## The Floure and the Leaf

WHEN that Phoebus his chair of gold so high
Had whirlèd up the starry sky aloft,
And in the Bull was ent'red certainly;
When shoures swete of rain descended soft°,
Causing the ground, felè times and oft,
Up for to givè many an wholesome air,
And everichè° plain was clothèd fair 1

With newè green, and maketh smallè floures
To springen here and there in field and mead –
So very good and wholesome be the shoures
That it reneweth that was old and dead
In winter time; and out of every seed
Springeth the herbè, so that every wight
Of this sesounè waxeth glad and light. 2

And I, so glad of the sesounè swete,
Was happèd thus upon a certain night:
As I lay in my bed, sleep full unmetè
Was unto me. But why that I ne might
Rest, I ne wist, for there nas earthly wight,
As I supposè, had more heartès-ease
Than I, for I n'ad sickness nor dis-ease. 3

Wherefore I marvail greatly of myself,
That I so long withouten sleepè lay;
And up I rose, three houres after twelf,
About the very° springing of the day –
And on I put my gear and mine array,
And to a plesaunt grove I 'gan to° pass,
(Long ere the brightè sun up-risen was), 4

In which were oakès great, straight as a line;
Under the which, the grass, so fresh of hue,
Was newly sprung; and (on eight foot or nine)
Every tree well fro' his fellow grew,
With braunches broadè, lade with leavès new,
That sproongen out ayen the sunneshien,
Some very red and some a glad light green; 5

Which (as methought) was right a plesaunt sight.
And eke the briddès-songès for to° hear
Would have rejoicèd any earthly wight;
And I (that couth not yet in no manére
Hear the nightingale of all the year)
Full busily hark'ned with heart and ear°
If I her voice perceive could anywhere. 6

And at the last a path of little brede
I found, that greatly had not usèd be,
For it forgrowen was with grass and weed
That well unneth a wight ne° might it see.
Thought I, this path some whider go'th, pardíe–
And so I followèd, till it me brought
To right a plesaunt herber, well ywrought, 7

That benchèd was and all° with turfès new
Freshly turf'd, whereof the greenè grass,
So small, so thick, so short, so fresh of hue,
That most like unto green velvétte it° was.
The hedge also that yeden in compáss
And closèd in of° all the green herbère,
With sycamore was set and eglantere, 8

Wreathen in-fere so well and cunningly
That every braunch and leaf grew by measúre,
Plain as a board, of an height, by and by.
Í sie neverè thing, I you ensure,
So well y-done; for he that took the cure
It for° to make, I trow, did all his pein
To make it pass all tho' that men have seen. 9

[1] *Phoebus's chair* ] Phoebus Apollo's chariot; the sun; *the Bull* ] Taurus; *fele* ] many.

[2] *reneweth that* ] reneweth that which; *wight* ] creature, person; *sesoune* ] season; *waxeth* ] grows.

[3] *full unmete* ] inaccessible (*unmete*) *or* remote (*un-meet*); *ne might* ] could not; *ne wist* ] know not; *nas* ] was not; *n'ad* ] had neither.

[4] *roos* ] rose.

[5] *ayen the sunneshien* ] against, toward, the sunshine.

[6] *couth* ] could; *manere* ] manner.

[7] *brede* ] breadth; *forgrowen* ] completely overgrown; *some whider* ] somewhere; *pardie* ] by God!; *herber* ] arbor or bower; *well y-wrought* ] well wrought; well-made (y- *indicates the past participle*).

[8] *benchèd ... new* ] with turf-topped earthen "benches"; *yeden in compáss* ] went round about; *eglantere* ] the eglantine or rose-tree.

[9] *in fere* ] together; *Plain...by* ] level, equal height, one after another; *sie* ] have seen; *cure* ] care.

And shapen was this herber, roof and all,
As is° a pretty parlour, and also
The hedge as thick as is° a castle wall,
That who that list without to stond or go,
Though he would all day pryen to and fro,
He should not see if there were any wight
Within or no – but oon within well might [1]

Perceive all tho' that yeden there-without
In the field, that was on every side
Covered with corn and grass, that (out of doubt),
Though oon would seek of° all the world wide,
So rich a field could not be espied
Upon° no coast, as of the quantitie;
For of all good thing there was great° plentíe. [2]

And I, that all this plesaunt sightè sie,
Thought sodainly I felt so swete an air
As° of the eglantere, that certainly
There is no heart, I deem, in such despair,
Ne yet° with thoughtès froward and contráire
So overlaid, but it should soon have bote,
If it had oonès felt this savour sote. [3]

And as I stood and cast aside mine eie,
I was ware of the fairest medle-tree
That ever yet in all my life I sie,
As full of blossomès as it might be –
Therein, a goldfinch leaping prettily
Fro bough to bough, and as him list he etè,
Here and there, of buds and floures swete – [4]

And to the herbere-sidè was joining
This fairest° tree, of which I have you told.
And at the last the brid began to sing,
When he had eaten what he etè would,
So passing swetely that (by many fold)
It was more plesaunt than I could devise.
And when his song was ended in this wise,

The nightingale with so merry a note
Answéred him, that all the woodè roong–
So sodainly that, as it were a sotte,
I stood astouned; so was I with the song
Thorough ravished, that, till late and long,
Ne wist I° in what place I was, ne where;
And ayén, methought, she soong even by mine ear–[5]

Wherefore about I waited° busily
On every side, if I her mightè see;
And at the last I 'gan full well espy
Where she sat in a fresh green laurer tree
(Ón the further side, even right by me!),
That gave so passing a delicious smell
According to the eglantere full well,

Whereof I had so inly great pleasire
That (as methought) I surely ravished was –
Into paradisè, wherein° my desire
Was for to be, and no further to° pass
As for that day. And on the sotè grass
I sat me down; for, as for mine intent,
The briddès-song was more convenìent

And more plesáunt to me, by many fold,
Than meat or drink, or any other thing;
Thereto the herber was so fresh and cold,
The wholesome savours eke so comfortíng,
That, as I deemèd, sith the béginning
Of the world was never seen, ere then,
So plesaunt a ground of none earthly man.

And as I sat, the briddès harkening thus,
Methought that I heard voices sodainly,
The most sweetest and most delicìous
That ever any wight (I trow truly)
Heard in their lifè. For the 'armony
And sweet accord was in so good musíquè
That the voice to angels most was like. [6]

At the last, out of a grove even by
That was right goodly and plesáunt to sight,
I sie where there came singing, lustily,
A world of ladies; but to tell aright
Their great beautíe, it lieth not in my might
(Ne their array). Nevertheless, I shall
Tell you a part, though I speak not of all.

In° surcoats white of velvet well-sittíng
They were y-clad, and the seams echoon,
As it were a manere garnishing,
Was set with emeraudès, oon and oon,
By and by; but many a richè stoon
Was set on the purfílès, out of doubt,
Of colours, sleeves, and trainès round about, [7]

---

[1] *pryen* ] observe closely.

[2] *yeden* ] went.

[3] *bote* ] remedy; *oonès* ] once; *sote* ] sweet.

[4] *eie* ] eyes; *medle-tree* ] the medlar tree, bearing small, brown-skinned fruit; often associated with sexual intercourse; *goldfinch* ] possibly a figure for Henry Tudor; *as him list he etè* ] as he wished he ate.

[5] *as it were a sotte* ] as if I were a sot; *astouned* ] astonished; overwhelmed; astounded.

[6] *trow truly* ] truly believe.

[7] *surcoats ... well-sitting* ] tailored surcoats of white velvet; with green laurel signifying devotion to the leaf; *seames* ] ornamental hems laid over the seams; *oon and oon* ] in rows, side by side; *purfiles* ] purfles; ornamental border on the surcoats.

As greatè pearlès, round and oriaunt,
Diàmondès fine and rubies red,
And many another stoon, of which I want°
The namès now; and everich on her head
A richè fret of gold; which, without dread,
Was full of stately, richè stoonès set.
And every lady had a chapèlettè [1]

On her head, of leavès° fresh and green,
So well y-wrought, and so marvèlously,
Thát it was a noble sight to seen.
Some of laurer, and some full plesauntly
Had chapèlets of woodbind; and sadliè,
Some of *agnus-castus* ware also
Chap'lettes fresh. But there were many of tho [2]

That duncèd and eke soong full soberly;
But all they yede in manere of compáss.
But oon there yede in mid the company
Sole by herself – but all followèd the pacè
That she kept – whose heavenly figured face
So plesaunt was (and her well-shaped persón)
That of beautíe she passed 'hem everichoon. [3]

And more richly beseen (by many fold)
She was also, in every manere thing:
Upon her head, full plesaunt to behold,
A crown of gold, rich for any king;
A braunch of *agnus-castus* eke bearíng
In her hand; and to my sight, truly,
She lady was of all° the company. [4]

And she began a roundel lustily,
That "Sues la feuille de vert mai" men call,
"Seant° mon joly cuer endormi."
And then the company answérèd all
With voices° sweet entunèd and so small,
That mé-thought it the sweetest melody
That ever I heard in my life, soothly. [5]

And thus they camè, dauncing and singíng,
Into the middès of the mead echoon,
Before the herber where I was sittíng,
And, God wot, mé-thought I was well begone,
For then I might avise 'hem, oon by oon,
Who fairest was, who best could° daunce or sing,
Or who most womanly was in all thing. [6]

They had not duncèd but a little throw
When that I heard, not far off, sodainly,
So great a noise of thundering trumpès blow
As though it should have départed the skie.
And after that, within a while, I sie,
From the same grove where the ladíes coom out,
Of men of armès coming, such a rout [7]

As all the men on earth had been assemblèd
In that place, well-horsèd for the nonce,
Steeríng so fast that all the earthè tremblèd.
But for to speak of richès and of° stones,
And men and horse, I trow, the largè wones
Of Pretir John, ne all his tresory,
Might not unneth have bought the tenth partíe. [8]

Of their array (whoso list, hear more),
I shall rehearse, so as I can, a littè.
Out of the grove that I spake of before
I sie come first, all in their cloakès white,
A company that ware, for their delight,
Chap'lettes fresh, of oakès-cereallè
Newly sproong. And trumpets they ware all, [9]

On every trump hanging a broad bannère
Of fine tartarium were full richly bete;
Every trump his lordès-armès bare°;
About their neckès, with great pearlès settè,
Colors broad. For cost they would not lett,
As it would seem, for their scutchóons echóon
Were set about with many a precious stoon [10]

---

[1] *oriaunt* ] from the Indian seas; brilliant, precious; *fret* ] a network of gold lace, set with gems and worn over the hair; *dread* ] doubt; *chapelette* ] chaplet; wreath for the head.

[2] *to seene* ] to see (*inflected infinitive, archaic*); *woodbind* ] woodbine, often employed (as here) to stand for loyalty, steadfast attachment; *sadlie* ] solemnly; *agnus castus* ] chasteberry, believed to preserve chastity.

[3] *compáss* ] round about.

[4] *Lady of the Leaf* ] poss. a figure for Elizabeth Woodville, queen dowager, mother of Elizabeth of York.

[5] *roundel* ] a rondeau (with repeated refrains); *Seant ... endormi* ] "While seated under the leaf of green May, / My pretty heart fell asleep." Adapted from "Dessoubz la branche d'ung verd moy / S'est mon jolli cueur endormy / En attendent le mien amy / Qui me debvoit revenir voir." (See A. Gaste, *Chansons* [1866], no. 97, p. 135). Source identified by Christine Reno; *small* ] high; *soothly* ] truly.

[6] *begone* ] beset; *avise hem* ] consider them.

[7] *departed* ] parted, split.

[8] *wones* ] estates, palaces (*OED* n.2); abundance (n.3); *Pretir John* ] Prester John, a legendary Christian king of the Far East (later, of Ethiopia); *tresory* ] treasury; *not unneth* ] not hardly (double neg.); *partie* ] part.

[9] *oakes-cerealle* ] oak-grain (denoting valor).

[10] *tartarium* ] tartar, a rich silken cloth; *were* ] *i.e.*, that was; *bete* ] overlaid with gold thread; *his lordes-armes* ] its lord's coat-of-arms; *lett* ] balk, hold back; *scutchóons* ] escutcheons; *i.e.*, a shield or shield-shaped surface on which a coat of arms is displayed.

(Their horse-harneìs was all white also).
And after 'hem, next, in oon company,
There° came nine° kings of armès, and no mo,
In cloakès of white cloth of gold, richly,
Chap'lets of green upon° their heads on high.
The crowns that they on their scutchoones bare
Were set with pearlè, ruby, and saphère, 1

And eke great diàmondès, many oon;
But all their horse-harneìs and other gear
Was in a suit according, everichoon,
As ye have heard the foresaid trumpets were;
And, by seemíng, they were no thing to lere,
All° their guidíng they did so manerely.
And after 'hem came a great companíe 2

Of heraudès and pursuivauntès eke,
Arrayèd in clothés of white velvétte;
And hardily, they were no thing to seek
How they on 'hem should the harneìs set;
And every man had on a chapèlet,
Scutchóons, and eke horse-harneìs, indeed,
That had in suit of 'hem that fore° 'hem yede. 3

Next after 'hem there° came (in armour bright,
All save their headès) seemèly knightès nine;
And every clasp and nail, as to my sight,
Of their harneìs were of red gold fine;
With cloth of gold and furrèd with ermine
Were the trappeurès of their steedès strong,
Wide and large, that to the ground did hong. 4

And every boss of bridle and peitrellè
That they had was worth, as I would ween,
A thousand pound; and on their headès (well
Dresséd) were crownès all° of laurer green,
The best y-made that ever I had seen.
And every knight had after him ridíng
Three henchè-men, upon° him awaitíng; 5

Of which, ever the oon, on° short trunchóun,
His lordès helmè bare, so richly dight
As° that the worst was worth the raunsoun
Of a king. The second, a shield bright
Bare at his back°. The thriddè° bare upright
A mighty spear, full sharp y-ground and keen.
And every child ware, of leavès green, 6

A fresh chap'let upon his hairès bright;
And cloakès white of fine velvétte they ware;
Their steedès, trappeurèd and 'rayèd right
Withouten difference, as their lordès were.
And after 'hem, on many a fresh coursére,
There came of armèd knightès such a rout
That they besprad the largè field about. 7

And all they warè (after their degrees)
Chapèlets new, made of laurer green,
Some of oak, and some of other trees.
Some in their hondès barè boughès sheen,
Some of laurer, and some of oakès kene,
Some of hawthorn, and some of woodbind,
And many mo, which I had not in mind. 8

And so they came, their horse freshly steeríng
With bloody sounès of 'heir trumpès loud.
There sie I many an uncouth disguisíng
In the arraying° of these knightès proud.
And at the last, as evenly as they could,
They took their place in middès of the mead,
And every knight turnèd his horse's head 9

To his fellów, and lightly laid a spear
Into° the rest, and so joustès began
On every part aboutè, here and there.
Some brake his spear, some drew down horse and man;
About the field astray the steedès ran.
And to behold their rule and governáunce,
I you ensure, it was a great plesáunce. 10

---

[1] *harneis* ] (här-nā'-ĭs) harness-work (*cf. 226, 237, 242*); *kings of armes* ] kings of arms; royal heralds, one to attend each of the Nine Worthies (line 240).

[2] *were . . . lere* ] had nothing more to learn.

[3] *pursuivauntes* ] attendants; *And . . . seek* ] and hardly did they need to inquire.

[4] *ermine* ] an animal of the weasel family, valued for its white fur; *trappeurès* ] trappers; defensive covering for the horse; *hong* ] hang.

[5] *boss* ] metal knob on the bridle; *peitrelle* ] peitrel; ornamental breastpiece for the horse, originally an armor-plate for battle; *ween* ] guess; *henchè-men* ] mounted squires.

[6] *ever the oon* ] every first one (of the henchmen); *lordes helme* ] lord's helmet; *raunsoun* ] ransom.

[7] *besprad* ] bespread.

[8] *hondes* ] hands; *sheen* ] beautiful; *kene* ] valiant, by association with those who bear the oak.

[9] *sounes* ] sounds; *'heir* ] their (*frequent* [MS *hir*]); *uncouth disguising* ] strange costume.

[10] *rest* ] a device fitted to the cuirass to hold the butt-end of the lance when charging; *steedes* ] riderless horses; *great pleasaunce* ] "While only men engaged in rigorous equine activies such as jousting, women were important spectators at those sports. During Elizabeth [of York]'s royal childhood, she watched her Wydeville uncles and cousins excel on the tilting fields, where they introduced the pageantry that later transformed English tournaments." (Okerlund, *Elizabeth of York,* 12).

And so the joustès last an hour and more;
But tho' that crownèd were in laurer greenè
Won the prize – their dintès were so sore
That there was none ayenst 'hem might sustein.
And then° the jousting all was left off clean,
And fro' their horse the nine° alight anon,
And so did all the remnant, everichoon. [1]

And forth they yede togider, twain and twain,
That to behold it was a worthy° sight,
To-ward the ladies on the greenè plain,
That soong and dauncèd, as I said now right.
The ladies, ás soon ás they goodly might,
They echoon° brake off both the song and daunce,
And yede to meet 'hem with full glad semblaunce.[2]

And every lady took full womanliè
By the hond a knight, and forth they yede
Unto a fair laurer that stood fast by,
With leavès lade, the boughès of great brede;
And to my doom there never was indede
A° man that had seen half so fair a tree;
For underneath it there might° well have be' [3]

An hundred persons at their own plesaunce,
Shadowèd fro' the heat of Phoebus bright,
So that they should have felt no grièvaunce
Of rain, ne haìl, that 'hem hurtè might.
The savour eke rejoice would any wight
That had be' sick or melancholious,
It was so very good and vertuous. [4]

And with great rev'rence they enclinèd° low
Unto° the tree, so sote and fair of hue;
And after that, within a little throw,
Théy began to sing and daunce of new;
Some soong of love, some plaining of untrue,
Environing the tree that stood upright,
And ever yede a lady and a knight. [5]

And at the last I cast mine eie aside,
And was ware of a lusty company
That came roamíng out of the field wide,
Hond in hond, a knight and a ladíe;
The ladies all in surcoats, that richlíe
Purfilèd were with many a riche stone;
And every knight of green ware mantles on, [6]

Embrouded well, so as the surcoats were.
And everich had a chapèlet on her head,
Which did right well upon the shining hair,
Made of goodly flourès, white and red.
The knightès eke, that they in hondè led,
In suit of 'hem ware chapèlets everichoon.
And before 'hem yedè° minstrels many oon, [7]

As harpès, pipès, lutès, and psautry,
All in green; and on their headès bare,
Of divers flourès, made full craftily,
All in a suit, goodlíe chap'lets they ware.
And so dauncíng into the mead they fare,
In mid the which they found a tuft that was
All oversprad with flourès in compáss, [8]

Whereunto° they enclinèd everichoon
With great rev'rence, and that full humbily.
And, at the lastè, there began anon
A lady for to sing, right womanly,
A bargeret in praising the daisíe;
For (as methought) among her notès swete
She said, "Si doucè est° la Margarete." [9]

Then they all answerèd her in-fere
So passingly well, and so plesauntly,
That it was a blissful noise to hear.
But I n'ot how° (it happèd sodainly),
As about noon, the sun so fervently
Wex hotè that the pretty tender flou'rs
Had lost the beauty of 'heir fresh colóurs, [10]

[1] *dintès* ] dints, blows; *sore* ] severe.

[2] *semblaunce* ] countenance.

[3] *doom* ] judgment; *have be'* ] have been.

[4] *rejoice . . . wight* ] would cheer any creature.

[5] *sote* ] sweet; *of new* ] anew; *plaining of untrue* ] lamenting a lover's unfaithfulness; *environing* ] standing round about.

[6] *purfilèd* ] bordered.

[7] *embrouded* ] embroidered; *so as* ] even as; *in suit of hem* ] like theirs.

[8] *psautry* ] psaltery; stringed instrument like a dulcimer; *tuft* ] grassy knoll; hillock.

[9] *bargeret* ] pastoral song; *Si ... Margarete* ] "How sweet is the margaret" (*the field-daisie*); *or* "Margarete" [Beaufort].

[10] *n'ot how* ] ne wot (don't know) how; (*the heat and storm may be a metaphor for the War of the Roses*); *Wex hotè* ] grew hot.

For-shroonk with heat; the ladies eke to-brent,
That they ne wist where they 'hem might bestow.
The knightès swelt; for lack of shade, nigh shent.
And after that, within a little throw,
The wind began so sturdily to blow
That down goeth all the flourès everichoon
So that in all the mead there laughed not oon, [1]

Save such as succourèd were among the leaves
Fro' every stormè that might 'hem assail,
Growing under hedges and thickè greaves.
And after that there came a storm of hail
And rain in-fere, so that, withouten fail,
The ladies ne the knightès n'ad a thread
Dry upon 'hem°, so dropping was 'heir weed. [2]

And when the storm was clean passèd away,
All° tho' in white that stood under the tree –
They feltè nothing of the great affray
That they in green without had in y-be:
To 'hem they yeden for ruth and pitíe,
'hem to comfórt after their great dis-ease,
So fain they were the helpless for to ease. [3]

Then I was 'ware how oon of 'hem in green
Had on a crownè, rich and well-sitting,
Wherefore I deemèd well she was a queen –
And tho' in green on her were a-waitíng.
The ladies then in white that were coming
To-ward 'hem, and the knightès eke° in-fere,
Began to comfort 'hem and make 'hem cheer. [4]

The queen in white, that was of great beautíe,
Took by the hond the queen that was in green
And said, "Suster, I have right great pitíe
Of your annoy, and of the troublous teen
Wherein ye and your company have been
So long, alas! and if that it you please
To go with me, I shall do you the ease [5]

In all the pleasure that I can or may."
Whereof the tother, humbly as she mightè,
Thankèd her (for in right ill array
She was, with storm and heat, I you behight).
And every lady, then, anonè-right,
That were in white, oon of 'hem took in-greene
By the hond; which, when the knights had seen, [6]

In likè wise ech of 'hem took a knightè
Clad in green, and forth with 'hem they fare
Unto° an hedge (where they, anonè-right
To make their joustes all° they would not spare
Boughes to hew down and eke treès square),
Wherewith they made 'hem stately fires great
To dry their clothès that were wringing wet. [7]

And after that, of herbès that there grew,
They made, for blisters of the sun-brenníng,
Very good and wholesome ointments new,
Where that they yede the sick fast anointíng.
And after that they yede about gad'ring
Plesáunt saladès, which they made 'hem eat
For to refresh their great unkindly heat. [8]

The lady of the Leaf then 'gan° to pray
Her of the Floure (for so to my deeming°
They shouldè be, as seemed° by their array)
To sup with her, and eke, for anything,
That she should with her all her people bring.
And she ayen, in right goodly manere,
Thanketh her of her most friendly cheer,

Saying plainly that she would obey
With all her heart all her commaundèment.
And then anon, without lenger delay,
The lady of the Leaf hath oon y-sent
For a palfrey, as° after her intent,
Rayed well and fair in harneìs of gold,
For nothing lackèd that to him 'long should. [9]

---

[1] *eke to-brent* ] likewise burned all over; *That ... bestow* ] in that they knew not where to shelter themselves; *swelt* ] sweltered; *nigh shent* ] near-ruined (exhausted).

[2] *greaves* ] shrubbery; *n'ad a* ] had not a; *so dropping... weed* ] so dripping were their clothes.

[3] *That . . . ybe –* ] That they had been in who were out-doors; *ruth* ] the quality of being compassionate.

[4] *in green* ] Lady Flora; possibly a figure for Margaret Beaufort, mother of Henry Tudor; *well-sitting* ] well-fitting.

[5] *troublous teen* ] troublesome sorrow.

[6] *tother* ] other; *I you behight* ] as I have declared to you; *anone-right* ] straightaway; *oon...In-greene* ] took in hand a lady dressed in green.

[7] *square* ] to cut off square.

[8] *yede . . . anointing* ] proceeded quickly to anoint those who were sunburned.

[9] *'long shold* ] should belong.

And after that, to all her company
She made to púrvey horse and everythingè
That they needed; and then, full lustily,
Even by the herber where I was sittíng,
They passèd all, so plesauntly singíng
That ít would have comfórted any wight.
But then I sie a passing wonder sight: [1]

For then the nightingale, that all the day
Had in the laurer set and did her might
The whole service to sing longing to May,
All sodainly began° to take her flight –
And to the lady of the Leaf forthright
She flew, and set her on her hond softlíe,
Which was a thing I marveled of greatlíe. [2]

The goldfinch eke, that fro' the medle-tree
Was fled for heat into the bushes cold,
Unto the lady of the Floure 'gan flie,
And on her hond he set him, as he would,
And pleasauntly his wingès 'gan to fold;
And for to sing they pained 'hem both as sore
As they had do' of all the day before.

And so these ladies rode forth a great pace,
And all the rout of knightès eke in-fere.
And I, that had seen all this wonder casè,
Thought I would assay, in some manére,
To know fullíe the truth of this mattére,
And what they were that rode so pleasauntly.
And when they were the herber passèd by, [3]

I dressed me forth, and happed to meet anone
Ríght a fair ladíe, I you ensure;
And she coom riding by herself alone,
All in white, with semblaunce full demure.
I salwèd° her, and bade good aventúre
Might° her befall, as I could most humblíe,
And she answerèd, "My doughter, gramercíe!"[4]

"Madáme," quod I, "if that I durst inquéire
Of you, fain would I°, of that companíe,
Wit what they be that passed by this herbére?"
And she ayen answerèd right friendlíe:
"My fair doughtér, all tho' that passed hereby
In white clothíng, be servants everichoon
Unto the Leaf, and I my self am oon. [5]

See ye not her that crownèd is?" quod she,
"All in white?" "Madáme," quod I, "yes."
"That is Diane, goddéss of chastity;
And for because that she a maiden is,
Is° in her hond the braunch she bareth – this
That *agnus castus* men call properly.
And all the ladies in her company

Which ye see of that herbè chap'lets ware,
Be such as han kept aye° 'heir maidenhead.
And all they that of laurer chap'lets bear
Be such as hardy were and won by deed°
Victorious name which never may be dead –
And all they were so worthy of their hond
As° in 'heir time, that none might 'hem withstond.

And tho' that ware chap'lettes on their head
Of fresh woodbind, be such as never were
To love untrue, in word, ne° thought, ne deed,
But aye steadfast; ne for plesáunce, ne fear,
Though that they should their heartès all to-tear,
Would never flit, but ever were steadfast,
Till that their livès there asunder brast." [6]

"Now, fair madáme," quod I, "yet I would pray
Your ladyship, if that it mightè be,
That I might knowè, by some manére way –
Sith that it hath y-likèd your beautíe
The trouth of these ladíes for to tell me –
What that these knightès be, in rich armour,
And what tho' be in green and ware the flou'r,[7]

And why that some did reverence to the tree
And some unto the plot of floures faire?"
"With right good will, my fair doughtér," quod she,
"Sith your desire is good and debonáire!
Tho nine crownèd be very exempláire
Of all honóur 'longing to chivalry,
And those, certáine, be called the Nine Worthíe– [8]

Which ye may see here° riding all before,
That in 'heir time did many a noble dede,
And for their worthiness ful oft have bore
The crown of laurer leavès on their head,
As ye may in your oldè bookès read;
And how that he that was a conquerour
Had by laurer alway his most honóur.

---

[1] *passing wonder* ] most wondrous.

[2] *set her on her hond* ] set herself on the lady's hand.

[3] *wonder case*] wondrous event.

[4] *salwèd* ] saluted; *gramercie* ] mild French oath used to express surprise.

[5] *durst inqueire* ] dare inquire; *Wit* ] to know.

[6] *asunder brast* ] burst asunder.

[7] *trouth of* ] truth about; troth of.

[8] *debonáire* ] virtuous; *Nine Worthie* ] three Hebrews: Joshua, David, Judas Macchabeus; three pagans: Hector, Alexander, Julius Caesar; three Christians: Arthur, Charlemagne, and Godfrey of Boulogne; conventional figures of nobility.

And tho' that barè boughes in their hondè
Of the precious laurer so notáble,
Be such as were, I woll ye understondè,
Noble knightès of the Roundè Table,
And eke the Dousèperis honourable –
Which they bear in sign of victory
As° witness of their deedès mightily. [1]

Eke there be knightès old of the Gartére,
That in 'heir timè did right worthily;
And the honour they did to the laurer
Is for there-by° they have their laud whollíe,
Their triumph eke and martìal gloríe;
Which unto 'hem is more parfit richésse
Than any wight imagine can or guess. [2]

For oon leaf given of that noble tree
To any wight that hath done worthily
(And it be done so as it ought to be),
Is more honóur than anything earthlíe.
Witness of Rome that founder was, truly,
Of all knighthood and deedès marvelous –
Record I take of Titus Livius.

And as for her that crownèd is in green,
It is Flora, of these floures goddésse.
And all that here on her awaiting be'n ,
It are such as han° lovèd idleness
And not delight had° of no busyness
But for to hunt and hawk, and play in meads,
And many other such-like° idle deeds.

And for the great delightè and plesáunce
They have unto° the floure, so reverently
They unto it do such obeìsaunce
As ye may see." "Now, faire madáme," quod I,
"If I durst ask, what is the cause and why
That knightès have the sign of 'heir° honóur
Rather by the leaf, than by the floure?"

"Soothlíe, doughtér," quod shee, "this is the truth –
For knightès euer should be persévering
To seek honóur without faintise or sloth,
Fro weal to better, in all manere thing;
In sign of which, with leavès aye-lastíng
They be rewarded after their degree,
Whose lusty green may not appairèd be, [3]

But aye keping their beauty fresh and green –
For there nis stormè that may 'hem deface,
Hail nor snow, wind nor frostès keen;
Wherefore they have this property and grace.
And for the floure within a little space
Woll be y-lost – so simple of natúre
They be, that they no grievaunce may endure [4]

And every storm will blow 'hem soon away,
Ne they last not but for a seàsoun –
That is the° cause, the very truth to say,
That they may not, by no way of reasóun,
Be put to no such occupatión."
"Madáme," quod I, "with all mine whole servíse
I thank you now, in my most humble wise;

For now I am ascértained thoroughly
Of every thing that° I desired to know."
"I am right glad that I have said – soothlíe –
Aught to your pleasure, if ye will me trow,"
Quod she ayen. "But to whom do ye owe
Your servicè? and which woll ye honóur,
Tell me, I pray, this year, the Leaf or Floure?"

"Madáme," quod I, "though I be° least worthíe,
Unto the Leaf I owe mine observáunce."
"That is," quod she, "right well done, certainly,
And I pray God to honour you avaunce
(And keep you fro' the wicked remembráunce
Of Male Bouch, and all his cruelty),
And all that good and well-conditioned be. [5]

For here may I no lenger now abide;
I must follów the greatè company
That ye may see yonder before you ride."
And forthright°, as I couth, most humbèly,
I took my leave of her, as she 'gan hiè
After 'hem, as fast as euer she might.
And I drow homeward (for it was nigh night) [6]

And put all that I had seen in writíng,
Under support of 'hem that lust it rede.
O little book, thou art so uncunníng,
How dar'st thou put thyself in press, for dread?
Ít is wonder that thou wex'st not rede,
Sith that thou wost ful light who shall behold
Thy rude langáge, full boistously unfold! [7]

---

[1] *Dousperis* ] *Les douze pers*, the 12 peers of France, Charlemagne's paladins.

[2] *parfit richésse* ] perfect riches.

[3] *faintise* ] deceit; weakness; *after their degree* ] according to their rank; *appairèd* ] injured, impaired

[4] *nis* ] is no.

[5] *avaunce* ] in advance; *Male Bouch* ] Slander (fr. *Romaunt of the Rose*).

[6] *drow* ] drove.

[7] *Under support ... rede* ] Trusting to the goodwill of those who wish to read it; *wex'st not rede* ] do not wax (grow) red with blushing; with pun on *rede* (590); *wost* ] knowest (*2d pers. sing. pres. of* wit, *to know*); *boistously unfold* ] coarsely, rudely to unfold.

# **Elizabeth of York** (1465/6-1503),

## Queen of Henry VII

*Loyalte me llye. Elyzabeth.*[1]

– Motto of Richard III, with signature of Elizabeth, in her hand; on a flyleaf of Boethius, *De consolatione philosophiae*

LIZABETH OF YORK, three weeks before her twentieth birthday, married the newly crowned Henry VII, first of the Tudor kings. Quoth the jubilant queen: "Mine heart is set upon a lusty pin! / I pray to Venus of good continuaunce, / For I rejoice the case that I am in." Elizabeth's wedding, on 18 January 1485/6, was said to unite the House of Lancaster with the House of York, thereby writing *finis* to the Wars of the Roses.

Princess Elizabeth was born at Westminster Palace on 11 February 1466, the eldest child of queen Elizabeth Woodville by her husband, King Edward IV. Elizabeth (the Lady "Bessie") grew up without any illusion that she would one day choose her truelove. At age three, she was betrothed by her father to George Neville, son of the earl of Northumberland. When Northumberland abandoned his allegiance to him, Edward IV called off that first engagement. A year later, having fled to France with his brother (Richard duke of Gloucester, later king), Edward IV ventured to disrupt the planned marriage of Anne Neville to Edward Prince of Wales (only son of Henry VI) by suggesting to his mother, Margaret of Anjou, that he be married to princes Elizabeth instead of to Anne.[2]

After his return to the English throne, King Edward next contracted to give Elizabeth in marriage to Charles, the French Dauphin. That engagement, lasting almost seven years, ended in 1482, when Louis XI reneged, looking to find his son a better match elsewhere.

No loss: Charles l'Affable was a notorious dimwit. Besides which, her engagement to the Dauphin, during those formative years, secured for Lady Elizabeth the best possible education. A few of her own childhood books have survived. In a copy of the *Testament de Amyra Sultan Nych Hemedy,* dated 12 Sept. 1481, the princess wrote: "Elysabeth the kyngys dowghter Boke."[3] An extant copy of the *Romance of the Saint Graal* is similarly subscribed on the flyleaf: "Elysabeth, the kyngys dowther." Her father the king saw to it that Elizabeth was tutored in French, Spanish, and – rare for a woman of the 15th century – Latin. Oxford scholars instructed her in the classics. From scriveners of the Westminster Abbey scriptorium, Elizabeth of York is reputed to have learned to write court hand as well as any professional scribe (this, at a time when many noblemen, though literate, wrote no more than their own name, depending on clerks for personal correspondence). Her training included horsemanship, archery, music, needlework, courtly dance. Her original verse may perhaps include *The Floure and the Leaf* (q.v.).

In April 1483, King Edward died, aged 41, naming his brother Richard, duke of Gloucester, as Lord Protector. Richard protected his two royal nephews by confining them in the Tower of London. Years later, Bernard André, chronicler of Henry VII's court, writes (in Latin) that Elizabeth had a love for her brothers and sisters that was unspeakable – almost unbelievable.[4] But she never saw them after May 1483: Edward V, aged 13, was disposed of in the Tower of London after a two-months reign, before he was even crowned. Prince Richard, age 10, was slain with him.

Alarmed by the Lord Protector's threatening behavior, dowager queen Elizabeth with her six daughters, and her brother Lionel, took sanctuary in Westminster Abbey, where they would spend the next year as political refugees, not knowing what had become of the two princes but fearing the worst.

---

[1] *Loyalte me llye* ] (French) *Loyalty binds me.*

[2] The marriage of Anne, 14, to Prince Edward, 17, went forward. This Edward (only son of Henry VI and Margaret of Anjou) was killed at the Battle of Tewkesbury; the 15-year-old widow, taken captive, a year later married King Edward's brother Richard (later king). Letters survive from Anne, written during her brief widowhood, to Elizabeth of York and to her mother the queen.

[3] *Testament de Amyra Sultan Nych Hemedy* ] an illuminated manuscript on vellum, containing a report of the death of Mohammed II; sent from Constantinople on 12 Sept. 1481 and presented to Edward (V), prince of Wales.

[4] Bernard André, *Henrici Septimi* (ed. Gardner, 1858), 38.

Elizabeth of York by the death of her brothers was legitimate heir to the throne. But not for long. In June, by an act of Parliament, Richard declared the marriage of Edward IV and Elizabeth Woodville to be invalid, their children to be bastards; and seized the throne for himself.

The vision of a happier future came from Margaret Beaufort (mother to Henry Tudor, the exiled earl of Richmond). While still in sanctuary, Elizabeth Woodville received from Margaret a political proposal: her son, Henry Tudor, of the House of Lancaster, would take to wife Edward's daughter, Elizabeth of York. Henry would raise an army and, with the Woodvilles' support, topple Richard III. Elizabeth and Henry would rule in his place. (Whether, on this plan, Elizabeth of York would be regnant queen seems not to have been spelled out with complete clarity.) The queen dowager signed on, as did Elizabeth, 17. Henry also subscribed: in December 1483, at Rennes Cathedral, Henry Tudor, earl of Richmond, solemnly vowed to marry Elizabeth of York. The Woodvilles in turn swore their allegiance to Henry Tudor.

Edward's widow and daughters now had only to wait for Henry's invasion. And wait. Richmond's assault on England, planned for spring 1484 (like his earlier attempt, in October) failed to materialize. A combination of bad weather, poor planning, and insufficient funds kept Henry anchored in Brittany.

When the long-suffering captives in Westminster Abbey became a political liability for Richard, he cut a deal: the king extended a written promise that Elizabeth Woodville and her six daughters would not be imprisoned, raped, or killed; the girls would receive annuities of 200 marks each; and the king would marry them to gentlemen born despite their having been proclaimed bastards (and property forfeit to the crown). On March first, in despair of rescue, Elizabeth Woodville surrendered herself and her daughters to the usurper's promised mercy.

Princess Elizabeth, the eldest, was brought to court, where she was given considerable freedom to enjoy the life to which she had been accustomed as a child. She was handled by courtiers, with respect; by Anne Neville (Richard's queen), with affection; and by the king himself, with much gallantry.

At one of the court festivities for Christmas 1484, Lady Elizabeth, 18, and queen Anne, 28, dressed as twins, causing tongues to wag that Elizabeth would be Richard's next wife – a conclusion that cannot have been the intended signal of the ladies' fashion choice that night; but in the historical moment, such observations stood for evidence. With each month that passed and still no sign of King Edward's much-beloved sons, antipathy for the usurper gave way to increased paranoia. Surely, any man who would kill or banish his brother's under-aged sons would also take his brother's (now bastardized) daughter to wife, and the Pope be damned.

Richard III and queen Anne
Salisbury Roll (B.L. Loan MS 90)

But for once, Richard was the victim rather than the source of rumor-mongering. (The gossip that said he intended to marry his niece was, in fact, so damaging politically that he issued a proclamation to deny it.)

And yet, Elizabeth's love-life during this period has remained a puzzle to historians. "Ricardians" (those seeking to recuperate the infamous king from Shakespeare's hatchet-job) have represented the princess as an unprincipled seductress who tried to seduce Richard; failed; and settled for Henry Tudor. Or else, as a mindless shuttlecock swept off her feet by Richard's charm. Historians as recently as 2009 have suggested that Elizabeth of York "may indeed have fallen in love with King Richard, who had restored her to the gaiety, privileges, and prerogatives of his Court"[1] (but who also killed her brothers; invalidated her parents' marriage; declared herself and her sisters bastards; stole her father's crown; and confiscated her inheritance).

[1] Arlene Okerlund, the most dependable of Elizabeth's biographers, remains uncommitted on this point. *Elizabeth of York* (2009), 38.

A third view, never considered: Elizabeth during that year under Richard's roof had many loved ones, herself not least, whose health and safety depended on her comportment with the king. If someone got played, it was Richard.

Elizabeth of York
Collection of the Earls of Essex (at Cashiobury)

Queen Anne died in March 1485. Elizabeth immediately distanced herself from Richard, whom she detested.[1] Rather than marry the widowed usurper, she made it her ambition to take him down. She knew what she wanted, by now, and she had a plan whereby to achieve it. Acting on Margaret Beaufort's scheme, Elizabeth would take to husband the exiled earl of Richmond – not for love, certainly (she had never met the man), but to depose Richard, avenge the murder of her brothers, and to secure her own future. Those goals could be achieved only by an alliance between Elizabeth of York, the Woodville family, and the House of Lancaster.

Shuffling for herself, Elizabeth found a reluctant ally in Sir Thomas Stanley. Though he was husband to Margaret Beaufort (and stepfather to her exiled son) Stanley had retained his position as steward of the royal household under Richard III (a fatal tactical error, on the king's part). Elizabeth considered Lord Stanley her best bet.

Humphrey Brereton (one of Lord Stanley's gentleman retainers) tells the story of Elizabeth's coup in "The Song of the Lady Bessy," a verse narrative of 1,082 lines written not long after Richard's fall and Henry's accession.[2] Brereton has no ear for English prosody. His eyewitness report mistakes a few dates and titles.[3] His story is not found in Shakespeare's *Richard III,* or in the major prose chronicles. The rhymed quotations are of course paraphrased or invented. But his tale is a largely dependable history of the catalytic role that the "wise and witty" Princess Bessie of York played in the defeat of Richard III.

The extracts printed here (in modern spelling) commence with a meeting that took place in April 1485; in which Elizabeth of York persuaded Sir Thomas Stanley, steward of the royal household, to assist her in raising funds and mobilizing troops for an armed rebellion against King Richard. In Shakespeare's version, wicked Richard is toppled by poetic justice. Omitted from his *Richard III* are two characters – Elizabeth of York, a princess; and Humphrey Brereton, a bad poet – who were key players in the original drama; without whose actions, history might well have taken a different course than what appears in the Tudor chronicles:

From **Song of the Lady Bessie**

"Help, father Stanley, I do you pray!
For of King Richard wroken I would be [4]
(He did my brethren to the death on a day
In their bed where they did lie)...
And help earl Richmond, that prince so gay,
That is exiled over the sea"
. . . . . . . . . . . . . . . . . . . . . . . . . . . . . . .

[1] *detested* ] the present editors have examined but do not find credible the 1619 allegation of George Buck, an apologist for Richard III, who states that Elizabeth of York in February 1485 wrote to John Howard duke of Norfolk, saying she was in love with the king and wished Norfolk's help in marrying Richard after Anne's death.

[2] *gentleman retainer* ] In the National Archives is a grant in fee from Overton to Sir Randle Brereton (13 Feb. 1468/9), with subscribed witnesses Thomas Lord Stanley, justice of Chester; Sir William Stanley, chamberlain of Chester; and Humphrey Brereton de Malpas; also, a quitclaim (16 Nov. 1478), signed by Sir Thomas Stanley, Sir William Stanley, Sir Randle Brereton, and Humphrey Brereton (DCH/C/949).

[3] *mistakes* ] e.g., Brereton twice calls princess Elizabeth, "countess" (becauses betrothed to the earl of Richmond); and he calls Lord Stanley "earl" [of Derby], though Stanley received that title the following October); the latter is not a mistake, but an ordinary courtesy (of referring to lords by their highest achieved title).

[4] *wroken* ] revenged (fr. Middle English preterit for *wreak*).

Then answered the earl again
(These were the words he said to Bessie):
"An' King Richard do know this thing,
We were undone, both thou and I! [1]

. . . . . . . . . . . . . . . . . . . . . . . . . . . . . . . .

She barred the door above and under,
That no man should come them nigh;
She set him on a seat so rich,
And on another she set her by.

. . . . . . . . . . . . . . . . . . . . . . . . . . . . . . . .

"Nothing," said Bessie, "I would have,
Neither of gold, nor yet of fee,
But fair earl Richmond (so God me save!),
That hath lyen so long beyond the sea."

Stanley though sympathetic seeks to excuse himself; Elizabeth persists, offering to write the letters herself:

"Alas, Bessie, that noble lord,
And thy boon, forsooth, grant would I thee,
But there is no clerk that I dare trust
This night to write for thee and me,
Because our matter is so high,
Lest any man would us bewray."
Bessie said, "Father, it shall not need:
I am a clerk, full good, I say."
She drew a paper upon her knee:
Pen and ink she had full ready,
Hands white and fingers long.
She dressed her to write, speedily.

Brereton reports that Elizabeth took the letters by dictation, then advised Lord Stanley to nap, while she prepared the fair copies:

"Go to thy bed, father, and sleep,
And I shall work for thee and me.
Tomorrow by rising of the sun
Humphrey Bre'ton shall be with thee."
She brought the lord to his bed,
All that night where he should lie;
Bessie worketh all the night;
There came no sleep in her eye.

The princess in a pre-dawn visit awakes Brereton and brings him to Lord Stanley. Explaining his mission, they dispatch Brereton to Stanley's allies in the West country. The letters that Bessie has written ask the recipients to attend a secret meeting on 3 May 1485, and to bring gold for the purpose of mounting a rebellion.

Brereton gives a detailed account of his journey, underscoring both the loyalty of Stanley's kin and their high regard for the princess Elizabeth. At Manchester, Lord Edward Stanley on reading his epistle is said to have exclaimed:

---

[1] *An'* ] If

"Women's wit is wonder to hear!
My uncle is turned by your Bessie!
And whether it turn to weal or woe,
At my uncle's bidding will I be."

To the May 3d meeting, Thomas Stanley and his allies bring quantities of gold and a promised number of fighting men. Brereton is then sent across the Channel on a ship owned by Lord Stanley. Sailing from Liverpool, he is accompanied by three packmules whose side-saddles are stashed with the hidden gold; he also carries letters from Henry's step-father Lord Stanley, and from the princess Elizabeth.

Arriving at a secret destination – an abbey in Brittany, not far from Sarzeau – Brereton is met at the gate by a porter who, like the poet himself, is a Cheshire man. Welcomed inside, Brereton is brought to some English gentlemen shooting at butts; among them, Henry Tudor (described as having a long face, with pale skin; a wart on his chin; and dressed in a coat of black velvet that came to his knees). Brereton introduces himself; then

Lowly he kneeled upon his knee;
He delivered the letter that Bessie sent,
And so he did, the mules three,
And a rich ring with a stone.

The earl of Richmond by this time knew that Queen Anne was dead. He may have also heard that his betrothed, the princess Elizabeth, would wed King Richard: On meeting Brereton, Henry remains wary and speechless until he sees the quantity of gold that Elizabeth and Lord Stanley have collected in his behalf; which makes a believer of him.

As Brereton waits at the abbey, a happy Henry Tudor hurries off to Paris to meet with Charles VIII (Elizabeth's childhood fiancé, now king of France). Returning with a promise of French support, Henry sends Brereton back to England with letters for his co-conspirators.

Events moved quickly. On August first, Henry with 2,000 fighting men sailed from Brittany, arriving on the 11th at Milford Haven, Wales. Marching eastward, he accepted the surrender of Dale Castle, Pembrokeshire, and pushed on to meet 6,000 troops raised by the Stanleys. King Richard on news of the invasion summoned fighting men to muster at Leicester, where there assembled a royal force of 10,000.

The story of the battle has been told many times: On 22 August, at Bosworth Field, Richard III was killed and his army defeated. In Brereton's account, the soldiers as if "wood" (insane) "hew" the usurper's corpse, then "dang" in his skull with a steel helmet ("basinet").

That same day, on a hill near Stoke Golding, Henry Tudor donned the crownet that King Richard wore into battle. He then led a triumphal procession to Leicester, where the dead king's naked body and royal armor were put on display for a few days while the dead and wounded were removed from the battlefield.

On news of the invasion, Richard had taken hostage the daughters of Edward IV. Elizabeth was dispatched to Sheriff Hutton, a distant and gloomy castle in north Yorkshire. Henry now sent Sir Robert Willoughby to Sheriff Hutton, to claim his bride. By the time Willoughby got there, she had already been liberated by a throng of jubilant citizens.

The city of Leicester, the halfway point between Sheriff Hutton and London, may be the place where Elizabeth first set eyes on Henry Tudor. It was here, in Brereton's account, that she last set eyes on King Richard. Brereton narrates a possibly ahistorical confrontation between the "merry" princess and Richard's mutilated corpse:

They carried him naked unto Leicester,
And buckled his hair under his chin.
Bessy met him, with merry cheer.
These were the words she said to him:
"How lik'st thou thy slaying of my brethren twain?"
(She spake these words to him aloud).
"Now are we wroken upon thee here –
Welcome, gentle uncle, home!"

The gloating ascribed to Elizabeth seems uncharacteristic of her behavior and language elsewhere, and may be either second-hand report, or artistic license. The editorial – "She spake these words to him *aloud*" – where one expects "alone," for the rhyme with *home* – may attest to Brereton's own unease with the attributed statement. In any case, the gracious nuns of Greyfriars received the king's corpse from Henry and buried it in their chapel of St. Mary's. And there it rested until September 2012, when Richard's remains were discovered beneath a Leicester car park and exhumed by British scientists; who report that he died of ten sword wounds, eight of them to the head and one upward thrust into the buttocks.

Ending his narrative with the royal wedding, Brereton is delighted with the outcome—

Great solace it was to see,
I tell you, masters, without lett,
When the Red Rose of mickle price
And our Bessie were met. [1]

Edward Hall, the first Tudor historian, reports that all England took comfort in their new king:

When these solempnities & gratifications were done & passed: accordyng as other kynges had been accustomed, he congregated together the sage councelers of his realme, in which counsail like a prince of just faith and true of promes, detestyng all intestine & cyvel hostilite, appoynted a daye to joyne in matrimony y^e lady Elizabeth heyre of the house of Yorke, with his noble personage heyre to y^e lyne of Lancastre: whiche thyng not onely rejoysed and comforted the hartes of the noble and gentlemen of the realme, but also gayned the favour & good myndes of all the commen people, much extollyng and praysyng the kynges constant fidelyte and his polletique devyce, thinkyng surely that the daye was now come that the seede of tumulteous faccions & the fountayne of civyle dissencion should be stopped, evacuate and clerely extinguished. [2]

[1] *without lett* ] without reservation; *Red Rose of mickle price* ] (Henry Tudor) a Lancaster of great worth.

[2] Edward Hall, *The Union of... Lancastre* [*and*] *Yorke* (1548), part 2, fol. 1v-2r. Portraits: *Henry VII*, National Maritime Museum (*Greenwich, London*); Elizabeth of York, by Malden, Sarah, Countess of Essex (1761-1838), from a 16th century copy of an earlier painting (public domain).

## The Epithalamion

The untitled poem here entitled "Epithalamion" celebrates the marriage of Princess Elizabeth to Henry VII. The scribal attribution, "quod Quene Elizabeth" (added by a later hand) is neither authoritative nor unambiguous: quod (or quoth) is a convention that in contemporary usage can signify either "written by" or "thus says" or "copied by." The "I" of the song, whose heart is "Delured from sorrow, annexed to plesaunce," speaks for Elizabeth of York, as represented in her own words. But one's reading of the poem depends in part on one's reading of "quod." If the epithalamion was composed by the queen, then the song emerges as a spontaneous overflow of personal happiness. If "quod Queen Elizabeth" signifies only that these lines are to be read *as if* by the queen, or were once copied by the queen (though composed by another), then some anonymous and unknown poet has presumed to articulate her feelings; and if so, he seems to have done a remarkably persuasive job of ventriloquism (31).

The "we" of line 20 can denote either "Mine heart and I" or "My husband and I" – which, in this context, amount to the same signified: *dear Henry and yrs truly* (not, primarily, *Elizabeth and the English nation*; and surely not *Elizabeth and her poet laureate*. (The epithalamion bears no resemblance to anything written by Bernard André, court poet to Henry and Elizabeth.) But it is not Henry Tudor who receives credit for having supplied the poet's habundaunce of comforte. Thanksgiving is directed to "the goodlihead / Of the most femyn and meek in countenaunce, / Very mirror and star of womanhead": Thanks be to Venus; or thanks be to the Virgin Mary; or to my mother (Queen Elizabeth Woodville); or his mother (Margaret Beaufort); or thanks be to the entire population, or condition, of womanhood: all, conflated here in the figure of transcendent femininity.) Whatever female divinity there may be, in heaven above, is called upon in the Epithalamion to ensure that Elizabeth's newfound happiness will endure: "This joy and I, I trust, shall neuer twin."

The poet in her first line recalls the duke of Suffolk's tribute to Margaret of Anjou, "How þe louer is sett to serve þe floure," written some forty years previous; even as "The Floure and the Leaf" recalls Suffolk's "Assembly of Ladies." With Elizabeth of York enlisted as the first-person speaker of both poems, the royal epithalamion "quod Elizabeth," and the nearly contemporaneous "Floure and the Leaf" might be taken as by the same poet; nor is it unthinkable that Elizabeth of York was the original author, of both.

### [Epithalamion]

MINE HEART is set upon a lusty pin!
I pray to Venus of good continuaunce,
For I rejoice the case that I am in:
Delúred from sorrow; ánnexed to plesáunce;
Of all comfórte, having hábundaunce.
This joy and I, I trust, shall neuer twin:
Mine heart is set upon a lusty pin. 1

I pray to Venus of good continuaunce,
(Sith she hath set me in the way of ease),
Mine heartly service with mine áttendaunce
So to continue that euer I may please,
Thus voiding from all pensiful dis-ease.
Now stand I wholè, far from all grieváunce.
I pray to Venus of good continuaunce, 2

---

[1] *set...pin* ] full of good cheer (*OED* pin 15); the origin of the conventional phrase, *set on a pin,* is obscure: *pin* may denote the peg or nail in the center of a target; the tuning pegs of a stringed instrument; the hand of a mechanical timepiece; a peak or apex (and Elizabeth is perhaps not too delicate for bawdy innuendo); *lusty* ] merry, pleasing; *Venus* ] Venus (2, 8, 14) *and* famous (41), *-est* verb endings, and the like are often elided in the fifteenth century, as here, where *Venus* may be pronounced as one syll., "I pray to Ven's," or with a shortened second syllable; *of* ] for; *Delúred* ] delivered (del-*yoord'*); *plesáunce* ] pleasance, pleasure; *hábundaunce* ] abundance; *again at 29*; *neuer* ] never (1 syll., *nyoor*); *twin* ] go asunder, part; *also*, find an equal.

[2] *Sith* ] since; *euer* ] ever; (1 syll., *yoor*; again at line 40); *voiding ... dis-ease* ] avoiding all melancholy discomfort.

For I rejoice the case that I am in,
My gladness is such, there grieveth me no pain –
And so to servè, neuer shall I blin;
And though I would, I may not me refrain.
Mine heart and I so sete° is certáine,
  We shall neuer slack, but euer new begin:
  For I rejoice the case that I am in, [1]

Delúred from sorrow, annexed to plesáunce,
That all my joy I set as aught of right,
To please (as after my simple súffisaunce),
To me the goodliest, most beauteous in sight,
A very lantern to ye all other light,
  Most to my comfort in her rémembraunce.
  Delúred from sorrow, annexed to plesáunce; [2]

Of all comfórte, having hábundaunce:
Ás when that I think the goodlihead
Of the most femyn and meek in countenaunce,
Very mirror and star of womanhead,
Whose right good fame so large abroad doth spread!
  Full glad to me, to havè cognisaunce
  Of all comfórte, having hábundaunce.

This joy and I, I trust, shall neuer twin:
So that I am so far forth in the trace,
My joys be'n double where other be but thin.
For I am stably set in such a place,
Where beauty 'creaseth, and euer welleth grace,
  Which is full famous and borne of noble kin.
  This joy and I, I trust, shall neuer twin. [3]

**Mine heartly service with mine attendaunce…**

Soon dispelled was any misperception that the earl of Richmond had fought for Princess Elizabeth's right to the crown: Henry was not to be her consort; she was to be his. Having climbed to the throne on his bride's shoulders, Henry refused to make Elizabeth regnant queen. Many citizens were surprised; and many Yorkists, outraged.

Lest there be further confusion concerning who was in charge, Henry deferred the wedding till after his coronation – a ceremony in which no mention was made of his betrothed.

Convening Parliament, Henry VII in one of his first acts as king created his mother a *femme sole,* thereby assigning to Margaret Beaufort the legal right to own property and to conduct business independent of her husband, Lord Thomas Stanley; and conferred upon her great quantities of real estate, for life. The king extended no such courtesy to Elizabeth, though she might have done well to request it.

The royal wedding, which occurred five months after Henry's victory at Bosworth, was a pinch-penny affair interpreted by some as an open insult to Elizabeth (and therefore to the Woodvilles, and the entire house of York and their allies). Adding salt, Henry denied Elizabeth a formal coronation even as his queen consort until 25 November 1487; by which time, in Lord Bacon's apt phrase, "danger taught him what to do." At the ceremony in Westminster Abbey and at the banquet afterward in the Hall, King Henry and his mother watched from their seats behind a latticework screen, so that they could keep an eye on the proceedings without seeming to attend the event.

---

[1] *blin* ] leave off, desist; *also*, to keep silence; *sete* ] settled.

[2] *aught of right* ] a due possession; *simple súffisaunce* ] the simple sufficiency that I had before.

[3] *So that* ] in that; *trace* ] path; course; dance.

**Full famous and borne of noble kin...**

If Elizabeth was forced to wait for satisfaction, Henry was not: at the time of their January wedding, she was already carrying Henry's child.

Expecting royal issue, the king directed his seers to examine the future; who dutifully consulted the oracles, or stars, or the Lord, and returned a prophesy that queen consort Elizabeth carried in her womb a son who would restore a golden age to England.

King Henry, former earl of Richmond, gave the heralds and royal genealogists as assigned task: they must trace his lineage as far back as Cadwaladr and the ancient British kings (thereby to strengthen his claim to the English succession). Filling in gaps where necessary, these able scholars, in their researches, discovered that Henry VII was indeed a direct descendant of the legendary King Arthur. Nor did the heralds dwell overmuch on the issue of bastardy.

For her lying in, Elizabeth was sent (with her sisters, and her mother, and her mother-in-law, and ladies in waiting) to Winchester, a city then believed to be the Camelot of King Arthur.

On 19/20 September 1486 a baby was born. It was a boy, as prophesied. Henry named his firstborn Arthur, in honor of his royal ancestor, and to marshal in the new Golden Age.

**Very mirror and star of womanhead,...**

A few weeks later, Henry arrested his mother-in-law for treason.

Francis Lord Bacon describes Elizabeth Woodville as "a busy, negotiating woman," one who believed "none could hold the book so well to the prompt, and instruct the stage-play, as she could." And she "was at this time extremely discontent with the king – thinking her daughter (as the king handled the matter) not *advanced,* but *depressed....* it was not her meaning (nor no more was it the meaning of any other of the better and sager sort that favored this enterprise, and knew the secret) that this disguised idol [Henry Tudor] should possess the crown."[1]

A rebellion erupted in Ireland in the fall of 1487: Elizabeth Woodville, discontented queen dowager of Edward IV, mother-in-law of Henry VII, was blamed for the uprising. King Henry therefore moved "to cloister the queen dowager in the nunnery of Bermondsey, and to take away all her lands and estate; and this by a close Council, without any legal proceeding, upon far-fetched pretenses." Bacon reports that "there was much wondering that a weak woman ... after so happy a marriage between the king and her daughter, blest with issue male, should, upon a sudden mutability or disclosure of the king's mind, be so severely handled."

**Most to my comfort ...**

Prince Arthur kept a busy schedule.

At age two, not yet in breeches, he was formally betrothed to the Infanta of Spain, Catherine of Aragon (a year elder than he).

At age three, on 29 November 1489, Arthur was brought to Westminster, where the king risking witticisms made him a Knight of the Bath. On the same day, Queen Elizabeth gave birth to a daughter, the Princess Margaret. The king showed scant interest: on the morrow, in the Parliament Chamber, he created his son Arthur Prince of Wales.

Wishing to ensure Arthur's proper training in kingship, and perhaps to demonstrate that the Prince of Wales was no more dependent on a woman than his father the king, Henry in 1492 removed Arthur from his mother's care and sent him to Ludlow Castle (in the Welsh Marches), where his education and his training in martial arts was supervised by the best Welsh and English tutors.

The other children, those who survived, were raised chiefly at Sheen Palace, under the watchful eye of their paternal grandmother, Margaret Beaufort, who was put in charge of the nursery.[2]

---

[1] Francis Bacon, *The Historie of the Reigne of King Henry the Seventh* (1629): 26 (again below); ed. DWF.

[2] Margaret, born 29 November 1489 (married, age 14, to King James IV of Scotland); Henry, born 28 June 1491 (future king of England, six wives; divorced two, killed two); Elizabeth, born 2 July 1492 (intended for the French prince, Francis, but died, age 3); Mary, born 18 March 1496 (at age 18, married 1. King Louis 12; age 19, married 2. Charles Brandon, duke of Suffolk); Edmund, born 21 February 1499 (died at 15 months); Katherine, born 2 February 1503 (died the same day).

**In her remembraunce...**

Elizabeth's mother spent the last five years of her life confined at Bermondsey Abbey. She wrote her will (she was penniless) on 10 April 1492; and died on 8 June. In accordance with her wishes she was buried beside her husband King Edward at Windsor; where she was laid to rest in the presence of all of her daughters except queen Elizabeth, who was either busy that day or forbidden by her husband the king to attend the funeral of her own mother.

**My simple suffisaunce...**

The privy purse expenses of Henry's queen, published by Sir Harris Nicolas in 1827, indicate that Elizabeth was generous to others, while slow to spend tuppence on herself. Her gowns were routinely mended to avoid the purchase of new ones. She wore shoes with tin buckles that cost twelve pence. What little she had, she shared with her sisters, who were destitute, and with others as she was able.

Tight-fisted Henry gave his wife so little to sustain her household that she fell deeply in debt; by 1495, after pawning her plate for £500, she was obliged to borrow another £2000 to satisfy her creditors (others loans followed, some for as little as £10).

That same year saw the death of Sir William Stanley, who with his brother Sir Thomas Stanley had led Henry to victory at the Battle of Bosworth Field. Disenchanted with King Henry, Sir William lent support to the "pretender," Perkin Warbeck, who claimed to be Queen Elizabeth's long-lost younger brother. King Henry beheaded Stanley in 1495, and hanged Warbeck in 1499.

**Where beauty 'creaseth, and euer welleth grace...**

After talks with Ferdinand and Isabella of Castile for nearly a decade, King Henry finally negotiated a marriage contract the Prince of Wales and the Princess of Castile: When she reached age fourteen, Catherine of Aragon would come to England and marry Prince Arthur (Pope willing); with a dowry of 200,000 gold crowns to be paid in installments.

In December, to express her joy, queen Elizabeth wrote in Latin to Queen Isabella (here, as in other state papers, called "Elizabeth," the English form of *Isabella*). The extravagant hyperboles of England's Elizabeth in addressing the Spanish queen illustrate diplomatic convention at a time when even the most ruthless state business was conducted under the gloss of elaborate courtesy.

## To Queen Isabella (3 December 1497) [1]

To the most serene and potent princess the Lady Elisabeth, by God's grace queen of Castile, Leon, Aragon, Sicily, Granada, &c., our cousin and dearest relation –

Elizabeth, by the same grace queen of England and France, and lady of Ireland wishes health and the most the world –

Although we before entertained singular love and regard to your Highness above all other queens in the world, as well for the consanguinity and necessary intercourse which mutually take place between us, as also for the eminent dignity and virtue by which your said Majesty so shines and excels that your most celebrated name is noised abroad and diffused everywhere–

Yet much more has this our love increased and accumulated by the accession of the most noble affinity which has recently been celebrated between the most illustrious Lord Arthur prince of Wales, our eldest son, and the most illustrious princess the Lady Catherine, the Infanta, your daughter. Hence it is that, amongst our other cares and cogitations, first and foremost we wish and desire from our heart that we may often and speedily hear of the health and safety of your serenity, and of the health and safety of the aforesaid most illustrious Lady Catherine, whom we think of and esteem as our own daughter, than which nothing can be more

[1] The original letter, one of the few in this volume that the editors of *Women's Works* have personally inspected, is reported by Mary Anne Everett Wood to be in Elizabeth's own hand. The Latin autograph was returned to England in 1836 by Don Paseval de Gayangos, and translated into English by Wood, 1.115-16.

grateful and acceptable to us. Therefore, we request your serenity to certify of your estate, and of that of the aforesaid most illustrious Lady Catherine our common daughter. And if there be anything in our power which would be grateful or pleasant to your Majesty, use us and ours as freely as you would your own; for (with most willing mind!), we offer all that we have to you, and wish to have all in common with you.

We should have written you the news of our state, and of that of this kingdom, but the most serene lord the King, our husband, will have written at length of these things to your Majesties.

For the rest may your majesty fare most happily according to your wishes.
From our palace of Westminster, 3[d] day of December, 1497.

Elizabeth the Queen

**Whose right good fame so large abroad doth spread...**

For King Henry, 1498 was a good year. Shortly after the pretender Perkin Warbeck was captured, the Pope issued a dispensation for Catherine of Aragon to be married to Arthur Prince of Wales. Ferdinand and Isabella sent an embassage to England, to make the wedding arrangements.

The Spanish ambassador, Pedro de Puebla, and the Sub-Prior of Santa Cruz, Fray Johannes de Matienzo, wrote separate reports of their encounters with the English royals. After meeting the king's mother, De Matienzo forwarded to Queen Isabella a special request for her daughter: it was the desire of Margaret the king's mother and (he was told) of queen Elizabeth, that Princess Catherine should learn French and speak only French on her arrival in England "since these ladies do not understand Latin, and much less, Spanish. They also wish that the princess of Wales should accustom herself to drink wine, since the water of England is not drinkable, and even if it were, the climate would not allow the drinking of it." [1] Both requests were superfluous: the Spanish princess already spoke French, and drank wine; while queen Elizabeth, and most of the King's male retainers, were conversant in Latin and, to some degree, Spanish (Elizabeth even retained a Spanish porter with whom to practice.) But the king's mother knew only French and English: when Arthur's bride arrived in England, Margaret Beaufort did not wish to be embarrassed or excluded from conversation.

Ambassador Sr. De Puebla reported to Queen Isabella on her future in-laws: "Henry is rich, has established good order in England, and keeps the people in such subjection as has never been the case before." Concerned that England might be sheltering refugees from the Spanish Inquisition, Henry had been reassuring: he "promised to punish soundly any Jew or heretic to be found in his realms" (they had "conversed a long time on this subject"). The king's favorite topic: "Henry likes to speak about the princess of Wales" (Catherine of Aragon).

In a shortlist of the persons who exercised the most influence on the king of England, de Matienzo placed Margaret Beaufort at the head of the list, omitting queen Elizabeth altogether; but added: "The queen is a very noble woman and much beloved. She is kept in subjection by the mother of the King." De Puebla found Elizabeth's situation pitiable. "It would be a good thing," he suggested to Isabella, "to write often to her, to show her a little love." [2]

**Thus voiding from all pensiful dis-ease...**

During the great epidemic of 1500, Henry moved his court to Calais, taking along Elizabeth and the children, the duke of Buckingham, two bishops, and some 300 others in his retinue.

Shortly after the family's safe home-return, queen Elizabeth composed a communion prayer, one of the few extant compositions from her 17-year marriage.

---

[1] G. A. Bergenroth, trans., Dr Rodrigo Gonzalez De Puebla to Ferdinand and Isabella (17 July 1598), *Calendar of Letters*, 156.

[2] Bergenroth, trans., Fray Johannes de Matienzo to Ferdinand and Isabella (17 July 1598), ibid., 163.

## Communion Prayer of Queen Elizabeth of York

*This devout prayer made the queen's grace, Elizabeth, late the wife of our sovereign the king, King Harry the Seventh, at Woodstock, the 27th day of November, the sixteenth year of our said sovereign lord and the year of our Lord God 1500*:

JESU, welcome my Maker, welcome my Redeemer. Welcome my Savior Jesu Crist, whom I here honor and make knowledge to be God and Man, in form of bread; the second person of the Trinity, Fader, Son, and the holy Ghost, three persons and very God; He that was born of the undoubted pure virgin, maiden, and moder, our blessèd Lady Saint Mary. Also, I knowledge thee to be He that suffered most painful death and passion for the redemption of sinners; and also, the third day after thy passion, rose from death to life; and after, ascended into Heaven and shall deem both quick and dead. [1]

Jesu, the giver of all grace and mercy, have mercy on me, most wretched and unkind sinner; and forgive me all that I have offended thee in, from the first hour of my birth until this hour, to me knowing or unknowing, in thoughts, wills, desires, deeds, or consents. For thy endless goodness, suffer me never to will, consent, nor do, that should be to thy displeasure or my dampnation. Graunt me above all earthly things to honor, love, and dread thee, and to keep thy precepts and commaundments. And of thy infinite goodness, send me sufficient confession and due satisfaction and to have full remission of my sins. [2]

O blessèd God and Man, I can no further but to flee in the holes of thy wounds, from the face of thy wrath. O good Lord, what should fall unto me if thou should deem me after thy rightwisness and not after thy mercy? Therefore, blessèd Jesu, as thou art the giver of all grace and mercy, have mercy upon me and look upon me with thine eyen of compassion. And forgive me all my wretched and most unkind sinful living and also of all those that ever I gave any occasion to offend thee by, and of all these that I am bound to pray for, and those that thou would'st that I shall pray for.

Now, good Lord, I make to thee oblation of my soul and body and of all things that to me appertaineth or belongeth, that I be this day, and ever, ordered and guided under thy will and protection, to the utter confusion of my ghostly enemy the Fiend, and to thy honor and to the increase of my merit everlasting.

Now, most blessèd Jesu, for thy glorious incarnation, nativity, and most painful death and passion, and for thy glorious resurrection, and for thy most marvelous ascension, for thy blessèd and holy living, and for thy love that thou hadst to all mankind when thou would'st willfully suffer passion for the redemption of sinners, have mercy upon me and upon all Cristen souls. Amen.

**We shall neuer slack, but euer new begin....**

Elizabeth's eldest son, Prince Arthur, met his bride, the Spanish Infanta, for the first time on 4 November 1501. He was fifteen, she was sixteen. Arthur liked what he saw. Ten days later, Arthur of England and Catherine of Aragon were happily wedded and bedded – the young groom, dressed in white, feeling "lusty and amorous."

Edward Hall, the first Tudor historian, reports of the bedding ceremony that "this lusty prince and his beautifull bryde were brought and joyned together in one bed naked, and there dyd that acte, whiche to the performaunce & full consummacion of matrimony was most requysite and expedient."

In the morning, reports Hall, Prince Arthur "called for drink, which he beforetimes was not accustomed to do – at which thing one of his chamberlains (marveling) required the cause of his drought. To whom he answered merely saying: 'I have, this night, been in the midst of Spain! – which is a *hot* region.'" [3]

---

[1] *deem* ] judge (the living and the dead).

[2] *that* ] that which; *that should be* ] anything that might be.

[3] Hall (1548), pt. 2, fol. 54r. This version of the honeymoon first became an issue in the 1520s, as grounds for Henry VIII's wished divorce from his brother's widow; at which time Catherine denied consummation with Arthur.

Arthur returned with his bride soon after the wedding to Ludlow Castle (where, already as a teenager, he served as President of the Council of Wales and Marches). Writing in Latin to his most serene and most powerful Spanish in-laws on 30 November, the Prince of Wales expressed his extreme bliss to be married to their most beautiful and most virtuous daughter; saying that he never felt so much joy in his life as when he first beheld the sweet face of his bride. He promised Ferdinand and Isabella that he would make Catherine a good husband.

The newlyweds' happiness, however, was brief. Before the winter was out, both Arthur and Catherine fell ill of an illness that their physicians were unable to diagnose or cure. Catherine survived. On 2 April 1502, Arthur died.

Henry and Elizabeth were at Greenwich Palace when the news came of the prince's death. When informed of her loss, the queen is reported to have spoken "pious words" of her submission to God's will, then retired to her chamber, and wept.

The prince's body lay in state at Ludlow for three weeks before being transported to Worcester for an inexpensive funeral. He was buried on 23 April, in the Abbey of St. Wolfstan. Catherine of Aragon, who remained ill from the same mysterious disease that killed her husband, was unable to attend Arthur's funeral. For reasons unknown, King Henry and Queen Elizabeth, his parents, also skipped the funeral. Historians have suggested that Worcester was considered too far for the king and queen to travel, or that Henry was simply too grief-struck to be seen in public.

Nine months and one week later, queen Elizabeth gave birth to the king's seventh child.

### Most femyn and meek in countenaunce...

Prince Arthur - *Royal Collection*

Queen Elizabeth, surnamed "the Good" for her gracious personality, many benefactions, and quiet passivity, gave birth on 2 February 1502/3. Princess Katherine died the same day. On 11 February, the queen also died, from a puerperal infection. She was 37.

Elizabeth's death came in the midst of fraught negotiations over the fate of Prince Arthur's teenaged widow. The king and queen of Spain, on news of Arthur's death and their daughter's illness, had asked that their Catherine be sent home; it was their expectation, after so brief a marriage, that England would return her dowry as well. Henry's position was that Spain still owed him the balance: the princess was going nowhere until the dowry was paid in full; and first, it must be seen whether his daughter-in-law was pregnant. She was not.

Both sides compromised: Catherine would be married to Arthur's younger brother, prince Henry, age 11, whose betrothal to Eleanor of Austria would be called off. The royal parents requested a papal dispensation (a necessary formality) authorizing Henry to marry his brother's widow, Catherine of Aragon, when he reached age 14. The dowry, however, remained a point of contention.

When queen Elizabeth died, King Henry felt obliged to inform King Ferdinand and Queen Isabella of his wife's death straightaway. In the same letter, he expressed his willingness to take the place of Henry, Jr., at the altar and marry Catherine himself. He was 46, she was 18. It seemed to him an excellent idea.

Queen Isabella, on receiving King Henry's letter, was apoplectic. In a letter to her ambassador, the Duke of Estrada, she expressed her surprise that "immediately after his bereavement, Henry could dare to think of a marriage to so young a princess, who was at the same time the widow of one son and the destined bride of another." As it would be "a very evil thing, the very mention of which offends the ears," Isabella stated she "would not for anything in the world that it should take place."[1] The king of England, she continued, must be told that there were two points on which she and King Ferdinand were now firmly resolved: "The first was, that the Princess Catherine should never marry King Henry; and the second, that she was immediately to return to Spain." They proved less resolute on the second point: a contract was concluded on 23 June 1503 for Catherine of Aragon to be married to Harry Junior.

King Henry survived his wife by seven years, dying in 1509. All biographies of Henry VII note that his character greatly deteriorated after his wife's death.

He was succeeded by Henry VIII.

DWF

---

[1] Bergenroth, *Calendar of Letters*, 156, xcv.

## **Margaret Beaufort** (1443-1509),
Countess of Richmond and Derby

*Souvent me souviens.*
—Lady Margaret's motto

MARGARET BEAUFORT was born in Bletsoe Castle, Bedfordshire, on 31 May 1443, the only child of John Beaufort, by his wife, Margaret Beauchamp. Her father, the duke of Somerset, was grandson to John of Gaunt (by a liaison with Katherine Swynford). Somerset's death at age 40, four days before Margaret's first birthday, is thought to have been a suicide. (Henry VI was about to charge Beaufort with treason, following a bungled military campaign in France.) His death left baby Margaret the wealthiest orphan in Europe.

Margaret's effigy in Westminster Abbey

When Somerset's widow remarried, Henry VI thought it best to keep the vast Beaufort wealth in the hands of the immediate royal family. In 1452 he assigned wardship of the Lady Margaret to his half-brother Edmund, earl of Richmond; and dissolved her (unconsummated) marriage to John de la Pole, so that Edmund, when he was ready, could take Margaret unto himself, in holy matrimony.

Honour called: Richmond left home to fight for King Harry and the Lancastrian cause. But first, he married his 12-year-old ward and got her pregnant, so as to secure his claim to her estate and income.

Captured and imprisoned by the Yorkists, Edmund was released from custody just in time to die of plague. Three months later, his widow, now thirteen, gave birth to Henry Tudor, future king of England.

Though she would bury four husbands before dying herself at the age of 66, Margaret Beaufort, countess dowager of Richmond, bore no other children. It may be that she was permanently injured by the birth of Henry, which cannot have been an easy delivery.

Lady Margaret doted on her son but she was not permitted to raise him. Edward IV – after defeating Henry VI and the House of Lancaster – removed Henry Tudor from Margaret's care and made him the ward of William, Lord Herbert, whose family seat was in Wales.

Herbert was put to death in 1469; after which, Margaret's son was bounced about from place to place. Finally taking refuge in Brittany, Henry Tudor sat out Edward's reign on the sidelines, eluding capture and evading extradition. Margaret cannot have seen him more than a few times between 1461 and 1485.

Everything about Margaret's life changed when her exiled son returned to England, defeated Richard III, and usurped the throne. Henry's triumph made Margaret Beaufort instantly one of the three most important women in England, together with the king's bride (Elizabeth of York, q.v.), and mother-in-law (Elizabeth Woodville).

Margaret moved quickly to subjugate the one and dispense with the other.

Once crowned, Henry studiously neglected his wife while making his mother's elevation paramount: His first Parliament in 1485 declared Margaret a *femme sole,* solely responsible for her actions at law. In addition, Margaret was awarded vast real estate holdings for life; over which, Margaret's husband (Lord Stanley, who helped Henry to the throne) had no say.

At Christmas 1487, Margaret wore robes and a crown matching those of Henry's queen—an explicit reminder to Elizabeth that she had once done much the same, dressing like Queen Anne for Richard III's Christmas festivities in 1483; but then as now, it was not Elizabeth who stood in the privileged position.

Margaret refused to give precedence to queen Elizabeth even in her own home. Whether at Sheen, Collyweston or Bishop's Hatfield, the king's mother remained in charge of the king's children, with sole discretion concerning who would be permitted to see them, or serve them. Wherever Margaret and the children went, Elizabeth was permitted or commanded to tag along: rarely were the king's wife and mother to be found under separate roofs.

While King Henry denied his queen any role in politics except as a gracious ornament at state functions, he established his mother as de facto vice-regent of England; in which capacity Margaret kept close watch, not only on Henry's wife and children, but on Henry's domestic and foreign policy.

Having been created a real-estate magnate without investing tuppence, Margaret acquired vast wealth. Her income, by 1504, amounted to £3000 per annum. At her favorite manor of Collyweston, she built a small empire, complete with its own equity court (of which she was the judge) and a debtor's prison. For herself and the grandchildren, she built a great palace. Her court was soon the largest in the realm after the king's, and far more lavish than his.

The annuity and allowance given to Queen Elizabeth, beyond what she received from her mother-in-law, was hardly enough to maintain herself and her small retinue. By 1495, she was wont to borrow petty cash from her own servants. Luxuries were few.

The privy purse expenses for Elizabeth's household do indicate several purchases of paper and ink, but it's not clear that the queen was ever permitted to use those supplies: the extant correspondence concerning the queen Elizabeth and her children was conducted between Margaret and King Henry.

What letters survive from Margaret Beaufort's pen are nicely varied. In one letter of uncertain date, we find her thanking the queen's chamberlain for fetching a pair of gloves she had left behind at a social gathering. In this letter appears Margaret's only recorded joke. She had set the gloves aside, she explains, because they were too big for her delicate hands – unlike the plump hands of those great ladies whose great wealth has supersized them into great personages:

**[To Thomas Butler, earl of Ormond, concerning her gloves** (25 April 1497?)°]

My Lord Chamberlain,

I thank you heartily that ye list so soon remember me with my gloves (the which were right good, save they were too mich for my hand!). I think the ladies in that parties be great ladies all, and according to their great estate, they have great personages.

As for news here, I am sure ye shall have more surety than I can send you. Blessèd be God: the king, the queen, and all our sweet children are in good hele. The *queen* hath been a little crazed, but now she is well, God be thankèd, her sickness is [not] so good as I would but I trust hastily it shall, with God's grace.[1] – Whom I pray give you good speed in your great matters, and bring you well and soon home. Written at Sheen, the 25 day of April,

M Rychmond
(To my Lord the Queen's Chamberlain) [2]

No great personage more deeply annoyed Margaret than the queen's mother. Dowager queen Elizabeth Woodville had thought that her daughter, Elizabeth of York, would by the death of Richard III become regnant Queen of England. Instead she had become a court decoration. The King's mother-in-law by this time was complaining bitterly of her daughter's treatment. Enough: in the autumn of 1497, King Henry on a pretext arrested Elizabeth Woodville for treason; sequestered her property; and banished her to a nunnery, where she died penniless five years later.

Margaret Beaufort also had her soft side. When her granddaughter and namesake, Margaret Tudor, was to be married at age nine to James IV of Scotland, the countess objected. King Henry VII therefore deferred the marriage, citing "many inconveniences," chiefly: resistance from his mother. "She has not yet completed the ninth year of her age," said King Henry of his daughter, "and is so delicate and weak that she must be married much later than other young ladies. ... Besides my own doubts, the queen and my mother are very much against this marriage. They say if the marriage were concluded we should be obliged to send the princess directly to Scotland – in which case, they fear the King of Scots would not wait, but injure her, and endanger her health.") [3]

As a result of that intervention, Princess Margaret was not married until 1503, when she was 13; nor was the marriage consummated until her fourteenth birthday. [4]

---

[1] *not so good* ] MS om. *not,* a Freudian slip of the pen ("her sykenes ys soo good as Y wuld..." MS).

[2] *chamberlain* ] Thomas Butler, earl of Ormond.

[3] Bergenroth, *Calendar of Letters*, 176.

[4] James IV was then 30 yrs old. Their 10-year marriage ended in 1513 with his death at the Battle at Flodden Field.

Margaret was a shrewd business woman. Her motto, *Souvent me souviens* – "I remember, often" – was not vindictive, in the sense of threatened revenge. It was just her way of saying: *If I think you owe me one, don't worry, I shall never let you forget.* Several letters survive between the king and his mother concerning Margaret's opportunistic claim to a ransom that was owing to her grandfather from the house of Orleans – a debt going all the way back to the Battle of Agincourt in 1415. Most of the ransom had been paid. Margaret was relentless in seeking the balance. While she pursued the matter in the French courts, she enlisted King Henry to assist, through diplomatic channels. (After protracted litigation in the French courts, the claim was finally settled after Margaret's death, by a 1514 agreement between Louis XII and Henry VIII.)

### **Margaret Beaufort to her son, Henry VII** (14 January 1499)

My own sweet and most dear King, and all my worldly joy:

In as humble manner as I can think, I recommend me to your Grace, and most heartily beseech our Lord to bless you. And my Good Heart, where that you say that the French King hath at this time given me courteous answer, and written letter of favor to his court of Parliament for the brief expedition of my matter, which so long hath hanged (the which, I know well, he doth especially for *your* sake); for the which, my [Lord, I humb]ly beseech your Grace that [you seek] to give him your favorable thanks, and to desire him to continue his in[tent to hear] me.[1] And, if it so might like your Grace, to do the same to the Cardinal [John Morton]; which, as I understood, is your faithful, true, and loving servant.

I wish, my Very Joy (as I oft have showed), an' I fortune to get this or any part thereof, there shall neither be that, or any good I have, but it shall be *yours* and at your commandment, as surely, and with as good a will, as any ye have in your coffers![2] And would God ye could know it as verily as I think it! But, my Dear Heart, I will no more encumber your Grace with further writing in this matter, for I am sure your chaplain and servant, Dr. Whytston, hath showed your Highness the circumstances of the same. And if it so may please your Grace, I humbly beseech the same, to give further credence also to this bearer.

And our Lord give you as long good life, health, and joy, as you in most noble heart can desire, with as hearty blessings as our Lord hath given me power to give you.

At Collyweston the 14th day of January, by your faithful, true beadswoman and humble moder,

Margret R.

As the end of a tumultuous century drew to a close, so did the conspiracies that had troubled Henry's reign. The king and his mother were able at last to relax and enjoy the fruits of their mutual labor. While Queen Elizabeth continued to pump out babies, Margaret settled into her work as vice-regent of England, and as business partner to the king. She even adopted a new signature, commensurate with her greatness; not just moving from cursive to block letters, but changing style of self-identification. Taking clever advantage of the "R" in *Richmond,* the countess changed her signature in 1499 from "M. Richmond" (the aristocratic form, which she had used since the 1460s), to "Margaret R" (the regal form), thereby to efface any difference between *Margaret, countess of Richmond*, and *Margaret, Regina.*[3] About this same time, Margaret altered her impresa, displaying her badge of the royal arms with the differencing removed from her shield, thereby to form a symbolic marriage between herself and her son that was signaled in heraldic imagery.

---

[1] The bracketed words are speculative interpolations of words or phrases no longer legible.

[2] *and I fortune* ] if I am so lucky as.

[3] The aristocratic form was to abbreviate one's Christian name followed by one's title, spelled out. In the regal form (Henry R., Elizabeth R.), the R. stood for Rex or Regina.

And a third life-change: Margaret in 1499 took a solemn oath before the Bishop of London, swearing thereafter to live separately from her husband, and to abstain from sexual intercourse. The first vow was the operative one – at 58, the countess dowager of Richmond was unlikely to turn suddenly promiscuous. Nor was the oath intended to embrace austerity: Margaret continued thereafter to live in the lap of luxury; but her own lap, from 1499, was off-limits. Lord Stanley, her husband, signed off on the arrangement with a good heart.

The oath of separation and chastity constituted Margaret Beaufort's final declaration of independence: "femme sole" was no longer just a legal status but a statement of identity. No woman in England could better stand on her own. That said, Margaret kept her son the king posted on her financial affairs, especially when she needed an assist with debt-collection.

In her letter of 28 January 1500/1 – a birthday greeting to the king while on a visit to Calais – Lady Margaret addresses both the ongoing litigation over the Orleans ransom, and her accounts receivable closer to home. In the autumn of 1500, her husband's receiver, Rev. William Wall, had been slow to deliver to Margaret her fair share of proceeds from the lordship of Kendall (with which she and her husband Sir Thomas Stanley had joint ownership). Margaret summarily fired the man, and proceeded to go after the sum in arrears. The dismissal caused some conjugal unhappiness in that Rev. Wall was not only Lord Stanley's accountant but also a good friend and his personal chaplain.

To forestall future domestic squabbles, Margaret needed a free hand to retain and dismiss whom she would, without kibitzing from her husband, a man whom she had promised the Bishop of London she would avoid. She therefore asks the king to supply her with a letter, under his royal seal, instructing her to employ only such men as were retained for the service of his younger son, Henry, duke of York (age 9; later, Henry VIII):

### **Margaret Beaufort to her son, Henry VII** (St. Agnes' Day, 28 January 1500/1)

My dearest, and only desired joy in this world:

With my most hearty loving blessings and humble commendations, I pray (our Lord to reward) and thank your Grace, for that it hath pleased your Highness so kindly and lovingly to be content to write your letters of thanks to the French king, for my great matter that so long hath been in suit (as Master Welby hath showed me your bounteous goodness is pleased). I wish, my Dear Heart, an' my fortune be to recover it, I trust ye shall well perceive I shall deal towards you as a kind loving moder; and if I should never have it, yet your kind dealing is to me a thousand times more than all that good I can recover (an' *all* the French king's might be mine withal!). My Dear Heart, ... all will I remit to your pleasure; and if I be too bold in this, or any of my desires, I humbly beseech your Grace of pardon, and that your Highness take no displeasure.

My good King, I have now sent a servant of mine into Kendall, to receive such annuities as be yet hanging upon the account of Sir William Wall, my lord's chaplain, whom I have clearly discharged, and if it will please your Majesty's own heart (at your leisure) to send me a letter and *command* me that I suffer none of my tenants be retained with no man, but that they be kept for my Lord of York, your fair sweet son, for whom they be most meet, it shall be a good excuse for me, to my lord and husband, ...

I now beseech you of pardon of my long and tedious writing, and pray almighty God to give you as long, good, and prosperous life as ever had Prince; and as hearty blessings as I can ask of God.

At Calais town (this day of Saint Annis, that I did bring into this world, my good and gracious prince, king, and only beloved son),

By your humble servant, beadwoman, and moder,
Margaret R.

The king always returned his mother's affection, as in this representative letter (written three months after the death of his eldest son, Prince Arthur, and seventeen months before the death of his wife, queen Elizabeth):

### **Henry VII to Margaret, countess of Richmond and Derby** (17 July 1501)

Madam, my most entirely well-beloved lady and Moder:

I recommend me unto you in the most humble and lowly wise that I can, beseeching you of your daily and continual blessings. And my Dame – not only in this but in all other things that I may know should be to your honor and pleasure, and weal of your soul – I shall be as glad to please you as your heart can desire it! And I know well that I am as much bounden so to do as any creature living, for the great and singular moderly love and affection that it hath pleased you at all times to bear towards me. Wherefore, my own most loving Moder, in my most hearty manner, I thank you, beseeching you of your good continuance in the same.... And I beseech you to send me your mind and pleasure in the same, which I shall be full glad to follow with God's grace, which send and give unto you the full accomplishment of all your noble and virtuous desires....

Written at Greenwich the 17 day of July, with the hand of your most humble and loving son.

H.R.

Margaret was no great scholar but she was an avid reader, and a patron of the printing press at a time when many aristocrats valued only manuscript volumes. Richard Pynson, William Caxton, and Wynkyn de Worde all printed books at Margaret's request and expense. Caxton in the year of her death styled himself "Prynter unto the moost excellent pryncesse my lady the kynges moder."

At the time of her death Margaret had in her collection of manuscript and printed books many volumes that she included by will in her legacies. Among these were "a great volume of vellum covered with black velvet, which is the second volume of Froissart"; a "book of vellum of Gower in English"; "a book of vellum of *Canterbury Tales*; "a French book of vellum with diverse stories, *At the Beginning: the Book of Genesis, with pictures limned*"; a "printed book called *Magna Carta* in French"; "a great volume of vellum of *The Siege of Troy* in English" (Wynken de Word, 1503), *The Great Ship of Fools of this World* (Sebastian Brant; trans. Henry Watson; Wynken de Word, 1509); and "a great volume of vellum named *John Bochas*, limned";[1] the last of which narrates "*the Fall of Princes, Princesses, and Other Nobles, beginning at Adam and ending with King John, taken Prisoner in Fraunce by Prince Edward*" (Pynson, 1494).

Margaret produced at least two original English translations of devotional texts, which she published. Her translation of the *Imitation of Christ,* Book 4 (into English, from a French version) was printed by Richard Pynson in 1503. Next, she translated into English a French version of the Latin *Speculum Aureum,* a late fifteenth-century text written by a Carthusian monk; this undated text was printed by Pynson, about 1506.

In her choice of what to translate, Lady Margaret hits upon texts with a highly misanthropic assessment of human worth and human sexuality (which is to say, highly orthodox; not least, her pejorative assessment of menstrual blood, and of the uterus as the site and source of human corruption):

This presente boke is called the Mirroure of golde to the sinfull soule / the whiche hath bin trã=slated at parice oute of laten in to frenche / and after the trãsla=cion seen & corrected / at length of many clarkis / Doctours / & maisters in divinite / and nowe of late translatede oute of frenche in to Englishe by the right excellẽt princesse Magarete moder to oure souerain lorde kinge Henry the vii. & Countesse of Richemond & derby. The wise man in his boke named / Ecclesi=astes consideringe the miserye and fraylete of the worlde saith / that it is vanite of all vanites / And all things that ben in the worlde present ought to be called vanites / & therfore saith the holy doctoure saint Gregory that there is noon more / acceptable sacrifice to god: then is gode zele / That it is to say an hernest desire to þ wayle of soules. For þ whi=che cause I haue willede to make & accomplysshe this present trety / gederinge and assemblinge ma ny diuerse autorites / of holy doctours of the chur=che / to thentent that the pore synfull soule troubled by the fraude of enmye and oft ouercome: May by holy manicions and auctorites / be addressed to the light of iustice and trouth / and so led by the meane of the holy goste that þ shepe that were perisshed may be reduced & led agayne to their grene paster And to the ende also that the pore soule redressed & reknowlegynge his erroure / knowynge his syne / and by Myrroure of golde. A.ii.

third printing (1522), sig. A2

[1] Charles Henry Cooper, *Memoir of Margaret: Countess of Richmond and Derby,* prints the entire inventory of Margaret Beaufort (original spelling); the books listed here are ones included in her legacies, pp. 129-35.

## From **The Mirror of Gold to the Sinful Soul:**

*Now of late translated out of French into English by the Right Excellent Princess Margaret, Moder to our Sovereign Lord King Henry the VII, and Countess of Richmond and Derby; of the Vileness and Misery of Man:*

NOW CONSIDER and behold, thou miserable man, what was of thee before thy nativity; and what is it of thee now, sith thou was born; and what shall be of thee to the hour of thy death; and what shall be of thee after this mortal life. Certainly, thou hast been from thy beginning a thing vile, stinking, detestable, and abhominable; conceived in filthy rottenness of flesh and stinking filthy concupiscence, and in th' embracement of stinking lechery; and, that worse is, conceived in the unclean spots of sin. [1]

And if thou behold and consider well what meat thou art nourished with in thy moder's womb, truly none other but with corrupt and infect blood (as well is known by many philosophers and other great clerks). And after thy nativity thou that hast been nourished of so foul and vile nature in thy moder's womb (as before is said), thou art also ordained to weepings and cryings and to many other miseries in the exile of this sorrowful world; and that that is more grievous, thou art also subject to thy death, the which every true Cristen man ought daily to remember and think upon. [2]

Behold then, and consider in thy life, that among all thing that almighty God hath created and formed, man is made of the most foul and abhominable matter; that is to know, of the slime of th' earth – the which (*earth*) is the least worthy of all other elements. God hath made the planets and stars, of the nature of the *fire*; the winds and birds, of the *air*; the fishes, of the *water*; the men and other beasts, of the *earth*.

Now consider then the thingès of old antiquity and thou shalt find thyself most foul. And when thou shalt know the other bodies which of the *fire* hath been made and brought forth, thou shalt among all other creatures repute thyself right vile and miserable. And thou shalt not, will or may, say or think, thyself semblable to celestial things; or shall be bold to prefer thyself before the thingès earthly. But if thou wilt 'company with any creature, accompany thee to the brute beastès, and thou shalt find thyself to them most semblable and like. For so sayeth wise Solomon: "Man and brute beastès semblably be comen of the earth and to th'earth they shall return." Know then, how "noble" thou art in this world, and take heed that the beauty, the praising of people, the strength and the heat of youth, the riches and th'honors of the world, may not keep thee from knowing of the *vility* of thy birth. [3]

Margaret Beaufort, as widow
*National Portrait Gallery (London)*

---

[1] *conceived in…sin* ] referencing the doctrine that the fertilized egg inherits from its Christian parents the contamination of sin, which makes the cells loathsome to God even before the fetus has broken any divine commandments.

[2] *infect blood* ] referencing the gynophobic belief that menstrual blood is poisonous.

[3] *vilety* ] vileness.

### Of the Vain Joy, Might, Dignity, Honors, and Riches of the World

If thou would know what is the joy, might, dignity, honors and riches of the world, understand and hearken the prophet Barak in his third chapter, the which demaundeth in this manner: "Where be the princes of the people, that had signory and domination of the beasts of th' earth, and that played and disported with the birds of heaven? Where be the men that gadereth gold and silver, and affy them in their treasure, never satisfied with *getting*? Iwis, they be all passed and dead and descended into Hell, and other be come in their places, which now joy and use of their goods that they lost" [Barak 3:16-19]. And where be the great clerks and the orators? or where be the great diners in excess and super-abundaunce of meats? – or they that have put their pleasaunce to nourish horses, palfreys, and such other? And where be the popes, emperors, kings, dukes, princes, marquis, earls, barons, noble burgeys, merchaunts, laborers, and folks of all estates? [1]

They be all in powder and rottenness! and of the most great, there is no more but a little memory upon their sepulchre, in letters contained.

But go see *in* their sepulchres and tombs, and look, an' thou canst well know and truly judge: which is the master? and which, the varlet? Which bones be of the poor and which be of the rich? Divide, if thou may, the laborer from the king, the feeble from the strong, the fair from the foul and deformed! [2]

### How Lechery Causeth Many Evils to Come to Man

Lechery is enemy to all virtues and to all goodness. And for that sayeth Boece in his third book of *Consolation* that "He is happy that liveth without lechery; for lechery is a sweet sickness and bringeth a man to death ere ever he perceive it." As witnesseth Valery in his ninth book, the which Valery also in his fourth book, telleth how Josephus in his age [was] demaunded of one if he were not lecherous; and he answered, "I pray, speak to me of some other thing. For as I am advised, I have had a great victory – that I may, by *age*, eschew lechery!" (For by lechery all evils cometh, and to that creature, all good things be troubled.)

Alas, what was the cause of the destruction of the people of Sichem but for violation of Dinah (the daughter of Jacob); the which, would go to see the dances; and there, [was] ravished (as it appeareth in the Book of Genesis, in the 34th° chapter). We read also of many, that is to say, moe than fifty thousand, were slain because of the lechery committed with the woman of Levite (as it appeareth in the twentieth chapter of the Book of Judges). And a man was slain for the lechery of Absalom his brother, forsomuch that he had defouled Tamar his sister (as it appeareth in the second book of Kings, in the tenth chapter). Abner by his lechery knew the concupiscence of his fader, Ish-Bosheth; but within short while after, they were both slain (as it appeareth in the second Book of Kings, in the fourth chapter). [3]

What was the cause of the deluge, but lechery? [4]

---

[1] *Where be* ] Where are they now? ("Ubi sunt") is a pervasive topos of medieval literature, much parodied in the modern period; *affy them* ] put their trust in; *burgeys* ] burgesses, citizens or freemen of a borough.

[2] *an' thou* ] if you; *varlet* ] menial servant.

[3] *the woman of Levite* ] one of the Bible's most appalling and morally ambiguous rape narratives; Book of Judges, chaps. 19-20; *a man* ] Ish-Bosheth; *tenth chapter* ] i.e., 2 Kings (2 Samuel), chaps. 3-4; where Ish-Bosheth is actually a son to King Saul, who scolds Abner, Saul's steward, for having had sex with Rizpah, one of the king's concubines; both Abner and Ish-Bosheth are murdered by David's men.

[4] *deluge* ] Noah's flood; "And when men began to be multiplied on earth, and had begat daughters, the Sons of God saw the daughters of men that they were fair, and took wives to them of all which they had chosen … Soothly giants were on the earth in those days. Forsooth, after that the Sons of God entered [in]to the daughters of men, and those daughters begat; these were mighty of the world and famous men of the world)." (Gen. 6:1-2, Wycliffe trans.).

*Margaret's fourth husband, Sir Thomas Stanley, first earl of Derby, died on 29 July 1504, aged 69. Rather than be tempted by the attractions of a fifth marriage, Margaret, 61, renewed her vow of chastity. The original text of 1499 has not survived, but her 1504 vow of renewal is preserved in the British Library:*

## The Lady Margaret her Vow°

IN THE PRESENCE of my Lord God Jesu Christ, and his Blessèd Mother the glorious Virgin Saint Mary, and of all the whole company of Heaven, and of you also my ghostly fader, I, Margaret of Richmond, with full purpose and good deliberation for the weal of my sinful soul, with all my heart promise from henceforth the chastity of my body; that is, never to use my body having actual knowledge of man after the common usage in matrimony; the which thing, I had before purposed in my lord my husband's days, then being my ghostly father the bishop of Rochester Master Richard FitzJames; and now eftsince I fully confirm it as far as in me lieth; beseeching my Lord God that He will this, my poor will, accept; to the remedy of my wretched life and relief of my sinful soul; and that He will give me His grace to perform the same. And also for my more merit and quietness of my soul, in doubtful things pertaining to the same, I avow to you, my lord of Rochester, to whom I am and have been, since the first time I see you admitted, verily determined (as to my chief trusty counselor) to owe my obedience in all things concerning the weal and profit of my soul.

*The matriarch of the House of Tudor died on 29 June 1509, two months after the death of her beloved son, King Henry, and four days after she attended the coronation of her grandson, Henry VIII. At the coronation banquet, Margaret either choked, or found too rich to digest, a plate of roasted swan. Henry Parker, Lord Morley, who served as her cupbearer at the ceremonies, reports that "she took her infirmity with eating of a cygnet."* [1]

• • •

The Coronation of Henry VIII
from the Parliamentary procession roll for Henry VIII (*British Library*, MS Add. 22306)

[1] BL MS Add. 12060, fol. 23v.

# Lady [—] Brian of Cheshire (fl. 1486-1489)

*Whed^er I were yours I cõnot tell.*
*To you I haue byn trew & lell...*
– Mistress Brian to Master Newton, fol. 93v

UMPHREY NEWTON of Pownall, Cheshire, was born on 3 October 1466, at Newton.[1] In 1490 he married Elena Fitton of Pownall, a union that produced four sons, six daughters, and a family dynasty. The Newtons of Pownall dominated the local economy until 1647 when the estates were broken up.

A meticulous records-keeper, Humphrey Newton in the early years of his marriage assembled a compendium of estate papers – deeds, accounts, leases, genealogical records – plus astrological predictions, correspondence, medical treatises, cooking recipes, and miscellaneous notes. His collection (further augmented by his son) was bound together in a hodgepodge volume that came to be known as the "Capesthorne manuscript," so-called because it was kept from 1656 until the mid-twentieth century at Capesthorne Hall. At one time, though now separated, it was bound with the St. Alban's 1486 print of Julian Barnes' *Book of Hunting.*

The Newton manuscript is housed today in the Bodleian Library (MS Lat. Misc. c.66). Tucked into the middle of the bound volume (92v-95) is a quire that preserves some two dozen poems, chiefly love lyrics from Humphrey Newton's youth – three of which, though copied in Newton's hand, are from a member of the Brian family, a young woman in whom he had a love interest. A correspondence was conducted in secret. Despite mutual affection, the courtship was abruptly terminated c. 1489, when the Brian parents betrothed their daughter to another.

Having lost his sweetheart, Newton found another and married into money, which had its compensations. Elena Fitton after her father's death brought to the marriage eight messuages, forty acres of meadow, twenty acres of wood, one hundred acres of pasture, plus two hundred acres of moss, peatbogs, and uncultivated "waste" in Pounall and Bollin – this, in addition to Newton's property, which included another six messuages, a water-mill, a fulling mill, a chapel, one hundred Cheshire acres of farmland, twenty acres of meadow, forty acres of pasture, plus a lake, a peat-bog, heathland, and waste.[2]

By his marriage to Elena Fitton, Humphrey Newton became one of Cheshire's wealthiest men. By his mid-forties he had acquired as well a strong sense of entitlement to the property of others. In July 1529, he armed Francis his son and nine accomplices, who "ryotously and with force and armes... cut down a parcell of the woode" belonging to Nicholas Browne, a less-wealthy neighbor; and there erected a weir, damming Browne's stream and diverting the water to Newton's mill.

An undated note in the Cheshire archives reports another quarrel, this one in the Mobberley alehouse of Randall Burgess, just four miles from Humphrey Newton's palace: Stopping by Randy's place for a beer – and observing Rev. Lawrence Leicester drunk and unable to stand – Newton remarked that the curate was fitter to preach from a midden (dungheap) than from a pulpit. Father Lawrence thereupon hurled a "black pot" at Newton's head. The priest's aim being impaired by alcohol, the missile happily missed Humphrey's noggin, bounced off the wall, and clattered to the floor. Newton survived the assault, forgave the drunken priest, and lived to the ripe age of 70. He died on 22 March 1536. His wife Elena survived him by six weeks.

The fate of Lady Brian is unrecorded.

---

[1] For information about Humphrey Newton the editors are indebted to Rossill Hope Robbins, "Poems of Humfrey Newton, Esq., 1466-1536," *PMLA* 65.2 (1950): 249-81. See also Ralph Hanna, "Humphrey Newton and Bodleian Library MS Lat. Misc. C.66, *Medium Aevum* (Fall 2000).

[2] Humfrey Norton, Cheshire Inq. p.m., 5 Sep. 1536, from Robbins; *Cheshire acres* ] 10,240 sq. yards, more than twice the size of the standardized modern acre.

**[Newton to Lady Brian:]**
***Go, litull bill…*** [1]

Go, little bill, and commend me heartily
Unto her that I call my true-lof and lady,
By this same true tokening:
That she saw me i' kirk on a Friday i' morning°,
With a sparhawk in my hond,
And my man° did by her stond. [2]

An old woman set her by
(That little Cold-of-Courtesy),
And oft, on her, she did smile –
To look on me, for a while.

And yet, by this, another token:
To the kirk she come, with a gentlewoman.
Even behind the kirkès-door°,
They kneelèd both upon° the floor
And fast they did pitter-pater—
(I hope they said matins togeder!) [3]

Yet once or twice, at the lest,
She did on me her eyen° kissed
I° hailsed on them, court'esly.
By all the tokens, truèly,
Commend me to her, heartily! [4]
[Humphrey Newton]

**[Newton to Lady Brian:]**
***I pray you M, to me be tru…*** [5]

I pray you, M, to me be true,
For I will be true as long as I live.
I will not change you, for old ne new,
Ne never lof other, whiles that I live.
And ye be avisèd this other year
Ye sent me a letter of lof so dear:
I was as glad of your writíng
As ever I was of any thing —
For I was sick the day before:
That letter healed! I was sick no more!
M, in space,
Comes fortune and grace.
I trust it so for to be.
M, be steadfast and true in thought,
For lof is the sweeter the [dearer 'tis°] bought.
And M, I hope, securèly,
There° is none that byes it so dear as we!
And in what place so ever ye be,
As oft as ye will, ye'll° me there see.

Therefore be ye true, True,
Or ellès sore I mun it rue!
Be ye steadfast and also true,
For I will not change for old [ne°] new.
And sith as° we may not togeder speak,
By writing, we shall our heartès break. [6]

**[Newton to Lady Brian:]**
**O ye my emp$^{er}$ice…**

O ye, my *em*press,
I, your servant, this to you I say:
My dearest queen, the which is Makèless,
My lady Most lovely, Methinks this'is no *nay*: [7]

My Masteress,
My Make, to me
Ye show great kindèness.
Ye are to me Meek and Mild, and More of cheer,
Ye are as bright of blee as blossom on brere.
Ye are sweeter than the flowers, to me Most-sweet,
Ye are the loveli'st in my heart: and More, to Meet.[8]

**[Newton to Lady Brian:]**
***Beaute of you burne in my body abydis…***

**B**eauty of you, burn in my body abidès.
**R**ight ruefully I sike, though I be far you fro'
**I**f ye be true, in truth, Love, it not slidès,
**A**nd I shall swear, the same, justly also.
**N**ought ye be wroth, though I say fain as I would do:[9]

My body I would betake into your gentleness,
With heart entire and spirit of meekèness.

---

[1] *bill* ] letter ("Go, little bill…" a conventional phrase, one of several employed by Newton).

[2] *sparhawk* ] a sparrow-hawk; *by her* ] by the sparhawk (i.e., he watched the hawk while I like a hawk watched the lady, my sparrow).

[3] *kirkes-door* ] church-door; *pitter-pater* ] chit-chat; with a pun on *pater noster*; *matins* ] morning prayers.

[4] *lest* ] least; *eyen kissed* ] kissed me with a glance of her eyes; *hailsed* ] saluted.

[5] *M* ] the lady's first name may have been *Margaret, Em, Madge* and *Meg* being common diminutives. Cf. next, where Humphrey riffs on the letter *M.*

[6] *mun it rue* ] must lament it; *break* ] disclose (perhaps also: it's heartbreaking that we must communicate only by writing).

[7] *Makeless* ] without equal, matchless.

[8] *blee* ] complexion, hue; *brere* ] briar.

[9] *Beauty of you* ] may modify either the speaker or her addressee; *burn* ] burning desire; and *berne* (warrior, man of valor, *OED* berne n.); possibly also Byrn, as a variant of Bryan; cf. "brid [*sic*] of paradise," fol. 95; *sike* ] sigh (*OED* sike n.2); *it not slidès* ] then love will not slip away; *Nought ye be wroth* ] Be not angry; *say fain* ] gladly say.

**[Lady Brian's Farewell:]**
***Farewell that was my lef so dere…***

Farewell, that was my lef so dear,
And fro' her that lovèd you so well.
Ye were my lef from year [to year°.]
(Wheder I were yours, I cannot tell.)
To you I have been true and lell,
At all timès, unto this day.
And now I say farewell, farewell,
I take my lef for ever and aye. 1

Your lof, forsooth, ye have not lost.
If ye loved me, I loved you, ywis,
But that I put you to great cost –
Therefóre I have you clipt and kissed.
But now, my love, I must needs cesse
And take me to him that me has ta'en.
Therefore, take ye another where ye list
I give you good lef, certáine. 2

Give ye me license to do the same:
This token, truly, I you betake,
Of my name in remembráunce °
Send me a token for my sake.
Wheder it be sent early or late,
I shall it keep for old 'quaintáunce.
And now, to Christ, I you be-take,
To save and keep, in whert and sans. 3

**[Newton's farewell:]**
***Alas a thousand sith alas…*** 4

Alas, a thousand sighs, alas,
For one that is of blee so bright,
That all my heart for euer she has,
To have and hold, as I her het. 5
Alas, I may not with her speak
That is so fair and fresh of face!
Alas, how should my heart be light?
Alas, a thousand sighs, alas!

But farewell, my rightwis joy and bliss—
Farewell, my worship and my weal—
Farewell, my mirth withouten miss—
Farewell, comfort of home and hele—
But farewell, truest, and most lell—
Farewell, as sweet as rose on hill—
Farewell, as oft as tongue can tell:
I take my leave again' my will. 6
[……………………………..] 7

Now farewell, the Sundays that [blessèd°] be–
Farewell the Wednesdays that roll so fast–
Farewell the stars upon the sky,
That night I sleep and take good rest—
Farewell, the arms that were so fair—
Farewell the hond-in-hond, I ween—
To *die* for her sake, me had liefér
Than fro' her euer that I would twain! 8

But farewell, queen that I love best
And violet that she worest on—
How that I fare, well mot she rest
And give her grace me to think on—
Farewell, the kirk that she in-kneeled,°
And the pillar made of stone–
There oft on me has she smiled.
But tales have forced me out of town. 9

But now farewell, looking and laughing both—
And farewell, shining° on each side—
To go fro' her then am I loath,
So the false tales I may not abide.
Farewell, farewell, a thousand sighs!
By this same true tokening
I tellèd you how long I would abide—
Ye said: "Alas, how shall I do so long?" 10

---

[1] *lef* ] love; life; *lell* ] loyal; *lef* ] 1. love; 2. leave; again in line 16.

[2] *ywis* ] surely; *clipt* ] embraced; *take … ta'en* ] she has evidently been pledged by her parents to another man; *where ye list* ] wherever you please; *good lef* ] good leave; good love.

[3] *This token* ] she with her love-poem has enclosed a lock of hair or some other remembrance, and requests one in return; *I you betake* ] I deliver to you; cf. line 23; *I you betake* ] I deliver you; *in whert and sans* ] in health and without (echoing the wedding liturgy, in sickness and in health).

[4] The MS is badly decayed; the editors are indebted to Rossill Robbins for her transcription, which entailed prolonged study of the text under ultraviolet light.

[5] *het* ] make or keep warm.

[6] *weal* ] prosperity; *hele* ] health; *lell* ] loyal.

[7] lines 17-32 of damaged MS are here omitted.

[8] *ween* ] believe, think; *liefer* ] prefer; *twain* ] separate.

[9] *violet* ] clothing of violet, the color of royalty; *How .. rest* ] However I fare, well may she remain; *kirk* ] church (where Humphrey and Brian had met on Sundays and Wednesdays).

[10] *how long* ] i.e., "for ever more".

# The Welsh Tradition

*Nerth gwraig yn ei thafod.*
–Welsh proverb (the strength of a woman is in her tongue)

ELSH women of the medieval period who composed verse remain largely unknown to modern scholarship. Allusions in the historical record, and circumstantial evidence, indicate that Celtic women throughout the centuries composed poems and songs and verse-narratives alongside the male bards, sometimes in competition with them; but they did so long before there was any perceived motivation to fossilize that oral tradition with a written record. And even when parchment and ink became plentiful, the male clerics and scribes who recorded Welsh verse privileged the work of professional bards, not folk-verses or women's songs. Ceridwen Lloyd-Morgan reports that of more than four thousand poets listed in the *Mynegai i farddoniaeth gaeth y llaqysgrifau,* covering extant manuscripts from the medieval period through the nineteenth century, fewer than seventy names are indisputably female, and many of those are figures from legend (such as Heledd), whose first-person narratives may have been sung or recited by women though composed by male bards. Moreover, of those few women-poets known by name from the earlier periods, almost nothing is known, and little has survived. Only six of the known woman poets before 1800 traced by Lloyd-Morgan have more than three poems preserved in the extant manuscript record.[1]

### Gwenllian ferch Rhirid Flaidd (fl. 1180-1200)

Gwenllian, the earliest woman poet known by name in the Welsh tradition, was the daughter of the male bard, Rhirid Flaidd, who was active c. 1160. Nothing else is known of her life and work. Because she was a contemporary of male poets whose work is preserved in the Red Book of Hergest, it is pleasant to think that we may have Gwenllian to thank for the Canu Heledd (q.v.). But in fact only one manuscript attribution to Gwenllian survives, which is for a four-line stanza written in reply to an insult.

Celtic poets often composed flyting verses in competition with one another, or to belittle their adversaries. When an otherwise unknown poet named Gruffudd ap Dafydd ap Gronw dismissed Gwenllian with a put-down, she is reported to have answered in kind:

**I'w Gwenllïan**

gan Gruffudd ap Dafydd ap Gronw

*Gwenllian druan, drwn ysgrafell – bren,*
*A wyr brynu bara gradell;*
*Doeth I Fon a'I hun fantell*
*Rhag newyn o Benllyn bell.*

**To Gwenllian**

trans. DWF

Nosed like a curry-comb – of wood – poor Gwenllian,
From her hunger in distant Penllyn [2]
Comes shrewdly to Fon in her only wrap: [3]
Looking to beg a griddle-loaf, per'aps?

**Englyn i ateb**

gan Gwenllïan

*Nid e da bara'n y byd – o'r diwedd*
*Y deuai ferch Ririd*
*At y gwas bras o Brysaeddfed;*
*Adnebydd dywyd dafad.*

**Englyn in reply**

trans. DWF

Not to beg any of your kind of bread
Did Rhirid's daughter at last come to
That uncouth knave of Prysaeddfed:
She knows too well what swells a ewe.

Perhaps Gwenllian has come to Prysaeddfed looking for child support from Gruffyd because he has gotten her pregnant, and he is in no mood to pay. Or perhaps Gruffud implies that Gwenllian has come from Anglesy hungry for sex; and she retorts she'll have no part of him (least of all his "griddle-loaf"), nor any child of his. Or perhaps the two poets are married: one of two surviving manuscript copies, both

---

[1] Ceridwen Lloyd-Morgan (1993): 184-5.

[2] lines 2 and 4 are here reversed for the translator's convenience.

[3] *Fôn* ] Môn (Fôn after a preposition): old Welsh name for Anglesy.

from the sixteenth century, identifies Gruffyd as Gwenllian's husband. The text and attribution may not even be accurate, appearing in the manuscript record nearly four hundred years after Gwenllian's death. But a known body of work ascribed to Gwenllian was still in circulation in the latter fifteenth century, for Gwerful Mechain in her "Cywydd to Jealous Wives," quotes from Gwenllian, expecting the allusion to be recognized. Having long since been threaded into the tapestry of the Welsh tradition, Gwenllian's original verses can no longer be traced.

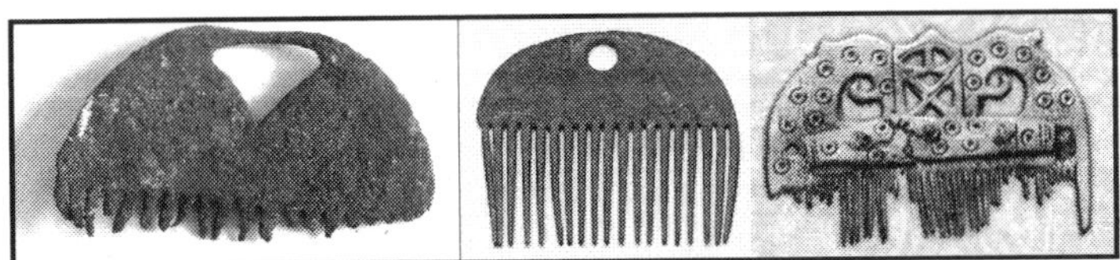

ancient Celtic curry-combs, of metal

**Gwerful Fychan** (c. 1430 - c. 1480)

Gwerful Fychan, daughter and heir of a nobleman, is identified under the Welsh patronymic system as Gwerful ferch Ieuan Fychan ap Ieuan ap Hywel y Gadair ap Gruffudd ap Madog ap Rhirid Flaidd. This Gwerful (in modern shorthand, Gwerful Fychan) was married to the better-known Tudur Penllyn, who wrote and performed at the time of the *Beirdd yr Uchelwyr*, the "poets of the nobility" who thrived during the late Middle Ages. Penllyn is a bardic name rather than a surname: a member of the minor gentry, Tudur is identified in the genealogies as Tudur ap Ieuan ap Iorwerth Foel. He worked for his day-job as a drover, trading the wool of his flocks in English markets; and by night, he wrote poems in praise of Welshmen who fought the English. (During the English Wars of the Roses, Tudur and Gwerful and are associated (through Tudur's known patrons) with support for the Lancastrian side.) Tudur and Gwerful lived in the parish of Llanuwchllyn at Caer-Gai, where the manor house they occupied (Gwerful's inheritance) still exists as a farm. Their son, Ieuan ap Tudur ap Ieuan, also became a poet.

Benefitting from the old double standard that deemed the work of male poets of more value than verse by women, much poetry by Tudur Penllyn was recorded for posterity while his wife's was forgotten. His extant work covers a range of themes, from eulogy to devotion to satire. In one well-known dialogue, Tudur represents himself trying out his crudest pickup lines on an English woman who understands his intent but not his Welsh obscenity (*gedor,* pussy) or his blasphemous identification of the Cross of Christ with her crossed legs. Tudur, in turn, is unsure whether or not his Celtic charm is having its desired effect on the English lady's virtue. The exchange is intended for the amusement of a bilingual Welsh audience:

**Mae'r Cymro a Saesnes**

gan Tudur Penllyn

"Dydd daed, Saesnes gyffes, gain
yr wyf i'th garu, riain."

"*What saist, mon*?" ebe honno,
*"For truthe, harde Welsmon, I tro*."

"Dyro wenferch loywserch lan,
amau gas, imi gusan."

"*Kyste dyfyl, what kansto doe*!
*Sir, let alons with sorowe*."

"Gad i'r llaw dan godi'r llen
dy glywed, ddyn deg lawen."

**The Welshman and the Englishwoman**

[English trans. DWF]

["Good day, fair English honey:
I'm in love—with your cunny."]

"*What sayest, man*?" [replies she now],
*For truth,* [*a*] *hardy Welshman, I trow*!"

["Come, sweet, fair lusty lassie,
Gimme kisses, don't be nasty."]

"*Kissed devil*! *what canst'ou do*?
*Sir, let* [*me*] *alone, with sorroow*." [1]

[I'll just slip a hand under your dress
For a fine feel, merry lady—yes?]

---

[1] *Kissed...do* ] perhaps also, "Kiss th' devil, [is] what you can do!"; *kansto* ] canst thou; *with sorrow* ] seriously; without this foolery.

"*I am nit Wels, thow Welsmon.*
*For byde the, lete me alone.*"

"*I am not Welsh, thou Welshman*!
*Forbid thee, let me alone*!"

"Na fydd chwimwth i'm gwthiaw,
cai arian llydan o'm llaw."

["What? *No*? Don't be rash!—
I have in hand a lot of cash."]

"*I holde thi mad byrladi.*
*Forth, I wyl do non for thi.*"

"*I hold thee mad, by'r Lady*!
*Forth*! *I will do none for thee*!"

"Pes meddwn, mi a roddwn rod,
myn dyn, er myned ynod."

["I'd give you quite a big load,
To get inside you, by god!"]

"*Tis harm to be thy parmwr,*
*Howld, hain, I shalbe kalde hwr.*"

"'*Tis harm to be thy paramour–*
*Hold! hang! I shall be called whore.*"

"Gad ym Saesnes gyffes, gu,
fondew fun, fynd i fyny!"

["Lead on, then, my fair English hoe!
Thick, stiff staff, up we go!"]

"*Owt, owt, bisherewe thy twtile*
*Sir, how? 'ware my sore hile.*"

"*Out, out! beshrew thy twattile,*
*Sir, how? 'ware my sore heel*!" [1]

"Na fydd ddig, Seisnig Saesnes,
yn wâr gad ddyfod yn nes."

["English Englishwoman, don't be cross:
Be gentle: let me come more close."]

"*By the rode I'll make the blodei.*
*anon I wyle plucke oute thyn ei.*"

"*By the Rood, I'll make thee bloody.*
*Anon, I will pluck out thine e'e.*" [2]

"Gad ym fyned I'th gedor,
Hyd y groes onid oes dor?"

["O let me come into thy puss'!
Have ye no opening to the Cross?"]

*"Thowe shalt not pas, be Saynt Asaf,*
*For thy lyf I have a knife, knave."*

*"Thou shalt not pass, by Saint Asaf,*
*For thy life. I have a knife, knave."*

"Io ddyn, ai caniadu'dd wyd
I Dudur ai nad ydwyd?"

["Yo, girl, was that a No?
—Or shall your Tudur have a go?"]

No verse certainly by Tudur's wife, Gwerful Fychan, has survived. It has been suggested that a cywydd in praise of a fine grey stallion may be hers ("Cywydd y March Glas"); another in which the poet seeks hay for an old horse. Certain of the englynion more commonly ascribed to Gwerful Mechain (her contemporary) find a competing attribution in the manuscript record to Gwerful Fychan. The two englynion here called "Snow" are given in sixteenth-century manuscripts both to both Gwerfuls. Recent Welsh scholarship has tipped in favor of Gwerful Fychan as the likeliest author:

**[*Y Eira*]**

gan Gwerful Fychan

*Gwynflawd°, daeargnawd – du oergnu y' mynydd*
*Manod wybren oerddu,*
*Eira'n blât, oer iawn ei blu,*
*Mwthlan a roed i'm methlu.*

*Eira gwyn ar fryn oer fry–a'm dallodd*
*A'm dillad yn gwlychu.*
*O Duw gŵyn, nid oedd geny'*
*Obaith y down byth i dy.*

**Snow**

trans. DWF

White flour on earth flesh, dark peak in cool fleece,
Flurry from a cold-black sky,
Coòl feathers, plate of snow,
A softness, sent to allure.

Above, snow white on high hill blinded me,
All my clothes are dripping wet.
Blizzèd God, I had no hope
E'er to make it home again. [3]

---

[1] *beshrew thy twattile* ] damn your twattle! (poppycock); *'ware my sore heel* ] beware my painful boot-heel

[2] *Rood* ] cross of Christ; *e'e* ] eyes.

[3] *blizzèd God* ] 1. blessed God; 2. blizzard god ("gwyn" denotes *blessed, pure,* and *white*).

## **Gwerful Mechain** (c. 1462 - c. 1505)

*Mor felys rhag marfolaeth* [*To Love is Sweeter than to Kill*]
—to Ieuan Dyfi (l. 26)

WERFUL MECHAIN is the only the female poet of medieval Wales with a substantial body of work to have survived. This may be so, in part, because the male scribes who controlled the transmission of Welsh poetry were amused by Gwerful's saucy and frank celebration of sexual intercourse; but it is also because Gwerful was respectful of the complex Welsh poetic meters. As noted by Katie Gramich, Gwerful does not represent a separate female tradition or feminine subculture but "belongs centrally to the Welsh bardic tradition"; she "engages in poetic dialogues with her male contemporaries, using similar forms, meter, tropes, and vocabulary."[1] Like Shakespeare's Beatrice a century later, but in real life, Gwerful Mechain transgressed conventional restrictions on feminine speech: in her verbal fencing with Dafydd Llwyd and Ieuan Dyfi, she gave as good as she got. One suspects that Gwerful could have held her own in any Cnapan locker room in fifteenth-century Powys.

"Mechain" is not a patronym, but a place: Gwerful was the daughter of a nobleman, Hywel Fychan ap Hywel, of Mechain, in Montgomeryshire (northern Powys). Her mother was named Gwenhwyfar. She had three brothers, Dafydd, Madog and Thomas; and a sister, Mawd. Gwerful is closely associated with Dafydd Llwyd of Mathafarn, who may have been her bardic master; he is also identified, in his verse and hers, as Gwerful's lover, either before or during her marriage John ap Llywelyn Fychan ap Llywelyn ap Deio (by whom Gwerful had a daughter, Mawd, evidently named after her sister).

The manuscript record ascribes a total of 38 poems to Gwerful Mechain, not all of which have been accepted by Welsh scholars, but this is partly to her credit. Gwerful was so highly esteemed in the two centuries after her death that some scribes attributed to her poems that were written by the great Dafydd ap Gwillym. Sadly, most scholars outside Wales have diverted their blushing gaze from Gwerful as if she were a whore scrawling obscenities on a latrine wall. Where Gwerful has been noted at all in scholarship, it is typically no more than a passing mention in which she is identified as a writer of "salacious verse." Leslie Harries edited some of Gwerful's poems as early as 1933 for his MA thesis, together with the work of male bards. But when Harries published his thesis, he dropped Gwerful, not wishing to be tainted by her feminine lubricity. That has everywhere been the story of Gwerful's legacy. As of this writing, Gwerful continues to be excluded from the Oxford Dictionary of National Biography, unlike her male contemporaries Tudur Aled, Dafydd ab Edmwnd Llywelyn Glyn Cothi, Gruffudd ab Ieuan, Dafydd Llwyd of Mathafarn, and Siôn Tudur (and others).

Happily, Gwerful's extant verses have recently been gathered and edited by Dafydd Johnston and (more completely) by Nerys Ann Howells.[2] The English translations published here for the first time are indebted to the Welsh texts of Johnston and Howells. Gwerful is represented in *Women's Works* by eight single *englynion*; a dialogue in five *englynion*; plus three *cywydd*. (The particular form of *englyn* preferred by Gwerful consists of four lines with a syllabic count of 10/6/7/7, linked by rhyme and the obligatory *cynghanedd* – internal rhyme and consonantal correspondence.)

Gwerful's most notorious poem, her "Cywydd y Cedor" (*Cywydd of the Bush*) is a poem in praise of her own "gont," a poem that answers or provokes Dafydd ap Gwillym's "Cywydd y gal" (*Cywydd of the Penis*). Gwerful lampoons the newly fashionable Petrarchan tradition of hyper-praising every female body part except the unmentionable one that the woebegone male lover has had in the back of his mind although not on the tip of his tongue. Gwerful's position: if the bards of Wales cannot supply some greater pleasure than to speak of star-like eyes and coral lips and pearl teeth, they need not apply.

---

[1] Katie Gramich and Catherine Brennan, *Welsh Women's Poetry, 1460-2001* (2003), xvii.

[2] Johnston, ed., *Canu Maswedd Yr Oesedd Canol* (1991); Howells, ed. *Gwaith Gwerful Mechain ac Eraill* (2001). The English translations published here for the first time emulate but do not strictly duplicate the internal rhyme and syllabic structure of Gwerful's originals; for which readers are referred to the Welsh texts of Johnston and Howells.

Gwerful's "Cywydd i Wragedd Eiddigeddus" (To Jealous Wives) makes a mockery of bourgeois commitments to monogamy while at the same time lampooning a double standard: literature throughout the medieval and early modern periods exhibits an obsessive masculine anxiety about cuckoldry, while affirming the husband's right to play around. Gwerful's narrator challenges virtuous housewives to let hubby chase a skirt when he so wishes – in fact, let it be her own skirt that he chases (because she's not a fast runner, when the moon is full and the man is well-hung).

The "Ymddiddan Rhwng Dau Fardd," or Conversation between Two Poets (Dafydd Llwyd and Gwerful Mechain) is a seduction poem on the model of Tudur Penllyn's "The Welshman and the Englishwoman"; but Gwerful's verse points toward a happier climax than between Tudur's repressed Englishwoman and his randy Welshman. It's possible that the "Conversation" was written entirely by Gwerful, or as a collaboration with Dafydd. (Not infrequently, dialogues of this sort began as an impromptu contest of wit between poets, composed on the spot, much as improvisational comics might do in our own culture, at a comedy club.)

Gwerful's "Cywydd in reply to Ieuan Dyfi for his cywydd to Anni Goch" invites a fuller introduction than these others. Until recently, not much was known about Ieuan Dyfi except that he composed five poems addressed to a certain "Anni Goch"; in one of which he cites Anni as a supreme example of the plain fact that women throughout history have been fickle and perfidious.

Llinos Beverley Smith reports the back story, drawing on historical research that ought to have won her a Pulitzer Prize: in 1501/2, two accused sinners were summoned to the Leominster Consistory Court, to answer allegations of adultery. The accused: Ieuan Dyfi, poet; and Anni Goch of Norton, the wife of John Lippard. Anni pleaded not guilty. She was given a few days to gather her "compurgators" – fellow Christians who would testify under oath, on pain of excommunication, that the accused was indeed innocent. Ieuan, however, freely confessed to having had sex with Anni Goch. His line of defense (Adultery is what Welsh poets *do*) cut no mustard with the Church magistrates. For his penance, and as an example to others, Ieuan Dyfi was sentenced to be whipped eight times around Presteigne Church.

Dyfi's unlooked-for confession put Anni Goch in a bind: she now stood at risk of punishment not only for adultery, but for perjury. In her second appearance in church court, Anni therefore brought four compurgators who swore that the sex with Ieuan Dyfi was non-consensual: Anni, they alleged, had been raped. The accused thereby escaped a whipping at the cost of Ieuan Dyfi's reputation. (Among the bards, rape was a crime committed by cowards, losers, and Englishmen; whereas adultery was a prime virtue, a strain of Welsh heroism, by both sexes, as old as the language itself.)

Ieuan, having confessed to good sex but not to sexual assault, responded with a cywydd fiercely denouncing womankind, and condemning dark-haired, dark-eyed Anni Goch in particular as a second Eve. Gwerful Mechain, outspoken champion of women's sexual freedom (and possibly a friend of Anni Goch), objected to Dyfi's generalized misogyny: in her "Cywydd in reply to Dyfi for his cywydd to Anni Goch," Gwerful praises women not just as the fair sex but as the smarter one; while mocking Ieuan Dyfi as a petulant buffoon.

In 1517 Anni Goch and John Lippard were back in Church Court. (Gwerful Mechain was now long dead, or at least retired; Anni Goch was still going strong.) Someone – possibly the father of the bride – accused Lippard of bigamy, alleging that he had contracted marriage to a local woman without ever having divorced his first wife, Anni Goch. Lippard, appearing before the church court, confessed to the betrothal, but he denied bigamy, on grounds that he disavowed his marriage to Anni Goch long ago, after she plotted to kill him.

Anni, answering a subpoena, confirmed that her cohabitation with John Lippard had lasted only six months, back in 1500/1. She now acknowledged having committed adultery with Ieuan Dyfi and two other randy fellows; whereupon her husband Lippard, she alleged, had *sold* her to Ieuan Dyfi. The poet was no longer available for comment.

Weighing the various testimonies, the church court judged Anni Goch's account the most credible: John Lippard for his penance was therefore obliged to be whipped around the churches of Presteigne, Norton, and Byton; a marathon hazing designed to show other Welshmen the Lord's displeasure with such husbands as John Lippard. Moreover, Lippard was commanded on pain of excommunication to restore full conjugal rights to his spurned wife, Anni Goch, within three days (Smith, 1993).

The "Cywydd in reply to Dyfi" is Gwerful's last known poem. She is presumed to have died not long after.

DWF

**Wyth Englynion**
gan Gwerful

[1. ***Llanc ym min y llwyn***]
*Rhown fil o ferched, rhown fwyn lances*
*Lle ceisiais i orllwyn,*
*Rhown gŵyn, mawr, rhown gan morwyn*
*Am un llanc ym min y llwyn.* 1

[2.] ***Y Gwahaniaeth***
*Dau beth odiaeth didol - siom gariad*
*(sy'n gyrru'n gynhwynoll):*
*Gwen ireiddwen gain raddol*
*sy ffrind a minnau sy ffôl.* 2

[3. ***Dyferu Wlyb***]
Fy mhais a wlychais yn wlych – a'm crys
A'm cwrsi sidangrych;
Odid Gŵyl Ddeinioel foelfrych 3
Na hin Sain Silin yn sych 4

[4. ***I'w Thad***]
*Gweles eich lodes lwydwen, eiddilaidd°,*
*Hi ddylai gael amgen:*
*Hi yn ei gwres, gynheswen,*
*Chwithau 'nhad aethoch yn hen.*

[5.] ***I'w Gwr am ei Churo***
*Dager drwy goler dy galon–ar osgo* 5
*I asgwrn dy ddwyfron,*
*Dy lin a dyr, dy law'n don,*
*A'th gleddau i'th goluddion.*

[6. ***Pwyllwch***]
*Dyn tanboeth annoeth ni bydd ynad – byth*
*tra fo bath ar ddillad*
*dyn distaw. A Duw yn dystiad,*
*ymaros a gaiff mawrhad.*

[7. ***Dianc y Bardd***]
*Ni wn o'r byd hwn I b'le tynna I ffwrdd,*
*na pha ffordd a gerdda;*
*Na pha wlad rad a rodia,*
*Na pha le rhag angau'r a.*

[8. ***Swydd Wag***]
*Och! lety, gwely gwaeledd, anniddan*
*Anheddle i orwedd –*
*Cloëdig, unig annedd,*
*Cas gan bwb yw cwsg y bedd.*

**Eight Englynion**
trans. DWF

**Boy in the Bush**
I'd give a thousand gals, a tender bride,
Most maids, beatitude besides,
Where I for ambush lie in wait,
For'a single lad by the bush-hedge. 1

**The Difference**
One sad ex, two exquisite love-extremes
(A man's instinctual drive, it seems):
Gwen, blest, so fresh and beautiful.
So one's the friend, and one, the gull. 2

**Dripping Wet**
My smock is wet and manky. My shirt is
Soaked. Crumpled, my silk hanky.
Hardly by Deiniol's Day will I – 3
Nor e'en by Saint Sulien's – be dry. 4

**To Dad (on his young girlfriend)**
Cute: I now have seen your grey-white match.
She'll find herself a substitute:
She has fire. You have – just desire.
You, Dad, can only act your age.

**To her Husband for Striking Her**
Through your heart's rough choler may a dagger 5
Plunge to the bone of your breast,
Your knee snap, your hand rot off,
Your own guts ensheath your blade.

**Keep Calm**
A fiery fool can never be a judge,
Even when he drapes himself
In silence. God be witness:
Patience is what wins respect.

**The Artful Dodger**
I don't know where on earth to hide my head,
Nor which pathway I might wend,
Nor what blessèd ground to tread,
Or where to go, to dodge the end—

**Vacancy**
Ugh! poor accommodations, lousy bed,
What a place to settle in –
Locked room, solitary, deep.
A common nuisance: cemetery sleep.

---

[1] *min y llyn:bush-hedge* ] *lit.*, edge (or lip) of the bush (or grove).

[2] *a...ffol* ] *literally*, and I, so foolish.

[3] *Ddeinioel:Deiniol* ] (d. 584), bishop of Bangor in the kingdom of Gwynedd; his feast day is Sept. 11.

[4] *Silin:Sulien* ] probably Sulinus or Sulien, the Breton saint of Cornouaille and Domnonée, whose feast day is 1 Oct.; but possibly St. Sulien/Sulian/Silin (29 July).

[5] *goler:choler* ] 1. heart's *collar* (rib); 2. *choler*, heart's anger.

**Cywydd y Cedor** [1]

gan Gwerful Mechain

Pob rhyw brydydd, dydd dioed,
Mul rwysg,° wladaidd rwysg erioed,
Noethi moliant, nis gwrantwyf,
Anfeidrol reiol, yr wyf,
Am gerdd merched y gwledydd
A wnaethant heb ffyniant ffydd
Yn anghwbl iawn, ddawn ddiwad,
Ar hyd y dydd, rho° Duw Dad.

Moli gwallt, cwnsallt ceinserch,
A phob cyfryw fyw o ferch,
Ac obry° moli heb wg
Yr aeliau uwchlaw° yr olwg;
Moli hefyd, hyfryd tew°
Foelder dwyfron feddaldew°
A breichiau° gwen, len loywlun,
Dylai barch, a dwylaw bun.

Yno, o'i brif ddewiniaeth
Cyn y nos canu a wnaeth,
Duw er ei radd a'i addef,
Diffrwyth wawd o'i dafawd ef:
Gadu'r canol heb foliant
A'r plas lle'r enillir plant,
A'r cedor clyd, hyder° claer,
Tynerdew°, cylch twn eurdaer,
Lle carwn i, cywrain iach,
Y cedor dan y cadach!

Corff wyd diball ei allu,
Cwrt difreg o'r bloneg blu.
Llyma 'ynghred, gwlad° y cedawr,
Cylch gweflau ymylau mawr,
Pant yw hwy na llwy na llaw,
Clawdd i ddal cal ddwy ddwylaw;
Cont yno wrth din fin ffloch,
Dabl y gerdd â'i dwbl o goch!°

Ac nid arbed, freisged frig,
Y gloywsaint, gwyr eglwysig
Mewn cyfle iawn, ddawn ddifreg,
Myn Beuno, ei deimlo'n deg. [2]
Am hyn o chwaen, gaen gerydd°,
Y prydyddion sythion sydd, [3]
Gadewch yn hael, gafael ged°
Gerddau cedor i gerdded.

**Cywydd of the Bush** [1]

trans. DWF

Every day, the poets, drunken fools,
Under mulish influence vainly mewl
Their naked verse (which I do only mock,
Being of gentle 'quaintance, ancient stock),
Their verse for pretty girls in every land.
Such barren praise I do not understand:
Daddy Dieu! Why write in verse, and if
He fails to praise her choicest part, and gift?

He commends a woman's hair, her "gown of love,"
And compliments the girlish bits above:
He praises merrily, without a frown,
Her brows, her eyes, her smile, and further down,
He duly notes those tender shapes, and chubby,
The smoothness of each soft, each snow-white bubbie.
Upon her beauteous, draping arms, he lingers–
Then pays respects unto her hands, and fingers.

Thus with his finest wizardry, and pen,
By night he sings his eulogies, and then
Pays homage, both to God and to his Muse
In barren eulogies of self-abuse,
But leaves unpraised the woman's blessèd twat,
The middle, where the babies are begot!
Hot and plump, bright-fervent broken ring,
A tight-thick spot for love, so quaint a thing–
Lustrous, warm, and firm, it has no match:
Beneath the damsel's skirt, the blessèd snatch!

Tireless power, feathered o'er with hair,
Thou keep'st a slick and ticklish court, in there.
The cunt's a country fair between the hips,
A circle edged about with plumpy lips,
A crevice, just a hand or teaspoon long,
But fit to sheath a manly two-span shlong:
O blessèd chink beneath the bouncing bum,
O double-pink, to music must thou come!

All the churchmen, all the saints a-glow,
Whene'er it chances them this bliss to know,
They never fail the blessèd gift to steal,
To cop (by Saint Beu*no*) a *bue*no feel. [2]
I charge, therefore, a public referendum
Let every proud and rigid male bard [3]
Raise hymns up to th' pubic – her pudendum! –
Or fail to get his coin, or coint, reward.

---

[1] cf. Roteland, *Ipomedon* (12th C Anglo-Norman romance composed 60 mi. south of Mechain): "Quant si beaus out les membres tuz, / K'en dites vus de cel desuz, / Ke nus apelum le cunet?" / "Je quit qe asez fut petitet" (2267-70).

[2] *Beuno* ] St. Beuno (d. 660?), abbot of Clynnog, said to have been born in Gwerful's home country of Powis-land; *bueno feel* ] ("*deimlo'n deg*") lit., a good feel.

[3] *sythion:proud and rigid* ] *sythion* = 1. proud; 2. stiff.

Sawden awdl, sidan ydiw, 1
Sêm fach, len ar gont wen wiw,
Lleiniau mewn man ymannerch,
Y llwyn sur, llawn yw o serch,
Fforest falch iawn, ddawn ddifreg,
Ffris ffraill, ffwrwr dwygaill deg,
Trwsglwyn merch°, drud annerch dro,
Berth addwyn! Duw'n borth iddo. 2

**Cywydd i Wragedd Eiddigeddus**
gan Gwerful Mechain

Bath ryw fodd, beth rhyfedda',
I ddyn, ni ennill fawr dda
(Rhyfedda' dim, rhyw fodd dig,
Annawn wyd yn enwedig),
Bod gwragedd, rhyw agwedd rhus,
Rhwydd wg, yn rhy eiddigus!
Pa ryw natur, lafur lun,
Pur addysg, a'i pair uddun?
Meddai i mi Wenllian
(Bu anllad gynt benllwyd gân!)
"Nid cariad" (anllad curiaw)
"Yr awr a dry ar aur draw";
Cariad gwragedd bonheddig
Ar galiau da (argoel dig). 3

Pe'm credid (edlid adlais):
Pob serchog caliog a'm cais —
Ni rydd un wraig rinweddawl,
Fursen, ei phiden a'i phawl.
O dilid gont ar dalwrn,
Nid âi un fodfedd o'i dwrn!
Nac yn rhad, nis caniadai,
Nac yn serth, er gwerth a gâi;
Yn ordain anniweirdeb
Ni wnâi ymwared â neb.

Tost yw na bydd, celfydd cain,
Rhyw g'wilydd ar y rhain
Bod yn fwy y biden fawr
No'i dynion, yn oed unawr,
Ac wyth o'i thylwyth, a'i thad,
A'i thrysor hardd a'i thrwsiad,
A'i mam, nid wyf yn amau,
A'i brodyr, glod eglur glau,
A'i chefndyr (ffyrt frodyr ffydd),
A'i cheraint a'i chwiorydd.
Byd caled yw bod celyn
Yn llwyr yn dwyn synnwyr dyn.

[1] *Sawden awdl, sidan ydiw:Rubáiyát* ] *literally*, A sultan's ode, silky-smooth

*Rubáiyát*: all is silky-smooth for him, 1
A curtained little seam, a fine, bright, quim,
A warm and cozy place to come, to meet,
A tart-wet shrub, and home to something great
There, all in one, a most tall tree (*l'amour*!),
A fine and furry rim for a sack of cods:
I salute a girl's thick glade, ring we adore:
O, glorious bush! – portal unto god. 2

**Cywydd to Jealous Wives**
trans. DWF

Amazing! what a way to fuss!
As if it were of any use
(It's marvelous, ridiculous,
A singular offense, obtuse)
That married gals – dour, oppressive,
So soon to frown – are so *possessive*!
In nature, what disturbing thought
Causes wives thus to be taught?
For as Gwenllian says (Now *there's*
A hoary lay from days of yore!)
"It is not *Love*" (lewd *throbbings-for*)
"Makes golden hours," I'm afraid:
The love of women (woeful omen)
Is merely to get laid. 3

I ought to know (*Jealous shrieks*):
Every well-hung amorous geek is
After me, yet no "good" prude will half
The comfort of her rod and staff.,
Lo, it stands inclined to chase the hare?
Fast she holds it in her grip!
"No sharing!" She won't let it slip –
Not for a cheapie, not for gold,
She'll cut no deal with any one:
"Unchastity" she'll not condone.

What a life! "Fine virtue"? Tush!
Should such a frau not rather *blush*?
One fat prick means more to her
Than her own family ever were,
Plus her daddy, plus eight kin,
Her pretty goods, her make-up bin,
Plus her (no doubt) saintly mother,
Plus her good (legitimate) brothers,
Cousins (kin of virtue stiff),
Her sisters, and her relatives.
'Tis pity that her husband's tool
Should make the wife a senseless fool.

[2] *Duw'n borth iddo:portal unto God* ] *literally,* God help it! – punning on "porth," *portal, gateway.*

[3] *galiau da:to get laid* : *literally,*[his] good cock.

Peth anniddan fydd anair:
Pwnc o genfigen a'i pair.
Y mae i'm gwlad ryw adwyth
Ac eiddigedd, lawnedd lwyth,
Ymhob marchnad, trefniad drwg,
Tros ei chal, trais a chilwg.
Er rhoi o wartheg y rhên,
Drichwech, a'r aradr ychen,
A rhoi (er maint fai y rhaid!)
(Rhull ddyfyn) yr holl ddefaid,
Gwell fydd gan riain feinir,
(Meddai rai) roi'r tai a'r tir,
A chynt ddull, rhoi ei chont dda,
(Ochelyd!) no rhoi'i chala;
Rhoi'i phadell o'i chell a'i chost
A'i thrybedd na'i noeth rybost; 1
Gwaisg ei ffull, rhoi gwisg ei phen 2
A'i bydoedd na rhoi'r biden!

Ni chenais fy nychanon,
Gwir Dduw, hynt ddim o'r gerdd hon,
I neb, o ffurfeidd-deb y ffydd, 3
A fyn gal fwy no'i gilydd.

Calumny's an evil force:
Sexual jealousy is its source.
Lovers of my country quest
For respite from the heaviest
Of plagues at markets all: the shock
That wifey broods to kill for cock.
She'll give the ox that pulls the plough,
She'll give away the eighteen cows,
And (no matter if he needed those!)
(Bad call) her lord's entire flock.
And though she's shapely, she will yield
(Some say) the buildings, grove and fields,
And sooner give her very twat
(Careful now!) than lose her cock;
Pans and pots, and fancy duds,
Her best dildo (a naked stud!), 1
All yours, and quick, plus hat and furs, 2
So long as hubby's cock is hers!

God's truth: this mock I do not sing
(No not one part, in anything)
So as to please the Virgin Mother— 3
But for a bigger, and another!

**Ymddiddan Rhwng Dau Fardd**

gan Gwerful Mechain a Dafydd Llwyd

*Dafydd*:
"Dywed ym, meinir, meinion, yw d'aeliau,
Mae d'olwg yn dirion;
Oes un llestr gan estron,
A gwain hir y gannai hon?"

*Gwerful*:
"Braisg yw dy gastr, bras gadarn, dyfiad
Fal tafod cloch Badarn; 4
Brisne cont, bras yn y carn,
Brasach yw na membr isarn.

Hwde bydew blew, hyd baudblin, Ddafydd,
I ddofi dy biden;
Hwde gadair i'th eirin,
Hwde, odoi hyd y din.

Haf atad, gariad geirwir, y macwy,
Dirmycer ni welir.
Dof yn d'ol oni'm delir
Y gwas dewr hael a'r gastr hir.

Gorau, naw gorau, nag arion – gwynio*n*
Gynio bun gyrru'n ireiddlan;
Gorau'n fyw gyrru'n fuan
A'r taro – cyn twitsio'r tân."

**Conversation between Two Poets**

trans. DWF

*David*:
"Say, lovely lass of slender brows,
Tender are your looks, [and hot].
Hath stranger room within her twat,
Sheath deep enough for what I've got?"

*Gwerful*:
"Indeed, your caster's stout, a dong
That's built like tongue of Padarn's bell, 4
Piercing pussy to the hilt,
A member (hammer-handle) strong!

I've here a fuzzy hole, Davitt, 'twill
Tire your busy pole: come have it!
A booty fit to cradle plums—
So thrust me up unto the bum!

My summer's true-love, have a go!
What isn't seen, they shouldn't knock.
If free, I shall return for moe,
My bold boy, for your great big cock.

More, nine times more, than pounds of sterling
Is't to pound a lovely darling!
Life's best good: a lusty one
In thrusting, ere he fires the gun."

---

[1] *noet rybost:naked stud* ] *lit.*, fine bare post.

[2] *gwisg ei phe:hat and furs* ] *lit.*, headdress.

[3] *Virgin Mother* ] *lit.*, beauty of the faith.

[4] *cloch Badarn:Padarn's bell* ] bell of St Padarn's Church, Llanbadarn Fawr (near modern Aberystwyth).

**Cywydd i ateb Ieuan Dyfi**
**am ei Gywydd i Anni Goch**

gan Gwerful Mechain

GWAE'R UNDYN heb gywreindeb!
Gwae'r un wen a garo neb!
Ni cheir gan hon ei charu
Un dda, er ei bod yn ddu.
Lliw yr un nid gwell o rod
Y nos pan elo'n isod.
Gwen fonheddig a ddigia,
Naws dydd, oni bydd was da
Nid felly y gwna'r ddu ddoeth: [1]
Ei drinio a wna drannoeth.

O dyfod Ieuan Dyfi!
Rhai drwg yn amlwg i ni:
Rhai o'r gwynion fydd gwenwyn
A rhai da a urdda dyn!

Merch a helethe Eneas [2]
Ddu rudd, ac oedd dda o ras.
Gwenddolen a ddialodd [3]
Ei bai am na wnaid ei bodd!
Gwraig Ddynfnwal yn gofalu
A wnâi les rhwng y ddau lu. [4]
Marsia ffel, gwraig Guhelyn, [5]
A ddaeth â'r gyfraith dda ynn.
A gwraig Werydd, ddedwydd dda, [6]
Heddychodd, hyn oedd iacha',
Rhwng dau lu, mawr allu maeth:
Mor felys rhag marfolaeth.
Mam Suddas oedd ddirawsr;
Cywir a gwych carai'i gwr.
A gwraig Beiled, pei credid,
Y gwir ddywad i gyd.
Elen merch Goel a welynt, [7]
Gwraig Gonstans, a gafas gynt
Y Groes lle y lladdwyd Iesu,
A'r gras, ac nis llas mo'i llu.

**Cywydd in reply to Ieuan Dyfi**
**for his cywydd to Anni Goch**

trans. DWF

WOE TO THE MAN without discretion!
Woe to maids with no affection!
If she be good, must maiden lack
Good lovin' just because she's "black"?
Complexion is not worth a jot
In darkness, when a woman's hot.
A rich and snow-white girl's unnerved,
(By day, a bitch) unless well-served.
The black one, wiser, brings no sorrow: [1]
She treats you right again tomorrow.

O [my god,], here's Evan Dyfi!
The root of evil isn't iffy:
The moaning that from *you* we've had
Poisons good men with the bad!

The girl who gave Aeneas grace [2]
A blueblood was, and black her face.
("Fair Gwendolena," when forsook, [3]
Against her rival *vengeance* took!)
The wife of Dyfnwal did the most
To end the strife of warring hosts. [4]
Cuhelyn's Marcia, widowed queen, [5]
Made the best laws ever seen.
Gwerydd's wife, being blest [6]
Between two foes brought healing peace.
She taught two forces woman's will:
To love is sweeter than to kill.
Judas was an evil louse;
His Mum, a correct and caring spouse.
The wife of Pilate uttered sooth
Unto his question, "What is 'truth'?"
Elen, child of old King Coel, [7]
Wife of Constans, got her goal:
The Cross upon which died our Lord,
Plus grace, and hosts that her adore.

---

[1] In the British Isles until the mid-17th century "black" [person] typically denoted anyone with black hair or dark complexion. But with respect to Africa: according to the racial mythology of the age, the northern races were said to be fair (white, beautiful) but unintelligent; while Africans were said to be wise. The ideology of white superiority developed in the 17th C., from a need to justify enslavement of Africans. As recently as 1607, (George Wilkins, *Three Miseries of Barbary*), the emperor is said to love his white wife for her (European) great beauty and his black wife for her great wisdom.

[2] *The girl* ] Dido, queen of Carthage in north Africa; Aeneas left her heartbroken (Virgil's *Aeneid*).

[3] *Gwendolena* ] King Locrine forsook Gwendolen ("White One") for Estrildis. She in revenge had Estrildis and her daughter Sabrina drowned in the River Severn.

[4] *Dyfnwal* ] Moelmud, grandson of Coel Odebog (5th C.), later mythologized as the founder of British law.

[5] *Marcia* ] Marcia Proba, 3d C. Celtic warrior-queen and law-giver. The Marcian Statutes are said to have been fair to all, giving equal status to women.

[6] *Gwerydd's wife* ] Gverissa (1st C.), wife of Gwerydd (Arviragus); mediated peace between Britain and Rome.

[7] *Elen* ] Elen the Fair, only child of Coel II, mother of Constantine I, is said to have traveled to the Holy Land where she discovered relics of the true Cross.

Wrth Gwlan, fu un waneg.
A ddoeth yr un fil ar ddeg
O'r gweryddon i'r gradde
Am odde a wnaeth, i Dduw Ne'. 1
Grwaig Edgar bu ddihareb,
A wnaeth yr hyn ni wnaeth neb:
Cerdded yr haearn tanllyd
Yn droednoeth, goesnoeth i gyd,
A'r tân ni wnaeth eniwed
I'w chroen, mor dda oedd ei chred.
Eleias a ddanfonasyd 2
At wraig dda i gael bara a byd
Gwraig a wnaeth pan oedd gaetha'
Newyn ar lawer dyn da,
O'r ddinas death at gasddyn
Dig i ddywedyd i'r dyn;
Troesai ei boen tros y byd,
Disymwth y doi symud.
Susanna yn son synnwyr, 3
Syn a gwael oedd son y gwyr
Mwy no rhai o'r rhianedd,
Gwell no gwyr eu gallu a'u gwedd.
Brenhines, daeres dwyrain,
Sy' abl fodd, Sibli fain, 4
Yn gynta' 'rioed a ddoede
Y down oll gerbron Duw Ne'; 5
Hithau a farn ar yr anwir
Am eu gwaith arddoedyd gwir.
Dywed Ifan, 'rwy'n d'ofyn,
Yn gywir hardd, ai gwir hyn?
Ni allodd merch, gorrderchwr,
Diras ei gwaith dreisio gwr.
Dig aflan, o doi gyfle,
Ymdynnu a wnâi nid am Ne'?
Gad yn wib godinebwr,
Galw dyn hardd gledren hwr?
Efô fu'n pech bob pen
Ac o'i galon pe gwelen'.
Dywed Ifan, ar dafawd,
Rhodiog wr, cyn rhydu gwawd,
Ai da i i ferch golli'i pherchen,
A'i phrynt a'i helynt yn hen?
Yr un ffwl a neidio wrth ffon
Neu neidio wrth lw anudon,
Aed ffeilsion ddynion yn ddig
Duw a fyddow dy feddyg.

Gwlan another – one so wise
Her goodness reached unto the skies:
Sinners sent her, with eleven
Thousand maids, to God in Heaven. 1
Edgar's wife made proverb good:
"She did what no warrior could."
She walked across those coals of fire
Barefoot, bare-leggèd, all, entire:
Her faith, it proved so strong within,
The fire dared not scorch her skin.
Elias, gone to Sidon, was fed 2
By a wife there with her bread.
When famine came at God's behest,
Her infant died upon her breast.
To th' hermit went she (far from town),
Angrily, to shout him down.
He turned her grief instead to life:
With a sudden start, her child revived.
Susanna spoke sense, every breath; 3
Surprise! – Her *accusers* suffered death.
Many a maid (I learn from books)
Exceed the male, in brains *and* looks.
The heiress of the Orient,
Queen Sybil, knew what omens meant. 4
She was the very first to say
That men should ponder Judgment Day. 5
(Because she warned men with her hymns,
Her name, and Truth, are synonyms.)
Speak, Evan! I am asking you:
Which sex is beautiful, and true?
What daughter e'er has aped the man,
Committed slaughter, raped a man?
When chance for down-and-dirty's given,
What man will e'er aspire to Heaven?
Is one who runs to promiscu'ty
A patron saint of woman's beauty?
The man who sins with every part –
Try looking once into his heart!
Speak, Evan! Do you think it's just
For a lazy spouse, with his rotting lust,
To deny rights, home, and heritage
To vex his wife because she's aged?
No wife will break an oath so quick
As an idiot with his jumping stick.
Angry men! I'll not endure them–
May God, as surgeon, fix to cure them!

[1] *Gwlan* ] i.e., St. Ursula, a legendary Romano-British princess killed at Cologne, by Huns, along with her 11,000 virgin handmaidens, while en route to be married to the pagan governor of Armorica.

[2] The story is told in 1 Kings 18:8-24; cf. Luke 4:25-26.

[3] Bk. of Daniel ch. 13: two peeping elders watch Susanna bathe in her garden, then libel her when she refuses to have sex with them.

[4] Heraclitus (frag. 92), earliest mention of the Sybils: "The Sibyl, with frenzied spech uttering things not to be scorned, unadorned and unperfumed, yet reaches across a thousand years with her voice by aid of the god."

[5] *Judgment Day* ] *lit.*, God [in] Heaven.

# Songs and Occasional Verse (ca. 1300 - 1500)

A woman is a worthy thynge
They do the washe and do the wring.
Lullay, lullay, she dothe thee singe,
And yet she hath but care and woe....
A woman is a worthy wight;
She serveth a man bothe daye and night;
Thereto she putteth alle her might;
And yet she hath but care and wo.
—British Library MS Harl. 4294, f. 81 (15th C.)

The woman singeth at her spinning-wheel
A pleasant chant, ballad, or barcarole;
She thinketh of her song, upon the whole,
Far more than of her flax; and yet the reel
Is full, and artfully her fingers feel
With quick adjustment, provident control.
The lines, too subtly twisted to unroll
Out to a perfect thread.
—Elizabeth Barrett Browning (*Sonnets of 1844*)

THE INDEX OF MIDDLE ENGLISH VERSE catalogues nearly one thousand anonymous lyrics under such headings as "To his mistress," "An unkind mistress," "On the absence of his mistress," "Verses expressing desire to serve his mistress." At least half of those texts contain no internal indication of gender; which means that, without emendation of pronouns, most of them might have been addressed or sung centuries ago by male or female: by a woman to a man, man to woman, man to man, woman to woman; by a soloist to a large company, by a mother to herself or to her infant. But to project onto the text an originary speaker who cannot be discovered, while failing to note the range of psychological or ideological work done by a lyric, is largely a waste of time – rather like a physicist who ignores the visible ripples of a thrown stone, in order to postulate what kind of rock it must have been that caused the original splash (an igneous white male aristocrat, almost always). Most surviving medieval lyrics were recorded by male scribes. And many, perhaps most, were composed by male poets, borrowing from others. But scholarship's pervasive assumption of male authorship and transmission too often imposes limited subjectivity on texts that had no such limitation in the minds of the original culture that produced the words and tune. Hardly inevitable is the familiar inference that medieval verse and music always articulate a masculine, usually aristocratic, always heterosexual voice.

Westron wynde, when wyll thow blow,
the smalle rayne downe can rayne.
Cryst, yf my love were in my armys
And I yn my bedde Agayne

West'ren wind, when wilt thou blow –
The small rain down can rain.
Christ, if my love were in my arms
And I in my bed again!

Just as one tune (e.g., "Greensleeves") may remain stable while the words are changed, so too could the original words of a lyric be performed to various tunes, or sung by male or female, rich or poor. We know that the musical setting for "West'ren Wind" was freely adapted in the sixteenth century for worship, same tune but with sacred lyrics (by John Taverner, Christopher Tye, John Shepherd); yet the text of "West'ren wind" is catalogued in the *Index of Middle English Verse* as a man's poem "Expressing yearning for his mistress." Rosemary Woolf (for one) elaborates further on the poet's social class: "There is no evidence that so masterly a verse ever sprang from the untrained imagination of the common people."[1] (The same might be said of *The Canterbury Tales,* if not already ascribed to the son of a London vintner; the same *has* been said of *Hamlet,* ascribed to the son of a provincial glover.) Setting aside our own "untrained" or perhaps over-trained imagination, we may do well to read and study late medieval charms, devotionals, lullabies, dance tunes, love lyrics, satires, without always hypostatizing a male aristocratic or clerical author. No single individual ever composed a poetic gem *ex nihilo.* Courtly composers drew on the imagination of the common people no less than commoners borrowed from courtly trends. So, too, for gender. Some lyrics best bespeak a masculine or feminine (or sexually transgressive) desire; some are best when performed in a cathedral, palace, nursery, or army barracks. But the original culture was under no constraint to read, perform, or preserve "West'ren Wind" as a masculine expression of desire for his absent female; if we cannot imagine a medieval woman singing or writing or even re-writing it, that may be our problem, not hers. Nor have we an obligation to assume that lullabies and poems of adoration for Jesus are by, or for, a woman's voice.) The verses following, of no known authorship, across centuries, from multiple genres, may facilitate fresh ways thinking about how a "master" or "mistress" inhabits the text; or, if class and gender do not inhere in the text but are constructed – then by whom?

DWF

[1] Rosemary Woolf, "Later Poetry: the Popular Tradition." In W. F. Bolton, *The Middle Ages.* London, 1970, p. 279.

## Charms

Sorcery, necromancy, and witchcraft were practices forbidden by church and secular law throughout the medieval period though rarely prosecuted prior to the fifteenth century (and then, chiefly, as a pretextual excuse for silencing religious dissidents and political enemies). An influential early case was that of Dame Alice Outlaw Kyteler, accused of sorcery in 1324. Kyteler was an Anglo-Irish aristocrat, but a cultural descendant of Anglo-Saxon cunning women. Raphael Holinshed reports in the *Chronicles* that she daily "swept the streets of Kilkenny between complin and twilight, raking all the filth towards the doors of her son, William Outlaw, murmuring secretly with herself these words":[1]

> To the house of William my son,
> Hie all the wealth of Kilkenny town.[2]

Living in an age when it was not uncommon for Christian men and women to dabble in white magic, and when most believed in the power of ritual prayer and related forms of magical speech, Dame Alice might have gone unobserved in her superstitions; but the hubris of her attempt to sweep all the town's goods to the door of her son – a fellow with the unpromising name of Master "Outlaw" – troubled local property owners, even as the growing heaps of manure about Outlaw's house must have troubled their noses.

The strategy seemed to be working: Dame Alice was four times married, each time to a man of power and wealth; and William, her eldest son by her first marriage, had by this time had grown prosperous as a moneylender. The citizens of Kilkenny, fearing the worst, accused Dame Alice of sorcery.

The local authorities who searched the Kyteler residence were in for a Satanic shock. "In rifling the closet of the lady, they are alleged to have found a wafer of sacramental bread having the devil's name stamped thereon instead of Jesus Christ." Moreover, the constables are said to have discovered the fuel and the aerial device on which Dame Alice flew her nightly rounds, "a pipe of ointment wherewith she greased a staff upon which she ambled and galloped, through thick and thin, when and in what manner she listed" (described thus as if it were a fourteenth-century dildo).[3]

Dame Alice was further "charged to have nightly conference [sexual congress] with a spirit called Robin Artison, to whom she sacrificed in the highway nine red cocks and nine peacocks' eyes." John de Ledred, Bishop of Ossory, enjoined penance upon Kyteler and upon two alleged accomplices, Basil and Petronilla (probably Kyteler's domestic servants). Holinshed writes that "This business about witches troubled Ireland the more for that the lady was supported by certain of the nobility, and lastly conveyed over into England, since which time it could never be understood what became of her."[4]

In point of fact, the story ended less happily than is reported in the *Chronicles*. Petronilla and Dame Alice relapsed into their familiar ways, whereupon they were again arrested, convicted, and this time burned at the stake.[5] (According to Friar Clyn, this was Ireland's first capital execution for the crime of sorcery.) Before she died, Petronilla accused William Outlaw, money-lender, who was subsequently arrested and shackled in solitary confinement; where he remained until he agreed to the penance of underwriting a new lead roof for St. Mary's Chapel, and all was forgiven.

Alice Kyteler's fate notwithstanding, men and women of all classes memorized charms and prayers whereby to ward off illness and evil, or to find a lost or stolen article. Such ritual incantations rested on a belief that if one uttered the right words in the right order, one obtained thereby a measure of control over what happened in the world. Numerous charms have survived from the late medieval period whereby the speaker sought to acquire, through words, the power to alter events. Of the extant charms surviving in manuscript, one cannot usually determine which were uttered by women and which by men, but it seems clear that men and women alike composed, pronounced, and transmitted charms from one generation to the next. The following charm against fever, probably the work of an English cleric, is typical of the form:

---

[1] Holinshed reports his name as William Outlaw and her name as Alice Kettle.

[2] *Kilkenny* ] an Irish town about 70 miles southwest of Dublin; *complin* ] the last worship service of the day.

[3] *listed* ] wished.

[4] Holinshed (1586) 2.69. A contemporary account of the proceedings against Dame Alice, unknown to Holinshed, is preserved in the B.L. MS Harleian 64, ed. Wright (1843).

[5] See Nichols, ed., *Proceedings* (1843).

### [By the Prayers of Saint Dorothy]

*Medicina pro morbo caduco et le fevre.*
*In nomine patris et fillii et spiritus sancti. Amen.*

*What manere of Ivell thou be,*
*in goddis name I coungere the.*
*I coungere the with the holy crosse*
*that Iesus was done on with fors.*
*I coniure the with nayles thre*
*that Iesus was nayled vpon the tree.*
*I coungere the with the crowne of thorne*
*that on Iesus hede was done with skorne.*
*I coungere the with the precious blode*
*that Iesus shewyd vpon the rode.*
*I coungere the with woundes fyue*
*that Iesus suffred be his lyue.*
*I coungere the with that holy spere*
*that longeus to Iesus hert can bere.*
*I coungere the neuertheless*
*With all the vertues of the masse,*
*And all the holy prayers of Seynt dorathe.*
*In nomine patris et filii et spiritus sancti.*
*Amen.*
(c. 1500)

[Medicine for Epilepsy and Fever
In the name of the Father and Son and Holy Spirit. Amen.]

What manner of evil thou be,
In Goddes-name I conjure thee. 1
I conjure thee with th' holy cross
That Jesus was done on with force.
I conjure thee with nails three
That Jesus was nailed upon the tree.
I conjure thee with the crown of thorn
That on Jesus' head was done with scorn.
I conjure thee with the precious blood
That Jesus shed° upon the rood. 2
I conjure thee with woundès five
That Jesus suffered by his life.
I conjure thee with that holy spear
That Longeus to Jesus' heart can bear. 3
I conjure thee, never-the-less,
With all the virtues of the Mass
And° th' holy prayers of St. Dorothy. 4
*In nomine patris et filii et spiritus sancti.*
Amen.

Whether uttered for profit to oneself ("white magic") or to inflict injury upon others ("black magic"), most medieval charms are lost to us. But various women's charms are preserved in extant court records of women prosecuted for witchcraft. For example, when Isabel Mure of Yorkshire stood trial in 1528 it was reported to the presiding justice that "She took fire, and two young women with her, and went to a running water, and lit a wisp of straw, and set it on the water, and said thus":

*Benedicite, se ye what I see...*
*I se the fier burne and water rynne*
*and the gryse grew, and see flew*
*and nyght fevers and all unknowth evils*
*that evil flee, and all other, God will.*

Benedicite! See ye what I see: 5
I see the fire burn, and water run,
And the grass grow, and sea flow –
And night fevers, and all unknowth evils.
That evil flee, and all other, God will.

"And after these words [she said] fifteen paternoster, fifteen ave Maria, and three creeds" – behavior that landed her before the local inquest on suspicion of witchcraft a half-century before witch-hunting became a national pastime.

## Devotional Verses

Not infrequently, erotic desire was sublimated into sacred words of adoration for the Holy Mother: medieval lyrics addressed to the Blessèd Virgin borrow freely from the language of courtly love. So, too, in women's devotional verses, which typically figure Jesus as a loving spouse. In Mother Mary's Lament, the singer pities the penetrated Christ in his Passion and longs to be made one with him in an agony of simultaneous and mutual consummation:

---

[1] *Goddes-name* ] ( = *old possessive*, God his name) God's name.

[2] *rood* ] cross.

[3] *Longeus* ] According to medieval legend, the soldier who speared Christ's body as it hung on the cross.

[4] *St. Dorothy* ] a virgin martyr of Alexandria in the third century.

[5] *Benedicite* ] bless ye (the Lord)!

### [Mother Mary's Lament]

*Wy haue ȝe no reuthe on my child*
*Haue reuthe on me ful of murnig*
*Taket doun on rode my derworþi child,*
*Or prek me on rode with my derling.*

*More pine ne may me ben don*
*þan laten me liuen in sorwe & schame;*
*Als loue me bindet to my sone*
*so lat vs deyȝen boþen i same*
(recorded 1372)

Why have ye no ruth on my child?
Have ruth on me full of mourning°—
Take down on rood my dear-worthy child
Or prick me on rood with my darling.

More pine ne may me be'n done
Than laten me liven in sorr'we and shame.
Als love me bindet' to my son
So let us dyen bothen y-same. [1]

Before the advent of printed lyrics, the words to popular tunes or conventional themes varied from one house to the next, from one generation to the next. The surviving versions are neither right nor wrong but simply the ones that someone copied down, among thousands that were sung and forgotten.

[1a.] **Jesu Christ my Leman Sweet**

Jesu Christ, my leman sweet,
That for me diedst on the rood-tree,
With all my might I thee beseech,
Fór thy woundès two and three,
That all-so-fastè mot thy love
Into mine heartè fichèd be,
As was the spear into thine heart
When thou suff'redest death for me.
(late 14th C.)

[1b.] **Jesu Christ my Leman Sweet**

Jesu Christ, my leman sweet,
That diedst on the roodè-tree
With all my might I thee beseech,
Fór thine woundès two and three,
That as deep into mine heart
Mot thy love y-stickèd be,
As was the spear into thine heart
When thou suff'redest death for me.
(late 14th C.)

[1c.] **Jesu Christ mine Leman Sweet**

Jesu Christ, mine leman sweet,
That for me dièds' on rood-tree,
With all mine heart I thee beseek,
Fór thy woundès two and three,
That all-so-fast into mine heart
Thy love rooted motè be,
As was the spear into thy side
When you suff'redes' death° for me. [2]
(15th C.)

[2.] **Jesu my Spouse**

Jesu, my spousè good and true,
Ne take me to none other new.
In thy keeping I me betake,
And thee I have chose to [be] my make.
Some token of love, thou send me blive
That I the Fiend away may drive. [3]
(15th C.)

## The Lullaby or Cradle Song

Early references (in poetry and sermons) to the English *lullay* mention it as a special grace of womanhood. Mothers while doing their work or when putting their children to bed sang lullays, some of which were well-known, while others were doubtless original compositions. Because we are dependent upon a literate clergy for those lullays that got written down, very few secular folk-lullays have survived: most surviving exemplars eulogize the Virgin Mary and the child Jesus, or express the Virgin's lamentation for her crucified son. (Sung to tunes designed to soothe rather than to entertain, the sacred lullay tradition survives in some modern Christmas carols, such as "Away in a Manger" and "Silent Night.")

---

[1] *ruth* ] pity; *on rood* ] from the cross; *prick* ] nail; *More ... done* ] No more pain may be inflicted upon me; *laten* ] to let; *Als ... son* ] Even as love binds me to my son.

[2] *leman* ] sweetheart, lover; *diedes' on rood-tree* ] died on the cross.

[3] *make* ] mate, spouse; *blive* ] quickly, soon; *Fiend* ] the Christian devil.

A few representative refrains, from extant medieval lullabies:

*Lullay, Jesu, lullay, lullay,*
*My own dear moder, sing lullay…*

*Lullay, mine liking, my dear son, mine sweeting,*
*Lullay, my dear heart, mine own dear darling…*

*Lullay my fader, lullay my brother,*
*Mine own dear son, lullay…*

*There was mickle melody, at that childès' birth,*
*All tho' weren in Heaven-bliss, they made mickle mirth…*

*Lullay, lullay, little child, child, rest ye a throw.*
*Fro' high hider art thou sent, with us to wonè low…*

*Lullay, lullay, little child, child, softè sleep, and fast,*
*In sorrow endeth every love but thine, at the last.*

The lullay "Why Weepest Thou" holds particular interest as the earliest extant example in the English vernacular (ca. 1300). It seems to be rooted less in biblical teaching or chivalric literature than in the tragic consciousness of the common folk, a sensibility that one finds also in the medieval ballad:

### [Lullay]

***Lullay lullay litel child, why wepest thou so sore…***

Lullay, lullay, little child, why weepest thou so sore?
Needes' must thou weep – hit was i-yarked thee yore
Euer to live in sorrow, and sich and mourn [therefore],
As thine eldren did ere this, while 'hey alivès wore.°
  Lullay, [lullay,] little child, child lullay, lullow,
  Into uncouth world y-comen, so art thou. 1

Beastès and those foulès, the fisses in the flood,
And eche sheff alivès, y-maked of bone and blood,
When 'hey cometh to the world 'hey doth 'hemself some good—
All but the wretchè broll that is of Adam'is blood.
  Lullay, lullay, little child, to care art thou be-met.
  Thóu n'ost not this world'is wield, before thee is y-set. 2

Child, if betideth that thou shalt thrive and thee,
Think, thou were y-fost'red upon° thy moder-knee.
Euer have mindè, in thine heart, of those thingès three—
When thou comest, when' thou art, and what shall come of thee.
  Lullay, lullay, little child, child lullay, lullay,
  With sorrow thou coom into this world,
  With sorrow shalt wend away. 3

Ne trust thou to this world: it is thy full foe.°
The rich he maketh poor, the poorer° rich also;
Hit turneth woe to weal, and ekè weal to woe.
Ne trust no man to this world while hit turneth so.
  Lullay, lullay, little child, the foot is in the wheel.
  Thou n'ost whoder turn, to woe [nor°] other weal. 4

---

[1] *hit* ] it (*again at 21, 22, et. seq.*); *i-yarked thee yore* ] (i-yarkt') appointed for you long ago; *Euer* ] (*1 syll.*, yoor) ever; *sich* ] to sigh; *eldren* ] elders, ancestors; *'hey* ] they; *alives wore* ] were alive; *uncouth* ] unpleasant.

[2] *fisses* ] fish; *eche* ] each; *sheff* ] creature; *y-maked* ] made; *wretche broll* ] wretched imp; *Adam'is* ] ( = *old possessive, Adam his*) Adam's; *be-met* ] measured out; *n'ost* ] ( = ne wost) knowest not; *world'is wield* ] world's meaning, significance.

[3] *betide* ] perchance; *thee* ] prosper (*vb.*); *when'* ] whence; *possibly read* what *for ms.* whan.

[4] *he* ] the world; *eke* ] also; *the wheel* ] the fabled wheel of Fortune, whereby the goddess reverses the fortunes of men and women; *n'ost whoder* ] wist (knowest) not whither.

Child, thou art a pilgrim, in wickedness y-bore
Thou wanderest in this false world – thou lookè thee before.
Death shall come, with a blast, out of a well-dim hore
Adam'is kin down to cast, himself hath y-do' before.
    Lullay, lullay, little child, só woe thee worth, Adam,
    In the laund of paradise, through wickedness of Sathan. 1

Child, thou n'art a pilgrim, but an uncouth guest.
Thy dayès be'th y-told; thy journey's be'th y-cast.
Whoder thou shalt wend, north [nor] other est,
Death thee shall betide, with bitter bale in breast.
    Lullay, lullay, little child, this woe Adam thee wrought
    When he of the apple ate, and Eve it him betaught. 2

As the lullay form developed from one generation to the next, it drew on both household and courtly traditions. The "Corpus Christi Lullaby" was recorded by a scribe about 1500:

### [**Corpus Christi Lullaby**]

    *Lulley lulley lully lulley,*
    *þe fawcon hath born my mak away.*

*He bare hȳ vp, he bare hȳ down*
*He bare hȳ in to an orchard brown.*
    *Lulley lulley lully lulley*, &c.
*In þat orchard þer was an hall*
*þat was hangid* $w^t$ *purpill & pall.*
    *Lully lulley*, &c.
*And in þat hall þer was a bede,*
*It was hangid* $w^t$ *gold so rede.*
    *Lully lulley*, &c.
*And yn þat bed þer lythe a knyght,*
*His wowndis bledyng day & nyght.*
    *Lully lulley*, &c.
*By þat bedis side þer kneleth a may*
*& she wepeth both nyght and day,*
    *Lully lulley*, &c.
*& by þat beddis side þer stondith a ston,*
*"Corpus Christi" wretyn þer on.*
    *Lully lulley*, [*lully lulley,*
    *þe fawcon hath born my mak away.*]

    Lully, lullay, lully, lullay,
    The falcon hath borne my make away.

He bare him up, be bare him down
He bare him into an orchard brown.
    Lully, lullay, lully, lullay, *etc.*
In that orchard there was an hall
That was hanged with purple and pall. 3
    Lully, lullay, *etc.*
And in that hall there was a bed;
It was hanged with gold so red.
    Lully, lullay, *etc.*
And in that bed there lieth a knight,
His woundès bleeding day and night. 4
    Lully, lullay, *etc.*
By that bedside there kneel'th a mai'
And she weepeth both night and day, 5
    Lully, lullay, *etc.*
And by that bedside there stondeth a stone,
"Corpus Christi" written thereon.
    Lully, lullay, [lully, lullay,
    The falcon hath borne my make away.]

---

[1] *woe thee worth* ] woe to you.

[2] *n'art* ] are not; *be'th y-told* ] have been counted; *y-cast* ] predestined; *wend* ] go; *nor other est* ] or else to the east; *bale* ] sorrow.

[3] *purple and pall* ] costly purple cloth.

[4] *knight* ] a figure for Jesus, wounded for others.

[5] *mai'* ] maiden; here standing for the Virgin Mary.

## Instructional verses

AS the principal educators of young children, women memorized catechisms and etiquettes in verse, and recited them over until the little ones had mastered their lessons. Julian Barnes's *Book of Hunting* is the best-known instructional poem from the late medieval period, but her verse-manual on hunting is hardly unusual apart from its good fortune to be printed as early as 1486. Bodleian Library MS Ashmole 61 contains another well-known exemplar, in a poem widely anthologized under the title, "How the Goodwife Taught her Daughter" (beginning, "Lyst and lyth a lytell space,...."); in which the maternal narrator is a dummy's voice for the holy patriarchy, drumming on the usual themes: the maiden's obligation to be chaste, silent, obedient, and tedious; to dress modestly, to attend Mass, and to pay tithes. More engaging is a second exemplar in the same Bodleian manuscript, in which the narrator's voice is more authentically maternal, addressing an audience of both girls and boys. "Dame Courtesy's Book for Children" illustrates the way in which children of wealthy parents acquired "manere," or good-breeding, from the schooling by a mother, nurse, or nun.

### Dame Courtesy's Book for Children

***Whosoeuer wyll thryue or the...***

WHOSOEUER will thrive or thea 1
Must virtues learn, and court'ous be—
For who in youth no virtues useth,
In age, all men him refuseth.
Clarks that can the science-seven
Says that courtesy came fro' Heaven
When Gabriel our Lady grete
And Elizabeth with her met. 2
Virtues° be closed in courtesy;
And all vices, in villainy. 3
  Arise betime out of thy bed,
And bliss thy breast and thy forehead; 4
Then wash thy hondès and thy face.
Kern thy head, and ask God gracè 5
Thee to help in all thy works—
Thou shall speed bett, whatso thy carks.° 6
Then go to church and hear a Mass:
Ask° mercíe for thy trespass.
  To whom thou meets come by the way,
Court'ously, "Good morn," thou say.
  When thou hast done, go break thy fast
With meat and drink of good repast.
Bliss thy mouth ere° thou it ete—
The better shall be thy diét.

Before thy meat say thou thy grace
(It occupies but little space):
"For our meat and drink, and us,
Thank we our Lord Ihesús." 7
  A paternoster and ave Marie
Say for the souls that in pain lie; 8
Then go labour as thou art bound,
And be not idle in no stound. 9
Holy Scripture, thus it sayeth
To thee that art of Christen faith:
"If thou labour, thou must ete
That with thy hondès thou dost get."
  Look thou be true in word and deed:
In all thy works then shall thou speed.
Truth doth neuer his master shame;
It keeps him out of sin and blame. 10
The ways to Heaven, they be'n thus twain,
Mercy and truth, as clarkès sayen.
Whoso will come to th' life of bliss,
To go these° ways he may not miss.
Make no promise but it be good,
And keep thou it with might and mood: 11
For euery promise, it is debt
That with no falsehood° must be lett. 12
God and thy neighbours love alway—
Well is thee, then, may thou say,

---

1 *Whosoeuer* ] (*hoo-so-yoor'*) Whosoever; *thea* ] prosper; fr. OE *þion* (again at 152).

2 *Clarks* ] (clerks) clerics, scholars); *can* ] ken, know; *science-seven* ] the seven arts or sciences: arithmetic, music, geometry, and astronomy (the quadrivium); grammar, rhetoric, and logic (the trivium); *our Lady grete* ] greeted our Lady, the Virgin Mary.

3 *villainy* ] rudeness; churlishness.

4 *bliss* ] bless.

5 *Kern* ] comb.

6 *bett* ] better (*cf. 62, 104, 133*); *carks* ] cares, burdens.

7 *Jesus* ] (*yeh-soos'*).

8 *paternoster* ] Lord's prayer ("Our Father..."); *ave Marie* ] a prayer based on the greetings of Gabriel and Elizabeth to the Virgin Mary. *See* Luke 1:28, 42.

9 *stound* ] station or position; state of bewilderment.

10 *neuer* ] (*1 syll.*, nyoor) never.

11 *might and mood* ] strength and spirit.

12 *lett* ] obstacle, hindrance.

For so thou keepès all the law,
Withouten any dread° or awe.
Uncalled, go thou to no counsel;
That 'longs to thee, with that thou mell. 1
Scorn not the poor, ne hurt no man.
Learn of him that thee teach can.
Be no glozer nor no mocker,
Ne no servants no way locker. 2
Be not proud, but meek and kind,
And with thy bett' go thou behind. 3
When thy better shows his will,
To he have said thou must be still. 4
When thou speaks to any man,
Hond, foot, and finger, keep° still then,
And look thou up into his face,
And courteous be in every place.
With thy finger show° no thing,
Nor be not lief to tell tidíng. 5
If any man say well of thee
Or of thy friends, [he] thanked must be.
Have few words, and wisely set,
For so thou may thy worship get. 6
Use no swearing, n'other lying,
In thy selling and thy buying: 7
For and thou do, thou art to blame,
And at the last thou will have shame. 8
Get thy good with truth° and win,
And keep thee out of debt and sin. 9
Be loath to grieve, and lief to please.
Seek the peace, and live in ease.° 10
Of whom thou speakès, where and when
Avise thee well, and to what men.
When thou comes unto a door,
Say "God be here," ere thou go far.
Where euer thou comes, speak honestly,
To sir or dame, or their meiníe. 11
Stand, and sit not first withal,
Till he bid thee that rules the hall.
Where he bids, there must thou sit
And for none other change ne flit;
Sit uppèright, and honestly.
Eat and drink, be fellowly; 12
Part with 'hem that sits thee by
(Thus teaches thee Dame Courtesy). 13
Take the salt with thy clean knife.
Be cold of speech and make no strife.
Backbite no man that is away:
Be glad of all men well to say.
Hear and see, and say thou nought:
Then shall thou not to 'proof be brought. 14
With meat and drink before thee set,
Hold thee pleased and ask no bett'.
Wipe thy mouth when thou will drink,
Lest it foul thy cuppès-brink. 15
Keep clean thy fingers, lips, and chin,
For so thou may thy worship win.
In thy mouth when thy meat is,
To drink, or speak, or laugh, iwis,
Dame Courtesy forbids it thee. 16
But praise thy fare, wheresoeuer thou be:
For be it good, or be it bad,
In good worth it must be had.
When thou spits, be well 'ware,°
Whereso thou spittès, nigh or far,
Hold thy hond before thy mouthe
When thou spits, and hide it couth. 17
Keep thy knife both clean and sharp,
And be not busy for to carp. 18
Cleanse thy knife with some cut bread
Not with thy cloth, as I thee rede. 19
With any filth to foul the cloth,
A courteous man, he will be loath.
In thy dish set not thy spoon,
N'other on the brink, as únlearn'd doen. 20
When thou suppès, make no noise°
With thy mouthè, as do boys.
The meat that on thy trencher is,
Put it not into thy dish. 21
Get thee soon a voìdeur,°
And soon avoid thou thy trenchour. 22

---

[1] *That* ] that which; *mell* ] mingle; concern thyself.

[2] *glozer* ] flatterer; *locker* ] fix with curled hair.

[3] *liened* ] deferent.

[4] *To he have said* ] until he is done speaking.

[5] *lief to tell tiding* ] eager to relate news or gossip.

[6] *wisely set* ] wisely expressed, well-ordered.

[7] *n'other* ] ( = *neither*) nor.

[8] *For and* ] for if.

[9] *win* ] profit; joy.

[10] *lief* ] desirous, eager.

[11] *Where euer* ] Wherever; *meinie* ] household; dependents.

[12] *fellowly* ] sociable.

[13] *part with hem* ] share with them.

[14] *'proof* ] reproof.

[15] *foul thy cuppes-brink* ] soil thy cup's rim.

[16] *iwis* ] surely.

[17] *couth* ] nicely.

[18] *carp* ] prate; *perhaps with a pun on* carf ( = *carve*).

[19] *rede* ] advise.

[20] *as unlearn'd doen* ] as the unlearned do.

[21] *trencher* ] a flat wooden platter on which meat was served .

[22] *voideur* ] voider; a receptacle into which meal scraps were gathered; *avoid* ] clear; *trenchour* ] trencher.

When thy bett take thee to cup
Drink thyself, and set it up; [1]
Take the cuppè with thy hondès,
Lest it fall there as thou stondès. [2]
When thy better speaks to thee,
Do off thy cap and bow thy knee.
At thy table, n'other cratch ne claw:
Then men will say thou art a daw. [3]
Wipe not thy nose nor thy nosthirls:
Then men will say thou comes of churls. [4]
Make thou n'other cat ne hound
Thy fellow at the table° round,
Ne play with spoon, trenchóur, ne knife.
In honesty and cleanness° lead thy life.
  This book is made for childèr young
At the school that bide not long. [5]
Soon it may be conned, and had,
And make them good if they be bad. [6]
God give them grace, virtuous to be.
For then they may both thrive and thea.

*finis*

## Dance Lyrics

Performed by all classes of society, indoors and out, the *carole* (singing-dance) was by far the most enduringly popular social dance in France and England in the 12th, 13th, and 14th centuries. The dancers formed a ring and moved left and right, in and out, as a leader (standing in the center) sang the verses. Everyone joined in the refrain. The *farandole,* also popular, was a snaking chain dance, all of the dancers holding hands and following the leader, sometimes ducking through the line. (New French and Italian dances came to England in the 15th century, which gradually developed into the varied, elaborate and graceful forms of courtly dance of the Renaissance period.)

Women are often depicted in late medieval art as singers and musicians, but most surviving dance lyrics are for a male voice, perhaps because male clerics controled which song verses were recorded for posterity. Lyrics that express feminine desire, pleasure, or agency generally went unrecorded. A few representativee survivivors:

**[The Irish Dancer: a fragment]**

*Ich am of Irlaunde...*
*ant of the holy londe*
*of irlande.*

*Gode sire, pray ich ge*
*for of saynte charite,*
*come ant daunce wyt me*
*In irlande.*
(14th C.)

Ich am of Irelaund,
And of the holy laund
Of Irelaund. [7]

Good sir, pray Ich thee,°
For-of Saint Charity,
Come and daunce wit' me
In Irelaund. [8]

1 *take thee to cup* ] hands thee a cup; *set it up* ] set it by.

2 *with thy hondes* ] with both hands.

3 *n'other cratch ne claw* ] neither scratch nor claw thyself; *daw* ] jackdaw; used as a derisive epithet, and applied most often to untidy women ( = *slattern* or *slut*).

4 *nosthirls* ] nostrils.

5 *childer* ] children; *At ... long* ] who don't stay long in school.

6 *conned, and had* ] memorized, and known.

7 *Ich* ] I.

8 *For-of saint Charity* ] For the sake of holy charity; or of St. Charity: according to legend, a Roman widow (Sophia, Wisdom) begot three daughters, Faith, Hope, and Charity, all of whom were martyred.

## [Black is Beautiful]

| | | |
|---|---|---|
| *Summe men sayonne þat i am blac:* | Some men sayon that I am black: | |
| *yt ys a colour for my þrow!* | It is a colour for my prow!° | |
| *þer y loue þer ys no lac.* | There I love, there is no lack. | |
| *I may not be so wyte as þou.* | I may not be so white as thou. | 1 |
| | | |
| *blac ys a colur þat ys god;* | Black is a colour that is good; | |
| *so say y & many mo.* | So say I and many moe. | |
| *blac ys my hat, blac is my hod,* | Black is my hat, black is my hood, | |
| *blac ys all that longet þer to.* | Black is all that 'longeth thereto. | |
| | | |
| *blac wol do as god a nede* | Black woll do as good a nede | |
| *as þe wyte at borde & bedde,* | As the white at board and bed, | |
| *& þer to also treu indede* | And thereto also true in deed; | |
| *& þer to y ley my lif to wedde.* | Thereto° I lay my life to wed. | 2 |
| | | |
| *Wynd & watur may steyne þe wyte;* | Wind and water may stain the white; | |
| *wyn wys þe blac yt may not so.* | Iwis° the black it may not so. | |
| *þer yse þe blac, ys al my delyte.* | There is the black, is my° delight. | |
| *y am yholde be schyle þer to.* | I am y-held by skill thereto. | 3 |
| | | |
| *Peper wyt oute, yt ys wel blac;* | Pepper wit'out, it is well black; | |
| *y wys, wyt inne yt ys not so.* | Iwis, within it is not so. | |
| *lat go þe colur, & tak þe smac:* | Let go the colour, and take the smack: | |
| *þis y sey by me & moe.* | This I say by me, and moe. | 4 |
| | | |
| *god saue ale [hem] þat buþ broune* | God save all 'hem that beèth° brown | |
| *for þey buth trew as any stel.* | For they beèth true as any steel. | |
| *god kepe hem boþe in feld & toune—* | God keep 'hem, both in field and town— | |
| *& þanne schal y be kept ful wel.* | And then shall I be kept full well! | 5 |

## [Trolly-Lolly]

| | | | | |
|---|---|---|---|---|
| *So well ys me be gone, troly lole.* | | So well is me begone, trolly-lolly. | | 6 |
| *so well ys me be gone, troly loly.* | | So well is me begone, trolly-lolly. | | |
| | | | | |
| Off seruing men I wyll begyne, | Troly loley, | Of serving men I will begin: | trolly-lolly, | |
| For they goo mynon trym, | Troly loley. | For they go minion trim | trolly-lolly.[7] | |
| Of mett & drink & feyr clothyng, | Troly loley, | Of meat and drink and fair clothíng, | trolly-lolly, | |
| By dere god I want none, | Troly loley. | By dear God I want [no thing°]. | trolly-lolly.[8] | |
| His bonet is of fyne scarlett, | Troly loley, | His bonnet is of fine scarlétte, | trolly-lolly, | |
| With here as black os geitt, | Troly lolye. | [His°] hair as black as jet, | trolly-lolly.° | |
| His dublett ys of fyne satyne, | Troly lolye, | His doublet is of fine satíne, | trolly-lolly, | |
| His shertt, well mayd & tryme, | Troly lolye. | His shirt, well made and trim, | trolly-lolly. | |
| His coytt itt is so tryme and rownde, | Troly lolye, | His coat it is so trim and round, | trolly-lolly, | |
| His kysse ys worth a hundred powynde, | Troly lolye. | His kiss is worth a hundred pound,° | trolly-lolly. | |

---

1 *prow* ] advantage; *There ... there* ] Where ... there; *may* ] would.

2 *nede* ] service; *wed* ] pledge; *Thereto ... wed* ] I will bet my life on it.

3 *Iwis* ] surely; *There ... black* ] Where the black is, there; *skill* ] reason, knowledge, experience; *yheld ... thereto* ] obliged in this by reason itself.

4 *wit'out* ] ( = *without* ] on the outside; *smack* ] taste, flavor within; *by me and moe* ] about myself and others.

5 *'hem that beeth* ] them that be.

6 *is me begone* ] am I furnished.

7 *minion trim* ] finely dressed.

8 *By ... none* ] I am not lacking, by God!

| | | | |
|---|---|---|---|
| His hoysse ys of london black, | Troly lolye. | His hose [it°] is of London black, | trolly-lolly. |
| In hyme ther is no lack, | Troly lolye. | In him there is no lack, | trolly-lolly. |
| His face yt ys so lyk a man, | Troly lolye. | His face it is so like a man, | trolly-lolly, |
| Who cane butt loue hyme than, | Troly lolye. | Who can but love him then, | trolly-lolly. |
| Wher so euer he bee, he hath my hert, | Troly lolye, | Wheresoe'er he be, he hath my heart, | trolly-lolly, |
| And shall, to death depart, | Troly lolye. | And shall, to death depart. | trolly-lolly. |

## Love Verses

Because single women were afforded so little agency in matters of love and marriage, it is perhaps unsurprising that the extant love lyrics – those that were composed by or for women – are more often wistful than joyful. The vast majority of women's songs and poetry from the late medieval period are ones that express disappointment, desolation, or at best a guarded hopefulness.

### [**As I could wish**]

*Wolde god that hyt were so*
*As I cowde wysshe by tuyxt vs too!*

*The man that I loued al ther best...*
*In al thys contre est other west*
*to me he ys a Strange gest*
What wonder es't thow I be woo?
[*Wolde god*, &c.]

*when me were leuest that he schold duelle*
[ ]
*he wold noȝt sey ones fare well*
*wen tyme was come that he most go.*

*In places ofte when I hym mete,*
*I dar noȝt speke, but forth I go.*
*with herte & eyes I hym grete,*
*so trywe of loue I know no mo.*

*Ás he is myn hert loue*
*My dyrward dyre, i blessyd he be*
*I swere by god that ys a boue,*
*Non hath my loue but only he.*

*I am i comfortyd in euery syde,*
*The coluers wexeth both fres and newe,*
*when he ys come & wyl a byde,*
*I wott ful wel that he ys trywe.*

*I loue hym trywely & no mo—*
*wolde god that he hyt knywe!*
*—And euer I hope hyt schal be so;*
*Then schall I chaunge for no new.*
[*Wolde god that hyt were so*
*As I cowde wysshe by tuyxt vs too!*]
(ca. 1500)

Wouldè God that hit were so
As I could wish betwixt us two!

The man that I loved alder-best°
In all this country, east other west,
To me, he is a strangè guest.
What wonder is't though I be woe? 1
[Woulde God, etc.]

When me were lief'st that he should dwell
[He would not bide a minute moe;°]
He would not say onès farewell
When time was come that he must go. 2

In places oft when I him meet,
I dare not speak, but forth I go.°
With heart and eyès I him greet,
So true of love I know no moe. 3

Ás he is mine heartès-love°
My dearward dear, y-blest he be.
I swear by God that is above,
None hath my love but only he.

I am y-comforted in euery side,
The colours wax° both fresh and new,
When he is come and will abide,
I wot full well that he is true. 4

I love him truly and no moe—
Wouldè God that he hit knew!
—And euer I hope hit shall be so;
Then shall I chaungè for no new.
[Wouldè God that hit were so
As I could wish betwixt us two!]

---

1 *alder-best* ] the best of all; *country* ] county, region; *other* ] or.

2 *when . . . liefest* ] when I most dearly wished; *moe* ] more; *He...moe* ] conjectural emendation for line om. in MS; *ones* ] once; *say ones* ] say, even once.

3 *no moe* ] no other.

4 *wax* ] grow; *wot* ] know.

Verse epistles between educated lovers, prior to marriage, may have been common practice among the educated classes. Most surviving exemplars were recorded without attribution. The stanzas here printed as a "Reply to her Lover" were composed in the early fifteenth century by an English lady, responding to a letter from a lovelorn suitor, possibly a royal one, in which he has solicited a secret tryst. In wooing her, the wooer has borrowed courtly phrases from the "doucet Frensshe," a nation which he is said otherwise to "spend." The seduction may thus have been attempted about 1416 by a noble warrior having returned victorious from Agincourt – perhaps the king himself, though it is difficult to imagine a woman of the court addressing King Henry V in such admonitory terms as we find in the maiden's reply. The woman poet, a well-educated aristocrat, probably a courtier, modestly declines to serve as a "royal ox" while being praised as a fair "swan." Resisting an unwanted sexual advance, she nevertheless gives her suitor reason to hope, if he can prove that his love is the real thing.

## [Reply to Her Lover:]

| | |
|---|---|
| *Ensamples fayre ye fynde in nature:* | Ensamples fair ye find in nature: |
| *Of plantys smale commeth trees huge and strong,* | Of plantès small cometh trees huge and strong; |
| *Of raggyd coltes palfreyes of plesure,* | Of ragged colts, palfreys of pleasure; |
| *The lytyll spryng groweth in the ryuer long.* | The little spring groweth (in the river) long. |
| *God and Nature worchyn nothyng wrong;* | God and Nature worken nothing wrong; |
| *And yet there must be had contynuaunce* | And yet there must be had continuaunce |
| *Or thynges may corn to her cheuysaunce.* | Ere things may corn unto° her chevisaunce. 1 |
| | |
| *Eftsones ye sey that I may do but lyte* | Eftsoons, ye say that I may do but litt'e |
| *For yow, but yef I can the tyme respyte* | For you, but yif I can the time espy° |
| *As for us to puruey suche respyte* | As for us to purvey such respíte° |
| *At tyme and place to mete so secretly* | At time and place to meet so secretly |
| *That the myght at good leyser asky* | That ye° might at good leisure ascry° |
| *The peynes all and all the bytter smert* | The painès all and all the bitter smart |
| *That presauntly so crampesheth your hert* | That presently so crampèsheth your heart. 2 |
| | |
| *Unto thys poynt, wolde your humanyte* | Unto this point, would your humanity |
| *I yow demaunde the thyng of my desyre,* | I, you, demaund – the thing of *my* desire? |
| *That were so fer ayenst femynyte?* | (That were so far 'gainst femininity!) |
| *How coude ye of me suche thyng requyre* | How could ye, of me, such thing require |
| *As shuld do nought but tonges set on fyre?* | As should do nought but tonguès set on fire? |
| *And eke yef I purueyed for that plesaunce* | (And eke, yif I purveyed for that plesáunce |
| *Ye myght well sey I coude of cheuesaunce.* | Ye might well say I *could*, of chevisaunce.) 3 |
| | |
| *And thynke well also as unto me* | And think well also (as unto me) |
| *Hit were noon case to wete your heuynesse;* | It were none case to wete *your* heaviness. |
| *Well bettyr hit ys that ye kepe syker* | Well better it is, that ye keep siccurly° |
| *Suche thynges as may nat your peynes redresse* | Such things as may not your pains redress |
| *Than shew hem to other folkes expresse,* | Than show 'hem to other folks express |
| *Suche as may shape no remedy.* | Such as may shape no remedy. |
| (*What "ease" ys hit sorow to multyply?*) | (What "ease" is it, sorrow to *multiply*?) 4 |

---

[1] *Ere* ] Before; *corn* ] yield the harvest; *her chevisaunce* ] Nature's fulfilment, full realization.

[2] *Eftsoons* ] Secondly, Moreover; *but yif* ] unless, except on; *ascry* ] cry out against; *crampesheth* ] cramps up.

[3] *Unto ... desire* ] perhaps: Would I demand you forfeit your humaneness (which I value) as you demand I forfeit my feminine chastity? That, too, would be against virtuous femininity; *nought but* ] nothing but; *set on fire* ] i.e., kindle gossip about you and me; *eke ...pleasaunce* ] also, if I *did* arrange for a plesant love-tryst; *Ye ... could* ] you might just tell me to do so (sacrifice my femininity, for pleasure).

[4] *none case* ] no reason; *to wete* ] to add sorrow to (*wet*); to know, experience (*weet*); *siccurly* ] securely, private; *express* ] openly, plainly stated as if for the record.

*But yet for to abrege your penaunce*
*And aswage somwhat couertly,*
*Yef that ye lyst to know the puruyaunce,*
*As I suppose ye know ryght verryly,*
*Of suche as be in loues Jeopardy,*
*Ye must in chyef lerne to be sufferaunt,*
*Seruyseable, secret, without auaunt.*

But yet, for to abridge your penáunce
And [to°] assuage somewhat covertly,
Yif that ye list to know the purveyáunce,
(As I suppose ye know right verily
Of such as be in Lovès' jeopardy),
Ye must in chief learn to be sufferaunt,
Serviceable, secret, without avaunt. 1

*And in case your masteres, yef I hit were,*
*Shewyd to yow countenaunce of delay,*
*Spare nat to serue trewly fro yere to yere.*
*Rome was nat bylt, men seyn, all in a day;*
*An owre may nat that lengor tyme may;*
*The drope by streyngth ne persheth nat the ston*
*But for so oft hit falleth theropon.*

And in case your masteress (yif I it were!)
Showed to you countenaunce of delay,
Spare not to serve truly fro' year to year
("Rome was not built," men sayen, "all in a day").
An hour may *not*, that lengor timè *may*.
The drop by *strength* ne perisheth not the stone
But for so *oft* it falleth thereupon! 2

*Ye must suffre when other be cherysshyd,*
*ffor loue standeth nat in countenaunce.*
*fful long ago that Ouyde hath dewsyd*
*All the craft and all the suffysaunce*
*Of louers law, with euery circumstaunce.*
*Ye wold joy hys doctryne for to here,*
*Or any wyght that lyst of loue to lere.*

Ye must suffer when other be cherishèd,
For love standeth not in countenaunce.
Full long ago that Ovid hath devisèd
All the craft and all the suffisaunce
Of lovers' law, with every circumstaunce.
Ye would 'joy his doctrine for to hear,
Or any wight that list of love to lere. 3

*At sondry tymes all other then men demeth*
*Ys set of loue, the wyt as well as I.*
*Hyt ys nat alwey so as hit semeth:*
*fful fer from hert somtyme stand full ny*
*Whereas the welbelouyd ys put by.*
*Thowgh ye be louyd full well, beleueth me,*
*Ye must go forth as though hit were nat ye*

At sundry times all other than men deemeth
Is set of love, ye° wit as well as I.
It is not alway so, as it seemeth:
Full far from heart, sometime, stand full nigh
Whereas the well-belovèd is put by.
Though ye be loved full well, believeth me,
Ye must go forth as though it were *not* ye. 4

*ffolke must fede so the world here and I,*
*That by fauour and frendely countenaunce*
*No wyght there shall perceue or spy*
*By any sygne, be utteraunce,*
*Whether ye please or cause displesaunce;*
*ffor and I loue yow, trust verryly,*
*I woll yow loue as though hit were nat I.*

Folk must feed so the world's° ear° and eye°,
That by favour and friendly countenaunce
No wight there shall perceive or 'spy
By any sign, by utteraunce,
Whether ye please or cause displeasáunce;
For, an' I love you, trust verily,
I woll you love as though it were *not* I. 5

*When ye be loued as though hit were nat ye*
*And ye loue me as though hit were nat I,*
*Trusteth well no suspecions shal be*
*In oure demenyng, and understandeth why:*
*The thyng ys guydyd than so thryftyly*
*To any wyght hit shall appere and seme*
*There nys no cause of us to speke or deme.*

When ye be loved as though it were not ye
And ye love me as though it were not I,
Trusteth well: no suspicìons shall be
In our demeaning. And understandeth why:
The thing is guided then so thriftily,
To any wight it shall appear and seem
There n'is no cause of us to speak or deem. 6

---

[1] *abridge your penaunce* ] minimize future remorse; *Yif ... purveyaunce* ] If you want to know the courtly manner (I'll teach you the drill, lover-boy: here are the rules); *sufferaunt* ] long-suffering, patient; *avaunt* ] boasting, arrogance.

[2] *masteress* ] the original sense of *mistress*: the woman who overmasters and is served by her male lover; *An...may* ] You may accomplish, in time, what an hour cannot accomplish.

[3] *For ... countenaunce* ] True love suffers it patiently, doesn't die, when she shows favor to a rival; You, or any wight (person) wishing to learn of love, would enjoy reading Ovid's teaching; *lere* ] learn.

[4] *At... deemeth* ] Love takes root at different times, or time-table, than; *wit* ] know, understand; *It* ] Love.

[5] *Folk* ] i.e., Those in love (must screen their feelings from view); *feed* ] (fede) satisfy.

[6] *thriftily* ] skillfully; *n'is* ] isn't; *speak or deem* ] gossip or conjecture (about us).

*Eke in your byll fynde I well comprysyd*
*Howe ye desyre mokry to eschew,*
*hyche me semeth passyngly deuysyd:*
*ffor who that loueth stedfast and trew*
*He wyll the cause of all mokry renew,*
*ffor well ye wote there be folkes that use*
*And euery thyng to mamer and to muse.*

Eke in your bill find I well-comprisèd
How ye desire mockery to eschew,
Which meseemeth passingly devisèd:
For who that loveth steadèfast and true
He will the cause of all mockery renew:
For well ye wot there be folkès that use
On° every thing to mammer and to muse. [1]

*And, wyll ye leue me, oo thyng I commende*
*In your persone whyche joy hit ys to here:*
*The doucet Frensshe, that otherwhyle ye spende;*
*Now lewde be he that lyst nat for to lere*
*Lo in the frute som tarrage wyll appere*
*When that the treys gentyll nature;*
*A plesaunt tre bereth frute of plesure.*

And, will ye 'lieve me, oo' thing I commend
In your persóne (which joy it is to hear
The doucet French, that otherwhile ye spend—
Now lewd be he that list not for to lere):
Lo, in the fruit some tarrage will appear
When that the [tree hath°] *tres-gentle* nature;
A pleasaunt tree beareth fruit of pleasure. [2]

*But, the "second Troyles," as I began*
*To be playne unto yow in my sentence,*
*And nat the Royal Ox for to be clepyd the swan,*
*Ne the swan that ys whyte in existence*
*To be cleped Coll–thys ys but apparence,*
*As in wordes trauersyng the kyng–*
*I pray to God, foule fall dissemblyng.*

But, the "second Troilus," as I began
To be plain unto you in my senténce,
And not the royal *ox* for to be clep'd the "swan,"
Ne the swan that's white in existénce
To be clepèd "coal"– this is but appearance.
As in wordès tráversing the King–
I pray to God, foul fall dissembèling! [3]

One woman poet a century later (name unknown, someone associated with the court of Henry VIII) was far less diplomatic in her assessment of the dissembling suitor whose oaths of true love cannot be trusted:

### [Double Dealing]

*Yowre counturfetyng with doubyll delyng*
*Avaylyth nothyng! and wote ye why?*
*For ye, with your fayning, hath such demyng*
*To make a beleuing? Nay, nay, hardely!*
*It were to grete pite that women truly*
*Hade so grete foly, that cowde nott tell*
*When that ye do lye, then speke ye so swetely,*
*And think the contrary. Thus know we well.*

Your counterfeiting with double dealing
Availeth nothing! And wot you why?
For ye, with your feigning, hath such deeming
To make a *believing*? Nay, nay, hardèly!
It were too-great pity that women truly
Had so great folly, that could not tell
When that *ye do lie*. Then speak ye so sweetly,
And think the contrary. Thus know we well.

---

[1] *bill* ] letter; *meseemeth* ] as it seems to me; *passingly* ] cursorily, perfunctorily, for the moment (you're not thinking); *You say you wish to avoid mockery; the steadfast lover is always the object of mocks;* *wot* ] know; *that use* ] whose practice is; *mammer* ] mutter, whisper; *muse* ] wonder about, ponder.

[2] *'lieve* ] believe; perhaps also *leave* (give me leave); *oo'* ] one (*oon*); *doucet* ] sweet; *spend* ] vanquish, consume (Glad to see you have written partly in the sweet language of the French people whom you overcome); *lewd ... lere* ] Boorish the man who will learn this; *tarrage* ] communicated taste (from the tree to the fruit; from the sweet French, to you).

[3] *ox* ] in 14th C. usage, either the bull or the cow; *cleped* ] called; *in existence* ] in actuality (the suitor having styled himself a "second Troilus," has called her a "swan" for her fair complexion, and the swan, by comparison, coal-black; which she modestly disclaims; *traversing* ] in opposition to, thwarting; *foul fall dissembeling* ] May dissembling in love, like all treasonous words spoken against the King, have ill luck.

## Songs of Lamentation

If women poets and singers of the late medieval and early Tudor periods had a shared theme to rival that of religious devotion, it was the experience of sorrow or fatigue, of trying to please one's earthly or heavenly Lord and never meeting with approval or grace.

### [Why Is It?]

*O blessed lord how may this be,*
*that y am thus in heuinesse?*
*and ȝet y haue do my besynesse*
*euer to plese hym wit all my myȝth,*
*bothe erly, late, by day & by nyȝth.*

O blessèd Lord, how may this be,
That I am thus in heaviness?
And yet I have do' my busíness
E'er to please him with all my might,
Both early, late, by day and by night.

Among the most popular form of women's verse was the song of lamentation. Most of these are in the form of prayer or self-reflection – one-way conversations, lacking the absent lord or lover's reply. The earliest extant example dates from about 1225:

### [The Night is Long]

*[ ]irie it is while sumer ilast*
*wið fughelès song,*
*Oc nu necheð windès blast*
*And weder strong.*
*Ej, ej, what! þis nicht long,*
*and ich, wid wel michel wrong,*
*soregh and murne and [ ]*

[M]erry° it is while summer y-last,
With fughelès song,
Oc nu necheth windès blast
And weather° strong. 1
Ei, ei, what! this nicht [is°] long,
And Ich, with well mickle wrong,
Sorrow and mourn and [fast°]. 2

Songs of lamentation typically imply a caveat on the vicissitudes of love: a maiden, seduced or raped, has lost her virginity before marriage. Now abandoned, perhaps pregnant, she is gripped with sorrow or remorse. Many of these are represented in the manuscript record only by the refrain, most frequently as quotations embedded in English or Latin homilies: "Welaway, why did I so? / Now Ich am in allè woe!" "Who shall to my leman say / That for his love me longeth aye?" "Welaway that Ich ne span / When I to the Ringè ran." This last, quoted in a fourteenth-century sermon, is from a lost song featuring a maiden who left her spinning to attend a bell-ringing festival, where she evidently lost her virginity. Another such is an English couplet embedded in a fifteenth-century collection of Latin exempla, introduced by the prompt, "Anglice dicitur" (*English is spoken*). The gift of a barred (ornamented) sash has led a maid to ruin: "Barrèd girdle, woe thee be: / My maidenhead I lost for thee."[3]

In 1324 – the same year in which he put to death Alice Kyteler and her friend Petronilla on charges of witchcraft – Richard Ledred, Bishop of Ossory, composed his "Cantilenae de Nativitate Domini." These are sixty Latin lyrics that Bishop Ledred wrote for the Vicars Choral of Kilkenny Cathedral, to be sung at the celebration of the Advent and other sacred festivals; so "that their throats and mouths, sanctified to God, might not be polluted with theatrical, indecent, and secular songs." Six of the bishop's Latin lyrics are set or adapted to English folk tunes, one being "Alas, How Should I Sing?" The original English lyric was evidently a lamentation sung by a maiden who is to be married against her will to an older man, though she loves another – precisely the kind of "indecent" lyric that Bishop Ledred could not endure; but he was good enough to provide us with a record of the burden (refrain) and first three lines:

---

[1] *fugheles* ] fowls, birds (possessive); *Oc nu* ] But now; *necheth* ] nigheth, threatens near.

[2] *nicht* ] night; *Ich* ] I; *mickle* ] much.

[3] 1. "*vaylaway whi ded y so/now ich am in alle wa*"; 2. "*Who schal to my lemman say / þat for his loue me longeþ ay*"; 3. "*Weylawey þat iche ne span / whan y to þe ringe ran.*" 4. "*Barred girdel wo þe be / mi maidenhed hi les for þe.*"

***Alas, hou shold y synge…***

*Alas hou shold y synge*
*Yloren is my playnge*

*Hou shold y wiþ þat olde man*
*To leuen and let my lemman*
*Swettist of al þinge…*

**Alas, How Should I Sing**

Alas, how should I sing?
Y-loren is my playing. [1]

How should I with that old man
To liven and lett my leman, [2]
Sweetest of all thing…

Another fragment in three stanzas is illuminating not because it was certainly written by a woman but because it takes for granted that a girl upon reaching age twelve is thereby fair game for the attention of amorous older men – twelve being the legal age at which girls could be married, according to Church canon law. Evidently a popular tune, "And I Were a Maiden" is called for in *Thersites,* a comic interlude written in 1537 on the occasion of the recent or anticipated birth of Prince Edward:

***And I war a maydn…***

*And I war a maydyn*
*As many one ys,*
*For all the golde in England*
*I wold not do amysse.*

*When I was a wanton wench*
*Of twelue yere of age,*
*Thes cowrtyers with their amorus*
*They kyndyld my corâge.*

*When I was come to*
*The age of fifteen yere*
*In all this lond, nowther fre nor bond,*
*Methought I had no peer.*

**And I Were a Maiden…**

And I were a maiden
As many-a-one° is,
For all the gold in England
I would not do amiss. [3]

When I was a wanton wench
Of twelve year of age,
These courtiers with their amours,
They kindled my corâge. [4]

When I was come to
The age of fifteen year
In all this lond, n'other free nor bond,
Methought I had no peer.

There is a generic likeness in these songs and verse epistles, most of which represent fictional women; many of which, though doubtless sung by many female voices of the age, are a transparent cover for a male, often clerical, point of view.

**[The Sooth I See]** [5]

*Were it vndo th$^{t}$ is ido,*
*I wold be war.*

*y louede a child of þis cuntre*
*& so y wende he had do me.*
*Now myself the sothe y see—*
*Th$^{t}$ he is far.*
*Were it vndo th$^{t}$ is ido, &c.*

*He seyde to me he wolde be trewe*
*& chaunge me for none oth$^{r}$ newe.*
*Now y sykke & am pale of hewe,*
*For he is far.*
*Were it vndo, &c.*

Were it undo' that is y-do', [6]
I would beware.

I loved a child of this country
And so I weened he had do' me.
Now myself the sooth I see—
That he is far. [7]
Were it undo' that is y-do', *etc.*

He said to me he would be true
And change me for none other new.
Now I sike and am pale of hue,
For he is far. [8]
Were it undo', *etc.*

---

[1] *Y-loren* ] lost, gone forever.

[2] *lett* ] prevent, bar access to; *leman* ] sweetheart.

[3] *And … maiden* ] If I were [still] a virgin.

[4] *corage* ] heart (*OED* n. 1a), desire (n.2a, 2e), boldness (n.4).

[5] *MS: this song is sung to the tune of* Brid on the briar I tell it; / To none other I ne dare [*Brid* = bird].

[6] *Were … y-do'* ] If what is done could now be undone.

[7] *weened* ] thought; *do'* ] done; *sooth* ] truth.

[8] *sike* ] sigh.

*He seide his saw$^{s}$ he wolde fulfulle;*
*Th$^{r}$fore y lat hī haue his wille.*
*Now y sikke and mourne stille,*
*For he is far.*
*Were it vndo, &c.*
(early 15$^{th}$ C.)

He said his saws he would fulfill;
Therefore I let him have his will.
Now I sike and mournè still,
For he is far. 1
Were it undo', *etc.*

### [Alas, What Remedy?]

[*Alas, what remedy,*
*That I cannot refreyne?*]

[Alas, what remedy,
That I cannot refrain?] 2

*Greuus ys my sorowe*
*Both euyne and moro*
*Vnto myselffe a lone.*
*Thus do I make my mowne*:
*That vnkyndnes haith kyllyd me*
*And putt me to this peyne.*
*Alas, what remedy,*
*That I cannot refreyne?*

Grievous is my sorrow
Both even and morrow
Unto myself alone.
Thus do I make my moan:
That unkindness hath killèd me
And put me to this pain.
Alas, what remedy,
That I cannot refrain?

*Whan other men doyth sleype,*
*Thene do I syght and weype,*
*All ragius in my bed,*
*As one for paynes neyre ded,*
*That vnkyndnes haue kyllyd me*
*And putt me to this payne.*
*Alas, what Remedy,*
*That I cannott refreyne?*

When other men doth sleep,
Then do I sigh't and weep,
All rageous in my bed,
As one for pains near dead,
That unkindness hath° killèd me
And put me to this pain.
Alas, what remedy,
That I cannot refrain?

*My harte, ytt haue no rest*
*but styll with peynes oppreste.*
*And yett, of all my Smart,*
*Ytt greuith moste my harte*
*That vnkyndes shuld kyll me*
*and putt me to this payne.*
*Alas, what remedy,*
*That I cannott refreyne?*

My heart, it hath° no rest
But still with pains oppressed.
And yet, of all my smart,
It grieveth most my heart
That unkindess should kill me
And put me to this pain.
Alas, what remedy,
That I cannot refrain? 3

*Wo worth trust vntrusty,*
*Wo worth loue vnlouyd!*
*Wo worth hape vnblamyd,*
*Wo worth fautt vn-namyd!*
*Thus vnkyndly to kyll me*
*And putt me to this payne,*
*Now, alas, what remedy,*
*That I cannott refrayne?*

Woe worth trust untrusty,
Woe worth love unloved!
Woe worth hap unblamed,
Woe worth fault unnamed!
Thus unkindly to kill me
And put me to this pain,
Now, alas, what remedy,
That I cannot refrain? 4

*Alas, I lyue to longe,*
*my paynes be so stronge,*
*for comfort haue I none.*
*god wott, I wold fayne be gone—*

Alas, I live too long,
My painès be so strong,
For comfort have I none.
God wot, I'ld fain be gone—

---

1 *saws* ] promises; *sike* ] sigh.
2 *refrain* ] 1. restrain ("this pain"); 2. abstain (from loving him anyway).
3 *smart* ] grief, pain.
4 *hap unblamed* ] faultless mischance.

*for vnkyndnes haith kyllyd me*
*And putt me to thys payne.*
*Alas, what remedy,*
*That I cannott refrayne?*

For unkindness hath killèd me
And put me to this pain.
Alas, what remedy,
That I cannot refrain? [1]

*Iff ony wyght be here*
*That byeth loue so dere,*
*come nere, lye downe by me*
*And wepe for company,*
*for vnkyndnes haith kyllyd me*
*And putt me to this payne.*
*Alas, what remedy,*
*That I cannott refrayne?*

If any wight be here
That buyeth love so dear,
Come near, lie down by me
And weep for company,
For unkindness hath killèd me
And put me to this pain.
Alas, what remedy,
That I cannot refrain?

*My foes, whiche loue me nott*
*Be vayle my deth, I wott,*
*And he that loue me beste*
*hym selfe my deth hath dreste.*
*What vnkyndes shuld kyle me*
*If this were nott my payne?*
*Alas, what remedy,*
*That I cannott refrayne?*

My foes which love me not
Bewail my death, I wot,
And he that loves° me best
Himself my death hath dressed.
What unkindess should kill me
If *this* were not my pain?
Alas, what remedy,
That I cannot refrain? [2]

*My last wyll here I make:*
*To god my soule I be-take,*
*And my wrechyd body*
*As erth in a hole to lye.*
*for vnkyndes to kyle me*
*And putt me to this payne!*
*Alas, what remedy,*
*That I cannot refreyne?*

My last will here I make:
To God my soul I betake,
And my wretched body
As earth in a hole to lie.
For unkindness to kill me
And put me to this pain!
Alas, what remedy,
That I cannot refrain?

*O, harte, I the bequyeth*
*To hyme that is my deth,*
*Yff that no harte haith he,*
*my heart his schalbe.*
*Thought vnkyndes haith kyllyd me*
*And putt me to this payne,*
*Yett yf my body dye,*
*My harte cannott refrayne.*

O, heart, I thee bequeath
To him that is my death,
If that no heart hath he,
My heartè his shall be.
Though't unkindness hath killèd me
And put me to this pain,
Yet if my body die,
My heart cannot refrain. [3]

*Placebo, Dilexi—*
*com, weype this obsequye,*
*My mowrnarus, dolfully,*
*come weype this psalmody*
*for vnkyndes haith kyllyd me*
*and putt me to this payne.*
*be hold this wrechid body*
*þat your vnkyndes haith slayne.*

"Placebo,—" "Dilexi—"
Come, weep this obsequy,
My mourners,° dolefully,
Come weep this psalmody
For unkindess hath killed me
And put me to this pain.
Behold this wretched body
That your unkindness hath slain. [4]

---

[1] *wot* ] knows.

[2] *dressed* ] prepared, made ready.

[3] *Though't* ] though (*again at xi.4*); *if* ] even if.

[4] Stanzas 10-14 (73 ff.) may originally have been intended as separaate poem to follow stanzas 1-9. *Placebo* ] first word of Vespers service; here, for the poet's funeral *Dilexi* ] first word of Matins.

*Now I be sych all ye*
*namely, þat louers be),*
*my loue, my deth, forgiue*
*and soffer hyme to lyue,*
*Thought vnkyndes haith kyllyd me*
*And putt me to this payne,*
*Yett haid I rether dye*
*for his sake ons agayne.*

Now I beseech all ye
(Namely, that lovers be),
My love, my death, forgive
And suffer him to live,
Though't unkindness hath killed me
And put me to this pain,
Yet had I rather die
For his sake once again. [1]

*My tomb, ytt schalbe blewe*
*In tokyne that I was trewe.*
*To bringe my loue from doubte*
*Itt shalbe writtynge abowtte*
*That vnkyndes haith kyllyd me*
*and put me to this pain.*
*be hold this wrechid body*
*That yor vnkyndes haith slayne.*

My tomb, it shall be blue
In token that I was true.
To bring my love from doubt
It shall be written° about
That "Unkindness hath kilлèd me
And put me to this pain.
Behold this wretched body
That your unkindness hath slain."

*O lady, lerne by me:*
*Sley nott loue wylfully,*
*for fer loue waxyth denty.*
[ ]
*vnkyndes to kyle me*
*or putt loue to this payne.*
*I ware the better dye*
*for loues sake a gayne.*

O ladies,° learn by me:
Slay not love wilfully,
For fear love waxeth denty.
[Sigh not that he sent me°]
Unkindness to kill me
Or put love to this pain.
I were the better die
For lovès sake again. [2]

*Grevus is my Soro,*
*but deth is my boro,*
*ffor to my selfe a lone*
*Thus do I make my mone:*
*That vnkyndes haith kyllyd me*
*And passyd is my payne.*
*Prey for this ded body*
*þat your vnkyndes haith slayne*
*amen.*
(ca. 1500)

Grievous is my sorrow,
But death is my borough,
For to myself alone
Thus do I make my moan:
That "Unkindness hath killed me
And passèd is my pain.
Pray for this dead body
That your unkindness hath slain." [3]
Amen.

"Lady Bryan's Lament" looks scarcely different from the cautionary lyrics composed by clerics for a female voice; and yet, the poet's personal tone and the self-affirming subscription in the unique surviving manuscript – "Bryan is my name yet" suggest that this next lyric may be autobiographical, having been composed, or at least appropriated, by a young woman who was raped by a nobleman ("Sir John") while "waking the well"; and who tried to make the best of a bad situation by accepting Sir John thereafter as a lover and marriage prospect. Instead, the knight has left her pregnant and forsaken.

The well-wake was an ancient festival of pagan origin that was at first combated, then assimilated, and finally suppressed by the Church. In the medieval and Renaissance periods, well-wakings were frequently conducted on St. John's Eve, being celebrated by revelers who danced, sang, and drank until dawn. Wakings continued into the seventeenth century. Vigorous and unrelenting opposition by the Puritans led to the suppression of well-wakes throughout England during the reign of Charles I.[4]

---

[1] *My love ... forgive* ] Forgive my lover for my death; *suffer* ] permit.

[2] *waxeth denty* ] grows rare; becomes hard to find; *Sigh ... me* ] conjectural reconstrution of omitted line.

[3] *borough* ] refuge.

[4] See R. C. Hope, *The Legendary Lore of the Holy Wells of England* (1893), xix and passim.

### [Lady Bryan's Lament]

*I haue for-sworne hit whil I life*
*To wake the well-ey.*

*The last tyme I the wel woke...*
*Ser Iohn caght me $w^t$ a croke.*
*he made me to swere be bel & boke*
*I shuld not tell.*
[*I haue for-sworne hit*, &c.]

*ȝet he did me a wel wors turne.*
*he leyde my hed agayn the burne.*
*he gafe my mayden hed a spurne.*
*And rofe my kell.*

*Sir Iohn came to oure hows to play.*
*Fro euensong tyme til light of the day;*
*we made as mery as flowres in may,*
*I was begyled-ay.*

*Sir Iohn he came to $o^r$ hows;*
*he made hit $wond^r$ copious,*
*he seyd that I was gracious*
*to beyre a childe-ey.*

*I go $w^t$ childe, well I wot.*
*I schrew the fadur þat hit gate,*
*With owten he fynde hit mylke & pape,*
*A long while-ey.*

[*I haue for-sworne hit whil I life*
*To wake the well-ey.*

*bryan hys my name iet*
(lattter 14th C.)

I have forsworn hit while I live 1
To wake the well-ay.°

The last time I the well y-woke,
Sír John caught me with a croke.
He made me to swear by bell and boke
I should not tell-ay.° 2
[I have forsworn it, etc.,]

Yet he did me a well-worse turn:
He laid my head again' the bourn;
He gave my maiden-head a spurn
And rove my kell-ay.° 3

Sir Iohn came to our house to play
Fro e'ensong time till light of the day.
We made as merry as flowers in May—
I was beguilèd-ay. 4

Sir John he came [un]to our house;
He made hit wonder copious.
He said that I was gracìous
To bear a child-ay. 5

I go with child, well I wot.
I shrew the fader that hit got
Withouten he find hit milk and pap
A long while-ay. 6

[I have forsworn hit while I live
To wake the well-ay.

*Bryan is my name yet.*

Peasant women often worked beside their husbands in the rigorous labor of plowing the fields. The man guided the ploughshare while the woman drove the oxen forward with a goad, perhaps while raising her voice in song. The singer of "I Will No More Go to the Plough" is a peasant woman overwhelmed with grief for the death of her mate. "Now I see I may be spared" suggests that she, too, has been ill. But she cannot endure a solitary return to the fields, having survived her husband; nor can she retire to her mother's home where as a child she was commanded from her play in order to spin wool or flax. Nothing remains but death-longing, a desire to be reunited with her spouse in the grave where she "might see [him] once a day" – i.e., continually. In alluding to the familiar lyric, "O West'ren Wind," the singer of "I Will No More Go to the Plough" associates the wind with a lovers' reunion, not in bed, but in the grave.

---

[1] *forsworn hit* ] sworn it off (*hit* = it).

[2] *croke* ] (*crook*) crooked staff; *by bell and boke* ] (used in the service of the mass) a frequent Medieval oath.

[3] *again' the bourn* ] against the well; *spurn* ] 1. blow; 2. act of contempt; *rove* ] rived, tore; *kell* ] 1. woman's headdress or hairnet; 2. maidenhead.

[4] *euensong:e'ensong* ] evening vespers.

[5] *wonder copious* ] furnished wondrously with gifts.

[6] *wot* ] know; *shrew ... got* ] curse the father that begot it; *Withouten* ] ( = *without*) that is, unless.

### [Come, Death]

**I wyll no more go to the plowe…**

*I wyll no more go to the plowe*
*I wyll go learne some other thynge*
*my mother knowythe it well inowghe*
*that I had rather play then spynne*

*O westerne wynd when wyllt thow blowe*
*& blowe the grene leves from the tree*
*O gentle dethe when wyllt thow coome*
*for off my lyff I am werye*

*My hart is in a prevy place*
*where as my body wold fayne be*
*and I my selff in a wofull case*
*wysshinge for dethe & can not dy*

*I aske of yowe no rytche araye,*
*nor yet no poynt of prevy playe,*
*but to the grownd that I might go*
*so that I myght se yow once a daye.*

*This have I here for an old reward,*
*some tyme to call, come tyme to crye.*
*for nowe I se I may be sparde,*
*I will go laye me doune & dye.*

**I will no more go to the plough…**

I will no more go to the plough
I will go learn some other thing
My mother knoweth it well enough,
That I had rather play than spin.

O Western Wind, when wilt thou blow,
And blow the green leaves from the tree?
O gentle Death, when wilt thou come? –
For of my life I am weary.

My heart is in a privy place
Whereas my body would fain be,
And I myself in a woeful case.
Wishing for death and cannot die.

I ask of you no rich array,
Nor yet no point of privy play,
But to the ground that I might go
That I might see you once a day.

This have I here, for an old reward,
Some time to call, some° time to cry.
For now I see I may be spared,
I will go lay me down, and die.

## Satire

For every sincere woman's lament recorded for posterity by male scribes, we have two or three extant parodies of the genre, many of which are in the form of the *carole,* and suited for a ring dance.

**Ladd Y the daunce**

*Alas, ales the wyle.*
*Thout Y on no gyle,*
*So haue Y god chaunce*
*Alas, ales the wyle,*
*That euer Y cowde daunce.*

*Ladd Y the daunce a Myssomur Day;*
*Y made smale trippus, soth for to say.*
*Jak, oure holy watur clerk, com be the way,*
*And he lokede me vpon: he thout he was gay*
*Thout ic on ne gile.*

*Jak, oure haly watur clerk, the yonge strippelyng,*
*For the chesoun of me, he com to the ryng,*
*And he trippede on my to and made a twynkelyng;*
*Euer he cam ner; he sparet for no thynge.*
*Thout Y on no gyle.*

**Led I the Dance**

Alas, alas the while!
Thought I on no guile.
So have I good chance:
Alas, alas the while,
That ever I could dance!

Led I the dance, a Mi'summer Day.
I made small trippès, sooth for to say.
Jack, our holy-water clerk, coom by the way,
And he looked me upon: he thought [I°] was gay
Thought Ich on no° guile. [1]
[Alas, alas the while, etc.]

Jack, our holy-water clerk, the young strippèling,
For the chesoun of me, he coom to the ring,
And he trippèd on my toe and made a twinkèling
Ever he came near. He sparèd for no-thing.
Thought I on no guile. [2]

---

[1] *trippès* ] dance-steps; *holy-water clerk* ] a monk who sells holy-water and relics; *coom* ] came; *gay* ] merry.

[2] *strippeling* ] (3 syls.), stripling just on the threshold of manhood; *twinkeling* ] winks; *Ever* ] whenever, every time.

*Jak, ic wot, preyede in my fayre face;*
*He thout me ful werly, so haue Y god grace.*
*As we turndun our daunce in a narw place*
*Jack bed me the mouth; a cussynge ther was.*
*Thout Y on no gyle.*

*Jak tho began to rowne in myn ere:*
*Loke that thou be priuey and graunte that thou the bere*
*A peyre wyth glouus ic ha to thyn were.*
*Gramercy, Jacke. That was myn answere.*
*Thoute yc on no gyle.*

*Sone after euensong Jak me mette:*
*Com hom aftur thy glouus that Ye the byhette.*
*Wan ic to his chambre com, doun he me sette.*
*From hum mytte Y nat go wan we were mette.*
*Thout Y on no gyle.*

*Schetus and chalonus ic wot a were yspredde*
*Forsothe tho Jack and yc wenten to bedde.*
*He prikede and he pransede, nolde he neuer lynne;*
*Yt was the murgust nyt that euer Y cam ynne.*
*Tout Y on no gyle.*

*Wan Jack had don, tho he rong the bell;*
*Al nyght ther he made me to dwelle.*
*Of y trewe we haddun yserued the reaggeth deuel of hell*
*Of othur smale burdus kep Y nout to telle.*
*Thout Y on no gyle.*

*The other day at prime Y com hom, as ic wene,*
*Meth Y my dame, coppud and kene.*
*Sey, thou stronge strumpeth, ware hastu bene?*
*Thy trippyng and they dauncyng wel it wol be sene.*
*Thout Y on no gyle.*

*Euer be on and by on, my damme reched me clot*
*Euer Y ber it privey wyle that Y mouth*
*Tyl my gurdul aros, my wombe wax° out.*
*Euel yspunne yern, euer it wole out.*
*Thout Y on no gyle.*

Jack, Ich wot, prayed in my fair face.
He thought me full werly, so have I good grace.
As we turn'den our daunce in a nar'we place
Jack bid me the mouth, a kissing there was.
Thought I on no guile. 1

Jack tho began to rown in mine ear
"Look that thou be privy and graunt that thou thee bear
A pair white glovès Ich ha' to thine wear."
"Gramercy, Jack!" That was mine answer –
Thought Ich on no guile. 2

Soon after evensong Jack me met:
"Come home after thy gloves that I thee be-het."
When Ich to his chamber coom, down he me set.
From him, might I not go when we were met.
Thought I on no guile. 3

Sheetès and chalonès Ich wot a'were y-spread
Forsooth, tho Jack and Ich wenten to bed.
He pricked and he pranced, n'ould he never lin.
It was the merriest°night that euer I came in.
Thought I on no guile. 4

When Jack had done, tho he rung the bell,
All night there he made me to dwell.
Oft° I trow we hadden y-served the rageth devil of hell.
Of other small bourdès keep I nought to tell.
Thought I on no guile. 5

The other day at prime I coom home, as Ich wene,
Met I my dame, coppèd and keen:
"Say, thou strong strumpet, where hast'ou been?
Thy tripping and thy dancing, well it woll be seen."
Thought I on no guile. 6

Ever, by one and by one, my dame reched me clout.
Ever I bore it privy while that I mote,
Till my girdle arose, my womb waxed° out.
Evil y-spun yern, euer it woll out.
Thought I on no guile. 7
[Alas, alas the while, etc.]

---

[1] *Ich* ] I; *werly* ] pretty? wary? (n/a *OED)*; *chesoun* ] reason; *Ever* ] whenever.

[2] *tho* ] then; *rown* ] whisper; *privy* ] secretive; *bear* ] receive as a gift; *nar'we* ] narrow (close-together).

[3] *be-het* ] behested, promised.

[4] *chalones* ] blankets; *wot* ] know; *n'ould ... lin* ] never would he let up.

[5] *I trow* ] I do believe; *rageth* ] rugged, shaggy (perhaps with a glance at *ragingest, most vehement*; *bourdès* ] idle pleasures, merriments; *keep* ] keep secret; *nought to tell* ] won't tell; use your imagination.

[6] *dame* ] mother, prioress, or other female superior; *prime* ] the first hour of prayer after dawn; about 6 a.m.; *I wene* ] I suppose (it was about 6 a.m.); *copped* ] peevish, irritable (*OED* 2.b); *hast'ou* ] hast thou (have you); *woll* ] will; *seen* ] discovered.

[7] *by ... one* ] again and again; *reached me clout* ] struck me with her fists; *mote* ] must; *girdle* ] sash, belt; *womb* ] belly, uterus; *wax* ] swelled; *Evil ... out* ] Spinning hastily into sin will always be discovered.

Among the best-known satirical songs on gender roles is "The Serving Maid's Holiday," a masculine fantasy, packed with bawdy innuendo, in the form of a carole for a holiday ring-dance:

**[The Serving Maid's Holiday]**

*Wybbe ne rele ne spynne yc ne may*
*ffor ioyȝe þat it ys holyday*

Web ne reel, ne spin Ich ne may
For 'joyès, that it is holiday! 1

*Al þis day, ich han souȝt,*
*spyndul, ne werue, ne wond, I nouȝt;*
*To myche blisse ich am brout*
*aȝen þis hyȝe holyday.*

All this day, Ich han sought,
Spindle, ne werve, ne wound, I not;
To mich bliss Ich am brought
Again' this high holiday. 2

*All vnswope ys owre vleth,*
*& our fyre ys vnbeth,*
*Oure ruschen ben vnrepe ȝeth,*
*aȝen þis hy halyday.*

All unswep' is our flet,
And our fire is unbet,
Our rushen be'n unrippè yet,
Again' this high holiday. 3

*yc moste feschun worton in*
*þredele my kerchef vndur my khyn –*
*leue iakke, lend me a pyn*
*To þredele me, þis holiday!*

Ic must fetchen worten in;
Threadle my kerchief under my chin –
Lovey Jack, lend me a pin
To threadle me, this holiday! 4

*Now yt draweþ to þe none*
*& al my cherrus ben vndone;*
*y moste a lyte solas mye schone*
*to make hem dowge þis holiday.*

Now it draweth to the noon
And all my chorès be'n undone;
I must a litt' solace my shooen
To make 'hem dough this holiday. 5

*y moste mylkyn in þis payl;*
*Outh me bred al þis schayl;*
*ȝut is þe dow vndur my nayl*
*as ic knad, þis holiday.*

I must milken in this pail;
Ought me brede, all this shale,
Yet is the dough under my nail
As Ich knead, this holiday. 6

*Iakke wol brynge me onward in my wey,*
*Wiþ me desyre, for to pleyȝe.*
*Of my dame, stant me none eyȝe*
*on neuer a god haliday.*

Jack will bring me on° my way,
With me desire, for to plaise.
Of my dame, stant me none ease
On neuer a good holiday. 7

*Iacke wol pay for my scoth,*
*a sonday atte þe ale-schoth;*
*iacke wol sowse wel my þrot*
*euery god haliday.*

Jack will pay for my scot,
A-Sunday, at the ale-shot;
Jack will saucè well my throat
Euery good holiday. 8

*sone he wolle take me by þe hond,*
*& he wolle legge me on þe lond,*
*þat al my buttockus ben of sond,*
*opon þis hye holyday.*

Soon he'll take me by the hand,
And he will leg me on the land,
That all my buttocks be'n of sand,
Upon this high holiday.

---

[1] *Web ... may* ] I need not weave, nor wind [thread], nor spin; *Ich* ] I.

[2] *I neither spindle nor weave nor wind* (thread); *Again'* ] (against) before, looking toward, in preparation for.

[3] *flet* ] floor, flat; *unbet* ] unbuilt; *rushen been unrippe yet* ] *floor-rushes are still uncut.*

[4] *fetche worten* ] gather herbs (e.g., rue or hyssop, abortifacients).

[5] *solace my shooen* ] give my shoes a rest; *dowghe* ] soft.

[6] *brede all this shale* ] bake the whole bowl(ful), make big (*OED* brede, v.2) the whole shell (nutshell, beanpod).

[7] *plaise* ] 1. play; 2. please; *Of my dame ... ease* ] My mother cannot stop my fun; *On neuer* ] not ever, on.

[8] *scot* ] tavern-tab; *ale-shot* ] ale-show, ale-feast.

*In he pult & out he drow,*
*& euer ic lay on hym y-low;*
*"by godus deth, þou dest me wow*
*vpon þis hey holiday!"*

*sone my wombe began to swelle*
*as greth as a belle;*
*durst y nat my dame telle*
*Wat me betydde þis holyday.*
(c. 1475)

In he pult and out he drow,
And euer Ich lay on him y-low;
"By Godès death, thou didst me woo
Upon this high holiday!" [1]

Soon my womb began to swell
As great as [any] bell;
Durst I not my damè tell
What me betid this holiday. [2]

"To my true love and able" parodies the courteous verse epistles often written to suitors by a coy mistress, and closes with an uncharacteristic obscenity:

**To my true love and able**
**(As the weathercock he is stable),**
**This letter to him be delivered**:

***Vnto you most froward þis letre I write…***

Unto you, most froward, this letter I write,
Which hath caused me so long in despair.
The goodliness of your person is easy to indite,
For he liveth not that can your person appair,
So comely, best shapen, of feature most fair,
Most fresh of countenaunce – even as an owl
Is best and most favored of ony oder fowl. [3]

Your manly visage, shortly to declare,
Your forehead, mouth, and nose so flat—
In short conclusion, best likened to an hare
Of all living things, save only a cat.
More would I say if I wist what—
That sweet visage full oft is – beshrew'd,
When I remember of some bawd so lewd. [4]

The proportion of your body commend well me aught
Fro' the shoulder down, behind and beforn:
If all the painters in a land togeder were sought
A worse could they not portray, though all they had it sworn.
(Keep well your patience, though I send you a scorn.)
Your garments upon you full gaily they hing—
As it were an old goose had a broke wing. [5]

Your thighs misgrowen, your shanks mich worse
Whoso behold your knees so crook'd,
(As each of 'hem bade oder Christ's curse)
So go they outward. Your hams be'n hooked,
Such a pair chambès I never on-looked.

---

[1] *pult ... drow* ] thrust (pulled) in and drew out; *woo* ] 1. woo; 2. woe.

[2] *durst ... dame* ] I dare not tell my mother.

[3] *froward* ] disagreeable; MS first line: "Vnto you most froward þis letre I write…"; *indite* ] express; *appair* ] deprecate; *ony oder* ] any other; a sarcasm (owls were considered the least handsome and most forboding of birds).

[4] *wist* ] knew; *beshrew'd* ] accursed; *bawd* ] pimp.

[5] *hing* ] hang.

So ungoodly your heels ye lift,
And your feet be'n crooked, with evil thrift. 1

Who might have the love of so sweet a wight,
She might be right glad that euer was she born.
She that onès would in a dark night
Ren for your love till she had caught a thorn,
I would her no more harm but hanged on the morn,
That hath two good eyen and y-chese her such a make
Or onès would lift up her hole for your sake. 2

Your sweet love – with bloody nails
Which feedeth moe lice than quails. 3

The poem here called "Woman's Work" (elsewhere printed as "The Tyrannical Husband") is an untitled song from a unique copy in the commonplace book of a London merchant of the latter fifteenth century (the paper is temp. Henry VII and Elizabeth of York). The text is manifestly corrupt, and the meter uneven, but the text is valuable for its caricature of the rigors of peasant labor. Beginning with a reminder that Mary's joy was not unrelated to the gentleness of her lord, the narrator announces that the story's purpose is to defend women from disrespectful men. The performance (by him or her) is addressed to a male audience ("Sirs"). Other items in the same manuscript include a "Life of St. Dorothy," "Assumptio sancte Marie," "Lyff of Seynt Anne," "Lyf of Seynt Katherin," "A Lamentation of Our Lady," and "A Prayar of Oure Lady."

### [Woman's Work]

***Ihesu that arte Jentyll, ffore joye off thy dam…***

Jesu that art gentle, for joy of thy dame,
As thou wrought this wild world, in Heaven is thy home,
Save all this company and shield them from shame,
That will listen to me and tend to this game.

God keep all women that to this town 'long,
Maidens, widows, and wivès among;
For much they are blamèd and sometime with wrong –
I take witness of all folk that heareth this song.

Listen, good sirs, both young and old,
By a good husband this tale shall be told;
He wedded a woman that was fair and bold,
And had good enow to wend as they would. 4

She was a good houswife, courteis and hend,
And he was an angry man, and soon would be tenned,
Chidin' and brawling, and fared like a fiènd,
As they that oft' will be wroth with their best friend. 5

---

[1] *shanks* ] lower legs; *mich* ] much; *As each ... curse* ] as if each knee were cursing the other; *pair chambes* ] pair of legs or buttocks; *thrift* ] luck.

[2] *wight* ] creature; *onès* ] once; *ren* ] run; *eyen* ] eyes; *y-chese* ] choose; *make* ] mate.

[3] *nails … quails* ] this puzzling witticism may perhaps imply, "I'll use my fingers to scratch your lousy flesh, not to serve you delicacies"; or it may suggest that the narrator is accustomed to scratching her own itching lice.

[4] *Bi* ] about a plowman (tenant farmer); *good* ] money.

[5] *courteis ... hende* ] courteous and handy/ready at hand; *tenned* ] irascible.

Till it befell upon a day (short tale to make),
The Goodman would to the plough, his horse 'gan he take;
He callèd forth his oxen, the white and the black,
And he said, "Dame, dight our dinner betime, for God's sake." [1]

The Goodman and his lad to the plough be gone
The Goodwife had much to do (and servant had she none):
Many small childern to keep beside herself alone,
She did more than she might, within her own wone. [2]

Home come the Goodman betime of the day,
To look that all thing were according to his pay,
"Dame," he said, "is our dinner dight?" "Sir," she said, "nay:
How would you have me do more than I may°?"

Then he began to chide and said, "Evil mot thou thea!
I would thou shoulds' all day go to plough with me,
To walk in the clots that be wet and mere,
Then shoulds' thou wit what it were a ploughman to be." [3]

Then swore the Goodwife, and thus 'gan she say,
"I have more to do than I do may;
An' ye should follow me fully on day,
Ye would be weary of your part, my head dare I lay."

"Weary! in the devil's name!" said the Goodman,
"What hast thou to do, but sits here at hame?
Thou goest to thy neighbor's house, by one and by one,
And sits there jangling with Jake and with Joan."

Then said the Goodwife, "Fare mot you fail!
I have more to do, whoso wist all;
When I lie in my bed, my sleep is but small,
Yet early in the morning ye will me up-call. [4]

When I lie all night waking with our child,
I rise up at morrow and find our house wild;
Then I milk our kine and turn them on the field.
While you sleep full still, also Christ me shield! [5]

Then make I butter, further on the day;
After make I cheese, - these, hold you a play?
Then will our children weep, and up must they,
Yet will you blame me for our good, an' any be away. [6]

When I have so done, yet there comès more e'en:
I give our chickens meat, or else they will be lean,
Our hens, our capons, and our ducks be-dene.
Yet, tend I to our goslings that goeth on the green. [7]

---

[1] *dinner* ] the midday meal (before returning to the fields).

[2] *wone* ] dwelling.

[3] *Evil ... thea* ] ill may you thrive; *mere* ] marshy, flooded.

[4] *Fare mot you fail* ] may you fare badly (be damned!); *who so wist all* ] if anyone really wants to know.

[5] *child* ] nursing infant (in addition to the others, l.51); *kine* ] milk-giving livestack (goats, dairy cows).

[6] *these ... play* ] you think those chores are fun?; *Yet you'll blame me if any goods goes missing.*

[7] *meat* ] food; *goslings...green* ] not just the poultry in the coup, but the goslings out on the green (common area).

I bake. I brew. It will not else be well.
I beat and swingle flax, as ever have I hele.
I heckle the tow. I kave, and I cool.
I tease wool, and card it, and spin it on the wheel." 1

"Dame," said the Goodman, "The Devil have thy bones!
Thou needst not bake nor brew in fortnight past once;
I say no good that thou dost within this wide wones,
But ever thou excusest thee with grunts and groans." 2

"Given, a piece of linen and woolen I make once a year,
For to clothe ourself and our children in-fere;
Else we should go to the market, and *buy* it, full dear.
I am as busy as I may, in every [year°]. 3

When I have so done, I look on the sun,
I ordain meat for our beasts again' that you come home,
And meat for ourself again' it be noon,
Yet I have not a fair word, when that I have done. 4

So I look to our good, without and within,
That there be none away – noder more nor min,
Glad to please you, to pay (lest any bate begin!)
And for to chide thus with me? I fight, *you* be in sin." 5

Then said the Goodman (in a sorry time),
"All this would a *good* housewife do, long ere it were prime;
And seeing the good that we have, is half-deal thine,
Thou shalt *labor* for thy part as I do for mine! 6

Therefore, Dame, make thee ready, I warn thee, anon –
Tomorrow, with my lad, to the plough thou shalt goen;
And I will be housewife and keep our house at home,
And take my ease as thou hast done, by God and Saint John!"

"I grant!" quod the Goodwife. "As I understand,
Tomorrow, in the morning, I will be walken'd:
Yet will I rise (while ye be sleepend),
And see that all thing be ready-led to your hand." 7

So it passed all to-th'morrow, that it was daylight.
The Goodwife thought on her deed, and up she rose right:
"Dame," said the Goodman, "I swear, by God's might,
I will fet home our beasts, and help that thee were dight." 8

The Goodman to the field hied him, full yern;
The Goodwife made butter (her deeds were full dern),
She took again' the butter-milk and put it in the chern,
And said, "Yet, of one *pint* our sire shall be to learn." 9

---

1 *beat .. swingle* ] pound and scrape (flax was grown by peasants, in their gardens); *hele* ] health; *heckle the tow* ] comb the raw fiber; *kave and kool* ] heat and cool the pot, in making linen from flax.

2 *needst ... once* ] need bake bread and brew beer no more than once every two weeks; wide wonès ] big house.

3 *in-fere* ] (cloth for all of us) together.

4 *the sun* ] i.e., I do all that before the sun comes up.

5 *none ... more nor min* ] nothing overlooked, neither great or small.

6 *sorry time* ] unpleasantly; *before prime* ] before high noon.

7 *walken'd* ] exhausted (yet I'll still need to rise and get everything ready for you).

8 *help ... with what you need to do.*

9 *hied him full yern* ] went quickly; *dern* ] secret (because he won't get it done); *to learn* ] *pint, for him to learn from.*

Home come the Goodman, and took good keep
How the wife had laid her flesh for to steep.
She said, "Sir, all this day ye need not to sleep,
Keep well our childern and let them not weep. [1]

If you go to the kiln, malt for to make,
Put small fire underneath, sir, for God'ès sake;
The kiln is low and dry: good tend, that ye take,
For an' it fasten on a fire, it will be evil to blake. [2]

Here sit two geese abroad. Keep them well from woe,
And they may come to good, that well wax sorrow enow."
"Dame," said the Goodman, "Hie thee to the plough!
Teach me no more housewifery, for I can enow." [3]

Forth went the Goodwife, curteis and hend,
She called to her lad, and to the plough they wend;
They were busy all day, a fitt here I find,
An' I had drunk once, ye shall hear the best, behind. [4]

The sequel relating how the Goodwife and Goodman fared at their cross-gendered labors is not extant. Insofar as the continuation employed familiar satirical conventions, one may speculate that the husband was a failure at the hearth, kiln, spindle, and churn; and that the wife and ploughboy completed their field-labors, with time to spare for a refreshing roll in the hay before Goodwife returned home for the Goodman's ill-made dinner.

"Jamie" (if written by a woman and not by Jamie himself, in modest self-mockery) signals the impatience of a maiden who perceived a discrepancy between the idealized courtly lover and the uncouth men of her own experience. The speaker, having surveyed the field, has lowered the bar. She names three criteria for the male suitor, without expecting a perfect score, of any man. Jamie, to the speaker's mind, scores 0 for 3:

### [**Jamie**:] ***He that will be a lover…***

*He that wil be a louer in euery wise,*
*He muste haue thre thingis whiche Ieame lackith:*
*The first is goodlyhede, at poynt deuise.*
*The secunde is manere, which manhoode makith;*
*The thryd is goode, þat no woman hatith.*
*Marke wel this þat louers wil be*
*Muste nedys haue oone of thes thre.*

He that will be a lover in every wise,
He must have three things, which Jamie lacketh:
The first is goodlyhead, at point devise.
The second is manner, which manhood maketh;
The thrid is good, that no woman hateth.
Mark well this: that lovers will be
Must needès have *oon* of these three. [5]

• • •

---

[1] *good keep* ] close attention; *flesh to steep* ] soak the salted meat.

[2] *fasten ... blake* ] catching fire, it will be burnt black.

[3] so they thrive, though they easily come to grief; *can enow* ] know enough already.

[4] *fitt* ] another canto; *drunk once* ] first, some ale; *behind* ] you'll hear the best part, after my beer.

[5] *goodlyhead, at point devise* ] handsome, from head to toe, and meticulously dressed; *manner* ] mannerliness, elegant manners; *good* ] money.

Birth of John the Baptist (detail) 1486-90, by Domenico Ghirlandaio (Cappella Tornabuoni, Santa Maria Novella)

Birth of the Virgin (unattrib., c. 1470) Alte Pinakothek (Munich)

# Vernacular Trotulas

*I wyl wright of women prevy sekenes the helpyng; and that oon woman may helpe another in her sykeness & nought diskuren her previtees to such vncurteys men.*
– MS Sloane 2463, fol. 194

TROTA of Salerno, a medical practitioner of the latter twelfth century, was the most famous of Italy's female physicians during that brief window when women in northern Italy were not simply tolerated, but respected for their special expertise, and licensed.[1] The *mulieres Salernis*, Trota in particular, had knowledge of birthing, feminine ailments, herbal remedies, abortifacients, and female anatomy; information that male physicians and scholars of the early Renaissance lacked, but coveted.

Trota's expertise was hard won and a long time coming. The Church quite literally blamed woman for all of the world's ills, and endorsed the miseries of childbirth as penance for the daughters of Eve. Both Church and State resisted any effort to ease the pains of childbirth or even to safeguard the mother's health. Hippocrates in the fourth century BCE advised Greek midwives to use boiled milk for a lavage, and boiled rainwater for the washing of hands – counsel that was discounted in the Christian era, running up against Jesus' statements in the New Testament that the washing of hands, even before eating, was a Pharisaical nicety not practiced by his disciples; as a result of which, hundreds of thousands of women, Gentiles especially, died from puerperal infections after giving birth to healthy babies.

Under Church canon law, a girl reached the legal age of consent to marry (under her father's authority) at age 7. Her husband, many years older, was entitled to consummate the marriage when his betrothed reached age 12. Thousands of child-brides therefore died in their first childbirth; or had their undeveloped bodies ruined for life by obstetric fistula (a wealthy few being confined to separate living quarters; the rest being turned out of doors to beg, abandoned by their husbands, eschewed by their community as social pariahs, and receiving notice in literature only in sick jokes, as in *The Tempest,* where Gonzalo remarks that his sinking ship is "leakier than an unstanch'd wench").

Mortality rates for both mother and child were so high throughout the middle ages, it's a wonder that any woman ever had the courage to become pregnant.

The most distinguished of ancient writers on obstetrics, having the unfortunate name of Soranus, practiced in Alexandria, later in Rome, in the early second century. His four-volume *Gynecology* (in Greek) contained counsel on such matters as prenatal care, delivery technique, and pediatrics. But few midwives from the third century through the twelfth had access to *Gynecology* (first printed in 1838), or even to the sixth-century Latin translation by Moscio. From the era of Constantine to the Italian Renaissance, the art of obstetrics made no advances except in midwives' highly secretive herbal practice.

Forbidden by the Church to read and write, midwives transmitted their obstetric expertise orally, young women learning the mystery of midwifery by apprenticeship. Trota, the first literate practitioner known to history by name, was unique in combining the Italian academy's renewed interest in Soranus with centuries of traditional midwifery and herbal knowledge. But professional midwives (perhaps Trota herself) continued to guard their area of expertise from incursions by men. Throughout the middle ages and well into the modern ea, doctors, clergy, even husbands, were *personae non gratae* in the birthing chamber. Deliveries were performed by the midwife, assisted by interns, female kin, and neighbors. Surgeons and priests were called upon only when the baby could not be delivered without a Caesarian section (a procedure that saved the baby's life only sometimes, and the mother's, never). Surgery and last rites were then performed with the dying mother's belly exposed but her genitals discretely covered.

Trota of Salerno was never accorded the honor of "master" as stated in some later sources; but her mastery was universally acknowledged by the master physicians at a time when scholars knew very little about women's bodies. Thus developed one of the great ironies of Western medical history: "Trotulas" – gynecological treatises ascribed to Trota (which survive in nearly 100 manuscripts) became the most widely disseminated medical texts in an era when women throughout Europe were being harassed and sometimes killed for practicing any medicine *except* herbal abortion and obstetrics. Trota wrote none of the extant works ascribed to her – all surviving Trotulas were written and disseminated by men, and were

---

[1] See John F. Benton, "Trotula, Women's Problems, and the Professionalization of Medicine in the Middle Ages," *Bulletin of the History of Medicine* 59.1 (1985): 30-53.

addressed overwhelmingly to male scholars and physicians.[1] "Trotula" became a household word because Trota's name lent to any late-medieval gynecological treatise the promised thrill of secret knowledge.

One distinctive feature of the many Trotulas that survive from England and the Netherlands is their mission of coeducation: many are expressly addressed to both men and women, or even to women alone. Traces of anxiety remain, as when *Woman's Privy Sickness* (MS Sloan 2463) shifts from English to Latin for sensitive material, as when the male scribe reports how to prevent an unwelcome erection (a secret recipe intended for the respite of celibate clerics, not for tired housewives). It's clear both from internal and external evidence that Trotulas were in great demand throughout the late Middle Ages, in Britain as elsewhere. As early as the mid-1200s, Anglo-Norman Trotulas circulated in England (in translation from such Latin precursors as Roger Frugard's *Chirurgia*); at least three of which expressly offer to inform women while screening their private needs from male scrutiny. Of the many English Trotulas preserved in research libraries, a few are pocket-sized, having been prepared not for a library but for ready reference; and those exemplars are well-worn.

In the meantime, professionalization of medicine in the twelfth and thirteenth centuries led to the exclusion of women from the medical profession. That movement reached Britain by 1422, when English physicians petitioned Parliament to bar from medical practice anyone who lacked a university education, on pain of imprisonment and a £40 fine – their petition being aimed expressly and chiefly at women practitioners (childbirth alone being exempted, since midwifery was not properly "medicine"). More extreme measures of suppression included the killing of midwives for alleged infanticide and witchcraft.

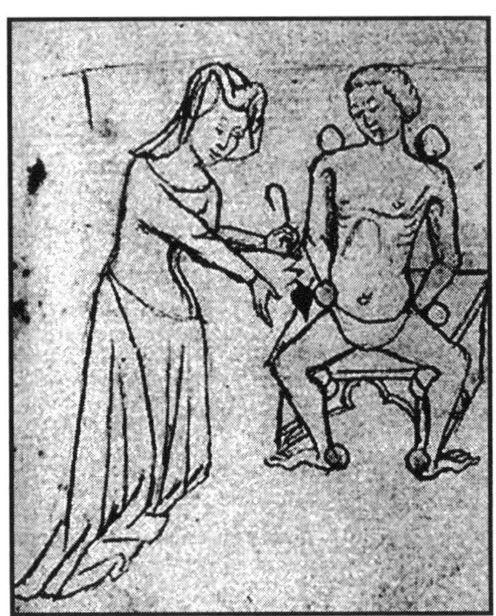

Woman medical practitioner drawing blood from a male patient (c. 1400-25)

Men now controlled both the practice and discourse of women's medicine, producing gynecological literature that incorporated classical learning, some physicians' experience, bits of women's lore, and a poor understanding of the female body. But women still controlled the lying-in, the birthing-chamber, and much secret information. Obstetrics thereby became a site of chronic, often bitter, gender-conflict. Scholars blamed high mortality rates on the incompetence of women in their conduct of a necessary service from which male physicians were excluded.

In 1522, a Dr. Wertt of Hamburg cross-dressed as a woman in order to observe childbirth and then record what he learned of the mystery of midwifery. Caught in the act, Wertt for his voyeuristic research was arrested and burned at the stake. Not until the renowned surgeon, Ambroise Paré, in the mid-sixteenth century was any male physician allowed to venture below a woman's navel to assist with difficult births. A sea-change came in the latter seventeenth century with Louis XIV, who used male physicians to deliver the illegitimate children of his mistresses; under whose influence the man-midwife became a thinkable thought. In the eighteenth century, male *accouchers* finally got their foot in the door by assisting deliveries in poorhouses; but the intrusion was still resented, as when one Haymarket midwife, Elizabeth Nihell, famously denounced William Snellie (1697-1763) as "a great horse-godmother of a he-midwife." Man-midwives were not accepted by married women, or even by married men, until well into the eighteenth century. The medical profession did not give up easily. In Britain the Midwife Act of 1902 greatly limited the practice and autonomy of midwives; in the USA and Canada, midwifery all but disappeared for much of the twentieth century: women other than the birth mother were no longer welcome in the birthing room except to assist the male obstetrician as nurses and technical assistants.

DWF

[1] Before she died, Trota is believed to have left a written practica from which surviving extracts appear in a *Practica secundum Trotum* (Madrid), and in *De aegritudinum curatione* (Wrocław), both from the early thirteenth century; but Trota wrote none of the many works ascribed to her. Most (prior to Vesalius) derive principally from Soranus.

### *The Knowing of Woman's Kind in Childing*
North Midlands (c. 1390, ms. c. 1510)

#### [Prologue]

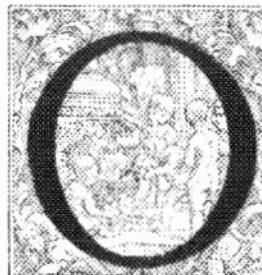

UR LORD GOD, when he stored the world of all creatures, he made man and woman and a reasonable creature, and bade 'hem wax and multiply and ordained that of 'hem two should come the third; and that of the man (that is made of hot and dry matter) should come the seed; and that the woman (that is made of cold matter and moist) should receive the seed; so that the temper of hot and cold, moist and dry, the child should be engend'red. Right as we seen trees, cornès, and herbès mou not grow without reasonable temper, of the four [humours°]. [1]

And forasmuch as women be'n more feeble and cold by nature than men be'n , and have great travail in childing, there fall often to 'hem moe divers sickness than to men; and namely, to the members that be'n-longing to gend'ring; wherefore in the worship of our lady and of all saints, I think to do mine intentive by signs, for to draw out of Latin, into English, divers causes of 'heir maladies; the signs that they shall know 'hem by, and the cures helping to 'hem; after the treatises° of divers masters that have translated 'hem out of Greek into Latin. And because women of our tongue do'en better read and understand this language than any other (and every woman, lettered, read hit to other, unlettered; and help 'hem and counsel 'hem in 'heir maladies withouten showing 'heir disease to man), I have this drawn and written in English. And if hit fall any man to read hit, I pray him and charge him in our Lady: behave that he read hit not in no despite ne slander of no woman, ne for no cause but for the heal and help of 'hem. [2]

Dreading that vengeance might fall to him as hit hath do' to other that have showèd her privities and slander of 'hem; understanding in certain that they have no other evils that now be alive than tho' women had that now be saints in Heaven.

Right as the Maker of all things ordained trees for to burgeon and flower and then afterward for to bear fruit, in the same manner he hath ordained to all women an espurgement, the which is called the flowres, withouten which may no child be engend'red ne conceived. For before that hit is comen, ne after hit is gone, may no woman conceive. For right as pollution by superhabundance of humors falleth to a man, so doth the flowres to a woman, as I shall tell you hereafter. [3]

From **Science of Cirurgie** (c. 1380),
Anon. trans., Lanfranco, of Milan (c.1250-1306),
*Chirurgia Magna* (1296)

**[Conception]**

I will tell the generation of embrion: that is to say, how a child is y-get in the moder-womb. Galen and Avicena tellen that of both the sperms of man and of woman, working and suff'ring togederes; so that each of 'hem work in other and suffer in other, embrion is beget.

But the working of man's kind is more mightier, and woman's kind more feebler. For right as the rundels of cheese hath by himself way of working, and the milk by way of suff'ring, so to the generation of embrion, man's sperm hath him by way of working, and woman's sperm by way of suff'ring.

And right as the rundels and the milk maken a cheese, so both the sperms of man and woman maken generation of embrion: though that all the small limbs of a child been y-geten of both two sperms, ne'theless, to clothe 'hem with flesh and with fatness, cometh to 'hem menstrue-blood.

The marice of woman hath an able complexioun to conceiven; and of her kind he casteth the sperms to the deepest place of her; and of her nature he closeth her mouth, that there might not enter the point of a needle; and then the formal vertue which almighty god hath geve to the marice ordaineth and divided every partie of these sperms in 'heir kind, till that the child be born. [4]

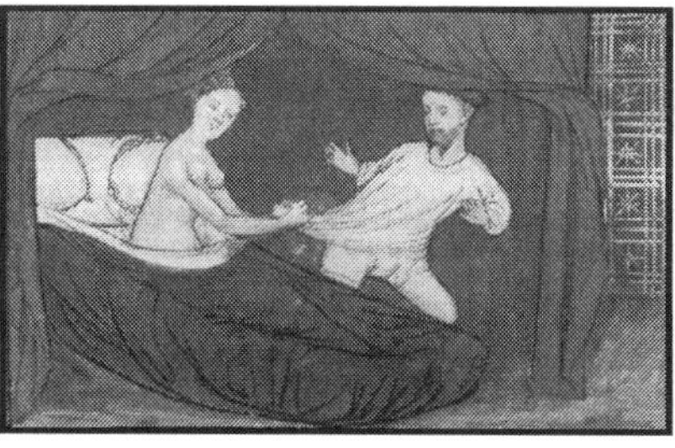

---

[1] *cornes* ] cereal grains; *humors* ] the four humors of Hippocratic medicne are blood (hot-wet), yellow bile (hot-dry), black bile (dry-cold), phlegm (cold-wet); an imbalance of which was thought to cause disorders; intellectual activity in women was said to be ill-suited to their supposed wet-and-damp constitution.

[2] *by signs* ] by noting the symptoms; *draw out of* ] translate; *divers masters* ] drawing partly on Muscio and Soranus ( the Greek medical writers of the early second century); *lettered ... unlettered* ] literate women may read the English text to illiterate others.

[3] *espurgement* ] purgation; *flowres* ] flows; menstruation.

[4] *marice* ] matrix, uterus; *complexion* ] in physiology, a combination of qualities; *mouth* ] (vaginal) opening.

Understond that the flesh and the fatness is made of menstrue-blood, the bones and gristles, ligaments and sinews, cords, arteries, veins, *pannicles* (that be'n small clothis); and the skin be'th engendred of both the sperms, as Avicen and other aucthorès tellen. [1]

If that any of the *limbs* that be'n engendred of the sperms be'n done away, he° moun never verilich be restored, for the matter of 'hem is the sperm of the fader *and* of the moder. But the flesh, the which matter is *blood*, that is alday engendred in us, may well and verilich be restored. [2]

These small limbs han divers forms, complexiouns, and helpings after the diversities of the proportions of the matter which that they be'n made of; for though that all the limbs be'n made of oon matter y-meddled, ne'theless in each of the small limbs there is a divers proportion of matter, for the which matter they taken divers forms and divers helpings. Almighty God giveth to each thing of his form after that his matter as° proportion deserveth....[3]

## [**Mammaries**]

Another manner flesh there is, that is *glandulous* (that is, as it were, *acorns*); and his juvament is that he turn *humiditès*, that is to say, *moistness*, to 'heir heat: the glandulous flesh of woman's breasts (the which that turneth the blood that is drawn from the marice, into milk); and the glandulous flesh of the ballocks (that turneth the blood into sperm); and the glandulous flesh of the cheeks (that engendreth spittle).... [4]

## [**Sexual anatomy**]

God almighty that all thingès knew to-fore the making of the world, other of man, He knew that a man should be made of moist substaunce, as of sperm, in which natural heat shall work. And for to receive the matter of sperm, it is necessary that a man have ballocks. He made ballocks as it was necessary, and gave 'em shape and complexion for to engender; and he gave a man great delight for to lie by a woman, so that a man should not have abhomination thereof, save a man shall do it with great will and with great love, so that generation might be multiplied with great delight.

Also, God almighty shop in man, a yard. And in the bigness thereof be'n cartilagineous and be'n made fast to the last bone of the ridgebone; and is made of nerves, veins and arteries, and is somewhat hollow, that he might be fulfilled with spirit. And in heed thereof is flesh that is feeling, and a skin that goeth over that skin; and of the flesh to-fore helpeth for to put out the sperm. The rising of a man's yard cometh of a man's heart, and wit of the brain, willing and great desire; and wat'ry humor cometh of the liver and hath two open holes. And through that oon hole goeth out urine (and cometh fro' the bladder); and thorough that other hole cometh sperm (and cometh fro' the ballocks). And these two holes be'n good for to know. [5]

And Avicen sayeth that there is the thrid hole; and through that hole passeth a manner of superfluity that a man feeleth not, as when he halseth a woman with his hands; save this thrid hole is not known of a chirurgeon. [6]

The marice in a woman is made nervous and is shape as it were a yard that were turned ayen her. And the neck of the marice is fleshy and brawny, and feeling, and gend'ring; and in the neck of the marice be'n veins that be'n to-broke when a woman loseth her maidenhood. And the bottom of the marice is shape as it were the case of a man's ballocks. [7]

And the marice hath two broad ballocks in the neck, and with the ilk two ballocks be'n made fast two vessels of sperm, and be'n more short than a man's vessels of sperm. And of these vessels, a woman's sperm goeth to the bottom of the marice. And in the time conceiving, the woman's sperm is meddled with a man's. And the marice of a woman hath within two great concavities. And the marice hath many veins, and thorough the ilk veins, when a woman hath conceived, cometh blood to the liver for to nourish the child. And when a woman is not with child, through the same veins cometh blood of the veins-menstrue, and is put out; and in this manner a woman is purged of superfluity of blood; and it is made fast betwixt the great gut and the bladder, and is higher than the bladder, and is made fast to the ridge with ligatures, and in time of childbearing the ligatures reacheth, and after that time [contract...°] [8]

---

[1] *pannicles – that been smalle cloths* ] membranes.

[2] *moun never verilich* ] may never truly; *alday* ] continually.

[3] *matter y-meddled* ] substance intermixed.

[4] *juvament* ] power to assist (of the glands).

[5] *shop* ] shaped, made; *yard* ] penis.

[6] *thrid* ] third; *superfluity* ] extra fluid (lubricant); *halseth* ] fondles; *known of* ] known to.

[7] *ayen* ] again, like a reverse penis.

[8] *broad ballocks* ] ovaries.

[**Breast cancer**]

God almighty made in a woman teats for the nourishing of a child.... In a woman's teats cometh many passions. For, as Egidius sayeth, that sometime there cometh thereto apostume of milk, and sometime ulcera. And commonly impostumes cometh of blood that is drawn° to the teats and may not turn into milk, or if a woman have too much blood and it cometh of feebleness of vertue (as it is aforesaid in the general chapter of impostumes). The cure of an hot impostume in the teats: first, thou shalt let her blood in *basilica*, or set a ventose upon her shoulders. [1]

And if the cause come of retention of menstrue, then thou shalt give her medicines for to bring out the menstrue; or thou shalt let her blood in the sophene, and anoint the place with oil of roses, and the fourth part of vinegar. And if this suffice not, then wet a linen cloth in the juice of solatre; and when thou has anointed the place with oil and vinegar, then lay this cloth thereupon. And look that all thingès that thou layest thereto be flash-hot. For there shall no cold thing be laid thereto, for the place is nervous, for cold thing would grieve it. [2]

If all these medicines sufficen not (save the matter beginneth to draw to quitture), then lay thereto maturatives. And if thou might not do it away with repercussives, ne with resolving thingès, and thou ne might not make it maturative, then it is dread lest the woman become in a passion that is clepèd "mania." Then her head mot be shave, and give her comfortive thingès for her head, and give her sotil dieting, and she shall drink no wine, ne eat no flesh; and thou must work full sotilly, for I saw a woman that had an impostume in her breast and come of blood; and so I taught her for to do as it is aforesaid. [3]

And tho there come a lewd cirurgeon and reproved me, and he laid thereupon maturatives: and the more that he laid thereupon maturatives, the more the matter waxèd great and the more burning; and the same cirurgeon would not hear my counsel. And the woman's friendès took more heed to the lewd cirurgeon than to me, and within three days mania come to her and was out of her wit, and so the frenzy fell on her; and this prognostication I said in the beginning, but they would not 'lieve my wordès. [4]

If it so be that it make quitture, then open it and do out the quitture, and then lay thereto a mundificative, and be well 'ware that thou put therein no great tent ne long, as many foolès doen; for a woman's teats be'n full of nerves, and if the nerves were pressèd with any tent, it would make great aching, and would lett the cure thereof. [5]

Also there be'n many fooli' leeches, when they finden in a woman's teat's flesh that is glandulous, then they ween that it be wicked flesh, and be'n therabout for to draw it out, and then they shendeth all the substance of the breast.

Thou shalt work wisely and thou shalt remove none hereof, for as it is aforesaid, *all* the flesh of the teats is glandulous ... and if it so be that the matter turn to hardness, and black or leady, then thou must beware that thou lay thereto no medicines that be'n too hot, for there may engender a cancre thereof full lightly. And if it be so , then thou thereabout, for to make it maturative, and do thou no cure thereto. And some men sayen that a woman may be curèd for to cut off all the breast, and that is all false.

From ***The Book of Rota* [i.e., Trota]** (c. 1550) [6]

[**Infertility**]

Another infirmity there is of the matrice of a woman, that is they may not conceive children as they would. And this may be sometime through the default of the man, and sometime it may be the default of the woman, and sometime through both. But to know in whether the fault is, take this medicine:

Take a little earthen pot (new) and put therein the man's urine and cast thereto an handful of bran and stir it fast with a stick about and take another new earthen pot and put therein the woman's urine and put bran thereto and stir it as the other. And let it stand so, nine days or ten. And look then, in whether pot that you find worms in, there is the default that is barren, be it the man or the woman: for the barren will be full of worms. The vessel that the barren urine is in will stink. And if neither vessel be with worms, than is neither of them barren. And then they may

---

[1] *apostume* ] abscess of purulent matter; *impostume* ] purulent swelling, or cyst; *basilica* ] basilic vein; *ventose* ] a cupping-glass that received the drawn blood.

[2] *sophene* ] small saphenous vein; *solatre* ] *flash-hot* ] lukewarm; *nervous* ] sensitive.

[3] *maturative* ] (n.) medicine promoting suppuration; *repercussive* ] an anti-inflammatory; *mot be shave* ] must be shaved; *sotill* ] soothing.

[4] *tho* ] then; Marginal note: *mea tamen prognosticatio multum exaltata extitit* (as I formerly very much prognosticated).

[5] *mundicative* ] mundificative, a cleansing medicine; *tent* ] probe; *lett* ] obstruct.

[6] *Rota* ] i.e., Trota.

be holpen with medicines; of the which, some I will speak of, to make a woman to conceive with child.

Take wool well-tossed and roast it well in ass-milk and bind it upon the woman's navel. And let hit lie so, till she have done with her husband for that journey, and she shall conceive.

Take the liver and the stones of a grise that a sow hath no moe of that litter but one; and dry that, and make it in powder, and give it to the woman to drink, and she shall conceive. And give a man the powder to drink and soon after he shall engender. (Some men say it is no force whether there be no moe of that farrow or no. [1]

And some men say it were good enough, if the stones of the grise were baken in a pie by 'em-selve, without any other flesh, and make a woman to eat of that pie; and the same night let it be known to her husband, and then company with him, and she shall conceive, as it hath been proved indeed.)

From **Woman's Privy Sickness** (c. 1525)[2]

[**Prologue**]

Forasmuch as there be'n many women that haven many divers maladies (and sicknesses nigh to the death); and because they also be'n shameful to showen and to tellen 'heir grievaunces unto any wight; therefore I shall somedeal write to 'heir maladies' remedy (praying to God full of grace to send me grace, truly to write to the pleasaunce of God, and to all women's helping). For charity asketh this: that every man should travail for helping of his brethren and his susteren, after the grace that he hath underfongen. [3]

And though women have divers evils and many great grievaunces (moe than all men knowen of), as I said, 'hem shamen, for dread of reprieving in times coming, and of discuring of uncourteis men who love women but for 'heir lusts and for 'heir foul liking. [4]

And if women be in dis-ease, such men have 'em in despite and think not how much dis-ease women have ere than they have brought 'em *into* this world. And therefore, in helping of women, I will write, of women's° privy sickness, the helping; and so° that one woman may help another in her sickness and not discuren her privities to such uncourteis men.

But nevertheless, whosoever he be that displeases a woman for her sickness (that she hath of the ordinaunce of God), he doth a great sin. For he despiseth not all-only 'em, but God that sendeth 'em such sickness, for her best. And therefore no man should despise other for the disease that God sendeth 'em, but to have compassion of 'em and relieven 'em yif he might.

[**Menstruation**]

Therefore, ye shall understond that women have less heat in 'heir bodies than men and more moisture (for default of heat that would dry 'heir moisture and 'heir humours); but ne'theless, of bleeding, to-make 'heir bodies clean and whole from sickness. And they have such purgations from the time of 12-winter age into the age of 50-winter. (But ne'theless, some women have it longer, such° as they that be'n high complexion, and be'eth nourished with hot meats and with hot drinks, and liven in much rest; and they have this purgation, in every month, once.) [5]

But it be women that be with child, or elles women that be of dry complexion, and travail much – for women after they be with child, or elles women that be of dry complexion foreto they be delivered – they ne' have this purgation; for the child in 'heir womb is nourissed with the blood that they should be purged of. And if they have purgation in this time, it is a token that the child refuseth that blood; and then, that child is fallen into some sickness, or it will die in his moder-womb. [6]

Women that be of an high complexion, and faren well and liven in much ease, haven this purgation ofter than once in a month. And this blood that passeth from women in time of her purgation cometh out of the veins that be'n in the marice that is cleped the *moder* and *nourisser* to the children right conceived in 'em. (The *moder* is a skin that the child is enclosed in his moder-womb. And many of the sicknesses that women haven comen of grievaunces of this moder that we clepen the "marice").[7]

---

[1] *stones of a grise* ] piglet's testicles; *i.e.* since a farrow of a single piglet is rare.

[2] MS once owned by Richard Ferris, Master of the Barbers' and Surgeons' Co. (in 1563) and Surgeon to Elizabeth I. Sold at his death for 48 s., fourpence.

[3] *wight* ] person; *susteren* ] sisters; *underfongen* ] received.

[4] They are ashamed, for fear of censure thereafter, and afraid to reveal their maladies to discourteous men who love women only to gratify foul lust.

[5] *hot meats ... much rest* ] rich foods, live in leisure.

[6] *with child* ] pregnant; *travail much* ] work hard (elsewhere, birth labor).

[7] *veins ... in 'em* ] veins in the uterus ("marice"), a membrane that is called the mother ("moder") and nourisher of the developing fetus.

## [Conception]

If [women] desire to conceive a male child, they must take a the marice of an hare, and the cunt, and dryen it ... and powd'ren it, and drink the powder thereof with wine. And if the woman desire a female child, let her dry the stones of an hare and (in the end of her flowres) make powder thereof and drink thereof to bedwards, then go play with her make.

## [Abortifacient herbs]

*If thou wilt know well and truly whether a woman be with child, other none* (*without looking of water*): If a woman be with child, take her to drink mead when she shall wend to bed; and if she shall have much woe in her womb, it is a sign that she is with child. Also, if the *trociscis* of myrrh – as Rhazes sayeth, with water that juniper be'n sodden in – and after that they be'n y-drunk (if she be with retention of her floures), then is right great sorrow following. [1]

And also, they cast out a dead child. And the cause, is for the *trociscis* maken sotill and viscous matter. Also, they open and they betten-out the marice. And also, they strengthen the virtue expulsive. And therefore they be'n good.[2]

Also, the things that shall casten out a dead child from the marice, they must be mightier than tho' that helpen to have easy birth. The things that helpen to have forth a dead child fro' the marice be'n three things:

The first is *galbanum*, two drachms (resolved in goat's milk, so° that the woman may easily usen a-two ounces of the milk, other three). The second is to make a suppository, thus. Rx: *ollis negri, stavesacre, aristolochia rotunda, bothon,*° *morien, granorum lauriole, pupe coloquintide, gummi armoniaci* (two drachms *ana*); and° *fel bovis* (one drachm). Make powder (save of *gummi aromatici*). Resolve it in juice *artemisia*; with the which, meddle all the other powders, and make a suppository (or else, with more of *fel bovis* and of the juice of *artemisia*). Make a pessary with a little oil. [3]

Also, a plaster that casteth out a dead child fro' the marice (one thereof), is this: Take galbanum (*li. sem.*); and temper it with the juice of mugweed; and lay it on a leather, in quantity of a palm and two fingers more in length; in breadth, of a little palm. And lay it under the navel, toward the privy member. [4]

Another: Take the juice of *rue* (*li. sem.*); *myrrh*, powdered (four drachms); powder of *coloquintide* (three drachms). And incorpore 'em togeder, in a nesh manner. Make a plaster and warm-lay it to-under the navel, on the womb. [5]

... And about that time of the moon that they shall have her purgation, if they have none, have 'em bleed a good quantity of blood at her great toe; and another day, at her other great toe. And everich week (once), let her usen to be'n y-bathed in such herbs as I spake of, rather; and she may be holpen, though her sickness have dured her long time.... yeve her this medicine – to make the matter that grieveth her the more able to pass

[1] *looking of water* ] a urine examination; *trociscis* ] (early 15th C.) pills (of myrrh), here drunk with juniper boiled (sodden) in water; *Rhazes* ] (*rā'*-zēz) Persian physician (c. 865-925), physician a free-thinking philosopher of Islam. He was chief physician at the Baghdad hospital; *if she be with retention of his floures* ] if she keeps from vomiting the seed-powder; *sorrow* ] discomfort, nausea.

[2] *they cast out* ] pills of myrrh will expel a fetus, if it's dead; *sotill* ] subtle (14th-15th C.), i.e., thin, runny; *sotill and viscous* ] the myrrh disrupts the woman's fluids (stimulates the uterus) and causes a miscarriage; *betten-out* ] relieve; *virtue expulsive* ] abortifacient power; *been good* ] are effective.

[3] *drachm* ] in the apothecary system of measurement, 1/8 fluid ounce; *other* ] or else; *resolved* ] dissolved in goat's milk to make the galbanum easier to swallow and hold down; *Rx* ] black olive oil, stavesacre, round birthwort [MS *bothor,* i.e., *bothon*], rosemary, marjoram, seeds of laurel, rosemary, marjoram, the *seeds of laurel*, the pulp of *colocynth*, and *gum ammoniac*, two drachms each (*ana.*); and one drachm of bull's gall; *save of* ] except for; *pessary* ] a device inserted to deliver medication.

[4] *li. sem.* ] half-pound; *mugweed* ] (mugwort) artemisia.

[5] *coloquintide* ] colocynth; *in a nesh manner* ] gently; dozens of abortifacient recipes survive from the medieval period, some of which were ineffective, others of which could cause hemorrhage and death.

lightly away from her.... [1]

And after that, let stew her and bathen her with such herbs as I said, rather; and after that this is sodden, let her drink a draught of wine and *savin*, other *mugwood*, other *madder* is sodden in; and meddle that wine with water that *polypody* is sodden in. And if they still° have no purgation, let 'em bleed a good quantity of blood (as I said afore). [2]

Suppositories be'n covenable medicines for these sicknesses. And they shall be put in woman's privy members as men putteth suppositories into a man's fundament for to purgen his womb. (But these suppositories that be'n ordained for women should be bound with a thread abouten one of her thighs, lest they were drawn° all into the moder.) And it is profitable to usen such suppositories a'four days, other a'five, before that time of the month that they shall have her purgation; and they mou the lightlier be'n y-purged.... Yif her womb be sore of such suppositories, let anoint within, with oil of roses or of violet, or with meat oil, or with fresh butter that is not salted. [3]

Other medicines there be'n, the which if a woman drink 'hem, they will make her to have a purgation; other, deliver of a dead child if there by any within her: as *balm-precious,* y-drunk; and the juice of *hyssop*; other, of *diptany;* and of leek; and of *tounkers*, the seed of tounkers y-powdered and y-drunken. [4]

But if this sickness come of anger, other of sorrow, let make her merry and yeve her comfortable meats and drinks, and let usen her to bathen her otherwhiles. And if it be of much fasting other of much waking, let diet her much with good meats and drinks that mou make her to have good blood, and let her make her merry and glad, and leaven the heaviness of her heavy thoughts.

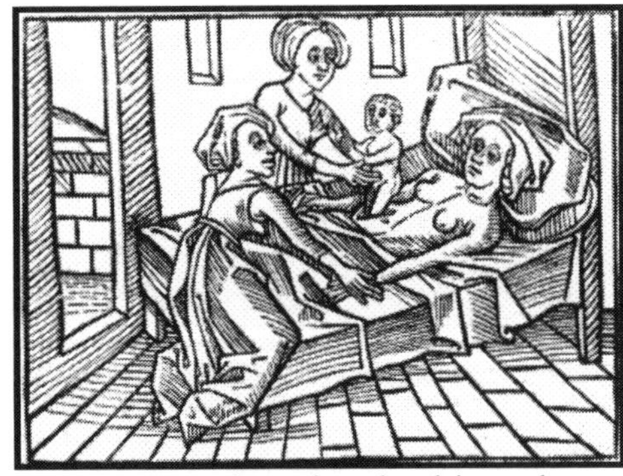

Caesarean section performed on dying mother
fr. *Seelenwurzgarten* (Augsburg, 1496)

### [Difficulty in childbirth]

*The tenth chapter is of the grievaunces that women have in bearing of 'heir children*: Grievaunces that women have in bearing of 'heir children cometh in two manners; that is to say, kindly and unkindly. When it is kindelich, the child cometh forth within a-twenty throws or within tho' twenty; and the child cometh in form as it should: first, the heved, and sithen the neck, and with the arms and shoulders and with his other members formably, as it should. [5]

And also in the second manner, the child cometh forth unkindly. ... For to deliveren a woman of a child and for to slay it if it may not be brought forth: take *rue*, *savin*, *southernwood*, and *gladon*, and let her drink it. And also, take the juice of *hyssop*, of *diptany* (*ana.* two drachms), *quicksilver* (two scruples) – and this medicine is proved. Also, take the juice of *iris* and *bull's gall* (*ana.* four drachms), of mete oil. Meddle all these togeders, and do it in a pessary, and serve the woman therewith, and this medicine will deliveren all corruptions of the marice. And it will delivereth her of a dead child, and it will deliver her of her secundines, and it bringeth forth his menstruis....[6]

[T]he root of iris, under-put into the marice (other sub-fumiga'ed with iris) maketh her to lesen lose her child. For iris roots be'n hot and dry, and have virtue to open, and to heat, and to

---

[1] *have 'em bleed* ] Bloodletting, from alternate legs (the use of irritant leaves, fasting, bloodletting, and moist heat on the abdomen, among the techniques described here, are recorded in Europe as early as 300 BCE, and were practiced throughout the Christian era; *rather* ] earlier (again below).

[2] *sodden* ] boiled; *savin* ] Juniperus sabina; *mugwood* ] mugweed (mugwort), or artemisia; *madder* ] madder root; *polypody* ] polypodium (a fern).

[3] *womb* ] belly (male or female); *they mou the lightlier been y-purged* ] women may thus be more easily purged; *mete oil* ] vegetable oil (15th century).

[4] *diptany* ] dittany, a restorative herb; *tounkers* ] nasturtiums.

[5] *kindly and unkindly* ] natural (head first) and unnatural (fetus in wrong position; hemorrhages, etc. The MS supplies a detailed account of how to cope with sixteen difficult deliveries, including twins; *kindelich* ] (c. 1400) natural, uncomplicated; *within a-twenty throws* ] during the first 20 contractions; *first, the heved* ] head-first.

[6] *gladon* ] stinking *Gladon*, a kind of flower-de-luce, so-called for its smell; *quicksilver* ] mercury (toxic); *his* ] its.

consume and waste. For when the woman is feeble and the child may not comen out, then it is better that the child be slain than that the mother of the child also die. And also, forth brings out the dead child marvelously, and the secundine and menstrua with it.... [1]

### [**The Ache of Loss**]

Ache of the moder cometh otherwhile of a dead-bore child that is bore rather than his time. Wherefore the moder hath a great liking and a comfort of the child that is within her; and when she leseth it, she maketh a kendelich mourning and sorrowing right as a cow doth when she hath lost her calf. And that sorrowing is ache of the moder.

### [**Obstetric fistula**]

Divers times it happeth of divers women a mischievous grievaunce in travailing of child, for defaut of good midwives, and that grievaunce keepen privy and it needeth for to be holpen. To some women happeth this grievaunce, that the peritoneon breaketh, that there is but one issue for both voidaunces. [2]

And of these women oft-times cometh out the marice, for the way is made so large in her travailing and so the marice waxeth hard and will not be set ayain in her own place but if it be holpen by medicine. And the health must be in this manner: Take good white wine and make it hot, and put butter in that wine that be fresh and not salt, and with wine softly moist the marice oft-times till it wax supple and soft and then easilich put it into the member there it should be.[3]

And after that, sew the breach of the peritoneon in three places or four with a double silken thread. Then put a linen clout into the member (after the quantity of the member), viz., vulva. And after that, line it above with hot tar; and that shall make the marice withdraw; and so, sit fast for the stinking of the tar.[4]

And then, shall the breach be healed and y-closed with powder of *comfrey*, and of *petit consew*, and of *canel*. And place the patient in her bed upright, so that her feet lie higher than her head; and let her lyen so, nine days. And so, without remeving fro' thence, do her needs. And make her eat liquid meats, measurablich, in that season, and drink also.[5]

And after nine days be'n passed, make her arise and measurablich let her keep herself fro' travail or busyness. And she mote keep her from baths, and fro' all meats that be'n evil to defyen, and fro' heavy meats, and fro' such meats as will engender the cough. Also, it is for to wit that there must be put into the arsehole a linen towel made of a linen clout to stop that the egestion go not out but when time of voidaunce be'n in the nine days foresaid.[6]

### [**Uterine prolapse**]

There be also other women in the which, oft-times her marice will come down (and sometime arise) for some cause; and it be'n such women, that mou not suffer a man's yard for the greatness thereof, and sometime they be constrained to suffer, will they, nil they. [7]

To such women we put the medicine foresaid, of the linen clout with the tar. And if we have no tar, we take a linen clout and moisten it with *oleo* (hot, of *puliol*) or *mousseline*; and we put it into the member, viz., the vulva, and we bind it there until the marice be settled. And the women be forbade meats that should make 'hem to cough, and drink also. [8]

Also it is to wit that the coming-out of the marice, in an old woman, is incurable; and also, in a young woman if it come out with much blood and so have be long time during.

---

[1] *fumiga'ed* ] fumigated, steamed; *lesen* ] lose; *secundine* ] the afterbirth, placenta and membranes; the MS follows with additional prescriptions.

[2] *one issue for both voidaunces* ] one orifice for the leakage of both menstrual blood and excrement (fistula today affects some two million women, chiefly child brides and poor women without access to Caesarean section; many of whom are abandoned by their husbands and despised like lepers).

[3] *oft-times ... medicine* ] Sometimes the rupture is made worse by a prolapsed or expelled uterus, which must be reinserted, and the patient stitched up.

[4] *linen clout* ] insert a linen rag into the vagina, as much as can be accommodated.

[5] *comfrey* ] healing ointment; *petit consew* ] *bellis minor*, or little daisy; *canel* ] cinnamon; *meats* ] foods; *measurablich* ] (14th c.) in moderation; a rare form that appears also in Lanfrank's *Science of Cirurgie* (c. 1380), p. 85.

[6] *mote keep her fro'* ] must avoid; *been evil to defyen* ] are hard to digest; *wit that* ] know that; *egestion* ] discharge.

[7] Due to uterine prolapse, such women cannot endure a man's penis (*yard*) because of the size of it, and sometimes they are forced to endure conjugal sex whether they would or not.

[8] *oleo ... mousseline* ] hot oil of wild thyme or musk.

But that that hath not long time dured, may be holpen thus: at the beginning we must moist the marice with the water that *mallows* and the *holly-hock* was sodden in. And after that we anoint the membra, viz. vulva, with *aragon*; and the share also. [1]

From ***Liber Trotuli*** (c. 1525)

**[Non-surgical treatment for fistula]**

Now it is to touch of some women that han their privy member so large and so evil-smelling, wherethrough their husbands forsaken 'em because of largeness and by the wicked smell, ne han no will to come near 'em.

For this vice of the woman, do make a water strictive that will make come togeder in this manner: Take the bark of the *pomegarnate* (and the galls *and* the bark of 'em), and the branches of *lentisci* and the leaves of *five-leaf* and the roots of the two *consounds* (the more and the less); and the leaves of the *lorer* and of the *rosemarin*. And seethe all these in rainy-water or in *aqua rosacea*, in which water do boil *mastik* and *frankincense*, *galbanum*, *sagapium* (that be'n gums), and *gumma arabica,* and parchmen' of a calf. And when these be'n well y-soth, do strain these and do to the leaves of the *lorer* and of *rosen*, that it smell sote. [2]

If that thou will so wash 'em with this water, have it ready and make 'hem, when that they go'th to bed with man, do 'em wash their instrument with this same water with their fingers within with wool y-wet in this water; and also wash well without, for it cleanseth and maketh swote the humors, both within and without. And then do 'hem dry with a linen cloth y-put within, and also do dry without, and then she may stride and let pass the moisture within, beneath. And then another time: do her put in, and dry it with a dry linen clout. [3]

And when that she will go sleep with any man, do her take these powders y-made of *dry roses*, of *cloves* and of *nutmegs*, of *galingale* and of the leaves of the *lorer*; and of this powder do take a little portion betwix' thine honds; and do frote the breast, and the teaten, and the privy member, and other that 'longeth thereto; and then do wash the face with *aqua rosacea*; and then do touch the man; and at she do frote her under the arm-holes and in other places where she see that it be do'. [4]

**[Other remedies]**

A powder y-proved for staunching of the blood at the nose and of the privy flowres: Take *saunk-de-dragoun* and *bolum armenicum* and *canel* and the rind of the *pomegarnet*, of *alum* and *mastik* of galls (*ana*, ounces two); and make powder of all these other (*ana*), and do 'em in a little water y-chafèd, and do this togeder; and sithen put in the hole that go'th to the marice. [5]

For to maken strait the privy member: Take a stone that is y-cleped "omahistos," and *gallas* and *bolum armenicum* and *saunk-de-dragoun,* and stamp 'em wonder-small, that they may be sourced through a linen clout, and temper then these powders with the juice of *plantain,* and then to dry it at soon, and then take a little of this power with the juice foresaid and do it in b a tent, and do make the woman somedeal lig wide-open, stretching out the legs (and this powder is good for woman that hath han part of man and would be held for a maiden. [6]

• • •

[1] *share* ] the pubic region (*OED* n.2).

[2] *water strictive* ] astringent liquid; *lentisci* ] mastic tree; *five-leaf* ] quintfoil; *consounds* ] the daisy (lesser) and comfrey (greater); *lorer* ] laurel; *rosemarin* ] rosemary; *aqua rosacea* ] rose-water; *galbanum* ] a gum resin; *sagpium* ] a gum resin, juice of *Ferula persica*; *gumma arabica* ] from a species of acacia; *parchmen'* ] skin; *y-soth* ] boiled, seethed; *sote* ] sweet.

[3] *stride* ] walk around; *pass* ] drain; *clout* ] cloth.

[4] *frote* ] rub; *arm-holes* ] armpits.

[5] *saunk-de-dragon* ] san-dragoun, red juice of the *Dacaena Draco*; *bolum armenicum* ] red earth (Armenian bole) *canel* ] cinnamon; *ana* ] of each; *y-chafed* ] warmed up; *do* ] mix; *sithen* ] then

[6] *maken strait* ] make tight.

# Dame Julian Barnes (fl. 1486)

*Say, chylde, where ye goo:*
*Yowre dame taght you so.*
– from *her Boke of Huntyng* (209–10)

ULIAN BARNES is reputed to be the first woman poet published in the British Isles. Her "boke of huntyng" appeared in the so-called "Book of Saint Albans," printed without title or title-page by an anonymous schoolmaster of St. Albans (Hertfordshire) in 1486, when movable type was still a novelty in Britain.[1] *The Book of Saint Albans* is of principal interest not as a text of female authorship, but as England's first printed elementary education textbook for the sons of nobility. A table of content for the original edition seems never to have been printed, until now (re-edited here from the original spelling):

| | |
|---|---|
| Book of Hawking | sigs. A2$^{r}$-D4$^{r}$ |
| Book of Hunting (verse) | sigs. D5$^{r}$-F4$^{r}$ |
| Beasts of the Chase: of the Sweet Feute and Stinking [2] | sig. F4$^{v}$ |
| The Names of Divers Manner Hounds | sig. F4$^{v}$ |
| The Properties of a Good Greyhound | sig. F4$^{v}$ |
| The Properties of a Good Horse | sig. F5$^{r}$ |
| [Moral axioms and proverbs, partly in verse] | sig. F5$^{r-v}$ |
| The Companies of Beasts and Fouls | sig. F6$^{r}$-7$^{r}$ |
| Of Breaking or Dressing of Divers Beasts and Fouls | sig. F7$^{v}$ |
| All the Shires and the Bishoprics of the Realm of England | sig. F8$^{r}$ |
| The Book of Cote Armours | sigs. Aa1$^{r}$-Bb5$^{v}$ |
| The Blasing of Arms | sigs. Cc1$^{r}$-Gg2$^{r}$ |

Of some interest for gender studies is the fifteenth-century curriculum appearing on sig. F5:

> A good horse should have fifteen properties and conditions. That is, to wit: three of a man, three of a woman, three of a fox, three of an hare, and three of an ass:
> Of a man: bold, proud, and hardy.
> Of a woman: fair breasted, fair of hair, and easy to lip upon.
> Of a fox: a fair tail, short ears, with a good trot.
> Of an hare: a great eye, a dry head, and well-running.
> Of an ass: a big chin, a flat leg, and a good hoof.
> (Well-traveled women nor well traveled horse were never good.)

On the last page is the 1486 equivalent of a jacket-blurb: "Here in this book afore are containèd the books of Hawking and Hunting, with other pleasures divers, as in the book appears; and also "Of Cote Armours," a noble work. And here now endeth the "Book of Blasing of Arms," translated and compilèd togeder at Saint Albans, the year from the Incarnation of our Lord Jesu Christ 1486."

In the original quarto, only one of these texts is ascribed to Julian: part 2 is introduced as a discourse on "the manere of huntynge for all manere of bestys." The text is constructed as a lesson taught by a "dame" to her children or students, and concludes:

**Explicit Dam Iulyans**
**Barns in her boke of huntyng.** (sig. F4r)

In the generations that followed, the Book of St. Albans was reprinted and augmented many times, under various titles. But Julian's "Book of Hunting" remained a central feature of every edition. In Wynkyn de Worde's 1496 reprint, the attributional note reads "Explicit [here ends] dame Iulyans Bernes doctryne in her boke of huntynge (sig. E2v). This second edition features three woodcuts, plus a "Treatyse of fysshynge wyth an Angle." (The treatise on angling was later ascribed to Dame Julian, together with everything else between the covers, except for those three woodcuts.)

---

[1] 1486 ed. untitled; known also as *The Book of Hawking, Hunting, and Blasing of Arms* (Wynken de Worde, 1496).

[2] *feute* ] the traces or track of an animal (from Old French *fuite*).

The remainder of Julian's biography has been filled in by imaginative and often mistaken historiography, after the manner of a saint's legend:

1. Julian was a nun. (Women upon taking vows in a holy order typically renamed themselves after saints, most of whom were men; *videlicet,* "Julian" of Norwich);

2. She was a prioress ("*Dame* Julian").

3. She was bound to the priory of Sopwell (founded in 1140 as a cell out of the Abbey of St. Alban's, where her book was first printed).

4. Dame Julian was prioress of Sopwell sometime between 1430 and 1480 (prioresses earlier than 1430, and from 1480-86, have been accounted for; but there is a gap in the records of Sopwell Priory for the critical period, 1430-1480).

5. Her original Christian name may have been "Juliana." Her surname was *Barnes* or *Bernes*.

Or rather, *Berners*. In Thomas Hearne's 1732 edition, the original contributor's note of 1486 is augmented by William Burton, who sums up past scholarship, adding fresh details:

> This Booke was made by the Lady Julian Berners, daughter of S$^{r}$ James Berners, of Berners Roding, in Essex, Knight, & Sister to Richard Lord Berners. She was Lady Prioress of Sopwell, a Nunnery neere St. Abons, in w$^{ch}$ Abby of S$^{t}$. Albons this was first printed 1486, 2 H[enry] 7. She was living 1460, 39 H[enry] 6, according to John Bale, *Centur.* 8, fol. 611.

In 1733, Thomas Rawlins reports to fellow scholar George Ballard that our author was "a Religious Sportswoman" whose *Boke of Huntyng* was actually her second publication, the first having appeared in 1481: Dame Barnes, he writes, was "a Gentlewoman of excellent Gifts, who wrote…also a *Book of y$^{e}$ Law of Arms and Knowledge*, appertaining to Heraldry in K$^{g}$ Edw$^{d}$ 4$^{th's}$ time; y$^{e}$ first of these Books was intituled *the Gentleman's Recreation*, or *Book of St. Albans*, so called because it was printed in y$^{t}$ Town, a thin Fol[io], in 1481…and in y$^{e}$ *Treatise of Hunting* she proposed for her model y$^{e}$ worthy Prince, y$^{e}$ Duke of York (Son of K[ing. Edw$^{d}$. 4$^{th}$), late called Mayster of Game, who hath described y$^{e}$ Mirths of Hunting."[1]

When Joseph Haselwood in 1811 issued a facsimile of the 1496 Winken de Worde text, he was able in his editorial introduction to supply an entire biography for Julian Barnes, complete with her family pedigree and notes on her character; while noting correctly that Dame Julian is credited in the original Book of St. Albans with only one item, the "boke of huntyng."

Julian's lesson plans are not original. For her source material, she draws principally on "Le Art de Venerie," by William Twici; and "The Craft of Hunting," by Twici as translated into English by John Gyfford. (Twici and Gyfford were employed the early fourteenth century, as huntsmen to England's Edward II.) The French lingers in Julian's text because hunting with horses and hounds was a pastime for wealthy bluebloods who traced their descent from the Normans; and whose hunting dogs generally fared better than Anglo-Saxon peasants.

At least one old hare-hunter from the Celtic period, Shakespeare's King Lear, when inviting his young subjects to begin the chase, takes his cue from the instruction of Julian Barnes: *"Sa, sa, sa, sa*!"

DWF

Edition of 1547, sig. F2r

[1] Thomas Rawlins to George Ballard (5 Feb. 1733). Bodleian Library MS Ballard 41, fol. 152. Ed. DWF.

## From ***Dame Julian Barnes Her Book of Hunting***

### [**Editor's Prologue** (1486)]

LIKEWISE as in the book of Hawking aforesaid are written and noted the termès of pleasure belonging to gentlemen having delight therein. In the same manner, this book following sheweth to such gentle persons the manner of hunting for all manner of beastès, whether they be beastès of venery, or of chase, or rascal. And also it sheweth all the termès convenient – as well to the houndès as to the beastès aforesaid. And in-certáine, there be many divers of them! – as it is declared in the book following: [1]

From [**Beasts of venery** and **Beasts of the Chase**, lines 1-14]

MY DEAR SONS where ye fare,   by frith or by fell,
Take good heed in his time   how Tristram woll tell
How maníe manner beasts   of ven'ry there were. 2
Listen to your Dame,   and she shall you lere:
Four manner beastès   of ven'ry there are.
First° of 'hem is a *hart*;   secóund° is an *hare*;
The *boar*'s oon of tho',   the *wolf* and no moe. 3
And where so ye comen   in play or in place
Now shall I tell you which   be'n *beastès of chase*
Oon of tho' [is] a *buck*,   another a *doe*;
The *fox* and the *marterin* and the *wild roe*. 4
And ye shall, my dear sonnès, other beasts all,
Whereso ye 'hem find,   *rascal* shall° 'hem call,
In frith or in fell   or in forest, I you tell.

[**Of the hunting of the hare**, lines 236-326]

Now to speak of the hare,   how all shall be wrought
When she shall with his hounds   be founden and sought:
The first word to his hounds   the hunt shall out-pit
Is at the kennel door   when he openès hit:
That all may him hear,   he say shall "*arrière*!" – [5]

For his hounds woulden come   out too hastilíe.
This ís the first word, my sons, of veneríe.
And° when he has couplèd°   his houndès echoon
And is forth with 'hem in   to the° fieldè gone, 6

---

[1] Scansion: although the 1486 text is defective, Barnes's prevailing meter is a line of eleven syllables, two anapests, beat, iamb, anapest, thus: "*my dear SONS where ye FARE* [beat] *by FRITH or by FEL*".

[2] *where* ] whether;   *fare . . . fell* ] dwell by deer-park or by moorlands (possibly with pun on *frith* as peace or security (*OED* n. 1), and on *fell* as bitterness or cruelty [*OED* n. 3]);   *were* ] be.

[3] *you lere* ] learn you (i.e., teach you).

[4] *be'n* ] be;   *marterin* ] marten; a carnivore related to the weasel and valued for its fur;   *wild roe* ] a small Eurasian deer.

[5] *his* ] the hunter's;   *hunt* ] hunter;   *out pit* ] put out; call out;   *hit* ] it;   *arrière* ] back!

[6] *woulden* ] would otherwise.

And there his couplès be'n cast at his will,°
Thén shall he speakè, and say his hounds till:
"*Hors du couple! Avant sus, avant*!" (twice so),
And then, "*Ça, ça, ci avant*" (high and nought low),
And then "*Só how, so hów, so how*!" (thrice and no mo),
And then "*Ça, ci, avant, ça, ci, avant, so how*."° 1

And if ye see your hounds have good will to ren
Drawen° a-wayward fro' you, says thus, I you ken:
"*Here, how, ami, how, ami*!" ayen 'hem calls so,
Then "*Souef, mon ami, souef*," to make them soft° go. 2

And if any of 'hem find there as° ho has been
That hight Richar or Beamond, thus to him bedene:
"*Oyez, à Beamond le vaillant*! and I you well avow
*Que quida trouver le couard à la° courte queue*!"
That is, "Beamond the worthy," without any fail
"Weens° to find th' coward with the short tail!" 3

And if ye seen the hare at pasture has been
If hit be in timè when cornès be'n green
And íf your hounds of her find that thou see'st°,
Then shall ye say, "*là, douce, la il ad esté*"
(And there with "*so how,*" all high and nought low)—
That is to say, "Sweet, there as ho has been!" 4
When they finden of her while the cornès be'n° green
And if your hounds chasen not well at your will,
Then three motes shall ye° blowè, loud and not still.
There oon, and there 'nother, there ho pastured has.
Then say, "*Illeoques, illeoques*!" in the same place. 5

So says to 'hem by kind while they of her find.
Then castès a sign all the field about
To see at her pasture wh'er she be in or out –
For at hér form gladly to be, her is not lief;
There ho has pastured but in time of° relief. 6

And if any of her find, or musing of her° mace
There ho has been, and ho be gone out of that place:
"*Ha, ci, tous, ci est-il*!" so shall ye say,
"*Venez arrière, so how*!" sayes as high as ye may,
"*Ça, ci ad esté, so how*!" after that,
"*Ça, ça, ci, avant*!" and thereof be not late. 7

---

[1] *there* ] there when; *cast* ] cast off (from their leashes); *Hors . . . avant*! ] Out of the couple! forward!; *Ça, ça, ci avant* ] On, on, go forward!

[2] *ren* ] run; *Draw* ] drawing (away from you);*says* ] say; *calls* ] call; *ayen hem calls so* ] call (ye) them again, like so; "*Souef, mon ami, souef*!" ] Softly, my friend, softly!

[3] *there as* ] where; *ho* ] she; *And...been* ] And if any hound finds a trace of the hare to indicate where she has been; *That...Beamond* ] And (for example) if he is named Richar or Beamond; *bedene* ] immediately, straightaway; *Oyez* ] Hear; *Que . . . queue* ] that he intended to find the coward with the short tail (*quider* = *penser*).

[4] *là . . . esté* ] La, my sweet, he has passed by.

[5] *motes* ] notes; *there ho* ] where he; *Illeoques* ] there!

[6] *wh'er* ] whether; *lief* ] eager, willing; *There* ] Where.

[7] *musing* ] (n.) passage through a fence or hedge; *mace* ] mass, body of the hare; *Ha . . . est-il* ] Ha, all of you, here he is!; *Venez arrière* ] Come back.

And when ye seen her into plain go at the last
In feld, arable londe, or into wood passed,
And your houndès there will of her finden, sayes° then,
"*Là, douce, ami, là est il*°!" and does as I you ken –
That is to say, "Sweet friend, there ho is comen low
For to dry her!" And thérewith say, "*Só how, so hów*!
*Illeoques, cí, douce, cí, vaillant, só how*!" (then twy).
Thus mou ye, my dear sons, learn of veneríe. 1

And when ye comen there as ye trow she will° dwell
And so seems to you well, then sayes as I you tell:
"*Là, douce, là est-il venu*" for to dwell there
And therewi' thrice "*So how, sessa*!" and no more. 2

And if hit seems you well to find her all in-fere
And ween well so to do, then says, "*Douce, how, here,*
*How, here, how, here, doucè, how, hereby sets*!"
Thus shall yé say, my childer, and for no man letts. 3

And áll manner beastès that euer chasèd were
Have óon manner of word, "*So hów*!" and no more.
To fulfill or unfill ech manner of chase,
The hunter euermore that word in his mouth has. 4

And íf° your hounds at a chase rennen there ye hunt
And the beast 'gin tó ruse, as hartès be'n wont,
Or to havelon as does the fox with his guile,
Or fór to cross, as does the roe other while,
Or dill, so that your houndès can no further go,
Then shall ye say, "*Hó so, ami, ça, so,*
*A coupler, ça arrière, so how*!" such is that play. 5

And "so how" is as much as "ça how" to say,
But "so how" is shorter in speech when forth-brought;
Therefore we sayn "so hów" and "ça how" say we not.

And íf your hounds chasen at hart or at hare
And they aren at defaute thus shall ye say there:
"*Ici, so how, assayne, assayne, sto*!" Then "*Ho hó,*
*Ça, assayne, arrière, so how*!" – these words and no moe. 6

---

1 *wode* ] woods; *Là...est il* ] "La, [*to the bitch*] my sweet one, [*to the male*] my friend, he's come there"; *does...ken* ] do as I instruct you; *dry her* ] dry herself; *twy* ] twice; *mou* ] may.

2 *Là . . . venu* ] La, my sweet, he has come there; *therewi'* ] therewith; also.

3 *all in-fere* ] all in one piece, not torn by the dogs; *hereby sets* ] sit right there; *childer* ] children; *for . . . letts* ] let no one hinder you.

4 *euer* ] (prn. *yooer*) ever.

5 *rennen there* ] run where; *And . . . wont* ] and the animal begins to double and turn as do harts when hunted, to evade the dogs; *to havelon* ] to use trickery; *Or . . . go* ] or hide, so that your hounds can go no further; *A coupler* ] "To the couples" – thereby commanding the hounds to stop and return in order to be coupled.

6 *aren at defaute* ] are at default; lose the scent; *assayne* ] a cry to menace the hounds and withdraw them (G. Tilander); *sto* ] stop.

And if your hounds ren well at fox or at doe
And so fallen at defaute, says thus fu'er ere ye go:
"*Ho, hó,* or, *souef, à lui, douce, à lui*!" that they hear,
"*Ho, how, assayne, assayne, ça, arrière,*
*So how, venez à coupler*!" and doès as I you ken.
The more worship ye mou have among all other men.
Your crafts let be kid: and doès as I you bid. 1

[**The reward for houndes**, lines 133-140]

When your houndès with strength have done her to death,
The hunter shall réward the hounds with her head,
With the shoulders and sides and the bowels all
And all thing within her, save only the gall.
Then the loins of the hare look ye not for-yet:
Bringès 'hem for the kitchen, to the lord's meat.
And of this ilkè hare mou speak we no mair. 2
. . . . . . . . . . . . . . . . . . . . . . . . . . . . . . . . . . . . . .
(Explicit Dame Julians Barnes° in her **Book of Hunting**)

Noblewomen hunting in a deer park (fr. Wikipedia Commons)

[1] *fu'er* ] further; *Ho, ho, or, souef, à lui* ] Ho, ho, so, soft, to him, [*etc.*]; *kid* ] made known; well-renowned.
[2] *dethe* ] (det) death; *with her head* ] with the head of the hare; *for-yet* ] forget.

# REFORMATION Period

And the woman sawe that it was a good tree to eate of and lustie vnto the eyes and a pleasant tre for to make wyse. And toke of the frute of it and ate and gaue vnto hir husband also with her and he ate. And the eyes of both them were opened, that they vnderstode…
—Gen. 3.5-6, Tyndale Bible (1525)

Es ist kein Rock noch Kleid, das einer Frau oder Jungfrau übler ansteht, als wenn sie klug sein will.

(No skirt or gown appearing on a woman or girl is more vile than the desire to be clever.)
—Martin Luther (1483-1546), *Tischreden 2* (1555)

THE "English Reformation," as a term for Henry VIII's declaration of independence from Rome, is a misnomer. A devout Catholic (not, to the bitter end, a Roman one), King Henry had zero tolerance for dissent of any kind, from anyone. Just two years after Martin Luther tacked his 95 Theses to a church door in Wittenberg, Henry VIII undertook a rebuttal; which, when published, passed through twenty editions, was translated into German, and earned Henry the gratitude of Pope Leo X, who granted him the official title, *Fidei Defensor* ("Defender of the Faith"). Making good on that honor, Henry expelled Tyndale from England in 1524, and put religious dissenters to death – John Frith in 1533, Tyndale (near Brussels) in 1536, John Lambert in 1538, Robert Barns in 1540, Anne Askew in 1546, and many more. Henry's differences with Rome were not over theology but over marriage canon law: the King determined that it was God's will for him to discard his wife, Catherine of Aragon, and his daughter Princess Mary, in order to wed Anne Boleyn and produce a male heir. But Pope Clement VII declined to cooperate with the requested annulment, the Vatican having less to fear from Henry than from Holy Roman Emperor Carlos V (Catherine's nephew). Undeterred, Henry took Anne into his arms, and canon law into his own hands: On 23 May 1533, a cooperative Archbishop of Canterbury, Thomas Cranmer, declared the king's 24-year marriage to Catherine of Aragon null and void; by which time, Anne was already pregnant, Henry having married her at Westminster Abbey on January 23[d].

Parliament in 1534 declared Henry the "only Supreme Head in Earth of the Church of England." That was rather like making Reynard the fox Supreme Head of the Chicken Coup. The king proceeded to confiscate the Church's vast wealth in goods, land, and rents. The Suppression of Religious Houses Act 1535/6 conferred upon the Crown all monasteries having annual income of less than £200. The second Suppression Act of 1539 took the rest. Meanwhile, the Reformation proceeded apace. All appeals to Rome on religious or other matters, and all bulls from the Vatican, were outlawed. Opposition was suppressed. Elizabeth Barton, a vocal critic of the king's second marriage, was among the first to lose her head. John Fisher, Bishop of Rochester, and Sir Thomas More, Henry's former Lord Chancellor, were beheaded for declining to take the oath of Supremacy. Dissenting monks were tortured first, then killed.

But if the "English Reformation" was about power, money, and the king's codpiece, dissent was not far behind. Conservatives who resented the break with Rome and the suppression of monasteries took part in the Lincolnshire Rising and the Pilgrimage of Grace. On the religious left were dissenters who pushed for doctrinal change. The litmus test for heresy was the Eucharist – whether Jesus meant it literally when he said of the bread, "This is my body, broken for you." Other flash points included Purgatory and the sale of indulgences; icons and relics as objects of veneration; prayer to saints; clerical celibacy; and the authority of Scripture. From the burning of John Hus until the close of the Thirty Years War in 1631, the settling of these debates took an estimated 10 to 13 million lives, chiefly on the Continent.

On the "woman problem," however, Protestant and Catholic spokesmen were in lock-step: Women's intelligence was to be discounted, feminine nature maligned, the female body commodified. During the witch-hunting craze of the fifteenth to seventeenth centuries, Protestant authorities competed with the Roman Church in putting accused women to death. Martin Luther taught that demons often impersonated women to have illicit sex with men or to abduct babies; and that "The Word and works of God are quite clear: women must serve, either as wives or whores" (*Works* 12.94). Female virtue was comprised of obedience, chastity, silence, and the production of children in Christian wedlock. All else was transgressive. Katharina Zell, Argula von Grumbach, and others registered thoughtful protest, but were forcibly silenced.

The printing press came to England in 1476, an opportunity for progress. Julian Barnes and Christine de Pizan were among the first authors published; Elizabeth of York and Margaret Beaufort were among Caxton's first patrons. But the first 150 years of moveable type did little to budge gender typology in Britain. Women were rigorously excluded from published discourse; misogynistic writing by men proliferated, across the genres. Except for tracts in support of the status quo, women's writing remained in manuscript or was driven underground. Literacy was now on the increase, providing a peaceful means to destabilize established hierarchies. But the time for a women's Reformation was not yet come.

# The Coffin-Welles Anthology (1517-1538)

*ytt shalbe to your understandyng*
*I haue nott all my wyll.*

—from "Even as merry as I make..."

MONG the rare manuscripts housed in the Bodleian Library of Oxford University is a large compilation of late medieval verse, Bodleian MS Rawlinson C.813, comprised of two separate manuscript volumes that were bound together in the seventeenth century. The earlier of these two collections (folios 1-98), here called the "Coffin-Welles anthology," was once owned by a man named Humphrey Welles, a courtier to Henry VIII and a member of Parliament. The manuscript may originally have belonged to William Coffin (*c.* 1492-1538), also a member of Parliament, who appears to have contributed many poems to the volume. The names of both men are written on the rear fly-leaf (98v). The Coffin-Welles anthology contains verses principally written in 1516-22 and 1535-38, by a variety of authors (mostly unidentified), and copied into the manuscript by three different hands (identified as Hands A, B, and C). The collection has been edited for publication, in a critical old-spelling edition, by Sharon Jansen and Kathleen Jordan.

As with the Findern manuscript, the Coffin-Welles anthology is of interest in that it contains a sampling of women's verse. Of these, only one is attributed – "The lamentatyon of the ladye gryffythe [ap Rhys]"[1] – but the "Lamentation" appears not to have been written by a woman, much less by Sir Griffith's grieving widow. Jansen and Jordan present a compelling case that "The Lamentation" was actually written by a male poet, here speaking in Lady ap Rice's persona – the same poet, possibly a Welshman at the court of Henry VIII, who wrote two other first-person laments in the Welles manuscript, the "The Epytaphe of Sir Gryffyth apryse" and "The lamentatyon of Edward [Stafford], late duke of Buckyngham."[2] The manner of the three poems is quite similar, and all three appear to have been copied into the Welles manuscript by the same person, probably at about the same time, c. 1521. "The Lamentation Lady Griffith" has therefore been omitted from the selections below.

More than half of the poems in the Coffin-Welles anthology are love-epistles, most or all of which arose from a single courtship between a west-country gentleman dwelling usually in London, and a teenaged beauty dwelling far away. The male suitor describes himself as "yonge bothe wyse and lustye / and eke descendyd of a gentyll lyne."[3] Although still a youth "of age butt tender," he has "gone through englond on euery syde / brettyn flanders with many an oder place."[4] He is now serving King Henry "yn þe courte Inperyall."[5]

The young woman, probably an aristocrat, is described by her suitor in conventional terms as having "fayr golden tressys ... her eyne grey, hur nose streyght and fayre, ... with a lyttyl pytte yn hur welfavoryd chyn."[6] The couple first met in London, evidently when the girl, then aged seventeen, was visiting the city with her parents.[7] The young man subsequently danced with the maid, in evening festivities held at court (or, possibly, at the Inner Temple) in a "hall gaye / wher þat diuerse base dances most swetly dyd

[1] "O Soorowe of all Sorowes my harte doeth cleve...," fol. 29v, immediately following the "Epytaphe."

[2] "When I revolve yn my Remembrance...," fols. 28v-29v; and "O dere god beholde þis worlde...," 49v-50v.

[3] Fol. 23r, lines 64-5 of epistle beginning, "Ryght gentyll harte of greane flouryng age..."

[4] Fol. 18r, line 157 of epistle beginning, "O my lady dere bothe regarde and See..."; and fol. 3v, lines 25-6 of epistle beginning "Iesue þat ys most of myght...."

[5] Fol. 18r, line 163 of epistle beginning, "O my lady dere bothe regarde and See..."

[6] Fol. 18r, line 4 of epistle beg., "O my swet lady and exelente gooddas"; fol. 17r, lines 112, 114, 120 of epistle beg., "O my lady dere bothe regarde and See".

[7] Fol. 16r, line 61 of epistle beginning, "O my lady dere bothe regarde and See..."; fol. 69r, lines 252 and 230 of epistle beginning, "Whatt tyme as parys Son of king priame..."

pley."[1] But alas, after having already fallen in love with her, the young suitor learned that his "swete mastress" could not remain in the city. Not long after their first evening together, the maid "partyd ryght ferre / yn hur owne cuntrye where she doth abyde."[2] Undaunted, the young man commenced a long-distance lovesuit, undertaken in a series of secret letters in which he pours forth his love and sorrow. Unfortunately, the maiden's parents had other plans, having already arranged a wealthy match in her behalf.

In a desperate effort to forestall this other marriage, the forlorn suitor dashed off a series of woeful love-letters, chiefly or entirely in verse – letters that were, however, greatly plagiarized from Chaucer, and from poetry then circulating at court. One of the suitor's epistles (fols. 48v-49v) is taken wholly from Chaucer's *Troilus and Criseyde*, while others borrow extensively from poems by Stephen Hawes' *The Comfort of Lovers* and *The Pastime of Pleasure*. The suitor introduces few changes and in so doing generally spoils the meter. In these earnest if unoriginal epistles, the lovelorn youth begs the maid to pursue the pleasures of love and not to marry "for lond or Substance."[3] The sympathetic maiden penned verse-epistles in reply, but she ultimately broke off the suit, having agreed to marry the man of her parents' choice. Her rejected suitor made a few last appeals, increasingly bitter in tone, but he finally gave her over as a lost cause. The maiden may have made a wise choice: her suitor, in plagiarizing Hawes, repeatedly omits phrases in which the speaker expresses his honorable wish to be married. The entire courtship appears not to have lasted for more than a few months, perhaps in 1516.[4]

Jansen and Jordan suggest that the youth who wrote the love-epistles may have been Humphrey Welles, sometime owner of the manuscript. Welles, a younger man than Coffin, was admitted to the Inner Temple in March 1522 – and the male poet's "old Temple" may reference to the Inner Temple.[5] But Welles was first recommended for the king's service in 1538, and so cannot have been writing as a courtier as early as 1522; by which time, in any case, the love affair had already commenced and may have been history.

Circumstances mentioned within the epistle and the external dating fit William Coffin himself: born and bred in the West Country as a native of Porthledgde, Devon, Coffin in 1513 served as a captain in the French war. Two years later he became a member of the Royal Household as a courtier to Henry VIII, with a £20 annuity and later that year was paid £20 on embassy to Flanders with other members of the Privy Council. He was appointed gentleman usher in 1519, sewer by 1526,[6] and master of horse to Queen Anne Boleyn in 1534; again to Queen Jane Seymour in 1536.[7] He died on 8 December 1538.

Master of Female half-lengths, c. 1520s, private collection

[1] Fol. 19r, lines 36-8 in epistle beg., "O my swet lady and exelente gooddas..."

[2] *cuntrey* ] i.e., county (fol. 17v, in epistle beg., "O my lady dere bothe regarde and See...").

[3] Epistle beg., "Ryght gentyll harte of greane flouryng age..." lines 74-91 (fol. 23r); cf. "What tyme as parys Son of king priame..." 204-245 (fols. 68v-69r).

[4] See Jansen and Jordan, "Dating," 7-9. Unrelated items in the MS, also in Hand A, may likewise be dated 1521-2.

[5] The lines concerning the "olde temple" are plagiarized nearly verbatim from Hawes's *The Pastime of Pleasure* (*PP* 2234-40); cf. fol. 16r, line 61 of epistle beginning, "O my lady dere bothe regarde and See..." (plagiarized from the same passage of *PP*) in which the "temple" has been called a "church."

[6] *sewer* ] official supervisor of meals in the Royal Household.

[7] Jansen and Jordan, p. 5.

Coffin in 1517 married Margaret (b. Dymock) Vernon, a wealthy widow in her late twenties.

Margaret cannot be the 17-year-old maiden of the lovesuit. But if the suitor is William Coffin – and he is the only available candidate – then he must have married widow Vernon on the rebound from his failed wooing of the maiden poet. This provides a fairly narrow window for the curtailed love affair, 1515-1516.

In some respects, it scarcely matters that we cannot identify with certainty the particular man and woman whose love-verses are preserved in the Coffin-Welles anthology. The maiden's verse reads well without knowledge of her identity; while the male suitor is at his best moments a plagiarist. But the manuscript fascinates as an early collection of love-verse from a particular courtship, a poetical exchange in which both male and female correspondents are represented.

The majority of the verse-epistles preserved in the manuscript are from the male suitor. None of the articles represents an original holograph copy; all may have been copied into the manuscript many years after the affair was over. Insofar as the Coffin-Welles collection is complete, the exchange of letters appears to have been initiated with the manuscript's first five entries (fols. 1-5, entered by Hand A). The remaining love-epistles are scattered in clusters throughout the manuscript, although not arranged in chronological order. This disarray in the manuscript has caused previous editors to overlook or to confuse the connectedness of one epistle to another, such as "Right best beloved" (fol. 71), written by the maid, which answers his "O my lady dere" and "O my swet lady," (fols. 15-21) and quotes another (fol.68v); or "Though I be sadde" (fol. 58), an epistle by her that answers his "My hart ys Sore" (fol. 57) (previously printed as one poem). The epistles are here printed for the first time in something close to their original order of composition.

The male suitor initiated this exchange of epistles shortly after the maiden returned to her home county. His ambitions as a lover and poet are represented by the following extracts, much of which he copied or adapted from Stephen Hawes:

### [From Her Suitor:] [1]

***Please ytt your grace dere harte to gyffe audyence…*** (fol. 1)

Please it your grace, dear heart, to give audience
Unto my woeful and piteous complaint,
How your fervent love without resistance
My careful heart hath made oft low and faint
And you thereof are all the whole constraint!
    Your beauty and kindness hath fett'red me so fast
    That without help my joy is near-hond past [2]

Ye have my heart without any lett:
I will neuer change you for any oder new.
So fervently on you my love is set
That, while I live, to you I will be true.
Wherefore, I pray you, once on me to rue –
    Sithen I am born so, to live in pain
    To love, and may not be loved again, [3]

[1] The first stanza of this verse epistle is adapted from *The Pastime of Pleasure,* 2052-8. The rest may be original. For a collation of the suitor's plagiarized epistles and his sources, see the Textual Notes.

[2] *your fervent love* ] I, your fervent lover, held in check by my cautious heart and your lack of pity; *near-hond* ] near-hand, nearly.

[3] *lett* ] obstacle; *rue* ] pity; *again* ] in return.

Yet, through governance there groweth grace!
I have heard say, both in town and street
How Fortune comes in to many a place –
And with good fortune, I trust shortly to meet.
I must walk forth, truelove to seek!
Into some place where it doth grow.
But on branch thereof, I will live with you! [1]

There is a vein up in your brow
Which is a truelove unto my sight:
For my true heart is set right dear on you
And euer shall, both day and night.
Thus with your love, now I am dight!
O my sweetheart, thus do I complain:
There is no moe but you, may help me of my pain. (c. 1516)

Having received his many protestations of "true love" (chiefly cribbed from *The Pastime of Pleasure*), the maiden at last replies to her suitor with a poem that offers to school him in the difference between true love and lust.

### [The Maiden to her Suitor]
***I loue So Sore I wolde fayne descerne…*** (fol. 61)

"I love so sore"? I would fain discern
(If that I could) what Love might be,
Or what should be his name. But tell, I ne can,
He is so far in the extremity.
There is but two manners of love, as seemeth me:
The one is true and sure, the other is false and slow.
But I will speak of truelove, and let the other go. [2]

This truelove, it is a marvelous, goodly flower,
One of the freshest during the year.
He is more goodly of his colóur
Than is the gold that is so clear.
This truelove hath four leavés sere
Which be fastenèd all in one root
For love, without truelove, nothing will boot. [3]

The first leaf of this truelove (after my opinion)
Is very pleasaunt to every wight
And may well be called *desire* or *affection*:
That of company cometh, and taketh his first sight,
And so to the heart he taketh his flight,
And there he doth rest. He will not depart
Till he have it stricken with his fiery dart. [4]

---

[1] *will* ] wish to.

[2] *slow* ] uncertain, faltering; *truelove* ] a greenish-yellow flower so called.

[3] *sere* ] separate, distinct; *boot* ] profit.

[4] *after* ] according to; *wight* ] person.

The second leaf of this truelove (whoso doth him seek)
May be callèd *meekness* or else *humility*,
In tokening that a true lover should be meek,
Courteìs, gentle and low in euery degree –
For if he lack these, he is nought set by.
  He must be still, say little, and keep close all
  But to his love alone, lest some misfortune fall.

The third leaf of this truelove (without any doubt)
May well be called *audacity* or *boldness*,
For he must show his love his whole mind and thought
And what is the cause of his great heaviness –
Or else he shall never his pains redress.
  For how should she know that he loveth her again
  If that he will (to her) never complain?

Then cometh the fourth leaf, which is last of all,
And to euery true lover he is most set by:
*Kindness most pure,* I may it well call:
That in the heart first springeth, truèly.
[From which there groweth true love, verily.]
  This leaf it cometh forth of the heart-root,
  For love, without kindness, nothing will boot. [1]

The nature of these four leaves now I have devised
And given them names like to their property.
I must seek a root wherein these leaves may be fastenèd
And set these leaves, euery one, in his degree
Wherein these leaves may stand in a suertie:
  This root is more pleasaunt than the leavès all,
  For *steadfastness that is sure* this root I may call. [2]

For if that a lover have the leavès all
And of his love be not steadfast and sure
Then the leaves stand so weak they must needs fall –
So that then love is lost. It may not endure.
Then farewell the leaves, both pleasaunt and pure.
  This steadfastness is master and rules all the leaves.
  For love without steadfastness nothing achieves.°

### [From Her Suitor:] [3]

***Ryght gentyll harte of greane flouryng age...*** (fol. 21v-24)

Right gentle heart of grenè flow'ring age,
The star of beauty and of famous port,
Consider well that your lusty *courágе*
*Age* of his *course* must, at the last, transport.
Now truth° of right doth my self exhort
  That ye your youth in idleness will spend
  Withouten pleasure to bring it to an° end.

[1] Speculative reconstruction. MS here omits a line that would complete the rhyme royal.

[2] *suertie* ] surety, fastness.

[3] This verse epistle from the suitor is a wholesale plagiarism from Hawes' *Pastime of Pleasure.*

What was the cause of your creatìon
But man to love, the world to multiply,
As to sow the seed of generatìon
With fervent love? So well, conveniently,
The cause of love engend'reth perfitly
Upon an° intent of fair Dame Natúre
Which hath you made° so fair a creàture.

Then of Dame Nature, what is the intent
But to accomplish her fair seed to sow
In such a place as is convenient
To God's pleasure, for to increase and grow?
(The kind of *her* ye may not overthrow!)
Say what ye list, ye can nothing deny
But otherwhile ye think (full privily)

What the man is and what he can do
Of chamber-work (as nature will agree).
Though by experience ye know nothing thereto,
[25] Yet oft ye muse and think what it may be.
Nature provoketh, of her strong degree,
You so to do as hath been her old guise.
Why will ye then the true love despise? [1]

. . . . . . . . . . . . . . . . . . . . . . . . .

One most ye love, it cannot be denied,
For hard it is to void you of the chaunce.
Then love him best that ye have so arrayed
With fiery chaiéns,° fettered in penáunce –
For he is ready, withouten° doubtáunce,
In everything for to fulfill your will.
[49] Now as ye list, ye may him save or spill. [2]

. . . . . . . . . . . . . . . . . . . . . . . . . . . . . . .

Is not he youngè, bothè wise and lusty
And eke descended of a° gentle line?
What will ye more have of him, truly,
Than you to serve as true love will incline?
But, as I think, ye do now determine
To fix your mind for worldly treasúre,
Though in your youth ye lesè° your pleasúre. [3]

Alas, remember first your beauty,
Your youth, your courage, and your tender heart.
What pain hereafter it may to you be
When ye lack that which is true lover's desert!
[75] I tell you this yourselfè to convert,
For little know ye of this pain, iwis:
To live with him in whom no pleasure is.

---

[1] *chamber-work* ] love-making.

[2] *most* ] 1. most; 2. must; *chaiens* ] chains; *penaunce* ] grief.

[3] *lese* ] lose.

Where that is lovè, there can be no lack—
Fie on that love for° land or substauncè!
For that° it mustè needs right soon aback
When that youth hath no joy nor pleasauncè
In the party with nature's suffisauncè.
 Then will ye, for the sin of avarice,
 Unto your youth do such a prejudice?.... [1]

In her reply, the maiden offers some encouragement to her suitor while deftly inquiring after his intentions, reformulating his conflation of "true-love" with "chamber-work":

**[The Maiden to her Suitor:]** [2]
***grene flouryng age of your manly countenance...*** (fol. 53v)

Green flow'ring age of your manly count'naunce,
Your youth, your lustiness, and your delectable courage
Causeth me to have it in remembraunce –
So that, day and night, in my heart I rage
For bycause I am so far out o' your presaunce –
Yet shall ye find me° true in your observaunce.
 In our heartès we may be right gladdén'd°
 For joy of our purpose aye° that shall wend.

Let never the love of true lovers be lost!
For, my amiable love, I am to you promisèd°
With all the sparkès of my heart unlacèd.
Howbeit, daily I am sorry and sad
And shall be till I know more of your mind,
 For my heart in your mind is closyde:
 In my body it will not abide! [3]

One of the maid's epistles concludes with a postscript, a quotation from the closing lines (379-86) of "The Churl and the Bird," a well-known poem by John Lydgate. Previous editors have been confused "as towching þis letter of translatyon / owt of frenche": the quotation does not imply that the maiden is (like Lydgate) professing to have translated her verses into English from an original draft in French. The lines are, in part, a conventional disclaimer concerning the quality of her own verses; but the quotation has been carefully chosen. In Lydgate's poem, the bird, having been encaged by the churl, refuses to sing ("Who loseth his freedom," she says, "in sooth, he loseth all"). On condition that she first be released from her cage, Lydgate's bird promises to give the churl three points of wisdom, to which he agrees. Her advice is, first, do not be over-credulous, nor give "hasty credence / To every tale" (197-8); second, do not desire the impossible ("Desire thou not by no conditions thing that is impossible to recur" [206-7]); and third, never sorrow for what is past (211-17). Lydgate advises:

For treasure lost, make never too great sorr'we
Which in no wisè may recurèd be –
For who taketh sorr'we for loss in that degree,
Reckne' first his loss, and after reckne' his pain.
Of o' sorr'we, he maketh sorr'wes twain.

---

[1] *Where that* ] Where there.

[2] A reply to "All plesure pastyme, lines 223-4 (fol. 68v), where the suitor advises the maid not "to Mispende your grene floring age / In peyne withowt Ioye plesure and corage"; which the suitor borrowed from Hawes, *Pastime of Pleasure*: "She wyll wyth love her grene flouryng age / Passe forth in joye, pleasure, and courage."

[3] *closyde* ] enclosed.

The maiden's postscripted quotation thus contains a warning that one romantic evening in London may not lead him to the fulfillment of his dreams:

**[The Maiden to Her Suitor:]**
***O resplendent floure prynte þis yn your mynde...*** (fol. 53v-54)

O resplendent flower, print this in your mind:
Hów as yet unto you I was neuer unkind
And therefore, dear heart, rote of tenderness,
To comfórth me of my care and cease my painès strong
Shortlie come speak with me, of your gentleness
Or else of discomfórth shall be my song. [1]

For in your confidence my word I have closéd:
Both lock and key ye have in your governáunce,
And to you in° my mind I have sailéd°
Of veráy pitíe, exile me not fro° remembráunce!
Thus I do finishè my simple bill.
At our meeting, ye shall know more of my will:
Unto you, I need not to write my name,
For she that loveth you best sent° you this same. [2]

"*Go, little quire, and recommendè me*
*Unto my master with humble affectìon*
*Beseeching him lowlie, of mercy and pitíe,*
*Óf my rude making to have compassìon.*
*And as touching this letter of translation*
*Out of French, howsoeuer the English be,*
*All this is said under correctìon*
*With th' supportatìon of your benignity.*" [3]

**[From her Suitor:]** [4]
***O my lady dere both regarde and See...*** (fols. 14v-18)

O my lady dear, both regard and see my heart:
Upon you so sore it is set,
That it is yours. It may none other be.
Ye have it caught in so sure a net
That if that I may not your favor get,
No doubt it is, the great pain of love
May not assuage till death it remove.

. . . . . . . . . . . . . . . . . . . . . . . . .

I will be true though I continue
All my whole life in pain and heaviness.
I will never change you for none other new.
Ye are my lady, ye are my masteress,
Whom I shall serve, with all gentleness.
Exile him never from your heart so dear
Which unto his heart hath set you most near.

---

1 *rote* ] root; *of your gentleness* ] if you please.

2 *veray* ] (vrī′) very, true; *bill* ] letter.

3 *quire* ] any little book or gathering of sheets of writing-paper, but properly a set of four sheets doubled so as to form eight leaves, a common form of medieval manuscript-tablet.

4 Lines 148-54 are plagiarized from Hawes' *Comfort of Lovers,* most of the rest from *Pastime of Pleasure.*

O my sweet lady, the bright-shining star
Of my true heart, wherever I go or ride,
Though that my body be from you afar,
Yet my heart only shall with you abide.
When that ye list, ye may for me provide:
My love is set upon a perfit ground.
No falsehood in me truly shall be found.

Alas, *madamè*, ye may say as ye list,
With your high beauty ye took my heart in snare;
Your lovely looks I could no whit resist.
Your virtuous manner increaseth my care,
That of all joy I am devoid and bare.
I see you right often as I am asleep
And when I waken do sike with tears deep [1]

O my sweet lady, the good perfit star,
Of my true heart take you now pitíe
Think on my pain which am from you afar
With your sweet eyes behold ye now and see
How thought and woe by great extremity
Hath changed my hue into pale and wan
(It was not so when to love you first I began!)

That I love you so sore it is no marvel why:
Your beauty clear and your lovely looks sweet
My heart did pierce with love so suddenly –
At the first time that I did you meet
In the middès of the church when I did you greet
– Your beauty my heart so surely assayed
That sith that time it hath to you ever obeyed.

. . . . . . . . . . . . . . . . . . . . . . . . . . . .

Thus fare ye well, there is no more to say —
Under my signet in the court imperial,
Of April the nine-and-twentieth day,
I closèd this letter and to me did call
Desire, my friend, so dear and especìal –
Commanding him as fast as he might
To my sweet lady to take it full right.
*Si trove soit hony soit qui mal y pense.* [2]

### [The Maiden's Reply to Her Suitor:]
***Right best beloved and most in assurance...*** (fols. 71-72v)

Right best belov'd, and most in assuráunce
Of my true hearte, I me recommende
Heart'ly unto you withouten variáunce
(And have received th' which ye t' me did sende,
Whéreby I perceive your loving heart and mind),
Desiring you i' th' same so to continue –
And then, for your "great painès," comfort may ensue.

---

[1] *sike* ] sigh.

[2] *Si ... pense* ] "If this letter should be discovered, evil be to him who imagines evil."

Thanking me for my kindness in times past,
Your desire is, I should keep in mind
The purpose I was in when ye spake with me last.
Truly, "unconstant" you shall me never find,
But ever to be true, faithful, and kind,
  And t' you bear my true heart withouten variaunce
  Desiring you to make *me* no dissembèlaunce!

Also, where you say that my beauty "so sore"
Should you inflame with "piercing violencè,"
That, with extreme love of me, you should be caught "in snare,"
I marvel thereof greatly, without doubtancè,
That it should have such might or puìssance! [1]
  For I know right well, I never was° so beauteous
  That I should you constrain to be so amorous!

Also, where you say that absencè should be
"The greatest painè that can be devisèd"
Únto one that is in "great extremity"
Ánd with painful love is° "sore tormented,"
It is of a truth. It cannot be denièd
  That° absence causeth oftè pensiveness –
  But I suppose you be in no such distress!

Also, it is truth that, through poverty,
Many 'oon "dare not" put himself "in prease" –
But I take you for none of them, truly,
But that you durst (if that it did you please)
Yourself put forth, your heartè for to ease!
  For how should I your sorrowès redress
  But if yet ye (to me) do them plainly express? [2]

Also, where you desire me that I should not shrink,
But that I should continue in "the samè minde"
That you left me in, so that° you "might think
That then° there were some truth in woman's kinde,"
Surely, in the same mind ye shall *me* still find,
  So that you shall not need me for to mistrust –
  (Though peradventure you *have* found *some* unjust!)

It is a true proverb, and of old antiquity:
"Dispraise not all, although° one have offended."
But they be worthy praise that steadfast, and true, be –
And they, dispraise, that oderways have intended.
(Yet say well by the worst, the best may be amended.)
  For my love is set upon a perfit ground
  No deceit in me truly shall be found. [3]

---

[1] *puissance* ] strength.

[2] *through poverty* ] on account of insufficient wealth; *many 'oon* ] many a one; *in prease* ] in competition, in the throng.

[3] Lines 48-49, 50-56 cite the suitor's previous epistle ("O my lady dere both regarde and See," lines 41-2, 29-35).

But I will be true, though I should continue
All my whole life in pain and heaviness.
I will never change you for any oder new.
You be my joy, my comfort, and gladnéss,
Whom I shall serve, with all gentleness.°
 Exile me never from your heart so dear –
 Which unto *my* heart have set *you* most near.

Finally, this schedule for to conclude,
My purpose is certáin, according to the same
Minding, for your sake, all fantasies to exclude
Of love feignèd; and the contrary, to attain.
And, by like uság of us, shall spring the fame
 Unto the presence of Venus, that goddess eternal –
 Who of her goodness grant joy to true lovers all! [1]

The suitor replies with a 168-line verse epistle, copied from Stephen Hawes's "The Comfort of Lovers" (lines 29-35, here quoted, duplicate *CL* 645-51):

***"O loue most dere o loue most nere my harte..."*** (fol. 24v)

....O most fair lady, young, good, and virtuous,
I know full well, never your countenance
Showed me any token to make me amorous,
But what for that? Your prudent governaunce
Hath embracèd my heart for to give attendáunce.
 Your excellent beauty could nothing lett
 To cause my heart upon you to set.... [2]

Perhaps with the following lines we arrive at something close to the suitor's own words (although it may be that these have simply been plagiarized from a text no longer extant):

Alas, how° great sorrow it is, and pain,
To live in dread, alway imagining
How her good grace that I might attain –
In thought and pensiveness alway desiring
At a good end my purpose for to bring.
 Thus do I live between hope and dread,
 Sometime trusting well and sometime not to speed.

Alas, good lady, hold me excused
If I desire the which I am not worthy
Love hath my heart so greatly abused
Above all other to love you specially.
To my hard fortune I can no ways reply
 But to submit me unto your grace and will –
 It is at your pleasure to save me or to spill....

[1] *schedule* ] letter.

[2] *lett* ] hinder.

The maiden at about this time chose indeed "to spill" her London suitor, and to marry instead the man chosen by her parents:

**[The Maiden's Reply to Her Suitor:]** [1]
***Evyn as mery as I make myght...*** (fol. 58v)

Even as merry as I make might
It is not as I would,
For to one I have my troth y-plight
And anoder hath my heart in hold.
He that hath my troth y-plight,
He dwellèth° with me awhile –
But he that hath my heart in hold,
I will him neuer beguile.
I must take as I have baked – °
Thereof I have my fill.
But I must drink as I have brew,
Wheder it be good or ill.
All my heart I have here written,
To send you in a bill:
It shall be to your understanding,
I have not all my will. (c. 1516)

Several poems from the suitor register his dismay over the maiden's decision to marry his rival, but to no avail. One of these farewell-epistles (printed below) has been described by editors, confused by its opening line, as "A letter from a lady to her fickle lover."[2] But when read in its larger context, the opening remark is rightly understood as a reproach to the maiden from her suitor. The poet avows that his love for his father is less than his love for the maiden; the reverse, he implies, is true of her, or else she would not have subjected her love to the authority of her father:

**[From Her Rejected Suitor:]**
***Swet harte I loue yow more feruent then my fader...*** (fol. 63)

Sweet heart, I love you more fervent than my sire,°
Yet know I well° your love so fervent is
In anoder place, that I dare not desire
Your love again, nor nought I will, Iwis.
But I beseke God of your love grant you bliss,
And preserve in grace both young and old:
Grant me in love – I ask no more, Iwis.
Among your new lovers, yet remember your old. [3]

[1] In *The Welles Anthology,* ed. Jansen and Jordan (1991) the maiden's reply is conflated with the lengthy poem from the suitor which precedes it in the manuscript.

[2] Rossell H. Robbins and John L. Cutler, eds., *Supplement to the Index of Middle English Verse* (Lexington: Univ. of Kentucky, 1965), p. 359.

[3] *fervent* ] fervently; *my sire* ] than I do my own father. The MS has "fader," but the rhyme calls for sire; *again* ] in return; *iwis* ] surely; *beseke* ] beseech.

Now will I say as I think in my heart
Of you, sweet heart (which I find so strange
As one of them that will not turn nor convert):
By my assent, ye shall be gi'en the range.
I was not ware ye cast you for to change.
  But for all this, I shall do my 'deavor
  To love you well, but trust ye me forever. 1
(c. 1516)

Expecting himself to die of a broken heart, the woebegone youth promises in a final series of poems, mostly plagiarized, that he will never love another. (If the suitor is William Coffin, he lived to love again: in 1517 he married Margaret [b. Dymocke], the wealthy widow of Richard Vernon.)

• • •

Among the later poems in the Coffin-Welles anthology is a comical verse epistle, described only as a "Letter Sent by One Young Woman to Another which aforetime were Fellows Together." The epistle was entered in the volume by Hand B, together with various other poems that appear to have been written and/or copied into the manuscript about 1534-1535. In previous winters the author ("one young woman") and her friend ("Bune") have lodged in the same manor house – one that possibly belonged to the poet's uncle – but the girls have since been separated. The author is not identified. Her "Letter" is followed in the Coffin-Welles anthology by a similar name-game epistle, "A Letter Sent by R.W. to A.C." R.W. identifies himself within the poem as a saddler of Ingestre, Staffordshire, writing from London to A. Chetwynd, also of Ingestre. R.W. may be a member of the Welles family in the employment of William Coffin. (Coffin was made master of horse to Queen Anne Boleyn in 1534 and to Queen Jane Seymour in 1536.) "Agnes Blackamore" was married to Thomas Blackmore (also Blakemire) of Lapley, Staffordshire before 1540. And Irpe, Cole, Thomson are surnames likewise found in the parish registers east of Stafford.

**[A lettre Sende by on yonge woman to a noder
Which Aforetyme were Felowes to geder:**

***My loving Frende amorous bune...*** (fols. 6v-7v)

My loving friend, amorous Bune,°
I come ambling to you by the same token 2
That you and I have be' togeder
And setten by the fire in cold weather
And with us no moe but our Gullét
With all the knackes in her bougét. 3
Her trumpet and her merry song
Now for to hear, I think it long.
Commend me to her, I you pray,
And to Agnes Irpe, as bright as day.
I would you were here to lock our gates,
But alas, it is too far to the Jakes. 4

---

[1] *strange* ] alien, unreceptive; *range* ] hunting-ground.

[2] *Bune* ] possibly Bowen or Bean (as a last name) or Bennet or Benedicta (as a first name) [documented spellings]; perhaps also *bun,* squirrel, as a term of endearment.

[3] *moe* ] more; *Gullet* ] 1. gullet; 2. Juliet (possibly a servant or musician employed by Bune, the addressee); *knackes ... bouget* ] baubles in her sack (with bawdy innuendo).

[4] *Jakes* ] 1. Jacques; 2. outhouse.

Farewell, fair Agnes Blackamore:
I would I had you here in store,
For you would come with all your heart:
Farewell, farewell, my lady dark.
Commend me to Willi'm, I you desire,
And pray him to wish us some of his fire,
For we have none but a Cole or a stick,
And so we drive away the weke. [1]
And commend me also to th' rough Holly
That turneth it oft into goddes-body, [2]
And to all your oder fellows beside,
As well as I had their names descried. [3]
[25] And pray John Cossall to be good and kind,
For the nextè year he will be blind.
And bid Humphrey do him no shrowd turn,
For then Sir John mustè him Worm. [4]
And commend me to Thomson, that tall man,
Which should have a ladder° to piss in a can.
And also to Nicholas with the black beard,
On whom to look it makes me affeared. [5]
My uncles and my aunt be merry and glad
And thanks be to God, I am not sad.
And Christopher your friend is of good cheer
And many times he wisheth him there.
Fair tokens I would have sent
But I lackèd money for to spend.
And thus, fare you well this good new year:
I pray you, be merry and of good cheer!
And for the love of sweet Saint Denyes
At this my letter think no unkindness,
For to make you all merry I do rhyme.
And now to leave I think it time.

At nine of the clock this was written:
I wouldè you were all beshetten! [6] (ca. 1534)

---

[1] *Cole* ] coal; apparently punning on a servant or friend having Cole as a surname; *drive ... weke* ] 1. pass the week (watching the coals); 2. drive away the weak (with a stick); and perhaps also 3. use up the (candle) wick.

[2] *rough Holly* ] apparently referring to a priest surnamed Holly, possibly with a pun also on Rafe as a first name; *turneth ... body* ] the holly, with its red berries, was often used in lessons as an emblem of Christ's crucified body ("goddes-body "); here probably a Rev. Holly who found his surname to be meaningful on account of its religious significance, or who employed it as a figure for the Eucharist.

[3] *As well* ] As well as if; *descried* ] 1. mentioned, declared; 2. disparaged.

[4] *bid ... turn* ] Forbid Humphrey (possibly Humphrey Welles) to play tricks on him; *Sir John* ] conventional epithet for a priest, but possibly punning here on a priest named John Worm.

[5] *affeared* ] MS *a Ferde*; possibly another name pun.

[6] *beshetten* ] shut up for the night (perhaps with scatalogical pun).

## **Mary Ostrewyk** (c.1470-1547)

*Of this life, says Love, we wish to speak...*
—Marguerite Porete of Hainault

IN the early twelfth century, women in the Low Countries who lived alone (many of them widows, or wives whose husbands had gone on the crusades) sustained one another in communal living and good works. The movement grew rapidly, without formal organization. Each community, or "Beguinage," was self-sustaining and had its own house rules. The emphasis, in most, was a decidedly mystical form of Christianity. Novitiates lived with a "Grand Maisteress," but after learning the discipline could have their own dwellings. The Beguines were not nuns and did not take vows. They were free to come and go as they pleased, or as the Spirit led. The women were bound together by shared ideals, dream visions, and by a common mission to minister to the poor and dispossessed. Some communities were exclusive, accepting only the social elite; others were comprised largely of beggars. The great Beguinage of Ghent, which accepted women of all social ranks, swelled to a community of many thousands.

The Beguines were influenced by The Brethren of the Free Spirit, a lay Christian movement declared heretical by Pope Clement in 1311/12. Early Beguine writers included Mechtild von Magdeburg (c. 1212-1285), a mystic who wrote an account of her visions called *The Flowing Light of the Godhead*, a popular text lost to history but rediscovered in the nineteenth century. Marguerite Porete (c. 1250-1310), author of a similar book called *The Mirror of Simple Souls,* and who wrote and preached of her visions, was burnt at the stake in 1310 for her refusal to recant.

Suppressed under Popes John XXII, Urban V, and Gregory XI, the Beguines were rehabilitated in the fifteenth century by Eugene IV, and again thrived. Marie Ostrewyk, also known as Marie van Hout, was born about 1470. Late in life, she met Gehrhard Kalckbrenner, a Carthusian monk from Cologne. Impressed with her spirituality, Kalckbrenner printed a spiritual exercise by Marie that reflected on the Five Wounds of Christ (in *Der rechte Wech zo der evangelischer Volkomenheit* [The Right Path to Evangelical Perfection], 1531); ascribing the vision to "a simple and pious person whose name is known unto God." A year later, the exercise was printed in a Latin version, attributed to "a certain virgin, close to God and most devout." The Latin text is the apparent source for the English version found in British Library MS Harley 494.

Mary Ostrewyk died on 30 September 1547.

### Certain Prayers Shewed unto a Devout Person called Mary Ostrewyk

First, in remembrance of the wound in the right hand of our Savior Christ Jesu, oon pater-noster and oon ave Maria – that God graunt us to have prompt° obedience.

The wound in the left hand, the second paternoster – for the profound meekness.
To the right foot, the thrid paternoster – for peacable patience.
To the left foot, the fourth paternoster – to be merciful and pitiful.
To the wound in the side, the fifth° – for parfit charity.

*All to be said standing, the arms spread abroad. This done, to continue, and immediately say five paternosters with so many aves, in remembrance of five principal sorrows of our Lady*:

The first, when she saw° the tender body of her Son beaten with scourges and other.
The second, when he was extended upon the cross.
The thrid,° when he was nailed and shed his precious blood upon the cross.
The fourth,° when he was fed with acer and gall.
The five, when the side was opened with the spear.
And then, kneeling, say *Veni, sancte spiritus*. *Emitte*. *Deus qui corda*. [1]

---

[1] *acer* ] vinegar; *Veni, sancte spiritus* ] Come, Holy Spirit; *Emitte* ] "Send forth [thy wisdom]..." *Deus qui corda* ] "God, [Thou] who [hast taught] the hears [of thy faithful]..." These Latin passages are a conventional prayer to the holy Ghost.

## **Eleanor (Sutton) Somerset** (c. 1489 – 1526/49), **Countess of Worcester**

RIOR to the advent of the printing press, only the most wealthy families could afford to own books. Early on in the history of book-lending, owners learned to identify their valued books to ensure that they would be returned when lent out to friends or relatives. In addition to distinctive bindings (often embossed with the family's coat of arms), book-owners sometimes composed bookplate-rhymes to remind the borrower to return lent volumes. Among the earliest surviving bookplates in English are verses by Eleanor Somerset, countess of Worcester. Somerset was the daughter of Edward Sutton, fifth lord Dudley, and of Cecily Willoughby Sutton; the fifth of sixteen children. She was the third wife of Charles Somerset (1460-1526), earl of Worcester. Lady Eleanor married secondly Lord Leonard Gray. The couple died without issue, Lord Gray being executed on Tower Hill on 28 July 1541 for having supported the rebelling Irish. Lady Eleanor may have died before him, certainly before 1549. She was buried at Ulverscroft Priory in Leicestershire. Her verses (on the left) probably date from about 1520.

**[Front Book-Plate:]**
This book is one,
And God's course is anoder
They that take the t'on
God give them the t'oder. [1]

**[Prayer to the Virgin]**
Most wisest lady,
Most chastest lady,
Most trustiest lady,
Most lowliest lady,
Most obedient lady,
Most gracious lady,
Most patient lady,
Most purest lady,
Most meekest lady,
Most sorrowful lady: Ave Maria.

**[Rear Book-Plate:]**
*This book is mine—Eleanor Worcester*
And I it lese, and you it find,
I pray you heartily to be so kind
That you will take a little pain
To see my book brought home again.
*Eleanor° Worcester* (early 16th C.)

Some additional examples of the bookplate from the 14th through 18th centuries:

This book is one,
Christ's curse is anoder
He that steeleth the t'on
I pray God send him the t'oder.
*quod Iohannes Wrightson* (14th C.)

*Thomas Shardelow ow'eth this book.*
God give him grace on it to look.
If I it lose and you it find
I pray you be not so unkind
But give to me my book again
And I will please you for your pain.
(In *Treasurie of Amadis of France,* 1572?)

[*owner unidentified*]
If it be lost and you it find
I pray you heartily be so kind
I pray you heartily be so kind
To send me my book home again. (late 16th C)

*I, Robert Barker, priest, did write this...*
If I it lose and you it find
I pray for you to be so kind
As for to let me have my book
Again and ye shall have no worse
But a penny to put in your purse.
(1626 Christian Bible)

Whosoever herein do look,
*Nicholas Kent of West Ketford*
*Oweth this Booke, 1689.*
If I it lose and you it find,
I pray be so good and kind
As for to give it me again,
More nor less but just one
Penny to put in purse. (in 1586 Bible)

*David Franks owns this book*
Witness for it, those that look
If it be lost and you it find
Return it for it is mine.
(18th C. Hebrew Bible inscribed Jan. 24, 1723/4)

---

[1] *course* ] lesson, with pun on *curse;* *that take the t'on* ] 1. that take this course; 2. that steal this book; *God ... t'oder* ] 1. May God give them his course as well; 2. May God give them a curse (for stealing).

# **Catherine of Aragon** (1485-1536),

Queen of Henry VIII

*Es una bestia feroz quien no comprende que*
*las ideas no pueden combatirse a cañonazos.*
—Catalina de Aragón

CATHERINE of ARAGON was the youngest daughter of Ferdinand of Aragon and Isabella of Castile. By the time "Catalina" was born, her parents had taken most of Spain from the Muslim emirate. An English royal on the mother's side, her great-grandmother as well as a great-great-grandmother were daughters of John of Gaunt (whose father was England's Edward III). Always on the move as an infant, the Spanish Infanta after Ferdinand's victory at Granada dwelt in splendor in the Alhambra. An avid reader, she learned to write in Spanish, Latin, and French. Her curriculum included religion, the Roman classics (some Greek), canon and civil law, and history. Her training in the arts and crafts of fifteenth-century Spain included music and dance, needlepoint, lace-making, and embroidery.

On 19 September 1486, when Elizabeth of York was delivered of a man-child, her husband Henry VII wasted no time: soon after sending the birth announcement, or perhaps with the same dispatch, the King of England proposed that Ferdinand and Isabella consider a match between their daughter and his newborn son, Prince Arthur. (When ambassadors from Spain arrived in England to discuss the betrothal, Catalina was not yet two years old, and Arthur not yet one.) A draft agreement was reached on 7 July 1488: Catalina's dowry was fixed at 200,000 Spanish escudos, to be paid in two installments. For her maintenance, the Infanta would receive 1/3 of Arthur's rents, hers to keep if the Prince of Wales predeceased her. After many delays, the prenuptials were signed on 1 January 1497/8.

Catalina, 16, after a stormy passage disembarked at Plymouth on 2 October 1498. An eventful progress across the country and down the Thames River brought her at last to London. In a grand procession on 12 November, Arthur's bride (English "Catherine" hereafter), entered the city seated upon a mule (as per Spanish custom), riding between the Duke of York and the papal ambassador. Her four Spanish damsels followed on mules, led by English ladies dressed in cloth-of-gold and riding on palfreys. The wedding was solemnized on 14 November at old St. Paul's Cathedral. A week of feasting, jousting, music, and dramatic pageants ensued; but Arthur was anxious to return to his duties in the Welsh marches. The newlyweds, able to converse only in Latin, departed for Ludlow Castle on 21 December.

The newlyweds had not cohabited for more than a few weeks when they both became gravely ill, possibly of the dreaded "sweating sickness," a virulent disease of the Tudor period. Prince Arthur died on April 2nd, at age 15. Catherine hung on, but remained gravely ill for weeks.

Much wrangling ensued between Spain and England. Resenting King Henry's miserly treatment of their ailing daughter, Ferdinand and Isabella demanded that she be returned home, along with her trousseau, plate, jewelry, and the 100,000 gold escudos already paid in dowry. Henry, taking the position that a deal's a deal, not only refused to return the 50% down-payment; he demanded another 100,000 escudos; and he denied the young widow Prince Arthur's rents until Spain settled the tab. These differences were resolved by the betrothal of Catherine to Arthur's younger brother Prince Henry, by a treaty signed 25 June 1503.

The papal bull approving the match did not reach England until March 1504/5, by which time both queen-mothers had died (Elizabeth in 1503, Isabella in 1504). Plus, shifting political alliances had by this time cooled Henry VII's desire for an alliance with Ferdinand; as a result, Prince Henry's ardor cooled as well: on 27 June 1505, the Prince of Wales renounced his 1503 betrothal to Catherine, stating that it was done without his consent – which Spain took for the latest negotiating tactic of his father the king.

Catherine of Aragon as a young woman
*Kunsthistorisches Museum* (*Vienna*)

Catherine was now living in poverty and said to be indulging in religious austerities, possibly in the form of anorexia, that were of concern to the English court. She was therefore removed to Richmond House, and kept under close watch on a shoestring budget, but without liberty to see Henry Jr. or Sr. or to associate with anyone but her Spanish retinue. Her opportunities to learn English improved somewhat in 1507, when King Ferdinand appointed his daughter, now 22, to head his embassy to the court of young King Henry VIII (making Catherine the first female ambassador in European history).

With the death of Henry VII on 21 April 1509, her fortunes suddenly improved – or seemed to: Henry VIII, 18, took Catherine to wife on June 11th. The marriage was happy at first, despite disappointments: Never robust after her 1501 illness, Queen Catherine from 1509-1516 had at least six pregnancies; of those infants that reached full term, none lived longer than 52 days except Mary, who was born on 18 February 1515/6. Another pregnancy in 1518, Catherine's last, ended in a stillbirth.

Already by 1514 a rumor had circulated in Rome that Henry intended to repudiate Catherine, in order to marry one of his mistresses; but the king made no recorded effort to dissolve his marriage until 1527, when Anne Boleyn insisted upon it; by which time Henry was still without a male heir, Catherine was beyond child-bearing age, and Anne Boleyn seemed his best ticket to a son. Henry banished Catherine in 1531; and when the Pope would not annul his marriage, and Anne Boleyn was pregnant, Henry took the divorce, and the English Church, into his own hands.

The 1533/4 Act of Succession declared Queen Catherine an incestuous adulteress (by virtue of her prior marriage to Arthur); "Lady" Mary, a bastard; and Princess Elizabeth the king's only legitimate child (and the heir apparent, until a brother was born). King Henry demanded that Mary swear her agreement to the Act. Mary stubbornly refused to sign. To coerce her compliance, Henry employed all tactics that were politically expedient. He dismissed her household and placed her in the custody of Queen Anne's Shelton kin, where Mary was deprived of her income and wardrobe, and forbidden to see visitors, including her mother. Still she refused.

On 25 March 1533/4, Parliament upped the ante by passing the Act of Supremacy, which made Henry, not the Pope, the supreme head of the English Church; and condemned as traitors all who declined to swear allegiance to the King in that capacity. Henry now demanded further that Mary take the oath of Supremacy. On this news, Catherine wrote to her daughter at once, in English. Fearing that Mary would be poisoned by the King if she did not comply, but damned to Hell if she did, Catherine in a smuggled letter advised her daughter to obey her father the King in all things except those which would offend God.

**[Queen Catherine of Aragon to her daughter, Princess Mary (April 1534)°]**

Daughter,

I heard such tidings today that I do perceive if it be true, the time is come that almighty God will prove you; and I am very glad of it, for I trust He doth handle you with a good love. I beseech you: agree of His pleasure with a merry heart; and be sure that, without fail, He will not suffer you to perish if you beware to offend Him. I pray you, good daughter, to offer yourself to Him. If any pangs come to you, shrive yourself. First make you clean. Take heed of His commandments and keep them as near as He will give you grace to do, for then you are sure armed. And if this lady [Anne Shelton] do come to you as it is spoken, if she do bring you a letter from the King, I am sure in the selfsame letter you shall be commanded what you shall do.[1] Answer with few words, obeying the King your father in everything, save only that you will not offend God and lose your own soul; and go no further with learning and disputation in the matter. And where soever, and in whatsoever company you shall come, observe the King's commandments.[2] Speak you few words and meddle nothing. I will send you two books in Latin; the one shall be *De Vita Christi* with a declaration of the Gospels, and the other the *Epistles* of St Jerome that he did write to Paul and Eustochium, and in them I trust you shall see good things. And sometimes for your recreation use your virginals or lute, if you have any.

But one thing I especially desire you, for the love that you do owe unto God and unto me: to keep your heart with a chaste mind, and your body from all ill and wanton company, [not] thinking or desiring any husband for Christ's passion; neither determine yourself to any manner of living till this troublesome time be past. For I dare make sure that you shall see a very good end, and better than you can desire. I would God, good daughter, that you did know with how good a heart I do write this letter unto you. I never did one with a better, for I perceive very well that God loveth you. I beseech Him of His goodness

---

1 *this lady* ] Anne Boleyn Shelton, who was assigned custody of princess Mary during Queen Anne's tenure.

2 *commandments* ] i.e., the command to endorse the Act of Supremacy and the Act of Succession.

to continue it; and if it fortune that you shall have nobody with you of your acquaintance, I think it best you keep your keys yourself, for howsoever it is, so shall be done as shall please them. And now you shall begin, and by likelihood I shall follow. I set not a rush by it; for when they have done the uttermost they can, than I am sure of the amendment. I pray you, recommend me unto my good lady of Salisbury, and pray her to have a good heart, for we never come to the kingdom of Heaven but by troubles.[1] Daughter, where soever you come, take no pain to send unto me; for if I may, I will send to you.

yours lovyng mother — Your loving mother,

Katherina the quene — Katherina the quene

• • •

On her mother's cue, Mary refused to buckle. Then came the 1534 Treason Act, which made it a capital crime not to take the oath of Supremacy. (Sir Thomas More was among those who were killed for failing to submit.) Still Mary held her course, willing to be martyred—until she lost her main stay of support:

**[Catherine to King Henry from her deathbed (6 Jan. 1535/6)°]**

My most dear lord, king, and husband,

The hour of my death now drawing on, the tender love I owe you forceth me, my case being such, to commend myself to you, and to put you in remembrance with a few words of the health and safeguard of your soul, which you ought to prefer before all worldly matters and before the care and pampering of your body, for the which you have cast me into many calamities and yourself into many troubles.

For my part, I pardon you everything, and I wish and devoutly pray God that He will pardon you also. For the rest, I commend unto you our daughter Mary, beseeching you to be a good father unto her, as I have heretofore desired. I entreat you also, on behalf of my maids, to give them marriage portions, which is not much, they being but three. For all my other servants, I solicit the wages due them, and a year more, lest they be unprovided for. Lastly, I make this vow, that mine eyes desire you above all things.

Katherine

Catherine as Henry's Queen
*National Portrait Gallery* (*London*)

*7 Jan.* "At dawn she heard mass, and took the Holy Sacrament with the greatest fervor and devotion that could be imagined; after which she went on repeating various prayers, begging those who were present to pray for the salvation of her soul, and that God would pardon and forgive the King, her husband, for the wrong he had done her, inspire him to follow the right path, and give him good counsel. After which, the Queen received extreme unction, she herself replying distinctly to all the questions of the ritual in a clear audible voice. Knowing that in England no woman surviving her husband can make a will, the Queen, for fear of infringing the law of the land, would not dispose of her property otherwise than by way of supplication and request to the King. ... The good Queen breathed her last at 2 o'clock in the afternoon."[2]

Six months later, by a sworn letter of submission, Mary finally caved. She lived another twenty-two years after that, but was never the same. In 1558, having reigned five years as Queen; having reestablished Roman Catholicism and restored many religious houses; having done penance by the burning of some 280 Protestants, Mary died, still fearing that her sinful soul would not see bliss, with her saintly mother.

---

[1] *Lady Salisbury* ] Margaret de la Pole, countess of Salisbury; Mary's governess and confidante; in 1533 Henry dismissed her; and in 1541, put her to death on a trumped-up charge of treason.

[2] Eustace Chapuys to Carlos V (21 Jan. 1535/6), *State Papers Spain*, 5.2 (1536–38), no. 9.

# **Elizabeth Barton** (1506?-1533),

## The Holy Maid of Kent

*go unto the kyng, that infydell prynce of Inglond,*
*and say that I comaund hym to amend his lyve...*
—angel of God to Elizabeth Barton (MS Cotton Cleop. E.iv. fol. 75)

LIZABETH BARTON, Benedictine nun and religious activist, was born in 1506 at Aldington, Kent. A commoner, she took employment as a domestic servant at Goldwell, a manor house owned by William Warham, archbishop of Canterbury. She was intensely devout; and at age 19, her spirituality found expression in a series of trances that lasted for days at a time. Though unable to read or write more than her own name, Barton while under the influence of the Holy Ghost described the geography of Heaven, Hell, and Purgatory; defended the doctrine of transubstantiation; proclaimed the necessity of the Roman Catholic Mass, pilgrimage, confession to priests, and prayer to the Virgin and the saints; railed against Protestantism and the Seven Deadly Sins; and uttered worrisome prophecies. The "Holy Maid of Kent" soon became a local celebrity as country folk gathered round her bedside to observe her fits and trances, and to be edified by her sermons, which seemed to come from a voice not her own, but from somewhere deep in her bowels.

When this activity in his own country manor was brought to the attention of Archbishop Warham, he authorized an inquiry, headed by Edward Bocking, a monk and Oxford scholar. The Commissioners were soon persuaded that the maid was of holy condition and that her visions were authentic: her chastity was assured beyond a reasonable doubt, and her revelations contained no hint of Lollardy or Lutheranism to indicate that her inspiration came from Satan rather than from God.

Afflicted with fits that contorted her face and wracked her body, Barton predicted that she would be healed of her infirmity during Lent 1526, at the Chapel of our Lady in the nearby village of Court-at-Street, where she had experienced her first vision, years before. This event, announced in advance, was attended by the Commissioners and by a lay audience of two to three thousand.

Soon after the miracle of her healing, Barton persuaded the Commissioners that it was God's will for her to become a professed nun – an honor usually accorded only to the daughters of aristocrats. She entered the Benedictine priory of Saint Sepulchre, Canterbury, as a postulant. Soon after, sans the usual dower but with Warham's blessing, she was admitted to the novitiate. The Maid asked that Bocking be appointed her confessor and spiritual advisor, and he agreed; under whose tutelage the Nun of Kent began to model herself on the lives and revelations of Saint Bridget of Sweden and Saint Catherine of Siena.

By the summer of 1527, Barton had taken her vows; but visitors were allowed free access to meet with her and to attend her revelations. Laymen and clergy came from all over England to consult with the Holy Maid about their lives and sins and future; and to seek her intercession for the sick, the dying, and the dead. Warham, having met with Barton, sent an account of her visions to Henry VIII. The king for a second opinion forwarded Warham's report to his Lord Chancellor, Sir Thomas More, who was the Maid's first recorded skeptic: "I found nothing in these words," wrote More, "that I could anything regard or esteem. For, saving that some part fell in rhyme (and that, God wot, full rude!), else for any reason (God wot) that I saw therein, a right simple woman might, in my mind, speak it of her own wit, well enough" (*Correspondence*, 481).

Barton demanded to meet with Cardinal Thomas Wolsey and with the King himself. In a letter dated 1 October 1528, Archbishop Warham recommended her to Wolsey as "a very well-disposed and virtuous woman (as I am informed by her susters)" and "very desirous to speak with your Grace personally. What she hath to say, or whether it be good or ill, I do not know; but she hath desired me to write unto your Grace and to desire the same (as I do) that she may come to your Grace's presence."[1]

The Cardinal twice met with Barton and was favorably impressed. It was probably through Wolsey's intercession that she was allowed face-time with King Henry as well, not just once, but on least three occasions.

---

[1] National Archives, State Papers 1/50, fol. 163.

Given the Maid's welcome support for the burning of heretics and hanging of rebels, Henry was at first tolerant of Elizabeth Barton's popularity, and he even extended signs of his favor.[1] What ultimately led to the Holy Maid's downfall was not public skepticism but her interest in affairs of State: when it was announced that Henry was suffering pangs of guilt over his twenty-year marriage to his brother's widow, and pangs of desire for Anne Boleyn, Barton received from the Virgin a warning that King Henry must never divorce Catherine of Aragon, much less divorce her in order to wed another.

Finding Warham and Wolsey well disposed to the king's marriage plans, Barton threatened them both with divine retribution. Wolsey, perhaps in response to that dire warning, began dragging his heels on the King's divorce. The delay infuriated Anne Boleyn without placating Elizabeth Barton; besides which, the Cardinal's repentance came too late to save him from his fate: In November 1530, Wolsey died on his way to London to be arraigned for treason.

Henry dismissed Catherine in July 1531; but while the nation waited on an annulment from the Pope, the Holy Maid of Kent gave his Majesty a piece of the Lord's mind: in one particularly unequivocal prophecy, she warned the nation that "in case his Highness proceeded to th'accomplishment of the said divorce and married another, that then his Majesty should not be king of this Realm by the space of one month after – and in the reputation of God should not be king one day nor one hour."[2]

Advised by Sir Thomas More and others to keep silent on matters of State, Barton boldly refused to hold her peace. An angel appeared to her, who said: "Go unto the King, that infidel prince of England, and say that I command him to amend his life, and that he leave three things which he loveth and purposeth upon: that is, that he take none of the Pope's right nor patrimony from him; the second, that he destroy all these new folks of opinion and the works of their new learning; the third, that if he married and took Anne to wife the vengeance of God should plague him." Barton was shown a vision of the exact place in Hell reserved for England's king if he should fail to submit to her good counsel. In another vision, Barton saw Anne Boleyn, Anne's father Thomas Boleyn, and King Henry conferring in a garden. The conspirators (as she beheld them) despaired of any means by which the annulment might be approved by Pope Clement and by the Holy Roman Emperor, Carlos V (Queen Catherine's nephew); but then "a little devil stood besides the queen [Anne], and put in her mind to say thus: 'You shall send my father unto th' emperor; and let him show the emperor your mind and conscience; and give him these many thousand ducats to have his good will, and thus it will be brought to pass." [3]

Anne's father was indeed dispatched to Europe; and he met at Bologna with Carlos. But thousands of ducats would not obtain the emperor's consent. (This was the same trip on which Sir Thomas famously declined to kiss the Pope's toe.) Henry meantime proceeded with his plans to dissolve the monasteries and appropriate their lands to the Crown; to divorce Catherine; and to marry Anne Boleyn; with or without the approval of the Pope, the Holy Roman Emperor, and the English nation.

In September 1532, the King traveled with Anne to Calais, there to meet with Francois I, king of France. Rumors were rife that the royal couple would return home married (as indeed they did, in the eyes of God, though there would be no wedding until January, by which time Anne was already pregnant).

While Henry and Anne were yet in France, the Holy Maid of Kent experienced a vision in which a priest serving Mass to the King in Calais had the Eucharistic host snatched from his hand by an angel, who brought it for Barton to receive instead. Returning from France, Henry and Anne passed through Canterbury on their way to London. Barton thrust herself into the presence of the King, anxiously proclaiming his eternal damnation. All England was thereby put on notice: one of them – either the King of England, or the Maid of Kent – was in favor with Almighty God; and the other was headed for a fall. The pious money was on Elizabeth Barton; the smart money was on King Henry.

Barton was by this time was no longer her own woman, having been co-opted by the King's critics and the supporters of Rome, who fed her inside information in order to receive feedback from the Lord. Barton communicated through translators with the papal ambassadors Silvestro Dario and Antonio de

---

[1] PRO, SP 1/80, fol. 138.

[2] 25 Henry VIII, c. 12, Statutes of the Realm, 446; cf. Thomas Cranmer to Archdeacon Nicholas Hawkins (20 Dec. 1534): "She said that the King should not continue King a month after that he were married, and within six months after, God would strike the realm with such a plague as never was seen. And then the King should be destroyed" (B.L. Harl. MS. 6148. fol. 38).

[3] MS. Cotton. Cleopat. E. iv. fol. 75.

Pulleo; and sent letters directly to Pope Clement VII, encouraging him to stand fast in his opposition to England's sinful King; stating that if the Pope ruled against Queen Catherine, "Almighty God would be displeased with him, and send plagues to him for it."[1]

In January, following the news of his marriage to Anne Boleyn, King Henry – long after his predicted demise – remained robustly healthy. The Maid's credibility, as well as the Pope's, thereby suffered a blow that was not easily mended. There ensued an all-out propaganda war. Bocking gathered Elizabeth's sayings into a book, and arranged to have seven hundred copies printed. The mendicant friars meanwhile spread report of the Maid's new revelation that Henry, though not slain outright, was no longer King of England in the Lord's eyes. Henry's agents responded with reports that Elizabeth Barton engaged in sex with priests and was mentally deranged.

William Warham having died in August 1532, Thomas Cranmer his successor was strong for the king – and out of patience with Elizabeth Barton. In July, Henry was excommunicated by Pope Clement; that gave renewed authority to the Maid of Kent's dire predictions for the nation of England. Moving to contain the damage, Archbishop Cranmer on 19 July wrote to the prioress of St. Sepulchre's with instructions for the Maid of Kent to be delivered to his manor at Otford for an interview; where Barton was duly interrogated, then released. A few weeks later, however, Bocking was arrested, his residence searched, and all of his writings confiscated; from which quotations were gleaned that were cited as treasonable. In November, Barton was arrested and interrogated by judges of the Star Chamber; on whose unconfirmed reports she was said to have confessed herself a fraud. Barton, five clergymen including Bocking, and two laymen, were forced to perform public penance – first at St. Paul's Cross, London, two weeks later at Canterbury – proclaiming themselves traitors and heretics; whereupon the alleged conspirators were returned to prison.

In March 1534, Barton and six of her supporters (priests and monks) were condemned of heresy and high treason, by attainder (without benefit of a trial). The seven felons were hanged at Tyburn on 20 April, then beheaded. Seven others, including the bishop of Rochester, were imprisoned, and forfeited their goods and property to the Crown. Sir Thomas More was accused but proved his innocence; he was therefore put to death instead for his refusal to sign the oath of supremacy, required by the First Succession Act.

from Hans Holbein, Dance of Death (1538)

The executions were supplemented with an unprecedented State publicity blitz: sermons were preached from the pulpit against the fraudulent Maid of Kent and her co-conspirators. Proclamations were read throughout the Realm giving citizens forty days to surrender any books or writings that touched upon Elizabeth Barton and her visions. The religious houses were condemned as dens of sedition, and the Dissolution praised. Many of Barton's former supporters, including the Carthusian monks of Charterhouse and Sheen, and the inmates of the monastery of Sion, outdid one another in their denunciations of the Maid whom they once considered a prophet inspired of God.

We have no eyewitness accounts of Elizabeth Barton's execution; but a thoughtfully crafted scaffold speech was delivered in her behalf, and circulated after, that struck all of the right notes, including a touch of self-justification and several authentic grammatical solecisms:

[1] ibid., fol. 79.

Hither am I come to die; and I have not been the only cause of mine own death (which most justly I have deserved!), but also I am the cause of the death of all these persons which at this time here suffer. And yet, to say the truth, I am not so much to be blamed, considering it was well known unto these learnèd men that I was a poor wench without learning; and therefore they might have easily perceived that the things that were done by me could not proceed in no such sort; but their capacities and learning could right well judge from whence they proceeded, and that they were altogether feigned. But because the things which I feigned was profitable unto them, therefore they much praised me, and bare me in hand, that it was the holy Ghost and not I that did them. And then I, being puffed up with their praises, fell into a certain pride and foolish fantasy with myself, and thought I might feign what I would; which thing hath brought me to this case; and for the which now I cry God and the King's Highness' most heartily mercy; and desire all you, good people, to pray to God to have mercy on me, and on all them that here suffer with me.

As a convicted felon, all of Elizabeth Barton's property, wardrobe, and furniture was forfeit to the State. An inventory survives of her worldly possessions at the time of her death:

## Inventory [of Elizabeth Barton, the Maid of Kent] (1534)

Stuff received the 16th day of February [1533/4], of dame Elizabeth Barton, by the hands of the prioress of Saint Sepulchre's-without-Canterbury, into the hands of John Anthony of Canterbury, as hereafter followeth:

- First, a cushion blade, and one old cushion.
- Two carpets, whereof one is cut into pieces.
- A old mattress, seven coarse sheets, a coverlet and a pair of blankets, with two pillows and a bolster.
- Two plates, four dishes, two saucers, and a little basin weighing twelve lbs., at fourpence a lb., which my lady prioress hath, and paid four shillings.
- A white corter, which my lady prioress hath, and paid twelve pence.[1]
- A little old diaper towel.
- Three pillow-beres.[2]
- Two can'sticks.
- A coat, which dame Katherine Wittsam hath, [and] paid five shillings.
- A piece of a plank for a table.
- A little chest.

Stuff which remaineth in the nunnery pertaining unto Dame Elizabeth Barton, at the request of my lady Prioress:

- First, two new cushions, given unto the church.
- A old mantle and a kirtle, unto the youngest nun.
- A Irish mantle, a collar, with two great chests, and two stools and a can'stick, to my lady Prioress.
- A coverlet, and a old kirtle, to dame Alice Coleman, at the request of my lady Prioress.

The headless corpse of Elizabeth Barton was buried at Greyfriars Church in Newgate Street. Her head was mounted on a spike on London Bridge. (Deemed a dangerous public enemy, the Holy Maid of Kent is the only woman ever to receive that distinction.) Her reputation ever since has been in the custody of Anglican historians who have typically represented Elizabeth Barton either as a pathetic dupe manipulated by Catholic churchmen or as a cunning charlatan who made love to her employment and who therefore got exactly what she deserved.

DWF

---

[1] *corter* ] bedspread.

[2] *pillow-beres* ] pillow cases.

# **Anne Boleyn** (1501?-1536),

## Queen of Henry VIII

*The Most Happy*
—motto of King Henry's second queen

NNE BOLEYN, daughter of Elizabeth (b. Howard), was a granddaughter to Elizabeth (b. Tilney) and Thomas Howard, the Duchess and Duke of Norfolk. Her father, Thomas Boleyn, a diplomat, was Viscount Rochford (later, earl of Ormonde and Wiltshire).[1] Anne spent much of her childhood on the Continent mastering the lifestyles of the rich and famous. In 1521, when tensions between England and France caused her to return home, her father secured her a coveted position as a maid-of-honor in the court of Catherine of Aragon. King Henry by that time had discarded Agnes Blewitt (his sixth mistress mentioned by name in the historical record). In the winter of 1519/20, having grown fond of Mary Boleyn, Henry possibly jousted in Mary's honor at the Field of Cloth of Gold in June. When he jousted two years later, on 2 March 1521/2, Henry rode a horse in silver trappings, embroidered with a wounded heart and the motto, "Elle mon coeur a navera" (*She has wounded my heart*).

Not wishing to stain her honor with a bastard, King Henry wedded Mary Boleyn to William Carey, a gentleman of the Privy Chamber; and paid Carey a generous pension so that he wouldn't mind lending his wife to the King, who kept her for four years. In the autumn of 1526, during a pregnancy, Henry's Rent-a-Wife returned to William Carey, to begin cohabitation with her husband.

When Mary Boleyn gave birth to Henry Jr. (4 March 1525/6), the King declined to acknowledge the lad. His heart had since been wounded by Joan Dingley, a royal laundress by whom the King begot a daughter (later wed to Sir John Harington, godson of Queen Elizabeth).

Anne Boleyn was not long at court before she attracted suitors, including two of England's most handsome and glamorous bachelors: the poet, Sir Thomas Wyatt, and Henry Percy, sixth earl of Northumberland. As early as 1523, Anne Boleyn and Henry Percy wished to marry, but the King interfered: Cardinal Wolsey, always ready to do his Lord's bidding, raised an impediment to their union. Young Northumberland was obliged to wed Mary Talbot instead.

That said, King Henry's suffering for Anne Boleyn cannot be dated earlier than the Shrove Tuesday jousting of 1526. (On that occasion, Henry wore the guise of a tortured lover, under the motto, "Declare, I dare not.") Playing hard to get, Anne retired to Hever Castle, resisting Henry's advances, which only increased his ardor. In a 1527 letter, Henry proclaims that his royal heart hath "been now above one whole year struck with the dart of love." Not until Henry pledged marriage did Anne capitulate.

When King Henry first pursued Anne Boleyn, it's not as if the king of England one night jumped from the bed of Mary Boleyn and into the arms of her sister. There was at least one affair, possibly more, that came between, plus a protracted petition for divorce. Nor is it true that Henry ever slept with the duchess of Norfolk: in 1535, when it was alleged the King had enjoyed sexual congress both with Anne's mother and sister, Henry replied, "Never with the mother."[2] King Henry had his standards. In fact, it was his passion for Anne Boleyn that first caused the King of England to have Hamlet-like moral scruples concerning the practice, widespread among European bluebloods, of having sex with multiple siblings: Specifically, it bothered King Henry in 1527 that Catherine of Aragon, his 42-year-old wife, had been married to his brother Arthur for a few weeks, back in 1502. It troubled his conscience so severely that he applied in August for a papal dispensation for annulment, so that he and Anne Boleyn could be married.

Preserved in the Vatican Library (of all places!) are seventeen of Henry's amorous epistles to Lady Anne from May 1527 to October 1528. (One suspects that the letters were purloined by a supporter of Queen Catherine sometime after October 1528, and sent to the Pope Clement VII in an effort to derail the King's plans for a divorce and second wedding.) The return correspondence, if there was any, is not extant. The Italian historian, Gregorio Leti, in his *Historia o vero Vita di Elisabetta, Regina d'Inghilterra* (1682-1693) printed much unique material, including one letter from Anne addressed to King Henry as early as 1527, another to Cardinal Wolsey dated 1529; but since the Italian text is not identical to Anne's original words; and since no English version of these letters is extant; and since Leti probably invented them from his own fertile mind, they are here omitted (which is too bad, because they're good letters).[3]

---

[1] William Camden, the Tudor historian, gives 1507 as her birth year; modern historians have argued for 1500/1.

[2] *Letters and Papers, Henry VIII*, 12/2, no. 952).

[3] For an English translation of Leti's Italian (1.60, 2.50) see Green, *Letters*, vol. 2, nos. 7, 19.

This 1528 epistle, from Anne to Cardinal Wolsey seeking help with "the King's great matter," is authentic:

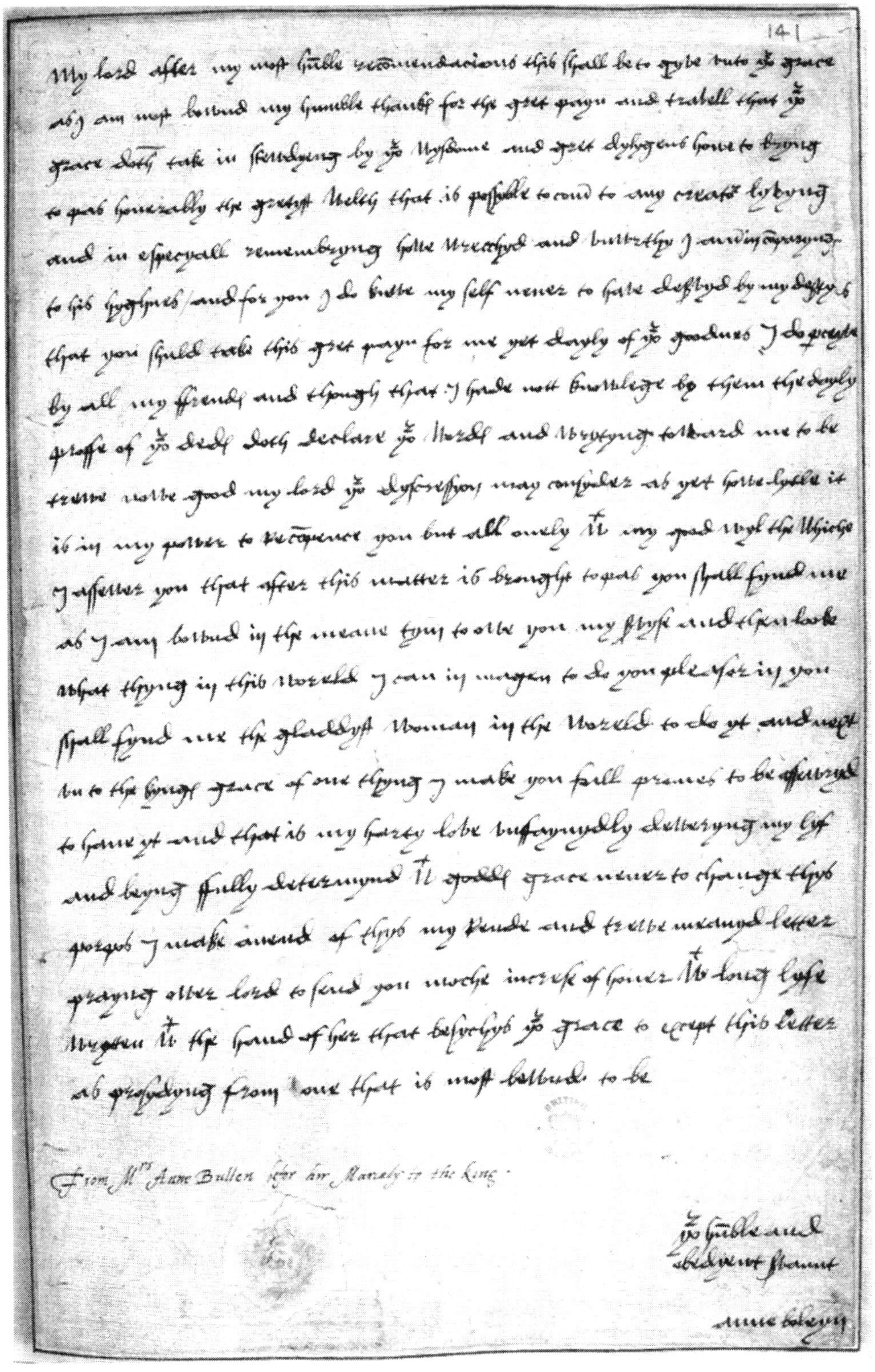
My lord after my most humble recommendacions this shall be to gyve unto yor grace
as I am most bownd my humble thankes for the gret payn and travell that yor
grace doth take in stewdyeng by yor wysdome and gret dyligens howe to bryng
to pas honerably the gretyst welth that is possyble to com to any creatur lyvyng
and in especyall remembryng howe wretchyd and unworthy I am in comparyng
to his hyghnes/ and for you I do know my self never to have deservyd by my desertes
that you shuld take this gret payn for me yet dayly of yor goodnes I do perceyve
by all my frends and though that I had not knowlege by them the dayly
proffe of yor deds doth declare yor words and wrytyng toward me to be
trewe nowe good my lord yor dyscressyon may consyder as yet howe lytle it
is in my power to recompence you but all onely wt my good wyl the whiche
I assewer you that after this matter is brought to pas you shall fynd me
as I am bownd in the meane tyme to owe you my servyce and then loke
what thyng in this world I can imagen to do you pleasor in you
shall fynd me the gladdyst woman in the world to do yt and next
unto the kyngs grace of one thyng I make you full promes to be assewryd
to have yt and that is my harty love unfaynydly duryng my lyf
and beyng fully determynd wt godds grace never to change this
porpos I make an end of this my rewde and trewe meanyd letter
praying ower lord to send you moche incresse of honor wt long lyfe
wryten wt the hand of her that besechys yor grace to except this letter
as prosydyng from one that is most bownd to be

From Mrs Anne Bullen before her Mariage to the King

yor humble and
obedient servaunt

Anne Boleyn

Anne Boleyn to Wolsey (holography, 1528), . BL MS Cotton Vespasian F XII, art. 92, fol. 80.
Courtesy of the Brish Library

Henry and Anne depended on Cardinal Wolsey to obtain Henry's annulment. But they soon found that Pope Clement's top value, with respect to England, was to placate Queen Catherine's nephew: Carlos V, Holy Roman Emperor. As negotiations dragged on, both Anne and Henry came to mistrust Wolsey's effectiveness and sincerity; by mid-1529, Anne counted the Cardinal an enemy (and vice versa). Preparations were made to take Wolsey's head, but on 26 November 1530, jas Sir William Kingston and 24 men stood ready to arrest him for treason, the ailing Cardinal died of illness and fatigue.

The idea that Henry, not an Italian Pope, should have supreme authority over the English Church is a doctrine largely of Anne's creation, in collaboration with Thomas Cranmer. After Wolsey's fall and Cranmer's rise, the clergy improved their cooperation with the King's ambition to displace the Pope. In February 1530/1, as an intermediate step towards independence from Rome, the clerical convocations declared King Henry "Supreme Head" of the English church "as far as the law of Christ allowed."

Queen Catherine all this while remained at court (not to sleep with the King, but to make his shirts and to perform other menial chores). Anne wanted her gone. In July 1531, Henry dismissed Catherine from his presence (for conscience' sake), and assigned the queen's chambers to Anne. On the political front, much of 1531-32 was spent in the struggle to secure general consent to Henry's claim of supreme authority over the Church. But for some things, Henry could not wait. By December 1532, six years after his initial flame, Henry had gotten Anne pregnant. A secret shotgun wedding followed, in January. Cranmer was installed as Archbishop of Canterbury on 30 March 1533, with a commission to examine the "King's Great Matter." On 23 May, having done so, he declared Henry's marriage to Catherine of Aragon null and void, as if it had never been; Princess Mary, a bastard; and Henry, free to wed whomever he pleased. Henry chose Anne Boleyn. She was publicly honored as Queen on Holy Saturday 12 April 1533, with the blessing of Holy Church, and just in the nick of time. She was really starting to show.

All of Henry's prognosticators and trusted clergy predicted a boy. A birth announcement "By the Queen" (though not written by her) was prepared in advance of her delivery, in multiple copies, bearing the news of King Henry's male heir. A blank was left for the date.

The child arrived on 7 September 1533. It was a girl. The birth announcements had to be twice altered from "prince" to "princes" (one *s* being as much as the space would allow).

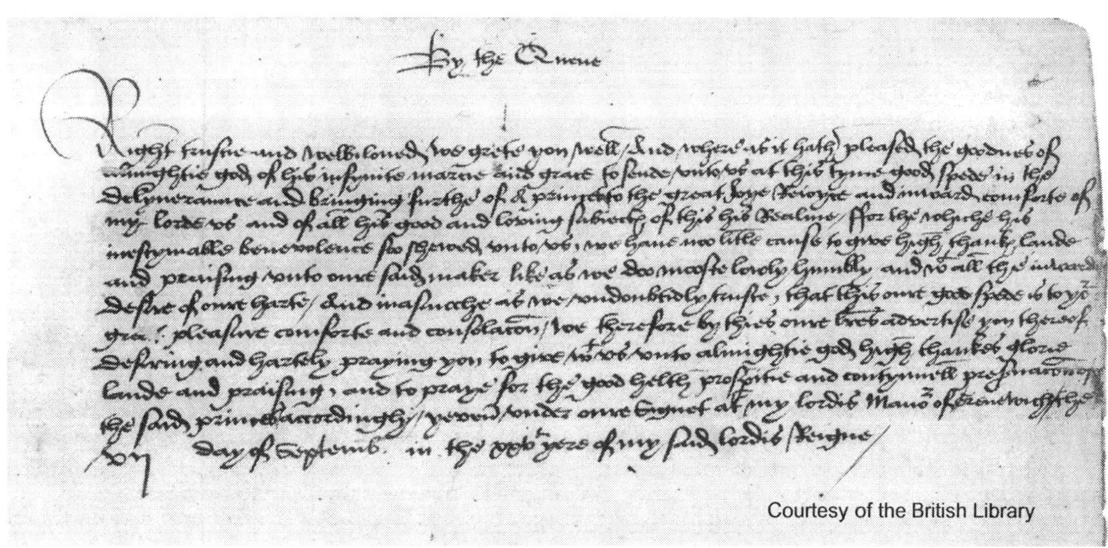

Courtesy of the British Library

By the Quene

Right trustie and welbeloued we grete you well / And where as it hath pleased the goodnes of almightie god of his infynite marcie and grace to sende unto vs at this tyme good spede in the Delyueraunce and bringing furthe of a prince[s]to the great Ioye Reioyce and inward comforte of my lorde vs and of all his good and loving subiect*es* of this his Realme / For the whiche his inestymable benevolence soo shewed unto us, we haue noo litle cause to gyve high thank*es*, laude and praising vnto oure said maker like as we doo mooste lowly humbly and $w^{t}$ all the inward Desire of oure harte / And inasmuche as we undoubtedlytruste, that this oure good speede is to $yo^{r}$ great pleasure comforte and consolac̄on / we therefore by thies oure lr̄es advertise you thereof,

> Desiring and hartely praying you to give w$^{t}$ vs unto almightie god high thankes, glorie, laude and praising, and to praye for the good helth prosperitie and contynuell preservacōn of the said prince[s]accordingly / yeven under oure signet at my lordis Mano$^{r}$ of grenewych the vij day of Septemb. in the xxv$^{t}$ yere of my said lordis Reigne. /

Three months after her birth, Elizabeth was sent to live with the queen's Shelton cousins, where she was soon joined by "the bastard," Princess Mary (whose household was disbanded so that she could be kept under the watchful eye of Queen Anne's kin). At about the same time, Margaret, the Sheltons' fourth daughter, was invited to become a maid of honor at court. Her parents consented, which was probably a mistake: By the winter of 1533/4, Madge Shelton had become the King's bedpartner (though without Queen Anne's knowledge until the following September, when there was a blowup).

Throughout her tenure as Queen, Anne was hated by religious conservatives who deplored England's break with Rome. The majority of English subjects pitied Henry's treatment of Catherine and resented the bastardization of Princess Mary. Anne was blamed for Cromwell's ruthless suppression of dissent; for the regime's gruesome slaughter of the monks of the London Charterhouse; for the dissolution of the monasteries; for the execution of Sir Thomas More; and more. But as long as Anne had the King's affection and Cromwell's support, her place as Queen was secure.

In the last week of January 1533/4 – some six or weeks after a conjugal visit – Anne gave king and court happy news: she was again pregnant. Her expected due date was mid-September.[1] Henry rejoiced: first, because the nation, this time, could expect the son that he demanded of Anne; second, because Anne during her confinement would be out of his hair, making it easier to fool around without her knowledge or jealous interference.

By April, Anne was seen at Court with a visible baby bump. A letter to Lady Lisle reports that "The Queen hath a goodly belly – praying our Lord to send us a prince." In July, Anne was reported to be "so far gone with child that she could not cross the sea with the King."[2] (Henry in the meantime consorted with his current favorite, Anne's cousin.)

Then, nothing – no baby, and no word of a miscarriage. By September, the court was abuzz with rumors that the alleged pregnancy was all of a piece with Anne's "trickiness" (*l'astuce*). And in retrospect, on incomplete information, the 1534 pregnancy looks indeed like a desperate ruse rather than a real or hysterical pregnancy; a stunt which, having arisen from wishful thinking or a lie, had no satisfactory conclusion. Having chosen as her queenly motto, "The Most Happy," Anne by September 1534 was no more happy than Catherine had been.

Anne Boleyn (copy c.1534 of earlier portrait)
*Hever Castle (Kent)*

• • •

*A Remembrance*. In the British Library is a volume catalogued as "Anne Boleyn's Prayer Book." This elaborate book of hours, often on exhibit, was created on the Continent many years before, possibly in Bruges, about 1500. The volume is illuminated with nearly fifty hand-painted illustrations. What distinguishes this one from all others, however, are two hand-written inscriptions. Under an image of the Man of Passion (Jesus, perspiring blood), King Henry wrote: "Si, selon mon affection la souvenance serai en vos prières ne sera guère oublié car votre suis Henry R., à jamais" [*If, according to my desire, there be remembrance in your prayers, I shall not long be forgotten, because I am your Henry Rex, for ever*].[3] Henry's message is clear: Just as Jesus suffered for his Church, I suffer for you, with a pain in my codpiece that will not go away. Remember that I am your Henry, king, always.

[1] Eustace Chapuys to Carlos V (28 January 1533/4), *L&P Henry VIII,* vol. 7 (1534), no. 114 (fr. the Vienna Archives).

[2] George Taylor to Lady Lisle (27 April 1534), *L&P Henry VIII,* vol. 7 (1534), no. 556 (fr. National Archives S.P. vii.565), Instructions to George Boleyn (July 1534), ibid., no. 958 (S.P. vii.565).

[3] "Si selon mon affection la sufvenāce sera / en voz prieres ne seray gers oblie / car v$^{re}$ suis Henry R. a Jamays" (231v).

images courtesy of the British Library

Under an image of the Annunciation, the king's correspondent has replied, "By daily proof, you shall me find, / To be to you both loving and kind."[1] From the lady's reply it has been inferred that the royal lovers inscribed their comments into this personal book of hours about 1528, at a time when Henry was still married to Catherine of Aragon but had finally won Anne Boleyn's consent to marry him, pursuant to a divorce; and that her inscription may be paraphrased thus: *Try me, any day of the week: I'll treat you right.* It is said that Anne Boleyn in her choice of illuminations has chosen the Annunciation as a hint of her youthful fertility and of better times to come: the Son and Savior whose birth the nation awaits shall indeed be born, and the willing Virgin is ready to make it happen.

This oft-told narrative, though endorsed even by the British Library's highly capable and well-trained archivists, contains two impediments to belief: 1. Anne's two authenticated prayerbooks are preserved at Hever Castle; no evidence points to her ownership of this third personal book of hours. 2. While the first inscription is in the hand of Henry VIII, the handwriting of the response is *not* that of Anne Boleyn.

Representative evidence: by 1528, Anne's lower-case *y* ends with a rightward hook, unlike those of Henry's correspondent, whose *y* trails off to the left. Nor is it Anne's characteristic spelling. In her adult correspondence, Anne almost always omits superfluous final *-e*, whereas the prayerbook annotation includes it at every opportunity (*prove* [for *proof*], *shalle, fynde, bothe, lovynge, kynde.* And where Anne habitually uses the modern spelling, *by,* Henry's correspondent writes "be" for *by,* her provincial pronunciation.[2]

Nor can Henry's correspondent be identified as Catherine of Aragon, Jane Seymour, Anne of Cleves, Katherine Howard, or Katherine Parr.

The puzzle is solved by an anedote of scandal appearing in the "Chronickille of Anne Bulleyne," by William Latimer; who reports that "a book of prayers (which belonged to one of her maids of honor called Mistress [Madge] Shelton) [was] presented unto her Highness, wherein were written certain idle poesies. She would not be satisfied by any means before she understood certainly to whom the book

[1] "be daly prove you shalle me fynde / to be to yow bothe lovynge and kynde" (66v).

[2] Many northern counties had not made this paricular vowel-shift. Cf. transcriptions (below) of verse by Mary Douglas and Mary Shelton, both of whom repeatedly write "be" to signify *by.* Like her Shelton cousins, Anne Boleyn was born in Norfolk but as a child lived in Austria and France before her preferment to Catherine's court.

pertained. The matter was covered awhile because of express threatenings of her majesty; but nothing can long escape the piercing eyes of princes, especially in their own palaces; so at length the pensive gentlewoman to whom the book appertained was discovered; whereupon the Queen her Majesty, calling her before her presence, wonderful rebuked her, that [she] would permit such wanton toys in her book of prayers (which [Queen Anne] termed 'a mirror, or glass' wherein [Shelton] might learn to address her wandering thoughts). And upon this occasion, [Anne] commanded the mother of the maidens to have a more vigilant eye to her charge, to th'end that at all times, and in time of prayers especially, they might comely and virtuously behave their selfs."[1] Latimer, clearly, did not know the whole story: it was not piety alone, but sexual jealousy, that fueled Queen Anne's rage over the prayerbook poeticisms.

Worse and worse: Henry by this time had begun to doubt that Anne was really pregnant, supposing it to be a tactic whereby to gain time, attention, or sympathy. He prided himself on his patience. But Anne's peremptory interference with his access to the maids of honor enraged him, and he let it be known. In September 1534, the fallout from this scandal was the talk of royal courts, not just in England but on the Continent. On 20 September, Count Cifuentes reported to Emperor Carlos V that Henry "was paying his courtship to another lady," whereupon Anne "incurred the royal displeasure," and is now "in disgrace with the King," so that "people have begun to utter words of much indignation against Anne."[2] Ambassador Chapuys elaborates: "Ever since the King began to doubt if his lady is really pregnant, he has rekindled and augmented the love that he has borne previously to another very handsome young lady of this court. The royal mistress [Anne] hearing of it, she tried to dismiss the damsel from her service.[3] The King has been very sad, and has sent her a message to this effect: that [Anne] ought to be satisfied with the opportunities he had given her; for if he had it do over, he would certainly not do as much; she ought to consider where she came from (and many other things of the same nature). Yet no great stress is to be laid on such words, considering the fickleness of this king, and the trickiness of the said lady, who knows perfectly well how to handle him."[4]

Six weeks later there was still no baby, now a month overdue. Meanwhile, Anne's sexy cousin, the King's "pretty Madge," remained at court, over Anne's objection. The queen could not even complain to her aunt and uncle, the girl's parents, because the Sheltons were guardians both of her own daughter Elizabeth, and of Henry's bastard daughter, Mary. No good outcome could arise from a quarrel involving the Shelton parents over the sexual behavior of *their* daughter with *her* royal husband.

On 13 October, Chapuys had news to report of Jane Boleyn, Lady Rochford, who has "lately been exiled from Court, due to her having joined in a conspiracy to devise a means to send away (through quarrelling or otherwise), the young lady to whom the King is now attached. As the credit of the latter is on the increase, and that of the King's mistress [Queen Anne] on the wane, she is visibly losing part of her pride and vainglory. [Mistress Shelton,] the lady in question has lately sent a message to the Princess [Mary], telling her to take good heart; that her tribulations will come to an end much sooner than she expected; and assures [Mary] that, should the opportunity occur, she will show herself her true friend and devoted servant."[5] (This confidential information Chapuys received directly from Princess Mary.)

Jane Boleyn was banished for only a few months; but her intimacy with Queen Anne, and with her own husband George, never recovered: resenting it that Sir George was closer and more deferential to his queen-sister than to herself, Jane thereafter counted herself Anne's foe, and Mary's ally. In the summer of 1535, Lady Rochford actually joined London citizens' wives in a public demonstration against Anne Boleyn; and in April 1536, by collaboration with Cromwell, she put both George and the queen in prison.

But that was still months away. In October 1535 came a blinding ray of hope: Anne was again pregnant.

---

[1] Latimer (ed. 1990), 62-3. Latimer writes "Mary" for *Madge* or *Marg.*, which has led to much confusion between Margaret Shelton (b. 1513) with her younger sister Mary (b. 1519); errors of this sort are very frequent in sixteenth-century documents (even with reference to the Boleyn sisters); *upon this occasion* ] because of this incident.

[2] *Calendar of State Papers, Spain*, Vol. 5.1 (1534-1535), no. 88; from S. Sec. de Guerra, Mar. y Tier (Spanish), L. 5. B.L. MS Add. 28,587, fol. 26.

[3] *royal mistress* ] i.e., Queen Anne; Chapuys, who detested Anne, always references her as Henry's "mistress" or "concubine" or "lady," reserving "queen" for Catherine Parr.

[4] Eustace Chapuys to Emperor Carlos V (23 Sep. 1534). French. Transcription and translation in *State Papers Henry VIII, Spain*, 5.1, no. 90 (from Wien, *Rep.* P.C., Fasc. 228, no. 57).

[5] Same to same (13 October 1534). French. Ibid., no. 96 (from Wien, *Rep.* P.C., *Fasc.* 228, no. 59). Lady Rochford's husband was George Boleyn; her sister, Margaret Parker, was married to Madge Shelton's brother, John Shelton Jr.

Then, on 7 January, came welcome news: Catherine of Aragon was dead. The messenger who brought these happy tidings from Kimbolton received a generous gift from Queen Anne, who was thrilled: England now had, indisputably, only one queen. Henry was no less pleased: on the morrow, with feasting and music, the entire court celebrated Catherine's demise. Henry dressed all in yellow (with a white feather in his cap); Anne dressed in yellow to match. They looked a happy couple. Among the other celebrants was a pale, tight-lipped spinster named Jane Seymour. Madge Shelton had since been discarded.

Anne's gaiety, however, was forced. Fond now of Jane Seymour, Henry had put his queen on notice: the child within her womb had better be a son, or he was through with her.

On January 29th, Queen Catherine was buried at St. Peterborough Cathedral. Because her queenly rites were scanted and because the King forbade Princess Mary to attend, Eustace Chapuys boycotted the funeral as well, staying home to send the Emperor an astonishing update: Queen Anne, days before, though pregnant, had been seen in tears. Today's news was that the King had remarked to his Privy Councilors that he was "seduced and forced into this second marriage by means of witchcraft and charms; and, for that reason, he held it as null. God (he said) had well shown his displeasure at it, by denying him male children. He therefore believes that he may take a third wife, which he said he wishes much to do."[1]

Not just Henry, but Anne's many enemies, plus Roman Catholic ambassadors from the Continent, and a majority of the King's own subjects, still held that Catherine was Henry's true wife; and Queen Anne, a concubine. With Catherine dead, the King (on this view) by renouncing Anne would be free to marry another, with the blessing of Holy Church, and Lady Anne be damned. But why Henry would speak to his Council of annulment while Anne was expecting remained a mystery.

By 10 February, Chapuys had news that solved the puzzle: Queen Anne on 29 January had suffered a miscarriage: "On the day of the interment of the Queen, the concubine had an abortion (which seemed to be a male child), which she had not borne $3^1/_2$ months."[2]

Anne's unconfirmed report that the undeveloped fetus "seemed to be a boy" can be discounted as wishful thinking. Rumors that the expelled fetus was examined by others and discovered to be monstrously deformed, as if by witchcraft, can be dismissed as rubbish. But neither was it an insignificant event. Henry had already pledged his affection to Jane Seymour, who was prepared to accept a marriage proposal in the event of Anne's death. Catherine's welcome demise gave Henry the motivation to speed Anne on her way; while Anne's acknowledged miscarriage gave him the ammunition: the King had only to deny to his Privy Council that he had copulated with her at any time in the past four months, and his queen was as good as dead. Henry's initial strategem whereby to dispose of her was to allege that Anne had a prior and consummated contract with the Earl of Northumberland, back in 1527. (Henry's unimaginative head, when thinking to divorce or kill a wife, had always the same theme: someone else got there first.) The more cynical plan, and the one that prevailed, was Cromwell's: accuse Anne of having committed adultery, citing as proof Anne's recent pregnancy and acknowledged miscarriage.

Cromwell needed only to whisper in the King's paranoid ear that Anne was known to have been horsing around, for the King to sign off on an inquest. In early questioning, Cromwell was told of a young court musician named Mark Smeaton who might have a crush on the queen. On 30 April, the youth was arrested. Taken to Cromwell's house in Stepney with a knotted cord tied around his eyes, Smeaton was interrogated and tortured. His absence at court went unnoticed.

Anne was kept out of the loop. Cromwell's strike, when it came, fell as a bolt from the blue.[3] Edward Hall reports:

*London. 2 May 1536°.* "On May Day were a solemn jousts kept at Greenwich. And suddenly from the jousts the King departed, having not above six persons with him; and came in the evening from Greenwich to his place at Westminster. Of this sudden departing many men mused,[2] but most chiefly, the

---

[1] Chapuys to Carlos V (29 Jan. 1535/6). *State Papers, Spain,* 5.2, no. 55 (fr. Wien, Rep. P. C., Fasc. 230, no. 29.

[2] Same to same (10 Feb. 1535/6), *L&P Henry VIII,* vol. 10 (Jan.-Jun. 1536), no. 282; *abortion* ] until the early twentieth century, *abortion* denoted any termination of a pregnancy, whether spontaneous or induced; the distinction developed out of the Church's historically recent campaign against induced abortion.

[3] Depictions of Anne Boleyn range from pathetic and hapless victim on the one hand, to conniving whore on the other. For a no-nonsense statement of the facts, see E.W. Ives, "The Fall of Anne Boleyn Reconsidered," *English Historical Review* 107, no. 424 (July 1992): 651-664.

queen, who the next day was apprehended and brought from Greenwich to the Tower of London; whereafter she was arraigned of High Treason, and condemned."

On the evening of Anne's sudden fall, Chapuys dispatched the day's news to the Emperor, not awaiting further details:

*London. 2 May 1536*°. "The concubine ... by the judgment of God has been brought in full daylight from Greenwich to the Tower of London, conducted by the duke of Norfolk and the two chamberlains (of the realm and of the chamber). Only four women have been left to her. The report is that it's for adultery, in which she has long continued with a spinet-player of her chamber ... The concubine's brother, named Rochford, has also been lodged in the Tower, but more than six hours after the others and three or four before his sister. And even if the said crime of adultery had not been discovered, this King (as I have been for some days informed by good authority) had already determined to abandon her; for witnesses testified that a marriage between her and the earl of Northumberland, nine years ago, was made and fully consummated. And the King would have declared himself earlier but that someone of his Council advised him that he could not separate from the concubine without tacitly confirming, not only his first marriage, but also (what he most fears) the authority of the Pope. These news are indeed *new*, but it is still more *wonderful* – to think of the sudden change from yesterday to today!" (Eustace Chapuys to Emperor Carlos V, 2 May 1536).°

*Those arrested*: on 30 April, Mark Smeaton; on 2 May, Queen Anne, Sir Henry Norris (Cromwell's principal rival at court), and George Boleyn (Queen Anne's closest ally); on 3-5 May, William Brereton, Thomas Wyatt, and Richard Page.

Brereton, a Cromwell critic, was charged with having committed adultery with Queen Anne on 27 November 1533, at Hampton Court, having been solicited by her on 16 November – Cromwell forgetting that the queen on those dates was still in Greenwich, in seclusion after having given birth to Princess Elizabeth; the court having remained at Greenwich until at least 25 November.

The arrest of Wyatt and Page was mere window-dressing. Months later, after their hearts were impressed with the fear of God and Lord Cromwell, both men were released, to illustrate to the nation that not all who were arrested were found guilty.

George Boleyn was accused of incest with the Queen on remarks made by his wife Jane – which was more than she intended to imply, but Henry and Cromwell were masters in the art of producing a mountain of evidence from a molehill of solicited innuendo. Cromwell then appointed Jane to attend Queen Anne in her prison cell, and to report all that was said.

During Anne's two-week confinement prior to her execution, Cromwell received daily updates from Sir William Kingston, Constable of the Tower, whose letters survive in a manuscript ravaged by the Ashburnham House fire of October 1731. (The phrases below within square brackets are conjectural emendations of the present editor, to supply text that is burnt away or damaged beyond recognition. The ellipses mark editorial elisions for the sake of brevity):

**[Sir William Kingston, Constable of the Tower, to Secretary Cromwell (3 May 1536)°]**

Sir,

This is to advertise you upon my Lord of Norfolk and the King's Council depart[ing] from the Tower, I went before the Queen into her lodging. And she said unto me, "Master Kingston, Shall I go into a dungeon?"

"No, Madam, y[ou] shall go into your lodging that you lay in at your Coronation."

"It is too good for me," she said. "Jesu, have mercy on me!" – and kneeled down, weeping a [little s]pace; and in the same sorrow, fell into a great laughing (and she hath done [the same] many times since). And then she desired me to move the King's Highness that she [might] have the sacrament in the closet by her chamber, that she mi[ght pray] for mercy: "for I am as clear from the company of man, as for c[ertain I] am clear from you, and am the King's true-wedded wife." And then she said, "Mr. Kingston, do you know wherefore I am here?"

And I said "Nay."

And then [she said,] "When saw you the King?"

And I said I saw him not, since I saw [him at] the Tilt-yard.

And then: "M[aster] K[ingston,] I pray you to tell me where my [father, Lord Roch]ford is."[1]

And I told her I saw him afore dinner, in the court.

"Oh, [where is] my sweet broder?"

I said I left him at York Place – and so I did.

"I [hear," sai]d she, "that I should be accused with three men! And I can say, ['How so,] nay, without I should open my body?'" – and therewith opened [her arms, saying, "O Nor]ris, hast thou accused me? Thou ar[t] in the Tower *with* me, and [thou and I shal]l die together. And Mark, thou art here, too? O, my mother, thou wilt die for sorrow!" – and much lamented my lady of Worcester for beca[use her child] did not stir in her body.[2]

And my wife said, "What should [be the cause?"][3]

[The queen] said, "for the sorrow she took for me." And then she said, "Master K[ingston, shall I die] without justice?"

And I said, "The poorest subject the king hath, has justice" – and therewith, she laughed.

All these sayings was yesterday ni[ght] … and this morning did talk with Mistress Cousin [and said that Nor]ris did say on Sunday last unto the queen's almon[er, that he would sw]ear for the queen that she was a good woman.[4]

[And then said Mistress Cousin, "Madam, why should there be any such matters spoken of?"

"Mary," said she, I bade him do so, for I asked him why he [did not consummate] his marriage.[5] And he made answer he would tarry [a while. Then said I, 'You] look for dead men's shoes! For if ought came[e to the king but good,] you would look to have *me.*' And he said if he [should have any such thought,] he would his head were off." And then she said [she feared so], and therewith they fell out.[6] But [she more feared Weston, for] on Whitsun ~~Monday~~ Tuesday last, [Weston told her] that Norris came more u[nto her chamber for her, than for M[adge Shelton….]

I was commanded to charge the gentlewomen that…attend upon the queen…they should have no communication with her unless my wife were present, and so I did it – notwithstanding, it cannot be, for my Lady Boleyn and Mistress Cousin lies on the queen's pallet; and I and my wife are at the door without, so [th]at they must needs talk, a[s we] be without. But I have everything told me by Mistress Cousin that she thinks meet for me to know; and t'other two gentlewomen lies without me. (And as I may know [the] King's pleasure in the premises, I shall follow.)

[*Kingston is called away to speak with the prisoner.*]

Sir, since the making of this letter, the Queen spake of West[on, that she] had spoke to him because he did love her kinswoma[n, Mistress Shelton; and that] he said he loved not his wife. And he made answer to her [again that he] loved *one* in her house better than them both. She asked, "Who is that?" He said] that "It is yourself!" – and then she defied him.[7]

William King[ston]

---

[1] *Lord Rochford* ] Thomas Boleyn, now earl of Wiltshire and Ormond; Anne's brother George having succeeded, Sir Thomas is still referenced often as Lord Rochford.

[2] Elizabeth (b. Browne) Somerset, countess of Worcester (died 1565); at Anne's 1533 coronation dinner, she stood to the Queen's left, "ready to hold a fine cloth in front of Anne's face whenever she wanted to spit"; 1533-6, lady-in-waiting to Queen Anne; May 1536, a principal accuser (a role not yet known to Anne). Named as a sometime mistress of King Henry VIII, the countess in April 1536 was several months pregnant with so sign of quickening, which is the cause of Anne's concern. It is alleged that when her brother scolded Elizabeth Somerset for sleeping with the King, she retorted she was ""no worse than the queen."

[3] *the cause* ] i.e., of Lady Somerset's failed pregancy, which Anne graciously supposes came from her friend's distress for Anne's unlucky falling-out with the king.

[4] *Mistress Cousin* ] Kingston's mistake for Coffin (first name unknown), a gentlewoman attendant on the queen who was one of Cromwell's paid spies; *queen's almoner* ] Rev. John Skip, the queen's loyal chaplain and her officer for the distribution of Anne's many generous alms (charitable benefactions).

[5] *his marriage* ] Norris, with Anne's encouragement, had betrothed himself to Margaret Shelton after the king discarded her; but he deferred consummation, perhaps because he sensed danger ahead.

[6] *fell out* ] quarreled.

[7] *Weston* ] Anne scolded Francis Weston, unhappily married, for his attempts on Margaret Shelton; then for saying (perhaps as a flirtation), that he loved the queen even better than he loved either Shelton or his wife.

*The flirtation of Francis Weston, which Anne had cited to illustrate her innocence, led to Weston's immediate arrest, on evidence that he and the queen were lovers.*

*A day or two later, thinking to introduce some reason to these mad proceedings, Queen Anne decided to prepare a written statement in her own defense:*

**[Sir William Kingston, Constable of the Tower, to Secretary Cromwell (6 May 1536)°]**

Sir,

After your departing yesterday, ... when I came to the chamber, the [queen heard] of me and sent for me – and said, "… I shall desire you to bear a letter from me [to Master] Secretary."

And then I said, "Madam, tell it me by [word of mouth and I] will do it"; and so gave me thanks, saying, "I ha[ve much marvel] that the King's Council comes not to me. And this [same day, it was] said we would have no rain till she [were delivered out] of the Tower. I pray you it may be shortly – be[cause of the fair weather, you know what I mean?"

The queen [said to]night that the King wist what he did wh[en he put such] two about her as my Lady Boleyn and Mistress [Cousin, for] they could tell her nothing of my [lord her father, nor] nothing else; but she defied them all.[1]

B[ut upon this, my Lady Boleyn] said to her, "Such desire as you have ha[d to hear such tales] has brought you to this!"

And then said she, "[Mark Smeaton] is the worst-cherishest of any m[an in the house, for he] wears yarns!" (She said that was [because he was no] gentleman.) "But he was never in m[y chamber but at Winchester, and] there she sent for him to pla[y on the spinet, for my] lodging was [by] the King's. [And yet,] I never spake with him since but upon Saturday before May Day. And then I found him standing in the round window, in my chamber of presence. And I asked him why he was so sad, and he answered and said it was no matter; and then she said [to him°], 'You may not look to have me speak to you as I should do to a nobleman – because you be an inferior person.' [He said,°] 'No, no, madam, a *look* sufficed me! And thus, fare you well.'…"

William Kingston

• • •

*Prior to her arrest, Anne had told one of her ladies-in-waiting – Jane Boleyn, Elizabeth Somerset, or both – of this brief encounter with a star-struck, ill-dressed, and penniless musician; which is why Smeaton was the first to be arrested on 30 April. Anne's confirmation of the anecdote – thinking to assert her innocence – was used by Cromwell at her mock trial to confirm an adulterous relationship.*

**[Sir William Kingston, Constable of the Tower, to Secretary Cromwell (c. 10 May 1536)°]**

Sir,

The queen hath much desired to have here in the closet the sacraments, and also her almoner (who she supposeth to be due); for one hour she is determined to die and the next hour much contrary to that. Yesterday, after your departing, I sent for my wife and also for Mistress Cousin to know how they had done that day. They said she had been very merry and made a great dinner; and yet soon after, she called for her supper, having marvel where I was all day. And after supper she sent for me. And at my coming she said, "Where have you been all day?" And I made answer I had been with prisoners. "So," she said, "I thought I heard Master Treasur[er]." I answered he was not here. Then she began talk and said, "I was cruelly handled, … a queen, and cruelly handled as was never seen – but I [think the king] does it to prove me" – and did laugh withal, and was very merry. And th[en she said, "Shall I have just]ice?"

And then I said, "Have no doubt there[in]."

Then she said, "If any man [accuse me, I can say but *N*]*ay*. And they can bring no witness." ... And then she said, "I [would God I had m]y bishops, for they would all go to the King for me, for I thi[nk the most part of] England prays for me. And if I die, you shall see the greate[st injustic]e within this seven year that ever came to England." And then s[he said, "I shall be with God, for] I have done many good deeds in my days. But yet, I think [much unkindness in the] King to put such about me as I never loved." I showed [er that the King took them] to be honest and good women. "But I would have had," [she said, "mine own women] which I favor most," etc.

William Kingston
(To Master Secretary)

---

[1] *wist well what he did* ] knew what he was doing.

• • •

*On 12 May, in rapid-succession charades of justice, Norris, Weston, Brereton and Smeaton were tried and sentenced to death for high treason, on grounds of adultery with the queen.*

*In a separate trial on 15 May (the duke of Norfolk presiding), Queen Anne and Lord Rochford were condemned for treason, adultery and incest. Chapuys reports that "The concubine was sentenced first to be burnt alive, or beheaded at the King's pleasure. When the sentence was read to her, she received it quite calmly, and said that she was prepared to die, but was extremely sorry to hear that others, who were innocent and the King's loyal subjects, should share her fate and die through her. She ended by begging that some time should be allowed for her to prepare her soul for death."*[1] *At the sentencing, it was determined that Smeaton would be hung, the four noblemen beheaded with an axe, and the queen beheaded with a sword.*

[**Sir William Kingston, Constable of the Tower, to Secretary Cromwell (16 May 1536)**°]

Sir,

… I shall desire you further to know the King's pleasure touching the queen, as well for her comfort as for the preparation of scaffolds and other necessaries concerning. The King's Grace showed me that my Lord of Canterbury should be her confessor (and was here this day with the queen);[2] and note, in that matter, sir, the time is short – for the King supposeth the gentlemen to die tomorrow, and my Lord of Rochford with the residue of gentlemen (and as yet without [confession,] which I look for). But I have told my Lord of Rochford that he be in a readiness tomorrow to suffer execution; and so he accepts it very well and "will do his best to be ready." …Sir, I pray you to have good remembrance in all this for us to do, for we shall be ready always, to our knowledge. (Yet this day at dinner, the queen said [th]at she "should go to Anvers," and is "in hope of life"!)[3]

William Kingston.

• • •

*The execution of Anne's alleged lovers went forward on 17 May, as scheduled. George Boleyn, Henry Norris, and Francis Weston were beheaded; William Brereton was beheaded and quartered. Smeaton, a commoner, was hung, disemboweled, cut down, castrated, and quartered. Chapuys reports that "To make matters worse for the concubine, it was arranged that she should witness their execution from the windows of her prison." Sir Thomas Wyatt, though never tried, was likewise obliged to watch from his prison cell. The spectacle remained with him, long after ("The bell tower showed me such sight / That in my head sticks day and night"). Anne's brother George "before dying declared himself to be innocent of all the charges brought against him, though he owned that he deserved death for having been contaminated with the new heresies, and having caused many others to be infected with them. He had no doubt (said he on the scaffold) that God had punished him for that; and, therefore, he recommended all to forsake heretical doctrines and practices, and return to true faith and religion."* [4]

*On the 18th Anne received word that her former ally, Thomas Cranmer, archbishop of Canterbury, had proclaimed her daughter Elizabeth a bastard, the court having determined that she was fathered on Anne's body by Henry Norris. This account was to be Anne's legacy in the annals of English history.*

*That same day, Kingston was directed to evacuate from the diplomatic chambers in the Tower of London all foreign visitors, so that there would be no unauthorized witness to Anne's execution.*

*On her last night, Anne slept little and spoke often with Kingston, twice swearing upon the sacrament that she was innocent.*

---

[1] Chapuys to Carlos V (19 May 1536) *Calendar of State Papers Spain,* 5.2 (1536–8), no. 55.

[2] *Lord of Canterbury* ] Thomas Cranmer, archbishop.

[3] *Anvers* ] French name for Antwerp, a city of tolerance and refuge for religious refugees.

[4] Chapuys, ibid.

**[Constable of the Tower to Secretary Cromwell (after midnight, 18/19 May 1536)°]**

Sir,

This shall be to advertise you I have received your letter, wherein yo[u would] have strangers conveyed out of the Tower – and so they be, by the means of Richard Gresham and William Locke and Withepole; but the number of str[angers passed] not thirty, and not many other; and the ambassador of the Emperor had a [servant] there, and honestly put out.[1] Sir, if we have not another (certain as it may be known in London), I think he[re] will be but few, and I think [a small] number were best: for I suppose she will declare herself to b[e a good] woman for all men but for the King, at the hour of her dea[th. This] morning she sent for me, that I might be with her at [such hour] as she received the good Lord, to the intent I should hear he[r speak as] touching her innocency alway to be clear.[2]

[*Kingston here was called away, while writing.*]

And in the writ[ing of this], she sent for me, and at my coming she said, "Mr. Kingston, I he[ard say I shall] not die afore noon, and I am very sorry therefore, for I thought [I would] be dead [an]d past my pain." I told her it should be no pain, it w[as little. And she said, "I] heard say the executioner was very good – and I have a li[ttle neck!" – and put he]r hand about it, laughing heartily.

I have seen [many men and] also women executed, and [th]at they have been in gre[at sorrow – and to my knowle]dge, this lady has much joy and pleasure, in death. [Sir, her almoner is conti]nually with her, and has been since two o' the clo[ck after midnight. This is] the effect of anything that is here at [this time, and thus fare you] well.

Your William Kingston
(To Master Secretary)

• • •

***Anne Boleyn's Last Letter.*** A letter addressed from "Anne Bullen" to Henry VIII and dated 6 May 1536, four days after Anne's arrest, has caused much debate: While conducting research for his *Life and Raigne of King Henry the Eighth* (1649), Sir Edward Herbert discovered amongst the papers of Lord Cromwell a letter from Anne Boleyn to Henry VIII, asserting her innocence. This document, which is not in the queen's own hand, has been dismissed by many scholars (including the editors of the *State Papers*) as an obvious forgery. This mistaken verdict, widely accepted, has served the rhetorical ends of those royalist historians who have sought to exonerate Henry VIII from a charge of uxoricide and to place upon Anne herself the onus for her execution. But the forgery allegation is of the same order as those concocted by the King: From the first, it's hard to imagine whose purpose could have been served by composing such a text in Anne's name and then to have concealed it: a contemporaneous forgery would contain incriminating disclosures while begging for mercy. If it were a seventh-century production, the rogue historian would not presume foreknowledge of confidential matters known to Anne in 1536; his text would look instead like one of Leti's transparent fictions of the 1680s. But in fact, the document was found by a credible witness among Secretary Cromwell's papers; it is written in a mid-sixteenth century hand, on sixteenth-century paper, in sixteenth-century syntax that finds parallels in Anne's known writing. Patronizing skeptics have stated, as a fact, that Anne would never have dared to address the King so boldly in her own defense (but Anne's presumptuous self-assertion is precisely what Henry most resented about her). Besides which, the forgery allegation is founded upon the historically naïve supposition that Anne while awaiting execution was allowed paper, ink, quill pens, and a post, to write whatever she pleased.

The facts: As with Katherine Howard's imprisonment five years later, anything Anne had to say following her arrest could not have been holograph (entirely in her own hand), but – at *most* – an autograph-letter (written by a scribe, and the copy of record signed by her). The reports of Sir William Kingston to Cromwell in May 1536 (testimony not previously considered) give the lie to the nineteenth-century forgery theory: Kingston clearly states both the occasion and mode of transmission for Anne's last letter to the king: Refusing to supply paper and ink, Kingston or an aide took the letter by dictation and delivered it to Cromwell. The scribe may not have gotten Anne's last letter exactly word for word, nor is the spelling hers. But we have no reason whatever to suppose the letter a fabrication, or indeed anything but an articulate defense by a remarkable woman, falsely accused, and slain by scoundrels.

---

[1] *ambassador of the emperor* ] Eustace Chapuys; the servant's name is unknown.

[2] *good woman for all* ] i.e., in the opinion of all; *received the good Lord* ] Anne wished for Kingston to be present at her final Mass, when she again swore her innocence (upon penalty of damnation, if she were lying).

**[Anne Boleyn to Henry VIII (6 May 1536)°]**

Sir,

Your Grace's displeasure and my imprisonment are things so strange unto me, as what to write, or what to excuse, I am altogether ignorant; whereas you send unto me, willing me "to confess a truth," and so to obtain favor by such a one whom you know to be my professed enemy; I no sooner received this message by him, than I rightly conceived your meaning.[1]

And if, as you say, confessing a truth indeed may procure my safety, I shall, with all willingness and duty, perform your command. But let not your Grace ever imagine that your poor wife will ever be brought to acknowledge a fault, where never yet so much as a thought thereof ever proceeded. And to speak a truth, never prince had wife more loyal in all duty and true affection, than you have ever found in Anne Boleyn, with which name and place I could willingly have contented myself, if God and your Grace's pleasure had so been pleased.

Neither did I at any time so much forget myself in my exaltation and received queenship, but that I always looked for such an alteration as now I find;[2] for the ground of my preferment being on no surer foundation than your Grace's fancy, the least alteration, I know, was fit and sufficient to draw that fancy to some other subject.

You have chosen me, from a low estate, to be your queen and companion, far beyond my desert or desire. If then you found me worthy of such an honor, good your Grace, let not any light fancy, or bad counsel of my enemies, withdraw your princely favor from me; neither let that stain, that unworthy stain of a "disloyal heart" towards your good Grace, ever cast so foul a blot on your most dutiful wife, and the infant princess your daughter:

Try me, good King, but let me have a lawful trial. And let not my sworn enemies sit as my accusers *and* judges. Yea, let me receive an open trial, for my truth shall fear no open shames. Then shall you see either my innocency cleared, your suspicion and conscience satisfied, the ignominy and slander of the world stopped; or my "guilt" openly declared – so that whatsoever God or you may determine of me, your Grace may be freed from an open censure; and my "offense" being so lawfully proved, your Grace is at liberty, both before God and man, not only to execute worthy punishment on me as an unfaithful wife, but to follow your affection already settled on that party, for whose sake I am now as I am (whose name I could some good while since have pointed unto: your Grace being not ignorant of my suspicion therein).[3]

But if you have already determined of me, and that not only my death, but an infamous slander must bring you the enjoying of your desired happiness; then I desire of God, that he will pardon your great sins herein, and likewise mine enemies, the instruments thereof; and that He will not call you to a strait accompt for your unprincely and cruel usage of me, at His general judgment seat, where both you and myself must shortly appear – and in whose just judgment, I doubt not (whatsoever the world may think of me) mine innocency shall be openly known, and sufficiently cleared.

My last and only request shall be, that myself may only bear the burthen of your Grace's displeasure, and that it may not touch the innocent souls of those poor gentlemen, whom (as I understand) are likewise in strait imprisonment for my sake. If ever I have found favor in your sight; if ever the name of Anne Boleyn hath been pleasing in your ears, let me obtain this request; and I will so leave to trouble your Grace any further, with my earnest prayer to the Trinity to have your Grace in His good keeping, and to direct you in all your actions.

From my doleful prison in the Tower, this 6th May.
Your most loyal and ever faithful wife,

Anne Boleyn

---

[1] *my professed enemy* ] Secretary Cromwell, who at first supported Anne but broke with her over disposition of the money acquired from the dissolution of the monasteries.

[2] *always looked for such an alteration* ] was always wary that this fall from your grace could occur.

[3] *that party for whose sake I am now as I am* ] i.e., Jane Seymour.

## Anne Boleyn's Speech at her Execution (19 May 1536, 8 o'clock in the Morning)°

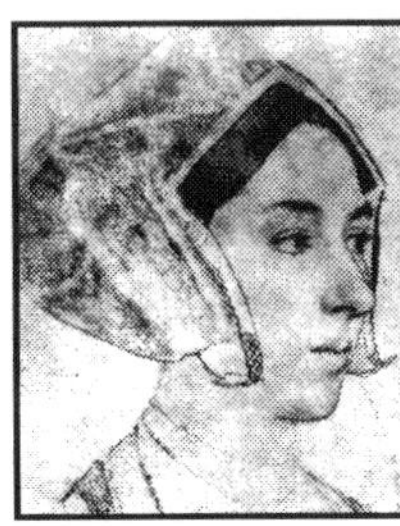

"Good Christen people, I am come hither to die. For according to the law, and by the law, I am judged to die, and therefore I will speak nothing against it. I am come hither to accuse no man, nor to speak anything of that whereof I am accused and condemned to die. But I pray God save the King and send him long to reign over you, for a gentler nor a more merciful prince was there never. And to me he was ever a good, a gentle and sovereign lord.[1] And if any person will meddle of my cause, I require them to judge the best. And thus I take my leave of the world and of you all, and I heartily desire you all to pray for me. O Lord, have mercy on me. To God I commend my soul."[2]

And then she kneeled down, saying, "To Christ I commend my soul. Jesu, receive my soul," divers times, till that her head was stricken off with the sword.

And on the Ascension Day following, the King wore white for mourning. The week before Whitsuntide, the King married Lady Jane, daughter to the right worshipful Sir John Seymour, knight, which at Whitsuntide was openly showed as Queen.

• • •

Eustace Chapuys was jubilant over Anne Boleyn's execution, while somewhat buoyed also by the citizens' distaste for Henry: "People speak variously about the King," he wrote, "and surely the slander will not cease when they hear of what passed and is passing between him and his new mistress, Jane Seymour. Already it sounds badly in the ears of the public that the King, after such ignominy and discredit as the concubine has brought on his head, should manifest more joy and pleasure now, since her arrest and trial, than he has ever done on other occasions; for he has daily gone out to dine here and there with ladies, and sometimes has remained with them till after midnight. I hear that on one occasion, returning by the river to Greenwich, the royal barge was actually filled with minstrels and musicians of his chamber, playing on all sorts of instruments or singing; which state of things was by many compared to the joy and pleasure a man feels in getting rid of a thin, old, and vicious hack in the hope of getting soon a fine horse to ride – a very peculiarly agreeable task, for this king.[3]"

Anne Boleyn lies buried in the Chapel of St. Peter Vincula in the Tower of London.

---

[1] That Anne from the scaffold praised the very man who libeled her and put her to death in order to marry another is a surprising and well-attested fact – more startling, if misunderstood as a full and dependable record of the queen's sincere thoughts and feelings. During the reign of Henry VIII, many thousands of citizens were put to death, often without the pretense of a trial (the king's displeasure being sufficient grounds for attainder and execution). Of all those scaffold speeches that have survived, whether authentic or propaganda, the one common feature is an encomium of the honor, justice, and merciful heart of the King. It may be inferred that these *de rigueur* compliments were extorted, possibly upon threat to the convicted felon's kin (who could be turned out of their homes, the felon's land and rents and moveables being forfeit to the Crown). William Tyndale in his *Practice of Prelates* writes that "When any great man is put to death, how his confessour entreateth him, and what penance is enjoyned him concerning what he shall say when he cometh unto the place of execution, I could guess at a practise that might make men's ears glow."[1] It is not beyond Henry and Cromwell to have advised Anne that the future of her daughter and other kin would depend on what she had to say about him from the scaffold on the occasion of her own murder.

[2] Another eyewitness reports, "The said Queen (unjustly called) finally was beheaded upon a scaffold within the Tower with open gates. She was brought by the captain upon the said scaffold, and four young ladies followed her. She looked frequently behind her, and when she got upon the scaffold was very much exhausted and amazed. She begged leave to speak to the people, promising to say nothing but what was good. The captain gave her leave, and she began to raise her eyes to Heaven, and cry mercy to God and to the King for the offense she had done, desiring the people always to pray to God for the King, for he was a good, gentle, gracious, and amiable prince. She was then stripped of her short mantle furred with ermines, and afterwards took off her hood (which was of English make) herself. A young lady presented her with a linen cap, with which she covered her hair, and she knelt down, fastening her clothes about her feet, and one of the said ladies bandaged her eyes. Immediately the executioner did his office; and when her head was off, it was taken by a young lady and covered with a white cloth. Afterwards the body was taken by the other ladies, and the whole carried into the church nearest to the Tower of London. It is said that she was condemned to be burned alive, but that the King commuted her sentence to decapitation" *Letters and Papers, Foreign and Domestic, Henry VIII,* Vol. 10 (Jan.-June 1536), no. 911 (from the Vienna archives).

[3] Chapuys to Carlos V (19 May 1536). *Cal. State Papers, Spain,* 5.2, no. 55 (fr. Wien, Rep. P. C., Fasc. 230, no. 29.

# **Margaret Douglas (Stuart)** (1515-1578),

Countess of Lennox

*Quhat ve resolue, Death shall dissolue.*
—motto on the Lennox jewel, designed by Margaret in memory of her murdered husband

ARGARET DOUGLAS was born on the run. Her mother, Margaret Tudor (1489-1541), was the niece and namesake of Margaret Beaufort; the daughter of Henry VII and Elizabeth of York; elder sister to Henry VIII; and from 1503, queen consort of King James IV of Scotland. When James and ten thousand Scots were killed at Flodden Field in September 1513, Margaret Tudor became regnant queen – but then forfeited her crown to marry Archibald Douglas, earl of Angus ("Anguish," in Scots). The duke of Albany, appointed Regent in her stead, besieged the queen at Stirling and got possession of the royal children; after which Margaret was forbidden access to her son, James V, for fear she would abscond with him to England. On 30 September 1515, nine months pregnant – having lost the regency, her revenues, her husband's love, and the custody of her children – dowager queen Margaret fled the country. She got as far as Harbottle Castle in Northumberland, where she gave birth on 7 October. The ordeal left Dame Margaret at the threshold of death for months. Baby Margaret was fed by a wet-nurse.

Margaret Tudor returned to Scotland in 1517, unhappily so. Her second marriage was now on the rocks. She was deprived of her estates, her revenues, and her son James. Baby Margaret was next to go: the earl of Angus kidnapped from his estranged wife the one child who had remained with her, and raised her thereafter without permitting maternal visits. Princess Margaret Douglas from early childhood was taught that her mother – whose wished annulment threatened to bastardize her – was her enemy.

In 1525 the earl of Angus overthrew the duke of Albany. He took custody of the 13-year-old James V (Margaret's half-brother); and kept him prisoner for three years, exercising power in the youth's behalf as the Regent of Scotland. After three years James finally escaped his stepfather's custody; assumed the reins of government; and forced Angus into exile. Margaret was then made the pawn of civil war between her stepfather, whom she loved, and her mother whom she hardly knew; with her royal brother taking the part of their mother against her father.

Divorced in March 1527/8, Margaret Tudor married, thirdly, Henry Stuart, Lord Methven. While James V sought to kidnap his sister from the earl of Angus, Dame Margaret took steps to find the girl a husband; offering her first (at age 12) to James Stuart (1499-1531), illegitimate son of James IV; and at age 13 to another James Stuart (1503-1547), the brother of her own third husband, Lord Methven (a man who, prior to that third marriage, was one of Margaret Tudor's own reputed lovers).

The earl of Angus, meanwhile, smuggled his daughter into England, to Norham Castle, the residence of her godfather, Cardinal Wolsey, where she became friends with the king's bastard son, Henry Fitzroy, duke of Richmond. On her own in England, Lady Margaret enjoyed better fortunes: following Wolsey's death in 1530, she was invited to Beaulieu to live with Princess Mary, who was only a few months younger than she. The two princesses became lifelong friends. Margaret was said also to be a favorite of her uncle, Henry VIII. Largesse followed: In 1532, the King settled on Archibald Douglas an annuity of 1000 marks, for the earl and his daughter. Angus requited that generosity with support for Henry's designs in Scotland.

The king's divorce from Catherine of Aragon and his marriage to Anne Boleyn put Margaret's future in doubt, but only briefly: soon after the birth of Princess Elizabeth, the king's niece was appointed first lady of honor to Queen Anne. While Princess Mary was banished to Hatfield as a proclaimed bastard, Margaret at age 18 became a central figure at Court; and she was every eligible courtier's dream bride.

On 26 November 1533, Fitzroy, 15, was wedded to Mary Howard, 13 (second daughter of Thomas Howard, third duke of Norfolk). Thereby created Duchess of Richmond, but judged too young to cohabit, Mary joined Margaret Douglas as a maid of honor to Queen Anne. In those happy days, Margaret's circle included George and Mary Boleyn, the queen's siblings; the queen's Shelton cousins; her Howard cousins, including Mary, duchess of Richmond, and Henry, earl of Surrey (Mary's brother); also, Surrey's friend and fellow poet, Sir Thomas Wyatt.

A romance developed between Lady Margaret and Thomas Howard (Anne Boleyn's youngest uncle: he was the eighth child of Thomas Howard, second duke of Norfolk; and cousin to Mary, duchess of Richmond). By Christmas 1535, there was an exchange of gifts: Howard gave Margaret a cramp ring; she gave him a miniature of herself. By Easter, they were betrothed. Then, disaster: on 2 May Queen

Anne was indicted for high treason; and on 19 May, beheaded. The Howard kin of Queen Anne fell from grace along with her. On 30 May, King Henry wedded his new sweetheart, Jane Seymour.

In the Parliament's haste to bastardize both Mary and Elizabeth in favor of any children born to Queen Jane, no one seemed to consider that the Act of Succession in the meantime rendered Margaret Douglas the obvious heir to the throne in the event of King Henry's death. Complicating the succession was the death of Henry Fitzroy, royal bastard, on 23 July 1536; whereupon Henry no longer had cause to show favor to any member of the Howard clan, not even to his daughter-in-law Mary, a virgin widow at 15.

King Henry expressed indignation upon learning that his niece, Margaret Douglas, was betrothed. He promptly had Thomas Howard arrested and imprisoned in the Tower of London while Parliament drew up reasons for putting him there. The indictment read: "The Lord Thomas Howard, ... being led and seduced by the Devil, not having God afore his eyes, nor regarding his duty of allegiance that he oweth to have borne the King, our and his most dread sovereign lord, hath lately ... without the knowledge or assent of our said most dread sovereign lord the King, contemptuously and traitorously contracted himself by crafty, fair, and flattering words to and with the Lady Margaret Douglas (being natural daughter to the Queen of Scots, eldest sister to our said sovereign lord; by the which it is vehemently to be suspected that the said Lord Thomas falsely, craftily, and traitorously hath imagined and compassed that in case our said sovereign lord should die without heirs of his body (which God defend!) then that the said Lord Thomas, by reason of marriage in so high a blood, and to one such which pretendeth to be lawful daughter to the said Queen of Scots, eldest sister of our said sovereign lord, should aspire by her to the imperial crown of this realm, or at the least making division for the same. By all likelihoods, having a firm hope and trust that the subjects of this realm would incline and bear affection to the said Lady Margaret Douglas, being born in this realm, and not to the King of Scots her brother…."[1]

Within days of Howard's imprisonment, Margaret, too, was arrested and confined in the Tower. But the same indictment that condemned Howard, declared Margaret to be the bastard offspring of an annulled marriage; unless Henry should name his niece as his successor (unlikely!) the indictment itself rendered moot the ambition ascribed to the accused. The legislature thereupon passed a statute making it high treason for any man to "marry or take to wife any of the King's children being lawfully born or otherwise, or commonly reputed for his children; or any of the King's sisters or aunts of the part of his father, or any the lawful children of the King's brothers or sisters (not being married) without consent of the King under the Great Seal; or to seduce any, not being married." Any such suitor "shall be deemed a traitor to the King and his realm, and with his abettors shall suffer the pains and execution of death, loss of privilege and sanctuary, and forfeitures of lands and hereditaments to all intents as in cases of high treason." Margaret, too, was made an outlaw: "[B]e it enacted that the woman (after the last day of this Parliament) so offending, being within the degrees before specified, shall incur like danger and penalty as is before limited, and shall suffer such-like death and punishment as appointed to the man offending."[2] Parliament in collusion with the Crown petitioned the King to condemn both Howard and Douglas to death for high treason; the King promptly signed Howard's death warrant, condemning him to die without benefit of a trial, for having broken a law that was not yet invented at the time of the betrothal. Margaret was "pardoned her life in that copulation had not taken place." The newlyweds were not without sympathy. Writing to Emperor Carlos V, ambassador Eustace Chapuys remarked that the bride deserved pardon "even if she had done much worse, considering the number of domestic examples she has seen and sees daily, and that she has been for eight years of age and capacity to marry. Since the case has been discovered she has not been seen, and no one knows whether she be in the Tower or some other prison." [3]

When the unhappy news of her daughter's arrest reached queen Margaret in Scotland, she wrote at once to her brother, astonished at the arbitrary behavior of a despot whose actions never ceased to amaze:

### [Margaret Tudor to Henry VIII (12 August 1536)°]

Dearest brother,

In our most heartly manner we recommend us to your Grace. Please you understand we are informed lately that our daughter, Margaret Douglas, should by your Grace's advice promise to marry Lord Thomas Howard; and that your Grace is displeased that she should promise or desire such thing; and that your Grace has delivered to punish my said daughter (and your near

---

[1] Great Britain, Records Commission, *Statutes of the Realm*, vol. 3 (1832), 610.

[2] ibid., 680-1.

[3] Chapuys to Carlos V, *S.P. Henry VIII,* 4.2, 4875.

cousin) to extreme rigor; which we can no way believe, considering that she is our natural daughter; your nepotess; and sister-natural to the king our dearest son, your nephew [James V], who will not believe that your Grace will do such extremity upon your own, ours, and his, being so tender to all three as our natural daughter is.

Dearest brother, we beseech your Grace of sisterly kindness to have compassion and pity of us your sister; and of our natural daughter and sister to the king your dearest nephew; and to grant our said daughter Margaret your pardon and favor; and remit of such as your Grace has laid to her charge; an' if it please your Grace, to be content she come into Scotland, so that in time coming she shall never come into your Grace's presence. And this, dearest brother, we (in our most heartily affectious, tender manner) beseeches your Grace to do, as we doubt not your wisdom will think to your honor, since our request is dear and tender till us, the gentlewoman's natural mother, and we, your natural sister, that makes this piteous and most humble request.

Further (please your Grace) this bearer will inform; and the eternal God conserve your Grace, as we would be ourself.

Written at Perth this 12th day of August, by your Grace's most loving sister,
Margaret R.

When Thomas Howard was sent to the Tower, he took with him *The Workes of Geffray Chaucer* (1532, edited by William Thynne), plus a manuscript commonplace book (mostly blank), for use as a prison journal – which he received as a gift from his newly widowed cousin, Mary Fitzroy, duchess of Richmond. Thomas Howard's prison journal, known today as the Devonshire Manuscript (British Library MS Add. 17492) has produced more mistaken and fanciful commentary than perhaps any other collection of sixteenth-century verse; but when rightly understood, it contains the record of a tragic love story.

For our purposes, the first entries of interest are five autograph poems by Howard, composed in July-August 1536 and addressed to Margaret Douglas, when Howard first came to grips with the catastrophe that had overtaken his life. (Whether the original of these verses reached Margaret is unknown.)

**Thomas Howard in prison** (holograph):
***Now may I morne as one off late...*** (fol. 26r)

Now may I mourn, as one of late
Driven by force from my delight,
And cannot see my lovely mate
To whom for euer my heart is plight.

Alas, that euer prison strong
Should such two lovers separate!
Yet, though our bodies suffereth wrong,
Our hearts shall be of one estate.

I will not swerve, I you ensure,
For gold nor yet for worldly feare.
But like as yron, I will endure –
Such faithful love to you I bear! [1]

Thus fare ye well, to me most dear
Of all the world, both most and least.
I pray you, be of right good cheer.
And think on me that loves you best.

And I will promise you again
To think of you – I will not lett,
For nothing could release my pain
But to think on you, my lover sweet. [2]

**Thomas Howard** (holograph)
***to morne off ryght yt ys my part...*** (f. 26v)

To mourn, of right, it is my part –
To weep, to wail, full grievously.
With sorrowful sighs and woundès-smart
My heart is piercèd suddenly. [3]

The bitter tears doth me constrain
Although that I would it eschew,
To wit, of them that doth disdain
Faithful lovers that be so true.

The one of us fro' th' other they do absent,
Which unto us is a deadly wound
Seeing we love in this intent,
In God'is laws for to be bound.

With sighès deep my heart is pressed,
'during of great pains among
To see her daily (whom I love best)
In great and untolerable sorrows strong. [4]

There doth not live no loving heart
But will lament our grievous woe,
And pray to God to ease our smart
And, shortly, together that we may go.

[To] Mar[gret] H[oward]

---

[1] *worldly feare* ] 1. mortal fear; 2. common mate (MS *fere*); *yron* ] 1. iron; 2. yearn (MS *yerne*).

[2] *lett* ] stop, cease.

[3] MS begins with lines 3-4 (*Wyth sorowful syghes*), then 1-2, with an arrow drawn to indicate the emended order.

[4] *'during* ] Enduring.

**Thomas Howard** (autograph):
***Who hath more cawse…*** (f. 28r)

Who hath more cause for to complain
Or to lament his sorrow and pain
Than I, which loves, and lovèd again,
Yet cannot obtain.

I cannot obtain that is mine own
Which causeth me still to make great moan
To see thus right with wrong o'erthrown,
As not unknown. 1

It is not unknown how wrongfully
They will me, her for to deny
Whom I will love most heartily
Until I die.

Until I die, I will not lett
To seek her out in cold and heat,
Which hath my heart as firmly set
As tongue or pen can that repeat. 2
*finis*

**Thomas Howard** (holograph):
***Alas that men be so ungent…*** (f. 27v)

Alas, that men be so un-gent,
    To order me so cruelly!
Of right, they should themself repent
    If they regard their honesty.

They know my heart is set so sure
    That all their words cannot prevail –
Though that they think me to allure
    With double tongue and flattering tale.

Alas, methinks they do me wrong,
    That they would have me to resign
My title, which is good and strong:
    That I am yours and you are mine.

I think they would that I should swear
    Your company for to forsake,
But once. There is no worldly fear
    Shall cause me such an oath to make!

For I do trust, ere it be long,
    That God of his benignity
Will send us *right* (where we have *wrong*),
    For serving him thus faithfully.

Now fare ye well, mine own sweet wife –
    Trusting that shortly I shall hear
From you, the stay of all my life –
    Whose health alone is all my cheer. 3
*finis*

[1] *that* ] that which.

[2] *lett* ] cease.

[3] *stay* ] support.

**Thomas Howard** (autograph, f. 27r):
***What thyng shold cawse me to be sad…***

What thing should cause me to be sad
As long ye rejoice with heart?
My part it is, for to be glad.
Since you have taken me to your part,
Ye do release my pain and smart,
Which would me very sore ensue
But that for you, my trust so true.

If I should write and make report
What faithfulness in you I find,
The term of life, it were too short,
With pen, in letters, it to bind;
Wherefore, whereas as ye be so kind,
As for my part, it is but due
Like case, to you: to be as true.

My love truly shall not decay,
For threat'ning nor for punis'ment:
For let them think and let them say,
Toward you alone I am full bent.
Therefore I will be diligent,
Our faithful love for to renew
And still to keep me trusty and true.

Thus, fare ye well, my worldly treasure! –
Desiring God that, of his grace,
To send no time his will and pleasure
And shortly to get us out of this place.
Then shall I be in as good case
As a hawk that gets out of his mew
And straight doth seek his trust so true. 4

• • •

Howard at last received a letter from Margaret (probably sent before she was herself arrested and incarcerated), containing verses that the hapless prisoner copied into his poetry book:

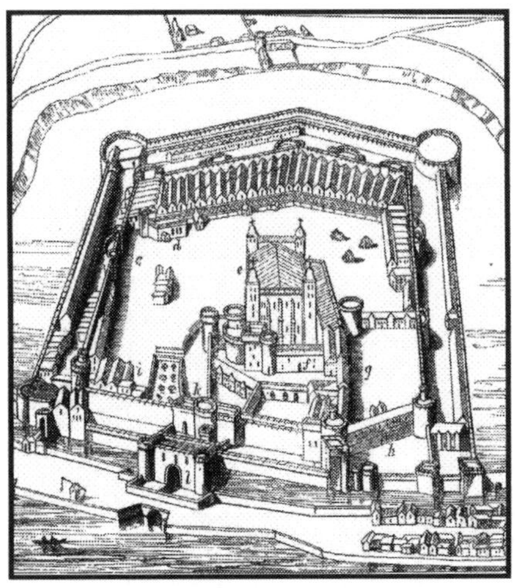

[4] *mew* ] cage for trained hawks.

**Lady Margaret to Thomas Howard** (entered into the book by Howard, in prison):

***I may well say*** $w^{t}$ ***Ioyfull harte…*** (fol. 28v)

*I may well say* $w^{t}$ *Ioyfull harte*
*as neuer woman myght say beforn*
*that I haue takyn to my part*
*the faythfullyst louer that ever was born*

*great paynes he suffereth for my sake*
*contynnually both nyght and day*
*for all the paynes that he doth take*
*from me hys loue wyll not decay*

*Wyth thretnynges great he hath ben sayd*
*off payne and yke off punnysment*
*yt all fere asyde he hath layed*
*to loue me best was hys yntent*

*Who shall let me then off ryght*
*onto myself hym to retane*
*and loue hym best both day and nyght*
*yn recompens off hys great payne*

*yff I had more more he shold haue*
*and that I kno he knowys full well*
*to loue hym best unto my graue*
*off that he may both bye and sell*

*And thus fare well my hartes desyer*
*the only stay off me and myne*
*onto god dayly I make my prayer*
*to bryng vs shortly both in one lyne*

**I may well say, with joyful heart…**

I may well say, with joyful heart
(As neuer woman might say beforn!),
That I have taken to my part
The faithfull'st louer that euer was born. [1]

Great pains he suffereth for my sake,
Continually, both night and day.
For all the pains that he doth take
From me, his love will not decay.

With threatenings great, he hath been said
Of pain and eke of punishment
Yet all fear, aside, he hath laid:
To love me best was his intent.

Who shall lett me then, of right
Unto myself, him to retain,
And love him best, both day and night,
In recompense of his grat pain? [2]

If I had more, more he should have,
And that I know he knows, full well.
To love him best unto my grave:
Of that, he may both buy and sell.

And thus farewell, my heart's desire
The only stay, of me and mine!
Unto God, daily, I make my prayer
To bring us shortly both in one line. [3]

Encouraged by Margaret's pledge of loyalty, Howard swore he would sooner die a hundred deaths than renounce his marriage vows:

**Thomas Howard to Lady Margaret** (holograph):

***To yowr gentyll letters an answere…*** (fol. 29r)

*To yowr gentyll letters an answere to resyte*
*both I and my penne there to wyll aply*
*and thowgh that I can not* $yo^{r}$ *goodnes aquyte*
*In ryme and myter elegantly*
*yet do I meane as faythfully*
*As euer dyd louer for hys part*
*I take god to record whych knowyth my hart*

*And where as ye wyll contynew myne*
*To reporte for me ye may be bold*
*That yff I had lyves as argus had yne*
*yet soner all them lyse I wold*
*then to be tempte for fere or for gold*

**To your gentle letters, an answer to recite…**

To your gentle letters, an answer to recite
Both I and my pen thereto will apply.
And though that I cannot your goodness acquit
In rhyme and meter elegantly,
Yet do I mean as faithfully
As euer did louer for his part.
I take God to record, which knoweth my heart.

And whereas ye will continue mine,
To report for me ye may be bold
That if I had lives as Argus had eyne,
Yet sooner all them lese I would
Than to be tempt, for fear or for gold,

---

[1] *internal rhyme*: in the 16th C, *ever* was commonly pronounced *yoo-er*; *lover* tended to be pronounced *loo-er*.

[2] *lett* ] stop, obstruct.

[3] *stay* ] support.

*yow to refuse or to forsake*
*wych ys my faythful and louyng make*

*wych faythfullnes ye dyd euer pretend*
*and gentylnes as now I see*
*off me wych was yowr pore old frend*
*yowr louyng husband now to be*
*synce ye desende from yo[r] degre*
*take ye thys unto yowr part*
*my faythful / trwe and louyng hart*

*for terme off lyfe thys gyft ye haue*
*Thus now adwe my none swete wyfe*
*from T. H. wych nowght doth crave*
*but yow the stay off all my lyfe*
*and the that wold other bate or stryfe*
*to be tyed wyth yn ~~yo~~[ower] louyng bandys*
*I wold the were on goodwyn sandys*

You to refuse or to forsake
Which is my faithful and loving make. 1

Which faithfulness ye did euer pretend
And gentleness as now I see
Of me which was your poor old friend,
Your loving husband now to be;
Since ye descend from your degree
Take ye this unto your part
My faithful, true, and loving heart:

For term of life this gift ye have.
Thus now adieu, mine own sweet wife,
From T.H., which naught doth crave
But you, the stay of all my life;
And they that would other bate or strife
To be tied within our loving bands,
I would they were on Goodwin Sands. 2

The young lovers from their separate chambers in the Tower were forbidden further communication. The weeks wore on to months. By October, Margaret had fallen ill. King Henry, who evidently wished for his niece to survive, provided her with medical care, at the Crown's expense; and promised more hospitable accommodations, provided that she renounce her marriage. Margaret Tudor on 20 October wrote to her brother the King, thanking him thereupon for the "nobleness" he had shown to her daughter, "who will never have my blessing if she do not all that you command her."[3] Lord Cromwell meanwhile wrote to Agnes Jordan, prioress, asking that she receive Margaret into the so-called lady-prison at Sion Abbey. His request coming at a time when the monasteries were under threat of dissolution. Dame Agnes was happy, at first, to comply: on 6 November 1536, she wrote back to Lord Cromwell, extending a welcome to the king's disgraced niece:

### [**Agnes Jordan, prioress of Sion Abbey, to Thomas, Lord Cromwell** (6 Nov. 1536)°]

Duty in most humble wise and thanks from the entires of our hearts unto your good lordship always premised. Pleaseth the same to be ascertained that, according to the will and pleasure of our liege lord and most gracious sovereign and prince, signified unto us by your lordship's letters as touching the Lady Margaret Douglas, I shall be ready and glad to receive her to such lodging, walks, and commodities as be or may be to her comfort and our prince's pleasure, in our precinct. And what service and pleasure shall be in us to do unto her, we shall be ever ready to do, at the will of our said gracious lord, to be opened unto us by your lordship's certificate, and that both for now and hereafter with all our powers. Yet I require of your good lordship that some person, such as you do trust and think apt, may come and see lodging and walks as be with us, and to judge which be most convenient for the purport. And thereupon all thing, to the most of my power, shall be ordered and directed by the help and grace of our Lord Jesu, who ever defend and bless you bodily and ghostly to His most merciful pleasure. From Sion, the 6[th] day of November, by your most bounden beadwoman and daily oratrice.

Agnes, Abbess

(To the right honorable and always our most assured good lord, my lord of the Private Seal, be these delivered with speed.)

---

[1] *lese* ] lose; *make* ] mate, spouse (*OED* make n.1).

[2] *that would other bate* ] who wish either quarrel; *bands* ] marriage bond; *Goodwin Sands* ] dangerous shoals off the coast of Dover.

[3] Margaret Tudor to Henry VIII (20 Oct. 1536), B.L. MS Add. 32646, fol. 89.

Dame Agnes and her sisters got more than bargained for. Once transferred to the abbey, Lady Margaret was permitted the same servants she had employed while at Court: Peter, a gentleman valet who maintained her wardrobe; Harvey, a common groom (for menial chores), another servant to clean and maintain her chamber; plus a Roman Catholic chaplain named Charles. These four were augmented by two former servants of Thomas Howard in need of work. Dame Agnes was unhappy to have men on the precincts who were not part of the abbey's own necessary staff, and complained.

Margaret in the meantime chose to cut her losses: she renounced her marriage to Thomas Howard and promised henceforth to make it her sole care to please the King. The King and Cromwell were of course mollified; but a few necessary actions were necessary to make her submission complete, the first of which was that she dismiss those two former servants of Thomas Howard. Margaret wrote again to promise her compliance and once again renounced her "fancy" for her betrothed husband.

[**Margaret Douglas to Thomas, Lord Cromwell** (December, 1536)°]

My Lord,

What cause have I to give you thanks, and how much bound am I unto you, that by your means hath gotten me, as I trust, the King's Grace's favor again, and besides that, that it pleased you to write and to give me knowledge wherein I might have his Grace's displeasure again (which I pray our Lord sooner to send me death, than that!); I assure you, my lord, I will never do that thing willingly that should offend his Grace.

And my lord, whereas it is informed you that I do charge the house [of Sion Abbey] with a greater number that is convenient, I assure you I have but two more than I had in the Court, which indeed were my lord Thomas's servants; and the cause that I took them for was for the poverty that I saw them in, and for no cause else. But seeing, my lord, that it is your pleasure that I shall keep none that did belong unto my lord Thomas, I will put them from me.

And I beseech you not think that any fancy doth remain in me touching him; but that all my study and care is how to please the King's Grace and to continue in his favor. And my Lord, where it is your pleasure that I shall keep but a few here with me, I trust ye will think that I can have no fewer than I have; for I have but a gentleman and a groom that keeps my apparel, and another that keeps my chamber, and a chaplain that was with me always in the Court.

Now, my lord, I beseech you that I may know your pleasure if you would that I should keep any fewer. Howbeit, my lord, my servants hath put the house to small charge, for they have nothing but the reversion of my board; nor I do call for nothing but that that is given me; howbeit I am very well intreated. And my lord, as for "resort," I promise you I have none, except it be gentlewomen that comes to see me, nor never had since I came hither; for if any "resort" of men had come, it should neither have become me to have seen them, nor yet to have kept them company, being a maid as I am. Now my lord, I beseech you to be so good as to get my poor servants' their wages; and thus I pray our Lord to preserve you both soul and body.

By her that has her trust in you,
Margaret Douglas

Upon her compliance, Margaret found that her situation improved at once: the Crown permitted her to receive gentlewomen visitors; underwrote the wages of her servants; and even funded an upgrade to her furnishings. Royal bequests to Margaret while she remained a prisoner at Sion abbey included Venetian silver fringe, crimson silk fringe, and two thousand gilded nails for the construction of an elegant and comfortable chair; and intermittent payments of £20 each for her "necessaries," over and above the wages and board-wages of her servants.[1]

Margaret's renunciation may have deferred the execution of Thomas Howard, but it broke his heart. In his misery, he took comfort from literature: into his commonplace book Howard copied dozens of quotations, many of them from Chaucer's *Troilus and Criseyde* – lines that deplore the vicissitudes of love, the infidelity of Criseyde, and the inevitable death of her forsaken lover. Other passages dear to Howard's cracked heart included Chaucer's Remedy of Love and Complaint of Anelida; plus various extracts from Hoccleve and Roos, all copied from Thynne's 1532 edition of Chaucer. To these, Howard added many verses of his own composition, thereby to supply for posterity a record of his misery.

[1] B.L. MSS Cott. Vesp. F.XIII, fol. 138; Arundel 97, fol. 7; *S.P. Dom. Henry VIII*, vol. 11, p. 406 and 13.2, pp. 5-41.

Having forfeited his freedom, property, and future for a woman who would no longer acknowledge him even as a friend, Howard like Chaucer's Troilus longed for better "hap" (luck). Else, a speedy death:

**Thomas Howard** (holograph, fols. 45-6):
***Yff reason govern fantasye aright…***

If reason govern fantasy
So that my fancy judge aright
Of all pleasures to man earthly,
The chiefest pleasure of delight
Is only this that I recite:
For friendship showed, to find at end
The friendship of a faithful friend.

If this be true, true is this too:
In all this pleasant evenness
The most displeasure chaunce may do
Is unkindness showèd for kindness –
For friendly friendship, frowardness.
Like as the one case, pleasant is;
Likewise, a painful case is this.

This, too, approved, approve the third:
That is to say, myself to be
In woeful case: for at a word
Where I show friendship and would see,
For friendship, friendship showed to me,
There find I friendship so far fainted
That I scantly may seem acquainted.

By this word, *friendship,* now here said,
My meaning, to declare truly,
I mean no whit the burning brand°
Of raging love most amorously,
But honest, friendly company;
And other love than this, I know,
Herself (nor yet no other) can show; 1

And since herself no farder knoweth
Nor I myself but as I tell;
Though false report doth graze, [it] groweth
That I love her exceeding well,
And that she takès my love as *ill.*
Since I indeed mean no such thing,
What hurt could honest friendship bring?

No staring eye, nor hearkening ear
Can hurt in this, except that she
Have other friends that may not bear,
In her presence, presence of me;
And that, for that her pleasure be
To show unkindness for none other
But banish me, to bring in other.

But since that fancy leads her so,
And leads my friendship from the light,
And walketh [my] darling to and fro
While other friends may walk in sight,
I pray for patience in that spite;
And thus fullfilled, her appetite
I shall example be, I trow,
Ere friends show friendship, friends to know.

*finis* / T. H.

**Thomas Howard** (holograph, fols. 46-7):
***What helpythe hope of happy hape…***

What helpeth hope of happy Hap,
When Hap will hap unhappily?
What helpeth hope to flee the trap
Which Hap doth set maliciously?
My hope and Hap hap contrary –
For as my hope, for right, doth long,
So doth my Hap award me wrong. 2

And thus my Hap my hope hath turned
Clear out of hope into despair.
For though I burn and long have burned
In fiery love of one most fair,
Where love for love should keep the cheer,
There my mishap is overpressed
To set disdain for my unrest.

She knoweth my love of long time meant.
She knoweth my truth (nothing is hid).
She knoweth I love in good intent
As ever man a woman did.
Yet love, for love in vain, askèd,
*What cloud hath brought this thunderclap*?
Shall I blame her? Nay, I blame Hap.

For whereas Hap list to arise,
I see both she and other can,
For little love, much love devise.
And sometime Hap doth love so scan,
Someone to love her faithful man.
Whom saving bondship nought doth crave
For him she ought, nor cannot, have.

How be it, that "Hap maketh you so do,"
So say I not, nor otherwise.
But what such haps, by Hap, hap to,
Hap daily showeth in exercise:
As power will serve, I you advise
To flee such Hap, for Hap that *growth.*
And pardon me, your man, Tom Troth.

---

[1] *braid* ] brand.

[2] *Hap* ] n. Fortune; *hap* ] v. to happen, to chance.

Some take no care where they have cure
Some have no cure and yet take care.
And so do I, sweetheart, be sure.
My love? – most care for your welfare!
I love you more than I declare.
But as for Hap happing this ill,
Hap shall I hate, hap what hap will.

**Thomas Howard**:
***This rotyd greff will not but growe…***
(holograph, fol. 47r)

This rooted grief will nought but grow,
To wither away is not its° kind.
My tears of sorrow, full well I know –
Which well I 'lieve will not from mind. [1]
T.H.

• • •

On 12 October 1537, Queen Jane gave birth to a baby boy. Throughout the realm, the news of Prince Edward's birth was greeted with joy and relief; and by Margaret Douglas not least. A male heir to the throne repaired a long-festering injury to King Henry's masculine narcissism, demonstrated the favor of God, and rendered Margaret's marriage of no immediate consequence to the English succession.

Queen Jane died on 24 October of a puerperal infection, but the baby prince remained healthy.

On 29 October, Margaret Douglas was released from custody and commanded to dress for Queen Jane's wake and funeral procession (as one of 29 mourners chosen to mark the late queen's 29 years of life). The solemnities lasted from 31 October until the queen's burial on 12 November. But the tears that stained Margaret's face were not for Jane Seymour: On 31 October – within 48 hours of Margaret's liberation from Sion – Thomas Howard was dead in the Tower. Charles Wriothesley reports blandly, "On All Hallow Even, the Lord Thomas Howard, brother to the duke of Northfolk, died in prison, in the Tower of London… Also, the Lady Margaret Douglas, that had lyen in prison in the Tower of London for love between him and her, was pardoned by the King and set again at her liberty. Howbeit, she took his death very heavily." [2]

The official version came from Thomas Wriothesley, Lord Chancellor: Howard perished of an "ague." But the fever was most probably caused by the same deadly poison that in 1531 was served to Bishop John Fisher and his guests. No charges appear in the account books for Howard's medical care, as for Margaret. None of his prison visitors report any signs of illness. Nor did the Howard family believe that the victim died of natural causes (he was, after all, under sentence of death). Lord Howard was dispatched, the family believed, as a royal inconvenience made more complicated by Margaret's release from prison.

What may be Howard's last two poems appear on fol. 58, one of them in his own hand, the other having been entered by his friend, Sir Edmund Knyvet; by which time Howard may already have received his last meal: [3]

**Thomas Howard**:
***Sum sum̄ say I love sum say I moke…***
(holograph, fol. 58v)

Some, some say I love. Some say I mock
Some say I cannot myself refrain.
Some say I was wrapped in a woman's smock.
Some say I have pleasure; some, I have pain.
Yet on my faith, if you will believe me:
None knows so well as I where my she grieves° me.

**Thomas Howard's Farewell:**
***O myserable sorow…***
(entered by Edmund Knyvet, fol. 58v)

O miserable sorrow, withouten cure!
If it please thee, Lord, to have me thus suffer,
At least let her know what I endure
And this, my last voice carry thou thither,
Where lived my hope, now dead, for ever.
For as ill-grievous is my banishment
As was my pleasure, when she was present.

[*To*:] *M*[*argaret*] *H*[*oward*]

Howard's mother, Agnes, dowager duchess of Norfolk, petitioned the king for her son's body. Edward Seymour, earl of Hertford – brother of the late queen, now Lord Protector – forwarded the king's response in a note to Cromwell: "My lord, I have showed the King's Highness of my Lord Thomas's

[1] *full…not* ] I know full well; a well-full of tears I know; *well… 'lieve* ] I well believe; 2. that well of sorrow, I believe.

[2] C. Wriothesley, *Chronicle,* 1.70.

[3] Additional poems on the theme of betrayal, disappointment and grief, possibly by Howard though entered into the book by another hand, appear on fols. 47v-54v and are here omitted.

death, as Master Wriothesley desired me; as also my lady his mother's request for the burying of him. His Grace is content she hath him according to your advice, so that she bury him without pomp. Your Lordship's loving friend, Hertford."[1] The family interred Lord Thomas at Thetford.

Howard's death, coming just when there seemed a hope of better times ahead, left Margaret angry and distraught – a dark period later documented in her original verses and a suicide letter (below). A plucky survivor, Margaret eventually overcame her despair. Restored to the king's favor following Prince Edward's birth and Lord Howard's death, she was appointed to serve as first lady of honor to Anne of Cleves, Henry's fourth wife. She resumed her friendship with Princess Mary, whose situation improved following the fall of Anne Boleyn and the birth of Prince Edward; and she renewed a wide circle of friends that included Anne Howard Fitzroy and her kin. In 1540, Thomas Howard, third duke of Norfolk and his extended family were restored to favor. And on 28 July, the same day that he put Cromwell to death, King Henry married Katherine Howard (daughter of Edmund Howard, a younger son of the second duke of Norfolk (she was a niece of Margaret's deceased husband). Divorced in favor of Queen Katherine, Anne of Cleves was exiled to Richmond as the king's adopted "sister." Margaret was assigned apartments at Hampton Court and was reappointed to serve as first lady of honor to the King's fifth wife.

When Charles Howard, Queen Katherine's brother, fell in love with Margaret Douglas, all went smoothly enough, at first. But ill Fortune again intervened: On 18 October 1541, at Methven Castle, Margaret Tudor died of a stroke. Unable to compose a will and testament, with her last words she professed the earl of Angus to be her rightful husband, and Margaret their legitimate daughter. She asked that her cash on hand (2500 marks), and jewelry and valuables, be given to Lady Margaret. (Her son, King James V, scorning his half-sister as a bastard, appropriated his mother's goods to the Scottish crown; and Henry VIII was only too happy to have his niece proclaimed a bastard by her own royal brother.)

That same month, King Henry learned that his beloved Katherine was not a virgin when she married, having had a prior undisclosed relationship with Francis Dereham. In the ensuing travesty of justice, Margaret was among those punished, on allegations she intended once again to marry one of the Howards without the king's permission. This time, there had been no betrothal, nor did Margaret to her dying day acknowledge a love interest in Charles. Nonetheless, she narrowly escaped a return to the Tower. Instead she was confined at Sion Abbey until 11 November, when the lady prison was needed for Queen Katherine. Margaret thereupon was sent with Anne Howard Fitzroy north to Kenninghall, being remanded to the (benign) custody of the duke of Norfolk. Before leaving Sion, however, Margaret was visited by Thomas Cranmer, Archbishop of Canterbury, with a warning from the King's Privy Council: the archbishop scolded her for "overmuch lightness"; he showed her "how indiscreetly she has acted," first with lord Thomas and then with Charles Howard; and he advised her to "beware the third time."[1]

It was during her friendly confinement with the Howard family in Norfolk that Margaret entered her additions to Thomas Howard's poetry book. (It's doubtful that Margaret ever saw the volume prior to her exile with Mary Fitzroy at Kenninghall.) At this point, the book's content included Howard's original verses and one poem by Margaret (entered by Howard in prison). Possibly at the same time, Margaret received additional loose sheets of verse by the deceased; all of which attested to his faithfulness in love. Assisted by her friend, Mary Shelton (a friend whose parents lived 18 miles to the east), Margaret undertook to copy into the poetry book Thomas Howard's loose verses – many of which were bitterly critical of her unfaithfulness. Margaret then transcribed several verses of her own (59r-68r).

**Thomas Howard**
***ther ys no cure ffor care off mind…***
(ent. after his death by Margaret Douglas, fol. 41r):

There is no cure for care of mind
But to forget (which cannot be!).
I cannot sail against the wind,
Nor help the thing past remedy.

If any such adversity
Do trouble other with such-like smart,
This shall I say, for charity:
I pray God help euery woeful heart!
*finis*

**Thomas Howard to Margaret Douglas Howard**:
***thy promese was to loue me best…***
(entered by Margaret Douglas, fol. 40)

Thy promise was to love me best
And that thy heart with mine should rest
And not to break this, thy behest –
Thy promise was, thy promise was.

Thy promise was not to acquit
My faithfulness with such despite,
But recompense it if thou might –
Thy promise was, thy promise was.

[1] Edward Seymour to Cromwell (1 Nov. 1537), *S.P., Henry VIII, Miscellaneous,* art. 1013.

Thy promise was (I tell thee plain)
My faith should not be spent in vain
But to have more, should be my gain –
Thy promise was, thy promise was.

Thy promise was to have observed
My faith like as it hath deserved
And not causeless thus to a-swerved –
Thy promise was, thy promise was.

Thy promise was, I dare avow,
But it is changed – I wot well how.
Though then were then, and now is now –
Thy promise was, thy promise was.

But since to change thou dost delight
And that thy faith hath ta'en his flight,
As thou deservest I shall thee 'quite,
I promise thee, I promise thee.

### Thomas Howard: *how shold I…*

(ent. by Margaret Douglas, fols. 43r)

How should I
Be so pleasant in my semblent
As my fellows be?
Not long ago, it chancèd so
As I walked alone,
I heard a man that now and then
Himself thus did bemoan:
"Alas," he said, "I am betrayed
And utterly undone.
Whom I did trust and think so just,
Another man has won.
My sorrows due and heart so true
On her I did bestow.
I never meant for to repent,
In wealth, nor yet in woe.
Love did assign her to be mine
And not to love none new.
But who can bind their fickle kind
That never will be true?"
The western wind has turned her mind
And blown her clean away.
Where be my wealth, my mirth, my health
Is turned to great decay.
Where is the troth? where is the oath
That ye to me did give?
Such crafty words and wily birds
Let no young man believe!
How should I
Be so pleasant in my semblent
As my fellows be?

### Thomas Howard: *I se the change…*

(ent. by Margaret Douglas, fols. 40-41)

I see the|e change from that that was,
And how thy faith hath ta'en his flight.
But I with patience let it pass
And with my pen, this do I write,
To show thee plain, by proof of sight:
I see the|e change. 1

I see the|e change of wearied mind,
And slipper hold hath quit my hire.
Lo, how by proof in thee I find,
Aborning faith in changing fire.
Farewell, my part: proof is no liar.
I see the|e change. 2

I see the|e change of chance in love:
Delight no longer may abide.
What, should I seek further to prove?
No, no, my trust, for I have tried
The following of a false guide.
I see the|e change.

I see the|e change, as in this case,
Has made me free from mine avow,
For now another has my place,
And ere I wist, I wot ne'er how,
It happ'neth thus, as ye hear now:
I see the|e change

I see the|e change – such is my chance,
To serve in doubt and hope in vain.
But since my surety so doth glance,
Repentance now shall 'quite thy pain,
Never to trust the like again.
I see the|e change.

### Thomas Howard: *as ffor my part…*

(ent. by Margaret Douglas, fol. 41r-v)

As for my part I know nothing,
Whether that ye be bond or free,
But yet of late a bird did sing
That ye had [gained] your liberty. 3

If it be true, take heed betime
And if thou may'st honestly fly,
Leave off and slack this foulest crime
That toucheth much thine honesty.

I speak not this to know your mind
Nor of your counsel for to be;
But if I were, thou should me find
Thy faithful friend, assuredly.

---

[1] *the|e* ] MS *the,* used for both *the* and *thee*; here, both.

[2] *slipper* ] slippery; *quit my hire* ] lost my requital.

[3] *gained* ] MS *lost*, an evident slip of Margaret's pen, in copying Howard's poem, for *won* or *gained.*

**Thomas Howard:**
***what nedythe lyff when I requyer…***
(entered by Margaret Douglas, fols. 43v-44r)

What needeth life when I require
Nothing but death to quench my pain?
Fast flyeth away, that I desire
And double sorrows return again.
By proof I see before mine eyne
Another hath, that once was mine.

That I was wont to have in hold 1
Is slipped away full suddenly
And craftily I am withhold
From all my life and liberty;
So that I see before mine eyne
Another hath that once was mine.

It is no news to find, I know,
For faithfulness, to find untruth
But I perceive the wind doth blow
A crafty way to cloak the truth.
By which I see before mine eyne
Another hath, that once was mine.

A proverb old I have heard oft,
That *A light love lightly doth go*.
Now am I low that was aloft,
That was my friend, is now my foe;
So that I see before mine eyne
Another hath, that once was mine.

Since right with wrong hath his reward
And feignèd faith doth truth oppress,
I let it pass; and it regard
As I have cause, no more nor less –
Because I see before mine eyne
Another has, that once was mine. 2

What heart could think more than was thought,
Or tongue could speak more than was spoke?
Yet what, for that? All was for naught,
For [s]he is gone, and slipped the knot –
Whereby I see before mine eyne
Another has, that once was mine. 3

**Thomas Howard**: ***and thys be thys ye may…***
(entered by Margaret Douglas, fol. 44)

And this (by this) ye may
Assure yourself of me:
Nothing shall make me to denay,
That I have promised thee.

[1] *That* ] That which; again in next, line 4.

[2] *his* ] its.

[3] *she* ] MS *he;* Margaret here makes a poignant slip in her transcription.

**Thomas Howard**:
***to my meshap alas I ffynd…***
(ent. by Margaret Douglas, fols. 42r-v) 4

To my mishap, alas, I find
That happy Hap is dangerous
And Fortune workès but her kind
To make the joyful, dolorous.
But all too late it comes in mind
To wail the want which made me blind –
So often warned! 5

Amends my mirth and pleasantness
Such chance is chancèd suddenly–
That in despair, to have redress,
I find my chiefest remedy
No new kind of unhappiness
Should thus ha' left me comfortless.
So often warned!

Who could have thought that my request
Should have brought forth such bitter fruit!
But now is happed that I feared *least*,
And all this grief comes by my suit –
For where I thought me happiest
Even there I found my chief'st unrest.
So often warned!

In better case was never none,
And yet unwares thus am I trapped.
My chief desire doth cause me moan
And to my pain my wealth is happed.
Was never man but I alone
That had such hap to wail and groan –
So often warned! 6

Thus am I taught for to beware
And not to trust such pleasant chance.
My happy Hap has bred this care
And turned my mirth to great mischance.
There is no man that Hap will spare,
But when she list, our wealth is bare
Thus am I warned.

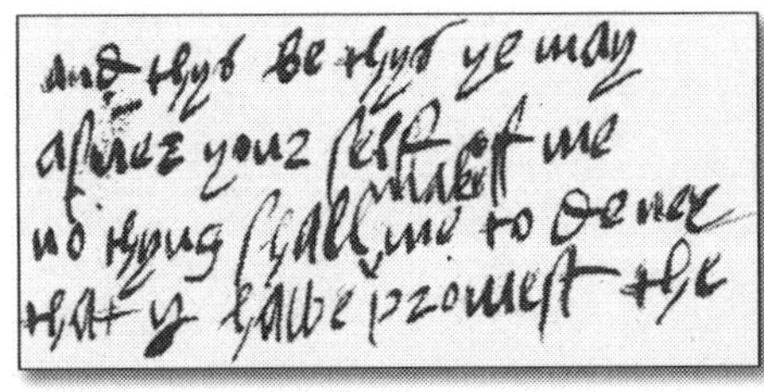

[4] This poem has been misattributed to Sir Thomas Wyatt on silly speculation that the first letter of the five stanzas, t-a-w-i-t, were intended as a scrambled lower-case anagram for T.WIAT.

[5] *happy Hap* ] good Fortune, luck.

[6] *And...happed* ] My very treasure (Margaret) has chanced to become my pain.

Some three or four years had lapsed since the trauma of Howard's death; but Margaret evidently wished that Lord Thomas's verse would not be the only lasting record of their ill-fated love. She next copied into the poetry book some verses of her own composition, which seem an authentic record of her emotional journey. The first of these, "My heart is set not to remove," may date from July-August 1536, during Margaret's initial resolve to keep her vows to Howard, come what may. Margaret entered the text, first, in pencil (fol. 58, reproduced below in original and modern spelling). When recording her final copy in ink (folio 65), Douglas made no substantive emendations but omitted the final stanza; perhaps because, on second thought, she realized that she was less prepared than she once believed for King Henry, Sir Thomas Wriothesley, and Thomas Lord Cromwell to "do their worst."

**Margaret Douglas, to the memory of Thomas Howard**

***my hart ys set not to remove...***
(holograph draft, in pencil, fol. 58v-59r)

*my hart ys set not to remove*
*ffor wher as I love ffath fully*
*I know he wyll not slak hys love*
*nor never chang hes ffantesy*

*I hawe delyt hym ffor to plese*
*yn all that towcheth onesty*
*hou felyth gref so yt hym ese*
*ples yt doth well my ffantesy*

*and tho that I be banest hym fro*
*hes spech hes syght and company*
*yt wyll I yn spyt of hes ffo*
*hym love and kep my fantesy*

*do what they wyll and do ther worst*
*ffor all they do ys wanety*
*ffor a sunder my hart shall burst*
*soworer than change my ffantesy*

**My heart is set not to remove**
(the same, in modern spelling)

My heart is set not to remove
For whereas I love faithfully:
I know he will not slack his love
Nor never change his fantasy.

I have delight, him for to please.
In all that toucheth honesty.
Who feeleth grief, so it him ease?
Please it doth well, my fantasy.

And though that I be banished him fro'
His speech, his sight and company,
Yet will I, in spite of his foe
Him love, and keep my fantasy.

<Do what they will, and do their worst
(For all they do is vanity),
For asunder my heart shall burst
Surer than change my fantasy.>

**Margaret Douglas, *When y bethynk my wonted ways...*** (holograph, fol. 58r)

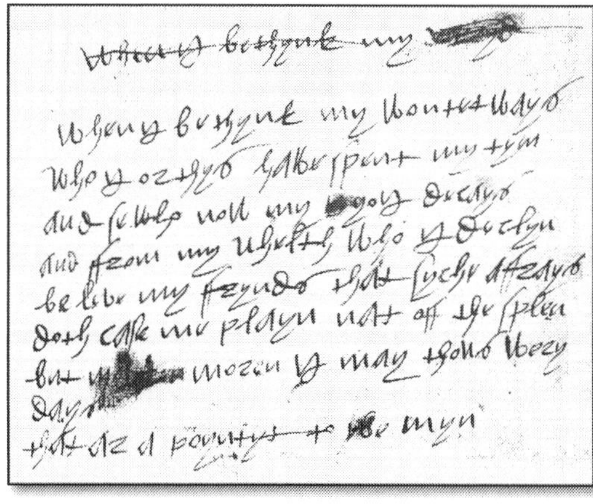

↑ Ent. by Mary Shelton, neater but with errors, fol. 59r

← Entered by Margaret Douglas, fol. 58r

**Margaret Douglas** (*holograph,* fol. 58r)
***when I bethynk my wontet ways…***

*when I bethynk my wontet ways*
*who I or thys hawe spent my tym* 1
*and se who now my ~~y~~ joy decays*
*and ffrom my whelth who I declyn* °
*be leve my ffrynds that syche affrays*
*doth case me playn nat off the splen*
*but moren I may thows wery days*
*that ar a poyntyt to be myn*

**When I bethink my wonted ways…**

When I bethink my wonted ways,
How° I, ere this°, have spent my time; 1
And see how° now my joy decays,
And from my wealth how° I decline°;
Believe, my friends, that such affrays
Doth cause me 'plain, not of the spleen, 2
But mourn I may those weary days
That are appointed to be mine.

**Margaret Douglas** (*holograph,* fols. 61-2)
***ffanecy fframed my hart ~~ffeu~~$^{ur}$st…***

*ffanecy fframed my hart ffeu$^{ur}$st*
*to bere good wyll and seke the same*
*I sowght the best and ffownd the wo$^{u}$rst*
*yet ffansy was no delle to blame*
*ffor ffancy hawe a dobell ne$^{a}$me*
*and has her ne$^{a}$me so ys her kynd*
*ffancy a ffoo and ffancy a ffrend*

*ffancy ffolowyd all my desyer*
*to lyk wher as I had best lust*
*what cold I mor off her requyr*
*than ffor that thyng wyche nedes I must*
*and fforsyt me styl ffor to be Iust*
*in thys she showyd her selff my ffrend*
*to mak me lord off my nown mynd*

*thys ffayned ffancy at the last*
*hath ca‸$^{u}$syd me ffor to beware*
*off wyndy words and bablyng blast*
*wych hath offtymes cast me in snare*
*and broght me ffrom my Joy to care*
*wherffor I mak thys promes now*
*to brek my ffancy and nat to bowe*

**Fancy framed my heart first…** 3

Fancy framèd my heart first
To bear good will and seek the same.
I sought the best and found the worst.
Yet Fancy was no deal to blame,
For Fancy hath° a double name
And as her name, so is her kynd:
Fancy, a foe; and Fancy, a friend.

Fancy followèd all my desire
To like whereas I had best lust
(What could I more of her require 4
Than for that thing which needs I must?),
And forced me still for to be just.
In this, she showed herself my friend: 5
To make me lord of mine own mind.

This feignèd Fancy, at the last,
Hath causèd me for to beware
Of windy words and babbling blast
Which hath oft-times cast me in snare;
And brought me from my joy, to care;
Wherefore I make this promise now:
To break my Fancy – and not to bow. 6

---

[1] *who:How* ] MS sp. *who* for *how*; again, lines 3 & 4; *how* in second copy, MS p. 59.

[2] *'plain* ] complain, lament; *the spleen* ] spitefulness.

[3] *Fancy* ] imagination, fondness, romantic fantasy.

[4] *her* ] Fancy, fondness, imagination.

[5] *she* ] Fancy.

[6] *break my Fancy and not to bow* ] (again below, "The Sudden Chance," l. 6); perhaps: disclose that I'm still in love with him and not to submit; more probably: to overcome my infatuation, renounce my vows, but with dignity (cf. the faithful wife of *Willobie his Avisa* (1594): "Though some there be that have done ill, / And for their fancy broke their faith, / Yet do not think that others will…").

**Margaret Douglas** (entered by Mary Shelton, fol. 65r):
***I ame not she be proweff off syt...***

*I ame not she be proweff off syt*
*kan make a yoy off al my woo*
*nor yn swche thyngs I do delyt*
*bot as the be so most the show*
*my nowen meshape hath hapt so ryt* [1]
*thys off my ffrynd to make my ffo*
*that than I wold yt loked nyt*
*to cloke my greffe wer yt doth grow*

**I am not she, by proof of sight...**

I am not she, by proof of sight,
Can make a joy of all my woe.
Nor in such things I do delight,
But as they be, so must they show.
Mine own mishap hath happed so righ
This of my friend, to make my foe,
That then, I would it lookèd night,
To cloak my grief where it doth grow.

**Margaret Douglas** (entered by Mary Shelton, fol. 65v)
***to cowntarffete a mery mode...*** [2]

*to cowntarffete a mery mode*
*yn mornyng mynd I thynk yt beste*
*ffor wen yn rayn I wor a hood*
*wel the war wet that bar hed ~~shod~~ stod*
*bot syns that clokes be good for dowt*
*the bagars prowarbe ffynd I good*
*betar a pach than a holle owte*

**To counterfeit a merry mood...**

To counterfeit a merry mood
In mourning mind, I think it best.
For when in rain I wore a hood
While they were wet that barehead stood.
But since that cloaks be good for doubt
The beggar's proverb find I good:
"Better a patch, than a hole out." [3]

**Margaret Douglas** (holograph, fol. 65v):
***myght I as well $w^{t}$in my songe be lay ...***

*myght I as well $w^{t}$in my songe be lay*
*the thyng I mene as in my hart I may*
*repentence showld dra ffrom thovs Ies*
*salt teres $w^{t}$ cryes remors and grow[n]es*

**Might I as well within my song belay ...**

Might I as well within my song belay
The thing I mean (as in my heart I may),
Repentance should draw from those eyes
Salt tears with cries, remorse, and groans.

**Margaret Douglas** (holograph, fol. 67):
***the sueden chance ded mak me mves***

*the sueden chance ded mak me mves*
*off hym that so lat was my ffrend*
*so straenely now the do me ues*
*that I well spy hes wavaryng mynd*
*wharffor I mak a promes now*
*to brek my ffansy and nat to bow*
*what cowld he say mor then he ded*
*or what aperrence mor covld he show*
*allways to put me owt off dred*

**The sudden chance did make me muse**

The sudden chance did make me muse
Of him that so late was my friend:
So strangely now they do me use
That I will spy his wavering mind
Wherefore I make a promise now
To break my fancy and not to bow.
What could he say more than he did,
Or what appearance more could he show,
All ways, to put me out of dread?

---

[1] Entered next and canceled: *~~that than I wold yt lake I myt~~* (line 7).

[2] Marginal note in Mary Shelton's hand: *ryme dogrel how many myle to meghelmes* (*i.e.,* rhyme doggerel [may be sung to the tune of] How Many Mile to Michaelmas).

[3] *Better ... out* ] proverbial: better to patch (conceal, cover up) a problem poorly than to let it show.

**Margaret Douglas** (entered by Mary Shelton, fol. 68): [1]

***my ywtheffol days ar past…***

*my ywtheffol days ar past*
*my plesant erese ar gon*
*my lyffe yt dothe bot wast*
*my grawe and I hame won*

*my morthe and al is flad*
*and I hame won yn woo*
*desyar to be dede /*
*my mescheffe to for goo*

*I born and ame acold*
*I ffresse amades the ffyar*
*I se the do w$^{t}$ hold ~~that~~*
*that most I do desyar*

*I se my helpe at hand*
*I se my dethe also*
*I se wer the dothe stond*
*I se my ffryndly ffoo*

*I se the know my hart*
*and how I kannot stan*
*I se the se me smart*
*and how I leff yn pane*

*I se how the dothe se*
*and yet the wel be blynd*
*I se yn helpeyng me*
*the se and wel not ffynd*

*I se haw the do wry*
*wan I begen to mon*
*I se wan I comby*
*how ffane the wold b gon*

*I se wat wold yow mar*
*the wold me gladly kel*
*and yow shal se therffar*
*that the shal hawe ther wel*

**My youthful days are past…**

My youthful days are past.
My pleasant years are gone.
My life, it doth but waste
My grave and I am one.

My mirth, and all, is fled
And I am one in woe,
Desire to be dead,
My mischief to forego.

I burn and am a-cold,
I freeze amidst the fire.
I see they do withhold,
That most I do desire.

I see my help at hand –
I see my death also –
I see where they doth stand –
I see my friendly foe.

I see they know my heart
And how I cannot stain
I see they see my smart
And how I live in pain.

I see how they doth see
And yet they wil be blind.
I see in helping me
They see and will not find.

I see how they do wry [2]
When I begin to moan.
I see when I come by
How fain they would be gone.

I see (what would you more?)
They would me gladly kill.
And you shall see therefore
That they shall have their will!

---

[1] At top of MS page: "Madame margeret / et madame de Richemont / Je vodroy bien quil fult" (Madame Margaret [Douglas and] Madame [Mary Fitzroy, duchess] de Richmond: Je voudrai bien, qu'il fuit [I desire to see, he flies]). The intended sense is perhaps: "The man I wish to see [Thomas Howard; Henry Fitzroy] has fled from me [in death]." By the time she copied the ensuing verses into the poetry book, Margaret had long since recovered from her despair. But her suicide poem, "My youthful days are past," resurfaced a decade later, in a revised text, in *Songs and Sonnets,* edited by Richard Tottel (1558, fol. 70r-v); and again, twenty years after that, in *A Gorgeous Gallery of Gallant Inventions,* edited by Thomas Procter (1578, sig. F3r). Margaret's poem suffers in revision: Margaret invokes death ("my mischief to forego") either to avoid further punishment, or in judgment for her own unfaithfulness in love. She resents those whom she thinks directly responsible for her husband's sudden demise, believing they would happily do the same to her: ("They would me gladly kill. / And you shall see therefore / That they shall have their will" – because I intend to do it myself). In both versions of the revised text (mutually dependent on some intermediate version), the sex of the original two lovers has been reversed, the text shortened, and the context altered: Margaret's rage and despair are imperfectly recast as the expression of a male suitor's frustrated sexual conquest. He threatens to kill himself to enforce pity from his coy mistress, a "she" who takes the place of Margaret's "they."

[2] *wry* ] turn aside.

*I kan not leffe w$^t$ stans*
*yt hes to hard a ffawde*
*I wol be ded at tons*
*yff yt myt do them good*

*the shal hawe ther rqwest*
*and I must hawe my nend*
*lo her my blody brest ~~to ples t~~*
*to ples the w$^t$ unkynd*

*M*

I can not live with stones –
It is too hard a food
I will be dead at once,
If it might do them good.

They shall have their request,
And I must have mine end:
Lo, here my bloody breast,
To please them with unkind.

M[argaret]

In November 1537, on word of Howard's death, Douglas resolved to take her own life, to satisfy those whom she represents as wishing to kill her. She went so far as to compose a verse epistle to be read at her funeral, recorded now in Howard's poetry book, years later, as a testament to the sincerity of her grief:

**Margaret Douglas** (holograph, fol. 88r):
***now that ye be assemblled heer…***

*now that ye be assemblled heer*
*all ye my ffrynds at my request*
*specyally you my ffather Dere*
*that off my blud ar the nerest*
*thys unto you ys my request*
*that ye woll pacyenlly hyre*
*by thys my last words exprest*
*my testement Intyer*

*and thynk nat to Interrupte me*
*ffor syche wyse provyded hawe I*
*that thoght ye welld yt woll nat be*
*thys touer ye se ys strong and hye*
*and the dooris fast barred hawe I*
*that no wyhght my purpose let shold*
*for to be quen off all Italy*
*nat on day lengere leve I wold*

*wherffor swet father I ~~I~~ you ~~pray~~ Pray*
*ber thys my deth w$^t$ pacyence*
*and tourment nat your herys gray*
*but frely pardonn myn offence*
*sythe yt presedeth off lowers ffervence*
*and off my harts constancy*
*let me nat ffrom the sweat presence*
*off hym that I haw case yt to dy*

**Now that ye be assembled here**

Now that ye be assembled here
All ye my friends at my request
Specially you my father dear
That of my blood are the nearest
This unto you is my request:
That ye will patiently hear
By this my last words expressed
My testament entire:

And think not to interrupt me
For such wise provided have I
That thought ye willed, it will not be
This tower ye see, is strong and high,
And the doors fast-barred have I
That no wight my purpóse let should –
For, to be queen of all Italy,
Not one day longer, live I would!

Wherefore, sweet father, I you pray,
Bear this my death with patience,
And torment not your hairès gray,
But freely pardon mine offense
Sith't proceeded of lovers' fervency
And of my heart's constancy.
Lett me not from the sweet presence [1]
Of him that I have causèd to die.

But that was then, and this was now. Exiled to Kenninghall to live with the Howard in-laws, confronted with poem after poem in which her late husband reproached her from his prison cell for having changed her fancy and broken faith – and having now recorded her own sincere and painful response to those difficult times – Margaret seems to have adopted a posture of defiant self-justification:

[1] *Lett me not* ] Do not obstruct me.

**Margaret Douglas** (holograph, fol. 59r):

***lo in thy hat thow hast be gone***

lo in thy ha[s]t thow hast be gone
to rage and rayll and rekuer how
and in thy rayge ffo~~r~~rth w[t] to run
fforther then resen can alov
but let them leve that lest to bow
or w[t] thy words may so be wone
ffor as ffor me I dare a woo
to do agen as I hawe done

***Lo, in thy haste, thou hast begun***

Lo, in thy haste thou hast begun
To rage and rail, and recure how;
And in thy rage forthwith to run
Further than Reason can allow.
But let them 'lieve that list to bow
Or with thy words may so be won:
For as for me, I dare avow
To do again as I have done. [1]

Margaret Douglas remained at Kenninghall until Henry VIII saw fit to employ her father once again to advance his political objectives in Scotland; whereupon he summoned his niece back to court. On 10 July 1543, Margaret Douglas was a bridesmaid at Henry's wedding to Katherine Parr.

(Margaret was now 28 years old, twice the age when noble and royal virgins were typically auctioned off to wealthy older husbands.)

A year later, King Henry and the earl of Angus contracted to wed Margaret to Matthew Stewart, earl of Lennox (this, in exchange for Stewart's promised support of Henry VIII's designs on Scotland). On 6 July 1544, at St James's Palace, Margaret Douglas, 29, was married to Matthew Stewart, 30. Lennox, one of Scotland's leading noblemen, is described by Robert Lindsay as "ane strang man of personage, weil-schapen in portratour,...weill-braint in legis, and armes weill-schoulderit, fair plessant faceit, with an goode and manlie contienance and zeid brent and right-wpe in his passage. Thairfor at that tyme he was most plessant for ane ladie."[2] On the day of his wedding, Lennox became a naturalized citizen of England, and received from the king bequests of property in London and Yorkshire, plus an annuity of 1000 crowns. Margaret was strong for the match, which proved to be a loyal and loving marriage for both parties (though the earl and countess of Lennox would often be separated by political affairs, or prison).

When Lennox was dispatched to Scotland, Margaret retired to Temple Newsham, Yorkshire, where she gave birth in February 1544/5 to a son (an earlybird), named after the king. The babe survived just nine months, dying a week before Margaret gave birth to her second son on 7 December 1545, also named Henry.

Margaret remained in Yorkshire for the last two years of Henry VIII's reign and for most of Edward's, while her husband wreaked bloody carnage on his own countrymen in what later came to be called the War of Rough Wooing (Henry's way of punishing Scotland for its reluctance to consent to a marriage between Mary Queen of Scots and his son Edward, prince of Wales).

On 8 September 1547, eight months after the death of Henry VIII, Lennox attacked and burned Annan. Two days later, Edward Seymour crushed the Scots at the Battle of Pinkie Cleugh. In March 1549, from Wressle Castle, Margaret wrote to her estranged father, remarking that he had only himself to blame for his difficulties. Among his offenses: the earl of Angus had named his brother George principal heir, and disinherited his only child, an act of disloyalty that Margaret could not easily forgive.

## [Margaret, Countess of Lennox, to Archibald Douglas, Earl of Angus (15 March 1548/9)°]

My Lord,

After my humble commendations, and desiring of your blessing, this shall be to signify to you the great unnaturalness which you show me daily, being too long to rehearse at all points; but some I will declare: Now the worst of all, my Lord, is that, being near you and most desirous to have spoken with you, yet you refused it and would not; wherein you showed yourself not to be so loving as you ought to be, or else so unstable that anyone may turn you. For divers times have you said you would be glad to speak with your son.[3] My Lord,

---

[1] *recure* ] seek remedy; *let ... how* ] let those who wish to submit believe you.

[2] *strang* ] strong; *weil schapen* ] well-shaped; *braint* ] brawned, muscled; *zeid brent* ] well-inclined; *right-wpe* ] upright; Robert Lindsay, *Historie and Cronicles of Scotland,* 2.16–18.

[3] *your son* ] i.e., son-in-law: Matthew, earl of Lennox, Margaret's husband.

remember: he hath married your own daughter – and the best child to you that you ever had, if you call to mind your being here in England. Howbeit, your deeds showeth the forgetfulness thereof, insomuch as you are so contrary to the King's Majesty's affairs that now is, his father being so good and so liberal a prince to you, which ought never to be forgotten.[1]

But now, my Lord, I hear say that you have protested never to agree with England, insomuch as the most part of your friends are slain; but whom can you blame for that but only your own self-will? For if you had agreed to this godly marriage [between Edward and Mary], there needed no Christian blood to be shed. For God's sake, remember yourself now in your old age, and seek to have an honorable peace, which cannot be without this marriage. And what a memorial it would be to you forever, if you could be an instrument for *that*.

If I should write so long a letter as I could find matter [for,] with the wrong of your part and the right of mine, it were too tedious for you to read; but forasmuch as I purpose (God willing) to come to Carlisle shortly after Easter, I will keep it in store to tell you myself: for I am sure you will not refuse coming to me (although my uncle George and the Laird of Drumlanrig speak against it, whom I know would be glad to see you in your grave although they flatter you to your face). My Uncle George hath said (as divers Scotchmen have told me) that though you had sons, he would be heir and make them all bastards; but my Lord, if God send you no more sons, and *I* live after you, he shall have little part thereof – or else many a man shall smart for it!

Thus leaving to declare to you farther of my mind till I may speak with you myself, I commit you to the keeping of Almighty God; who send you long life with much honor.

From the King's Majesty's castle of Wressil, the 15th of March.
By your humble daughter,
Margaret Lennox

The desired union of the Queen of Scots with England's Edward VI was rendered moot by Edward's death at age 16 of tuberculosis. Princess Mary succeeding Edward, Margaret returned to London, and to the center of Court life as the first lady of honor. Her husband the earl of Lennox was appointed to the Privy Council. Margaret, royal cousin and best friend, received from Queen Mary opulent apartments in Westminster Palace; an annuity; board and wages for her servants; tax revenues of 3000 per annum on the wool trade; and a steady shower of gifts in jewelry, gold, gowns, furniture, and tapestries. Lacking a child of her own and despising her half-sister, Queen Mary viewed her cousin, the countess of Lennox, as the heir presumptive to the English throne. Margaret heartily shared the queen's assessment, considering Princess Elizabeth a bastard born to a Protestant harlot.

When Queen Mary died in 1558, there was surprise throughout Europe that the succession passed to the daughter of Anne Boleyn and not to the daughter of Margaret Tudor; but the excesses of Mary's reign, and her marriage to a foreigner, left the English nation with no appetite for another Roman Catholic sovereign. Out of favor with Elizabeth, the Lennoxes retired again to Yorkshire; where their household became conspiracy central for English recusants. Hoping to restore England someday to the old religion, Roman Catholics looked to Mary, Queen of Scots; to Margaret, countess of Lennox; and to her son, Henry Stewart, Lord Darnley, as their last best hopes.

Scottish Mary first set eyes on Darnley in February 1561, while she was in mourning for her first husband, King François II of France: on that sad occasion, Margaret dispatched her son to Paris, to express condolences and to present himself as a future marriage prospect. Over six feet fall, Darnley impressed the grieving widow as "the lustiest and best proportionit lang man" that she had ever seen.[2]

Mary Stuart returned to Scotland in August 1561 and resumed government of Scotland as regnant queen. The Lennoxes lobbied hard for a marriage: Lord Darnley and the Queen of Scotland were both descended from Henry VII, through Margaret Tudor. Both were Roman Catholics. And the children of their marriage would be next in line not only for the throne of Scotland, but of England. Darnley did his part: the Devonshire manuscript – Thomas Howard's commonplace book, which remained in Margaret's

---

[1] *his father* ] King Edward's father, Henry VIII, who had been Archibald Douglas's greatest benefactor; and for whose generosity to her father, Margaret claimed credit.

[2] Sir James Melville, *Memoirs*, MS p. 72; (1827), 134.

possession – contains a poem of two eight-line stanzas, written perhaps as early as 1561, in which Henry confesses his love for Mary ("My hope is you for to obtain, / Let not my hope be lost in vain...," fol. 57v).

When spies in the Lennox household reported on Darnley's ambition, Elizabeth I acted quickly to forestall a union that might threaten the security of her own Protestant regime: Lennox was imprisoned without trial in the Tower, and Margaret at Sheen, in the home of the queen's Boleyn cousin, Sir Richard Sackville. From her confinement, Margaret plied William Cecil, Elizabeth's chief minister, with one letter after another (some dozen are extant), pledging her allegiance to Elizabeth and begging compassion: she and her husband were subjected to this misery, she wrote, without having committed a crime.

In November 1562, the earl was at last permitted to join his wife at Sheen; but not until February next were the offenders released from custody – by which time Queen Elizabeth believed that the danger was past: during their incarceration, the earl and countess of Lennox were reduced to poverty. Their rents were sequestered by the English crown (from which funds, Margaret and her husband were forced to pay for their own imprisonment). Meantime, their estates, managed by Elizabeth's deputies, fell into disrepair. Their goods were put to pawn, their livestock dispersed, their servants dismissed without wages. Moreover, Lennox was long since declared a traitor in his own native land for his services to Henry VIII. His Scottish titles and lands had been forfeited to the Scots crown. By 1563, it appeared to Elizabeth as if Mary queen of Scots would marry her own favorite, Robert, earl of Leicester, and show no further interest in poor Henry Stewart. But Elizabeth underestimated Margaret's tenacity and Henry's charm.

Lennox when released from custody returned (with Elizabeth's permission) to Scotland, where he sought and obtained Mary's goodwill: in December 1564 the Scottish queen pardoned him, and in April approved the restoration of his lands and titles. Darnley followed his father north, meeting Queen Mary in February 1565, at Wemyss Castle. Romance blossomed: in June, word reached London that the Scots queen was betrothed to Henry Stewart, Lord Darnley, the darling of Scottish and English Catholics.

A furious Queen of England summoned Lennox and Darnley to London, on suspicion of treason. Fearing imprisonment, they refused to obey. Elizabeth therefore sent Margaret to prison instead, this time for the offense of her son's betrothal. On 20 June 1565, the countess of Lennox was arrested at Settrington, Yorkshire. Her 9-year-old Charles was left behind to fend for himself. Margaret was transported to London, and locked up in the Tower.

Married on 29 July, Mary Queen of Scots soon became pregnant, though by whom is unsure. The child's paternity was credited, by some, to Darnley; and by popular opinion, to David Rizzio, Mary's private secretary and reputed lover. On 9 March 1565/6, in the presence of his pregnant and terrified queen, a jealous Darnley murdered his Italian rival. Mary survived the shock and on 19 June gave birth to a son, James VI of Scotland (whose destiny it was to succeed Elizabeth I as James I of England).

While estranged from the queen, Lord Darnley, king consort, found comfort in the usual manner of British aristocrats but with the wrong partner: by January 1566/7, he was suffering from second-stage syphilis; while Mary, having fully recovered from childbirth, was thought to be in bed with a new lover, James Hepburn, fourth earl of Bothwell.

Mary visited her ailing husband in Glasgow and returned with him to Edinburgh, where she lodged him in the Provost House of a church called Kirk o'Field, just inside the city walls. On 9 February Mary paid him a visit there, returning then to Holyroodhouse, the royal palace at Edinburgh. About two a.m. that same night, Provost House was destroyed by a tremendous explosion and fire. When the smoke cleared, Darnley and his male page were found in the orchard, dead by strangulation, evidently killed while trying to escape the flames. The architect of this daring assassination is thought to have been the earl of Bothwell. Many believed he was urged on by Mary, to revenge the death of David Rizzio.

Lady Margaret was still in prison on 19 February when word was brought to her of her elder son's murder; at which time she was told that Lennox was slain as well. These ill tidings, though half wrong, nearly killed her. In failing health, the countess was released from the Tower and remanded once again to the custody of Richard Sackville, at Sheen.

On April 24, the earl of Bothwell's wife sued for divorce, on grounds of his alleged adultery, not with Queen Mary but with his maidservant. That same day, with or without Mary's advance knowledge, Bothwell abducted the queen, carried her to Dunbar Castle, and raped her; whereupon she agreed to marry him, pursuant to his divorce. (Mary told the bishop of Dunblane two weeks later, "Albeit we found his doings rude, yet his words were gentle.")[1]

---

[1] Teulet, ed., *Lettres*, 2.31.

Lennox in disgust left Scotland to rejoin Margaret in England, come what may. Queen Elizabeth, without restoring their property, permitted the Lennoxes to dwell in the empty, damp, and dilapidated royal palace of Coldharbor.

Mary and Bothwell, meantime, were forced by their rebellious subjects to flee the country. Hepburn sailed for Scandinavia (thinking to raise an army); Mary fled to England, and was apprehended.[1] On news of Mary's capture, Margaret appeared before Queen Elizabeth in mourning clothes. "Blubbered with tears, in her own name and her husband's also, she besought Queen Elizabeth that [Mary] might be arraigned for the death of her son. Comforting Margaret with courteous words, [Elizabeth] willed her not to lay such a crime upon so great a princess, her nearest cousin, which could not be proved by any certain evidence; that the times were malicious, and unjust spite blind, which doth lay crimes upon innocent persons."[2] (With Northern Catholics now divided against themselves, Elizabeth saw no pressing need to put her badly behaved cousin-queen on trial for murder; Mary was kept in English custody for nearly twenty years; and finally beheaded in February 1586/7 not for the murder of Darnley but for her complicity in the Babington plot.)

The earl and countess of Lennox, praying for revenge (detail)

Though desperately short of cash, Margaret commissioned a 5' x 7' mural portrait depicting herself, her husband Matthew, their son Charles, and grandson James VI, kneeling beside the corpse of Lord Darnley, praying for revenge. This "Memorial of Lord Darnley," with its many inscriptions, narrates Henry Stewart's death and charges both Charles (Henry's only surviving brother) and young James VI (his nephew) never to rest until Darnley's murder was avenged.

What happened instead: on 23 January 1570/1, James Stewart, Regent for the infant King James, was assassinated. With Queen Elizabeth's backing, Matthew Stewart, earl of Lennox, was appointed the next Regent. (Margaret was detained at Windsor, ostensibly as Elizabeth's first lady of honor but in actuality a hostage, together with her son Charles, to ensure Lennox's cooperation in Scotland.) Lennox's rocky tenure as Regent was abruptly terminated on 4 September 1571: during a raid led by Mary's supporters, the earl was shot in the back. With his dying words, he is said to have begged protection for the six-year-old King James, and asked his colleagues "to remember my love to my wife, Meg."[3]

Margaret erected an elaborate monument at Stirling Castle, where Lennox was buried. As a further tribute, she designed and commissioned the famous Lennox jewel, a heart-shaped gold locket, set with a large sapphire and copiously decorated with allegorical figures. Now in the Royal Collection, the locket bears enigmatic inscriptions, never deciphered, that may pertain to Margaret's future hopes for James VI, and for Charles Stewart, the only one of her eight children who remained alive.

In 1574 Margaret obtained the queen's permission to visit Scotland with her son Charles, to see her eight-year-old grandson, James VI, now under the cruel regency of the earl of Morton, a Bothwell collaborator. Elizabeth was suspicious of her cousin's intentions: Margaret having long since become persuaded of Mary's innocence in the matter of Darnley's murder, Elizabeth feared that Margaret might now be colluding with Mary's Roman Catholic supporters in the North. But whatever Margaret's original intentions may have been, love intervened: on a layover at Huntington, Suffolk (at the home of the duchess of Suffolk), Charles Stewart met and fell in love with Elizabeth Cavendish, daughter to Bess of Hardwick, countess of Shrewsbury (the richest woman in England after the queen herself). The young lovers were both 19 years old. With the encouragement of their widowed mothers, a marriage was clapped up on the spot. (Among the gifts that the couple received, either as a wedding present or soon after, was the Howards' poetry book, containing the sad record of Lady Margaret's first love.)

When news of the marriage reached Elizabeth on 17 November, she exploded. A letter from the earl of Leicester was dispatched to Huntington, bearing the queen's command that Margaret and her son, and the countess of Shrewsbury and her daughter, must return at once to London, to answer to the Queen's rage. Margaret wrote in haste to William Cecil, seeking his intervention: "My very good lord, Assuring myself of your friendship, I will use but few words at this present, other than to let you understand of my

[1] Captured off the coast of Norway, Bothwell spent the last decade of his life in Dragsholm Castle, as the guest of Denmark's Frederick II; chained to a stake amidst his own excrement, Bothwell died insane in 1578.

[2] Ed. DWF from Udall, *The Historie of the ... Queene of Scotland* (1624), 49.

[3] Spottiswoode, *History* (1851), 2.166.

wearisome journey, and the heavy burden of the Queen's Majesty's displeasure, which I know well I have not deserved.... Your Lordship's assured loving friend, Margaret Lennox." To the earl of Leicester, Margaret wrote another, first excusing herself of collusion with Mary Queen of Scots; adding then: "Now, my lord, for the hasty marriage of my son, after that he had entangled himself so that he could have none other, I refer the same to your lordship's good consideration, whether it was not most fitly for me to marry them, he being mine only son and comfort that is left me. And your lordship can bear me witness how desirous I have been to have had a match for him (other than this), and the Queen's Majesty, much to my comfort, to that end gave me good words at my departure." A week later, Margaret and Charles had returned as far as Hackney, outside London. Fearing imprisonment, she wrote again to Leicester, pleading, "[S]urely, my lord, as touching the marriage, other dealing or longer practice there was none but the sudden affection of my son." She begs Leicester "to be a mean unto her Majesty to pity my cause and painful travel, and to have compassion on my widowish estate, being aged, and of many cares."[1]

A few days after their arrival in London, both mothers were arrested and locked up in the Tower, the blame being officially placed on Mary Queen of Scots, who was accused of having procured the match. From prison Margaret corresponded regularly with Mary, on one occasion sending her a gift lace interwoven with her own white hairs. All of Margaret's correspondence was of course opened and read, but no evidence of treason was found therein.

The countess of Shrewsbury was released first, Margaret being kept in the Tower until September, at which time she took up residence at Stepney, with Charles and Elizabeth and their infant daughter (Arbella Stuart). Margaret was now virtually destitute of income, deeply in debt, and anguished by the failing health of her only surviving child: in 1576, Charles died of tuberculosis. Margaret waged a successful campaign to claim the earldom of Lennox for Arbella, but thereafter had little enthusiasm for life. Her death came sooner than expected: on 7 March 1577/8, she became suddenly ill after hosting a dinner for Robert Dudley, earl of Leicester. Poison was suspected, but nothing proved. Two days of vomiting and dysentery led to her death on March 9th.

William Udall in his *History of Mary Stuart* provides a death notice: "Margaret Douglas – Countess of Lennox; niece to Henry the Eighth by his eldest sister; widow of Matthew, Earl of Lennox; grandmother unto James King of Great Britain, overliving her eight children – departed to the joys of Heaven in the threescore and third year of her age and was buried at Westminster with a solemn funeral, at the Queen's charge: a matron of worthy piety, patience, and chastity, who was thrice cast into prison (as I have heard her speak it) not for matter of treason, but for love-matters – first, when Thomas Howard … (being in love with her) died in the Tower; then for the love of Henry Dar'ly, her son, to the queen Mary of Scotland; lastly, for the love of Charles her younger son to Elizabeth Ca'ndish, mother to Arbella" (Udall 123-4).

A quarter of a century after her death, Margaret's grandson James – king of Scotland, England, Ireland, and Wales – erected a lavish monument to her memory. But the greatest memorial to Margaret Douglas is the one that she created herself, in Thomas Howard's poetry book, a poignant confirmation of the old adage that the course of true love, for the daughters of royalty, never did run smooth.

Margaret's effigy in Westminster Abbey

margaret lennox and anguyse

[1] Margaret Douglas Stewart to William Cecil (3 Dec. 1574); to Robert Dudley, earl of Leicester (3 Dec. 1574); to Leicester (10 Dec. 1574). *S.P. Dom. Elizabeth I*, vol. 99 (1856), 12-13.

## **Mary Shelton** (1519-1570/1),
### Lady Heveningham

*ondesyard sarwes reqwer no hyar*
—Shelton annotation, fol. 7r

ARY SHELTON was the ninth and youngest child of Lady Anne Boleyn (1483 -1555) by her husband, Sir John Shelton (c. 1472-1539), of Shelton, Norfolk. In 1533, King Henry's divorce and second marriage must have looked to the Sheltons like a godsend: Lady Shelton was a beloved aunt to her niece and namesake, Henry's new queen; while the Sheltons' son and heir, John Jr., was married to Margaret Parker, sister-in-law to George Boleyn, the queen's brother.

King Henry's favor was soon extended: In December 1533, three months after Queen Anne gave birth, her infant daughter Elizabeth was placed at Hatfield under the supervision of Anne and John Shelton. The King next dissolved the household of his elder daughter, Mary (who at age 16 was no longer permitted to call herself "princess," having been proclaimed a bastard). She, too, was placed in the Sheltons' care. Sir John Shelton was appointed comptroller of accounts; and his wife, Anne Boleyn Shelton, the controller of Mary's behavior. Together with her sister, Lady Alice Clere, Lady Shelton served as governess to the King's two daughters – and govern she did. Princess Mary while under the Sheltons' supervision was kept nearly destitute of clothing and other necessities, and forbidden to attend Mass (this, according to Eustace Chapuys, the Ambassador from the Holy Roman Emperor). On instructions from Queen Anne, Lady Shelton never permitted Mary to be alone except in the privy; nor ever permitted her to correspond with the outside world (but Chapuys was eventually able to bypass that restriction, with bribes). In October 1535, when the French ambassadors paid a visit to Princess Elizabeth at Eltham, they were told that Lady Mary greatly wished to see them as well, but that Lady Shelton had shut her up in her room, and caused all of the windows to be nailed down. Mary steadfastly refused to renounce her mother's marriage and declare herself a bastard; whereupon the Sheltons were authorized to give the obstinate girl discretionary beatings. It is to be doubted that they did so, but there were many altercations, including one public incident in which Mary, having refused to ride behind Princess Elizabeth, was roughly forced into the litter, and boxed on the ear.

Mary Shelton, by Hans Holbein, c. 1547
Courtesy of the Royal Collection, Windsor

Princess Elizabeth, dwelling under the same roof, was given every indulgence (entirely too much, according to Lady Bryan, who objected to an infant dining in state with the adults, drinking wine and eating fruit before she had teeth).

Princess Mary during these years was often sick and severely depressed, which her physician attributed to "ill treatment"; but reports differ: First, Queen Anne, then George Boleyn and the duke of Norfolk, reprimanded Lady Shelton for showing entirely too much kindness to Mary; who replied that even if Mary were the bastard of a poor gentleman, she deserved respect and fair treatment commensurate with her virtues. And though Mary may have felt no affection for her guardians, she was least forgiving: in 1538, again in 1543/4, Mary gave small gifts to the Shelton daughters; years later, as queen, Mary retained a Shelton son in her retinue, and settled an annuity on Lady Anne in her widowhood. At the time, however, Mary was (for many reasons) desperately unhappy; and from September 1534, even Lady Shelton went about in tears, following false reports that she had tried to poison Mary with pills obtained from an apothecary that were intended to relieve Mary's menstrual irregularities but nearly killed her.

During Ann Boleyn's tenure as queen consort, at least two, probably all three, of the older Shelton daughters – Amy, Elizabeth, and Gabriella – were already in religious orders; Gabriella, at the prestigious Barking Abbey. Mary, the youngest, was placed at St. Helen's Priory, possibly in 1533 when she turned fourteen. Anne, the fifth daughter, was married to Sir Edmund Knyvet (since 1527), with children. But Margaret, the Sheltons' fourth daughter, was sent to court, where she was appointed a maid of honor to Queen Anne; and she had a lively time of it. Margaret's flirtation with King Henry may have been initiated by Queen Anne, as a scheme to distract Henry from chasing other women. If so, the King took the bait and ran with it: in 1534, during Queen Anne's mysterious pregnancy of 1534, Henry and his "pretty Madge" were inseparable.

In December 1535, Queen Anne was again pregnant. As a substitute during her lying-in, Henry's interest shifted from Margaret Shelton to Jane Seymour; whereupon others stepped up to woo Margaret: she was courted in the winter of 1535/6 by Sir Francis Weston (who was married), and by Sir Henry Norris (a widower). Queen Anne chided Weston for his illicit wooing, and chided Norris for not wooing hard enough. Hoping perhaps to put cousin Madge out of the King's reach, Queen Anne demanded that Norris marry Margaret as he had once promised; but he demured.

In the end, neither man had her: King Henry in May 1536 beheaded both Weston and Norris, together with George Boleyn (Anne's brother), on allegations that Queen Anne had cuckolded him with those men (and with Mark Smeaton, and with Sir William Brereton). It was Lady Shelton, in January 1535/6, who gave Princess Mary the news that her mother, Catherine of Aragon was dead (Mary went to pieces); and it must have been Lady Shelton who conveyed similar if euphemized news to three-year-old Elizabeth, whose mother was beheaded in London on 19 May. The Sheltons continued to care for Mary and Elizabeth until autumn when they were then relieved of their duties; then returned home to Norfolk.

During all this time, there is no record that Mary Shelton – often confused by historians with Margaret – ever appeared at Court.[1] For all or most of Anne Boleyn's marriage, Sister Mary remained at St. Helen's, not returning home until November 1538, when her nunnery was surrendered to the Crown and Mary was sent packing with an annual pension of £4.

With the execution of Anne Boleyn and of Margaret Shelton's known suitors, pretty Madge was no longer a desirable property at court. In October 1537 (following Jane Seymour's death), Court gossip suggested that the King might yet revive interest in Mistress Shelton, but it was not to be. Margaret was married in 1539 to Captain Thomas Wodehouse, a military man. (By 1547, when Woodhouse was slain at the Battle of Musselborough, Margaret had given birth to six children; her glory days, a distant memory.)

Mary Shelton, when not confused with her elder sister, is best remembered today for her collaboration in the Howards' poetry book. Mary's autograph, and Margaret Douglas's, both appear on the torn front flyleaf of the bound volume; but the 200 poems contained therein do not appear in the chronological order in which they were written, which has caused much confusion. Mary Shelton's first interest in the volume comes not from her later friendship with Margaret Douglas but months earlier. About two years after her return home from the convent, Mary Shelton attracted the sexual interest of a Norfolk gentleman; a Howard family retainer who suffered from a cruel and unrequited passion to get Mary Shelton into bed. Among the earliest poems on this subject is an acrostic he wrote on the Shelton surname:

---

[1] The confusion arises from two texts, one Latimer's *Chronickille of Anne Bulleyne* (ed. Camden Society, 62-3), the other a letter of court gossip preserved with the Lisle letters after the death of Queen Jane: "The election [of Henry's next wife] lieth betwixt Mistress Mary [i.e.. Madge] Shelton and Mistress Mary Skipwith. I pray Jesu send such one as may be for his Highness' comfort and the wealth of the realm. Herein I doubt not but your Lordship will keep silence till the matter be surelier known" (John Husee to Lord Lisle [3 Jan. 1537/8]). The Shelton children: 1. *Amy* a.k.a. *Emma* and *Amice* (b. 1500, a nun; 1536, after the first dissolution, returned to Norfolk; 1565, mentioned as lady in waiting to Elizabeth I with annuity of £30; will dated 1566, proved 1579); 2. *Elizabeth* (b. 1502; possibly a nun c. 1516-1539; said to be destitute in 1561; died after 1566, unmarried); 3. Sir *John* (b. 1503, m. 1529 Margaret Parker; 1553, joined Mary I at Kenninghall, opposing rival claim of Queen Jane; d. 1558); 4. *Ralph* (b. 1506, m. 1530 Amy Woodhouse, sister of Thos. Woodhouse; d. 1561); 5. *Gabriella* (b. 1508, nun at Barking Abbey c. 1522-Nov. 1539; granted a pension of £6 in will of her brother-in-law Edmund Knyvet, 1550; died unmarried 1558); 6. *Thomas* (b. 1510, died unmarried 1562); 7. *Margaret* (b. 1513, reputed to be Henry's mistress 1533-34; m.1539 Capt. Thomas Woodhouse [d. 1547], 1556 omitted fr. mother's will]; died after 1561); 8. *Anne* (b. 1516, m.1 1527 Edmund Knyvet [d. 1551]; m.2 1552 Christopher Coote; 1556 om. mother's will; d. Feb. 1563/4); 9. *Mary* (b. 1519; nun at St. Helen's Priory, 1536-39; betrothed to Sir Thomas Clere [d. 1545]; m.1, 1546 Sir Anthony Heveningham [d. 1557]; m.2. 1558 Philip Appleyard [d. 1570]; d. Jan. 1570/1).

**EDMUND KNYVET** (holograph, 6v-7r)

***Suffryng in sorow in hope to attayn…***

*Suffryng in sorow in hope to attayn* [1]
*desyryng in fere & dare not cōplayn*
*trew of beleffe in whome ys all my trust*
*do thow apply to ease me off my payn*
*els thus to s$^{er}$ve & suffer styll I must*

*Hope ys my hold yet in Dyspayre to speke* [2]
*I dryve from tyme to tyme & dothe not Reke*
*how long to lyve thus after loves lust*
*in studye styll of that I dare not Breke* [3]
*wherfore to s$^{er}$ve & suffer styll I must*

*Encrease of care I fynd bothe day & nyght*
*I hate that was sūtyme all my delyght*
*the cawse theroff ye know I have dyscust*
*& yet to Reffrayn yt passythe my myght*
*wherfore to s$^{er}$ve & suffer styll I must*

*Love who so lyst at lengthe he shall well say*
*to love & lyve in fere yt ys no play*
*Record that knowythe & yf thys be not Iust*
*that where as love dothe lede there ys no way*
*But s$^{er}$ve & suffer euer styll he must*

*Then for to leve w$^{t}$ losse of lybertye*
*at last p$^{er}$chawnce shall be hys Remedye*
*& for hys trewthe Requit w$^{t}$ fals mystrust*
*who wold not rew to se how wrongfullye*
*thus for to s$^{er}$ve & suffer styll he must*

*Vntrew be trust oftymes hathe me betrayd*
*mysvsyng my hope styll to be delayd*
*fortune allways I have y$^{e}$ fownd unIust*
*& so w$^{t}$ lyke rewarde now am I payd*
*that ys to s$^{er}$ve & suffer styll I must*

*Neu$^{r}$ to cesse nor yet lyke to attayn*
*as long as I in fere dare not complayn*
*trew of beleff hathe allways ben my trust*
*& tyll she knowythye the cawse of all my payn*
*content to s$^{er}$ve & suffer styll I must*

*ffynys*

**Suff'ring in sorrow, in hope to attain…**

Suff'ring in sorrow, in hope to attain,
Desiring in fear and dare not complain.
True-of-belief, in whom is all my trust,
Do thou apply to ease me of my pain –
Else thus to serve and suffer still I must.

Hope is my hold, yet in despair to speak,
I drive from time to time and doth not reck
How long to live thus, after love's lust:
In study still, of that I dare not break;
Wherefore to serve and suffer still I must.

Encrease of care I find both day and night.
I hate that, was sometime all my delight.
The cause thereof, ye know, I have discussed –
And yet to refrain, it passeth my might;
Wherefore to serve and suffer still I must.

Love, whoso list! at length, he shall well say,
*To love and live in fear – it is no play*!
Record, that knoweth – and if this be not just,
That whereas love doth lead, there is no way
But to serve and suffer, still he must.

Then, for to live with loss of liberty,
At last, perchance, shall be his "remedy";
And for his truth, requite with *false mistrust*:
Who would not rue, to see how wrongfully
Thus for to serve and suffer still he must?

Untrue-be-trust oft-times hath me betrayed,
Misusing my hope, still to be delayed.
Fortune, always I have thee found unjust –
And so, with like reward, now am I paid:
That is, to serve and suffer still I must.

Neu'r to cease, nor yet like to attain,
As long as I, in fear, dare not complain;
True-of-belief hath always been my trust,
And till she *knoweth* the cause of all my pain,
Content to serve and suffer still I must.

*finis*

[in Mary Shelton's hand:]

***on* [ ] *sarwe*** [4]

*ondesyard sarwes*
*reqwer no hyar*
*– Mary Shelton*

**On [*E.K. his*] *"Service"*** [5]

*Undesired service*
*require no hire* [6]
*– Mary Shelton*

---

[1] marginal note by Shelton: "*fforget thys*" [*Forget this!*].

[2] marginal note, by Shelton: "*y$^{t}$ ys worhy*" [*That is worthy*].

[3] *that* ] that which; *break* ] disclose (*OED* v.22).

[4] barely visible: *Knyvet's initials, rubbed out.*

[5] *service* ] cf. *deserwed … obsarwed … desarwest* (deserved, observed, deservest, 40r); *to sarwe* (serve, 41r); *my sarwes due* (service, 43r).

[6] *hire* ] compensation.

Shelton's marginal notes – "Forget this!" (stanza 1); and "Undesired service require[s] no hire" (bottom) – have been described in the scholarly commentary as "curt," "sharp," and "waspish" – but when Shelton penned these notes in the book, she had no thought of pleasing 21st-century literary scholars; besides which, her notes express disapproval, not of the poet's courtly style but of his character: it has been overlooked in previous scholarship that the author of this seductive acrostic was Sir Edmund Knyvet; that Knyvet was Mary's brother-in-law; and that Knyvet's "SHELTUN" poem was addressed not to his wife of thirteen years but to her little sister, 21-year-old Mary. Knyvet's proffered "service" was to have sex with no thought of marrage. Sister Mary felt no obligation to pity his tears; hence the "waspish" marginal comments. Shelton reserves her one line of praise – "That is worthy" (stz. 2) – for Knyvet's remark that he is in "despair to speak" – her courteous way of saying, *Good, now shut up.* But Knyvet would not take no for an answer.

**[Sir EDMUND to Sister MARY]** (holograph, 8v-9r)

***Bownd am I now & shall be styll …***

*Bownd am I now & shall be styll*
*euer my lyff contynually*
*she shall be sure off my good wyll*
*so shall none els but she onlye*
*enduryng paynes In hope of pyttye*

*Trusty & true she shall me fynd*
*in worde & dede neuer to offend*
*alas accepte myn Inward mynd*
*altho my power do not extend*
*I wyll be trew to my lyves end*

*Oh what payn yt ys to me*
*yf chawnce I cum in her p[re]synce[1]*
*when I wold speke yt wyll not be*
*my hart ys there my wyttes be thence*
*I am in fere w[t]owt offence*

*Marvell yt ys to se the lyff*
*whyche I do lede from day to day*
*my wyttes & wyll allways in stryff*
*I know not what to do nor say*
*but yeld me to her g[r]ace allway*

*A thowsand hartes yff that I had*
*she shuld be sure of them all*
*ther were nothyng cold make me sad*
*yff in her favowre I myght fall*
*who hathe my hart & euer shall*

*sso fervently I do her love*
*as hart can thynke or tong expresse*
*my paynes they ar all other above*
*thus love putes me to grett dystresse*
*& noways can I fynd Relesse*

*How shuld I do my paynes to cesse*
*alas whyche dare not me ~~me~~ cõplayn[3]*
*Ryght sore my sorows shall encrease*
*vnles I may her love optayn*
*I must endure allways in payn.*
*fynys*

**Bound am I now and shall be still …**

Bound am I now and shall be still,
Euer my life continually.
She shall be sure of my goodwill
(So shall none else, but she only),
Enduring pains, in hope of pity.

Trusty and true she shall me find
In word and deed, neuer to offend.
Alas, accept mine inward mind:
Although my power do not extend,
I will be true to my life's end.

O, what pain it is to me
If chance I come in her presénce!
When I would speak, it will not be –
My heart is there, my wits be thence!
I am in fear, without offense.

Marvel it is, to see the life
Which I do lead from day to day –
My wits and will, always in strife.
I know not what to do nor say,
But yield me to her grace, alway.

A thousand hearts, if that I had,
She should be sure of them all.
There were nothing could make me sad [1]
If in her favor I might fall,
Who hath my heart – and euer shall!

So fervently I do her love
As heart can think or tongue express.
My pains, they are all other above.
Thus love puts me to great distress,
And no-ways can I find release.

How should I do, my pains to cease,
Alas, which dare not me complain?
Right sore my sorrows shall increase –
Unless I may her love obtain,
I must endure, always, in pain.
*finis*

[1] *sure* ] shoo-er (two syllables).

Sir Edmund Knyvet, sister Anne's amorous husband, was the son of Sir Thomas Knyvet (courtier and naval commander), by his wife Muriel Howard (sister to the Thomas Howard who died in prison on 31 Oct. 1537 for his 1536 betrothal to Margaret Douglas). In 1536 Knyvet joined with his uncle the third duke of Norfolk in suppressing the Pilgrimage of Grace uprising; in 1538, he was knighted for his service to the King. In 1539, Knyvet was appointed high sheriff of Norfolk and Suffolk; which is about the time he had developed a passion for his virginal sister-in-law. Knyvet's ardor peaked in the winter of 1540/1, when he was still on intimate terms with the duke of Norfolk, Mary Duchess of Richmond, and with her brother Henry Howard, earl of Surrey (the poet). As visitors and sometime residents at Kenninghall, both Knyvet and Shelton were permitted to make entries in Lord Thomas Howard's poetry book, which came to serve as a covert venue for Knyvet's poetry of desire and Shelton's resistance.

**[Sir EDMUND to Sister MARY]** (holograph, 7v)

***My ferefull hope from me ys fledd…***

*My ferefull hope from me ys fledd* [1]
*whyche of long tyme hathe ben my gyde*
*now faythefull trust ys in hys stedd*
*& bydes me sett all fere asyde*

*O trewthe yt ys I not denye*
*all lovers may not lyve in ease*
*yet sum by hap dothe hyt truly*
*so lyke may I yff that she please*

*Why so yt ys a gyfft ye wott* [2]
*by nature one to love another*
*& syns y$^{t}$ love dothe fall by lott*
*then why not I as well as other*

*yt may so be the cawse ys why*
*she knowythe no part to my poore mynd*
*but yet as one assuryddly*
*I speke nothyng but as I fynd*

*yff nature wyll yt shall so be*
*no reason Rulythe fantasy* [3]
*yet in thys case as semythe me*
*I take all thyng Indyfferently*

*yet uncertayn I wyll Reioyce*
*& thynk to have tho yet thow hast*
*I put my chawnce unto her choyce*
*w$^{t}$ pacyence for power ys past*

*No no I knowe the lyke ys fayre*
*w$^{t}$ owt dysdayn or cruelltye*
*& so to end from all dyspayre*
*vntyll I fynd the contrarye*

*fynys q$^{d}$ Nobodye*

**My fearful hope from me is fled …**

My fearful hope from me is fled,
Which of long time hath been my guide.
Now faithful trust is in his stead,
And bids me set all fear aside.

O truth it is, I not deny,
All lovers may not live in ease.
Yet some, by hap, doth hit truly –
So, like, may I, if that she please.

Why, so it is a gift, ye wot, [2]
By nature, one to love another.
And since that love doth fall by lot,
Then why not I, as well as other?

It may so be the cause is why,
She knoweth no part to my poor mind:
But yet as one assuredly
I speak nothing but as I find.

If Nature will, it shall so be:
No reason ruleth fantasy. [3]
Yet in this case, as seemeth me,
I take all thing indifferently.

Yet uncertain, I will rejoice –
And *think* to have, though yet thou hast.
I put my chance unto her choice,
With patience – for power is past.

No, no, I know the like is fair,
Without disdain or cruelty:
And so to end, from all despair,
Until I find the contrary.

finis, quod Nobody

The lovelorn "Nobody" (i.e., Sir Edmund Knyvet) did indeed "find the contrary": Shelton in her reply warned her reckless brother-in-law to back off, or he would know more pain than ever he felt from the pangs of courtly romance. Knyvet copied her reply into the poetry book, ascribing it to "Somebody."

---

[1] Marginal note: P$^{ri}$m*us* [*First*].

[2] *ye wot* ] you know.

[3] *fantasy*: inclination, liking, desire (*OED* n.7).

[**MARY SHELTON to Sir Edmund**] (entered by Knyvet, fol. 8r)

***Yowre ferefull hope cannot p$^{re}$vayle ...***

*Yowre ferefull hope cannot p$^{re}$vayle* [1]
*nor yet faythfull trust Also*
*sum thynke to hytt oftymes do fayle*
*wherby they change theyre welthe to wo*

*What tho In that yet put no trust*
*but allways after as ye see*
*for say yo$^{r}$ wyll & do yo$^{r}$ lust*
*there ys no place for yow to be*

*No sure therin ye ar farr owte*
*yo$^{r}$ labor lost ye hope to save*
*but ons I put ye owt off dowte*
*thet thyng ys had that ye wold have*

*tho to Remayn w$^{t}$owt Remorce*
*& petyles to be opprest*
*yet ys the coorse of love by force*
*to take all thynges unto the best*

*Well yet beware yff thow be wysse*
*& leve thy hope thy hete to coole*
*ffor fere lest she thy love dyspyse*
*reputyng the but as a ffole*

*Syns thys to folow of force thow must*
*& by no Reason can Refrayn*
*thy chawnce shall change thy lest mystrust*
*as thow shalt prove unto thy payn*

*When wythe suche payn thow shalt be payd*
*the whyche shall passe all Remedy*
*then thynke on thys that I have sayd*
*& blame thy folysshe ffantasy*

*fynys q$^{d}$ s[umbodi]e* [2]

**Your "fearful hope" cannot prevail...**

Your "fearful hope" cannot prevail,
Nor yet, "faithful trust" also.
Some think to "hit," oft-times do fail –
Whereby they change their wealth to woe.

What though! In that, ye put no trust,
But always, *after*, as ye see:
For say your will, and *do* your lust,
There is no place for you to be.

No, sure! Therein ye are far out;
Your labor lost, ye hope to save.
But once I put ye out of doubt,
That thing is had, that ye would have:

Though to remain without remorse,
And pitiless to be oppressed,
Yet is the course of *Love*, by force,
To take all things unto the *best*.

Well, yet beware (if thou be wise),
And leave thy hope, thy heat, to *cool*
(For fear lest she thy love *despise*,
Reputing thee but as a fool).

Since this to follow, of force, thou *must*,
And by no reason can refrain,
Thy chance shall change thy least mistrust:
As thou shalt prove unto thy pain –

When with such pain thou shalt be paid,
(The which shall pass all remedy),
Then think on this that I have said,
And blame thy foolish fantasy.

finis, quod Somebody

Rebuffed in his sexual advance, Knyvet's rhetoric turns derisively misogynistic:

[**Sir EDMUND KNYVET**] (holograph, 59v)

***To dere is bowght the doblenes...***

*To dere is bowght the doblenes*
*that perith owte in trowthes sted*
*for faut of faith newfangilnes*
*is cheff ruler in womanhed*

*for trusty love they vse hatred*
*and change is all ther stedfastnes*
*wherfor he trustith to womans faith*
*folium eius non defluet.* [3]

**Too dear is bought the doubleness**

Too dear is bought the doubleness
That peereth out in truth's stead.
For fault of faith, newfangledness
Is chief ruler in womanhead.

For trusty love, they use hatred,
And change is all their "steadfastness."
Wherefore trusteth he to woman's faith?
*Folium eius non defluet.* [3]

[1] Marginal note: Second ("*Secūdus*").

[2] much of "sumbodie" has been rubbed out.

[3] *Folium ... defluet* ] "His leaf shall not wither"; cf. Psalm 1:3: "And his leaf shall not fall off: and all whosoever he shall do shall prosper" (Rheims).

**[Sir EDMUND: To Men, on Womankind]** (ent. Shelton, 60r )

***to men that knows ye not…***

*to men that knows ye not*
*ye may aper to be*
*ffol cher and w^t owt spot*
*bot sewarly un to me*
*so ys yowar wontied kynd*
*be proffe so sewarly knowen*
*that I wel not be blynd*
*my nys shal be my ~~nowe~~ nowen*

*I wel not wynke and se*
*I wel not ples the so*
*I wel not ffawar the ] favor*
*I wel not be thy ffo*
*I wel not be that man*
*that so shal the de~~ffa~~wowar*
*I wel not thow I kan*
*I wel not show my pore*

*bot I ham he that wel ~~wel~~*
*se stel as I hawe sen*
*thy goodnes ffrom thy el ill*
*my nyes shal stel be chere*
*ffrom mot~~h~~ys off blyndyd lowe*
*wche wowthy men somtym*
*to trost or the do proffe ~~and ffal wan~~*
*and ffal wan the wold clym*

**To men that knows ye not…**

To men that knows ye not
Ye may appear to be
Full [clear°], and without spot.
But surely, unto me,
So is your wonted kind –
By proof so surely known,
That I will not be blind.
Mine eyes shall be mine own.

I will not wink and see
(I will not please thee so).
I will not favor thee;
I will not be thy foe.
I will not be that man
That so shall thee devour.
I will not, though I can,
I will not show my power.

But I am he that will
Be still, as I have seen
Thy goodness from thy ill.
Mine eyes shall still be [clean°]
From motes of blinded love,
Which worthy men, sometime,
Do trust ere they do prove –
And fall, when they would climb.

"To Men" appears also in the Arundel-Harington MS, where it is expressly attributed to Knyvet (fol. 18v). Shelton copies her brother-in-law's self-pitying diatribe into the Howards' poetry book without attribution. Notable is that she twice misquotes Knyevtt's original: At line 3, finding "clere" (*clear*) in her copytext, she has changed the word to "cher" (*cheer*). In line 20, where Knyvet evidently had "clene" (i.e., *clean*; also easily mistaken for "clere"), Shelton again wrote "chere" (*cheer*). While concealing Knyvet's identity, Shelton emends his text, probably on purpose, to ensure that the poem if read by prying eyes would not be mistaken for something from the pen of her fiancè, Sir Thomas Clere. Knyvet, meanwhile, kept trying:

**[Sir EDMUND to MARY]** (holograph, fol. 63r)

***If y^t I cowlde in versis close…***

*If y^t I cowlde in versis close*
*thowghtes y^t in my hart be shett*
*hart so hard was new^r yet*
*that vulde not pitie I suppose*
*vnhappy Eys my Ioy I lose*
*by strokes of love throw you so frett*
*that no defence can make w^t sett*
*for nowght but sorow I cãn chose*
*syns that your sight so bright did shew*
*w^t in my hart by fiery gleames*
*as in a glas the sonny streames*
*suffise the then̄ for as I trow*
*of Right he may desir deth*
*that fyndith his foo by frendly faith*

*E K*

**If that I could in verses 'close…**

If that I could in verses 'close
Thoughts that in my heart be shet,
Heart so hard was never yet
That would not pity, I suppose.
Unhappy eyes! My joy I lose
By strokes of love through you, so fret
That no defense can make with-set. [1]
For nought but sorrow I can choose
Since that your sight so bright did show
Within my heart, by fiery gleams,
As in a glass the sunny streams.
Suffice thee then, for (as I trow)
Of right he may desire death,
That findeth his foe by friendly faith.

E. K.

---

[1] *with-set* ] opposition, prevention.

**Sir EDMUND to Sister MARY** (holograph, 62v)
***In places Wher that I company…***

*In places wher that I company*
*I go sayng I lywe full merely*
*yet offtymes to cloke my care and payn*
*I make my contenance to be glad and fayn*
*whe̅n th^t my hert wepith and sithyth full bitt^r ly*

**In places where that I company**

In places where that I company
I go saying I live full merrily.
Yet oft-times to cloak my care and pain,
I make my countenance to be glad, and feign,
When that my heart weepeth and sigheth full bitterly.

**Sir EDMUND to Sister MARY** (holograph, 60)
***Myn unhappy chaunce to home shall I playn…***

*My̅n unhappy chau̅nce to home shall I pla̅yn*
*for wher as I love no grace do I fynd*
*displesur I haue w^t woo and payn*
*tormented I am I wot not wher to wynde*
*shall it be my fortune thus to be assynd*
*that wher as I vulde be faynest beloved*
*to be w^t disday̅n Cruelly rewardid*

*Offt haue I shoyd my lovyng hert*
*w^t wordes unfayned and eke by lett^r*
*by message all so sent o̅n my p^r t*
*and all to cause her love the grett^r*
*but yet of no̅wght I am the bett^r*
*for the more I sho to be beloved*
*the more w^t disday̅n I am rewardyd*

*My truth nor yet my lowynge chere*
*my harty mynd ~~nor~~ and stedfastnes*
*my woofull lyff whiche I haue here*
*w^t all my ~~payf~~ paynfull hewynes*
*cannot <not> her cause for to redresse*
*my hart whiche is to her unfayned*
*but w^t disdayn to be rewardyd*
*Causeles*

**Mine unhappy chaunce! to whom shall I 'plain?**

Mine unhappy chance! to whom shall I 'plain?
For whereas I love, no grace do I find.
Displeasure I have, with woe and pain;
Tormented I am, I wot not where to wind.
Shall it be my fortune, thus to be assignèd,
That whereas I would be fainest belovèd,
To be with disdain cruelly rewarded?

Oft have I showed my loving heart
With words unfeigned and eke by letter,
By message also, sent on my part;
And all to cause her love the greater –
But yet of nought I am the better,
For the more I show to be beloved,
The more with disdain I am rewarded.

My truth nor yet my loving cheer,
My hearty mind and steadfastness,
My woeful life which I have here
With all my painful heaviness,
Cannot her cause for to redress
My heart which is to her unfeigned,
But with disdain to be rewarded
Causeless

**Sir EDMUND to Sister MARY** (holograph, fol. 59v)
**[Farewell:] *Wyly no dought ye be a wry***

*Wyly no dought ye be a wry*
*for wher ye thought a fole to fynd*
*fole farwell / my tale is at a nend*

*E knywet*

**[Farewell:] Wily, no doubt, ye be awry…**

Wily, no doubt, ye be awry:
For where ye thought a fool to find
Fool, farewell – My tale is at an end.

E. Knyvet

Disgusted with Mary Shelton's intractable chastity, Knyvet went off to London in a huff, where Mary's love-interest, Sir Thomas Clere, was serving as a courtier. Crossing paths one day on the tennis courts behind King Henry's residence, the two men exchanged insults; whereupon Knyvet punched Clere in the face, giving him a nosebleed. The combatants were arrested on 28 February 1541, indicted on April 27th.

A quest before the King's Justices at Greenwich on 10 June found Knyvet to be the aggressor. Under a recent statute deploring violence, he was sentenced to have his right hand amputated. On 13 June 1541, the convicted pugilist was led by the executioner onto a scaffold for the scheduled surgery; at which time Knyvet delivered a gallant speech honoring the King, closing with a last-minute appeal that his right hand be spared and his left hand taken, so that "I may hereafter do such good service to his Grace as shall please him."[1] Henry Howard, earl of Surrey – Sir Thomas Clere's employer and closest friend – carried Sir

[1] Cobbett, *State Trials*, vol. 1, pp. 139-40.

Edmund's request to the King. Meantime, the statute called for some preliminary entertainments: these went forward as planned: The king's Master Cook had brought a meat cleaver; the Sergeant of the Poultry, a cock; and the Sergeant of the king's Larder, beer and ale. While waiting for the King's response to Knyvet's petition, Master Cook duly chopped off the rooster's head, thereby to supply an object lesson for the crowd and to test the sharpness of the king's cutlery. Surrey returning, he whispered a few words to the high sheriff of London regarding King Henry's gracious answer; whereupon Knyvet was obliged to kneel beside the dead chicken, with his left hand tied securely to the chopping block. When "all the other mysteries [were] done, even to pretending to deal the blow," the sheriff cried "Hold!" – and he announced Knyvet's royal pardon.[1]

It was at about this time that Mary Shelton and Sir Thomas Clere became engaged. They had no property and therefore no money to marry. They saw one another only when Surrey returned to Norfolk with his loyal squire at his side. (It was during this interval, during Lady Margaret's exile to Kenninghall, that the Shelton-Douglas friendship blossomed.) When Henry Howard was sent with English troops to aid Carlos V in his wars on northern France, Clere went, too. Mary never saw him again. On 19 September 1544, at the siege of Montreuil, Surrey in his eagerness to inspire the troops charged the city wall. He reached the town gate having outrun his support and would have been slain but for Thomas Clere, who risked his own life to save Surrey's: Clere carried his friend to safety while being fired upon – but in doing so, received a wound from which he never recovered. Clere died in April, of gangrene. Mary Shelton grieved his death for a year, then married Sir Anthony Heveningham.

On 7 January 1545/6 Surrey suffered a defeat at St. Étienne. He returned home in disgrace with the King. The following year he was arrested for treason, on trumped-up charges that he intended to usurp the throne following Henry's death; the evidence for which was that Surrey had displayed in his heraldry the royal arms of King Edward the Confessor (which Surrey claimed as an unchallenged right, immemorially borne by his ancestors, the dukes of Norfolk). Sir Edmund Knyvet, who remained at enmity with his Howard kin, was among those who testified against Surrey at trial; stating that the accused traitor had associated with foreigners; that he had employed an Italian buffoon, who was probably a spy; and that he affected French manners and dress that savored of dissimulation and vanity. Among additional allegations investigated by the Privy Council: "many secrets" had passed between Henry Howard and Mary Shelton Heveningham.[2] Surrey was beheaded on 19 January 1546/7; Mary escaped punishment; and Sir Edmund Knyvet was handsomely rewarded with a cheap lease of Howard lands forfeited to the Crown. Knyvet went on to become knight of the shire for county Norfolk, a longtime ambition.[3]

Anthony and Mary Shelton Heveningham had three sons and six daughters. Sir Anthony dying in 1557, his will names as his executrix his wife Mary; as a witness, Philip Appleyard, whom Lady Heveningham married a year later. Appleyard died in 1570. Surviving her second husband by only a few weeks, she was buried at Heveningham, Norfolk, on 8 Jan. 1570/1, aged 51.

---

[1] Charles de Marillac, ambassador, to King François (14 Jun. 1541). *Letters and Papers, Henry VIII*, vol. 16, p. 312.

[2] ibid., vol. 21, pt 1, p. 1426.

[3] Long after Mary Shelton's rejection, Knyvet's woman troubles continued, with Anne Calthorpe Radcliffe, second wife of the earl of Sussex. The countess was a key figure on Thomas Wriothesley's hit list of dangerous Protestants: she had been associated with Anne Askew (whom Wriothesley burned at the stake) and with Queen Katherine Parr (whom he wished to burn). Wriothesley's agents, having the countess under surveillance, reported in 1546 that she was having an affair – information that the lord chancellor happily forwarded to the earl. Outraged at his horning, Radcliffe on Wriothesley's information called Lady Anne a whore and evicted her from their London home—as she later reported to her mother, without "money, men, women, meat, nor more than two gowns of velvet uncomely for my misery to be worn" (Green, 3.240-1). Lacking income and a place to stay, Anne Radcliffe found solace in the arms of Sir Edmund Knyvet, with whom she seems to have cohabited until her arrest two years later, on charges of bigamy. Knyvet, still married to Anne Shelton, was arraigned as well: in Feb. 1548/9, he was bound for £1000 to appear before Lord Protector Somerset and the Privy Council to answer charges against him. Knyvet died in 1551. His widow, Anne Shelton Knyvet, soon remarried. Anne Radcliffe, less lucky, was arrested again the year after and kept in the Tower for six months on charges of witchcraft and treasonable prophecies. On Mary's accession, she fled to France to avoid religious persecution. Henry Radcliffe divorced her in absentia and asked that Parliament bastardize his children by his second marriage. Returning to England in 1557 after the earl's death, Lady Anne was again arrested on those outstanding charges of bigamy (mere harassment: both husbands were now dead). Released from prison, she married Andrew Wyse, in Ireland, by whom she had two children and lived into her seventies.

# **Jane Seymour** (c. 1508-1537),
## Queen of Henry VIII

*Bound to Obey and Serve*
—Jane Seymour's motto

ANE SEYMOUR, third wife of Henry VIII, was the eldest of ten children born to Margery (b. Wentworth) Sir John Seymour of Wolf Hall, Wiltshire. Nothing is known of her childhood. She was introduced at court about 1529 and served thereafter as a lady-in-waiting, first to Catherine of Aragon, then to Anne Boleyn. Eustace Chapuys, the imperial ambassador to the Holy Roman Emperor, Carlos V, describes Jane as a woman "of middling stature, no great beauty, and of a complexion so white that one would call her rather pale"; "not a woman of great wit, but she may have good understanding ... It is said she tends to be proud and haughty."[1] King Henry seems to have taken no interest in her until September 1535, when on a royal progress he made a stopover at Wolf Hall. Entertained by the Seymours and their ambitious brood, Henry was chiefly attracted to Jane, the Seymours silent and deferential eldest daughter; who by Tudor standards, at 27, was a middle-aged spinster.

After Queen Katherine's death on January 7th and Queen Anne's miscarriage on the 29th, Henry unleashed the floodgates of his largesse and affection for Jane Seymour. Among his gifts was a locket containing his portrait – which Queen Anne is said to have spotted: "espying a jewel pendant about her neck, [Anne] snatched thereat (desirous to see, the other unwilling to show it) and casually hurt her hand with her own violence."[2] Anne on another occasion is said to have found Jane sitting on what remained of her obese husband's lap, sparking a furious tantrum that is often cited as a cause of Anne's miscarriage.

By February 1535/6, diplomatic dispatches buzzed with rumors of King Henry's new romance. Chapuys, the imperial ambassador, reports on 1 April that the King sent Jane Seymour a purse full of gold sovereigns, with a love-letter. Jane kissed the letter and returned it unopened to Henry's messenger; then fell to her knees, saying that she had a reputation to consider; and "that if the King wished to make her a gift of money, she requested him to reserve it for such a time as God pleased to send her a good marriage" (Chapuys considers Jane's refusal on this occasion to have been motivated by cunning rather than virtue: "I hear that the young lady has been well tutored, and warned by some of this King's courtiers who hate [Anne] the concubine, that [Jane] must not in any way surrender to the King's fancy unless he makes her his Queen.")[3]

Jane's concern for her honor, and her coy refusal of a purse of gold, further inflamed Henry's passion. Jane was happy to see him, but insisted on a chaperone, until marriage. To accommodate her sense of honor, Henry installed Edward and Anne Seymour in rooms that connected through a hidden passage to his own royal apartments; this permitted his interviews with Jane to be conducted without scandal. Henry moved Queen Anne to Greenwich Palace, in rooms vacated by Thomas Cromwell.

Jane Seymour, 1536
Hans Holbein the Younger
*Kunsthistorisches Museum (Vienna)*

[1] Chapuys to Antoine Perrenot (19 May 1536) Great Britain, *Letters and Papers Henry VIII,* vol. 10, no. 901.

[2] Thomas Fuller, *History of the Worthies of England,*

[3] Chapuys to Carlos V (1 Apr. 1536) *Calendar of State Papers Spain, 1536–8*, no. 84.

On 2 May, Anne was arrested for high treason and adultery, and beheaded on 19 May.

As soon as Anne was out of the way, a jubilant King Henry gave Jane jewelry and a jointure of lands and lordships in counties across England. Her siblings and kin were appointed to lucrative posts vacated by Howards and Boleyns. Jane's sister Elizabeth was married to Gregory, the son and heir of Cromwell. To Jane's brothers, Henry gave generous grants of real estate. Edward Seymour, Jane's elder brother, was appointed to be a Privy Councilor; created Viscount Beauchamp in 1536, earl of Hertford in 1537 (and after Henry's death, Lord Protector).

Queen Jane chose an apt motto – *Bound to Obey and Serve*. Mindful of the fates of queens Catherine and Anne, and indeed of anyone who crossed the King's will, Jane countered Anne Boleyn's spunk with utter docility. She made no pronouncements on religion or politics. In public, she spoke hardly at all. She wrote nothing. Biographer Agnes Strickland observes that Queen Jane's written corpus is comprised of a single autograph, appended to an order addressed to the park keeper at Herving-atte-Bower, commanding him "to deliver to her well-beloved the gentlemen of her sovereign lord the king's chapel-royal, two bucks of high season"; signed—

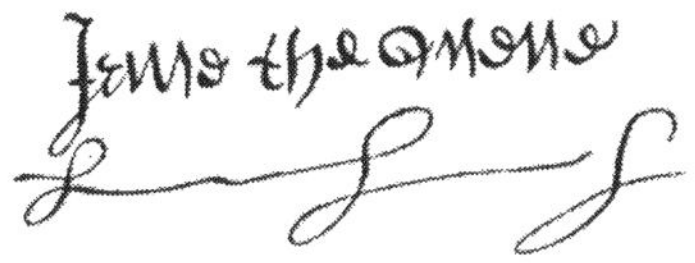

—and "For this very trifling exercise of the power and privileges of a queen of England, she names the king's warrant and seal as her authority, as if her own were insufficient."[1] In July, having received a gift of quails from Lady Lisle, Queen Jane via John Husee sent a note of qualified appreciation ("The Queen thanks you for the quails. Those sent hereafter should be fat, or they are not worth thanks.").[2] Those two notes, one of which has survived, are the total sum of Jane Seymour's known literary production.

With the ladies in waiting and maids of honor, Queen Jane was much more assertive than with the keeper of the royal deer park. She laid down a strict code for her retinue. Each candidate was required to have at least one gown of black satin, another of red velvet – in the English style. (All French apparel was forbidden.) Smocks had to be of fine linen, not course cloth. Sashes and headdresses were to be fully set with pearls, no fewer than 120 visible pearls when one wished to appear in the Queen's presence; without which, admittance was refused.

Unlike previous queens, Jane's name rarely appears in the State correspondence in any capacity at all, except for such mundane matters as the acknowledgement of receipts. Henry's third queen made it her one purpose in life to beget the King of England a male heir; and in that, she succeeded.

Not until January did Jane become pregnant, announced in April. In May, Queen Jane felt the "quickening" – which in the medieval and Tudor periods was associated with the infusion of a human soul). The nation rejoiced at the news, with bonfires and celebrations throughout London. At various points in the city, the royal vintner distributed six hogsheads of the king's own wine, to be "drunk freely," thereby to help lubricate the festivities.

On 16 September, Jane removed to her chambers at Hampton Court for her lying-in. Her water broke on October 8$^{th}$, but it would prove a difficult delivery. Some 55 torturous hours later, the queen gave birth to Henry's wished-for son.

The royal birth announcement – at least two copies have survived – was distributed under the queen's signet. The document was neither written by her, nor signed by her, but is best understood as a kind of Tudor press release, the main point of which was to cite the long-awaited heir to Henry's throne as a sign of God's blessing on the king's third marriage.[3]

---

[1] A. Strickland, *Lives of the Queens of England* (1844) 4.290; signature from B.L. MSS Cotton Vespasian F.iii.

[2] John Husee to Lady Lisle (17 July 1537), no. 269.

[3] Dunham Massey MS. Photograph courtesy of the Dunham Massey estate. Cf. B.L. MSS Harl. 283, fol. 155, Cotton Nero C.x.1.

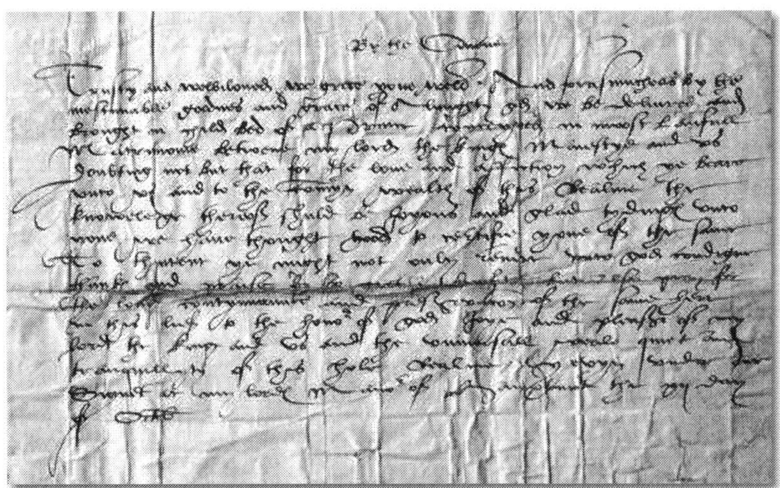

*By the Queen*

*Trusty and well beloved, we greet you well. And forasmuch as by the inestimable goodness and grace of Almighty God, we be delivered and brought in childbed of a prince, conceived in most lawful matrimony between my lord the King's Majesty and us, doubting not but that for the love and affection which ye bear unto us and to the commonwealth of this realm, the knowledge thereof should be joyous and glad tidings unto you, we have thought good to certify you of the same. To th' intent ye might not only render unto God condign thanks and praise for so great benefit but also pray for the long continuance and preservation of the same here in this life, to the honor of God, joy and pleasure of my lord the king and us, and the universal weal, quiet and tranquility of this whole realm. Given under our signet at my lord's manor of Hampton Court the 12th day of October.*

The christening ceremony began in the Queen's bedchamber on October 15: Jane, wrapped in robes, was carried on a litter to the King's chapel in Hampton Court to attend the baptism. Princess Mary, still a proclaimed bastard, stood as godmother. Elizabeth, a year-old toddler proclaimed a bastard in June 1536, was carried in the arms of Jane's brother, Thomas Seymour (the same man who would be put to death by Jane's elder brother twelve years later for his indiscreet attempts to seduce Elizabeth as a teenager).

Baby Edward was robust. (Lord, he "sucketh like a child of his puissance!" exclaimed the wet-nurse [*S.P.* 8.1]). But the long ordeal of his christening left his birth-mother weak and exhausted. Soon after, the queen developed a fever, probably from a puerperal infection caused by unsanitary assistance in childbirth. She was soon delirious. Physicians performed bleedings while attendants plied her with sweets and wine, but their efforts were ineffectual. Her mission in life complete, Queen Jane passed about midnight on 24 October. She died without a will.

Jane Seymour was buried in a vault beneath the floor of St. George's Chapel. King Henry planned a sumptuous monument in her memory, but he got distracted and it was never built. When Henry died, his coffin was placed beside her (his "true wife," as per his will, her three successors notwithstanding).

The chapel vault was opened again in January 1649, to receive the body and head of Charles I; again in the 1698, to receive a stillborn son of Queen Anne. In 1813, the shameless Hanovers opened the vault out of mere curiosity; knocked a hole in the coffin of Henry VIII to see his skull; and pried open the coffin of King Charles, whose head was removed and examined, and his severed neck bones carried about Windsor Palace as a curiosity. The less interesting Queen Jane was allowed to rest in peace.

DWF

# **Anne of Cleves** (1515-1557),

## Queen of Henry VIII

*I besiche your grace hūbly when yoe loke on ~~d~~ this remēber me, yo$^{r}$ graces assured anne the dowghter off cleues.*
—in a prayerbook presented to Henry VIII by Anne of Cleves

NNE of CLEVES, fourth wife of Henry VIII, was the second daughter of Johann, third duke of Juliers-Cleves (1490–1539), by his wife, Maria (1491–1543). Her mother claimed descent from Edward I of England and Jean II of France. Lady Maria supervised her daughters' household education, which emphasized needlework. Musical training was forbidden as too frivolous (though in later years Anne became quite fond of card games). In 1527, before her twelfth birthday, Lady Anne was betrothed by her parents to ten-year-old François, heir to the duchy of Lorraine; after an engagement of eight years, he repudiated her, without having consummated the union.

Following the death of Jane Seymour, King Henry scouted about for a fourth wife. Two weeks after the queen was buried, Cromwell wrote to John Hutton (English ambassador to Mary of Hungary, Regent of the Netherlands), demanding an inventory of continental Protestants suitable for King Henry to wed. On 4 December Hutton retuned his short list: the widow of Count Egmont was a "fair woman of good report." Next, the Duke of Cleves had a marriageable daughter, but he heard "no great praise either of her personage or beauty." Third was Christina, Duchess of Milan, "whom I have not seen, but who is reported to be a goodly personage of excellent beauty." (Christina, now dowager duchess of Milan, was the youngest surviving daughter of Christian II of Denmark; her husband the Duke of Milan had died in 1534, leaving her a 14-year-old widow.) Five days later Hutton wrote again, to announce that the Duchess of Milan on December 8$^{th}$ had come to Brussels, and was received by a great company of honorable gentlemen: "She is, I am informed, of the age of sixteen years, very high in stature for that age – higher, in fact, than the Regent – and a goodly personage of competent beauty, of favor excellent, soft of speech, and very gentle in countenance. She weareth mourning apparel, after the manner of Italy. The common saying here is that she is both widow and maid. She resembleth much one Mistress [Madge] Shelton that sometime waited in Court upon Queen Anne. She useth most to speak French, albeit it is reported that she can speak both Italian and High German." That same evening, having set eyes on his quarry, Hutton added a few details: "there is none in these parts of personage, beauty, and birth, like unto the Duchess of Milan!" gushed Hutton. "She is not so pure white as was the late Queen [Jane], whose soul God pardon, but she hath a singular good countenance. And when she chanceth to smile, there appeareth two pits [dimples] in her cheeks and one in her chin, the which becometh her right excellently well."[1]

Christina, 16, dowager duchess of Milan (1538)
(the one that got away)
By Hans Holbein the Younger
Courtesy of the National Gallery

[1] Hutton to Cromwell (4 Dec. 1537), *L&P Henry VIII*, vol. 12.2, no. 1172 (National Archives S.P. viii.5); and Hutton, in a postscript addressed to Sir Thomas Wriothesley (then ambassador to Brussels) (9 Dec. 1537), vol. 8, p.7.

Henry, however, was now viewed with contempt throughout Europe: having been excommunicated by the Pope, he was also a notorious cuckold, or a psychopath, or both. And since Anne Boleyn was not his only victim – Holinshed reports that 72,000 were put to death during Henry's 38-year reign, many of them bluebloods who displeased the king, plus clergymen by the dozen – Christina had her reservations about becoming his wife.

On 10 March 1537/8, Hans Holbein accompanied by English diplomats arrived in Brussels to paint a portrait of the widowed duchess. Christina dutifully posed for three hours. The sketch completed, she sent the embassage back to London without encouragement. When Henry saw the completed portrait, he swore he would have the duchess, even if she came to him without a farthing; but Christina had no such intention. In a conversation at the court of Nancy, she quipped with a dimpled smile: "I possess only one head; if I had two, one might have been at his Majesty's disposal." Henry nevertheless persisted in his lovesuit until March 1539, when Thomas Wriothesley advised Henry that he should "fix his most noble stomach in some other place."[1]

Anne, 24, the daughter of Cleves, 1539
By Hans Holbein the Younger
Courtesy of the Louvre (Paris)

Cromwell turned his attention to the single daughters of the duke of Cleves. Hans Holbein was sent to paint portraits of Anne, now 24, and of her sister, Amalia, 22. When the pictures were presented to King Henry, with testimonials of the younger sister's great beauty, Henry chose Anne. When the negotiations proceeded more slowly than Cromwell anticipated, he reported to the king: "Every man praiseth the beauty of [Lady Anne], as well for the face as for the whole body, above all other ladies excellent. One, amongst other purposes, said ... that 'She excelleth as far the duchess, as the golden sun excelleth the silver moon.'"[2] The poeticism comes from Cromwell's agent, Christopher Mont; but Cromwell in his vetting neglected to mention to Henry that Mont with his hyperbole was comparing Anne not to the lovely 16-year-old duchess of Milan, but to Anne's married elder sister Sybille, the duchess of Saxony, married with four kids.

On the word of Anne's great beauty, Henry upped his ante. By a marriage treaty signed on 4 October 1539, Anne's brother, Wilhelm, duke of Juliers-Cleves, granted his sister Anne a fictional dowry of 100,000 gold florins (25,000 English marks sterling); a sum that he could not afford and that Henry waived, in order to take the daughter of Cleves to wife without a farthing. From Henry, Anne received a jointure of more than 4000 marks sterling.

That same week, Anne left her home in Dusseldorf for her new life in England.

Delayed by bad weather, Anne and her entourage landed at Dover on 27 December. After a few days rest, she was transported to Canterbury, where she was received by the archbishop and lodged at the royal palace of St. Austin's. Her next stop was Sittingbourne. On New Year's Eve, the duke of Norfolk escorted her to Rochester Abbey, where she stayed the night.

King Henry, wishing to inspect the commodity before receiving the goods, decided to prank his German bride before she came to London:

*Rochester* (1 January 1539/40). "On New Year's Day at afternoon, the King's Grace with five of his privy chamber, being disguised with cloaks of marble with hoods [so] that they should not be known, came privately to Rochester, and so went up into the chamber where the said Lady Anne looked out a window to see the bull-baiting that was [at] that time [underway] in the court[yard].[3] And suddenly he embraced her, and kissed, and showed her 'a token that the King had sent' her for her New Year's gift.

[1] Thomas Wriothesley to Cromwell (3 March 1538/9), National Archives, *S.P.* viii.159 (cf. viii.127). A few years later, Christina gave her hand in marriage to the Duke of Lorraine, the same man who in 1535 jilted Anne of Cleves.

[2] *State Papers, Henry VIII,* I. 605.

[3] *of marble* ] mottled cloth.

And she being abashed and not knowing who it was, she thanked him. And so he communed with him, but she regarded him little, but always looked out the window on the bull-baiting. And when the King perceived that she regarded his coming so little, he departed into [an]other chamber and put off his cloak; and came in again in a coat of purple velvet. And when the lords and knights did see his Grace, they did him reverence. And then she, perceiving the lords doing their duties, humbled her Grace lowly to the King's Majesty. And his Grace saluted her again, and so [they] talked together lovingly. And after, [he] took her by the hand and led her into another chamber where they solaced their Graces that night, and till Friday at afternoon…"[1]

Henry appointed Anne's English retinue: six great ladies of the household (including Margaret Douglas, unmarried, and Mary Howard Fitzroy, widowed duchess of Richmond); five ladies of the privy chamber; five gentlewomen-in-waiting; and six maids of honor, one of whom was the pretty and vivacious Catherine Howard, future queen.

On Saturday, at Greenwich, Anne was welcomed by a crowd of five to six thousand – aristocrats, aldermen, guildsmen, servants – who came out for the event in their best outfits, with banners and music. There was great feasting. "And on Twelfth Day, which was Tuesday, the King's Majesty was married to the said Queen Anne, solemnly, in her closet at Greenwich. His Grace and she went a procession openly that day, she being in her hair with a rich coronet of stones and pearl, set with rosemary on her Grace's head, and a gown of rich cloth-of-silver, and richly be-hanged with stone and pearl; with all her ladies and gentlewomen following her Grace; which was a goodly sight to behold."[2]

On her wedding ring was engraved the posy, "God send me well to keep." But all was not well. Anne had a fuller figure and less vivacity than Henry had expected. To Cromwell, Henry grumbled that his German bride's features were "Nothing so well as she was spoken of";[3] and to Sir Anthony Browne, "I see nothing in this woman as men report of her, and I marvel that wise men would make such report as they have done." The King was so disappointed that he deferred giving Anne his New Year's present, a partlet furred with sables and sable skins, with a furred muffler and cap: Henry ordered Browne to deliver the gifts to Anne the next day, with a "cold message." At this point, reports Browne, the royal groom and bride had not yet spoken twenty words together.[4] After their first few nights in bed, Henry began to muse aloud, to his councilors, that Anne of Cleves must have lost her maidenhead to the duke of Lorraine. On 11 February, Henry grumbled to Anthony Denny of the privy chamber that "he could not induce himself to have affection to the queen, for that she was not as she was reported, but had her breasts so slack, and her other parts in such sort, that he suspected her virginity; and concluded that her body was of such indisposition to his that he could never in her company be provoked and stirred to know her carnally."[5]

From January 9th, Henry paid Anne conjugal visits "nightly or every second night"; only to complain in the morning, to anyone who cared to listen, that he "never liked her," and how he "had been evil served of them that [he] had put in trust; insomuch as, so often as [he] went to bed to her, he ever grudged, and said plainly, he mistrusted her to be no maid, by reason of the looseness of her breasts and other tokens."[6]

By February 10 Henry was spreading word that, by feeling Anne's breasts and belly and other parts, he had determined that she was not a virgin when she came to England, although he had not himself consummated a union due to an "obstacle": the good Lord, to prevent him from having sexual relations with a frau who belonged to another, had afflicted Henry with selective impotence, toward one woman only, Anne of Cleves, due to "the hanging of her breasts and looseness of her flesh." [7]

Anne, meanwhile, studied English and did all in her power to please her morbidly obese husband, both in public and in his nightly visits, which continued through April. But by that time, Henry had given up: his heart was set on Katherine Howard, maid of honor, a niece to the Duke of Norfolk.

On 20 June, Anne told her brother's ambassador, Carl Harst, of Henry's affair with Katherine Howard, of which Harst was already aware (he reported to the Duke of Cleves that the affair had been going on for months). On 24 June, the Privy Council abruptly ordered Anne's removal to Richmond

---

[1] Ed. from Charles Wriothesley, *Chronicle,* 109-10.

[2] Ibid., 111.

[3] Cromwell testimony, B.L. Cotton Titus B.I, fol. 409; Cotton Otho C.X, fol. 242.

[4] "Deposition of Sir Anthony Browne, Master of the Horse," Strype, *Memorials* (1816), 1.2, pp. 215-16.

[5] "Deposition of Mr. Anthony Denny," ibid., 1.2, pp. 216-7.

[6] "Deposition of Thomas Henneage," ibid., 1.2, pp. 217-8.

[7] "Deposition of Dr. Butts," ibid., 1.2, 221.

Palace. Events thereafter moved quickly. King Henry developed a scruple in his conscience that – quite apart from his selective impotence – his marriage to Anne of Cleves was not legal, given her prior betrothal to the duke of Lorraine. When Henry brought this moral dilemma before the Privy Council and the Parliament, they quickly shared his concern. On 6 July a parliamentary delegation petitioned Henry to permit an ecclesiastical inquiry into the validity of his marriage. That same day, the king sent five lords and a German-English interpreter to Richmond, to explain to Anne that her previous marriage contract impeded her marriage to King Henry. On their arrival, Anne fainted, perhaps fearing she was to be arrested and taken to the Tower. When she revived, she was told that Parliament had obtained documents relating to her Lorraine marriage that were of deep concern (she was refused permission to see them). She learned that the English Church was weighing the legality of her marriage to King Henry; and when that verdict came down, she must not dissent.

Having warned Anne that she must send no further messages to the king, the lords returned to Henry with Anne's reply: she had taken him as her husband and lord, and nothing could part them, but death.

On the afternoon of 9 July, the convocation of clergy ruled the King's marriage illegal, null and void.

Two days later, Suffolk, Southampton, and Wriothesley returned to Richmond to present Anne with a bag of gold – Henry's token of thanks for her cooperation, so far. They then presented her with the King's offer: Their marriage would be annulled, due to Anne's prior betrothal and Henry's own alleged inability to consummate the union. Henry would adopt Anne as his sister. He would endow her with estates to the value of £3,000 a year, and an allowance of 8,000 nobles for her household, thereby making her one of the wealthiest women in England. A yes or no would be insufficient. She would need to sign a letter of consent – which the councilors had in hand, in English. Addressed from Anne to the King, the letter was written by a barrister, in Anne's behalf. The councilors withdrew while Anne's interpreter reviewed the letter with her:

### [**Letter of Consent: Anne of Cleves' to Henry VIII** (11 July 1540)°]

Pleaseth your most excellent Majesty to understand that, whereas, at sundry times heretofore, I have been informed and perceived by certain lords and others your Grace's Council, of the doubts and questions which have been moved and found in our marriage; and how hath petition thereupon been made to your Highness by your nobles and commons, that the same might be examined and determined by the holy clergy of this Realm; to testify to your Highness by my writing, that which I have before promised by my word and will, that is to say, that the matter should be examined and determined by the said clergy; it may please your Majesty to know that, though this case must needs be most hard and sorrowful unto me, for the great love which I bear to your most noble person, yet, having more regard to God and his truth than to any worldly affection, as it beseemed me at the beginning to submit me to such examination and determination of the said clergy, whom I have and do accept for judges competent in that behalf; so now being ascertained how the same clergy hath therein given their judgment and sentence, I acknowledge myself hereby to accept and approve the same, wholly and entirely putting myself, for my state and condition, to your Highness' goodness and pleasure; most humbly beseeching your Majesty that, though it be determined that the pretended matrimony between us is void and of none effect, whereby I neither can nor will repute myself for your Grace's wife, considering this sentence (whereunto I stand) and your Majesty's clean and pure living with me, yet it will please you to take me for one of your humble servants, and so determine of me, as I may sometimes have the fruition of your most noble presence; which as I shall esteem for a great benefit, so, my lords and others of your Majesty's council, now being with me, have put me in comfort thereof; and that your Highness will take me for your sister; for the which I most humbly thank you accordingly.

Thus, most gracious prince, I beseech our Lord God to send your Majesty long life and good health, to God's glory, your own honor, and the wealth of this noble realm.

From Richmond, the 11th day of July, the 32nd year of your Majesty's most noble reign.
Your Majesty's most humble sister and servant,

[signed,] "*Anne dochtter the Cleyffys*"

The King's councilors were happily surprised when Anne, having had the text explained to her in German, agreed to sign. The lords then demanded another document: she must write to her brother, the Duke of Cleves, stating her satisfaction with the King's offer. This, Anne refused to do, saying she would not write to her brother until he had written to her, so that she would know what to say. Southampton, Suffolk, and Wriothesley decided not to press her until they inquired further of the King's pleasure.[1]

On July 13, the same day on which Archbishop Cranmer and Holy Church proclaimed Henry's marriage to Anne of Cleves null and void, the King replied to his councilors concerning the required documents: before leaving Richmond, they must obtain from Anne a signed letter of consent addressed to her brother. So that she and interpreter would know what to say, the king enclosed a "Minute" in English. The councilors were further commanded to obtain a signed German translation of Anne's letter to the King. ("The translation is to prevent her saying hereafter that she did it ignorantly. The letter to her brother is to prevent her swerving from her conformity, in case her brother, having recourse to the Emperor [Carlos V], should encourage her to do so. She must not put it off till her brother writes to her. Otherwise, all agreements will remain uncertain upon a woman's promise to abandon the condition of a woman.")[2]

## The Minute in English of the letter sent by the lady Anne to her brother (21 July 1540)°

My dear and well-beloved brother,

After my most hearty commendations – where, by your letters of the 13th of this month, which I have seen written to the King's Majesty of England (my most dear and most kind brother), I do perceive that you take the matter, lately moved and determined between him and me, somewhat to heart. Forasmuch as I had rather you knew the truth by mine advertisement, than, for want thereof, you should be deceived by vain reports, I thought meet to write these present letters unto you, by the which it shall please you to understand that, being substantially advertised how the nobles and commons of this Realm desired the King's highness to commit the examination of the matter of marriage between his Majesty and me, to the examination and determination of the whole Clergy of this Realm, I did then willingly consent thereunto. And since the determination made, [I] have also, upon intimation of their proceedings, allowed, approved, and agreed unto the same, wherein I had more respect (as beseemed me) to truth than to any worldly affection that might move me to the contrary. And [I] did the rather condescend thereunto, for that my body remaineth in the integrity which I brought into this Realm.

And being the matter thus finished, [I write] to advertise you how I am used: Surely the King's Highness, whom I cannot now justly have nor will repute as my husband, hath nevertheless taken and adopted me for his *sister*; and as a most kind, loving, and friendly brother [he] useth me with as much or more humanity and liberality, as you, I myself, or any of our kin or allies, could well wish or desire. Wherewith I am, for mine own part, so well satisfied, that I much desire that my good mother and you should know this my state and condition, not doubting but when you shall thoroughly weigh all things, you will so use yourself towards this noble and good Prince, as he may continue his friendship towards you, which, on his Highness' behalf, shall nothing be impaired or altered for this matter, unless the fault should be in yourself (whereof I would be most sorry!). For so it hath pleased his Highness to signify unto me, which I have thought necessary to write unto you, and also that, God willing, I purpose to lead my life in this Realm, having his Grace so good Lord as he is towards me.

–Lest, for want of true knowledge of my mind and condition, you might otherwise take this matter than you ought, and in other sort care for me than you have cause. Thus, etc.—

Richmond, 21 July
Anna, duchess born of Cleves; Jülich-Gelders-et-Berg, the loving sister

Two copies were prepared, one in German, signed and sent to the Duke of Cleves, the other in English, for Henry's files. Once again a free man, King Henry made Katherine Howard his next unlucky bride.

---

[1] Suffolk, Southampton, and Wriothesley to the King (12 July 1540). B.L. MS Cotton Otho. C.x, 248.

[2] King Henry to Suffolk, Southampton, and Wriothesley (13 July 1540) National Archives, SP 1/638; quotation is not from the original but from the abstract in *Letters and Papers, Henry VIII*, vol. 15 (1540), no. 883.

### The Book of Hours

Anne gave Henry a gift, a book of hours, now preserved at the Folger Shakespeare Library; in which is inscribed: "I beseech your Grace humbly, when you look on this, remember me, your Grace's assured Anne, the daughter of Cleves." *Remember* (think of) *me* could have been written even before she met the King; and the inscription was penned by a scribe; but the note is no less poignant, for that.

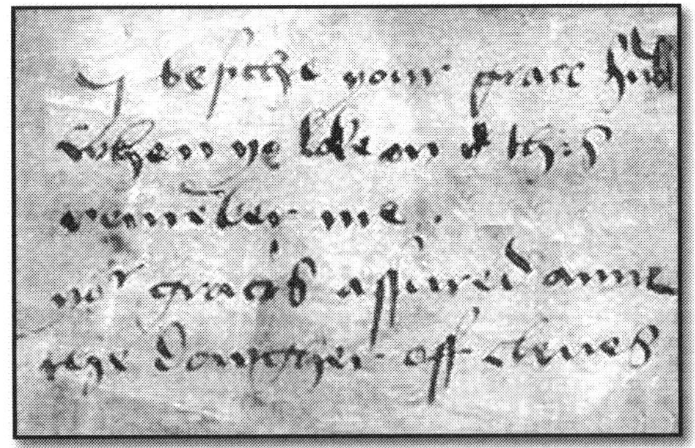

Image courtesy of the Folger Shakespeare Library

The only extant holograph letter by Anne of Cleves is addressed to Queen Mary. Having lived in seclusion at Hever Castle for fourteen years with only rare visits to court, Anne humbly requests permission to visit Mary and Philip:

## [Anne of Cleves to Queen Mary (4 August 1554)°]

After my humble cōmendacons vnto your
Ma$^{tie}$, w$^{t}$h like thankes for your approvid
gentilnes and lawfful favor showed vnto
me yn my laste sute, praying your highnes
of your lovinge cōtynuance

It may please your highnes to vnderstande
that I am enformed of your grasis returne
to loundon againe beyng desyrous to do my
dwyetie to se your ma$^{tie}$ and the kynge yf yt
may so stande w$^{th}$ your hyghnes plesure
and that I may knowe whenne and where y
shall wayte vppon your ma$^{tie}$ and his

wyshinge you bothe muche ioye and felecitie
w$^{th}$ encrease of children to godes glory and to
the preservacon off your prosperous estates
longe to con¯tinwe w$^{th}$ honor in all gody vertue

from my powre house off hever the 4 off August.

Yo$^{r}$ highnes to cōmande,
ANNA the dowghter off Cleues
(to the queens ma$^{tie}$)

After my humble commendations unto your
Majesty, with like thanks for your approved
gentleness and loving favor showed unto
me in my last suit, praying your Highness
of your loving continuance:

It may please your Highness to understand
that I am informed of your Grace's return
to London again, being desirous to do my
duty to see your Majesty and the King, if it
may so stand with your Highness' pleasure
and that I may know when and where I
shall wait upon your Majesty and his—

Wishing you both much joy and felicity, with
increase of children to God's glory, and to the
preservation of your prosperous estates, long to
continue with honour in all godly virtue.

From my poor house of Hever, the 4 of August.

Your Highness' to command,
Anna, the Daughter of Cleves
(*To the Queen's Majesty*)

After the death of Henry, Anne openly expressed her desire to return home to the Rhineland but she was obliged to remain in England. During the reigns of Edward VI and Mary I, much of the financial settlement she received from Henry evaporated. She died at Chelsea Old Manor on 16 July 1557, aged 41, probably of cancer. Anne, daughter of Cleves, was the last surviving wife of Henry VIII and the only one of his six consorts to be buried in Westminster Abbey. Her tombstone supplies a concise biography:

ANNE OF CLEVES
QUEEN OF ENGLAND
BORN 1515 DIED 1557

Birthing Chamber
In the style of Lucas Cranach the Younger (Wittenberg 1515 - Weimar 1586)
Courtesy of *Sphinx Fine Art*

# The Birth of Mankind; or the Woman's Book (1540-1654)

By Richard Jonas and Thomas Raynald

> the womã in her kynde and for thoffice and purpose wher= fore she was made, is euen as absolute and perfect as man is in his kynd, neither is woman to be called (as some do) vnperfecter then manne.
>
> —*The Byrth of Mankynde* (1560), fol. xviii

HE BIRTH OF MANKIND, published in 1540, is a translation by the English schoolmaster, Richard Jonas, and published by Thomas Raynald, a London physician.[1] Jonas based his work on *De Partu Hominis* (1532), by Eucharius Röesslin the younger; which was a Latin translation, by Röesslin, of his father's German best-seller *De swangern Frauwen und Hebammen Roszgarten* (Strasburg, 1513); which was itself a compilation from earlier sources, from Soranus of Ephesus to Muscio to Trotula to Savanarola. Röesslin the elder wrote his *Pregnant Women's and Midwives' Rosegarden* for the instruction of German midwives, looking to improve a dismal mortality rate in Frankfurt-am-Main and Worms, where he was a state physician. Unimpressed, Martin Luther wrote: "Death in childbirth is nothing more than to die in a noble labor of obedience to God. If women become exhausted or die, that harms nothing. Let them bear until they perish, that's why they're here."[2] Other readers disagreed. Filling a need, *Rosegarten* by mid-century was translated into all the languages of Western Europe. Throughout the sixteenth and seventeenth centuries, midwives risked being put to death as witches. That, too, was a legacy of Röesslin. Viewing human reproduction as a masculine prerogative from first to last, Röesslin denounces midwives who "through neglect and oversight...destroy children far and wide." He warns midwives that God will call them to account for every fatality in childbirth. "And since no midwife that I've asked / Could tell me anything of her task I'm left to my medical education."[3]

Jonas and Raynald dedicated their English *Birth of Mankind* to Queen Katherine (Howard), whose predecessor, Queen Jane, had died from an infection received in her delivery of Prince Edward. Unlike the Röesslins' *Rosegarten* and *De Partu Hominis*, however, *The Birth of Mankind* was pitched to the entire female population, not just to medical practitioners. The first edition, in 166 pages, was divided into three parts: 1. "all such things the which chance to women in their labor"; 2. "infirmities which happen unto the infants after they be delivered"; and 3. "the conception of mankind, and how many ways it may be letted or furthered."[4] (Book 3 was based not on Röesslin but on the Hippocratic corpus.)

Jonas and Raynald had done well to have sought a different patron: their book was not long in print before Katherine was arrested and beheaded for alleged adultery and high treason. *The Byrth of Mankynde* was suppressed. But Raynald three years after Katherine's execution issued a revised and augmented version, 300 pages in four books, called *The Birth of Mankind, otherwise named The Woman's Book* (1545), which provided English readers for the first time with a basic understanding of female anatomy.[5] Omitting the original dedication, Raynald addressed his new edition "To the Women Readers." His additions included a new first book of 18,000 words, reporting the anatomical discoveries of Andreas Vesalius (which were first published, in Latin, in a costly folio text [1543]); plus an appendix containing cosmetic recipes. The fourth edition (1560) was further expanded to include woodcut illustrations of the fetus in utero, borrowed from Vesalius; and a sketch of the latest continental technology, a birthing chair.

---

[1] Richard Jonas (Jones, Jonys) was master of St. Paul's School from 1522-1532 and died in 1549.

[2] "Der Tod im Kindbett ist nichts weiter als ein Sterben im edlen Werk und Gehorsam Gottes. Ob sie sich aber auch müde und zuletzt tot tragen, das schadet nichts. Laß [sie] nur tot tragen, sie sind darum da." (Luther, Sermon, 1526, Weimarer Ausgabe, 20.84).

[3] Röesslin, verse preface, trans. Wendy Arons (1944).

[4] *all such ... furthered* ] from the title page (1540), ed. DWF; *letted* ] prevented or hindered.

[5] For a scholarly edition of *The Birth of Mankind,* with collations and commentary, see Hobby (2009).

*The Birth of Mankind* follows the Röesslins in providing remedies whereby to stimulate menstruation following a missed period, or to expel a dead fetus, using abortifacient herbs.[1] At the time, *abortion* and *aborcement* were still used to denote any miscarriage, whether accidental or induced ("Aborcement or untimely birth is when the woman is delivered before due season and before the fruit be ripe (as in the third, fourth, or fifth month, before the birth have life..."). Raynald in 1545 expands on Jonas's pharmacology, providing "divers remedies where to provoke the terms or flowres [*menstruation*], when that needeth"; while adding a caveat: "The abusion of this book (in my simple judgment) consisteth only in these two points: Th'one is, lest that some wickedly disposed person should abuse such medicines as be here declared for a good purpose, to some devilish and lewd use. (What I mean by the 'lewd use' of them, they that have understanding right soon will perceive.) The second point is, lest that this book happening into an light merchant's hands, should minister matters ... to devise of these things at unset and unseemly times."[2] It's hard to take the disclaimer at face value: Raynald advises his readers to visit his business partner, apothecary William Normville, at the sign of the Three Doves in Bucklersbury Street, "in whose shop I have caused the said things faithfully to be made"; so that pregnant aristocrats ("such as will not spare for any cost to acquire and obtain of the best") may obtain the finest "drugs in their kind that may be gotten for money" (Book 2, conclusion); while those with any other ailment whatsoever could purchase Raynald's quack elixir called Oil Imperial, which prevented or cured such ills as "the pestilence," "the falling sickness," "oft belchings and curling, murmuring or rumbling in the guts"; "impotency to the works of generation"; "toothache"; and "the swelling about the throat called the King's Evil."[3]

But if Raynald had his eye on profits, his book nevertheless contained the best gynecological practice available at the time, and his handbook is more sympathetic to women than any gynecological manual since Trota. In his 1545 prologue, Raynald writes, "I know nothing in woman so privy ne so secret, that they should need to care who knew of it; neither is there any part in woman more to be abhorred than in man....Sith the first setting forth of this book, right many honorable ladies and other worshipful gentlewomen, which have not disdained th'oftener by the occasion of this book to frequent and haunt women in their labors, carrying with them this book in their hands, and causing such part of it as doth chiefly concern the same purpose to be read before the midwife and the rest of the women then being present....wherewith the laboring woman hath been greatly comforted and alleviated of her throngs and travail" (C6r-D1r).

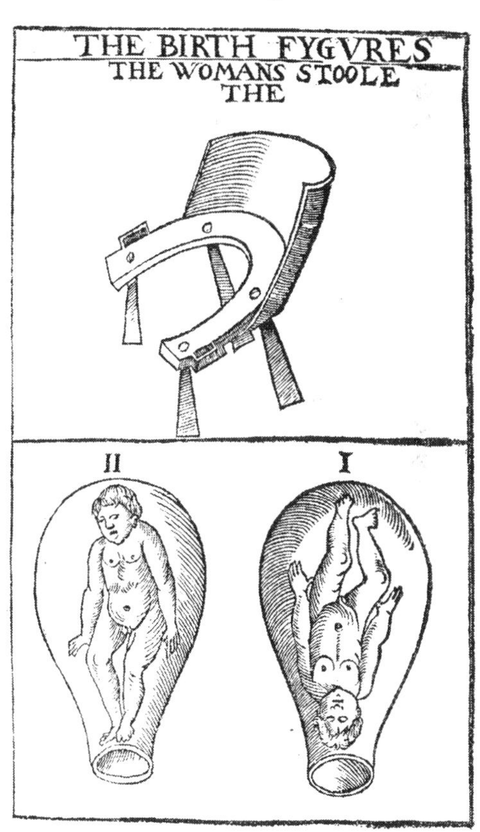


*The Birth of Mankind, or the Woman's Book* passed through thirteen editions by 1654, a commercial success rarely equaled by a book on any topic; being supplanted at last *A Directorie for Midwives* by Nicholas Culpep[p]er (1651); and *The Compleat Midwife's Practice,* written by four midwives, two of whom have been identified as Diana Ireland of St. Brides, licensed in 1638, and Catherine Turner of St. Martin's in the Fields, licensed in 1632.

---

[1] "Of aborcements or untimely births, and the causes of it, and by what remedies it may be defended, holpen [*helped*], and eased"; and "Of dead births, and by what ... means it may also be expelled" (Jonas, Bk. 1, chaps. 8-9; Raynald Bk 2, chaps. 7-8); and "Of Conception, and How may ways it may be hindered or letted" (Jonas, Bk. 3; Raynald Bk 4); "But if all these medicines profit not, then must be used more severe and hard remedies with instruments as hooks, tongs, and such other things made for the nonce" (Jonas, N3r).

[2] Ed. DWF, fr. Prologue, eds. 1545, 1552, 1560 et al.

[3] Thomas Raynald, *A compendious declaration of the excellent virtues of a certain lately invented oil, called for the worthiness thereof Oil Imperial; with the manner how the same is to be used, to the benefit of mankind against innumerable diseases* (London, 1551).

From ***The Birth of Mankind; or, The Woman's Book***

[Preface and dedication to the 1540 edition]

**An Admonition to the Reader**

FORSOMUCH as we have enterprised the interpretation of this present book,[1] offering and dedicating it unto our most gracious and virtuous Queen Katherine only, by it minding and tendering the utility and wealth of all women, as touching the great peril and dangers which most commonly oppresseth them in their painful labors, I require all such men in the name of God, which at any time shall chance to have this book, that they use it godly, and only to the profit of their neighbors, utterly eschewing all rebawd and unseemly communication of any things contained in the same, as they will answer before God, which (as witnesseth Christ) will require account of all idle words – and much more, then, of all rebawd and uncharitable words.

"Everything," as sayeth Solomon, "hath his time"; and truly, that is far out of time, yea, and far from all good honesty, that some use at the common tables, and without any difference before all companies, rudely and lewdly to talk of such things, in the which they ought rather to know much and to say little (but only where it may do good), magnifying the mighty God of nature in all his works, compassionating and pitying our even-Christians the women, which sustain and endure for the time so great dolor and pain for the birth of mankind and deliverance of the same into the world.

Praise God in all his works.

Delivery using a birthing chair
*Rosegarten,* chap. 4 (1513)

[1] *interpretation* ] translation.

**Unto the most gracious, and in all goodness most excellent virtuous lady, Queen Katherine, wife and most dearly beloved spouse unto the most mighty sapient Christen prince, King Henry the Eight, Richard Jonas wisheth perpetual joy and felicity**

HEREAS of late, most excellent virtuous Queen, many goodly and proper treatise ... [are] set forth in this our vulgar English tongue, to the great enriching of our mother language, and also the great utility and profit of all people using the same, ... there is, in the Latin speech, a book entitled *De Partu Hominis* (that is to say, *Of the Birth of Mankind*), compiled by a famous doctor in physic called Eucharius; the which he wrote in his own mother tongue (that is, being a German, in the German speech); afterward, by another honest clerk, at the request and desire of his friend, transposed into Latin; the which book for the singular utility and profit that ensueth unto all such as read it – and most specially, unto all women (for whose only cause it was written) – hath been sith in the Dutch and French speech set forth and imprinted in great number; so that there be few matrons and women in that parts but (if they can read) will have this book always in readiness.[2]

Considering, then, that the same commodity and profit which they, in their regions, do obtain by enjoying of this little book (in their maternal language) might also ensue unto all women in this noble realm of England (if it be set forth in the English speech). As concerning this, I have done my simple endeavor (for the most bound service the which I owe unto your most gracious Highness) to translate the same into our tongue; Most humbly desiring first your grace's Highness, and then consequently all noble ladies and gentlewomen with other honest matrons, to accept my pains and goodwill employed in the same; the which thing, as I do not doubt for the wont and incomparable benignity, goodness, and gentleness inset and planted in your Grace's nature, so shall it be no little encouraging unto me hereafter, with farther deliberation and pains, to revise and oversee the same again and with much more diligence to set it forth.[3]

[2] *set forth* ] published in print; *vulgar* ] common; *clerk* ] scholar; *physic* ] medicine; *sith* ] since then.

[3] *wont ... benignity* ] characteristic graciousness.

For considering the manifold daily and imminent dangers and perils the which all manner of women (of what estate or degree soever they be) in their labor do sustain and abide, yea, many times with peril of their life (of the which, there be too many examples, needless here to be rehearsed), I thought it should be a very charitable and laudable deed, yea, and thankfully to be accepted of all honorable and other honest matrons, if this little treatise so fruitful and profitable for the same purpose were made English; so that, by that means, it might be read and understond of them all. For as touching midwives, as there be many of them right expert, diligent, wise, circumspect, and tender about such business, so be there again many moe full undiscreet, unreasonable, churlish, and far-to-seek in such things, the which should chiefly help and succor the good women in their most painful labor and throngs.[1] Through whose rudeness and rashness only, I doubt not but that a great number are cast away and destroyed (the more pity!).

For this cause and for the honor of almighty God, and for the most bound service the which I owe unto your Grace, most gracious and virtuous Queen, I have judged my labor and pains in this behalf right well bestowed, requiring all other women of what estate soever they be, which shall by reading of the same find light and comfort to yield and render thanks unto your most gracious Highness; wishing greatly that it might please all honest and motherly midwives diligently to read and over-see the same; of the which, although there be many which do know much more peradventure than is here expressed, yet am I sure in the reading of it their understanding shall be much cleared and have somewhat farther perceiverance in the same.[2] It is no small charge the which they take upon them: for if, when any strange or perilous case doth chance, the midwife be ignorant or to-seek in such things which are to be had in remembrance in that case, then is the party lost and utterly doth perish for lack of due knowledge requisite to be had in the midwife. Wherefore I beseech almighty God that this my simply industry and labor may be through your Grace unto the utility, wealth, and profit, of all Englishwomen, according to my utter and hearty desire and intent; to whom also I daily pray, long to preserve and prosper your most gracious Highness, both to the continual comfort and consolation of our most redouted and without comparison most excellent Christen prince, and also the joy and gladness of all his loving subjects.[3] Amen.

### From **Part 1, Chapter 10**

### Who be Unperfecter, the One than the Other

The woman in her kind, and for the office and purpose wherefore she was made, is even as absolute and perfect as man in his kind. Neither is woman to be called (as some do) unperfecter than man (for because that man is more mightier and strong, the woman weaker and more feeble). For by *this* reason, the horse, the lion, the elephant, camel, and many other beasts should be called more "perfect" than man, to the which man is not able to compare in natural might and strength.

But truly, comparing one man to another, such as be gelded and want the genitories be much feebler, weak, and effeminate than other; in voice, womanlike; in gesture and condition, nice; in softness of skin and plumpness of the body, fatter and rounder; in strength and force, impotent, nothing manly ne bold: the which imbecility, in them, may well be named "imperfection." For *imperfection* is when that any particular creature doth lack any property, instrument, or quality which commonly by nature is in all other, or the more part, of that kind (comparing it to other of the same kind and not of another kind).

### From **Part 1, Chapter 11**

### The Pricks of Nature [4]

In women having great and fervent desire to any man, [her] seed doth issue ... down along to the woman's privy passage, moisturing all that part as it were with a dew. Aristotle and other moe do suppose that this seed in woman serveth for no other purpose, but only to excite, move, and stir the woman to pleasure. But some, peradventure, would think that "This were but a simple, and an idle or slender purpose!" Which, if they did more nearly consider the matter, should perceive it to be a just, great, and necessary cause. For if that the God of nature had not instincted and inset in the body of man and woman such a vehement and ardent appetite and lust, the one lawfully to company with the other, neither man ne woman would never have been so attentive to the works of generation and increasement of posterity – to the utter decay, in short time, of all mankind.

---

[1] far-to-seek ] clueless; *throngs* ] afflictions, travail.

[2] *perceiverance* ] perception (perhaps with a pun on perseverence, in labor).

[3] *redouted* ] revered.

[4] *pricks* ] prompts, stimuli.

### No Joy without Some Sorrow

For ye shall hear some women, in time of their travail (moved through great pain and intolerable anguish), forswear and vow themself never to company with a man again. Yet after-that the pangs be passed, within a short while, for entire love to their husbands, and singular natural delight between man and woman, they forget both the sorrow passed and that that is to come. Such be the privy works of God, and such be the pricks of nature, which never createth no special pleasure unaccompanied with some sorrow. Neither is there for the most part any sorrow, but that it hath annexed some joy or comfort, less or more, to alleviate and lighten the burthen and weight of displeasure.

### Part 1, Chap. 14: The *Terms* be of so Wholesome Blood, as Any other Part of the Body [1]

Here ye shall note, that they be greatly deceived and abused, which call the *terms* the woman's "purgation," or the "cleansing of their blood"; as who should say, that it were the *refuse, dross,* and *viler* part of the other blood remaining in the body, naturally every month sequestrate and separated from the purer, for the vility and evil quality therein comprehended. For undoubtedly, this blood is even as pure and wholesome as all the rest of the blood in any part of the body else. Is it to be thought that Nature would feed the tender and delicate infant in the mother's woman with the *refuse* of the blood, or not rather with the *purest* of it? ...

Yet much more are to be detested and abhorred the shameful lies and slander that Pliny, Albertus Magnus (*De Secretes Mulierum*), and divers other moe have written, of the "venomous" and dangerous "infective" nature of the woman's *floures* or *terms* – the which, all be but dreams and plain dotage. To rehearse their fond words, here, were but loss of ink and paper;[2] wherefore, let them pass, with their authors.

### Part 2, Chap. 1: The Due Fashion of Birth

The due fashion of birth is this: first, the head cometh forward. Then followeth the neck and shoulders, the arms with the hands lying close to the body toward the feet, the face and forepart of the child being toward the face and forepart of the

---

[1] *terms* ] menstrual periods.

[2] *floures*; a woman's "flows," or menstrual blood; *dotage* ] foolishness; *fond* ] silly; *pass* ] pass away; be forgotten.

Albertus Magnus (pseudo-Albert), in English: "Women are so full of venom in the time of menstruation that they poison animals with a glance; they infect children in the cradle; they spot the cleanest mirror; and when a man has sexual intercourse with them, he is made leprous and sometimes cancerous" (widely cited in late medieval and early modern literature).

Pliny, *Natural History,* 7.15: "But to come again to women, hardly can there be found a thing more monstrous than is that flux and course of theirs. For if during the time of this their sickness, they happen to approach or go over a vessel of wine, be it never so new, it will presently sour: if they touch any standing corn in the field, it will wither and come to no good. Also, let them in this estate handle any grasses, they will die upon it: the herbs and young buds in a garden if they do but pass by, will catch a blast, and burn away to nothing. Sit they upon or under trees whiles they are in this case, the fruit which hangeth upon them will fall. Do they but see themselves in a looking glass, the clear brightness thereof turneth into dimness, upon their very sight. Look they upon a sword, knife, or any edged tool, be it never so bright, it waxeth duskish, so doth also the lively hue of ivory. The very bees in the hive, die. Iron and steel presently take rust, yea, and brass likewise, with a filthy, strong, and poisoned stink, if they lay but hand thereupon. If dogs chance to taste of women's flowres, they run mad therewith: and if they bite anything afterwards, they leave behind them such a venom that the wounds are incurable. Nay, the very clammy slime bitumen, which at certain times of the year floateth and swimmeth upon the lake of Sodom called *asphaltites* in Jewry (which otherwise of the own nature is pliable enough, soft and gentle and ready to follow what way a man would have it), cannot be parted and divided asunder, for by reason of the viscosity, it cleaveth and sticketh like glue and hangeth all together, pluck as much as a man will at it, but only by a thread that is stained with this venomous blood. Even the silly pismires ([ants,] the least creature of all others) hath a perceivance and sense of this poison, as they say: for they cast aside and will no more come to that corn which they have once found by taste to be infected with this poison. This malady, so venomous and hurtful as it is, followeth a woman still every thirty days: and at three months' end, if it stay so long, it cometh in greater abundance.
Ed. fr. Philemon Holland, trans. (London, 1601), 163.

mother (*as it appeareth in the first of the birth figures*). For as hath been said already in the first book, before the time of deliverance, the child lieth in the mother's womb the head upward and the feet downward; but when it should be delivered, it is turned clean contrary – the head downward, the feet upward, and the face toward the mother's belly; and that, if the birth be natural. Another thing also is this: that if the birth be natural, the deliverance is easy without long tarrying or looking for it.

The birth not natural is when the mother is delivered before her time or out of due season, or after any other fashion than is here spoken of before; as when both the legs proceed first, or one alone with both the hands up, or both down, other else the one up and the other down, and divers otherwise (as shall be hereafter more clearly declared).

From **Part 2, Chapter 2: Of Easy and Uneasy, Difficult or Dolorous Deliverance and the Causes of It; with the Signs How to Know and Foresee the Same**

Very many be the perils, dangers and throngs which chance to women in their labor, which also ensue and come in divers ways, and for divers causes, such as I shall here declare.

First, when the woman that laboureth is conceived over-young, as before twelve or fifteen years of age (which chanceth sometime, though not very often),[1] and that the passage be over-angust, strait, or narrow (other naturally, or else for some dis-ease and infirmity which may happen about that part, as *apostumes, pushes, piles*, or *blisters*, and such other);[2] through the which causes, nature cannot but with great dolor and pain open and dilate itself, to the expelling and deliverance of the child; and sometime the *vesike* (or "bladder"), or other entrails being about the matrix or womb, be also apostumate and blistered; which, being grieved, the matrix or womb, likewise, for vicinity and neighborhood, is grieved with them. And that hindereth greatly the deliverance....

If the woman feel pain only in the back and above the navel, and not under, it is a sign of hard labor; likewise, if she were wont in times past to be delivered with great pain, is an evidence and likelihood of great labor always in the birth.

Now, signs and tokens of an expedite and easy deliverance be such as be contrary to all those that have been rehearsed before: as for example when the woman hath been wont in times past easily to be delivered, and that in her labor she feel but little throng or dolor; or, though she have great pains, yet they remain not still in the upper parts, but descend always downwards to the nether parts or bottom of the belly.

And to be short, in all painful and troublesome labors, these signs betoken and signify good speed and luck in the labor: unquietness, much stirring of the child in the mother's belly, all the throngs and pains tumbling in the forepart of the bottom of the belly, the woman strong and mighty of nature, such as can well and strongly help herself to the deliverance of the birth. And again, evil signs be those: when she sweateth cold sweat, and that her pulses beat and labor oversore, and that she herself in the laboring faint and swoond, these be unlucky and mortal signs.

From **Part 2, Chapter 3: On the Management of Normal Childbirth**

Now when the woman perceiveth the *matrix* or *mother* to wax lax and loose, and to be dissolved, and that the humors issue forth in great plenty, then shall it be meet for her to sit down, leaning backward, in manner upright; for which purpose, in some regions (as in France and Germany), the midwives have stools for the nonce, which being but low and not high from the ground, be made so (compass-wise and cave or hollow in the middest), that they may be received from underneath which is looked for; and the back of the stool, leaning backward, receiveth the back of the woman.[3]

And when the time of labor is come, in the same stool ought to be put many clothes or cloths or clouts in the back of it, the which the midwife may remove from one side to another, according as necessity shall require. The midwife herself shall sit before the laboring woman, and shall diligently observe and wait, how much, and after what means the child stirreth itself: also shall, with hands first anointed with the oil of almonds

[1] *twelve or fifteen* ] Rösslin's original *Rosegarten* follows church canon law in citing 12 years as the earliest appropriate age of consummation; Jonas's emendation reflects a growing sensitivity to the damage done to the bodies of brides under the age of 18-20.

[2] *over-angust* ] compressed; *other* ] either; *apostumes, pushes, piles*, or *blisters* ] abcesses, pimples, hemorrhoids, vesicatory swelling.

[3] *disssolved* ] softened; *meet* ] appropriate, beneficial; *compass-wise and cave* ] round and concave.

or the oil of white lilies, rule and direct everything as shall seem best. [1]

Also the midwife must instruct and comfort the party, not only refreshing her with good meat and drink, but also with sweet words, giving her good hope of a speedful deliverance, encouraging and enstomaching her to patience and tolerance, bidding her to hold in her breath so much as she may; also, stroking gently with her hands her belly above the navel, for that helpeth to depress the birth downward.

But and if the woman be anything gross, fat, or fleshy, it shall be best for her to lie grovelling; for by that means the matrix is thrust and depressed downward; anointing also the privy parts with the oil of white lilies. And if necessity require it, let not the midwife be afraid ne ashamed to handle the places, and to relax and loose the straits (forsomuch as shall lie in her), for that shall help well to the more expedite and quick labor. [2]

But this must the midwife above all things take heed of, that she compel not the woman to labor before the birth come forward and show itself. For before that time, all labor is in vain, labor as much as ye list. And in this case, many times it cometh to pass that the party hath labored so sore before the time, that when she should labor indeed, her might and strength is spent before in vain, so that she is not now able to help herself, and that is a perilous case. [3]

### On the Rupturing of the Forewaters

When the secundine or "second birth" (in the which, the birth is wrapped and contained) doth once appear, then may ye know that the labor is at hand. If the bag do not burst of its own accord, it shall be the midwife's part and office (with her nails, easily and gently) to break and rend it; or if that may not conveniently be done, then raise up between your fingers a piece of it, and cut it with a pair of sheers, or a sharp knife, but so that ye hurt not the birth with the cut.... Next followeth immediately, the birth.

### On the Management of Abnormal Presentation

But when the birth cometh not naturally, then must the midwife do all her diligence and pain (if it may be possible) to turn the birth tenderly with her anointed hands, so that it may be reduced again to a natural birth. As for example: sometime it chanceth the child to come, the legs and both arms and hands downward, close to the sides, first forth.... In this case, she must do all her pain and tender handling and anointing to receive forth the child, the legs being still close together.... Howbeit, it were far better (if it may be done by any possible ways or means) that the midwife should turn these legs coming first forth, upwards again by the bellyward, so that the head might descend downward by the back part of the womb; for then naturally again and without peril might it proceed and come forth, as the first.

### From **Part 3: Of the Nurse and her Milk**

As concerning the bringing up, nourishment, and giving of suck to the child, it shall be best that the mother give her child suck herself. For the mother's milk is more convenient and agreeable to the infant than any other woman's; and more doth it nourish it, for because-that in the mother's belly, it was wont to the same, and fed with it; and therefore also it doth more desirously covet the same (as that, with the which it is best acquainted). And to be short, the mother's milk is most wholesomest for the child....

If it be so that the mother cannot give the infant suck herself, either for because of sickness, or that her breasts be sore and her milk corrupted, then let her choose a wholesome nurse with these conditions following:

First, that she be of a good color and complexion, and that her bulk and breast be of good largeness. Secondly, that it be not too soon ne too long after her labor, so that it be two months after her labor at the least, and that (if it may be) such one which had a man child. Thirdly, that she be of mean and measurable liking, neither too fat, ne too lean. Fourthly, that she be good and honest of conversation, neither over-hasty or ireful, ne too sad or solemn, neither too fearful or timorous (for these affections and qualities be pernicious and hurtful to the milk, corrupting it, and pass forth through the milk into the child, making the child of like condition and manners). Also, that they be not over-light and wanton of behavior. Fifthly, that her breasts be full, and have sufficient plenty of milk, and that they be neither too great, soft, hanging, and flagging, ne too little, hard, or contract; but of a measurable quantity.

---

[1] *clouts* ] rags.

[2] *groveling* ] prostrate, face down.

[3] *labor as much as ye list* ] no matter how hard you try.

## Part 4, Chapter 6: Bellifying Receipts [1]

### Remedies of Dandruff of the Head

Some say, that they which use oft washing of their heads shall be very prone to headache. That is not true.... Oft washing shall purify the skin of the head, and steadfast the hair from falling, 'lleviate and lighten the head with all the sense therein contained, and greatly comfort the brains.

### To Take away Hair from Places Where it is Unseemly

In many maidens and women, the hair growth so low in the foreheads and the temples that it disfigureth them. For this ye may use three ways to remove them.

Either, to pluck up one after another with pincers (such as many women have for the nonce).

Either else, with this lye following: Take new-burnt lime, four ounces; of arsenic, one ounce. Steep both these in a pint of water, the space of two days, and then boil it from a pint to the half. And to prove whether it be perfect, dip a feather therein, and if the plume of the feather depart off easily, then is it strong enough. With this water then anoint so far the place that ye would have bare from hair, as it liketh you. And within a quarter of an hour, pluck at the hairs, and they will follow. And then wash that place much with water wherein bran hath been steeped....

The third way to remove hair is with a plaster made of very dry pitch, and upon leather applied to the place; the hairs being first shaven, or cut as near as can be with a pair of scissors....

### To Clear and Clarify the Skin in the Hands, Face, or Other Part

For this is nothing better than to take one spoonful of the oil of tartar, and six spoonfuls of water. With these commixed together, wash the hands, face, and other parts, for it scoureth, cleanseth, and purifieth the skin sovereignly, and will suffer no filthiness to remain in the pores of the flesh.

### To Supple and Mollify the Ruggedness of the Skin

Anoint the skin with the oil of sweet almonds. The same is very good also for chappings of the lips or hands. Item, deer suet is very proper for the same purpose; especially, being well washed, and tempered with rosewater wherein hath been dissolved two or three grains of pure musk.

### To Keep and Preserve the Teeth Clean

First, if they be very yellow and filthy, or blackish, let a barber scour, rub, and pick them clean and white. Then after, to maintain them clean, it shall be very good to rub them every day with the root of a mallow, and to pick them clean, that no meat remain and putrefy between the teeth.

Item, take of the small white pebblestones which be found by the watersides, and beat them in very small powder. Hereof, take an ounce; and of mastic, one dram. Mingle them together, and with this powder once in fourteen days rub exactly your teeth. And this shall keep your teeth fair and white. But beware ye touch not ne vex the gums therewithal.

Item, to stable and steadfast the teeth, and to keep the gums in good case, it shall be very good every day in the morning to wash well the mouth with red wine.

### Of Stinking Breath

Stink of the breath cometh either by occasion bred in the mouth, or else in the stomach. If it come from the stomach, then the body must be purged by the farther advice of a physician. If it be engendered in the mouth only, then most commonly it cometh of some rotten and corrupted hollow teeth, which in this case much be plucked out, and the gums well scoured and washed with vinegar wherein hath been sodden cloves and nutmegs. The cleanly keeping of the teeth doth confer much to the savoriness of the mouth.

### Of the Rank Savor of the Armhole

This vice in many persons is very tedious and loathsome, the remedy whereof is to purge first he choleric and eager humors, original causers of the same; and afterward, to wash the armholes often times with the water wherein wormwood hath been sodden together with camomile and a little quantity of alum.

Item, authors do write that roots of artichokes (the pith picked out), sodden in white wine and so drunk, doth cleanse the stench of the armholes and other parts of the body, by the urine.... And thus here I make an end of this fourth and last book.

*finis*

---

[1] *Bellifying Receipts* ] beautification recipes.

# **Katherine Howard** (1521-1542),
## Queen of Henry VIII

*Non autre volonté que la sienne.*[1]
—motto of Queen Katherine

ATHERINE HOWARD, fifth wife of Henry VIII, was the daughter of Joyce (Culpepper) Howard by her husband, Lord Edmund. She was a granddaughter of the second duke of Norfolk, a niece of the third duke, and a cousin of Anne Boleyn. Joyc Howard died when Katherine was quite young. Her father remarried; but as the third son in a large family, when the duke his father died in 1524, Edmund received little inheritance. Always cash-strapped, he had to beg handouts from his elder brother; until, on the preferment of Anne Boleyn in 1531, he was appointed Controller of Calais.

Before leaving for France, Edmund Howard made Katherine a ward of his stepmother, Agnes (Tilney) Howard, dowager duchess of Norfolk.[2] After seven years service, in his last witty dispatch, he speaks of returning to London; but he died in Calais on 19 March 1538/9. Orphaned, Katherine depended thereafter on the charity of a generous but aloof step-grandmother with whom she shared no blood-ties.

Katherine was numbered among some dozen wards entrusted by noble families to the custody of Dame Agnes, ostensibly for a courtly upbringing under headmistress Jane, Lady Rochford, the widow of George Boleyn. Katherine was taught to play the virginals and lute, and tutored in reading and writing. But she received little supervision either from her headmistress or step-grandmother, and no protection from a predator, who arrived in the person of her music teacher, Henry Mannock.[3] Katherine was not more than twelve years old when Mannock, 21, began fondling her. On one occasion, Lady Agnes found Katherine and Mannock engaged in unseemly behavior, whereupon she gave Katherine a sound beating ("all to-corned her"); but Mannock retained his position and continued to abuse the girl (probably, as Katherine later testified, heavy petting without penetration; which in Mannock's view, made it okay).

Katherine Howard (? disputed) at age "XVII"
In the style of Hans Holbein
Metropolitan Museum of Art, NY

About Michaelmas 1537, when Lady Norfolk removed her household to Lambeth, Mannock followed, but he was soon replaced in Katherine's affection by Francis Dereham, a kinsman who had been a gentleman pensioner to the duke of Norfolk, now secretary to widow Agnes at Lambeth. By the autumn of 1538, Dereham was paying clandestine visits to the shared bedroom of Katherine Howard and her cousin, Katherine Tilney, and was once seen upon the bed with both women at the same time.

The dowager duchess one day coming into a room where young women of the household devoted themselves to needlework, she found Katherine embracing and kissing Dereham. Lady Norfolk beat them both. Joan Bulmer received a box on the ear for sitting by and permitting such conduct (who took it in stride; Joan, 17, was now the lover of Dereham's best friend, Edward Waldegrave, cousin to Mannock).

According to Katherine's subsequent testimony, Dereham eventually raped her; but their intimacies lasted for several years, and they seem to have considered themselves husband and wife.

---

[1] No other will but his.

[2] Agnes (Tilney) Howard (1477-1545), 2d wife of the duke; 5 sons, 8 daughters; patron of John Skelton; godmother to Princess Mary; bore Anne Boleyn's train at her coronation; godmother to Princess Elizabeth; Jan. 1542, convicted of misprision of treason and imprisoned in the Tower; pardoned in May; died 1545.

[3] Henry Mannock ("Manox" in the court records); b. 1515 in Oxford, the son of George and Catherine (Waldegrave) Mannock; c. 1540, wedded Margaret Munday (1520-1546), widow of (a younger) Edmund Howard; d. c. 1542, possibly in prison; gave incriminating testimonty but was not mentioned among those executed (CLDS, IGI).

Dame Agnes one day received an anonymous letter (written by jealous Mannock and his friend Barnes), advising her that if she would rise after going to bed and visit the gentlewomen's chamber, she would be displeased. The drama that ensued came to nothing: Agnes scolded Dereham, and the two Katherines, and Joan Bulmer; and commanded Lady Rochford to lock the girls' quarters after dark; but she seems not to have interfered greatly with the amorous activities of Dereham, her kinsman. Thereafter, when Dereham was looked for and not found, she would say, "'An you seek him in Katherine's chamber, or in the gentlewomen's chamber, there shall you find him."[1]

About November 1539, near Katherine's eighteenth birthday, Dereham left for Ireland, to serve the English occupation – employment that may have been secured by the Howards, to get him out of the way (although Dame Agnes denied that). On his departure, he left £100 with his "wife" Kate for safe-keeping. About the same time, the Howards preferred Katherine to a place at court (possibly by submitting a portrait, which Henry typically required in place of a C.V.). By 19 December, she was on the payroll with a maid of honor's stipend. Katherine, with other newly appointed maids of honor, attended the January wedding festivities in Greenwich, when Henry dragged his feet to the altar to make Anne of Cleves his fourth wife – at which time the King's mind was evidently already fixed on young Kate Howard: Dame Agnes later testified that his Majesty was besotted with Katherine from the first time he set eyes on her.

The King thereafter had opportunity to see his vivacious maid of honor whenever he pleased. His interest cannot have gone unnoticed by her Howard kin. What began as flirtation led soon to substantial benefactions: on 24 April 1540, Henry signed over to Katherine lands and rents that had belonged to executed killers and were forfeit to the Crown – an unromantic gift, though welcome to a single girl without property. On 18 May, the King gave Katherine a costly sarcenet quilt, so that she might repose in a luxurious bed; but by that time, the King had made his ardor for Kate Howard apparent to everyone, including his wife, Anne of Cleves, a hefty German frau whom Henry detested and soon repudiated.

Katherine, 18, cannot have found the King sexually attractive. Pushing fifty, he now weighed twenty-one stone (about 300 lbs.); and he suffered, upon his obese thigh, a foul-smelling, suppurating ulcer that had to be drained daily (probably a symptom of Type II diabetes). Under such circumstance, gossip that King Henry was also sexually impotent would not have been considered a drawback, by most women.

That Katherine was forced by her uncle the duke or by the dowager duchess to accept the King's sexual advances may be doubted; but she certainly received plenty of encouragement, both from the King and from her Howard kin. From the duke of Northumberland's point of view, Henry's affection for Katherine was a gift from God: the Howards' position had been substantially weakened by Anne Boleyn's fall, and further undermined by Archbishop Cranmer and Thomas Cromwell, who viewed the old-school, old-Church Howard clan as an obstacle to their own dynastic ambitions. A marriage between King Henry and Katherine would make all good again.

On 9 July 1540 the English Church, of which King Henry was the Supreme Head, annulled his 6 January marriage to Anne of Cleves – on grounds of the Queen's childhood betrothal to another man and the King's alleged *Frau*-specific sexual dysfunction.

When the King's fourth marriage was annulled, Katherine's Lambeth friends were quick to come calling; the first of whom was Joan (Ackworth) Bulmer (1519-1590). On July 12th Joan wrote to Katherine from Yorkshire, predicting Katherine's marriage to the king, and looking for a for a position at court: "for I trots [*trust*] the coin [*Queen*] of Bretane wyll not forget her secretary."[2]

King Henry took Katherine to wife in a private ceremony at Oatlands palace on 28 July, the same day on which his deputies beheaded his chief minister, Thomas Cromwell – not for his many crimes against humanity but for the mistake of having saddled King Henry with Anne of Cleves, a virtuous but unhandsome bride.

Thomas Cromwell, beheaded 28 July 1540
by Holbein (detail) Frick Collection (NY)

---

[1] Alice Wilks, Katherine Tilney, Joan Bulmer (12 July 1540). *L&Ps, Henry VIII*, vol. 16: 1540-1, no. 1469.

[2] Joan Bulmer to Katherine Howard (12 July 1540). *Letters and Papers, Henry VIII*, vol. 15: 1540 no. 875.

On August 8, after a short honeymoon at Windsor, the royal newlyweds returned to Hampton Court, where Henry's teen bride was introduced as the new and true Queen of England. There was to be no coronation until Queen Katherine was delivered of a son; but the King doted on her, calling her his "rose without a thorn." Henry gave his bride lavish gifts of jewelry, clothing, and gold, by the cartload.

Over the Christmas holidays of 1541/2, Henry was as happy as anyone had seen him in years: he even brought Anne of Cleves to court, to meet Katherine. On command, Anne kneeled before Henry's new wife; acknowledged her as queen, and later danced with her. (Sympathetic Katherine gave ex-queen Anne the gift of two lap dogs she had received from Henry and did not want; plus a ring.)

Miniature of Katherine as queen, wearing jewels of Jane Seymour
Miniature by Hans Holbein
(Royal Collection)

When Queen Katherine appointed her ladies in waiting and maids of honor, she retained at least four former friends from Lambeth: Katherine Tilney, Joan Bulmer, Alice Restwold, and Margaret Morton. Incredibly, she also hired Henry Mannock to serve as a court musician.

If Mannock hoped to resume former intimacies now that Dereham was away in Ireland, he was disappointed: Katherine in the spring of 1541 became enamored of a handsome roisterer named Thomas Culpepper, a distant cousin who from childhood had been brought up with Henry VIII, even sleeping together (when young) in the same bed. As an adult Culpepper remained a gentleman of the Privy Chamber, and was one of the King's favorites. (In 1539, when Henry shut down Cumbwell Priory, he gave the property as a gift to Culpepper; and when Culpepper raped a park-keeper's wife and murdered a provincial constable, Henry quickly pardoned him.)

During Lent 1541, Culpepper and Paston and three servants were jailed in the Fleet, briefly, after a night of breaking windows and quarreling in Southwark. The King ordered their release on 20 March, just before leaving for Dover on the 21st – the same day on which Katherine comforted Culpepper for his troubles with the gift of a velvet cap with aglets, a token of her affection. The Queen and Culpepper now began seeing one another privately. Their meetings may never have gotten much farther than flirtation; but when Culpepper attended on the Queen, none of her attendants except her best friends, Katherine Tilney and Jane, Lady Rochford, were allowed inside the Queen's chambers. There was talk.

The whispers did not immediately reach Henry's ears. The King was now preoccupied with the Catholic uprising in the North (a rebellion against Henry's claimed supremacy over the Church). Henry blamed the unrest on Cardinal Reginald Pole, a religious conservative. Seeking revenge on the Cardinal, Henry in May abruptly ordered the death of Pole's elderly mother, the countess of Salisbury, already in custody. (On trumped-up charges of treason, old Lady Pole had been lodged in the Tower for a year, her lands and rents and titles forfeit to the Crown.)

At 7 o'clock in the morning on 27 May, Margaret Pole was awakened and told that her head was to be struck off, post-haste. The usual executioner was off-duty, but Sir William Kingston had conscripted an athletic young man, possibly a fellow prisoner, as a substitute. The countess, aged 77, said she was no traitor, and refused to die. The constables dragged her fighting and kicking to Tower Green, where some 150 spectators had gathered in a circle around the chopping block (no scaffold was erected). The countess boldly refused to lay her head upon the block, stating that if the young man wished to have her head, he would have to do it where she stood; whereupon the old lady was forced to lie on her belly, neck on the block, with attendants pinning her down. Perhaps they got in the way. Or perhaps the countess moved: With his first blow, the "wretched and blundering youth" whose job it was to remove her head with one blow, sank his axe into the old lady's shoulder – which didn't kill her. In a panic, he then proceeded with ten more blows to chop her head into fragments.[1]

The countess was buried in the Tower, in the Chapel of St. Peter ad Vincula (the last resting place of Anne Boleyn). In less than a year, she would be joined there by Queen Katherine, Henry's teen bride.

• • •

[1] Chapuys to the Queen of Hungary (10 June 1541), *State Papers, Spain* (1538–42), no. 166 (from the Vienna Archives); confirmed by Queen Victoria's government in 1876 during its orgy of exhumations 1876 to 1901; Lady Pole's skeleton was removed for study; it was determined that the countess was quite tall, for her age (Bell, 1877).

With the plague hot in London, Henry was advised that his august presence in Yorkshire would quell the unrest: so he embarked on a progress to the north. Departing in late June, his retinue included Queen Katherine; Jane Boleyn, Lady Rochford; Katherine Tilney; and Thomas Culpepper.

Love was now in full bloom: Katherine and Thomas arranged a social tryst at Lincoln; another Pontefract Castle on or about August 23. Mistress Luffkin, a chamberer, was asked to depart and kept outside for a private meeting between Katherine and Culpepper that lasted five or six hours.

On her third or fourth day at Pomfret, Katherine received an unexpected blast from the past in the person of Francis Dereham. Having returned from Ireland looking for work, Dereham had been sent by Dame Agnes to follow the royal progress and (with her letters of support) to seek a position with the Queen. Rather than send him packing, Katherine made the unwise decision of appointing Dereham her personal secretary, in place of Joan Bulmer; which must have made assignations with Culpepper more difficult, or at least more risky. And yet, when the King's entourage reached York, the Queen assisted by Jane Boleyn arranged still another private social engagement. (Katherine said later she tried to break off the relationship at this meeting, before it went too far.)

As the royal court wended its way homeward, trouble was brewing in London. Mary (Lascelles) Hall, now married, had been chambermaid to Lady Norfolk at Horsham and at Lambeth House during the period of Katherine's activities, first with Mannock, then with Dereham – and she had told her brother, the reformer John Lascelles, all about it. Lascelles in October 1541 told Cranmer, who was most interested. Without waiting for the King's return, the Archbishop began his investigation by interviewing Mary Hall, who gave him an earful.

King Henry, returning to London in high spirits, hosted an All Hallows feast at Hampton Court. At that dinner, Cranmer took the King aside, expressing his fears that his Majesty had perhaps been cuckolded by Katherine. The bull-headed Henry angrily dismissed this unwelcome intelligence as a Protestant conspiracy; but he authorized Cranmer to proceed with a full investigation.

That night and for the next two weeks, Katherine and her ladies were confined to the Queen's chambers, incommunicado, with guards posted at all exits; being told only that the King was indisposed.

Arrested on 3 November, Dereham and Mannock were doubtless treated to the usual unpleasantries upon the rack, being interviewed by Sir Thomas Wriothesley (who was known to enjoy turning the crank himself). Mannock denied he had ever been intimate with the queen, but he accused Dereham. Dereham acknowledged his sexual encounters but hoped for mercy as he had no way of knowing, at the time, that his Kate would one day be Queen of England; nor had he touched her since.

It took just 24 hours for Cranmer to return to Hampton Court, with these confessions in hand, for a meeting with the King and Privy Council. As Cranmer made his presentation, the King broke down and wept like a broken-hearted child. The Council remained in session for most of the next several days. First Norfolk, then Cranmer, were sent to the queen's chambers with interrogatories. Cranmer described the Queen as almost delirious with fright, sobbing and suicidal. But by promising her the King's pardon, and by pretending to be her sympathetic holy confessor, the archbishop extracted from Katherine a satisfactory confession:

## [Confession of Catherine Howard taken by Cranmer (7 November 1540)°]

*Confession of Q[ueen] Katherine Howard, anno 33 Henry VIII, afore the King's Council at Hampton Court*

I, your Grace's most sorrowful subject and most vile wretch in the world, not worthy to make any recommendations unto your most excellent Majesty, do only make my most humble submission and confession of my faults. And where no cause of mercy is given upon my part, yet of your most accustomed mercy extended unto all other men undeserved, most humbly on my hands and knees do desire oon sparkle thereof to be extended unto me, although of all other creatures most unworthy either to be called your wife or subject. My sorrow I can by no writing express; nevertheless, I trust your most benign nature will have some respect unto my youth, my ignorance, my frailness, my humble confession of my fault, and plain declaration of the same, referring me wholly unto Your Grace's pity and mercy.

First: at the flattering and fair persuasions of Mannock, being but a young girl, [I] suffered him at sundry times to handle and touch the secret parts of my body, which neither became me with honesty to permit, nor him to require.

Also, Francis Dereham by many persuasions procured me to his vicious purpose, and obtained first to lie upon my bed with his doublet and hose; and after, within the bed; and finally, he lay with me naked, and used me in such sort as a man doth his wife, many and sundry times (but how often, I know not). And our company ended almost a year before the King's Majesty was married to my Lady Anne of Cleve[s] and continued not past one quarter of a year, or little above.

Now the whole truth being declared unto your Majesty, I most humbly beseech the same to consider the subtle persuasions of young men and the ignorance and frailness of young women. I was so desirous to be taken unto your Grace's favor, and so blinded with the desire of wor'dly glory that I could not, nor had grace to, consider how great a fault it was to conceal my former faults from your Majesty – considering that I intended ever during my life to be faithful and true unto your Majesty after. And nevertheless, the sorrow of mine offenses was ever before mine eyes, considering the infinite goodness of your Majesty toward me from time to time ever increasing and not diminishing. Now I refer the judgment of all mine offenses with my life and death wholly unto your most benign and merciful Grace, to be considered by no justice of your Majesty's laws but only by your infinite goodness, pity, compassion and mercy, without which I 'knowledge myself worthy of the most extreme punishment.

Kateryn Howard

In a conversation with Marillac, ambassador to François I, Katherine's uncle Norfolk said that the young queen "supposed that after her free confession they would make no further inquiry. But finding the contrary, she refuses to drink or eat and weeps and cries like a madwoman, so that they must take away things by which she might hasten her death—which will not be long if the last point which is yet in presumption is proved": Norfolk spoke with tears in his eyes of "the King's grief (who loved her much)," and of the misfortune to his "own house (because of her and Queen Anne, his two nieces)."[1]

When Katherine's confession was presented to the King, his Majesty is said to have "changed his love for the Queen into hatred, taking such grief at being deceived, that at last it was thought he had gone mad (He called for a sword to kill her whom he had loved so much). Still sitting in Council, he called suddenly for horses without saying where he would go. Sometimes he said, *hors de propoz*: 'That wicked woman had never such pleasure in her inchastity as she shall have torture in her death!' And finally he broke into tears, regretting his bad luck in meeting with such ill-disciplined wives (and blaming his Council for this latest mischief).

"The ministers," Marillac continued, "have done their best to make him forget his grief, and he is gone 25 miles from here with no company but musicians and ministers of pastime."[2] (With only a few close advisors and professional entertainers, Henry had retired to Oatlands Manor, with instructions for the Council to arrest everyone who assisted, or knew about, or who might have known about, Queen Katherine's amours with other men.)

The worst, for Katherine, was yet to come: Dereham while being interrogated had denied touching her since his return from Ireland; not least (he said) because he was displaced in her affections by another. With some encouragement, Dereham gave up a name: Sir Thomas Culpepper, a Privy Councilor and the King's lifelong friend. With the threat of torture and the gallows to back him up, Archbishop Cranmer proved a relentless detective. He soon learned that Katherine and Culpepper had been together, unsupervised, some half dozen times – once, for five or six hours during the King's recent progress, with Jane Boleyn standing watch.

There was not yet sufficient evidence to convict Lady Rochford. On Nov. 12, the Privy Councilors met again in the King's absence; at which time they brought the Queen from her chambers to be interrogated in their presence. At this interview, Cranmer and Wriothesley informed a weepy Katherine that the King and Council already knew the facts concerning her past indiscretions; to which, one more name had been added: Thomas Culpepper. Lady Rochford was named as the Council's principal source for this tip (a lie). Feeling betrayed, Katherine in turn gave evidence against Lady Rochford.

---

[1] Ambasador Marillac to François I (14 Nov. 1540), ed. Kaulek (1885), 355. In French.

[2] Same to same (7 Dec. 1541), ibid., 370. In French.

### [Examination of Queen Katherine before the King's Privy Council (12 November)°]

*1541, November 12. Hampton.* The queen sayeth that my lady Rochford hath sundry times made instance to her to speak with Culpepper, declaring him to bear her goodwill and favor; whereupon she did, at the last, grant he should speak with her (my lady of Rochford affirming that he desired "nothing else but to speak with her," and that she durst "swear upon a Book he meant nothing but honesty").

And so he spake with her in a little gallery at the stairhead, at Lincoln, when it was late in the night about 10 or 11 o'the clock, an hour and more; another time in her bedchamber at Pomfret; and another time in my Lady Rochford's chamber at York.

Item, she sayeth that she would ever say to my Lady Rochford when she moved her for him, "Alas, madam, this woll be spied, oon day, and then we be all undone!" – whereunto my Lady Rochford would say: "Fear not, madam, let me alone, I warrant you."

Item, she sayeth that when Culpepper was talking with her, my Lady Rochford would many times, being ever by, sit somewhat far off, or turn her back; and she would say to [Lady Rochford], "For God's sake, madam, even near us."

Item, she sayeth since the Council came, [Lady Rochford] hath advised her sundry times in no wise to disclose this matter, saying, "They would speak fair to you and use all ways with you, but and if you confess, you undo both yourself and others. And for my part," said my Lady Rochford, "I woll never confess it, to be torn with wild horses."

Item, she confesseth that she gave [Culpepper] once a cap with aglets, and a chain; and my Lady Rochford took a cramp ring from her and sent him after; and after, had another of hers, to match it; and that my Lady Rochford prayed her she might buy somewhat to send him, when he sent certain pheasants.

Item, she sayeth that my Lady Rochford would at every lodging search the back doors and tell her of them if there were any, unasked. And sithens the progress, [Lady Rochford] told her that when [the Queen] came to Greenwich she knew an old kitchen wherein [the Queen] might well speak with him.

Item, she sayeth that my Lady Rochford told her also that she thought [Thomas] Paston bore her favor (but he never spake with her).

Item, she sayeth that lately (but the time, she remembereth not) my Lady Rochford spake of Culpepper; whereunto the queen answered, "Alas, madam, woll this never have end? I pray you, bid him desire no more to trouble me or send to me";

Whereupon "She told me [*sic*] that she had done my message. His answer was that he besought me to send him no such word, for he would take no such answer; but still sent to me as he might have a messenger." At which time she called him "Little sweet fool."

Item, her Grace sayeth that when she took her rites last, she gave [Lady Rochford] warning to trouble her no more with such light matters; whereunto [Lady Rochford] answered, "Yet must you give men leave to *look* – for they *will* look upon you!"

[subscribed by signatures of Katherine (not in her own hand) and eleven members of the Privy Council:]

T. Cant[erbury], T. Norfolk, W. Southampton, Robert Sussex, E. Hertford, J. Russell, Stephen Winton, Anthony Browne, Anthony Wingfield, Thomas Wriothesley, Rafe Sadler

• • •

Lady Rochford was now summoned and presented with the queen's allegations. Feeling betrayed, Jane accused Katherine and Culpepper of contriving the affair themselves and forcing her to act as a go-between.

On 13 November, Wriothesley visited Hampton Court, where he assembled all employees of the queen in the Great Hall; read to them a litany of the queen's alleged sexual offenses; and fired the staff, en masse. That same day, Culpepper was arrested and taken to the Tower; as was Jane Boleyn, Lady Rochford, for her alleged services as a bawd.

On the 14th, Katherine was transported to Sion Prison—formerly Sion Priory, now surrendered to the Crown and put to its fullest use as a prison for special guests. The Queen was permitted four gentlewomen and two chamberers – at least one of whom (Lady Bainton) was a paid Wriothesley spy. Katherine at this juncture still believed that her life might be spared, given the King's great love for her; but Wriothesley and Cranmer had up their sleeve a trump card: they had obtained a letter, in the Queen's own hand, addressed to her little sweet fool, Thomas Culpepper:

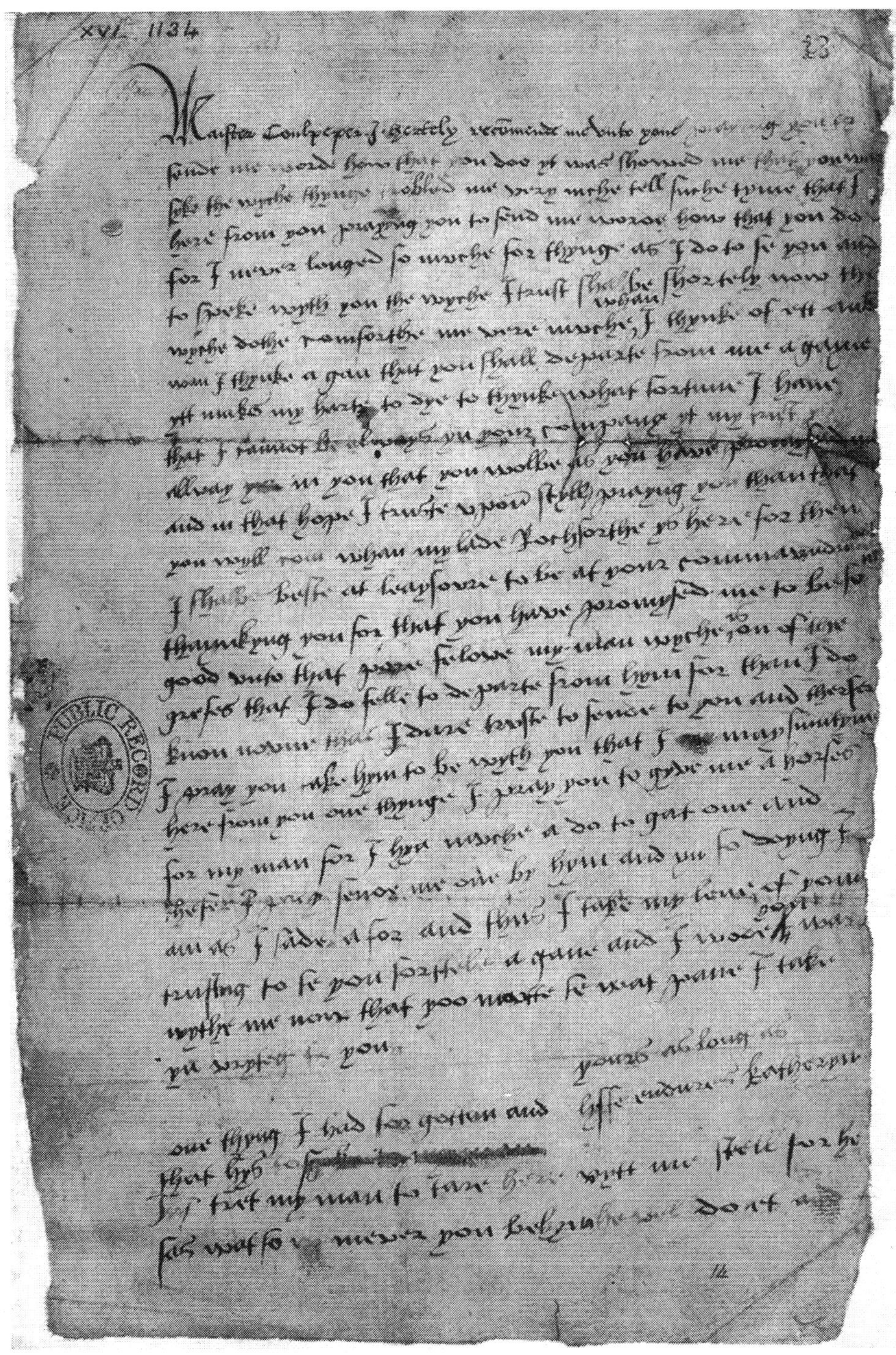

XVI. 1134

Master Colpeper I hartely recomend me unto you praying you to
sende me worde how that you doo yt was showed me that you was
seke the wyche thynge trobled me very muche tell suche tyme that I
here from you praying you to send me worde how that you do
for I never longed so muche for thynge as I do to se you and
to speke wyth you the wyche I trust shalbe shortely now the
wyche dothe comforthe me very muche when I thynke of ytt and
when I thynke agane that you shall departe from me agayne
ytt makes my harte to dye to thynke what fortune I have
that I cannot be always yn your company yt my trust ys
always in you that you wolbe as you have promysed me
and in that hope I truste upon styll praying you than that
you wyll come whan my lady Rochforthe ys here for then
I shalbe beste at leysoure to be at your commandment
thankyng you for that you have promysed me to be so
good unto that pore felowe my man whyche ys one of the
grefes that I do felle to departe from hym for than I do
knoe noone that I dare truste to sende to you and therfor
I pray you take hym to be wyth you that I may sumtyme
here from you one thynge I pray you to gyve me a horse
for my man for I hade muche a do to gat one and
therfor I pray sende me one by hym and yn so doyng I
am as I sayde afor and thus I take my leve of you
trustyng to se you shortely agane and I wold you was
wyth me now that yoo myt se what pane I take
yn wryteng to you

yours as long as lyffe endures Katheryn

one thynge I had forgotten and that ys to instruct
my man to tarre here wyth me stell for he
sas whatsomever you bed hym he wyl do et

14

Courtesy of the National Archives, State Papers 1/167 fol. 14.

### [Queen Katherine to Master Thomas Culpeper (August? 1541)°]

Master Culpepper,

I heartily recommend me unto you, praying you to send me word how that you do. It was showed me that you was sick, the which thing troubled me very much till such time that I hear from you; praying you to send me word how that you do, for I never longed so much for [a] thing as I do to see you and to speak with you, the which I trust shall be shortly now – that which doth comforth me very much when I think of it. And when I think again that you shall depart from me again, it makes my heart to die to think what fortune I have that I cannot be always in your company.

Y[e]t my trust is alway in you that you woll be as you have promised me, and in that hope I trust upon still, praying you then that you will come when my Lady Rochforth is here; for then I shall be best at leisure to be at your commandment, thanking you for that you have promised me to be so good unto that poor fellow my man – which is one of the griefs that I do feel, to depart from him, for then I do know no one that I dare trust to send to you; and therefore, I pray you, take him to be with you that I may sometime hear from you one thing. (I pray you to give me a horse for my man: for I had much ado to get one and therefore, I pray, send me one by him.)

And in so doing I am as I said afore, and thus I take my leave of you, trusting to see you s[h]ortly again – and I would you was with me now (that you might see what pain I take in writi[n]g to you!).

Yours as long as life endures,

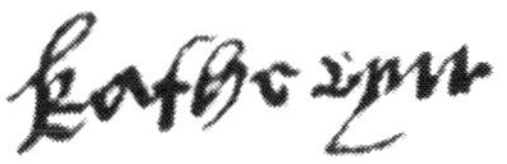

Katheryn

[*P.S.*] One thing I had forgotten and that is to instruct my man to tarry here wit[h] me still, for he says whatsomever you bid him, he will do it ~~and~~

• • •

On the first of December, at the London Guildhall, Dereham and Culpepper were tried and condemned by Cranmer's hand-picked jury. The Lord Mayor of London played the part of presiding judge, with Lord Chancellor Audley on his right hand and the duke of Norfolk on his left; together with Henry Brandon, duke of Suffolk; Thomas Wriothesley, Lord Privy Seal; the earls of Sussex and Hertford (Henry Radcliffe and Edward Seymour); and other cooperative members of the king's Council.

The trial was over before it began. When the accusations had been read and the defendants had entered their plea of Not Guilty, the duke of Norfolk announced the sentence with noted pleasure: both Culpepper and Dereham were to be dragged through the streets of London to Tyburn, where they were to be "hanged, cut down alive, and disemboweled; and, while still living, their intestines cut out, then burnt; the corpses then to be beheaded and quartered."[1] Citing his knighthood and his lifelong friendship with the King, Sir Thomas Culpepper requested and received a commuted sentence: he would be beheaded only, without the extra ceremonies.

Dereham and Culpepper were executed at Tyburn on December 10th. Their heads were mounted on spikes on London Bridge. No sooner were they dispatched than their place in the Tower was taken by the dowager duchess of Norfolk. Dame Agnes, 65, was known to have opened two of Dereham's coffers. Accused of evidence tampering, she had said she was looking to help the investigation, not seeking to destroy incriminating documents; but no one believed her. Arrested again on 10 December, she was confined in the Tower. Also imprisoned were her eldest son William and his wife Margaret; her daughters, Anne Howard and Katherine Howard Daubeney; Katherine and Malin Tilney, ladies in waiting; Alice Restwold, Margaret Bennet, Joan Bulmer, chamberers; Joan's former lover, Edward Waldegrave; Robert Davenport and William Ashby, gentleman retainers, and others: all of whom were indicted for misprision

---

[1] National Archives (Dec. 1541), "Baga de Secretis," Pouch XIII., Bundle 1, no. 41. In Latin, tr. DWF.

of treason for having concealed Katherine's sexual history from the King.

"As to the old duchess of Norfolk," wrote the French ambassador, "some say she shall die, others that she shall keep perpetual prison.... A few days will show. All her goods are already confiscated – and are of *astonishing* value, 400,000 or 500,000 crowns (for ladies in this country succeed for life to the movables of their deceased husbands). Norfolk [her stepson, Thomas Howard] is greatly interested, since the greater part came to her through his late father; yet the times are such that he dare not show that the affair touches him, but approves all that is done."[1] (Not wishing to join his family in prison, Thomas Howard, third duke, on 14 December wrote a letter to the king, denouncing his siblings and stepmother, hoping thereby to escape sharing their fate and perhaps have something left to inherit after the law took Dame Agnes's life and property.)

On 16 January, the accused were convicted by attainder (without a trial). Their sentence: "all of them shall forfeit their goods to the King, and be imprisoned for life, and the King shall take the revenues of their lands."[2] (The Crown made out, as usual, like a bandit; though many were later pardoned.)

The Queen all this while remained in Sion Prison, in limbo. The bill of attainder drawn up against her on 16 January made illegal the "intent" to commit treason by an act of adultery involving the King's wife; which rendered moot the question of actual adultery. On 7 February, Parliament passed another bill making it punishable by death for a queen consort to fail to disclose her sexual history to the King prior to marriage; or to incite any man thereafter to commit adultery with her. No trial was necessary: Pronounced guilty on both counts, Katherine was appointed to die at 7 a.m. on 13 February.

King Henry's fifth queen was brought by barge to the Tower of London on the 10th: "The lord Privy Seal, with a number of Privy Councilors and servants went first in a great barge. Then came the Queen with three or four men and as many ladies, in a small covered barge; then the Duke of Suffolk, in a great barge, with a company of his men." Katherine's barge passed under London Bridge where she could see the rotting heads of her accused lovers (whose grinning skulls would remain there until the death of King Henry in 1547). "On their arrival at the Tower, the lords landed first; then the Queen, in black velvet; and they paid her as much honor as when she was reigning. On Sunday the 12th, towards evening, she was told to prepare for death, for she was to die next day. That evening she asked to have the block brought in to her, so that she might know how to position herself; which was done, and she tried it out."[3]

Next morning, the Archbishop who helped to ensure Katherine's death arrived promptly to hear the queen's confession and to administer the holy Eucharist. Katherine confessed her many sins, conceding that she deserved to die; but she still denied, on pain of damnation, having committed adultery. The Archbishop was unimpressed.

Queen Katherine was beheaded before a large audience on Tower Green, the site of Anne Boleyn's execution, her head being removed with a single stroke of the axe. Covered with a black cloth, her head and body were "removed by her ladies" (perhaps on a cart) while Jane Boleyn was brought forth to die. Lady Rochford had gone mad in prison but was now recovered sufficiently to speak at length from the scaffold, extending her life by some few minutes. Then she, too, was beheaded.

The remains of Katherine Howard and Lady Rochford were brought to the Chapel of St Peter ad Vincula for burial, and laid to rest with the bones of Anne Boleyn.

Ambassador Marillac reports: "The King has been in better spirits since the execution. During the last three days before Lent there has been much feasting. Sunday was given up to the lords of his Council and Court, Monday to the men of law, and Tuesday to the ladies, all of whom slept at [Hampton] Court. He himself in the morning did nothing but go from room to room to order that lodgings be prepared for these ladies, and he made them great and hearty cheer."[4]

DWF

---

[1] Ambasador Marillac to François I (13 Feb. 1541/2), ed. Kaulek (1885), 388. In French.

[2] National Archives, Parliament Rolls, 33 Hen. VIII. (16 Jan. 1541/2). Most were later released from prison. Margaret Douglas (widow of Lord Thomas Howard) and Mary Howard Fitzroy (widow of Henry VIII's bastard son, Henry Fitzroy) were dismissed from court to dwell with the duke of Norfolk at Kenninghall until further notice (they had been ladies in waiting to the Queen but were not suspected of complicity in her lovelife). Mannock, having denied any wrongdoing, and having turned State's evidence, was released from custody, though his sexual abuse of a thirteen-year-old is what set the tragic machinery in motion.

[3] Chapuys to Carlos V (25 Feb. 1541/2), *S.P. Henry VIII, Spanish,* 6.1, no. 232; *L&P Henry VIII* 17 (1542), no.124.

[4] ibid.

# **Katherine Parr** (1512-1548), Queen of Henry VIII

> [W]e, outlawes, the chyldren of Eue, wepe and waile the bitter tediousnesse of our daye, that is of this present life, shorte and euil, full of sorowe and anguishe...
> —from *Prayers Stirryng the Mynd* (1545), sig. B8[v]

ATHERINE PARR, the last of King Henry's six wives, was the eldest surviving daughter of Maud (b. Green) by her husband, Sir Thomas Parr, who rose to prominence with Henry's 1509 accession. Thomas became a favorite courtier, though some thirteen years older than the king; and Maud was made a lady-in-waiting to Catherine of Aragon. When a baby girl was born in 1512, the Parrs named her after the queen, who stood as godmother.

When Katherine was just five years old her father died, leaving by will £800 as a marriage portion to be divided between his two daughters; and he left Maud with enough money to raise the children like aristocrats. Katherine was tutored in reading and writing, arithmetic, Latin, French, and Italian, dancing, etiquette, medicine, and prayers; also, sewing and needlework (which she is said to have disliked.)

The earliest extant writing by Katherine Parr appears beneath the image of St. Catherine of Alexandria in a Book of Hours that belonged first to her father, and after his decease to her Uncle, Sir William Parr of Horton. She was about eight years old:

| | |
|---|---|
| oncle wan you do on thys loke | Uncle, When you do on this look, |
| I pray you remember wo wrete thys in your boke | I pray you, remember who writ this in your book: |
| your louuynge nys Kathren Parr | Your loving niece, Katherine Parr |

At age 15 Katherine was married to Edward Borough, who died in 1533. A year later she married John Neville, Lord Latimer, a man twice her age but a member of the peerage. In 1536, during the Pilgrimage of Grace uprising, the rebels dragged Neville from his home at Snape Castle, Yorkshire, demanding he join their cause; and later held his family held hostage. The terror of that experience may have firmed up Katherine's support for King Henry's policies. But Henry also toyed for a very long time with the idea of putting Lord Latimer to death; Neville saved him the trouble on 2 March 1542/3, leaving Lady Katherine again a widow, and very rich. Renewing her friendship with Princess Mary, Katherine joined her household, where she fell in love with Thomas Seymour, younger brother of the late Queen Jane. Henry had recently beheaded his fifth wife, Katherine Howard, and was shopping for a sixth when his fancy was attracted to Katherine Parr. To remove his rival, the King dispatched Seymour to a post in Brussels. The King then asked Katherine to marry him, who considered it her Christian and civic duty to accept his offer over that of Seymour, the man she loved; and Seymour knew better than to object. The marriage took place on 12 July 1543, with eighteen people present.

Ever gracious, Katherine developed an affectionate relationship with the king's son and two daughters, treating them as her own children; and was influential in Henry's approval of the Third Succession Act, which restored both Mary and Elizabeth to the line of succession. All three of Henry's children came to love her dearly.

When Henry left England in July 1544 for the last of his unsuccessful military campaigns in France, he appointed Katherine regnant queen. For three months, Katherine handled the responsibilities of the kingdom more capably than Henry ever did. She supervised the provision, finances and musters for Henry's military; signed five Royal proclamations; maintained good communication with her lieutenants throughout the counties; and kept the borders secure, even in the troubled north. She wrote often to the king, to report on the state of the realm – more often, to express her humble affection, as in this representative letter, written while Henry was engaged in pointless killing at the siege of Boulogne:

Katherine Parr, unattrib., *National Portrait Gallery*

### [Katherine, Queen Regnant, to King Henry VIII (31 July 1544)°]

Although the discourse of time and account of days neither is long, nor many, of your Majesty's absence, yet the want of your presence (so much beloved and desired of me!), maketh me that I cannot quietly pleasure in anything until I hear from your Majesty. The time, therefore, seemeth to me *very* long, with a great desire to know how your Highness hath done since your departing hence, whose prosperity and health I prefer and desire more than mine own. And whereas I know your Majesty's absence is never without great respects of things most convenient and necessary, yet love and affection compelleth me to desire your presence.

And again, the same zeal and love forces me also to be best content with that which is your will and pleasure. And thus, love maketh me in all things to set apart mine own commodity and pleasure, and to embrace most joyfully his will and pleasure whom I love. God, the knower of secrets, can judge these words not only to be with ink, but most truly impressed in the heart.

(Much more I omit, lest it be thought I go about to praise myself, or crave a thank; which thing to do, I mind nothing less but a plain, simple relation of my zeal toward your Majesty, proceeding from the abundance of the heart.[1] Wherein I must needs confess I deserve no worthy commendation, having such just occasion to do the same.)

I make like account with your Majesty as I do with God for His benefits and gifts heaped upon me daily, 'knowledging myself all ways a great debtor unto Him, in that I do omit my duty toward Him, not being able to recompense the least of His benefits; in which state I am certain and sure to die.[2] But yet I hope in His gracious acceptation of my goodwill. And even such confidence I have in your Majesty's gentleness, knowing myself never to have done my duty as was requisite and meet to such a noble and worthy prince; at whose hands I have found and received so much love and goodness, that with words I cannot express it.

Lest I should be too tedious unto your Majesty, I finish this my scribbled letter, committing you into the governance of the Lord with long and prosperous felicity here, and after this life to enjoy the kingdom of His elect.

From Greenwich, by your Majesty's humble and obedient servant,

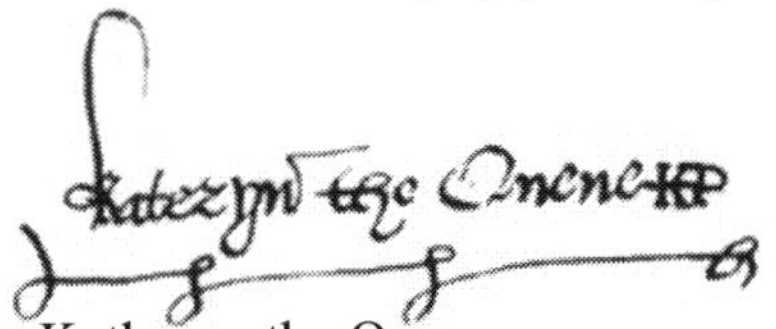

Katheryn the Quene

• • •

Katherine Parr was the first English queen to publish under her own name. Her *Prayers Stirrying the Mynd*, which appeared in 1545, was reprinted more than a dozen times in the century that followed (under variant titles). Her second book, *The Lamentacion of a Sinner* (1547; rep. 1548, 1563) is more transparently Protestant in its sympathies than the 1545 *Prayers*; in it, Katherine stresses the Calvinist doctrine of salvation by grace alone, and the Lutheran doctrine of the total depravity of women. (During Mary's reign, the *Lamentation* of sinful Katherine was expressly banned.) Influenced by Anne Askew's *Examinations,* but without Askew's deft irony and bold self-assertion, Queen Katherine in both books advocates an almost Buddhistic renunciation of the will. Her ideal of spiritual kenosis was strongly gendered: it is the woman's duty to nullify her will so that she may be wholly subsumed as an instrument of her heavenly and earthly Lords.

(*Caveat:* The modern reader may find Katherine Parr deeply annoying in her expressions of abject self-denial, unless one remembers that she was never the spineless milksop to which her rhetoric aspires.)

---

[1] *mind nothing less but* ] intend nothing other than.

[2] *sure to die* ] sure to be blessed until the day I die.

## From ***Prayers Stirring the Mind***

MOST BENIGN LORD JESU, grant me thy grace, that it may alway work in me and perséver with me unto the end.[1] Grant me that I may ever desire and will that which is most pleasant and most acceptable to thee. Thy will be my will, and my will be to follow alway thy will. Let there be alway in me one will and one desire with thee, and that I have no desire to will, or not to will, but as thou wilt. Lord, thou knowest what thing is most profitable and most expedient for me. Give therefore what thou wilt, as much as thou wilt, and when thou wilt. Do with me what thou wilt, as it shall please thee, and as shall be most to thine honor. Put me where thou wilt, and freely do with me in all things after thy will. Thy creature I am, and in thy hands. Lead and turn me where thou wilt. Lo, I am thy servant, ready to all things that thou commandest; for I desire not to live to myself, but to thee.

Lord Jesu, I pray thee, grant me grace, that I never set my heart on the things of this world, but that all worldly and carnal affections may utterly die and be mortified in me. Grant me above all things that I may rest in thee, and fully quiet and pacify my heart in thee. For thou, Lord, are the very true peace of heart and the perfect rest of the soul; and without thee, all things be grievous and unquiet. My Lord Jesu, I beseech thee, be with me in every place and at all times, and let it be to me a special solace; gladly (for thy love) to lack all worldly solace: and if thou withdraw thy comfort from me at any time, keep me, O Lord, from desperation and make me patiently to abide thy will and ordinance.

O Lord Jesu, thy judgments be righteous, and thy providence is much better for me than all that I can imagine or devise; wherefore do with me in all things as it shall please thee, for it may not be but well, all that thou dost. If thou wilt that I be in light, be thou blessed; if thou wilt I be in darkness, be thou also blessed. If thou vouchsafe to comfort me, be thou highly blessed; if thou wilt I live in trouble, and without comfort, be thou likewise ever blessed. Lord, give me grace gladly to suffer whatsoever thou wilt shall fall upon me, and patiently to take at thy hand good and bad, bitter and sweet, joy and sorrow; and for all things that shall befall unto me, heartily to thank thee.

Keep me, Lord, from sin, and I shall then neither dread death nor Hell. O what thanks ought I to give unto thee, which hast suffered the grievous death of the Cross to deliver me from my sins and to obtain everlasting life for me! Thou gavest us most perfect example of patience, fulfilling and obeying the will of thy Father even unto the death. Make me (wretched sinner) obediently to use myself after thy will in all things and patiently to bear the burden of this corruptible life. For though this life be tedious, and as an heavy burden to my soul; yet nevertheless through thy grace, and by example of thee, it is now made much more easy and comfortable than it was before thy incarnation and passion. Thy holy life is our way to thee; and by following of thee, we walk to thee, that art our head and savior. And yet, except thou hadst gone before and showed us the way to everlasting life, who would endeavor himself to follow thee? – seeing we be yet so slow and dull, having the light of thy blessèd example and holy doctrine to lead and direct us.

O Lord Jesu, make that possible by grace that is impossible to me by nature. Thou knowest well that I may little suffer, and that I am anon cast down and overthrown with a little adversity; wherefore I beseech thee, O Lord, to strengthen me with thy spirit, that I may willingly suffer for thy sake all manner of trouble and affliction. Lord, I will acknowledge unto thee all mine unrighteousness, and I will confess to thee all the unstableness of my heart. Oftentimes a very little thing troubleth me sore, and maketh me dull and slow to serve thee. And sometime I purpose to stand strongly, but when a little trouble cometh, it is to me great anguish and grief, and of a right little thing riseth a grievous temptation to me.

Yea, when I think myself to be sure and strong, and that (as it seemeth) I have the upper hand, suddenly I feel myself ready to fall with a little blast of temptation. Behold therefore, good Lord, my weakness, and consider my frailness, best known to thee. Have mercy on me, and deliver me from all iniquity and sin, that I be not entangled therewith. Oftentimes it grieveth me sore, and in manner confoundeth me, that I am so unstable, so weak, and so frail in resisting sinful motions – which, although they draw me not alway to consent, yet nevertheless their assaults be very grievous unto me; and it is tedious to me to live in such battle (albeit I perceive that such battle is not unprofitable unto me – for thereby I know the better myself, and mine own infirmities, and that I must seek help only at thy hands).

---

[1] *persever* ] (par-sev'-er) persevere.

O Lord God of Israel, the lover of all faithful souls, vouchsafe to behold the labor and sorrow of me, thy poor creature. Assist me in all things with thy grace, and so strength me with heavenly strength, that neither my cruel enemy the fiend, neither my wretched flesh (which is not yet subject to the spirit), have victory or dominion over me. [1]

O what a life may this be called, where no trouble nor misery lacketh and where every place is full of snares of mortal enemies! For one trouble or temptation overpassed, another cometh, by and by; and the first conflict yet during, a new battle suddenly ariseth; wherefore, Lord Jesu, I pray thee, give me the grace to rest in thee above all things, and to quiet me in thee above all creatures; above all glory and honor, above all dignity and power, above all cunning and policy; above all health and beauty; above all richesse and treasure; above all joy and pleasure; above all fame and praise; above all mirth and consolation that man's heart may take or feel besides thee. For thou, Lord God, art best, most wise, most high, most mighty, most sufficient, and most full of all goodness, most sweet and most comfortable, most fair, most loving, most noble, most glorious, in whom all goodness most perfectly is. And therefore whatsoever I have beside thee, it is nothing to me; for my heart may not rest, ne fully be pacified but only in thee. [2]

O Lord Jesu, most loving spouse, who shall give me wings of perfect love, that I may fly up from these worldly miseries, and rest in thee? O when shall I ascend to thee, and see and feel how sweet thou art? When shall I wholly gather myself in thee so perfectly that I shall not for thy love feel myself, but thee only above myself, and above all worldly things, that thou may'st vouchsafe to visit me in such wise as thou dost visit thy most faithful lovers? [3]

Now I often mourn and complain of the miseries of this life, and with sorrow and great heaviness suffer them; for many things happen daily to me, which oftentimes trouble me, make me heavy, and darken mine understanding. They hinder me greatly and put my mind from thee, and so encumber me many ways that I cannot freely and clearly desire thee, ne have thy sweet consolations which with thy blessèd saints be always present. I beseech thee, Lord Jesu, that the sighings and inward desires of my heart may move and incline thee to hear me.

O Jesu, king of everlasting glory, the joy and comfort of all Christen people that are wandering as pilgrims in the wilderness of this world: my heart crieth to thee by still desires, and my silence speaketh unto thee and sayeth: How long tarryeth my Lord God to come to me? Come, O Lord, and visit me, for without thee I have no true joy. Without thee, my soul is heavy and sad. I am in prison and bound with fetters of sorrow, till thou, O Lord, with thy gracious presence, vouchsafe to visit me and to bring me again to liberty and joy of spirit, and to show thy favorable countenance unto me.

Open my heart, Lord, that I may behold thy laws; and teach me to walk in thy commandments. Make me to know and follow thy will, and to have always in my remembrance thy manifold benefits, that I may yield due thanks to thee for them. But I 'knowledge and confess for truth, that I am not able to give thee condign thanks for the least benefit that thou hast given me. [4]

O Lord, all gifts and virtues that any man hath in body or soul, natural or supernatural, be thy gifts, and come of thee, and not of our self, and they declare the great richesse° of thy mercy and goodness unto us. And though some have moe gifts than other, yet they all proceed from thee; and without thee, the least cannot be had. [5]

O Lord, I account it for a great benefit not to have many worldly gifts, whereby the laud and praise of men might blind my soul and deceive me. Lord, I know that no man ought to be abashed or miscontent that he is in a low estate in this world and lacketh the pleasures of this life, but rather to be glad and rejoice thereat – for so much as thou hast chosen the poor and meek persons, and such as are despised in the world, to be thy servants and familiar friends. Witness be thy blessèd apostles, whom thou madest chief pastors and spiritual governors of thy flock, which departed from the counsel of the Jews, rejoicing that they were counted worthy to suffer rebuke for thy name. Even so, O Lord, grant that I thy servant may be as well content to be taken as the least, as other be to be greatest; and that I be as well pleased to be in the lowest place as in the highest, and as glad to be of no reputation in the world, for thy sake, as other are to be noble and famous.

---

[1] *strength me* ] strengthen me.

[2] *during* ] enduring; lasting; *richesse* ] riches, opulence; *comfortable* ] comforting; *ne* ] nor.

[3] *wise* ] ways (*throughout*).

[4] *'knowledge* ] acknowledge; *condign* ] adequate.

[5] *moe* ] more.

Lord, it is the work of a parfit man never to sequester his mind from thee, and among many worldly cares to go without care – not after the manner of an idle or a dissolute person, but by the prerogative of a free mind, alway minding heavenly things and not cleaving by inordinate affection to any creature. I beseech thee therefore, my Lord Jesu, keep me from the superfluous cares of this world, that I be not inquieted with bodily necessities, ne that I be not taken with the voluptuous pleasures of the world, ne of the flesh. Preserve me from all things which hindereth my soul-health, that I be not overthrown with them. [1]

O Lord God, which art sweetness unspeakable, turn into bitterness to me all worldly and fleshly delights, which mought draw me from the love of eternal things, to the° love of short and vile pleasures. Let not flesh and blood overcome me, ne yet the world with his vainglory deceive me, nor the fiend with his manifold crafts supplant me; but give me ghostly strength in resisting them, patience in suffering them, and constance in persévering to the end. Give me, for all worldly delectations, the most sweet consolation of thy Holy Spirit, and for all fleshly love endue my soul with fervent love of thee. [2]

Make me strong inwardly in my soul, and cast out thereof all unprofitable cares of this world, that I be not° led by unstable desires of earthly things, but that I may repute all things in this world (as they be) transitory, and soon vanishing away, and myself also with them, drawing toward mine end; for nothing under the sun may long abide, but all is vanity and affliction of spirit. Give me, Lord, therefore, heavenly wisdom, that I may learn to seek and find thee, and above all things to love thee. Give me grace to withdraw me from them that flatter me, and patiently to suffer them that unjustly grieve me. Lord, when temptation or tribulation cometh, vouchsafe to succor me, that all may turn to my ghostly comfort; and patiently to suffer, and alway to say, "Thy name be blessed."

Lord, trouble is now at hand. I am not well, but I am greatly vexed with this present affliction. O most glorious Father, what shall I do? Anguish and trouble are on every side. Help now, I beseech thee, in this hour. Thou shalt be lauded and praised when I am perfectly made meek before thee, and when I am clearly delivered by thee. May it therefore please thee to deliver me? – for what may I (most sinful wretch) do? Or whither may I go for succor but to thee? Give me patience now at this time in all my troubles. Help me, Lord God, and I shall not fear ne dread what troubles soever fall upon me. And now what shall I say, but that thy will be done in me? I have deserved to be troubled and grieved; and therefore it behooveth that I suffer as long as it pleaseth thee. But would to God that I might suffer gladly till the furious tempests were overpassed, and that quietness of heart might come again! Thy mighty hand, Lord, is strong enough to take this trouble from me, and to assuage the cruel assaults thereof, that I be not overcome with them; as thou hast oftentimes done before this time – that when I am clearly delivered by thee, I may with gladness say, "The right hand of him that is highest hath made this change." Lord, grant me thy singular grace, that I may come thither where no creature shall lett me ne keep me from the perfit beholding of thee. For as long as any transitory thing keepeth me back or hath rule in me, I may not freely ascend to thee. [3]

O Lord, without thee nothing may long delight or please; for if anything should be liking and savory, it must be through help of thy grace, seasoned with the spice of thy wisdom. O everlasting light, far passing all things, send down the beams of thy brightness from above, and purify and lighten the inward parts of my heart. Quicken my soul, and all the powers thereof, that it may cleave fast and be joined to thee in joyful gladness of ghostly ravishings. O, when shall that blessèd hour come that thou shalt visit me and glad me with thy blessèd presence, when thou shalt be to me all in all? Verily, until that time come, there can be no perfect joy in me.

But alas, mine old man, that is, my carnal affections, live still in me, and are not crucified, nor perfitly° dead; for yet striveth the flesh against the spirit, and moveth great battle inwardly against me, and suffereth not the° kingdom of my soul to live in peace. But thou, good Lord – that hast the lordship over all, and power of the sea to assuage the rages and surges of the same – arise and help me! Destroy the power of mine enemies, which always make battle against me. Show forth the greatness of thy goodness, and let the power of thy right hand be glorified in me; for there is to me none other hope nor refuge but in thee only. My Lord, my God, to thee be honor and glory everlasting. [4]

---

[1] *parfit* ] perfect; *inquieted* ] disquieted; *ne that* ] and that.

[2] *mought* ] might; *ne yet* ] nor let; *ghostly* ] spiritual.

[3] *lett me* ] obstruct me; *perfit* ] perfect.

[4] *old man* ] human frailty.

O Lord, grant me that I may wholly resign myself to thee, and in all things to forsake myself, and patiently to bear my cross, and to follow thee. O Lord, what is man, that thou vouchsafest to have mind of him and to visit him? Thou art alway one, alway good, alway rightwise and holy, justly and blessèdly disposing all things after thy wisdom. But I am a wretch, and of myself alway ready and prone to evil, and do never abide in one state, but many times do vary and change. Nevertheless, it shall be better with me when it shall please thee, for thou, O Lord, only art he that mayest help me; and thou mayest so confirm and 'stablish me, that my heart shall not be changed from thee, but be surely fixed, and finally rest and be quieted in thee. I am nothing else of myself but vanity before thee, an unconstant creature and a feeble; and therefore, whereof may I rightfully glory? or why should I look to be magnified? [1]

Whoso pleaseth himself without thee, displeaseth thee; and he that delighteth in men's praisings, loseth the true praise before thee. The true praise is to be praised of thee and the true joy is to rejoice in thee; wherefore thy name (O Lord) be praised, and not mine. Thy works be magnified and not mine, and thy goodness be always lauded and blessed. Thou art my glory and the joy of my heart. In thee shall I glory, and joy in thee and not in myself, nor in any worldly honor or dignity (which, to thy eternal glory compared, is but a shadow and very vanity).

O Lord, we live here in great darkness, and are soon deceived with the vanities of this world, and are soon grieved with a little trouble; yet if I could behold myself well, I should plainly see that, what trouble soever I have suffered, it hath justly comen upon me, because I have often sinned and grievously offended thee. To me therefore confusion and despite is due; but to thee, laud, honor and glory. [2]

Lord, send me help in my troubles, for man's help is little worth. How often have I been disappointed, where I thought I should have found friendship? and how often have I found it, where as I least thought? – wherefore it is a vain thing to trust in man, for the true trust and health of man is only in thee. Blessed be thou, Lord, therefore, in all things that happeneth unto us, for we be weak and unstable, soon deceived, and soon changed from one thing to another. [3]

O Lord God, most righteous judge, strong and patient, which knowest the frailty and malice of man, be thou my whole strength and comfort in all necessities, for mine own conscience, Lord, sufficeth not; wherefore to thy mercy I do appeal, seeing no man may be justified ne appear righteous in thy sight, if thou examine him after thy justice.

O blessèd mansion of thy heavenly city, O most clearest day of eternity, whom the night may never darken! This is the day, alway clear and merry, alway sure, and never changing his state. [4]

Would to God this day might shortly appear and shine upon us, and that this world's° fantasies were at an end! This day shineth clearly to thy saints in Heaven with everlasting brightness, but to us pilgrims in earth, it shineth obscurely, and as through a mirror or glass. The heavenly citizens know how joyous this day is; but we outlaws, the children of Eve, weep and wail the bitter tediousness of our day, that is, of this present life, short and evil, full of sorrow and anguish – where man is oftentimes defiled with sin, encumbered with affliction, inquieted with troubles, wrapped in cares, busied with vanities, blinded with errors, overcharged with labors, vexed with temptations, overcome with vain delights and pleasures of the world, and grievously tormented with penury and need. O when shall th'end come of all these miseries? When shall I be clearly delivered from the bondage of sin? When shall I, Lord, have only mind on thee, and fully be glad and merry in thee? When shall I be free without letting, and be in perfect liberty without grief of body and soul? When shall I have peace without trouble, peace within and without and on every side, steadfast and sure?[5]

O Lord Jesu, when shall I stand and behold thee and have full sight and contemplation of thy glory? When shalt thou be to me all in all? and when shall I be with thee in thy kingdom, that thou hast ordained for thine elect people from the beginning? I am left here poor and as an outlaw, in the land of mine enemies, where daily be battles and great misfortunes. Comfort mine exile, assuage my sorrow, for all my desire is to be with thee. It is to me an unpleasant burden, what pleasure soever the world offereth me here. I desire to have inward fruition in thee, but I cannot attain thereto. I covet to cleave fast to heavenly things, but worldly affections pluck my mind downward. I would subdue all evil affections, but they daily rebel and rise against me, and will not be subject unto my spirit. Thus I (wretched

---

[1] *one* ] constant; *rightwise* ] righteous; *whereof may I rightfully glory?* ] what right have I to gloat?

[2] *despite* ] spite.

[3] *where as* ] where.

[4] *his* ] its; *this... day* ] the day of the biblical Last Judgment; the end of the world.

[5] *letting* ] hindrance.

creature) fight in myself, and am grievous to myself, while my spirit desireth to be upward, and, contrary, my flesh draweth me downward.

O, what suffer I inwardly! I go about to mind heavenly things, and straight a great rabble of worldly thoughts rush into my soul. Therefore Lord, be not long away, ne depart not in thy wrath from me. Send me the light of thy grace. Destroy in me all carnal desires. Send forth the hot flames of thy love, to burn and consume the cloudy fantasies of my mind.

Gather, O Lord, my wits and the powers of my soul together in thee, and make me to despise all worldly things, and by thy grace strongly to resist and overcome all motions and occasions of sin. Help me, thou everlasting truth, that no wordly guile nor vanity hereafter have power to deceive me. Come also, thou heavenly sweetness, and let all bitterness of sin flee far from me. Pardon me, and forgive me, as oft as in my prayer my mind is not surely fixed on thee. For many times I am not there, where I stand or sit; but rather there whither my thoughts carry me. For there I am, where my thought is; and there as customably is my thought, there is that that I love. [1]

And that oftentimes cometh into my mind, that by custom pleaseth me best, and that delighteth me most to think upon. Accordingly as thou dost say in thy gospel: "Where as a man's treasure is, there is his heart"; wherefore if I love Heaven I speak gladly thereof, and of such things as be of God and of that that appertaineth to his honor, and to the glorifying of his holy name. And if I love the world, I love to talk of worldly things and I joy anon in worldly felicity – and sorrow and lament soon for worldly adversity. If I love the flesh, I imagine oftentimes that [which°] pleaseth the flesh. If I love my soul, I delight much to speak and to hear of things that be for my soul-health. And whatsoever I love, of that I gladly hear and speak, and bear the images of them still in my mind. Blessed is that man that (for the love of the Lord) setteth not by the pleasures of this world, and learneth truly to overcome himself, and with the fervor of spirit crucifieth his flesh, so that in a clean and pure conscience he may offer his prayers to thee, and be accepted to have company of thy blessèd angels, all earthly things excluded from his heart.

Lord and holy Father, be thou blessed, now and ever; for as thou wilt, so is it done, and that thou dost is alway best. Let me, thy humble and unworthy servant, joy only in thee and not in myself, ne in anything else beside thee; for thou, Lord, art my gladness, my hope, my crown, and all mine honor. What hath thy servant, but that he hath of thee (and that, without his desert)? All things be thine; thou hast created and made them.[2]

I am poor, and have been in trouble and pain ever from my youth, and my soul hath been in great heaviness through manifold passions that come of the world and of the flesh; wherefore, Lord, I desire that I may have of thee the joy of inward peace. I ask of thee to come to that rest which is ordained for thy chosen children that be fed and nourished with the light of heavenly comforts; for without thy help, I cannot come to thee. Lord, give me peace, give me inward joy, and then my soul shall be full of heavenly melody, and be devout and fervent in thy lauds and praisings. But if thou withdraw thyself from me (as thou hast sometime done), then may not thy servant ren the way of thy commandments as I did before, for it is not with me as it was when the lantern of thy ghostly presence did shine upon my head and I was defended under the shadow of thy wings from all perils and dangers. [3]

O merciful Lord Jesu, ever to be praised, the time is come that thou wilt prove thy servant, and rightful is it that I shall now suffer somewhat for thee. Now is the hour comen that thou hast known from the beginning: that thy servant for a time should outwardly be set at nought, and inwardly to lean to thee; and that he should be despised in the sight of the world, and be broken with affliction, that he may after arise with thee in a new light and be clarified and made glorious in thy kingdom of Heaven. [4]

O holy Father, thou hast ordained it so to be, and it is done as thou hast commanded. This is thy grace, O Lord, to thy friend: to suffer him to be troubled in this world for thy love, how often soever it be, and of what person soever it be, and in what manner soever thou wilt suffer it to fall unto him. For without thy will or sufferance, what thing is done upon earth? It is good to me, O Lord, that thou hast meeken'd me, that I may thereby learn to know thy righteous judgments and to put from me all manner of presumption and stateliness of heart. It is very profitable for me that confusion hath covered my face, that I may learn thereby rather to seek to thee for help and succor, than to man. I have thereby learned to dread thy secret and terrible judgments, which scourgest the righteous with the sinner (but not without equity and justice).

---

[1] *there as customably* ] there where habitually.

[2] *that* ] that which; *again below* ("but that he hath ... ").

[3] *ren* ] run.

[4] *prove* ] test, examine.

Lord, I yield thanks to thee that thou hast not spared my sins, but hast punished me with scourges of love and hast sent me affliction and anguishes within and without. No creature under Heaven may comfort me but thou, Lord God, the heavenly leech of man's soul, which strikest and healest, which bringest a man nigh unto death and after restorest him to life again, that he may thereby learn to know his own weakness and imbecility, and the more fully to trust in thee, Lord. Thy discipline is laid upon me, and thy rod of correction hath taught me, and under that rod I wholly submit me. Strike my back and my bones, as it shall please thee, and make me to bow my crooked will unto thy will. Make me a meek and an humble disciple as thou hast sometime done with me, that I may walk after thy will. To thee I commit myself to be corrected – for better it is to be corrected by thee here than in time to come. [1]

Thou knowest all things, and nothing is hid from thee that is in man's conscience. Thou knowest all things to come before they fall, and it is not needful that any man teach thee or warn thee of anything that is done upon the earth. Thou knowest what is profitable for me, and how much tribulations helpen to purge away the rust of sin in me. Do with me after thy pleasure. I am a sinful wretch, to none so well known as to thee. Grant me, Lord, that to know, that is necessary to be known; that to love, that is to be loved; that to desire, that pleaseth thee; that to regard, that is precious in thy sight; and that to refuse, that is vile before thee. Suffer me not to judge thy mysteries after my outward senses, ne to give sentence after the hearing of the ignorant, but by true judgment to discern things spiritual, and above all things alway to search and follow thy will and pleasure.

O Lord Jesu, thou art all my richesse; and all that I have, I have it of thee. But what am I, Lord, that I dare speak to thee? I am thy poor creature and a worm most abject. Behold, Lord, I have nought, and of myself I am nought worth. Thou art only God, righteous and holy. Thou orderest all things, thou givest all things, and thou fulfillest all things with goodness. I am a sinner, barren and void of godly virtue. Remember thy mercies, and fill my heart with plenty of thy grace, for thou wilt not that thy works in me should be made in vain. How may I bear the misery of this life, except thy grace and mercy do comfort me?

Turn not thy face from me! Defer not thy visiting of me, ne withdraw not thy comforts, lest haply my soul be made as dry earth without the water of grace. Teach me, Lord, to fulfill thy will, to live meekly and worthily before thee – for thou art all my wisdom and cunning. Thou art he that knowest me as I am, that knewest me before the world was made and before I was born or brought into this life. To thee, O Lord, be honor, glory, and praise forever and ever. Amen.
*Laudes deum in eternum.* Amen.

• • •

In 1546, when the torture and burning of Anne Askew led to evidence that Queen Katherine and her circle were reading and circulating Reformist literature, Thomas Wriothesley (Lord Chancellor) and Stephen Gardiner (Bishop of Winchester) came to view Katherine as a potential menace, in the event of Henry's death. Wishing to avoid a minority regency by Edward's left-leaning stepmother, Wriothesley tried assiduously to poison her relationship with the King. One day the queen, in Gardiner's presence, dared to challenge Henry on religion. Henry dismissed her; and Gardiner began working on the King. Within 24 hours a warrant was drawn up for the Queen's arrest. Katherine learning of the warrant managed to escape prison by persuading the King she had debated with him only to take his mind off his physical disabilities, and to receive the benefit of his superior wisdom. When Wriothesley and his thugs arrived to arrest her, Henry called them knaves and sent them packing.

Henry's waistline now measured 54 inches. Mechanical devices were required to get him in and out of bed. The end came at Whitehall on 28 January 1546/7. (His dying words: "Monks! Monks! Monks!") Henry's massive and pocky corpse was laid to rest besides that of Queen Jane, beneath the floor of St. George's Chapel in Windsor Castle, without a marker.

Three days after King Henry's death, Edward Seymour made himself duke of Somerset and Lord Protector. Contrary to her expectations, Katherine was altogether excluded from the regency, and refused access to King Edward, whom she viewed as her adoptive son. Off-setting that disappointment was an annuity granted by the king's will of £7,000 (an enormous income, even for a woman with a large household).

The queen was expected to mourn the king for two years. But Thomas Seymour, brother of the Lord Protector and Katherine's former lover, waited in the wings. After Henry's death it was only a matter of time until that old flame was rekindled—in fact, not more than a week.

[1] *leech* ] physician (by association with the leeches that physicians used to draw blood).

**[Katherine Parr to Lord Thomas Seymour (February 1546/7)°]**

My Lord,

I send you my most humble and hearty commendations, being desirous to know how ye have done since I saw you. I pray you be not offended with me in that I send sooner to you than I said I would (for my promise was "but once in a fortnight"). Howbeit, the time is well abbreviated! – by what means I know not, except weeks be shorter at Chelsea than in other places.

My lord your brother hath deferred answering such requests as I made to him till his coming hither, which he sayeth shall be immediately after the term. (This is not his first promise I have received of his coming, and yet unperformed. I think my lady hath taught him that lesson; for it is her custom to promise many comings to her friends, and to perform none. I trust in greater matters she is more circumspect.)[1]

And thus, my lord, I make my end, bidding you most heartily farewell, wishing you the good I would myself. From Chelsea.

[*P.S.*] I would not have you to think that this mine honest goodwill toward you to proceed of any sudden motion of passion: for as truly as God is God, my mind was fully bent the other time I was at liberty to marry you, before any man I knew. Howbeit, God withstood my will therein most vehemently for a time; and through His grace and goodness made that possible which seemed to me most impossible – that was, made me to renounce utterly mine own will, and to follow His will most willingly. It were too long to write all the process of this matter. If I live, I shall declare it to you myself. I can say nothing, but as my lady of Suffolk sayeth, "God is a marvelous man!"[2]

By her that is yours to serve and obey during her life,
Kathryn the Queen, K.P.

**[Lord Thomas Seymour to Dowager Queen Katherine (March 1546/7)°]**

The like humble and hearty recommendations I send your Highness that I received. And being more desirous to hear from you than (as I thought) ye desired to hear from [me,°] as yesterday in the morning I had written a letter unto your Highness ... which letter being finished, and my hand thereat, remembered your commandment to me; wherewith I threw it into the fire, by minding to keep your requests and desires. And, for that it hath pleased you to be the first breaker of your appointment, I shall desire you Highness to receive my thanks! ... I beseech your Highness to put all fancies out of your head that might bring you in any one thought that I do think that the goodness you have showed me is of "any sudden motion" – as at leisure your Highness shall know, to both our contentations...

From the body of him whose heart ye have,
T. Seymour

**[Dowager Queen Katherine to Lord Thomas Seymour (April 1547)°]**

My Lord,...

Whereas ye charge me with a promise written with mine own hand, "to change the two years into two months," I think ye have no such plain sentence written with *my* hand! I know not whether ye be a paraphraser or not. If ye be learnèd in that science, it is possible ye may of one word make a whole sentence – and yet not at all times after the true meaning of the writer – as it appeareth by this your exposition upon my writing.

When it shall be your pleasure to repair hither, ye must take some pain to come early in the morning, that ye may be gone again by seven o'clock, and so I suppose ye may come without suspect. (I pray you, let me have knowledge near night at what hour ye will come, that your porteress may wait at the gate to the fields for you.)

And thus, with my most humbly and hearty commendations, I take my leave of you for this time, give you like thanks for your coming to the court when I was there. From Chelsea....

By her that is and shall be your humble, true, and loving wife during her life,
Katherine the Queen KP

---

[1] Katherine demanded that her jewels (mostly gifts from Henry) be returned to her; Somerset and his wife said she could not have them, that the jewels belonged to the Crown and would someday be worn by Edward's queen.

[2] *my lady of Suffolk* ] Katherine Parr's friend and confidante, Katherine Brandon, duchess of Suffolk.

### [Lord Thomas Seymour to Dowager Queen Katherine (17 May 1547)°]

...I received from your Highness (by my sister Herbert) your commendations; which were more *welcome*, than they were *sent.*[1] And (after the same) she waded further with me touching my being with your Highness at Chelsea – which I denied (being with your Highness); but that, "Indeed, I went by the garden, as I went to see the Bishop of London's house" – and at this point, stood with her for a time till at the last she told me further tokens, which made me change colors, who like a false wench, took me with the manner![2]

...If I knew by what means I might gratify your highness for your goodness to me, showed at our last meeting together, it should not be slacked to declare mine to you again. And to that intent that I will be more bound unto your Highness, I do make my request that (if it be not painful to your Highness) that once in three days I may receive three lines in a letter from you (and as many lines and letters more as shall seem good unto your Highness!). Also, I shall desire your Highness to give me one of your small pictures, if you have any left – who, with his silence,[3] shall give me occasion to think on the friendly cheer that I shall receive when my [love]suit shall be at an end! And thus, for fear of troubling your Highness with my long and rude letter, I take my leave of your Highness – wishing that my hap may be once so good, that I may declare so much, by mouth, at the same hour that this was writing, which was twelve of the clock in the night! This Tuesday, the seventeenth of May, at Saint James....

From him whom ye have bound to honor, love, and such in all lawful thing obey,
T. Seymour

### [Dowager Queen Katherine to Lord Thomas Seymour (c. 24 May 1547)°]

My Lord, ...I think to see the king one day this week; at which time I would be glad to see you (though I shall scarce dare ask or speak).[4] I shall most willingly observe your commandment of writing to you once in three days, thinking myself not a little bound to you (that it hath pleased you, too, so to command me!). I have sent in haste to the painteress for one of my little pictures, which is very perfect, by the judgment of as many as hath seen the same. The last I had myself, I bestowed it upon my lady of Suffolk. (This letter had been sooner with you but for tarrying the coming of the picture, the which I am not certain to receive at this time. If I cannot perform your request at this season, I shall not fail to accomplish the same shortly.)

My Lord, whereas you desire to know how ye might "gratify" my goodness showed to you at your being here, I can require nothing for the same, more than ye say I have, which is your heart and goodwill during your life: praying you to perform that, and I am fully satisfied. When you be at leisure, let me hear from you; I dare not desire to see you for fear of suspicion. I would the world were as well pleased with our meaning as, I am well assured, the goodness of God is. But the world is so wicked that it cannot be contented with good things. And thus, with my most humble and hearty commendations, I take my leave for this time, wishing your well-doing no less than mine own.

From Chelsea, by her that is yours to serve and obey during her life
Katherine the Queen KP

### [Dowager Queen Katherine to Lord Thomas Seymour (c. 25 May 1547)°]

My Lord, This shall be to advertise you that my lord your brother hath this afternoon a little made me warm:[5] it was fortunate we were so much distant, for I suppose else I should have bitten him! What cause have they to fear you having such a wife? It is requisite for them continually to pray for a short dispatch of that hell! Tomorrow, or else upon Saturday at afternoon about three o'clock, I will see the King; where I intend to utter all my choler to my lord your brother, if you shall not give me advice to the contrary. For I would be loath to do anything to hinder your matter.... From Chelsea in great haste.

Your humble, true, and loving wife in her heart,
Katherine the Queen KP

---

[1] *my sister Herbert* ] i.e., Katherine's sister, Anne (Parr) Herbert (1515-1552), countess of Pembroke, a survivor who served as lady-in-waiting to each of Henry's six queens; Katherine and Seymour are now betrothed.

[2] *colors ... manner* ] by my blushing, Anne Herbert caught me in the act of fibbing.

[3] *his silence* ] i.e., of the silent picture (possessive *its* was not yet entered into English).

[4] *the king* ] after Henry's death, Katherine was permitted only by appointment to see her stepson, King Edward VI.

[5] *warm* ] angry (When Edward Seymour learned of the betrothal, he wrote Katherine with a reprimand).

**[Lord Thomas Seymour to Dowager Queen Katherine (c. 31 May 1547)°]**

After my humble recommendations (with thanks that ye have admitted me one of your counselors), I perceive that your Highness hath been "warmed" – whereof I am *glad,* for that ye shall not think on the "two years" ye wrote of in your last letter before this! …

From him that is your loving and faithful husband during his life,
T. Seymour

In May or June, Thomas Seymour took Katherine to wife, in defiance of the Privy Council and of his brother, the Lord Protector Somerset – and to the great displeasure of Princess Mary, who held that true love was no excuse for a 35-year-old widow to abbreviate her period of mourning for her father the King.

By December, the dowager queen was pregnant, which came as a surprise: her three previous marriages had never resulted in a pregnancy. Katherine Parr was now at the height of her happiness.

Her husband, however, was not. When Edward Seymour seized the reins of government, he appointed his brother Lord High Admiral; but Sir Thomas was deeply unsatisfied with his limited role in the new regime. Always a schemer, he took steps to advance himself. The plan at first went well enough. In January 1546/7, immediately after Henry's death, Princess Elizabeth, 13, had been sent to live with dowager queen Katherine, at Whitehall and Chelsea. That spring, the parents of Lady Jane Grey (age 10, and fourth in line to the succession) sent her to live with Katherine as well. Seymour then cut a secret deal with Lady Jane's father: the contract granted Seymour legal custody of Lady Jane in exchange for £2000 and Seymour's promise to effect her betrothal to King Edward.

In September, when Somerset went north to fight the Scots (scoring a major victory at Pinkie on 10 September), brother Thomas took the opportunity to curry King Edward's favor with generous gifts. (Edward remarked, "My Uncle of Somerset dealeth very hardly with me and keepeth me so strait that I cannot have money at my will. But my Lord Admiral both sends me money and gives me money.")[1] Seymour was now cohabiting with Princess Elizabeth, Lady Jane, and pregnant Katherine. Confident that he had his hands securely on the reins of his advancement, he soon had his hands all over Princess Elizabeth. Katherine being indisposed by her pregnancy, Seymour tried his charms on his royal stepdaughter, who responded warmly (a story told, partly from Elizabeth's own testimony, in *Women's Works,* volume 2). Katherine, in despair over this flirtation but seeking to keep hubby happy, joined in the horseplay, on occasion; but in May 1548, after Seymour had been found in Elizabeth's arms or bed one too many times, the 13-year-old princess was exiled to Hatfield, for fear of a pregnancy – which by June was (falsely) rumored throughout London already to have happened.

Katherine, six months pregnant, did what she could to awaken Seymour's sense of responsibility, and to recover his affection:

**[Katherine to Thomas Seymour, on the baby's movement (11 June 1548)°]**

My Lord,

…I gave your little knave your blessing, who like an honest man stirred apace, after and before. For Mary Odell, being abed with me, had laid her hand upon my belly to feel it stir. It hath stirred these three days every morning and evening so that I trust when ye come it will make you some pastime! And thus I end, bidding my sweetheart and loving husband better to fare than myself.

From Hanworth this Saturday in the morning…by your most loving, obedient, and humble wife,
Katherine the Queen KP

Two days later, to prepare for her lying in, Katherine removed (with Lady Jane) to her husband's castle of Sudeley, Gloucestershire, then one of the most magnificent palaces in England. And on 30 August 1548, she gave birth to her only child, a daughter, Mary Seymour. The queen, taking infection, never recovered. By 3 September, Katherine knew she was dying. Her former lady-in-waiting, Elizabeth Tyrwhitt, at her bedside till the end, reports an unhappy scene when Seymour appeared to pay his last respects:

[1] Sir Thomas Seymour, Hatfield House (Hertfordshire), Salisbury (Cecil) MS 150, fol. 112r.

### [The Confession of Elizabeth Tyrwhitt concerning the Death of Katherine Parr°]

[T]wo days afore the death of the Queen, at my coming to her in the morning, she asked me where I had been so long, and said unto me, she did fear such things in herself, that she was sure she could not live: Whereunto I answered as I thought, that I saw no likelihood of death in her. She, then having my Lord Admiral by the hand (and divers others standing by), spake these words, partly, as I took it, idly: "My Lady Tyrwhitt, I am not well handled, for those that be about me careth not for me, but standeth laughing at my grief, and the more good I will to them, the less good they will to me."

Whereunto my Lord Admiral answered, "Why sweetheart, *I* would you no hurt!"

And she said to him again aloud, "No, my Lord, I think so" – and immediately she said to him in his ear, "but, my Lord, you *have* given me many shrewd taunts!" Those words I perceived she spoke with good memory, and very sharply and earnestly, for her mind was far unquieted.

My Lord Admiral perceiving that I heard it, called me aside, and asked me what she said; and I declared it plainly to him. Then he consulted with me, that he would lie down on the bed by her, to look if he could pacify her unquietness with gentle communication; whereunto I agreed.

And by that time he had spoken three or four words to her, she answered him very roundly and shortly, saying "My Lord, I would have given a thousand marks to have had my full talk with [Dr.] Huicke, the first day I was delivered, but I durst not, for displeasing of *you*." And I, hearing that, perceived her trouble to be so great, that my heart would serve me to hear no more. Such-like communication she had with him the space of an hour; which they did hear that sat by her bedside.

Elizabeth Tyrwhitt

• • •

On 5 September 1548, Katherine died of puerperal fever, the result of unsanitary conditions at her delivery, the same thing that killed queens Elizabeth of York (1503) and Jane Seymour (1537).

Before she passed, Katherine dictated her last will and testament, bequeathing to her well-beloved husband all of her possessions, "wishing them to be a thousand times more in value than they were." Seymour wasted no time taking the inventory.[1] Katherine's net worth at her death is beyond calculation. But Seymour lost more than Katherine's royal pension £7,000; he lost the protection of King Edward, who loved his late stepmother better than he loved the Lord Admiral her husband; especially after rumors that Seymour had seduced Elizabeth during Katherine's pregnancy – a project that Seymour after Katherine's death pursued with renewed urgency. But in his haste to wed and bed Princess Elizabeth, the Lord Admiral overstepped himself. Condemned for treason, Thomas Seymour was beheaded on March 20th.

In 1782, the body of Queen Katherine, wrapped in cerecloth within a leaden envelope, was discovered by ladies exploring the ruins of Sudeley Castle. They peeled back the lead from her face and breast, and were surprised to see her features, "particularly the eyes, in the most perfect state of preservation. Alarmed with this sight, and with the smell which came from the cerecloth, they ordered the earth to be thrown in immediately, without closing over the cerecloth and lead that covered the face....In the same summer Mr. John Lucas, the person who rented the land on which the ruins of the chapel stand, removed the earth from the leaden coffin...Mr. Lucas had the curiosity to rip up the top of the coffin, and found the whole body, wrapped in six or seven linen cerecloths, entire and uncorrupted...He made an incision through the cerecloths which covered one of the arms of the corpse, the flesh of which at that time was white and moist."[2] After taking a few locks of her hair for a souvenir, Lucas closed the coffin and shut up the crypt. It was opened a year later by Emma Dent, "to satisfy my own curiosity."[3] This story being bruited abroad, Katherine's body became a late-night tourist attraction for ruffians. "In 1784 the body was again dug up and treated in the most irreverent manner"; again in 1786; again in 1792 by drunks who, for a laugh, turned the coffin upside down.[4] In 1810, Lord Rivers of Stratfield Saye sold the ruined castle to Richard Temple Nugent Brydges Chandos Grenville, Duke of Buckingham. Katherine's remains being included with the sale, Lord Chandos in 1817 again opened the coffin for a peek – by which time only a skeleton remained, and no jewelry. In 1965, a lock of Queen Katherine's hair, removed from the corpse, was put on display in the British Library. She has not been seen since.

---

[1] Will of Katherine Parr Seymour, National Archives, PROB 11/32, fol. 19; inventory at Sudeley Castle archives; for details, see Richard Davey, *The Nine Days' Queen* (1909), 141-2. Lady Jane Grey was chief mourner at the funeral.

[2] *British Architect and Engineer* (25 August 1876): 119.

[3] Emma Dent (1877), 315-17.

[4] *Architect,* ibid., and Dent, 318-20.

# Anne Askew (ca. 1520-1546)

*He answered that I was a woman, and that he was nothynge deceyved in me.*
— from *The First Examination*

NNE ASKEW, Protestant evangelist and martyr, was the daughter of Sir William Askew of Stallingborough, Lincolnshire, by his first wife, Elizabeth Wrottesley. Her father, knighted by Henry VIII in 1513, was appointed high sheriff of Lincolnshire in 1521; he sat as MP from Grimsby in 1529, and was very old school. About 1534, Sir William betrothed his elder daughter Martha to Thomas Kyme of nearby Friskney. When Martha died before the wedding, Askew substituted Anne, against the girl's will. Johan Bale reports that "Notwithstanding, the marriage once past, she demeaned herself like a Christen wife," giving birth to at least two children before religious convictions led to domestic unrest: "In process of time," writes Bale, "by oft reading of the sacred Bible, she fell clearly from all old superstitions of papistry, to a perfit belief in Jesus Christ" (H8r).[1] Well read and a skilled debater, Anne Kyme soon developed local notoriety. Concerned friends advised her to avoid Lincoln, for the priests there would assault her and put her to great trouble "as thereof they had made their boast" (E7r). Rising to the challenge, Anne traveled to Lincoln in December 1544 and remained there for six days, reading her Bible in the Cathedral, without serious incident. But "she so offended the priests" that Thomas Kyme "at their suggestion violently drove her out of his house" (E8v). There was no going home to Mom and Dad: both of her parents were now dead; and her siblings were in London.

The Jesuit polemicist Robert Parsons, years later, mocks Bale for calling Askew "a young wench of a worshipful house, and of elegant beauty and rare wit." "But when Bale calleth Anne Askew *iuvencula,* a young heifer or steer that abideth no yoke," quips Parsons, "he seemeth not to be far amiss! for-that she was a coy dame, and of very evil fame for wantonness, in that she left the company of her husband to gad up and down the country, a-gospelling and gossipping where she might (and ought not!). And this, for divers years before her imprisonment."[2]

Anne had connections in London: her brother Edward had been a gentleman retainer to Archbishop Cranmer and was now cupbearer to King Henry; her half-brother Christopher had been a gentleman of the Privy Chamber until his death in 1543. The family had various connections with barristers and JPs at the Inns of court, and with wealthy sympathizers who were suspected of funneling money into the Reform movement. Given Katherine Parr's reputed support for the reformists, Askew doubtless entertained at least some hopes of hitching her wagon to a star.

Receiving a loan from one of her brothers, Askew in the winter of 1544/5 set out for London with Joan Bocher, a maidservant. Having renounced her married name, Askew resolved to seek a divorce on grounds of abandonment. The petition for divorce went nowhere; but with so many kindred spirits in the capital, the two women chose to stay on.

With King Henry in declining health and Prince Edward's intentions unclear, paranoia reigned on both sides of the Church aisle. Protestant martyrs in 1543/4 included William Anderson, James Finlayson, James Hunter, and Robert Lamb, hanged in Perth; Henry Filmer, Anthony Pearson, and Robert Testwood, burnt at the stake in Windsor; James Raveleson, burnt at the stake in Perth; Helen Stark, forcibly drowned in Perth; and Adam Danlin, hung, drawn, and quartered in Calais. Catholic martyrs that same year included Thomas Ashby, Martin Coudres, German Gardiner, John Ireland, John Larke, and Robert Singleton, executed at Tyburn. The safest thing was to go about one's business, and express no opinions.

Askew was soon brought to the attention of the orthodoxy police. Parsons reports that "she did in secret seek to corrupt divers people, but especially women."[3] An agent of Sir Thomas Wriothesley, Lord Chancellor, took lodgings next to Askew's chamber at the Inner Temple, where she lived with her brother; and kept watch on her activities, day and night. Her residence was repeatedly searched; and for a time she was forced into hiding. But Wriothesley's spy finally had no evil to report of her except that the woman from Lincolnshire spent entirely too much time praying at an open window.

---

[1] Sig. refs. are to Johan Bale, ed., *The first examinacio̅ of Anne Askewe* (1546), *STC* 1470.

[2] Robert Parsons, *The Third Part of a Treatise ... of Three Conversions of England* (1604), 2:493-5.

[3] ibid., 2.493.

What finally led to Askew's arrest was an intercepted letter, one that evidently incriminated her in the distribution of Reformist literature at Court, which raised the ire of the King. Edward Askew reports that "Mine aunt after many threats and great search made for her by the prelates her persecutors, was by casual intercepting of her own letter discovered; and so unwillingly delivered into their bloody hands by him that both loved her and the religion she professed."[1] "Overcome with fear (for he had much to lose, lest haply, by concealing what was known he knew, he might so have brought himself into trouble)," the unnamed kinsman agreed to turn State's evidence. On 10 March 1544/5, under the Six Articles Act, the Aldermen of London ordered the arrest of Anne Askew on suspicion of heresy. Interrogated at Sadler Hall, she was then imprisoned in the Counter for twelve days, where she declined to be shriven except by Reformist priests. Her cousin, Christopher Britain, a barrister, was finally allowed to visit her and to begin negotiations concerning bail. But when a doubt arose concerning the credibility of the State's only witness, the charges against her were dropped. Askew returned to her chambers at the Temple and sat down to write an account of her ordeal.

*The First Examinacyon of Anne Askewe* (1546) was printed at Wesel in Germany, with introduction, conclusion, and notes by Johan Bale; copies of which were then smuggled back into England. A year later, Bale published *The Lattre Examinacyon of Anne Askewe*. By that time, Henry VIII was dead and Protestants were in the ascendancy. It was not until after the Marian persecutions, and the publication of John Foxe's *Actes and Monuments of the Christian Church,* that Anne Askew emerged as one of the great heroes of the Protestant Reformation in England; but she is also one of the movement's great prose stylists. With every encounter, Askew proved herself both intellectually and morally superior to her persecutors, all the while maintaining the speaking position of a modest Christian woman who claimed no right to speak except when called upon the authorities.

The *Examinations* of Anne Askew proved what Wriothesley and his ilk most feared: educated and articulate women represented a threat to the patriarchal authority of both Church and State. In the end, Anne Askew's wit, no less than her interpretation of Scripture, was the crime for which she died. Moreover, others took inspiration from her. Parsons a half-century later cites Anne Askew thereby to illustrate how one woman's heresy leads inevitably to more, and worse: "[T]he proud and presumptuous answers, quips and nips, which she gave – both in matter of religion and otherwise to the King's Council and bishops when they examined her and dealt with her seriously for her amendment – do well show her intolerable arrogancy. And if she had lived but few years longer, it is very likely she would have come to the point that her dear sister, disciple, and handmaid Joan of Kent (alias Knell, alias Bocher) did: Whom she used most confidently in sending heretical books hither and thither, but especially into the Court." Joan Bocher "*denied openly*, within four years after, *that our Savior took flesh of the blessèd Virgin*! And being condemned to the fire by Cranmer and other bishops, and Councilors in King Edward's days for the same, ... she said scornfully unto them: 'It is not long ago since you condemned and burned that notable holy woman, Anne Askew, for a piece of bread. And now you will burn *me*, for a piece of flesh. But as ye are now come to believe that yourselves which ye condemned in her, and are sorry for her burning, so will the time come quickly, that you will believe that which now you condemn in me, and be sorry for this wrong done unto me.'"[2]

Applauding the use of the rack for such women, Parsons reports that King Henry from the interrogation of Askew learned so much about his sixth wife, Katherine Parr, that he wisely "purposed to have burned her, too, if had he lived." And indeed, shortly after the execution of Askew, a warrant was issued for the arrest of Katherine Parr. She persuaded his Majesty that she wished only to learn from his wisdom. When Wriothesley arrived to arrest her, King Henry sent him away, calling him a fool and beast. "The principal occasion against her," writes Parsons, "was for heretical books found in her closet brought or sent her in by Anne Askew; whereof the witnesses were the Lady Herbert, Lady Lane, Lady Tyrwhitt, and others. And by *that* occasion was the said Anne Askew put to the rack: *for the discovery of the Truth*."[3]

DWF

---

[1] Edward Ayscu, *A Historie* (London, 1607), 308.

[2] Parsons, *A Treatise of Three Conversions of England* (1603; repr. 1688), 202-3.

[3] ibid., 493. Parsons further cites as one of his sources Sir Francis Englefield, a retainer in Princess Mary's household and later one of Mary's Privy Councilors.

## The First Examination

By Anne Askew

TO SATISFY YOUR EXPECTATION, good people,° this was my first examination, in the° year of our Lord 1545, and in the month of March. First Christopher Dare examined me at Sadler's Hall, being one of the quest, and asked if I did not believe that the sacrament hanging over the altar was the very body of Christ really. Then I demanded this question of him, wherefore St. Stephen was stoned to death? And he said he could not tell. Then I answered that no more would I assoil his vain question.[1]

Secondly, he said that there was a woman which did testify that I should read how God was not in temples made with hands. Then I showed him the seventh and the seventeenth chapter of the Apostles' Acts, what Stephen and Paul had said therein – whereupon he asked me how I took those sentences. I answered that I would not throw pearls among swine, for acorns were good enough. [2]

Thirdly, he asked me wherefore I said that I had rather to read five lines in the Bible than to hear five masses in the temple. I confessed that I said no less – not for the dispraise of either the epistle or gospel, but because the one did greatly edify me, and the other nothing at all; as Saint Paul doth witness in the fourteenth chapter of his first epistle to the Corinthes,° where as he doth say, "If the trump giveth an uncertain sound, who will prepare himself to the battle?" [3]

Fourthly, he laid unto my charge that I should say if an ill priest minist'red, it was the devil and not God. My answer was that I never spake such thing; but this was my saying, that whatsoever he were which minist'red unto me, his ill conditions could not hurt my faith; but in spirit I received, nevertheless, the body and blood of Christ.

Fifthly, he asked me what I said concerning confession. I answered him my meaning, which was as St. James sayeth, that every man ought to acknowledge° his faults to other, and the one to pray for the other.

Sixthly, he asked me what I said to the king's book. And I answered him that I could say nothing to it, because I never saw it. [4]

Seventhly, he asked me if I had the spirit of God in me. I answered, if I had not, I was but a reprobate or castaway. Then he said he had sent for a priest to examine me, which was there at hand. The priest asked me what I said to the sacrament of the altar, and required much to know therein my meaning. But I desired him again to hold me excused concerning that matter. None other answer would I make him, because I perceived him a papist.

Eighthly, he asked me if I did not think that private masses did help souls departed. And I said it was great idolatry to believe more in them than in the death which Christ died for us.

Then they had me from° thence unto my Lord Mayor. And he examined me as they had before, and I answered him directly in all things, as I answered the quest afore. [5]

Besides this, my Lord Mayor laid one thing unto my charge which was never spoken of me, but of them – and that was, whether a mouse eating the host received God, or no? This question did I never ask; but, indeed, they asked it of me, whereunto I made them no answer, but smiled. [6]

Then the Bishop's chancellor rebuked me – and said that I was much to blame for uttering the Scriptures: for St. Paul (he said) forbode° women to speak or to talk of the Word of God. I answered him that I knew Paul's meaning so well as he, which is (1 Cor. 14)° that a woman ought not to speak in the congregation by the way of teaching. And then I asked him how many women he had seen go into the pulpit and preach. He said he never saw none. Then I said he ought to find no fault in poor women, except they had offended the law. [7]

---

[1] *Sadler's Hall* ] situated in Cheapside, London; *quest* ] inquest; *assoil* ] examine and solve.

[2] *should* ] (throughout) *in modern usage*, would.

[3] i.e., to read five lines in the English Bible than to hear five Latin masses. The Coverdale version was printed in 1535 and 1537; the Matthew, in 1537; the Taverner, in 1539; and the Great Bible seven times from 1539 -1541.

[4] *the king's book* ] i.e., *The Erudition of a Christian Man* (1543), the second (greatly revised) edition of *The Institution of a Christian Man* (1537), which set forth the dogmas of the English Church.

[5] *Lord Mayor* ] Sir Martin Bowes, mayor of London.

[6] *spoken of me ... of them* ] spoken by me ... by them; *host* ] the consecrated bread of the eucharist.

[7] *bishop's chancellor* ] Thomas Bawghe alias Williams (ca. 1501- ca.1558), archdeacon of Surrey.

My Lord Mayor, Sir Martin Bowes, sitting with the Council (as most meet for his wisdom, and seeing her standing upon life and death): "I pray you," quoth he, "my lords, give *me* leave to speak with this woman." Leave was granted.

*Lord Mayor.* Thou foolish woman, sayest thou that the priests cannot make the body of Christ?
*A. Askew.* I say so, my lord. For I have read that God made man, but that man can make God, I never yet read, nor I suppose ever shall read it."
*Lord Mayor.* *No*, thou foolish woman? After the words of consecration, is it not the Lord's body?
*A. Askew.* No, it is but consecrated bread, or sacramental bread.
*Lord Mayor.* What if a mouse eat it, after the consecration? What shall become of the mouse? What sayest thou, thou foolish woman?
*A. Askew.* What shall become of her say *you,* my lord?
*Lord Mayor.* I say, that mouse is *damned.*
*A. Askew.* Alack, poor mouse!

By this time, my lords heard enough of my Lord Mayor's divinity; and perceiving that some could not keep in their laughing, proceeded to the butchery and slaughter that they intended afore they came hither.

(John Strype, *Ecclesiastical Memorials,* 1.387, from John Louth, archdeacon of Nottingham)

Then my Lord Mayor commaunded me to ward. I asked him if sureties° would not serve me. And he made me short answer, that he would take none. Then was I had to the counter, and there remained twelve days, no friend admitted to speak with me. [1]

But in the meantime, there was a priest sent to me which said that he was commaunded of the bishop to examine me and to give me good counsel (which he did not). But first he asked me for what cause I was put in the counter. And I told him I could not tell. Then he said it was great pity that I should be there without cause, and concluded that he was very sorry for me. Secondly, he said it was told him that I should deny the sacrament of the altar. And I answered him again, that that I had said, I had said. Thirdly, he asked me if I were shriven. I told him no. Then he said he would bring one to me for to shrive me. And I told him, so that I might have one of these three, that is to say, Dr. Crome, Sir Gillam, or Huntington, I was contented, because I knew them to be men of wisdom: "As for you or any other, I will not dispraise, because I know ye not." [2]

Then he said, "I would not have you think but that I or another that shall be brought you shall be as honest as they; for if we were not, ye may be sure the king would not suffer° us to preach." Then I answered by the saying of Solomon, "By communing with the wise I may learn wisdom; but by talking with a° fool I shall take scathe" (Prov. 1). Fourthly, he asked me if the host should fall, and a beast did eat it, whether the beast did receive God or no? I answered, "Seeing ye have taken the pains to ask this question, I desire you also to take so much pain more as to assoil° it yourself; for I will not do it, because I perceive ye come to tempt me." And he said it was against the order of schools that he which asked the question should answer it. I told him I was but a woman, and knew not the course of schools. Fifthly, he asked me if I intended to receive the sacrament at Easter, or no? I answered, that else I were no Christen woman, and that° I did rejoice that the time was so near at hand. And then he departed thence, with many fair words.

And the twenty-third day of March my cousin Britain came into the counter to me, and asked there whether I might be put to bail, or no? Then went he immediately unto my Lord Mayor, desiring of him to

---

[1] *ward* ] custody; *sureties* ] persons bonded to be responsible for another; *counter* ] prison attached to the city court.

[2] *bishop* ] Edmund Bonner (1500-1569), bishop of London 1540-49, 1553-59; chiefly responsible for the persecution of Protestants during Mary's reign (1553-58); refused oath of supremacy at accession of Elizabeth; died in prison; *shriven* ] confessed and given absolution; *Dr. Crome* ] Dr. Edward Crome (ca. 1584-1562), rector of St. Mary Aldermary, London (a benefice obtained for him in 1539 by Anne Boleyn), and a reformist; *Sir Gillam* ] or, Sir Guilliam; not certainly identified; *Huntington* ] John Huntington, author of *The Genealogy of Heretics* (1542, not extant; repr. in Johan Bale, ed., *A Mysterye of Inyquyte* [Geneva, 1545]); converted to the Reformist cause between 1542 and 1545.

be so good lord unto me, that I might be bailed. My lord answered him and said that he would be glad to do the best that in him lay; howbeit, he could not bail me without the consent° of a spiritual officer – so requiring him to go and speak with the chancellor of London – for, he said, like as he could not commit me to prison without the consent of a spiritual officer, no more could he bail me without consent of the same.

So, upon that, he went to the Chancellor, requiring of him as he did afore of my Lord Mayor. He answered him that the matter was so heinous, that he durst not of himself do it, without my lord of London were made privy thereunto; but he said he would speak unto my lord in it, and bade him repair unto him the next morrow and he should well know° my lord's pleasure.

And upon the morrow after, he came thither and spake both with the Chancellor and with my lord Bishop of London. My lord declared unto him that he was very well contented° that I should come forth to a communication, and appointed me to appear afore° him the next day after, at three of the clock at afternoon. Moreover he said unto him that he would there should be at that examination such learnèd men as I was affectioned to, that they might see and also make report that I was handled with no rigor. He answered him that he knew no man that I had more affection to than other. Then said the Bishop, "Yes, as I understand, she is affectioned to Dr. Crome, Sir Gillam, Whitehead, and Huntington, that they might hear the matter, for she did know them to be learnèd and of a godly judgment." [1]

Also he required my cousin Britain that he should earnestly persuade me to utter even the very bottom of my heart. And he sware by his fidelity that no man should take any advauntage of my words, neither yet would he lay aught to my charge for anything that I should there speak; but if I said any manner of thing amiss, he, with other more, would be glad to reform me therein with most godly counsel.

On the morrow after, my lord of London sent for me at one of the clock, his hour being appointed at three. And as I came before him, he said he was very sorry of my trouble, and desired to know my opinion in such matters as were laid against me. He required me also in any wise boldly to utter the secrets of my heart, bidding me not to fear in any point; for whatsoever I did say within his house, no man should hurt me for it. I answered, "Forsomuch as your lordship appointed three of the clock, and my friends shall not come till that hour, I desire you to pardon me of giving answer till they come."

Then said he that he thought it meet to send for those four men which were afore-named and appointed. Then I desired him not to put them to the pain, for it should not need, because the two gentlemen which were my friends were able enough to testify that I should say. Anon after, he went into his gallery with Master Spilman and willed him in any wise that he should exhort me to utter all that I thought. [2]

In the meanwhile he commaunded his archdeacon to commune° with me, who said unto me, "Mastress, wherefore are ye° accused?" I answered, "Ask° my accusers, for I know not as yet." Then took he my book out of my hand and said, "Such books as this is hath brought you to the trouble ye are in. Beware," sayeth he, "beware – for he that made it was brent in Smithfield." Then I asked him if he were sure that it was true that he had spoken. And he said he knew well the book was of John Frith's making. Then I asked him if he were not ashamed for to judge of the book before he saw it within, or yet knew the truth thereof. I said also that such unadvised and hasty judgment is a token apparent of a very slender wit. Then I opened the book and showed it him. He said he thought it had been another (for he could find no fault therein). Then I desired him no more to be so swift in judgment till he throughly knew the truth; and so he departed.[3]

Immediately after came my cousin Britain in, with divers other, as Master Hall° of Gray's Inn, and such other like. Then my lord of London persuaded my cousin Britain as he had done oft before, which was that I should utter the bottom of my heart in any wise. [4]

My lord said (after that) unto me that he would I should credit the counsel of my friends in his behalf, which was that I should utter all things that burdened my conscience. For he ensured me that I should not need to stand in doubt to say anything; for like as he promised them, he said, he promised me, and would perform it – which was that neither he, nor any man for him, should take me at advauntage of any word I

---

[1] *Whitehead* ] David Whitehead (1492?-1571), Protestant divine.

[2] *to testify that I should say* ] to bear witness of what I say.

[3] *brent* ] burned at the stake; *John Frith* ] (1503-33) Protestant clergyman who aided Tyndale in translating the New Testament; left England in 1528 to escape persecution; returned in 1532, whereupon he was imprisoned and subsequently burned at the stake; *throughly* ] thoroughly.

[4] *Master Hall* ] Edward Hall, the chronicler (d. 1547).

should speak. And therefore he bade me say my mind without fear. I answered him that I had nought to say; for my conscience, I thanked God, was burdened with nothing.

Then brought he forth this unsavory similitude, that if a man had a wound, no wise surgeon would minister help unto it before he had seen it uncovered. "In like case," sayeth he, "can I give you no good counsel unless I know wherewith your conscience is burdened." I answered that my conscience was clear in all things, and for to lay a plaster unto the whole skin, it might appear much folly.

"Then ye drive me," sayeth he, "to lay to your charge your own report, which is this: Ye did say, 'He that doth receive the sacrament by the hands of an ill priest, or a sinner, he receiveth the devil and not God.'" To that I answered that I never spake such words; but as I said afore, both to the quest and to my Lord Mayor, so say I now again, that the wickedness of the priest should not hurt me, but in spirit and in faith I received no less the body and blood of Christ. Then said the Bishop unto me, "What a saying° is this! 'In spirit'! I will not take you at that advauntage!"

Then I answered, "My lord, without faith and spirit I cannot receive him worthily." Then he laid° unto me that I should say that the sacrament remaining in the pyx was but bread. I answered that "I never said so, but indeed the quest asked me such question – whereunto I would not answer, I said, till such time as they had assoiled me this question of mine, wherefore Stephen was stoned to death? They said they knew not. Then I said again, no more would I tell them what it was." [1]

Then laid it° my lord unto me that I had alleged a certain text of the Scripture. I answered that I alleged none other but St. Paul's own saying to the Athenians in the seventeenth chapter of the Apostles' Acts, that God dwelleth not in temples made with hands. Then asked he me what my faith and belief was in that matter. I answered him, "I believe as the Scripture doth teach me." Then inquired he of me, "What if the Scripture doth say that it is the body of Christ?" "I believe," said I, "like as the Scripture doth teach me." Then asked he again, "What if the Scripture doth say that it is *not* the body of Christ?" My answer was still, "I believe as the Scripture informeth me." And upon this argument he tarried a great while, to have driven me to make him an answer to his mind. Howbeit, I would not, but concluded thus with him, that I believed therein, and in all other things, as Christ and his holy apostles did leave them.

Then he asked me why I had so few words. And I answered, "God has given me the gift of knowledge, but not of utterance. And Solomon sayeth that 'A woman of few words is a gift of God'" (Prov. 19).

Thirdly, my lord laid unto my charge that I should say that the Mass was idolatry. I answered him, "No, I said not so. Howbeit," I said, "the quest did ask me whether private masses° did relieve souls departed, or no. Unto whom then I answered, 'O Lord, what idolatry is this, that we should rather believe in private masses, than in the healthsome death of the dear Son of God!'" Then said my lord again, "What an answer was that!" "Though it were but mean," said I, "yet was it good enough for the question."

Then I told my lord that there was a priest which did hear what I said there before my Lord Mayor and them. With that the Chancellor answered, "Which was the same priest?" "So – she spake it in very deed," sayeth he, "before my lord the mayor and me." Then there were certain priests, as Dr. Standish and other, which tempted me much to know my mind. And I answered them always thus, "That that° I have said to my lord of London, I have said."

And then Dr. Standish desired my lord to bid me say my mind concerning the same text of St. Paul. I answered that it was against St. Paul's learning, that I, being a woman, should interpret the Scriptures, specially where so many wise learnèd men were.

Then my lord of London said he was informed that one should ask of me if I would receive the sacrament at Easter, and I made a mock of it. Then I desired that mine accuser might come forth, which my lord would not. But he said again unto me, "I sent one to give you good counsel, and at the first word ye called him papist." That I denied not, for I perceived he was no less (yet made I none answer unto it). [2]

Then he rebuked me, and said that I should report that there were bent against me threescore priests at Lincoln. "Indeed," quoth I, "I said so: for my friends told me, if I did come to Lincoln, the priests would assault me and put me to great trouble, as thereof they had made their boast. And when I heard it, I went thither indeed, not being afraid, because I knew my matter to be good. Moreover, I remained there six° days, to see what would be said unto me. And as I was in the minster, reading upon the Bible, they resorted unto me, by two and by two, by five and by six, minding to have spoken to me; yet went they their ways again, without words speaking." [3]

---

[1] *pyx* ] covered vessel that held the bread of the eucharist.

[2] *should ask* ] did ask.

[3] *minster* ] English monastery church.

Then my lord asked if there were not one that did speak unto me. I told him yes, that there was one of them at the last which did speak to me indeed. And my lord then asked me what he said. And I told him his words were of so small° effect, that I did not now remember them.

Then said my lord, "There are many that read and know the Scripture, and yet do not° follow it nor live thereafter." I said again, "My lord, I would wish that all men knew my conversation and living in all points; for I am so sure of myself this hour, that there are none able to prove any dishonesty by me. If you know any that can do it, I pray you, bring them forth."

Then my lord went away and said he would entitle somewhat of my meaning. And so he writ° a great circumstance; but what it was, I have not all in memory, for he would not suffer me to have the copy thereof. Only do I remember this small portion of it: "*Be it known,*" sayeth he, "*of all men, that I, Anne Askew, do confess this to be my faith and belief, notwithstanding any° reports made afore to the contrary: I believe that they which are houseled at the hands of a priest, whether his conversation be good or not, do receive the body and blood of Christ in substance really. Also I do believe it° after the consecration, whether it be received or reserved, to be no less than the very body and blood of Christ in substance. Finally, I do believe in this, and in all other sacraments of holy church, in all points according to the old catholic faith of the same. In witness whereof I, the said Anne, have subscribed my name.*" There was somewhat more in it, which, because I had not the copy, I cannot now remember. [1]

Then he read it to me and asked me if I did agree to it. And I said again, "I believe so much thereof as the holy Scripture doth agree to.° Wherefore I desire you that you will add that thereunto." Then he answered that I should not teach him what he should write. With that, he went forth into his great chamber and read the same bill afore the audience, which inveigled and willed me° to set to my hand, saying also that I had favor showed me.

Then said the bishop I might thank other, and not myself, of the favor° I found at his hand; for he considered, he said, that I had good friends, and also that I was come of a worshipful stock. Then answered one Christopher (a servant to Master Denny), "Rather ought ye, my lord, to have done it in such a case for *God's* sake than for man's." [2]

Then my lord sat down and took me the writing to set thereto my hand, and I writ after this manner: "*I, Anne Askew, do believe all manner things contained in the faith of the catholic church.*" Then, because I did add unto it "the catholic church," he flung into his chamber in a great fury. With that my cousin Britain followed him, desiring him for God's sake to be good lord unto me. He answered that I was a woman, and that he was nothing deceived in me. Then my cousin Britain desired him to take me as a woman, and not to set my weak woman's wit to his lordship's very great wisdom. [3]

Then went in unto him Doctor Weston and said that the cause why I did write there "the catholic church" was that I understood not "the church" written afore. So with much ado they persuaded my lord to come out again, and to take my name with the names of my sureties° (which were my cousin Britain and Master Spilman of Gray's Inn).

This being done, we thought that I should have been put to bail immediately, according to the order of the law. Howbeit, he would not so suffer° it, but committed me from thence to prison again, until the next morrow. And then he willed me to° appear in the Guildhall; and so I did. Notwithstanding, they would not put me to bail there neither, but read the bishop's writing° unto me, as before, and so commaunded me again to prison.

Then were my sureties appointed to come before them on the next morrow in Paul's church; which did so indeed. Notwithstanding, they would once again have broken off with them, because they would not be bound also for another woman, at their pleasure, whom they knew not; nor yet what matter was laid unto her charge. Notwithstanding, at the last, after much ado, and reasoning to and fro, they took a bond of them of recognisance for my forthcoming. And thus I was, at the last, delivered. [4]

Written by me, Anne Askew (1545; pub. 1546)

---

[1] *entitle somewhat of my meaning* ] record my testimony in part; *circumstance* ] circuitous account; *houseled* ] given the eucharist.

[2] *worshipful stock* ] honorable family.

[3] *catholic* ] universal (not here to be understood as Roman Catholic).

[4] *would not be bound* ] Britain and Spilman were asked to stand surety for a second woman, unknown to them, and they refused; Askew was arraigned on 13 June 1545, along with Joan Sawtrey and Robert Lukine. All three were accused of speaking against the Eucharist. But when the only witness against them was judged unreliable, they were released.

### The Ballad which Anne Askew Made and Sang When She Was in Newgate [1]

Like as the armèd knight appointed to the field,
With this world will I fight – and faith shall be my shield.
Faith is that weapon strong which will not fail at need.
My foes therefore among therewith will I proceed:
As it is had in strength and force of Christès way.
It will prevail at length though all the devils say nay.
Faith in the fathers old obtainèd rightwisness,
Which makes° me very bold to fear no world's distress.
I now rejoice in heart and hope bids me so to do:°
For Christ will take my part and ease me of my woe.
Thou sayest, Lord, whoso knock, to them wilt thou attend.
Undo therefore the lock, and thy strong power, *send*!
More enemies now I have than hairs upon my head.
Let them not me deprave, but fight thou in my stead.
On thee my care I cast, for all their cruel spite.
I set not by their hate°, for thou art my delight.

I am not she that list my anchor to let fall [2]
For every drizzling mist. My ship's° substantìal.
Not oft use I to write in prose, nor yet in rhyme –
Yet will I shew one sight that I saw in my time:
I saw a royal throne° where justice should have set° –
But in her stead was one of moody, cruel wit.
Absorbed° was rightwisness, as of the raging flood. [3]
Satan, in his excess, sucked up the guiltless blood.
Then thought I, "Jesus, Lord, when thou shalt judge us all,
Hard is it to record on these men what will fall!"
Yet, Lord, I thee desire: for that they do to me,
Let them not taste the hire of their iniquity.

(1545)

On 24 May 1546, letters were sent to Thomas Kyme requiring him to stand before the king's Privy Council at Greenwich, together with his wife. On 19 June Kyme appeared with Anne, who denied that Kyme was her husband. He returned home; Anne was detained. In *The Latter Examination* Askew describes the interrogation to which she was then subjected by the Council. Present were Sir Thomas Wriothesley, Lord Chancellor; Stephen Gardiner, bishop of Winchester; John Dudley, viscount Lisle; William Parr, earl of Essex; and Sir William Paget, the king's secretary. Threatened with burning, Askew refused to recant. She was subsequently imprisoned in Newgate, in "extremity of sickness," and on 28 June arraigned for at the Guildhall for thought crimes against Christian orthodoxy. Nicholas Shaxton (former bishop of Salisbury) and two other men were indicted with her. Shaxton abjured – for which he was not only pardoned, but received the honor of preaching the sermon at Askew's burning, two weeks later. Hoping that Askew would implicate closet Protestant sympathizers in Queen Katherine's court, the Council not only approved for Askew to be stretched on the rack and tortured; Lord Wriothesley and Sir Richard Rich appropriated to themselves the sadistic pleasure of turning the crank.

---

[1] *Newgate* ] Newgate prison.

[2] *list* ] chooses.

[3] *rightwisness* ] righteousness.

## The Latter Examination

### The Sum of my Examination afore the King' Council at Greenwich

YOUR REQUEST, as concerning my prison fellows, I am not hable to satisfy, because I heard not their examinations. But the effect of mine was this: I, being° before the Council, was asked of Master Kyme. I answered that my Lord Chancellor knew already my mind in that matter. They with that answer were not contented, but said it was the king's pleasure that I should open the matter to them. I answered them plainly that I would not so do, but, if it were the king's pleasure to hear me, I would show him the truth. Then they said it was not meet for the king with me to be troubled. I answered that Solomon was reckoned the wisest king that ever lived, yet misliked not he° to hear two poor common women – much more his grace a simple woman and his faithful subject. So, in conclusion, I made them none other answer in that matter.[1]

Then my Lord Chancellor asked me of my opinion in the sacrament. My answer was this: "I believe that so oft as I, in a Christen° congregation, do receive the bread, in remembrance of Christ's death and with thanksgiving, according to his holy institution, I receive therewith the fruits also of his most glorious passion." The bishop of Winchester bade me make a direct answer. I said I would not sing a new song to the Lord in a strange land. [2]

Then the bishop said I spake in parables. I answered it was best for him: "—for if I show the open truth," quoth I, "ye will not accept it." Then he said I was a parrot. I told him again I was ready to suffer all things at his hands – not only his rebukes, but all that should follow besides, yea, and° that gladly. Then had I divers rebukes of the council because I would not express my mind in all things as they would have me. But they were not in the mean time unanswered, for all that – which now to rehearse were too much, for I was with them there above five hours. Then the clerk of the Council conveyed me from thence to my Lady Garnish.

### The Sum of the Condempnation of me, Anne Askew, at Guildhall°

They said to me there that I was an heretic, and condempnèd by the law if I would stand in my° opinion. I answered that I was no heretic, neither yet deserved I any death by the law of God; but as concerning the faith which I uttered and wrote to the council, I would not, I said, deny it, because I knew it true. Then would they needs know if I would deny the sacrament to be Christ's body and blood. I said, "Yea, for the same Son of God that was born of the Virgin Mary is now glorious in Heaven and 'will come again from thence at the latter day, like as he went up' (Acts 1.12°). And as for that ye call your God, is but a piece of bread. For a more proof thereof (mark it when ye list) let it lie in the box but three months, and it will be moldy,° and so turn to nothing that is good. Whereupon I am persuaded that it cannot be God."

After that they willed me to have a priest, and then I smiled. Then they asked me if it were not good. I said I would confess my faults to God, for I was sure that he would hear me with favor. And so we were condempnèd, without a quest.

### The Effect of My Examination and Handling since My Departure from Newgate

On Tuesday I was sent from Newgate to the sign of the Crown, where as Master Rich and the bishop of London with all their power and flattering words went about to persuade me from God; but I did not esteem° their glozing pretenses. Then came there to me Nicholas Shaxton, and counseled me to recant (as he had done). Then I said to him that it had been good for him never to have been born; with many other like words.[3]

---

[1] *hable* ] able; *common women* ] harlots; *simple* ] innocent; honest; *Solomon ... women* ] I Kg. 3:16-28.

[2] *bishop of Winchester* ] Stephen Gardiner (1483?-1555), bishop of Winchester (1531-51, 1553-55) and chancellor of Cambridge (1540-47, 1553 ff.); imprisoned during reign of Edward VI, reinstated under Mary; supported the persecution of Protestants and the imprisonment of Elizabeth.

[3] *Master Rich* ] Richard Rich (later, Baron Rich); Lord Chancellor (1548-51); perjured himself in the trial of Sir Thomas More; aggrandized himself by the suppression of monasteries; supported Lord Protector Somerset (1548-49); deserted to Warwick and helped to overthrow Somerset; signed proclamation for Lady Jane Grey (1553) and immediately after declared for Mary; active during Mary's reign in the persecution of Protestants; *glozing* ] specious; *it ... born* ] Jesus' remark about Judas Iscariot (Mark 14.21, Mat. 26.24).

Then Master Rich sent me to the Tower, where I remained till three of the clock. Then came Rich and one of the council, charging me upon my obedience to show unto them if I knew man or woman of my sect. My answer was that I knew none. Then they asked me of my lady of Southfolk,° my lady of Sussex,° my lady of Hertford, my lady Denny, and my lady Fitzwilliams. I said, if I should pronounce anything against them, that I were not hable to prove it. [1]

Then said they unto me that the king was informed that I could name, if I would, a great number of my sect. Then I answered that the king was as well deceived in that behalf as dissembled with in other matters.

Then commaunded they me to show how I was maintained in the counter, and who willed me to stick by my opinion. I said that there was no creature that therein did strengthen me. And as for the help that I had in the counter, it was by the means of my maid – for as she went abroad in the streets, she made° to the 'prentices, and they by her did send me money. But who they were, I never knew.

Then they said that there were divers gentlewomen that gave me money. But I knew not their names. Then they said that there were divers ladies which had sent me money. I answered that there was a man in a blue coat which delivered me ten shillings, and said that my lady of Hertford sent it me, and another in a violet coat did give me eight shillings, and said that my lady Denny sent it me. Whether it were true, or no, I cannot tell; for I am not sure who sent it me, but as the men did say.

Then they said there were of the Council that did maintain me. And I said no. Then they did put me on the rack, because I confessed no ladies nor gentlewomen to be of my opinion – and thereon they kept me a long time; and because I lay still and did not cry, my Lord Chancellor and Master Rich took pains to rack me with° their own hands till I was nigh dead. [2]

Then the lieftenant caused me to be loosed from the rack. Incontinently I swoonded, and then they recovered me again. After that I sat two long hours reasoning with my Lord Chancellor, upon the bare floor, where as he with many flattering words persuaded me to leave my opinion. But my Lord God (I thank his everlasting goodness) gave me grace to perséver, and will do (I hope) to the very end.

Then was I brought to an house and laid in a bed, with as weary and painful bones as ever had patient Job (I thank my Lord God thereof). Then my Lord Chancellor sent me word: if I would leave my opinion, I should want nothing; if I would not, I should forth to Newgate, and so be burned. I sent him again word that I would rather die than to break my faith. Thus the Lord open the eyes of their blind hearts, that the truth may take place! Farewell, my dear friend, and pray, pray, pray....

By me, Anne Askew (1545; pub. 1547)

*Bale*: Touching the order of her racking in the Tower, thus it was. First, she was led down into a dungeon, where Sir Anthony Knyvet, the Lieutenant, commanded his jailer to pinch her with the rack. Which being done so much as he thought sufficient, went about to take her down, supposing he had done enough. But Wri'sley the Chancellor (not contented that she was loosed so soon, confessing nothing), commanded the Lieftenant to strain her on the rack again. Which because he denied to do, tendering the weakness of the woman, he was threatened therefore grievously of the said Wri'sley, saying, that he would signify his disobedience unto the king; and so, consequently upon the same, he and Mr. Rich, throwing off their gowns, would needs play the tormenters themselves; first asking her if she were with child.

Sir Thomas Wriothesley by Holbein (Louvre)

[1] *my lady of Southfolk* ] Catherine (*b.* Willoughby) Bertie Brandon (1520-1580), widow and 4th wife of Charles Brandon, duke of Suffolk (d. 1545); *Sussex* ] Anne (*b.* Calthorp) Radcliffe, 2d wife of Henry Radcliffe, 2d earl of Sussex; imprisoned in the Tower of London 1552, on suspicion of "sorcery" (more probably for her protestantism); divorced by husband 1555, to debar her dower; fled to France 1556; returned and confined in the Fleet prison 1557; *Hertford* ] Anne (*b.* Stanhope) Seymour (1497-1587), 2d wife of Edward Seymour, 1st earl of Hertford (from 1547, duke of Somerset); *Denny* ] Joan (b. Champernoun) Denny (*d.* 1533), wife of Sir Anthony Denny (1501-1549); divorced by him for religious differences and noted in his will as his "unkind wife"; *Fitzwilliams* ] Jane (*b.* Ormond) Fitzwilliam, widow and 3d wife of Sir William Fitzwilliam (alderman of London, *d.* 1534), and the grandmother of Lady Anne Bacon, to whom Bacon's translation of *The Apology of the Church of England* is dedicated.

[2] *Council* ] King Henry's Privy Council (a few of whom inclined to Protestant doctrine); *that* ] some that.

To whom she answering again, said: "Ye shall not need to spare for that, but do your wills upon me!" – and so quietly and patiently praying unto the Lord, she abode their tyranny till her bones and joints almost were plucked asunder; in such sort, as she was carried away in a chair.[1]

*Anne Askew was appointed to be burned at the stake along with three other unrepentant Protestants, John Lascelles, John Adams, and Nicholas Belenian. Her broken body was transported to Smithfield sitting upon a chair in a dung cart.*

*16 July 1546.* [Anne Askew] now had been so tormented that she could neither live long in so great distress, neither yet by her adversaries be suffered to die in secret. The day of her execution being appointed, she was brought into Smithfield in a chair, because she could not go on her feet, by means of her great torments. When she was brought unto the stake, she was tied by the middle with a chain, that held up her body.

When all things were thus prepared to the fire, Dr. Shaxton, who was then appointed to preach, began his sermon; Anne Askew hearing, and answering again unto him where he said well, confirmed the same; where he said amiss, "There," said she, "he misseth, and speaketh without the Book."

The sermon being finished, the martyrs standing there tied at three several stakes ready to their martyrdom, began their prayers. The multitude and concourse of the people was exceeding the place where they stood, being railed about to keep out the press. Upon the Bench under Saint Bartholomew's Church sat Wri'sley, Chancellor of England; the old duke of Norfolk; the old earl of Bedford; the Lord Mayor; with divers other moe. Before the fire should be set unto them, one of the Bench hearing that they had gunpowder about them, and being afraid lest the faggots, by strength of the gunpowder, would come flying about their ears, began to be afraid, but the earl of Bedford – declaring unto him how the gunpowder was not laid under the faggots but only about their bodies to rid them out of their pain; which, having vent, there was no danger, to *them*, of the faggots – so diminished that fear.

Then Wri'sley Lord Chancellor sent to Anne Askew letters, offering to her the king's pardon if she would recant; who refusing once to look upon them, made this answer again: that she came not thither to deny her Lord and Master.

Then were the letters likewise offered unto the other; who in like manner following the constancy of the woman, denied not only to receive them but also to look upon them. Whereupon the Lord Mayor commanding fire to be put unto them, cried with a loud voice: "FIAT JUSTITIA!"[2]

The manner of burning Anne Askew, Iohn Lacels, Iohn Adams, & Nicolas Belenian, with certane of ÿ counsell sitting in Smithfield.

[1] John Foxe, *The Actes and Monuments* (1570), 1419.

[2] Ed. DWF from Foxe, 1420.

## A Timeline of Women's History
(Asterisked dates are approximate)

2000 BCE
* Bronze is first used in Britain
* Stonehenge is built

1800-1200 BCE
* Political power in Britain passes from priests to those who control the manufacture of metal objects.
* Emergence of a powerful warrior class in Britain

1570 BCE
* Queen Ahmose Nefertari, sister and principal wife of King Ahmose, honored as "god's wife," a position enacted into law by the king (Egypt)

1490 BCE
* Queen Hatshepsut rules as pharaoh after the death of her husband, King Thutmose II (Egypt)

1360 BCE
* Queen Nefertiti co-rules with her spouse, pharaoh Akhenaten (Egypt)

1360 BCE
* Hebrew law, later canonized as holy writ for Christians, treats wife, daughter, concubine, or female slave as a man's personal property (e.g., Genesis 3:16, Exodus 20:17, 21:7-11, Leviticus 27:3-7, Numbers 30); mandates the death of rape victims

1000 BCE
* Fortified farmsteads and hill-forts begin to appear in Britain; increasing sophistication of arts and crafts

750 BCE
* Iron is used in Britain

650 BCE
* The Celts develop iron tools and weapons

620 BCE
* Birth of Sappho (Isle of Lesbos, Greece)

600 BCE
* Construction of Old Sarum (Britain)
* Sappho of Lesbos establishes a *thiasos,* an academy for young, unmarried women (Greece);: published ten books of verse published by the third and second centuries BCE. All copies were lost during the Christian book-burnings of the Dark Ages. One complete poem from Sappho survives, and a few quoted fragments, the longest of which is 16 lines.
* Women of Sparta are able to own property, pursue learning, and participate in athletics (Greece)

550 BCE
* Death of Sappho (Greece)

100 BCE
* Roman laws allows a man to determine the payment his wife is owed in the event of divorce, and to claim his children as property; also, authority to kill his spouse if she is found in the act of adultery

69 BCE
• Birth of Cleopatra VII Philopator (Egypt)

36 BCE
• Cleopatra weds Antony (Egypt)

30 BCE
* Death of Cleopatra VII Philopator (Egypt). Defeated by Octavian, she kills herself rather than be humiliated in Rome as prize booty.

19 BCE
* Sulpicia I, writer of elegiac poems, eleven of which survive (Rome)

5 BCE
• Rome acknowledges Cymbeline, king of the Catuvellauni, as king of Britain
* Birth of Jesus of Nazareth (Gospel of Matthew)

- - - - - - - - - - - - - - - - - - - - - - - - - - - - - - - - - - - - -

6 CE
* Birth of Jesus of Nazareth (Gospel of Luke)
* Birth of Paul (Saul) of Tarsus (modern Turkey)

18 CE
• Emperor Augustus decrees the *Lex Julia,* with penalties for childless Roman citizens, adulterers, and those who marry outside of their social rank or status.

30
* Death of Jesus of Nazareth

43
• Eleven British tribes surrender to Claudius

49
* The Paulists split with Jewish Christians over whether circumcision is required for male converts; debate continues over kosher laws

61
• Boudica, queen of the Iceni, rises against the Roman occupation, burning Colchester, St. Albans, and Londinium; defeated in battle by Suetonius, she and her daughters are said to have killed themselves

66
* Death of Paul the apostle, author of fourteen epistles later canonized as holy writ; epistles to Timothy and Titus, and to the churches at Ephesus and Corinth, mandate the inferiority and subjection of women to men, and of a wife to her husband; women are forbidden to speak in assembly

70 - 80
* Gospels of Mark, Matthew, and Luke report that the Crucifixion was attended by women disciples while the male disciples hid themselves

75-77
* Wales is finally subdued; Roman conquest of Britain is now complete

100
* Martial mentions women poets named Theophila (whom he compares to Sappho) and Sulpicia II

240
* Birth of Zenobia (Syria)

267
• Zenobia becomes sovereign queen of the Palmyrene Empire following Odaenathus' death; led a revolt against Rome; by 269, she expanded the empire, conquering Egypt and expelling the Roman prefect; ruled for five years before being defeated by Aurelian and taken in golden chains to Rome

270 ff.
• Network of forts built along the eastern coast, to defend against the invading Saxons; Rome in decline

324
• Constantine gains full control of an undivided empire; makes Christianity the official religion of the empire

340
• The Synod of Gangra in North Africa condemns women belonging to the sect of Eustathius who put on a male dress and cut off their hair to show independence from their husbands.

354 ff.
* Burning of non-Christian libraries in throughout the Roman empire, by order of emperor Constantine

364
• Emperor Jovian orders the burning of the library of Antioch.

365 ff.
* Tens of thousands of books are burnt in the squares of the cities of the Eastern Empire.

370
* Birth of Hypatia (Egypt), scholar, philosopher, mathematician, astronomer; salaried head of the Platonist school at Alexandria

372
• Valens orders the governor of Minor Asia to exterminate the Hellenes and to destroy all of their literature

381
• At the Council of Constantinople the 'Holy Spirit' is declared 'Divine' thus adding a third personality to the God of Christianity. Theodosius directs for pagan temples and libraries to be looted or burned.

391
• After a bloody siege, the Christians occupy and burn down the world-famous Alexandrian library.

395
• Goths converted to Christianity burn down the Eleusinian Sanctuary and burn alive all its priests

398
• The Fourth Church Council of Carthage prohibits even Christian bishops from the study of

407
• Last Roman soldiers leave Britain

408
• Honorius (emperor of the Western Empire) and Arcadius (emperor of the Eastern Empire) order bishops to continue burning books until "pagan" thought and learning are utterly extirpated.

410
• The Goths, under Alaric, sack Rome. Britain gains independence from Rome.

415
• In Alexandria, a Christian mob, urged on by Bishop Cyril, attacks and cuts Hypatia to pieces. The pieces of her body, carried by the Christians through the streets of the city, are finally burned together with her books at Cynaron.

441
* Gallic Chronicle records, prematurely, that "Britain, abandoned by the Romans, has passed into the power of the Saxons." 441-490, the Britons continue to fight the invading Picts, Irish (Scots). Vortigern welcomes the Saxons as mercenaries, who crush the Picts but stay on as conquerors, moving westward from Kent

500
* Salians (Germanic Franks living in Gaul) issue a code of laws which prohibit women from inheriting land; the law is used for centuries to prevent women from ruling in France; referenced in Shakespeare's *Henry V* as the Salique law
* Spread of Celtic monasticism throughout Europe; 530-40, mass migration of Celtic monks to Brittany (the "third migration")

519
• Kingdom of the West Saxons (Wessex) founded under Cerdic

548
* Death of the empress Theodora, who co-ruled the Byzantine Empire with her husband Justinian. Advanced laws to establish homes for prostitutes and to prohibit sexual slavery of women; also, laws granting women new rights in divorce

556
• Justinian orders the inquisitor Amantius to go to Antioch, to find, arrest, torture and exterminate the last non-Christians there, and to burn down all private libraries

584
• Anglo-Saxon kingdom of Mercia is established
• Council Of Macon (584, at Lyons).

590
• Gregory orders bishops to desist from the "wicked labor" of teaching grammar and Latin to lay people. He forbids the laity to read the Bible and orders the burning of the Palatine Apollo library so that its secular literature "will not distract" the clergy from religious devotion. With education reduced to theology (and even that forbidden to all but clerics), the church now rules over illiterate society throughout Europe

597 ff.
* The Roman brand of Christianity is brought to Britain by Augustine, a missionary sent from Pope Gregory to convert the Saxons. Augustine founded a monastery and the first church at Canterbury, and was proclaimed its first Archbishop.

600
* Legislation permits men to publicly punish and shame women as "scolds," a practice that will continue for 1,000 years

664 ff.
• Synod of Whitby; Oswy accepts the faith of Rome; decline of the Celtic Church

680
* Barking Abbey founded

721
• Charlemagne criminalizes prostitution.

793
• Vikings first attack Britain

797
• Empress Irene of Athens (c. 752-803) is crowned sole ruler of the Byzantine empire, the first woman to rule the (East) Roman Empire.

800
• The poet Kasia loses her opportunity for a place at court for having retorted to a sexist remark made by the Emperor Theophilus

855
• The legendary Pope Joan
• Latter ninth century CE. The englynion of the Canu Heledd are recorded

871
• The Danes attack Wessex; Alfred defeats the Danes at Edington in 878 and captures London from the Danes in 886.

10th Century
* The Exeter Book (containing "Wulf" and "Lamentation," and the Vercelli Book (containing Cynewulf's "Elene" are compiled)

912 ff.
• King Alfred's eldest daughter Aethelflaed (Ethelfleda) fights the Vikings and rules Mercia. 912-15, builds fortresses at Shergate, Tamworth, Stafford, Eddesbury, Warwick, and Runkorn

924 ff.
• King Athelstan enacts laws against witchcraft

935
• Birth of Hrotsvitha (aka Hrotsvit or Roswitha) (Germany)

980
* The Danes renew their attacks on Britain, fighting continues between the Danes and Saxons for the next quarter-century

1000
* *Beowulf* manuscript compiled

1003
* Death of the canoness, chronicler, and poet-dramatist, Hrotsvitha ("Strongvoice") of Gandersheim (Germany); composed comedy and poetry that influenced the creation of miracle plays.

1022
• Heretics burned at Orleans (France)

1040
• Duncan, king of Scotland, is killed by Makbeth

1057
• King Makbeth is slain

1065
• Westminster Abbey consecrated

1066
• The Norman conquest. Battle of Hastings. William the Conqueror crowned king of Britain on December 25. The privileged class of Saxon women have their freedoms curtailed; but chattel slavery of the underclasses gradually disappears.

1067
• Work on Tower of London begins

1077
• Bayeux Tapestry completed, depicting the Battle of Hastings

1085
• Domesday Book is commissioned. Census finds that more than 10% of England's population were slaves.

1087
• Death of William the Conqueror

1096
• Oxford University is founded
• First Crusade against the Muslims to win control of Palestine. Thousands of Jews slaughtered along the way. One division slaughtered 10,000 Jews in the Rhineland. Godfrey Bouillon, leader of the First Crusade, vowed "to leave no single member of the Jewish race alive."

1097
• fl. Trota of Salerno, a midwife or physician. A compilation of medical texts includes by Trota, sometimes called "Trotula," provided standards for guiding gynecological and obstetrical practice which were observed for centuries afterward

1098
• Birth of Hildegard von Bingen (Germany)
• Crusades begin against Muslims and Jews

1099
• Christians capture Jerusalem. Godfrey of Bouillon, elected King of Jerusalem, orders the synagogue burned to the ground with its entire Jewish congregation trapped inside.

1100
* Love songs by women troubadours become popular in France; by some 20 aristocratic poet-composers; some two dozen of their songs survive, including four by Beatrix (the countess of Dia)

1102
• The Council of London issues a decree: "Let no one hereafter presume to engage in that nefarious trade in which hitherto in England men were usually sold like brute animals."

1110
• Matilda, da. of Henry I, crowned empress of the Germans

1114
• Matilda (Maud), daughter of Henry I of England, weds Emperor Henry V

1115
* The *Leges Henrici Primi*, which records the legal customs of medieval England in the reign of King Henry I, describes pre-quickening abortion as a misdemeanor, and post quickening abortion as quasi-homicide, carrying a lesser penalty than homicide

1122
• Birth of Eleanor of Aquitaine (France)
• Heretics burned at Soisson (France)

1126
• Henry I settles the English succession on widowed da. Matilda

1139
• Matilda claims the throne of England; civil war with Stephen

1141
• Disputed reign of Matilda, Holy Roman Empress and daughter of Henry I of England. Matilda captures Stephen at the battle of Lincoln; she is deposed by a popular rising and Stephen restored

1147
• The Second Crusade. Eleanor of Aquitaine accompanies her husband, French King Louis VII, on the Second Crusade. After their marriage ends in 1152, she weds the future King Henry II of England.

1148
• Death of Anno Comnena (b. ca. 1083). Documented the life and reign of her father the Emperor Alexius I Comnenus of Byzantium; a 15-volume history written in Greek, which also included information on medicine, astronomy, and accomplished women of Byzantium.

1160
* Estimated date of Marie de France's birth

1152
* Abbess Hildegard of Bingen completes *Scivias*, a narrative of her visions, confirmed as authentic by a committee of theologians.

1160
* estimated birth of Marie de France

1170
* The nun of Barking writes the Life of St. Edward the Confessor
* Marie de France writes the Fables, perhaps also at Barking Abbey
* Marie of Champagne (1145-1198), daughter of King Louis VII of France and Eleanor of Aquitaine, cosponsors "courts of love" to debate points on the proper conduct of knights toward their ladies. Marie encourages Chrétien de Troyes to write *Lancelot,* and Andreas Capellanus to write *The Art of Courtly Love.*

1176
• Heretics burned at Rheims (France)

1179
• Death of the poet Hildegard von Bingen (Germany)

1180
* Marie de France writes the Lays

1180s
• Rich people in England have glass windows for the first time since the Roman era

1190
• Christian massacre of Jews at York, at Bury St Edmunds, and elsewhere

1190
• Death of Herrad of Landsberg (b. ca. 1130), abbess and scientist, author of *Hortus Deliciarum* (*Garden of Delights*). Nun, then abbess, at the convent of Hohenberg
* Marie de France writes the Life of St. Audrey

1200
* Estimated death of Marie de France, the earliest known female French writer and author of *lais;* lived in England, wrote in French.

1200-1230
* The AB Texts (*The Ancrene Wisse*, the "Katherine Group" texts, the "Wooing Group" prayers, are composed for anchoritic readers

1204
• Death of Eleanor of Aquitaine (France)

1209
• Migrant scholars establish Cambridge University
• The Pope excommunicates King John following attacks on Church property

1209. The Cathars are massacred in the Albigensian crusade. (The Albigensians taught that by her baptism and by her study, a woman could become the equal of male believers, achieve perfection. In 1208, the Pope declared a Crusade to exterminate them. Thousands were slaughtered – many first blinded, mutilated, dragged behind horses or used for target practice.

1212
• First Great Fire of London

1213
• The Pope declares King John deposed; he resigns his kingship to the Pope and receives it back as a holding from the Roman legate, thereby ending the interdict.

1214
• Oxford University is chartered

1215
• Signing of Magna Carta; English barons force John to agree to a statement of their rights

1220
• At the University of Paris, women are banned from practicing medicine.

1231
• Escalation of execution for heretical opinions

1258
• Pope authorizes citizens to hunt witches as heretics

1274
• Death of Thomas Aquinas), theologian & misogynist

1275
• Angele, Lady of Labarthe, first victim known by name to be burnt as a witch (at Toulouse, Italy).

1285
* Death of Mechtild von Magdeburg (b. ca. 1212), a Beguine and medieval mystic who wrote The Flowing Light of the Godhead, an account of her visions rediscovered in the nineteenth century.

1290
• Edward I expels all Jews from England; many are slain

1300
• Glass windows and chimneys are becoming common among the merchant class • (Most people have only a hole in the roof to let out smoke).

1309
• Death of Angela of Foligno, author of the *Book of Visions and Instructions* (1298). Angela was celebrated for her Christian penance, which included habitual drinking of water that had been used to wash lepers. Beatified in 1701.

1310
* Death of Marguerite Porete (b. 1250), a Beguine mystic who wrote and preached of her visions, burnt at the stake for her refusal to recant her views or remove from circulation her book, *A Mirror for Simple Souls*

1315-1316
• Great famine across England

1316
• Papal bull *Super illius specula* encourages the hunting of heretics and witches, and accuses people at court of sorcery

1320
• Pope John XXII authorizes the Inquisition to prosecute alleged sorcerers

1321
• Death of Dante Alighieri, author of the *Comedia*

1322
• Jacqueline Felicie de Almania is prosecuted for practicing medicine without a license. Male physicians of Paris force her to close her women's clinic.

1324
• Dame Alice Kyteler is tried for witchcraft in Ireland

1326
• Queen Isabella and Roger Mortimer sail from France with an army to rebel against Edward II of England. Parliament in 1327 declares Edward II deposed; his son accedes as Edward III.

1327
• Queen Isabella and Roger Mortimer order the death of Edward II

1328
* The French cite the Salic Law, which was promulgated in the early medieval period and prohibits women from inheriting land, as the authority for denying the crown of France to anyone—man or woman—whose descent from a French king can be traced only through the female line.

1328
• Isabel Mure of Yorkshire hanged as a witch

1337
• Hundred Years' War bet. England and France begins

1347
• Birth of Geoffrey Chaucer

1342
* Birth of Julian of Norwich (1342-1417?)

1346
• Mystic St. Birgitta of Sweden (c.1303-1373) founds the Roman Catholic Order of St. Savior, whose sisters are called the Brigittines. She writes *Revelations,* an account of her supernatural visions.

1347
• Birth of Caterina Benincasa (later St. Catherine of Siena) (Italy)
• First wave of the Black Death kills millions in Europe

1348
• Black Death reaches England, killing 30-45% of England's populace

1351
• England's Treason Act considers any murder that subverts the usual hierarchies, such as a servant killing his master or a wife killing her husband, to be petty treason against the State

1363/5
* Birth of Christine de Pizan (Venice)

1363-1376
* fl. Katherine of Sutton, abbess of Barking

1373
* Birth of Margery Kempe (King's Lynn, Norfolk)
• Julian of Norwich experiences her first visions

1375
• Alice Perrers, mistress of King Edward III of England, is accused of witchcraft

1380
• Death of (St.) Catherine of Siena (Italy)

1384
• The Peasants' Revolt

1384
• Jadwiga is crowned "king" of Poland.

1387
• Chaucer, first *Canterbury Tales*

1388
* Birth of [Julian] Barnes
• Julian of Norwich has second series of visions

1390
• London licensing law for medical practice requires a university education, thus barring women from the profession.

1393
* Julian of Norwich (1342?-1416?) writes her *Revelations of Divine Love*
* Margery Kempe marries

1397
• Chaucer gives recital of *Canterbury Tales* at King Richard's court

1397
• Under the Kalmar Union, Denmark, Sweden, and Norway are united under Queen Margaret I as their sole monarch.

1399
* Christine de Pizan writes her "Letter to the God of Love," initiating the *querelle des femmes*, a debate on women continued by European poets and scholars for centuries.
• Death of John of Gaunt, whose son, Henry of Bolingbroke, deposes Richard II.

1400
• Death of Geoffrey Chaucer.

1401
• Persecution of Lollards begins in earnest.

1401
• Christine de Pizan, *Le Livre de la Cité des Dames*

1413
• Accession of Henry V
* Margery Kempe visits Julian of Norwich at her cell

1415
• Henry V invades France, victory at Agincourt

1420
• Charles VI cedes France to Henry V, Treaty of Troyes
* Death of Leonor López de Córdoba (b. ca. 1362), after being banished from the Castilian Court, she wrote the first known autobiography in Spanish, called *Memorias* by an early editor

1429
• Joan of Arc (1412-1431), supported by Queen Yolande, begins her military and religious campaign against the English. At the Battle of Orléans she leads the French army to victory.

1430
• Birth of (queen) Margaret of Anjou
* Birth of Gwerful ap Fychan (Wales)
• Burgundians capture Jeanne d'Arc and hand her over to the English, who burn her at the stake, as a heretic and witch, in 1431; canonized as a saint in 1920.

1431
• Henry VI of England crowned king of France in Paris
• The English execute Joan of Arc
• Death of Christine de Pizan (France)

1432
• Margery Jourdain and Eleanor Cobham accused of witchcraft, as the witch-hunting craze reaches England

1436
* Margery Kempe through an amanuensis records her autobiography

1440
* Death of Margery Kempe
* Death of Frances of Rome (1384-1440), celebrated for her penance in wearing cilices and iron devices that tore the flesh of her genitals; canonized 1608

1432
• Birth of Margaret Beaufort

1445
• Wedding of Henry VI and Margaret of Anjou
• John Talbot, earl of Shrewsbury, as a wedding gift presents Margaret of Anjou with MS B.L. Royal E.VI, which includes Christine de Pizan's *Book of the Deeds of Arms and Chivalry*

1447
* William de la Pole, attrib., "The Assembly of Ladies"

1448
• Margaret of Anjou, the wife of Henry VI of England, establishes Queens' College, Cambridge.

1450s
• Printing press developed in the Holy Roman Empire

1453
• Henry VI goes insane. The Hundred Years War ends. England loses all its territory in France except Calais.

1454
• Duke of Suffolk impeached and murdered
• Johannes Gutenberg develops printing with movable type (Germany)

1455-1485
• Henry, recovered, resumes power. The Wars of the Roses between the Yorkist and Lancastrian factions
• May. First Battle of St. Albans

1460
* fl. Julian Barnes, poet and translator
* fl. Gwellian ferch Rhirid Flaidd
* The Findern MS (1460s)

1461
• Lancastrians defeated at Towton; Edward IV proclaimed king

1462
• Margaret of Anjou invades Northumberland
* Birth of Gwerful Mechain (Wales)

1465
• Birth of Cassandra Fedele (Italy)

1466
• Birth of Elizabeth of York

1469
• Birth of the humanist scholar, Laura Cereta (Italy)

1470
• Henry VI briefly restored to throne

1471
• May. Yorkists defeat Margaret of Anjou and the Lancastrians at Tewkesbury, killing Edward prince of Wales (only son of Henry VI and Margaret of Anjou)

1473
• Death of Sir Thomas Malory

1473
• William Caxton in Bruges publishes the first printed books in English, including his own trans, of Aesop's *Fables* and *The recuyell of the historyes of Troye*.

1476
• Margaret of Anjou ransomed to France
• Caxton sets up a printing press in Westminster

1477
• "Dictes of Sayengs of the Philosophres," first book printed in England
• first printing of Chaucer's *Canterbury Tales*.

1477-81
• Letters and verse by the Brews-Paston women

1480
* Anon (the Leaf Poet), "The Floure and the Leaf"

1482
• Death of (queen) Margaret of Anjou

1483
• Jane Shore confesses to witchcraft (England)
• 9 April. Death of Edward IV
• Princes murdered in the Tower; usurpation by Richard

1484
• Pope Innocent VIII authorizes inquisitors to systemize the persecution of witches; from 1480-1650, an estimated 40,000 to 60,000 were put to death, in Protestant as well as Catholic countries

1485
• Caxton prints the *Morte d'Arthur*
• 1 Aug. Henry Tudor (Richmond) returns to England
• 22 Aug. Richard III defeated and killed at Battle of Bosworth. Henry is proclaimed king.
• Birth of Veronica Gambara (Italy). Her court becomes an important center of the Italian Renaissance, and Gambara earns distinction as an author of Petrarchan sonnets as well as for her patronage of the artist Corregio.
• Death of Eustochia Smeralda Calafato of Messina (b. 1434), who did penance on a self-torture rack of her own construction; beatified in 1782, canonized 1988
• Birth of (queen) Catherine of Aragon
* *The Floure and the Leafe*

1486
• 16 Jan., Henry VII weds Elizabeth of York, poet
• 20 Sept., Birth of Arthur, prince of Wales
• Caxton prints the Julian Barnes, *Boke of Huntyng*
• *Malleus Maleficarum* (*The Hammer of Witches*), a witch-hunting manual, is published in Germany. Declares women's greater susceptibility to evil, and contributes to the escalating demonization and execution of women as witches. Midwives are among those accused of committing witchcraft.

1486-89
* fl. Lady – Brian, poet

1487
• 11-year-old Arthur of England is betrothed to 12-year-old Catherine of Aragon

1490s
* fl. Gwerful Mechain, Welsh poet

1491
• Birth of Henry VIII

1492
• Birth of Marguerite de Navarre (France)
• Queen Isabella I of Spain finances Columbus's voyage of exploration

1499
• Death of Laura Cereta (b. 1469), scholar, essayist, and poet (Italy)

1500
* Death of the poet and musician, Gwerful Mechain; birth of Alis ferch Gruffud (Wales)

1501
* Birth of (queen) Anne Boleyn
• Caxton prints extracts from the *Book of Margery Kempe*

1502
* Death of Prince Arthur; his widow, Catherine of Aragon, is betrothed a year later to prince Henry

1503
• Death of queen Elizabeth of York
• James IV of Scotland weds Margaret Tudor, da. of Henry VII and Elizabeth of York

1508
* Birth of (queen) Jane Seymour

1509
• Death of Henry VII; Henry VIII succeeds; weds Katherine; during the reign of Henry VIII, about 72,000 citizens will be put to death on various charges.

1510
• King Henry said to be coupling with Anne Stafford

1512
• Birth of (queen) Katherine Parr

1513
• King Henry said to be coupling with Etiennette de la Baume

1514
• King Henry said to be coupling with Elizabeth Bryan

1514-16
• King Henry said to be coupling with Jane Popincourt

1515
• Birth of Margaret Douglas (Stuart)
• Birth of Teresa de Alhumadawas (later St. Teresa de Ávila) (Spain)
• 22 Sept. Birth of (queen) Anne of Cleves

1515-38
* The Coffin-Wells anthology

1516
• Birth of (Queen) Mary

1517
• Luther posts His 95 Theses at Wittenberg; the Protestant Reformation begins; Luther outdoes Rome in calling for the extermination of witches

1517-22
• Henry couples with Bessie Blount (acknowledged)

1519
* Birth of Elizabeth (Oxenbridge) Tyrrwhit [vol. 2]
• Bessie Blount gives birth to Henry Fitzroy, the king's illegitimate son
• Mexican Indian princess and slave Doña Marina becomes translator and mistress of Hernán Cortés as he conquers New Spain

1520
* Birth of Isabella Whitney [vol. 2]
* Birth of (queen) Katherine Howard
• King Henry said to be coupling with Agnes Blewitt

1521
* Birth of Anne Askew

1522-24
• King Henry couples with Mary Boleyn (acknowledged)

1524
• Birth of poet Gaspara Stampa (Italy)
• King Henry ceases to cohabit with Catherine of Aragon

1525
• Mary Boleyn gives birth to a son, christened Henry; Henry declines to acknowledge him
• Henry VIII seeks annulment of his marriage to Catherine of Aragon in order to wed Anne

1525-27
• King Henry is said to beget two sons by Mary Berkeley

1526
• In what is now South Carolina, the African slaves revolt against Spanish colonists and seek refuge among Native Americans; most of the Spanish perish of an epidemic; survivors abandon the colony, leaving behind the escaped slaves.

1527
• Birth of poet Veronica Franco (Italy)
• King Henry said to have coupled with Joan (Dobson) Dingley, laundress, begetting da. named. Ethelreda

1527-33
• King Henry seeks divorce, pursues Anne Boleyn

1529
• King Henry dismisses Cardinal Wolsey for his failure to obtain papal consent to a divorce from Catherine

1530
• Birth of Katherine Cook [Killigrew] (vol. 2)
* Death of Frances (Manners) Neville (vol. 2)
• Italian physician and poet Girolamo Fracastoro, describing the "Great Pox" or "French Disease," gives it the name "syphilis." The epidemic spreads throughout Europe

1532
• Anne Boleyn becomes pregnant

1533
• Henry VIII marries Anne Boleyn and is excommunicated by the Pope
• Henry and Margaret Shelton said to be a couple during Anne's pregnancy
• 7 Sept. Birth of (Queen) Elizabeth, daughter of Anne Boleyn. Henry is disappointed. Chapuys mentions Henry's renewed interest in an unnamed beautiful damsel of Anne's court

1534
• Act of Supremacy: Henry VIII makes himself head of the Church of England; Thomas Cranmer appointed Archbishop of Canterbury
• Papal Bull *Licet ab initio* established the Holy Office of the Inquisition (which endures until 1965)
• Elizabeth Barton, the Holy Maid of Kent, is beheaded
• Buggery Statute

1535
• First English Translation of the Bible is printed
• Anne is again pregnant, Feb.-July; King and Margaret Shelton are said again to be a couple

1536
• Death of Henry's first ex, Catherine of Aragon
• Henry VIII libels, condemns, and beheads his second wife, Anne Boleyn; weds Jane Seymour
• Death of Joan (Fitzalan) Lumley [vol. 2]

1536-1540
• Calvinism spreads to Germany, the Lowlands, England Scotland, Wales
• Henry VIII closes and sells the monasteries and abbey

1537
• Jane Seymour dies after giving birth (Edward VI)
• Princess Elizabeth is declared a bastard and excluded from the succession
• Birth of Lady Jane Grey (Queen Jane I, 1553)
* Birth of Joane Fitzalan [Lumley]
• Luther publishes his anti-Semitic screed, *On the Jews and their Lies,* advocating extermination

1540
• 6 Jan. Henry VIII weds Anne of Cleves
• 9 July. Henry VIII divorces Anne of Cleves
weds 19-year-old Catherine Howard
• *Birth of Mankind; or, the Woman's Book*

1542
- 7 Feb. Katherine Howard\is condemned by attainder; 13 Feb., beheaded
- Witchcraft Act regulates the penalties for witchcraft.
- Death of the poet Veronica Franco (Italy)
- Princess Mary Stuart is born at Linlithgow (8 Dec.); death of her father a week later makes her queen of Scotland as a newborn infant; succession crisis
- Rome's Inquisition is established

1543
- Henry VIII weds Katherine Parr
- Coronation of Mary Queen of Scots

1546
- 18 Feb. Death of Martin Luther
- 24 May. Death of Copernicus, same day he was presented with an advance copy of *On the Revolution of Celestial Spheres*
- 16 July Anne Askew burned at the stake

1547
- 28 Jan. Death of Henry VIII; Edward VI succeeds, with Duke of Somerset as Protector
- Princess Elizabeth lives with Katherine Parr and her husband Thomas Seymour
- 31 March. Death of King François I, of France; Henry II succeeds; Mary Stuart Queen of Scots at age 5 is betrothed to Henry II's son François, the dauphin

1548
- Mary Stuart Queen of Scots at age 6 is sent to France
- 5 Sept. Death of Katherine Parr after childbirth

1549
- Death of Marguerite de Navarre, poet, literary patron; queen consort of Henry II of France

* Birth of Isabella Whitney
- Rebellion in Norfolk, major uprising

1550
- Death of poet Veronica Gambara (Italy)

Henry VIII (c. 1520)
artist unknown
*National Portrait Gallery* (*London*)

Judith with the head of Holofernes
By Luis Cranach the Elder (c. 1530)
*Jagdschloss Grunewald* (*Berlin*)

## Church Doctrine, 600-1550 CE

"Woman is slow in understanding. Her unstable and naive mind renders her by way of natural weakness to the necessity of a strong rule by her husband. Her use is twofold; copulation and motherhood."
—Pope Gregory I (540-604), *Patrologiae cursus completus, ser. Graeca*, ed. J.P. Migne (1857-66), 59, 268.

"If men could see beneath the skin, the sight of women would make them nauseous....Since we are loath to touch spittle or excrement even with our fingertips, how can we desire to embrace such a sack of shit as a woman?" —St. Odo of Cluny (c. 878-842): *Patrologia Latina,* 221 vols. (1844-1864), vol. 133, col. 556.

"Woman is a fearsome snake, a harsh wolf, a cheap brute ...She has a lion's head, a serpent's tail, and everything in between is nothing but a burning fire."
—Marbode (1035?-1123), Bishop of Rennes: "On the Wicked Woman," *Book of Ten Chapters,* part 3.

"A frail thing is woman, constant only in sin, never on her own desisting from harm. Woman is a devouring flame, extreme madness, disaster unparalleled. She learns and teaches every possible way to harm us. Woman is a cheap commodity, available to all, born to deceive, for whom success is the ability to commit sin. Woman is a grim yoke, a grievance against what is right and just. She thinks herself debased only when she cannot debase others. The more she works in private, the more oppressive, she. With gifts and voice and hand she entices to sin. All-consuming in vice, she is consumed by every vice. Preying on men, she makes herself their prey. She exhausts the flesh, loots resources, afflicts minds..."
—Hildebert of Lavardin (c. 1055-1133), Bishop of Le-Mans, Archbishop of Tours: "De tribus titiis: Muliebri amore, avaritia, ambitione." *Patrologia Lat.,* vol. 171.

"If a woman's bowels were cut open, you would see what filth is covered by her white skin. If a fine crimson cloth covered a pile of filthy excrement, would anyone be foolish enough to love shit, because of the covering?" —Roger de Caen (d. 1095), Bishop of Salisbury: *Carmen de mundi contemptu*

"Woman is filthy, woman is treacherous, woman is frail. She pollutes what is clean, peers into the unholy, exhausts men's gains.... No woman is good, but if some one should happen to be so, even her goodness is evil... Woman works to deceive, is born to betray. She is skilful in deluding...most depraved of vipers. She is excrement with a pretty surface."
—St. Berno of Cluny (12th C): *De contemptu mundi*

"Consider that the most lovely woman has come into being from a foul-smelling drop of semen, then consider her midpoint, how she is a container of filth; and after that consider her end, when she will be food for worms."
—Petrus Cantor (c. 1150-1197), Dean of Rheims: *Patrologia Latina,* vol. 205, col. 265.

"Between Adam and God in Paradise there was only one woman: and she could not rest until she had managed to banish her husband from the Garden of delights and condemn Christ to the tortures of the Cross."
—Jacques de Vitry (c.1170-1240), Bishop of Acre: Lüttich UB 416, 204rb-va; Paris, B.N. lat. 17509, 139ra

"Woman is less qualified [than man] for moral behavior. Because the woman contains more liquid than man, ... women are inconstant and curious. When a woman has relations with a man, she would prefer to be lying with another man at the same time. Woman knows nothing about fidelity. ...Prudent men share their plans and actions least of all with their wives. Woman is a misbegotten man and has a faulty and defective nature unlike his. Unsure in herself, what she cannot get she seeks to obtain through lying and diabolical deceit. And so, to put it briefly, one must be on one's guard with every woman, as if she were a poisonous snake and the horned devil. If I could say what I know about women, the world would be astonished... Woman strictly speaking is not more clever, but more cunning, than man.... Her feelings drive woman toward every evil, just as reason impels man toward all good."
—St. Albert Magnus (c.1206-1280), *Quaestiones super de animalibus*, XV q. 11.

"Woman is defective and misbegotten, for the active force in the male seed tends to the production of a perfect likeness in the masculine sex; while the production of woman comes from defect in the active force or from some material indisposition, or even from some external influence, such as that of a south wind, which is moist."
—St. Thomas Aquinas (1225-1274), *Summa Theol.*, I.q.92.a.1

"When you see your wife commit an offense, ...scold her sharply, bully and terrify her. And if this still doesn't work, take up a stick and beat her soundly, for it is better to punish the body and correct the soul than to damage the soul and spare the body."
—Friar Cherbino of Siena (fl. 1450-81): *Rules of Marriage*

"All wickedness is but little to the wickedness of a woman....What else is woman but a foe to friendship, an inescapable punishment, a necessary evil, a natural temptation, a desirable calamity, a domestic danger, a delectable detriment, an evil of nature, painted with fair colors." —*Malleus Maleficarum* (1486), 1.6

"No smock or gown more ill suits a woman or girl than the desire to be wise...Men have a broad chest and narrow hips, so they have more intelligence than women, who have a narrow chest and wide hips and buttocks, their purpose being to stay at home, to keep house, to bear and raise children.... The greatest honor a woman has, altogether, is that she gives birth to men."
—Martin Luther (1483-1546*), Tischreden*

"Woman is more guilty than man, because she was seduced by Satan, and so diverted her husband from obedience to God that she was an instrument of death leading to all perdition. It is necessary that woman recognize this, and that she learn to what she is subjected; and not only against her husband. This is reason enough why today she is subjugated and that she bears ignominy and shame within her."
—Jean Calvin (1509-1564): *The Institutes of the Christian Religion* (1536)

## Textual Notes

**WELCOME to *Women's Works***

**I am rose**. Ed. DWF from Cambridge University Library MS Hh.6.11 (Contains "I am rose," fol. 67r).

**CELTIC**

**Canu Heledd:** Ed. and trans. DWF from Jesus College Oxford MS. 111 (Llyfr Coch *Hergest*) col. 1044-1049
41 nabydyd ] nabydy *MS*
60 Etlit ] Elit *MS*
78 Hidyl vyn neigyr men] meu *MS*
86 yr ] y *MS*
95 Kyndrwyn ] Kyndrwyn *MS*
101 ef ] *MS om.*
101 gwyar ] gwyr *MS*
101 Heno ] *MS om.*
120 a gereis ] *MS om.*
139 Kyndrwynin] Kyndrwyn *MS*
146 Heno ] *MS om.*
146 yr ] y *MS*
168 y ] *MS om.*
171 llesseint ] lesseint *MS*
202 haval] havl *MS*
205 croennen] croen *MS*
215 mawr ] *MS om.*
219 gwyr anchwant] gwyr a Uchuant *MS*
222 eduynt ] eduyn *MS*
223 gwarthegyd ] warth gwarthegyd *MS*
234 yt ] yth *MS*
235 brodyr ] bro *MS*
237 yt ] yth *MS*
242 olygon ] *MS om.*
264 tru ] *MS om.*
268 Hedyn ] ehedyn *MS*
274 wn y ] wy *MS*
281 ystle ] ystle *MS*
286 dihat ] *MS om.*
295 buum ] bum *MS*

**Chwiorydd Heledd**
From B.L. MS Add. 14867, fol. 166v. Trans. DWF.
bu diddan ] bydiddan *MS*

**Kynddyllan y Kynwraith**
Ed. and trans. DWF fr. B.L. MS Add. 14867, fol. 166v-167r.

**ANGLO-SAXON**

Extract from **Charm for a Sudden Stitch**
BL MS Harley 585, circa 1050, fols. 75-6. Trans. DWF.

***Wulf/Wolf***: Ed./trans. DWF fr Exeter Cath. Lib. MS *Codex Exonensis*, facs., 1933), 100v-101r.
*title* ] *DF*; *omit MS*
16 Eadwacer ] *Thor and most later eds*; eadwacer *MS*
16 earmne ] *Holthausen* (1893), *Kennedy* (1960); earne *MS* (cf. ear[g]ne *Mackie* (1934).

**Heofung:/Lamentaion (The Wife's Lament):** Ed./ trans. DWF fr. Exeter Cathedral Library MS *Codex Exonensis*, facs., 1933), fol. 115. *title* ] *DF*; *MS om.*
3 aweox ] *Sieper* (1915), *Mackie* (1934), *Leslie* (1961); weox *MS, Hamer* (1970).
10 wræcca ] *Sieper, Leslie, Hamer*; wre, cca *MS, Mackie*
15 her eard ] *Sieper, Leslie, Hamer*; her heard *Mackie*; herheard *MS*
20-21 hycgendne. / Bliþe gebæro ] *Thorpe* (1842) *and most subsequent eds*.; hycgende / bliþe gebæro *MS, Sieper*
24 nu fornumen] *Leslie, Hamer*; nu *MS, Mackie. The greater portion of line 24a has been lost; no emendation can be made with confidence*
25 Sceal ] *Thorpe and most subsesquent eds*.; seal *MS*
37 sittan] *Thorpe and most subsequent eds*.; sittam *MS*
50 min wine ] *MS*; wine min *Sieper*

**Æcerbot / Field Blessing**
Ed. and trans. DWF from B.L. MS Cotton Caligula, A. VII, fol. 176a-178a, late tenth or early eleventh century.

**To Induce Delayed Labor, After the Quickening, After a Stillbirth or Infant Death, To Produce Breast Milk:** Ed., trans. DWF fr. BL MS Harl. 585, fol. 185.

**MARIE de FRANCE**

***Fables***: Ed. and trans. Harriet Spiegel (1987); reprinted by permission of the University of Toronto Press. Readers interested in Marie's *Fables* are urged to consult Spiegel's edition, which includes all 103 Fables, invaluable introduction and notes, textual collations, and manuscript illuminations.

***Lay le Frein***
Lines 1-120, 133-340 ed. DWF from MS Advocates 19.2.1 ("the Auchinleck Manuscript"), in the online transcript at auchinleck.nls.uk. The MS dates from the early 14th C, and is badly damaged. Lines 121-132 and 133-340 are here supplied by the reconstruction of Henry William Weber (1810); ed. DWF.
15 song ] *MS om.*
19 Now…y'fall ] Now of þis auentours þat weren yfalle *MS*
22 Ich'll tell you ] Ichil gou telle *MS*
24 made a ] made *MS*
28 past time ] time *MS*
29 knights ] knigtes *MS*
33 nought ] & haþ nouȝt *MS*
53 maid-child ] maidenchild *MS*
57 graunted ] & graunted *MS*
69 tuay ] to *MS*
77 one ] woman *MS*
78 women ] *MS* om.
81 she euer should child ] hye euer ani child schuld
82 her ] hir schuld *MS*
83 thereaft' ] therafter *MS*
88 her ] hir was *MS*
92 speak another ] speken ani other *MS*
104 three ] þre þinges *MS*
105 I had ] Ich had a
121- 133, Weber's recconstruction of missing text
139 child ] maiden *MS*
141 she it ] iy *MS*
142 lace ] a lace *MS;* y-plit ] plit *MS*
150 clear ] was clere *MS*
153 thereafter ] after *MS*
159 street ] steete *MS*
163 Abode the maiden ] Þe maiden abod *MS*
169 Thou ] *MS om.*
198 Home ] And hom *MS*
203 Ac ] & *MS*
216 her ] him *MS*

219 a-wondered ] was awonderd *MS*
228 fontston] funston *MS*
258 sigge] sey *MS*
276 sigge ] said *MS*
283 damsel] damilel *MS*
285 swithe] swhe *MS*
298 love ye] lovi *MS*
318 whose ] was *MS*
322 Fresne ] sche *MS*
326 They ] & *MS*
341-408, Weber's recconstruction of missing text

**KATHERINE of SUTTON**: ***The Easter Play of the Nuns of Barking Convent***

The unique copy of the play is found in University College (Oxford) MS 169, written at the direction of Sibille Felton, Abbess of Barking from 1394 to 1419 and presented to the convent by her in 1404. The manuscript was given the title *The Ordinale and Customary of the Benedictine Nuns of Barking Abbey* when it was edited by J.B.L Tolhurst for the Henry Bradshaw Society, vols. 65-66 (London: Harrison and Sons, 1927). The play itself was edited by Karl Young in his *Drama of the Medieval Church* (Oxford: Clarendon, 1933), v. 1, pp. 165-66, 381-84. Young locates most of the verses for the play from the incipits; Professor Ruth Steiner of Catholic University of America directed the present translator to the versicle "Dicite in nacionibus" in the *Corpus Antiphonalium Officii*, ed. Renato-Joanne Hesbert (Rome: Herder, 1963-79), number 8013. English translation by Michael O'Connell, from the Latin text of the "Visitatio" in University College MS 169, sæc. xv, pp. 121-4. First publication.

**JULIAN of NORWICH**

From ***Revelations to One who Could not Read a Letter***

Julian's spiritual autobiography survives in two versions. The shorter version, found in British Library MS Additional 37790 [*MS-a*], fols. 97r-115r, is thought to represent the original text of 1373 (a.k.a. "the Amherst MS," after the name of its last private owner); *MS-a* begins, "Here es a visiõn schewed be the goodenes of god to a deuoute womãn ..."). The longer version, deriving from Julian's revision ca. 1393, survives in five manuscripts. The most authoritative of these (here chosen as copytext) is British Library MS Sloane 2499 (with the scribal heading, "Revelations to one who could not read a letter") [*MS-s*]; this is a mid 17$^{th}$-century MS that was apparently transcribed from a 14$^{th}$-century copy quite close to the original. The scribal hand for much of *MS-s* appears to be that of Anne Cary (in religion, Clementina), daughter of Elizabeth Tanfield Cary. Somewhat earlier than *MS-s*, and likewise copied from a 14$^{th}$-century manuscript (but in a normalized text that flattens Julian's dialectical forms and that contains some interpolations) is Paris Bibliothèque Nationale MS Fonds anglais 40 ("a reuelacion of loue") [*MS-bn*]. The first printed text, published by Dom Serenus Cressy as *XVI Revelations of Divine Love* (1670) (215 pp.), was apparently printed from *MS-bn*. Also of interest as exemplars of the long version (but not collated herebelow) are British Library MS Sloane 3705 [*MS-s*], which is an 18$^{th}$-century MS copied from *MS-s*, with some checking against Cressy; also the MS copies owned by St. Joseph's College (Upholland) (ca. 1650) and by the Westminster Archdiocesan Archives (extracts only, fols. 1r, 25r, 35$^v$, 72, 112$^v$; ca. 1500, with 17$^{th}$-century annotations). For a complete transcript of *MS-a* and of *MS-bn* (with extensive collations for the latter), see Colledge and Walsh (1978).

Ed. DWF from *MS-s* and partially collated with *MS-bn.* A few words are here added for clarity (*so*, *Shewing*, etc.); these are noted below. Also noted are a few substantive errors in Glasscoe's generally accurate edition of *MS-s* (1976); repr. 3$^d$. ed. (1981). Folio numbers are from the archivist's numbering of the ms. rather than from the old page numbers.

The title "A Revelation of Love" is borrowed from *MS-bn*, and the epigraph following ("Botte for I am a womann,...") from *MS-a* (fol. 101r).

**Chapter 2**, fols. 1r - 2r

eighth ] viij$^{th}$ *MS-s*; xiii *MS-bn*
three ... second ... third ] iij ... ij ... iij *MS-s* (*not noted hereafter*
As for ] For *MS-bn*
of ] *MS-bn; omit MS-s*
were ] *MS-bn*; *omit MS-s*
tempests ] *MS-s*; temptations *MS-bn*
saying ] *mS37*; sey *MS-s* (*at end of line,* -ing *omitted*); for me thought this was not the cõmune vse of prayer; therfor I sayd *MS-bn*

**Chapter 3**, fols. 2r - 3r

thought't ] *DF*; thought *MS-s*; *again at 2.23*
sweem ] *glossed in margin by scribe:* regret
that ] *MS-bn*; thes *MS-s*
so ] *DF* (*for clarity*); *omit MS-s*
thought't ] *DF*; thought *MS-s*
God's will ] gods will *MS-bn*; God will *MS-s* (*cf.* Gods will *MS-s, in second sentence following*)
[6] shortness of ond ] shortness of onde *MS-s* (*and glossed in margin by scribe:* scarcely
[6] winde); shortnes of breth *MS-bn*
[7] liefer ] leuer *MS-s* (*and glossed in margin by scribe:* rather)

**Chapter 4**, fol. 3.
that was ] *DF* (*for clarity*); *omit MS-s*
homely ] *glossed in margin by scribe*: familiar
flesh ] *MS-bn adds*, Thus I toke it for that tym that our lord Ihesu of his Curteys loue would shewe me comfort before the tyme
her ] hir *MS-s*; his *Glas3* (*but final* r *in MS-s frequently looks like* s; *e.g.*, hir *at 44*r*, line 3*)
manhood ] *MS-bn; omit MS-s*

From **Chapter 5**, fols. 3$^v$ - 4r
halseth ] *MS-bn*; *MS-s partly obscured;* hedseth [*sic*] Glas3
becloseth ] *MS-bn*; *MS-s obscured*
till ] *MS-bn*; that *MS-s*; till [*sic*] *Glas3*

**Chapter 24**, fols. 17$^v$ - 18r

From **Chapter 58**, fols. 41$^v$ - 42$^v$
on two ] onto *MS-s*
kindly ] *MS-bn*; kindy *MS-s*
yielding ] yeldyng *MS-bn*; reldyng *MS-s*
endlessly ] *MS-bn*; endless *MS-s*

From **Chapter 59**, fols. 42$^{v}$ - 43r
have ] *MS-bn; omit MS-s*

From **Chapter 60**, fols. 43r - 44r
Shewing ] *DF* (*for clarity*); *omit MS-s*
seckirest ... truth ] suerest: nerest for it is most of kynd, redyest for it is most of loue, and sekerest for it is most of trewth *MS-bn*
but ] *MS-bn; omit MS-s*
bear ] *MS-bn*; beryng is *MS-s*
alone ] *MS-bn*; al love *MS-s*
so ] *DF* (*for clarity*); *omit MS-s, MS-bn*
he shewed ] he shewid *MS-s*; shewid he [*sic*] *Glas3*; shewd he *MS-bn*
so ] *DF* (*for clarity*); *omit MS-s, MS-bn*
Tenth ] x *MS-bn*; ix *MS-s*
Shewing ] *DF* (*for clarity*); *omit MS-s*
willeth ] *DF*; will *MS-s*

**Chapter 86**, fol. 57
all togeder ] all to gedyr *MS-bn*; all to God *MS-s*
learned ] *MS-bn*; lerid *MS-s* (*which may, however, represent the author's original form*)
ne ] *MS-bn*; no *MS-s*

### MARGERY (BRUNHAM) KEMPE

From ***The Book of Margery Kempe***: Ed. DWF from British Library MS Additional 61823 ("the Boke of Margerie Kempe") [*MS*] (ca. 1450; a.k.a. the "Salthows MS," so called after the name of the scribe who prepared it); here collated with the transcription by Meech (1940) [*Meech*]. For a full listing of the marginal and interlinear additions, see *Meech*. The revisions and corrections in *MS* are in at least four different hands, chiefly in red ca. 1500 and probably by a Carthusian monk at the the Mount Grace Priory. I have found no substantive errors in Meech's extraordinarily careful transcription.

**THE FIRST BOOK** (fol. 5r ff.):

**Chapter 1**, fols. 3$^{v}$-5r. (paragraph numbers in brackets)
[1] burgess ] of Lynne *in red in inner margin after* burgeys *MS*
[2] gan ] be, *in red, inserted above* gan *MS* (*repeated for most occurrences of* gan)
[3] spirits. He said ] spyrit$^{ys}$ seyd *MS*; spyrit$^{ys}$, seyd *Meech*
[6] And she took ] And [sche] toke *Meech*; And toke *MS*

**Chapter 2**, fols. 5r-6r.
[2] pun'shed ] ne *in red, above, before* pu$^{n}$ched *MS*
[4] one thing ] [o thyng] *Meech*; *omit MS*
[4] mercy ] m$^{e}$rce, *in red, in outer margin MS*

From **Chapter 3**, fol. 6.
[2] eten ] haue, *in red, above* etyn *MS*
[3] counseled ] lyvyd chast *canceled in red before* cownseld *MS*

From **Chapter 4**, fols. 7v-8v.
[2] devil's suasions ] Deuel suasynons, *with first* n *canceled in original ink MS*

From **Chapter 11**, fols. 12r-13r.

From **Chapter 13**, fol. 14.

From **Chapter 18**, fol. 21.
[3] may and ought ] *DF*; m< > *MS*; m[uste], *with note,* "ust *or* uste *and perhaps a two letter word,* as *or* so, destroyed" *Meech*. *But cf.* may & owyth to leuyn *in next sentence*
[3] Jerome ] S [*for* St.] *in red, supra, before* Jerome *MS*

From **Chapter 39**, fol. 46r.

**Chapter 46**, fol. 54.
[1] that ] that *in red, in outer margin, MS*
[1] fire of love ] fyer of lofe *in red, in inner margin, MS*
[6] of ] of *in red, above, before* Lyn *MS*
[11] the ] þe, *in red, above, before,* man *MS*

From **Chapter 47**, fols. 54r-55r.
[8] best ] therin *in red, in margin, after* beste *MS*

**Chapter 48**, fols. 55v-56v.
[3] didden her swearen ] dedyn *canceled in red, with* made *in red in outer margin immediately before it, MS*; dedyn hir sweryn *Meech* (*with note*)

From **Chapter 52**, fols. 59v-62r.
[17] thou — ] wrecche, *in red, above* þou *MS*
[22] thought it was ] thowt is was *MS*; thowt [it] was *Meech*
[23] thou ne shalt ] þu xalt *MS*; þu [ne] xalt *Meech*
[30] hinder ] hymyr *MS*
[39] five shillings ] v s. *MS* (*again below*)

From **Chapter 53**, fols. 62r-63r.
[2] he ] sche *MS, with* sc *canceled in red*
[7] saint ] saint *in red in outer margin, MS*

From **Chapter 54**, fols. 63r, 64v-65r.
[3] My ] my *in red above* Ercheb *MS*

From **Chapter 75**, fols. 86v-87r.

**Chapter 76**, fols. 87r-88r.
[4] hurt ] hurt *MS written above in red, with caret before* fayling *MS*

From **Chapter 88**, fols. 104v-105r.

From **Chapter 89**, fol. 106.

**THE SECOND BOOK**

From **Chapter 10**, fols. 120v-123r.
[1] wistly as I would not ] wistly not *MS*; wistly [as I wolde] not *Meech*
[5] thee ] *MS* hym *canceled in red after* plesyn *and* the *in red above*
[8] will ] *MS* wyll *in red, above*
[13] we ] < >*MS, letters destroyed at beginning of line; Meech* [we]

### AWISIA MOON

***The Abjuration of Hawisia Moon***: Ed. DWF from Westminster Cathedral Diocesan Archives MS B.2, fols. 102-3; as transcribed by Tanner (1977), pp. 138-54

### MARGERY BAXTER

***The Story of Margery Baxter:*** Ed. DWF from John Foxe, *Actes and Monuments* (1431; pub. 1563), pp. 407-08. Foxe omits portions of the original deposition, which is found in Westminster Diocesan Archives MS B.2. The portions of Cliffland's deposition omitted by Foxe are here represented within square brackets, English trans. DWF from Tannner (1977), pp. 44-51.
call ] *DWF*; called *Foxe*

**VERNACULAR TROTULAS**

***The Knowing of Woman's Kind in Childing:*** Ed. DWF from Bodleian Library, MS Douce 37, North Midlands (c. 1390, ms. c. 1510)

**Prologue**, fols. 1-2]
humors ] *MS om.*
treatises ] tretys *MS*

**Science of Cirurgie** (c. 1380): Ed. DWF from Bodleian MS Ashmole 1396.

**Conception**, pp. 20-22
he ] *MS om.*
as ] is *MS*

**Mammaries**, p. 28

**Sexual anatomy**, pp. 173-75
contract ] *DF* (*a word or phrase is lacking MS*)

**Breast cancer**, 265-67
drawn ] drawe *MS*
From ***The Book of Rota*** (c. 1550): Ed. DWF from Cambridge University Library *MS MS* Ii.vi.33.

**Infertility,** fols. 3-5, 11v-13.

From **Woman's Privy Sickness** (c. 1525): Ed. DWF from B.L. MS Sloane 2463

**Prologue**, fol. 194r.
women's ] women *MS*
and so ] and *MS*

**Menstruation**, fol. 194v]
such as ] as *MS*

**Conception**, fol. 205v

**Abortifacient herbs**, fol. 216r, 197-8]
so that ] that *MS*
bothon ] bothor *MS*
and ] *MS om.*
still have ] haue *MS*
drawn ] drawe *MS*

**Difficulty in childbirth,** fol. 216v-7r, 219r, 207r.

**The Ache of Loss,** 215r.

**Obstetric fistula**, 229r.

**Uterine prolapse,** fols. 229v-230r.

From ***Liber Trotuli*** (c. 1525): Ed. DWF from B.L. MS Add. 34111.

**Non-surgical treatment for fistula**, fol. 211-12v.

**Other remedies**, fol. 212.

**JULIAN BARNES**

From the ***Boke of Huntyng***: Ed. DWF from Bodleian Library MS Rawl. poet. 143 [*MS-r*] (latter 15th century; for scribe, cf. Bodleian MSS Douce 324 and Rawl. C.86), fols. 1r-11av; extracts from fols. 1r, 3v-5r. Collated with Lambeth Palace Library MS 491 [*MS-lp*], fols. 287r-290v (incomplete, with no heading or subscription); with [*The Boke of St. Albans*] (1486) [*Q1*] and (1496) [*Q2*] (*Qq* where they agree); and with G. Tilander, ed. (1964) [*Til*]. Barnes's source, Twety's "Le Venery" (as recorded in British Library MS CB.xii [15th century] supplies some corrections [*Twet*]. For convenient cross-reference, line-numbering is adopted from *Til* rather than being keyed to *MS-r*.
*title* ] *adapted from the colophon in Q1; omit mRp14*

**Prologue**
prologue ] *Q1*; *omit MS-r*
pr.2 therein ] therm *Q1*
pr.6 book ] boooke *Q1*

**Beasts of venery** ] Bestys of venery *Qq* (heading for lines 1-8, *Qq* sec. I); *omit MS-r*

**Beasts of the chase** ] Bestys of the chace *Qq* (heading for lines 9-16, *Qq* sec. II); *omit MS-r; 1-16 continuous in MS-r, fol. 1*r.
1 sons ] sone *MS-lp*; My dear sons where ] Wheresouere ye fare *Q1*
2 Take ... tell ] Takith good heed how Tristam woll tell *MS-lp*; take hede how Tristram dooth you tell *Q1*
3 manie ] maide *MS-lp*
4 your ] yowre *Qq*; *MS-r* oure; Listen ... lere ] Q1Lystyn to yowre dame and she shall yow lere
Listene ... here ] lystenith ˙e to ˙or dame and y [*sic*] shal yow lere *MS-lp*; Lystyn to yowre dame and she shall yow lere *Q1*
5 manie ] maide *MS-lp*
6 First of them ] The first of theym *Qq;* secound ] the secund *Qq;* an ] the *Qq, MS-lp*
8 wolf ] wolf eke [eke *written above*] *MS-lp*; no moe ] not oon moo *Qq*; eke [eke *canc.*] no mo *MS-lp*
9 so ] so eure *MS-lp*; that *Qq*; comen ] come *MS-lp*, cum *Qq*; play ] playne *Qq*
10 Now shall I tell you ] I shall tell yow *MS-lp*; I shall yow tell *Qq*; be'n ] ben *MS-r,* be *MS-lp*; of chase ] of the chace *MS-lp*; of enchace *Qq*
11 Oon ... doe ] One of tho a Buk another a doo *MS-r*; Oon of theym is the bucke, a nother is the doo, *Qq*; On of hem is the buk the tothir is the do *MS-lp*
12 sonnes ] chylde *Qq;*
13 Whereso ] Wherso eure *MS-lp*; ye shall ] *Qq; omit MS-r, MS-lp*
14 Or in forest I you tell. ] *followed next in MS-lp by* Ane for to speke of þe hart...

**Of the hunting of the hare** ] Of the huntyng of the haare *Qq* (heading for lines 235-328, *Qq* sec. 22). Continuous verse *MS-r*, without heading, fols. 3v-5r; *MS-lp*, fol. 288v.
237 he ] sche *MS-lp*; his houndes ] *omit* his *Qq*
238 houndes ] houndis that *Qq*;
239 openes ] opnynis *MS-lp*; opnes *MS-r*; openys *Q1*; openyth *Q2*; hit ] it *Q1*
240 say shal ] shall say *Qq*; shal soy *MS-lp*
241 woulden ] wold(e) *Qq*, *MS-lp*; oute ] *omit Qq*
242 This ] That *Qq*, *MS-lp*; sons ] son(n)e *MS-lp*, *Qq*
242-43 *MS-r wrongly inserts lines corresponding to Til 153-160* ( = *Qq* [XV] Whiche beestis shall be reride with the lymer)
243 And ] *Qq*; *omit MS-lp*, *MS-r*; has coupled ] hath cowplid *MS-lp*; hath couplyd *Qq*; has complet *MS-r*
244 into the fielde ] into þe feld *MS-lp*; into felde *MS-r*; to the felde *Qq*
245 And…will ] And there his couples ben of Cast at his will *MS-r*; And his couplis Whan he hath cast at his will *MS-lp*; And when he has of cast his cowples at will *Qq*
246 till ] *Qq*; thus til *MS-r*
247 sus ] se [=*ci*] *Qq*; twice ] sey twyes *MS-lp*; thries *Qq*
248-9 *Qq transposes; MS-lp omits lines 248, 250*
248 And ... low) ] And then say . Sa sa cy auaunt So how . I you pray *Qq*

249 thrice ] iij *mR14*; thries *MS-lp*
250 *Qq, MS-lp omit line*
252 Drawen ] And draw *MS-lp*, *Qq*; says thus ] say as *MS-lp*, *Qq*
253 calls ] call *MS-lp*, *Qq*; Here ... so ] Here how amy . agayne hem call so *Qq*
254 souef ... souef ] swef ... shefe *Twet*; soft go ] *Q1*; soth to go *MS-r*; soft to go *MS-lp*; soft thoo *Q2*
255 there as ho ] *DF*; þe hare *MS-lp*; there he *MS-r, Qq; cf. line 267*; And ... been ] And iff any fynde of the hare ther he hath bene *Q1*; hath go *Q2*
256 That hight ] That hate *MS-r*; And he hight *Qq*; And hight *MS-lp*; Richar ] Richarde *Q2*; rigge *MS-lp*; thus ] *Qq*; þus sais *MS-r*; sey þus *MS-lp*; bedene ] crye loo *Q2*
257 you well ] shall you *Qq, MS-lp*
258 trouver ... à la ] trouere ... ou le *Twet*; trouer le couard oñ le *MS-r*; troner la cowarde on la *Q1*; trouer le coward one le *MS-lp*
259 is ] *omit Qq*; worthy ] which *MS-lp*
260 weens ] That wenyth *Qq, MS-lp*
261 seen ] se where *Qq*; se *MS-lp*; has ] hath *Qq*
262 in ... green ] in tyme when cornes ben grene *MS-r*; in tyme whan þe corne is grene *MS-lp*; in the tyme of the corne grene *Qq*
263-67 And ... green ] *omit Qq*
263 thou see'st ] ye see *MS-lp* (cf. *este,* 264)
265 all ] on *MS-lp*
266 sweet … ho ] þe sweete þer she *MS-lp*
267 finden ] find *MS-lp*; cornes be'n green ] *DF*; corn(e) is grene *MS-lp, MS-r; cf. line 262*
268 chasen not well ] chace not wele *MS-lp*; chace weel *Qq*
269 ye ] *MS-lp*, *Qq*; he *MS-r*; Then ... still ] Then III motis shall ye blaw booth lowde and shill *Q1*, *Q2*; Then blow three notes loude and shrill *Qq*3
270 and ] *omit MS-lp;* ho ] she *MS-lp*; has ] hath *Q2*
271 Then say ] *Qq*; And þen say *MS-r*; says ] say *Qq*; illeoques ] illeosque *Twet*; place ] path *Q2*
272 by ] *MS-lp*; be *MS-r*; in *Qq*; While...find ] Whil þei wele of her fynde *MS-lp*; unto tyme that ye hir fynde *Qq*
273 Then castes ] And caste *MS-lp*; And then cast *Qq*; a sign ] assygge *Twet*
274 be ] hath be *Qq*
275 For … to be, her ] ffore at hir form glalle to be hir *MS-r*; Oder at hir forme for gladli to be she *Qq*; Or at her fourme for gladly to be is her *MS-lp*
276 There … relief ] *DF*; There ho has pastured but in tyme releve *MS-r*; Ther as she hath pasturid but yn tyme of relefe *MS-lp*; Ther she hath pasturid in tyme of relefe *Qq*, pasturid [but] in tyme *Til*.
277 And ... mace ] *DF*; And if eny of hir fynde or musyng mase *MS-r*; And any hounde fynd or musyng of hir mace *Qq*; And if eny hound fynd or musyng of her make *MS-lp*; And [if] any hounde [of hir] fynde or musyng of hir mace *Til*
278 There ... gone ] Ther ho has ben*n* and ho be gone *MS-r*; þr as she haþ bene & she be goñe *MS-lp*; Ther as she hath byne and is goon *Q1*; be [*for* byne] *Q2*
280 arrière ] arier *MS-lp*; arere *Twet, MS-r*; avez *Q1*; arer *Q2*; sayes ] sa *Qq*; so as *MS-lp*; as high ] also lowde *Qq*
281 ad esté ] *MS-lp, Q1*; and est *MS-r*
283 seen ... last ] *DF*; seen hir into playne go oute at þe last *MS-r*; se her into þe playn gone at þe last *MS-lp*; se unto the playne her at the last *Qq*
284 feld, arable ] feld or arable *MS-lp*; felde or in errabull *Qq*; wode ] *MS-lp, Twet*; wold *MS-r*; the wode *Qq*
285-86 houndes … then ] houndes there wel of hir þen / Says *MS-r*; houndis þr will fynd of her þan *MS-lp*; hounde will fynde of her ther, then / Say *Qq*
286 douce ... est il ] douce amy la est il *MS-lp*, *Twet, Til*; douce amy il est *MS-r*; la douce amy la est a *Qq*
287 ho is comen ] ther he come *Qq*; þr she is come *MS-lp*
288 And ] *omit MS-lp*; say ] ye shall say *Qq*; þow shalt sey *MS-lp*; so how, so how ] *DF*; so how *MS-r*, *MS-lp*, *Qq*
289 ci...ci ] si...si *MS-r, MS-lp*; ey...ey *Q1*; cy...cy *Q2*; so how ] *MS-r*, so how, so how *MS-lp*, *Qq* (*2nd Qq* so how *belongs with 290*); twy ] *MS-lp*, *Q1*; twey *MS-r*; twyse *Q2*
290 mou ] may *MS-lp, Qq*; my ] now *Qq*; venery ] veneryce *Q2*
291 as ye trow she will ] as best ye trowe she wel *MS-r*; as ˙e wene she wolle *MS-lp*; as ye trow he will *Qq*
292 seemes…says ] semeth…say *Q2*; semith…seith *MS-lp*
293 Là … venu ] La douce la est il venuz *MS-r, MS-lp*; La douce la est a venuz *Qq*; là, douce amy, là est-il venuz *Twet, Til*
294 thrice "So how, sesse!" and ] iii sohowe cese and *MS-r*; thries sohow and þan *MS-lp*; .iii. sohow . say ye *Qq*; thryes sohowe cese say ye *Q2*; seems ] semith *MS-lp*; semyth *Q2*; if…all ] And iff it semes well yow to fynde all *Q1*; And if it semith yow fo [*sic*] fynd her al *MS-lp*
296 ween ] wenen *Qq*; well ] *omit Qq;* says ] say *Qq*; sey *MS-lp;* how here ] how here how here *Qq*
297 How here, how here, douce, how ] How here douce how here how *Qq*; how douce how here how here *MS-lp*; hereby settes ] here by settes *MS-r*; here he sittys *Q1*; here he syttyth *Q2*; be her sette *MS-lp*
298 Thus ] So *Qq*; childer ] chyldre *Q1*; chyldren *Q2*; dere childryn *MS-lp*; man lets ] man lette *MS-lp*; thyng lettes *Qq*; thyng lettyth *Q2*
299 ff. *MS-lp inserts passage here about skinning and cooking the hare; lines 301 following do not appear, in that fols. 289-92 are lacking;* And all ] All *Qq;* were ] *DF*; wore *MS-r*, *Q1*; be *Q2*
300 and no more ] I tell the *Q2*
301 unfill ... of ] *DF*; unfulfill eche maner *MS-r*; unfill eche maner of *Qq*
302 hunter … has ] hunt euermoore in his mowth that worde he haas *Qq*
303 if ] iff *Qq*; of *MS-r*; rennen ] renne *Qq*
304 ruse ] reuse *MS-r*; renne *Qq*; be'n ] be *Qq*
305 to havelon ] for to hanylon *Qq*; does ] doos *Q1*; doth *Q2*; does the roe ] the roo dooth *Qq*
307 dill ] dwell *Qq*; can … go ] can no ferre ga *MS-r*; cannot owte go *Q1*, goo *Q2*
308 say, "Ho, ça…" ] sey ho so *MS-r*; say . ho sa *Qq*
309 coupler ] *Twet, Til*; compler *MS-r*; complex *Q1*; couples *Q2*; such ] sich *Q1*; that ] the *Qq*
310 is … as ] is as moche as *MS-r*; as moch is as *Qq*
311 But … forth-brought ] *DF*; But so how is shorter in speche whan it is forth bro˙t *MS-r*; Bot for . sohow . is short in speche when it is brought *Qq*
312 sayn ] say *Qq*; and ] but *Q2*
313 chasen ] chase *Qq*; they aren ] thay renne *Qq*
314 shall ye say ] ye shall say *Q1*; there ] there tare *Q2*

315 sto ] ston *Q1*; stou *Q2*; then ] *omit Qq*
315-20 assayne ] hossame, hossame ... hossame ... ossayn *Twet*
318 fallen ] fayle *Qq*; says ... go ] *DF*; saies þus fyrre er ye go *MS-r*; say thus ferther or ye goo *Qq*
319 souef à lui, douce, à lui ] *DF*; swife ale douce ale ale *MS-r*; swef a luy douce a luy *Q1*
320 ho, how ] ho hawe *MS-r*; ho hoy *Qq*; ça ] sa *Qq*; so *MS-r*
321 So how, venez à coupler ] so, venez à couplere *Twet*; So how venez à compler *MS-r*; So how so how venez a coupler *Qq*; does ] do *Qq*
321 ye mou ] may ye *Qq*; other ] *omit Qq*
323 let be kid ] let not be hydde *Q2*; does ] do *Qq*; *Qq adds* [*327-28*]: All my sonnys in same / and thus may ye konne of game.

**The reward for houndes** ] The rewarde for howndys *Qq* (heading for lines 133-1448, *Qq* sec. XIII). Continuous verse, without heading, *MS-r* , sig. 3r; *MS-lp*, fol. 288r.
133 have ] hath *Qq*
134 the hounds ] his houndes *MS-lp*; hem then *Qq*; her ] the *Qq, MS-lp*
134-5 *Qq adds between 134 and 135*: The paunche also, / yeve hem noon of thoo, / Wich rewarde, when oon the erth it is dalt, / With all goode hunteris the halow it is calt. *Q1*, dealyd ... namyd [*for* dalt ... calt] *Q2; cf. MS-lp, which inserts the following between lines 146 and 147*: The paunche also ˙eve hem none of þe roo / The which rewarde on erthe whan it is dalt / Wiþ all good hunters þe halow is calt; *omit Rp14*
135 sides and boweles ] the sides and the bowelles *MS-r*; the sides and with the bowellis *Qq, MS-lp*
136 within her ] with in the wombe *Qq, MS-lp*
137 look ye ] like þei be *MS-lp*
141 for-yet ] foryete *MS-r, MS-lp*; forgete *Qq*
142 Bringes 'hem for ] Bot bryng hem to *Qq*; But bryng hê home to *MS-lp*
143-44 And ... mair ] And of this sayd beest to trete here it shall be lete *Q2*; *MS-lp omits, and continues instead with lines corresponding to Qq 235 ff.*
144 Mou speak ] Speke we *Q1*
Explicit ... Hunting ] Explicit Dam Iulyans Barnes in her boke of huntyng *Q1*, Bernes *Q2*; Explicit expliceat ludere scriptor eat *MS-r*

**The reward for houndes** ] The rewarde for howndys *Qq* (heading for lines 133-1448, *Qq* sec. XIII). Continuous verse, without heading, *MS-r* , sig. 3r; *MS-lp*, fol. 288r.
133 have ] hath *Qq*
134 the hounds ] his houndes *MS-lp*; hem then *Qq*; her ] the *Qq, MS-lp*
134-5 *Qq adds between 134 and 135*: The paunche also, / yeve hem noon of thoo, / Wich rewarde, when oon the erth it is dalt, / With all goode hunteris the halow it is calt. *Q1*, dealyd ... namyd [*for* dalt ... calt] *Q2; cf. MS-lp, which inserts the following between lines 146 and 147*: The paunche also ˙eve hem none of þe roo / The which rewarde on erthe whan it is dalt / Wiþ all good hunters þe halow is calt; *omit Rp14*
135 sides and boweles ] the sides and the bowelles *MS-r*; the sides and with the bowellis *Qq, MS-lp*
136 within her ] with in the wombe *Qq, MS-lp*
137 look ye ] like þei be *MS-lp*
141 for-yet ] foryete *MS-r, MS-lp*; forgete *Qq*
142 Bringes 'hem for ] Bot bryng hem to *Qq*; But bryng hê home to *MS-lp*
143-44 And ... mair ] And of this sayd beest to trete here it shall be lete *Q2*; *MS-lp omits, and continues instead with lines corresponding to Qq 235 ff.*
144 Mou speak ] Speke we *Q1*
Explicit ... Hunting ] Explicit Dam Iulyans Barnes in her boke of huntyng *Q1*, Bernes *Q2*; Explicit expliceat ludere scriptor eat *MS-r*

**MARGARET of ANJOU and The Flower Poet**

**William de la Pole, attrib., *To Serve the Flower***: Ed. DWF from Bodleian MS Fairfax 16 (formerly Bod. MS 3896) [*MS*], fols. 325v -327r (indexed as "How þe louer is sett to serve þe floure," fol. 2r); "Anno 1450" written at top of fol. 1r; with heraldic arms on fol. 14v beneath illustration of Mars and Venus. Collated with MacCracken, "An English Friend of Charles of Orléans" (1911) [*MacC*], 168-71; Hammond, *English Verse between Chaucer and Surrey* (1927) [*Hamm*], 200-01; and Robbins, *Secular Lyrics*, 2nd ed. (1955) [*Rob55*], 186-89 ("In Praise of Margaret the Queen: By the Duke of Suffolk"), follow *MS* except as noted.
5 thee ] the *MS*; *Hamm mistakes* the *as def. article and emends to* ye
14 to ] *Rob55*; *omit MS*
19 *marg. note, in later hand*: Chaucer
21 Of ] *DF*; And of *MS*
19 *marg. note, in later hand*: lidgate of bury
22 go' ] go *MS*; gon *Rob55, with note*; gon [*sic*] *MacC*
29 to ] *DF*; *omit MS*
35 choose ] chese *MS*
55 'hemself ] thaym self *Hamm*
56 their ] thair *MS*; [to] their *MacC*
57 by ] be *MS*
58 moved ] myued *MS, Rob55*; myned [*sic*] *MacC*; myned [*sic*, from *MacC*] *emended to* [meuyd] *Hamm*
65 thou ] *MS*; thom [*sic*] *MacC*; thom [*sic, from MacC*] *"emended" to* thou *Hamm, Rob55*
69 thee ] the *MacC, Rob55*; *omit MS*
76 shall be ] is *MS, Rob55*; is [out] *MacC*
78 If ] It [*sic*] *Rob55*
78-82 *In MS, line 79 is wrongly situated between lines 81 and 82, with scribal marks for transposition*

**William de la Pole, attrib., *The Assembly of Ladies:*** Ed. DWF from Trinity College (Cambridge) MS R.3.19 (latter 15th century) [*MS-tc*], fols. 55r-65v; partly collated with Longleat House (Warminster) MS 258 (ca. 1500) [*MS-lh*], a later MS copy with which *MS-tc* is closely related [*MS-lh*], fols. 58r-75v (*MS-t/l* where *MS-tc* and *MS-lh* agree). Collated also with British Museum MS Addit. 34360 (late 15th century) [*MS-a*], fols. 37r-49r; and the more noteworthy variants in Thynne's collected Chaucer (1532, first publication of *AL*) [*Thyn*], fols. 294a-298b. Thynne's emendations, which are far too numerous for detailed notice here, are given as adopted; Skeat (1897) [*Sk*] generally follows *Thyn.* Pearsall (1962) [*Pear*] follows *mAd* except as noted. For a full description of *MS-tc* see M. R. James, *Western MSS. in the Library of Trinity College, Cambridge* (4 vols., 1900-4), 2.69-74; for a description of *MS-lh* see

Eleanor P. Hammond, "MS. Longleat 258 – A Chaucerian Codex." *MLN* 20.3 (1905), 77-9.
8 fair ] fayre *Thyn*; foure *MS-a*
11 fantasies ] fantasyse *Thyn, Pear*; fantasy *MS-tc*; fantise *MS-a, MS-lh*
18 ne wrought ] *omit* ne *MS-a, MS-t/l, Thyn*; of nothing wrought *Sk*; Pearsall: *cf. CT* 4.685: "He wente his wey, as hym no thyng ne roghte" (*Riverside Chaucer*)
19 that ] *Thyn; omit MS-t/l, MS-a; cf. 67, 175*
29 an ] *MS-t/l, Thyn, Pear; omit MS-a*
33 And...intent ] *omit MS-a*; *Pear supplies from MS-tc*
33 our ] *Thyn*; other *MS-t/l*
34 weened ] wend *Thyn*; went *MS-t/l, MS-a*
50 methought ] my thought *MS-a*; me thought *Pear*
51 proportion ] *MS-a*; dew proporcioun *MS-t/l*
53 masonry ] *MS-t/l, Thyn, Pear*; mesure *MS-a*
55 with ] a *MS-a*
57 With ] *MS-t/l, Thyn, Pear*; Was *MS-a*
61 *Ne...also* ] *MS-a*; Ne momblynes and souenes also *MS-tc*; Ne momblysnesse and souenesse also *MS-lh, Thyn*
64 beneath ] beneth *MS-a*; & benche *MS-t/l, Thyn*
77 I fell ] fil *MS-a*
86 sovenez] *MS-a*; stones *MS-t/l, Thyn*
88 loialment] *MS-a*; et loyalment *MS-t/l, Thyn*
105 Pertayning is unto *Sk*; P$^{e}$rteyneng unto *MS-a*; Appertaining is to ] *Thyn*;
109 which ... anon ] whiche shuld be anone *MS-a*
111 furthermore ] more *MS-a*
112 no ] *DF*; *omit MS-t/l, MS-a, Thyn; cf. 124*
121 As many ] *MS-t/l, Thyn*; As many as *MS-a* (as *inserted above, in different ink*)
124-5 *transposed in MS-a*
125 sore ] *DF*; *omit MS-t/l, MS-a, Thyn; cf. 466, 584*
137 mannere ] maners *Thyn*; maner is *MS-a*
149 they ] *MS-a*; I *MS-t/l, Thyn*
153 questions … large ] questions nothyng may I be large *MS-a*
154 meddle…charge ] meddle me no further than my charge *Thyn*; medle me no further than is my charge *MS-a*
162 and ] *MS-t/l, Thyn, Pear*; *omit MS-a*
163 bay ] *MS-t/l, Thyn, Pear*; *omit MS-a*
167 every ] *MS-t/l, Thyn, Pear*; euer *MS-a*
430 Therefore ] There for *MS-t/l, Thyn, Pear*; They for *MS-a*
437 when as ] when *MS-t/l, MS-a, Thyn*; *cf. 109, 438, 611*
437 had ] had so *Thyn*
450 Susters ] Systers *Thyn*; Suster *MS-a*
454 eche ] eche a *MS-a*
455 was ] is *MS-a*
458 love ] *MS-t/l, Thyn*; the love *MS-a*
461 how ] *omit MS-a*
461 right ] a ri˙t *Thyn*; *omit MS-a*
463 how that Melusine] how Melusine *Pear*; how Enclusene *MS-a*; Hawes the shene *MS-t/l, Thyn*
474 furthermore ] *MS-t/l, Thyn*; further *MS-a*
475 withouten ] *Sk*; without *MS-t/l, MS-a, Thyn*
484 right ] *Thyn*; full *MS-a*
491 as ] *MS-t/l, Thyn, Pear*; al *MS-a*
496 with ] bi *MS-a*
501 stand ] stande *Thyn*; gan stande *MS-a*
509 needeth ] nedeth *Thyn*; must *MS-a*
519-32 And furthermore ... every wise ] *omit MS-a; Pear supplies from MS-tc*
532 full ] *Sk*; *omit MS-t/l, MS-a, Thyn*
533 serp ] serpe *Pear*; sorte *MS-a, MS-t/l, Thyn*
534 In ] *MS-t/l, Thyn, Pear*; Of *MS-a*
545 after her ] *Thyn*; after in theyr *MS-a*
720 court ] *MS-t/l, Thyn, Pear*; comfort *MS-a*
728 bring ... by ] bryng it yow bi *MS-a*; hyt yow tell by *MS-tc*; it tel you by *Thyn*
745 here ] *MS-t/l, Thyn, Pear*; her *MS-a*
747 great ] *MS-t/l, Thyn, Pear* (grete); *omit MS-a*
748 now ] *MS-t/l, Thyn, Pear;* how *MS-a*

**MARGARET of ANJOU**
Letters. Ed. DWF from transcripts by Cecil Monro (1863).

**The Queen to Robert Kent**, no. 60, pp. 89-90.

**To the Master of St. Giles in the Fields**, no. 64, 95.

Upham ] Vhome *MS, Monro*

**To Dame Jane Carew**, no. 65, 97-98.

**To the Executors of Cardinal Beaufort's Will**, no.70, p. 102.

**To Nicholas Straunge of Iseldo**n, no.93 p. 125.

Islington ] Iseldon *MS, Monro* (caption and address)

**To Sir John Forester**, no. 95, 127-28.
now ] *DWF*, MS; you *Monro* [sic]

**To William Gaskrik**, no.122, pp. 153-54.

Gaskrik ] Gastrik *Monro* (Cf. Gaskrik, e.g. Close Rolls)

**Letter of Recommendation…Nuneaton**, no. 134, p. 164.

**To the Citizens of London** (1461): Ed. DWF from British Library Harl. MS 543, fol. 147.
*York* ] n. *MS* (Margaret in her rough draft leaves space for York's title marked with an *n.* (for *nomen*), to be filled in later)

**(Balthasar of Syrie, to England [c. 1470, parody]):** Ed. DWF from Monro transcript, no. 136

**The FINDERN MANUSCRIPT**
Ed. DWF from Cambridge MS Ff.1.6 (the sole textual authority for the poems printed here). Nos. 1-4, 6, 7, and 9 collated with Robbins, *PMLA* 69 (1954) [*Rob54*]; no. 5 with R. H. Robbins, *Secular Lyrics* (1955) [*Rob55*], 156-57. Nos. 1, 5, 6.

**Farewell to His Betrothed**: ***I may well sygh for greuous ys my payne…***), fol. 20
10 unto ] *DF*; to *MS*
19 I ] *DF*; *MS om.*

***Margery Hungerford, Without Variaunce*:** "Where y haue chosyn...," fol. 20v [=*Rob54*, no. 8].
7 endure ] in lyfe endure *MS* (*perhaps deriving from* in lyfe [*lined out*] indure *in an earlier ms. copy*)
13 By ] *MS*; þy [*sic*] *Rob54.* Conflated in Person, *Cambridge Middle English Lyrics* (1962) with the ensuing quatrain on fol. 20v:
Ye are to blame to sett yowre hert so sore
Seþen þat ye wot that hyt [ys] rekeurles *MS om.* ys
To encrece yowre payne more & more –
Syn þat ye wot þat she is merceles.

***Sorrow***: "*This ys no lyf a las y*[t] *y do lede…,* "fol. 153r.

***Goodbye***: "Yit wulde I nat the causer faryd a mysse…," fol. 153v-154r
8 in ] *DF; MS om.*

***Alas, Why***: "Alas, alas, and alas – why...," fols. 137v-138r [=*Rob54*, no. 35; *Rob55,* no. 167].
7 thy ] *Rob54*, *Rob55*; *omit MS*
of ] *DF*; *omit MS*
17 take me o'er ] *DF*; me owre *MS* (*word missing; cf.* owr-take, *below, "Of a Star," line 47* )
19 earthly ] *DF*; erly *MS*

[***Of a Star***:] "For to pent...," fols. 143v-144r [*Rob54*, no. 40].
1 pent ] pente *MS*; preuente *Rob54* (*on account of superscript line above* pente)
4 ways ] *DF*; wass *MS*
7 sweat for feint ] *DF*; sweyte ffor ffent *MS*
13 star ] star˙e *MS*
14 compare ] compasse *MS, Robb*
16 beams ] *DF*; beyme *MS*
17 yseems ] *DF*; ys En (*with trailing line*) *MS*; ys Eu[c]r *Rob54*
24 hit ] Hyl [*canceled*] hyt *MS*
24 mine eie ] my nee *MS*
25 cloud ] chirh [*canceled*] cloud *MS*
29 shone ] Scwon *MS*
30 Streaming ] Streymyn *MS*; Etremeyt [*sic*] *Rob54*
31 *MS* But *at top of page, uncanceled, as line by itself preceding line 31*
47 o'ertake ] owr take *MS*; owr-take *Rob54*
51 When ] Whell *corrected to* When *MS*; When *Rob54*

***Continuaunce***: "Continuaunce / Of remembraunce…" fols. 138v-139.

***Men***: "Whatso men sayen...," fol. 56r [*Rob54*, no. 17].
31 begeled ] *DF*; be-gelid *MS*

***Absence***: "My woeful heart ...," fol. 69v [*Rob54*, no. 23]; first printed in Halliwell, *Reliquæ Antiquæ* (1845) [*Hall*], 1.169.
1 thus ] thus *Hall*; this [= thus] *MS, Rob54*
10 make me fain ] *DF*; make me to be fayn *MS*
12 all ] *DF*; *omit MS*

***Love Cycle***: "Welcome be ye, my souereine…"
From fols. 135r-136r [=*Rob54*, no. 31].
Miscopied in MS from four 13-line stanzas rhyming *aabbaabaabba;* 1.7 lacking, I-IV in MS ordered 4,1,2,3
I.1 your ] from *MS*
I.1=7 woll ] woul *MS*
IV.2 causer ] *DF* (*cf.* causer *in* ["*Goodbye*,"] *line 1*); cause *MS*
IV.7 My…pain ] *DF* (conjectural, to supply line lacking in the MS)

***Good Fortune***: "Sith Fortune hath me set thus in this wyse…," fol. 137r.
2 I callèd ] MS callyd

**The PASTON LETTERS:** Ed. DWF from MSS as noted. Quotation from uncaptioned letters are documented where they appear, in the footnotes.

**Elizabeth Clere to John P. I (29 June [1449]):** Ed. DWF from B.L. MS Add. 34888, fol. 34

**Elizabeth Paston Poynings to Agnes Paston** (3 Jan. [1458/9]): Ed. DWF fr. B.L. MS Add. 34888, fol. 136.

**Agnes Berry Paston to William P. I (3 Jan. [1458/9]):** Ed. DWF from B.L. MS Add. 34888, fol. 136.

**Margaret (Mautby) Paston to John Paston I (14 December [1441])]°:** Ed. DWF from B.L. MS Add. 43490, fol. 34.

**Margaret (Mautby) Paston to John Paston I (28 September [1443])**: Ed. DWF from B.L. MS Add. 34888, fol. 8.
ye ] *MS om.*
hers ] *MS;* here [*sic*] *ed. Davis*

**Agnes Berry Paston to William P. I (3 Jan. [1458/9]):** Ed. DWF from B.L. MS Add. 34888, fol. 136.

**John Paston III to Sir John Paston (May 1469):** Ed. DWF from B.L. MS Add. 34889, fol. 77.

**Richard Calle to Margaret Paston (August? 1469):** Ed. DWF from B.L. MS Add. 34889, fols. 78-9.

**Margaret Paston to Sir John P. (10-11 Sept. 1469):** Ed. DWF from B.L. MS Add. 34889, fol 83v.
Richard Calle ] he *MS*

**Margaret Paston to Sir John P. (12 Sept. 1469):** Ed. DWF from B.L. MS Add. 34889, fol. 88.
is ] *MS om.*

**Sir John Paston to Margaret Paston (15 Sept 1469):** Ed. DWF from B.L. MS Add. 34889, fol. 83v.
Caister ] *MS om.*

**Margaret Paston to Sir John Paston (30 Sept 1469):** Ed. DWF from B.L. MS Add. 34889, fols. 95v-96r.
send ] *MS om.*

**Sir John Paston to John P. III (9 March 1476/7):** Ed. DWF from B.L. MS Add. 27445, fol. 106.

**John Paston III to John P. II (1 March 1469/70):** Ed. DWF from B.L. MS Add. 34889, fol. 193r.

**Elizabeth Brews to John P. III (ca. Jan. 1476/7)**: Ed. DWF from B.L. MS Add. 27445, fol. 105.
unto ] un *MS*
mine husbond and ye ] and mine husbond and ye MS
an ] and *MS*

**Margery Brews to John P. III (9/10 Feb. 1477)**: Ed. DWF from B.L. MS Add. 43490, fol. 23.

**Elizabeth Brews to John P. III (9/10 Feb. 1477)**: Ed. DWF from B.L. MS Add. 43490, fol. 22.
is ] *DWF*; omit MS; cf. letter from Thomas Kela to John Paston (Feb. 1477): "And I harde my lady sey þ[t] it was a febill oke, þ[t] was kut down at the first stroke" (B.L. MS Add 43490, fol. 25; Davis 2.436).

**Margery Brews to John P. III (14? Feb. 1477)**. : Ed. DWF from B.L. MS Add. 43490, fol. 24.
all ] *DWF*; *om. MS*
God ] Good *MS*
it ] *DWF*; is *MS*

**Sir John Paston to John P. II (9 March 1476/7):** Ed. DWF from B.L. MS Add. 27445, fol. 106.
your man, John ] you man, I *MS*
Thomas Grey ] T. Grey *MS*

**John Paston II to Sir John P. (9 March 1476/7):** Ed. DWF from B.L. Add. 27445, fol. 107.

**Sir John Paston to John P. III ([28 March 1477]),** Ed. DWF from B.L. MS Add. 27445, fol. 110.

**Margaret Paston to Elizabeth Brews (11 Jun 1477)** : Ed. DWF from B.L. MS Add. 27445, fol. 112.
known ] knowe *MS*

**"Margaret Paston" to John P. III (29 June 1477).]** : Ed. DWF from B.L. MS Additional 27445, fol. 113v.

**Sir John Paston to Margaret P. (7 Aug. 1477).** : Ed. DWF from B.L. MS Add. 27446, fol. 1.

**Margery Paston to Sir John Paston (11 Aug. 1477).** : Ed. DWF from B.L. MS Add. 27446, fol. 2.
Cockett a penny ] hym peny *MS*
May God ] God *MS*

**John Paston III to Sir John P. (21 Jan. 1477/8)**: Ed. DWF from B.P. MS Add. 27446, fol. 8.

**John Paston III to Margaret P. (3 Feb. 1477/8)** : Ed. DWF from B.P. MS Add. 27446, fol. 9.
her ] & her soiornaunt E. Paston recomandyth him *MS*

**Margery Brews Paston to John P. III (1 Nov. 1481 or '82)**: Ed. DWF from B.P. MS Addit. 27446, fol. 51;
you ] *MS om.*
it ] *MS om.*

**Margery Brews Paston to John P. III (4 Nov. 1481 or '82)**: Ed. DWF from B.P. MS Addit. 27446, fol. 52.

**Margery Brews Paston to John P III (21 Jan. 1485/6):** Ed. DWF fr. B.P. MS Addit. 27446, fol. 62.

**The LEAF POET**

***The Floure and the Leaf***: Ed. DWF from Speght (1598) [*Sp1*], fols. 365v-368v; with collations from Speght, 2[nd] ed., (1602) [*Sp2*], fols. 344r-346v; Urry (1721) [*Urr*], pp. 473-78; Skeat (1854) [*Sk*], 361-79; and Pearsall (1962) [*Pear*], 85-102. *Sp2* and *Pear* follow *Sp1* except as noted (with many orthographical differences in *Sp2*). The emendations of Urry and Skeat, which are far too numerous for a detailed listing here, are generally given only as adopted for this ed. All substantive emendations adopted for this ed. from *Urr* are adopted also by *Sk*, except as noted otherwise (albeit with many orthographical differences in *Sk*).
4 soft ] *Urr, Pear*; oft *Sp1*
7 everiche ] *DF*; euery *Sp1*
9 mead ] *Urr*; in mede *Sp1*
25 very ] *Sk*; *omit Sp1*
27 gan to ] *Urr*; gan *Sp1, Sk; cf. 94, 319, 385, 414, 446*
37 briddes songes for to ] birdis songis for to *Urr*; briddes song fort *Sp1*; briddes song for to *Sp2, Pear*
41 heart and ear ] hert and ere *Urr*; hart and with eare *Sp1*
46 ne ] *DF*; *omit Sp1*; ther *Sk*; *cf. 203*
50 all ] *Sk*; *omit Sp1*
53 unto green velvette ] *DF*; unto green welwet *Pear*; unto grene wel wot I *Sp1*; to grene woll wot I *Urr*; *cf. 141, 233, 261*
54 yeden in ] *Urr*; yede as in *Sk*; yede in *Sp1*
55 of ] *DF*; *omit Sp1; cf. 40, 74, 448*
56 eglantere ] *Sk*; eglatere *Sp1* (*cf. Sp1* eglentere *80, 112*)
61 ydone ] y-don *Urr*; done *Sp1*
62 for ] *Urr*; *omit Sp1*
65 is ] *Urr*; *omit Sp1*
66 is ] *Urr*; *omit Sp1*
74 seek of all ] *DF*; seeke all *Sp1*; sekin all *Urr; cf. 40, 55, 448*
76 Upon ] *Urr*; On *Sp1*
77 great ] greet *Sk*; *omit Sp1*
80 As of ] *DF*; Of *Sp1*; Come of *Sk*; *cf. 76*
82 Ne yet with ] *Urr*; Ne with no *Sk*; Ne with *Sp1*; *cf. 39, 87*
93 fairest ] *Urr*; faire *Sp1, Sk; cf. 86*
102 astouned ] *DF*; astonied *Sp1*
104 Ne wist I ] *Sk*; I ne wist *Sp1*
106 about I waited ] *Sk*; I waited about *Sp1*
109 laurer ] *Sp2, Sk*; laurey *Sp1*
110 wherein ] *Urr*; where *Sp1, Sk*; *cf. 390*
116 to pass ] to pas *Urr*; passe *Sp1*
119 briddes ] birdis *Urr*; birds *Sp1*
127 briddes ] birdis *Urr*; birds *Sp1*
141 In ] *Sk, Pear*; The *Sp1*
142 were yclad ] *Sk*; were clad *Sp1*; were in clad *Sp2*; werin clad *Urr*
150 want ] *Sk*; went *Sp1*
155 leaves ] leves *Sk*; *omit Sp*; braunchis *Urr*
156 ywrought ] *Urr*; wrought *Sp1*
160 ware ] *Sk*; were *Sp1* (*again at 208*); werin *Urr*
161-65 But … But … But … but ] *perhaps one or more of these should read* and
175 all ] *Urr*; *omit Sp1*
178 Seant ] *DF*; Seen & *Sp1*; seen, et *Sk*
180 voices ] *Urr*; voice *Sp1*
188 best could ] *Urr*; coud best *Sp1, Sk*
192 trumpes ] trumpis *Urr*; trumps *Sp1*
195 coom ] *DF*; come *Sp1*; *again at 458*
200 of ] *Sk*; *omit Sp1*
209 cerealle ] seriall *Sp1*
213 trumpe his lordes-armes ] *DF*; trumpet his lords armes *Sp1*; trumpet his lordes armes *Sk*
213 bare ] bere *Urr, Pear*; here *Sp1*
219 hem ] *Sk*; them *Sp1*; *again at 371, 377, 384, 398, 400, 524, 561, 587, 590*
220 There came ] *DF*; Came *Sp1*; *cf. 136, 265, 368*
220 nine ] *Pear*; *omit Sp1*
222 upon ] *DF*; on *Sp1*
230 All ] *DF*; And *Sp1*
238 fore hem ] *DF*; before him *Sp1*; before hem *Sp2, Sk, Pear*
239 there ] *DF*; *omit Sp1; cf. 136, 265, 368*
249 all of ] al of *Sk*; of *Sp1*; of the *Urr*
250 ymade ] *Urr*; made *Sp1*
252 upon ] *Sk*; still upon *Urr*; on *Sp1*
253 ever the oon on ] *DF*; euery on a *Sp1*; ever (first) on a *Urr*; the first upon a *Sk*; ever the on on a *Pear*
254 lordes helmet ] lord'is helmet *Urr*; lords helme *Sp1*
255 As ] *DF; omit Sp1*
257 back ] necke *Sp1*; thridde bare ] *Sk*; thred bare *Sp1*
258 spear ] spere *Sp3*; sphere *Sp2*; speare *Pear*
258 yground ] *Sk*; ground *Sp1*
262 trappeured and rayed ] *DF*; trapped and raied *Sp1*; trappid and arayid *Urr*
263 withouten ] *Sk*; without *Sp1*; *cf. 23, 369*
267 ware ] were *Sp1* were; werin *Urr*
274 horse ] *Urr, Pear*; hors *Sk*; horses *Sp1* (*cf. l. 281*)
277 arraying ] *DF*; array *Sp1*
279 place ] *Urr*; places *Sp1, Sk*
280 horse's ] horsis *Urr*; horse *Sp1*
282 Into the rest ] *Urr*; In the rest *Sp1*; In the arest *Sk*

283 aboute ] about *Sp1*; aboutin *Urr*
292 then ] than *Sk*; *omit Sp1*
293 nine ] *Urr*, *Pear*; ninth *Sp1*
296 worthy ] *Sp2, Urr, Pear*; wordly *Sp1*, *Sk*
300 echoon brake ] *DF*; breken *Sk*; brake *Sp1*
307 A ] *Urr*; *omit Sp1*
308 it there might ] *Urr*; there might it *Sp1*
316 enclined ] enclinid *Urr*; enclining *Sp1; cf. 344*
317 Unto ] *Urr*; To *Sp1*
336 before hem yede ] *DF*; before hem went *Sp1*; hem before went *Sk* (went *is not found elsewhere in AL against 13 instances of* yede-)
344 Whereunto ] *Sk*; Whereto *Sp1*
350 douce est ] *Urr, Pear*; douset & *Sp1* (*with gloss*: douce est)
354 how ] *Urr*, *Pear*; *omit Sp1*
369 in-fere ] in fere *Urr*; in feare *Sp1*
371 upon hem ] *Sk*; on them *Sp1*
373 All tho ] *DF*; Tho *Sp1*; Tho clad *Sk*; *cf. 63, 71, 382, 467, 497*
376 yeden ] *DF*; yede *Sp1*
384 To-ward hem ... knightes eke ] *Sp1*; Toward them ... knights; *Sk* Towardis them . . . knightis *Urr*; *cf. 454*
402 Unto ] *Sk*; To *Sp1*
403 all ] *DF*; lo! *Sk*; *omit Sp1*
414 gan ] *Urr*; began *Sp1; cf. 27, 108, 414, [438], 444, 446, 586*
415 deeming ] *DF*; seeming *Sp1; cf. 81, 124-25, 381*
416 seemed ] *DF; omit Sp1; cf. 216, 229*
425 as ] *Sk*; *omit Sp1*
426 Rayed ] *DF*; Araied *Sp1; cf. 262*
438 began ] *Urr*; gan *Sp1*
445 her ] *Urr*; hir *Sp1*
460 salwed ] salued *Sk*; saluted *Sp1*
460 bade good ] bad good *Sk*; bad her good *Sp1*
461 Might ] *Sk*; Must *Sp1*; Mote *Sp2, Urr;* (mote *does not appear in* Sp1, *and* must *appears only once* [*583, as an imperative*], *against 19 occurrences of* might)
464 fain wold I ] *DF;* I wold faine *Sp1*
474 Is in ] *DF*; In *Sp1, Sk*; Into *Urr*
478 aye ] ay *Sk*; alway *Sp1*
480 and won by deed ] *DF*; and wan by deed *Pear*; and manly indeed *Sp1*; in manly dede *Urr*; and wan indede *Sk*
483 As ] *Sk*; *omit Sp1*
486 ne thought ] *Sk*; thought *Sp1*; in thought *Urr; cf. 487*
494 yliked ] *Sk*; liked *Sp1*
505 here ] *Sk*; *omit Sp1*
518 As ] *Urr*; It is *Sp1*
522 for there-by ] *DF*; forby *Sp1*; for by it *Urr*
536 as han ] that *Sp1*; folk that *Urr*; *cf. 478, 480, 485, 514, et. al.*
537 delight had ] delyte had *Sk*; delite *Sp1*
539 such-like ] such like *Urr*; such *Sp1*
541 unto ] *Sk*; to *Sp1*
541 so] *Sk*; and so *Sp1*
545 'heir ] *DF*; *omit Sp1*; al *Sk*
553 may ] *Urr*; May may *Sp1*
559 ylost ] *Sk*; lost *Sp1*
563 is the ] *Sp2*, *Urr*, *Pear*; if their *Sp1*
569 that ] *DF*; *omit Sp1*
574 Flou'r ] Flour *Urr*; the flour *Sp1*
575 be ] *Sk*; *omit Sp1*
585 forthright ] *Sk*; forth *Sp1;* forthwith *Urr; cf. 439*
590 it rede ] *Urr;* it to rede *Sp1*

**ELIZABETH of YORK**

**(Humphrey Brereton: Song of the Lady Bessie)**: Ed. DWF from *Bishop Percy's Folio Manuscript. Ballads and Romances,* ed. J.W. Hales and F.J. Furnivall, 3 vols. (London, 1868), III, pp. 319-363.

**Epithalamion**: Ed. DWF from Bodleian MS Rawl. C.86 [*MS*], fols. 155v-156r; with collations from flawed transcriptions by E. Flügel (1895) [*Flüg*] and R. Cords (1916) [*Cord*].
3 delured ] delyu^c^rd *MS*; *again at 22, 28*
12 pensiful ] pensful *MS, Flüg*; penfful [*sic*] *Cord*
16 there ] þ^c^r *MS, Cord*; y^t^ [*sic*] *Flüg*
19 setè ] set *MS*
20 slack ] slake *MS*
25 goodliest, most beauteous ] *omit* most [*sic*] *Cord*
27 in] on [*sic*] *Flüg*
31 meek in ] *omit* in [*sic*] *Flüg*

**To Queen Isabella (3 December 1497)**
Trans. M.A.E. Wood, from BL Egerton 616, fol. 7. In *Letters of Royal and Illustrious Ladies,* 1.115.

**Communion Prayer:** Ed. DWF from Trinity College (Cambridge) MS O.2.53, fols. 53-4.

**MARGARET BEAUFORT**

**Margaret Beaufort to Thomas Butler, earl of Ormond, concerning her gloves** (25 April 1597?): Ed. DWF from State Papers SC1/51/189 (holograph).

**To her son, Henry VII (14 January 1499):** Ed. DWF from BL Cotton Vesp. F.XIII, fol. 60 (holograph); pr. Cooper, p.64, from Henry Ellis, *Letters,* Series 1, p.46.

**To her son, Henry VII** (St. Agnes' Day, 28 January 1500/1): Ed. DWF from Leonard Howard, ed., *A Collection of Letters* (1753) 155-7.

**(Henry VII to Margaret, countess of Richmond and Derby** [17 July 1501]): Ed. DWF fr. B.L. MS Harl. 7039, fol. 34.

From **"The Mirror of Gold to the Sinful Soul"** : Ed. DWF from Margaret Beaufort, trans., *The mirroure of golde* (1504)

**Of the Vileness and Misery of Man**, p. 5

**How Lechery Causeth Many Evils**, pp. 8-9
was ] *MS om.*
was ] *MS om.*
chap. 34^th^ ] twenty-third *MS*

**Of the Vain Joy**, p. 32
**The Lady Margaret her Vow:** Ed. DWF from B.L. MS Cole 24, fol. 244v.

**Lady BRIAN and Humphrey Newton**
**To Humphrey Newton:** Ed. DWF from Rossill Robbins' transcription of Oxford Bodleian Library MS Lat. Misc. c. 66.

**H. Newton to Lady Brian: *Go, litull bill…*** fol. 94r
i' … i' ] i*n* a … i*n* a *Robbins*
man ] mone *Robbins*
upon ] *DWF*; on *Robbins*
kirkes-door ] kirk dore *Robbins*
eyen ] *DWF;* ee *Robbins*
I ] *DWF*; *and Robbins*

**H. Newton to Lady Brian: I pray you M,…** fol. 93v
15 dearer tis ] DWF; der þat it is bogt MS
There ] The; The[re] *Robbins*
ye'll ] ye shall MS
old ne new ] old new MS
sith as ] sithen as MS

**Newton to Lady Brian: O ye my emp$^{e}$rice…** fol. 94r

**Newton to Lady Brian: *Beaute of you burne in my body abydis…*** fol. 93v

**Lady Brian's Farewell: Farewell that was my lef so dere…** fol. 93v
3 year to year ] *Robbins;* year *MS*
26 Of my name, in remembraunce] *DWF;* In remembrance of my name *Robbins*

**Newton's farewell: Alas a thousand sith alas…**fol. 94v
33 blessed ] *DWF*; *illeg.* MS; *om. Robbins*
45 in-kneeled ] *DWF; illeg. MS;* did in kneled *Robbins*
50 shining ] *DWF; illeg. MS;* skinning *Robbins*

**TUDUR PENLLYN, The Welshman and the Englishwoman.** Trans. DWF. Witnesses include B.L. MS Add. 1.f.5, fo.79b; 14936, fo.72a; 31095, fo.150b; 31058, fo.90a; Cardiff Lib. MS 2.616, fo.275; MS 2.14, fo.431; MS 5.44, fo.282b; NLW Llansteffan 134, fo.506; Llans. 122, fo.58; Llans. 133, fo.600; Llans. 47, fo.461; Llans. 6, fo.166; MS Methyr Tudful, fo.537; NLW MS 13066, f.142; NLW MS 13061, f.195b; NLW MS 6706, fo.89; MS Peniarth 104, fo.71, South Glamorgan Lib. MS Thelwall 283; not collated.

**DAFYDD AP DAFYDD to Gwenllian**
Trans. DWF (not fully collated). Witnesses include NLW MS Wrexham 1, fo.384 B.L. MS Add. 14875, fo.51; Cardiff Lib. MS 13, fo.108; South Glamorgan Lib. MS Hafod 26, fo.454; NLW MS Mostyn 131, fols. 230, fo.481; NLW 872, fo.382; NLW 96, fo.23.

**GWENLLIAN in reply to Dafydd**

Trans. DWF (not fully collated). Witnesses include Bangor (Univ. Coll. of No. Wales) 7268, fo.2; NLW MS Cwrtmawr 12, fo.218; NLW 670, fo.4; NLW MS Peniarth 101, fo.270; Pen. 67, fo.39; Pen. 99, fo.390.

**GWERFUL ap FYCHAN**

***Y Eira* / Snow**. Ed./trans. DWF from N.L.W. MS Cwrtmawr 24 [*MS-cw*] (latter 17th century), p. 12. Collated with MS Llansteffan 165 [*MS-ll*] (ca. 1680), 141 and Cardiff Library MS 1.2 [*MS-cl*]. Additional MS copies, without substantive variants, are found in Cwrtmawr 25, p. 11, and NLW 16B, p. 262. For full collation, see Howells.
1 gwynflawd ] gwnflawd (white flour) *MS-cw, MS-ll; Oerflawd* (cold flour) *MS-cl, Howells*
1 y' mynydd ] i mynydd *MS-ll*; i mynwdd *MS-cw*
4 methlu ] mathlu *Ll 165*; mathlw *MS-cw*

**GWERFUL MECHAIN**
Welsh texts edited and translated from MS sources as noted. First publication. As is usual in editing early Welsh poetry, the orthography of the Welsh texts has been modernized. Editorial emendations and readings adopted from manuscripts other than that of the base text are indicated in the notes. Variants in other manuscripts are shown only if the reading of the base text is in need of emendation.

**1. Boy in the Bush**. Ed. and trans. DWF from MS N.L.W. 1553A, p. 694.

**2. The Difference.** Ed. and trans. DWF from MS Mostyn 131, p. 405.

**3. Dripping Wet:** Ed. and trans. DWF from MS NLW Llansteffan 173, p. 177; cf. NLW Llansteffan 167, p. 34, N.L.W. 7191, p. 169.

**4. To her Dad:** Ed. and trans. DWF fr. NLW MS 436, fo. 104v. Anr. copy appears in Peniarth 203, p. 138.
1 eiddilaidd ] eiddilaid *MS*

**5. To Her Husband for Striking Her:** Ed. and trans. DWF from NLW MS Peniarth 94 (ca. 1600), p. iii. Heading from NLW Llansteffan 145, p. 90. Additional copies include NLW MSS 3039B (=MS Mostyn 131, ca. 1605-1618) (two copies, pp. 404, 406), and Llansteffan 119 (ca. 1646), p. 138. Heading from NLW Llansteffan 145, p. 90.

**6. Keep Calm**: Ed. and trans. DWF from NLW MS Llansteffan 167, p. 177. Cf. N.L.W. MSS 3039B (=Mostyn 131), p. 405

**7. The Artful Dodger**: Ed. and trans. DWF from MS Minor Depost 56B (=Swansea 2, the Cefn Coch Manuscripts); photocopy in Lloyd-Morgan, 165.

**8. Vacancy**. Ed. and trans. DWF from MS Cwrtmawr 117, p. 211. Och ] *Howells;* Ces *MS*
gwely gaweledd anniddan ] gely ag aelwyd a than *MS*

**Cywydd i'r Cedor**
Ed. and trans. DWF from National Lib. of Wales MS 1206 (Tan-y-bwlch), fol. 145, with emendations suggested by Dafyd Johnston. For collation of thirteen witnesses, see Howells? 103-5.
2 rwysg wladaidd ] *DJ;* Brwysg wladaidd *MS*
7 hyd y dydd, rho ] *DJ*; rhyd y dydd i rho *MS*
11Ac obry ] *DJ;* Ago ben *MS*
12 uwchlaw yr ] uwchlaw'r *MS;* uwch yr *DJ*
13 hyfryd tew ] *DJ;* dyfryd twf *MS*
14 dwyfron feddaldew ] *DJ;* dwyfron fyddaldwyf *MS*
15 breichiau ] (arms, branches) *MS*; A moli (praise) *DJ*
23 hyder ] (reliable) *DJ;* (more) rhagor *MS*
24 Tynderdew ] (bright, thick) *MS*; Tynderdeg (bright, fair) *DJ;* twn eurdaer ] *DJ;* twyn y taer *MS*
25 Lle carwn i, cywrain ] *DJ;* Llei carwn lliw, cowrain *MS*
29 gwlad ] (country) *DJ;* teg (fair, comely) *MS*
31 Pant ] *MS;* Cont *DJ*
31 Pant ] *DJ* (as line 47)*;* Cont *MS*
31-3 yw ... ffloch ] *MS* (corresponding to lines 47-8, *DJ*; *at l.31,* Cont ddwbl yw, syw seingoch *DJ*
39 gaen gerydd ] *DJ;* chwaen chwerydd ] *MS*
41 yn hael, gafael ged ] *DJ;* heb ffarl er cael ced *MS*
42 cedor i ] *DJ;* i gedor *MS*
47-8 See note to lines 31-3
50 Trwsglwyn merch ] (girl's glade) *DJ;* Breisglwyn berth (grove-bush) *MS*

**Cywydd i Wragedd Eiddigeddus / To Jealous Wives**
Ed. and Trans. DWF from Mostyn 147, p. 360.

**Ymddiddan Rhwng Dau Fardd**
Ed. and trans. DWF from NLW 1553A, p. 473.

**Cywydd i ateb Ieuan Dyfi am ei Gywydd i Anni Goch:** Ed. DWF based on the text ed. Howells, from B.L. MS Add. 14896, fol. 25r. English trans. DWF.

**SONGS AND OCCASIONAL VERSES:** Ed. DWF from MSS as noted.

**Westron Wynde**
British Library MS Royal App. 58, fol. 5.
2 can ] *alt. spelling for* gan (began)

**Charms**

**Dame Alice Kyteler, A Charm for Wealth:** "To the house": Ed. from Raphael Holinshed (1587): *Ireland*, p. 69.

**Isabel Mure, *Benedicite*:** Ed. DWF from J. Raine, ed., *The Fabric Rolls of York Minster*. Surtees Society, no. 35 (Durham: for the Society, 1889), 273.

**Mother Mary's Lament: *Why have ye no ruth on my child…:*** Ed. DWF from Faculty of Advocates Library 18.7.21 (early 14th century), fol. 24r.
2 mourning ] murnig *MS*

**By the Prayers of Saint Dorothy: *What manner of evil thou be…:*** Ed. DWF from B.L. MS Sloane 747, fol. 57r; written as prose. Collated with R. H. Robbins, *Secular Lyrics* (2nd ed., 1955), pp. 60-1.
10 shed ] shewyd *MS*
13 thee ] the *Robbins*; *omit MS*
17 And the ] And all the *MS* (*wrongly repeating* all *from 16*)

**O Sweet Jesus: *Jesus Christ mine leman sweet…***
(Version on left) Ed. DWF from Bodleian MS Eng. poet. a.1 (SC 3938) [Vernon MS], fol. 114vb (stz. 1), 300rb (stz. 2).
(Version on right) Ed. DWF from B.L. MS Harleian 2316 (early 14th century [*MS-h*]), fol. 25r. Written as prose.
8b death ] ded *MS-h*

**Jesu, my spouse good and true** (lower right): Ed. DWF from Lambeth Palace MS 78, fol. 223v.

***To onpreyse wemen yt were a shame*:** Ed. DWF from B.L. MS Harleian 4294, fol. 81r; quotes: lines 7-12.

**Lullaby: *Little child, why weepest thou so sore?*** Ed. DWF from B.L. MS Harleian 913, fol. 32.
1 Lullay, lullay ] Lollai ·/· *MS*
1 weepest thou ] wepistou *MS*
3 therefore ] euere *MS*
4 while 'hey ] whil hy *MS*
4 wore ] were *MS*
5 lullay ] *MS omits repetition sign*
6 art thou ] ertow *MS*
14 upon ] up *MS*
19 trust thou ] tristou *MS*
19 foe ] io *MS*
20 poorer ] pore *MS*
24 woe nor ] *omit* nor *MS* (*cf. line 33*)
33 north nor ] *omit* nor *MS*

**Corpus Christi Lullaby: *The falcon hath born my make away…:*** Ed. DWF from Balliol College (Oxford) MS 354, fol. 165v. For another version, see MS Sloane 2593, fol. 63r: "*A new ger, new ger, a chyld was yborn…*"

**Reply to Her Lover: *Ensamples fair ye find in Nature*:** Ed. DWF from Trinity College (Cambridge) MS R.3.19, fols. 7v-8v.
7 unto ] to *MS*
9 espy] respyte *MS* (*fr. line 3*)
12 ye ] ys *MS*
12 ascry] asky *MS*
24 siccurly ] syker *MS*
30 to ] *MS om.*
51 ye ] the *MS*
57 world's ear and eye ] world here and I *MS*
77 On ] And *MS*

**Why Is It? *O blessed Lord, how may this be…*:** Ed. DWF from BL MS Addit. 5665, fol. 69v.

**Night is Long: *[M]erry it is while sumer ylast…*:** Ed. DWF from Oxford University MS Rawlinson G22 (SC 14755), fol. 1v.
1 Merry ] irie (M *effaced*) *MS*
4 weather ] w der *MS* (*i.e.*, w [ e ] der)
5 is ] *om. MS*
7 fast ] *lacking in MS, lower part of leaf cut away*

**Fragment: *Welaway, why did I so?*** Ed. DWF from Balliol College 220, fol. 220vb.

**Fragment: *Who shall to my leman say…*:** Ed. DWF from Bibliothèque Ste Geneviève 3390, fol. 106.

**Fragment: *Welaway that Ich ne span…*:** Ed. DWF from B.L. Addit. 33956, fol. 98.

**Fragment: Anglice dicitur**: *Barrèd girdle, woe ye be…* Embedded in a in Latin prose *Summa de vii viciis* of Thomas Aquinas.: Ed. DWF from Durham Cathedral Library (Durham) B.I.18, fol.. 116vb. A second copy appears in B.L. Harl. 3823, fol. 354v.

**Fragment: *Alas, How Should I Sing?…*:** Ed. DWF from Representative Church Body Library (Dublin) MS D11.1.2 [Red Book of Ossory], fol. 71va.

**Fragment: *And I Were a Maiden…*:** Ed. DWF from B.L. Addit. 31922, fols. 106v-107.
Other witnesses (not inspected for this volume): Bodleian Library Eng. poet. e.1 (SC 29734), fol. 54v. and B.L. Egerton 3537, fol. 59.

**Lady Bryan's Lament: *The last tyme I the wel woke…*:** Ed. DWF from Cambridge Univ. Library MS Ff.5.48, fol. 114v. I.1. *burden* well-ay ] well *MS*
4 tell-ay ] tell *MS*
10 kell-ay ] kell *MS*

**The Sooth I See: *y louede a child of þis cuntre…*:** Ed. DWF from Caius College (Cambridge) MS 383 [*MS*], p. 210. In *MS*, the tune is indicated before the first burden: [sung to the tune of] *bryd on brere y telle yt, to non oþ*$^{u}$*r y ne dar*.
9, 15 seke ] sykke *MS*

**Alas, What Remedy?: *Grevus ys my sorowe…*:** Ed. DWF from B.L. MS Sloane 1584 [*MS*], fol. 85r-87r; with collations from R. H. Robbins, *Secular Lyrics*, 2nd ed. (1955) [*Rob55*], 214-18.
13 hath] haue *MS*
17 hath] haue *MS*
51 loves ] loue *MS*
75 mourners ] mowrmarus *MS*; [mowrnarus] *Rob55*
77 Of ] [For] *Rob55* (unnecessary emendation)
92 written ] writtynge *MS*

97 ladies ] lady *MS*
100 Sigh ... me ] *DF, to supply line missing in MS*

**As I could wish**: ***The man that I loued al ther best…***: Ed. DWF from Cambridge University Library MS Addit. 5943 [*MS*], fol. 178v; with collations from Greene, *Early English Carols* (1st ed., 1935 [*Gre35*], 306); 2nd ed., 1977 [*Gre77*], 275), and R. H. Robbins, *Secular Lyrics* (2nd ed., 1955), 16-17.
1-22 *pronouns in opposite gender, for a male speaker, are interlined in a different hand, MS*: sche *for* man, *1*; sche *for* he *3, 5-8, 13, 14, 16, 19, 20, 22*
1 all-the-best ] altherbest *MS*
8 He … moe ] *DF*; he maketh haste fro me to go *Gre35* (*speculative subststitution for error in MS, which duplicates line 9*), *Rob55* (fr. *Gre35*); *Gre77 omit, and repeat line 7 as in MS*
14 I go ] *MS* speke but forth *written twice, second time lined out*, I go *inserted*
19 heartes-love ] *DF*; hert love *MS*
26 was ] *DF*; waxeth *MS*

**Come, Death: *I Will No More Go to the Plough…:*** Ed. DWF from Trinity College, Dublin 490, fol. 179v.

**Double Dealing: *Your counterfeitng with double dealing…***: Ed. DWF fr. B.L. MS Add. 5465 (Fairfax MS), fol. 22v.

**The Serving Maid's Holiday: *Web ne reel, ne spin Ic ne may…:*** Ed. DWF from Caius College (Cambridge) MS. 383 (Contains Anon., ["The Serving Maid's Holiday"]).
on ] onward in *MS* ; with collations from R. H. Robbins, *Secular Lyrics,* 2nd ed. (1955), 24-25.
any ] a *MS, Robb55*

**The Irish Dancer: *Ich am of Irelaund,…***: Ed. DWF from Bodleian Lib. MS Rawlinson D. 913, art. I.g.
4 thee ] ˙e *MS*

**Black is Beautiful: *Some men sayon that I am black…***: Ed. DWF from Caius College (Cambridge) MS 383 [*MS*], p. 190; with collations from R. H. Robbins, *Secular Lyrics,* 2nd ed. (1955), 30-31. *Rob55* follows *MS* except as noted.
2 prow ] *Rob55*; þow *MS*
11 in deed ] in dede *MS*
12 Thereto ] *DF*; & þer-to *MS* (*dup's* & þer-to *line 11*)
14 Iwis ] y-wys *Rob55*; Wyn wys *MS* (*partly duplicating* Wynd &, *line 13*)
15 my ] *DF*; al my *MS*
21 beeth ] buþ *MS*

**Trolly-Lolly: *Of serving men I will begin…***: Ed. DWF from B.L. MS Sloane 1584 (a commonplace book of Canon John Gysborn) [*MS*], fol. 45v; with collations from Greene, *Early English Carols,* 1st ed. (1935) [*Gre35*], 303-4; 2nd ed. (1977) [*Gre77*], 272; and R. H. Robbins, *Secular Lyrics*, 2nd ed. (1955) [*Rob55*], 32-33. The "Trolly-lolly" refrain is common in songs of the early 16th century.
2 minion ] mynyon *MS*; mynon [*sic*] *Rob55*
4 no thing ] none *MS*
3-4 So well *etc.* ] *DF* (again at 10, 16, 19, 22, 25-6; in *mS15, the burden appears above, in red*
9 His ] *DF*; W[t] *MS*
9 trolly ] *Gre, Rob55*; Torly *MS*
15 hundred pound ] C[l] *mS15*
17 it is ] *DF*; is *Gre, Rob55*; *MS omit*

**Dame Courtesy's Book for Children**: Ed. DWF from Bodleian Library MS Ashmole 61 (ca. 1500), fols. 20r-21v. The MS text has no heading; it is subscribed "Amen quod Rate," Rate being the name of the scribe. For another version, see "The Lytylle Childrenes Lytil Boke," beginning, "Litill children here may ye lerne…"; in 54 couplets, Balliol College MS 354, fols. 142-3
2 court'ous ] c'tas *MS*
9 Virtues ] *DF*; All v[e]rtus *MS*
16 speed bett whatso thy carks ] *DF*; spede bett[e]r what so þ[u] carpes *MS*; *cf.* bett (*H* bette), *line 104*
18 Ask ] Ther Aske *MS*
23 ere ] or *MS* (*again at 86*)
46 these ] *DF*; þe *MS*
50 falsehood ] falsed *MS*
54 any dread ] *DF*; Any fer[e], dred, or awe *MS*
66 keep ] *DF*; kepe þ[u] *MS*
69 shew ] *DF*; shew þ[u] *MS*
72 he ] *DF*; *omit MS*
79 truth] *DF*; treweh *MS*
82 live in ease] lyfe is es *MS*
94 thou ] *DF*; & be *MS*
115 'ware ] were *MS*
127 noise ] *DF*; nose *MS*
131 a voideur ] A voyd[e]r *MS*
144 the table] þhi tabull *MS*
146 lead ] *DF*; lede thou þ[u] *MS*

**Ladd Y the daunce (Led I the Dance)**
Ed. DWF from Gonville & Caius College (Cambridge) MS 383/603, p. 41
1.4 I ] that he *MS*
1.5 no ] ne *MS*
6.4 merriest ] murgust *MS*
7.3 Oft I trow] Of Y trew *MS*
9.3 waxed ] wax *MS*

**Women's Work: *Jesu that art gentle, for joy of thy dame…:*** Ed. DWF from Chetham Lib. MS 8009, fols. 370-372.
28 may ] *DWF*; can *MS*
68 year ] *MS om.*

**Jamie: *He that will be a lover…***: Ed. DWF from B.L. MS Royal 18 A.VI, fol. 22.

**CHRISTINE de PIZAN**

**Christine Reno: Christine de Pizan in England (Reno, 2013)**

Prologue to ***The Feat of Arms and Chivalry***: Ed. DWF fr. *The boke of the fayt of armes and of chyualrye* (1484).

***The Body of Policy:*** Ed. DWF from [*T*]*he body of polycye* (1521) [*Q1*]; collated with Cambridge Univ. Lib. mS Kk.1.5, fols. 69r-71v (a very close transcription of the printed text); collated only where the MS corrects obvious misprints in the printed text)
Orace ] Orose *Q1* (mistaking Horace for Orosius, church historian)
his ] DWF; his *Q1, mCUL* (a printshop misreading of MS hir for *his*)
weary ] very *Q1*
chose ] *mCUL* ; chase *Q1*

applyeth ] *mCUL* applied *Q1*
disports ] disportes *mCUL* disported *Q1*

***The City of Ladies***: Ed. DWF fr. *The Boke of the Cyte of Ladyes* (1521) [*Q1*].

**1.1**
me ] my *Q1*
there ] *DF* (for clarity); *Q1 om.*
and ] in *Q1*
come ] came *Q1*
been and be ] ben & ben *Q1*
it ] it it *Q1*
**1.2**
that I ] I that *Q1*
I ] *Q1 om.*
sovereign ] soueraynely *Q1*
thou ] that *Q1*
yet ] syth
**2.12**
Lady Rightwisness ] *Q1 om*
not ] *Q1 om*
who are wives ] *Q1 om*
writing ] written *Q1*
women] they *Q1*
if ] *Q1 om*
the ] that the *Q1*
**2.36**
are ] *Q1 om*
that which ] that *Q1*
that which ] that *Q1*
**2.64**
he ] *Q1 om.*
**2.68**
to ] *Q1 om.*

## HOLY SISTERS

***Ancren Wisse***: Trans. DWF from B.L. Cotton Nero A.xiv, fols. 101, 116v-117r.

**Barking Abbey, Cellaress: *Work Orders***
Ed. D. Foster fr. B.L. MS Cotton Julius D8, fols. 41-44.
The Cellaress must ] *DWF*; Whereof, what part of the said sum she must *MS*

**Rothwell, 1421/1422: Mandate of Solemn Excommunication:** Trans. DWF fr. *Visitations, 1420-1436* [Reg. Flemyng], fol. 225, ed. Hamilton Thompson (1914), 1.107-9.

**Markyate (1433): The Resignation of Dame Denise Lowelich:** Trans. DWF from *Visitations, 1420-1436* [Reg. Gray, fol. 149], ed. Thompson (1914), 1.82-85.

**Sewardsley (1435): Commission of Inquiry (23 February 1434/5):** Trans. DWF from *Visitations, 1420-1436* [Reg. Gray, fol. 173], ed. Thompson (1914), 1.111-12.

**Stainfield (1436): Commission for Enclosure (23 January 1435/6)**
Trans. DWF from *Visitations, 1420-1436* [Reg. Gray, fol. 186, ed. Thompson (1914), 1.113-15.

**Heynings (1440): Visitation, 7 April 1440:** Trans. DWF from *Visitations, 1436-1449* [Reg. Alnwick, fol. 23], ed. Thompson (1918), 2.132-35.

**Legbourne (1440): Visitation, 3 July 1440:** Trans. DWF from *Visitations, 1436-1449* [Reg. Alnwick, fol. 68], ed. Thompson (1918), 2.183-87.

**Joan Missenden to Lord Cromwell**: Ed. DWF from Thomas Wright, ed., *Three Chapters of Letters from the Suppression of Monasteries*. Camden Old Series vol. 26 (September 1843): 116-117 116.

**Grace Dieu (1441): Visitation, 21 January 1440/1:** Trans. DWF from *Visitations, 1436-1449* [Reg. Alnwick, fol.109], ed. Thompson (1918), 2.119-29.

**Ankerwicke (1441):] Visitation, 10 October 1441:** Trans. DWF from *Visitations, 1436-1449* [Reg. Alnwick, fol. 57], ed. Thompson (1918), 2.1-9.

**Catesby (1442): Visitation** (17 July 1442): Trans. DWF from *Visitations, 1436-1449* [Reg. Alnwick, fol. 94], ed. Thompson (1918), 2.46-53.

**Joyce Berkeley, to Lord Cromwell (c. April 1536):** Ed. DWF from Misc. Corresp. Second Series v. 180.

**Commissioners in Northamptonshire to Lord Cromwell (12 May 1536)**: Ed. DWF from B.L. MS Cotton Cleopatra E.iv. fol. 209.

**Littlemore (1445): Visitation, 1 June 1445:** Trans. DWF from *Visitations, 1436-1449* [Reg. Alnwick, fol. 31], ed. Thompson (1918), 2.217-18.

**Littlemore (1517): Visitation, Edmund Horde:** Trans. DWF from *Visitations, 1517-1531* [Reg. Atwater], ed. Thompson, 2.9-10.

**Littlemore (2 Sept. 1518): Visitation, William Atwater, bishop:** Trans. DWF from *Visitations, 1517-1531* [Reg. Atwater], ed. Thompson, 2.11-12.

**Godstow (1432-34): Visitation, 16 July 1432; Injunctions, 7 June 1434:** Trans. DWF from *Visitations, 1420-1436* [Reg. Gray, attachment at fol. 167,] ed. Thompson (1914), 1.66-68.

**Godstow (1445):] Visitation, 29 May 1445:** Trans. DWF from *Visitations, 1436-1449* [Reg. Alnwick, fol. 28], ed. Thompson (1918), 2.113-16.

**Prologue to the English Register of Godstow Abbey [c.1450]:** Ed. DWF from Andrew Clark (1911), 25.
**Abbess Katherine Bulkeley to Thomas Cromwell, 5 November 1536:** Ed. DWF from MS Cotton Cleop. E.iv., fol. 229.

**Abbess Katherine Bulkeley to Thomas Cromwell, 26 Nov. 1536:** Ed. DWF from Ellis, *Letters,* 3d Ser. 3.233.

**Bishop Longland's Injunctions to the Priory of Nun Cotham, 30 April 1530:** Ed. DWF from transcription by Peacock (1883): 51-3.

**Elstow Abbey (1422): Injunctions (17 Jan. 1421/22)**

Trans. DWF from *Visitations, 1420-1436* [Reg. Fleming, fols. 231], ed. Thompson (1914), 1.48-52.

**Bishop Gray's Injunctions to Elstow Abbey [October or November, 1432]**: Trans. DWF from *Visitations, 1420-1436* [Reg. Gray, fol. 203], ed. Thompson (1914), 1.52-54.

**Injunctions of the bishop of Lincoln to Elstow Abbey, [October] 1530.** (English.): Ed. DWF from transcription by Peacock (1883): 51-3.
sisters ] *MS om.*

**Visitation of the Vicar General of Lincoln to Elstow Abbey, 1 July 1531:** Trans. DWF from *Visitations, 1517-1531* [Reg. Long-land, fols. 51-53], ed. Thompson (1914), 2.130-3.

**Form of Confession**: Ed. DWF from Cambridge University Library MS Add. 3042, fols. 79r-80v.
*took* ] take *MS*

**ELIZABETH BARTON, Holy Maid of Kent**
**Cranmer's Account of Elizabeth Barton**: Ed. DWF from B.L. Harl. 6148, fol. 40.

**Scaffold Speech**: Ed. DWF from Edward Hall, *Vnion* (1550), p. 224.

**Inventory of Elizabeth Barton**: Ed. DWF from B.L. MS Cotton Cleopat. E.iv. fol. 84.

**KATHERINE OF KENT**
**For Nun Would I Never be None** (c. 1500): Ed. DWF from B.L. MS Cotton Vesp. D.ix, 177r-182v, 190r-v.
1.3 rode o'er ] roden over *MS*
1.6 That ] And that *MS*
2.8 were they ] they were *MS*
3.3 *And ... Mass* ] conjectural insertion for line *MS om.*
4.8 cheer ] gode chere *MS*
5.6 that ] *MS om.*
6.5 To ] And to *MS*
6.7 And woll ] And I woll *MS*
6.7 without ] wythe owten *MS*
7.1 repents ] repenteth *MS*
7.3 My ] Than my *MS*
8.1 morn ] mornyng *MS*
8.7 a ] *MS om.*
9.4 showers ] flowres *MS*
9.6 birds singing ] birde syngyng *MS*
10.2 sang ] syngyng *MS*
10.4 all made ] all they maden *MS*
10.4 in ] into *MS*
10.7 pitous ] *MS om.*
11.3 liven ] lyve *MS*
11.4 Fro' the ] For the *MS*
16.3 Then ] And than *MS*
17.2 Then ] And than *MS*
18.2 without ] wythowten *MS*
18.6 behold ] beholden *MS*
19.1 'rayed ] arrayed MD
19.2 Comforteth ] Sche comfortythe *MS*
19.3 Be not dismayed ] in dyvers wyse *MS* (rep. of l. 2)
19.4 Methought ] And me thowght *MS*
21.6 ] promise ] promyt *MS*
21.7 Bring ] And bryng *MS*
22.1 Methought ] Than me thowght *MS*
22.3 stond ] ryse *MS*
22.4 she ] *MS om.*
23.1 Methought ] Than me thowght *MS*
24.4 thou ] you *MS*
26.5 comes of ] cometh of the *MS*
27.8 So ] And so *MS*
28.1 There ] But there *MS*
28.1 hight ] that hygh *MS*
28.5 see'th ] seythe I *MS*
28.7 look'd ] loke *MS*
29.5 She ] And sche *MS*
29.5 with but ] but wythe *MS*
30.1 Which ] The whyche *MS*
30.3 'nother ] another *MS*
30.8 'habited ] enhabyted *MS*
30.9 took ] token *MS*
32.1 Which ] The whyche *MS*
32.3 But woll ] But I wolle *MS*
32.4 'tis ] yt ys *MS*
32.6 all ] alle that *MS*
32.6 see'th and heareth ] herethe and seethe *MS*
32.8 He'll ] He schalle *MS*
32.9 wisdom leareth ] wysdum us lerethe *MS*
33.3 myself ] *MS om.*
33.9 seld ] seldom *MS*
34.1 Dame Patience ] Than Dame Pacience
34.1 Charity ] Chariteте *MS*
34.3 I'd ] I wolde
34.3 not ] nought *MS*
34.7 dwelt ] dweldyn *MS*
35.4 that ] *MS om.*
35.5 subjects ] sugettys *MS*
36.1 Of ] And of *MS*
36.3 Hit was the one most ] Hyt was one of the most that *MS*
36.6 All religious rule witnesseth
36.8 When ] And when *MS*
36.8 in her ] her in *MS*
36.9 s'bide ] abyde *MS*
37.3 had they ] they hadden *MS*
37.6 at ] a *MS*
38.2 set ] setten *MS*
38.3 beheld ] we behelde *MS*
38.4 talkèd ] talkeden *MS*
38.6 I prayed ] And than I prayed *MS*
38.6 me ] for *MS*
39.6 I said I'd ] And I seyde, I wolde cese *MS*
39.9 I've showed ] I have schewed *MS*
39.9 I've ] I have *MS*
40.1 yond ] yonder *MS*
42.2 I thought ] And I thowght *MS*
43.1 But peradventure some would ] But here peraventure sum man wolde *MS*
43.3 soon forsook ] forsoke sone *MS*
43.4 And forfeited what might have been ] conjectural; *MS* line om.
43.5 Dream ] a dreme *MS*
43.6 Dream ] For dreme *MS*
43.7 'Twas ] Hyt was *MS*
43.8 To keep me from apostasy ] conjectural; *MS om.*
44.1-8 lacking in *MS*
45.1 w[ell doth agree ] w.... *MS* (damaged)
45.2 when you will ] wh... *MS* (damaged)
46.4 holy be ] be holy *MS*
46.9 Wherefore ] And therefore *MS*
46.9 folk ] people *MS*
48.1-6 ....yng...nde gode levyng, / ...yf they be wythin the contrary *MS* (damaged)
49.1 ladies, heed ] ladyes, taketh gode hede to *MS*
49.3 Behold ] And beholde *MS;* goodly ] goodly *MS*
49.6 Which ] The whyche *MS*
49.7 lived ] levedyn *MS*
50.2 Scholastica ] Seynte Scolastica *MS*
50.3 were ] weren *MS*
51.1 Saints Audrey, Freswith, Esmereld ] Seynte Audre, Seynte Freswyth, and Seynte Emerelde *MS*

51.2 Saint Withburga and Saint Mildered ] Seynte Wythbuge and Seynte Myldrede, *MS*
51.3 Saint Sexburga and Saint Ermengild ] Saint Sexburge and Saint Ermenylde: *MS*

**The COFFIN-WELLES ANTHOLOGY**: Ed. DWF from Bodleian Library MS Rawl. C.813. Jansen and Jordan (1991) [*JaJo* ] follow *MS* except as noted. Epistles from the suitor are largely plagiarized from a prior manuscript text of Hawes' *Pastime of Pleasure* (not extant) that closely matches the first printed text (London, 1554). Substantive variants betwen *Rawl. C.813* [*MS*] and the 1554 printed text of Hawes [*PoP*].

**From Her Suitor**: "Please ytt your grace dere harte to gyffe audyence…." fol. 1
1 dear heart ] dere harte *MS*; *for* Pop
3 your ] *MS*; om. *PoP*
4 oft ] *MS*; om. *PoP*
5 all ] *MS*; om. *PoP*
6 Your…fast ] your beaute truely / hath me fettred faste *PoP*
7 That … past ] Without youre helpe / my lyfe is nerehande past *PoP*

**From Her Suitor**: ***Ryght gentyll harte of greane flouryng age…***, fols. 21v-23v. Collated with Stephen Hawes, *Pastime of Pleasure* [*PoP*], lines 3951-78, 3592-99, 4007-4027.
5 truth ] *PoP*, *JaJo* (from *PoP*); *omit MS*
5 my ] our *PoP*
6 ye ] you *PoP*; again at lines 28, 43, 66, 74, 83
7 an ] *PoP*; a *MS*
13 an ] *PoP*; a *MS*
14 hath you made ] you haue made *PoP*
46 chaiens ] cheyens *MS*; chaines *PoP*
47 withouten ] without *MS*
65 a ] the *PoP*
70 lese ] *PoP*; losse *MS*
79 for ] for the *PoP*
80 that ] *DF*; om. *MS*
82 suffisaunce ] suffycysaunce *PoP*

**The Maiden to Her Suitor**: ***grene flouryng age of your manly countenance***..., fol. 53v.
6 me ] *DF*; *omit MS*
7 gladden'd ] *DF*; glad *MS*
8 aye ] I *MS*
10 am ... promised ] do ... promise *MS*
11 unlaced ] unlasyde *MS*

**Maiden to her Suitor, on Truelove**: ***I loue So Sore I wolde fayne descerne...***, fol. 61.
56 achieves ] avayles *MS*

**The Maiden to Her Suitor**: ***O resplendent floure prynte þis yn your mynde***..., fols. 53v-54r; with collations from R. H. Robbins, *Secular Lyrics* (2nd ed., 1955) [*Rob55*], 218-19.
9 in ] *DF*; *omit MS*
9 sailed ] *DF*; sayllyde *MS*'; sayssyde [*sic*] *Rob55*
10 fro ] *DF*; owt of *MS*
14 sent] *DF*; send *MS*

**From Her Suitor**: ***O my lady dere both regarde and See***..., fols. 14v-18r. Collated with Stephen Hawes, "The Pastime of Pleasure" [*PoP*] (MS copy not extant; pub. London, 1554, 1555), lines 2066-72, 2122-28, 2136-40, 218304, 2150-6, 2220-6, 2234-4, 4084-90. Not printed here are lines 148-54, taken from Hawes's "The Comfort of Lovers," and lines 78-82 (appearing also in poem 38. "O my swete harte...," lines 22-26), taken from Chaucer's *Troilus and Criseyde*, 5.1072-6. The remainder of the poem is taken entirely from *PoP*.
1-2 O ... set ] Then stode I up and ryght so dyde she / Alas I sayde than my herte is so sette *PoP*
4 Ye ... caught ] Yourselfe hath caught it *PoP*
29 I will be true ] That shall I not *PoP*
30 whole ] *omit PoP*
31 will never ] shall not *PoP*
32 ye ... ye ] you ... you *PoP* (*again at 40*)
35 heart ] *omit PoP*
35 set ] sette *PoP*
36 O...star ] Alas, madame, now the bright lode star *PoP*
41-2 My ... found ] *omit PoP* (1555); *PoP* (1554) (*from lines 1998 a-b*)
44 high ] *omit PoP*
44 my ] mine *PoP*
45 looks ] lokes *PoP*; (*again at 58*)
45 no whit ] not *PoP*
49 waken do sike with tears ] wake doe sigh with teres *PoP*
50 my ] *omit PoP*
52 from you afar ] tofore you here *PoP*
53 ye ] you *PoP*
56 to love you first I ] I to loue *PoP*
57 That I love you so sore ] My good dere herte *PoP*
61 middes of the church ] olde temple *PoP*
63 ever ] *omit PoP*
162 Thus ] And *PoP*
163 the court imperial ] þe courte Inperyall *MS*; our courte ryall *PoP*
164 Of April...day ] Of Septembre the two and twenty day *PoP*
165 I ... me ] She ... her *PoP*
165 this ] the *PoP*
166 Desire, my friend, ] Cupyde her sone *PoP*
168 my sweet ... right ] labell pucell for to take his flyght *PoP*

**The Maiden's Reply to Her Suitor**: ***Right best beloved and most In assurance***..., fols. 71r-72v.
20 never was ] *DF*; was neuer *MS*
25 is ] *DF*; *omit MS*
27 That ] *DF*; butt that *MS* (*taking* butt *from next line*)
38 that ] þat then *MS*
39 That then ] that *MS*
44 although ] *DF*; though *MS*
54 gentleness ] *DF*; dilligence *MS* (*See 13. From her suitor, line 33*)

**From Her Suitor**: ***O loue most dere o loue most nere my harte***..., fols. 24v-27v.
127 how ] *JaJo*; gow *MS*

**Her Reply to Her Lover**: ***Evyn as mery as I make myght***..., fol. 58v. *JaJo* conflates No. 49 [b.] with 49 [a.] ("My harte ys Sore but yet noo forse..."), which immediately precedes 49 [b.], and is by the suitor.
10 dwelleth ] *DF*; dwellyd *MS*
13 bakes ] *DF*; bake *MS*

**From Her Rejected Suitor**: ***Swet harte I loue yow more feruent then my fader***..., fol. 63r.

1 sire ] fader *MS*
2 well ] wyll *MS*
14 me make ] make me *MS*
25 is ] *omit MS*
27 That ] But that *MS*
38 that ] þat then *MS*
39 That then ] that *MS*
54 gentleness ] dilligence *MS* (*cf. poem [13.], line 33, above*)

***A Letter Sende by on yonge woman to a noder***, fol. 6v.
1 Bune ] *possibly read* Bene *as rhyme-word*
9 Commend ] Come amble *MS* (*picked up from* come ambling *in line 2*)
30 ladder ] lather *MS*

**MARY OSTREWYK**
***Certain Prayers***
From British Library MS Harleian 494 (15th century), fols. 61v-62r.
1 have prompt ] hane prompte *MS*
3 thrid ] threde *MS*
5 fifth ] vth *MS* (*again below*)
7 she saw ] shew sawe *MS*
9 thrid ] iij (*cf.* threde *above*)
10 The fourth ] Tho iiij *MS*

**ELEANOR (SUTTON) SOMERSET**
**Book-Plates:** Ed. DWF from B.L. MS Harl. 1251.

[***Front Bookplate***:] **"This book is one,..."** fol. 1r.
6 Eleanor ] Er *MS*

[***Prayer to the Virgin***:] **"Most wisest lady..."** fol. 182r.

[***Rear Book-Plates***] and **"And I it lose, and you it find,..."** fols. 184v-185r.

**J. Wrightson, bookplate:** Ed. DWF from St. John's Coll. MS 76, fol. 5v

**T. Shardelow, bookplate:** Ed. DWF from Huntington Lib. MS HEH RB 12924, flyleaf.

**Anon. bookplate (If it be lost...):** Ed. DWF from R. Johnson Walker, *N&Q* 10th ser. (24 March 1906): 230.

**R. Barker, bookplate:** Ed. DWF from B.L. MS Harl. 5036, fol. 44

**N. Kent, bookplate:** Ed. DWF from Mass. for Renaissance Studies, Bible (London: Barker, 1586)

**D. Franks, bookplate:** Ed. DWF from transcript by N. Taylor Phillips, *Am. Jewish Quarterly,* vol. 4 (Dec. 1894): 197.

**Queen CATHERINE of ARAGON**

**Letter of Catharine of Aragon to her daughter, Princess Mary** (April 1534): Ed. DWF from B.L. MS Arundel 151, fo. 194.

**Catherine to King Henry from her deathbed** (7 Jan. 1535/6). Vienna Archives England, fasc. 9. From Garrett, *Catherine of Aragon.* New York: Little Brown, 1941. 429-30.

**Queen ANNE BOLEYN**

**To Cardinal Wolsey (1528)**. Ed. DWF fr. MS Cotton Vespasian F XII, art. 92, fol. 80.

**Birth Announcement**: Transcription DWF from BL MS Harl. 283, fol. 75r. This copy superscribed, "To oure right trustie and welbiloved, the Lord Cobham."

**The Arrest of Anne Boleyn** (2 May 1536): Ed. DWF from Edward Hall, *Vnion* (1550), fols. 227-228.

**Eustace Chapuys to Emperor Carlos V** (2 May 1536): Ed DWF from LP Henry VIII, Vol, 10 (Jan.-June 1536), no. 782 fr. the Vienna Archives.

**Kingston to Cromwell** (3 May 1536): Ed DWF fr. MS Cotton Otho C.x. fol. 225.

**Kingston to Cromwell** (6 May 1536): Ed DWF fr. B.L. MS Cotton Otho C.x. fol. 222.
to him ] (*inserted for clarity*) *MS om.*
He said, ] (*inserted for clarity*) *MS om.*

**Kingston to Cromwell** (c.10 May 1536): Ed. DWF from B.L. MS Cotton Otho C.x. fol. 224v.

**Kingston to Cromwell** (16 May 1536): Ed. DWF from B.L. MS Harl. 283, fol. 134.

**Kingston to Cromwell** (19 May 1536).: Ed. DWF from B.L. MS Cotton Otho, C.x, fol. 223.

**Anne Boleyn to Henry VIII (**6 May 1536): Ed. DWF from B.L. MS. Cott. Otho C. x. fol. 232r (16th C copy)

**Anne Boleyn's Scaffold Speech** (19 May 1536). Ed. DWF from Edward Hall, *Vnion* (1550), fol. 228.

**MARGARET DOUGLAS**

**Margaret Tudor to Henry VIII** (12 August 1536): Ed. DWF from *State Papers, Henry VIII,* vol. 5 (art. 293), 58; Scotland Royal Letters, Vol. 1. Art. 28.

**T.H.,** ***Now may I morne as one off late*** (holo., f. 26r)

**T.H.,** ***to morne off ryght yt ys my part ...*** (holo., f. 26v)

**T.H.,** ***Who hath more cawse*** (holo., f. 28r)

**T.H.,** ***Alas that men be so ungent*** (holo., f. 27v)

**T.H.,** ***What thyng shold cawse me to be sad*** (holo., f. 27r)

**M.D.,** ***I may well say w<sup>t</sup> Ioyfull harte*** (ent, T.H., f. 28v)

**T.H.,** ***To yowr gentyll letters an answere*** (holo., f. 29r)

**Agnes Jordan, prioress of Syon Abbey, to Cromwell** (6 Nov. 1536): National Archives, State Papers 1/110, fol. 186r. For Henry to Margaret, see *Letters and Papers,* 11:1373.

**Margaret Douglas to Thomas, Lord Cromwell** (Winter, 1536/7). B.L. MS Cotton Vespasian F.xiii, fol. 134b [173] (holograph).

**T.H.,** ***Yff reason govern fantasye aright*** (hol., fols. 45-6)
44b my ] me *MS*

**T.H.,** ***What helpythe hope of happy hape*** (holo., fols. 46-7)

**T.H.,** ***This rotyd greff will not but growe*** (holo., f. 47)
2 its ] *or*: his; ys *MS*

**T.H.,** ***Sum sum̄ say I love*** (holo., f. 58v)
6b grieves ] grewe *MS*

**T.H.,** ***O myserable sorow*** (ent. Edmund Knyvet, f. 58r)

**T.H.,** ***thy promese was to loue me best*** (ent. M.D., f. 40)
15a asward ] *DWF*; awarvd *MS*

**T.H., *how shold I*** (ent. M.D., fols. 43r)

**T.H., *I se the change*** (ent. M.D., fols. 40-1)

**T.H., *as ffor my part I know no thyng*** (ent. M.D., f. 41)

**T.H., *To my mishap, alas I find*** (ent. M.D., f. 42r-v)

**T.H., *and thys be thys ye may*** (ent. M.D., f. 444)

**T.H., *what nedythe lyff*** (ent. M.D., f. 43v-44r)

**M.D., *my hart ys set not to remove*** (*holo., f.* 58v-59r,

**M.D., *when I bethynk my wontet ways*** (*holo., f.* 58r)
Collated with second copy in Mary Shelton's hand, p. 59r
1 bethink ] bethynk *MS Douglas*, fol. 58r; be thyng *MS Shelton*; ways ] was *Shelton*
2, 3, 4 how ] *spelled* who *by Margaret Douglas, intending* how, *as per Shelton copy*
2 ere this ] or thys *MS Douglas*; anon *MS Shelton*
4 declyn ] *MS Douglas*; or myn *MS Shelton*
5 affrays ] *MS Douglas*; assais *MS Shelton*

**M.D., *ffanecy fframed my hart*** (*holo.,* fols. 61-2)

5 hath ] hawe *MS*

**M.D., *I ame not she be proweff off syt*** (ent. Mary Shelton, f. 65r)

**M.D., *to cowntarffete a mery mode*** (ent. Shelton, f. 65v)

**M.D., *myght I as well w^t in my songe be lay*** (holo., f. 65v)

**M.D., *the sueden chance ded mak me mves*** (holo., f. 67)

**M.D., *my ywtheffol days ar past*** (ent. Shelton, f. 68)

**M.D., *now that ye be assemblled heer*** (holo., f. 88r)

**M.D., *lo in thy hat thow hast be gone*** (holo. fol. 59 v)
1 haste ] hat *MS*

**MARY SHELTON**

**E.K., *Suffryng in sorow in hope to attayn*** (f. 6v-7r)

**E.K., *My ferefull hope from me ys fledd*** (7v)

**M.S., *Yowre ferefull hope cannot p^re vayle*** (8r)

**E.K., *Bownd am I now & shall be styll …*** (8v-9r)

**E.K., *to men that knows ye not*…** (60r)

**E.K., *Myn unhappy chaunce to home shall I playn*…** (60)

**E.K., *To dere is bowght the doblenes*…** (holograph, 59v)

**E.K., *In places Wher that I company*** (holograph, 62v)

**E.K., *If y^t I cowlde in versis close*** (holograph, fol. 63v)

**E.K., *Wyly no dought ye be a wry*** (holograph, fol. 59v)

**Queen JANE SEYMOUR**

**Birth Announcement:** Ed. DWF from the Dunham Massey MS, discovered in Feb. 2012, which is substantively identical to B.L. Harl. MS 283, fol. 155, a later copy. Image courtesy of Dunham Massey MS (picture courtesy of the Dunham Massey estate).

**Queen ANNE of CLEVES**

**Conset Letter to Henry VIII** (11 July 1540). Ed. DWF from National Archives SP 1/161, art. 204.

**The Minute in English of the letter sent by the lady Anne to her brother (21 July 1540)**
Ed. DWF from National Archives SP 1/645. English and German copies (not examined) are preserved with the Hatfield MSS. (HMC Calendar 1.13)

**Inscribed Book of Hours** (Salisbury [1533?], *STC* 15982). Image courtesy of Folger Shakespeare Library.

**[Anne of Cleves to Queen Mary (4 August 1554)]**
Ed. DWF from National Archives SP SP 1/161, fol. 97.

**Queen KATHERINE HOWARD**
**Confession of Queen Katherine** (7 Nov. 1541): Ed. DWF from HMC *Longleat* (1907) 2.8-9.

**Examination of Queen Katherine** (12 Nov. 1541): Ed. DWF from HMC *Longleat* (1907) 2.9-10.

**Letter to Thomas Culpepper** (1541): Ed. DWF from National Archives (Kew) State Papers 1/167, fol. 14; *Letters And Papers*, vol. 16, 1134.

**Birth Of Mankind; or The Woman's Book:** Ed. DWF from Rösslin, *Byrth of Mankynde*, ed. 1540, trans. Jonas (Preface, Dedication to Queen Katherine Howard, both by Jonas) and ed. 1560, trans. Raynalde.

**Queen KATHERINE PARR**

**Book of Hours inscription** (c. 1520). Cambridge Univ. Lib. Inc. 4.J.1.2, sig. ciii(v).

**Letter to Henry VIII (31 July 1544):** Ed. DWF from B.L. MS Lans. 1236, fol. 9r

**1. *Prayers Stirring the Mind*:** Ed. DWF from *Prayers Stirryng the mynd* (1545) [*Q1*]; collated with 2^nd ed., entitled *Prayers or Meditacions* (1545) [*Q2*] (*Qq* where both eds. agree).
[11] richesse ] *Q2*; riches *Q1* (*cf. richesse, par. 32*)
[13] the ] *Q2*; *omit Q1*
[17] perfitly ] perfectly *Q2*
[23] this world's ] this worldely *Q1*
[26] that which ] *DF* (*for clarity*); that *Qq*

**Katherine to Thomas Seymour (February 1546/7):** Ed. DWF fr. Sudeley Castle MS Dent-Brocklehurst (holograph); from ed. Mueller, 129-30.

**Thomas Seymour to Katherine (March 1546/7):** Ed. DWF fr. S.P. Dom. Supplementary, Edward VI, 46/1/14 (holograph); from ed. Mueller, 131-2.
me ] *DF* (*for clarity*); him *MS*

**Katherine to Thomas Seymour (April 1547):** Ed. DWF fr. Bodleian MS Ashmole 1729, art. 4, fol. 5 (holograph).

**Thomas Seymour to Katherine (17 May 1547):** Ed. DWF fr. SP 10/1/41, fols. 128r-129r (holograph).

**Katherine to Thomas Seymour (c. 21 May 1547):** Ed. DWF Bodleian Library Rawl. MS D1070, art. 2, fols. 4r-5r (17^th-C. copy).

**Katherine to Thomas Seymour (c. 25 May 1547):** Ed. DWF fr. Hatfield House (Hertfordshire), Salisbury (Cecil) Papers, 133/3/248, fols. 4r-5v (holograph).

**Thomas Seymour to Katherine (c. 31 May 1547):** Ed. DWF fr. SP 10/1/43, fol. 132 (holograph)

**Princess Mary to Thomas Seymour (4 June 1547)**Ed. DWF fr. B.L. Lansdowne 1236, fol. 26 (holograph).

**Katherine to her husband (11 June 1548):** Ed. DWF fr. Hatfield House (Herts.) Salisbury (Cecil) Papers 133/3, fol.s 6r-7v (holograph)

**Elizabeth Tyrwhitt's Confession (Feb. 1548/9):** Ed. DWF from Samuel Haynes, *A Collection of State Papers* (1740), 103-4. Original no longer extant.

**ANNE ASKEW (KYME)**

***The First Examination*:** Ed. DWF from *The first examinacyon*, ed. Bale [Wesel, 1546] [*Q1*], sigs. A1r-E8v, but with the interpolated commentary of Johan Bale omitted. Collated with *The first examincyõ* (*The Latter Examination.*), ed. Bale (Marpurg, 1546-1547) [i.e., London? 1547?] [*Q2*], sigs. B2r-F5v; and with *The firste Examinacyon* (*The latter Examination.*) [1548] [*Q3*], sigs. A1r-B3r (the first ed. with Bale's commentary omitted). *Qq* is given where all three eds. agree.

[1] people ] people (saith she) *Qq;* (saith she), *Bale*
[1] the ] thy *Q3*
[3] Corinthes ] Corinthians *Q3*
[5] acknowledge ] knowledg *Q3*
[9] from ] *omit Q3*
[11] forbode ] forbade *Q3*
[11] Cor. ] *DF*; Corinthiorum *Qq*
[12] sureties ] suretees *Q1, Q2b*; suerties *Q3*
[13] not suffer ] noe suffer *Q3*
[13] a ] *omit Q3*
[13] to take so much pain more as to assoil ] to assoil *Q3*
[13] that ] thear *Q3*
[14] consent ] on sent *Q3*
[15] know ] *Q3*; knowne *Q1, Q2b*
[15] contented ] *Q2b, 48*; contended *Q1*
[16] afore ] before *Q3*
[20] commune ] commê *Q1, Q2b*; *Q3* cõmon
[20] Ask ] *Q3*; Axe *Q1, Q2b*
[21] Hall ] Hawe *Q1, Q2b*; Hawle *Q3*
[24] what a saying ] *omit* a *Q3*
[25] laid ] sayed *Q3*
[25] laid it ] *omit* it *Q3*
[27] masses ] masse *Q3*
[28] that that ] *DF* (*for clarity*); that *Qq*
[31] six ] vi *Q1, Q2b*; ix *Q3*
[32] so small ] *omit* so *Q3*
[33] do not ] *omit* do *Q3*
[34] writ ] wrote *Q3*
[34] any ] *DF*; my *Qq*
[34] it ] it, Q1, Ex 47b; y[t] Q3 (*in later eds.*, that)
[35] to ] unto *Q3*
[35] willed me ] *omit* me *Q3*
[36] favor ] fauour that *Q3*
[38] sureties ] suerties *Qq*; *again at* [*9.11*]
[39] so suffer ] *omit* so *Q3*
[39] to appear ] tappere *Q3*
[39] writing ] wrytynge *Q2b, 48*; witynge *Q1*

**Ballad which Anne Askew Made and Sang:** Ed. DWF from *The lattre examinacyon* [Wesel,] (1547) [*Q2a*].

8 makes ] make
9 bids me so to do ] byd me do so Q1
16 hate ] hast Q1
18 ship's ] *DF*; shyppe *Q2a*
21 throne ] trone *Q2a* (as pronounced)
21 set ] sytt *Q2a*
23 Absorbed ] Absorpt *Q2a*

***The Latter Examination:*** Ed. DWF from *The lattre examinacyon* (1547) *Q2a*, with collations from *Q2b* sigs. G4r-P2r, and *Q3*, sigs. B4v-D1r (this being the first ed. without Bale's commentary).

**The Sum of My Examination** (*Q2a*, pp. 14r-17r; *Q2b*, sigs. H7r-I2r; *Q3*, sigs. B6v-C1r)

[1] being ] *omit Q2b*
not he ] he not *Q3*
[2] Christen ] Christian *Q3*
[3] yea, and ] yea, and all *Q3*

**The Sum of the Condempnation** (*Q2a*, pp. 31r-32v; *Q2b*, sigs. K6r-L5r; *Q3*, sig. C2).

*tit*] Guildhall ] Guilde Halle *Q3*; yelde hawle *Q1, Q2a-b*
[1] my ] mîe *Q3*
[1] Acts 1.12 ] Acto. i *Qq*
[1] moldy ] mouldy *Q3*; moulde *Qa-2b*

From **The Effect of My Examination and Handling since My Departure from Newgate** (*Q1a*, 38r-49r; *Q2b*, sigs. L5r-N7r; *Q3*, sigs. C4r-6r)

[1] esteem ] estem *Q3*; exteme *Q2a-b*
[2] Suffolk ] *Q3* Suffolke; *Q2* Sothfolke
[2] of Sussex ] Sussex *Q3*
[2] hable ] able *Q3*
[4] made ] made mone *Q3*
[6] with ] w[t] *Q1a*; *omit Q2a-b*

Young Englishwoman,
costume study by Hans Holbein, 1526-28
*Ashmolean Museum* (*Oxford*)

## Bibliography of Works Cited

### I. Manuscripts

**Balliol College** (Oxford). MS Balliol College 220,. ("vaylaway whi ded y so" [Welaway, why did I so?" fol. 220vb.)

—. MS 354. (["Corpus Christi Lullaby,"] fol. 165v.)

**Bibliotheque d'Amiens** (France). MS 460. (Contains a Latin version antecedent to English "I am rose," fol. 93). See Coyecque, p. 221.

**Bibliothèque Ste Geneviève** (Paris). MS 3390. ("Who schal to my lemman say…," fol. 106.)

**Bodleian Library** (Oxford). MS Ashmole 61. (Dame Courtesy, pseud., ["Dame Courtesy's Book for Children,"] fols. 20r-21v.)

—. MS Ashmole 1396 (Contains "Science of Cirurgie,"anon. trans. of Lanfranco of Milan, *Chirurgia Magna* [1296]).

—. MS Ashmole 1729 (K. Parr to T. Seymour [April 1547], art. 4, fol. 5).

—. MS Ballard 41, fol. 152 (Thomas Rawlins to George Ballard, 5 Feb. 1733, fol. 152.)

—. MS Douce 37, North Midlands (c. 1390, ms. c. 1510) ("The Knowing of Woman's Kind in Childing," fols. 1-37v).

—. MS Eng. poet. a.1 (SC 3938) [Vernon MS] ([O Sweet Jesus:] Jhesu crist my lemmon swete [14th C. versions], fols. 114vb, 300rb); cf. B.L. 2316.

—. MS Fairfax 16 (formerly Bodleian MS 3896). (Contains W.Pole, attrib., "How þe louer is sett to serve þe floure," fol. 325v -327r; indexed title, fo. 2r.

—. MS Rawlinson C.86. (Elizabeth of York, ["Epithalamion"], fols. 155v-156r).

—. MS Rawl. C. 813 [Findern Manuscript]. ("Please ytt your grace dere harte to gyffe audyence…"; "O my lady dere both regarde and see...," fols. 14v-18r; "Ryght gentyll harte of greane flouryng age...," fols. 21v-23v; " I loue So Sore I wolde fayne descerne..., fol. 61; "O loue most dere o loue most nere my harte..." fols. 24v-27v; "grene flouryng age of your manly countenance...," fol. 53v; "I loue So Sore I wolde fayne descerne...," fol. 61; "O resplendent floure prynte þis yn your mynde...," fols. 53v-54r; "Right best beloved and most In assurance...," fols. 71r-72v (all in Hand A); and "A Letter Sende by on yonge woman to a noder," fols. 6v-7v [in Hand B].)

—. MS Rawlinson D.913 (["The Irish Dancer,"] art. I.g).

—. MS Rawlinson D1070 (K. Parr to T. Seymour [c. 24 May 1547], art. 2, fols. 4r-5r).

—. MS Rawlinson G22 (SC 14755). ([M]irie it is while sumer ilast…, fol. 1v)

—. MS Rawlinson poet. 36 (SC 14530). ("To my true love and able," fols. 3v-4.)

—. MS Rawl. poet. 143. (J. Barnes, "Boke of Huntyng," fols. 1r-11av.)

**British Library** (London). MS Add. 5465 (Fairfax MS). (Yowre counturfetyng with doubyll delyng," fol. 22v).

—. MS Additional 5665. (["Explain Thyself"], fol. 69v).

—. MS Add. 12056 ("Science of Cirurgie" anon. trans., Lanfranco, of Milan, *Chirurgia Magna* [1296]).

—. MS Additional 12060 (report of Margaret Beaufort's death, fol. 23v).

—. MS Add. 14875 (Dafydd to Gwenllian, fol. 51).

—. MS Additional 17492 (the "Devonshire Manuscript.") (Poems by Margaret Douglas, Thomas Howard, , Mary Shelton, et al.)

—. —. [digital facsimile and transcription]. *The Devonshire Manuscript: A Digital Social Edition*. Ed. Ray Siemens, et al. (Devonshire MS Editorial Group).

—. MS Additional 27445 (selections from the Paston Letters, as noted).

—. MS Additional 27446 (selections from the Paston Letters, as noted).

—. MS Additional 33956 ("Weylawey þat iche ne span…," fol. 98r).

—. MS Additional 34111 ("Liber Trotuli" fol. 197 ff.).

—. MS Additional 34360 (["The Assembly of Ladies,"] fols. 37r-49r).

—. MS Additional 34888 (selections from the Paston Letters, as noted).

—. MS Additional 34889 (selections from the Paston Letters, as noted).

—. MS Additional 37790 (Julian of Norwich, ["A Revelation of Love":] "Here es a visiõn schewed be the goodenes of god...," fols. 97r-115r).

—. MS Additional 37977 (Sir James Melville, *Memoirs of his own Life.*)

—. MS Additional 43490 (selections from the Paston Letters, as noted).

—. MS Additional 61823 (a.k.a. the "Salthows MS," so-called for the name of the scribe who prepared it ca. 1450) (Kempe, "The Boke of Margerie Kempe").

—. MS Arundel 151 (Catharine of Aragon to Princess Mary, April 1534, fol. 194).

—. MS Arundel 318 (A. Howard, ["Oratio":] "Oratio elianore percie / Ducissa Buckhammie," fol. 152).

—. MS Cole 24 (Margaret Beaufort, "The Lady Margaret her Vow," fol. 244v).

—. MS Cotton Caligula A.vii ([Æcerbot: Field Blessing], fols. 176a-178a).

—. MS Cotton Caligula A.ix (["Owl and Nightingale,"] 233c-244v.)

—. MS Cotton Cleopatra E.iv. (Commissioners in Northamptonshire to Lord Cromwell [12 May 1536], fol. 209; Abbess Katherine Bulkeley to Th. Cromwell [15 November 1536], fol. 229; George Gifford to Cromwell [19 June 1536], fol. 213).

—. MS Cotton Julius D.viii (Cellaress of Barking Abbey, ["Work Orders"] fols. 41-44).

—. MS Cotton Nero A.xiv (Ancrene Wisse)

—. MS Cotton Otho C.x (William Kingston to Lord Cromwell [19 May 1536], fol. 223; and Anne Boleyn to Henry VIII [6 May 1536], fol. 232r [16th C copy]).

—. MS Cotton Vespasian D.ix ("Nun will I Never None, fols. 177r-182v, 190r-v).

.—. MS Cotton Vespasian F.iii. (signature of Queen Jane Seymour.)

—. MS Cotton Vespasian F.xiii. (Margaret Beaufort to her son, Henry VII [14 January 1499], fol. 60; and Margaret Douglas to Thomas Cromwell [1536], art. 188, fol. 173).

—. MS Egerton 616 (Elizabeth of York, To Queen Isabella [3 December 1497], fol. 7).

—. MS Harleian 64 (a narrative of the proceedings against Dame Alice Kyteler, 1324 CE).

—. MS Harleian 283 (Anne Boleyn, Birth Announcement [Elizabeth I], fol. 75r; Jane Seymour, Birth Announcement [Edward VI], fol. 155).

—. MS Harleian 494 (M. Ostrewyk, ["Certain Prayers":] "Certane prayers shewyd unto a devote person callyd Mary Ostrewyk," fols. 61v-62r).

—. MS Harleian MS 543 (Margaret of Anjou, Citizens of London (1461), fol. 147).

—. MS Harl. MS 585 (Anglo-Saxon Charms, fol. 185).

—. MS Harl. 913 ("Lullay, lullay, little child," fol. 32).

—. MS Harleian 978 (Marie de France, [Fables,] fols. 40a-67b).

—. MS Harleian 2316 (["O Sweet Jesus":] "Jhesu crist my lemmon swete…" [15th C. version], fol. 25. Cf. Bodleian MS Eng. poet. a.1 (14th C.).

—. MS Harleian 3823 ("Anglice dicitur," fol. 354v).

—. MS Harleian 4294, fol. 81r ("To Onpreyse Wemen yt were a shame," , fol. 81r).

—. MS Harleian 5036 (Robert Barker, book-plate, If it be lost…, fol. 44).

—. MS Harleian 6148 (Cranmer on Elizabeth Barton, fol. 40).

—. MS Harleian 7039 (Henry VII to Margaret, countess of Richmond [17 July 1501], fol. 34).

—. MS Lansdowne 1236 (Queen Katherine Parr to Henry VIII [31 July 1544], fol. 9r).

—. MS Royal 18 A.VI (["Jamie: *He that wilbe a lover in euery wise…*," fol. 22).

—. MS Royal 20.A.xix (Boethius, *De consolatione philosophieœ,* anon. trans. into French verse; Elizabeth of York, "Loyaltye me lye. Elyzabeth" [holo. motto on fly-leaf,] fol. 195r).

—. MS Royal App. 58 (Westron wynde, fol. 5).

—. MS Royal *Fr.* 46919 (formerly CB.xii). (W. Twety, "Le Venery," fols. 15v-18v).

—. MS Sloane 747 (["By the Prayers of St. Dorothy,"] fol. 57r).

—. MS Sloane 1584. (["Of Serving Men,"] fol. 45v; ["Alas, What Remedy?] 85r-87r).

—. MS Sloane 2463. ("Woman's Privy Sickness").

—. MS Sloane 2499 (Julian of Norwich, ["A Revelation of Love."]).

—. MS Sloane 3705. (Julian of Norwich, ["A Revelation of Love"]).

**Caius College Library** (Cambridge). MS 383. (["The Serving Maid's Holiday" and "Led I the Dance,"] p. 41; "Black is Beautiful,"] 190; ["Maiden's Complaint,"] 210).

**Cambridge University Library** (Cambridge). MS Add. 3042 ("Form of Confession," fols. 79r-80v).

—. MS Add. 5943. (["As I Could Wish,"] fol. 178v).

—. MS Ff.1.6 ("The Findern Manuscript"). (["Margery Hungerford, Without Variaunce":] "Where y haue chosyn...," fol. 20v. ["Men":] "What so men seyn...," fol. 56r; ["Absence":] "My woofull hert...," fol. 69v; ["A Love Cycle":] "Welcome be ye, my souereine," fols. 135r-136r; ["Alas":] "Alas, alas, and Alas, why…," fols. 137v-138r; ["Grievaunce":] "Continvaunce / Of remembraunce...," fols. 138v-139r; ["Of a Star":] "ffor to pente…," fols. 143v-144r. ["This is No Life":] "This ys no lyf, alas, þat y do lede…," fol. 153v; ["Goodbye":] yit wulde I nat the causer faryd a-mysse," fols. 153v-154r; ["A Promise":] "Veryly / And truly / I schall nat fayne...," fol. 154r).

—. MS Ff.5.48 (["Bryan's Complaint,"] fol. 114v).

—. MS Hh.6.11 (Contains "I am rose," fol. 67r).

—. MS Ii.vi.33 (["Infertility."] *The Book of Rota,* fols. 3-5, 11v-13).

—. MS Inc. 4.J.1. (Parr Book of Hours, with inscription c. 1520, sig. 103v).

—. MS Kk.1.5 (Marie de France, *Bodye of Policy*, fols. 69r-71v; anon. trans., as transcribed from the first print edition (London, 1521).

**Cardiff Free Library** (Cardiff, Wales). MS 1.2 (Gwerful ap Fychan, ["Snow,"] p. 405; Tudur Penllyn, ["The Welshman and the Englishwoman,"] MSS 2.616, fol. 275; 2.14, fol. 431; 5.44, fol. 282b; Dafydd to Gwenllian, MS 13, fol. 108.

**Chetham Library** MS 8009 (["Woman's Work"], fols. 370-72).

**Dunham Massey** (Altrincham, Greater Manchester). MS copy of the birth announcement of Edward VI (12 Oct. 1537). Cf. B.L. MS Harleian 283.

**Durham Cathedral Library** (Durham) MS B.I.18 ("Anglice dicitur," fol.. 116vb).

**Exeter Cathedral Library** (Exeter) *Codex Exoniensis.* (["Wulf,"] fols. 100v-101r; ["Lamentation" a.k.a. "The Wife's Lament,"] fol. 115).

**National Archives** (Kew) MS SC1/51/189 (Margaret Beaufort, To Thos. Butler, earl of Ormond [25 April 1597?]).

—. —. MS 1/110 (Agnes Jordan, prioress of Syon to Thos, Ld Cromwell [6 Nov. 1536], fol. 186r).

—. —. MS 1/113 (note of parcels received to supply chamber of M. Douglas at Syon Abbey, fol. 49r).

—. —. MS 1/167 (Katherine Howard to Thos Culpepper, fol. 14; pr. in *Letters & Papers*, 16, no. 1134).

—. —. MS DCH/C/949 (quitclaim, 16 Nov. 1478, noted under Elizabeth of York).

**Hatfield House** (Hertfordshire), Salisbury (Cecil) Papers, 133/3/248 (K. Parr to T. Seymour [31 May 1547], fols. 4r-5v).

**Huntington Library** (San Marino). MS HEH RB 12924 (T. Shardelow, bookplate, flyleaf).

**Lambeth Palace Library** (London) MS Lambeth 491. (J. Barnes, "The Boke of Huntyng.")

—. MS 78 ("Jesu, my spouse good," fol. 223v).

**Leicestershire Record Office** (Leicester) MS 6D32/2 ("*Omnis amor clerici amor clerici*," p. 38).

**Library of Scotland** (Edinburgh) MS Advocates 19.2.1 ("The Birth of Freine," anon. trans. of Marie de France, the lai le Fresne).

**Longleat House** (Warminster). MS 258 (formerly housed at Trinity College, Cambridge). ("The Assembly of Ladies:] the Boke of Assemble de dames," fols. 58r-75v).

**National Library of Wales** (Aberystwyth). MS Cwrt. 12 (Gwenllian, Reply to Gruffudd, fol. 218).

—. MS Cwrtmawr 24. (Gwerful Fychan, ["Snow"], 12).

—. MS Cwrtmawr 25 (ca. 1650). (Gwerful Fychan, ["Snow,"] 11).

—. MS Cwrtmawr 117 (Gwerful Mechain, ["Vacancy"], 211).

—. MS 16B, p. 262 (Gwerful Fychan, ["Snow"], 12).

—. MS 278. (Gwerful Mechain, ["Keep Calm,"] p. 11).

—. MS 436 (Gwerful Mechain, ["To her Dad"] 104).
—. MS 670 (Gwenllian, Reply to Gruffudd, fol. 4).
—. MS 1553A (Gwerful Mechain, ["Boy in the Bush,"] 694).
—. MS 7191 (Gwerful Mechain, ["Dripping Wet,"] 169).
—. MS Llansteffan 119 (Gwerful Mechain, ["To her Husband,"] 138).
—. MS Llansteffan 145 (Gwerful Mechain, ["To her Husband,"] 90).
—. MS Llan. 165 (Gwerful ap Fychan, ["Snow,"] 141.
—. MS Llansteffan 167 (Gwerful Mechain, ["Dripping Wet"], 34; ["Keep Calm"], 177).
—. MS Llansteffan 173 (Gwerful Mechain, ["Dripping Wet"] 34).
—. MS 3039B (=Mostyn 131) (Gwerful Mechain, ["The Difference"], 405; ["To her Husband"], two copies, 404, 406; [Keep Calm], 405; Gruffudd to Gwenllian, fols. 230, fo.481).
—. MS Peniarth 67 (Gwenllian, Reply to Gruffudd, fol. 39).
—. MS Peniarth 73 (Gwerful Mechain, ["Keep Calm,"] p. 115).
—. MS Peniarth 94. (Gwerful Mechain, ["To her Husband"], p. iii).
—. MS Pen. 99 (Gwenllian, Reply to Gruffudd, fol. 390).
—. MS Pen. 101 (Gwenllian, Reply to Gruffudd, fol. 270).
—. MS Peniarth 203. (Gwerful Mechain, ["To her Dad"], p. 138).
—. MS Minor Depost 56B (=Swansea 2, the Cefn Coch Manuscripts). (Gwerful Mechain, ["The Artful Dodger,"] 365. Pr. C. Lloyd-Morgan, 195).
**Public Record Office**. *See* Great Britain. National Archives.
**Representative Church Body Library** (Dublin) MS D11.1.2 [Red Book of Ossory]. ("Alas hou shold y synge," fp;. 71va.)
**St. John's College** (Cambridge) MS 76 (J. Wrighton, bookplate, fol. 5v).
—. MS G.30 (epigraph, O.F/M.E., p. 413.)
**St. Joseph's College** (Upholland). (Julian of Norwich, ["A Revelation of Love."])
**Sudeley Castle** (Gloucestershire) MS Dent-Brocklehurst (K. Parr to T. Seymour [Feb. 1546/7]).
**Trinity College** (Cambridge). MS O.2.53 (Elizabeth of York, "Communion Prayer," fols. 53-4).
—. MS R.3.19. ("The Assembly of Ladies":] "the Boke callyd Assemble de Damys," fols. 55r-65v; [Reply to her Lover,] fols. 7v-8v).
**Trinity College** (Dublin). MS 490. (*"I wyll no more go to the plowe...*, fol. 179v.)
**University College** (Oxford). MS 169, sæc. xv. (Katherine of Sutton, "The Easter Play of the Nuns of Barking Convent," pp. 121-24.)
**University College of North Wales** (Bangor). MS 7268 (Gwenllian, Reply to Gruffudd, fol. 2).
**Westminster Archdiocesan Archives** (Westminster). Unnumbered MS. (Julian of Norwich, extracts from ["A Revelation of Love,"] fols. 1, 25, 35, 72, 112.)
—. MS B.2. (Avisa Moon, "The Confession of Hawisia Moone," fols. 102-3.)

## II. By Author or Editor

Albertus Magnus, attrib. (pseudo-Albert). ["On Menstrual Blood"]. Trans. DWF 2013.
André, Bernard. *De Vita atque gestis Henrici Septimi Historia.* Ed. James Gardner. London, 1858.
ANNE (Boleyn), queen. *See* MSS B.L. Cotton OthoC.X, Cotton Vesp. F.XII; Harl. 283; also Hall, *Union* (1548, 1550) and Leti, *Vita di Elisabetta.*
ANNE (of Cleves), queen. *See* State Papers 1/161.
Archer, Margaret, ed. *Register of Bishop Philip Repingdon 1405-1419* Vol. 1. Lincoln Record Society Pubs., vol. 57. Hereford: for the Society, 1963.
ASKEW (Kyme), ANNE. *The first examinacyon*, ed. Johan Bale [Wesel, 1546].
—. —. *The first examincyõ* (*The Latter Examination*). Ed. Bale (Marpurg, 1546-1547) [i.e., London? 1547?].
—. —. *The firste Examinacyon* (*The latter Examination.* [1548]).
["The ASSEMBLY OF LADIES."] *See* de la POLE.
Bacon, Francis. *The Historie of the Reigne of King Henry the Seventh*. London, 1629.
Bambas, Rudolf C. "Another View of *The Wife's Lament*." *NM* 69 (1968): 72-90.
Barker, Robert. [Bookplate.] Ed. R. Johnson Walker, *N&Q* 10[th] ser. (24 March 1906): 230.
BARNES, JULIAN (a.k.a. Berners, early 15th C.). [*Book of Hunting*.] "Dam Iulyans Barnes in her boke of huntyng." In [*The Book of St. Albans*] [1486]. Sigs. D5r-F4r. [Many times reprinted. See *STC*.].
BARTON, ELIZABETH, Maid of Kent. *See* B.L. MSS Harl. 6148, Cotton Cleopat. E.iv.
BAXTER, MARGERY. *See* Westminster Diocesan Archives MS B.2; ed. Foxe (1563), 407-08.
BEAUFORT, MARGARET (1443-1509). *See* B.L. MSS Add. 12060; Cotton Vesp. F.XIII; Cole 24; Harl. 7039; PRO SC1/51/189; Howard, ed., *Letters.*
—, trans. *The mirroure of golde for the synfull soule.* London, 1504.
Bell, Dotke C. "Notices of the historic persons buried in the chapel of St Peter ad Vincula in the Tower of London" *Archaeologia* 34 (1877): 507.
Bentley, Samuel ed. *Excerpta Historica.* London, 1831. (Margaret Beaufort to Thos Ormond, p. 285.)
Bowker, Margaret, ed. *An Episcopal Court Book for the Diocese of Lincoln.* Lincoln Record Society, Pubs, Vol. 21. Lincoln: for the Society, 1967.
BREWS, Dame ELIZABETH DEBENHAM (fl. 1477-1487). *See* B.L. MSS Add; pr. Davis, ed., *The Paston Letters* (1971-76).
BREWS PASTON, MARGERY (1457-1495). *See* B.L. MSS Add; pr. Davis, *The Paston Letters* (1971-76).
BRIAN, Lady. *See* Bodleian Library MS Rawl. C.813.
*British Architect and Engineer*. "Proposed Exhumation of Shakespeare." Anon. (25 August 1876): 119.
Burnet, Gilbert. *History of the Reformation of the Church of England.* 6 vols. London: Priestly, 1820.
CATHERINE (of Aragon) (1485-1536), queen. *See* MSS B.L. MS Arundel 151, fo. 194; *Letters & Papers,* vol. 6, no. 1126.
Chambers, E. K., and Frank Sidgwick, *Early English Lyrics.* London: Sidgwick, 1937.

CHRISTINE de PIZAN. *Here begynneth the booke whiche is called the bodye of polycye.* Anon. trans. London: John Skot, 1521.

—. *Here begynneth the table of the rubryshys of the boke of the fayt of armes and of chyualrye.* London, Caxton, 1484.

—. *The morale prouerbes of Cristyne.* Anon. trans. London: William Caxton, 1478.

—. *Here begynneth the boke of the cyte of ladyes.* Anon. trans. London: Henry Pepwell, 1521.

Clark, Andrew, ed. *The English Register of Godstow Nunnery, near Oxford, written about 1450.* London: Early English Text Society, 1911.

Clinker, Janet [i.e., Humphrey]. *The History of the Haverel Wives* (1787). Ed. William Harvey. *Scottish Chapbook Literature.* Paisley, 1903.

Colledge, Edmund, and James Walsh, eds. *A Book of Showings to the Anchoress Julian of Norwich.* 2 vols. Toronto: Pontifical Ins. of Medieval Studies, 1978.

Cooper, C.P., ed., *Chancery Proceedings.* Vol. 1. London, 1832.

Cooper, Charles Henry. *Memoir of Margaret: Countess of Richmond and Derby.* Cambridge Univ. Press, 1874 (inventory of Margaret Beaufort, pp. 129-35).

Cords, Rose. "Fünf me. Gedichte aus den Hss. Rawlinson Poetry 36 und Rawl. C.86." *Archiv* 135 (1916): 300-302. (Elizabeth of York, ["Epithalamion,"] 302.)

Cox, Charles. "The Parish Churches of Northamptonshire Illustrated by Wills, Temp. Henry VIII." *Archaelogical J.,* 58 (ser. 2, vol. 8) (1901): 113-32.

Coyecque, E., ed. *Catalogue Général des Manuscrits des Bibliothèques publiques de France.* Vol. 19: (Amiens) Paris, 1893.

Cressy, Dom R. F. Serenus, ed. *XVI Revelations of Divine Love* (1670). *See* JULIAN of Norwich.

Davis, Norman, ed. *The Paston Letters and Papers.* 2 vols. Oxford: Clarendon, 1971-1976.

Dent, Emma. *Annals of Winchcombe and Sudeley.* London, 1877.

Desmond, Marilynn. "The Voice of Exile." *Critical Inquiry* 16 (Spring 1990): 572-90.

DOUGLAS (Stuart), MARGARET. *See* B.L. MS Add 17492 ("Devonshire Manuscript"). MacCracken, Henry Noble. "An English Friend of Charles of Orléans." *PMLA* 26 (1911), 142-80.

ELIZABETH of York (1465-1502), queen. ["Epithalam-ion."] *See* MS Rawl. C.86; pr. Cords, ed. (1916); Flügel, ed. (1892, 1895).

Ellis, Henry. *Original Letters, Illustrative of English History.* 1st ser. 3 vols. London: Harding et al., 1824.

—. 3d series. 4 vols. London, R. Bentley, 1846.

The EXETER BOOK. *Codex Exoniensis. A Collection of Anglo-Saxon Poetry.* Ed. Benjamin Thorpe. London: for the Society of Antiquaries, 1842, 1908.

—. [Facsimile reproduction.] *The Exeter Book of Old English Poetry.* London: P. Lund and Humphries for the dean and chapter of Exeter Cathedral, 1933.

—. *See also* Thorpe, Benjamin, ed. *Codex Exoniensis* (1842; repr. 1908); Mackie, ed. (1934); F. Holthausen (1893), E. Sieper (1915), C. Kennedy (1960), R. Leslie (1961), R. Hamer (1970).

FINDERN ANTHOLOGY. *See* MS Rawl. C. 813.; cf. Robbins, ed., "The Findern Anthology" (1954).

"The Floure and the Leaf." Anon. In *The Workes of ... Geffrey Chavcer.* Ed. Thomas Speght. London, 1598. Fols. 365v-68v. Repr. revd. ed., London: A. Islip, 1602. Fols. 344r-46r.

—. —. *See* eds. Pearsall, Skeat, Thynne, Urry.

Foxe, John. *Actes and Monuments of the Christian Church.* London, 1563.

Franks, David. [Bookplate]. Ed. N. Taylor Phillips, *Am. Jewish Quarterly,* vol. 4 (Dec. 1894): 197.

FYCHAN. *See* GWERFUL.

Gasté, Armand. *Chansons Normandes du XV^e siècle.* Caen: E. Le Gost-Clérisse, 1866.

Gilbert, Sandra, and Susan Gubar. *Norton Anthology of Literature by Women,* 3d ed., vol. 1. Norton, 2007.

Glasscoe, Marion, ed. *A Revelation of Love.* By Julian of Norwich. Exeter: Univ. of Exeter, 1974; 3d ed., 1981.

Great Britain. Historical Manuscripts Commission. *Calendar of the Manuscripts of the Marquis of Bath ... at Longleat.* Vol. 2. London: HMSO, 1907.

—. State Paper Office. *Calendar of State Papers, Spain, 1585-1558.* 13 vols. HMSO, 1862-1954.

—. —. *State Papers, Henry VIII,* 11 vols. Part I: Corrspondence between the King and Cardinal Wolsey, 1518-1530. HMSO, 1830-1852.

—. —. *Letters and Papers, Foreign and Domestic, Henry VIII.* 2nd series. 21 vols. in 28. London: HMSO, 1864-1910.

GWENLLIAN ["Reply to Gruffudd."] *See* MSS Univ. Coll. of North Wales, and N.L.W.

GWERFUL ap FYCHAN. *See* MSS Cardiff Free Library and National Library of Wales.

GWERFUL MECHAIN. *See* N.L.W.; and eds. Howells (2001), Lloyd-Morgan (1990, 1993).

Hales, J.W., and F. J. Furnivall, eds. *Bishop Percy's Folio Manuscript.* 3 vols. London, 1868.

Hall, Edward. *The Vnion of the Two Noble and Illustre Famelies of Lancastre & Yorke.* London: 1548, 1550.

Halliwell, James O., and Thomas Wright, eds. *Reliquæ Antiquæ.* 2 vols. London: Smith, 1845.

Hamer, Richard, ed. *A Choice of Anglo-Saxon Verse.* London: Faber and Faber, 1970.

Hammond, Eleanor Prescott. "A Reproof to Lydgate." In *Mod. Language Notes* 26.3 (1911), 74-6 (W. de la Pole, ["To Serve the Flower," 200-01).

Hanna, Ralph. "Humphrey Newton and Bodleian Library MS Lat. Misc. C.66, *Medium Aevum* (Fall 2000): 279-91.

Haselwood, Joseph, ed. *The Book Containing the Treatises of Hawking, Hunting, Coat-Armour, Fishing, and Blasing of Arms.* [*1496*]. Facsimile. London: Harding and Wright, 1810 [i.e., 1811].

Haynes, Samuel. *A Collection of State Papers, Relating to Affairs, from the Year 1542-1570* [fr. the Salisbury (Cecil) papers.] London, 1740.

Hobby, Elaine. *The Birth of Mankind.* Burlington, VT: Ashgate, 2009.

Holinshed, Raphael. *The Chronicles of England, Scotlande, and Irelande.* fol. 3 vols. London, 1587.

Holthausen, Ferdinand. "Zu alt- und mittelenglischen Denkmälern. *Beiblatt zur Anglia* 15 (1893): 187-203. (textual notes for ["Wulf,"] 188-9.)

Hope, Robert C. *The Legendary Lore of the Holy Wells of England.* London: E. Stock, 1893.

Howard, Katherine, queen. *See* KATHERINE (Howard).

Howard, Leonard. *A Collection of Letters: from the original manuscripts of many princes.* London: Withers, 1753.

Howells, Nerys Ann, ed. *Gwaith Gwerful Mechain ac Eraill.* University of Wales Centre for Advanced Welsh and Celtic Studies, 2001.

JANE (SEYMOUR) (1508-1537), queen. B.L. MS Cotton Vespasian F.III.

Jansen, Sharon L., and Kathleen H. Jordan, ed.s, *The Welles Anthology.* Binghamton, NY: Medieval and Renaissance Texts and Studies, 1991 (a transcription of Bodleian Library MS Rawl. C.813).

Johnston, Dafydd. *Canu Maswedd Yr Oesedd Canol* Cardiff: Tafol, 1991.

JULIAN of Norwich (1342-1417?), anchorite of Norwich. ["A Revelation of Love."] *XVI Revelations of Divine Love.* [London?:] R.F.S. Cressy, 1670.

—. *See also* College and Walsh, eds. (1978); Glasscoe, ed. (1974; 1981).

KATHERINE (HOWARD) (c. 1520-1542), queen. *See* MSS National Archives (Kew) State Papers 1/167; ed. Great Britain. HMC *Longleat* (1907), vol. 2; *Letters & Papers of Henry VIII*, vols. 14-17. *State papers ... Henry VIII*, 11 vols. (1830–52).

KATHERINE of Kent (fl.c. 1500). [Nun would I never be None."] *See* B.L. MS Cotton Vespasian D.ix.

KATHERINE of Sutton. *See* University College (Oxford) MS 169.

KATHERINE (PARR) (1512-1548), queen. *See* B.L. MS Lans. 1236; Sudeley MS Dent-Brocklehurst; *S.P. Dom. Supplementary, Edward VI,* 46/1/14; Bodleian MS Ashmole 1729; Nat'l Archives, S.P. 10/1/41-43, 10/2; Bodleian Library Rawl. MS D1070; Hatfield House (Hertfordshire) 133/3; Hearne, ed., *Epistolarum*; Haynes, ed., *State Papers.*

—. [*Prayers.*] *Prayers Stirryng the mynd unto heauenly medytacions.* London: Berthelet, 1545.

—.—. [Anr. ed.] *Prayers or Meditacions, wherin the mynde is styrred paciently to suffre all afflictions here,* etc. London: T Berthelet, 1545.

Kaulek, Jean, ed. *Correspondence politique de MM. de Castillon* et de *Marillac.* Paris, 1885.

KEMPE, MARGERY (BRUNHAM) (1373-1438?). *See* B.L. MS Additional 61823 (the "Salthows MS"); and see Meech, ed. (1940).

Kennedy, Charles W., ed. *An Anthology of Old English Poetry.* New York: Oxford Univ. Press, 1960. (["Wulf,"] 84-85.)

Klinck, Anne L. "Lyric Voice and the Feminine in Some Ancient and Mediaeval *Frauenlieder,*" *Florilegium* 13 [1994:] 13-36.

Latimer, William. *William Latymer's Chronickille of Anne Bulleyne.* Ed. Maria Dowling. Camden Miscellany, no. 30, 4th ser., vol. 39. London: for the Society, 1990: 62-3.

Leslie, R. F. *Three Old English Elegies: The Wife's Lament, The Husband's Message, The Ruin.* Manchester: Manchester Univ. Press, 1961.

Leti, Gregorio. *Historia, overo Vita de Elizabetta, Regina d'Inghilterra.* 2 vols. Amsterdam, 1693.

Lewis, C.S. *The Allegory of Love.* Oxford UP, 1936.

Lloyd-Morgan, Ceridwen. "'Gwerful Ferch Ragorol Fain': Golwg Newydd ar Gwerful Mechain." *Ysgrifau Beirniadol* 16 (1990), 84-96.

—. "Women and their Poetry in Medieval Wales." *Women and Literature in Britain, 1150-1500.* Cambridge: Cambridge Univ. Press, 1993. 183-201.

Lucas, Angela M. "The Narrator of *The Wife's Lament*," *NM* 70 (1969): 282-97.

Lysons, Daniel and Samuel. *Magna Britannia: Derbyshire.* London, 1817.

Mackie, W. S., ed.. *The Exeter Book. Pt. II: Poems 9-32.* London: Oxford Univ. Press for the Early English Text Society, 1934. (["Wulf,"] 86-87; ["Lamentation,"] 152-55.)

Mandel, Jerome *Alternative Reading in Old English Poetry.* New York: Land, 1987.

Map, Walter. Dissuasio Velerii ad Rufinum. In *Texts, Documents, and Extracts Chiefly from Manuscripts in the Bodleian and other Oxford Libraries.* Ed. Montague R. James. Cambridge: Clarendon, 1914.

MARGARET of Anjou (1430-1482), queen. *See* MS Harleian MS 543; and *Letters*, ed. Monro.

MARIE de France (fl. ca. 1155-1190). [Fables.] *See* Spiegel, trans., *Fables* (1987).

Mathieu of Boulogne. Les Lamentations de Matheolus. Ed. A. G. Van Hamel, Paris, 1905.

MECHAIN. *See* GWERFUL.

Meech, Sanford Brown, ed. *The Book of Margery Kempe* London: Oxford University Press, 1940.

Melville, Sir James. *Memoirs of his own Life.* Bannantyne Club, 1827. (B.L. Add. MS 37977.)

Meyer, Kuno, ed. *Cáin Adamnáin: an old-Irish treatise on the law of Adamnan.* Oxford: Clarendon, 1905

Monro, Cecil, ed. *Letters of Queen Margaret of Anjou.* London: Camden Society, 1863.

MOON, AWISIA. *See* Westminster Archdiocesan Archives MS B2.

Nichols, J. G., ed. *Narratives of the days of the Reformation*, Camden Society, old ser., 77 (1859).

Okerlund, Arlene Naylor. *Elizabeth of York.* London: Macmillan, 2009.

OSTREWYK, MARY. *See* MS Harleian 494.

PARR, KATHERINE. *See* KATHERINE [PARR].

PASTON WOMEN. *See* B.L. MS Add.; and Davis, ed., *The Paston Letters* (1971-76).

Peacock, Edward. "III. Injunctions of John Longland, Bishop of Lincoln, to Certain Monasteries of his Diocese." In *Archaeologia: or Miscellaneous Tracts relating to Antiquity,* vol. 47 (1883): 49-64.

Pearsall, Derek A., ed. *The Floure and the Leafe and The Assembly of Ladies.* London: Nelson, 1962. ("The Floure and the Leaf," 85-102, from ed. Speght (1598); and "The Assembly of Ladies," 105-26, from British Library MS Add. 34360.)

—. "The Floure and the Leafe: Introduction." *The Floure and the Leafe; The Assembly of Ladies; The Isle of Ladies.* Ed. Pearsall. Kalamazoo: Medieval Institute, 1990; repr. 1992; online, www.lib.rochester.edu/camelot/teams/flourint.htm.

Pliny. *Natural History.* Trans. Philemon Holland. London, 1601.

Pole, William de la, duke of Suffolk, attrib. ["The ASSEMBLY OF LADIES."] *See* B.L. MS Add.

34360; Longleat 258; Trinity College MS R.3.19. *See* eds. Pearsall, Skeat, Speght, Thynne, Urry.

—. ["To Serve the Flower":] "How þe louer is sett to serve þe floure." In MacCracken, "An English Friend of Charles of Orléans" (1911), q.v., 168-71.

—.—. "A Reproof to Lydgate." In Hammond, *English Verse* (1927), q.v., 200-01.

—. —. "In Praise of Margaret the Queen: By the Duke of Suffolk." In Robbins (1955), q.v., 186-89.

Pontfarcy, Yolande de. "Si Marie de France était Marie de Meulan." *Cahiers de Civilisation Medievale (Xe-XIIe Siecles)* 38 (1995): 353–61.

Raine, James, ed., *The Fabric Rolls of York Minster.* Surtees Society, no. 35. Durham: for the Society, 1889. (Isabel Mure witch trial [1528,] p. 273).

—. *Historical Letters and Papers from the Northern Registers* (Rolls Series) London, 1873.

Remley, Paul G. "Mary Shelton and her Tudor Literary Milieu" In Peter C. Herman, ed., *Rethinking the Henrican Era*. Univ. of Illinois Pr., 1994. 40-77.

Robbins, Rossell Hope. "The Findern Anthology." *PMLA* 69 (1954): 610-42. (["Margery Hungerford, Without Variaunce," #8, 632; ["Absence,"] #23, 633-4; ["A Love Cycle,"] #31, 635-6; ["Of a Star,"] #40, 636-8; ["Goodbye,"] #52, 638-9.)

—, ed.. "Poems of Humfrey Newton, Esq., 1466-1536," *PMLA* 65.2 (1950): 249-81.

—, ed. *Secular Lyrics of the XIVth and XVth Centuries.* 2nd edition. Oxford: Clarendon, 1955.

—, and John L. Cutler, eds., *Supplement to the Index of Middle English Verse*. Univ. of Kentucky Pr, 1965.

Rossi, Carla. *Marie de France et les érudits de Cantorbéry*. Paris, 2009.

Rösslin, Eucharius. *The Byrth of Mankynde, newly translated out of Laten into Englysshe* by T[homas] R[aynalde] (from *Der swangern Frauwen vnd Hebamen Rosegarten*). London, 1540; repr. 1560 et al.

—. Trans. Wendy Arons. *When Midwifery became the Male Physician's Province*. Jefferson, NC: McFarland, 1994.

Ryland, W. et. al. *Victoria County History of Northamptonshire*. Vol. 2. London: Constable, 1906.

Scrope, Geo. *History of...Castlecombe*. London, 1852.

SHELTON, MARY, Lady Heveningham. *See* B.L. MS Add 17492 (the "Devonshire Manuscript").

Sieper, Ernst, ed. *Die altenglische Elegie*. Strassburg: Trübner, 1915. (["Wulf"] and ["Lamentation"]).

Skeat, Walter W., ed. *The Complete Works of Geoffrey Chaucer*. 7 vols. Oxford: Clarendon, 1894-97. (["Assembly of Ladies,"] and ["Floure and the Leaf].)

Smith, Llinos Beverly. "Olrhain Anni Goch," *Ysgrifau Beirniadol* 19, ed. J.E. Caerwyn Williams. Dinbych: Gwasg Gee, 1993, pp. 107-26.

Speght, Thomas, ed. *The Workes of our Antient and lerned English Poet, Geffrey Chavcer, newly Printed.* Edited by Thomas Speght. London: [A. Islip,] imp. G. Bishop, 1598. (["Assembly of Ladies,"] and ["Floure and the Leaf].) Repr. 1602.

Spiegel, Harriet, ed. and trans. *Marie de France: Fables* [Parallel text, English and Old French.] Toronto and London: Univ. of Toronto Press, 1987.

Spottiswoode, John. *History of the Church of Scotland*, vol. 2. London, 1851.

Storey, Robin *The End of the House of Lancaster.* London: Sutton, 1986.

Strype, John. *Ecclesiastical Memorials.* 5 vols., 1721; 3 vols. 1733; 6 vols., London, 1816-1822.

Stafford, Pauline. "Women and the Norman Conquest," *Transactions of the Royal Historical Society*, 6th Series, vol. 4, (1994), 221-249.

Tanner , Norman P., ed. *Heresy Trials in the Diocese of Norwich, 1428-31...from Westminster Diocesan Archives MS. B.2.* Camden, 4th ser., vol. 20. London: Royal Historical Society, 1977.

Teulet, Alexandre, ed., and trans. *Lettres de Marie Stuart.* Paris, 1859.

Thompson, A. Hamilton. *Visitations in the Diocese of Lincoln,* 1517-1531. Vol. 1. Lincoln Record Society, Pubs, no. 33. Hereford: for the Society, 1940.

—. *Visitations in the Diocese of Lincoln,* 1517-1531 Vol. 2. Lincoln Record Society, Pubs, no. 35. Hereford: for the Society, 1938.

—. *Visitations in the Diocese of Lincoln,* 1517-1531. Vol. 3. Lincoln Record Society, Pubs, no. 37. Hereford: for the Society, 1947.

—. *Visitations of Religious Houses in the Diocese of Lincoln,* 1420-1436. Vol. 1. Lincoln Record Society, Pubs. no. 7. Horncastle: for the Society, 1914.

—. *Visitations of Religious Houses in the Diocese of Lincoln,* 1436-1449. Vol. 2.1. Lincoln Record Society, Pubs, no. 14. Horncastle: for the Society, 1918.

—. *Visitations of Religious Houses in the Diocese of Lincoln,* 1436-1449. Vol. 3.2. Lincoln Record Society, Pubs, no. 21. Horncastle: for the Society, 1923.

Thorpe, Benjamin, ed. *Codex Exoniensis.* London: for the Society of Antiquaries, 1842; repr. 1908. (["Wulf,"] fols. 100v-101r; ["Lamentation,"] 115.)

Thynne, William, ed. The workes of Geffray Chaucer (1532). ("The Assembly of Ladies," fols. 294r-299.) Repr. 1542, 1550?, 1561.

Tilander, Gunnar, ed. *Boke of huntyng [by] Julians Barnes.* Karlshamm, [Sweden:] Johannsons, 1964.

Tolhurst, John B. L. ed. *The Ordinale and Customary of the Benedictine Nuns of Barking Abbey.* Pubs of the Henry Bradshaw Society. Vol. 65. London, 1927.

Tyndale, William. *The Practyse of Prelates.* London, 1530.

Udall, William. *The Historie of the Life and Death of Mary Stuart Queene of Scotland.* London, 1624.

Urry, John, ed. *The Works of Geoffrey Chaucer.* London: for B. Lintot, 1721. (["Assembly of Ladies,"] and ["Floure and the Leaf].)

Warnicke, Retha. "Three Forged Letters of Anne Boleyn," *J. of the Rocky Mountain Medieval and Renaissance Association* 11 (1990): 33-48.

Wood, Mary Anne Everett, ed., *Letters of Royal, and Illustrious Ladies of Great Britain.* 3 vols. London, Colbourn, 1846. (Elizabeth of York to Queen Isabella, 3 Dec. 1497, 1.115-16).

Wright, Thomas ed., *A Contemporary Narrative of the Proceedings against Dame Alice Kyteler.* Camden Society, vol. 24. London: Nichols, 1824.

—. *Three Chapters of Letters from the Suppression of Monasteries.* Camden Old Series. Vol. 26 (Sept. 1843): 116-117.

Wriothesley, Charles. *A Chronicle of England during the Reigns of the Tudors.* Ed. Douglas Hamilton. Cambden Soc., 1875.

**Acknowledgments**

*Women's Works*, volumes 1-4, is the product of twenty-five years' labor, with travel to more than thirty libraries and private collections in England, Scotland, Wales, Ireland, France, and the United States. Grateful acknowledgement is made to Michael O'Connell, for his translation of the Easter play of Barking Abbey (and introduction); to Christine Reno, for her commentary on Christine de Pizan in England; to Harriet Spiegel and the University of Toronto Press for permission to reprint selections from Prof. Spiegel's edition and translation of the Fables. Vassar students assisted with development, many of whom have since gone on to careers in academia or publishing. Special thanks are due to Vassar colleagues Mark Amodio, Rachel Friedman, Rachel Kitzinger, Bert Lott, Christine Reno, for much help and many excellent suggestions. Prof. Joseph Walunywa (1988), Ms. Pamela Seay Appleby (1990), Ms. Karin Cook (1990), Prof. Elizabeth Rivlin (1992), Prof. John Paul Spiro (1996), Ms. Lexa Hillyer (2002), Ms. Tobian Banton (2011-2013), and Ms. Emma Russell (2013) helped with primary research, transcription, editing, formatting, and fact-checking. Sarah Nelson (2005), Philosophy Walker (2008), and Erica Hersh (2010) assisted with correspondence and citations. Anastasia Stevens (2015) helped with the cover design. Blake Foster and Baynard Bailey assisted with Web design. The editors are much obliged.

We are grateful as well to the many institutions that have provided access to original manuscripts, printed texts, and graphics. For the selections in Volume 1, special thanks are owing to the archivists and staff of British Library, the National Archives (Public Record Office), the London Guildhall Office, University College (London), the Leicestershire Record Office, the Chetham Library; Longleat House; the libraries of Durham Cathedral, Exeter Cathedral, and Lambeth Palace; the Westminster Archdiocesan Archives; the Bodleian Library and the libraries of Balliol and University colleges (Oxford). Cambridge University Library; the libraries St. John's, Caius, and Trinity colleges (Cambridge); and St. Joseph's College (Upholland). In Wales, the National Library of Wales and Cardiff Free Library. In Edinburgh, the Library of Scotland. In Dublin, the Representative Church Body library and Trinity College library; in France, the Bibliothèque Ste Geneviève; in the USA, the Huntington Library (San Marino). Invaluable digital resources include Early English Books Online (Ann Arbor), British History Online, and Archive.org. The decorative caps were supplied by FromOldBooks.org and Early English Books Online.

For permission to use images (artwork and photographed documents), the editors wish to thank the Llyfrgell Genedlaethol Cymru (National Library of Wales, Aberystwyth), Llyfrgell Ganolog Caerdydd (Cardiff Central Library), the BBC, National Galllery, National Portrait Gallery, British Library and Museum (London); National Maritime Museum (Greenwich, London); National Archives (Kew); the Royal Collection (London and Windsor); Sphinx Fine Art (London); Ashmolean Museumthe Barking and District Historical Society (Essex); Dunham Massey estate (Cheshire); Collection of the Earls of Essex (Cashiobury, Herts.); Hever Castle (Kent); Musée du Louvre (Paris); Jagdschloss Grunewald (Berlin, Germany); Alte Pinakothek (Munich); Kunsthistorisches Museum (Vienna); Museo del Prado and the Museo Thyssen-Bornemisza (Madrid, Spain); Galleria Nazionale d'Arte Antica (Rome); the Cloisters, the Frick Collection, and the Metropolitan Museum of Art (New York, NY); the Folger Shakespeare Library (Wash., D.C.); Cummer Museum of Art and Gardens (Jacksonville, FL); and David Badke's Medieval Bestiary (online, bestiary.ca).

*Women's Works* has been funded by grants from the Mellon Foundation, the Ford Foundation; and by research support from Vassar Colllege.

A hearty communal thanks to my colleagues at Vassar, and at academic institutions across North America and the United Kingdom, who have read drafts and made thoughtful suggestions; and to my academic collaborators in the production of Wicked Good Books.

Enjoy!

DWF (2013)

*Women's Works* would have been impossible without the prior labor of others. The scholars and writers noted here have supplied facts, ideas, and source material. Many have shared their research or assisted with fact-checking. To all, many thanks:

Elizabeth Abel, Katherine Acheson, David Adams, Mark Amodio, Bernadette Andrea, Maya Angelou, Raymond Anselment, Margaret Arnold, Kate Aughterson, David Baldwin, Ariane Balizet, Linda Bamber, Carol Barash, Irice Baron, Alexandra Barratt, Emily Bartels, Madeline Bassnett, Jamie Reid Baxter, Charles Beem, Elaine Beilin, Alexandra Bennett, Pamela Iona Bell, Joseph Benson, R. Howard Bloch, Lynda Boose, Diane Bornstein, Keith Botelho, Barbara Bowen, Emily Bowles-Smith, Virginia Brackett, Catherine Brennan, Michael Brennan, Karen Britland, Cedric Brown, Robert Bucholz, Glyn Burgess, Irene Burgess, Victoria Burke, Deborah Burks, F.D.A. Burns, Catherine Burroughs, Keith Busby, Martin Butler, Caroline Bynum, Patricia Cahill, Julie D. Campbell, Jennifer Lee Carrell, Clare Carroll, Jane Cartwright, Jocelyn Catty, Jean Cavanaugh, Sheila Cavanagh, S.P. Cerasano, Jane Chance, Danielle Clarke, Elizabeth Clarke, John Considine, Thomas Corns, Marguérite Corporaal, Julie Crawford, Patricia Crawford, Eugene Cunnar, Karen Cunningham, Peter Davidson, Norman Davis, Leanda De Lisle, Mary DeShazer, Carolyn Dinshaw, Michael Ditmore, Frances Dolan, Jane Donahue Eberwein, Michelle Dowd, Martha Driver, Peter Dronke, Heather Dubrow, Jane Dunn, Sarah Dunnigan, Mary Eagleton, Jacqueline Eales, Julie Early, John Edwards, Laurie Ellinghausen, Robert C. Evans, Margaret Ezell, Susan Felch, Margaret Ferguson, Joan Ferrante, Nona Fienberg, Iva Figes, Alison Findlay, Caitlyn Finlayson, James Fitzmaurice, Angus Fletcher, Julia Fox, Antonia Fraser, Arthur Freeman, Susan Frye, John Garrison, Margaret George, Claire Gheeraert-Graffeuille, B.J. Gibbons, Jonathan Gibson, Sandra Gilbert, Marion Glasscoe, Suzanne Gossett, Melinda Gough, Laura Gowing, Katie Gramich, Catharine Gray, Stephen Greenblatt, Amy Greenstadt, Germaine Greer, Phillipa Gregory, Erin Griffey, Marshall Grossman, Isobel Grundy, Susan Gubar, Nancy Gutierrez, Judith Haber, Heidi Brayman Hackel, Elizabeth Hageman, Anita Hagerman, Kim Hall, Pamela Hammons, Margaret Hannay, Robert Hanning, Elizabeth Hansom, Cathy Hartley, Susan Hastings, Jane Hedley, Jennifer L Heller, Diana Henderson, Katherine Usher *Henderson*, Margo Hendricks, Cynthia Herrup, Caroline Hibbard, Eleanor Hibbert, Jennifer Higginbotham, Susan Higginbotham, Anne Hildebrand, Elaine Hobby, Barbara Hodgdon, Stephanie Hodgson-Wright, Lisa Hopkins, Jean Howard, Cynthia Huff, Jennett Humphreys, Heidi Hutner, Lorna Hutson, Eric Ives, Frances James, Sharon Jansen, Dafydd Johnston, Michael K. Jones, Kathleen Jordan, David Scott Kastan, David Kathman, N.H. Keeble, Nely Keinanen, Sean Kelsey, Angus Kennedy, Gwynne Kennedy, Newton Key, Younkyung Kim, Arthur Kinney, Noel Kinnamon, Clare Kinney, Victoria Kirkham, Jean Klene, Rebecca Krug, Chris Kyle, Mary Ellen Lamb, Ian Lancashire, Rebecca Laroche, Katherine Larson, Jin-Ah Lee, Jongsook Lee, Barbara Kiefer Lewalski, Keith Lindley, Margaret Lloyd, Nora Lofts, Paula Loscocco, Ben Lowe, Christina Luckyj, Liz Herbert McAvoy, Kari Boyd McBride, William McCarthy, Anita McConnell, Kristen McDermott, Barbara *McManus*, Lynne Magnusson, Nadia Margolis, Zoltan Markus, Helen Marlborough, Priscilla Martin, Randall Martin, Helen Maurer, Stephen May, Elizabeth Mazzola, Heather Meakin, Carol Meale, Jeslyn Medoff, Sara Mendelson, Stephanie Merrim, G.J. Meyer, Marianne Micros, Jacqueline Miller, Naomi Miller, Nancy Weitz Miller, Jill Seal Millman, Toril Moi, William Monter, Deborah Montuori, Janel Mueller, Jessica Murphy, Anne M. Myers, J.E. Neale, Karen Nelson, Miranda Garno Nesler, David Norbrook, Marianne Novy, Michael O'Connell, Elisa Oh, Arlene Okerlund, Susan G. O'Malley, Stephen Orgel, Lena Cowen Orlin, Anita Pacheco, Helen Ostovich, John Ottenhoff, Anita Pacheco, George Parfitt, Pamela Corpron Parker, Elizabeth Patton, Helen Payne, Patricia Pender, Thomas Penn, Régine Pernoud, Patricia Phillippy, Joanna Picciotto, Meg Powers Livingston, Linda Porter, Anne Lake Prescott, Roger Prior, Diane Purkiss, Maureen Quilligan, Ayesha Ramachandran, James Ramey, Christine Reno, Judith Richards, Claire Ridgway, Anna Riehl, William Ringler, Elizabeth Rivlin, Josephine Roberts, Karen Robertson, Mark Robson, Katharine Rogers, Mary Beth Rose, Margaret Rosenthal, Laura Runge, Joanna Russ, Jesse Russell, Paul Salzman, Melissa Sanchez, Arnie Sanders, Julie Sanders, Amelia Zurcher Sandy, Melinda Sansome, Louise Schleiner, Roy Schreiber, Kimberly Schutte, Sharon Seelig, L.E. Semler, Desmond Seward, Anne Shaver, Lauren Shohet, Elaine Showalter, Elizabeth Skerpan-Wheeler, Nigel Smith, Rosalind Smith, Anne Somerset, Patrica M. Spacks, Richard Spence, Jane Spencer, Dale Spender, Harriet Spiegel, John-Paul Spiro, Liberty Stanavage, Kay Stanton, Nathan Comfort Starr, Sara Jayne Steen, Jane Stevenson, Kirilka Stavreva, Matthew Steggle, Barbara Taft, Ayanna Thompson, Audrey Tinkham, Janet Todd, Sophie Eliza Tomlinson, Valerie Traub, Betty Travitsky, Giles Tremlett, Suzanne Trill, Mary Trull, Amos Tubb, Deborah Uman, Malcolm Underwood, Steven Urkowitz, Linda Vecchi, Geraldine Wagner, Alison Wall, Wendy Wall, Gary Waller, Retha Warnicke, Joseph Walunywa, Robin Warren, Diane Watt, Valerie Wayne, Alison Weir, Barry Weller, Christopher Whitfield, Barbara Wiedemann, Anna Whitelock, Helen Wilcox, Charity Cannon Willard, Gweno Williams, Katharina Wilson, B.A. Windeatt, Brandon Withrow, Heather Wolfe, Susanne Woods, Ramona Wray, Jillian Wright, Marion Wynne-Davies, Laetitia Yeandle, Samantha Zacher, Georgianna Ziegler, and Judith Zinsser.

*Thank you*!

Made in the USA
Charleston, SC
29 April 2013